Warman's
ANTIQUES
AND THEIR PRICES

24th Edition

*The Standard Price Reference for antiques
and collectibles, for collectors, dealers
and professionals in the trade.*

Edited by
Harry L. Rinker

**Completely illustrated
and authenticated**

**Wallace-Homestead Book Company
Radnor, Pennsylvania**

ISBN 0-87069-560-6
ISSN 0196-2272
Library of Congress Catalog Card No. 82-643542
Manufactured in the United States of America

2 3 4 5 6 7 8 9 0   9 8 7 6 5 4 3 2 1 0

Additional copies of this book may be obtained from your book-
store or directly from Wallace-Homestead Book Company, 201
King of Prussia Rd., Radnor, PA 19089. Enclose $13.95 plus
$2.00 for postage and handling for the first book and $.50 for each
additional book. Residents of AL, AR, AZ, CA, CT, DC, FL,
GA, IA, IL, KS, LA, MA, MD, ME, MI, MN, MO, NJ, NV,
NY, OH, OK, PA, RI, SC, TN, TX, UT, WA, WI and WY add
applicable sales tax.

EDITORIAL STAFF, 24TH EDITION

Regis and Mary Ferson
122 Arden Rd.
Pittsburgh, PA 15216
(412) 563-1964
Milk Glass

Doug Flynn and Al
Bolton
Holloway House
P. O. Box 210
Lititz, PA 17543
(717) 627-4567
*British Royalty
Commemoratives*

Ron Fox
Fox-Terry Steins, Inc.
416 Throop St.
N. Babylon, NY 11704
(516) 669-7232
Mettlach, Steins

Walter Glenn
Geode Ltd.
3393 Peachtree Rd.
Atlanta, GA 30326
(404) 261-9346
Frankart

Dan Golden
5375-C Avendia Encinas
Carlsbad, CA 92008-
4362
(619) 438-8383
Telephones

Ted Hake
Hake's Americana &
Collectibles
P. O. Box 1444
York, PA 17405
(717) 848-1333
*Disneyana, Political
Items*

John High
415 E. 52nd St.
New York, NY 10022
(212) 758-1692
Stevengraphs

Joan Hull
1376 Nevada
Huron, SD 57350
(605) 352-1685
Hull Pottery

David and Sue Irons
Irons Antiques
R. D. #4, Box 101
Northampton, PA 18067
(215) 262-9335
Irons

William J. Jenks
Golden Webb Antiques,
Inc.
P. O. Box 1274
Wilkes-Barre, PA 18703
(717) 288-3039
Pattern Glass

Judy Knauer
1224 Spring Valley Lane
West Chester, PA 19380
(215) 431-3477
Toothpicks

Edward W. Leach
381 Trenton Ave.
Paterson, NJ 07503
(201) 684-5398
Shaving Mugs

Ron Lieberman
The Family Album
R. D. #1, Box 42
Glen Rock, PA 17327
(717) 235-2134
Books, Americana

Elyce Litts
P. O. Box 394
Morris Plains, NJ 07950
(201) 361-4087
Geisha Girl

Elaine J. Luartes
Athena Antiques
100 Beta Drive
Franklin, TN 37064
(615) 377-3442
Jewelry

Clarence and Betty
Maier
The Burmese Cruet
P. O. Box 432
Montgomeryville, PA
18936
(215) 855-5388
*Burmese Glass, Crown
Milano, Royal Flemish*

James S. Maxwell, Jr.
P. O. Box 367
Lampeter, PA 17537
(717) 464-5573
Banks, Mechanical

Joan Collett Oates
5912 Kingsfield Dr.
W. Bloomfield, MI
48322
(313) 661-2335
Phoenix Bird Pattern

Evalene Pulati
National Valentine
Collectors Association
P. O. Box 1404
Santa Ana, CA 92702
Valentines

John D. Querry
R. D. 2, Box 137B
Martinsburg, PA 16662
(814) 793-3185
Gaudy Dutch

INTRODUCTION
"Warman's Is The Key"

Warman's provides the keys needed by auctioneers, collectors, and dealers to open the doors to understanding and dealing with the complexities of the antiques market. A price list is only one of the many keys needed today. **Warman's 24th Edition** contains many additional keys including histories, reference books, periodicals, collectors' clubs, and museums. Useful buying and collecting hints also are provided.

Warman's has been designed to be your first key to the exciting world of antiques. As you use the keys provided to advance beyond this book in specialized collecting areas, **Warman's** hopes you will remember with fondness where you received your start. When you encounter items outside your area of specialty, remember **Warman's** remains your key to unlocking the information you need, just as it has for over forty-one years.

ORGANIZATION

Listings: Objects are listed alphabetically by category, beginning with ABC Plates and ending with Zsolnay Pottery. If you have trouble identifying the category in which your object belongs, use the extensive index in the back of the book. It is designed to guide you to the proper category.

We have attempted to make the listings descriptive enough so that specific objects can be identified. We also have placed emphasis on those items which are actively being sold in the marketplace. Nevertheless, some harder-to-find objects are included in order to demonstrate the market spread.

Each year as the market changes, we carefully consider which categories to include, which to drop, and which to add. **Warman's** is a direct response to the developing trends in the marketplace. To further help collectors and dealers, Wallace-Homestead has published *Warman's Americana & Collectibles*, an excellent source for information and prices on 20th century collectibles and items of nostalgia.

History: Every collector should know something about the history of his object. We have presented a capsule background for each category. In many cases the background contains collecting hints or tips to spot reproductions.

References: Special references are listed for each category to help collectors learn more about their objects. Included are author, title, publisher [if published by a small firm or individual, we have indicated "published by author"], and date of publication or most recent edition.

Finding these books may present a problem. The antiques and collectibles field is blessed with a dedicated core of book dealers who stock these specialized publications. You will find them at flea markets, antiques shows, and advertised in leading publications in the field. Many dealers publish annual or semi-annual catalogs. Ask to be put on their mailing lists. Books go out-of-print quickly, yet many books printed over twenty-five years ago remain the standard work in a category. Used book dealers often can turn up many of these valuable reference sources.

Periodicals: Generally, the newsletter or bulletin of a collectors' club focuses on the specific publication needs within a category. However, there are other publications, not associated with collectors' clubs, of which the collector and dealer should be aware. These are covered under specific categories.

In addition, there are general interest newspapers and magazines which deserve to be brought to our user's attention. These are:

Antique Review, P. O. Box 538, Worthington, OH 43085
Antique Trader Weekly, P. O. Box 1050, Dubuque, IA 52001
Antique Week, P. O. Box 90, Knightstown, IN 46148
Antiques (The Magazine Antiques), 551 Fifth Avenue, New York, NY 10017
Antique & The Arts Weekly, Bee Publishing Company, 5 Church Hill Road, Newton, CT 06470
Antiques & Collecting Hobbies, 1006 South Michigan Avenue, Chicago, IL 60605
Collector News & Antique Reporter, Box 156, Grundy Center, IA 50638
Collectors Journal, P. O. Box 601, Vinton, IA 52349
Collectors' Showcase, P. O. Box 837, Tulsa, OK 74101
Maine Antique Digest, P. O. Box 358, Waldoboro, ME 04572
MidAtlantic Monthly Antiques Magazine, P. O. Box 908, Henderson, NC 27536
New England Antiques Journal, 4 Church Street, Ware, MA 01082
New York-Pennsylvania Collector, Drawer C, Fishers, NY 14453
Southern Antiques, P. O. Box 1107, Decatur, GA 30031
West Coast Peddler, P. O. Box 5134, Whittier, CA 90607
Yesteryear, P. O. Box 2, Princeton, WI 54968

It is impossible to list all the national and regional publications in the antiques and collectibles field. The above is merely a sampling. A check with your local library will bring many other publications to your attention.

Collectors' Clubs: The large number of collectors' clubs adds vitality to the antiques and collectibles fields. Their publications and conventions produce knowledge which often cannot be found anywhere else. Many of these clubs are short-lived; others are so strong that they have regional and local chapters.

Museums: The best way to study a specific field is to see as many documented examples as possible. For this reason, we have listed museums where significant collections in that category are on display. Special attention must be directed to the complex of museums which make up the Smithsonian Institution in Washington, D.C.

Reproductions: Reproductions are a major concern to all collectors and dealers. Most reproductions are unmarked; the newness of their appearance is often the best clue to uncovering them. Specific objects known to be reproduced are marked within the listings with an asterisk (*).

Index: A great deal of effort has been expended to make our index useful. Always try to find the most specific reference. For example, if you have a piece of china, look first for the maker's name and second for the type. The key is to ask the right questions of yourself.

Photographs: You may encounter a piece you cannot identify well enough to use the index. Consult the photographs and marks. If you own the last several editions of **Warman's**, you have assembled a valuable photographic reference to the antiques and collectibles field.

PRICE NOTES

In assigning prices we assume the object is in very good condition. If otherwise, we note this in our description. It would be ideal to suggest that mint, or unused, examples of all objects do exist. The reality is that objects from the past were used, whether they be glass, china, dolls, or toys. Because of this, some normal wear must be expected. In fact, if an object such as furniture does not show wear, its origins may be more suspect than if it does show wear.

Whenever possible, we have tried to provide a broad listing of prices within a category so you have a ''feel'' for the market. We emphasize the middle range of prices within a category, while also listing some objects of high and low value to show the market spread.

We do not use ranges because they tend to confuse rather than help the collector and dealer. How do you determine if your object is at the high or low end of the range? There is a high degree of flexibility in pricing in the antiques field. If you want to set ranges, add or subtract 10% from our prices.

One of the hardest variants with which to deal is the regional fluctuations of prices. Victorian furniture brings widely differing prices in New York, Chicago, New Orleans, or San Francisco. We have tried to strike a balance. Know your region and subject before investing heavily. If the best prices for cameo glass are in Montreal or Toronto, then be prepared to go there if you want to save money or add choice pieces to your collection. Research and patience are key factors to building a collection of merit.

Another factor that affects prices is a sale by a leading dealer or private collector. We have tempered both dealer and auction house figures.

PRICE RESEARCH

Everyone asks—where do we get our prices? They come from many sources.

First, we rely on auctions. Auction houses and auctioneers do not always command the highest prices. If they did, why do so many dealers buy from them? The key to understanding auction prices is to know when a price is high or low in the range. We think we do this and do it well.

Second, we work closely with dealers. We screen our contacts to make certain they have a full knowledge of the market. Dealers make their living from selling antiques; they cannot afford to have a price guide which is not in touch with the market.

Over forty antiques and collectibles magazines, newspapers, and journals come into our office regularly. They are excellent barometers of what is moving and what is not. We don't hesitate to call an advertiser and ask if their listed merchandise sold.

When the editorial staff is doing field work, we identify ourselves. Our conversations with dealers and collectors around the country have enhanced this book. Teams from **Warman's** are in the field at antiques shows, flea markets, and auctions recording prices and taking photographs.

Collectors work closely with us. They are specialists whose devotion to research and accurate information is inspiring. Generally, they are not dealers. Whenever we have asked them for help, they have responded willingly and admirably.

BOARD OF ADVISORS

Our Board of Advisors are specialists, both dealers and collectors, who feel a commitment to accurate information. You'll find their names listed in the front of the book. Several have authored a major reference work on their subject.

Members of the Board of Advisors file lists of prices in their categories for which they are responsible. They help select and often supply the photographs used. If you wish to buy or sell an object in their field of expertise, drop them a note along with an SASE. If time or interest permits, they will respond.

BUYER'S GUIDE, NOT SELLER'S GUIDE

Warman's is designed to be a buyer's guide to what you would have to pay to purchase an object on the open market from a dealer or collector. **It is not a seller's guide to prices.** People frequently make this mistake. In doing so, they deceive themselves. If you have an object listed in this book and wish to sell it to a dealer, you should expect to receive approximately fifty percent (50%) of the listed value. If the object is not anticipated to be resold quickly, expect to receive even less.

A private collector may pay more, perhaps seventy to eighty percent of our list price. Your object will have to be something needed for his or her collection. If you have an extremely rare object or an object of exceptionally high value, these guidelines do not apply.

Examine your piece as objectively as possible. As an antiques and collectibles appraiser, I spend a great deal of time telling people their treasures are not ''gold'' at all, but items readily available in the marketplace.

In respect to buying and selling, a simple philosophy is that a good purchase occurs when the buyer and seller are happy with the price. Don't look back. Hindsight has little value in the antiques field. Given time, things tend to balance out.

COMMENTS INVITED

Warman's Antiques and Their Prices continues to be the leader in the antiques and collectibles price guide field because we listen to our readers. Readers are encouraged to send their comments and suggestions to Harry L. Rinker, Consulting Editor, Wallace-Homestead, c/o Rinker Enterprises, Inc., P. O. Box 248, Zionsville, PA 18092.

ACKNOWLEDGMENTS

With this 24th edition, **Warman's** enters its fifth decade of service to the antiques and collectibles profession. It is a tradition and heritage that continues to grow in excellence due to a dedicated staff, board of advisors, and numerous individuals from all levels of the field whose expertise and opinions are found throughout this volume. But, most importantly, this volume is what it is because of you, our user. When you demand the best, you get the best.

This edition marks both an ending and a beginning. **Warman's** grew and prospered during the 1980s through the diligent managerial efforts of Stanley and Katherine Greene. In fall 1989 Wallace-Homestead Book Company, a division of Chilton Book Company, purchased Warman Publishing Company. Our new beginning also means new opportunities. Watch for the Warman name to appear in a number of new places.

The day to day compiling of listings for this volume rests upon the capable shoulders of Ellen Schroy and Terese Oswald. I could not ask for two more competent and loyal employees. Dean, Terese's husband, is currently battling leukemia. His good health is our constant wish; we ask that you include him in your wishes as well.

This past year two new employees proved welcome additions to the staff at Rinker Enterprises, Inc. Lois Anastas is responsible for a never ending list of things that need to be done. Jocelyn Butterer, one of our former associate editors, has returned as keeper of the research files.

Copy alone never makes a book. My staff and I are privileged to work with Frank Righter, Bruce Nesbitt, and the employees at Ruttle, Shaw & Wetherill, our typesetters, and Edna Jones, Kathryn Conover, Tony Jacobson, and Troy Vozzella, members of the Chilton Book Company production staff.

What do you say to a wife who has provided support and encouragement during the past nine years that I have served as editor for **Warman's**? Certainly not: ''If you had it to do all over again, would you still marry me?'' I wouldn't dare. The answer might not be the same.

Finally, a general note of thanks to all those who sent price lists and letters, allowed their material to be photographed, and took time to discuss the business with me when I talked with them on the phone or saw them in the field.

Rinker Enterprises, Inc.   Harry L. Rinker
P. O. Box 248   Editor
Zionsville, PA 18092
February, 1990

STATE OF THE MARKET

The 1980s were a boom time for the antiques and collectibles business. No one, even those whose involvement in the field extends back into the 1940s and 1950s, remembers a period of such sustained growth over such a wide portion of the market. Many, and I am one, feel a technical correction in pricing is long over due. Signs of such a correction do not appear on the horizon. Let the good times roll.

There are two main groups fueling the current market: foreign investors and the baby boomers of the late 1940s and early 1950s. Their diverse collecting interests are responsible for the overall strength of the market.

While attending the D.S. Clarke Miami Antique Show in Miami's Coconut Grove and the Miami Beach Convention Center in early February 1990, I was amazed at the tremendous number of foreign buyers and dealers. These two shows cater to this international clientele by heavily emphasizing jewelry, silver and silver plate, and eighteenth and nineteenth century furniture and decorative accessories. Traditional European collecting habits are not well understood by most American dealers. It is time to learn them.

Foreign buyers were not limited to Europeans. Japanese and South Americans were well represented. The Japanese influence in the fine arts market has been actively reported. Not so well documented is that they are major players in the antiques and collectibles market as well. South American buyers are an unknown quantity to almost all American dealers and collectors. Opportunity abounds.

A major toy show took place in Miami the same weekend as the two antiques shows. Foreign buyers were very much in evidence. It is important that American collectors and dealers realize that American culture was imported worldwide beginning in the 1950s. Anyone, whether they live in Des Moines, Iowa, or Stockholm, Sweden, who wants to buy back their childhood can find all the examples they need in the American market.

If you are fifty or younger (a baby boomer), your childhood is the post-World War II period. I feel more strongly than ever that 1940 is the dividing line between an ''antique'' and ''collectible'' and is viewed as such by the vast majority of collectors and dealers in the field, although I am not certain that they would admit this openly.

The baby boomer influence in our market is taking place in three key areas. First, post-1945 collectibles are ''hot.'' This includes everything from television memorabilia to 1950s furniture. Second, because most cannot afford the rapidly escalating prices of period colonial furniture, they are buying the factory made stylistic copies of the 1880s through the 1930s. They also react favorably to the more elegant china and glassware of the 1920-1940 era. Third, baby boomers have fallen in love with the Victorian era. Victorian is the ''in'' look for the first years of the 1990s.

Major auctions in January 1990 at Christie's and Sotheby's in New York City resulted in many record prices for American furniture, decorative accessories, and folk art. Be careful how you interpret what happened and its long term implications. My personal feeling is that many of the pieces did far better than they deserved.

What I think these sales indicate is: (1) auction hype, practiced so masterfully by the major houses, still successfully manipulates the market and (2) many collectors are getting very bad advice on the quality of the material they are buying, if, in fact, they are getting any advice at all. I also want to sound my annual warning about the infatuation with the folk art market. The results of the Barenholtz sale must be viewed as the exception, not the rule.

The vast majority of collecting categories in the antiques and collectibles field enjoys a stable pricing structure, i.e., prices do not rise or fall more than five percent of the norm. However, there always are areas gaining and declining in value. You may not agree with my conclusions, but you would be well advised to think about them.

Gaining	*Declining*
Aluminum, Handwrought	Baseball Cards
American Furniture, Colonial Revival Styles	Clothing Accessories
	French Country, Especially Bleached Pine Furniture
Art Glass, Especially Galle	Furniture, Painted
Bottles, All Types	Holiday Collectibles
Paperback Books	Lace and Linen
Prang Prints	Limited Edition Anything
Psychedelic Collectibles	Majolica
Robots, Battery-Operated	Paperweights
Silver Plate, Nineteenth and Early Twentieth Centuries	Stoneware, Blue and White
Staffordshire, Dark Blue Historical Views	Stuffed Toys, Including Teddy Bears
Toys, Friction	Weller Pottery
Wrist Watches	

Two areas of the field received strong doses of negative publicity as the decade of the 1980s ended. The national media reported extensively on the financial difficulties experienced by a number of leading buyers of paintings and their inability to resell their purchases at a price that allowed recovery of their purchase price at auction. Serious questions were raised about pricing levels for many aspects of the fine arts field.

Baseball cards and baseball memorabilia were the subject of several exposés in print and on television concerning the large number of fakes and forgeries that had worked their way into the market, the flooding of the market with special issues and other marketing devices, and the control and manipulation of star players and their products by greedy speculators. A tremendous quantity of new material is stored each year with expectations of large future gain. If this material comes into the market all at once, the entire market will collapse.

The antiques mall continues to play a stronger and stronger role in the sale of antiques. We are now developing professional mall dealers, dealers who have booths in six to ten malls scattered over a large geographic area and spend their time rotating their merchandise between their locations.

Finally, it is clear that a major redefinition of the antiques and collectibles market will take place in the 1990s. The collector of 2001 will differ significantly from his 1990 counterpart.

AUCTION HOUSES

The following auction houses cooperated with Wallace-Homestead Book Company by providing catalogues of their auctions and price lists. This effort is most appreciated.

Sanford Alderfer Auction
Company
501 Fairgrounds Rd.
Hatfield, PA 19440
(215) 368-5477

W. Graham Arader III
1000 Boxwood Court
King of Prussia, PA
19406
(215) 825-6570

Ark Antiques
Box 3133
New Haven, CT 06515
(203) 387-3754

Arman Absentee
Auctions
RR 1 Box 353A
Woodstock, CT 06281
(203) 928-5838

Arthur Auctioneering
R. D. 2
Hughesville, PA 17737
(717) 584-3697

Noel Barrett Antiques
and Auctions Ltd.
Carversville, PA 18913
(215) 297-5109

Robert F. Batchelder
1 West Butler Avenue
Ambler, PA 19002
(215) 643-1430

Richard A. Bourne Co.,
Inc.
Corporation St.
P. O. Box 141
Hyannis, MA 02647
(617) 775-0797

Butterfield's
1244 Sutter St.
San Francisco, CA
94109
(415) 673-1362

Christie's
502 Park Avenue
New York, NY 10022
(212) 546-1000

Christie's East
219 E. 67th St.
New York, NY 10021
(212) 546-1000

Marvin Cohen Auctions
Box 425, Routes 20 &
22
New Lebanon, NY
12125
(518) 794-7477

Marlin G. Denlinger
RR 3, Box 3775
Morrisville, VT 05661
(802) 888-2774

William Doyle Galleries,
Inc.
175 E. 87th St.
New York, NY 10028
(212) 427-2730

Early Auction Co.
123 Main St.
Milford, OH 45150
(513) 831-4833

Fine Arts Co. of
Philadelphia, Inc.
2317 Chestnut St.
Philadelphia, PA 19103
(215) 564-3644

Ron Fox
F. T. S. Inc.
416 Throop St.
N. Babylon, NY 11704
(516) 669-7232

Garth's Auction, Inc.
2690 Stratford Rd.
P. O. Box 369
Delaware, OH 43015
(614) 362-4771 or 369-
5085

Guerney's
Tuxedo Park, NY 10987
(212) 794-2280

Hake's Americana and
Collectibles
P. O. Box 1444
York, PA 17405
(717) 848-1333

Harmer Rooke
Numismatists, Inc.
3 East 57th St.
New York, NY 10022
(212) 751-1900

Harris Auction Galleries,
Inc.
873-875 N. Howard St.
Baltimore, MD 21201
(301) 728-7040

Leslie Hindman, Inc.
215 West Ohio St.
Chicago, IL 60610
(312) 670-0010

James D. Julia, Inc.
Route 209
RFD 1, Box 830
Fairfield, ME 04937
(207) 453-7904

Mid-Hudson Auction
Galleries
One Idlewild Ave.
Cornwall-On-Hudson,
NY 12520
(914) 534-7828

Milwaukee Auction
Galleries
4747 West Bradley Rd.
Milwaukee, WI 53223
(414) 355-5054

Neal Alford Company
4139 Magazine St.
New Orleans, LA 70115
(504) 899-5329

New England Auction
Gallery
Box 8087
East Lynn, MA 01904
(617) 581-5366

New Hampshire Book
Auctions
Woodbury Rd.
Weare, NH 03281
(603) 529-1700

Nostalgia Publications,
Inc.
21 South Lake Dr.
Hackensack, NJ 07601
(201) 488-4536

Pettigrew Auction
Company
405 S. Nevada Ave.
Colorado Springs, CO
80903

David Rago Arts &
Crafts
P. O. Box 3592
Station E
Trenton, NJ 08629
(609) 585-2546

Lloyd Ralston Toys
447 Stratfield Rd.
Fairfield, CT 06432
(203) 366-3399 or 335-
4054

R. Niel & Elaine
Reynolds
Box 133
Waterford, VA 22190
(703) 882-3574

Roan Bros. Auction
Gallery
R.D. 3, Box 118
Cogan Station, PA 17728
(717) 494-0170

Savoia's Auction
Services
Route 23
South Cairo, NJ 12482
(518) 622-8000

Robert W. Skinner Inc.
Bolton Gallery
Route 117
Bolton, MA 01740
(617) 779-5528

Smith House Toy Sales
26 Adlington Rd.
Eliot, ME 03903
(207) 439-4614

Sotheby's
1334 York Avenue
New York, NY 10021
(212) 472-8424

Swann Galleries, Inc.
104 E. 25th St.
New York, NY 10010
(212) 254-4710

Waverlys Auctions
7649 Old Georgetown
Rd.
Bethesda, MD 20814
(301) 951-0919

Winter Associates
21 Cooke St., Box 823
Plainville, CT 06062
(203) 793-0288

Wolf's Auction Gallery
13015 Larchmere Blvd.
Shaker Heights, OH
44120
(216) 231-3888

Woody Auction
Douglass, KS 67039
(316) 746-2694

ABBREVIATIONS

The following are standard abbreviations which we have used throughout this edition of **Warman's**.

ah =	applied handle	ls =	low standard
C =	century	MIB =	mint in box
c =	circa	mkd =	marked
circ =	circular	MOP =	mother of pearl
cov =	cover	NE =	New England
d =	diameter or depth	No. =	number
dec =	decorated	opal =	opalescent
DQ =	Diamond Quilted	orig =	original
emb =	embossed	os =	orig stopper
ext. =	exterior	pat =	patent
FE =	first edition	pcs =	pieces
ftd =	footed	pr =	pair
ground =	background	rect =	rectangular
h =	height	sgd =	signed
hp =	hand painted	sngl =	single
hs =	high standard	SP =	silver plated
imp =	impressed	SS =	Sterling silver
int. =	interior	sq =	square
irid =	iridescent	w =	width
IVT =	inverted thumbprint	yg =	yellow gold
j =	jewels	# =	numbered
K =	karat		
l =	length		
litho =	lithograph		

ABC PLATES

History: The majority of early ABC plates were manufactured in England, imported into the United States, and achieved their greatest popularity from 1780 to 1860. Since a formal education was limited in the early 19th century, the ABC plate was a method of educating the poor for a few pennies.

ABC plates are found in glass, pewter, porcelain, pottery, and tin. Porcelain plates range in diameter from 4⅜ to slightly over 9½ inches. The rim usually contains the alphabet and/or numbers; the center features animals, great men, maxims, or nursery rhymes.

Reference: Susan and Al Bagdade, *Warman's English & Continental Pottery & Porcelain, 1st Edition,* Warman Publishing Co., Inc., 1987; Mildred L. and Joseph P. Chalala, *A Collector's Guide to ABC Plates, Mugs and Things,* Pridemark Press, 1980.

Porcelain, 8½″ d, Staffordshire, $75.00.

GLASS

Arabic and roman Numerals, 7¾″, clear	50.00
Clock, 7″, blue	35.00
Dog's Head, 6″, blue	45.00
Ducks, 6″, amber	45.00
Elephant, howdah, 3 figures on howdah waving flag, 6″, sgd R & C (Ripley & Co.) on howdah	150.00
Emma, girl's head center, beaded rim, Higbee	85.00
Floral Bouquet with bow, clear	50.00
Garfield, 6″, clear	65.00
Hen and Chicks, 6″, clear	40.00
Rabbit running, 6″ frosted	50.00
Rabbit in Cabbage Patch frosted center, stippled edge	40.00
Sancho Panza and Dabble, frosted center, clear border	52.50
Santa on Chimney, "Christmas Eve," 6″, clear	65.00
Star Medallion, 6″, clear	40.00
Stork, carnival	65.00

PORCELAIN OR POTTERY

American Sports, Baseball, Out on the Third Base, 7⅛″, black transfer, Staffordshire	60.00
Baby Bunting and Little Dog Bunch	55.00
Baker, The, 7″, worker putting loaves of bread into brick oven, Staffordshire	135.00
Boy, fishing, 6″, Staffordshire	35.00
Campbell Kid	50.00
Christmas, snowman, children	55.00
Deaf and Dumb, sign language, 6½″, pink transfer, hands making signs of alphabet on inner rim, 2 elegantly dressed cats in center, H. Aynsley & Co., London, England, c1904	150.00
Dog and Bird, 7⅝″, black transfer, Staffordshire	60.00
Elephant, fishing 2 little girls, pink transfer, Staffordshire	85.00
Franklin Maxim	
Dost Thou Love Life, Then Do Not Squander Time, brown transfer, polychrome enameling	68.00
Like Rest Consumes Faster Than Labor While the Used Key is Always Bright	80.00
Goat Herd Boy, horn, dog and goat center, 5″, emb border	75.00
Going to Market, chromolithograph, c1840	60.00
Harvest Home, hay wagon, 5½″, emb border, J.G. Meakin, c1870	75.00
Men Fighting on Donkeys, 7″	65.00
Niagara From The Edge Of The American Falls, 7¼″ d, Staffordshire	125.00
Nursery Rhyme, 7¼″, D.E. McNicol	25.00
Organ Grinder, 8¼″, Staffordshire	40.00
Punch and Judy, 7″, Ironstone, blue transfer, mkd Allertons, England	75.00
Robinson Crusoe at Work, 7¼″, transfer, printed alphabet border, Brownhills Pottery Co., Tunstall, c1875	55.00
Shepherd Boy, horn, dog, goat, 5¼″	75.00
Sly Old Fox	65.00
Stag's Head, 6″	25.00
Washington, 7¼″, Staffordshire	90.00
Wild Horse Hunt, 7½″, multicolored transfer center, emb alphabet border, Staffordshire	70.00

TIN

Animals and bird, 8"	40.00
Bear and children border, sea horse center, 8", hp	25.00
Cat with yarn, 4"	35.00
Children center, alphabet rim, 2"	65.00
Girl on swing, 3½"	40.00
Hey Diddle Diddle, 8"	55.00
Jumbo the Elephant, 6"	90.00
Mary had a Little Lamb, 8"	90.00
Tom thumb, 3"	40.00
Who Killed Cock Robin, 7⅞"	45.00

ADAMS ROSE

History: Adams Rose, made c1820–40 by Adams and Son in the Staffordshire district of England, is decorated with brilliant red roses and green leaves on a white ground.

G. Jones and Son, England, made a variant known as "Late Adams Rose." The colors are not as brilliant and the ground is a "dirty" white. It commands less than the price of the early pattern.

Reference: Susan and Al Bagdade, *Warman's English & Continental Pottery & Porcelain, 1st Edition,* Warman Publishing Co., Inc., 1987.

Cup and Saucer, early, 6" d, $200.00.

Bowl, 8¾", early	600.00
Creamer, early	340.00
Cup and Saucer, handleless, late	65.00
Cup Plate, 4¼"	48.00
Milk Pitcher	
4⅞", c1840	75.00
6¾", bulbous, emb	130.00
Plate	
7¼", early	145.00
7½", late	35.00
8½", late	45.00
8¾", late	50.00
9¼", early	175.00
9½", late	65.00
10½", early	225.00

Platter, 15", oval, early, c1820	300.00
Soup, flange rim, late	75.00
Sugar, cov, late	150.00
Teapot, late	210.00
Vegetable Dish, cov, 12⅝" l, c1850	500.00
Wash Bowl and Pitcher, early	1,000.00

ADVERTISING

History: Before the days of mass media, advertisers relied on colorful product labels and advertising giveaways to promote their products. Containers were made to appeal to the buyer by the use of stylish lithographs and bright colors. Many of the illustrations used the product in the advertisement so that even an illiterate buyer could identify a product.

Advertisements were put on almost every household object imaginable and were constant reminders to use the product or visit a certain establishment.

References: Al Bergevin, *Food And Drink Containers And Their Prices,* Wallace-Homestead, 1988; Ray Klug, *Antique Advertising Encyclopedia,* Vol. 1 (1978) and Vol. 2 (1985), L-W Promotions; Ralph and Terry Kovel, *Kovels' Advertising Collectibles Price List,* Crown Publishers Inc., 1986; Robert W. and Harriet Swedberg, *Tins "N" Bins,* Wallace-Homestead, 1985.

Collectors' Clubs: The Ephemera Society of America, P. O. Box 224, Ravena, NY 12143; Tin Container Collectors Association, P.O. Box 440101, Aurora, CA 80014.

Periodical: National Association of Paper and Advertising Collectibles, P.O. Box 500, Mount Joy, PA 17552.

Additional Listings: See *Warman's Americana & Collectibles* for more examples.

Coffee Can, Our Jewel Roasted Coffee, Ericsson's Mills, Brooklyn, NY, dark blue ground, lighter blue, cream, silver, and red dec, blue knob, $250.00.

Ashtray
  Fatima Cigarettes, orig pack of ciga-
    rettes, marked "Made in Austria" . **75.00**
  Providence Ins. Co., brass **15.00**
Bank, First National, Portland, OR . . . **100.00**
Basket, "Kool-Aid–2 cents" painted on
  top, picnic type **35.00**
Blotter
  Mazda, 3½ x 6", cardboard, full color
    illus, 1912 copyright by General
    Electric Co, unused **5.00**
  Morton's Salt, 4 x 9", full color illus
    pair of animals headed into arc un-
    der torrential rain as salt continues
    to pour, c1930, unused **15.00**
Bookends, Hartford Fire Ins Co, bronze,
  dated 1935 . . . . **100.00**
Bookmark, Cracker Jack, black, white,
  and tan litho, tin Scotty dec **20.00**
Box, Gold Dust Twins Washing Powder,
  unopened **55.00**
Calendar
  Anti-Kammia Tablets, 1912, young
    girl, calendar on back **10.00**
  C. F. Rich and Co, Boston, 1912, 13
    x 18", colored man and woman on
    horses, full pad **50.00**
  Deering Harvesters, 1906, 13 x 20",
    lady seated on farm wall eating
    cherries, metal band top **150.00**
  Selz Shoes, 36 x 11½", beautiful lady,
    red dress, white feather fan, wood
    frame **135.00**
Calendar Plate, 1909, Foran Furniture
  Co. New London, CT, calendars on
  outer rim, bird holding ribbon in beak **55.00**
Can, A & P Baking Powder, litho tin,
  grandmother Ginna, 1800s **100.00**
Candy Box
  Powerhouse, picture of boy **20.00**
  Zagnut **15.00**
Candy Pail, Lovell & Kovell, historical
  scene **350.00**
Cigarette Lighter
  Dow Oven Cleaner, can shape top . **10.00**
  Zarkin Machines, chrome, black glass **15.00**
Clipboard, Indianapolis Lumber Insur-
  ance Agency, metal, 5¢ tablet **15.00**
Clock
  Calumet Baking Soda, "Let Us Bake
    Your Calumet Cake", 39" h, wall
    type, calendar **675.00**
  King Alfred Cigar, 10" h, base **375.00**
Cookie Cutter, Winnie Winkle, Pillsbury,
  comic, 1937, boxed **25.00**
Crock, Heinz, orig label, "Preserved
  Red Raspberries" **450.00**
Cup and Saucer, Vah Dole's Hot Choc-
  olate, green and purple irid porcelain,
  c1930, marked "Made in Japan" . . . **15.00**
Demitasse Spoon, Log Cabin Syrup . . **15.00**

Display, Counter
  Pall Mall Herbert Tareyton, 10½ x 6
    x 9½", wood case, plastic front,
    black, gold lettering, orig paper la-
    bel, "Duranol" **20.00**
  Vellastic Underwear, 10 x 7", oval
    frame, Art Deco litho, brown stand,
    shows family in underwear, orig pa-
    per label dated 1918 . . . . **165.00**
Doll, Vermont Syrup, vinyl **45.00**
Doll House, Dunham Coconut **300.00**
Door Push
  Junge's Bread, 9 x 4", porcelain over
    steel, gray lettering, yellow ground **30.00**
  Vicks, porcelain **100.00**
Fan
  New Home Sewing Machine, two little
    blond haired girls holding doll . . . **55.00**
  Schlitz Beer, early 1900s **10.00**
  Wacker Brewing Co, 7½ x 9", diecut,
    cardboard, full color illus, 1930s . . **25.00**
Flour Sifter, Calumet **15.00**
Fly Swatter, Schell's Beer, wood and
  screen **30.00**
Glass
  Busch Extra Dry Ginger Ale, vertical
    panels, "A-B" logo in shield **20.00**
  7-Up, set of 4 . . . . **40.00**
Globe, Mobil Oil Gaygoyle, one piece . **450.00**
Horseshoe, raised "Take Simmons
  Liver Regulator," 6" h, 6" w **40.00**
Japanese Lantern, adv for Patterson
  Brothers, dealers in boots and shoes,
  Lansing, MI, illus panels of General
  U. S. Grant, three puppies, young girl,
  wilderness scene, and adv logo . . . **175.00**
Jar
  Ansom Dairy, Wadhams, New York,
    cow and barn **15.00**
  National Biscuit Company, 10 x 11",
    emb clear glass, red metal top . . . **100.00**
  Planters Peanut, football shape **185.00**
Juice Mixer, Snow Crop **5.00**
Key Holder
  American-Maid Bread, brass, figural,
    loaf of bread design, ... **10.00**
  Dr. Pepper, 1930 . . . . **5.00**
Lamp, John Anderson Co, 21¾" h, cast
  white metal, brass finish, newsboy by
  street lamp, cigar cutter in base, white
  globe **650.00**
Lapel Pin,⅞", Top-Round Shoes, three
  cherubs carrying shoes up a ladder
  to the top of the world, c1900 . . . . . **25.00**
Letterhead, matching envelope, Pond's
  Bitters Co. **20.00**
Letter Opener, 10½", Boyertown Burial
  Casket Co., dark finish brass, raised
  illus of a casket on both sides of han-
  dle, early 1900s **25.00**
Measuring Cup, Kellogg's, glass, green **15.00**
Menu Holder, Borden's Ice Cream, Elsie **50.00**

Mirror, Queen Quality Shoes, oval, black and white, woman in Federal era dress, $35.00.

Mirror
Dockash Stoves	18.00
Gilford-Strauss, Chicago	35.00
Horlicks Malted Milk, woman with cow	25.00
KoKo Tulu Chewing Gum, 11 x 7½", wood frame, beveled glass, white lettering	60.00
Noxall Clothing, pocket type	20.00
Silverman Bros, Chicago, Wool Commission Merchants, sheep, bright green colored grass, red and black lettering	75.00
Wadsworth Bros, Fashionable Furniture, hand, 9" l, paper label on wood	10.00
Mold, Hershey Chocolate	100.00

Mug
Hamm's Krug Klub, set of 6, marked "Red Wing"	325.00
Hires Root Beer, stoneware, branch handle, ornate	250.00
Needle Holder, Hires Condensed Milk, 1½ x 2½", cardboard, full color illus, 1899 copyright	15.00
Needle Threader, Prudential Insurance	10.00
Notebook, Hunt's Supreme Quality Sliced Lemon Cling Peaches, diecut, can shape, celluloid cov, yellow peaches, blue and gold bowl, bright red ground, 1915 calendar, brass rings	25.00

Paperweight
Henry Werner Boots and Shoes, Columbus, OH, ceramic, blue, orig box	90.00
Smith & Welker Hardware, Kane, PA	20.00
Pencil, Ace Pencil Co, USA, 62" l, yellow	100.00

Pill Holder, Phillips Milk of Magnesia, cylinder type, patent date April 15, 1902, belt type	35.00

Pinback Button
Edison Records	35.00
Limetta-The Drink of Drinks, little girl riding dog	55.00
Toledo Scales, "Made in Canada"	20.00

Poster
Prince Albert Tobacco, 43 x 95", canvas, "The National Joy Smoke"	110.00
Travelers Insurance Co, C. G. C. Plummer, Agent, 26 x 19¾", litho by Major & Knapp, center river scene with Beacon Hill, people, train, stage coach, and wagons in foreground, modern frame	1,000.00

Pot Scraper, tin, Sharples Tubular Cream Separator, red cream separator, blue book with adv, sepia tones, company locations on reverse, 1909, 3½" h, 2¼" w, $250.00.

Punchboard, Planter's Cocktail Peanuts, 7½ x 8 x ¾", full color peanut can, unused, punching tool still sealed under paper label	75.00
Puzzle, Heinz 57 Varieties, 10 x 12", diecut, numerals, 1940s juvenile grocery store setting, orig mailing envelope	50.00
Rolling Pin, Crockery, Sheldahl, Iowa	150.00
Shaving Mug, glass, Golden Knight Soap	25.00

Sign
Baker's Vanilla, 46 x 34", porcelain	170.00
Cheltenham Tailoring, 11 x 8½", reverse on glass, free standing	25.00
Drivers Hardware Store, 33 x 99¾", wood, mustard yellow, red, and black	200.00

Ex-Lax, 8 x 37″, porcelain **150.00**
Fisk Tires, boy with tire **2,000.00**
Good Gulf, 10½″, round, metal **45.00**
Hajoca Kitchen Products, 18 x 13½″,
   metal, orange and black **55.00**
Keyler's Pharmacy, Bloomfield, NJ,
   15 x 10″ **20.00**
Nu Grape, 12 x 36″, tin, yellow and
   blue, dated March 9, 1920 . . . . . . **100.00**
Nichol 5¢ Kola, multicolored, early
   1930s **100.00**
Mohawk Beverages, 28 x 20″, tin,
   emb **60.00**
Peter Schulyer Cigar, 46 x 30″, paper **35.00**

**Sign, Rex Smoking Tobacco, emb tin
litho, yellow ground, 19½″ l, 9″ h,
$150.00.**

R. G. Sullivan Cigar, 23 x 10½″, por-
   celain **100.00**
Tasty Dixie Milk, 22″, neon **350.00**
T. R. Havan Cigars, 30 x 20″, tin,
   cardboard backed, royal blue
   ground, gold trim and bottom let-
   tering, full color picture of Teddy
   Roosevelt in center, gold and or-
   ange frame **450.00**
Ward's Vitovim Bread, 27″ d **55.00**
York Harbor Garage, 30 x 16″, tin,
   black writing, green frame, wood
   "Carroll S. Bridges-Manager"
   hangs below **90.00**
Spittoon, Redskin Cut Plug Chewing
   Tobacco, brass **110.00**
Spool Cabinet, Clark's, two drawer, oak **350.00**
Tape Dispenser, Karo Syrup, porcelain,
   white **40.00**
Tape Measure
   Allentown Dairy Co, 1½″, round, cel-
     luloid, red, white and blue **20.00**
   Colgate's Fab, celluloid, 1930s laun-
     dry product, inscribed bottom **12.00**
   International Harvester **10.00**
Thermometer
   Prestone Anti-Freeze, 35″, off-white
     ground, blue square at top, red oval
     at bottom, white lettering **65.00**

Old Brown Forman's King Whiskey . **250.00**
Orange Crush, bottle shape, brown . **45.00**
Thimble, Butternut Coffee **4.00**
Tin
   Allen's Toffee, 12″ h, Statue of Lib-
     erty, Golden Gate, California **45.00**
   Baker's Cocoa, orig paint, 19th C . . **40.00**
   Blanke's Coffee, 2 lb, dome type can-
     ister, woman on horse **150.00**
   Culture Smoking Tobacco **90.00**
   Frontenag Brand Peanut Butter, 4 x
     3″, red and blue lettering trimmed
     in gold, white ground **35.00**
   Hancock Old Black Joe Axle Grease,
     4½ x 3″, orig contents, picture of
     Old Black Joe on front and back,
     cane on either side **45.00**
   Jarvina Coffee, 6 x 4″, black and red
     lettering, silver trim, red ground . . **35.00**
   Mt. Cross Coffee, 10 lb., litho, re-
     cessed lid, bail, marked "Product of
     Denver, Colo" **85.00**
   Pennzoil United Air Lines Motor Oil,
     air liner, owls, and Liberty Bell . . . **45.00**

**Tin, peanut butter pail, Staple Brand,
Syracuse Candy & Specialty Co, Syracuse, NY, Canco, $45.00.**

Rexall Drugs Foot Powder, dome top **25.00**
Thomas Writing Fluids, black cat on
   one side **110.00**
Universal Buck Powder, black and
   white Kewpies, "For White & Col-
   ored Kids" **75.00**
Virginia clubs Cigarette, London . . . **10.00**
Tip Tray
   "Compliments of Dixie Loan Co-
     Money When You Need It," 4″,
     round, gold letters, black rim, lady
     with pink roses in hair **75.00**
   Geo. Ehret's Hellgate Brewery, NY,
     13½ x 16¾″, oval, tin **25.00**
   Hopski Soda, litho, frog pouring
     drinks **50.00**

Moxie, purple flowers and lady	**150.00**
Token, Evans Dairy, Davenport, IA ...	**5.00**
Tray	
Hanley's Peerless Ale, 11½" d, tin ..	**150.00**
Miller High Life, girl sitting on moon .	**25.00**
Mott Robertson Ice Cream, 11½ x 17½"	**135.00**

Tray, Anheuser–Busch, tin litho, marked "Standard Adv Co., Conshocton, Ohio," 1909, 16½" h, 13½" w, $1,250.00.

Old Reading Beer, red border, white lettering, blue ground	**50.00**
Peerless Ice Cream	**85.00**
Rockford Watches, 3½ x 5", tin, girl in green dress	**115.00**
Wall Plaque, Hartford Insurance Co, bronze and oak, dated 1909	**125.00**
Watch Fob	
Keystone Steel and Wire Company, Peoria, Ill, brass, silvered, red porcelain bale of wire fence with three columns numbered 1-2-3 superimposed on front	**95.00**
Old Dutch Cleanser, blue, white, and yellow	**100.00**
Paul Revere Insurance	**15.00**
Whistle	
Buster Brown Shoes, 1¼", Buster holding shoe, "First Because Of The Last," c1910	**75.00**
Red Goose Shoes, 1½", yellow and red litho, 1930s	**15.00**

ADVERTISING TRADE CARDS

History: Advertising trade cards are small, thin cardboard cards made to advertise the merits of a product and usually bear the name and address of a merchant.

With the invention of lithography, colorful trade cards became a popular advertising media in the late 19th and early 20th centuries. They were made especially to appeal to children. Young and old alike collected and treasured them in albums and scrapbooks. Very few are dated; 1880 to 1893 were the prime years for trade cards; 1810 to 1850 cards can be found, but rarely. By 1900 trade cards were rapidly losing their popularity. By 1910 they had all but vanished.

References: Kit Barry, *The Advertising Trade Card*, Book 1, Iris Publishing Co., 1981; John and Margaret Kaduck, *Advertising Trade Cards*, privately printed; Robert Jay, *The Trade Card In Nineteenth-Century America*, University of Missouri Press, 1987; Jim and Cathy McQuary, *Collectors Guide To Advertising Cards*, L-W Promotions, 1975; Murray Card (International) Ltd., *Cigarette Card Values: Murray's 1988 Guide To Cigarette & Other Trade Cards*, published by author, 1988.

Additional Listings: See *Warman's Americana & Collectibles* for more examples.

CLOTHING

Bonner & Co, NYC, ext. and int. views of store, adv on back for clothing department with directions for ordering by mail, Sackett, Wilhelms & Betzig, NY, 5¾ x 3⅝"	**7.50**
Koch Bros, Allentown's Leading Clothing Makers, girl with umbrella holding fan, boy in sailor suit, Maud Humphrey, 1902	**12.00**
Duplex Corset, The Secret Out At Last/ Why Mrs. Brown Has Such A Perfect Figure, adv on back, c1890, 3½ x 5½"	**10.00**
F. Mayer Boot & Shoe Co, Milwaukee, three boys playing hopscotch, shoe emblem on front with Ella Wheeler Wilcox poem "Jimmy's First Boots," shoe adv on reverse	**3.00**
Kline & Bros, Hatter, Allentown, PA, man before mirror trying on derby, Ketterlinus, Philadelphia, 2¾ x 4¼"	**2.50**

COFFEE

Grandma's Coffee, cat and dogs, 3 x 5"	**3.50**
Great Atlantic & Pacific Tea Company, black landlord and renter discussing A & P teas and coffees, adv on back, 1884, 8 x 9"	**35.00**
Lion Coffee Co, girl in picture hat, basket of cherries	**5.00**

FARM MACHINERY

DeLaval Cream Separators, diecut, litho, Jersey cow, adv on back, c1900, 3 x 5"	**25.00**

Eclipse Halter, multicolored, tethered black and white cow in stall, adv on back for Montrose, PA harness dealer, 1884, 3 x 5" 5.00
Moline Wagon Co, Moline, IL, "A Mobile Bridal Trip," couple in Moline wagon 3.50
Wm. Deering & Company, Agricultural Equipment Manufacturer, two young girls and dog transform into sockets of skull, adv on back, c1890, 4 x 6½" 20.00

Farm Machinery, McCormick Reaping Machines, 6¼ x 4⅛", $15.00.

FOOD

Anheuser Busch, Christopher Columbus bust, girl with flag, large beer cask, Columbian Expo 18.00
B. F. Clark, Ice Cream, Fruit, Confectionery, Phila, Mother Goose flying through sky 1.00
Daniels & Smith, groceries, canned, dried, and green fruits, vegetables, La Crosse, pink rose, buds, and foliage 2.00
Hires' Root Beer, diecut, boy holding glass standing in front of bicycle, c1897, 3 x 5" 15.00
Maiden Blush Vinegar, children playing 3.00
Mellin's Food, diecut of baby in high chair, white dress, pink bow, adv on back, c1915, 4 x 5½" 8.00
Sanford's Ginger, black girl rocking baby 75.00
Troy Branch of the Bennett Tea House of Vesey St. Troy, NY, blonde girl lying in grass daydreaming, red umbrella, basket of flowers 3.00
Woolson Spice Co, multicolored, Christmas scene with Santa carrying large sack over shoulder, "The Woolson Spice Co. Wishes You A Merry Christmas and A Happy New Year," adv on back for Lion Coffee in black and white, 5" sq 45.00

MEDICINE

Chesebrough Manufacturing Co, Vaseline, girl in apron playing with cat and two puppies 2.50
Dr. J. C. Ayer & Co, Lowell, MA, Ayer's Cherry Pectoral for the cure of coughs, colds, asthma, croup, bronchitis, whooping-cough, and consumption, girl gazing at robins in cherry tree 3.00
Dr. Seth Arnold's Cough Killer, girl holding puppy, "It Works Like Magic" ... 5.00
German Corn Remover, man dancing, c1890, 3" sq closed, 3 x 5" open ... 10.00
Lydia E. Pinkham, portrait sgd "Yours for Health, Lydia E. Pinkham" on one side, virtues of vegetable compound on reverse 2.50
Kendall's Spavin Cure, black jockey and race horse, testimonials on back, c1890, 4 x 6" 8.00
Morse's Pills, girl in orchid dress feeding two kittens, 1890 .... 3.00
Warner's Safe Yeast, woman before window, logo at right, factory in shield cut at bottom left, title "Up With The Sun," Mensing & Stecher, NY, 3⅞ x 5½" 7.50

MISCELLANEOUS

Buckeye Force Pumps, Mast, Fous & Co, Springfield, OH, boy pumping water in front of burning house, Krebs Lithograph Co, Cinncinnati 8.00
Forepaugh Wild West Show, multicolored, scenes of Battle Of The Little Big Horn/Death Of Custer, adv on back, c1890, 4 x 5" 20.00
Lehigh Lumber Scale, cello, double faced, mechanical, inner spinner wheels to measure lumber and proportions for mixing cement and concrete, c1930, 2½ x 4½" 20.00
National Cash Register, mechanical .. 45.00
Solon Palmer Perfumer, New York, diecut, paint pallet shape, side view bust of a young girl, flowers 6.00
Wanamaker's Ladies' and Gents' Dining Room, Phila, cream pink rose buds, green foliage 4.00

SOAP AND CLEANERS

Bell Soap, white buffalo pulling children in soap box, adv on back 4.00
Enoch Morgan & Sons, "Sapolio," boy wearing fancy clothes 2.50
Pearline Soap Co, Pyle's Pearline, court jester in pain 2.00

Thread, Clark's O. N. T. Spool Cotton, Jumbo Aesthetic, sepia, 4¾ x 3″, $5.00.

THREAD AND SEWING

Golden Eagle Knitting Wools, Willey & Pearson, Ltd, Trafalgar Works, Halifax, woman in front of mirror wearing green dress	2.00
James Chadwick & Bros, girl sitting on spool of thread holding a small chalkboard, reverse looks like a school chalk board, Stahl & Jaeger, 1887	7.00
New Home Sewing Machine Co, multicolored, diecut, mother holding bouquet of flowers with daughter and doll seated next to sewing machine, c1890, 7 x 9″	20.00
Willimantic thread, cupid tying thread around world	3.00

TOBACCO

Mail Pouch, oval cut out on front opens to show baby slipping hand under diaper, title Just Found His Mail Pouch, adv on back, 1938, 3½ x 5″	15.00
Smoke La Pastora, kittens in top hat, Currier & Ives	20.00

TRANSPORTATION

Pittsburgh Locomotive Works, three trains, steel engraving, Western Bank Note Co, Chicago, 1884	25.00
Ryders Excursion, Thompsonville to Rockaway Beach, shows paddlewheel, 1881	20.00
State Line, ship anchored in foreign harbor, Europe	10.00

AGATA GLASS

History: Agata glass was invented in 1887 by Joseph Locke of the New England Glass Company, Cambridge, Massachusetts.

Agata glass was produced by using a piece of peachblow glass, coating it with metallic stain, spattering the surface with alcohol, and firing. The result was a high gloss, mottled appearance of oil droplets floating on a watery surface. Shading usually ranged from opaque pink to dark rose. Pieces are known in a pastel opaque green. A few pieces have been found in a satin finish.

Whiskey Taster, 2⅝″ h, $600.00.

Bowl, 5⅜″ d, crimped rim	600.00
Celery Vase, 6½″ h, scalloped rim	1,300.00
Creamer	1,200.00
Finger Bowl, 5¼″ d, 2⅝″ h, crushed raspberry shading to creamy pink, all over gold mottling with bits of blue mottling	1,250.00
Juice Glass, 3¾″ h	825.00
Pitcher, 6⅜″ h, crimped rim	1,650.00
Spooner, 4½″ h, green opaque, gold band and mottling	650.00
Toothpick, 2¾″, cylindrical	550.00
Tumbler, 3¾″ h, wild rose color fading to cream at base, profuse mottling	545.00
Vase, 4½″ h, sq, pinched sides, ruffled 4 scalloped rim	550.00
Whiskey Taster, 2⅝″	600.00

AMBERINA GLASS

History: Joseph Locke developed Amberina glass in 1883 for the New England Glass Works. "Amberina," a trade name, describes a transparent glass which shades from deep ruby to amber color. It was made by adding powdered gold to the ingredients for an amber glass batch. A portion of the glass was reheated later to produce the shading effect. Usually it was the bottom which was reheated to form the deep red; however, reverse examples have been found.

Most early Amberina is of flint quality glass, blown or pattern molded. Patterns include Diamond Quilted, Daisy and Button, Venetian Diamond, Diamond and Star, and Thumbprint.

In addition to the New England Glass Works, the Mt. Washington Glass Company of New Bedford, Massachusetts, copied the glass in the 1880s and sold it at first under the Amberina trade name and later as "Rose Amber." It is difficult to distinguish pieces from these two New England factories. Boston and Sandwich Glass Works never produced the glass.

Amberina glass also was made in the 1890s by several Midwest factories, among which was Hobbs, Brockunier & Co. Trade names included "Ruby Amber Ware" and "Watermelon." The Midwest glass shaded from cranberry to amber and resulted from a thin flashing of cranberry applied to the reheated portion. This created a sharp demarkation between the two colors. This less expensive version caused the death knell for the New England variety.

In 1884 Edward D. Libbey was assigned the trade name "Amberina" by the New England Glass Works. Production occurred in 1900, but ceased shortly thereafter. In the 1920s Edward Libbey renewed production at his Toledo, Ohio, plant for a short period. The glass was of high quality. Amberina from this era is marked "Libbey" in script on the pontil.

Reproduction Alert: Reproductions abound.

NEW ENGLAND

Bowl
7½" d, DQ, roll over scalloped edge   **180.00**

Vase, New England, Inverted Thumbprint, 7¼" h, $285.00.

7", bulbous, 4 feet, blown, melon ribbed	**325.00**
8½", cradle shaped, Daisy & Button	**250.00**
9" sq, berry, Daisy & Button	**230.00**
Butter Tub, cov, Daisy & Button, amberina, cov lid has flakes	**475.00**
Celery	
5¾", scalloped sq top, pinched paneled sides	**120.00**
7", scalloped top, DQ	**375.00**
Compote, 8¾" d, thumbprint	**325.00**
Cruet	
6", amber stopper, applied amber handle	**200.00**
6¾", 3" d, amber cut faceted orig stopper, amber applied handle	**225.00**
Curtain Tiebacks, pr, orig shanks	**150.00**
Cuspidor, 9 x 5", hourglass shape, ruffled rim, Swirl, gold trim	**375.00**
Finger Bowl, 5½", ruffled rim, slightly paneled	**125.00**
Ice Cream Plate, 5⅝" sq, Daisy & Button	**110.00**
Lemonade Glass, 5¼", swirled, gold dec, applied handle	**225.00**
Parfait, 6½", ftd, swirled, gold leaf and bud dec	**275.00**
Pickle Jar	
5½", pewter cov, wavy lines and thumbprints, silver and gold bowl of fruit dec	**400.00**
6¾", pewter cov, IVT, enameled floral dec, Mt. Washington	**225.00**
Pitcher	
5¾", bulbous, IVT, applied amber reeded handle, Mt. Washington	**160.00**
8½", triangular top, IVT, amber reeded applied handle, Mt. Washington	**225.00**
Punch Cup, DQ, applied reeded handle, Libbey	**100.00**
Ramekin underplate, 2¼" h, 4¼" d, slightly ribbed, New England Glass Works	**200.00**
Sauce Dish, sq, fuchsia, Daisy & Button	**110.00**
Spoon Holder, 5", pinched scalloped top, DQ	**135.00**
Syrup, orig pewter top, IVT, New England Glass Works	**325.00**
Toothpick Holder	
2½", baby DQ, New England Glass Co. label, Pat July 24, 1881	**375.00**
2¾", ftd, Daisy & Button	**250.00**
Tumbler, Venetian Diamond, New England Glass Works	**90.00**
Vase	
5⅛", lily, orig Libbey label	**325.00**
5¾", fold over rim, IVT, 5 applied feet, Mt. Washington	**125.00**
6", trumpet	**250.00**
Whiskey Glass, 2½", DQ	**120.00**

MID-WESTERN

Berry Dish, 5" sq, Daisy & Button	90.00
Bowl, 4½" sq, Hobnail	120.00
Carafe, 7⅛", IVT, reversed color, swirled neck	150.00
Creamer, 4½", Hobnail, clear reeded handle	175.00
Cruet, 6", IVT, orig amber stopper ...	225.00
Dish, 5" sq, Daisy & Button	120.00
Ice Cream Dish, 5¾", sq, Daisy & Button, scalloped corners	100.00
Lamp, hand, 10¾" h overall, 5" base, Baby Hobnail, 6 applied shell feet, 5 amber leaf-like extensions rising to middle of lamp, applied amber branch handle	475.00
Muffineer, Baby Thumbprint	155.00
Pitcher	
6½", Coin Spot Opalescent	220.00
6¾", Hobnail, Hobbs, Brockunier & Co.	165.00
7", 5½" d, bulbous, round mouth, IVT, applied amber handle	175.00
7⅝", bulbous crackle, amber reeded applied handle	175.00
Punch Cup, DQ, applied reeded handle	85.00
Sauce Dish, 5½" sq, Daisy & Button, Hobbs, Brockunier & Co	200.00
Vase	
5½" h, 4⅛" d, bulbous, IVT, applied amber leaf feet	145.00
6¾", ribbed lily	150.00
Whiskey bottle, 11", double pouring spout, matching stopper	120.00

Cruet, applied amber handle, faceted amber stopper, 6¾" h, $3,200.00.

Pitcher, milk, applied amber handle, orig "Aurora" label	7,000.00
Punch Cup, vertical ribs, applied handle	1,500.00
Salt Shaker, orig top	1,000.00
Syrup Pitcher, orig top, applied handle	5,500.00
Tumbler, 3¾", vertical ribs	2,250.00
Vase	
7¼", lily shape	2,500.00
9¾", lily shape	5,500.00

AMBERINA GLASS—PLATED

History: The New England Glass Company, Cambridge, Massachusetts, first made Plated Amberina in 1886; Edward Libbey patented the process for the company in 1889.

Plated Amberina was made by taking a gather of chartreuse or cream opalescent glass, dipping it in Amberina and working the two, often utilizing a mold. The finished product had a deep amber to deep ruby red shading, a fiery opalescent lining, and often vertical ribbing for enhancement. Designs ranged from simple forms to complex pieces with collars, feet, gilding, and etching.

A cased Wheeling glass of similar appearance had an opaque white lining, but is not opalescent and the body is not ribbed.

Celery	2,600.00
Cruet, 6¾" h, faceted amber stopper .	3,200.00
Lamp Shade, 14", hanging, swirled, ribbed, 4,750.00	
Parfait, applied amber handle, c1886 .	1,250.00

AMPHORA

History: The Amphora Porcelain Works was one of several pottery companies located in the Teplitz-Turn region of Bohemia in the late 19th and early 20th centuries. It is best known for art pottery, especially Art Nouveau and Art Deco pieces.

Several markings were used, including the name and location of the pottery and the Imperial mark which included a crown. Prior to WWI Bohemia was part of the Austro-Hungarian Empire so the word "Austria" may appear as part of the mark; after WWI the word "Czechoslovakia" may be part of the mark.

Reference: Susan and Al Bagdade, *Warman's English & Continental Pottery & Porcelain, 1st Edition*, Warman Publishing Co., Inc., 1987.

Additional Listings: Teplitz.

Basket, 9", Art Nouveau style, purple, beige, green, and gold, large applied flowers, basketweave, imp mark . . . **345.00**

Bowl, 9 x 8", four handles, gray, enameled poppies, sgd **50.00**

Center Bowl, 17" d, oval, undulating rim, applied scrolled handles, green glaze, grapevines and bunches dec, four scrolled feet, imp "Amphora 8192/56," c1900 . . . . **325.00**

Centerpiece, 18½ x 18½", matt glazed, figure, baby Dionysius wearing wreath of grapes on head, holding two thyrsos, sitting on ram with two empty basket molded containers, rect base, painted amber and green, gilt highlights, cream ground, imp "Amphora" and crown mark **420.00**

Vase, grape motif, multi–handled top, triangle mark "EDDA," impressed "Amphora/8675/56," 16¾" h, $275.00.

Ewer
  9½" h, handles, spout, oval reserve of gladiator **125.00**
  13" h, children in forest dec **100.00**

Figure
  8" h, girl, selling roses, marked "Amphora–Teplitz" **150.00**
  10" h, lion stalking over rocky cliff formation **275.00**

Vase
  7", beige, purple and red gooseberries, sgd **150.00**
  9" h, bottle form, gilt rim and highlights, green thistles, royal blue ground, base imp "Amphora/Austria/Turn/Pans 1900 RSTK," pr . . . **425.00**
  11½", stylized floral dec, polychrome, sgd "Amphora, Austria" **225.00**

ARCHITECTURAL ELEMENTS

History: Architectural elements are those items which have been removed or salvaged from buildings, ships, or gardens. Many are hand crafted. Frequently they are carved in stone or exotic woods. Part of their desirability is due to the fact that it would be extremely costly to duplicate the items today.

The current trend of preservation and recycling architectural elements has led to the establishment and growth of organized salvage operations who specialize in removal and resale of elements. Special auctions are now held to sell architectural elements from churches, mansions, office buildings, etc. Today's decorators often design an entire room around one architectural element, such as a Victorian marble bar or mural, or use several as key accent pieces.

References: J. L. Mott Iron Works, *Mott's Illustrated Catalog of Victorian Plumbing Fixtures For Bathrooms and Kitchens,* Dover Publications, 1987; Alan Robertson, *Architectural Antiques,* Chronicle Books, 1987; J. P. White's Pyghtle Works, Bedford, England, *Garden Furniture And Ornament,* Apollo Books, 1987.

Additional Listings: Stained Glass.

Atheniennes, 29½", 53½", cast iron, Neo–classical style, circular dished brazier, ornamented band of guilloche, slender tapering legs, hock capitals with lion masks, husks, and monopodia terminals, incurvate triangular plinth, maker's plate marked "W. Addis, Leicester Street, Leicester Sq, London," English registry mark within casting, Victorian, mid 19th C, pr **17,000.00**

Aviary, 60 x 144", iron and wirework, faceted onion dome top, rect vertical cage, arched sides, radiating spandrels, painted white, French **4,500.00**

Baluster, 18½", walnut and inlaid ivory, late Georgian, early 19th C **110.00**

Bird Bath, 43 x 84", cast iron, figural, two sections, putto with upraised arms supporting shell, octagonal basin on acanthus and cabochon cast baluster standard, painted green, inscribed "Salin Fondeur" **3,500.00**

Capital, 13½ x 12", white marble, carved scrolls above acanthus panels, weathered, Roman style . . . **130.00**

Ceiling, pressed copper, 31 x 5', elaborate floral dec **1,200.00**

Ceiling Cornice, 62', carved wood, cyma recta form, bas relief bean like fronds and organic motifs **800.00**

Cistern
  English, George III, third quarter 18th C, garden, lead, rect, molded

scrolling cartouche panels, armorial dec, initials "W C," date "1762," 34" w, 12" d, 28" h, pr **4,000.00**

Italian, 18th C, majolica, removable shell form cov, applied leafy cattails, pentagonal, inverted blue and manganese dolphin form spout, 16½" w, 21½" h **1,320.00**

Conservatory Gazebo, 92" h, rattan, semicircular latticed domed top, four supports, circular base inset with woven rush seat platform, Chinese style **500.00**

Conservatory Tub, Georgian style, coopered mahogany, oval, brass bound, 33½" w, 21" d, 9" h **2,600.00**

Door, Genoese Rococo, giltwood, mirrored, two pairs, animal paw footed swagged stool with profile sphinx, leafy strapwork, dragon and animal mask beneath partially draped winged female figure gazing at nude seated male, ribbon tied cornucopia, winged cherub in cresting, 28" w, 108" h, suite of four **181,500.00**

Door Hinges, cast iron, signature "WOR...," good, rusted surface, 20" l, pr **45.00**

Doorway, 126" h, exterior, pine, pitched projected cornice, fan light with incised dec, reeded pilasters, painted, Federal, Trenton, NJ, c1800, 1928 measured drawing **6,500.00**

Fanlight, 52 x 22", hinged, wooden fan shaped frame, mullioned glazed panels, beaded swags dec, Federal, New England, c1810 . . . . **3,200.00**

Festoon, Italian, late Baroque, carved giltwood, three parts, central arch with fruits, flowers, leaves, and pods, sides with pendant blossoms and leaves, 65" w, 36" h **10,000.00**

Figure
Doe, cast metal, ears pointing up, weathered rect plinth, American, late 19th C, 48" h **1,875.00**

Stag, cast iron, traces of pink and brown pigment, weathered rect plinth inscribed "Robert Wood & Co, Philadelphia," late 19th C, 4'6" l, 6'1" h **5,500.00**

Finial, Italian, Baroque, early 18th C, parcel gilt, iron, urn form, gadrooned, leafy berried knop, three applied fleur–de–lis, 7¾" h **1,200.00**

Fireplace, 40¾ x 39¼", brown marble, shaped shelf and apron, oval central cartouche, angled fluted stiles, orig brickwork, Napoleon III style, c1870 **1,350.00**

Garden Bench, cast iron
48" l, fern back, pierced seat, splayed legs, late 19th C **500.00**

58" l, reeded scroll ends, grotesque masks, animal leg form supports, painted, Regency **425.00**

Garden Urn, late Georgian, 19th C, cast lead, baluster form, scrolling S handles, griffin head terminals, raised molded socle base, 13" d, 23" h, pr . **4,000.00**

Gate, 34¾ x 82½", wrought iron, arched, tall tree with sprays of leafy branches, flowers, and tendrils, Continental, 19th C **725.00**

Mailbox, 44" h, painted metal, pagoda form, front and sides molded in relief of equestrian postmen, foliage cast baluster pedestal, rect base, painted dark green, Victorian **675.00**

Mantel, 59 x 42¼", veined white marble, serpentine shelf, molded edge, scalloped front, gilt bronze shell flanked by acanthus scrolls, and floral sprigs, scrolled jambs mounted with floral sprig pendants, Louis XV style, c1900 **6,500.00**

Mask, carved walnut, woman, plumed headdress, pierced bow behind suspending fruit and flower pendant swag, 15" h **385. 00**

Overdoor Panel
French, 18th C, oil on board, female mask above scallop, flanked by multicolored leafy scrolls, later stained oak frames, 31 x 23¼", pr **3,850.00**

Louis XVI, late 18th C, parcel black painted giltwood, rect bead carved molding, leafy roundels, center trophy symbolizing love, carved crossed quiver and flambeau, bow, hearts, and pair of lovebirds, 30" l, 20" h **1,760.00**

Pedestal, marble, sq, gray veined Carrara cornice, Roman composite capital, Verde Antico shaft, molded circular base raised on sq plinth, 34¼" h **2,750.00**

Pediment Ornament, eagle, 38" wingspan, wooden, hard carved, full feathers, gold paint, 19th C **450.00**

Pilasters, Neoclassical, carved and painted beechwood, upward carved sinewy fern tendrils and flowerheads, late 18th C, 6¾" w, 75" h, pr **1,540.00**

Radiator Grill, Art Deco, French, c1930, later oak top with canted corners, molded edge, pierced wrought iron grill, rounded rect grate, center rect bosses, 39" w, 45½" h **900.00**

Torus Molding, Louis XVI, Austrian, last quarter 18th C, parcel gilt, painted gray, center summer nosegay flanked by flowerheads, concentric leafy vines, 45" l, 11" h **1,200.00**

Transom Window, 9 x 30¾", leaded glass, finely plated, dusty pink and

deep purple wisteria blossoms, green
leaves, mottled lavender branches,
twilight ground, marked "Tiffany Stu-
dios," oak frame **2,500.00**
Wall Bracket, eagle, 31½" wingspan,
carved oak, late 19th C **600.00**
Wallpaper Border, French Gouache,
early 19th C, fragment, rect, burnt–
umber, crimson, and off white, stylized rosettes and leafy scrolls, 10 x
22", framed **120.00**

ART DECO

History: The Art Deco period was named for an
exhibition, "L'Exposition Internationale des Arts
Decoratifs," held in Paris in 1927. It is a later period
than Art Nouveau, but sometimes the two styles
overlap since they were closely related in time.

Art Deco designs are angular and of simple
lines. This was the period of skyscrapers, movie
idols, and the cubist works of Picasso and Legras.
Art Deco motifs were used for every conceivable
object being produced in the 1920s and 1930s,
including ceramics, furniture, glass, and metals,
not only in Europe, but in America as well.

References: Victor Arwas, *Glass: Art Nouveau
To Art Deco*, Rizzoli, 1977; Lillian Baker, *Art Nou-
veau & Art Deco Jewelry: An Identification & Value
Guide*, Collector Books, 1981; Bryan Catley, *Art
Deco And Other Figures*, Antique Collectors' Club;
Tony Fusco, *The Official Identification And Price
Guide To Art Deco*, House of Collectibles, 1988;
Mary Gaston, *Collector's Guide To Art Deco*, Col-
lector Books, 1989; Katherine Morrison McClinton,
Art Deco: A Guide For Collectors, reprint, Clark-
son N. Potter, 1986; Wolf Uecker, *Art Nouveau and
Art Deco Lamps and Candlesticks*, Abbeville
Press, 1986.

Additional Listings: Furniture and Jewelry.
Also check glass, pottery, and metal categories.

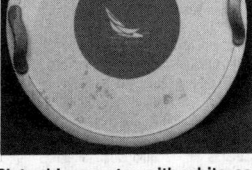

**Plate, blue center with white sailboat,
blue handles, marked "Sailboat, Japan," 11¾" d, $25.00.**

Ashtray
4" d, three rearing malachite green
horses, heavy glass dish, Czecho-
slovakia **150.00**
10" h figural nude holding tray over-
head, copper colored metal,
marked "Rembrandt" **185.00**
32" h, Jeeves, wooden, figural, butler **125.00**
Bookends, pr. figural
Nudes, 5 x 7", cast iron, full figure
nude woman kneeling, leg extended forward, body arched back,
bronze finish **70.00**
Race Horse and Jockey, white metal,
bronze finish **75.00**
Box, 2½ x 3½", porcelain, luster finish,
lady forms cov, skirt forms bowl,
marked "Japan" **40.00**
Candelabra, pr, 9¾" h, sterling silver,
three light, chamfered flaring central
shafts, circular base, engraved cipher
monogram, Elgin Silversmith Inc.,
c1945 . . . . **175.00**
Centerpiece, 24¼", triangular wrought
iron base, delicately fashioned blossoms and leaves, blue porcelain
Sevres bowl, French, c1925 . . . . . . **600.00**
Cigarette Case, 3 x 3½", hinged rect
case, silver, horizontal reeded bands
with 14K red and green gold bands,
medallion with engraved monogram,
Elgin, c1915–30 . . . . **300.00**
Clock
6½", alarm, blue mirrored glass and
chromed metal circular case, rect
chromium base, designed by Gilbert Rohde for Herman Miller Clock
Co, Zeeland, MI, c1932 . . . . **600.00**
8", lamp, two figural bronze washed
white metal ladies hold 6" d center
clock, glass lamp shade **150.00**
15¼" h, mantel, arched marble case,
black marble banding, gilt bronze
floral dec, four circular gilt bronze
feet, French, c1925 . . . . **800.00**
Cocktail Shaker, chrome, alternating
hammered and smooth horizontal
panels, dec black wood handle,
marked "Farber Bros" **20.00**
Cologne Bottle, acid treated glass,
enameled cobalt blue and yellow stylized flowers, large mushroom stopper **175.00**
Doorstop, 7 x 9", bronze, woman standing, holding out skirt of clinging gown **165.00**
Dresser Set, Coquille d'Oeuf, sq tray,
brush, mirror, cov box, make up tray,
black ground, eggshell linear dec, box
sgd "Jean Dunand," 6 pcs **3,250.00**
Figure
8¼" h, male dancer, purple costume,
female dancer in pale yellow and

Figure, Goldschneider, artist Lorenzl, marked "6211/344/10 72/700," 16¼" h, $1,500.00.

coral costume, sgd "C Werner, Hutschenreuther" 345.00
14⅛" h, bronze, young woman, standing on toes, arms extending high at sides, enameled jewel band dec on forehead, brown enameled hair, gray and red marble plinth base, inscribed "Grundmann," Germany 575.00
18⅛" h, man playing tennis, wood, chrome, and rubber, bald, wearing T shirt and baggy pants, flattened circular base, imp "SK" within a triangle, c1930 .... 1,100.00
Fish Bowl, 4½ x 8¼ x 9", pale amber glass, molded figural chalkware base, orig label 65.00
Furniture
    Buffet, American, burl walnut, 66" l, c1925 .... 1,000.00
    Chest of Drawers, 44½ x 35", parchment covered, rect top, three tapering drawers, pyramidal mirrored stiles, bracket feet, back branded "Quigley," French, c1925 .... 2,750.00
    Game Table, American, oak, hinged leaf, felt lined inner compartment, 48" l, 30" h 600.00
    Magazine Stand, 15" h, bronze, two centaurs 225.00
    Vanity, 43 x 23¾", rect top, two drawers, cupboard doors flanking recessed door, mirrored glass panels 425.00
Lamp, table
    14½" h, electroplated, bell form shade suspended over tapering cylindrical

shaft, circular base, inscribed "Perzel" 725.00
19¾", stylized young nude woman, drape suspended from waist, walking on toes, both hands behind her head holding rouge frosted glass fan shaped shade, Cubist style floral motif, green patina, stepped rect plinth base, pr 1,500.00
Perfume Bottle, 3¼ x 6½", cased cranberry glass, deep cut opposing triangles, high matching stopper 125.00
Powder Box, 5½", black glass base, silverplated cov, wolf hound finial 65.00

Sugar Shaker, cone shaped, black, dark green, light green, and white, marked "Bizarre/Clarice Cliff/Newport Pottery," 5¼" h, $125.00.

Vanity Set, lady's, traveling, 14 karat gold, engine turned striated design, center oval medallion on each pc engraved with cipher, 11¾" hand mirror, fitted blue leather carrying case, McChesney Co, Newark, NJ, retailed by Cartier, c1920–31, 18 pcs 6,500.00
Vase
    6" h, lacquer, spherical, black ground, gold, gray, and red fanciful animals, lacquered "Jean Dunand" 2,400.00
    6¼" h, sterling silver, oval, flared sides, applied bands of parcel gilt scalloping, detachable silverplate liner, Jeans E Puiforcat, Paris, c1940 .... 7,100.00
    6½" h, lacquer, spherical, black, red, and silver, vertical stripes and light-

ning bolts, silver gilting highlights, lacquered "Jean Dunand" **5,000.00**

9¼" h, silver, tapering, squat stems pierced with scrolling blossoms and cast fruit, circular spreading feet, La Paglia for International, c1935, pr   **1,200.00**

ART NOUVEAU

History Art Nouveau is the French term for the "new art" which had its beginning in the early 1890s and continued for the next 40 years. The flowing and sensuous female forms used in this period were popular in Europe and America. Among the most recognized artists of this period were Galle, Lalique, and Tiffany.

Art Nouveau can be identified by its flowing, sensuous lines, floral forms, insects, and the feminine form. These designs were incorporated on almost everything produced at that time, from art glass to furniture, silver, and personal objects.

References: Victor Arwas, *Glass: Art Nouveau To Art Deco*, Rizzoli, 1977; Lillian Baker, *Art Nouveau & Art Deco Jewelry: An Identification & Value Guide*, Collector Books, 1981; Giovanni Fanelli and Ezio Godoli, *Art Nouveau Postcards*, Rizzoli International Publication, Inc., 1987; Albert Christian Revi, *American Art Nouveau Glass*, reprint, Schiffer Publishing, 1981; Wolf Uecker, *Art Nouveau and Art Deco Lamps and Candlesticks*, Abbeville Press, 1986.

Additional Listings: Furniture and Jewelry. Also check glass, pottery, and metal categories.

Architectural Element, molded plaster, scrolled cartouche, high relief female head, flowing and intertwined whip-lash hair, jeweled forehead band,

Match Safe, sterling silver, woman with flowing hair and flowers, American, 1⅝ x 2½", $150.00.

imp "Agianni & Guerineau, Paris," c1900, 39½" l, 20" h **2,000.00**

Basket, 9½" l, sterling silver, monogram, marked "Frank W Smith Silver Co Inc. for Bailey, Banks, and Biddle Co" . .   **350.00**

Billiards Table, 121 x 66 x 32", walnut, leather playing surface, six leather pockets with rosewood borders, six flared sq form legs, geometric patterns of ebony and MOP, Brunswick, c1916 . . . .   **8,500.00**

Bust, porcelain

26" h, finely molded face, downcast eyes, long light brown hair looped into chignon, narrow mauve head band with oval irid glass jewel, gilt draped gown, narrow mauve straps set with matching jewel, incised "Montenave," Goldscheider seal molded in relief, imp "Reproduction/Reservee" and numerals **2,750.00**

28¼" h, Daphne, finely featured, garland in hair, self base, molded name **1,700.00**

Calling Card Tray, 4½ x 7", pewter, relief molded woman with flowing hair . . .   **75.00**

Centerpiece, 20½" h, 22" w, resilvered metal standard of female, three ruffled overshot rubena bowls **1,500.00**

Clock, 7¼", gilt bronze, enameled dial, tapering tall case, trailing fruiting vines repousse, marked "Susse Freres, Paris," c1900 . . . .   **575.00**

Figure

9½" h, nymph skipping rope, gilt bronze, rouge marble circular base, inscribed "A Marionnet," French, c1910 . . . .   **385.00**

14½" h, girl, gilt bronze, long skirt, low girdle and breastplates over mesh bodice, draped beaded necklace, ivory head, arms, and feet, coved circular gray–green and black marble base, incised "A Gori" **3,200.00**

Fireplace Tools, poker, shovel, and broom on stand, silver alloy, looped handles terminating in wavy tendrils, marked "S Hart," 40" h **2,750.00**

Furniture

Dining Suite, c1900, walnut, 96" h buffet, 55" h credenza, 28¾" h table, and four side chairs, buffet with arched crest over rounded rect beveled glass mirror, flanked by leaf and pod sprigs, two glazed cabinet doors, lower section with molded edges, two drawers with berried gilt bronze pulls, two cupboard doors with arched panels and central leaf carved supports, stiles continuing to form slightly splayed feet, 7 pcs **2,475.00**

Etagere, Galle, c1900, marquetry, inlay depicting life cycle of plant form, back panel cut with outline and inlaid with large cluster of cow parsley, second cluster inlaid below, shaped rect burled top, two small parsley shaped flanking platforms, stalk form support, three rect shelves, molded legs joined by pierced carved scrolling leafy vine, 36" w, 62½" h **13,200.00**

Fireplace Screen, Majorelle, c1900, carved walnut, shaped rect, arching open crest, central V form of intersecting wood bands of carved clematis vines, two orig ivory and white silk upholstered panels, molded downswept supports, 29" l, 42" h **2,200.00**

Mirror, silverplate, German, rect, easel back, figure of woman in long flowing gown, cast torso on right, holding left arm to her hair, right hand extended to flowering tree, train extending along base, 10½" w, 14½" h **1,980.00**

Parlor Suite, Majorelle style, escargot pattern, carved mahogany, 55" l settee, two armchairs, two side chairs, molded and dipped crestrails, carved and pierced stiles, rect upholstered seats, cabriole legs, 5 pcs **4,125.00**

Table
Occasional, French
Oak and marquetry, Galle, two tiers, shaped rect top, conforming undertier, inlaid thistles, splayed fluted supports, 21" w, 24" h **1,200.00**
Walnut and marquetry, shaped circular top, reeded stepped edge enclosing scene of magpie perching among oak leaves and acorns, four waisted reeded clustered tapering supports, 24¼" d, 22" h . . **800.00**
Side, nest of four, rect top, marquetry, pierced organic trestle supports, shaped stretcher, marquetry includes landscape, seascape, three cats, and flowers, 22½" l, 27½" h **2,250.00**

Garniture, sterling silver, Iris pattern, Shreve & Co, San Francisco, c1909, 15½" cov vase, two flanking vases, inverted pyriform bodies, domed circular feet, applied chased bearded iris dec, bell mark, 3 pcs **2,475.00**

Lamp, table
20½" h, 10" d shade, peacock form, gilt brass and parcel gilt, fourteen cabochon shaped emerald green foil with cobalt blue enameled center jeweled eyes, beak clasping gilt ring suspending parasol shaped etched glass shade, ext. enameled with blue and green gilt peacock feathers **4,675.00**

22¼" h, patinated metal, figural, maiden wearing flowing gown terminating in inverted lily blossom, full blown lily behind head, upheld arms supporting single lily lights, green patina, inscribed "J Causse 1900" **825.00**

29" h, patinated metal, figural, slender girl with butterfly wings, holding arching branch with applied enameled green leaves, two stems ending in leaf form light sockets, hanging frosted green grape cluster shades, green and brown patina, marble base, inscribed "J Causse," applied metal tag imp "Papillon/par J Causse (Statuaire)" **1,210.00**

Magnifying Glass, 2⅛" d glass, 6¼" l, sterling silver hollow handle, scrolled leaves dec, marked "Blackinton, 1904" **110.00**

Match Holder, 5" h, painted bronze, figural, imp marks, Franz Bergman, c1910 . . . . **475.00**

Pitcher, 14½" h, glass, silverplated mountings, cylindrical body, bulbous base, hinged lid, scrolled handle, green leaves, fuchsia blossoms, and band of iris, four scroll feet **330.00**

Plaque, 13½" w, 25⅛" h, earthenware, rect, molded, maiden in profile, garland of blossoms and berries in hair, large blossom and cluster on left, earth tones, designer sgd "Lamassi," Goldscheinder mark, c1900 . . . . . . **1,000.00**

Postal Scale, 4¼" h, desk type, sterling silver, cased, monogram, marked "Shreve & Co," c1900 . . . . **250.00**

Textile, throw pillow, 16½" sq, dark blue velour, grape appliques, scrolled plum stitched pattern, self welt, pr **250.00**

Tray, 16¼ x 26½", bowed rect, raised gallery, marquetry, inlaid scene of silhouetted castle, fruiting grapevine cascading in foreground, spread winged crane form handles, signed "Galle" in marquetry **500.00**

Vase
6" h, bronze, cast cherub faces in swirling sea, brown patina, gilded faces, artist sgd "Jules Meliedon 1896, Louchet" **315.00**
9⅛" h, glass, gold luster, threaded, applied dec, feather design, bogus Tiffany signature **1,200.00**

14¼" h, pottery, cylindrical, flared bulbous base, low circular foot, relief molded hollyhocks and leaves, white matte glaze, translucent green glazed int., inscribed monogram, marked "L. C. Tiffany Studios," c1900–28 . . . . **3,575.00**

14½" h, glass, jack in the pulpit, amethyst and gold luster, feather veining **210.00**

Wall Shelf, 21" l, demilune, fruitwood, pale gray glass overlaid in shades of purple, meandering river and forest scene, shaped demilune shelf and bracket, signed "Jacques Gruber" in cameo, c1900 . . . . **2,250.00**

ART PEWTER

History: Pewter objects produced during the Art Nouveau, Arts and Crafts, and Art Deco periods are gaining in popularity. These mostly utilitarian objects, e.g., tea sets, trays, and bowls, were elaborately decorated and produced in the Jugendstil manner by German firms, such as Kayserzinn, and Austrian companies, such as Orivit. In England, Liberty and Company marketed Tudric Pewter, which often had a hammered surface and was embellished with enameling or semi-precious stones. Most pieces of art pewter contain the maker's mark.

FIEN ZINN

Bowl, 9½", large open rim handles, marked "S Rothhan, Fien Zinn" . . . **50.00**
Pitcher, 12", marked "Wien, Fien Zinn" **85.00**

JUGENDSTIL

Tray, 9" l, 8½" w, shaped triangular harp form, relief dec, standing figure of woman with one bare arm resting on top of harp, diaphanous flowing gown swirling at feet, two slender branches form handles, leaves spreading across dished surface, imp "B" and "OX" **335.00**

KAYSERZINN

Candy Dish, leaf shape, marked #4065 **100.00**
Chamberstick, Art Nouveau floral dec . **75.00**
Vase, 7¾" h, wheat and butterflies dec, marked #4310 . . . . **125.00**

ORVIT

Pitcher, claret type, green glass insert, Art Nouveau vines and floral dec . . **90.00**
Wine Cooler, 8 x 10½", floral dec **275.00**

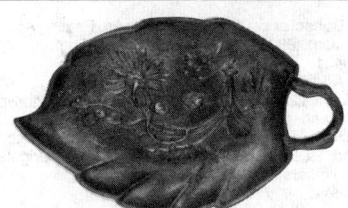

Kayserzinn, candy dish, emb daisies and foliage, marked "4065," $100.00.

TUDRIC

Centerpiece, 9¾" d, two handles, circular dish, raised base, sinuous blossoms and stems, inscribed, stamped "Tudric," c1900 . . . . **500.00**
Clock, 5½" h, desk, rect, repousse winding vines and berries dec, Arabic numerals enameled in red, green, and blue, stamped "Tudric" **350.00**
Vase, 6" h, floriform, double tendril handles, small bulbous bowl, slender tapering stem, spreading circular foot, imp "English Pewter/029/2," designed for Liberty, c1903 . . . . **825.00**

URANIA

Candelabra, 13¼" h, flattened oval pierced standard, low relief casting, linear motifs, flanking branches at right angles, conical cup, tapering cylindrical nozzle, imp "Urania/Hutton, Sheffield/1376," pr **550.00**

ART POTTERY (GENERAL)

History: The period of art pottery reached its zenith in the late 19th and early 20th century. Over a hundred companies produced individually designed and often decorated wares which served a utilitarian as well as an aesthetic purpose. Artists moved about from company to company, some forming their own firms.

Quality of design, beauty in glazes, and condition are the keys in buying art pottery. This category covers companies not found elsewhere in the guide.

References: Paul Evans, *Art Pottery of the United States, Second Edition,* Feingold & Lewis Publishing Co., 1987; Lucile Henzke, *Art Pottery of America,* Schiffer Publishing; Ralph and Terry Kovel, *The Kovels' Collector's Guide to American Art Pottery,* Crown Publishers, Inc., 1974.

Periodical: *Arts & Crafts Quarterly,* Station E, P.O. Box 3592, Trenton, NJ 08629.

Collectors' Club: American Art Pottery Association, 9825 Upton Circle, Bloomington, MN 55431.

Additional Listings: See Cambridge, Clewell, Clifton, Cowan, Dedham, Fulper, Grueby, Jugtown, Marblehead, Moorcroft, Newcomb, North Dakota School of Mines, Ohr, Owens, Paul Revere, Peters and Reed, Rookwood, Roseville, Van Briggle, Weller, and Zanesville.

Swastika Keramics, pitcher, copper luster, green leaves, 10¼″ h, $375.00.

Arc-En-Ciel, (1903–05), Zanesville, OH
  Vase
    10″, waisted, poppy relief, gold irid   **250.00**
    10½″, tree bark body, purple and gold irid luster **200.00**
Arequipa, (1911 to 1918), Fairfax, CA
  Bowl
    1½ x 4¾″, octagonal, gray matte, die mark **125.00**
    9 x 4¾″, flower and leaf mold, black and white **150.00**
  Vase
    3¼″, carved leaf and berries, purple matte, imp mark **380.00**
    5⅝″, irregular green matte glaze . **240.00**
Batchelder, center bowl, 18½″ d, wide everted rim, int. glazed in pale green, purple ext., inscribed "5 EA Batchelder/Kinneloa/Kiln" **625.00**
California Faience
  Bookends, pr, eagle, blue matte . . . **675.00**
  Bowl, 10½″, black matte, turquoise int., frog, pedestal base **150.00**
  Box, 1½ x 4½ x 3½″, raspberry tile top, cloisonne dec **100.00**
  Potpourri Jar, 4½″ h, Oriental shape, yellow matte, incised mark **225.00**

Vase
  6½″, red glossy glaze, large stylized carved leaves **180.00**
  10″, baluster, salmon ground, tan drip dec **200.00**
Chelsea Keramic Art Works (1872–89), Chelsea, MA
  Pitcher, 8″, geometric rim and handle motif, hp birds, three line mark . . **285.00**
  Vase, 4½″, octagonal, elephant head handles, brown flambe **375.00**
Kenton Hills ((1939–42), Erlanger, KY
  Ashtray, 7 x 6½″, stylized horse head shape, turquoise glossy glaze, marked **45.00**
  Bowl, 3½″, olive glossy glaze **100.00**
  Vase, 7 x 6″, brown irid glaze **120.00**
Massier, Clement, c1900, vase, 6″ h, cylindrical, sq mouth, outwardly tapering body, four applied angular strap handles at base, clusters of irid voilet and gilt lilies radiating above each handle, scattered flowers on shaded, streaked gilt and voilet irid ground, inscribed "C. M./Golfe Juan/ A. M." **250.00**

Pewabic Pottery, vase, irid, high glaze, purple and turquoise, orig paper label, 5″ d, 4″ h, $265.00.

Pewabic Pottery (1903–61), Detroit, MI
  Plate, 9″, hp, cottage scene border . **150.00**
  Tile, 2¾″, floral nosegay dec, blue luster, matte white ground **65.00**
  Vase, 5 x 4″, high glaze, purple and turquoise, orig paper label **265.00**
Pisgah Forest (1913–present), Mt. Pisgah, NC
  Creamer, blue, pink int. **15.00**

Cup and Saucer, yellow and pink .. **25.00**
Pitcher
  6½", green **55.00**
  9", yellow and pink, 1956 ...... **120.00**
Urn, 4¼", white crackle, pink int.,
  1936 .... **35.00**
Vase
  7", turquoise, 1949 .... **85.00**
  10", bulbous, green mottled glaze,
  1928 .... **128.00**
Swastika Keramos (1902–04), Owens
China Co., Minerva, OH
Ewer, 11", green grapes, copper
  leaves, gold ground, wide base .. **200.00**
Vase, 7½", round body, cone top,
  large red luster flower, gold ground **180.00**

Teco (1886–30), Terra Cotta, IL
Ash Bowl, frog overlooking 4½" bowl,
  cream matte finish, sgd **200.00**
Vase
  Copper green glaze, 12" h, ovoid
  sectioned into four swelling
  molded panels, border of six horizontal rings, short molded foot,
  designed by M G Garden, c1903,
  base incised "Teco" vertically
  twice **5,500.00**
  Matte green, #262, designed by
  M P White **17,100.00**
Wall Pocket, 14½", green, deep gray
  spatter, marked **175.00**

Vance/Avon Pottery (1892–1908), Til-
tonville, OH and Wheeling, WV
Basket, 6½", gourd shape, vine handle, sgd "R Lorber" **65.00**
Pitcher, 10¼", tankard shape, multicolored troubadour dec, marked
  "Wheeling" **100.00**

Voklmar Pottery (1882–1903), Tremont,
NY
Charger, 12" d, Washington's Headquarters, Newburgh, emb sgd ... **100.00**
Tile, 9 x 5", hp, Yale College scene,
  set of 2 .... **200.00**
Vase, 8 12", thickly textured variegated green glaze, medium green
  underglaze, thick matte gunmetal
  gray spots, marked **300.00**

Walrath Pottery (1900–1920), Rochester, NY
Bowl, 4¾", green florals, brown
  ground **225.00**
Figure, 6", lion, seated, one paw
  lifted, 1913 .... **250.00**
Mug, 6", brown florals, green matte
  ground, sgd "RB," incised mark .. **250.00**
Pitcher, 10", two colored stylized floral
  band, brown matte **250.00**
Vase, 4¾", cylindrical, hp buds and
  leaves, green ground **750.00**

ARTS AND CRAFTS MOVEMENT

History: The Arts and Crafts Movement in
American decorative arts took place between 1895
and 1920. Leading proponents of the movement
were Elbert Hubbard and his Roycrofters, the
brothers Stickley, Frank Lloyd Wright, Charles and
Henry Greene, George Niedecken, and Lucia and
Arthur Mathews.

The movement was marked by individualistic
design (although the movement was national in
scope) and re-emphasis on handcraftsmanship
and appearance. A reform of industrial society was
part of the long range goal. Most pieces of furniture
favored a rectilinear approach and were made of
oak.

References: Steven Adams, *The Arts & Crafts
Movement*, Chartwell Books, Inc., 1987; David M.
Cathers, *Furniture Of The American Arts and
Crafts Movement*, New American Library, 1981;
Paul Evans, *Art Pottery Of The United States, 2nd
Edition*, Feingold & Lewis Publishing, 1987; Mal-
colm Haslam, *Collector's Style Guide: Arts and
Crafts*, Ballantine Books, 1988; Bruce Johnson,
*The Official Identification And Price Guide To Arts
And Crafts*, House of Collectibles, 1988; Wendy
Kaplan, *The Art That Is Life: The Arts And Crafts
Movement In America 1875-1920*, Boston Mu-
seum of Fine Arts, 1987; Coy L. Ludwig. *The Arts
and Crafts Movement In New York State, 1890s–
1920s*, Gallery Association of New York State,
1983.

Periodical: *Arts and Crafts Quarterly*, Station E,
P.O. Box 3592, Trenton, NJ 08629.

Museum: Museum of Modern Art, New York,
NY.

Additional Listings: Roycroft Items, Stickleys,
and art pottery categories.

Ashtray, 6¼" d, round, puffed out rim,
  hammered copper, aged patina,
  marked "Benedict Studios" **180.00**

**Foot Stool, leather cover, Roycroft, 10
x 15", $225.00.**

Candlestick, brass, candle nozzle with flared collar, slender standard, flared foot, Jessie Preston, c1908 . . . . **3,850.00**

Cocktail Service, silver plated, 13″ h cocktail shaker, thirteen 5¼″ h goblets, 23¾″ l tray, peened finish, pierced handles, marked "Meriden Silver Plate Co (For International), Meriden, CT" **250.00**

Cocktail Tray, rect, silver, hammered surface, pierced ends for handles, R Wallace & Sons, Wallingford, CT . . . **2,200.00**

Dinner Service, silver, hammered surface, applied edges, cursive monogram, Durgin for Gorham, Concord, NH, c1906

  Bread and Butter Plates, 6⅞″ d, set of twelve **1,870.00**

  Gravy Boat, 8¼ x 4″ **300.00**

  Ramekins, 5″ d, 1¾″ h, silver frames and matching saucers, twenty four porcelain gilt edged liners marked "Lenox," set of twelve **1,760.00**

  Service Plates, 11″ d, set of twelve . **7,150.00**

  Serving Dish, 11½″ d, tripartite divided, reversible cover with concave center well **1,000.00**

  Soup Frames, 5¾″ d, 2¾″ h, twenty two porcelain gilt edged liners marked "Lenox," set of twelve . . . **2,000.00**

  Teacup Frames and Saucers, twenty one porcelain gilt edged liners marked "Lenox," set of twelve . . . **1,875.00**

  Wine Goblet, 6½″ h, gilt int., set of twelve **1,775.00**

Furniture

  Chair, dining, Frank Lloyd Wright, designed for Ray Evans Chicago House **26,400.00**

  Stand, oak, sq overhanging top, four tapered legs, keyed tenons, four shelves bracketed on either side by vertical slats attached to wood rivets, Mission, American, 33¼″ h . . **1,000.00**

  Table, oak, copper top, low, eight angled legs, vertical stretchers, arched aprons, Mission, American, 32¼″ d, 22″ h **500.00**

Lamp, 16″ h, 13″ d shade, mica, patinated brass standard, Dirk Van Erp . . **8,800.00**

Lamp Shade, 17½″ d, 7½″ h, hammered copper frame, three shaped mica panels, central aperture with cut and slightly everted edge, three riveted vertical supports spade shaped at top, molded lower rim, dark brown patination **1,550.00**

Lamp Base, 16″ h, ceramic, ovoid body, glaze simulates darkened copper overlaid with brass, three oval panels extending from shoulder to base, large scrolled dec devices, top

pierced by cylindrical patinated metal shaft with two sockets, orig paper label imprinted "Koven Mfg Co, San Francisco" **300.00**

Salad Serving Set, fork and spoon, silver, Peacock pattern, applied raised central section with panel of champleve enameled blue and green peacock feather, pierced sides, peened surface, marker B enclosed by C, c1910, 6 ozs, 8 dwts **825.00**

Serving Dish, 16¼″ l, 11″ d, 2¾″ h, silver plated, hand wrought, rect, deep bowl, flaring horizontal border, four ivory feet, monogrammed, slightly peened finish, marked "Dirk Van Erp, San Francisco," c1929–30 . . . . **2,475.00**

Smoking Stand, 30½″ h, four slender cylindrical shafts riveted to circular convex base, circular dish top, four scalloped cigarette rests, hammered copper, imp windmill mark above closed box enclosing "Dirk Van Erp" **715.00**

Tray, 11¾″ d, circular, sloping cavetto, narrow flat border, hammered copper, imp windmill mark above broken box enclosing "Dirk Van Erp" and "San Francisco" **275.00**

Vase

  9¾″ h, shouldered ovoid, wide mouth, hammered copper, imp windmill mark above broken box enclosing "Dirk Van Erp" and "San Francisco" **1,000.00**

  21″ h, ovoid, wide mouth, copper, hammered int. **825.00**

AUSTRIAN WARE

History: Over a hundred potteries were located in the Austro-Hungarian Empire in the late 19th and early 20th centuries. Although Carlsbad was the center of the industry, the factories spread as far as modern day Czechoslovakia.

Many of the factories were either owned or supported by Americans; hence, their wares were produced mainly for export to the United States. Responding to the 1891 law that imported products must be marked as to country of origin, many wares do not have a factory mark, but only the word "Austrian."

Reference: Susan and Al Bagdade, *Warman's English & Continental Pottery & Porcelain, 1st Edition,* Warman Publishing Co., Inc., 1987.

Additional Listings: Amphora, Carlsbad, Royal Dux, and Royal Vienna.

Biscuit Jar, cov, 7″, hp, white and pink roses, green ground **90.00**

Book Cover, brass, reserved and deli-

Figure, Arab warrior and horse, impressed "Amphora, Teplitz," 10″ h, 9¾″ oval base, $385.00.

cately tooled, sinous blossoms,
stems, and pendant hearts **800.00**
Bowl, 10½″, glazed pottery, gnarled
branch section, grape bunch at one
end, incised "Austria, 8967," c1900 .   **300.00**
Cactus Holder, 6½″ h, glazed pottery,
molded figure of half kneeling man
grasping sq container with right arm,
knee resting on base, canted sq
holder on top of head, held by left
hand, blue clothes, relief molded zig
zag stripes, raspberry and chartreuse
spots, mottled sq blue and red base,
imp "Wiener Werkstatte, Made in
Austria," artist's cipher of Erna Ko-
priva, c1925 . . . .   **500.00**
Candelabrum, 11¼″ h, hammered
brass, seven light, curved and angled
arms supporting frilled drip pans and
candle nozzles, spherical standard,
domed foot, stamped maker's mark,
Secession style **2,750.00**
Celery Tray, 12″, scalloped border, pink
roses, green leaves, gold trim **45.00**
Compote, 9″ d, irid, metal mounts **175.00**
Creamer, moose head **12.00**
Decanter, 19¼″ h, glass, cranberry,
gold dec, applied porcelain flowers,
steeple stopper, pr **275.00**
Dish, 8¼″ h, brass, deep, conical, fitted
cov with stylized figure and begging
dog finial, green patina **550.00**
Ewer
8¾″, glass, cranberry, heavy gold and
floral dec **90.00**
10¾″, gold and floral dec, cobalt blue
ground **75.00**
Figure, 8″ h, Oriental subduing rearing
horse, painted blue, green, red, and
yellow, ovoid socle, crazed clear

glaze, imp "WW560," Weiner Werk-
statte, attributed to Susi Singer **600.00**
Lamp, 20½″ h, figural, bronze, turbaned
slaver showing nude female, standing
on Turkish carpet, musical instruments hanging from masts, Moorish
lantern, stamped maker's mark and
"Made in Austria" **1,750.00**
Pitcher
5½″, floral **15.00**
13½″, hp floral dec, gold dragon han-
dle, marked "Hapsburg Austria" . .   **225.00**
Plate
8″, purple edge, gold trim, floral rim
dec, gold floral center, marked "OE
& G," "Royal" in wreath, set of 6 .   **50.00**
9¼″, game bird, pearl luster border,
marked "MZ Austria," set of 6 . . .   **75.00**
9½″, pink and yellow roses, green
leaves in center and border, gold
scalloped rim, marked "MZ Aus-
tria," set of 6 . . . .   **75.00**
Powder Box, 3 × 4″, yellow flowers,
green leaves, white ground, marked
"O & E G" **35.00**
Relish Dish, 9 × 6″, oval, pink flowers,
white ground, gold trim, marked "MZ
Austria" **65.00**
Stamp Box, 4¼″ × 3⅛″, cov, ftd, 2
compartments, hp roses, gold trim .   **35.00**
Sugar Shaker, yellow flowers, green
leaves, pale yellow ground, gold
metal top **40.00**
Tureen, cov, floral dec, marked "O & E
G" **60.00**
Vase
6″, handles, woman in portrait med-
allion **60.00**
7″, enamel, bulbous, four handled, Art
Deco type poppy dec, matte
ground **65.00**
8½″, irid, waisted with four dimpled
sides, blue striations dec **625.00**
9″ h, glass, Secession, attributed to
Otto Prutscher, conical, undulating,
clear, honeycomb dec, black
enamel highlights **450.00**
14″, gold and green, transfer scene
of classical ladies, beehive mark .   **125.00**

AUTOGRAPHS

History: Autographs occur in a wide variety of
formats—letters, documents, photographs, books,
and cards, etc. Most collectors focus on a particular person, country, or category, e.g. signers of
the Declaration of Independence.

The condition and content of letters and documents bears significantly on value. Collectors
should know their source since forgeries abound,
and copy machines compound the problem. Fur-

ther, some signatures of recent presidents and movie stars are done by machine rather than by the persons themselves. A good dealer or advanced collector can help one spot the differences.

The leading auction sources for autographs are Swann Galleries, Sotheby's, and Christie's, all located in New York City.

References: Mary A. Benjamin, *Autographs: A Key To Collecting,* reprint, Dover, 1986; Bob Benett, *A Collector's Guide To Autographs With Prices,* Wallace-Homestead, 1986; Charles Hamilton, *American Autographs,* University of Oklahoma Press, 1983; George Sanders, Helen Sanders, Ralph Roberts, *Collector's Guide To Autographs,* Wallace-Homestead, 1990; George Sanders, Helen Sanders, Ralph Roberts, *The Price Guide To Autographs,* Wallace-Homestead, 1988.

Collectors' Clubs: Manuscript Society, 350 Niagara Street, Burbank, CA 95105; Universal Autograph Collectors Club, P.O. Box 6181, Washington, DC 20044-6181.

Additional Listings: See *Warman's Americana & Collectibles* for more examples.

The following abbreviations denote type of autograph material and their sizes.

ADS	Autograph Document Signed
ALS	Autograph Letter Signed
AQS	Autograph Quotation Signed
CS	Card Signed
DS	Document Signed
LS	Letter Signed
PS	Photograph Signed
TLS	Typed Letter Signed

Sizes (approximate):

Folio	12 x 16 inches
4to	8 x 10 inches
8vo	5 x 7 inches
12mo	3 x 5 inches

COLONIAL AMERICA

Ellsworth, Oliver, pay order to Capt. William Coit, "for his company last year in the Colony's service and for losses of clothing and arms they sustained in action at Bunker Hill" sgd August 7, 1776 . . . . **950.00**

Greene, General Nathaneal, ALS, 2 pgs, integral leaf, 4to, Camp Springfield, June 1779, to Col James Abale, orders supplies to be sent, mentions General Washington, sgd "Nath Greene Qmr," framed **1,600.00**

Gridley, Richard, Revolutionary War General, order to James Fitter, Pay Office, Horse Guards, for payment of 42 sterling to Jonathan and John Amory, sgd Boston, June 25, 1771 . **450.00**

Hamilton, Alexander, ALS, 1 pg, 4to, Philadelphia, August 1794, requesting tents and camp equipage to be sent to New Jersey Militia **850.00**

Hancock, John, PDS, 1 pg, oblong 4to, Watertown, November 1775, sgd by Hancock and Charles Thomson, Secretary, appointing Edward Wigglesworth colonel in Continental Army, worn along folds, repaired on verso . **3,000.00**

Ingersoll, Jared, signer of Constitution, ALS, regarding disposition of Mr. Taylor's claim against Callender's estate, Philadelphia, October 13, 1788 . . . . **875.00**

Otis, James, orator and patriot, DS, appointing James Warren as sheriff of Plymouth County, over 100 words . . **325.00**

Washington, George
   ALS, 1 page, folio, Headquarters, Middle Brook, 19 March 1779, to Colonel Wiggelsworth, re resignation, strengthened along folds, copy of 1 page 8vo resolution, sgd by Chas Thompson (sic) **9,000.00**
   DS, 1 page, oblong 4to, June 1894, countersigned by Thomas Jefferson, ship's paper for Brig Eagle, passepartout frame **5,250.00**

EUROPEAN

Charles X, King of France, DS, folio, sgd as Comte d'Artois, conferring decoration, Paris, September, 1816, creased, foxed along folds **100.00**

Duke of Wellington, DS, appointing Samuel Paul Baghott a Lieutenatnt in the 80th Regiment of Foot for Staffordshire Volunteers, October 9, 1821 **675.00**

Francisco, Franco, PS, bust length, military dress, inscribed on mat, 14 x 10" **325.00**

Hitler, Adolf, PS, standing with Pres Paul Von Hindenburg and Franz Von Papen, sgd on mat by each, c1933, 18 x 22" **7,000.00**

Hugo, Victor, French poet, ALS, expressing regrets that he is too busy to help Madame Reynaud but expressing the hope that General Lamoriciere will grant her request, written and sgd September 13, 1848 . . **265.00**

Lafayette, Gilbert Marquis De, ALS, 1 page, 4to, Paris, January, 1820, sgd "Lafayette," discusses news from Spain, framed with engraved portrait **550.00**

Louis XV, King of France, military commission appointing d'Bellisle de Vieleastel a Captain in the "Regiment Dauphine," August 1, 1743 . . . . **385.00**

Mussolini, Benito, PS, bust length, mil-

itary uniform, sgd on mat "Benito
Mussolini Roma 23 Mayo 1928–VI,"
12 x 8" **1,700.00**
Napoleon Bonaparte, DS, names Jean
C. Lorine a Knight of the Empire, seal
attached, rolled in a tin sleeve, April
2, 1812 . . . . **2,875.00**
Vespucci, Amerigo, manuscript, 5 pgs,
8vo, stiff paper wrappers, Nuremberg,
c1505 . . . . **1,300.00**

GENERAL

Barnum, P. T., check, payable to S. H.
Hurd for $500, October 17, 1865 . . . **390.00**
Bell, Alexander Graham, 3½" sq mag-
azine picture, sgd lower white margin **275.00**
Edison, Thomas, check, to Walter N.
Archer, January 16, 1929 . . . . **425.00**
Hopkinson, Joseph, ANS, to the Mayor
of Philadelphia John Scott, introduc-
ing J. W. Audubon, September 30,
1833 . . . . **390.00**
Lewis, Meriweather, promissory note,
"No. 6," 8vo, Gov of Louisiana Terri-
tory, drawn by hand payable to
Thomas Prather, Louisville, February
15, 1808 . . . . **1,100.00**
Montezuma, Carlos, PS, sgd on back
with an attached signature of the front **175.00**
North, Luther, Indian fighter and friend
of Buffalo Bill, ALS, 2 pgs, 4to, Columbus, NE, March 22, 1931, to
Agnes Urbank giving his ancestry and
mentioning Winnebago Indians **240.00**
Patton, George, ALS, to Lt. Gen. John
C. H. Lee, remarks I had the honor of
being among the first people to cross
over the Mainz railway bridge, also
recommends Col. Harry Hulen for the
Legion of Merit or a DSM, April 15,
1945 . . . . **1,175.00**
Penn, William, DS, 12¼ x 15", vellum,
August 12, 1705, wax seal in orig
case, land grant in Philadelphia to
Francis and Elizabeth Fox **810.00**
Pope Pius X, PS, silver print photograph
showing him seated, also sgd by
Archbishop of Balisa and the Bishop
of Sao Paulo, 1906 . . . . **1,275.00**
Rockwell, Norman, ALS, to John D.
Lippy Jr., answering a request for as-
sistance in locating a Rockwell pic-
ture, envelope **360.00**
Warhol, Andy, black and white glossy
postcard, boldly sgd in felt tip **40.00**

LITERATURE

Cooper, James Fenimore, check, #316,
Copperstown, filled in and sgd, No-
vember 19th, 1839 . . . . **260.00**

Doyle, Arthur Conan, ALS, Haslemere,
May 5, 1904, to Mackenzie Bell about
Charles Martineau, framed with en-
velope **175.00**
Fitzgerald, F. Scott, CS, to Paul Clute
about his poems **250.00**
Grey, Zane, State of Oregon hunting li-
cense, dated September 2, 1925,
signed in three places **890.00**
Longfellow, Henry Wadsworth, ALS, to
Cary & Hart, Philadelphia, concerning
the details of publication of various of
his works, dated December 3, 1844 **475.00**
O'Neill, Eugene, book *Dynamo*, 1929,
limited edition of 775, No. 331, bound
in blue-green vellum, gilt lettering,
purple board box **175.00**
Torrence, Ridgley, ALS, May 6, 1922,
mentions "fortunate experience" in
Miami, etc **35.00**
Twain, Mark, CS, framed with photo-
graph **200.00**

MUSIC

Carmichael, Hoagy, AMQS, 8vo, 1 pg,
no date, three bars from "Stardust" . **150.00**
Crosby, Bing, TLS, "Bing," 4to, 2 pgs,
November 21, 1960, to Charles
Graves in London, personal and men-
tions gold **45.00**
Gershwin, George, 4to sheet music,
Rhapsody in Blue for Jazz Band and
Piano, orig color wrappers, inscribed
on title page, NY, 1925 . . . . **4,600.00**
Farrar, Geraldine, PS, 4to, sepia **50.00**
Presley, Elvis, PS, 4to, bust pose in
white sequined costume holding mi-
crophone performing last time in Las
Vagas, signed **500.00**
Salieri, Antonio, orig autograph musical
manuscript, oblong folio, 2 pgs, titled
"Il maestro e la scolaro" **950.00**
Strauss, Richard, AQS, signature and 2
bars of music on approx 6 x 5" blank
side of Excelsior Hotel-Italie Florence **1,000.00**

PRESIDENTIAL, AMERICAN

Buchanan, James, four language ship's
paper, for Francis E. Strawburg, master of the ship "Congress" bound for
the Pacific Ocean, sgd August 2,
1858 . . . . **1,275.00**
Eisenhower, Dwight D., ALS, White
House letterhead to the Overseas
Press Club of America, March 25,
1958 . . . . **685.00**
Grant, Ulysses S, DS, 1 pg, 4to, Wash-
ington, September 1871, order to affix
seal on pardon for John Wiggins,
framed with engraved portrait **400.00**

Harding, Warren G, and Herbert Hoover, DS, 4to, 1 leaf from register of Ritz–Carlton Hotel, Atlantic City, 1921, sgd by Harding, who also signs for Mrs. Harding, Hoover, and George B Christian, Jr., framed with newspaper clippings 225.00

Hoover, Herbert

PS, seated, surrounded by eleven cabinet members, sgd by all, 9½ x 6½" 500.00

TLS, 1 page, 4to, Washington, January 1925, sgd as Secretary of Commerce, slightly browned, framed . 100.00

Jefferson, Thomas, ALS, written to Mrs. Eleanor Worthington acknowledging the receipt of the seeds of the Serpentine Cucumber and the debts of an old friendship, April 22, 1826 ... 2,950.00

Lincoln, Abraham, ADS, 1 page, folio, vellum, paper seal, Washington, March 1863, appointing Winslow L. Kidder Assistant Adjutant General of Volunteers, countersigned by Edwin M. Stanton, small tears on edges, laid down, framed with engraved portrait 3,200.00

Madison, James, check, Office of Pay and Deposit of the Bank of Columbia, Washington, March 27, 1816 .... 1,585.00

Monroe, James, DS, 13 x 8", 1819, land grant "Chillicothe" with seal intact .. 395.00

Pierce, Franklin, appointment of Edwin C. Bailey as Deputy Postmaster at Boston, September 23, 1853, seal attached 650.00

Roosevelt, Eleanor, PS, full length, evening gown, by Harris & Ewing, 6 x 9", signed on image 250.00

Roosevelt, Franklin D, TLS, 1 page, 4to, White House, Washington, December 1944, framed with photograph 325.00

Taft, William, H. ALS, appointing Rear Admiral Charles F. Stokes a member and vice-chairman of the War Relief Board of the American National Red Cross, dated December 11, 1912 .. 450.00

Wilson, Woodrow, TLS, 1 page, 8vo, White House, 29 December 1917 .. 175.00

SHOW BUSINESS

Crawford, Joan, TLS, 8vo, 1½ pgs, September 8, 1959, to Walter Smally, objects to statement saying she was noisy during a performance of someone else 75.00

Fields, W. C., PS, 14 x 11", standing in costume worn in *Poppy*, sgd "Bill Fields," inscribed to Arthur Samuels, author of *Poppy*, Oct 1928 .... 1,700.00

Garbo, Greta, check, Chase Manhattan Bank, filled in and signed, envelope **2,500.00**

Hart, William S., PS, sepia, 7 x 8", full pose, large sentiment and full signature in lower right corner 200.00

Kern, Jerome, PS, seated at piano, sgd and inscribed, 11 x 14" 1,700.00

Monroe, Marilyn, and Joe DiMaggio, menu, cut to 4 x 3", matted, 9 x 7" black and white glossy photo, sgd "Warmest Regards/Marilyn Monroe &," his signed full name underneath, dated Saturday, May 16, 1953 .... 2,000.00

Novarro, Ramon, PS, 10 x 13", silent film star, close-up bust portrait 250.00

Robinson, Edward G., program for "Darkness at Noon," given at Princeton, NJ in 1951, sgd on front cover 25.00

Aaron, Hank, autographed baseball, $20.00.

SPORTS

Cobb, Ty, check, oblong 8vo, 1945, drawn on First National Bank of Nevada, filled in and sgd by Cobb as "Tyrus R. Cobb," cancellation markings 100.00

Dempsey, Jack, SP, sepia, 4to, full length pose in boxing stance, sgd "Best regards/Jack Dempsey/Nov. 22, '27" 75.00

Ruth, Babe, 1939 Commemorative U. S. Postage Stamp, The Centennial of Baseball 375.00

STATESMAN, AMERICAN

Acheson, Dean, TLS, 4to, 1 page, Jan 23, 1954, to Ellis of Four Freedoms Foundation thanking him for photographs 25.00

Clinton, De Witt, DS, appointment of Elisha Waters as an Ensign in the

24th Regiment of Infantry, March 27, 1819 . . . . **95.00**
Colfax, Schuyler, envelope, addressed in another hand, franked by Colfax at upper right, Washington postmark at left, Vice Pres under Grant **75.00**
Davis, Jefferson, ALS, endorsement on a letter concerning the Allegheny Valley R. R. Co., April 28, 1853 . . . . . . **485.00**
Hall, A. Oakley, Mayor of NYC, ALS, 8vo, 4pp, Executive Depart., City Hall, response to inquiry re: "the new charter," envelope included **300.00**
Holmes, Oliver Wendell, calling card, February 13, 1913 . . . . **490.00**
Jay, John, DS, appointing Henry Saltsman Pay Master of the Regiment of Militia in the county of Montgomery, April 18, 1800 . . . . **790.00**
King, Preston, ALS, 4to, 8 pgs, Washington, Feb 6, 1851, to Gideon Welles, Lincoln's Sec. of Navy, political letter concerning the presidential election to be held the following year **275.00**
Sumner, Charles, ALS, 12mo, 1 page, "Senate Chamber, Aug. 25," n.y., stating he has not received letters from Webster on specific subject . . . **25.00**

AUTOMOBILES

History: Automobiles can be classified into several categories. In 1947 the Antique Automobile Club of America devised a system whereby any motor vehicle (car, bus, motorcycle, etc.) made prior to 1930 is an "antique" car. The Classic Car Club of America expanded the list focusing on luxury models from 1925 to 1948. The Milestone Car Society developed a list for cars in the 1948 to 1964 period.

Some states, such as Pennsylvania, have devised a dual registration system for older cars—antique and classic. Models from the 1960s and 1970s, especially convertibles and limited production models, fall into the "classic" designation depending how they are used.

References: Quentin Craft, *Classic Old Car Value Guide, 23rd Edition,* published by author, 1989; Editors of Old Cars Weekly, *Old Cars Auction Results Worldwide Model Years 1905–1988, 1989 Edition,* Krause Publications, 1989; Beverly Kimes and Henry Austin Clark, Jr., *Standard Catalog of American Cars, 1805–1942, Second Edition,* Krause Publications, 1989; *The Official Price Guide To Collector Cars, 7th Edition,* House of Collectibles, 1986; *Standard Guide to Cars & Prices, 1989 Edition,* Krause Publications, 1989.

Periodicals: *Hemmings Motor News,* Box 100, Bennington, VT 05201; *Old Cars Price Guide,* 700 E. State Street, Iola, WI 54990; *Old Cars Weekly,* 700 E. State Street, Iola, WI 54990.

Collectors' Clubs: Antique Automobile Club of America, 501 W. Governor Road, Hershey, PA 17033; Classic Car Club of America, P. O. Box 443, Madison, NJ 07940; Milestone Car Society, P. O. Box 50850, Indianapolis, IN 46250.

Note: The prices below are based upon a car in running condition, with a high percentage of original parts, and somewhere between 60 and 80% restored. *Prices can vary by as much as 30% in either direction.*

Many older cars, especially if restored, now exceed $15,000.00. Their limited availability makes them difficult to price. Auctions, more than any other source, are the true determinant of value at this level. Especially helpful are the catalogs and sale bills of Kruse Auctioneers, Inc., Auburn, IN 46706.

AUTOMOBILES

Allen, 1914, Touring, 4 cyl. **5,000.00**
AMC, American DeLuxe, Sedan, two door, 6 cyl. **2,500.00**
Auburn
  1915, Model 4-36, Touring, 4 cyl. . . **17,000.00**
  1935, Model 653, Sedan, 6 cyl. **8,500.00**
Austin-Healy, 1964, Model 3000 MK II, Convertible, 6 cyl. **7,500.00**
Bentley
  1953, Park Ward, Convertible, 4.6 Litre **28,000.00**
  1963, S3, four door sedan, right hand drive, repainted sand and sable, taupe leather int. **16,500.00**
Brewster, 1914, Town Car, Limousine, 4 cyl. **22,000.00**
Bricklin, 1975, Model SV-1, Gullwing Coupe **8,000.00**
Bugatti, 1932, Type 46, Sedan, 8 cyl., 5 Litre **32,000.00**
Buick
  1908, Model 10, Touring, 4 cyl. **12,000.00**
  1941, Roadmaster, Sedan, 8 cyl. . . . **15,000.00**
  1967, Riviera GS, Coupe, 8 cyl. . . . **25,000.00**
Cadillac
  1908, Model H, Touring, 4 cyl. **11,000.00**
  1931, Model 370, Cabriolet, V-12 . . **42,000.00**

Monza, 1963, Spyder, convertible, 6 cylinders, $3,750.00.

1942, Model 62, Fast Back, V-8 . . . **8,000.00**
1968, Calais, 2 door, V-8 . . . . **3,500.00**
Chandler, 1927, Big Six, Sedan, 6 cyl. **4,800.00**
Chevrolet
  1912, Classic Six, Touring, 6 cyl. . . **8,800.00**
  1933, Eagle, Rumble Seat Coupe, 6
    cyl. **6,000.00**
  1958, Corvette, Roadster, V-8 . . . . .**15,000.00**
  1965, Corvair, Convertible, 6 cyl. . . . **4,000.00**
Chrysler
  1928, Imperial, Sedan, 6 cyl. **9,000.00**
  1932, Royal CT, Sedan, 8 cyl. **10,000.00**
  1959, Saratoga, Sedan, V-8 . . . . . . **3,000.00**
Columbia, 1925, Six, Sedan, 6 cyl. . . . **8,000.00**
Cord, 1968, Warrior, Roadster Convert-
  ible, V-8 . . . . **6,800.00**
Cunningham, 1929, Model V9, Roads-
  ter, 6 cyl. **20,000.00**
Daniels, 1920, Submarine, Speedster,
  V-8 . . . .**24,500.00**
Dayton, 1913, Tandem, Cycle, 2 cyl. . **3,000.00**
Delahaye, 1935, Superlux, Roadster, 6
  cyl. **12,000.00**
DeSoto
  1913, Model 55, Touring, 6 cyl. **5,000.00**
  1931, Model 31, Rumble Seat Coupe,
    6 cyl. **4,200.00**
  1952, Firedome, Convertible Coupe,
    V-8 . . . . **6,000.00**
Dodge
  1921, Model 21, Touring, 4 cyl. **3,500.00**
  1949, Wayfarer, Roadster, 6 cyl. . . . **4,000.00**
  1966, Charger, Coupe, V-8 . . . . **2,200.00**
Dort
  1915, Model 5, Touring, 4 cyl. **5,000.00**
  1924, Model 27, Touring, 6 cyl. **4,000.00**
Dragon, 1906, Model 25, Touring, 4 cyl. **5,500.00**
Drexel, 1916, Model 7-60, 7 passenger
  touring, 4 cyl. **5,000.00**
Drummond, 1915, Town, 4 cyl. **4,200.00**
Duesenberg, 1931, LeBaron-J, Con-
  vertible Berline, 8 cyl. **125,000.00**
Durant, 1928, Model M, Sedan, 4 cyl. . **4,800.00**
Edsel, 1958, Ranger, 2 door hardtop,
  V-8 . . . . **2,400.00**
Eureka, 1899, High-Wheel, Surrey, 3
  cyl. **5,000.00**
Excalibur SS, 1973, Model SSK,
  Roadster, V-8 . . . .**11,500.00**
Falcon, 1922, Touring, 4 cyl. **5,000.00**
Ferrari, 1956, Tipo 375, Touring, V-12 **27,000.00**
Ford
  1903, Model A, Runabout, 2 cyl. . . .**11,500.00**
  1926, Model T, Coupe, 4 cyl. **2,800.00**
  1940, Deluxe, Sedan Delivery, V-8 . **6,800.00**
  1958, Thunderbird, Hardtop, V-8 . . . **3,500.00**
  1960, Galaxie, Victoria, V-8 . . . . . . **3,000.00**
  1966, Mustang, Convertible, 6 cyl. . . **6,000.00**
Fox, 1921, Model A, Sedan, 6 cyl. . . . **5,000.00**
Franklin
  1930, Model 14, Convertible Sedan,
    6 cyl. **20,000.00**

1933, Olympic, Cabriolet, 6 cyl. **7,000.00**
Frazer, 1951, Manhattan, Convertible, 8
  cyl. **5,000.00**
Fritchle, 1916, Touring, 4 cyl. **5,000.00**
Fuller, 1907, Model 60, Touring, 6 cyl. **15,000.00**
Gardner, 1929, Model 130, Roadster, 8
  cyl. **12,000.00**
Graham-Paige
  1935, Crusader, Sedan, 6 cyl. **3,500.00**
  1941, Hollywood, Convertible Coupe,
    6 cyl. **10,000.00**
Grant, 1921, Model HZ, Sedan, 6 cyl. . **4,500.00**
Grout, 1899, Runabout, Steam **10,000.00**
Haynes, 1923, Special, Speedster, 6
  cyl. **10,000.00**
Hillman, 1967, Huskey, Station Wagon,
  1.7 Litre **1,200.00**
Hudson, 1948, Super 6, Convertible
  Coupe, 6 cyl. **5,000.00**
Jaguar
  1951, Mark VII, Sedan, 6 cyl. **3,600.00**
  1966, XKE, Sport Racing, 4.2 Litre . **6,500.00**
Jeep, 1968, Jeepster, Convertible, V-6 **3,000.00**
Jordan, 1920, Playboy, Roadster, 6 cyl.**12,000.00**
Julian, 1922, Model 60, Coupe, 8 cyl. .**10,000.00**
Kissel, 1925, Gold Bug, Speedster, 6
  cyl. **18,000.00**
Lambert, 1909, Roadster, 6 cyl. **8,000.00**
LaSalle
  1932, Model 345B, Victoria Coupe, 8
    cyl. **9,500.00**
  1940, Model 52, Club Coupe, V-8 . . **5,000.00**
Lexington, 1915, Minute Man, Roadster,
  6 cyl. **12,000.00**
Lincoln, 1935, Dietrich, Convertible
  Coupe, V-12 . . . .**28,000.00**
Lotus, 1966, Mark 46 Europa, Coupe,
  1.5 Litre **2,000.00**
Marmon, 1917, Cloverleaf, Roadster . .**14,000.00**
Mercedes-Benz
  1935, Model 170-V, Limousine **15,000.00**
  1956, Model 190SL, Convertible, 4
    cyl. **9,000.00**
Mercury
  1940, Series 09A, Convertible, 8 cyl.**10,000.00**
  1955, Monterey, Sedan **1,500.00**
  1963, Comet S-22, Convertible, 8 cyl. **2,400.00**
MG, 1961, MGA, 1600 Coupe, 4 cyl. . **4,000.00**
Nash
  1954, Ambassador, 2 door hardtop, 8
    cyl. **1,200.00**
  1962, Metropolitan, Convertible, 4 cyl. **2,300.00**
Oldsmobile
  1942, Model 66, Station Wagon, 6 cyl. **4,000.00**
  1966, Toronado, Coupe, V-8 . . . . . . **3,000.00**
Opel
  1926, Laubfrosch, Sedan, 4 cyl. . . . **1,800.00**
  1938, Admiral, Drophead Coupe, 3.6
    Litre **1,700.00**
Packard
  1901, Model C, Runabout, 1 cyl. . . .**25,000.00**
  1928, Model 426, Roadster, 6 cyl. . .**14,000.00**

1940, Darrin, Convertible Victoria, 8
cyl. 25,000.00
Peugeot
1939, Darl mat, Coupe, 2.1 Litre ... 1,200.00
1964, Model 505, Sedan, 1.5 Litre . 900.00
Pilot, 1922, Model 50, Touring, 6 cyl. . 8,000.00
Pittsburgh, 1911, 7 Passenger Touring,
6 cyl. 6,500.00
Plymouth
1928, Model Q, Sport Roadster, 4 cyl. 8,500.00
1942, Model P145, Sedan, 6 cyl. .. 2,500.00
1957, Fury, Convertible, V-8 cyl. ... 4,000.00
Pontiac
1958, Bonneville, 2 door hardtop,
V-8 .... 2,800.00
1966, GTO, Convertible, V-8 ...... 5,200.00
Porsche
1948, Type 356, Roadster, 4 cyl. ... 8,500.00
1969, Model 911 T, Coupe, 4 cyl. .. 6,800.00
Premier, 1911, Model 440, 5 Passenger
Touring, 6 cyl. 8,000.00
Renault, 1955, Fregate, Convertible, 2
Litre 2,000.00
REO, 1923, Model T6, Sport Touring, 6
cyl. 9,500.00
Rolls Royce
1929, Pall Mall, Touring, 6 cyl. 60,000.00
1952, Silver Dawn, Touring Limou-
sine, 6 cyl. 18,000.00
1964, Silver Cloud III, two door sedan, left hand drive, Tudor gray
over silver gray, red leather int. ..24,200.00
Stanley, 1905, Large Model, Runabout,
Steam 15,000.00
Studebaker
1933, President, Convertible, 8 cyl. .10,000.00
1949, Champion, Convertible, 6 cyl. 4,800.00
1963, Avanti, Coupe, V-8 .... 5,000.00
Stutz
1914, Bearcat, Roadster, 6 cyl. 45,000.00
1927, Black Hawk, Speedster, 8 cyl. 8,000.00
Sun, 1924, Touring, 4 cyl. 4,200.00
Sunbeam, 1958, Alpine, Sport, 4 cyl. . 2,800.00
Triumph, 1949, Model 2000, Roadster,
2 Litre 4,500.00

MISCELLANEOUS

Fire Engine
American LaFrance, 1951, 700 Series, pumper 4,000.00
Diamond T, 1947, pumper 2,500.00
Dodge
1932, pumper 3,500.00
1945, pumper, 6 cyl., American
LaFrance 2,500.00
Ford
1925, Model TT 7,000.00
1929, Model AA 4,800.00
1940, pumper, flat V-8 .... 6,500.00
Mack, 1936, pumper, Hale pump ... 4,000.00

Motorcycle
BMW, 1966, Thumper R27 .... 1,800.00
BSA, 1943, Military 3,800.00
Harley-Davidson
1952, Model K 1,800.00
1961, DuoGlide 4,500.00
Henderson, 1929, KJ Streamline ... 2,500.00
Indian
1930, Scout, Model 101 .... 5,500.00
1948, Chief 7,500.00
Triumph
1921, Baby 1,500.00
1949, Springfield Scout 4,200.00
Vincent, 1942, Comet, Series C ... 6,800.00

Truck, Chevrolet, 1932 Huckster, $6,000.00.

Truck
Chevrolet
1928, Pickup, 1 Ton, V-8 .... 2,300.00
1937, Sedan Delivery, 6 cyl. 5.500.00
1957, Pickup,½ Ton, Short Bed,
V-6 .... 2,300.00
Dodge
1937, Pickup,¾ Ton, Slant 6 .... 2,000.00
1940, ¾ ton, 6 cyl 2,500.00
1957, Sweptside,½ Ton, V-8 .... 800.00
Ford
1920, Model A, Custom Cab, 4 cyl. 4,500.00
1941, F-1 Stake, 8 Foot Bed, V-8
Lemi 2,500.00
1956, F-100, Custom Cab, V-8 .. 2,500.00
1962, Falcon, Ranchero, 6 cyl. .. 2,500.00
G.M.C., 1956, Pickup, Fiberglass
Bed, V-8, 3-Speed 1,800.00
Plymouth, 1938, Pickup, High Side,
Slant 6 .... 2,400.00
Stewart, Pickup, 1 Ton, 4 cyl. 3,200.00
Studebaker, 1948,½ ton Pickup, 6 cyl. 5,000.00
VW, Pickup, Short Bed, 1600 cc ... 1,400.00
White, 1915, "C" cab panel 3,500.00
Willys
1902, Runabout, 2 cyl. 3,000.00
1928, Model 70, Sedan, 6 cyl. 1,800.00
1941, Americar, Sedan, 4 cyl. 1,800.00
1952, Wagon 3,750.00

AUTOMOBILIA

History: The amount of items related to the automobile is endless. Collectors seem to fit into three groups—those collecting parts to restore a car, those collecting information about a company or certain model for research purposes, and those trying to use automobile items for decorative purposes. Most material changes hands at the hundreds of swap meets and auto shows around the country.

Reference: Scott Anderson, *Check The Oil: Gas Station Collectibles With Prices,* Wallace-Homestead, 1986; Brian Jewell, *Motor Badges & Figureheads,* Midas Books, 1978.

Periodical: *Hemmings Motor News,* Box 100, Bennington, VT 05201.

Steam Gauge, Boyce Moter Meter, DeLuxe, 3½″ d, $10.00.

Advertising
  Ashtray
    Evergreen Tubes, green glazed
      Weller pottery insert, tire shape   40.00
    Goodrich Silvertowns, rubber tire
      shape, glass insert 15.00
    Kaiser–Frazer, aluminum, car in re-
      lief 55.00
  Paperweight
    Goodyear Rubber Co., celluloid tur-
      tle, cast iron base 25.00
    Yellow Taxicab Service, 3″, round   30.00
  Sign
    Dunlop Tires, 60 x 13½″, tin, verti-
      cal 28.00

Ford Parts, porcelain, c1924 . . . .   90.00
Invincible Motor Insurance, tin,
  1928 . . . . 50.00
Mobil Gas, 12 x 12″, shield with
  flying horse, porcelain 45.00
Thermometer, Ford Auto, 24 x 6″, tin   45.00
Carburetor
  Buick, 1931 . . . . 90.00
  Oakland, 1926 . . . . 75.00
Engine
  Overland, 1916, 6 cyl., carb., and
    mag. 325.00
  Ford, 1938, 21 stud engine 275.00
Grille
  Ford, 1931, painted red 125.00
  Nash, 1937, LaFayette 400 . . . . 145.00
  Plymouth, 1950 . . . . 50.00
Headlights, pr
  Chevrolet, 1934 . . . . 85.00
  Franklin, 1928 . . . . 230.00
Horn
  Autolite, H-1001 . . . . 45.00
  Spartonet, non-electric, push down
    handle 60.00
  Trojan United, electric 50.00
  Yoders Super Goose, chrome, bulb
    type 35.00
Hood Ornament, Hudson, 1936 . . . . . 50.00
Hubcap
  Durant, 6½″ 60.00
  Edsel, spinner type 35.00
Jack
  Hudson, 1930 . . . . 25.00
  Jaguar 30.00
Lamp
  Gray–Davis, 7″ face, side, early Cad-
    illac 125.00
  Neverout, No. 67, headlamp with fork   200.00
Literature
  Brochure
    Buick for 1930 . . . . 45.00
    Chevrolet & GMC Trucks, 1948, 8
      pgs 8.00
    Oldsmobile, 1948, 8 pgs 8.00
    Standard Oil, Walt Disney illus . . . 30.00
    Studebaker, 1934 . . . . 48.00
  Catalog
    DeVilbiss Automotive, 60 pgs . . . 18.00
    Oldsmobile, 1946, 24 pgs 20.00
    Western Auto, Ford Supply Co.,
      1929 . . . . 25.00
  Owner's Manual
    American Motors, Rambler, 1958 . 20.00
    Chevrolet, 1942 . . . . 18.00
Magneto
  Cadillac, 1904 . . . . 500.00
  Liberty, 1940, 12 cyl. 750.00
Radiator Ornament
  Jewell, 1923 . . . . 125.00
  Packard, 1938 . . . . 50.00
Radio, Lincoln Town and Country, 1957   75.00
Temperature Gauge, Chevrolet, 1933 .   42.00

BACCARAT GLASS

History: The Sainte-Anne glassworks at Baccarat in the Voges, France, was founded in 1764 and produced utilitarian soda glass. In 1816 Aime-Gabriel d'Artiques purchased the glassworks, and a Royal Warrant was issued in 1817 for the opening of Verrerie de Vonche á Baccarat. The firm concentrated on lead crystal glass products. In 1824 a limited company was created.

From 1823 to 1857 Baccarat and Saint-Louis glassworks had a commercial agreement and used the same outlets. No merger occurred. Baccarat began the production of paperweights in 1846. In the late 19th century the firm achieved an international reputation for cut glass table services, chandeliers, display vases and centerpieces, and sculptures. Products eventually included all forms of glass ware. The firm still is active today.

Additional Listing: Paperweights.

Vase, cobalt blue ground, white lace dec, 6⅛" h, $250.00.

Ashtray, 4½" d, Pinwheel, sgd	85.00
Biscuit Jar, vaseline, shaded frosted to clear, swirling flowers, sgd	200.00
Bowl	
8", Rose Tiente, scalloped, ftd, sgd .	100.00
14" d, 3½" h, wide flattened rim, narrow knopped annual foot, etched "Baccarat, France"	500.00
Candlestick	
9¾", triple cut overlay, deep blue cut to white to clear	150.00
10¾", Eiffel Tower pattern, Rose Tiente, pr	225.00
Celery, 3½ x 9½", Rose Tiente	50.00

Champagne Bucket, 9¼" h, tapering cylindrical, rect stop fluted molded sides, stamped "Baccarat, France" .	400.00
Cigar Lighter, Rose Tiente, SP top . . .	125.00
Cologne Bottle	
5½" h, Rose Tiente, Diamond Point Swirl, orig stopper	75.00
6¾", overlay, white cut to cobalt blue, gold striping, orig stopper	100.00
Compote, 4½ x 3¾", Rose Tiente, Swirl pattern	60.00
Decanter, 9¾", Rose Tiente, orig stopper	115.00
Dresser Jar, 5⅜" d, round, double cut overlay, pink cut to clear over opaque white, cut vertical panels, gold dec .	125.00
Epergne, 15" h, scalloped edges, Rose Tiente, 3 pcs	450.00
Fairy Lamp	
3⅞" h, shaded white to clear	275.00
5¼ x 4", Rose Tiente, emb Sunburst pattern, matching saucer base . . .	235.00
Finger Bowl	
4¾" d bowl, 6¼" d underplate, ruby, medallions and flowers gold dec .	325.00
5", Rose Tiente, Swirl pattern	115.00
Goblet	
Perfection pattern	36.00
Vintage pattern, cone shaped amber bowl, etched grape design, cut stem and base, set of 6	100.00
Jar, cov	
3 x 5", Rose Tiente, Swirl pattern . .	75.00
7", cameo glass, gilt metal mounts, imp "Baccarat"	350.00
Jewelry Box, 4" d, 2¾" h, hinged lid, Button and Bow pattern, sapphire blue, brass fittings	125.00
Lamp	
Fluid, crystal and gilt metal, electrified	800.00
Table, crystal and gilt metal	
Column form, pr	3,200.00
Urn form, pr	3,000.00
Pitcher, 9¼", Rose Tiente, Helical Twist pattern	275.00
Rose Bowl, 3" h, cranberry, lacy enamel dec	150.00
Sweetmeat Jar, cranberry colored strawberries, blossoms, and leaves, cut back to clear ground of ferns, SP cov and handle, sgd	350.00
Toothpick Holder, 2½", scalloped, Rose Tiente	100.00
Tray, 11¼" d, scalloped, Rose Tiente .	85.00
Tumble-Up, Rose Tiente, Swirl pattern, carafe and tumbler	200.00
Tumbler, Rose Tiente, Swirl pattern . .	40.00
Vase	
8¼", bamboo stalk form, relief molded leaf sprig at side, coiled snake around base, enameled and gilt insects, early 20th C, sgd	500.00

Vase, 10¾", waisted tapering cylindrical, miter molded top and bottom, Isabelle pattern, etched "Baccarat, France" **650.00**

BANKS, MECHANICAL

History: Banks which display some form of action while utilizing a coin are considered mechanical banks. Although mechanical banks are known which date back to ancient Greece and Rome, the majority of collectors center their interests in those made between 1867 and 1928 in Germany, England, and the United States. Recently there has been an upsurge of interest in later types, some of which date into the 1970s.

Initial research suggested that approximately 250 to 300 different or variant designs of banks were made in the early period. Today that number has been revised to 2,000–3,000 types and varieties. The field remains ripe for discovery and research.

Over 80% of all cast iron mechanical banks produced between 1869 and 1928 were made by J.E. Stevens Co., Cromwell, Connecticut. Tin banks tend to be German in origin.

While rarity is a factor in value, appeal of design, action, quality of manufacture, country of origin, and history of collector interest also are important. Radical price fluctuations may occur with an imbalance of these factors. Rare banks may sell for a few hundred dollars while one of more common design with greater appeal will sell in the thousands.

The prices on our list represent fairly what a bank sells for in the specialized collectors market. Some banks are hard to find and establishing a price outside auction is difficult.

The prices listed are for original old mechanical banks with minor repairs, in sound operating condition, and with a majority of the original paint intact.

References: Al Davidson, *Penny Lane, A History Of Antique Mechanical Toy Banks,* Long's Americana, 1987; Bill Norman, *The Bank Book: The Encyclopedia of Mechanical Bank Collecting,* Collectors' Showcase, 1984.

Reproduction Alert: Reproductions, fakes, and forgeries exist for many banks. Forgeries of some mechanical banks were made as early as 1937, so age alone is not a guarantee of authenticity. In our listing two asterisks indicate banks for which serious forgeries exist and one asterisk indicates banks for which casual reproductions have been made.

Advisor: James S. Maxwell, Jr.

Frogs, Two, J & E Stevens Co, Cromwell, CT, $550.00.

Australian William Tell, brass, wood, and tin	1,200.00
Automatic Coin Savings, tin, strong man in leopard skin holding man by hair .	2,000.00
Bank of Education & Economy	550.00
Barking Dog, wood and steel	1,400.00
** Bear, standing, iron	350.00
** Billy Goat, iron	1,000.00
** Bismark, iron	2,350.00
Bowing Man in Cupola, iron	3,000.00
** Boy & Bull Dog, iron	550.00
** Boy on Trapeze, iron	875.00
* Boy Scout Camp, iron	2,000.00
** Boys Stealing Watermelons, iron	850.00
British Lion, tin	850.00
** Bull & Bear, iron 12,000.00
* Bull Dog, iron, coin on nose	650.00
Bull Dog Savings, iron, key wind	2,000.00
Bull Tosses Boy in Well, brass	2,200.00
Bureau, Freedman's, wood	650.00
Bureau, tin, ideal	475.00
Bureau, wood, Serrill Pat. Appld. For .	400.00
Bureau, wood, stenciling on front	350.00
** Butting Buffalo, iron	950.00
Butting Ram, man thumbs nose	1,700.00
** Calamity, iron	4,500.00
** Called Out, orig unpainted iron 10,000.00
Called Out, lead master pattern	12,000.00
Calumet with Calumet Kid, tin can ...	150.00
Calumet with Soldier, tin can	1,000.00
Calumet with Sailor, tin can	1,200.00
** Cannon, U.S. & Spain	1,850.00
Cat & Mouse, iron and brass, cat standing upright	12,000.00
Cat Chasing Mouse in Building, tin ...	2,400.00
Chandlers, iron	250.00
Child's Bank, Clark Thread	350.00
** Chimpanzee, iron and tin	1,150.00
Chinaman, iron, reclining	1,650.00
Chocolat Menier, tin	75.00
** Circus Ticket Collector, man at barrel .	800.00
Clown & Dog, tin	850.00
Clown, tin, black face	250.00
** Clown, Harlequin, Columbine, iron ...14,500.00
** Clown on Globe, iron	775.00
Coin Registering, iron, domed building	300.00
Confectionery, iron	2,800.00
Crescent Cash Register, iron	125.00

Alligator, grabs coin in mouth, tin **1,150.00**
** American Sewing Machine, iron **2,000.00**
* Artillery, four-sided block house **550.00**

Crowing Rooster, tin	275.00
Dapper Dan, tin	450.00
Darky Bust, tin	450.00
** Dentist, iron	2,200.00
Dog Goes Into House, lead and brass	3,800.00
Dog, pot metal, spring jawed	275.00
** Dog With Tray, iron, oval base	1,000.00
Ducks, lead, two	650.00
Electric Safe, steel	150.00
Elephant Baby, lead, with clown at table	3,700.00
** Elephant With Howdah, iron, man pops out	375.00
** Elephant With Locked Howdah, iron, oval base	600.00
** Elephant, iron, "Light of Asia" on wheels	675.00
Elephant, tin, Royal Trick	850.00
** Elephant On Wheels, iron, trunk moves	700.00
** Elephant, iron, trunk moves, raised coin slot	120.00
Face, wood	875.00
** Feed the Kitty, iron	400.00
** Ferris Wheel, iron and tin, marked "Bowen's Pat."	1,400.00
Fire Alarm, tin	1,250.00
Flip The Frog, tin	950.00
Football, iron, black man and watermelon	14,000.00
Fortune Teller Safe, iron	450.00
Freedman (man at desk)	38,500.00
** Forty-Niner, iron	400.00
Frog On Arched Track, tin	2,000.00
Frog on Rock, iron	350.00
Fun Producing Savings, tin	275.00
Germania Exchange, iron, tin and lead	2,800.00
** Giant Standing, iron	6,800.00
** Girl in Victorian Chair, iron	2,350.00
Give Me A Penny, wood	700.00
** Glutton, brass, lifts turkey	425.00
Golden Gate Key, aluminum	125.00
Grasshopper, tin, wind-up	5,000.00
Guessing, lead and iron, man's figure	2,000.00
Hall's Excelsior, iron and wood, policeman figure	1,400.00
Hall's Lilliput, Type II	250.00
Hall's Yankee Notion, brass	850.00
Harold Lloyd, tin	950.00
Hillman Coin Bank, wood, iron, and glass	3,200.00
** Hold The Fort, iron, five holes	1,400.00
Home, iron	375.00
Home With Dormer Windows, iron	475.00
** Horse Race, iron, tin horses, flanged base	2,000.00
** Humpty Dumpty, iron	425.00
I Always Did 'Spize a Mule, black, sitting on bench	575.00
Huntley And Palmers Readings	250.00
* Indian And Bear, iron, white bear	750.00
** Initiating First Degree, iron	2,800.00
Jack on Roof, tin	300.00
Joe Socko, tin	275.00

John R. Jennings Money Box, wood	2,800.00
Jolly Joe Clown, tin	400.00
** Jolly Nigger, aluminum, string tie	100.00
** Jolly Nigger, iron	150.00
Jolly Nigger, iron, high hat	250.00
Jonah And Whale, iron, ftd base	12,500.00
Key, iron, World's Fair	300.00
Kick Inn, paper on wood	275.00
** Leap Frog, iron	1,250.00
** Lighthouse, iron	600.00
Lion Hunter, iron	1,650.00
Little High Hat, iron	500.00
Little Jocko Musical, tin	900.00
Little Moe, iron, tip hat	450.00
Long May It Wave, iron and wood	400.00
Lucky Wheel Money Box, tin	150.00
** Magic Safe, iron	175.00
** Magician, iron	1,650.00
** Mama Katzenjammer, iron, 1930s	550.00
Mama Katzenjammer, iron, 1905–08, low cut dress with white fringe	3,700.00
Man on Chimney	550.00
** Mason, iron	1,450.00
Merry-Go-Round, mechanical	4,500.00
Metropolitan, iron	150.00
Mikado, iron	7,500.00
Minstrel, tin	450.00
Model Railroad Stamp Dispenser, tin	650.00
Model Railroad Sweet Dispenser	650.00
Model Savings, tin	500.00
* Monkey & Coconut, iron	750.00
Monkey & Parrot, tin	200.00
Monkey With Tray, tin	350.00
Moonface, iron	20,000.00
Mosque, iron	450.00
* Mule Entering Barn, iron	650.00
Musical Church, wood, rotating tower	2,500.00
Musical Savings, wood house	1,200.00
New, iron, lever in center	450.00
New Creedmoor Bank, iron	450.00
** Novelty, iron	400.00
Old Woman In The Shoe	180,000.00
* Organ, iron, cat and dog	475.00
** Organ Grinder With Performing Bear, iron	1,600.00
Owl, iron, slot in head	250.00
Owl, turns head, iron	225.00
* Paddy & Pig, iron	875.00
Pascal Savings, tin	250.00
** Peg Leg Begger, iron	600.00
** Pelican With Rabbit, iron	700.00
** Piano, iron, old conversion to musical	2,200.00
Pig In High Chair, iron	450.00
Pistol, stamped metal	325.00
Postman, tin, English	250.00
Presto, iron, penny changes to quarter	3,700.00
Pump & Bucket, iron	425.00
* Punch & Judy, iron	750.00
Punch & Judy, tin	1,500.00
Queen Victoria Bust, iron	5,000.00
** Rabbit, iron, large	275.00
Rabbit In Cabbage	250.00

** Red Riding Hood, iron	5,500.00
Rival, iron	5,000.00
Roller-skating, iron	4,000.00
Safety Locomotive, iron	250.00
Saluting Sailor, tin	500.00
Sam Segal's Aim to Save Target, iron	4,500.00
Savo, tin, round, children	125.00
Scotchman, tin	375.00
Sentry, tin, raises rifle	550.00
Sentry, wood, c1910	450.00
Shoot The Hat, brass	2,500.00
Signal Cabin, tin	150.00
Snake & Frog In Pond, tin	1,200.00
* Speaking Dog, iron	750.00
Sportsman, iron, fowler	4,500.00
** Squirrel & Tree Stump, iron	800.00
Stollwerk, tin, Victoria	250.00
Sweet Thrift, tin	150.00
* Tammany, iron	275.00
* Tank & Cannon, aluminum	200.00
Target, iron, fort and cannon	2,750.00
Ten Cent Adding Bank, iron	400.00
Thrifty Tom's Jigger, tin	400.00
Tiger, tin	950.00
Time Lock Savings, iron	1,100.00
Toboggan, SP Britannia metal	850.00
Treasure Chest Music, pot metal	375.00

Trick Dog, Hubley Mfg Co, Lancaster, PA, $450.00.

** Trick Dog, iron, solid base	450.00
* Trick Pony, iron	675.00
Trick Savings, wood, front drawer	125.00
Try Your Weight Scale, tin	250.00
** Uncle Remus, iron	1,650.00
** Uncle Sam Bust, iron	475.00
Uncle Tom, iron, star base	250.00
United States Bank, iron, picture pops up	875.00
Viennese soldier, lead	1,800.00
Volunteer, iron	450.00
Watch Dog Safe, iron	250.00
Weeden's Plantation, tin, wind-up	650.00
Wimbledon, iron	1,600.00

Wishbone, brass	6,000.00
Woodpecker, tin, 1920s	850.00

BANKS, STILL

History: Banks with no mechanical action are known as still banks. The first still banks were made of wood, pottery, or from gourds. Redware and stoneware banks, made by America's early potters, are prized possessions of today's collectors.

Still banks reached a "golden age" with the arrival of the cast iron bank. Leading manufacturing companies include Arcade Mfg. Co., J. Chein & Co., Hubley, J. & E. Stevens and A. C. Williams. The banks often were ornately painted to enhance their appeal. During the cast iron era, banks and other businesses used the still bank as a form of advertising for attracting customers.

The tin lithograph bank, again frequently with advertising, did not reach its zenith until the 1930 to 1955 period. The tin bank was an important premium, whether it be a Pabst Blue Ribbon beer can bank or a Gerber's Orange Juice bank. Most tin advertising banks resembled the packaging shape of the product.

Almost every substance has been used to make a still bank—diecast white metal, aluminum, brass, plastic, glass, etc. Many of the early glass candy containers also converted to a bank when the candy was eaten. Thousands of varieties of still banks were made, and hundreds of new varieties appear on the market each year.

References: Earnest Ida and Jane Pitman, *Dictionary of Still Banks*, Long's Americana, 1980; Andy and Susan Moore, *Penny Bank Book, Collecting Still Banks*, Schiffer Publishing, Ltd., 1984; Hubert B. Whiting, *Old Iron Still Banks*, Forward's Color Productions, Inc. 1968, out of print.

Collectors' Club: Still Bank Collectors Club of America, P. O. Box 356, Bradford, VT 05033. *Penny Bank Post.*

Museum: Margaret Woodbury Strong Museum, Rochester, NY.

GLASS

Atlas Mason Jar	15.00
Barrel, emb	8.00
Dog, 3¼" barrel	75.00
House	
3¼", Save With Pittsburgh Paints, clear, pressed	25.00
4", brick, orig brown paint, milk glass, orig mustard label on bottom	40.00
Kewpie, 3⅛" h, pressed glass with polychrome	75.00
Liberty Bell, dated 1919	20.00
Log Cabin, 4", milk glass	20.00
Milk Bottle, 4½", Elsie The Borden Cow	25.00
Monkey, 5"	35.00

Owl, 7", carnival glass, marigold 25.00
Schoolhouse, milk glass 50.00

Metal, First National Bank, Albright, W. VA, coin and paper slots, $35.00.

METAL. Cast Iron unless otherwise stated.

Animal
Boston Bull, 4⅜" h, seated, polychrome 85.00
Camel, 7¼" l, gold, red and orange . 215.00
Cat with ball, 5⅝" l, gray, gold ball . 150.00
Deer, 9½", antlers 55.00
Donkey, 6¾" 100.00
Elephant, 4", gold trim 115.00
Goose, 3¾", "Red Goose School Shoes" adv 100.00
Hippopotamus, 5" l, black 200.00
Newfoundland, 3⅝" h, black 40.00
Pig, 2½", "Decker's Iowana," gold . . 65.00
Possum, 2¹/₁₂", gold or silver 165.00
Scottie, 3⁵/₁₆", black 70.00
Seal, 3⅜" h, gold 240.00
* Sheep, 5¼", gold 65.00
Turkey 70.00
Other
Baseball Player, 5¾", gold or blue . . 75.00
Battleship, "Maine", 4½", japan finish 125.00
Beehive 60.00
Bicentennial, 1776–1976, 6 x 6" . . . 40.00
Boy Scout, 5¾", gold 65.00
Building, 7", "Columbia," nickel finish 80.00
Bungalow, 3¾" h, polychrome, porch 175.00
Captain Kidd, 5⅝", c1901 . . . . 225.00
Castle, 3" h, brown japanning, gold trim 250.00
Clock, "Time Is Money," 3³/₁₆", black 55.00
Colonial House, 3" h, gold and green 95.00
Devil, 4¼", two faced, red 285.00
Dutch Girl, 5¼", flowers 35.00
Fireman 95.00
Frowning Face, 5¾" h, unpainted . . 485.00
Garage, 2½" h, aluminum, two car, red 135.00
Gingerbread House, 2½", tin, German 35.00
Gothic Bank, 4⅜", early tin, American 40.00

Globe, 5¾", on stand, eagle finial, red 90.00
Goodyear Zeppelin Hanger, 2⁵/₁₆", aluminum 130.00
Helmet, German, 4⅞" l, lead, olive drab, key trap 175.00
High Rise, 5½" h, silver, gold trim . . 65.00
Hot Water Heater, Rex, 7¾" h, green litho finish 20.00
Independence Hall, Tower Bank, bell 220.00
* Junior Cash Register, 5¼", nickel finish 75.00
Mary, 4⅜", lamb 190.00
Mutt and Jeff, 5⅛" h, gold 85.00
Pass Around The Hat, 2⅜", black . . 60.00
Plymouth Rock, 3⅞", dated "1620," white metal 20.00
Porky Pig, 4⁷/₁₆", tree trunk, white metal 60.00
Radio, 4½", "Majestic," steel back . . 45.00
Rose Window, 2¼" h, brown japanning 145.00
Safe, 4", "Mascot," tin 25.00
Statue of Liberty, 6⅜", silver 75.00
Stop Sign, 4½", painted 140.00
Stove, 5⅜", "Gas Stove Bank," black 80.00
Taxi, 4", "Yellow Cab," Arcade 240.00
Teddy Roosevelt, 5" h, gold, red and silver trim 145.00
U.S. Mailbox, 4¾", silver 30.00
"White City Puzzle Pail," 3⅛", nickel finish 45.00
Windmill, 3⅜", brass, silvered 60.00

Pottery, pig, brown ground, cream colored spots, attributed to McCoy Pottery Co., 5½" l, $35.00.

POTTERY

Apple, 2½", redware 80.00
Bear, 12", ceramic, black and white, Hamm's 30.00
Cat
4", head, amber glaze, brown and tan sponging, emb features 110.00
5½", sitting in basket, blue and green 35.00
Donkey, white, staffordshire 40.00
Duck, 2¾", blue and white spongeware 65.00
Elephant 25.00

Frog, 4″ **40.00**
Incense Burner **25.00**
Kewpie, chalkware, black **50.00**
Mail Box, 3¾″, U.S. Mail, red, white, and
  blue **40.00**
Owl, 6¾″, brown glaze, yellow eyes .. **70.00**
Peach, 2⅝″, pale yellow and peach .. **50.00**
Peacock, 5″, multicolored glaze **75.00**
Pig
  6″ l, blue and brown sponge spatter **100.00**
  10″, sewer pipe, tooled eyelashes .. **400.00**
Shoe, 5″, high button, tan **80.00**
Sphere, 4⅞″, dark albany slip glaze,
  pedestal base, dog finial **130.00**

BARBER BOTTLES

History: Barber bottles, colorful glass bottles found on shelves and counters in barber shops, held the liquids barbers used daily. A specific liquid was kept in a specific bottle which the barber knew by color, design, or lettering.

The bulk liquids were kept in utilitarian containers under the counter or in a storage room.

Barber bottles are found in many types of glass: art glass with varied decoration, pattern glass, and commercially prepared and labeled bottles.

References: Richard Holiner, *Collecting Barber Bottles*, Collector Books, 1986; Ralph & Terry Kovel, *The Kovels' Bottle Price List, Eighth Edition* Crown Publishers, Inc. 1987; Philip L. Krumholz, *Value Guide For Barberiana & Shaving Collectibles*, AdLibs Publishing Co., 1988.

Note: Prices are for bottles without original stoppers unless otherwise noted.

Amber, hobnail **75.00**
Amethyst
  6¾″, orange dot pattern, white
    enamel flowers, pontil **50.00**

**Cranberry, vertical white opalescent
stripes, square base, 8½″ h, $250.00.**

7¼″ h, paneled, applied lip **100.00**
Blue, 8″ h, horizontal brown band design, applied white enamel floral pattern above and below the band, sheared lip, exposed pontil **100.00**
Clambroth, 8″ h, emb "WATER" in red across front, porcelain stoppers ... **40.00**
Clear Glass
  6½″ h, ribbed style, decorated band around center, gold trim, raised enamel dot pattern, pontil **50.00**
  7″ h, recessed under glass label ... **25.00**
Cobalt Blue, 8½″ h, bell shape, raised white and orange flowers, sheared lip, exposed pontil **50.00**
Cranberry, 7″, melon base, fern pattern, white design, rolled lip, pr **250.00**
Cut glass, 5″, pewter top **50.00**
Frosted, 8″ h, raised floral enamel design, pontil ground, pr **75.00**
Handpainted
  7½″ h, red, frosted oval areas, purple and white flowers, green leaves, pontil, pr **200.00**
  11″ h, frosted glass, gold medallion, raised enamel around it, blue highlight, gold lip, pontil **25.00**
Hobnail
  7¼″ h, blue, four neck rings, uneven rolled lip, pontil **40.00**
  7½″ h, irid Art Deco, greenish coating over cobalt blue, pontil ground ... **200.00**
Mary Gregory, 8″ h, cobalt blue, one with woman holding a bird, other hunter with bird on hand, gold trimmed lips, pr **300.00**
Milk Glass, 9″ h, hp, "BAY RUM," pink and white flowers, green leaves, pastel ground, rolled lip, pontil **125.00**
Opalescent
  7″, blue, stars and stripes pattern, pontil **200.00**
  7½″ h, cranberry, melon based, vertical stripes, rolled lip, pontil **100.00**
  8½″ h, white, fern pattern, rolled lip, sq base **55.00**
Porcelain, 9″ h, flowers decorated on three sides, one is emb "TONIC" in black, other is "WITCH HAZEL," pr . **200.00**
Purple, deep color, blown, white enameled matching scenes, bulbous base, shaped neck, tooled rim, pr **300.00**
Spatter glass, 8¼″, red and white **150.00**
Wedgwood, tri-color, four cameos of classical scenes **750.00**

BAROMETERS

History: A barometer is an instrument which measures atmospheric pressure which, in turn, aids weather forecasting. Low pressure indicates the coming of rain, snow, or storm; high pressure signifies fair weather.

Most barometers use an evacuated and graduated glass tube which contains a column of mercury and are classified by the shape of the case. An aneroid barometer has no liquid and works by a needle connected to the top of a metal box in which a partial vacuum is maintained. The movement of the top moves the needle.

Banjo, A & V Cattania, hygrometer, thermometer, barometer with balancing level, mahogany case, York, England, 38½" l, $400.00.

Aneroid, 7¼", Boston Brand, highly polished brass case 245.00
Banjo
  38", George III, mahogany, split baluster, hygrometer, barometer, thermometer, barometer spirit level, convex mirror, inscribed "Cicera & Pini, Endinburgh" 500.00
  39¼"
    George III, inlaid mahogany, silvered brass register dials, inlaid in Sheraton taste with fruitwood stringing, oval reserves of berries and foliage, broken arched pediment, urn finial, inscribed "Domenicho Gatty, No 94, High Holborn, London," c1810 .... 1,000.00

Regency, mahogany, sgd "A Intross & Co, Chaltham," early 19th C 500.00
40", Louis XVI, carved giltwood, circular dial inscribed "Robert Op, passage St. Pierre 4 a Versailles," centigrade thermometer, pierced foliate scrolls and swagged drapery, pair of lovebirds under laurel arbor cresting, restoration to gilding, late 18th C 1,210.00
Desk, tin, figural, Weather House, painted dec, chalk man and woman, sgd "Alvan Lovejoy, Boston," label on back 165.00
Portable, 37¾", Victorian, American, walnut, plain case, printed paper barometer, vernier gauge, silver metal thermometer, marked "H. A. Simmons, Fulton, NY, Patent Nov 13, 1877" 1,000.00
Stick
  37", Victorian
    American, walnut, marked "John M Merrick & Co., Worcester, Massachusetts," mid 19th C 400.00
    Irish, rosewood, engraved ivory register scales and vernier gauge, cov pediment, circular cistern cov, marked "W Gilbert, Belfast" 995.00
  37½", Georgian, late, mahogany, bow front, silvered brass register plates with vernier gauge, ebony striped borders, ebonized cistern cov, marked "John Walker, One South Molton Street, London," second quarter 19th C 1,650.00
  38¾", George III, inlaid mahogany, silvered brass register plates, broken arch pediment, brass finial, checker strung borders, ivory inlaid cistern cov, marked "Roncheti & Gatty Fecerunt," c1790 .... 1,320.00
Wheel, 39", shell inlaid mahogany, marked "Jennings, Ipswich, England," mid 19th C 500.00

BASKETS

History: Baskets were invented when man first required containers to gather, store, and transport goods. Today's collector, influenced by the country look, focuses on baskets made of splint, rye straw, or willow. Emphasis is placed on handmade examples. Nails or staples, wide splints which are thin and evenly cut, or a wire bail handle denote factory construction which can date back to the mid-19th century. Painted or woven decorated baskets rarely are handmade, unless American Indian.

Baskets are collected by (a) type–berry, egg, or field, (b) region–Nantucket or Shaker, and (c) composition–splint, rye, or willow. Stick to examples in very good condition; damaged baskets are a poor investment even at a low price.

References: Frances Johnson, *Wallace-Homestead Price Guide To Baskets, Second Edition,* Wallace-Homestead, 1989; Martha Wetherbee and Nathan Taylor, *Legend of the Bushwhacker Basket,* published by author, 1986; Christoph Will, *International Basketry For Weavers and Collectors,* Schiffer Publishing, 1985.

Reproduction Alert: Modern reproductions abound, made by diverse groups ranging from craft revivalists to foreign manufacturers.

Storage, rye and straw, 18½" d, $175.00.

Berry
  8 x 9½ x 5", splint and red, melon rib, old red paint **200.00**
  10 x 10½ x 6", plus wooden handle, woven splint, buttocks, good age and color **80.00**
  10¾ x 11½ x 5½", plus wooden handle, woven splint, buttocks **125.00**
Cheese, 24" d, woven splint, gray scrubbed finish, blue paint traces . .   **475.00**
Drying, 11 x 15 x 6¼", woven splint, open work bottom, open rim handles   **48.00**
Egg
  10½ x 12 x 6", plus bentwood handle, woven splint, radiating ribs, old varnish finish **60.00**
  11 x 11 x 6", splint, finely woven, bentwood handle **140.00**
  12 x 15 x 7", splint, handle **100.00**
  13 x 14 x 7½", splint, radiating ribs design, bentwood handle **100.00**
  15 x 7", woven splint, radiating ribs, bentwood handle **75.00**
  15 x 17", woven splint, weathered gray scrubbed finial, bentwood handle **55.00**

Gathering
  10 x 10½ x 6", reed, splint melon ribs, bentwood handle, "H.P." carved into handle **100.00**
  14 x 25", woven splint, bentwood handle marked "Lookout Mt" **30.00**
  17 x 23 x 7¾", woven splint, oblong, built up rim handles, good age and color, minor rim wear **70.00**
  18 x 9 x 13", woven splint, well shaped bentwood handles, faded red and blue design **75.00**
  19 x 27", splint, oval, plaited rim, bentwood handles **120.00**
Kitchen, 12 x 14 x 6½", plus handle, woven splint, buttocks, woven in 3 shades of splint **150.00**
Laundry, 19 x 31 x 13½", Shaker, woven splint, bentwood rim handles **100.00**
Loom, 9½" w, 9½" h, woven splint, faded green and yellow **65.00**
Market, 13½ x 19 x 8½", splint and cane, bentwood carved handle **80.00**
Miniature
  3¾" d, 2¼" h, splint, cylindrical, plain plaiting, double handles, wrapped rim with blue paint **150.00**
  4¾" d, 2½" h, woven splint, damaged handle **30.00**
Nantucket
  6½" d, circular, faint signature on bottom, date "1909" **600.00**
  7½" d, circular, swing handle **650.00**
  8¼" l, oval, swing handle **500.00**
  13" d, swing handle Ferdinand Sylvaro **1,250.00**
Picnic, 7¾ x 15 x 6", splint, double hinged lid, int. with pattern of green and natural, faded ext., bentwood handle **100.00**
Sewing, 8¼ x 8½ x 3¼", plus handle, finely woven splint, bands of curlicues and woven grass, attached small oval basket and pincushion **45.00**
Sower's
  12 x 14½ x 7", plus wooden handle, woven splint **50.00**
  12 x 16½ x 8", plus wooden handle, woven splint **60.00**
Storage
  10" h, rye straw, oval shape **50.00**
  11½" h, woven splint, bentwood rim handles **65.00**
Wall, 8 x 6 x 5", oak, c1900 . . . .   **65.00**

BATTERSEA ENAMELS

History: Battersea enamel is a generic term for English enamel-on-copper objects of the 18th century.

In 1753 Stephen Theodore Janssen established

a factory to produce "Trinkets and Curiosities Enamelled on Copper" at York House, Battersea, London. Here the new invention of transfer printing developed a high degree of excellence, and the resulting trifles delighted fashionable Georgian society.

Recent research has shown that enamels actually were being produced in London and the Midlands several years before York House was established. However, most enamel trinkets still are referred to as "Battersea Enamels," even though they were probably made in other workshops in London, Birmingham, Bilston, Wednesbury, or Liverpool.

All manner of charming items were made, including snuff and patch boxes bearing mottos and memory gems. (By adding a mirror inside the lid, a snuff box became patch box). Many figural whimsies, called "toys," were created to amuse a gay and fashionable world. Many other elaborate articles, e.g., candlesticks, salts, tea caddies, and bonbonnieres, were made for the tables of the newly rich middle classes.

Reference: Susan Benjamin, *English Enamel Boxes*, Merrimack Publishers Circle, 1978.

Advisors: Barbara and Melvin Alpren.

Patch Box, black and white King Charles Spaniel, pink ground, floral dec, 2½ x 1¾ x 1½", $2,550.00.

Bougie Box, (wax jack container), 1¼" d, 2" h, turquoise, raised all-over flowers, Bilston, c1770	950.00
Box, 1¾ x 1½ x 1", "A Trifle from Mother," black lettering, gold, white, and blue	575.00
Candlesticks, pr, 11" h, white ground, cobalt reserves, all-over spring flower dec, Bilston, c1780	3,500.00
Cloak Hooks, pr, 1¼" d, pastoral scenes, Battersea, c1770	500.00
Patch Box	
1¼" l, oval	
"A Pleasing Gift" inscribed with bowknots, pink ground, Bilston, c1780	600.00
"Esteem the Giver" inscribed within large heart surrounded by garlands of flowers and lovebirds, Bilston, c1780	500.00
1¼", round, white ground, realistic roses on top and sides, Birmingham style, c1790	600.00
1⅞" l, oval, historical, "A Trifle from Bath, North Parade," natural colors, pink base, Bilston, c1770	500.00
2", oval, "Remember Me, When This You See," lovers, ship, and wreath on lid, green base, South Staffordshire, c1780	600.00
Scent Bottle Holder, ½ x 1¼ x 2¼", white ground, purple dec, green leaves, rose and blue flowers, bow and arrow sheaf on reverse	400.00
Scent Flask, 2⅜" h, hinged cov, orig glass scent bottle inside, white ground, blue and green trellis work, Birmingham, c1770	1,000.00
Snuff Box	
1¼", The Gift of A Friend, green, white lid, black script inscription	155.00
2 x 1½", rect, yellow, painted cabbage rose, rare color, South Staffordshire, c1780	1,000.00

BAVARIAN CHINA

History: Bavaria, Germany, was an important porcelain production center, similar to the Staffordshire district in England. The name Bavarian China refers to companies operating in Bavaria, among which were Hutschenreuther, Thomas, and Zeh, Scherzer & Co. (Z. S. & Co.). Very little of the production from this area was imported into the United States prior to 1870.

Reference: Susan and Al Bagdade, *Warman's English & Continental Pottery & Porcelain, 1st Edition*, Warman Publishing Co., Inc., 1987.

Salt, ftd, white int., blue ext., pink roses, gold rim and feet, 1⅝ x 1", $15.00.

Bowl, 9½", hp strawberries, flowers, and
leaves on green ground, artist sgd . . . 45.00

Celery Tray, 11" l, basket of fruit in center, luster edge, c1900 . . . . 35.00

Charger, scalloped rim, game bird in
woodland scene, bunches of pink and
yellow roses, connecting garlands . . 75.00

Chocolate Set, chocolate pot, cov, 6
cups and saucers, shaded blue to
white, large white leaves, pink, red,
and white roses, crown mark 235.00

Cup and Saucer, roses and foliage, gold
handle 20.00

Figurine, 10½" h, dark blue and pale
orange marabou standing beside tan
and navy cactus, marked "Hutschenreuther Selb-Bavaria, K. Tutter" . . . 250.00

Fish Set, thirteen plates, matching
sauceboat, artist sgd 400.00

Hair Receiver, 3½ x 2½", apple blossom
dec, marked "T. S. & Co" 50.00

Pitcher, 9" bulbous, blackberry dec,
shaded ground, burnished gold lizard
handle, sgd "D. Churchill" 110.00

Plate
6", salad, gold and white 10.00
8½", hp, poinsettia dec 45.00
9", portrait, side view of lady, sgd "L.
B. Chaffee, R. C. Bavarian" 70.00
9½", red berries, green leaves, white
ground, scalloped border 25.00

Platter, 16", Dresden flowers 90.00

Punch Bowl, hp roses int. and ext.,
pedestal base, marked "H & C" . . . 250.00

Ramekin, underplate, ruffled, small red
roses with green foliage, gold rim . . 40.00

Salt and Pepper Shakers, pink apple
blossom sprays, white ground, reticulated gold tops, pr 25.00

Shaving Mug, pink carnations, marked
"Royal Bavarian" 50.00

Sugar, cov, white, green grapes dec . . 30.00

Sugar Shaker, hp, pastel pansies 50.00

Toothpick Holder, barrel shape, pink
roses 30.00

Vase, 4¾", hp, florals, sgd 20.00

BELLEEK

History: Belleek, a thin, ivory colored, almost
iridescent-type porcelain, was first made in 1857
in county Fermanagh, Ireland. Production continued until World War I, was discontinued for a period of time, and then resumed. The Shamrock

pattern is most familiar, but many patterns were
made, including Limpet, Tridacna, and Grasses.

Irish Belleek has several identifying marks, e.g.,
the Harp and Hound (1865–80) and Harp, Hound,
and Castle (1863–91). After 1891 the word "Ireland" or "Erie" was added. Some pieces are
marked "Belleek Co., Fermanagh."

There is an Irish saying: If a newly married couple receives a gift of Belleek, their marriage will be
blessed with lasting happiness.

Several American firms made a Belleek-type
porcelain. The first was Ott and Brewer Co. Tren-
ton, New Jersey, in 1884, followed by Willets.
Other firms included The Ceramic Art Co. (1889),
American Art China Works (1892), Columbian Art
Co. (1893), and Lenox, Inc. (1904).

Reference: Mary Frank Aston, *American Belleek*, Collector Books, 1984.

Additional Listings: Lenox.

Abbreviations: 1BM = 1st Black Mark;
2BM = 2nd Black Mark; 3BM = 3rd Black Mark;
4GM = 4th Green Mark; 5GM = 5th Green Mark.

Advisor: Mary Beth Appert.

**Cup and saucer, scalloped edge, white
ground, gold dec, Willets mark, $80.00.**

AMERICAN

Bowl, 9" d, Wavecrest, green, heavy
gold trim, white curled handle, Lenox
green wreath mark 90.00

Cup and Saucer, 6" h, square pedestal
base, undecorated, Willets brown
mark 35.00

Demitasse Cup, liner, gold band border,
SS holder with saucer, Lenox green
wreath mark 55.00

Dresser set, cov powder box, pin tray,
buffer and container, nail brush, pin
cushion, hp violets, artist sgd "M.R.",
Willets brown mark, 6 pcs 550.00

Figure
4"
Elephant, white, Lenox green
wreath mark 315.00
Swan
Green, Lenox green wreath mark 65.00
Pink, Lenox green wreath mark 50.00

Loving Cup, three handles, wine keeper
in wine cellar, artist sgd, SS repousse
collar, CAC mark **185.00**
Mask, 7½", lady's face, black, Lenox
green wreath mark **175.00**
Mug
  7", William Penn, Lenox green wreath
  mark **175.00**
  7½", grapevines and olive green
  grapes, SS overlay, CAC mark . .   **225.00**
Perfume, figural, rabbit, white, Lenox
green wreath mark, pr **525.00**
Pitcher, 5½", body indentation, tree
branch shaped handle, gold paste flo-
ral dec, Willets brown mark **375.00**
Powder Box, 4 x 6"
  Pink, gold wheat on lid, Lenox green
  wreath mark **40.00**
  White, hp, portrait of dog on lid, artist
  sgd "Nosek" **600.00**
Salt
  1"
    Gold rim, Willets brown mark **15.00**
    Pink roses, gold rim, CAC mark . .   **18.00**
  2", gold ftd, green ground, pink rose
  ext., single pink rose int., gold rim,
  CAC mark **25.00**
Salt and Pepper Shakers, pr, 1" d salt,
2" h egg shape pepper, pink roses,
Lenox green palette mark **35.00**
Vase
  8½", bulbous shape, pine cone and
  branches decor, Lenox green
  wreath mark **55.00**
  12" h, 8½" d, applied handles, floral
  ground, artist sgd, CAC mark . . .   **475.00**

IRISH

Ashtray, 4½", shamrock horseshoe,
4GM **45.00**
Basket, 9" d, Sydenham **450.00**
Butter Plate, leaf, No. 1, 5GM **20.00**
Cup and Saucer, 6" d, 2" h, Shamrock
pattern, 2BM **200.00**
Cake Plate
  Limpet pattern, 2BM **175.00**
  Shamrock pattern, 3BM **125.00**
Creamer, Lotus pattern, green handle,
2BM **75.00**
Creamer and Sugar
  Lily pattern, 5GM **45.00**
  Lotus pattern, 5GM **45.00**
  Tridacna, green rim, 3BM **115.00**
Dish, 6½", heart shape, 3BM **95.00**
Figure
  3½", Terrier, 4GM **35.00**
  4½", Swan, 3BM **65.00**
  14⅝"
    Affection, multicolored, 1BM **2,500.00**
    Meditation, multicolored, 1BM . . . **2,500.00**
Flower Holder, 3½" h, Seahorse, one

with white head, other with brown,
1BM, pr **1,200.00**
Sandwich Tray, Mask pattern, 2BM . . .   **275.00**
Sugar
  Cleary pattern, 3BM **60.00**
  Shamrock pattern, cov, 3BM **65.00**
Tea and Dessert Service, Eugene
Sheran, partially decorated, c1887,
32 pcs **7,900.00**
Tea Set
  Limpet pattern, 7" teapot, 3¼" creamer, 4½" covered sugar, 3BM, 3
  pcs **350.00**
  Neptune pattern, teapot, creamer,
  sugar, six cups and saucers, and
  six dessert plates, 2BM, 15 pcs . . **1,500.00**
Tub, 3¼" d, Shamrock pattern, 3BM . .   **55.00**
Vase
  5½", Shamrock spill, 4GM **35.00**
  5⅜", ftd, flower spill, applied flowers,
  3BM **325.00**
  6¼", Shamrock tree trunk, 2BM . . .   **145.00**
  6½", Harp, Shamrock pattern, 5GM .   **40.00**
  7⅞", Panel, shamrocks with yellow
  gilt, 6GM **65.00**

BELLS

History: Bells have been used for centuries for
many different purposes. They have been traced
as far back as 2697 B.C., though at that time they
did not have any true tone. One of the oldest bells
is the "crotal," a tiny sphere with small holes and
a ball or stone or metal inside. This type now
appears as sleigh bells.

True bell making began when bronze, the mixing
of tin and copper, was discovered. There are now
many types of materials of which bells are made—
almost as many materials as there are uses for
them.

Bells of the late 19th century show a high degree
of workmanship and artistic style. Glass bells from
this period are examples of the glass blower's talent and the glass manufacturer's product.

Collectors' Club: American Bell Association,
Rt. 1, Box 286, Natronia Heights, PA 15065. *The
Bell Tower.*

Additional Listings: See *Warman's Americana
& Collectibles* for more examples.

Altar, sanctus, four varied sized bells
with three clappers each, four birds,
twig type handle, 2½", Bevin Bros,
CT, c1930 . . . .   **50.00**
Church Steeple, cast iron, Hollsboro,
OH, 1886, N2 yoke **220.00**
China
  Limoges, cow shape, pale blue, pink
  roses, gilded handle, 4" **40.00**
  Staffordshire, figural, girl, blue, white,
  and gold, 6" **90.00**

Desk
  Brass, face in top center of fancy-
    work, operating gong on each side,
    7″ 120.00
  Bronze, white marble base, side tap,
    c1875 .... 45.00
  Silverplate, open filigree skirt, wind-
    up, top knob 85.00
Glass
  Bohemian, ruby flashed, Deer & Cas-
    tle, clear handle and clapper, 4½″ 80.00
  Burmese, shaded deep pink to ivory,
    satin finish, 6¼″ 70.00
  Carnival, figural, Southern Belle,
    white imperial 38.00
  Custard, souvenir, "Alamo - Built
    1718, San Antonio, TX," gilt band 90.00
  Cut, clear, pinwheels, notched han-
    dle, Brilliant Period 290.00
  Heisey, frosted, Victorian Belle 125.00
  Milk, smocking, marked "Akeo, Made
    in USA" 22.00
Hand, brass, figural
  Dickens man with pipe, 3⅞″ 70.00
  Lady, bust, quilted pattern on bell,
    3⅝″ 35.00
  Monk, carries umbrella and basket, 5″ 75.00
  Old Woman carrying pot, feet form
    clapper, 5″ 70.00
  Turtle, bell bracket and striker on
    shell 30.00
  Liberty, nickel steel base, green, 4⅜″ . 70.00
  Locomotive, brass, emb "E.M.D.", cast
    iron ball clapper, mounted on steel tri-
    pod, 12″ d 270.00
  School, brass, wood handle 55.00
  Silver, German, florentine, emb figures,
    2¾″ 75.00

Sleigh bells, orig leather strap, $75.00.

Sleigh, brass
  Twenty, 36″ pigskin strap 75.00
  Thirty-three, leather strap 80.00
  Thirty-six, crotal type, 89″ leather
    strap 180.00

Table, 4⅝″, SS, cupid blowing horn, figural handle, frosted finish, foliate
  strap work border, Gorham Mfg Co,
  c1870 .... 725.00
Trolley Car, brass 125.00

J. NORTON
BENNINGTON
VT.

BENNINGTON AND
BENNINGTON-TYPE POTTERY

History: In 1845 Christopher Webber Fenton
joined Julius Norton, his brother-in-law, in the manufacturing of stoneware pottery in Bennington, Vermont. Fenton sought to expand the company's
products and glazes; Norton wanted to concentrate solely on stoneware. In 1847 Fenton broke
away and established his own factory.

Fenton introduced the famous Rockingham
glaze, developed in England and named after the
Marquis of Rockingham, to America. In 1849 he
patented a flint enamel glaze, "Fenton's Enamel,"
which added flecks, spots, or streaks of color (usually blues, greens, yellows, and oranges) to the
brown Rockingham glaze. Forms included candlesticks, coachman bottles, cow creamers, poodles,
sugar bowls, and toby pitchers.

Fenton produced the little known scroddled
ware, commonly called lava or agate ware. Scroddled ware is composed of different colored clays,
mixed with cream colored clay, molded, turned on
a potter's wheel, coated with feldspar and flint, and
fired. It was not produced in quantity, as there was
little demand for it.

Fenton also introduced Parian ware to America.
Parian was developed in England in 1842 and
known as "Statuary ware." Parian is a translucent
porcelain which has no glaze and resembles marble. Bennington made the blue and white variety
in the form of vases, cologne bottles, and trinkets.

Five different marks were used, with many variations. Only about twenty percent of the pieces
carried any mark; some forms were almost always
marked, others never. Marks: (a) 1849 mark (4
variations) for flint enamel and Rockingham; (b) E.
Fenton's Works, 1845–47, on Parian and occasionally on scroddled ware; (c) U. S. Pottery Co.,
ribbon mark, 1852–58, on Parian and blue and
white porcelain; (d) U. S. Pottery Co., lozenge
mark, 1852–58, on Parian; and (e) U. S. Pottery,
oval mark, 1853–58, mainly on scroddled ware.

The hound handled pitcher is probably the best
known Bennington piece. Hound handled pitchers
also were made by some 30 potteries in over 55
different variations. Rockingham glaze was used

by over 150 potteries in 11 states, mainly the Mid-West, between 1830 and 1900.

References: Richard Carter Barret, *How To Identify Bennington Pottery,* Stephen Greene Press, 1964; Laura Woodside Watkins, *Early New England Potters And Their Wares,* Harvard University Press, 1950.

Museums: Bennington Museum, Bennington, VT; East Liverpool Museum of Ceramics, East Liverpool, OH.

Additional Listings: Stoneware.

Bennington, pitcher, seated hunter and hounds, Fenton, 9″ h, $175.00.

BENNINGTON POTTERY

Bottle, 10⅜″ h, coachman, Rockingham glaze, professional hat restoration, dated "1849" on bottom **200.00**
Candlestick, 6¾″, columnar, yellow-brown, flint enamel, blue glaze **400.00**
Coffeepot, 12¾″ h, flint enamel, olive and mottled amber glaze, fluted finial, c1849–58 . . . . **1,700.00**
Creamer, 5½″ h, figural, cow, Rockingham glaze, imp "N" **300.00**
Dish, 9¼″, flint enamel, 1849, marked "Fenton Co" **400.00**
Flask, book type
7½″, "Ladies Companion," flint enamel, dark brown, amber, blue and green glaze, 2 qt **1,000.00**
8″, "Departed Spirits," flint enamel, light cream glaze, blue and amber flecks, 2 qt **1,000.00**
10¾″, "Bennington Companion," flint enamel, dark brown, amber, blue and green glaze, 4 qts, repaired . **700.00**
Foot Bath, 19½″ l, flint enamel, brown and cream mottled glaze, blue and amber highlights, Scalloped Rib pattern, crack beside handle **700.00**
Goblet, 4½″ h, Rockingham glaze **275.00**
Mantle Ornament, 9½ x 8½″, poodle,

Rockingham glaze, holding basket of colored fruit in mouth, applied coleslaw dec, c1849–55 . . . . **3,600.00**
Picture Frame, 8¾ x 9¾″, opening size 3⅜ x 4¼″, oval, Rockingham glaze, old repairs, pr **325.00**
Pitcher
8″, Parian, white, tulip and sunflower pattern, c1852 . . . . **225.00**
9½″, Rockingham glaze, glaze imperfection **1,000.00**
Snuff Jar, 4″, toby hat, Rockingham glaze, Fenton, 1849 mark **400.00**
Soap Dish, 5¼″, flint enamel, olive brown and cream, glazed, green flecks, dated "1849" on bottom **125.00**
Teapot, 7⅜″ h, flint enamel, Alternate Rib pattern, marked **500.00**
Vase
8⅞″ h, Belleek type, eagle form, two small chips **200.00**
9¾″, tulip, scroddled, variegated brown clays **1,500.00**
Washbowl and Pitcher Set, 13 x 4⅜″ bowl, 10½″ pitcher, Diamond pattern, flint enamel glaze, orange, yellow, and green, 1849 mark **950.00**

Bennington–type, figure, monkey, 3″ h, $125.00.

BENNINGTON-TYPE

Bottle, 6″, figural, pair of high button shoes, Rockingham glaze **175.00**
Bowl, 14¼ x 5¼″, mixing, Rockingham glaze **190.00**
Food Mold, 6⅝″, Turk's head, Rockingham glaze **90.00**
Pitcher, 10½″, Rockingham glaze, paneled, c1850 . . . . **225.00**
Soap Dish, 4 x 2½″, round, Rockingham glaze **100.00**

BISCUIT JARS

History: The biscuit or cracker jar was the fore-runner of the cookie jar. They were made of various materials by leading glassworks and potteries of the late 19th and early 20th centuries.

Note: All items listed have silver plated mountings unless otherwise noted.

Wavecrest, square, ball corners, two horizontal wavy lines across body, shaded green to white, transfer and painted floral design, silver plated top, $230.00.

Bisque, 4⅞", figural, boy's head **150.00**
Cranberry, 9 x 6¼", clear feet, flower prunt underneath, and ribbed finial knob with prunt, two clear ring applied handles **170.00**
Crown Milano, 7 x 5¼", satin finish, flower and leaves outlined with gold dec, white lining, orig "M.W." paper label **700.00**
Florentine Cameo, white floral dec . . .   **225.00**
Jasperware, 5⅜ x 6¾", deep blue, white classical ladies with cupid, SP rim, lid, handle, and ball feet, marked "Wedgwood" only **150.00**
Mother of Pearl, 11" h, 5" d, DQ, rose satin, SP dome shaped lid, sturdy collar, and bail, four tiny feet **735.00**
Nippon, 4½ x 7¼", sq, white, multicolored floral bands, gold outlines and trim, marked "E. E." **85.00**
Pairpoint, 9½", burnt orange, large floral dec, blown-out floral base, sgd **325.00**
Royal Bonn, 6 x 7½", beige and cream ground, pink, blue, rose, and orange flowers, gold outlines, emb swirls, SP rim, lid, and handle, marked **125.00**
Satin Glass
  7¼", pink, shell pattern base, enameled floral dec, SP lid and handle   **300.00**
  9 x 5", flared base, rainbow, DQ, MOP, shiny finish, SP cov, and handle, marked "Patent" **950.00**
Schlegelmilch, R. S. Prussia, pearlized luster, lily of the valley dec, ftd scalloped base, red mark **285.00**
Silverplated, 8 x 8", round, hinged lid, bright cut floral dec, pierced ftd base, late 19th C **165.00**
Stevens and Williams, 5½ x 7¾", amber and green applied leaves, cream opaque ext., deep pink int., SP rim, lid, and handle **275.00**
Wave Crest, 5½ x 9", long stemmed yellow roses, molded multicolored Helmschmied swirls ground, incised floral and leaf dec on lid, marked "Quadruple Plate" **385.00**

BISQUE

History: Bisque or biscuit china is the name given to wares that have been fired once and are not glazed.

Bisque figurines and busts were popular during the Victorian era, being used on fireplace mantels, dining room buffets, and end tables. Manufacturing was centered in the United States and Europe. By the mid-20th century the Japanese were the principal source of bisque items, especially character related items.

Reference: Susan and Al Bagdade, *Warman's English & Continental Pottery & Porcelain, 1st Edition,* Warman Publishing Co., Inc., 1987.

Basket, 8", barefoot boy with wide brimmed hat seated on rim, marked "Germany" **50.00**
Box, egg shape, relief windmill scene, ftd **45.00**
Cigar Holder, 6" h, figural, French soldiers, match holder, French **150.00**
Dish, cov, 9 x 6½ x 5½", dog, brown and white, green blanket, white and gilt basketweave base **500.00**
Figure
  8", Bonnie Prince Charlie, French . .   **30.00**
  14½" h, girl with kitten in left arm, white blouse, pink trimmed blue dress, blue hat with pink bow, German, c1920 . . . .   **250.00**
  20¾" h, pr, man offering lady a rose, Victorian costumes, polychrome, German, late 19th C **300.00**

Flower Pot, carriage, four wheels, royal
   markings dec, pale blue and pink,
   white ground, gold dots, blank back   **135.00**
Match Holder, figural, Dutch girl, copper
   and gold trim, includes striker **35.00**
Night Light, owl head, 3½", 2⅞", gray,
   brown glass eyes, blue bow around
   neck **175.00**
Nodder, 2½ x 3½", jester, seated hold-
   ing pipe, pastel peach and white, gold
   trim **75.00**

**Figurines, pr, one playing French horn,
blue coat, white pants, other with tambourine, blue pants, white coat, rust
lapels and cuffs, white hats, 8¾" h,
$550.00.**

Piano Baby
   7", seated, holding gold watch to ear,
      fancy gown, German **150.00**
   8", boy, seated, blue hat, holding
      drum, marked "Royal Rudolstadt,
      Germany" **350.00**
Planter, girl with water jug, sitting by
   well, coral and green **48.00**
Salt, 3" d, figural, walnut, cream, branch
   base, matching spoon **70.00**
Tobacco Jar, figural, little boy, hair forms
   cover, marked "Heubach" **150.00**
Toothpick Holder, lady with flower **35.00**

BITTERS BOTTLES

History: Bitters, a "remedy" made from natural
herbs and other mixtures with an alcohol base,
often was viewed as the universal cure-all. The
names given to various bitter mixtures were imag-
inative, though the bitters seldom cured what their
makers claimed.

The manufacturers of bitters needed a way to

sell and advertise their products. They designed
bottles in many shapes, sizes, and colors to attract
the buyer. Many forms of advertising, including
trade cards, billboards, signs, almanacs, and novelties proclaimed the virtues of a specific bitter.

During the Civil War a tax was levied on alco-
holic beverages. Since bitters were identified as
medicines, they were exempt from this tax. The
alcohol content was never mentioned. In 1907
when the Pure Foods Regulations went into effect,
"an honest statement of content on every label"
put most of the manufacturers out of business.

References: Carlyn Ring, *For Bitters Only,*
1980; J. H. Thompson, *Bitters Bottles,* Century
House, 1947; Richard Watson, *Bitters Bottles,*
Thomas Nelson and Sons, 1965.

Periodical: *Antique Bottle and Glass Collector,*
P. O. Box 187, East Greenville, PA 18041.

**Grenade Sauvinet Malakoff Seine, emb
name, natural colored pottery, 3¾" h,
$25.00.**

Abbott's Bitters, amber, 8" **8.00**
African Stomach Bitters, amber, 9½" . .   **40.00**
Angostura Bark Bitters, amber, 7" **90.00**
Atwood's Quinine Tonic, aqua **35.00**
Barto's Great Gun Bitters, "Reading,
   Pa." in center circle, cannon shop bot-
   tle, olive amber, 11 x 3¼" **785.00**
Bender's Bitters, aqua **50.00**
Bird Bitters, Phila, PA, clear **75.00**
Brown's Celebrated Indian Herb Bitters,
   Indian queen, yellow, rolled mouth,
   12" **750.00**
Calabash Bitters, aqua **75.00**
Castilian Bitters, light honey amber . . .   **100.00**
Catawba Wine Bitters, cluster of grapes
   in front and back, green, 9" **65.00**
Clayton's & Russell's Bitters, "Cele-
   brated Stomach Bitters," sq **68.00**
Climax Bitters, pale gold amber **75.00**
Columbo Peptic Bitters, amber **30.00**
Constitution Bitters, deep amethyst,
   sloping collared mouth, 9⅛" **725.00**
Dandelion Bitters, rect bottle, clear, am-
   ber, tapered top, 8" **32.00**
Doyle's Hop Bitters, amber, sloping col-
   lared mouth, 9⅜" **25.00**

Drake's Plantation, cabin shape, six
logs, olive amber **140.00**
Eagle Aromatic Bitters, amber **25.00**
Emerson Excelsior Botanic Bitters,
"E.H. Burns, Augusta, ME," amber, 9″ **75.00**
English Femal Bitters, clear **70.00**
Excelsior Aromatic Bitters, smoky am-
ber **100.00**
Gilbert's, Dr., Rock and Rye Bitters,
bluish-green **100.00**
Globe, The, Tonic Bitters, amber, slop-
ing collared mouth, 10″ **65.00**
Goff's Bitters, H on bottom, clear and
amber, 5¾″ **25.00**
Hart's Star Bitters, Philadelphia, PA . . **175.00**
Hentz's Curative Bitters, pale green . . **100.00**
Holtzermann's Patent Stomach Bitters,
rect cabin, yellow amber, sloping col-
lared mouth, 9½″ **425.00**
Hutching's Dyspepsia Bitters, aqua,
sloping collared mouth, 8⅜″ **75.00**
Kimball's Jaundice Bitters, golden amber, sloping collared mouth, iron pon-
til, 7″ **150.00**
King Solomon's Bitters, amber **150.00**
Lorimer's Juniper Bitters, sq, blue
green, 9½″ **60.00**
McKeever's Army Bitters, on shoulder,
drum shaped bottom, cannonballs
stacked on top, tapered top, amber,
10¼″ **600.00**
Moffit, John, NY, Phoenix Bitters, olive
amber, eight sided, round collar pon-
til, 6⅜″ **2,500.00**
Night Cap Bitters, clear, three sided . . **80.00**
Old Homestead Wild Cherry Bitters, sq
cabin, deep golden amber, sloping
collared mouth, 9½″ **150.00**
Oregon Grape Root Bitters, round,
clear, 9¾″ **48.00**
Phoenix Bitters, olive amber, rolled
mouth, 5⅛″ **250.00**
Porter's, Dr., Medicated Stomach Bitters **70.00**
Radium Bitters, rect, clear **35.00**
Rothenberg, S.B., Sole Agent, U.S., gin
shape, milk glass, applied collared
mouth, 9″ **100.00**
Sazerac Aromatic Bitters, lady's leg,
milk glass, applied mouth, 12¼″ . . . **275.00**
Seaworth Bitters, lighthouse shape . . . **275.00**
Suffolk Bitters, pig, yellow amber, dou-
ble collared mouth, 10″ **325.00**
Sunny Castle Stomach Bitters, light am-
ber **60.00**
Toneco Stomach Bitters, "Appetizer &
Tonic," clear, sq **60.00**
Traveller's Bitters, man standing with
cane, oval, amber, 1834–1870, 10½″ **260.00**
Turkish Bitters, amber **75.00**
Uncle Tom's Bitters, light amber **75.00**
Von Humboldt's Stomach Bitters, sq,
amber **80.00**

BLOWN THREE MOLD

History: The Jamestown colony in Virginia introduced glass making into America. The artisans
used a "free blown" method.

Blowing molten glass into molds was not introduced into America until the early 1800s. Blown
three mold glass used a pre-designed mold that
consisted of two, three, or more hinged parts. The
glass maker placed a quantity of molten glass on
the tip of a rod or tube, inserted it into the mold,
blew air into the tube, waited until the glass cooled,
and removed the finish product. The three part
mold is the most common and lends its name to
this entire category.

The impressed decorations on blown mold glass
usually are reversed, i.e., what is raised or convex
on the outside will be concave on the inside. This
is useful in identifying the blown form.

By 1850 American made glassware was in relatively common usage. The increased demand led
to large factories and the creation of a technology
which eliminated the smaller companies.

Reference: George S. and Helen McKearin,
American Glass, reprint, Crown Publishers, 1941,
1948.

Bottle
Light Green, sq, orig ribbed ball stop-
per, McKearin GII-28, stopper type
20, ex-William Elsholz collection . **2,000.00**
Olive green, pint, McKearin GIII-16 . **375.00**
Bowl, 5⅝″ d, 1³⁄₁₆″ h, clear, folded rim,
pontil, twelve diamond base, Mc-
Kearin GII-6 . . . . **85.00**
Celery Vase, Pittsburgh, G-V-21 . . . . . **650.00**
Cologne, 6″, sapphire blue, paneled,
smooth plain base **160.00**
Cordial, clear, 2⅞″ h, ringed base-pontil,
somewhat hollow stem, flat heavy cir-
cular foot, blown into small whiskey
glass mold and formed free hand,
McKearin GII-16 . . . . **450.00**
Creamer, deep purple-blue, 3½″, ap-
plied handle, McKearin GII-11, ex-
William Elsholz collection **1,750.00**
Cruet
Cobalt Blue (deep), 7¾″ h, scroll
scale pattern, ribbed base-pontil,
applied handle, French **250.00**
Sapphire Blue (deep), 6¾″ h, solid
"Tam" stopper, pontil, McKearin
GI-7, type 2 . . . . **220.00**
Decanter
Clear
Pint, 8½″, period sunburst stopper
which may be original, possibly
Irish, McKearin GII-7 . . . . **140.00**
Quart, 10½″ h, 3½″ d, prior to ex-
pansion in the tree mold, piece
was molded in sixteen vertical rib
mold, applied spiral threading

around neck, flanged neck, pontil, McKearin GIII-5, 1/2" piece of applied threading flaked off, stopper McKearin GII-18, ex-McKearin, Guggenheim, Logan, and Gotjen collections **1,500.00**

Olive Amber

Pint, 5 5/8" h, 3 1/4" d, diamond sunbursts between swirled flutes, flanged neck, pontil, product of Mount Vernon Glass Co., McKearin GIII-2, type 1, minutes shallow pinpoint flake on underside of flange, ex-Gotjen collection **1,400.00**

Quart, Keene, NH, McKearin GIII-19, unusual in that this has flanged lip as opposed to funnel shaped mouth, slight int. stain . **850.00**

Olive Green, 7" h, geometric, no stopper, McKearin GIII-16 . . . . **325.00**

Dish

7 1/4" d, 1 3/8" h, clear, folded rim, diamond base, pontil, McKearin GII-21, ex-Culbertson collection **100.00**

8" d, clear, New England, McKearin GII-18 with McKearin base #21 . . **120.00**

Flask

4 4/8" h, 3 7/8" w, chestnut shape, light yellow tint, one-half pint, sheared mouth-pontil, McKearin GII-24, mouth roughness (two tiny shallow flakes on top of mouth rim), 1 x 1/2" oval shallow sliver/smooth broken bubble off underside of base (in making), ex-Tiffany and Gotjen collections **1,100.00**

5 1/4" h, clear, pattern of arches, then diamonds within diamonds, then inverted arches resting upon small dots, sheared mouth, pontil, Continental, slight interior haze **300.00**

7 1/4", deep yellow-green, pint, plain base, slight wear, slight chemical deposit on one rib, McKearin GI-22, ex-William Elsholz and George S. McKearin collections **1,250.00**

Beaver Hat, purple–blue, rayed base, G–III–23, type IV, $465.00.

Flip, clear

5 1/8" h, 4 1/2" d, sixteen diamond base, pontil, McKearin GII-18 . . . . **150.00**

6", barrel shaped, eighteen diamond base, McKearin GII-18, ex-Culbertson collection **220.00**

Glass, clear, 3 1/4" h, plain base pontil, McKearin GI-24 . . . . **65.00**

Hat, Beaver

Cobalt Blue, 2 7/16" h, McKearin GIII-4, ex-William Elsholz collection . . . **1,100.00**

Sapphire Blue (deep), 2 3/16" h, McKearin GIII-25, ex-William Elsholz collection **600.00**

Inkwell

1 3/4" h, 2 3/4" d, olive amber, ringed base, pontil, flat collar, McKearin GII-18E **65.00**

1 5/8" h, 2" d, sapphire blue, smooth base, short ground neck, possibly Boston and Sandwich Glass Company, McKearin GI-7, tiny open bubble on one rib, ex-Tiffany and Gotjen collections **300.00**

Lamp, clear

Font, 4 7/8" h, pressed sq stepped lacy base, conical shape ending in a melon knop, McKearin GI-7, type 1, small chip in one corner of pressed base, slight residue inside font . . . **650.00**

Peg, 3 7/8" h, 3 1/8" w, ball shaped, short sheared neck and solid applied peg, McKearin GII-21, ex-Tiffany and Gotjen collections **1,400.00**

Sparking, 2 1/8" h, blown in stopper mold, applied sheared handle with tiny flake, iron pontil, drop burner, stopper illustrated in McKearin 114-6 . . . . **800.00**

Mustard, 4 1/4"h, clear, pontil, cork stopper, orig paper label, "SWEET SPIRIT OF NITRATE..../H M Baldwin and Son/West Stockbridge, Mass.," McKearin GI-15 . . . . **40.00**

Pitcher

7 1/4" h, light aquamarine, quart, Mt. Vernon Glass Co., McKearin GIII-2, Type 1, ex-William Elsholz, George S. McKearin, and Crawford Wettlaufer collections **7,500.00**

8 1/8", clear, Horn of Plenty pattern, applied hollow blown handle, McKearin GV-17, ex-William Elsholz and George S. McKearin collections **2,400.00**

Punch Bowl, 8 3/4" d bowl, 5 1/4" d foot, 7 3/8" h, clear McKearin GII-18, foot pattern GIII-21, ex-William Elsholz collection **4,000.00**

Salt

1¹¹⁄₁₆″ h, sapphire blue, low ftd, flaring rim, McKearin GIII-25, ex-William Elsholz and George S. McKearin collections **500.00**

2⁹⁄₁₆″ h, clear, made from tumbler mold, hollow foot, McKearin GII-9 **110.00**

2½″ h, cobalt blue, galleried, fifteen diamond base, McKearin GII-18 . . **550.00**

Sauce Dish, 4⁹⁄₁₆″, deep purple-blue, McKearin GIII-23, ex-William Elsholz and Crawford Wettlaufer collections . **3,250.00**

Sugar Bowl, cov, 5¾″, clear, galleried rim, McKearin GII-18, ex-William Elsholz collection **3,000.00**

Toilet Bottle, 5⅞″, light yellow-green, orig stopper, McKearin GI-3, Type 2, ex-William Elsholz collection **700.00**

Vase, 6⅝″ h, clear, patterned from pint decanter mold, McKearin GII-18, ex-William Elsholz collection **2,000.00**

Vinegar Bottle, cobalt blue, period stopper, McKearin GI-VII-4 . . . . **275.00**

Whiskey Tumbler, 2⅞″ h, 2⅞″ d, amber, pontil diamond base, McKearin GII-18, ex-McKearin collection, illus plate #8, Girl Scout Loan Exhibition Catalog, 1929 . . . . **2,700.00**

BOHEMIAN GLASS

History: The once independent country of Bohemia, now a part of Czechoslovakia, produced a variety of fine glassware: etched, cut, overlay, and colored. Their glassware was first imported into America in the early 1820s and continues today.

Bohemia is known for its "flashed" glass that was produced in the familiar ruby color, as well as amber, green, blue, and black. Common patterns include "Deer and Castle," "Deer and Pine Tree," and "Vintage."

Most of the Bohemian glass encountered in today's market is of the 1875–1900 period. Bohemian–type glass also was made in England, Switzerland, and Germany.

Reproduction Alert.

Beaker

4³⁄₁₆″, clear, cut and engraved, initialed, dated 1836 . . . . **80.00**

5½″, amber flashed, engraved, animals and building, C scroll panels, flared foot, c1860 . . . . **75.00**

Bowl

9″, ruby, Deer and Pine Tree **75.00**

12½″, double cut overlay, cobalt blue cut to clear **250.00**

Box

3½″, domed lid, ruby flashed, Vintage, engraved clear and frosted

Bowl, ten panels, shaped top, leaf and grape design, 3⅛″ d, 2″ h, $45.00.

grape clusters and vines, gilt brass fittings **125.00**

3¾″, domed hinged lid, ruby flashed, engraved clear and frosted buildings, scrolling foliate bands, brass fittings **90.00**

Candy Dish, cov, ruby flashed, Deer and Castle, clear and frosted **90.00**

Celery Dish, ruby flashed, Deer and Castle, clear and frosted **80.00**

Cologne Bottle, 3¾ x 7¼″, double cut overlay, ruby cut to clear, clear frosted base, ruby stopper **115.00**

Compote

7″ d, amber flashed, cut leaf and floral dec, green band at top, pedestal base **100.00**

9½ x 6½″, amber flashed, Deer and Castle, engraved clear and frosted animals, castle, and trees **150.00**

Decanter

11⅛″, clear, ruby glass overlay, thumb cut faceted sides swirling to base . **50.00**

14¾″, crystal, octagonal, greenish tint, engraved forest and deer scene, orig stopper **80.00**

Flip Glass, 6 x 6″, clear, cut, engraved forest scene with fox and birds **100.00**

Goblet

7½″, cranberry, gold and enamel dec, artist sgd **125.00**

11″, ruby flashed, gilt dec, scalloped scent bottle top **175.00**

Jar

7″, cov, barrel shape, bands of clear engraving, red satin discs, barrel finial **125.00**

9½″, cov, ruby **145.00**

Mantel Lusters, 6½″ d, 12¼″ h, cranberry cut overlay, cut scalloped tops, white overlay panels, multicolored flowers, all over gold flowers and scrolls, clear cut prisms, pr **1,000.00**

Mug, 6″, ruby flashed, engraved castle and trees, applied clear handle, sgd "Volmer, 1893" **80.00**

Perfume Bottle

5¼", ruby, paneled sides, cut stopper **110.00**

7", ruby flashed, Deer and Castle, clear and frosted, gold dec **90.00**

Pickle Jar, cov, 6", ruby flashed, Deer and Castle, clear and frosted **50.00**

Powder Box, 4¼" d, round, straight sides, flat top, ruby flashed, etched cov with leaping stag, forest setting, landscape and birds on sides, clear base **100.00**

Rose Bowl, 8½" d, ruby flashed, Deer and Castle, clear and frosted **225.00**

Stein

2¾ x 4½", ruby flashed, engraved dog and deer in forest, "Souvenir de Luchon" on front, pewter mounts **225.00**

3 x 6½", ruby flashed, engraved cathedral panel, leaves, and scrolls, pewter mounts, ruby inset lid **300.00**

Sugar Shaker, ruby flashed, Bird and Castle, clear and frosted **70.00**

Teapot, 11" w, cranberry cut to clear, panels of flowers, gilt spout and handle **185.00**

Tumbler

4", ruby flashed, cut design, gold dec, set of 4 . . . . **125.00**

4¼", engraved scene, early 19th C . **150.00**

Vase, 11" h, gold rose dec, late 19th C **175.00**

Whiskey Glass, pr, 3¼", engraved, clear, early 19th C **225.00**

BOOKS, AMERICANA

History: America's fascination with local, regional, state, and national history owes it origin to the nation's centennial in 1876. The next thirty years witnessed a proliferation of histories, atlases, genealogies, and photographic studies. Historical groups organized and published pamphlets or annual studies. A renewal of interest in local history occurred with the historic preservation movement of the 1950s forward. As communities and states celebrated the 50th, 75th, 100th, 150th, 200th, and more anniversary of their establishment, committees organized celebrations, one by-product of which was a local history publication.

The number of books and pamphlets range in the hundreds of thousands. Pennsylvania has been chosen as a typical example. Readers are asked to compare what they have to the items cited. The prices are approximately the same nationally for the identical type of material. More recent publications, i.e., those published within the last twenty-five years, rarely are valued above their initial selling price.

On October 9 and 10, 1984, Sotheby's in New York held a major sale of over 1,000 early cookbooks. One buyer was primarily responsible for driving up prices from 5 to 70 times above catalog estimates. Cookbooks caught fire and are now among the hottest items in the antique book market.

Please remember that condition is perhaps the greatest factor in properly pricing a book. Also, local and region books will bring slightly higher prices in the areas to which their subjects relate.

References: Linda J. Dickinson, *Price Guide to Cookbooks & Recipe Leaflets,* Collector Books, 1990; *Old Book Value Guide, Second Edition,* Collector Books, 1990.

See *Warman's Americana and Collectibles* for additional listings in the Books: Antiques and Collectibles, Cookbooks, Paperback Books, and Pulp Magazine categories.

Advisor: Ron Lieberman

PENNSYLVANIANA

Ashburton Coal Company, *Prospectus & Reports On The Company's Estate In Schuykill And Luzerne Counties, Pennsylvania,* New York, 1864, 16 pgs, map, plain paper wraps **25.00**

Barber, Edwin Atlee, *Tulip Ware Of The Pennyslvania-German Potters,* Philadelphia, 1903, 233 pgs, color frontis, illus, printed wraps **60.00**

Birmingham Friends, *250 Years of Quakerism at Birmingham, Chester County, PA, 1690–1940,* West Chester, 1940, 128 pgs, illus **25.00**

Browning, Charles H., *Welsh Settlement of Pennsylvania,* Philadelphia, 1912, 631 pgs, illus, library binding **35.00**

Callender, James, *The Political Progress of Britain...Tending to Prove the Ruinous Consequences of the Popular System of Taxation, War, & Conquest,* 1st Pt. Folwell, Philadelphia, 1795, 120 pgs, later marbled wraps **85.00**

Carmer, Carl, *The Susquehanna,* Rivers of America Series, NY, 1955, 493 pgs, illus, dj, sgd by author **35.00**

Colby, George, *The Horseman's Friend,* Wible, Gettysburg, 1868, 31 pgs, advertisements, 24 mo **40.00**

Cumberland And Adams Counties, PA, Chicago, 1886, illus and maps **120.00**

Dahlinger, Charles W., *Pittsburgh: A Sketch of Its Early Social Life,* Zadok Cramer, publisher, 1916, 216 pgs . . **35.00**

East Stroudsburg Centennial, 1870– 1970, 200 pgs, wraps, 4to **15.00**

Eshleman, H. Frank, *Lancaster County Indians, Annals of the Susquehannocks and Other Indian Tribes of the Susquehanna Territory from 1500– 1763, the Date of their Extinction,*

Lancaster, 1908, 415 pgs, new wraps, limited to 550 copies **60.00**

Gibson, John, *History of York County, PA...,* Chicago, 1886, 979 pgs, litho plates, thick 4to,½ morocco binding . **150.00**

Hain, H. H., *History of Perry County, PA,* Harrisburg, 1922, 1088 pgs, illus . . . **125.00**

Jones, Charles H., *History Of The Campaign For The Conquest Of Canada In 1776,* Philadelphia, 1882, 234 pgs, illus, detailed study of PA regiments **35.00**

King, Moses, *Philadelphia & Notable Philadelphians,* bound with *King's Views of Phila.,* Philadelphia, 1902, 218 pgs, portraits and views, folio, full morocco **50.00**

Lewis, John F., *Redemption Of The Lowe Schuylkill...,* Philadelphia, 1924, 171 pgs, illus, sgd by author . **16.00**

McKeesport, PA, The First 100 Years, Abbott & Harrison, McKeesport, 1894, 178 pgs, illus **30.00**

Nutting, Wallace, *Pennsylvania Beautiful,* Garden City, NY, 1935, 296 pgs, dj **25.00**

Pennypacker, Samuel Whitaker, *Annals of Phoenixville & Its Vicinity...,* Philadelphia, 1872, 295 pgs, illus, orig morocco cloth, military of history of Chester and Montgomery counties . **75.00**

Punkin, Jonathan, (Pseud.), *Downfall of Freemasonry...& The Origin & Increase of Abolition,* Philadelphia, 1838, 48 pgs, caricature plates, ds . **40.00**

Report of the National Sesquicentennial Exhibition Commission, Philadelphia, 1927, 536 pgs **25.00**

Rupp, Israel Daniel, *History Of The Counties Of Berks And Lebanon: Containing a Brief Account of the Indians,* Lancaster, 1844, 513 pgs, plates, full leather binding **100.00**

Sellers, Charles Coleman, *Benjamin Franklin In Portraiture,* Yale, New Haven, 1962, 254 pgs, 45 pgs illus . . . **60.00**

Sewel, William, *The History of the Rise, Increase & Progress of the Christian People Called Quakers...,* 3rd ed, corrected, Issac Collins, Trenton, 1774, 828 pgs, folio, worn orig leather **275.00**

Shoemaker, Henry Wharton, *North Mountain Mementos: Legends And Traditions Gathered In Northern Pennyslvania,* Altoona, 1920, 383 pgs, illus, clothbound **35.00**

Sutton, George M., *Birds of Pennsylvania,* Harrisburg, 1928, 168 pgs, illus, dj **20.00**

Thayer, William M., *The Printer Boy. "How Benjamin Franklin Made His Mark...,"* London, 1860, 264 pgs, illus, hand colored **15.00**

Venango County: Centennial Celebration of the Bench & Bar, Franklin, 1905, 169 pgs, illus **20.00**

Walker, J. H., *Rafting Days In Pennsylvania,* Altoona, 1922, 122 pgs, illus . **40.00**

COOKBOOKS

Bitting, A. W., *Appetizing; or, The Art of Canning: its History and Development,* 4to, 1st ed, cloth, San Francisco, 1937 . . . . **75.00**

Bradley, Martha, *The British Housewife: or, the Cook, Housekeeper's, and Gardiner's Companion,* 2 volumes, London, c1790 . . . . **200.00**

Brillat-Savarin, J. A., *The Physiology of Taste; or, Meditations on Transcendental Gastronomy,* 4to, Garden City, 1926, one of 500 numbered copies . **40.00**

Brown, Eleanor and Bob, *Culinary Americana: Cookbooks published during the Years from 1860 through 1960,* 8vo, 1st ed, dj, New York, 1961 **75.00**

Dumas, Alexandre, *Grand Dictionnaire de Cuisine,* 8vo, 1st ed, Paris, 1873 **250.00**

Edwards, Clarence E., *Bohemian San Francisco: its Restaurants and their most Famous Recipes,* 8vo, cloth, dj,San Francisco, 1914 . . . . **35.00**

Escoffier, Auguste, *Le Guide Culinaire,* 8vo, Paris, 1907 . . . . **100.00**

Eustis, Celestine, *Cooking in Old Creole Days,* 8vo, New York, 1904 . . . . **120.00**

Francatelli, Charles, *The Modern Cook,* large 8vo, Philadelphia, c1850 . . . . **50.00**

Glasse, Hannah, *The Art of Cookery, Made Plain and Easy,* 4to, 5th ed, London, 1755 . . . . **150.00**

Graham, Thomas John, *Sure Methods of Improving Health, and Prolonging Life,* 12 mo, straight-grain morocco gilt, London, 1827 . . . . **80.00**

Haraszthy, Agoston, *Grape Culture, Wines, and Wine-Making,with Notes upon Agriculture and Horticulture,* 8vo, New York, 1862 . . . . **300.00**

Henderson, William Augustus, *The Housekeeper's Instructor; or, Universal Family Cook,* 8vo, London, c1790 **125.00**

Kitchiner, William, *The Cook's Oracle,* 12 mo, New York, 1825, dedication page sgd by author **60.00**

Lawlor, C. F., *The Mixicologist; or, How to Mix All Kinds of Fancy Drinks,* 12mo, orig wrappers, Cincinnati, 1899 . . . . **50.00**

Packman, Ana, *Early California Hospitality: The Cookery Customs of Spanish California,* 8vo, Glendale: Arthur Clark, 1938 . . . . **85.00**

Pennell, Elizabeth Robins, *My Cookery*

Books, 8vo, Boston, 1903, one of 330 numbered copies **100.00**

Quennell, Nancy, *The Epicure's Anthology, with an Essay by A. J. A. Symons,* illus by Osbert Lancaster, 8vo, Golden Cockerel Press, London, 1936, one of 150 numbered copies sgd by illus **50.00**

Redding, Cyrus, *A History and Description of Modern Wines,* 8vo, London, 1836 . . . . **80.00**

Richardson, A. E., and Eberlein, H.D., *The English Inn Past and Present,* 8vo, 1st ed, London, 1925 . . . . **30.00**

Rundell, Maria Eliza, *A New System of Domestic Cookery,* 12mo, New York, 1814 . . . . **75.00**

Seldes, Gilbert, *The Future of Drinking,* 8vo, 1st ed, Boston, 1930 . . . . **25.00**

Wayland, Virginia and Harold, *Of Carving, Cards, and Cookery,* 8vo, Raccoon Press, Arcadia, California, 1962, one of 275 numbered copies . **75.00**

Wells, J. R. *The Family Companion,* 12mo, Boston, 1846 . . . . **50.00**

BOOTJACKS

History: Bootjacks are metal or wooden devices that facilitate the removal of boots. Bootjacks are used by placing the heel of the boot in the "U" shaped opening, putting a foot on the back of the bootjack, and pulling the front boot off the foot.

Cast iron, lyre shape, 10¼″ l, $48.00.

Brass, beetle, 10″ **90.00**
Cast Iron
  Cricket, emb lacy design, 11¾″ l . . . **25.00**
  Horse, stylized **110.00**
  Lyre shaped, 10¼″ l **50.00**
  Mule's head **40.00**
  Naught Nelly, old worn polychrome repaint, 9¾″ l **45.00**
  Tree center, two footed, 12″ l **30.00**
  Vine design, 12″ l **35.00**
  Wishbone, curling ends on arched feet **130.00**
Wood
  Folk Art, monkey, painted suit, 15″ l, c1900 . . . . **30.00**

Maple, hand hewn, 13″ l **15.00**
Pine, oval ends, sq nails, 25″ l **28.00**
Tiger Stripe Maple, 4 x 10″ **20.00**
Walnut, portable, carpeted top, cast iron frame **50.00**

BOTTLES, GENERAL

History: Cosmetic bottles held special creams, oils, and cosmetics designed to enhance the beauty of the user. Some also claimed, especially on their colorful labels, to cure or provide relief from common ailments.

A number of household items, e.g., cleaning fluids and polishes, required glass storage containers. Many are collected for their fine lithograph labels.

Mineral water bottles contained water from a natural spring. Spring water was favored by health conscious people between the 1850s and 1900s.

Nursing bottles, used to feed the young and sickly, were a great help to the housewife because of graduated measures, replaceable nipples, ease of cleaning, sterilizing, and reuse.

References: Ralph & Terry Kovel, *The Kovels' Bottle Price List, Eighth Edition,* Crown Publishers, Inc., 1987; Carlo & Dorothy Sellari, *The Illustrated Price Guide To Antique Bottles,* Collector Books, 1989.

Periodicals: *Antique Bottle And Glass Collector,* P.O. Box 187, East Greenville, PA 18041.

Additional Listings: Barber Bottles, Bitter Bottles, Figural Bottles, Food Bottles, Ink Bottles, Medicine Bottles, Poison Bottles, Sarsaparilla Bottles and Snuff Bottles. Also see the bottle categories in *Warman's Americana & Collectibles* for more examples.

COSMETICS

De Vry's Dandero-Off Hair Tonic, clear, 6½″ **10.00**
Hyacinthia Toilet Hair Dressing, rect, crude applied lip, open pontil, aqua, 6″ **22.00**
Kranks Cold Cream, milk glass, screw top, 2¾″ **4.00**
Pompeian Massage Cream, amethyst, 2¾″ **4.00**
Van Buskirb's, aqua, 5″ **3.00**

HOUSEHOLD

Alma Polish, aqua, name emb on shoulder, 5″, marked "M & Co" on base . **5.00**
Gordon's Chafola Furniture Polish, emb, open pontil **150.00**
Lake Shore See Co, aqua, 5¾″ **6.00**
Osborn's Liquid Polish, round, open pontil, amber **325.00**
Standard Oil Co, clear, orig label, 6″ . . **6.00**

MINERAL OR SPRING WATER

American Kissinger Water, aqua, pt . .	50.00
Boardman, J & Co, cobalt	50.00
Crystal Spring Water, Saratoga, NY, horseshoe shape, green, qt, 9½" . . .	85.00
Geyser Springs, emerald green, 7⅝" .	550.00
Indian Spring, aqua, emb Indian head, 10½"	15.00
Round Lake Mineral Water, red-amber, 9¼"	750.00
Rutherford's Premium Mineral Water, ground pontil, dark olive, 7½"	60.00
San Francisco Glass Works, tapered neck, blob top, sea green, 6⅞"	15.00
Veronica Mineral Water, amber, sq . . .	8.00
Vichy Water Cullums Spring, Choctaw Co, AL, dark olive, 7¼"	35.00
Witter Medical Spring Co, amber, 9½"	8.00

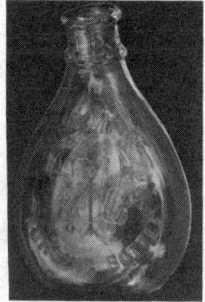

Nursing, clear glass, emb "The Empire Nursing Bottle," 5½", $45.00.

NURSING

Empire Nursing Bottle, 6½", bent neck, emb name	50.00
Hygenic Feeder, emb, open on both ends	30.00
Marguerite Feeding Bottle, inside screw, daisy on top	32.00
Mother's Comfort, clear, turtle type . . .	20.00
Teddy's Pet, Peaceful Nights, clear, emb, turtle shape, 4 oz	70.00

BRASS

History: Brass is a durable, malleable, and ductile metal alloy consisting mainly of copper and zinc. It achieved its greatest popularity for utilitarian and decorative art items in the eighteenth and nineteenth centuries.

References: Mary Frank Gaston, *Antique Brass: Identification and Values,* Collector Books, 1985; Peter, Nancy, and Herbert Schiffer, *The Brass Book,* Schiffer Publishing, Ltd, 1978.

Additional Listings: Bells, Candlesticks, Fireplace Equipment, and Scientific Instruments.

Reproduction Alert: Many modern reproductions are being made of earlier brass forms, especially in the areas of buckets, fireplace equipment, and kettles.

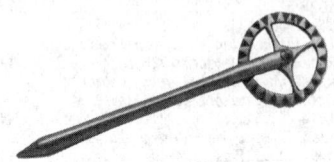

Pie crimper, 5½" l, $15.00.

Alms Dish, 18" d, repousse leaf and shell border, 19th C	110.00
Andirons, 20", pr, ring turned shafts, faceted finials, scrolled legs	275.00
Basinette, 43" l, 35" h crozier, Edwardian, crozier suspending a knotted rope basket, oval brass basin, decorative stand, scrolled legs	1,150.00
Bed Warmer	
43" l, tooled design on lid, turned wood handle	325.00
58" l, pierced lid, turned handle	150.00
Book Stand, 9" h, folding, pierced and scrolled, rect base, English	160.00
Bowl, handles, Dutch	50.00
Box, 6¾" l, hanging, emb floral dec . .	25.00
Bucket, 12" h, tapered, swing handle, Georgian, c1800	650.00
Call Bell, 6¼" h, red granite base	25.00
Candle Box, hanging, scalloped back, 12" l, minor dents	150.00
Candle Jack, 6" h, Dutch, late 18th C .	150.00
Candlesticks, pr 6⅝" h, pushups, Victorian	110.00
Chamberstick, pr	
3¾" h, pushups	80.00
6⅝" h, pushups, Victorian	110.00
Clock, 18 x 14", wall, round, enameled Roman numeral dial, ball and ring hanging, Georgian style, late 19th C	600.00
Coal Scuttle, 15" h, wrought iron swing handle, c1900	110.00
Dish, 15½" d, ftd, Dutch, late 19th C . .	50.00
Door Handles, pr, 16" l, sq elongated form, cast floral dec	10.00
Doorstop, 13" h, pineapple, cast	115.00
Fireplace Fender, 48" l, reticulated screen, lion paw feet	275.00
Fireplace Fan, 38" w, 25" h, folding, griffin detail	65.00

Girondoles, pr, 45" h, lyre form, seven curved arms with prisms and faceted swags, late 19th C 950.00

Inkwell

5½" l, triple, three monkeys, hear no evil, see no evil, and speak no evil pose, hinged heads, Victorian, late 19th C 80.00

11" l, pierced scrolled back plate, two ink pots, pen tray, Victorian style . 110.00

Jam Kettle, 11½" d, Ansonia Brass Co, 1865–66 patent 80.00

Jardiniere, 6" h, globular form, incised geometric and floral motif, 19th C . . 20.00

Lamp

Desk, 17½" h, green overlay shade, labeled "Amronlite, Pat 1917" . . . 110.00

Gimbal, 6" h, whale oil burner 85.00

Lantern, 22" h, repousse, Dutch style, rect form, scroll and leaf motifs 170.00

Mortar and Pestle, 2½" h 40.00

Pitcher, 7" h, Continental, late 19th C . 50.00

Plant Stand, gilded, white onyx shelf and top 50.00

Planter, 14" d, oval, two handles, Victorian, late 19th C 200.00

Salt, cov, 3" d, 4¾" h, paw feet 85.00

Samovar, 25½" h, tray, Russian 390.00

Sconces, pr

12" l, scrolled form, English, 19th C . 120.00

14" h, French Empire style, mounted swan supporting wreath in mouth holding three candle arms 550.00

20" l, Louis XVI style, rose sprigs, two candle arms tied with bow knot . . 250.00

Scuttle, 7" h, repousse floral dec, scoop, Victorian 100.00

Shelf, hanging, 20 x 14 x 8", reticulated unicorn and vine pediment, glazed oval sides, drawer, late 19th C 70.00

Wafer Iron, 4" d, 17" l, geometric floral design, wrought iron handles 65.00

Wash Bowl, Georgian

14" d, 18th C 50.00

15" d, circular handle, 19th C 90.00

Watch Holder, 8½" h, Rococo style, scroll, leaf, and floral dec 80.00

Water Carrier, 17" h, two spouts, Continental, early 19th C 80.00

BREAD PLATES

History: Beginning in the mid-1880s, special trays or platters were made for serving bread and rolls. Designated by collectors as "bread plates," these small trays or platters can be found in porcelain, glass (especially pattern glass), and metals.

Bread plates often were part of a china or glass set. However, many glass companies made special plates which honored national heroes, com-

memorated historical or special events, offered a moral maxim, or supported a religious attitude. The theme on the plate could be either in a horizontal or vertical format. The favorite shape for these plates is oval, with a common length being ten inches.

Reference: Anna Maude Stuart, *Bread Plates And Platters*, published by author, 1965.

Additional Listings: Pattern Glass.

Venus and Psyche pattern, clear glass, 11 x 7½", $45.00.

Aluminum, hand wrought, pine cone dec 12.00

China

Noritake, 10", gold handled, hp scene in center, wide border, hp stylized flowers, maroon wreath 65.00

Silhouette, Crooksville 80.00

Pattern Glass

A Pleasure To... . . . . 38.00

Aurora, 10" round, large star in center, ruby stained 35.00

Baltimore, 12½" 70.00

Be Industrious, 12 x 8¼", oval, clear, handled 50.00

Butterfly & Fan, clear 40.00

Canadian, 10", clear 45.00

Continental, 11¾" l, clear, c1870 . . . 90.00

Cupid and Venus, amber 75.00

Daisy and Button, 13", apple green . 60.00

Deer and Pine Tree, blue 100.00

Egyptian, Mormon Temple 300.00

Fern 30.00

Good Luck 45.00

Grace 60.00

Horseshoe, 14 x 10", double horseshoe handles 65.00

Iowa, motto 80.00

Lion, 12", frosted, including lion handles, GUTDODB 125.00

Moon and Star, rect, clear 45.00

One Hundred One, 11", farm implement center 75.00

Palmette, 9", handled 30.00

Polar Bear, frosted 150.00

Queen Anne	**50.00**
Rock of Ages, 12⅞″ l, clear and opalescent, colored and clear combinations, c1870	**175.00**
Shell and Tassel, round	**55.00**
Tennessee, colored jewels	**75.00**
Three Presidents, frosted center	**85.00**
U.S. Coin, frosted coins	**300.00**
Westward Ho	**180.00**
Sterling Silver, repousse, 10½ oz troy, Loring Andrews Co, Cincinnati OH	**250.00**

BRIDE'S BASKETS

History: A ruffled edge, glass bowl in a metal holder was a popular wedding gift in the 1880–1910 era, hence, the name of "bride's basket." The glass bowls can be found in most glass types of the period. The metal holder was generally silver plated with a bail handle, thus enhancing the basket image.

Over the years bowls and bases became separated, and married pieces resulted. When the base has been lost, the bowl is sold separately.

Reference: John Mebane, *Collecting Bride's Baskets And other Glass Fancies,* Wallace-Homestead, 1976.

Reproduction Alert: The glass bowls have been reproduced.

Note: Items listed have silver plated holder unless otherwise noted.

Cased glass, white ext., shaded pink int. with gold floral dec, clear ruffled rim, stand marked "Superior Silver Co, Quad Plate 1000," 9⅜″ d, $100.00.

Cameo, 8″ sq, pink cut to white, floral sprays, Mt Washington, period SP holder, minor damage	**175.00**
Cased	
9″ d, shaded white to blue, green pontil, Pairpoint holder	**275.00**
10 x 14¼″, white int., cobalt blue ext., enameled gold flowers and leaves, ruffled rim, SP frame, emb leaves	**400.00**

11 x 11¼″, shaded pink, white ext., quadruple plate stand, Middletown	**150.00**
Custard, 10″ sq, melon ribbed bowl, enameled daisies, applied rubena crystal rim, twisted and beaded handle, ftd emb SP frame, marked "Wilcox"	**425.00**
Hobnail, 10½″, pink, enameled flowers, ruffled rim, reticulated SP frame	**225.00**
Loetz, 8 x 10½″, irid gold, blue, and purple, recessed indentations, ruffled, ground pontil, ftd metal stand	**300.00**
Opalescent, 9¼″, blue, crimped rim, reticulated SP holder marked "Wallingford, Biggins & Rodgers Co"	**165.00**
Satin	
10½″, butterscotch fluted, ruffled bowl, ornate SP pedestal holder with four floral arms	**375.00**
11 x 15½″, deep rose, enamel dec, swan surrounded by flowers, heavy bronze holder with birds perched on top	**400.00**
11¼″, emerald green, shaded light to dark bowl, enameled dec, ornate ftd SP frame	**265.00**
Spangled, 10⅜″, multicolored, ruby, cranberry, and green, ivory and yellow base, silver flecks	**100.00**
Spatter, yellow, brown, and purple, ruffled and crimped, SP holder	**235.00**
Stevens and Williams, tapestry ware, threaded ext., creamy white MOP inner layer, pink lining, two shades of gold enamel dec, foliate branch, fully opened blossoms, and butterfly, twisted white thorn handle, four white applied feet, Oscar Pierre Erard dec, sgd "972/1 B332," c1892	**1,250.00**

BRISTOL GLASS

History: Bristol glass is a designation given to a semi–opaque glass, usually decorated with enamel and cased with another color.

Initially the term referred only to glass made in Bristol, England, in the 17th and 18th centuries. By the Victorian era firms on the Continent and in America copied the glass and its forms.

Bottle	
Blue, gold dec	**25.00**
Caramel, enamel flowers, matching stopper and holder	**110.00**
Box, 1½″, round, Victorian lady and gentleman dec, brass trim	**48.00**
Cake Stand, celadon green, enameled herons in flight, gold trim	**125.00**
Candlestick, 7″ h, soft green, gold band, pr	**60.00**

Vase, shaded light pink to dark pink ground, painted enamel dec, 8½" h, $50.00.

Cologne Bottle, 2⅛ x 5¼", green, pink roses, blue, and white flowers, white scrolls and gold trim, matching ball shaped stopper 75.00
Cruet, 2¼ x 4¾", blue, white flowers, gold leaves, applied blue handle, matching ball stopper 90.00
Decanter, 8", blue, matching stopper . .   75.00
Dresser Set, two cologne bottles, cov powder jar, white, gilt butterflies dec, clear stoppers 50.00
Ewer, 17", white, enameled cupid scene   80.00
Fairy Lamp, 4 x 4½", opaque white shade, blue shading to yellow and pink, clear marked "Clarke" base . .   140.00
Hatpin Holder, 6⅛", ftd, blue, enameled jewels, gold dec 100.00
Perfume Bottle, 3¼", squat, blue, gold band, white enameled flowers and leaves, matching stopper 100.00
Pickle Castor, pink, flower dec 300.00
Puff Box, cov, round, blue, gold dec . .   30.00
Rose Bowl, 3½", shaded blue, crimped edge 60.00
Sugar Shaker, 4¾", white, hp flowers .   60.00
Sweetmeat Jar
  3 x 5½", deep pink, enameled flying duck, leaves, blue flower dec, white lining, SP rim, lid, and bail handle   100.00
  5¾ x 4½", green, enameled garlands of pink, white, yellow, blue, and green flowers, four butterflies, SP rim, lid, and bail handle 120.00
Vase
  10" h, baluster, oval reserve with figure, Neoclassical style robes, trailing drapery, black, white, and gilt border, pr 200.00
  15" h, pr, baluster form, polychrome bird, leaf, and floral dec, pink ground, Victorian, c1880 . . . .   90.00

BRITISH ROYALTY COMMEMORATIVES

History: British commemorative china, souvenirs to commemorate coronations and other royal events, dates from the 1600s, with the early pieces being rather crude in design and form. The development of transfer printing, c1780, led to a much closer likeness of the reigning monarch on the ware.

Few commemorative pieces predating Queen Victoria's reign are found today at popular prices. Items associated with Queen Elizabeth II and her children, e. g., the wedding of HRH Prince Andrew and Miss Sarah Ferguson and the subsequent birth of their daughter HRH Princess Beatrice are very common.

Some British Royalty commemoratives are easily recognized by their portraits of past or present monarchs. Some may be in silhouette profile. Other royal symbols include crowns, dragons, royal coats of arms, national flowers, swords, scepters, dates, messages, and initials.

References: Malcolm Davey and Doug Mannion, *50 Years of Royal Commemorative China 1887-1937*, Dayman Publications, 1988; Peter Johnson, *Royal Memorabilia: A Phillips Collectors Guide*, Dunestyle Publishing Ltd., 1988; John May, *Victoria Remembered, A Royal History 1817–1861*, London, 1983; John and Jennifer May, *Commemorative Pottery 1780–1900, A Guide for Collectors*, Charles Scribner's Sons, 1972; Josephine Jackson, *Fired For Royalty*, Heaton Moor, 1977; David Rogers, *Coronation Souvenirs and Commemoratives*, Latimer New Dimensions, Ltd., 1975; Sussex Commemorative Ware Centre, *200 Commemoratives*, Metra Print Enterprises, 1979; Geoffrey Warren, *Royal Souvenirs*, Orbis, 1977; Audrey B. Zeder, *British Royal Commemoratives*, Wallace-Homestead, 1986.

Additional Listings: See *Warman's Americana & Collectibles* for more examples.

Advisors: Douglas Flynn and Alan Bolton.

Beaker
  Charles/Diana, Wedding, 3¾", sepia portraits, Royal Doulton 45.00
  Edward VIII, Investiture as Prince of Wales, 1911, 3½", color portrait, Royal Wintonia 140.00
  George V/Mary, Coronation, 4⅜", color portraits along with Prince of Wales (later Edward VIII), unmarked 80.00
Bowl
  Elizabeth II, Coronation, 8" d, 4¼" w at bottom, crown shape, pressed glass 40.00
  George VI/Elizabeth, 1937 Coronation, sepia Marcus Adams portrait, color dec, 6" sq, J & G Meakin . .   40.00
  Edward VIII, 1937 Coronation, profile in well, 10" d, pressed glass 65.00

Spoon, Queen Victoria, Diamond Jubilee, sterling silver, gold wash, coronation scene in bowl, elaborate dec on both sides of handle, 6¼" l, $150.00.

Victoria, 1897 Jubilee, 19¼" d, pressed glass, amber 65.00

Box
   Elizabeth II, 25th Anniversary of Coronation, 4¼" d, Coalport 40.00
   Elizabeth, The Queen Mother, 80th Birthday, color portrait, 4" d, Crown Staffordshire 65.00

Cup and Saucer
   Charles/Diana, 1981 Wedding, Royal Albert 25.00
   Charles, 1969 Investiture as Prince of Wales, Duchess 50.00
   George V/Mary, 1911 Coronation, color portraits, no mark 55.00
   Edward VII/Alexandra, 1902 Coronation, Foley 45.00

Jug
   Edward VII, In Memoriam, brown and green, relief portrait, 6¼" h 65.00
   Edward VIII, character, 8" h, Bretby . 125.00
   Elizabeth II, 1953 Coronation, color portrait, 3¾" h, Royal Stafford ... 60.00

Lithophane
   Alexandra, 1902, cup, crown, and cypher, 2¾" h 175.00
   Edward VII, 1902, mug, crown, and cypher, 2¾" h 90.00
   George V, 1911, mug, crown, and cypher, 2¾" h 140.00
   Mary, 1911, cup, crown, and cypher, 2¾" h 250.00

Loving Cup
   Charles/Diana, 1981 Wedding, brown on white portraits, Royal Doulton, limited edition 5,000 .... 85.00

Elizabeth II, 1972 Silver Wedding Anniversary, 3" h, Paragon 150.00
Elizabeth, The Queen Mother, 80th Birthday, gold profile, 3" h, Royal Crown Derby, limited edition 500 . 235.00
Victoria, 1897 Jubilee, brown portrait, 4" h, Victoria 175.00
William, 1982 Birth, 3" h, paragon .. 110.00

Mug
   Andrew/Sarah, 1986 Wedding, color portraits, 3¾" h, Calclough 24.00
   Duke/Duchess of Windsor, In Memoriam, black and white portraits; birth, marriage, accession, abdication, death dates, 3⅜" h, Dorincourt 50.00
   Edward VII/Alexandra, 1902 Coronation, 3" h, Johnson Brothers 55.00
   Edward VIII, 1937 Coronation, sepia portrait, 3½" h, Empire 40.00
   Elizabeth II, 60th Birthday, color portrait, 3½" h, Coronet 20.00
   Henry, 1984 Birth, blue design, silver trim, 4¼" h, R. Guyatt design, Wedgwood, limited edition 1,000 . 65.00

Mug, Queen Elizabeth II coronation, multicolored dec, white ground, gold banding, marked "Issfield Pottery," 3⅞" h, $15.00.

Victoria, 1887 Jubilee, black and white portrait, 3" h, CTM 100.00
Victoria, 150th Anniversary of Coronation, 3⅝" h, Caverswall 40.00
William 3rd Birthday, Henry 1st Birthday, black and white portraits, 2⅝" h, Dorincourt, limited edition 150 . 50.00

Paperweight
   Edward VIII, 1937 Coronation, black and white portrait, 4¼ x 1⅛" 25.00
   George VI/Elizabeth, 1937 Coronation, black and white Marcus Adams portrait, 2½" d 35.00
   Victoria/Albert, black and white portraits, color and glitter, 2⅞" 30.00

Pin Tray
   Edward VII/Alexandra, 1902 Coronation, sepia portraits, 4" d 40.00

Edward VIII, 1937 Coronation, 4⅞ x
3¾", Hammersley **48.00**
Elizabeth II, 1959 Canada visit, sepia
photograph, 4¼" sq **28.00**
Victoria, 1897 Jubilee, sepia portrait,
5" d **40.00**

Pitcher
Elizabeth II, 1953 Coronation, brown
portrait, 6¼" h, Royal Doulton . . . **175.00**
Victoria, 1887 Jubilee, black and
white portrait, 5" h **120.00**

**Plate, Edward VIII, marked "Wedg-
wood, England," numbered, 8⅜" sq,
$50.00.**

Plate
Andrew/Sarah, 1986 Wedding, silhouette portraits, 8½" d, Caver-
swall, limited edition 1,500 . . . . . . **45.00**
Charles, 1969 Investiture as Prince of
Wales, sepia portrait, 8" d, Coronet **65.00**
Edward VII/Alexandra, 1902 Corona-
tion, blue and white portraits,
10¼" d **170.00**
Edward VII/Alexandra, 1902 Corona-
tion, 7" d, Royal Copenhagen . . . **190.00**
Elizabeth II, 60th Birthday, large color
portrait, 10½" d, Coalport, limited
edition 20,000 . . . . **80.00**
George V/Mary, 1911 Coronation,
8½" d, C.T. Maling **65.00**
George VI/Elizabeth, 1937 Corona-
tion, sepia portraits, 9½ x 8¼",
Shelley **75.00**
Victoria, 1887 Jubilee, orange and
white portrait, 10½" d, Royal
Worcester **125.00**
Victoria, 1897 Jubilee, color dec, 7¼"
d, Foley **40.00**
Victoria, 1897 Jubilee, color portrait,
servicemen, ships, 8" d **165.00**
Victoria, 150th Anniversary of Coro-
nation, gold portrait, 10½" d, Cav-
erswall, limited edition 150 . . . . . **135.00**

Playing Cards
Edward VIII, 1919 Canada visit, color
portrait, single deck, C. Goodall &
Co **75.00**
Elizabeth II, 1977 Jubilee, sepia por-
trait, single deck, Waddingtons . . . **25.00**
George V/Mary, 1911 Coronation,
color portraits, double deck **75.00**
George VI/Elizabeth, 1937 Corona-
tion, color portrait, double deck,
Canadian Playing Card Co **65.00**

Shaving Mug
Edward VII/Alexandra, 1902 Corona-
tion, color portraits, 3¾" h **100.00**
Edward VIII, 1937 Coronation, sepia
portrait, 4" h, no mark **90.00**
Elizabeth II, 1953 Coronation, dolor
portrait, 4" h **65.00**
George VI/Elizabeth, 1937 Corona-
tion, sepia portraits, 4½" h, Shelley **100.00**

Teapot
Charlotte, In Memoriam, black and
white dec, 6" h **250.00**
Edward VII/Alexandra, 1902 Corona-
tion, color portraits, 4¾" h, no mark **70.00**
Elizabeth II, 1953 Coronation, relief
portraits, white on royal blue Jasperware, 5" h, Wedgwood **225.00**
George V/Mary, 1911 Coronation,
color portraits (also Prince of
Wales), 6" h, bone china, no mark **250.00**
Victoria, 1897 Jubilee, color portraits,
4" h **130.00**
Victoria, 1897 Jubilee, color coat of
arms, 6" h, Aynsley **220.00**

Tea Set, Elizabeth II, 1953 Coronation,
teapot, creamer, and sugar, relief portraits, light blue on white Queen-
sware, Wedgwood **275.00**

Tin
Edward VII/Alexandra, 1902 Coronation, color portraits, hinged, 4¼ x
5½" **65.00**
Edward VII/Alexandra, 1907 Cardiff
visit, color portraits, 6 x 3½", J. S.
Fry & Sons **48.00**
Edward VIII, 1937 Coronation, color
portrait, hinged lid, 5¾ x 3¾", Ri-
ley's Toffee **45.00**
Elizabeth II, 1953 Coronation, color
portrait, 10 x 7", E. Sharp **30.00**
George V/Mary, 1935 Jubilee, color
portrait, 6¾ x 4½" **45.00**
George VI/Elizabeth, 1937 Corona-
tion, gold portraits, 3" h, Oxo **18.00**
Victoria, 1897 Jubilee, color portraits
(young, mature), hinged lid, 3¼ x
3" **100.00**

Vase, Edward VII, Memorial, 3¼", includes birth, accession, and death
dates, Goss **120.00**

BRONZE

History Bronze is an alloy of copper, tin, and traces of other metals. It has been used since Biblical times not only for art objects, but also for utilitarian purposes. After a slump in the Middle Ages, bronze was revived in the 17th century and continued in popularity until the early 20th century.

Reference: Anita Jacobsen (ed.), *Jacobsen's Painting and Bronze Price Guide*, published by author.

Notes: Do not confuse a "bronzed" object with a true bronze. A bronzed object usually is made of white metal and then coated with a reddish–brown material to give it a bronze appearance. A magnet will stick to it.

A signed bronze commands a higher market price than an unsigned one. There also are "signed" reproductions in the market. It is very important to know the history of the mold and the background of the foundry.

Vase, mottled green ground, sterling silver overlay, marked "Pat. Aug 27, 1912, Pu Fla Macy & Co #3806," 11¼" h, $350.00.

Animal
Flamingos, pr, marble base	250.00
Moose, 14" l, marble base	200.00
Turtle, 4¾" l, sgd "Scippa," marked "34/250"	110.00

Ashtray, 7½" d, circular leaf form, applied salamander, c1910 . . . . 100.00

Basket, Victorian, ornate, cranberry bowl 225.00

Bust
13" h, young woman, striped scarf wrapped around head, gilt, inscribed "Georges Van Der Straeten," imp "B2828," patinated bronze founder's seal of the Society of Bronzes, Paris, Sienna marble socle, late 19th C 525.00
14½", youth, cast from model found in ruins of Pompeii, green patina . 2,000.00

Candelabra
15", man holding wheel, sgd "H Maras" 575.00
21" h, pr, three acanthus and scrolled arms, reeded urn form candle sockets, turned and floral banding, French Empire 1,700.00

Candlesticks, pr
9½", parcel gilt, Empire Revival 275.00
10½", Louis XVI style, gilt, turned standard, molded stepped base . . 850.00

Cauldron, 12" h, scrolled handle, three legs, Continental 65.00

Chandelier, 34" h, gilt, baluster form standard, pendant crystal beadwork swags, nine scrolling candle arms, turned nozzles, ruffled bobeches, faceted prisms, Rococo Revival, mid 19th C 2,500.00

Clock, mantle
17½" h, four turned Corinthian columns, enameled Roman numeral dial center, rect base, toupee feet, French Empire, late 18th C 500.00
18", gilt and patinated, "Le Jardinier Fatique" figure holding water sack and tools, steadying Versailles pot with enamel dial and movement, molded base, Empire, early 19th C 1,600.00

Dish, 4¼ x 6¼", oval, girl picking apples, naughty view reverse 35.00

Figure
7¾" h, David with head of Goliath . . 155.00
13" h, woman, nude, draped, Neo-Classic, sgd "Canova" 1,200.00
16⅛" h, whistling boy, after V Szczaeblewski, 1889, sailor's blouse, beret, rolled up pants, bare feet, hands in pockets, light brown patina 950.00
49½" h, Venus, nude, diadem in plaited hair, downcast head, drapery hung vase on pedestal to her left, sq plinth, gray painted fluted pedestal base, swivel Portor marble top, after Giovanni Da Bologna 3,850.00

Fire Tools, 34" h, Renaissance style gilt, mounted iron, matching stand 1,150.00

Furniture
Stand, 15½" d, 56" h, gilt and patinated, swan form supports, molded incurvate triangular base, four circular verde antico marble surfaces, Empire, mid 19th C 9,000.00
Table, 42" d, Louis XVI style, three scrolling gilt bronze supports, paw feet, circular marble top, late 19th C 4,500.00

Garnitures, pr, 5½ x 8½" gilt, compressed urn, spirally engine turned column, sq base, Empire, early 19th C 1,800.00

Inkstand, 10″ l, figural, classical figure beside basket, French, c1900 . . . . . **750.00**

Jardiniere, pr, 37 x 26″, rect well, berry swags and ribbons dec, raised cabriole legs with X-stretchers and paw feet, c1900 . . . . **5,000.00**

Lamp, 16″ h, hanging, globe form, openwork lily pads and vines, Chinese . . **120.00**

Letter Opener, Chinese pattern, dore finish, marked "Tiffany Studios, New York" and numbered **145.00**

Matchsafe, Zodiac pattern, matching ashtray, sgd "Tiffany Studios, New York" and numbered **160.00**

Music Box, 4″, gilt, filigree dec, German **425.00**

Paperweight, 3″ h, McKinley bust, relief **150.00**

Pen Tray, Zodiac pattern, brown patina, sgd "Tiffany Studios, New York" and numbered **125.00**

Pencil Holder, 9½″ l, cast detail **45.00**

Sconces, pr, 23″, figural, Louis XVI style, Roman soldier figure backplate, naturally modeled branches ending in candle nozzles, 19th C **3,800.00**

Spoon Mold, 19th C **150.00**

Tray, 8″ d, Greek Key pattern, dore finish, pedestal base, sgd "Tiffany Studios, New York" and numbered **170.00**

Urn, 16″ w, 13″ h, gilt, Louis XVI style, squatty bulbous body, high relief casting of frolicking putti, animal mask handles, swirl fluted socle, shaped sq base, green patina to base and parts of socle, 19th C **1,760.00**

Vase
  5½″ h, verdigris dec finish, gilt stripes, marked "Carl Sorensen" **75.00**
  11¾″ h, urn form, paneled etched body, double flacon mask handles, circular foot **200.00**
  16″ h, globular form, relief bats, applied ring handles, 19th C **200.00**

BUFFALO POTTERY

History: Buffalo Pottery Co., Buffalo, New York, was chartered in 1901. The first kiln was fired in

October 1903. Larkin Soap Company established Buffalo Pottery to produce premiums for its extensive mail order business. Wares also were sold to the public by better department and jewelry stores. Elbert Hubbard and Frank L. Wright, who designed the Larkin Administration Building in Buffalo in 1904, were two prominent names associated with the Larkin Company.

Early production consisted mainly of dinner sets of semi–vitreous china. Buffalo was the first pottery in the United States to produce successfully the Blue Willow pattern, marked "First Old Willow Ware Mfg. in America." Buffalo also made a line of hand decorated, multicolored willow ware, called Gaudy Willow. Other early items include a series of game, fowl, and fish sets, pitchers, jugs, and a line of commemorative, historical, and advertising plates and mugs.

In 1908–09 and 1921–23, Buffalo Pottery produced the line for which it is most famous, Deldare Ware. The earliest of this olive green, semi–vitreous china depicts hand decorated scenes from the English artist Cecil Aldin's *Fallowfield Hunt.* Hunt scenes only were done in 1908–09. English village scenes also were characteristic and found throughout the series. Most are artist signed.

In 1911 Buffalo Pottery produced Emerald Deldare, which used scenes from Goldsmith's *The Three Tours of Dr. Syntax* and an Art Nouveau type border. Completely decorated Art Nouveau pieces also were made.

In 1912 Abino was born. Abino was done on Deldare bodies and showed sailing, windmill, and seascape scenes. The main color is rust. All pieces are artist signed and numbered.

In 1915 the pottery was modernized, giving it the ability to produce vitrified china. Consequently, hotel and institutional ware became their main production, with hand decorated ware de–emphasized. Buffalo china became a leader in producing and designing the most famous railroad, hotel, and restaurant patterns. These wares, especially railroad items, are eagerly sought by collectors.

In the early 1920s fine china was made for home use, e.g., the Bluebird pattern. In 1950 Buffalo made their first Christmas plate. They were given away to customers and employees from 1950–60. Hample Equipment Co. ordered some in 1962. The Christmas plates are very scarce.

The Buffalo China Company made "Buffalo Pottery" and "Buffalo China," the difference being one is semi–vitreous ware and the other vitrified. In 1956 the company was reorganized, and Buffalo China became the corporate name. Today Buffalo China is owned by Oneida Silver Company. The Larkin family no longer is involved.

Reference: Seymour and Violet Altman, *The Book Of Buffalo Pottery,* reprinted by Schiffer Publishing, 1987.

Note: Numbers in parenthesis refer to plates in the Altman's book.

Advisor: Seymour & Violet Altman.

Milk pitcher, blue geranium dec, 5⅝″ h, $90.00.

ABINO WARE

Candlestick, 9″, sailing ships, 1913 (251)	475.00
Pitcher 7″, Portland Head Light (256)	700.00
Plaque	
12¼″, sailing ships (241)	1,000.00
13½″, pasture scene (244)	2,500.00
Tankard, 10½″, sailing scene (255)	900.00

BLUE AND WHITE WILLOW

Blue Willow	
Creamer, double lip (30)	15.00
Plate, 9¼″ (75)	25.00
Relish (27)	45.00
Gaudy Willow	
Pitcher, 8″ (C*)	350.00
Plate, 10½″, (28)	125.00

CHRISTMAS PLATES

1950 (260)	50.00
1956 (266)	50.00
1962 (271)	225.00

COMMERCIAL SERVICES

Cake Plate, Roycroft Inn, 10″ (288)	150.00
Plate	
B & O Railroad, Harpers Ferry, 9½″ (282)	300.00
Mont Clair Hotel, 10½″ (293)	100.00
Platter, George Washington Service, (275)	600.00

DELDARE

Bowl, Ye Village Street, 8″, fern, insert (153)	450.00
Cake Plate, 10″, Ye Village Gossips, 1908 (142)	325.00
Calendar Plate, 1910	1,800.00
Calling Card Tray, Ye Lion Inn (173)	300.00
Chocolate Pot, 9″ (163)	1,500.00

Dresser Tray, 9 x 12″, Dancing Ye Minuet, 1909 (144)	550.00
Humidor, 7″, octagonal, Ye Lion Inn (174)	675.00
Mug, 3½″, Fallowfield Hunt, 1909 (122)	235.00
Nut Bowl, 8″ Ye Lion Inn (175)	475.00
Pitcher, 9″, With A Cane Superior Air (167)	525.00
Plate	
6½″, Fallowfield Hunt, 1909 (132)	120.00
9½″, Ye Olden Times, 1908(145)	160.00
Powder Jar, cov, Ye Village Street (143)	300.00
Relish Dish, Fallowfield Hunt, The Dash (135)	350.00

Deldare, bowl, Ye Village Tavern, 1908, 9″ d, 3¾″ h, $400.00.

Sugar, cov, village scenes, 1925 (138)	200.00
Tea Tile, 6″, Traveling In Ye Olden Days (140)	300.00
Teapot	
3¼″, Scenes of Village Life, 1909 (138)	250.00
5¼″, Scenes of Village Life in Ye Olden Days	375.00
Vase, 8″, fashionable men and women (162)	675.00

DELDARE SPECIALS

Humidor, 8″, There Was An Old Sailor (227)	750.00
Mug, 4½″, Indian scene (231)	500.00
Salt and Pepper Shakers, pr, Art Nouveau	500.00

EMERALD DELDARE

Cup and Saucer, Dr. Syntax At Liverpool (181)	275.00
Fruit Bowl, octagonal, Art Nouveau dec, matching underplate (183)	3,550.00
Humidor, 7″ Dr. Syntax Returned Home	850.00
Inkwell, Art Nouveau dec (196)	5,000.00
Plaque, 13½″, Penn's Treaty With The Indians, 1911 (217)	1,500.00
Tea Tray, 10¼ x 13¾″, Dr. Syntax Mis-	

takes A Gentleman's House For An
Inn (180) **875.00**

GAME SETS

Plate
   9", fish, striped bass (60) **70.00**
   9½", Champion-Bromley Crib Dog
     (73) **500.00**
Platter, oval, Buffalo Hunt, 1907 (62) . **175.00**

HISTORICAL, COMMEMORATIVE, AND ADVERTISING WARE

Mug, 4½"
   Calumet Club (111) **75.00**
   Fraternity Hall (109) **75.00**
Plate
   7½", Gate Circle, buffalo, NY (97) .. **90.00**
   9", Women's Christian Temperence
     Union, 1908 (86B) **150.00**
Pitcher, Holland **250.00**

MISCELLANEOUS

Canister Set, cov, 1906, each (353) .. **40.00**
Dinner Set, 100 pcs, Kenmore (315) .. **500.00**
Jug, Landing of Roger Williams (36) .. **550.00**
Plate, 10¼", eleven Roosevelt Bear
   scenes, 1906 .... **700.00**
Punch Set, Tom and Jerry (352) **150.00**
Rose Bowl, Geranium, 3¾", 1907 (358) **75.00**
Teapot, Argyle, matching teaball (336) **190.00**

BURMESE GLASS

History: Burmese glass is a translucent art
glass originated by Frederick Shirley and manufactured by the Mt. Washington Glass Co., New
Bedford, Massachusetts, from 1885 to c1891.

Burmese glass shades from a soft lemon to a
salmon pink. Uranium was used to attain the yellow color and gold was added to the batch so that
on reheating one end turned pink. Upon reheating
again, the edges would revert to the yellow coloring. The blending of the colors was so gradual that
it was difficult to determine where one color ended
and the other began.

Although some of the glass has a surface that
is glossy, most of it is acid finished. The majority
of the items were free blown, but some were blown
molded in a ribbed, hobnail, or diamond quilted
design.

American–made Burmese is quite thin, fragile,
and brittle. The only factory licensed to make Burmese was Thos. Webb & Sons in England. Out of
deference to Queen Victoria, they called their
wares "Queen's Burmese."

Reproduction Alert: Reproductions abound in
almost every form. Since uranium can no longer
be used, some of the reproductions are easy to
spot. In the 1950s Gunderson produced many
pieces in imitation of Burmese.
   MW = Mount Washington
   Wb = Webb
   a.f. = acid finish
   s.f. = shiny finish
   Advisors: Clarence and Betty Maier.

Toothpick Holder, glossy finish, 2⅝" h, $250.00.

Bon Bon, 2", MW, a.f. tricorner **290.00**
Bowl, 5" d, MW, a.f. ball shape, four fold-
   down edges on top, berry pontil, four
   applied feet **450.00**
Champagne Glass, 5½" h, raspberry to
   yellow shading, circular base, two
   handles **250.00**
Creamer and Sugar, 2¾" h, MW, a.f.,
   applied handle on creamer, two applied handles on sugar bowl **790.00**
Cruet, MW, a.f., melon ribbed, enamel
   dec **2,450.00**
Epergne, 9½" h, Wb, a.f., two undecorated fairy lamps with sgd Clarke
   bases, twin bud vases, centered
   metal standard holding upright vase,
   SP stand **1,400.00**
Fairy Lamp, Wb, a.f.
   Dome shaped shade, urn shaped
     base, double prunus blossoms dec,
     sgd Clarke candle cup and candle
     cup holder, 9½" **950.00**
   Twin undecorated fairy lamps, clear
     sgd Clarke glass candle cups,
     brass stand, centered brass dol-
     phin **750.00**
Hat, 1¼" h, Pairpoint Corp, s.f., c1930 **450.00**
Lamp Shade, 5", gaslight
   MW, a.f. **225.00**
   MW, s.f. **290.00**
Plaque, 11¾", MW, a.f., cottage, birds
   and daisies dec **750.00**
Pitcher
   2½" h, Wb, a.f., prunus blossom dec **540.00**
   9" h, MW, a.f. tankard, rural scene
     and florals, Longfellow verse **3,250.00**

Rose Bowl, 3″ d, Wb, a.f., prunus blossom dec ... **370.00**
Rose jar, 5¼″ h, MW, cov, floral dec .. **400.00**
Salt, Wb, a.f., 2¾″ d, bittersweet colored blossoms, gold branches **450.00**
Sweetmeat, 7″ h, Wb, a.f., cylindrical, bittersweet and gold foliage, SP collar, lid, and bail handle, sgd **450.00**
Toothpick Holder, MW

2½″, a.f., cylindrical, trefoil top, floral dec, optic diamond quilting **420.00**
2¾″, a.f., cylindrical, crimped top, optic diamond quilting, paper label .. **490.00**
Tumbler, prunus blossom dec, thin walls **885.00**
Vase

7″, MW, a.f., flower form, undecorated, metal holder, putti holding vase in upraised arms, Pairpoint mark **490.00**
9″, MW, a.f., petticoat shape, long neck, trefoil top, undecorated **590.00**
10½″ Pairpoint, s.f., urn shape, pedestal base, c1930 .... **665.00**
12″, MW, a.f.

Chinese manner dec, florals, geometrics, and two dragons, two applied handles **1,750.00**
Jack-in-the-pulpit, pie crust crimped edge, heavy enamel floral dec **1,150.00**
13″, MW. a.f., raised gold stylized floral dec, geometric design **1,150.00**

BUSTS

History: The portrait bust has its origins in pagan and Christian tradition. Greek and Roman heroes, and later images of Christian saints, dominate the early examples. Busts of the "ordinary man" first appeared in the Renaissance.

Busts of the nobility, poets, and other notable persons dominated the 18th and 19th centuries, especially those designed for use in a home library. Because of the large number of these library busts, excellent examples can be found at reasonable prices, depending on artist, subject, and material.

Reference: Anita Jacobsen (ed.), *Jacobsen's Painting and Bronze Price Guide*, published by author.

Additional Listings: Ivory, Parian Ware, Soapstone, and Wedgwood.

Bisque, Sir Walter Scott, 8″ h **250.00**
Bronze, girl, inscribed signature, 22″ h **1,050.00**
Lead, Goddess, Hera, diadem in parted hair, loose tunic tied at shoulders, 18th C, 28″ **1,150.00**
Majolica, Charles V, full beard, Order of the Golden Fleece around neck, intaglio dec, scrolling foliage, mustard,

Plaster, George Washington, black, sgd, dated 1861, 9″ h, $75.00.

rust, and green edged epaulets, 16th C, 29½″ **2,500.00**
Marble, Emperor Augustus, short curly hair, white marble socle, 18th C, 37″ **9,000.00**
Metal, Hermes, cast, 21″ h **150.00**
Plaster, Marquis de Mejanes, white, poetic pose, high brow, receding hairline, long hair resting on back, drilled eyes, open necked chemise, socle base, after Jean–Antoine Houdon, 19th C, 35½″ h **3,850.00**
Terra Cotta

Court Lady, Louis XVI style, sgd "Coustou," 30″ **500.00**
Young maiden, French **600.00**
Wood

Mahogany, Daniel Webster, carved from single piece of wood, 16½″ . **650.00**
Oak, Benjamin Franklin, old brown alligatored finish, "Harris" carved in black, 15″ **725.00**

BUTTER PRINTS

History: Butter prints divide into two categories: butter molds and butter stamps. Butter molds are generally of three piece construction—the design, the screw-in handle, and the case. Molds both mold and stamp the butter at the same time. Butter stamps are of one piece construction, sometimes two pieces if the handle is from a separate piece of wood. Stamps decorate the top of butter after it is molded.

The earliest prints were one piece and hand carved, often thick and deeply carved. Later prints were factory made with the design forced into the wood by a metal die.

Some of the most common designs are sheaves of wheat, leaves, flowers, and pineapples. Animal designs and Germanic tulips are difficult to find. Rare prints include unusual shapes, such as half-rounded and lollipop, and those with designs on both sides.

Reference: Paul E. Kindig, *Butter Prints And Molds,* Schiffer Publishing, 1986.

Reproduction Alert: Reproductions of butter prints date as early as the 1940s.

MOLD

Acorn, carved wood, outer case, 3¼″ d	**150.00**
Anchor, carved, wood, 2¾″d	**175.00**
Pineapple, carved, wood, 4⅜″ d	**325.00**
Sheaf of wheat and rosette, carved, wood, 3⅞″ d	**150.00**
Sunflower, carved, wood, 3½″d	**50.00**
Thistle, carved, wood, 3⅝″ d	**100.00**

Stamp, scallop design, reeded border, 3½″ d, 2⅝″ h, $90.00.

STAMP

Compass Star, round, 4″	**55.00**
Cow, turned handle, 4¼″ d	**150.00**
Cow and fence, turned screw-in handle, 5½″ l	**160.00**
Eagle, shield, and stars, 4½″ d, missing handle	**200.00**
Floral design	
3⅞″, round, stylized, turned handle	**55.00**
4½″ d, stylized, turned handle	**55.00**
5″ d, concave, stylized, knob handle	**190.00**
5¼″ l, wheel type	**100.00**
Flower, stylized, turned handle, 4½″ d	**55.00**
Foliage design, knob handle, 4″ d	**105.00**
Leaf	
3¼″ d, turned inserted handle, refinished	**45.00**
5½″ d, stylized, turned handle	**65.00**
Scrolls, lollipop shape, 7″ l	**200.00**
Sheaf of Wheat, 6¼″ l, semicircular	**60.00**

Star and floral, stylized, round, rect handle, 5″	**100.00**
Thistle design, turned handle, 2½″ d	**45.00**

CALENDAR PLATES

History: Calendar plates were first made in England in the late 1880s. They became popular in the United States after 1900, the peak years being 1909 to 1915. The majority of the advertising plates were made of porcelain or pottery with a calendar, the name of a store or business, and either a scene, portrait, animal, or flowers. Some also were made of glass or tin.

Additional Listings: See *Warman's Americana & Collectibles* for more examples.

1911, compliments of Hilding Nelson, New Britain, CT, 7½″ d, $30.00.

1906, 9″, flowers, York, Pennsylvania	**40.00**
1907, Christmas snow scene	**50.00**
1908, 9″, fruit	**25.00**
1908, 9½″, two monks drinking wine	**65.00**
1908, 9¾″, hunting dog, Pittston, PA	**35.00**
1909, 7½″, Santa in zeppelin dropping presents to children	**50.00**
1909, 8¼″, flowers	**18.00**
1909, 9″, woman and man in patio garden	**22.00**
1910, 8″, The Old Swimming Hole	**45.00**
1910, 8¼″, Gibson Girl	**30.00**
1910, Betsy Ross, Dresden	**30.00**
1910, ships and windmills	**20.00**
1911, 7½″, pink flowers, Byers, Hagerstown, MD	**30.00**
1911, 8″, hunt scene, Markell Drug Co., Chelsea	**25.00**
1911, deer in meadow, scenic panels between months	**35.00**
1912, 7½″, bowl of pink roses	**30.00**
1912, 9¼″, Martha Washington	**35.00**
1913, 9″, roses and holly	**25.00**

1914, 6¾", Point Arena, CA	25.00
1915, 7", Panama Canal	25.00
1915, 9", black boy eating watermelon	32.00
1916, 7½", man in canoe, Iowa	25.00
1916, 8¼", eagle with shield and American flag	32.00
1920, "The Great War," MO	25.00
1921, 9", bluebirds and fruit	25.00
1922, dog watching rabbit	30.00
1924, 9", steeplechase scene	28.00
1929, 6¼", flowers, Valentine, NE	25.00
1929, 7½", boy with dog	28.00

CALLING CARD CASES AND RECEIVERS

History: Calling cards, usually carried in specially designed cases, played an important social role in the United States from the period of the Civil War until the end of World War I. When making a formal visit, a caller left their card in a receiver (card dish) in the front hall. Strict rules of etiquette developed. For example, the lady in a family was expected to make calls of congratulations, visits to the ill, and condolence.

The cards themselves were small, embossed or engraved with the caller's name, and often carried a floral design. Many hand done examples, especially in Spencerian script, can be found. The cards themselves are considered collectible and range in price from a few cents to several dollars.

Note: Don't confuse a calling card case with a match safe.

Calling Card Case, coin silver, shaped edges, engine turning dec, 3½ x 2½", $75.00.

CALLING CARD CASES

Abalone, 3 x 4", pearl, diamond design	**35.00**
Ivory, 3¼", deeply carved scene of tale of William Tell, German	**185.00**
Mother of Pearl, 4 x 2¾"	**35.00**
Pearl, carved, classical woman profile, floral engraving	**35.00**
Silver	
Plated, floral engraving	**35.00**
Sterling	
2½ x 3½", rect, rounded corners, hinged lid, repousse and chased, cathedral against punched ground, reverse with fortress in landscape, marked "Leonard & Wilson, Phila.," c1845	**200.00**
3" h, Unger Bros, rect, each side chased, bathing maiden scene .	**75.00**
Tortoise Shell, Oriental carving	**70.00**

CALLING CARD RECEIVERS

Cast Metal, figural lady, painted green, Art Deco	**85.00**
China	
Hand Painted, 10", roses, gold handles	**30.00**
Nippon, 7½", white and pink flowers, green leaves, rolled edges, cobalt ground, gold tracery, blue mark . .	**150.00**
Crystal, blown out flowers, pedestal base	**35.00**
Silver	
Plated, ornate, upright, marked "Wilcox"	**75.00**
Sterling, American, marked "S Kirk & Sons," 1880	**125.00**

CAMBRIDGE GLASS

History: Cambridge Glass Company, Cambridge, Ohio, was incorporated in 1901. Initially the company made clear tableware, later expanding into colored, etched, and engraved glass. Over 40 different hues were produced in blown and pressed glass.

Five different marks were employed during the production years, but not every piece was marked.

The plant closed in 1954. Some of the molds were later sold to the Imperial Glass Company, Bellaire, Ohio.

References: National Cambridge Collectors, Inc., *The Cambridge Glass Co., Cambridge, Ohio* (reprint of 1930 catalog and supplements through 1934), Collector Books, 1976; National Cambridge Collectors, Inc., *The Cambridge Glass Co., Cam-*

bridge, Ohio, 1949 Thru 1953 (catalog reprint), Collector Books, 1976; National Cambridge Collectors, Inc., *Colors In Cambridge Glass,* Collector Books, 1984; Mark Nye, *Cambridge Stemware,* published by author, 1985.

Collectors' Club: National Cambridge Collectors, Inc., P. O. Box 416, Cambridge, OH 43725. *Crystal Ball* (monthly).

Bon Bons	
6¼", Cleo etch	25.00
7", Mt. Vernon	45.00
Bottle, dressing, Wildflower, marked "Oil"	90.00
Bowl	
Caprice, 12½" crystal, bell form	30.00
Cleo, 12", blue-green, flared	30.00
Decagon, light blue	
6½", cereal, wide rim	20.00
10", two handles	40.00
Diane, 11"	22.50
Seashell, 11"	50.00
Celery Dish, Rosepoint, 11"	48.00
Cigarette Holder, Diane, crystal	65.00
Compote, Crown Tuscan, sea shell shape, 9", marked "Cambridge"	125.00
Cocktail Shaker, 48 oz, Pristine	35.00
Condiment Set, 2 oz oil and vinegar, tray, SP	55.00

Console Bowl, Heliotrope, 10" w, $65.00.

Creamer and Sugar	
Rosepoint, small	45.00
Tally Ho, amber, ftd	25.00
Wildflower	38.00
Cup and Saucer, Tally Ho, amber, ftd	10.00
Dish, oval, Crown Tuscan, sea shell shape, 8", four ftd	90.00
Flower Figures (Frogs)	
8½", Draped Lady	
Amber	150.00
Crystal	55.00
Pink	100.00
9" Heron	65.00
Goblet	
Caprice, pink	35.00

Cascade	15.00
Chantilly	20.00
Mt. Vernon, crystal	6.00
Roselyn	27.50
Ice Bucket, Gloria etch, pink, tongs, sgd	90.00
Iced Tea	
Cleo, light blue	22.00
Portia	23.00
Rosepoint, ftd	25.00
Ivy Ball, Crown Tuscan, nude stem	135.00
Jar, Yardly, Crown Tuscan, lid	15.00
Lamp, 12", Seashell Vase	275.00
Mayonnaise Set, 3 pcs, Portia	40.00
Mustard, Farberware, 4½" amber insert	8.00
Plate	
7½", salad, Decagon, pink	5.00
8", Laurel Wreath	8.50
8½", Lorna, pink, sgd	8.00
8⅜", Decagon, green	5.00
Platter	
10½", Decagon, pink	30.00
12½", Decagon, light blue	42.00
14", Gloria, pink	75.00
Relish	
Chantilly, three part	18.00
Ebony, four part	25.00
Elaine, five part	35.00
Rosepoint, three part	42.00
Rose Bowl, 5", Caprice, blue	90.00
Salt and Pepper Shaker, pr	
Diane	40.00
Rosepoint	80.00
Sherbert	
Cleo, green ftd	14.00
Elaine, crystal	16.00
Portio, flared rim, tall stem	20.00
Rosepoint	18.00
Wildflower	15.00
Swan	
3¼", green	30.00
6½", black	90.00
9½", topaz	145.00
10½", crystal, frosted	110.00
Torte Plate, Diane, crystal	40.00
Tray, 9", Caprice, oval, blue, handles	35.00
Tumbler	
Cascade, crystal, 12 oz	18.00
Elaine, crystal, ftd, 10 oz	18.00
Mt. Vernon, crystal, flat, 5 oz	5.00
Rosepoint, ftd, 10 oz	25.00
Vase	
Crown Tuscan, 8½", candlelight, pedestal, gold dec	70.00
Portia, 8", gold encrused	45.00
Rosepoint, 10", bud, crystal	55.00
Wine	
Apple Blossom, yellow	25.00
Chantilly	30.00
Decagon, light blue	30.00
Portia	22.50
Pristine, 3 oz	15.00

CAMBRIDGE

CAMBRIDGE POTTERY

History: The Cambridge Art Pottery was incorporated in Ohio in 1900. Between 1901 and 1909 the firm produced the usual line of jardinieres, tankards, and vases with underglazed slip decorations and glazes similar to other Ohio potteries. Line names included Terrhea, Oakwood, Otoe, and others.

In 1904 the company introduced Guernsey kitchenware. It was so well received that it became the plant's primary product. In 1909 the company's name was changed to Guernsey Earthenware Company.

All wares were marked.

Vase, Oakwood, mold 235, saucer base, extended body, applied shaped handles, high glaze, tones of yellow, green, and brown, 8″ h, $140.00.

Bank, 6 x 3¼″, pig shape, dark glaze .	95.00
Bowl, 8½″ d, 5¾″ h, matte green glaze, ftd, four imp acorn marks	115.00
Custard Cup, Guernsey mark	30.00
Pitcher, 5″ h, ewer shape, Oakwood, marbleized green, brown, and yellow	85.00
Tankard, 16½″, mold #263, two ears of corn, incised signature	650.00
Tile, 6″ sq, majolica type glaze, high relief florals	85.00

Vase
5½″ h, ovoid, grapes and leaves, artist sgd	125.00
6½″ h, tapering sides, inward flaring collar, raised sq motif with raised circles, green matte finish, acorn mark	100.00
8″, Oakwood, mold #235, saucer base, extended body, applied shaped handles, high glaze, tones of yellow, green, and brown	140.00

CAMEO GLASS

History: Cameo glass is a form of cased glass. A shell of glass was prepared; then one or more layers of glass of a different color(s) was faced to the first. A design was then cut through the outer layer(s) leaving the inner layer(s) exposed.

This type of art glass originated in Alexandria, Egypt, 100-200 A.D. The oldest and most famous example of cameo glass is the Barberini or Portland vase which was found near Rome in 1582. It contained the ashes of Emperor Alexander Serverus who was assassinated in 235 A.D.

Emile Gallé is probably one of the best known artists of cameo glass. He established a factory at Nancy, France, in 1884. Although much of the glass bears his signature, he was primarily the designer. On many pieces assistants did the actual work, even to signing his name. Glass made after his death in 1904 has a star before the name Gallé. Other makers of French cameo glass include D'Argental, Daum Nancy, LeGras, and Delatte.

English cameo does not have as many layers of glass (colors) and cuttings as do French pieces. The outer layer is usually white, and cuttings are very fine and delicate. Most pieces are not signed. The best known makers are Thomas Webb & Sons and Stevens and Williams.

References: Victor Arwas, *Glass Art Nouveau to Art Deco*, Rizzoli International Publications, Inc., 1977; Ray and Lee Grover, *English Cameo Glass*, Crown Publishers, Inc., 1980; Albert C. Revi, *Nineteenth Century Glass*, reprint, Schiffer Publishing, 1981; John A. Shuman, III, *The Collector's Encyclopedia of American Art Glass,* Collector Books, 1988.

AMERICAN

New England Glass Co.
Lamp, fluid, 10¾″ h, 8″ d, pink birds and flowers, white ground, iron base, brass font	300.00

Tiffany
Vase
8½″, ovoid, white calla lilies, lime green leaves, and insects, pearly irid body, inscribed "L.C.T. X1175," c1892–1928	5,500.00

17⅞", slender trumpet, bulbous neck, brilliant blue irid, trailing green stems and leaves, circular white etched blossom frieze, inscribed "L. C. Tiffany Favrile 7209J," c1915 . . . . **6,500.00**

ENGLISH

Stevens and Williams
Lamp, 8", red fuchsias and leaves, yellow ground, sgd **2,500.00**
Vase, 5⅝", baluster, translucent lime green ground, etched pendent dogwood blossoms, flowering rose bushes, lower section with reserved arched frieze of alternating blossoms and squares, similar frieze on waisted neck **2,450.00**
Unknown Maker
Biscuit Jar, 5½" d, 6½" h, frosted vaseline ground, opaque white carved berries and leaves, SP top, rim, and handle **2,000.00**
Rose Bowl, 3", white morning glories, brown ground **350.00**
Vase, 4½", carved white lilac sprays, lotus trim at neck baluster shape, citron ground **380.00**
Webb, Thomas & Sons
Compote, 10 x 4", pink and white flowers, blue ground, sgd **1,800.00**
Inkwell, 3½ x 4", bluish-white flowers, frosted amber ground, SS hinged top, sgd **900.00**
Scent Bottle, 4", white irises, frosty blue ground, Gorham SS hinged top, sgd **500.00**
Vase, 4⅛", white flowers, frosted raspberry red ground, sgd **675.00**

French, Daum Nancy, vase, rect, iris dec, 7¼" h, $525.00.

FRENCH

Arsall, vase, 7" h, 5¼" w, bulbous baluster, deep cut rust and brown autumn leaves, gray frosted ground, signed in cameo on leaf, inscribed numerals on base, expertly cut down . **575.00**
D'Argental, pieces sgd "D'Argental" in cameo
Flask, 6", pink bleeding hearts **400.00**
Vase, 6¾" h, shaped ovoid, swelling at base, pink splashed white overlaid in dark burgundy and pink, wide landscape framed by small groves of trees and shrubbery, pond in foreground, sgd in cameo, c1920 . . . . **500.00**
Daum Nancy, pieces sgd "Daum Nancy" in gilt intaglio
Bowl
5 x 3", oval, pointed ends, natural colored berries and leafy vines, mottled yellow ground, sgd **300.00**
9 x 3½", blue winter plants, mottled frost ground, crimped top **950.00**
Box, cov, 4¾ x 2¾", green grapes and leaves, tan ground **450.00**
Creamer, 4¼", colorful enameled tulips, mottled green and peach ground, cameo cut handle, sgd . . **325.00**
Flask, 6", lavender flowers, yellow frosted ground **500.00**
Jar, 3¼", red flower buds, green leaves, lavender and opalescent ground, sgd **200.00**
Lamp, 22", winter scene, orange ground, sgd **3,600.00**
Perfume Bottle, 10", iris, gold enamel highlights, green ground, incised label "Parfum de Vertus," sgd . . . **325.00**
Pitcher, 5", mottled rusty-orange base shading to lemon yellow, applied handle, body overlaid with clear glass, bellflower blossoms, buds, and foliage, naturalistic enamel coloration, gold brushed lip, name sgd in gold with Cross of Lorraine logo **990.00**
Salt
1⅛ x 1¼ x 2", leafy green and pink trees, pink mountains, frosted ground, sgd **500.00**
2", blackbirds in snow, sgd **225.00**
Toothpick, 2 x 1¼", acid etched and enameled violets, leaves, and stems, mottled ground shading from white to deep violet, sgd . . . **300.00**
Vase
4⅝", sq, translucent amber ground, etched and enameled black and white winter scene, enameled "Daum Nancy" **1,100.00**

9½", conical, circular foot, translucent green and amber martele ground, etched poppies, leaves, and stems, etched "Daum Nancy" **3,800.00**

10", scalloped rim, circular foot, overlaid and wheel etched fruited branches, etched "Daum Nancy" **2,400.00**

Degue
Vase

15¾", baluster, acid etched matte black and polished red mottle, band of red lappets, wide red zig zag border on shoulder, rounded foot, incised "Degue" **1,225.00**

23¼", frosted ground, red and purple overlay, etched orange blossoms, vines, and leaves, sgd "Degue" in cameo **2,225.00**

Delatte, vase, 4⅛" h, spherical, short rounded neck, molded butter yellow overlaid in brown at base, etched continuous polished border of iris blossoms and buds, sgd in cameo "A Delatte/Nancy," c1923 .... **800.00**

Devez/Patin, vase, 8", cylindrical, pink ground, blue overlay mountains and lake scene, sgd "Devez" in cameo . **750.00**

Galle
Decanter, 7½" h, shouldered cylindrical form, everted lip, outwardly tapering salmon body, overlaid purple morning glory vine, ovoid stopper in deeper shade of red, mottled light purple ground, sgd in cameo near base, c1900 .... **1,150.00**

Vase

4¾", flattened ovoid, lime green ground, overlaid deeper green shading to lavender, floral etching, sgd in cameo **1,100.00**

5¼", baluster, waisted at base, short circular foot, frosted surface overlaid in red, foot shading to rose, floral spray and budding branch cutting, sgd in cameo .. **1,650.00**

7⅛", flask, frosted body, lavender and olive green overlay, etched pendent wisteria and leaves, sgd in cameo **1,300.00**

9", slightly flattened ovoid, yellow and gray body, brown cut to leafy trees, continuous riverscape, sgd in cameo, c1900 .... **3,000.00**

10"

Flask, white frosted ground, overlaid ochre, etched poppy clusters, sgd in cameo **2,400.00**

Trumpet, translucent frosted ground, amber and augergine overlay pendent blossoms,

stems, and leaves, wheel polished, sgd in cameo **1,700.00**

13", oviform, conical base, lemon yellow ground shading to brilliant green, relief molded pendent plum boughs, sgd in cameo ... **12,000.00**

16", modified trumpet, circular foot, translucent ground, lavender overlay, etched pendent wisteria, leaves, and stems, sgd in cameo **2,100.00**

18½", trumpet, Chinese manner, translucent ground, orange overlaid, etched blossoms, stems, and leaves, wheel polished, sgd in cameo **2,600.00**

Legras
Vase

14¼", flattened baluster, orange and green lake scene, cameo etched "Legras" **1,000.00**

25¼", elongated pyriform, high waisted neck, slightly bulbous mouth, acid etched pink glass, internally dec lower half, mottled white, carved ext., enameled fuchsia flowers and leaves, inscribed "Legras," **1,800.00**

Le Verre
Ewer, 12" orange geometric design, white ground, blue handle and rim, sgd **450.00**

Night Light, horse chestnut shape shade, mottled brown horse chestnuts, sunset colored ground, sgd on shade, made-up base **250.00**

Vase

5¾", frosted orange and lavender

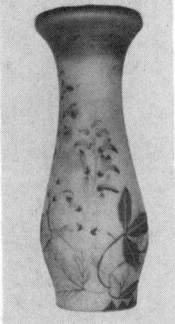

French, Richard, vase, chartreuse ground, amber dec, sgd "Richard," 12½" h , $990.00.

ground, etched stylized dec, inscribed "Le Verre Francais" ... | 550.00
14", ovoid body, wide mouth with yellow overlaid in dark mottled amber and orange, cut to stylized leaves and fruit, flaring round orange foot, inscribed "Le Verre Francais" .... | 975.00
14", shouldered ovoid, waisted neck and base, mottled yellow and orange, etched surface cased with orange foot and staggered band of orange hexagons, top overlaid in purple–blue shading to orange, cut pendant leaves and stylized flowerheads, foot incised "Le Verre Francais" .... | 1,200.00

Mabut, J, 7½" d, 11" h, acid cut green ground, large flowers, heavy gold dec, sgd on base .... | 900.00
Richard, vase, 3", purple flowers, frosted ground, sgd .... | 200.00

St. Louis
Box, 5 x 2¾", cranberry flowers, green ground .... | 350.00
Ice Bucket, 5¾ x 5¾", red poppies, vaseline ground, gold highlights, brass handle and mountings, sgd | 500.00
Vase, 12", carved purple iris at neck, translucent yellow ground overlay flowerhead borders, sgd .... | 500.00

Vallerystahl
Cologne Bottle, 6¾", fuschia flowers and leaves, frosted cranberry ground, gold colored collar and screw stopper, sgd "Cristaherie Le Gantin" .... | 475.00
Vase, 12", amberina, gold daffodils, sgd .... | 3,500.00

CAMERAS

History: The collecting of cameras, except in isolated instances, started about 1970. Although photography generally is considered to have had its beginning in 1839, it is very unusual to find a camera made before 1880. These cameras and others made before 1925 are considered to be antique cameras. Most cameras made after 1925 that are no longer in production are considered to be classic cameras. American, German, and Japanese cameras are found most often.

Value of cameras is affected by both exterior and mechanical conditions. Particular attention must be given to the condition of the bellows if cameras have them.

References: Jim and Joan McKeown, *Price Guide To Antique And Classic Still Cameras*, Seventh Edition, 1989–90, published by authors,

1990; *Jason Schneider On Camera Collecting, Book Three*, Wallace Homestead, 1985; Myron Wolf, *Blue Book Illustrated Price Guide to Collectible & Useable Cameras, Second Master Edition*, Photographic Memorabilia, 1985.

Periodical: Photique Magazine, One Magnolia Hill, West Hartford, CT 06117.

Collectors' Clubs: National Stereoscopic Association, P. O. Box 14801, Columbus, OH 43214; Photographic Historical Society, P. O. Box 9563, Rochester, NY 14604.

Museum: George Eastman Museum, Rochester, NY; Smithsonian Institution, Washington, DC.

Additional Listings: See *Warman's Americana & Collectibles* for more examples.

Weno Hawk–Eye Box, #7, Eastman Kodak, Rochester, NY, $25.00.

Ansco (Binghamton, NY; merged with Agfa in 1928), folding camera, Model 7, postcard size roll film, red bellows, brass Wollensak lens .... | 30.00
Argus, Model A, 35 mm, f4.5/50mm fixed focus anastigmat lens, c1936–1941, (Ann Arbor, MI) .... | 20.00
Baldinette, folding 35mm, f2.9/50, Schneider Radionar, Balda-Werke, 1950, (Dresden, Germany) .... | 48.00
Bell & Howell, Filmo Turret Movie Camera, 8 mm, triple lens holder, variable speeds, 16–64 frames, c1938, (Chicago, IL) .... | 15.00
Busch, Verascope F-40, f3.5/40 Berthiot lens, guillotine shutter to 250, RF, 1950s, (Chicago, IL) .... | 375.00
Ciro, Ciroflex B, c1948, (Delaware, OH) | 15.00
Coronet, midget, bakelite, black, 15 mm roll film, c1935, (Birmingham, England) .... | 35.00
Devry, 16 mm movie camera, c1932, (Chicago, IL) .... | 25.00
Dossert Detective Camera, box, 4 x 5" plate, reflex viewing, leather cover designed to look like satchel, c1885,

Dossert Detective Camera Co. (New York, NY) 675.00
Dubroni, Le Photographe de Poche, wooden box, porcelain int. for in-camera processing, cl860, (Maison Dubroni, Paris) 3,000.00
Eastman Kodak (Rochester, NY)
Automatic Kodak Junior, No. 2C, c1916–27 .... 15.00
Boy Scout Camera, 1⅝ x 2½", 127 roll film, green vest pocket, emblem on bed, 1930–34 .... 40.00
50th Anniversary Box Camera, brown with silver seal, c1938 .... 25.00
Medalist II, 2¼ x 3¼", 620 film, f3.5/ 100mm Ektar, flash supermatic shutter, 1946–52 .... 150.00
No. 2, Folding Pocket, 101 roll film, 3½ x 3½", 1899–1903 .... 15.00
No. 4 Bullet, box, c1896 .... 50.00
Foth, Derby 11, folding, (Berlin, Germany) 40.00
Genie, brass magazine-box, string-set shutter, push-pull action changes plates and actuates exposure counter, c1892, (Philadelphia, PA) 450.00
Ingento, 3A Folding, Burke & James, (Chicago, IL) 35.00
Kalimar A, 35 mm, non-RF, f3.5/45mm Terionar lens, c1950, (Japan) 25.00
Leitz (Wetzlar, Germany)
Leica E (Standard), black, c1932–46 275.00
Leica M2, black, c1950 .... 400.00
Nikon, Nikon F Photomatic, 35 mm, c1965, (Tokyo, Japan) 150.00
Revere, Ranger Model 81, 8 mm movie camera, c1947, (Chicago, IL) 10.00
Seneca, Busy Bee, box, c1903, (Rochester, NY) 70.00
Tom Thumb Camera Radio, Automatic Radio Mfg Co, 1948, (Boston, MA) . 110.00
Tynar, 10 x 14mm exposures on specially loaded 16mm cassettes, single speed guillotine shutter, c1950, (Los Angeles, CA) 40.00
Universal Camera Corp (New York, NY)
Buccaneer, 35mm, Tricor lens, Chronomatic shutter 10-300, c1945 18.00
Roamer 63, 100 mm f6.3 lens, 120 roll film 10.00
Univex AF, compact, collapsing for Number 00 roll film, cast metal body, 1930s 15.00
Vitar 35 mm, Flash Chronomatic shutter 15.00
Vidmar, Vidax, folding, 120 roll film, c1951, (USA) 250.00
Voigtlander Superb, Twin Lens Reflex, 120 film, f3.5/75mm Skopar, 1930s, Voigtlander & Sons (Braunschweig, Germany) 125.00

CAMPHOR GLASS

History: Camphor glass derives its name from its color. Most pieces have a cloudy white appearance, similar to gum camphor; the remainder has a pale colored tint. Camphor glass is made by treating the glass with hydrofluoric acid vapors.

Vase, fan shaped, frosted, clear leaf design, 8" h, 10" w, $85.00.

Bottle
6½", stopper 30.00
8½", perfume, pinch type, mushroom stopper 35.00
Bowl, 10", fluted rim, polished pontil .. 125.00
Box, 5", hinged, holly spray 75.00
Candlestick, pr, 7", roses, hp 70.00
Creamer, 3¾" 20.00
Cruet, hp, enameled roses, orig stopper 30.00
Miniature Lamp, 4½", hp, violets 75.00
Place Card Holder, 3¾", ftd 35.00
Plate
6½", Easter Greeting 25.00
7¼", owl dec 30.00
Powder Jar, cov, 4½", pink-salmon, emb flowers on lid, figural love birds finial 48.00
Rose Bowl, hp violets, green leaves .. 45.00
Salt and Pepper Shakers, blue, Swirl pattern, orig tops, pr 40.00
Sugar Shaker, 3½", yellow, pressed leaf dec, SP top 50.00
Toothpick Holder
Bucket 25.00
Swirled, ruffled top 30.00
Vase
8", fan shape, clear leaf design and trim 80.00
10½", Grecian shape, double handle, clear base 100.00

CANDLESTICKS

History: The domestic use of candlesticks is traced to the 14th century. The earliest was a picket type, named for the sharp point to hold the candle. The socket type was established by the mid-1660s.

From 1700 to the present, candlestick design mirrored furniture design. By the late 17th century, a baluster stem was introduced, replacing the earlier Doric or clustered column stem. After 1730 candlesticks reflected rococo ornateness. Neoclassic styles followed in the 1760s. Each new era produced a new grouping of candlesticks.

However, some styles became universal and remained in production for centuries. For this reason, it is important to examine the manufacturing techniques of the piece when attempting to date a candlestick.

Reference: Margaret and Douglas Archer, *The Collector's Encyclopedia Of Glass Candlesticks,* Collector Books, 1983.

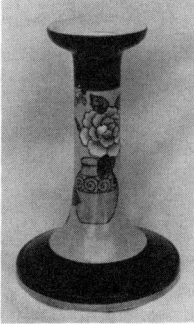

Noritake, black bands, purple flowers, yellow ground, 6⅜″ h, $40.00.

Bennington, 8¼″, Rockingham glaze	320.00
Brass	
4½″, chamber stick, pushup	100.00
5½″, sq ftd base, Spanish, c1600–50	250.00
8¼″ h, shell pattern, English, 18th C, pr	2,000.00
8½″ h, mid drip, Heemskerk, c1650	700.00
14½″ h, columnar, raised dec of grapes and vines	150.00
Glass	
Amber, pr, 10″, pressed	120.00
Cut, 10″ h, hollow center, frosted butterfly and flowers	85.00
Imperial, 7½″, pressed, crystal, orig stickers	30.00
Opalescent, 6″ h, rose dec, pr	50.00
Rose Point, ram's head, Cambridge	195.00
Sandwich, flint, clear dolphin, petal sockets, pr	450.00
Steuben, 8¾″, clear glass, tear drop, baluster form, model #7792, inscribed	600.00
Pewter	
4″, chamber stick, pushup, pr	190.00

6½″ h, snuffer provision, weighted base, c1700	225.00
8¾″ h, pushup ejectors, English, c1800–25	375.00
9⅞″ h, trumpet shape, Henry Hopper, New York, 1842–47	300.00
Sterling Silver	
4½″, circular, gadrooned mouth and base, Empire	55.00
9″, baluster shafts surmounted by urns, beaded base, drip pan, Goodnow & Jenks	220.00
11⅛″, octagonal base with reeded border and engraved formal dec, engraved and initialed fluted tapered stem, fluted vase shape socket, detachable wax pan with reeded border, Bigelow, Kennard & Co, Boston, 1920, pr	350.00
Tin	
3¼ x 6¼, chamber stick, white porcelain insert, wide drip pan	80.00
4 x 5½″, saucer base with lift, ring handle, c1840	60.00
Wood	
7½″, turned base with four turned columns, tin collar and socket, adjustable by turning thumb screw on bottom	160.00
25″, baroque style, tapering shaft carved with spiraling berried foliage, carved acanthus and cartouches triform base	440.00
Wrought Iron, 7″, spiral, lip hanger, pushup, wood base	100.00

CANDY CONTAINERS

History: In 1876 Croft, Wilbur and Co. filled a small glass Liberty Bell with candy and sold it at the Centennial Exposition in Philadelphia. From that date until the 1960s glass candy containers remained popular and served to outline American and American transportation history.

Jeannette, Pennsylvania, a center for the packaging of candy in containers, was home for J. C. Crosetti, J. H. Millstein, T. H. Stough, and Victory Glass. Other early manufacturers included: George Borgfeldt, New York, New York; Cambridge Glass, Cambridge, Ohio; Eagle Glass, Wheeling, West Virginia; L. E. Smith, Mt. Pleasant, Pennsylvania; and, West Brothers, Grapeville, Pennsylvania.

Candy containers with original paint, candy, and closures command a high premium, but be aware of reproduced parts and repainting. The closure is a critical part of each container; its loss detracts significantly from the value.

Small figural perfumes and other miniatures often are sold as candy containers.

References: George Eikelberner and Serge

Agadjanian, *The Compleat American Glass Candy Containers Handbook,* revised and published by Adele L. Bowden, 1986; Jennie Long, *An Album Of Candy Containers*, published by author, Volume I: 1978, Volume II: 1983.

Collectors' Club: Candy Container Collectors Of America, P.O. Box 1088, Washington, PA 15301. *The Candy Gram* (bimonthly).

Museums: Cambridge Glass Museum, Cambridge, OH; L. E. Smith Glass, Mt. Pleasant, PA.

Additional Listings: See *Warman's Americana & Collectibles* for more examples.

Airplane, US P-51, 5″, emb wing, cardboard closure 30.00
Automobile
  Coupe, 5¼″ l, 3″ h, clear, pressed, long hood, snap on tin closure ... 75.00
  Limousine, 4⅛ x 1¹⁵⁄₁₆ x 2½″, clear, pressed, black painted tin wheels, open top, c1912–1914 .... 70.00
Bath Tub, 4¾″ l, 1⅞″ h, clear, pressed, open top, traces of white paint, "Dolly's Bath Tub" marked on sides, Victory Glass Co, Jeannette, PA, USA 2,200.00

Battleship, clear, 5½″ l, $25.00.

Bird on stump, 5″ h, wood, composition, and chalk, polychromed 25.00
Boat, S. S. Colorado, 6½″ 325.00
Bureau, clear, pressed, inserted mirror, painted gold and black trim, tin slideon closure 125.00
Bus, Victory Lines Special, gray paint, cardboard closure 50.00
Candlestick, clear, pressed, handled, candle socket, tin screw-on cap ... 150.00
Cash Register, 3 x 1½ x 2⅝″, clear, pressed, gold paint, tin slide closure, Dugan Glass Co, Indiana, PA 325.00
Clock, 3¼ x 2½ x 1¾″, opaque milk white, pressed, painted gilt scrolls, pink rose and green leaf spray, tin slide closure 150.00
Dice, 3⅜″ sq, 3¼″ h, clear, pressed, traces of green paint, slightly concave, self closure lid,"Bristol–Diced–Mints" on lid, Brandel & Smith Co, Phila, USA 20.00

Dog, 3½″ h, begging, clear, pressed, round open base 150.00
Elephant, 2¾″, G.O.P. 110.00
Felix, 3¼″ h, 2⅛″ d, pedestal base with block letters, painted black body, white eyes, smiling mouth, metal screw cap 2,200.00
Football, tin, Germany 18.00
Girl, 5¾″ h, clear, pressed, two geese, oval base, c1950 .... 20.00
Goblin, head, 3⅝″ h, clear, pressed, orange face, green with orange splash raised leaves, white bulging eyes, white incised teeth, gold tin screw lid 350.00
Gun, 3⅝″ l, 2″ h, clear, molded, cream enamel screw cap, waffle type pattern grip 12.00
Hat, clear, opaque white and stained colors, screw-on tin brim 60.00
Horn, musical, tin whistle, cardboard tube
  Clarinet 30.00
  Piccolo 45.00
Kettle, 2″ h, 2¼″ d, clear, pressed, three feet, cardboard closure, T.H. Stough Co 45.00
Lantern, glass barn type frame, tin bottom, friction closure 50.00
Man on motorcycle, side car, clear, pressed, painted, red tin snap closure, Victory Glass Co, Jeannette, PA 350.00
Mailbox, 3¼″ 50.00
Nursing Bottle, clear, pressed, natural wood nipple closure, T. H. Stough Co, c1940–45 .... 15.00
Opera Glasses, 3⅝″, swirl rib 45.00
Owl, 4⅜″ h, clear, pressed, stylized feathers, gold tin screw cap 80.00
Phonograph, clear, pressed, gold tin horn, molded arm, black painted glass record disc, gold slide closure 225.00
Puppy, 2½″ h, papier mache, white paint, black muzzle, glass eyes 30.00
Purse, 4⅛ x 2½ x 3⅝″, clear, pressed, light emerald, alligator leather design, gilded metal parts, gold souvenir panel, aluminum closure 275.00
Rabbit, 8⁷⁄₁₆″, fur covered, Germany, 1910–20 .... 85.00
Radio, emb tune-in, tin closure, V.G. Co. 85.00
Refrigerator, clear, pressed, painted white, gilded hinges, handles, and latches, four legs, USA–V.G. Co.–Jeannette, PA 1,000.00
Rooster, 6½″ h, papier mache, orig polychrome paint 10.00
Santa, 12″, crepe paper, cotton, white, gold snowflakes, painted plaster feet, face, German 225.00
Soldier, 5⅛″ h, molded, holding sword, painted, stepped plinth type base, tin slide closure 800.00

Squirrel on stump, 5″ h, clear, pressed, sitting upright holding nut, emb leaves, twig, and acorn design, tree bark ground, metal screw cap **1,200.00**
Statue of Liberty, 5⅜″ h, lead top, clear glass bottom **1,100.00**
Suitcase, 3⅝″, emb straps, tin closure, wire handle **35.00**
Telephone, desk, French, Crosetti . . . **20.00**
Traffic Sign, 4½″, "Don't Park Here" . . **60.00**
Turkey, 3¾″, papier mache, lead feet . **15.00**
Wolf, 4⅝″, with book **50.00**

CANES

History: Canes and walking sticks were important accessories in a gentleman's wardrobe in the 18th and 19th centuries. They often served both a decorative and utilitarian function. Collectors frequently view carved canes in wood and ivory as folk art and pay higher prices for them. Glass canes and walking sticks were glass makers' whimsies, ornamental rather than practical.

Reference: Catherine Dike, *Cane Curiosa*, published by author, 1983.

CANES

Glass
46⅜″, clear, int. twist, red, white, and blue **75.00**
59″, aqua, twisted handle, straight rib **90.00**
Ivory, 40″, whale, dove of peace carved handle, wings outlined in incising, perched atop knob and shaft, c1860 **4,200.00**
Scrimshaw
31″, lady's, whalebone, carved walrus, ivory dog's head handle **150.00**
33¾″, wood shaft, carved walrus ivory handle of knee with laced legging and boot, tassel **200.00**
36″, Lady's, whalebone with whalebone ivory knob, baleen and shell inlays, c1850 . . . . **375.00**
Sword, 35″, horn handle in shape of dog's head **150.00**
Wood
35½″, birch, light shade, inlaid handle of torsia floral and leaves **115.00**
42″, commemorating 100 years, Newburgh, NY, Stanhope, Washington's headquarters, c1883 . . . . **75.00**

WALKING STICKS

Bone, 35½″, tapered fluted to round shaft, carved ivory fist **500.00**
Curly Maple, 35¾″, tapered octagonal shaft **55.00**
Ebony, 25½″, ivory head, short stiletto sword **125.00**

Folk Art, 38″, carved snake, wood burned and red and black ink detail . **80.00**
Glass
54½″, clear, gold int. **70.00**
63″, Nailsea type, clear with swirls of blue, red, white, and pale green . . **200.00**
Wood
33″, Mahogany, ivory tip, paneled, bulbous knob **250.00**
36″ l, pine, folk art, carved clenched fist, cuff and cuff link, V. W. Williams, and snake, old varnish finish **100.00**
39½″, simple chip carved designs . . **20.00**

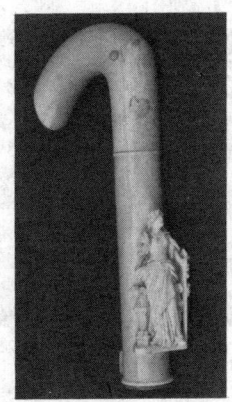

Handle, ivory, figure of Liberty, 5½″ h, $175.00.

HANDLES

Gold, 14K, plain **85.00**
Ivory, 6″ h, carved, modeled as phrenology head, 19th C **950.00**

CANTON CHINA

History: Canton china is a type of oriental porcelain made in the Canton region of China from the late 18th century and early 19th century to the present and produced largely for export. Canton china is hand decorated in light to dark blue underglaze on white. Design motifs include houses, mountains, trees, boats, and a bridge. A design similar to "willow china" is the most common.

Borders on early Canton feature a rain and cloud motif (a thick band of diagonal lines with a scalloped bottom). Later pieces usually have a straight line border. The markings "Made in China" and "China" indicate wares which date after 1891.

Early plates are very heavy and often have an unfinished bottom, while serving pieces have an overall "orange peel" bottom. Early covered pieces, such as tureens, vegetable dishes, sugars, etc., have strawberry finials and twisted handles. Later ones have round finials and straight, single handles.

Reference: Sandra Andacht, *Oriental Antiques & Art: An Identification And Value Guide,* Wallace-Homestead, 1987.

Reproduction Alert: Several museum gift shops and private manufacturers are issuing reproductions of Canton china.

Advisor: Mark Saville.

**Dish, water edge scene, 9 x 11¼ x 1¾",
$250.00.**

Basket, 9¾" l, fruit, reticulated, matching undertray, c1840	1,100.00
Bowl, 10"	
Round, scalloped, c1830	775.00
Square, cut corners, c1830	1,200.00
Butter Dish, 3 pcs, c1840	700.00
Butter Pat, early	80.00
Candlesticks, pr, 7", trumpet shape	2,850.00
Charger, 14", early, c1835	800.00
Coffeepot, 10", domed lid, c1850	900.00
Creamer, 4", pear shape, c1840	235.00
Egg Cup, 2½", early, c1840	125.00
Ginger Jar	
4", c1840	135.00
6", cov, c1840	275.00
Hot Water Dish, 8½", c1845	400.00
Kettle Stand, 7", c1830	225.00
Pie Dish, early, c1840	
7"	300.00
9"	425.00
Plate, early, c1820–30	
6", butter	60.00
7½", salad	75.00
8"	
Desert	90.00
Pierced	275.00
9", lunch	110.00
10", dinner	150.00
Platter, early, c1830–40	
13", rect	375.00
16", rect	650.00
17", Well-in-tree	750.00
Salt, master, c1830	500.00
Saucer	
Straight line border, late, c1875	75.00
Twig shape handle, c1850	105.00
Serving Dish, early, c1840	
10", open	300.00
12", rect, open	450.00
Leaf shape	285.00
Spoon, firemarks, early, c1835	50.00
Sugar, Cov, twisted handles	360.00
Teapot	
6", drum shape, c1830	500.00
7", lighthouse shape, c1825	650.00
Tile, sq, early, c1820	325.00
Tureen	
8", undertray	750.00
13", undertray, c1820	2,400.00
Vegetable Dish, cov, 8½ x 9½", sq, c1840	475.00
Water Pitcher, 10", c1830	1,300.00

CAPO-DI-MONTE

History: In 1743 King Charles of Naples established a soft paste porcelain factory near Naples which made figures and dinnerware. In 1760 many of the workmen and most of the molds were taken to Buen Retiro, near Madrid, Spain. A new factory opened in Naples in 1771 and added hard paste porcelains. In 1834 the Doccia factory in Florence purchased the molds and continued their production in Italy.

Capo-di-Monte was copied heavily by factories in Hungary, Germany, France, and Italy. Many of the pieces in today's market are of recent vintage. Do not be fooled by the crown over the "N" mark; it also was copied.

Reference: Susan and Al Bagdade, *Warman's English & Continental Pottery & Porcelain, 1st Edition,* Warman Publishing Co., Inc., 1987.

Ashtray, 6", crown mark	20.00
Bowl, cov, multicolored allegorial scene, goddesses in relief	125.00
Box, 4½ × 7", cov, circular, relief figures of children and trees, paw feet, fruit finial on cov	75.00
Candleholder, 3", raised flowers and nude figures	100.00
Compote, cov, 9", oval, relief molded	

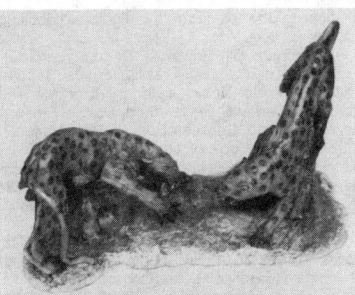

Figurine, Fighting Leopards, marked "G. Qurius," 17½" l, $160.00.

cherubs on sides, cherub finial and handles **225.00**
Cup and Saucer, florals, hp, sgd **40.00**
Demitasse Set, 17 pcs, covered pot, creamer, sugar, six ftd cups and saucers, large round ftd tray, artist sgd . **250.00**
Ewer, 14", semi-nude maiden in relief . **110.00**
Ferner, 11", oval, relief molded and enameled allegorial figures, full relief female mask at each end **100.00**
Figurine
   5", bisque, masked jester, black and orange costume, holding sword, gold and white pedestal **100.00**
   9", flower girl, c1880 .... **325.00**
   9 x 8", soldier on horseback, dated 1840 .... **350.00**
Jewel Box, 9¾", oval, relief molded and brightly painted frieze of drunken cherub being carried away by baby satyrs, domed cov with Venus, entwined rose garland and feather borders, 19th C **350.00**
Lamp, table, pr, 26" h, urn form, cream cupids dec, forest green ground, gilt bronze dolphin feet **150.00**
Perfume, 3", cherub in garden, blue crown mark **65.00**
Plaque, 22½ x 16½", harvest scene, high relief, velvet covered molded frame **290.00**
Plate, semi-nudes bathing beside brook relief, floral festoon border **100.00**
Snuff Box, 3¼", hinged lid, cartouche shape, molded basketweave and flowerhead ext., painted int. with court lady and page examining portrait of gentleman, gold mountings, c1740, minor restoration **1,650.00**
Stein, garden scene, adults and children, lion on cov, sgd **120.00**

Urn, 28 x 12", cov, three cherubs seated blowing trumpets finial and on base, heavy relief on sides **675.00**

CARLSBAD CHINA

History: Because of changing European boundaries, German–speaking Carlsbad found itself located in the last hundred years first in the Austro-Hungarian Empire, next in Germany, and currently in Czechoslovakia. Carlsbad was one of the leading pottery manufacturing centers in Bohemia.

Wares from the numerous Carlsbad potteries are lumped together under the term "Carlsbad China." Most pieces on the market are post-1891, although several potteries date to the early 19th century.

Reference: Susan and Al Bagdade, *Warman's English & Continental Pottery & Porcelain, 1st Edition,* Warman Publishing Co., Inc., 1987.

Biscuit Jar, twig handle, gold trim, stamped "Victoria, Carlsbad," angel scepter mark, 6⅜" h, 5½" d, $50.00.

Berry Dish, 5¾", white, pink, and yellow roses, green buds and leaves, shaped gold rim, c1905 .... **20.00**
Bowl
   8¾", shallow, gold center with death of King Lear,green border, artist sgd **70.00**
   10", portrait, green border, gold tracings, sgd "Boucher, Victoria Carlsbad, Austria" **60.00**
Butter Pat, 2", round, white, blue floral dec **10.00**
Cake Plate, 11" d, pierced handles, center pink poppies and green leaves, white ground, emb gilt rim, marked "Austria Imperial Carlsbad" **65.00**

Chocolate Pot, 10", blue, scenic portrait,
marked "Carlsbad Victoria" **110.00**
Creamer and Sugar, Bluebird pattern,
marked "Victoria Carlsbad" **55.00**
Cup and Saucer, set of 6, rosebuds,
vines, and leaves, c1875 . . . . **125.00**
Ewer
6", cream, pastel pink, gold, floral dec **75.00**
14", handles, light green, floral dec,
gold trim, marked "Carlsbad, Vic-
toria" **80.00**
Hair Receiver, 4" d, white, cobalt blue
flowers, gold trim, emb basketweave
at top **30.00**
Oyster Plates, set of 10, 8¾", white, lavender flowers, gold outlining **100.00**
Pin Tray, 8½", irregular scalloped
shape, white, bunches of small roses,
green leaves, marked "Victoria,
Carlsbad, Austria" **30.00**
Pitcher, 8", ornate handle, soft cream,
gold floral dec **60.00**
Plate
7", white, fancy reticulated border,
c1860 . . . . **15.00**
9", cherries, hp, sgd **25.00**
Portrait Plate, 8½", Melle La Vallerie,
blue mark L.S.& S./Carlsbad/Austria **35.00**
Powder Box, cov, 5" d, Bluebird pattern,
Victoria, Carlsbad **45.00**
Soup Tureen, cov, large white, deep
pink and yellow roses, green leaves,
gold trim buckle handles and finial,
imp mark **65.00**
Sugar Shaker, 5½", egg shape, floral
dec **60.00**
Vase, 9½" h, center medallion of four
Grecian figures, dark blue–green
ground, ornate cream handles **48.00**
Vegetable Dish, cov, 6¼ x 9½", sq,
chamfered corners, pink and yellow
roses, green buds and leaves, gold
trim, buckle handles and finial, c1900 **70.00**

CARNIVAL GLASS

History: Carnival glass, an American invention,
is colored pressed glass with a fired on iridescent
finish. It was first manufactured about 1905 and
was immensely popular both in America and
abroad. Over 1,000 different patterns have been
identified. Production of old carnival glass patterns
ended in 1930.

Most of the popular patterns of carnival glass
were produced by five companies—Dugan, Fenton, Imperial, Millersburg, and Northwood. Northwood patterns frequently are found with the "N"
trademark. Dugan used a diamond trademark on
several patterns.

In carnival glass color is the most important factor in pricing. The color of a piece is determined
by holding the piece to the light and looking
through it.

References: Bill Edwards, *The Standard En-
cyclopedia of Carnival Glass, Revised Second
Edition*, Collector Books, 1988; Bill Edwards, *The
Standard Carnival Glass Price Guide, Revised
Seventh Edition*, Collector Books, 1989; Marion T.
Hartung, *First Book of Carnival Glass to Tenth
Book of Carnival Glass* [series of 10 books], pub-
lished by author, 1968 to 1982; Thomas E. Sprain,
Carnival Glass Tumblers, New and Reproduced,
published by author, 1984.

Collectors' Club: American Carnival Glass Association, Box 3514, Plymouth, MA 02360; Heart
of America Carnival Glass Association, 3048 Ta-
marak Drive, Manhatten, KS 66502; International
Carnival Glass Association, Inc., R.D. #1, Box 14,
Mentone, IN 46539.

Acanthus, Imperial
Bowl
7", green **20.00**
8", marigold **60.00**
Plate
9", marigold **145.00**
10", smoky **185.00**
Acorn, Fenton
Bowl
5", blue, ribbon candy rim **60.00**
7", amber, ruffled **110.00**
9", purple, ribbon candy rim **50.00**
Apple Blossom Twigs, Dugan
Banana Boat, peach opalescent, ruf-
fled **175.00**
Bowl
8", marigold **50.00**
10", purple **250.00**
Plate, 9", blue **110.00**
Vase, amethyst **50.00**
Autumn Acorns, Fenton
Bowl, 9"
Blue **75.00**
Green **40.00**
Marigold **50.00**
Barrel, bottle, smoky **160.00**
Basket, Northwood, aqua opalescent . **450.00**
Beaded Shell, Dugan
Berry set, master and three ftd
sauces, purple **185.00**
Creamer, marigold **60.00**
Mug, purple **65.00**
Rose Bowl, green **40.00**
Spooner, marigold **40.00**
Table Set, marigold, 4 pcs **250.00**
Tumbler
Blue **45.00**
Lavender **95.00**
Marigold **70.00**
Blackberry Spray, Fenton
Bonbon, marigold **30.00**
Compote, green, 5½" **40.00**
Hat, red **240.00**

Blueberry, Fenton
Pitcher, blue 500.00
Tumbler
  Blue 75.00
  Marigold 35.00
  White 185.00
Carolina Dogwood, Westmoreland
Bowl, 8½″
  Aqua opalescent 375.00
  Peach opalescent 150.00
Bride's Bowl, peach opalescent 325.00
Plate, peach opalescent, 8½″ 475.00
Cherry, Fenton
Bonbon, aqua, two handles 275.00
Bowl, green 150.00
Calling Card Tray, aqua 125.00
Plate, marigold, 6″ 40.00
Cherry Chain, Fenton
Bonbon, marigold, two handles 40.00
Bowl
  5″, marigold, Orange Tree pattern
    ext. 25.00
  8″, white 100.00
Plate, 6″, blue 115.00
Coin Dot, Northwood
Bowl
  6″, green 20.00
  8″, aqua, stippled 45.00
  9″, vaseline, ruffled 55.00
Pitcher, marigold 150.00
Plate, purple 60.00
Rose Bowl, marigold 45.00
Tumbler, marigold 50.00
Corinth, Dugan
Banana Boat, marigold 30.00
Rose bowl, ice blue 110.00
Corn, Northwood, vase, ice green,
marked "N" 350.00
Country Kitchen, Millersburg
Bowl, 5″, marigold, ruffled 80.00
Butter Dish, cov, purple 350.00
Spooner, marigold 100.00
Crab Claw, Imperial
Bowl, marigold 270.00

Tumbler, marigold 40.00
Water Set, pitcher and six tumblers,
  marigold 300.00
Daisy, Fenton
Bonbon, marigold 85.00
Nut bowl, blue 220.00
Daisy and Plume, Northwood
Candy Dish, green 65.00
Compote, aqua 60.00
Rose Bowl, marigold 80.00
Diamond and Sunburst, Imperial
Bowl, 8″, marigold 50.00
Decanter, aqua 150.00
Wine, amethyst 65.00
Dragon and Lotus, Fenton
Bowl, blue 75.00
Plate, 9½″, marigold 650.00
Drapery, Northwood
Bowl, 8″, pastel 50.00
Candy Dish, marigold 150.00
Rose Bowl, green 85.00
Vase, ice green 55.00
Elks Club, Fenton, bowl, 1910, green   925.00
Embossed Mums, Northwood
Bonbon, pastel 100.00
Bowl, 9″, marigold 45.00
Plate, irid 1,750.00
Feather Stitch, Fenton, bowl, blue . . .   290.00
Fleur–de–lis, Millersburg, bowl, mari-
gold 60.00
Flowers and Frames, Dugan, bowl,
blue 175.00
Flute, Imperial and Millersburg
Breakfast Set, individual size, green   115.00
Goblet, marigold 15.00
Sauce, green 60.00
Sherbet 25.00
Toothpick, amethyst 55.00
Good Luck, Northwood
Bowl
  7″, green, ruffled 200.00
  8″, purple, piecrust 235.00
Plate, 9″
  Green 500.00

Left: Dragon and Lotus, bowl, blue, flat, collared base, 8″ d, $75.00; center: Louisa, rose bowl, purple, $70.00; right: Orange Tree, mug, purple, $50.00.

Marigold	225.00

Grape and Cable, Fenton and Northwood

Banana Boat, blue	335.00
Berry Set, master and six sauces, green	200.00
Bowl, aqua opalescent, stippled	2,600.00
Butter Dish, cov, amethyst	95.00
Compote, cov, purple, small	250.00
Creamer and Sugar, amethyst	85.00
Cup and Saucer, marigold	250.00
Ice Cream Bowl, white	130.00
Plate, green	85.00

Heart and Flowers, Fenton

Bowl, ice blue	300.00
Compote, aqua opalescent	475.00

Hobnail, Millersburg

Butter Dish, cov, marigold	350.00
Cuspidor, purple	475.00
Rose Bowl	
Amethyst	475.00
Marigold	50.00

Hobstar and Feather, Millersburg

Punch Bowl, two pcs, marigold, vaseline base, chip on inside rim	525.00
Punch Cup, green	30.00
Rose Bowl, green	1,500.00

Holly, rose bowl, large, blue | 290.00

Horse Heads, Fenton

Bowl, blue	100.00
Jack In The Pulpit Vase, vaseline	135.00
Nut Bowl, vaseline	210.00
Plate, 8″, marigold	145.00
Rose Bowl, marigold	110.00

Jeweled Heart, Dugan

Bowl, white	165.00
Calling Card Tray, peach opalescent, turned up sides	45.00
Pitcher, marigold	650.00
Sauce, purple	40.00
Tumbler, amber	115.00

Leaf and Beads, Northwood

Candy Bowl, green, ftd	60.00

Nut Bowl, purple, handles	65.00
Rose Bowl, marigold	50.00

Leaf and Flower, Millersburg, compote, green | 190.00

Lion, Fenton

Bowl	
5″, marigold, low	80.00
7″, blue	300.00
Plate, 6″, marigold	600.00

Little Flowers, Fenton

Berry Set, master bowl and three sauces, blue	80.00
Bowl	
5″, aqua	100.00
8″, blue	100.00
10″, lavender, ruffled	115.00
Nut Bowl, marigold	65.00
Plate, 6″, marigold	150.00

Loganberry, Imperial, vase, amethyst | 450.00

Lotus and Grape, Fenton

Bonbon, green, two handles	50.00
Bowl	
5″, blue, ftd	40.00
7″, marigold, ftd	45.00
Ice Cream Bowl, 8½″, Persian blue	400.00
Plate, 9″, green	1,500.00

Louisa, Westmoreland

Bowl, 8″, green, ftd	45.00
Nut Bowl, marigold, ftd	30.00
Plate, 9½″, teal blue, ftd	100.00
Rose Bowl, lavender, ftd	70.00
Salt and Pepper Shakers, pr, marigold	20.00

Many Stars, Millersburg

Bowl, 8″, marigold	130.00
Ice Cream Bowl, 10″, green	375.00

Nautilus, Dugan

Bowl, ftd, amethyst	130.00
Creamer, purple	170.00
Sugar Bowl, peach opalescent	250.00

Night Stars, Millersburg

Bonbon, marigold	950.00
Calling Card Tray, purple	300.00

Left: Peacock At The Fountain, butter dish, purple, $225.00; center: Singing Birds, mug, purple, $120.00; right: Three Fruits, plate, marigold, $160.00.

Orange Tree, Fenton

Berry Set, master and four sauces, white	165.00
Bowl, 10", purple	175.00
Breakfast Set, individual size, purple	125.00
Compote, green	85.00
Goblet, blue	50.00
Hatpin Holder, marigold	150.00
Ice Cream Bowl, marigold	25.00
Mug, vaseline	55.00
Pitcher, blue	325.00
Plate, white	200.00
Powder Jar, purple	125.00
Tumbler, white	135.00
Wine, marigold	30.00

Palm Beach, United States Glass Co

Banana Boat, purple	115.00
Bowl, 5", marigold, turned in sides	90.00
Butter Dish, cov, white	200.00
Creamer, marigold	70.00
Pitcher, marigold	400.00
Rose Bowl, amber	125.00
Sauce, white	40.00
Spooner, white	85.00
Tumbler, marigold	200.00

Peacock and Urn, Fenton and Millersburg

Bowl

Blue	300.00
Marigold, with bee	350.00
Compote, 5", aqua	325.00
Ice Cream Bowl, 10", purple	250.00
Plate, 6½", marigold	165.00
Sauce, green	75.00

Peacock at the Fountain, Northwood

Berry Set, master and six sauces, marigold	200.00
Butter Dish, cov, purple	225.00
Compote, marigold	400.00
Creamer, purple	90.00
Punch Bowl and Base, marigold	350.00
Punch Cup, blue	50.00
Sauce, ice blue	75.00
Sugar Bowl, white	180.00
Water Set, pitcher, six tumblers, cobalt blue	600.00

Peacock on Fence, Northwood

Bowl

8", blue, piecrust rim	375.00
9", marigold, ruffled rim	200.00

Plate, 9"

Ice green	2,100.00
Purple	600.00
White	400.00

Persian Medallion, Fenton

Bonbon, amber, two handles	60.00

Bowl

Blue	65.00
Ice blue	150.00

Compote, 6½"

Marigold	60.00
Purple	100.00

Hair Receiver, marigold	50.00
Plate, 9", marigold	115.00

Plaid, Fenton

Bowl, blue	90.00
Plate, 9", marigold	125.00
Pony, Dugan, bowl, marigold	115.00

Rose Show, Northwood

Bowl, 8¾", marigold	125.00
Plate, aqua opalescent	2,000.00

Singing Birds

Creamer, marigold	40.00
Sugar, marigold	45.00

Stag and Holly, Fenton

Bowl, amethyst	160.00
Rose Bowl, marigold	375.00

Three Fruits, Northwood

Bonbon, green	80.00
Bowl, aqua opalescent	400.00
Compote, marigold	50.00
Plate, marigold	160.00

Two Flowers, Fenton

Bowl, large, blue	100.00
Rose Bowl, marigold	100.00

Wide Panels, United States Glass Co

Plate, red	90.00
Salt, marigold	40.00

Wishbone, Northwood

Bowl, ftd, amethyst	130.00
Epergne, aqua	275.00

Zig Zag, Fenton and Millersburg

Bowl, marigold	100.00
Pitcher, marigold, dec	185.00
Tumbler, blue	50.00

CAROUSEL FIGURES

History: By the late 17th century carousels were found in most capital cities of Europe. In 1867 Gustav Dentzel carved America's first carousel. Other leading American manufacturers include Charles I. D. Looff, Allan Herschell, Charles Parker, and William F. Mangels.

Original paint is not critical, since figures were repainted annually. Park paint indicates layers of accumulated paint; stripped means paint removed to show carving; restored involves stripping and repainting in the original colors.

References: Charlotte Dinger, *Art Of The Carousel,* Carousel Art, Inc., 1983; Tobin Fraley, *The Carousel Animal,* Tobin Fraley Studios, 1983; Frederick Fried, *The Pictorial History Of The Carousel,* Vestal Press, 1964; William Manns, Peggy Shank, and Marianne Stevens, *Painted Ponies: American Carousel Art,* Zon International Publishing, 1986.

Periodical: *Carrousel Art,* P.O. Box 992, Garden Grove, CA 92642.

Collectors' Clubs: The American Carousel Society, 470 South Pleasant Avenue, Ridgewood, NJ 07450; National Amusement Park Historical Association, P.O. Box 83, Mount Prospect, IL 60056;

National Carousel Association, P.O. Box 307, Frankford, IN 46041.

Camel, Bactrian, carved and poly-chromed wood, later glass eyes, res-toration, 45″ l, 43½″ h, American, 19th C **2,750.00**
Chicken, old paint, needs some repair, Herschell/Spillman, c1910 .... **4,000.00**
Donkey, jumper, stripped, restored, Dentzel, c1908 .... **10,000.00**
Giraffe, ornate carving, Phila Toboggan Co **24,000.00**

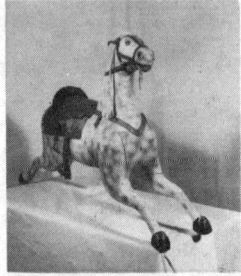

Horse, wood, painted white, orig halter, leather saddle, and corduroy blanket, Eastern origin, c1840, 29¼″ h, 46″ l, $850.00.

Horse
  Galloping, 58″ h, 54″ l, painted, gray, red, yellow, and gold trim, butterfly at rear of brown saddle, eleven glass jewels, paperweight glass eyes, mounted on brass pole and wood base **6,000.00**
  Jumper
    Outer row, park paint, raised head, jeweled trappings, Carmel, c1911 .... **13,000.00**
    Row two, head down, stripped to bare wood, Dentzel **6,250.00**
  Prancer
    Inner row, head down, park paint, Dentzel **4,500.00**
    Outer row, park paint, Looff **6,750.00**
  Standing
    Outer row, Muller style, figural on side, Dentzel, c1890–1903 .... **15,000.00**
  Track machine style, American flag on side, restored, primer paint, Armitage/Herschell, c1900 .. **2,500.00**
Mirror, three 18th C figures and flowers dec, 37″ w, 42½″ h, Ralph Cahoon dec **600.00**
Mule, galloping, left ear forward, right

ear back, wood, carved, orig paint, mounted on spiral brass pole, 53″ l, 54½″ h, Phila Toboggan Co **5,000.00**
Rooster, restored, Herschell/Spillman, c1907 .... **5,800.00**
Shield, clown face, park paint, needs repair, Herschell **500.00**

CASTLEFORD

History: Castleford is a soft paste porcelain made in Yorkshire, England, in the 1800s for the American trade. The ware has warm, white ground, scalloped rims (resembling castle tops), and is trimmed in deep blue. Occasionally pieces are decorated further with a coat of arms, eagles, or Liberty.

Teapot, blue dec, 9″ l, 5¼″ h, $200.00.

Creamer, 4¼″, white, parian, deep blue striping, emb classical scenes of cherubs **100.00**
Milk Jug, 4¾″ h, oval, relief of American Eagle on one side, Liberty and cap on reverse, acanthus leaf border ... **150.00**
Sugar, cov, relief of classical figure lean-ing on urn, acanthus leaf panel, blue enamel border, scalloped edge, three enamel bands on cov **245.00**
Tea Set, cov teapot, milk jug, cov sugar bowl, relief panels of mythological fig-ures, animals, and shell, bead border, fluted base, dolphin knob, blue enamel line border, glazed int. **400.00**

CASTOR SETS

History: A castor set consists of matched con-diment bottles within a frame or holder. The bottles are for condiments such as salt, pepper, oil, vine-gar, and mustard. The most commonly found cas-tor set consist of three to five glass bottles in a silver plated frame.

Although castor sets were known as early as the 1700s, most of the sets encountered today date from the 1870 to 1915 period when they enjoyed great popularity.

3-bottles, Bristol glass, cream, opaque, enameled leaves and fruit dec, SP frame **115.00**

3-bottles, clear, Daisy and Button bottles, toothpick holder in center, matching glass holder **100.00**

3-bottles, clear, Ribbed Palm pattern, pewter tops and stand **170.00**

3-bottles, cranberry glass, SP crescent moon shaped stand, orig spoon ... **175.00**

4-bottles, clear, bulbous, floral etching, cut honeycomb and circles dec, shaker, two cruets, mustard, SP frame, ladies heads on base and handle, cherub holding up handle, sgd "Rogers Bros" **150.00**

4-bottles, clear, King's Crown pattern bottles, matching glass stand, metal center handle **100.00**

4-bottles, cranberry glass, IVT pattern bottles, enameled floral dec, SP stand, marked "Meriden" **100.00**

4-bottles, green cut to clear, sq bottles, sq SP stand **335.00**

Five bottles, Gothic Arches pattern, flint glass, pewter standard, attributed to Sandwich Glass, c1860, 10½" h, $225.00.

5-bottles, Baccarat glass, Rose Tiente, SP frame **175.00**

5 bottle, 11¼" h, Bellflower pattern, pewter frame **300.00**

5-bottles, china, Willowware pattern, matching china stand **115.00**

5-bottles, clear, cut, all over lunar and geometric cutting, SS mounts and stand, Warwick form, shell shaped foot, English hallmarks, c1750, 8½" h **600.00**

5-bottles, clear, cut, Honeycomb pattern and etched floral bottles, SP stand, marked "Tufts" **185.00**

5-bottles, cut, three ball and claw feet, open cartouche circular handle, SS stand, English hallmarks, c1861 ... **375.00**

5-bottles, clear, etched glass bottles, revolving SP stand, 16" **125.00**

5-bottles, ruby cut to clear glass bottles, SP stand **185.00**

6-bottles, clear, fluted glass, SS stand, circular, vertical fluted border, central ring of cast antheminon and ivy leaf dec, sgd "Tiffany & Co, NY," c1865, 11" h **1,250.00**

8-bottles, pressed glass, SP tops and holder, Simpson H. Miller Co **225.00**

CATALOGS

History: The first American mail order catalog was issued by Benjamin Franklin in 1744. This popular advertising tool helped to spread inventions, innovations, fashions, and other necessities of life to rural America. Catalogs were profusely illustrated and are studied today to date an object, identify its manufacturer, study its distribution, and determine its historical importance.

References: Don Fredgant, *American Trade Catalogs: Identification and Value Guide,* Collector Books, 1984; Lawrence B. Romaine, *A Guide To American Trade Catalogs 1744–1900,* R. R. Bowker, 1960.

Additional Listings: See *Warman's Americana & Collectibles* for more examples.

Marshall Field & Company, Chicago, 1907–1908, $50.00.

Arcade Cast Iron Toys, 12 pgs, 5 x 7¼",
1927 .... **65.00**
Ario's Cowboy Catalog, 66 pgs, 1942 . **15.00**
Autos Chalmers, Deluxe, color, 32 pgs,
7¼ x 9¼", 1914 .... **50.00**
Bannermann Military Goods, 1931 ... **140.00**
C. Fischer, 120 pgs, 9½ x 12½", 1902 **100.00**
Chandler and Barber Metal Working
Tools, 1907 .... **15.00**
Chicago Engineer Supply Co, hard
cover, 528 pgs, 1915 .... **25.00**
Colt, 1909 .... **30.00**
Crane Co., Valves, Fittings, 743 pgs,
1923 .... **15.00**
DuPont, American Game Birds, Lynn
Bogue Hunt **30.00**
FAO Schwartz Christmas, 151 pgs,
1965 .... **20.00**
Fenestra Windows, c1920 .... **15.00**
George Gibson, Belfast, Irish linens, 22
pgs, 1930 .... **20.00**
Heywood Wakefield Furniture, c1927 . **55.00**
International Trucks, Model SL, 8 pgs,
9 x 12" **20.00**
John Plain Co., fine jewelry and
watches, 97 pgs, 1925 .... **25.00**
Kewannee Book of Laboratory, Voca-
tional, Home Economics, Furniture,
391 pgs, 1937 .... **35.00**
Laboratory Supply, hard cover, 1,000
pgs, 1938 .... **25.00**
Lincraft Rustic Furniture, Fences, c1920 **15.00**
Lloyd's Cane Furniture, 1925 .... **75.00**
Mills Novelty, 1898 .... **6.00**
Mitchell Motion Picture Cameras, 44
pgs, 9 x 11½", 1937 .... **35.00**
Montgomery Ward, 1925 .... **30.00**
Oliver (Hart-Parr) Tractor and 36 H.P.
Engines, 144 pgs, 1929 .... **20.00**
Olson Rugs, color, 1931 .... **10.00**
Phillip Bernard Co. Farm Equipment #7 **15.00**
Remington, pocket type, 1935 ...... **25.00**
Restaurant Supplies, 1923 .... **25.00**
Rubber Swim Caps, color, c1920 .... **18.00**
Savage Grocery, 1928 .... **10.00**
Scranton Lace Curtains, 1918 ...... **12.00**
Stevens, 1907 .... **65.00**
Stromber, Carburetors, 1939 ...... **50.00**
The Mershow Co. Firearm Accessories
and Police Equipment, 1940 ...... **20.00**
The Winton Six, hard cover, 54 pgs, 5¼
x 8", 1913 .... **50.00**
Thomas Register of American Manufac-
turers, 5,200 pgs, 1937 .... **145.00**
Victor Red Seal Records, 1924 ..... **20.00**
Wiedke Flue Tools, 1915 .... **10.00**

CELADON

History: The term celadon, meaning a pale
grayish green color, derives from a theatrical char-

acter Celadon, who wore costumes of varying
shades of grayish green, in Honore d'Urfe's 17th
century pastoral romance, "L'Astree." French Jes-
uits living in China applied it to a specific type of
Chinese porcelain.

Celadon divides into two types. Northern celadon, made during the Sung Dynasty up to the
1120s, has a gray to brownish body, relief decoration, and monochrome olive green glaze.

Southern (Lung-ch'uan) celadon, made during
the Sung Dynasty and much later, is paint decorated with floral and other scenic designs and
found in forms which would appeal to the European and American export market. Many of the
Southern pieces date from 1825 to 1885. A blue
square with Chinese or pseudo-Chinese characters appears on pieces after 1850. Later pieces
also have a larger and sparser decorative pattern-
ing.

Reproduction Alert.

**Brush Washer, 2″ h, 2¼″ d,
$80.00.**

Bowl, 8½", blue and white dragon in
center **65.00**
Brush Bowl, 2¼ x 2", slightly bulbous,
crackle **100.00**
Cake Stand, 10½ x 4½", Canton,
19th C **300.00**
Censer, 3¾", lobed body, short neck,
out turned rim, ruyi scroll work, key
fret neck band, two rope twisted handles, three burnt orange flared feet . **275.00**
Charger, 14¼ x 10¾", octagonal, pea-
cock, flowers **175.00**
Dish, 6¼", pale, incised single floral
spray in center **200.00**
Fish Bowl, 8⁷⁄₁₆", flattened rim, carved
petals, int. with two small fish swimming left and right, luminous glaze . **350.00**
Ginger Jar, 6", bulbous, multicolored relief floral dec, dark green leaves, gold
trim **125.00**
Incense burner, 10″ h, 7″ w, figural,
Chinese **175.00**

Jar, 14", ovoid, underglaze blue dec, large phoenix, flowering and fruiting plants, inset lid, knob finial **100.00**

Jardiniere, pr, 12", circular, pale green glaze, molded as alternating shaped medallions with stags and owls, bird and floral border **475.00**

Lamp, pr, 25", baluster shape vase base, white relief dec, prunus, chrysanthemum, and lotus, Ch'ien Lung . **825.00**

Libation Cup, 3¾", steep tapering sides, foliate rim, dragon and clouds, blue-green glaze, 19th C **65.00**

Plate, 6", birds, butterflies and roses dec **85.00**

Planter
5", spherical, incised peony blossoms, foliate tendrils, glazed white int., pr **150.00**
7½", cylindrical body, molded, bundle of bamboo stalks tied together with blue and white ribbon, stylized calligraphy, glazed deep celadon . . . **200.00**

Vase
7¾", Hu form, low relief, handled . . **1,750.00**
23" h, shouldered baluster, small loop handles, incised flowers, Korean, Koryo period, 12th/13th C, mounted as lamp **1,100.00**

Wall Pocket, 12" l, blue iris dec, Japanese **60.00**

CELLULOID ITEMS

History: In 1869 brothers J. W. Hyatt and I. S. Hyatt developed celluloid, the world's first synthetic plastic, as an ivory substitute because elephant herds were being slaughtered for their ivory tusks.

Known as "Ivorine" or "French Ivory," celluloid was made of nitrocellulose and camphor. Early pieces have a creamy color with stripes and grooves to imitate the texture of ivory or bone. The 1897 Sears catalog featured celluloid items. Celluloid was used widely until synthetics replaced it in the early 1950s. Celluloid often is used as a generic term for all early plastics.

Advertising
Bookmark, figural, teddy bear, 1½" x 3", "Buckwalter Stove Co., Royersford, PA" **15.00**
Pencil Box, Red Goose Shoes **75.00**

Animal
Bison, 2" h **20.00**
Peacock on pedestal, 5½" h **25.00**
Swan **10.00**

Baby's Set, brush, comb, jar, cov, and rattle, orig box **35.00**

Candlestick, 5", creamy ivory **10.00**

Cane Handle, carved dog's head, glass eyes **30.00**

Collar Box, white chrysanthemums and green leaves on cov, velvet lined . . . **45.00**

Comb, lady's, creamy ivory **18.00**

Doll, 10", French, elaborate costume, marked "270" **50.00**

Door Knob, creamy ivory **35.00**

Dresser Set, 10 pcs, amber, black and gold overlay, beveled edge mirror . . **90.00**

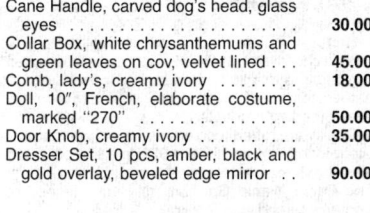

Toy, Prince on Pig, jointed legs, 4½" l, 4" h, $30.00.

Figure
Felix, black, hands behind back, c1930 . . . . **50.00**
Soldier carrying gun **18.00**

Frame, 4 x 3", creamy ivory, reticulated border, easel back **25.00**

Glove box, hp floral dec on cov, pink lining, dated 1869 . . . . **35.00**

Jewelry Box, creamy ivory, red roses on cov **30.00**

Nail File, folding, emb floral dec **12.00**

Napkin Ring, creamy ivory **10.00**

Necktie Box, 2½ x 3 x 4", creamy ivory, gold and floral dec on cov **42.00**

Rattle, blue and white, c1930 . . . . **12.00**

Roly Poly, chicken **10.00**

Scissors, manicure, 4", creamy ivory handle **12.00**

Stick Pin, color portrait of woman, yellow and green ribbons, "Welcome to Eugene, Oregon" **25.00**

Toy, wind-up
Betty Boop, 7", orig box **150.00**
Clown, 7½", marked "Occupied Japan" **60.00**
Penguin, 3", marked "Made In Japan" **30.00**
Rabbit, marked "Irwin" **20.00**

Tatting Shuttle **8.00**

CHALKWARE

History: William Hutchinson, an Englishman, invented chalkware in 1848. It was a substance used by sculptors to imitate marble. It also was used to harden plaster of Paris, creating a confusion between the two products.

Chalkware often copied many of the popular Staffordshire items of the 1820 to 1870 period. It was cheap, gayly decorated, and sold by vendors. The Pennsylvania German "folk art" pieces are from this period.

Carnivals, circuses, fairs, and amusement parks used chalkware pieces as prizes during the late 19th and 20th centuries. They often were poorly made and gaudy. Don't confuse them with the earlier pieces. Prices for these chalkware items range from ten to fifty dollars.

References: Thomas G. Morris, *Carnival Chalk Prize,* Prize Publishers, 1985; Ted Soufe, *Midway Mania: A Collectors Guide To Carnival Plaster Figurines, Prizes, and Equipment 1900–1950,* L-W, Inc., 1985.

Additional Listings: See Carnival Chalkware in *Warman's Americana & Collectibles.*

Dish, figural, doll holding shell, pink velvet hat, brown hair, 7″ h, $48.00.

Bank, 11″ h, dove, worn orig polychrome paint . . . . | **350.00**
Bookends, pr, boy and girl, seated, reading . . . . | **65.00**
Bust, Hiawatha, 20″, 1890s . . . . | **115.00**
Church, 9½ x 18″, molded, white, pierced with decorative holes, colored glass insert window, PA, 19th C . . . | **1,050.00**
Figure
  Belsnickle, 5″, German . . . . | **60.00**
  Bird on plinth, 6″ h, worn orig polychrome paint . . . . | **150.00**

Deer, 10½″ h, reddish paint, black trim . . . . | **250.00**
Dog, 8½″ h, Boston Bull, orig red, white, and black paint . . . . | **150.00**
Horse, 10⅜″ h, orig brown and green paint . . . . | **900.00**
Rooster, 5⅜″ h, polychrome repaint . | **100.00**
Snake, curled, c1910 . . . . | **15.00**
Squirrel, 7″, holding nut, orig white, yellow, red, black, and brown paint | **285.00**
Stag, reclining, 5⅜″, orig olive amber with black stripes, red and black features, oblong base . . . . | **300.00**
Garniture, fruit basket with pair of love birds, 7¾″, yellow, red, and black . . | **400.00**
Match Holder, 6″, figural, man with long nose and beard, adv "Northwestern National Insurance Co.," c1890 . . . . | **95.00**
Nodder, cat, 6″, orig red and black dec | **325.00**
Wall Pocket, basket shape . . . . | **15.00**
Watch Holder, 13¾ x 8¼″, figural, woman, blue shawl, spotted dress, red apron, carved leaves on bottom, glass enclosure . . . . | **550.00**

CHARACTER AND PERSONALITY ITEMS

History: The use of the "star" product endorser began in the late 19th and early 20th centuries. By the 1930s the system was entrenched.

Two groups evolved. The first was the characters found in cartoons or portrayed on radio, in the movies, or on television by actors. Some characters, e.g., Tony The Tiger, were created by the advertising industry solely for advertising use.

The second group consists of "real" people, e.g., actors, sports personalities, heroes, or political figures. The 1960s and 70s witnessed the pinnacle of star endorsed products.

References: Sandra Andacht, *Joe Franklin's Show Biz Memorabilia,* Wallace Homestead, 1985; David Longest, *Character Toys and Collectibles,* Collector Books, 1984; David Longest, *Character Toys And Collectibles, Second Series,* Collector Books, 1987; Richard O'Brien, *Collecting Toys, A Collector's Identification & Value Guide, No. 5,* Books Americana, 1990.

Additional Listings: See *Warman's Americana & Collectibles* for expanded listings in Cartoon Characters, Cowboy Collectibles, Movie Personalities and Memorabilia, Shirley Temple, and Space Adventurers.

CHARACTERS

Betty Boop
  Match Safe, 1¼″, sq, celluloid, c1930 | **150.00**
  Pin, gold colored metal with attached link chain to Scotty dog, Fleisher

Studios copyright, 1930s, attached to orig sample retail card **150.00**
Brownies, stickpin, black, white, and green enamel, c1896 . . . . **20.00**

Character, Buster Brown, plate, multi-colored transfer, gold rim, 5¼″ d, $40.00.

Buster Brown
Bank, iron, horseshoe shape, Buster Brown, Tige, and horse **125.00**
Clicker, 1¾″ litho metal, "Brown Shoe Co." inscription, c1930 . . . . **15.00**
Drawing Book, 8 pgs, thin film tracing sheets between each illus page, six neatly traced sheets, issued by Emerson Piano Co **45.00**
Pitcher, 4″ h, white, china, full color illus, early 1900s **75.00**
Campbell Kids
Child's knife, fork, and spoon, SP . . **50.00**
Reverse Painting on Glass, 7½ x 9½″, kids loading baskets in a vegetable patch, "C" on shirt, 11 x 12½″ gray wood frame, c1970 . . . **60.00**
Thermometer, tin, figural, adv **35.00**
Captain Marvel
Pennant, felt, dark blue, maroon picture **20.00**
Wristwatch, red strap, orig box, copyright 1948, Fawcett Publications . **125.00**
Charlie McCarthy, ring, plastic, green, black and white photo, c1940 . . . . . **30.00**
Dennis The Menace
Mug, 4″ h, plastic, picturing Dennis, 1950s **15.00**
Spoon, 6″ l, SP, emb figure at top of handle, name vertically on handle, 1950s **25.00**
Dick Tracy
Camera, 3 x 5″, plastic, black, Seymore Products, Chicago **45.00**
Game, Dick Tracy Electronic Target Game, battery operated, silent ray

gun, shoots a beam of light at a revolving cardboard drum, electronic photocell bullseye, automatic scorekeeper, 11″ black plastic pistol, instruction sheet, American Doll & Toy Corp, 1961 copyright, unused **100.00**
Salt and Pepper Shaker, pr, plaster, Dick and Junior **35.00**
Elsie The Cow
Button, 2¼″, emb brass, raised head, c1940 . . . . **25.00**
Doll, cloth, stuffed **25.00**
Ring, plastic, green, color inset picture, Borden Company copyright, c1950 . . . . **50.00**
Felix The Cat
Doll, 8½″ l, wood, jointed, decals, leather ears, Schoenhut, c1920 . . **200.00**
Place Card Holder, celluloid 1¾″ Felix figure, ½″ h arched back black cat, base, glossy black holder, Japanese, 1930s **80.00**
Valentine, diecut, jointed cardboard, full color, valentine pictured on his tail, "Purr Around If You Want To Be My Valentine" inscription, Pat Sullivan copyright, c1920 . . . . **15.00**
Yarn Holder, 6½ x 6½″, diecut wood, black images, inscription "Felix Keeps On Knitting," "Pathe Presents" symbol in center, c1920–30 **35.00**
Andy Gump, nodder, bisque **65.00**
Hopalong Cassidy
Badge, metal, silver, star shape, raised portrait at center, c1950 . . . **20.00**
Ring, adjustable, silvered brass, portrait on top with initials and the Bar 20 symbol, c1950 . . . . **30.00**
Shirt, button, red trim slit pocket and collar, six different images, red inscription, "Little Champ Of Hollywood" label, size 12, early 1950s **150.00**
Tablet, 8 x 10″, color photo cov, facsimile signature, unused, early 1950s **20.00**
Howdy Doody
Marionette, 16″ h, wood and stuffed cloth, composition hands, movable lower mouth, plastic jiggle eyes, fully strung, hand control board, printed instructions **200.00**
Record Spindle Spinner, 4″ h plastic figure, movable mouth, figure mounted on 3″ d plastic base, center hole for placement over record player spindle, inscription "Hi Ya Kids/Watch Me Go Round On Your Record" on base, Kagran copyright, 1951–56 . . . . **50.00**
Wall Light Shade, parchment like heavy paper, plastic edge lacing,

soft blue, red, and yellow illus, off white background, Kagran copyright c1951–56, orig wall mount .. **75.00**

Sonja Henie, pinback button, 1¼", pink and brown, "Skate for Pleasure," 1937 .... **15.00**

Little Orphan Annie
Clicker, red, white, and black, Mysto members, 1941 .... **35.00**
Gravy Boat, lusterware, white, orange, yellow, and black **175.00**
Nodder, 3½" h, painted bisque, stamped on back "Orphan Annie," 1930s **150.00**
Pastry Set, miniature baking utensils, two aluminum mixing spoons, wood pestle shape rolling pin, flour cup, and 6 x 8" rolling board, boxed, Transogram "Gold Medal" Toy, 1930s **75.00**
Whistle, tin, signal, three tones **30.00**

Lone Ranger
Holster, 9" stiff cardboard, colored to resemble tan leather, steer design, brand initials "GA", inscription in rope script, khaki web army style belt, includes a 7" l aluminum single shot cap pistol with white plastic grips, boxed, 1942 copyright **75.00**
Pencil Case, 1 x 4 x 8¼", textured stiff cardboard, gold cov design is lightly emb, dark blue background, American Lead Pencil Co, Lone Ranger copyright, 1930s **40.00**
Rifle, 24" l, plastic, simulated metal and wood parts, gold script inscription, emb Indian head and bear in woods on sides of stock, clicking sound, sighting scope, c1960 ... **25.00**

Mr. Peanut
Bank, 8½" h, molded tan plastic, coin slot in top of hat, inscription on hat brim, c1950 .... **40.00**
Pencil, mechanical, 5¼", red and white plastic, cylinder at top contains miniature tan figure, inscription on side, c1940–50 .... **15.00**

Annie Oakley
Coloring Book, 11 x 14", Whitman, soft color, 1955, unused **18.00**
Suspenders, 4½ x 12", card, multicolored, elastic, Annie Oakley on one, Tagg on other, c1960 ..... **15.00**

Popeye
Charm, celluloid **5.00**
Lamp, figural, 16" h, dark maroon with gold accent striped shade, gray metal base with 8" h figure, arms around brown lamp pole **150.00**
Watch, 1¼", silver colored metal case, dial pictures Popeye holding

spinach can, gray leather bands, c1960 .... **50.00**

Red Ryder
Book, *Red Ryder and Circus Luck,* Whitman Better Little Book #1466, 1949 .... **25.00**
Glove Case, black enameled metal and cardboard, illus on lid, leather carrying handle, elastic straps for holding supplies, silvered metal spring clip fasteners, 1951 salesman program, Wells-Lamont Glove Company **150.00**
Skippy, ice cream sign, 24 x 36", diecut cardboard, "Fro-joy" ice cream container, color, 1930s **200.00**

Straight Shooter, (Tom Mix)
Coloring Book, 8½ x 11", health and hygiene, Ralston premium, unused **75.00**
Ring, brass, checkerboard logo on top with steer head and gun design on sides, 1935 .... **50.00**

Yellow Kid
Cigar Box, 3½ x 4¼ x 9", wood, illus and name inscription in bright gold, brass hinges, label inside "Smoke Yellow Kid Cigars/Manuf'd By B. R. Fleming, Curwesville, Pa." tax label strips on back, c1896 .... **200.00**
Postcard, 3¾ x 6", full color illus for month of October, issued as reminder from Ohio hardware company, 1911 post mark **40.00**

PERSONALITIES

Amos and Andy
Poster, 13 x 29", multicolored, Campbell's Soup ad, radio show listings, framed **125.00**
Sheet Music, 6 pgs, "Three Little Words," from movie "Check and Double Check, 1930 copyright ... **25.00**

Jack Armstrong
Flashlight, bullet **25.00**
Telescope **10.00**

Gene Autry
Cap Pistol, 6½", silver, cast iron, bright red plastic grips, "Gene Autry" script on each side, uses roll caps, 1940s **75.00**
Wallet, 4 x 4½", brown, leather, zippered, "Gene Autry" in script on front and back, 1940s **25.00**

Edgar Bergen
Pinback Button, ¾", celluloid, black and white portrait of Charlie, c1930 **65.00**
Notepad, 5½ x 9", black, white, and green, lined paper, 1938 .... **20.00**

Eddie Cantor, tin, brass, diecut, depicts Cantor in large red top hat, 1930s .. **25.00**

Charlie Chaplin
    Coloring Book, 11 x 15", Saalfield, 52
        pgs, 1941 .... 30.00
    Pennant, felt, 1¼ x 2", dark plum with
        a pink tinted black and white photo,
        tan lettering and design, c1915–20 40.00
Dionne Quintuplets
    Ink Blotter, 4 x 9", color photo of two-
        year old quints, birth date and
        weights at birth, unused, 1936 ... 25.00
    Fan, 8 x 9", diecut cardboard, wood
        handle, Elvgren illus celebrating
        their fifth birthday 8.00
    Thermometer, 3⅞" x 6", cardboard,
        multicolored, Cupp's Dairy 25.00
Gabby Hayes, target set, 18" sq card-
    board target, 6½" l plastic dart pistol,
    two rubber cup plastic darts, orig box,
    Haecker Industries, c1950 .... 100.00
Charles Lindbergh
    Book, *Trophies and Decorations,* 8 x
        11", soft cov, 64 pgs, black and
        white photos, Missouri Historical
        Society, 1933 copyright 40.00
    Bunting, 1¼", "Lucky Lindy," red
        white and blue, gold horseshoe,
        black and white photo 40.00
Willie Mays, photo, 2" black and white,
    Willie in New York Giants cap, red,
    white, and blue ribbon, green plastic
    bat, and white ball attached below,
    c1961 .... 50.00
Roy Rogers
    Bank, 3 x 5 x 5", metal, boot shape,
        copper color, raised Roy on rearing
        Trigger illus 25.00
    Nodder, 6½" h, composition figure,
        head mounted on neck spring, sig-
        nature decal on base, 1962 copy-
        right and "Japan" stamped on bot-
        tom 40.00
    Watch, 1 x 1¼" dial face illus in
        brown, red, black, and white, sig-
        nature in black, red numerals, sil-
        vered metal with floral pattern
        edges on case, stainless steel ex-
        pansion band, 1940s 100.00
Babe Ruth
    Figure, 8" h, realistically detailed,
        white uniform with dark blue
        sleeves, insignia, outer stockings
        and cap, removable bat in orange
        tone, Hartland 150.00
    Score Counter, playing diamond and
        disc wheels are turned to record
        runs, strikes, balls, on one side,
        other side 1¾" black and white
        photo, 1920–30 .... 60.00
Shirley Temple
    Button, 1¼", brass, black and white
        photo, c1930 .... 50.00
Handkerchief, 8½" sq, linen, white,

brown and orange illus on corners,
    Little Colonel copyright **25.00**
Pin, 1⅛", diecut, brass, white, blue,
    and red enameling **125.00**

CHELSEA

History: Chelsea is a fine English porcelain designed to compete with Meissen. The factory began operating in the Chelsea area of London, England, in the 1740s. Chelsea products are divided
into four periods: (1) Early period, 1740s, with incised triangle and raised anchor mark; (2) The
1750s, with red raised anchor mark; (3) The
1760s, the gold anchor period; and (4) The Derby
period from 1770–1783. In 1924 a large number
of the molds and models of figurines were found
at the Spode-Copeland Works, and many items
were brought back into circulation.

Reference: Susan and Al Bagdade, *Warman's
English & Continental Pottery & Porcelain, 1st Edition,* Warman Publishing Co., Inc., 1987.

**Pastille Burner, red, pink, blue, and yel-
low pastel flowers, gold outlining, purple ground, gold anchor mark, 5½" h,
4⅛" w, $250.00.**

Beaker, 2⅝", octagonal, iron-red, ori-
    ental floral sprays, rose, green, blue,
    and yellow, red anchor mark, c1750 **1,400.00**
Bowl, 6½" d, molded leaves on ext., flo-
    ral spray in center, red anchor **1,000.00**
Candlestick, pr, 7½", figural, draped
    putti seated on tree stump holding
    flower, wax pan, scroll molded base
    encircled in puce, gilt **825.00**

Cup and Saucer, white, multicolored exotic birds, gold anchor, c1765 ..... **750.00**
Dish
  6³⁄₁₆", pr, silver form molded edge, sprays of flowers and leaves, red anchor mark, c1755 .... **350.00**
  6½", ten sided, Flying Dog, Kakiemon style, red anchor mark, c1755 ... **1,250.00**
Figure, pr, 14" h, fruit and flower sellers, multicolored clothing, standing, attended by animals, shaped socles, gold anchor mark, late 18th C **600.00**
Plate, 9" d, botanical, Hans Sloane type, red anchor period, c1756, set of six **4,675.00**
Scent Bottle, 2½", figural, cauliflower head, pink ribbed green leaves, thick olive green stem, white florette stopper, gold mounts, red anchor, c1756 **3,400.00**
Seal, cupid, 1¼", cupid disguised as a barrister, set with a sardonyx intaglio, inscribed "Je Plait Pour Ma Belle," c1760 .... **450.00**
Soup Plate, 9⅜", octagonal, center painted with iron-red and gold phoenix in flight, yellow breasted blue and iron-red pheasant, turquoise rock, iron-red, blue, turquoise, and gold flowering tree, ridged rim, iron-red floral border, red anchor, c1753 ..... **2,000.00**
Tureen, cov, 3½" l, melon shape, yellow, green, and brown, snail finial, iron-red anchor, tureen marked "45," cover marked "31," c1755 .... **1,220.00**

"CHELSEA" GRANDMOTHER'S WARE

History: "Chelsea" Grandmother's ware identifies a group of tableware with raised reliefs of either grapes, sprigs of flowers, or thistles on a white ground. Some examples are lustered.

The ware was made in the first half of the 19th century in England's Staffordshire district by a large number of manufacturers. The "Chelsea" label is a misnomer, but commonly accepted in the antiques field.

Berry Bowl, 6", Grape	**8.00**
Butter Pat, 4" d, Sprig	**12.00**
Cake Plate, 10", Grape	**40.00**
Creamer, Sprig	**50.00**
Coffeepot, cov, Grape	**145.00**
Cup and Saucer, Sprig	**25.00**
Egg Cup, Grape	**25.00**
Pitcher, milk, Sprig	**50.00**
Plate	
8", Grape	**20.00**
9", Sprig	**30.00**
Ramekin, blue, underplate, Sprig	**12.00**
Sauce Dish, Sprig	**5.00**

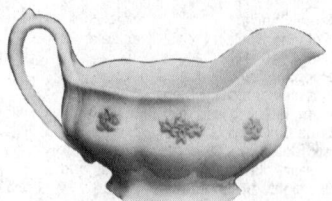

Sauce Boat, Grape pattern, marked "Adderleys/England/Ltd," $30.00.

Sugar, cov, 7½", Sprig	**110.00**
Teapot, 10", octagonal, Grape luster ..	**125.00**
Tureen, cov, applied handles, Grape, c1840	**75.00**

CHILDREN'S BOOKS

History: Because there is a bit of the child in all of us, collectors always have been attracted to children's books. In the 19th century books were popular gifts for children, with most of the children's classics written and published during this time. These books were treasured and often kept throughout a lifetime.

Developments in printing made it possible to include more attractive black and white illustrations and color plates. The work of these artists and illustrators has added value beyond the text itself.

References: Barbara Bader, *American Picture Books From Noah's Ark To The Beast Within*, Macmillan, 1976; Virginia Haviland, *Children's Literature, A Guide To Reference Sources*, Library Of Congress, 1966, first supplement, 1972, second supplement, 1977, third supplement, 1982.

Libraries: Free Library of Philadelphia, PA; Library of Congress, Washington, D.C.; Pierpont Morgan Library, New York, NY; Toronto Public Library, Toronto, Ontario, Canada.

Additional Listings: See *Warman's Americana & Collectibles* for more examples and an extensive listing of collectors' clubs.

Note: dj = dust jacket; wraps = paper covers; pgs = pages; unp = unpaged; n.d. = no date; teg = top edges gilt

Advisor: Margaret L. Tyrrell.

Allingham, William, *In Fairy Land,* Richard Doyle, illus, Longmans, Green, 1870, 31 pgs, 1st ed **550.00**
Barrows, Marjorie, *Muggins Mouse,* Deith Ward, illus, Reilly & Lee, 1932, 60 pgs **50.00**
Buck, Pearl S., *Johnny Jack and His Beginnings,* Werth, illus, John Day, 1954, 47 pgs, 1st ed, dj **30.00**

Burnett, Frances, Hodgson, *Sara Crewe or What Happened at Miss Minchin's,* Reginald Birch, illus Scribner's, 1888, 83 pgs, 1st ed 75.00

Chapin, Anna, *True Story of Humpty Dumpty,* Ethel Betts, illus, Dodd, 1905, 206 pgs, 1st ed 95.00

Clyne, Geraldine, *The Jolly Jump-ups And Their New House,* McLoughlin, 1939, unp, 6 pop-ups 35.00

Disney, Walt, *Dance of the Hours from Fantasia,,* Harper, 1940, unp, 1st ed . . 40.00

Dr. Seuss, *Bartholomew and the Oobleck,* Random House, 1949, unp, 1st ed, sgd 75.00

Field, Rachel, *Hitty: Her First Hundred Years,* Dorothy Lathrop, illus, Macmillan, 1929, 207 pgs, 1st ed, sgd by Lathrop 70.00

Garer, Elvira, *Ezekiel,* Holt, 1937, unp, 1st ed, dj 35.00

Greenaway, Kate, *Almanac for 1889,* Routledge, n.d. unp. a.e.g. 100.00

Harris, Joel Chandler, *The Tar Baby and other Rhymes of Uncle Remus,* A. B. Frost & E. W. Kemple, illus, D. Appleton, 1904 190 pgs, 1st ed . . . 70.00

Hoffmann, Heinrich, *Slovenly Peter,* Fritz Dredel, illus, German to English by Mark Twain, limited edition club, 1935, 34 pgs, numbered ed in box . 135.00

Kipling, Rudyard, *Just So Stories,* Macmillan, 1902, 249 pgs, 1st ed 125.00

Lenski, Lois, *The Easter Rabbit's Parade,* Oxford, 1936, 32 pgs, 1st ed . 45.00

The Hungry Tiger of Oz, **Ruth Plumly Thompson, John R Neill, illus, Reilly & Lee Co, Chicago, publishers, copyright 1926, 261 pgs, 7 x 9½ x 1½", $100.00.**

McCready, T.L., *Biggity Bantam,* Tasha Tudork, illus, Ariel/Farrar Straus, Young, 1954, unp, 1st ed, dj 55.00

Moore, Clement, *The Night Before Christmas,* Elizabeth MacKinstry, illus, Dutton, 1928, unp, 1st ed 65.00

Newberry, Clare, *Babette,* Harper, 1937, 30 pgs, 1st ed, dj 43.00

Nura, *Nura's Garden of Betty & Booth,* Morrow, 1935, 41 pgs, 1st ed 50.00

Owen, Dora, *The Book of Fairy Poetry,* Warwide Goble, illus, Longmans, 1920, 129 pgs, 1st ed 95.00

Phillpotts, Eden, *The Girl and the Fawn,* Frank Branquyn, illus, London, 1916, 78 pgs, dj 125.00

Pyle, Howard, *The Garden Behind the Moon,* Scribner's, 1895, 192 pgs, 1st ed 115.00

Sarg, Tony, *Where is Tommy?* Greenberg, 1932, unp, 1st ed 55.00

Southwold, Stephen, *The Book of Animal Tales,* Honor/C. Appleton, illus, Crowell, n.d. c1930, 286 pgs 50.00

Tarcov, Edith, *Rumpelstiltskin,* Edward Gorey, illus, Four Winds, 1974, 46 pgs, 1st ed, dj 45.00

Tate, Sally Jane, *Sally's ABC Sewed in a Sampler in 1795,* Dugald Stewart Walker, illus, Harcourt, Brace, 1929, unp, 1st ed 65.00

Thompson, Kay, *Eloise,* Hilary Knight, illus, Simon and Schuster, 1955, 65 pgs, 1st ed, dj 50.00

Upton, Bertha, *The Golliwogg's Desert Island,* Florence K. Upton, illus, Longmans and Green, 1906, unp, 1st ed . 100.00

Wilder, Laura Ingalls, *On The banks Of Plum Creek,* Helen Sewell & Mildred Boyle, illus, Harper & Row, 1937, 239 pgs, 1st ed 65.00

Zaffo, George, *Peter On The Paddleboat,* Saalfield, 1946, unp, spiral, dj, animated 25.00

CHILDREN'S FEEDING DISHES

History: Unlike toy dishes meant for play, children's feeding dishes are the items actually used in the feeding of a child. Their colorful designs of animals, nursery rhymes, and children's activities are meant to appeal to the child and make meal times fun. Many plates have a unit to hold hot water, thus keeping the food warm.

Although glass and porcelain examples from the late 19th and early 20th centuries are most popular, collectors are beginning to seek some of the plastic examples from the 1920s to 40s, especially those with Disney designs on them.

References: Doris Anderson Lechler, *Children's Glass Dishes, China and Furniture,* Collector Books, 1983; Doris Anderson Lechler, *Children's Glass Dishes, China, Furniture, Volume II,* Collector Books, 1986; Lorraine May Punchard, *Child's Play,* published by author, 1982; Margaret & Kenn Whitmyer, *Children's Dishes,* Collector Books, 1984.

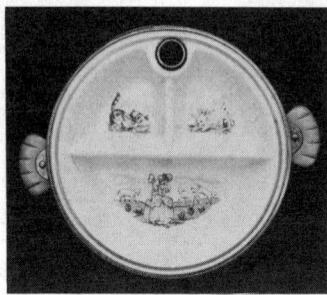

Divided, hot water reservoir, multicolored nursery rhyme transfer dec, handles, $70.00.

Baby Dish, warming type, circus, 8″ red decals, white ground, divided, marked "Hazel Atlas" 8.00
Bowl
  6¾″, Beach Baby, marked "P. K. Unity, Germany" 42.00
  9″, Sing A Song of Sixpence 40.00
Breakfast Set, plate, bowl, and creamer, white, blue design of children playing 75.00
Creamer
  Bunnykins, marked "Royal Doulton" 40.00
  Buster Brown 50.00
Cup and Saucer
  Boy, girl, and bunny, red mark, Germany 12.00
  Century of Progress, nursery rhyme dec, marked "Shenango," 1933 . . 48.00
  Old Mother Hubbard, marked "Royal Doulton" 50.00
  Sand Baby, marked "Royal Bayreuth" 75.00
Egg Cup, Bunnykins, marked "Royal Doulton" 10.00
Mug
  China
    2¾″, portraits of boy and girl, marked "Germany" 35.00
    3½″, Little Bo Peep, transfer print of scene and rhyme, marked "England" 70.00
  Glass, Dog and Bird, beaded handle 35.00
  Sterling Silver, christening, hallmarked, "R. Redgrave, R. A.," London, c1865 . . . . 500.00

Plate
  4½″, children playing, Kate Greenaway illus 75.00
  6½″, Sunbonnet Babies, babies sewing, marked "Royal Bayreuth" . . . 165.00
  7½″, hexagon, emb floral border, green transfer of child and cat, marked "Davenport" 85.00
  8½″, Uncle Wiggily 50.00
Sugar, Bunnykins, marked "Royal Doulton" 20.00

CHILDREN'S NURSERY ITEMS

History: The nursery is a place where children live in a miniature world. Things come in two sizes. Child scale designates items actually used for the care, housing, and feeding of the child. Toy or doll scale denotes items used by the child in play and for creating a fantasy environment which copies that of an adult or his own.

Cheap labor and building costs during the Victorian era enabled the nursery to reach a high level of popularity. Most collectors focus on items from the 1880 to 1930 period.

References: Doris Anderson Lechler, *Children's Glass Dishes, China, and Furniture,* Collector Books, 1983; Doris Anderson Lechler, *Children's Glass Dishes, China, Furniture, Volume II,* Collector Books, 1986; Anthony and Peter Miall, *The Victorian Nursery Book,* Pantheon Books, 1980; Lorraine May Punchard, *Child's Play,* published by author, 1982.

Additional Listings: Children's Books, Children's Feeding Dishes, Children's Toy Dishes, Dolls, Games, Miniatures, and Toys.

Bathtub, tin 40.00
Blocks, set of 36, 1¾″, polychrome, alphabet, animals, and stripes 110.00
Bride's Basket, miniature, 5¾ x 5½″, ruffled cranberry bowl, SP holder marked "Reliance Quadruplate Silver" 200.00
Carriage, 52″ l, open, push type, wooden wheels, wooden and iron frame, bentwood handle, adjustable fringed top, cast iron frame, orig worn brown and black paint and striping . 275.00
Chamber Set, wash bowl, pitcher, chamber pot, cov soap, toothbrush and comb holder, slop bucket, hp, floral dec, 8 pcs 175.00
Doll Carriage, 24 x 12 x 28″, wicker, stick and ball design, wood spoke wheels, velvet cushion 320.00
Furniture
  Bed, baby, turned posts and legs, four rails with lattice slats, solid board bottom, old green paint over red, 29 x 48 x 30½″ 75.00

Chair

    Chippendale, mahogany, armchair,
salmon colored linen upholstered
slip seat, 24" **800.00**

    Hepplewhite, Martha Washington
style, armchair, upholstered back
and seat, 30" **650.00**

Cradle

    Walnut, 37" l, dovetailed, cut out
rockers, shaped sides, hand
holds **225.00**

    Wicker, ornate basket suspended
between two supports, swings,
ornate shelf, high crown mount-
ing at head end to hold netting . **2,000.00**

Cupboard, pine, orig dark brown finish, stenciled gold and silver dec,
decoupage, top with double doors,
glass pane in each, drawers and
doors in base, late wire nail construction, 17 x 12½ x 30¾" **200.00**

Highchair, oak, pressed back, cane
seat, Victorian, converts to stroller **400.00**

Rocker, ladder back, turned arms,
three slats, turned finials, old dark
finish, 26" h **150.00**

**Rocking Horse, wood head, red burlap
cov, straw filled, wood legs, red paint,
red felt and leather saddle, hair mane,
marked "Cebasco, Made in Germany,"
40" h, 34" l, 58" l rockers, $975.00.**

Mug

  China

    Copper Luster, putty colored band,
"Eliza," 2½" **50.00**

    Staffordshire, purple transfer, poly-
chrome enamel dec, children
playing, 2½" h **75.00**

  Glass, complete raised alphabet,
raised scene of little girl looking at
Christmas tree and boy at desk . . **125.00**

Quilt

    Child size, 40 x 58", nursery rhyme
characters, embroidered names . . **100.00**

    Crib, crazy pattern, patchwork and
applique, velvet, satin, and cotton
patches, elaborate embroidery . . . **450.00**

Rattle, celluloid, 3½" h, puffin bird . . . **10.00**

Sled, Victorian, stenciled "No. 52, Paris
Mfg Co., So. Paris, Maine," maple
and steamed oak, center board red
with stenciled flowers and transfer
portrait of Indian, 27½" **1,000.00**

Tea Set, ironstone, red transfer of
Punch and Judy, three 5¾" d plates,
5⅜" h teapot, 3¾" d waste bowl,
sugar, four cups and saucers, minor
stains **165.00**

Teether, 5¼", SS, Father Christmas,
bag of toys emb on back, MOP
teether, English **275.00**

Tricycle, wooden frame and wheels,
orig red paint, black striping **500.00**

Trunk, 12 x 5", camel back, heavy cardboard, brass handles, hinges, and
lock **40.00**

CHILDREN'S TOY DISHES

History: Dishes made for children often served
a dual purpose—play things and a means of learn-
ing social graces. Dish sets came in two sizes.
The first was for actual use by the child when
entertaining her friends. The second, a smaller
size than the first, was for use with dolls.

Children's dish sets often were made as a side
line to a major manufacturing line either as a com-
plement to the family service or as a way to use
up the last of the day's batch of materials. The
artwork of famous illustrators, such as Palmer Cox,
Kate Greenaway, and Rose O'Neill, can be found
on porcelain sets.

References: Doris Anderson Lechler, *Chil-
dren's Glass Dishes, China and Furniture,* Collec-
tor Books, 1983; Doris Anderson Lechler, *Chil-
dren's Glass Dishes, China, Furniture, Volume II*
Collector Books, 1986; Lorraine May Punchard,
Child's Play, published by author, 1982; Margaret
& Kenn Whitmyer, *Children's Dishes,* Collector
Books, 1984.

Akro Agate

  Dinner Service

    Green and white swirl, large, four
cups and saucers, cereal bowls,
creamer, cov sugar, cov teapot . **285.00**

    Interior Panel, small, green Tran-
soptic, four cups and saucers,
four plates, creamer, cov teapot **80.00**

  Water Service, Stippled Band, amber,
pitcher and six tumblers **65.00**

Pattern Glass, condiment set, Hickman pattern, bowl, cruet, and shaker on shaped tray, $60.00.

Bohemian Glass, decanter and glasses, ruby flashed, Vintage dec, 5 pcs . . .	125.00
China	
Chocolate Pot, Model T car with passengers	85.00
Cup, Willow Ware, blue, 1 x 1¾", marked "Occupied Japan"	6.00
Dinner Set	
23 pcs, Moss Rose	85.00
25 pcs, Blue Willow	145.00
Mugs, Babes in Woods, marked "Shelley"	48.00
Tea Set, children playing grown–ups, teddy bears, German	225.00
Tureen, attached tray, marked "Porcelaine Empire"	8.50
Milk Glass	
Creamer, Wild Rose	65.00
Cup, Nursery Rhyme	20.00
Ice Cream Platter, White Rose	60.00
Punch Cup, Wild Rose	15.00
Punch Set, White Rose, lemon stain, punch bowl, six cups	200.00
Spooner, Wild Rose	45.00
Pattern Glass	
Berry Set, Nursery Rhyme, master berry, six small bowls	185.00
Butter, cov	
Hobnail with thumbprint base, blue	95.00
Pennsylvania, green, gold dec . . .	145.00
Cake Stand	
Fine Cup and Fan	35.00
Palm Leaf Fan	30.00
Rexford	25.00
Candlesticks, Moonlight Blue, pr . .	20.00
Condiment Set, Hickman, open salt, pepper shaker, cruet, and leaf shaped tray	60.00
Creamer	
Buzz Saw	10.00
Drum	70.00

Sandwich	50.00
Twin Snowshoes	15.00
Whirligig	15.00
Cup and Saucer, Lion	45.00
Mug, Grapevine	20.00
Pitcher	
Colonial, clear	10.00
Oval Star, clear	15.00
Punch Set, Star Arches, punch bowl, six cups	75.00
Rose Bowl, Star, 2½"	25.00
Saucer, Puss in Boots	7.00
Spooner	
Diamond and Panels	15.00
Tulip and Honeycomb	10.00
Whirligig	15.00
Sugar	
Beaded Swirl	35.00
Drum	60.00
Menagerie, bear, blue	225.00
Tulip and Honeycomb	25.00
Table Set, 4 pcs	
Little Lamb	435.00
Lion, frosted	550.00
Nursery Rhyme	315.00
Water Set, Nursery Rhyme, pitcher, six tumblers	225.00
Tin	
Coffeepot, graniteware	70.00
Dinner Set, 16 pcs, four dinner plates, dessert plates, cups, and saucers, strawberry dec, white ground, marked "J. Chein"	30.00
Ice Cream Freezer, 5½" h, hand crank, Baby Jeannette Freezer, Jeannette Toy & Novelty Co, Jeannette, Pa, includes instructions . .	80.00

CHRISTMAS ITEMS

History: The celebration of Christmas dates back to Roman times. Several customs associated with modern Christmas celebrations are traced back to early pagan rituals.

Father Christmas, believed to have evolved in Europe in the 7th Century, was a combination of the pagan god Thor, who judged both the good and punished the bad, and St. Nicholas, the generous Bishop of Myra. Kris Kringle originated in Germany and was brought to America by the Germans and Swiss who settled in Pennsylvania in the late 18th Century.

In 1822 Clement C. Moore wrote "A Visit From St. Nicholas" and developed the character of Santa Claus into what we know today. Thomas Nast did a series of drawings for *Harper's Weekly* from 1863 until 1886 and further solidified the character and appearance of Santa Claus.

Reference: Robert Brenner, *Christmas Past,* Schiffer Publishing, 1986; George Johnson,

Christmas Ornaments, Lights & Decorations, Collector Books, 1987, 1990 value update; Francine Kirsch, *Christmas Collectibles*, Wallace-Homestead, 1985; Nancy Schiffer, *Christmas Ornaments: A Festive Study,* Schiffer Publishing, 1984; Margaret & Kenn Whitmyer, *Christmas Collectibles,* Collector Books, 1987; 1990 value update.

Periodicals: Golden Glow of Christmas Past, P.O. Box 14808, Chicago, IL 60614; Hearts to Holly, The Holiday Collectors Newsletter, P.O. Box 105, Amherst, NH 03031; Ornament Collector, R.R. #1, Canton, IL 61520.

Additional Listings: See *Warman's Americana & Collectibles* for more examples.

Advisor: Lissa L. Bryan-Smith and Richard M. Smith.

Bank, 12″, Santa by chimney, carnival chalkware	15.00
Candy Container, 7″ h, snowman, papier mache, black broom and hat	18.00
Christmas Fence	
Metal and wire, green and red, 8 sections, orig box	100.00
Wooden	
Folding, red and green	40.00
Lighted, red, 6 sections and gate	65.00
Church, musical, wind-up, plays "Silent Night," mica covered, wood	28.00
Deer	
5″ h, metal, brown, marked "Germany"	35.00
6″ h, glass, silvered, blown glass base, German	40.00
Doll House, two story, wooden, homemade, furnished	365.00
Light Bulb	
Betty Boop	40.00
Kewpie	35.00
Red Riding Hood	40.00
Santa, with tree	20.00
Star	8.00
Teddy Bear	30.00
Light Set, bubble, one string, orig box	20.00
Ornament	
Chromolithograph	
Angels, group of three, cellophane and tinsel	22.00
Child, sleeping, surrounded by toys, tinsel	28.00
Father Christmas, blue coat, head and shoulders, tinsel	40.00
Father Christmas, red coat, standing, toys attached to belt	35.00
Young Couple, arms linked, tinsel	20.00
Cotton Batting	
Baby, composition face, skis with poles, 3½″ h, Japan	70.00
Dog, standing on back legs	20.00
Girl, composition face, skis with poles, 5½″ h, Japan	110.00
Peach, rose blush	12.00

Ornament, glass, Christmas Tree, orange highlights, base with red capped mushrooms and Santa face, 3¼″ h, $75.00.

Santa, composition face, faded red coat, black legs	100.00
Dresden	
Crescent Moon, gold, 3″ h	20.00
Fish, silver, two sided	150.00
Owl, on branch, three dimensional, realistic coloring	300.00
Star, gold, 2″ h	15.00
Washtub, gold, chromolithograph children, 4″ h	100.00
Glass	
Accordion	18.00
Airplane, spun glass wings	175.00
Angel, head	75.00
Bell, red, white, and blue	25.00
Cat in Shoe	95.00
Champagne Bottle	28.00
Crown, gold	16.00
Deer, silvered, glass hook	40.00
Devil, head and neck	130.00
Graf Zeppelin	250.00
Los Angeles Zeppelin	275.00
Punch and Judy, stage	155.00
Santa	
Clip on	40.00
Gold coat	40.00
Red suit, green tree	35.00
Stork, clip	42.00
Sugar Bowl	22.00
Teapot	23.00
Urn	25.00
Kugels	
2″ h, oval, ribbed	22.00
4″ d, round, blue	60.00
Wax, early, angel	
Large	75.00
Small	40.00
Pinback Button, "Christmas at Butlers"	25.00

Post Card, Santa Claus, red outfit, silver ground, outline relief, c1908, printed in Germany, $12.00.

Putz Material
  Animal
    Camel
      5″ h, composition, Japanese . . .   12.00
      7″ h, composition body, hide covering, wood legs 50.00
    Cow, 6″ h, composition body, cloth cov, wood legs 40.00
    Ram, 4″ h, celluloid 10.00
    Sheep
      2″ h, composition on stuffed body, cotton covering, wood legs 25.00
      8″ h, composition on stuffed body, cotton covering, wood legs 85.00
    House, 4″, cardboard and mica, Japanese 6.00
    Village, cigar box, four houses and church 100.00
  Santa
    1¼″ h, bisque, green pack, Japanese   18.00
    2″ h, 4″ l, celluloid, driving station wagon, one piece, Japanese 30.00
    2½″ h, chenille, red, composition face, Japanese 22.00
    4½″ h
      Father Christmas, white mica coat, holding feather tree 400.00
      Santa, celluloid, metal skis, wood poles, Japanese 42.00
  Sheet Music, "Silver Bells," E. T. Paul   25.00
  Toy
    Pop-Up Santa, litho cov cardboard, chimney, top opens, cloth cov

Santa, composition face, c1910, German **110.00**
Wilson Walkie, Santa, red, orig box .   **40.00**
Tree
  6″ h, brush, red, snow, glass balls, Japanese **8.00**
  12″ h, brush, green, snow, Japanese   **10.00**
  24″ h, feather, white, sq red base, West Germany **90.00**
Tree Stand, cast iron, painted black and gold, marked "North Bros Mfg Co, Philadelphia, PA" **65.00**

CIGAR CUTTERS

History: Counter and pocket cigar cutters were used at the end of the 19th and the beginning of the 20th centuries. They were a popular form of advertising. Pocket-type cigar cutters often were a fine piece of jewelry that was attached to a watch chain.

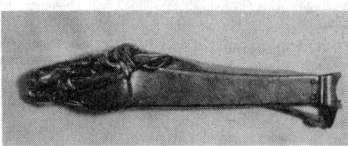

Silver plated horse head, 5¾″ l, $100.00.

CIGAR CUTTERS

Advertising
  Brunholl Co, cast iron, emb ash base, 9 x 6″ **150.00**
  East Rock Cigars, glass top with mountain scene **80.00**
  Gentlemen's Preference, El Santo, glass base **115.00**
  Great Ohio 5¢ Cigar, cast iron, pig shape **425.00**
  Strauss & Hamburger, Chicago, oak, match holder, lighter, cigar cutter, and container, 7½″ x 11″ **100.00**
Figural
  Bulldog, cast iron, desk type **40.00**
  Donkey, cast iron, tail plunger cutter   **200.00**
  Horse's head, bridle, flowing mane, SP, 5¾″ **100.00**

POCKET

Advertising
  Lord Closter Cigars, pipe tamper, metal **20.00**
  New Bachelor, brass **20.00**
  Swift & Co, watch chain **45.00**

Figural

Dog's head, silver metal, 5¾" l	65.00
Log, bakelite, wood grain	15.00

Knife Type

Brass

Bottle	40.00
Girl on potty	90.00
Revolver, black onyx handle, 3½"	150.00
Ivory, boar tusk, SS mount	200.00
Scissors Type, SS, floral	25.00

CIGAR STORE FIGURES

History: Cigar store figures were familiar sights in front of cigar stores and tobacco shops from about 1840. Figural themes included Sir Walter Raleigh, sailors, Punch figures, ladies, and Indians, the most popular.

Most figures were carved in wood, although figures also were made in metal and papier mache for a short time. Most carvings were life size or slightly smaller and brightly painted. A coating of tar acted as a preservative against the weather. Of the few surviving figures, only a small number have their original bases. Most replacements are due to years of wear and usage by dogs.

Use of figures declined when local ordinances were passed requiring shop keepers to move the figures inside at night. This soon became too much trouble, and other forms of advertising developed.

Reference: A.W. Pendergast and W. Porter Ware, *Cigar Store Figures*, The Lightner Publishing Corp., 1953.

Indian

Brave, 52" h, carved and painted, wearing gold bandeau, blue costume, holding bunch of cigars in one hand, other grasping bunch of tobacco leaves, sq base on black lacquer stand, 19th C **24,200.00**

Maiden, 28" h, pine, carved and painted, wearing three feathered headdress, standing on circular base, missing one arm, c1870 . . . **3,575.00**

Princess

79" h, carved and painted, holding various tobacco products, molded and painted composition base, stepped and rolled pedestal, inscribed "Cigars 5¢-10¢," c1890 . . . . **15,400.00**

98¼" h, pine, carved, wearing feathered headdress, feather trimmed costume and cloak, holding cigars in right hand, tobacco leaves in other, green painted rolling base, inscribed "Cigars, Tobacco, Fine Cut," . . **38,500.00**

Racetrack Tout, 78" h, holds can in left

Warrior, polychrome, 108" h, $11,000.00.

hand offers race sheets in right, four cigars in jacket pocket, black top hat, repainted, stood in front of Opera House Restaurant, Nantucket, 19th C **42,500.00**

CINNABAR

History: Cinnabar is a ware made of numerous layers of a heavy mercuric sulfide and often referred to as vermillion, the red hue in which it is most commonly found. It was carved into boxes, buttons, snuff bottles, and vases. The best examples were made in China.

Reference: Sandra Andacht, *Oriental Antiques & Art: An Identification And Value Guide*, Wallace-Homestead, 1987.

Box

5¾ x 4 x 2½", intricate carving, reserved on lid of birds and florals, Greek key border, sgd in Oriental script on brass base **65.00**

11 x 10", camel shape, carved figural scene **225.00**

Cigarette Case, 6⅛" l, rect hinged top, cinnabar lacquer and ivory, carved courtly scene, key fret band border . **350.00**

Dish, 14½", carved, three maidens in palace courtyard scene, lotus scrolls on sides, barbed and lobed rim **225.00**

Ginger Jar, 9", ivory, marked "China," pr **650.00**

Plate, 7", carved village scene 185.00
Snuff Bottle, 3½", carved scene, figures
  in garden, carved matching stopper,
  c1825 .... 250.00
Sweetmeat Box, 4½ x 9 x 9", carved,
  openwork cov, eight Buddhist Emblems, latticework platform galleried
  base, diaper ground 1,320.00

Snuff Bottle, lapis lazuli top, late 19th C, 2¾" h, $285.00.

Table Screen, 22¼", figural scene with
  monk rowing boat, reverse with 3
  dragons above rock, flower scroll border, stand 300.00
Tray, 8 x 12", carved garden scene .. 225.00
Vase
  10", landscape, eight people in gar-
    den 250.00
  12¼", six lobed per shape, carved
    with flowering plants, flower scrolls
    at neck, 19th C 200.00

CLAMBROTH GLASS

History: Clambroth glass is a semi-opaque, grayish-white glass which resembles the color of the broth from clams. Pieces are found in both a smooth finish and a rough sandy finish. Sandwich Glass Co. and other manufacturers made clam-broth glass.

Barber Bottle 25.00
Candlesticks, pr
  7¼", hexagonal petal top, Sandwich 225.00
  8¾", reeded, scalloped base 100.00
Ewer, 10⅞" h, green applied handle and
  band, pewter fittings 55.00
Ladle, 9½" 30.00
Lamp Shade, pr, sgd "Northwood" ... 45.00
Mug, Lacy Medallion, souvenir 35.00

Pomade Jar, 3¾" h, bear, made for
  F. B. Strouse, NY 375.00
Salt, master, Sawtooth, Sandwich,
  c1850 .... 50.00

Salt, open, pedestal, $32.50.

Soap Dish, cov, orig insert, Robin and
  Wheat pattern 100.00
Talcum Shaker 20.00
Toothpick Holder, souvenir 30.00

CLEWELL POTTERY

History: Charles Walter Clewell was first a metal worker and second a potter. In the early 1900s he opened a small shop in Canton, Ohio, to produce metal overlay pottery.

Metal on pottery was not a new idea, but Clewell was perhaps the first to completely mask the ceramic body with copper, brass, "silvered" and "bronzed" metals. One result was a product whose patina added to the character of the piece over time.

Most of the wares are marked with a simple incised "CLEWELL" along with a code number. Because Clewell used pottery blanks from other firms, the names "Owens" or "Weller" are sometimes found.

Since Clewell operated on a small scale with little outside assistance, only a limited quantity of his art work exists. He retired at the age of 79 in 1955, choosing not to reveal his technique to anyone else.

References: Paul Evans, *Art Pottery of the United States, 2nd Edition,* Feingold & Lewis Publishing Corp., 1987; Ralph and Terry Kovel, *The Kovels' Collector's Guide To American Art Pottery,* Crown Publishers, Inc., 1974.

Bowl, 8", blue-green patina 125.00
Box, round, riveted, imp "Clewell, Can-
  ton, OH" 275.00
Mug, 5", riveted design 125.00

Vase, twisted flask body, relief flower design, marked "Z/Owens/120," 4¾" h, $400.00.

Pitcher, 5¾", copper clad Owens blank,
green patina **150.00**
Punch Bowl Set, 12" pedestal bowl,
matching cups, riveted design, brown
patina **1,200.00**
Vase, copper clad, leaves and flowers
dec, 1910 . . . . **1,100.00**

CLIFTON

CLIFTON POTTERY

History: The Clifton Art Pottery, Newark, New Jersey, was established by William A. Long, once associated with Londhuna Pottery, and Fred Tschirner, a chemist.

Production consisted of two major lines: Crystal Patina, which resembled true porcelain with a subdued crystal-like glaze, and Indian Ware or Western Influence, an adaptation of the American Indians' unglazed and decorated pottery with a high glazed black interior. Other lines included Robin's Egg Blue and Tirrube. Robin's Egg Blue is a variation of the crystal patina line but in blue-green instead of straw colored hues and with a less prominent "crushed crystal" effect in the glaze. Tirrube is on a terra cotta ground, features brightly colored, slip decorated flowers, and is often artist signed.

Marks are incised or impressed. Early pieces may be dated and shape numbers impressed. Indian wares are identified by tribes.

References: Paul Evans, *Art Pottery Of The United States, 2nd Edition,* Feingold & Lewis Publishng Corp, 1987; Ralph and Terry Kovel, *The Kovels' Collector's Guide To American Art Pottery,* Crown Publishers, Inc., 1974.

Indian Ware, bowl, brown, stamped "Clifton Indian Cooking Ware," 8⅞" d, 4" h, $50.00.

Bowl
3¾", Indian Ware, redware, black Indian dec, marked "Florida" **50.00**
6", Tirrube **90.00**
Candleholder, 7 x 4", two handles . . . **115.00**
Coffeepot, cov, Indian Ware **75.00**
Humidor, 4½ x 4¼", Indian Ware, brown **50.00**
Teapot, cov, 7", Indian Ware **65.00**
Vase
3", Indian Ware, dark rust, black dec,
unmarked **25.00**
5", bulbous gourd shape, 1906 . . . . **100.00**
7⅞", Indian Ware, redware, black and
beige thunderbirds, marked "Hom-
olobi" **150.00**
13", Crystal Patina, bulbous, narrow
neck, 1907 . . . . **220.00**

CLOCKS

History: The sundial was the first man-made device for measuring time. Its basic disadvantage is well expressed in the saying: "Do like the sundial, count only the sunny days."

With need for greater dependability, man developed the water clock, oil clock, and the sand clock respectively. All these clocks worked on the same principle—time was measured by the amount of material passing from one container to another.

The wheel clock was the next major step. These clocks can be traced back to the 13th century. Many improvements on the basic wheel clock were made and continue to be made. In 1934 the quartz crystal movement was introduced.

Recently an atomic clock has been invented that measures time by the frequency of radiation and only varies one second in a thousand years.

Identifying the proper model name for a clock is critical in establishing price. Condition of works also is a critical factor. Examine the works to see how many original parts remain. If repairs are needed, try to include this in your estimate of purchase price. Few clocks are purchased purely for decorative value.

References: *Collectors Guide To Clocks Price Guide,* L-W Promotions, 1973 (revised 1986 price list); Roy Ehrhardt, *Clock Identification And Price Guide: Book I,* rev. ed., Heart of America Press, 1979; Roy Ehrhardt, *Clock Identification And Price Guide: Book II,* Heart of America Press, 1979; Roy Ehrhardt, ed., *The Official Price Guide To Antique Clocks,* House of Collectibles, Third Edition, 1985; Robert W. & Harriett Swedberg, *American Clocks and Clockmakers,* Wallace-Homestead, 1989.

Collectors' Club: National Association of Watch and Clock Collectors, Inc., P. O. Box 33, Columbia, PA 17512. Dues: $20.00. *Bulletin* (bimonthly).

Museum: American Clock & Watch Museum, Bristol, CT; Museum of National Association of Watch and Clock Collectors, Columbia, PA.

MISCELLANEOUS

Advertising
 Chelsea Exchange Bank, New York City, mantel, brass and metal, New Haven Clock Co. 50.00
 Foster & Co., Beloit, WI, USA, 1910, The World's Best Shoes For Men, pocket watch shape, nickel plated, dial inscribed, back of case opens, 30 hour spring driven balance wheel movement, 10¼" 150.00
 Hollow Tile Fire Proofing, Henry Maurer & Son, 420 E. 23rd St., New York, nickel case, 30 hour time movement, sgd on dial, German, 1940, 4" 35.00
 Keller & Sons, Jewelers, Allentown, PA, E. Ingraham & Co, c1890, regulator, refinished case, lower tablet with name in gold leaf, paper on zinc dial, 8 day time movement with key and pendulum, gold painted bezel, 36" 500.00
 Old Mr. Boston, Gilbert Clock Co., Winstead, CT, 1900, replica of bottle, painted sheet iron, 8 day balance wheel movement, maker's signature on dial, 21½" 275.00
 The Blade, Keen Sharp, Toledo, Ohio, Baird Clock Co., Plattsburg, NY, 1875, case painted pale red, white letters, paper on zinc dial inscribed by maker, 8 day time movement, 30¾", case repainted and refinished, label missing 2,300.00

Alarm
 Ansonia Clock Co., Ansonia, CT
  Cast white metal, Good Luck, 30 hour time and alarm lever movement, paper dial with maker's trademark, 7" 150.00
  Nickel plated case, black and gold dial, pressed brass dial surround with image of Father Time, 30 hour time and alarm movement striking bell in bottom of case, trademark on dial and back of case, patent 3/27/77, 8" 100.00
 Boat Clock, used on Erie Canal, 1900, American oak case, conical dial, 30 hour time and alarm movement, 6¾" 125.00
 Kroeber Clock Co., New York City, 1890, "Brass Plaque #4," gilted pressed tin front, four inset colored glass prisms, clock face with red velvet background, applied porcelain numerals, 30 hour time and alarm movement, brass hands, 12" 100.00
 La Salle, IL, 1940, gilded cast white metal, War Alarm, nude woman holding clock, paper dial, 30 hour time and alarm movement, 8½" . . 125.00
 Lux Clock Mfg. Co., Waterbury, CT, 1930, animated, dial with scene of man and woman at home, woman at work at spinning wheel, wheel turns in conjunction with movement escapement, colorful dial with dog in front of fireplace, painted black tin case, 30 hour time and alarm movement, maker's signature on dial, 4½" 125.00
 Rolling Bell, c1800, nickel plated case with bell on top which swings back and forth when alarm is triggered, blue velvet panels, 10½" 150.00
Candlestand, Terryville Mfg Co, Terryville, CT, 1854, 30 hour spring movement, torsion bar control, silvered pressed brass dial inscribed "Ansonia Clock Co, Ansonia, Ct. U.S.A.," back cov marked by Terryville Mfg Co, milk glass base, orig glass dome, 10¼" . 1,250.00
Desk
 Ansonia Clock Co., New York, patent 1878, white metal case in shape of front of train, including engineers, amber reflector, and numerals "45," 30 hour balance wheel movement, paper dial, gilt highlights, maker's signature on dial, 8" 600.00
 Lux Clock Mfg. Co., Waterbury, CT, 1930, animated, painted scene of Church on dial, bell in tower moves with escapement, 30 hour movement, maker's signature on dial, 4" 75.00

Octavia Clock Co., Switzerland, 1900, gold plated, engraved, 15 jewel watch movement, porcelain dial with seconds bit, maker's signature on movement, 4″ **100.00**

Miscellaneous, gas light, porcelain face, marked "Theodore B Starr, NY," orig leather case, 5⅛″ d, $150.00.

Gaslight, Waltham, opaque glass dial, balance wheel movement, 5½″ **165.00**

Novelty

Ansonia Clock Co., New York

Armor #25, 1900, pressed nickel plated case, orig leather belt for hanging, case includes removable helmet and two spears, 30 hour time balance wheel movement, 11″ **275.00**

Cherub, 1890, two cast white metal figures supporting 30 hour time balance wheel movement, unusual winding mechanism, porcelain dial, hairline crack in dial, gilting removed, 4¼″ **80.00**

Lux Clock Mfg. Co., Waterbury, CT, 1890, figural, town hall, painted, 30 hour weight driven movement that strikes on hour and half hour, as clock strikes, bell in steeple rocks back and forth, 12″ **475.00**

New Haven Clock Co., New Haven, CT, 1900, banjo shape, detailed white metal case, 30 hour balance wheel movement in lower section, sgd on dial, 10½″ **200.00**

Parker Clock Co., Meriden, CT

Model #11, brass case with chains supporting works, 30 hour balance wheel movement with calendar mechanism, patent Nov 28, 1876 on rear of case, maker's signature on back plate, dial faded, 9½″ **400.00**

Travel type, carrying handle, brass case, 30 hour balance wheel

movement, beveled glass over dial, sgd on back of case, 1890, 7″ **250.00**

Seth Thomas, Plymouth Hollow, CT, 1860, alarm mechanism by G. K. Proctor & Co., Beverly, MA, rosewood veneered case, 30 hour time and alarm movement, painted zinc dial, mirror tablet, orig "S T" hands, mechanism at top ignites a small lamp at the moment the alarm strikes, maker's signature on label on back, veneer missing from base, minor paint loss on dial, 11½″ . . . **650.00**

Unidentified Maker, Connecticut, 1860, "Topsy," eyes move with escapement of movement, 30 hour time, unsigned, dial repainted, 16½″ **1,600.00**

Welch, E. N., Bristol, CT, 1860, Briggs rotary patent, rotary escapement mounted on turned wood base, cast feet, orig glass dome, unsigned, base repainted, 8″ **375.00**

Western M.F.G. Co., La Salle, IL, 1900, black painted tall case clock with child pulling up the weights, 30 hour movement, maker's signature on dial, feet missing from case base, 8¼″ **45.00**

Picture, Le Roy, Paris, France, 1875, painting of mountain village and church in foreground, small porcelain dial in steeple, 8 day time and strike movement inscribed by maker, later cylinder musical mechanism with pull cord, 35¼″ w, 39½″ h **950.00**

Time Recorder, Simplex Time Recorder Company, Gardner, MA, 1920, oak case fitted with mechanism to punch time cards, double wind move time only movement, 15 day, painted dial inscribed by maker, 30½″ **160.00**

Travel, New Haven Clock Co, New Haven, CT, 1880, ebonized iron case, applied gilded trim, inlaid mother of pearl, paper dial, 30 hour time and strike movement, lever escapement, 9″ **200.00**

SHELF CLOCKS

Acorn, J. C. Brown, Bristol, CT, laminated case, rosewood facings, 8 day brass time and strike movement with fusees, orig paper label, "Forestville Mfg. Co." sgd on dial 19⅛″ **3,000.00**

Balloon, Gilbert Clock Co., Winstead, CT, c1900, mahogany case, pattern inlay around edge, porcelain dial, 8 day movement with lever escapement, 9″ **150.00**

Shelf, Ansonia, mirror sides, walnut, 8 day movement, two gold gilded cherubs, 24″ h, $485.00.

Beehive
  Brewster & Ingraham, Bristol, CT,
    1850, rosewood veneered case,
    orig painted tablet, painted zinc
    dial, 8 day time and strike move-
    ment with strike advance method of
    raising the strike hammer, maker's
    signature on label, movement, and
    dial, case refinished, 18¾″ 400.00
  Jennings Bros, Brush Brass Novelty
    No. B5437, filigree panel beneath
    face, 5″ 90.00
  New Haven Clock Co.
    Mahogany and rosewood veneered
      case, 1865, orig painted tablet,
      painted zinc dial, 30 hour time,
      strike, and alarm movement,
      maker's signature on paper la-
      bel, columns re-veneered, 19½″ 200.00
    Rosewood veneered case, 1860,
      painted beehive tablet, painted
      zinc dial, 8 day time and alarm
      movement, maker's signature on
      paper label, some veneer loss,
      tablet replaced, 19″ 175.00
    Seth Thomas, stenciled mahogany
      and rosewood veneered case,
      black and gold tablet, painted zinc
      dial, 8 day time, strike, and alarm
      Seth Thomas movement (not orig
      to case), sgd "Chauncey Jerome"
      on label on case, 19″ 225.00
Box or Cottage
  Ansonia Clock Co., c1910, veneered,
    8 day time and strike movement,
    9½″ 150.00

Gilbert, William L Clock Co., "Rose
  Cottage Time," gilt rose dec, 30
  hour, 9⅞ x 7¾″ 125.00
Terry, S. B., Plymouth, CT, 1860, mahogany and pine case, door with
  orig stenciled tablet, painted wood
  dial, 30 hour ladder movement with
  alarm, unsigned, 11½″ 325.00
Waterbury Clock Co., c1858, painted
  green wood case, 30 hour brass
  spring movement and alarm, 12″ . 175.00
Bracket
  Bosley, Joseph, London, c1750,
    George II, mahogany and gilt
    bronze bell topped case, pineapple
    finials, crown wheel escapement,
    musical, 21¼″ 3,850.00
  Dent, London, George II, gilt metal
    and bronze mounted red japanned,
    2nd half 18th C, 17″, 5¾″ d pewter
    dial, black-painted Roman numer-
    als, movement gong striking on
    hour, strike silent mechanism in
    cresting, lantern-form case, dec all-
    over with chinoiseries in gold, tones
    on a vermilion ground, various gilt
    enrichments 2,475.00
  European, 1880, brass case, cast
    with pierced frets and ornamenta-
    tion, replaced red velvet backing,
    silver engraved dial, 8 day time and
    strike fusee movement striking on
    hour and half hour, opens in rear,
    14 x 27½″ 1,000.00
  Japanese, 1800, rosewood or teak-
    wood case, mother of pearl and
    brass inlay, brass finials, early 8
    day time and strike fusee move-
    ment with crown wheel escape-
    ment, engraved brass dial with an-
    imals of the zodiac, sweep second
    hand, some veneer loss, modern
    reproduction dial, hands do not
    match, 18½″ 500.00
  Payne, London, c1810, Regency, gilt
    bronze mounted burr yew wood,
    acanthus chased bail handle, an-
    chor escapement, glazed on all
    sides, fluted border at top, ogee
    molded base, four gilt ball feet, 10″ 2,125.00
Calendar
  Ansonia, Banker's Inkstand, bronze,
    nickel finish, Egyptian motif, 1 day,
    12″ 375.00
  Feishtinger, C. W., Fritztown, PA,
    1895, walnut case, door with orig
    glass tablet with silver dec, two
    painted zinc dials, 8 day time and
    strike movement, day indicator
    roller in base, lower dial with point-
    ers to indicate date and month,
    pendulum seen through small ap-

erture in bottom of calendar dial, orig instruction label on back, case refinished, tablet cracked, 22″ . . . **350.00**

Ithaca Calendar Clock Co., oak, 1880, No 17 Mantel Index, solid oak case with carved dec, door opens to two paper on zinc discs, 8 day time and strike spring driven movement sgd E. N. Welch, calendar mechanism showing day of week, date, and month, maker's label on back, sgd on calendar dial, case refinished, 28¾″ **500.00**

Southern Calendar Clock Co., St. Louis, Missouri, 1879, Fashion Model #3, solid walnut case, moldings, columns, and finials, glass door with orig gold leaf inscription, 8 day time and strike Seth Thomas movement, separate calendar mechanism and dial, black paper label in back of case, 32″ **1,700.00**

Union Clock Co, produced by Wm L Gilbert, rosewood veneered case with paper on zinc dial, black and gold paper label, 8 day time, strike, and calendar spring movement marked by Gilbert, fancy pendulum, minor re-veneered, clear lower glass, 25¾″ **200.00**

Waterbury, Office Calendar, Double Dial No. 40, walnut case, time, strike, and alarm movements, 24″ **625.00**

Welch, E. N., Forestville, CT, 1875, Aditi Model, D. J. Gale's patent perpetual calendar, walnut case, two paper on zinc dials, lower with day and month indicators, 8 day time and strike movement, maker's signature on paper label on back, cast int. label, and movement, case refinished, upper dial faded, 27½″ . . **700.00**

Carriage

Black Starr & Forest, c1900, champleve enamel, platform lever movement, porcelain dial, multicolored, 5½″ **1,200.00**

French, Paris, 1900, Anglaise Riche, brass case, pierced, engraved, and silvered panels around dial and case sides, 8 day jeweled lever with hour strike and repeat movement, polished case, 6½″ **1,000.00**

Le Roy et Fils, c1900, gilt metal, detached lever movement, alarm, patented bottom wind, fitted leather case, 5¼″ **1,425.00**

Limoges, 1898, Grande Sonnerie, gilt metal, platform lever movements, repeating, alarm, case with four free standing columns with Corinthian capitals and acanthus chased

Carriage, French, brass, four beveled glass panels, 2½ x 3¼ x 4½″, French patents, $450.00.

urn finials, inset with enamel panels painted with classical women holding a jewel box, basket of flowers, gilt highlights, maroon ground, fitted leather case with key, 6¾″ . . . **10,000.00**

Seikosha, Tokyo, Japan, 1900, pressed brass case, porcelain dial with date and day indicators, 8 day balance wheel movement, 7″ **175.00**

Voak, London, c1840, gilt metal, engraved, diamond endstone, lever movement mounted on back, 4¾″ **1,225.00**

Waterbury, 1890, porcelain dial, jeweled movement with hour and half hour strike and repeat mechanism, sgd on dial and movement, 6″ . . . **175.00**

Chime, A. Wagstaff, London, England, 1880, elaborate inlaid brass dec, brass case hardware, dial engraved with rings and applied spandrels, 8 day fusee 3 train movement striking Westminster or Whittington chimes on gongs and musical tones, nest of eight bells, 30″ **3,200.00**

Crystal Regulator

Ansonia Clock Co., 1880, brass case, beveled glass panels, porcelain dial, 8 day time and strike movement, visible Brocot escapement, 2-jar simulated mercury pendulum, 9¾″ **275.00**

French, 1860, painted case, elliptic front, 8 day time and strike movement, orig mercury filled pendulum, 10½″ **750.00**

Gilbert, W. L., Tunis, 8 day, half hour strike **675.00**

Seth Thomas, 1890, brass case, beveled glass panels, porcelain dial inscribed "Mitchell Vance & Co., NY," 8 day time and strike movement inscribed "R. Kaiser, Seth Thomas," 11" **225.00**

Waterbury, Bordeau, gold plated, 8 day, half hour strike **850.00**

Figural

Ansonia Clock Co.

Cupid, 1880, gold plated ormolu, 30 hour time movement, porcelain dial, maker's signature on dial, quiver of arrows finial, 8¼" ... **250.00**

Swinging Doll, 1890, brass cased alarm clock and support with ceramic figure of boy which swings with the movement, 30 hour time movement, paper dial with maker's name and trademark, 11½" **400.00**

German, 1890, Diana, cast white metal figure supports watch movement which swings its own pendulum, 30 hour time movement, maker's signature on back of movement, "Made In Germany," 13½" **350.00**

Gilbert Clock Co., chariot, gold plated ormolu, 30 hour time movement, paper dial, patent 1891, 6½" **225.00**

Kennedy, T., CT, 1860, John Bull, blinking eyes, 30 hour time only balance wheel movement, "T. Kennedy, Patent applied for 1856" stamped on base, dial repainted, 16½" **1,200.00**

Unknown Maker, violin, mahogany case shaped like violin on base, paper on zinc dial, 8 day time and strike movement, black and gold glass, some restoration, 28" **500.00**

Gingerbread (Kitchen)

Ansonia, c1890, Kentucky, ash, rosewood trim, 6" dial, 8 day strike, spring wound, 22" **215.00**

Gilbert, William L., Clock Co., 1899, Excelsior No. 2, oak, 8 day half hour strike, 16½" **200.00**

Ingraham, 1905, Cayuga, solid oak, emb, 8 day half hour strike, 22" .. **225.00**

New Haven Clock Co., pressed oak case, door glass with gold design, 8 day time, strike, and alarm movements, paper label on back "Our Pride 8 day Striking Alarm," sgd on movement and paper label, case refinished, 25" **175.00**

Waterbury, Ideal O, black walnut, 8 day, cathedral gong, wire bell ... **300.00**

Welch, E. N., 1880, walnut, white dial, brass alarm bell, 8 day, 23⅜ x 14½ x 15⅛" **265.00**

Mantel

Brush Brass, B5436, Waterbury movements, 5½" **60.00**

Chelsea Clock Co., E. A. Brown, Boston, MA, c1910, fruitwood case, 8 day movement **80.00**

Gilbert Clock Co., 1890, marbleized wood case, gilted white metal feet and bell mount, 8 day time and strike movement striking hours and half hours on gold painted bell mounted on top, paper dial inscribed by maker, 17½ x 17¼" .. **150.00**

Kroeber Clock Co., 1875, solid walnut Victorian case, dec tablet, porcelain dial, 8 day time and strike spring movement, fancy glass pendulum, paper label on back of case, dial chipped and repaired, 19½" .. **225.00**

New Haven Clock Co., 1910, tambour, mahogany case, porcelain dial, 30 hour time movement, maker's signature on dial, 6¾" **50.00**

Sessions Clock Co., 1920, inlaid mahogany case, porcelain dial, 30 hour time movement, maker's signature on dial, one ball foot missing, 8¼" **80.00**

Seth Thomas

Brass and glass, 1900, fancy case, copper plated white metal base and top, porcelain dial, 8 day time and strike movement, maker's signature on dial and movement, 12" **250.00**

Wood, 1875, solid walnut case, painted gold tablet, orig paper dial, 8 day time and alarm movement which sounds with two hammers on a gong and bell, maker's signature on label and dial, case refinished, 21¾" **275.00**

Waltham Watch Co., 1920, hardwood tambour case, 8 day movement adjusted with 15 jewels, removable front bezel, sgd on dial and movement, 5¾" **100.00**

Marble, French, 1870, 16", black marble case, inlaid panels of light colored marble, brass mounts, porcelain dial, 8 day time and strike movement with pendulum **125.00**

Massachusetts Shelf

Boston Clock Co., Chelsea, MA, 1888, Empire style painted black wood case, four columns with brass capitals, brass dec on top and bottom of case, etched and cut glass tablet with flaming leaf motif, emb brass rim surround on paper dial, one year, torsion escapement patented by Aaron Crane, fusee powered, tin and strike, orig label, minor stains on dial, one fusee cord broken, possible brown spring on strike side, 21″ **2,500.00**

Hubbard, Daniel, Medfield, MA, c1820, Federal, mahogany and eglomise, shaped crest, urn and foliate form finial, rect eglomise door dec with lyres and foliate motifs, gold painted dished dial, hinged eglomise door with mill and waterfall scene, molded base, giltwood ball feet, 36″ **42,000.00**

Unknown Maker, miniature, iron case, mother of pearl inlay, painted gold dec, orig dial, 30 hour time only movement, with S. B. Terry patent torsion balance, marked "Oct 5th, 1852," 8½″ **1,500.00**

Willard, Aaron, Boston, c1820, Federal, mahogany and eglomise, shaped crest, brass eagle finial, door dec with polychrome foliate and lyre motifs, white painted dished dial above eglomise panel painted with corner lyre motifs, oval mirror, brass ball feet, 34½″ **9,500.00**

Metal

Brass, cast, France, 1875

Figural, male and female figures, porcelain dial, 8 day time and strike movement, pendulum missing, replaced dust cov, 18½″ **175.00**

Mantel, cast case with orig gilt surface, dec blue porcelain panels on front, sides, and urn, 8 day time and strike movement with pendulum, 20½″ **650.00**

Bronze

Ansonia, figural, MacBeth, seated in ornate chair, 8 day, half hour strike, sounding board, patent regulators, white 5″ dial, 11½″ . **250.00**

Du Buc, Paris, c1805, gilt bronze, surmounted by spread winged American eagle, shield, arrows and olive branch on top of a globe and plinth inscribed "E Pluribus Unum," white enameled dial centering inscription "Du Buc, Rue Michel-le-Comte No. 33, A Paris," and "Washington, the first in war, first in peace, and in his countrymen's hearts," flanking standing figure of Washington holding scroll in right hand, sword and gloves in left hand, lower section with gilt-metal mount centering female's head, chased flattened ball feet **25,300.00**

Jennings Bros, 1906, gold finish, 2″ ivory dial, 1 day time, 4⅝″ **65.00**

Seth Thomas, Duchess, cottage style, emb flowers, foliage, and scrolls, 4½ dial, 9¾″ **185.00**

Cast Metal, Germany, 1900, cast figure of Lady Diana supporting 30 hour time movement with swinging pendulum, porcelain dial, broken jeweled support arm, 13½″ **325.00**

Copper, New Haven, CT, 1885, hammered ground, SS ornaments of lily and lily pad, fold over corners, easel back, 1 day time, 8½″ **165.00**

Iron

Ansonia Clock Co., 1890, porcelain dial, 30 hour balance wheel time movement, musical mechanism in bottom of gold painted case, busts of Beethoven and Wagner, musical motifs, sgd on dial, 10¾″ **125.00**

New Haven Clock Co., 1890, cast iron, gilted white metal ornamentation, mother of pearl inlay, painted dec, 8 day time and strike movement, unsigned, 8″ . **200.00**

Muller, Nicholas, 1886, figural, boy pushing wheelbarrow containing clock, 1 day time, small movement, 6½″ **165.00**

Noah Pomeroy & Co., 1860, mother of pearl inlay and painted dec, 30 hour balance wheel movement with nickel plated balance wheel that shows through opening in dial, maker's signature on movement, 10″ **600.00**

Terry Clock Co., 1875, round top, zinc dial with applied paper, 8 day time and strike movement with fixed pendulum, maker's label on case, case repainted black, 9″ **100.00**

Unidentified American Maker, 1890, circular clock, pedestal on rect base, porcelain dial, 30 hour balance wheel movement, 12″ . **75.00**

Waterbury Clock Co., 1860, case marked "Muller, NY," 30 hour time and strike movement and pendulum opening to lower part of case, maker's signature on paper label and case, 16¾″ **100.00**

Nickel Plated Brass, Seth Thomas Clock Co., Thomaston, CT, 1900, kite shape, pressed front with floral designs and inscription "Time Flies," three feet form stand, maker's signature on dial, 8″ **200.00**

Pot Metal

Unidentified Maker, 1910, gilted metal case supported by pressed glass columns, 30 hour balance wheel movement, case repainted, 16¼" **50.00**

Westclox, 1918, gray silver finish, emb Dutch figures, 1 day movement, 4½" **60.00**

Mirror Side

Ansonia, Triumph, silvered cupids, bronze ornaments, 8 day movement, 24½" **325.00**

New Haven, Occidental, walnut, gilt ornaments, 8 day strike, 24" **375.00**

Ogee

Ansonia, 1891, central panel of petit point etching with cupid holding basket of flowers, 1 day, strike, and alarm movements, 26" **225.00**

Brewster, E. C., Bristol, CT, 1840, mahogany veneered case, repainted tablet, heavy painted zinc dial, spring driven movement with cast iron back plate, maker's label, 26" **200.00**

Forestville Manufacturing Co., Bristol, CT, 1850, mahogany case with choice figured veneers, double door, painted floral tablet in lower door, painted zinc dial inscribed with maker's name, 8 day time and strike movement, 31" **275.00**

Gilbert, Wm. L., c1870, goldfinch dec, 30 hour weight, strike, 25⅞" **175.00**

Hills, George, Plainville, CT, inverted ogee mahogany veneer, mirror, 30 hour brass time only movement, replaced dial, 36½" **450.00**

Hunt, John, Farmington, CT, 1835, mahogany and rosewood veneered case, four orig feet, glazed door, orig wood dial, replaced glass tablet, brass 8 day time and strike movement retaining orig weights, partial paper label, minor veneer loss, 30¼" **300.00**

New Haven Clock Co., 1880, zebra case, etched lyre and foliage dec, 1 day strike, orig weights, 26" . . . **225.00**

Jerome & Co., New Haven, CT, 1860, mahogany veneered case, double doors, lower with frosted design, painted zinc dial, 8 day time and strike weight driven movement, maker's label **275.00**

Walton, Hiram, Terryville, CT, 1850, mahogany veneered case, wood painted dial, orig painted glass tablet with floral motif, vertical oval center, 30 hour time and strike brass weight driven movement, orig weights, paper label, some flaking to tablet, 26" **235.00**

Pillar and Scroll

Clark, Herman, Plymouth, CT, 1820, mahogany and veneered case,

painted iron dial sgd "H Clark, Plymouth," painted glass tablet with harbor scene of boats, leaf like surround, 8 day brass weight driven time and strike movement, orig paper label, right ear piece out, tablet restored, 3 contemporary finials, 20¼" **5,600.00**

Hoadley, S., Plymouth, CT, 1825, mahogany case, scrolled ears, turned columns, cut out feet, orig painted wood dial, orig painted tablet, orig upper glass, ivory brushed 30 hour wood upside down movement, orig weights, maker's label with picture of Benjamin Franklin and motto "Time is Money," finials missing, 28¾" **2,500.00**

Ives, Joseph, Bristol, CT, 1820, tiger maple pillar with reeded back columns, brass plates, iron posts, tin keystone, 8 day movement, single winding arbor, time, and strike, bell strikes hourly, 29¾" **6,500.00**

Leavenworth & Son, Mark, Waterbury, CT, 1820, mahogany case, painted wood dial, orig glass with landscape of mansion and lake, 30 hour wood time and strike, orig paper label, orig brass urn finials, 28½" **2,125.00**

North, Norris, Torrington, CT, c1820, 30 hour wood time and strike movement (east-west), orig dial and finials, paper label, 29¾" **2,000.00**

Seth Thomas, 1820, mahogany case, turned columns, scrolled feet and crest, glazed door with replaced painted tablet, enameled wood dial and maker's label, 30 hour time and strike movement with iron weights, finials replaced, 31" **850.00**

Terry, Eli, Plymouth, CT, 1817, tiger maple and mahogany case, dial dec with eagle and crossed flags, 30 hour movement, outside escapement, time, and strike, 30½" . **10,000.00**

Unidentified Maker, CT, 1825, mahogany case, painted wood dial and glass tablet, 30 hour time and strike weight driven wood movement, door reveneered, label done, glass repainted, 16½ x 28¾" **500.00**

Porcelain or China Case

Ansonia, 1890

Royal Bonn, porcelain dial with visible escapement, Roman numerals, 8 day time and strike movement, brightly colored blue case, floral dec, case marked "Royal Bonn, Germany, La Vogue," hair-

line cracks in dial, minor loss of
gilt dec, 12¾″ **375.00**

Winnebago, porcelain dial, 8 day
time and strike spring movement
with pendulum, deep green case,
gold and floral dec, back move-
ment cover missing, 11¾″ **175.00**

Germany, 1880, off white and pale
green china case, paper dial and
brass rim, 8 day time wheel balance movement supported by two
columns, 16″ **75.00**

Gilbert, Wm. L., 1900, Cameo, white
landscape and florals, green
ground, 2″ dial, 1 day time, 6¼″ . .   **80.00**

Kroeber, F., NY, 1888, lever movement, urn shape, gilt foliate handles
and finial **225.00**

Waterbury, 1903, boudoir, clover dec,
pastel ground, 2″ dial with beveled
glass, 1 day lever time, 5⅝″ **85.00**

Shelf

Atkins & Porter, Bristol, CT, 1850, mahogany and rosewood veneered
case, orig painted tablet and zinc
dial, 30 hour time and strike weight
driven movement, maker's label on
case int., case refinished, 24½″ . .   **250.00**

Birge & Peck, Bristol, CT, 1850, mahogany veneered case with gilted
and painted dec split columns and
splat, painted tablet in lower door,
mirror in center section, orig dial
and paper label in top section, 8
day weight driven time and strike
movement with rolling pinions,
case refinished, 35½″ **475.00**

Birge, Mallory & Co., 1840, choice
mahogany case, carved crest,
turned columns, ball feet, orig
painted tablet in lower door, two
clear glasses in upper door, orig
painted wood dial, maker's label,
and large strap brass 8 day weight
driven time and strike sgd movement, case refinished, tablets
cracked, 38½″ **800.00**

Boardman & Wells, Bristol, CT, 1830,
mahogany case with gilted split columns, stenciled splat with maker's
name, painted tablet with naval battle scene, 30 hour time and strike
wood movement, orig weights,
black and gold wood dial, paper la-
bel, 32¾″ **275.00**

Brewster & Ingraham, 1850, round
laminated and turned mahogany
case, convex glass, painted zinc
dial, 8 day horizontal movement,
sgd on dial, case refinished, 11¼″   **500.00**

Clark & Morse, Plymouth, CT, 1825,
mahogany veneered case with four

columns flanking two doors, lower
with orig painted tablet, upper with
orig glass, painted iron dial inscribed by maker, high quality 8 day
brass weight driven Salem Bridge
movement with orig weight,
scrolled crest and three brass fini-
als, 30¾″ **2,800.00**

E. Ingraham & Co.

Grecian Model, 1870, walnut case,
turned and laminated bezel, applied paper face on zinc dial, 8
day time, strike, and alarm movement, sgd on paper label, case
refinished, 14¾″ **250.00**

Venetian, rosewood veneered case
with turned split columns,
painted tablet inscribed "E Pluribus Unum" with eagle and American shield, Joseph Ives 8 day
time and strike tin plate movement with squirrel cage roller escapement and rolling pinions,
maker's signature on label, case
refinished, one hand replaced,
18″ **2,100.00**

Venetian #2 (Candy Striper), 1875,
mosaic front, alternating light and
dark woods, orig table, paper on
zinc dial, unsigned, 18″ **225.00**

French, 1850, walnut inlaid case,
painted dial, 8 day spring driven
time movement with fixed pendulum, maker's instruction label on
case int. and label of "Jesse Smith,
262 Essex St., Salem," 8″ **130.00**

Hotchkiss & Benedict, Auburn, NY,
1820, mahogany case with choice
veneers, columns with carved capitals, upper door opens to painted
wood dial, lower door with mirror
and orig paper label, detailed inscription of maker, shaped crest, 8
day time and strike movement with
orig lead weights, second hand
shaped like human hand with finger
pointing, sgd on dial and label, pat-
ent by Asa Munger, 38″ **1,150.00**

Jerome & Co., 1870, rosewood veneered case, door with gutta percha pressed and gilted design,
painted zinc dial, 8 day time, strike,
and alarm movement, blue paper
maker's label, 14¾″ **225.00**

Jerome, Gilbert & Grant, 1840, mahogany case with rounded sides,
two painted tablets, painted zinc
dial, 30 hour time and strike weight
driven movement, maker's label,
22¼″ **275.00**

Marsh, George, Bristol, CT, 1830,
Empire mahogany case, carved

crest, columns, and feet, door with mirror and painted tablet, repainted wood dial, paper maker's label, unusual time and strike wood movement with very small winding drums and ivory bushings, old lead weights, minor veneer damage, finials missing, movement not orig to case, 38" **450.00**

Mills, J. R. & Co., NY, c1845, mahogany veneered case with grained columns, gilt capitals, painted glass dial with pressed brass surround, 30 day weight driven time and strike movement with A. D. Crane's Patent torsion escapement and three ball pendulum, paper label, door, glass dial, weights, and suspension spring replaced, 22" **1,600.00**

Mitchell, George, Bristol, CT, 1830, mahogany case with stenciled columns and crest, door with replaced mirror tablet, enameled wood dial, paper label, 30 hour time and strike weight driven wood movement, period weights, 35" **250.00**

Munger, Asa, Auburn, NY, 1830, mahogany and walnut case, molded cornice and base, carved columns on door, orig dec metal plate around dial, mirror, 8 day time and strike weight driven movement with exceptional brass hands, period iron weights and orig eagle pendulum, case refinished, 38¼" **2,225.00**

Roberts, Titus, Bristol, CT, 1840, mahogany veneered case, paint dec and gilted columns, painted wood dial, black and gold tablet, 30 hour time and strike weight driven wood movement, maker's signature on paper label with inscription "For Henry Hart," gilted ball feet, 32¾" **375.00**

Seth Thomas
Column Front, c1850, mahogany veneered case, painted zinc dial, split gilded columns, choice painted tablet with eagle on dark blue ground, 30 hour time and strike brass weight driven movement, paper label, orig iron weights and pendulum, 25" ... **200.00**

Round Top, 1875, rosewood veneered case, painted zinc dial, paper label, 8 day time and strike movement, maker's signature on label and dial, 15" **175.00**

Sleigh Front, 1865, rosewood veneered case with gilted and paint dec columns, two painted tablets, painted zinc dial, 8 day time and strike weight driven movement, maker's label, 32½" **1,650.00**

Stratton, Charles, Worcester, MA, 1860, mahogany veneered reverse ogee case, mirror tablet, painted zinc dial, 30 hour time and strike weight driven movement with orig weights, over pasted maker's label, 23½" **225.00**

Terry & Andrews, Ansonia, CT, rosewood veneered case with painted dec, two painted tablets, painted zinc dial, 8 day time and strike lyre movement, blue paper maker's label, 15½" **700.00**

Shelf, Eli Terry & Sons, 8 day movement, stencil dec, claw feet, $450.00.

Terry, Eli & Sons, Plymouth, CT, 1830, mahogany case with orig gold stenciling on splat and quarter columns, replaced painted tablet, painted wood dial, 30 hour time and strike weight driven wood movement, maker's signature on paper label, 29¾" **350.00**

Terry, Henry, & Co., Plymouth, CT, 1830, mahogany case with split columns, carved pineapples, carved crest, black and gold painted wood dial, 30 hour time and strike wood movement with orig weights, maker's label, bottom door glass missing, 33¾" **225.00**

Terry, Silas B., choice mahogany case, black and gold painted wood dial, orig mirror tablet, round movement, sgd on label, labeled and sold by Williams, Orton, Prestons & Co., Farmington, CT, 1840, ivory escutcheons missing, 32¾" **350.00**

Waterbury Clock Co., 1875, rosewood veneered case with applied rippled molding, painted zinc dial with seconds indicator, 30 hour time and strike balance wheel movement, maker's signature on movement, case refinished, 11¾" **250.00**

Welch, Spring & Co, Forestville, CT, 1875, Patti No. 1, solid rosewood case with glass sides, gold dec tablet, 8 day time and strike movement by Sessions, paper on zinc dial, replaced movement and dial, 19" . . **225.00**

Whiting, Riley, Winchester, CT, 1830, mahogany case with carved eagle crest and columns, replaced mirror tablet, black and gold painted wood dial, 30 hour time and strike movement, orig weights, maker's label, 35¼" **475.00**

Skeleton

Terry Clock Co., 1875, miniature, porcelain dial, pressed brass ornamentation including maker's name, 8 day double wind time movement, base with painted dec and marbleization, maker's signature on plate above dial, under dome, 8¾" **1,150.00**

Unidentified Maker, CT, 1850, mounted on walnut base, cov with glass dome, painted zinc dial, 30 hour time movement with S. N. Botsford Patent escapement with horizontal balance wheel, some marriage of parts, 12¾" **175.00**

Solar

Arkell, James & A. G. Richmond, Canjohaire, NY, 1880, patented by Lewis Paul Juvet, Glenn Falls, NY, globe on solid cast base, globe with paper covering rotates once every 24 hours, beveled glass time dial with reverse gold leaf numerals, 30 hour movement, compass hangs from base of the pole, maker's signature on globe, 12" d globe, 48" h **4,250.00**

Whiting, Dr. Lewis, Saratoga, NY, 1863, patent by Thedore Timby, Baldwinsville, NY, walnut case, 8 day movement, globe made and installed by Gilman Joslin, Boston, MA, 12 hour dial above globe and minute dial below, believed to be one of only 600 made, lower dial, lower door, and one drop acorn replaced, 27" **2,600.00**

Steeple

Boardman, Chauncey, patent 1847,

mahogany veneered case, painted tablet with Windsor castle, painted zinc dial, 30 hour time and strike fusee movement, maker's signature on movement and paper label, 20" **475.00**

Brewster & Ingraham, Bristol, CT, 1845, Gothic, round, twin steeples, rosewood veneered case, cut glass tablet, painted zinc dial, maker's label and rare repeating 8 day time and strike movement with strike snail and retaining both brass springs, maker's signature on label and movement, case refinished, base reveneered, two finials missing, 20" **800.00**

Roswell Kimberly, 1850, standard 8 day time and strike movement, silver and black painted tablet of an eagle, inscription on top of case "Patented Oct 11th 1850 by R. Kimberly, Ansonia, Ct," case refinished, 20½" **700.00**

Smith & Goodrich, Bristol, CT, 1850, mahogany veneered case with turned finials, painted tablet, painted zinc dial, 30 hour time and strike fusee movement, maker's label, case and dial refinished, 19¾" **275.00**

Terry, Silas Burnham, Terryville, CT, 1845, mahogany and rosewood case, painted scene in door, painted wood dial with seconds aperture, heavy strap brass movement, 30 hour time and strike with two large wooden fusee cones, minor veneer loss, old replaced tablet, 24¾" **3,750.00**

TALL CASE CLOCKS

Beckel, Charles, Bethlehem, PA, c1820, 97½", yellow pine case, elaborate carved crest, turned finials, turned hood columns, fluted quarter columns, waist door with carved shell, bracket feet, 30 hour time and strike pull up movement, orig weight and pendulum, painted iron dial with bird in arch, calendar indicator, inscribed "C. F. Beckel, Bethlehem," case stripped **1,000.00**

Burnap, Daniel, East Windsor, CT, c1780, 88", Chippendale carved cherrywood, molded hood surmounted by a pierced cresting centering three ball and spirally twisted finials above glazed door opening, engraved brass dial, inscription "Daniel Burnap, East Windsor," minute and date registers, waisted case with hinged shaped door flanked by fluted quarter columns, molded base **13,200.00**

Effingham Embree, New York, c1800, 94¾", Federal inlaid mahogany, molded hood centering and eagle inlaid tympanum above arched door opening, white painted dial with minute and date registers, painted bucolic scene above inscription "EF-FINGHAM EMBREE, NEW YORK," waisted case with bookend inlaid frieze and fan inlaid door, fluted quarter columns, fan inlaid base on bracket feet, restored hood molding **22,000.00**

Garrett, Philip, Philadelphia, PA, c1775, 100¾", Chippendale carved mahogany, bonnet with swan's neck pediment ending in carved rosettes, three urn and flame finials, arched glazed door, painted face with minute and date registers, painted arch panel of sporting scene, maker's name and location below date register, waisted case with shaped and recessed oval panel door, fluted quarter columns, 8 day, scalloped recessed panel in base flanked by fluted quarter columns, ogee bracket feet, rear feet replaced **14,500.00**

Harland, Thomas, Norwich, CT, 1785, 91", Chippendale cherry case, molded arched bonnet with three flame finials, and whale's tail fret, fluted columns with brass capitals flank glazed door, silvered brass dial, inscribed "Thomas Harland, Norwich" in arch, seconds bitt, calendar aperture, 8 day, brass time and strike movement, orig weights, wood pendulum rod, and brass bob, waisted case with tombstone door, molded base with scroll pattern applied to top and side panels, double molded base, ogee bracket feet, hardware on door not orig, old replacement in fret, two finial replacements **20,000.00**

Hill, Samuel, Harrisburg, PA, c1780, 103½", Chippendale carved mahogany, bonnet with molded broken arch pediment ending in carved rosettes and centering three carved urn and pierced flame finials, arched glazed door, white painted dial with floral spandrels and birds in fountain in arch, minute and date registers, "SAML HILL" at base of number, "VI," fluted columns flanking bonnet door, waisted case, molded shaped hinged door, fluted quarter columns in waist and base, molded shaped panel on base, ogee bracket feet **14,500.00**

Kepplinger, Samuel, Baltimore, MD,

c1810, 106", carved and inlaid satinwood and plum pudding mahogany, bonnet with molded swan's neck cresting ending in inlaid roundels, acorn wood center finial, arched glazed door, white painted dial, moon phases, 8 day, minute and date registers, inscription "Samuel Kepplinger BALTIMORE" between registers, waisted case, rect cock beaded door, satinwood inlaid frieze, line inlaid quarter columns, line inlaid base with plum pudding mahogany panel, ogee bracket feet **8,000.00**

Pratt, John, Washington, NJ, 1824, Federal carved curly maple, hood with swan's neck crest above a carved teardrop relief and hinged glazed door opening, white painted dial with moon phases, minute and date registers, inscription "John Nicholl," waisted case with shell carved hinged door flanked by canted corners, molded base with shaped skirt, turned feet, case sgd, "January 25th, 1824, made by John S. Pratt, Washington," moon phases repainted, slight repair to crest **7,150.00**

Rogers, Paul, Berwick, ME, c1800, 85", flat top, pine case, long slender arched waist door and upper glazed door, 8 day, double molded base, brass gears and iron plates, engraved brass dial inscribed "Paul Rogers, Berwick" **4,000.00**

Rota, Jacob, Berks County, PA, c1770, 94½", Chippendale, carved, inlaid, and turned walnut, molded swan's neck cresting bearing initials "MF," ending in floral carved rosettes, centered by three turned finials above arched white painted dial, dec with bird and flowers, turned colonettes flanking, case with arched and hooded door flanked by fluted quarter-columns, base with molded rect panel, molded base and ogee bracket feet, orig printed operating instructions, six month warranty printed in Germany by J. Ritter & Co., Reading to clock maker, Jacob Rota **19,250.00**

Spaulding, Edward, Providence, RI, c1760, Chippendale, mahogany, block and shell carved, bonnet with arched molded cornice, three fluted urn and flame carved finials, arched glazed door, brass engraved dial, "Edward Spaulding/Providence" in arch, brass spandrels, 8 day, calendar aperture and second dial, four fluted columns, waist with arched door centering a block figured mahogany panel and carved shell, molded base with figured front, ogee bracket feet, refinished, numerous minor repairs **27,500.00**

Waterbury Clock Co, Waterbury, CT, 1890, 75″, Victorian, oak case with carved shells, rope columns, and figureheads, cast brass dragons, scrolled dec and rosettes, brass dial and 8 day time and strike weight driven movement, brass weights and pendulum, lower door opening to int. compartment, numerals painted over **1,450.00**

Willard, Aaron, Boston, MA, c1800, 88″, Federal inlaid mahogany, hood with pierced shaped crest centering three brass finials above line inlaid glazed hinged door opening, white painted dial with moon phases, minute and date registers, painted wing spread eagle above inscription "Aaron Willard Boston," brass stop-fluted quarter columns flanking fan inlaid base centering satinwood conch inlaid oval reserve, ogee bracket feet, slight repair to pierced crest, reduced feet . . **46,750.00**

Unknown, European, 1775, 90½″, carved solid oak case, painted black, inscription "M. 1676 S." on upper door, 8-day time and strike, silvered engraved brass dial with attached spandrels, iron weights and period pendulum, case needs regluing, back board replacement, missing feet . . . **3,000.00**

Unknown, New York or New Jersey, c1800, 101½″, Federal inlaid mahogany, molded swan's neck crest centering three brass finials hinged glazed door opening, white painted dial, oval inlaid door on waisted case, inlaid base, shaped feet, restored base and crest **4,675.00**

Unknown, Pennsylvania, 1825, 92½″, cherry case, broken arch hood, turned feet, 30-hour pull up movement, dial and period pendulum, hood surmounted by carved finial from a lyre or banjo clock, ears pieced out on hood, minor paint loss on dial, finial not original, minor repairs **1,700.00**

WALL

Banjo

Curtis & Dunning, Burlington, VT, c1815, 32¾″, mahogany, giltwood case, foliate waist, brass fillets, naval battle **7,000.00**

Howard & Davis, Boston, MA, 1850, 32″, grain painted poplar case, two black and gold tablets with open centers, gilded pendulum rod and

brass bob, paper on zinc dial inscribed by maker, 8 day time movement inscribed "Howard & Davis, Boston," iron weight, orig pendulum, lower glass cracked, weight pan and bottom board replaced . . **800.00**

Howard Type, MA, c1870, 28¾″, walnut, black and gold glasses, painted zinc dial, 8 day time movement, iron weight and pendulum, old replacement glasses, replaced hour hand **450.00**

Little and Eastman, Boston, MA, 1900, 32″, mahogany, brass sidearms, bezel, and eagle finial, two painted tablets, lower tablet Mt Vernon, painted zinc dial, 8 day time movement, lead weight and pendulum, movement stamped "Little and Eastman, Boston," case refinished, replaced finial **500.00**

Low, John J. & Co., Boston, MA, c1828, 39½″, Empire, painted stenciled case, landscape scene, eagle on ball finial **3,000.00**

Seward, J., Boston, MA, 1835, 29½″, gold front, painted tablets, brass side arms and bezel, painted iron dial inscribed "Seward," acorn finial, 8 day time movement with orig weight, cracked throat tablet, finial not original, gilted rope missing . . **1,600.00**

Tifft, Horace, North Attleboro, MA, c1840, 33¼″, mahogany and mahogany veneered case, two black and gold tablets, carved side arms, painted zinc dial inscribed "H Tifft," 8 day time movement with orig weight and pendulum, initials "HT" cast in orig weight, orig finial and plinth, one side arm replaced, replaced lower glass **600.00**

Unknown, MA, 1820, 32″, mahogany case with two painted tablets one "Girard's Bank," painted iron dial inscribed "Zacheus Gates," 8 day time movement with period cast iron weight, brass side arms, bezel and eagle finial, replacements, minor veneer damage **900.00**

Waltham Watch Co, Waltham, MA, 1930, 41″ h, presentation, mahogany case, two painted tablets of George Washington and Mt Vernon, 8 day time weight driven movement marked by maker, deadbeat escapement, period weight and pendulum, engraved painted dial, gilded finials, top finial replaced **1,100.00**

Willard, S., MA, c1820, 11½″ w, 37½″ h, Federal, mahogany and eglomise, giltwood acorn finial, circular glazed door opening to white painted dial, eglomise throat panel depicting female figure of Justice flanked by brass side arms, hinged door centering eglomise panel depicting Neptune and Father Time with inscription "S. Willard's Patent," eglomise panels restored . . . **2,250.00**

Willard School, Boston, 1810, 29½", mahogany case with dovetailed bottom, cross banded frames, 4" movement, painted iron dial, brass bezel and side arms, gilted acorn finial, two painted tablets, period lead weight, dial inscribed "A. Willard," movement inscribed, "Cleaned by E. Taber, 1834,", replaced finial, wheel, and glass, minor veneer damage **1,000.00**

Williams, David, Rhode Island, 1820, 34", mahogany case, two modern tablets, painted iron dial, 8 day "A frame" movement, brass finial, sidearms, bezel, sgd repainted dial, replacements, repainted, and reveneered **900.00**

Wall, calendar, Ingraham, mosaic, rosewood case, 30″ l, $850.00.

Calendar

Ansonia Brass & Copper Co., Ansonia, CT, 1875, 26", round drop, rosewood veneer case, turned wood bezel, dial inscribed by maker and "Terry's Patent," black and gold tablet, turned finials, 8 day time and strike movement, attached calendar mechanism, one finial replacement, re-veneered lower door **900.00**

Gilbert, William, Winsted, CT, c1890, 37", Observatory model, solid oak, pressed designs, black and gold dec upper tablet, paper on zinc dial, 8 day time movement with period pendulum, orig paper label on back, upper glass flaking, lower glass replaced **225.00**

Ithaca Calendar Clock Co., Ithaca, NY, 1881, 33", walnut case with bracket, molding, carved crest, 8 day time and strike movement, calendar dial and mechanism, 5" time dial, 7" calendar dial, orig paper instruction label, sgd label and calendar dial, replacements, loose hood molding **1,000.00**

New Haven Clock Co, New Haven, CT, 1890, 33", regulator, long drop, pressed oak case, "Regulator" tablet, paper on zinc dial with calendar, paper label, 8 day time movement, pendulum and calendar gear missing **275.00**

Prentise, Empire, walnut, 60 day, two springs **1,875.00**

Waterbury Clock Co., Waterbury, CT, 39½", oak case, pressed and reeded dec, turned finials, two painted zinc dials inscribed, "Pat. July 30th 1889" on calendar dial, paper label, 8 day time and strike movement with large brass bob . . **950.00**

Cuckoo

American Clock Co., Philadelphia, PA, c1930, 17 x 14 x 7½", Victorian, carved wood case, carved spread eagle at top, red, blue, and black painted cuckoo, 8 day brass movement **150.00**

Keebler Clock Co., Philadelphia, PA, 1920, 5 x 4 x 1¾", pressed log design, leaves, flowers, nest of birds, brass spring pendulum **75.00**

Kroeber, F., c1888, 18", walnut case, brass movement, two weights, pendulum **250.00**

Gallery

Ingraham, 12", chestnut, 8 day **250.00**

Sempire, No 8, 21⅛", electric, oak . **265.00**

Thomas, Seth, Wardroom, c1905, 5½" d **225.00**

Girandole, Lemuel Curtis, 1815, 13½" w, 46" h, Federal, eglomise and giltwood mahogany, giltwood spread wing eagle finial above metal circular hinged door mounted with spherules, opening to gilt and white painted dial with inscription "L. Curtis, Patent," eglomise throat panel dec with standing female figure above spread wing American eagle, shield, and flag above tomb inscription "Washington, Lawrence, Ludlow, Durrows," gilt metal sidearms flanking, circular eglomise panel below dec with allegorial scene of female figure on boat with gentleman in background, giltwood acanthus form pendant below, slight repair to pendant, lower eglomise panel repainted **19,800.00**

Lantern, England, 1700, pierced and engraved dolphin frets, engraved brass dial and alarm dial, 30 hour time and alarm, 1 handed movement converted to anchor escapement, period pendulum and lead weight, replaced bell escapement and side doors, unpolished surface, 16" **1,700.00**

Lyre
   Ives, Joseph, c1840, 38¼", elaborately carved and gilted Lyre front, gilted dial with raised dec panel, entire clock is very ornate, brass 8 day time and strike movement, dial replaced, upper glass replaced, lower door hinge replaced **5,000.00**
   Sawin, John, Boston, MA, 1830, 36½", carved mahogany case, brass bezel, painted iron dial inscribed "Sawin," eagle finial, painted tablet, 8 day weight driven time movement, replaced finial and plinth, refinished and reglued, some replacements **1,000.00**

Mirror
   Dewey, I, Chesea, VT, c1830, 44¾", wood case, scroll crest, three urn finials, 8 day **2,500.00**
   Ives, Joseph, 36½", wood case, pineapple finials, carved capitals with fluted columns, scenic panel below mirror, wood movement **1,500.00**
   Unsigned, NH, 1820, 30", half round gilted and black painted columns, brass rosettes in corners, mirror in lowers section, primitive tablet of rose and trefoil leaf motif, 8 day time and strike brass weight driven movement, rat trap striking mechanism, orig dial, dovetailed case . **3,750.00**

Miscellaneous
   Jerome, C., New Haven, CT, 1860, 21¾", rosewood veneered case, rippled molding, carved dec, brass pendulum, painted zinc dial, 8 day time fusee movement, blue paper

maker's label, case needs regluing, veneer loss and damage, paint touch-up on dial **900.00**
   New Haven Clock Co., New Haven, CT, 1875, 35¼", Winnipeg model, Victorian, walnut case, turned finials, 8 day time and strike movement, painted zinc dial, brass pendulum bob, orig maker's label on back of case, orig glass on door with painted dec **650.00**

Regulator
   Ansonia Clock Co., CT, 1880, 49¼", walnut case, carved and reeded dec, porcelain dial with maker's trademark, brass pendulum and regulator gauge, 2-weight time movement, two period brass weights, replacements, refinished case **800.00**
   Chelsea Clock Co, Boston, MA, 1920, 38", #2 Model, walnut case, painted zinc dial with seconds indicator inscribed by maker, 8 day movement with deadbeat escapement and maintaining power, orig pendulum, weights missing **1,000.00**
   Howard, E., #70, oak, 8 day, weight, time only **1,250.00**
   New Haven, Prussian Oak, 51½", 90 day **600.00**
   Terry, S. B., Plymouth, CT, 1835, 34½", mahogany case, turned wood bezel opens to painted wood dial, crotch mahogany panel lower door opens to paper label, 8 day weight driven time movement, round front plate, sgd label, replaced weight, replaced upper glass, minor veneer damage **3,500.00**
   Thomas, Seth, Thomaston, CT, 1900, 36", #2 Model, quality oak case, molded bracket, paper label on case int., painted zinc dial with seconds indicator and maker's name, 8 day time weight driven movement, brass pendulum, deadbeat escapement and maintaining power, weight missing **700.00**
   Waltham Clock Co, Waltham, MA, 1900, 38", carved walnut case, fine quality movement, deadbeat escapment and maintaining power inscribed "Waltham Clock Co," replaced hands, weights and pendulum missing, case partially stripped **250.00**
   Waterbury, Regulator B24, 83", 8 day, Swiss movement, weight **3,750.00**
   Willard, Jr., A., Boston, MA, 1830, mahogany case with applied rippled moldings, turned laminated

bezel, painted zinc dial, 8 day banjo
type movement, orig lead weight,
sq pendulum rod, replaced weight
pan, minor touch-up on dial **1,400.00**
School House
Atkins Clock Co., Bristol, CT, 1855,
25" h, 17" w, rosewood veneer case,
octagonal shape top, rippled molding around edge, lower door with
black and gold glass, 30 day fusee
time and strike movement, orig label, missing ivory knob on lower
door **2,000.00**
Gilbert, Wm. L., 26¾", Standard Ad-
miral, oak case, 8 day strike **325.00**
Imperial, Regulator No 4T120E,
34½", electric, oak finish **425.00**
New Haven, 24", 12" Mosaic Drop,
octagon top, 8 day **250.00**
Thomas, Seth, Litchfield, 31", mahog-
any finish, 30 day, spring Graham
deadbeat escapement **525.00**
Waterbury, 27¾", English Drop No 2,
calendar, veneered oak case **450.00**
Wag on Wall
Dutch, 19th C, oak case, removable
hood, arched glazed door, painted
iron dial, 30-hour movement, pendulum, three pressed brass paint
dec finials, case needs regluing,
window broken, missing pendulum,
weights, hands, brass mount and
side windows **750.00**
English, B. Gray and J. Vulliamy, Lon-
don, 1750, engraved brass, makers' names inscribed on boss in
arch, single hand and alarm indicator, 30 hour weight driven time
and alarm movement with crown
wheel escapement, old brass
weight, movement protected in
later tin case, orig dust protectors
missing, 7½" **1,500.00**

CLOISONNÉ

History: Cloisonné is the art of enameling on
metal. The design is drawn on the metal body;
wires, which follow the design, are glued or soldered on the body. The cells thus created are
packed with enamel and fired; this step is repeated
several times until the level of enamel is higher
than the wires. A buffing and polishing process
brings the level of enamels flush to the surface of
the wires.

This art form has been practiced in various
countries since 1300 B.C. and in the Orient since
the early 15th century. Most cloisonné found today
is from the late Victorian era, 1870–1900, and was
made in China and Japan.

**Vase, extended outward tapering neck,
robin's egg blue on body and collar,
shield designs with phoenix's and abstract serpents, cartouche designs on
top of body, 9½" h, $750.00.**

Beaker, 19½", spheroid body, stepped
foot, long flaring neck, galleried rim,
brocade dec, green ground, Japa-
nese, mid 19th C, pr **800.00**
Bowl
2½ x 8", yellow dragons, flaming pearl
around rim and int. black ground,
brass stand **125.00**
12" d, 3½" h, turned in rim, marine
blue, variety of large lotus blossoms, clusters of small circle cloisonnes, cobalt border with silk-
worm cloisonnes, overlapping
pomegranates on bottom, un-
marked Chinese **400.00**
Brush Pot, 5", asters and butterfly dec,
light blue ground, sgd "Takeuchi,"
Japanese, c1875 . . . . **200.00**
Button, black and white flying birds, red
ground, brass base **65.00**
Censer, 10" l, bear form, crouching, inlaid turquoise eyes, white ground
body with geometric multicolored
black, brown, and pastel enamel
whorls, bear form lid, Chinese, c1990,
pr **1,870.00**
Charger, 10¾", geometric border, red
roses, pink daisies, blue flowers and
butterflies, green leaves, turquoise
ground **335.00**
Cigarette Case, green, three dragons,
multicolored, Chinese **125.00**
Figure, 22¾", horse, enameled body,
multicolored, turquoise ground,
molded collar, gilt metal mane, re-

movable saddle and blanket, standing on stylized wood base, pr **1,250.00**

Humidor, 5¾ x 8", cov, multicolored flowers, brick red ground, light blue border, double "T" fret cloisonnes, figural brass Foo dog finial, ornate teakwood base **225.00**

Incense Burner, multicolored floral dec, cobalt blue ground, three cobalt blue round feet, cut out butterflies on brass lid **225.00**

Jardiniere, 12½", turquoise, flowering branches, butterflies, birds, gilt rim, Chinese, early 19th C **250.00**

Libation Cup, 5½" l, figural ram's head, blue, multicolored swirl and dragon design **225.00**

Plate, 9¾", marine blue, 2 white cranes in scenic terrain, peonies, foliage, etc, unmarked, Japanese **300.00**

Potpourri Jar, cov, 4¼", 4⅛", panels around top, multicolored with flowers and butterflies, black, gold, and blue below with flowers, Japanese **265.00**

Sauceboat, green handle, turquoise artichoke dec, marked "China" **115.00**

Stamp Box, 4¼" l, green, multicolored flowering branch **25.00**

Sugar, 4½", handle, black, multicolored, yellow dragons **85.00**

Tea Jar, 4⅝", bulbous, Totai, cobalt, multicolored flowers, large reserves of flowers, butterfly and bird, sgd, c1870, 3 pcs **300.00**

Teapot, cov, 4½" h, 4½" w, tree bark ground, dragon, artist sgd, Japanese **365.00**

Temple Jar, cov, 13" h, 24" d, black ground, 2 yellow five-toes dragons fighting over flaming pearl, blue, red, white, and pink **400.00**

Tile, 5¾" h, 4¼" w, Totai, cobalt, multicolored, bird, flower, diapering, sgd "Kinkozan," imp "c1870" **225.00**

Vase
3¾", bulbous, gold stone, floral and scrolled leaf, reserves of butterflies, floral, Japanese, unmarked **110.00**

5", blue ground, Japanese lady among butterflies and leaves, Japanese, 19th C **475.00**

9¾", shield shape panels, exotic dragons, blue ground, green and goldstone dec, small butterflies around top, Japanese **400.00**

10½", pr, bluebirds, clouds **600.00**

12" h, flared body, tapering neck, sq base, two applied handles, late 19th C **200.00**

21" h, sq baluster body, high foot, birds, flowers, and insects, bright blue ground, Japanese, 19th C .. **450.00**

29" h, pr, baluster form, overall trailing flowers, black ground, mounted as lamps, Chinese **750.00**

CLOTHING

History: While museums and a few private individuals have collected clothing for decades, it is only recently that collecting clothing has achieved a widespread popularity. Clothing reflects the social attitudes of an historical period.

Christening and wedding gowns abound and, hence are not in large demand. Among the hardest items to find are men's clothing from the 19th and early 20th centuries. The most sought after clothing is by designers, such as Fortuny, Poirret, and Vionnet.

Note: Condition, size, age, and completeness are critical factors in purchasing clothing. Collectors divide into two groups: those collecting for aesthetic and historic value and those desiring to wear the garment. Prices are higher on the west coast; major auction houses focus on designer clothes and high fashion items.

References: Maryanne Dolan, *Vintage Clothing 1880–1960*, Second Edition, Books Americana, 1987; Tina Irick-Nauer, *The First Price Guide to Antique and Vintage Clothes*, E.P. Dutton, 1983; Sheila Malouff, *Clothing With Prices*, Wallace-Homestead, 1983; Terry McCormich, *The Consumer's Guide To Vintage Clothing*, Dembner Books, 1987; Diane McGee, *A Passion For Fashion: Antique, Collectible, and Retro Clothes*, Simmons-Boardman Books, 1987.

Periodical: *Vintage Clothing Newsletter*, P.O. Box 1422, Corvallis, OR 97339.

Collectors' Club: The Costume Society of America, P.O. Box 761, Englishtown, NJ 07726.

Museums: Los Angeles County Museum (Costume and Textile Dept.), Los Angeles, CA; Metropolitan Museum of Art, New York, NY; Museum of Costume, Bath, England; Philadelphia Museum of Art, Philadelphia, PA; Smithsonian Institution (Inaugural Gown Collection), Washington, D.C.

Additional Listings: See *Warman's Americana & Collectibles* for more examples.

Blouse
Cotton, lace, high neck **70.00**

Silk, brocade, embroidered, Chinese kimono style **100.00**

Silk, taffeta, pale green, handmade bobbin lace trim, 1900 .... **400.00**

Bodice, satin, beige, fully lined, nine satin-lace covered buttons, pleated tail-back, 22" fitted waist line, 9½" ruffled cuff trim, semi-high neckline, lace overlay **25.00**

Cape
Brocade, black, 3" jet beaded neck band, 2" tassels at hem **75.00**

Blouse, evening, turquoise sequins, $20.00.

Gauze, black, stenciled foliate scrolls, tied at shoulders, hem threaded with striped Venetian glass beads, Fortuny, 36″ l **400.00**

Satin, evening, semi-circular, hip length, ivory, brocade poppies, pink satin lining, ruffled pink and ivory silk organdy trim, ivory ostrich feather neck dec **200.00**

Chemise, silk, cream, Valenciennes lace trim, garlands of flowers embroidered in French knots, V neck, pale yellow ribbon **275.00**

Christening Dress, cotton, white, eyelet inset and trim, 1920–30 .... **40.00**

Coat, lady's

Brocade, evening, bat-wing shape, gold leaf and flower design, collared V neck, appliqued scroll embroidered closures, c1915 ...... **200.00**

Gabardine, lavender-gray, flaring form, panels of blue and gray silk, floral embroidery, gray rabbit fur collar **120.00**

Leather, wrap style, lavender, long, tie belt, cuffed dolman sleeves, slash pockets, irid taffeta lining **125.00**

Wool twill, blue, single breasted, wide lapels, slightly fitted waist, two clear plastic buttons, two false pockets, 15″ w at shoulders, 40″ l, designed by Galanos **25.00**

Dress

Day

Cotton, turquoise, high neck, lace inserts, ruffled sleeves, 1895 .. **200.00**

Rayon, pink, blue piping, padded shoulders, 1935–45 .... **35.00**

Silk, irid green, lace trim, handmade, 1890–1900 .... **225.00**

Evening

Chiffon, brown and beige, velvet and rhinestone appliques, matching scarf, 1925–30 ..... **85.00**

Gabardine, royal blue, net and silk satin, self-colored piping, white lace, black velvet trim, 1890–1900 .... **225.00**

Lace, silk, 2 piece, nile green, long waisted, snug fitting bodice, layered rows of ruffled skirt, hip length jacket, 1928 .... **50.00**

Silk, pleated, black, dolman sleeves, V neck, black, white, and blue Venetain glass beads, Fortuny, 57″ l **2,000.00**

Taffeta, black, sequin flowers, label "Jeanne Lanvin, Paris Hiver," 1938–39 .... **325.00**

Jacket

Cotton, calico print, brown and white, pearl buttons, 1900 .... **40.00**

Fur, brown fox, label "Henry Marshall, Brooklyn," 1940–50 .... **250.00**

Silk, irid blue moire, full-length sleeves and cording, c1855 ..... **70.00**

Wool, pinstripe, black and white, silk lined, 1910–20 .... **55.00**

Robe

Gauze, black, gilt foliate scrolls and medallions, Fortuny, 44″ l **1,000.00**

Silk, blue ground, eight couched gold dragons chasing flaming pearls, stylized clouds and bats, boashan haishui band at hem, Chinese, mid 19th C **1,700.00**

Skirt

Cotton, cord, white, Victorian **40.00**

Felt, gray, velvet embroidered border, c1880 .... **40.00**

Satin, red, peasant-type, black velvet stripes, braiding, lace apron, 1906 **100.00**

Smoking Jacket, velvet, brown, silk quilted collar, cuffs, and pockets, silk lined, 1900–10 .... **75.00**

Suit, lady's

Gabardine, red, padded shoulders, 1940 .... **50.00**

Rayon, white and black print, padded shoulders, peplum, 1935 .... **65.00**

Sweater

Cashmere, black, fox collar, 1960–70 **80.00**

Knit, cream, pastel floral embroidery and beads, 1960–65 ..... **45.00**

Orlon, white, rabbit collar, 1960–70 . **60.00**

Tuxedo, wool, black, cutaway coat, pants button in front, 1900–10 .... **100.00**

Uniform, Red Cross, lady's, summer, light blue cotton seersucker dress, buttoned to hem, Red Cross insignia and rank badge on pocket, matching cap, size 20, accompanied by postcard with black and white photo of

owner, pencil inscription on back,
1944 . . . .   **35.00**

CLOTHING ACCESSORIES

References: Rod Dyer & Ron Spark, *Fit To Be
Tied: Vintage Ties Of The Forties And Early Fifties*,
Abbeville, 1987; Evelyn Haetig, *Antique Combs &
Purses*, Gallery Graphics Press, 1983; Richard
and Teresa Holiner, *Antique Purses*, Second Edition, Collector Books, 1987.
Additional Listings: See *Warman's Americana
& Collectibles* for more examples.

**Shawl, Egyptian motif, sterling silver
woven into net, 72″ l, 24″ w,
$125.00.**

Apron, cotton, hand sewn, patchwork
design, waist length, ties **25.00**
Bonnet, baby, newborn, crochet, ribbon
insert **15.00**
Fan
14″ w, deep purple–blue feathers,
spreading floral spray with small robin painted pink, red, and white,
green leaves, pierced ivory sticks
and guards **35.00**
15½″ w, Spanish lace, enameled center organdy cartouche with painted
scene titled "El Caemarrero," faux
MOP gilt and rose pique sticks and
guards, paper label inscribed "Aleixandre" **35.00**
16″ w, green silk and white net
shaped ground, green silk leaf bordered with gilt sequin flowerheads,
gilt dec edges, gilt pique faux ivory
guards and sticks, minor damages
and discoloration, Continental . . .   **35.00**
16½″ w, faux tortoiseshell, brown silk
ribbon **20.00**
Gloves, pr
Infants, leather, white kidskin, silvered
metal button snap, imp "Dent's,"
4¾″ l **25.00**
Handbag, evening, faille, black, marcasite set mount, green onyx monogram, c1930 . . . .   **60.00**
Hat
Braid, shiny, black, sweetheart brim,

black ribbon trim, label "Bullocks
Wilshire" **35.00**
Felt, skull cap, black, elaborate ostrich trim, French, label "Lorelei Designs" **25.00**
Milan Braid, garden, black, ecru appliques, black feather edged ribbon
trim **25.00**
Shoe, leather
Child's, two tone, Freed Bros, c1900   **65.00**
Lady's, black, high button **50.00**
Spats, men's, gray **20.00**

COALPORT

History: In the mid-1750s Ambrose Gallimore
established a pottery at Caughley in the Severn
Gorge, Shropshire, England. Several other potteries, e.g., Jackfield, developed in the area.
About 1795 John Rose and Edward Blakeway
built a pottery at Coalport, a new town founded
along the right-of-way of the Shropshire Canal.
Other potteries located adjacent to the canal were
those of Walter Bradley and Anstice, Horton, and
Rose. In 1799 Rose and Blakeway bought the
"Royal Salopian China Manufactory" at Caughley.
In 1814 this operation was moved to Coalport.
A bankruptcy in 1803 led to refinancing and a
new name, John Rose and Company. In 1814
Anstice, Horton, and Rose was acquired. The
South Wales potteries at Swansea and Nantgarw
were added. The expanded firm made fine quality,
highly decorated ware. The plant enjoyed a renaissance in the 1888 to 1900 period.
World War I, decline in trade, and shift of the
pottery industry away from the Severn Gorge
brought hard times to Coalport. In 1926 the firm,
now owned by Cauldon Potteries, moved from
Coalport to Shelton. Later owners included Crescent Potteries, Brain & Co., Ltd., and finally, in
1967, Wedgwood.
References: Susan and Al Bagdade, *Warman's
English & Continental Pottery & Porcelain, 1st Edition*, Warman Publishing Co., Inc., 1987; Michael
Messenger, *Coalport 1795-1926*, Antique Collectors' Club, 1990.
Additional Listings: Indian Tree Pattern.

Bough Pot, 11½″ h, hp landscape scene
with two British soldiers, gilt floral dec,
yellow ground, c1809 . . . .   **350.00**
Compote, 12″ d, round, pedestal on sq
ft, gilt scroll molded rim, flower sprays

Plate, ecru ground, gold dec, bell flower bands, scalloped edges, raised wreath and impressed mark, 9½″ d, $35.00.

within, gilt and foliage surrounds, red
  ground, c1830 . . . .   450.00
Cup and Saucer, Harebell pattern 25.00
Dish, leaf shape, apple green, garden
  flower bouquet, gilt foliage, c1820 . .   90.00
Figure, 4½″ h, Doris, marked "Coalport"   45.00
Ginger Jar, cov, Blue Willow pattern . .   70.00
Plate, 9″, pink roses, green garlands,
  heavy gold, artist sgd, made for Davis
  Collamore, NY 90.00
Soup Plate, 10″ d, flowering branch centering oval reserve, gilt scalloped rim,
  burgundy band 20.00
Spill Vase, 5″, set of 3, pink, garden
  flowers and gilt scroll bands, bird's
  head handles with gilt rings, flared
  rim, sq base, c1830 . . . .   875.00
Tureen, 12½″, cov, iron red, yellow and
  gilt scattered flower sprays, gilt handles, flowerhead finial, c1850 . . . . .   400.00
Vase, 7″, waisted, pierced lip dec with
  leaf sprays and applied flowerheads,
  body with gilt highlighted leaf scrolls
  which form pierced handles, painted
  butterflies and floral sprays, magenta
  glazed lower section, scroll molded
  foot, quatrefoil base, underglaze blue
  mark 165.00

COCA-COLA ITEMS

History: The originator of Coca-Cola was John Pemberton, a pharmacist from Atlanta, Georgia. In 1886 Dr. Pemberton introduced a patent medicine to relieve headaches, stomach disorders, and other minor maladies. Unfortunately, his failing

health and meager finances forced him to sell his interest.

In 1888 Asa G. Candler became the sole owner of Coca-Cola. Candler improved the formula, increased the advertising budget, and widened the distribution. Accidentally, a "patient" was given a dose of the syrup mixed with carbonated water instead of still water. The result was a tastier, more refreshing drink.

As sales increased in the 1890s, Candler recognized that the product was more suitable for the soft drink market and began advertising it as such. From these beginnings a myriad of advertising items have been issued to invite all to "Drink Coca-Cola."

Dates of interest: "Coke" was first used in advertising in 1941. The distinctive shaped bottle was registered as a trademark on April 12, 1960.

References: Deborah Goldstein Hill, *Wallace-Homestead Price Guide to Coca-Cola Collectibles,* Wallace Homestead, 1983; Allan Petretti, *Petretti's Coca-Cola Collectibles Price Guide,* The Nostalgia Company, 1989; Al Wilson, *Collectors Guide To Coca-Cola Items, Volume I,* (revised: 1987) and *Volume II,* (1987), L-W Book Sales.

Collectors' Club: The Coca-Cola Collectors Club International, P.O. Box 546, Holmdel, NJ 07733.

Museum: Schmidt's Coca-Cola Museum, Elizabethtown, KY.

Additional Listings: See *Warman's Americana & Collectibles* for more examples.

Change Tray, Elaine, 1917, 4⅜ x 6⅛″, $55.00.

Apothecary Jar and Bottle Set 200.00
Bank, 5½″, metal, figural vending ma-
  chine, red paint 70.00
Bingo Game, 7 x 14″ box, red and white,
  c1940 . . . .   25.00
Bookmark, Lillian Russel, 1904 . . . . .   70.00

Bottle Carrier, 6 unused bottles, removable lucite protector, 1929 .... 110.00
Bottle Opener, sword shape, emb "Drink Bottled Coca-Cola" 18.00
Calendar
1921, 12 x 31", "Girl in Garden" ... 250.00
1933, 12 x 30", "The Village Blacksmith" 175.00
Carrying Case, salesman's samples, 1939 .... 75.00
Cigarette Box, glass, frosted, 50th Anniversary, 1936 .... 210.00
Clock, 16 x 16", wood frame, sq, 1939 90.00
Doll, Santa Claus, 15", vinyl, 1958 ... 40.00
Door Handle, 8" l, plastic, 3 dimensional 28.00
Fan, cardboard, wood handle, "Save With Ice," 1915 .... 65.00
Glass, 6 oz, acid etched, 1935 ...... 15.00
Hat, Soda Jerk, cloth, c1920 .... 10.00
Ink Blotter, 4 x 9", cardboard, red and white, c1930 .... 12.00
Jump Rope, 4" wood handles, inscribed "Drink Coca-Cola in Bottles, Pure as Sunlight," c1930 .... 20.00
Knife, pocket, Chicago World's Fair, 1933 .... 30.00
Menu Board, wood and masonite, 1939 90.00
Mirror, 1¾ x 2¾", celluloid, aqua blue ground, black letters, red "Icy-O" logo, black soda dispenser, red and white Coca-Cola bottle, made by Parisian Novelty, Chicago 500.00
Napkin, paper, matted, c1911 .... 35.00
Notebook, 3 ring, Sales Management Conference, 1958 .... 15.00
Pencil Sharpener, figural, cast iron, Germany 75.00
Perfume Bottle, miniature, glass, 1930 25.00
Pocket Mirror, oval, Elaine, 1916 .... 100.00
Postcard, Bottling Plant, 1910 ...... 40.00
Pretzel Dish, 8" d, aluminum, three aluminum 4" h Coke bottles around sides, 50th Anniversary, Brunhoff Mfg Co, 1936 .... 75.00
Radio, 8", bottle shaped, plastic case, made in Hong Kong 30.00
Ruler, wood, "Compliments The Coca-Cola Bottling Company," reverse side "The Golden Rule," 1940 .... 5.00
Safety Marker, 1900 .... 125.00
Sign
Bottle, 35", figural, tin, 1923 ...... 85.00
Cheerleader, 15 x 27", cardboard frame, 1944 .... 80.00
Triangle, advertisement on 2 sides, porcelain, 1935 .... 300.00
Thermometer, 30", tin, bottle shape, 1958 .... 30.00
Tie Clip, metal, enamel, "All Star Dealer Campaign Award," 1950s 30.00
Thimble, aluminum, "Drink Coca-Cola in Bottles" 25.00

Tray
1905, 10½ x 13¼", oval, "In Bottles/At Fountain" 850.00
1907, Relieves Fatigue, change ... 325.00
1914, Betty, 10½ x 13¼" 350.00
1921, Autumn Girl, 10½ x 13¼" ... 425.00
1934, couple on beach 325.00
1939, Spring Board Girl, Sunblom, artist, 14 x 10" 50.00
1958, picnic cart, 13½ x 19" 15.00

COFFEE MILLS

History: Coffee mills or grinders are utilitarian objects designed to grind fresh coffee beans. Before the advent of stay-fresh packaging, coffee mills were a necessity.

The first home size coffee grinders were introduced about 1890. The large commercial grinders designed for use in stores, restaurants, and hotels often bear an earlier patent date.

Reference: Terry Friend, *Coffee Mills,* Collector Books, 1982.

Crescent Mfg Co, Louisville, KY, wooden body, metal handle and grinder, marked "Crescent #705, Superior Coffee Mill," $65.00.

COUNTERTOP (COMMERCIAL)

Fairbanks-Morse, two wheels, white paint, brass finial, 38" h 350.00
Landers, Frary, Clark, New Britain, CT, 1901, 12" h 450.00
Woodruff and Edwards Co, cast iron, adv, "Elgin National Coffee," 14⅞" wheel, 24" h 325.00

FLOOR MODELS (COMMERCIAL)

Enterprise Mfg Co, 72", mint condition   **1,300.00**
Star Mill, brass urn top, iron wheels,
  works, and base, orig scoop, marked
  "Star Mill/Philadelphia," 43½" h **700.00**

LAP (DOMESTIC)

Delmew, Simons Hardware, St. Louis .   **75.00**
Elma, tin, wood handles **35.00**
Kendrick, cast iron, brass name plate,
  porcelain lined cup, iron drawer . . .   **75.00**
Universal 109, tin, Pat Feb 14, 1905,
  Landers, Frary, Clark **50.00**

TABLE (DOMESTIC)

Challenge Fast Grinder, wooden base,
  drawer, cast iron hopper, crank, and
  handle, wooden base, 6½ x 6½ x 7½"   **80.00**
Grand Union Tea Co, cast iron **175.00**
Hobart, aluminum hopper, electric . . .   **150.00**
Wrights Hardware Co, black and gold
  decal "Brighton Coffee Mill; Manufactured by Wrights Hardware Company," base and top 6½ x 6½", box
  5¾ x 5¾ x 5½", grinding mechanism
  by Logan & Strobridge **60.00**

WALL (DOMESTIC)

Grand Union Tea, red tin, adv, gold trim,
  cast iron grinder **90.00**
Lunbrack, Czechlovokia **70.00**
Mystic, tin "V" shaped hopper, cast iron
  grinder **25.00**
National Specialty Co, Philadelphia,
  cast iron, orig red scroll, gilt dec . . .   **85.00**
Parker, #50, cast iron, black, tin emb
  eagle **50.00**

COIN OPERATED ITEMS

History: Coin operated items include amusement games, pinball, jukeboxes, slot machines, vending machines, cash registers and other items operated by coins.

The first jukebox was developed about 1934 and played 78 RPM records. Jukeboxes were important parts of teenage life before the advent of portable radios and television.

The first pinball machine was introduced in 1931 by Gottlieb. Pinball machines continued to be popular until the advent of solid state games in 1977 and advanced electronic video games.

The first three-reel slot machine, the Liberty Bell, was invented in 1905 by Charles Fey in San Francisco. In 1910, Mills Novelty Company copyrighted the classic fruit symbols. Improvements and ad-

vancements have lead to the sophisticated machines of today.

Vending machines for candy, gum, and peanuts, were popular from 1910 until 1940 and can be found in a wide range of sizes and shapes.

Because of the heavy usage these coin operated items received, many are restored and at the very least have been repainted by either the operator or manufacturer. Using reproduced mechanisms to restore pieces is acceptable in many cases, especially when the restoration will be able to perform as originally intended.

References: Jerry Ayliffe, *American Premium Guide To Jukeboxes And Slot Machines, Gumballs, Trade Stimulators, Arcade,* Books Americana, 1985; Richard Bueschel, *Pinball I: Illustrated Historical Guide To Pinball Machines, Volume I,* Hoflin Publishing Ltd., 1988; Richard Bueschel, *Slots 1: Illustrated Guide to 100 Collectible Slot Machines, Volume 1,* Hoflin Publishing Ltd., 1989; Nic Costa, *Automatic Pleasures: The History Of The Coin Machine,* Kevin Francis Publishing Ltd., 1988; Bill Enes, *Silent Salesmen: An Encyclopedia Of Collectible Gum, Candy & Nut Machines,* published by author, 1987; Stephen K. Loots, *The Official Victory Glass Price Guide To Antique Jukeboxes, 1988 (Third) Edition,* Jukebox Collector Newsletter, 1988.

Periodical: *Coin-Op Newsletter,* 909 26th Street, N. W., Washington, DC 20037; *Jukebox Collector Newsletter,* 2545 SE 60th Street, Des Moines, IA 50317.

Additional Listings: See *Warman's Americana & Collectibles* for separate categories for Jukeboxes, Pinball Machines, Slot Machines, and Vending Machines.

GAME

Bally Hoo, amusement, tilted wood
  case, glass top, plunger at front,
  31" l **75.00**
Challenger, target practice, 10 shots for
  1¢, ABT Mfg Corp, Chicago, USA, or-
  ange, black, and gold, key **275.00**
Foxhunt, pinball, 5¢, 65 x 21 x 51", Pat
  1936, orig instruction card, 1940 . . .   **175.00**
Kiss-o-Meter, 5¢, Exhibit Supply Co,
  c1930 . . . .   **450.00**
Play Football, arcade, Chester Pollard
  Amusement Co, c1924 . . . .   **800.00**
Select-Em, dice game, Exhibit Supply
  Co, Chicago **275.00**
Uncle Sam Grip Test, Caille, 1¢, 1910,
  restored **3,200.00**

JUKEBOX

Seeburg
  Model P148, light up side columns,
    top changes colors with revolving

lights, blue glass mirrored tile front,
5 plays for a quarter, 1948 ..... **1,450.00**
Wurlitzer
Model 850, peacock front, restored . **6,500.00**
Model 1015, bubble tubes framing
glazed front, veneered wood case,
50" h, c1947 .... **2,700.00**
Model 1650, 48 selections, 55" h, light
up side columns, 1954 .... **500.00**

**Slot Machine, The Puritan Ball, nickel
play, 9⅛" d, 7⅜" w, 10 1 /4" h,
$135.00.**

SLOT MACHINE

Bally Reserve, 5¢, award card and key **160.00**
Indian, life size, carved wood with headdress, holding Bursting Cherry slot
machine, 3 reels, restored **2,500.00**
Jennings, Silver Moon, 5, countertop,
1941, restored **1,200.00**
Jubilee, 1, 3 reels, blue, wood sides,
diamond dec on right side **500.00**
Liberty Bell, 5¢, 3 reel, orig red, white,
and blue, decal **160.00**
Mills
The Owl, 5¢, one wheel upright, oak
cabinet carved with owl and foliage
below color wheel, 5 way cast
metal coin head, 64", c1905, restored **7,000.00**
War Eagle, 5¢, 3 reel, double jackpot,
c1931 .... **1,800.00**
Pace, Comet Deluxe, 3 reel, twin jackpots, restored, c1939 .... **1,500.00**
Wattling, Blue Seal, 5¢, 3 reel, double
jackpots, 24", c1932, restored **1,500.00**

VENDING

Adams, 1¢, gum, 10 x 4 x 22½", Art
Deco lady on label **100.00**
Advance, 1¢, peanuts, football style
globe, c1923 .... **140.00**
Columbus, 1¢, Gumball Machine, 15" h,

8" d, cast iron, porcelain paint, light
and dark green, orig key **300.00**
Hawkeye, 1¢, gum, cast metal, 6 sided,
red paint, c1931 .... **120.00**
Lucky Strike Cigarettes, 1¢, Wilson Mfg **800.00**
Mansfield, 5¢, gum, 12" h, 10½" sq,
etched glass front, glass sides **400.00**
Master, 1¢, peanuts, 16" h, 8" sq, cast
metal, red and black paint, complete
with orig keys, c1930s **120.00**
Nut Jewel, 5¢, 2 columns, peanuts,
Lawrence Mfg Co **100.00**
Pulver Yellow Kid, 1¢, gum, clockwork
movement of Yellow Kid with insertion
of penny **550.00**
Stuart & Maguire, 1¢, Art Deco style,
restored **175.00**

MISCELLANEOUS

Cash Register
McCaskey, 23 x 23 x 27", oak, orig
decal of manufacturer, metal account files, 2 drawers below, refinished **150.00**
National, Model 542, brass, keys up
to $99.99, receipt machine at side,
running totals at other side, crank
operated, brass cash drawer, 24" h **600.00**
Fare Box, Jonson, hand crank, patent
1914, restored **225.00**
Hotel Radio, "25 for 2 hours," 14 x 8 x
7½", gray metal case, Corado, c1940 **65.00**
Piano, Seeburg style A, mandolin attachment, oak case with art glass
panel **6,750.00**
Wall Phone, Western Electric, oak, uses
dimes, nickels, and quarters, c1920 . **475.00**

CONTINENTAL CHINA AND PORCELAIN (GENERAL)

History: By 1700 porcelain factories existed in
large numbers throughout Europe. In the mid-18th
century the German factories at Meissen and
Nymphenburg were dominant. As the century
ended, French potteries assumed the leadership
role. The "golden age" of Continental china and
porcelains was from the 1740s to the 1840s.

Americans living in the last half of the 19th century eagerly sought the masterpieces of the European porcelain factories. In the early 20th century this style of china and porcelain was a "blue
chip" among the antiques collectors.

References: Susan and Al Bagdade, *Warman's
English & Continental Pottery & Porcelain, 1st Edition,* Warman Publishing Co, Inc, 1987; Rachael
Feild, *Macdonald Guide To Buying Antique Pottery & Porcelain,* Wallace-Homestead, 1987.

Additional Listings: France—Haviland, Limoges, Old Paris, Sarregeumines, and Sevres; German—Austrian Ware, Bavarian China, Carlsbad China, Dresden/Meissen, Rosenthal, Royal Bayreuth, Royal Bonn, Royal Rudolstadt, Royal Vienna, Schlegelmilch, and Villeroy and Boch; Italy—Capo-di-Monte.

French Faience, plate, green and blue dec, marked, 9⅝″ d, $125.00.

FRENCH

Chantilly
Dish, 8½″, kakiemon palette, c1735 . **400.00**
Snuffbox, 3¼″, heart shape, butterfly on lid, modern gold mounts **250.00**
Faience
Figure, 21″, bisque, nymph, standing, polychrome, curled pale brown hair, wreath of fruiting sprigs, blue sash, floral print drape, tree trunk, mound base, imp factory mark, c1900 . . . **1,000.00**
Jardiniere, 22½″ d, yellow, green, and blue, painted chrysanthemums, scalloped rim **475.00**
Jacob Petit
Clock Case, 15¾′, portrait of French courtesan, sgd, c1840, chips **1,000.00**
Vase, pr, 7″ h, cornucopia shape, multicolored floral garland, green ground, molded foliate scrollwork, shaped rect base with scroll molding and emb floral sprigs and gilt highlighting, underglaze blue "J. P." mark **400.00**
Mennency
Figure, 9″, lady, seated, polychrome and gilt dec, c1755, minor damage **3,300.00**
Gravy Boat, 9″, marked "DVA", 18th C **950.00**
St. Cloud
Bonbonniere, cov, cat form, SS mountings, late 19th C **225.00**
Chamber Pot, cov, 4½″, SS mountings, c1740 . . . . **1,200.00**

Cup and Saucer, pr, trembleuse, c1750 . . . . **600.00**
Samson
Jar, cov, pr, 12¼″ h, armorial porcelain, fitted as lamps, Chinese Export **1,000.00**
Jardiniere, pr, bisque, tapering cylindrical body, relief molded continuous frieze of dancing putti holding floral garland, white foliate scroll border, blue ground, gilt ram's heads, pseudo interlaced L's enclosing AA mark, late 19th C **6,000.00**
Plate, 9″, set of 8, octagonal, porcelain, armorial center, floral dec cavetto, gilded rim, Chinese Export, late 19th C **1,700.00**
Sauce Tureen, cov, 8½″, armorial porcelain, Chinese Export **1,600.00**
Vieux Paris
Clock, 13″ h, vase form, yellow ground, minor chips, c1820 . . . . . **950.00**
Tray, 13½″, sq, mythological dec, iron red factory mark, Duc d'Angouleme factory, c1800 . . . . **450.00**
Vase, pr, 14¾″, floral medallion, lavender ground, handles, sq marble plinth base, mounted as lamp, c1815 . . . . **3,125.00**

GERMAN

Berlin
Plaque, 1-½ x 14¼″, domestic int. scene, painted in the manner of Felix Schlesinger, c1870 . . . . **3,750.00**
Frankenthal
Figure, 8″ h, lyre player, 18th C **475.00**
Tea Service, teapot, milk jug, four cups and saucers, polychrome dec of two lovers, rococo garden ornament, floral sprays, underglaze blue crowned monogram, modeler's, gilder's, and artist's marks, c1762–95 . . . . **3,200.00**
Furtsenberg
Cup and Saucer, purple dec, underglaze blue "F" mark, c1765 . . . . . **500.00**
Plate, pr, 9½″ d, underglaze blue script "F" mark, painted by C G Albert, c1770 . . . . **1,200.00**
Platter, 14″ d, circular, laurel leaves edge band, polychrome bird in tree center, late 18th C **650.00**
Hochst
Figure, 11″, group of lovers, rococo arbor entwined with grapes, underglaze wheel mark, incised triangle, c1765, minor restoration **9,250.00**
Platter, 17½″ l, oval, scrolling handles, pierced border, polychrome

floral spray, underglaze blue wheel
mark **1,700.00**
Sugar Bowl, 6¼" d, Meissen type dec,
polychrome village scene, ran-
domly scattered sprigs and sprays,
underglaze blue crowned wheel
mark **600.00**

Hutschenreuther
Plaque, 4" h, rect, profile portrait of
beauty, long flowing hair, blue drapery, white diaphanous, sgd "Wagner" in lower left corner, imp factory
monogram in circle, ornately
carved gilt wood frame, c1900 . . . **1,000.00**
Portrait Plate, 9⅝" d, Princess de
Lamballe, yellow roses and pink
ribbons in hair, white ruffled dress,
gray ground, imp factory mark, blue
"lamb Dresden 135.K," artist sgd
"Vorberger" **800.00**

Ludwigsburg
Figure, 5", peasant, modeled by
Pierre Francois Lejeune, painted
by D Chr Sausenhofer, underglaze
blue crowned interlaced C's, c1765 **1,100.00**
Teapot, cov, 3½", painted, green,
brown, blue, and iron-red, underglaze blue crowned interlaced C's,
c1765 . . . . **1,100.00**

Nymphenburg
Cup and Saucer, painted large bouquet and scattered sprays, brown
rims, imp shield mark, c1765 . . . . **200.00**

Saxony
Vase, cov, pr, 21½", polychrome floral
dec, applied flowers and putti, gilt
dec, massive floral finial, blue mark,
19th C, slight damage **1,250.00**

Unknown Manufacturer
Plaque, 4 x 5¼", oval, cupid portrait,
tousled brown hair, blue eyes, pale
blue clouds, gilt foliate frame, imp
"12," c1900 . . . . **275.00**
Torcheres, pr, figural, standing bac-
chant holding cornucopia, playful
putti dancing, polychrome and parcel gilt dec, rockwork base, Ba-
roque, late 17th or early 18th C . . **25,000.00**

Volkstedt
Teapot, swelled circular, faint ridging,
dome cov, applied purple berry finial, purple floral sprigs, applied
scroll handle, underglaze blue
crossed pitchforks mark, handle re-
stored, mid 18th C **250.00**

Wallendorf
Figure, pr, 13", Adam and Eve, standing before tree holding forbidden
fruit, white, molded base, blue "W"
mark, c1775 . . . . **525.00**

ITALIAN

Doccia
Charger, 15¾", Imari style, cobalt
blue, iron-red, and gold, branches
of flowering prunus and peonies,
trellis, diaper, and floral panel bor-
ders, c1755 . . . . **300.00**
Cup, U form body, painted scene,
Turk kneeling beside river, gilt edge
cartouche, purple panels, c1750 . **200.00**
Tea Bowl, 3¼", chinoiserie figures,
c1770 . . . . **450.00**

Naples
Ewer, 20", relief dec, bacchic scene
in orchard, female rising from leaf
ornaments handle, late 19th C . . . **350.00**
Vase, pr, 13½", Francis I of Bourbon
and his consort portraits, rubbed
gilding, sgd "Raffaele Giovine,
1823" **6,000.00**

COPELAND

COPELAND AND SPODE

History: In 1749 Josiah Spode apprenticed to
Thomas Whieldon and in 1754 worked for William
Banks in Stoke-on-Trent. In the early 1760s Spode
started his own factory, making cream colored earthenware and blue printed whiteware. In 1770 he
returned to Banks' factory as master, purchasing
it in 1776.

Spode pioneered the use of steam powered pottery making machinery and mastered the art of
transfer printing from copper plates. Spode
opened a London shop in 1778 and sent William
Copeland there about 1784. A number of larger
London locations followed. At the turn of the century Spode introduced bone china. In 1805 Josiah
Spode II and William Copeland entered into partnership for the London business. A series of partnerships between Josiah Spode II, Josiah Spode
III, and William Taylor Copeland resulted.

In 1833 Copeland acquired Spode's London operations and the Stoke plants seven years later.
William Taylor Copeland managed the business
until his death in 1868. The business remained in
the hands of Copeland heirs. In 1923 the plant
was electrified; other modernizations followed.

In 1976 Spode merged with Worcester Royal Porcelain to become Royal Worcester Spode, Ltd.

References: Susan and Al Bagdade, *Warman's English & Continental Pottery & Porcelain, 1st Edition,* Warman Publishing, 1987; D. Drakard & P. Holdway, *Spode Printed Wares,* Longmans, 1983; L. Whiter, *Spode: A History Of The Family, Factory, And Wares, 1733–1833,* Barrie & Jenkins, 1970.

Mug, multicolored transfer titled "The Chase/The First Over," $25.00.

Butter Dish, cov, Spode's Tower, blue, Copeland Spode	60.00
Butter Pat, hunt scene, blue transfer . .	20.00
Creamer, 4", Spode's Tower, blue transfer	48.00
Cup and Saucer, Rosalie	8.00

Dinner Set
  Felspar, 95 pcs, royal blue border outlined with gilt, puce printed Spode Felspar marks, iron-red Pat #3951, c1810 . . . . **1,600.00**
  Indian Tree, service for eight, 51 pcs, cov butter dish, vegetable bowl, 12" pedestal cake plate, Spode **375.00**
Dish, 11½" w, 2 handled, mushroom ground, gilt foliage, gilt scroll molded handles, puce Spode Felspar mark, c1800 . . . . **125.00**

Figure
  17" l, 17½" h, bisque, seated young woman, bending over to mend fishing net draped over her lap, oval base inscribed "Mending The Net," Edward W. Lion, Sculptor, 1873, Art Union of London Copyright Reserved, Copeland L74" **1,750.00**
  21½" h, parianware, barefoot boy wearing breeches and jacket, scarf tied at throat, sickle lying on ground, pointing to letter concealed in tree stump, titled "The Trysting Tree," incised "C Halse, Sc/Pubd

1874," imp "Copeland/Copyright Reserved"	600.00

Jar, cov, 10", globular, handled, Oriental style, apple green, birds on flowering peony branches, iron-red, pink, and gilt, gilt knob finial, Spode mark, Pat #3086, c1820 . . . . **700.00**

Jardiniere, pr, 14 x 10¼", rect gilt bronze frame inset with four porcelain panels, rose ground, transfer printed and enameled reserves of two ladies in 17th C costume, cartouche shaped border, gilt foliate C scrolls with polychrome floral festoons, four gilt bronze bun feet, brass liner, circular factory mark imprinted on each panel "Copeland & Garrett/Late Spode," c1833–47 . . . . **4,400.00**

Jug, 6 /12" d, 8¼" h, bright blue ground, raised ivory figures on front and back, raised leaf trim around top, Copeland, made for Columbian Expo, 1893 . . . **200.00**

Pitcher, 7½" h, deep blue glaze, raised white figures, tavern scenes and berries **210.00**

Plaque, 5" w, turquoise, printed multicolored sporting trophy, gilt scroll and foliage surround, green Copeland mark, late 19th C **30.00**

Plate
  8¾", creamware, pink shell motif, gilt flowering foliage, brown net pattern ground, gilt rim, imp Spode mark, c1820 . . . . **80.00**
  9½", bird perched on snowy branch, holly leaves and berries **100.00**
  10¼" d
Rosalie	13.00
Rose Briar	12.00

Platter
  9½", oval, birds on gnarled tree trunk issuing oriental flowers, peonies, chrysanthemums, and foliage border, imp Copeland Spode oval mark, Pat #4639, 19th C **100.00**
  10½" l, oval, creamware, pierced rim, Spode, marked, c1820 . . . . **75.00**

Potpourri Jar, 10", pierced cov, flared rim and foot, Imari style, flowering plants, gilt knop finial, Spode mark, Pat #967, c1810 . . . . **600.00**

Soup Plate, black transfer printed, multicolored insert and flowering plants, scrolling floral foliage borders, Spode mark, pattern #2148, c1810, set of 12 . . . . **450.00**

Spill Vase, pr, 4¾", flared rims, pale lilac, gilt octagonal panels with portrait of bearded man, band of pearls on rims and bases, Spode, c1820 . . . . **400.00**

Tray, 11½", sq, rose spray center, floral bouquet in corners, blue ground with

gilt scale pattern, Pat #1163, iron-red
Spode, c1800 .... **350.00**
Tureen, cov, matching stand, 13″ h,
compressed baluster, loop handles
and finials, three peonies and fowl,
rocky landscape, marked "Spode
Stone China," mid 19th C **350.00**

COPPER

History: Copper objects, such as kettles, tea
kettles, warming pans, measures, etc., played an
important part in the 19th century household. Outdoors, the apple butter kettle and still were the two
principal copper items. Copper culinary objects
were lined with a thin protective coating of tin to
prevent poisoning. They were relined as needed.

Great emphasis is placed by collectors on
signed pieces, especially those by American
craftsmen. Since copper objects were made
abroad as well, it is hard to identify unsigned examples.

References: Mary Frank Gaston, *Antique Cop-
per*, Collector Books, 1985; Henry J. Kauffman,
Early American Copper, Tin, and Brass, Medill
McBride Co., 1950.

Additional Listings: Arts and Crafts Movement
and Roycroft.

Reproduction Alert: Many modern reproductions also exist.

**Pub Measure, one quart, Georgian,
marked "1826" and "N–P" on spout,
6⅛″ h, $225.00.**

Basin, circular form, loose ring handles,
ftd, Continental, c1890 .... **170.00**
Bed Warmer
35″ l, wrought iron ferule, replaced
wood handle **65.00**
38½″ l, engraved lid, wood handle,
wrought iron ferule, European ... **75.00**

Boiler
23″ l, oval, lid, two handles, inner
strainer, Victorian, mid 19th C ... **425.00**
27″ l, oval, reticulated insert int., impressed diamond seal, two han-
dles, English, mid 19th C **650.00**
Bowl, tooled, 15¼″ d, cast brass handles, Middle Eastern **25.00**
Bucket
Coal, 12″ h, 10″ d, swing and side
handles, German, late 19th C ... **70.00**
Log
Continental, 12″ h, 13″ d, swing
handle, late 19th C **350.00**
English, swing handle, early 19th C **475.00**
Cauldron, 17″ h, 26″ d, tapered form,
wrought iron swing handle, Victorian,
mid 19th C **350.00**
Coal Bucket, 12″ h, tapered form, lid,
swing handle, Victorian, late 19th C **225.00**
Coffee Can, 14″ h, swing handle, En-
glish, late 19th C **325.00**
Creamer, 3¾″ h, luster, polychrome flo-
ral band **65.00**
Crumb Scoop, marked "Manning-Bow-
man Quality" **15.00**
Food Mold, 10″ d, turk's head, geometric design **55.00**
Funnel, 10″ d, Victorian, mid 19th C .. **200.00**
Haystack Measure, 12″ h, dovetailed
construction, marked "gallon" **115.00**
Jardiniere, 11″ d, tapered form, Victorian, late 19th C **210.00**
Jug
9″ h, ribbed form, Victorian, mid 19th
C **225.00**
14½″ h, iron hoop base, Continental,
late 19th C **500.00**
16″ h, Continental **350.00**
Lantern, 15″ h, hexagonal beveled glass
panels, circular handle, 19th C **250.00**
Milk Pail, 12″ h, swing handle, stamped
"1870," Dutch **500.00**
Milk Pitcher, Victorian, mid 19th C
14″ h, tapered, marked "4 Gallons,"
impressed Victorian weights and
measures seal **375.00**
16″ h **700.00**
Pan, 23″ l, rect, two hinged handles,
Victorian, 19th C **425.00**
Planter, 15″ l, oval, two ring handles, ftd,
Victorian, late 19th C **150.00**
Pot, 17½ x 22″, 6½″ h, diamond shape,
lift out rack **190.00**
Sauce Pan, 11½″ l, oval, lid, Victorian,
mid 19th C **250.00**
Skillet, 9″ d, dovetailed, cast iron han-
dle, marked "Solari" and "E.M. 128
S. 5th Ave, NY" **55.00**
Still, 24″ h, domed cauldron, arched
spout, applied armorial crest, two
handles, spigot, English, mid 19th C **375.00**

Stock Pot, 9½″ d, iron swing handle, stamped "A.L.," Victorian, mid 19th C   **500.00**

Tea Kettle
    9¾″ h, dovetailed construction, gooseneck spout, acorn finial, shaped handle **45.00**
    10½″ h, rect, gooseneck spout **100.00**
    12″ h, swivel handle, soldered repair   **100.00**

Teapot, 7½″ h, luster, polychrome enameled floral dec **175.00**

Wash Tub, 13⅓″ h, 27″ w, oval, double handles, American, mid 19th C **20.00**

Weather Vane Figure, 18″ h, crowing rooster **45.00**

CORALENE

History: Coralene is a glass or china object which has the design painted on the surface of the piece and tiny glass colorless beads applied with a fixative. The piece is placed in a muffle which fixes the enamel and sets the beads.

Several American and English companies made glass coralene in the 1880s. Seaweed or coral was the most common design. Other motifs were "Wheat Sheaf" and "Fleur-de-Lis." Most of the base glass was satin finished.

China and pottery coralene, made from the late 1890s to the post WW II era, is referred to as Japanese coralene. The beading is opaque and inserted into the soft clay. Hence, it is only half to three-quarters visible.

Reproduction Alert: Reproductions are on the market, some using an old glass base. The beaded decoration on new coralene has been glued and can be scraped off.

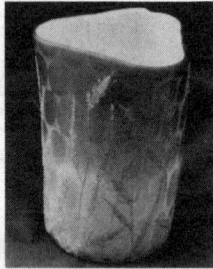

Tumbler, tricorn, satin glass, elongated thumbprint pattern, orange–apricot shaded to white ground, yellow sheaves of wheat coralene, white mother of pearl lining, 3¾″ h, $250.00.

CHINA

Condiment Set, open salt, cov mustard, pepper shaker, white opaque ground, floral coralene dec, SP stand **245.00**

Pitcher, 4½″, 1909 pattern, red and brown ground, beaded yellow daffodil dec **950.00**

Vase
    4¾″, tan, morning glories, cobalt blue trim **130.00**
    7 x 7″, two handles, pedestal, bulbous body, narrow neck, ornate scalloped collar, green, brown, and rust flowers and leaves, red patent applied form mark, Japanese **200.00**
    8″ h, 6¾″ w, melon ribbed, sq top, yellow drape coralene, rose shaded to pink ground, white int. .   **830.00**

GLASS

Bowl, 5½″, ruffled, peachblow **100.00**

Pitcher, 6¼″, Seaweed pattern, shaded yellow, white int. **350.00**

Tumbler, 3¾″, gold coral dec, satin glass, medium to light pink, white int., gold rim **225.00**

Vase
    4½″ h, 3⅜″ d, DQ, MOP, shaded pink, yellow beaded coralene stars in centers of diamonds, white enamel dot beading around top edge **475.00**
    5½″, deep peachblow, satin finish, coral coralene dec **300.00**
    10″, large medallions front and back, pink flowers, two tone green beads, beaded gold swirls **350.00**

CORKSCREWS

History: The corkscrew is composed of three parts: (1) handle, (2) shaft, and (3) worm or screw. The earliest known reference to "a Steele Worme used for drawing corks out of bottles" is 1681. Samuel Henshall, an Englishman, was granted the first patent in 1795.

Elaborate mechanisms were invented and patented from the early 1800s onward, especially in England. However, three basic types emerged: "T" handle (the most basic, simple form), lever, and mechanism. Variations on these three types run into the hundreds. Miniature corkscrews, employed for drawing corks from perfume and medicinal bottles between 1750 and 1920, are among the most eagerly sought by collectors.

Nationalistic preferences were found in corkscrews. The English favored the helix worm and tended to coppertone their steel products. By the mid-18th century English and Irish silversmiths were making handles noted for their clean lines and practicality. Most English silver handles were hallmarked.

The Germans preferred the center worm and nickel plate. The Italians used chrome plate or massive solid brass. In the early 1800s the Dutch and French developed elaborately artistic silver handles.

Americans did not begin to manufacture quality corkscrews until the late 19th century. They favored the center worm and specialized in silver mounted tusks and carved staghorn for handles.

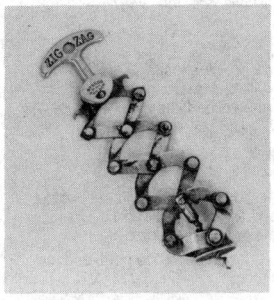

Zig Zag, marked, $70.00.

LEVER

Chrome plated steel, Italian (Vogliotti-Torino), double, wire helix, marked "Japan" and "Christian-Brothers—San Francisco 1908" 125.00
Nickel plated steel, helical worm, stamped "Patent, Weir's Patent 1280425 Sept, 1884/J. Helley & Son Maker" 75.00
Steel, hinged, retractable, scalloped casing, nickel plated corkscrew, marked "The Handy" and "Patented Feb 24, 1891," round shaft with center worm 35.00

MECHANISM

Bronze Frame, rosewood handle with brush, marked "G. Twigg's Patent, c1868 . . . .   400.00
Bone handle, polished, English rack and pinion corkscrew (King's Screw), brush and hanging ring, four plain post open barrel, narrow rack, long wire helix, side handle, sgd "Verinder," c1800 . . . .   400.00
Brass, solid, 4 triangular posts, open cage, uncyphered solid cutworm, probably Italian, c1890 . . . .   220.00
Nickel plated steel, open cage, swivel

over collar on handle to raise shaft, hanging ring, cyphered center worm, German Pat 1892 . . . .   40.00
Wood barrel handle enclosed by metal caps, thick steel cylindrical sheath leading to metal rim stamped "Magic Cork Extractor Pat March 4–79, May 10–92," Mumford 300.00

MINIATURE

Brass, figural elephant, 2″, tail is corkscrew, marked "Perage England, c1930" 30.00
Chrome, two finger pull, wire helix, enamel City of Clacton 25.00
Meissen, porcelain head of Johann Von Schiller (1759–1805), poet and philosopher, uncyphered center worm, head marked with crossed swords under glaze, c1870 . . . .   385.00
Nickel plated cut steel, 3″ peg and worm, fluted wire helix, mid 18th C .   80.00

NOVELTY

Brass, "Old Snifter," Senator Volstead depicted standing, corkscrew and bottle opener, helical worm, fixed hat   200.00
Celluloid, white, lady, figural, folding, helical worm, stamped "Ges. Gech," Germany 525.00
Silver, carved, boar's head, scroll mount, monogrammed, Archimedean screw, nickel plated bell cap 265.00

T-HANDLE

Brass, Thomason type, bone handle with brush, helical worm 150.00
Staghorn handle, 5½″, figural, carved horsehead with flowing mane and spirited glass eyes, tapered shaft, center worm with point, c1880 . . . .   250.00
Steel, scrolled handle, Archimedean screw 55.00

COSMOS GLASS

History: Cosmos glass is a milk glass pattern made by the Consolidated Lamp and Glass Company, c1900.

Cosmos glass is identified by its distinctive pattern. The ground is a molded cross-cut design. Relief molded flowers are painted in pink, blue, and yellow. Cosmos glass comes in an extended tableware line which includes several sizes and shapes of lamps.

Basket, ftd 120.00
Butter Dish, cov 115.00

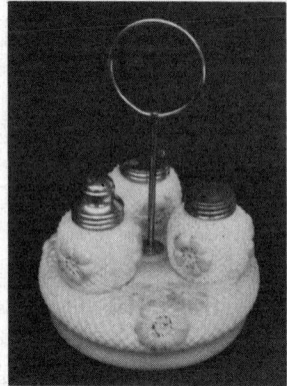

Condiment Set, salt and pepper shakers, and mustard, Cosmos pattern frame with pink band, metal ring handle, $300.00.

Condiment Set, salt, pepper, and mustard, orig handled Cosmos pattern frame, pink band 300.00
Creamer and Sugar, cov 315.00
Miniature Lamp, 7½″ h 290.00
Pickle Castor, pink band, ftd SP frame 400.00
Pitcher, water, 9″, pink band 225.00
Powder Box, cov 200.00
Salt and Pepper Shakers, tall, pink band, orig tops, pr 150.00
Spooner 120.00
Sugar, cov 150.00
Tumbler, 3¾″, pink band 90.00

COWAN POTTERY

History: R. Guy Cowan founded the Cowan Pottery in 1913 in Cleveland, Ohio. The establishment remained in almost continuous operation until 1931 when financial difficulties forced closure.

Early production was redware pottery. Later a porcelain-like finish was perfected with special emphasis placed on glazes. Lustreware is one of the most common types. Commercial wares marked "Lakeware" were produced from 1927 to 1931.

Early marks include an incised "Cowan Pottery" on the redware (1913–17), an impressed "Cowan," and an impressed "Lakewood". The imprinted stylized semicircle with or without the initials R. G. was later.

References: Paul Evans, *Art Pottery of the United States, 2nd Edition,* Feingold & Lewis Publishing Corp., 1987; Ralph and Terry Kovel, *The Kovels' Collector's Guide to American Art Pottery,* Crown Publishers, Inc., 1974.

Bowl
  7¼ x 2¼″, blue luster 40.00
  9½ x 4″, blue luster glaze, flared top, seahorse pedestal 45.00
Candlesticks, pr
  4″, pink 20.00
  8″, triple light, ivory glaze 75.00
Charger, 11″, bottle green glaze, pierced for hanging, sgd 45.00
Cigarette Holder, seahorse, ivory 30.00
Figure, 9″, man, blue, irid gold, and maroon 45.00

Flower Frog, figural, c1920, marked "Lakewood, Ohio," 7″ h, $125.00.

Flower Frog, nude, #686 . . . . 125.00
Soap Dish, 4″, seahorse, blue 35.00
Teapot, 7¼″, white glaze 75.00
Trivet, 6½″, scalloped rim, bust of young girl framed by flower, sgd 250.00
Vase
  6 x 5″, blue and green glaze, hand mushroom dec 350.00
  7¼″ h, seahorse standard, green glaze, imp mark 50.00
  9″, hp, dragonfly and cattails 80.00

16", red clay, orange luster glaze, hand sgd "R.G. Cowan" **450.00**

CRANBERRY GLASS

History: Cranberry glass is transparent and named for its color, achieved by adding powdered gold to a molten batch of amber glass which then is reheated at a low temperature to develop the cranberry or ruby color. The glass color first appeared in the last half of the 17th century, but was not made in American glass factories until the last half of the 19th century.

Cranberry glass was blown, mold blown, or pressed. Examples often are decorated with gold or enamel. Less expensive cranberry glass was made by substituting copper for gold and can be identified by its bluish-purple tint.

Reference: William Heacock and William Gamble, *Encyclopedia Of Victorian Colored Pattern Glass: Book 9, Cranberry Opalescent from A to Z,* Antique Publications, 1987.

Additional Listings: See specific categories, such as Bride's Baskets, Cruets, Jack-in-the-Pulpit Vases, etc.

Reproduction Alert: Reproductions abound. These pieces are heavier, off-color, and lack the quality of older examples.

Water Bottle, blown, reverse ribbing, c1880, 6¼" h, $160.00.

Bonbon Dish, 6¼ x 6", applied clear shell trim, SP basket **125.00**

Bowl

- 3⅞ x 3¾", three crystal star shape appliques with berry centers, heavy foil pcs in glass, three crystal scroll applied feet, berry pontil **150.00**
- 7¾", paneled, flower dec, brass standard, mirrored base **100.00**

Box, 4½ x 2⅝", round, hinged, enameled colonial girl, white wig, black and white dress, basket of flowers **135.00**

Butter Dish, cov, round, Hobnail pattern **100.00**

Celery Vase, Swirl pattern, satin finish **100.00**

Cologne Bottle, 3 x 7", dainty blue, white, and yellow flowers, green leaves, gold outlines and trim, orig clear ball stopper **180.00**

Cornucopia, 9½" h, gilt dec, prisms, pr **600.00**

Creamer, 2⅞", blue, white, and coral flowers, lacy gold foliage, applied clear handle **125.00**

Cruet

- 5", bulbous, IVT, flower dec, pontil, applied clear ribbed handle, clear stopper **65.00**
- 9½", engraved flowers and leaves, applied clear handle, clear wafer foot, clear cut stopper **160.00**

Cup and Saucer, 2½ × 4⅛", gold bands, enameled purple and white violets, gold handle **125.00**

Decanter

- 16¾", double cut overlay, cranberry cut to clear, orig matching stopper, applied clear handle, clear ftd base **100.00**
- 19¼" h, gold dec, applied raised porcelain flowers, steeple stopper, Austrian, pr **275.00**

Dresser Jar, 4¼" d, round, hinged lid, medallion of young girl in white playing lyre, yellow foliate dec **150.00**

Epergne, 21½" h, 10" d bowl, three hanging baskets, four trumpets, applied pale vaseline handles, stems, and rigaree, clear twisted canes ... **1,850.00**

Finger Bowl, scalloped, matching underplate, attributed to New England Glass Co **125.00**

Humidor, 4¼" d, 6" h, enameled white and blue dec, gold trim, brass lid .. **355.00**

Jam Dish, 4½" d, applied clear rim, SP holder **100.00**

Liqueur Cruet, 3¼" d, 7¾" h, sq bulbous, applied clear handle, orig clear ball stopper, enameled blue and white flowers, green leaves, four 1¼" d x 1⅞" h matching mugs, clear handles, 8" cranberry tray **265.00**

Miniature Lamp

- 8¼", bulbous, swirled, hobnail dec . **300.00**
- 10½", cylindrical, flared out shade, opal stripes **625.00**

Muffineer, twelve section **110.00**

Perfume Bottles, 5½" h, pr, enameled, beveled glass house shaped casket, gilt brass fittings **335.00**

Pin Dish, 3¾ x 3" h, enameled white daisies and flowers, ftd ormolu holder **85.00**

Pickle Castor, 3¼ x 10⅛", enameled

white band of flowers and leaves,
  gold trim, SP frame, lid, and tongs . **235.00**
Pitcher
  5¼", Hobnail, applied clear handle . **75.00**
  6", Coin Spot, white int. **225.00**
  7", tankard, applied clear handle, adv
    "Daniel Crawford Scotch Whiskey" **150.00**
  10", bulbous, long neck, applied am-
    ber handle, enameled flowers and
    leaves **315.00**
Rose Bowl
  3½", melon ribbed **125.00**
  4¾", egg shape, applied clear swags,
    scroll feet, berry pontil **250.00**
Salt, master
  2¾ x 1¾", cut to crystal on sides, star
    design on base **70.00**
  2⅞ x 1¾", gold band, enameled blue
    and white flowers, green leaves . . **55.00**
  3½ x 1½", SP holder, lion's mask and
    claw feet **75.00**
  3½ x 2⅛", four applied clear shell
    feet, applied clear shells trim **70.00**
Shrimp Dish, 4⅛ x 3¾", intaglio cut to
  clear, attached clear underplate . . . **100.00**
Sugar Shaker
  6", Spanish Lace, opalescent pattern,
    nickel plated top **125.00**
  6¼", Venetian Diamond pattern **100.00**
  6½", Drape pattern, SS hallmarked
    top **85.00**
Sweetmeat Dish, 5¾", fluted, applied
  clear shell trim, SP basket holder . . **90.00**
Syrup Pitcher, opalescent, hobnail,
  Hobbs, Brockunier & Co, orig pewter
  top sgd "Pat Mar 20 83" **385.00**
Toothpick, 3¾" h, applied vaseline ri-
  garee **114.00**
Tumbler
  3¾", all over multicolored enameling,
    gold trim **55.00**
  4", IVT, enameled white daisy, blue
    forget-me-not, and white lily-of-the-
    valley dec **35.00**
Urn, 5 x 12½", cov, deep all over cutting,
  raised diamonds, bands of bull's
  eyes, cut clear glass stem, sq pedestal base, cut dome cov, clear acorn
  finial **275.00**
Vase
  3" d, 5¾" h, sanded enamel white
    scallops, grapes, and leaves, gold
    ormolu feet, pr **225.00**
  3½ x 9" h, enameled white daisies
    and leaves, facing pr **250.00**
  5¼" d, 13⅛" h, enameled dainty white
    flowers, gold berries, scrolls, and
    leaves, applied clear shell trim . . . **225.00**
Water Set, 5½ x 10" pitcher, six 2⅞ x 4"
  tumblers, pressed, spade between
  flowers, band of emb flowers, gold
  trim, applied clear handle **225.00**

CROWN MILANO

History: Crown Milano is an American art glass
produced by the Mt. Washington Glass Works,
New Bedford, Massachusetts. The original patent
was issued in 1886 to Frederick Shirley and Albert
Steffin.

Normally it is an opaque white satin glass finished with light beige or ivory color ground embellished with fancy florals, decorations, and elaborate heavy raised gold. When marked, pieces
carry an entwined CM with crown in purple enamel
on the base. Sometimes paper labels were used.
The silver plated mounts often have "MW" impressed or a Pairpoint mark as both Mount Washington and Pairpoint supplied mountings.

Advisors: Clarence and Betty Maier.

**Vase, diamond quilted body, scalloped
top, gold and enamel floral dec, crown
mark, 4″ d, 4⅝″ h, $625.00.**

Biscuit Jar, 5" h, cylindrical, SP floral
  emb lid, butterfly finial **945.00**
Creamer and Sugar, sq shape, jeweled
  flowers, gold and green leaves outlined in raised gold, gold ribbed han-
  dles, pr **700.00**
Ewer
  9¾" h, autumn colored oak leaves
    and acorns, outlined in heavy gold,
    turquoise twisted handle extending
    around neck, sgd **1,750.00**
  13" h, flowers and trailing vines,
    heavy raised gold, gold shadow
    scrolling, trefoil fold-down top, un-
    signed **900.00**
Syrup Pitcher, oak branch, acorns, and
  leaves dec outlined in raised gold,
  melon ribbed body, SP lid **985.00**

Tumbler, 3⅞" h, shiny finish, gold swag
and ribbon dec, sgd **460.00**
Vase
6" h, onion shape, molded swirl pattern, fern leaf dec, white int., attached SP stand **385.00**
8" h, sq, rounded corners, dragon's
head medallions and floral dec in
gold, ivory ground, two delicate ap-
plied handles **900.00**
8¼" h, enameled chrysanthemum
and thistle dec, raised gold bor-
ders, sgd **2,200.00**
9" h, shiny finish, applied scroll han-
dles, large flowers dec, heavy gold
highlighting, Albertine, (early
Crown Milano) signature **1,000.00**

CRUETS

History: Cruets are small glass bottles, used to
hold oil, vinegar, wine, etc., for the table. The high
point of cruet use was during the Victorian era
when a myriad of glass manufacturers made
cruets in a wide assortment of patterns, colors,
and sizes. All cruets had stoppers; most had handles.

Reference: Dean L Murray, *More Cruets Only,*
Killgore Graphics, Inc., 1973; William Heacock,
*Encyclopedia of Victorian Colored Pattern Glass:
Book 6, Oil Cruets From A To Z,* Antique Publi-
cations, 1981.

Additional Listings: Pattern Glass and specific
glass categories such as Amberina, Cranberry,
and Satin.

**Herringbone pattern, cranberry
ground, opalescent white stripes, clear
faceted stopper, Hobbs, Bruckunier &
Co, $350.00.**

Amber, 8 x 4", gold, four dimpled sides,
sapphire blue bubble stopper and
handle **110.00**
Amberina
5¾", IVT, applied amber handle and
stopper, Mt Washington **325.00**
7 × 3½", IVT, three petal top, amber
applied handle and cut faceted
stopper **175.00**
Blue, hobnail, applied amber handle,
amber stopper **70.00**
Cranberry, double cut overlay, cranberry
to clear **80.00**
Custard, Argonaut Shell **425.00**
Emerald Green
Beaded Ovals In Sand, dec, orig
stopper **135.00**
Esther, 5¾", gold dec, orig stopper . **150.00**
Opalescent, Intaglio, blue and white . . **125.00**
Pattern Glass
Broken Column, orig stopper **48.50**
Flora, clear, gold trim, orig stopper . **150.00**
Peachblow, 7", enameled fish, water lil-
ies, and cattails, gold outlines, acid
finish, applied amber handle, orig fac-
eted amber stopper **1,100.00**
Ruby Stained, Royal Crystal, orig stop-
per **165.00**
Satin, 7", yellow, DQ, applied frosted
handle, faceted clear stopper **250.00**
Spatter, 4½" h, red and white, tricorn
top, applied clear handle **135.00**

CUP PLATES

History: Many early cups and saucers were
handleless, with deep saucers. The hot liquid was
poured into the saucer and sipped from it. This
necessitated another plate for the cup, the "cup
plate."

The first cup plates made of pottery were of the
Staffordshire variety. In the mid-1830s to 40s,
glass cup plates were favored. Boston and Sandwich Glass Company was one of the main contrib-
utors to the lacy glass type.

It is extremely difficult to find glass cup plates in
outstanding (mint) condition. Collectors expect
some marks of usage, such as slight rim roughness, minor chipping [best if under rim], and in
rarer patterns a portion of a scallop missing.

Reference: Ruth Webb Lee and James H.
Rose, *American Glass Cup Plates,* published by
author, 1948, reprinted by Charles E. Tuttle Co.,
Inc. in 1985.

Notes: The numbers used are from the Lee-
Rose book in which all plates are illustrated.

Prices are based on plates in "average" condition.

GLASS

LR 4-A, 4⅛", clear, swirled red and white latticinio, gold flecks in rim, attributed to Nicholas Lutz, ex-William Elsholz collection 150.00

LR 11, 2¹³⁄₁₆", clear, New England origin, small shallow rim chips and roughage   60.00

LR 22-B, 3⁷⁄₁₆", clear, pontil, New England origin, slight roughage 80.00

LR 26, 3⁹⁄₁₆", clear, attributed to Sandwich or New England Glass Co 150.00

LR 37, 3¼", opalescent, attributed to Sandwich or New England Glass Co, two heat checks in rim, light roughage   150.00

LR 45, 3⁹⁄₁₆", pale opalescent, attributed to Sandwich or New England Glass Co, mold overfill, slag deposit near center 100.00

LR 51, 3¾", clear, pontil, eastern origin, moderate rim roughage, few shallow flakes 175.00

LR 58, 3⅜", clambroth, unlisted, eastern origin, ex-William Elsholz collection .   275.00

LR 61, 3⅜", opalescent, attributed to New England Glass Co 250.00

LR 75-A, 3¹³⁄₁₆", clear, attributed to New England Glass Co, one tiny rim flake   70.00

LR 80, 3¾", opalescent, New England origin, ex-William Elsholz, Harry S. High, James H. Rose collections . . .   250.00

LR 81, 3¾", fiery red opalescent, New England origin, ex-William Elsholz, Louise S. Esterly, James H. Rose collections 350.00

LR–82, Acorn and Leaves pattern, silver opaque blue, fiery opalescent, $500.00.

LR 88, 3¹¹⁄₁₆", deep opalescent opaque, attributed to Sandwich and New England Glass Co, two minute under rim flakes 175.00

LR 95, 3⅝", opalescent opaque, attrib-

uted to New England, tiny under rim nick 150.00

LR 100, 3¼", clear, attributed to Philadelphia area, unseen flake under rim, normal mold roughness 75.00

LR 107, 3⅜", clear, lacy, attributed to Philadelphia area, very slight rim roughage 50.00

LR 121, 3¹⁄₁₆", clear, lacy, midwestern, slight rim roughage, two minor nicks, mold overfill 100.00

LR 242-A, 3½", black amethyst, lacy, eastern origin, mold underfill and overfill 650.00

LR 247, 3⁷⁄₁₆", emerald green, lacy, attributed to Sandwich or New England Glass Co, small chip on one scallop   750.00

LR 253, 3⁹⁄₁₆", bluish-green, Roman Rosette, midwestern origin, two very small rim nicks 300.00

LR 259, 3⁷⁄₁₆", clear, eastern origin, small chip on one point and one scallop, normal mold roughness 85.00

LR 276, 3⁷⁄₁₆", blue, lacy, Boston and Sandwich Glass Co., slight opalescence bloom 325.00

LR 279, 2⅞", light green, lacy, eastern origin, two chipped scallops 250.00

LR 291, 3", amethyst, ex-William Elsholz collection 300.00

LR 319, 3⁵⁄₁₆", clear, one scallop missing, five have small flakes, normal mold roughness 100.00

LR 399, 3⁵⁄₁₆", clear, eastern origin, normal mold roughness 60.00

LR 433, 4⅛", clear, two chips, mold roughness 75.00

LR 440-B, 3½", gray-blue, attributed to Sandwich, nine scallops flaked, one missing 100.00

LR 445, 3⁷⁄₁₆", cloudy, midwestern origin, four bull's eyes missing, five chips, mold roughness 265.00

LR 459M, jade opaque, twelve hearts, near mint 450.00

LR 516, 3¼", amethyst, attributed to Sandwich, rim chip on underside, surface spalls, and rim roughage 425.00

GLASS HISTORICAL

LR 568, 3⁷⁄₁₆", clear, attributed to Sandwich, one scallop tipped, mold roughness 50.00

LR 580-B, 3¾", clear, English origin, underfill covering 1½ of rim 275.00

LR 586-B, clear, Ringgold, Palo Alto, stippled ground, small letters, Philadelphia area, 1847–48, trace of mold roughness 650.00

LR 595, 3¼", amber, attributed to Sandwich, three small mold spalls, one

scallop missing, six scallops tipped, one spall on underside, average mold roughness **265.00**
LR 615-A, 3⅜", clear, unknown origin, Constitution **650.00**
LR 691-A, 3³⁄₁₆", clear, midwestern origin, normal mold roughness **450.00**
LR 695, 3", clear, midwestern origin two scallops tipped, normal mold roughness **125.00**

PORCELAIN OR POTTERY

Gaudy Dutch, Butterfly pattern **750.00**
Leeds, 3¾", softpaste, gaudy blue and white floral dec,very minor pinpoint edge flakes **240.00**
Staffordshire, Historical
  Franklin Tomb (so called), 3½", dark blue, Wood, faint hairline **600.00**
  Landing of Lafayette, 4⅜", dark blue, full border, Clews **425.00**
  The Tyrants Foe...Lovejoy, 4", light blue, unknown maker, minute pinpoint on foot rim **275.00**
  Unidentified View of Country Estate, 4⅝", grapevine border series, dark blue, Wood **60.00**
Staffordshire, Romantic
  Balantyre, twelve sided, J Alcock .. **50.00**
  Garden Scenery, twelve sided, pink, Mayer **30.00**

CUSTARD GLASS

History: Custard glass was developed in England in the early 1880s. Harry Northwood made the first American custard glass at his Indiana, Pennsylvania, factory in 1898.

From 1898 until 1915, many manufacturers produced custard glass patterns, e.g., Dugan Glass, Fenton, A. H. Heisey Glass Co., Jefferson Glass, Northwood, Tarentum Glass, and U.S. Glass. Cambridge and McKee continued the production of custard glass into the Depression.

The ivory or creamy yellow custard color is achieved by adding uranium salts to the molten hot glass. The chemical content makes the glass glow when held under a black light. The higher the amount of uranium, the more luminous the color. Northwood's custard glass has the smallest amount of uranium, creating an ivory color; Heisey used more, creating a deep yellow color.

Custard glass was made in patterned tableware pieces. It also was made as souvenir items and novelty pieces. Souvenir pieces are marked with place names or hand painted decorations, e.g., flowers. Patterns of custard glass often were highlighted in gold, enamel colors, and stains.

Reference: William Heacock, *Encyclopedia Of Victorian Colored Pattern Glass, Book IV: Custard Glass From A to Z,* Peacock Publications, 1980.

Reproduction Alert: L. G. Wright Glass Co. has reproduced pieces in the Argonaut Shell and Grape and Cable patterns. It also introduced new patterns, such as Floral and Grape and Vintage Band. Moser reproduced toothpicks in Argonaut Shell, Chrysanthemum Sprig, and Inverted Fan & Feather.

Additional Listings: Pattern Glass.

Chrysanthemum Sprig, Northwood, jelly compote, 5" h, $90.00.

Berry Bowl
  Individual
    Fan **40.00**
    Louis XV, gold trim **40.00**
  Master
    Fan **135.00**
    Louis XV, gold trim **135.00**
Berry Set, Chrysanthemum Sprig, 11" oval unsigned master, six individuals sgd "Northwood" script **675.00**
Butter, cov
  Chrysanthemum Sprig, 6" h **275.00**
  Georgia Gem, enamel dec **135.00**
  Intaglio **175.00**
  Louis XV **120.00**
  Victoria **280.00**
Celery
  Georgia Gem **175.00**
  Ring Band **300.00**
Cologne Bottle, Grape, nutmeg stain, orig stopper, marked "N" **400.00**
Compote, jelly
  Argonaut Shell **160.00**
  Beaded Circle **350.00**
  Intaglio, green trim **100.00**
Condiment Set, Creased Bale, 4 pcs . **180.00**
Creamer
  Grape, nutmeg stain **100.00**
  Heart with Thumbprint **80.00**
Cruet
  Argonaut Shell, orig stopper **425.00**

Chrysanthemum Sprig, clear stopper, goofus dec	60.00
Intaglio, green dec	400.00
Ribbed Drape	350.00
Custard Cup, Winged Scroll	50.00
Dresser Tray, Winged Scroll, hp dec	165.00
Goblet, Grape and Gothic Arches, nutmeg stain	65.00
Hair Receiver, Winged Scroll	125.00
Humidor, Winged Scroll	175.00
Ice Cream Bowl, Peacock & Urn, individual size, Northwood	35.00
Nappy	
Northwood Grape	50.00
Prayer Rug, 6" d	50.00
Pickle Dish, Beaded Swag	250.00
Pin Tray, Chrysanthemum Sprig	50.00
Pitcher, water, Argonaut Shell	300.00
Plate, 7½" d	
Prayer Rug	20.00
Three Fruits	22.00
Punch Cup	
Inverted Fan and Feather	250.00
Northwood Grape	48.00
Rose Bowl, Grape and Gothic Arches	75.00
Salt and Pepper Shakers, pr	
Chrysanthemum Sprig	150.00
Heart	60.00
Punty Band	85.00
Vine with Flowers	50.00
Sauce	
Cane Insert	30.00
Intaglio	35.00
Jefferson Optic, dec	15.00
Spooner	
Chrysanthemum Sprig, blue, gold trim	220.00
Geneva	50.00
Sugar	
Everglades	150.00
Fluted Scrolls	150.00
Heart and Thumbprint, individual	75.00
Victoria	175.00
Syrup	
Ring Band	300.00
Winged Scroll	350.00
Table Set, cov butter, creamer, cov sugar, spooner	
Argonaut Shell	400.00
Intaglio	500.00
Toothpick	
Argonaut Shell	275.00
Chrysanthemum Sprig, blue	300.00
Maple Leaf	550.00
Ribbed Drape	150.00
Tumbler	
Cherry Scale	40.00
Geneva, red and green enamel dec	50.00
Grape and Gothic Arches, gold, carnival finish	55.00
Inverted Fan and Feather	100.00
Ring Band	65.00

Wild Bouquet	25.00
Tumbler	
Chrysanthemum Sprig, set of 6	300.00
Louis XV, gold trim	55.00
Vase	
Diamond Peg, 8" h	100.00
Grape Arbor, nutmeg stain	65.00
Water Pitcher, gold and green intaglio	350.00
Water Set, Fluted Scroll, gold trim, 5 pcs	350.00

CUT GLASS, AMERICAN

History: Glass is cut by the process of grinding decoration into the glass by means of abrasive-carrying metal wheels or stone wheels. A very ancient craft, it was revived in 1600 by Bohemians and spread through Europe, to Great Britain, and to America.

American cut glass came of age at the Centennial Exposition in 1876 and the World Columbian Exposition in 1893. The American public recognized American cut glass to be exceptional in quality and workmanship. America's most significant output of this high quality glass occurred from 1880 to 1917, a period now known as the "Brilliant Period."

About the 1890s some companies began adding an acid-etched "signature" to their glass. This signature may be the actual company name, its logo, or chosen symbol. Today, signed pieces can command a premium over unsigned pieces since the signature clearly establishes the origin.

However, caution should be exercised in regard to signature identification. Objects with forged signatures have been in existence for some time. To check for authenticity, run your finger tip or finger nail lightly over the area with the signature. As a general rule, a genuine signature cannot be felt; a forged signature exhibits a raised surface.

Many companies never used the acid-etched signature on the glass and may or may not have affixed paper labels to the items originally. Dorflinger Glass and the Meriden Glass Co. made cut glass of the highest quality, yet never acid-etched a signature on the glass. Furthermore, cut glass made before the 1890s was not signed. Many of these wood polished items, cut on blown blanks, were of excellent quality and often won awards at exhibitions.

Consequently, if collectors restrict themselves to signed pieces only, many beautiful pieces of the highest quality glass and workmanship will be missed.

References: E. S. Farrar & J. S. Spillman, *The Complete Cut & Engraved Glass Of Corning*, Crown Publishers [Corning Museum of Glass monograph],1979; J. Michael Pearson, *Encyclopedia Of American Cut & Engraved Glass*, Volumes I to III, published by author, 1975; Albert C. Revi, *American Cut & Engraved Glass*, Thomas Nelson, Inc., 1965; Martha Louise Swan, *American and*

Engraved Glass, Wallace-Homestead, 1986; H. Weiner & F. Lipkowitz, *Rarities In American Cut Glass*, Collectors House of Books, 1975.

Collectors' Club: American Cut Glass Association, 1603 SE 19th, Suite 112, Edmond Professional Bldg., Edmond, OK 73013.

Museums: The Corning Museum of Glass, Corning, NY; High Museum of Art, Atlanta, GA; Huntington Galleries, Huntington, WV; Lightner Museum, St. Augustine, FL; Toledo Museum Of Art, Toledo, OH.

Basket, 8 x 11″, Harvard, hobstars, and prism cut	475.00
Bell	
5¾″ h, dinner size, hobstars, fans, strawberry diamond	255.00
6¾″ h, strawberry diamond and fan sharply cut, pattern cut on knob at end of stem as well	550.00
Bowl	
7 x 2″	
Figured blank, hobstars and fans	75.00
Grecian, sgd "Hawkes"	625.00
8 x 2″, cross-cut diamond and fan	60.00
8 x 3″, Iris, sgd "Hawkes Gravic"	250.00
8 x 4″, Ellsmere, sgd "Libbey"	600.00
9″	
Palm, five sided, Taylor Bros	450.00
Russian, cane, feather, and hobstars	140.00
9 x 4″, Prima Donna, sgd "Clark"	375.00
9¾ x 6¾ x 3¾″, orange, hobstars and strawberry diamond	180.00
10″, Kohinoor, blown-out type blank, swirled pattern design, sgd "Hawkes"	1,250.00
10 x 4″, Nautilus, blown blank, Hawkes	2,400.00
10 x 4½″	
Chrysanthemum, wood polished, Hawkes	650.00
Venetian, wood polished, Hawkes	500.00
10 x 8″, Sultana, folded-in sides, Dorflinger	525.00
Box	
4 x 11″, glove, hinged lid, silver fittings, Harvard border around intaglio cut floral	750.00
5 x 3″, intaglio pears and cherries, sgd "Heisey"	110.00
6 x 5″, round, green cased to clear, SS repousse lid, hobstar base, vertical punties and prism columns	500.00
8″ d, hinged, round, Florence hobstar lid, miter cut sides	320.00
Bread Tray, 11 x 5″, hobstars, sgd "Clark"	275.00
Butter, cov, 5″ h	
7″ d plate, Russian and floral	385.00
8″ d plate	
Hobstar chain cut on figured blank	325.00

Hobstars and fans, sgd "Libbey"	**425.00**
Butter Pat	
Pair, Cypress, Laurel, each	32.00
Set of 4, sgd "Hawkes," each	20.00
Set of 6, well cut hobstars, each	30.00
Candlestick	
8″ h	
Hollow teardrop stems, rayed bases, hobstars, hobnail, and diamonds, pr	975.00
Teardrop stems, floral and Harvard, pr	250.00
9½″ h, teardrop stem, hobstar base, hobstars	230.00
11″ h, teardrop stem, notched prisms, 24 pt hobstar base, pr	600.00
12″ h, Adelaide, amber, Pairpoint, pr	250.00
14″ h, teardrop stems, cut and engraved, sgd "Sinclaire," pr	325.00

Canoe, Plaza pattern, Pitkin and Brooks, Chicago, IL, 11¼″ l, 4¾″ d, $275.00.

Canoe	
11″ l, Harvard	240.00
13½ x 4½″, floral and leaves	75.00
Carafe	
Clear button Russian	325.00
Harvard	160.00
Hobstars and notched prisms	110.00
Wedgemere, 9″ h, Libbey	1,000.00
Casserole, cov, 8½ x 7″ h, Palm, sgd "Taylor Bros"	1,300.00
Celery	
11″, hobstars, double miters, strawberry diamond on blown blank	150.00
11½ x 5″, hobstars, cross hatch, and notched prisms on figured blank	60.00
12″, hobstars, flashed double vesicas, sgd "Alford"	250.00
Champagne Bucket, 7 x 7″, sgd "Hoare"	350.00
Cheese and Cracker Dish, Double Lozenge	275.00
Cheese Dish, cov	
9½″ d plate, hobstars, prisms, clear tusks	550.00
Encore, Straus	375.00
Hobstars, deep miters, cane	450.00

Cigar Jar
7½", Middlesex, hollow stopper, lid to
  hold sponge, Dorflinger **475.00**
9"
  Monarch, pattern cut lid hollow for
    sponge, hobstar base, Hoare . . **625.00**
  Pattern cut lid hollow for sponge,
    hobstars, beaded split vesicas,
    hobstar base **550.00**
Cigarette Holder, 4" l,¾" w, nailhead diamond, strawberry diamond, fans, and
  honeycomb **630.00**
Cocktail Shaker, strawberry diamond
  and fan, SS top, sgd "Hawkes" **275.00**
Cologne
  5", bulbous, strawberry diamond, fans
    and hobstars **150.00**
  6" h, Hob and Lace, green cased to
    clear, pattern cut stopper, Dorflin-
    ger **600.00**
  7½ x 2¾", Parisian, sq shape, Dor-
    flinger, pr **620.00**
  Ruby cased to clear, all over cane . . **250.00**

**Compote, Arbutus pattern, Clark, tear
drop in stem, 7¾" h, 6" d, $265.00.**

Compote
  5" h, 7" d, hobstars, rayed foot, sgd
    "Maple City" **150.00**
  7" h, 8½", two notch cut handles, hob-
    star base, teardrop stem, hobstars **400.00**
  8" h, daisies and leaves **80.00**
  9"h, 6" d, Ribbon Star, rayed foot . . **275.00**
  9 x 9", teardrop stem, hobstars and
    diamonds **275.00**
  9¾" h, cov, Arcadia, Bergen **1,850.00**
  14 x 10", Design #100, notch cut
    teardrop stems, hobstar base, El-
    mira, pr **2,700.00**
Console Center Set, Victoria, pedestal
  bowl, pair candlesticks, 3 pc **325.00**

Cookie Jar
  6½" h, hobstars, fans, double "X" cut
    vesicas, strawberry diamond,
    curved-in sides, matching pattern
    cut glass lid rests into SS rim . . . **800.00**
  Hobstars, strawberry diamond, cane
    and fans, pattern cut glass lid . . . **900.00**
Cordial Set, Flute, green cased to clear,
  9" h handled decanter with ringed
  neck and matching colored stopper,
  set of 8 cordials, Dorflinger **875.00**
Creamer, 4", prism and punties **65.00**
Creamer and Sugar
  Clear button Russian, hobstar bases,
    cut creamer handle, cov sugar with
    wafer foot, pattern cut lid **800.00**
  Hobstar clusters, blown blanks, El-
    mira **275.00**
  Hobstars and fans, figured blanks,
    plain handles **90.00**
  Hobstars, fans, and strawberry dia-
    monds, notched handles **145.00**
  Intaglio fruit and geometric cutting . . **75.00**
  Pedestal, 7" h cov sugar, pinwheel,
    hobstar, fans, rayed bases **975.00**
Cruet
  6" h, Chrysanthemum, tri-pour spout,
    cut handle and stopper, Hawkes . **350.00**
  7", Butterfly and Daisy, Pairpoint . . . **85.00**
  9½" h, Alhambra, honeycomb handle,
    tall pyramidal shape **675.00**
  Ship's cruet, wide bottomed, tri-pour **150.00**
  Squat oil, hobstars and cross-cut dia-
    monds **100.00**
Decanter
  7" h, Lotus, ship's, pattern cut stop-
    per, Egginton **380.00**
  10" h, bulbous, hobstars and straw-
    berry diamonds **275.00**
  11" h
    Argand, SS flip-top lid and handle,
      Hoare **700.00**
    Stopper cut in matching geometric
      pattern, sgd "Hawkes" **525.00**
  12" h, Russian and Pillar, pattern cut
    stopper **1,100.00**
  13½" h, Brazilian, heavy blank, bul-
    bous, wood polished, Hawkes . . . **650.00**
Dish, 10 x 7", hobstar button Russian,
  heart shape **220.00**
Door Knob, facet cut **25.00**
Fernery
  8" d, hobstar and fan, three ftd **80.00**
  Expanding Star, three ftd **325.00**
  Royal, three ftd, Hunt **195.00**
Finger Bowl
  5" d, cross-cut diamond and fan, pr . **70.00**
  Glenwood, Bergen **60.00**
  Strawberry diamond and fan, set of 4 **175.00**
Flask, ladies, 6 x 3½", SS lid, cross-cut
  diamond, strawberry diamond and
  fan **180.00**

Flower Center

6" d, 5" h, flat-bottomed, hobstars, flashed fans, hobstar chain and base 300.00

10" d, 7½" h, hobstars in diamond shape fields, fans, strawberry diamond, honeycomb neck 775.00

Flower Pot, 6 x 6", hobstars and fans, pyramidal starred fields 775.00

Hair Receiver

4" d, 3" h, engraved SS top, floral and leaves, rayed base 75.00

5" d, 3½" h, Harvard 150.00

Humidor

6¾" h, all over notched prism, glass lid 350.00

8" h, Monarch, SS repousse lid 650.00

Hanging Globe, 12" d, cross-cut diamond and fan, 20" to top of brass finial, orig brass chain and mounting fixture 475.00

Ice Bucket

6" d, Jewel, hobstar bases, two handles, 8½" d underplate, Clark 525.00

6" d, 6" h, hobstar and cross-cut panels, tab handles 350.00

7" d, 5½" h, Harvard, tab handles .. 440.00

Ice Cream Set, 13 x 8" tray with curved ends, six 5" sq bowls, rayed button Russian, 7 pc 1,100.00

Ice Cream Tray

14 x 7", cut glass, Nelson pattern variation, all over cutting, sgd "Fry" . 270.00

14" x 10", rect, Devonshire, sgd "Hawkes" 925.00

Jar

1¾" sq

Prism and cane, rayed base, SS repousse lid, marked "Unger Bros" 75.00

Rouge, cut panels, engraved SS tops, pr 75.00

4" h, 5" d, glass lid, sgd "Libbey" .. 260.00

6" h, Holland, hobstar lid, sgd "Hawkes" 300.00

Kerosene Lamp, 7" h to top of chimney, geometric pattern 425.00

Ketchup Bottle

6½" h, Ramona, Pairpoint 450.00

8½" h, hobstars 240.00

Knife Rest

4", pr, facet panel cut, orig box 100.00

4½", all over strawberry diamond and miter 75.00

4¾", nailhead diamonds and strawberry diamonds 85.00

Ladle

11½" l, SP emb shell, cut and notched prism handle 150.00

15", hobstars, strawberry diamond, and fans in teardrop handle, sgd "Bergen" 400.00

17" l, double pouring spout, hobstars and notched prisms, sgd "Meriden" 500.00

Lamp

13" h, 6½" d, mushroom shade, St. Louis Diamond neck, notched prism and hobstars, flashed fans . 400.00

18" h, mushroom shade, hobstars, cane vesicas, fans, pr 4,300.00

21" h, 12" shade, La Rabida, double light, Straus 3,200.00

22½" h, Sultan's hat shade, Harvard and late floral 500.00

23" h, 2" shade, hobstars, beaded double miters, fans, double light . 2,800.00

27" h, pointed top, Harvard, hobstars 2,750.00

Light Shade, 7½" h, 7" w, hobstar button Russian 225.00

Loving Cup, 5½" h, SS rim, monogrammed, dated 1900 .... 400.00

Mayonnaise Set, two pc

Bowl and matching underplate, punties, flashed pinwheel 135.00

Hobstars, cane, and strawberry diamond on blown blanks 275.00

Prism and hobstars 190.00

Medicine Bottle, globe shape, clear button Russian, pattern cut top 625.00

Mug, 4" h, Tyrone, handled, Pairpoint . 235.00

Mustard

Hobstars and notched prisms, figured blank, cov 60.00

Renaissance, cov, underplate 135.00

Silverplate hinged lid and handle, strawberry and fan 60.00

Napkin Ring, hobstars and bow tie fans 85.00

Nappy

5" d, hobstars and cross-cut diamond, handle 35.00

6" d

Cane and cross hatching, two handles 125.00

Figured blank, hobstar cluster, no handle 50.00

Good Wishes, engraved, handled, Harvard 200.00

Paste Pot, vertical notched prisms, crossing miters 170.00

Perfume

3½" l, pistol shape, SS fittings 230.00

4" h, 2½" sq, atomizer, gold washed top, Harvard 125.00

5¾" h, three panels Harvard and three panels floral 125.00

Picture Frame, 4¾ x 6¾", heavy cut corners with florals on each panel, pr 250.00

Pitcher

6", milk, hobstars and fans 200.00

8", tankard, sunburst, hobstar bands, rayed base, sgd "Libbey" 275.00

8½", tankard, Brunswick, sgd "Hawkes" 500.00

9", tankard, Orpheus, pattern cut handle, sgd "Hawkes" **1,250.00**
10", Keystone Rose **135.00**
11", Harvard, rayed base, double punty handle, sgd "Hawkes" **315.00**
11 x 5", tankard, hobstar and ovals filled with cane and nailhead diamond, hobstar base **350.00**
Planter, 12 x 4 x 4", close notched rim, cut all over, 3½" d sunflowers, hobstar center, small rayed flowers, heavy detailed ferns, cut rayed base, American Brilliant period **345.00**

Plate
7"
Gladys, sgd "Hawkes" **115.00**
Grecian, Hawkes **750.00**
Hindoo, Hoare **115.00**
Hunt, 16 point hobstars, fans, prisms radiants **100.00**
Lace, Hawkes **330.00**
10"
Corinthian, Libbey **285.00**
Rosaceae, sgd "Tuthill" **1,000.00**
Thirty two point hobstar center, hobstar band near rim **160.00**

Powder Jar
4 x 3", SS Art Nouveau lid **90.00**
5 x 3", Harvard **150.00**
7" d, sgd "Hawkes" **170.00**

Punch Bowl
One piece, 14" d
Dauntless, Bergen, 1 pc **575.00**
Hobstar chain, notched prisms, zipper, mitered panels, sgd "Clark," 1 pc **1,210.00**
Two piece
10 x 9", hobstars and pinwheels, 2 pc **400.00**
12 x 11½", Temple, sgd "Maple City," 2 pc **1,000.00**

Punch Cup
Set of 6, pedestal, handled, hobstars, each **75.00**
Set of 10, "Monarch" **300.00**
Set of 11, pedestal, handled, hobstars, rayed base, each **60.00**
Punch Set, 16 x 14½", Ribbon Star, ten cups, 2 pc **3,200.00**
Ramekin Set, ruby cased to clear, clear button Russian, 2 pc **600.00**

Relish
6", pinwheel, hobstars, fans, and prisms **65.00**
7½ x 5½", flat, oval, Vintage, hobstar gallery, sgd "Tuthill" **275.00**
8 x 3½", hobstars **35.00**

Rose Bowl
6" d, Russian **450.00**
6 x 5½", vesica, fan, and cross-cut diamond **400.00**
6 x 7", fan, cane, and prisms **310.00**

7"
Clear button Russian **525.00**
Pedestal, Bruswick, sgd "Hawkes" **1,025.00**
9", Queens, Hawkes **1,400.00**
Rum Jug, 7½" h, all over notched prism **325.00**
Salad Set, SP, fork and spoon, cross-cut diamond glass handles **300.00**

Salt and Pepper Shaker
Garland, 4", green, SS lids **55.00**
Notched prism columns **25.00**

Salt Dips
Feather **14.00**
Master and 8 individual, notched prism **100.00**
Notched prism, set of 6 . . . . **65.00**

Spooner
Floral, double handled **135.00**
Hobstars and strawberry diamonds . **160.00**

Stemware
Champagne
Double teardrop stems, strawberry diamonds and fans, set of 6 . . . **300.00**
Flared bowls, hobstar chain and bases, set of 9 . . . . **450.00**
Kalana Lily, Dorflinger **50.00**
Monarch, saucer shape, set of 12 **1,200.00**
Cordial, cut and engraved, sgd "Hawkes" **65.00**
Sherbet, Chicago, 4" h, Fry **65.00**
Supreme, 6½" h, hobstar, strawberry diamonds, and fans, hobstar bases, set of 6 . . . . **270.00**
Water
Clear button Russian, facet cut teardrop stem, rayed base, set of 8, each **125.00**
Double Lozenge, set of 9 . . . . . . **950.00**
Double teardrop stems, 6½ x 3½", strawberry diamond, and fans, wood polished, set of 12 . . . . . **780.00**
Double teardrop stems, hobstar bases, cane, hobstars, fans, strawberry diamonds **1,400.00**
Rayed button Russian, 6" h, teardrop stems, sgd "Hawkes," set of 9 . . . . **1,170.00**
Wine
Amberina bowl, hobstar button Russian, honeycomb stem **650.00**
Cross-cut diamond and fans, 5" h, set of 8, each **33.00**
Hobstars, fans, and strawberry diamonds, pr, each **30.00**
Imperial, teardrop stem, sgd "Libbey," pr, each **80.00**
Rayed button Russian, knobbed teardrop stem, rayed bases, set of 4 . . . . **350.00**
Rayed button Russian, teardrop stem, pattern cut base **200.00**
Ruby bowl, rayed button Russian,

teardrop stem, Brooklyn star
base, Dorflinger **700.00**
Yellow bowl, hobstar and straw-
berry diamond, teardrop stems,
hobstar base **110.00**
String Holder, fancy notched prism, Gorham SS top **125.00**
Sugar Cube Tray, 9″, cane **75.00**
Syrup Pitcher
4″, SP, hinged lid and handle, fancy
vertical notched prisms **70.00**
Strawberry diamond and fan, SS top **120.00**
Tantalus, 13″ h, frame, Quadruple plate
on copper frame, two 9½ x 3″ sq bottles, honeycomb and engraved florals, sgd "Hawkes" on frame and
glass **250.00**
Toothbrush Holder, cane **140.00**
Toothpick Holder
2½″ h, prism cut **35.00**
3″ h, pedestal, hobstars **90.00**
Floral **25.00**
Tray
11½ x 13½″, oak leaf shape, flashed
fancy notched prisms, vesicas,
cane Pitkins and Brooks **1,025.00**
12″
Corinthian, sgd "Libbey" **625.00**
Hobstars, cane, and strawberry
diamonds **300.00**
Pinwheels, hobstars, and floral . . **110.00**
13″, Alhambra **1,300.00**
13 x 8½″, rect, handled, sunbursts
and leaves **250.00**
14″, Kohinoor surrounding intaglio cut
medallions, hobstar center, cane,
and vesicas **2,000.00**
18″ l, oval, Carolyn, thick heavy blank,
well cut, Hoare **1,600.00**
18 x 10½″, hobstars sharply cut, clear
blank **1,700.00**
Tumble Up, handled pitcher with tum-
bler over top, geometric and floral . . **410.00**
Tumbler
Bristol Rose, Mount Washington, set
of 3 . . . . **210.00**
Champagne, rayed button Russian,
Russian bases, set of 6 . . . . **480.00**
Clear button Russian, set of 8, each **95.00**
Harvard, rayed base, set of 3 . . . . . **120.00**
Hobstars, set of 5, each **35.00**
Hobstars, strawberry diamonds, fans,
hobstar cluster and base, set of 6 **330.00**
Notched prism, hobstar, cane **55.00**
Panel, sgd "Hawkes," rare **400.00**
Star of David, 4″, set of 4 . . . . **260.00**
Whiskey, 3½″ h, 2½″ d rim, hobstar
chain and cane **125.00**
Umbrella Stand, 24″ h, hobstar chain
around top, middle, and base with
vertical notched prism bars between **1,600.00**

Vase
4½″ h, bud, trumpet shape, daisy, sgd
"Sinclaire," pr **170.00**
12″
Corset shape, cosmos and cane . **75.00**
Russian and pillar **900.00**
Trumpet, punty, hobstar, and straw-
berry diamond **75.00**
12 x 4″, cylindrical, Queens, Hawkes **825.00**
12 x 4½″, chalice, butterflies, and
flowers, facet cut knob near base,
pattern cut base **375.00**
14″, trumpet, Queens, sgd "Hawkes" **825.00**
14 x 5″
Assyrian, sgd "Sinclaire" **1,300.00**
Lotus, rayed base, Egginton **395.00**
15″, Queens, facet cut knob, hobstar
base, slight glass tint, sgd
"Hawkes" **1,000.00**
16″, trumpet, Teutonic, sgd "Hawkes" **500.00**
Violet Vase
Fancy notched prism bowl, rayed
base **190.00**
Hobstars and strawberry diamonds . **225.00**
Hobstars and zipper **80.00**
Wall Placket, 9″, Mums, sgd "Hawkes
Gravic" **150.00**
Water Carafe, ruby cut to clear, all-over
cutting, many rayed stars, cut double
flutes and notches on neck, American
Brilliant period **350.00**
Water Set
Floral and butterfly, pitcher and four
tumblers **200.00**
Hobstars, rose hatching, 9″ pitcher
and six tumblers **250.00**
Hobstars, tankard pitcher and six
tumblers, sgd "Libbey" **475.00**
Poppy, tankard pitcher and six tum-
blers, sgd "Tuthill" **2,000.00**
Queens, tankard pitcher and six tum-
blers, Hawkes **1,800.00**
Whiskey Jug, 8½″, swirled bands of
strawberry diamond and cane, hob-
star chain, fans **500.00**

CUT VELVET

History: Several glass manufacturers made cut
velvet during the late Victorian era, c1870–1900.
An outer layer of pastel color was applied over a
white casing. The piece then was molded or cut
in a ribbed or diamond shape in high relief, ex-
posing portions of the casing. The finish had a
satin velvety feel, hence the name "cut velvet."

Biscuit Jar, pink, SP mountings **230.00**
Creamer, 3½″, cranberry, DQ, applied
multicolored enamel dec **350.00**

Ewer, 4¾", deep blue, DQ, applied
  frosted handle **140.00**
Finger Bowl, 4½" d, blue, DQ **125.00**
Rose Bowl, 4¼", blue, DQ, crimped top   **175.00**
Toothpick, 3⅝", yellow, DQ, sq mouth .   **180.00**

**Vase, blue, diamond quilted, ruffled
and crimped top, twisted reeding on
neck, spherical pedestal base, 9½" h,
$250.00.**

Vase
  5¼", blue, quatrefoil top **100.00**
  6¼", opaque white, faint pink int., rib-
    bon candy rim **100.00**
  6¾", pink, DQ, ruffled **200.00**
  8¼", blue **190.00**
  8⅜", pale blue **250.00**
  9", blue, DQ, ruffled **235.00**

CZECHOSLOVAKIAN ITEMS

History: Objects marked "Made in Czechoslovakia" were produced after 1918 when the country
claimed its independence from the Austro-Hungarian Empire. The people became more cosmopolitan, liberated, and expanded their scope of life.
Their porcelains, pottery, and glassware reflect
many influences.

A specific manufacturer's mark may be identified
as being much earlier than 1918, but this only
indicates the factory existed in the Bohemian or
Austro-Hungarian Empire period.

Reference: Ruth A. Forsythe, *Made in Czechoslovakia*, Richardson Printing Corp., 1982.

GLASS

Basket, 6½" h, 5" d, clear with red and
  yellow spangle, applied clear handle   **50.00**
Bowl, cased, yellow int., black ext., polished pontil **45.00**
Decanter Set, figural owl decanter, four

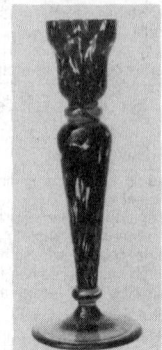

**Candlestick, tortoise glass, brown and
white, marked "Made in Czechoslovakia," 7¾" h, $100.00.**

  matching cups, blue glass, painted
  eyes **155.00**
Dish, filigree, frosted, cameo inset, ftd   **45.00**
Lamp, mushroom shape, frosted glass
  shade, glass base with silhouette of
  lady and gentleman, small raised
  roses and beading on shade **350.00**
Lamp Shade, beaded, Forsythe "659"   **35.00**
Perfume Bottle
  5", amber glass, engraved design,
    frosted flowers, stopper **25.00**
  5¼", cut crystal, yellow with round,
    flat, cut dauber **35.00**
Powder Box, cov, round, yellow, black
  knob top **55.00**
Vase
  8", yellow, black snake, ruffled top . .   **175.00**
  12½", flask shape, Burmese, birds
    perched on stems, foliage, moon,
    sgd "Tischer #426" **500.00**

POTTERY AND PORCELAIN

Bookends, Pouter Pigeon, pr **45.00**
Cologne Bottle, 4", glossy blue, bow
  front **12.00**
Creamer, 4½", figural, parrot, multico-
  lored **35.00**
Pitcher, 4", red black handle **15.00**
Plate, 10", Art Deco, maiden, black and
  yellow, 1920s **50.00**
Salt Box, Dutch scene **50.00**
Teapot, cov, and underplate, Chelsea
  style, delicate florals, marked "Em-
  phila Czechoslovakia" **40.00**
Vase, 8¼", brown to yellow, cobalt han-
  dle **50.00**

DAVENPORT
LONGPORT
STAFFORDSHIRE

DAVENPORT

History: John Davenport opened a pottery in Longport, Staffordshire, England in 1793. His ware was of high quality, light weight, and cream colored with a beautiful velvety texture.

The firm made soft-paste (Old Blue), luster trimmed ware, and pink luster with black transfer. There have been pieces of Gaudy Dutch and Spatterware found with the Davenport mark. Later Davenport became a leading maker of ironstone and early flow blue. His famous "Cyprus" pattern in mulberry became very popular. His heirs continued the business until the factory closed in 1886.

Reference: Susan and Al Bagdade, *Warman's English & Continental Pottery & Porcelain, 1st Edition,* Warman Publishing Co., Inc., 1987.

Cup and Saucer, Clifford Pattern, $100.00.

Butter Pat, flow blue	**20.00**
Charger, 17½", oval, Venetian harbor scene, light blue transfer	**70.00**
Compote, 2½ x 8½", turquoise and gold band, tiny raised flowers, hp scene with man fishing, cows at edge of lake, c1860, pr	**175.00**
Creamer, tan, jasperware, basketweave, incised anchor mark	**50.00**
Cup and Saucer, Amoy pattern, flow blue, 3¾" cup, 6" saucer, incised anchor mark	**70.00**
Cup Plate, teaberry, pink luster	**30.00**
Dish, ftd, tricorn, Belvoir Castle dec . .	**85.00**
Ewer, 9", floral dec, multicolored, c1830	**185.00**
Mustard Pot, 3½", hinged SP cov, turquoise, gilt foliage and florals, 1870–86	**65.00**
Pitcher, 8"	
Cathedral, pink luster, black transfer	**200.00**
Country scene, gold wheat and berries trim	**85.00**
Plate	
8", octagonal, floral dec, gold rim . .	**40.00**
9⅛", Legend of Montrose, transfer, 1850–70	**50.00**
Plate, 10½", Rose and Lily pattern, marked "Davenport"	**60.00**
Platter	
17¼", Tyrol Hunter, brown transfer .	**100.00**
18", white, blue border, anchor mark, c1820	**200.00**
20" l, rect, blue and white, transfer printed exotic bird and flower pattern, c1840	**300.00**
Punch Bowl, 14" d, int. painted iron-red, blue, and gilt, chrysanthemum and rockwork, iron-red trellis border, rim with flowering foliage on blue ground, ext. with band of seaweed pattern in gilt on pale blue ground between bands of dark blue foliage, puce mark "Davenport, Manufacturers To Their Majesties, Long Port, Staffordshire," c1830	**2,200.00**
Sauce Dish, cov, ladle, creamware, molded leaves, lime green veining, early	**425.00**
Tazza, 9½", octagonal, ftd, Imari pattern, c1860	**110.00**
Tea Set, teapot, creamer, and ftd sugar, blue and white, marked "Davenport, Godden No. 1194," c1880	**100.00**
Tureen, 12", Blue Willow pattern	**150.00**
Vegetable Dish, Berry pattern, imp signature, anchor mark	**50.00**

DECOYS

History: Carved wooden decoys, used to lure ducks and geese to the hunter, have become widely recognized as an indigenous American folk art form in the past several years.

Many decoys are from the 1880–1930 period when commercial gunners commonly hunted using rigs of several hundred decoys. Many fine carvers also worked through the 1930s and 1940s.

The value of a decoy is based on several factors: (1) fame of the carver, (2) quality of the carving, (3) species of wild fowl–the most desirable are herons, swans, mergansers, and shorebirds, and (4) condition of the original paint (o.p.).

The inexperienced collector should be aware of several facts. The age of a decoy, per se, is usually of no importance in determining value. Since very few decoys were ever signed, it will be quite difficult to attribute most decoys to known carvers. Anyone who has not examined a known carver's work will be hard pressed to determine if the paint on one of his decoys is indeed original.

Repainting severely decreases a decoy's value. In addition, there are many fakes and reproductions on the market and even experienced collectors are occasionally fooled.

Decoys listed below are of average wear unless otherwise noted. o.p. indicates original paint.

Reference: Henry A. Fleckenstein, Jr., *American Factory Decoys*, Schiffer Publishing; Art, Brad and Scott Kimball, *The Fish Decoy,* Aardvark Publications, Inc., 1986; Carl F. Luckey, *Collecting Antique Bird Decoys: An Identification & Value Guide,* Books Americana, 1983.

Periodicals: *Decoy Hunter Magazine*, 901 North 9th, Clinton, IN 47842; *Decoy Magazine*, P.O. Box 1900, Montego Bay Station, Ocean City, MD 21842; *The Wild Fowl Art Journal*, Ward Foundation, 655 South Salisbury Blvd, Salisbury, MD 21801.

American Merganser Drake, Hurley Conklin, hollow carved, sleeping position	**475.00**
Black Breasted Plover	
Harry V. Shourds, orig paint	**2,600.00**
Unknown maker, metal spike bill, tack eyes, split tail, orig paint, branded "EP Smith" on bottom	**1,000.00**
Black Duck	
A. E. Crowell, sleeping position, rect brand on bottom	**1,000.00**
Charles Thomas, Massachusetts, glass eye, orig paint	**350.00**
Gus Wilson, Maine, calling and rocking head style, carved wings, orig paint	**3,500.00**
Ira Hudson, preening, raised wings, outstretched neck, scratch feather paint	**8,500.00**
Mason Factory, Challenge Grade, snakey head, orig grade stamp on bottom	**1,600.00**
Ward Brothers, balsa body, head turned to left, orig paint	**1,200.00**
Blue-Wing Teal Drake	
Harry Jobes, carved, sleeping position	**90.00**
Mason Factory, Premier Grade, orig paint	**475.00**
Unknown Maker, standard grade, tack eyes, orig paint	**425.00**
Blue-Wing Teal, mated pair, Charles E.	

Bluebill Drake, Rozell Bliss, Stratford, CT, 1910, $250.00.

Wheeler, hollow carved, sleeping position	**16,000.00**
Bluebill Drake	
C. Ralph Welles, carved, branded "CRW" on bottom, c1930	**2,400.00**
Ira Hudson, Virginia, orig paint	**325.00**
Ward Brothers, pinch breast style, sgd "Lem and Steve" under tail, stamped on bottom, c1930	**850.00**
Brant	
A. E. Crowell, carved, three dimensional feathered paint pattern, brass tack eyes	**6,000.00**
Ward Brothers, Maryland, hollow carved, head turned left, sgd "Lem and Steve," dated "1971"	**1,500.00**
Bufflehead Drake	
A. A. Waterfield, orig paint, stamped signature on bottom	**80.00**
Harry M. Shourds, hollow carved, painted eyes	**1,800.00**
Unknown Maker, hollow carved, old paint	**500.00**
Canada Goose	
A. E. Crowell, carved, feathered paint pattern, brass tack eyes, oval brand on bottom	**4,750.00**
Doug Jester, Virginia, old paint	**450.00**
Harry V. Shourds, New Jersey, hollow carved, repaint	**600.00**
Hurley Conklin, hollow carved, swimming position, branded "H. Conklin" on bottom	**600.00**
Curlew	
Harry V. Shourds, orig paint	**2,000.00**
Unknown Maker, New Jersey, iron spike bill, orig paint	**550.00**
William Gibian, carved wings and feathers, head turned back, carved neck muscle, sgd on bottom	**500.00**
Eider Drake, unknown maker, Maine, carved bill, inlet neck, chip carved body, up-turned tail, orig paint	**700.00**
Golden Plover, unknown maker, orig paint, carved "JHS" initials on bottom	**600.00**
Goldeneye Hen, Lothrop Holmes, orig paint, flaking on one side	**450.00**
Green Wing Teal	
Harry Jobes, carved, sleeping position	**90.00**
Hurley Conklin, pr, hollow carved, carved wing tips, turned heads, branded "H. Conklin"	**700.00**
J. T. Coolidge Jr., miniature, sgd and dated 1942 on bottom	**200.00**
Green Wing Teal Hen, Lem Ward, hollow carved, raised feathers and wing tips, head turned left, sgd and dated "1959"	**2,000.00**
Gull, Hurley Conklin, New Jersey, hollow, stickup carving, raised wing tips, branded "H. Conklin" on bottom	**550.00**

Heron, unknown maker, carved wing
and tail, wrought iron legs **900.00**
Knot, John Dilley, New York, carved
wings, burnt orange breast, multico-
lored feather detail **6,000.00**
Mallard Drake
Bert Graves, hollow carved, orig
weight on bottom, branded "E. I.
Rogers" and "Cleary" **900.00**
Mason Factory, Standard grade,
glass eyes, orig paint **350.00**
Mallard Hen
Bernard Ohnmacht, orig paint **1,150.00**
Robert Elliston, hollow carved, orig
paint **1,700.00**
Unknown maker, premier grade, head
turned to right, orig paint **1,650.00**
Merganser Drake
Mason Factory, Challenge Grade,
orig paint **675.00**
Unknown Maker, challenge grade,
up-turned head, swirled paint,
glass eye **2,000.00**
Merganser Hen
Capt Small, Massachusetts, hollow
carved, orig paint, c1900 . . . . **825.00**
George Boyd, head turned slightly,
feathered paint **7,000.00**
Hurley Conklin, hollow carved, carved
wing tips, branded "H. Conklin" on
bottom **350.00**
Mason Factory, up turned head,
swirled feathering **1,600.00**
Pintail Drake
A. E. Crowell, Massachusetts, orig
paint, oval brand on bottom **1,600.00**
Mason Factory, Premier Grade, slop-
ing breast, orig paint **750.00**
Tony St. Germain, orig paint, c1940 **1,800.00**
Pintail Hen, Mason Factory, Premier
Grade, sloping breast, orig paint,
marked "Big Point Co./Pathcourt,
Ont/John S. Meredith/member 1900–
1920" **2,300.00**
Plover
Joe Lincoln, winter plumage feather
painting, orig paint **750.00**
Unknown Maker, iron spiked bill,
glass eyes, winter plumage paint
pattern **3,400.00**
Red Breasted Merganser Drake
Amos Wallace, Maine, inlet neck,
carved crest, detailed feathered
paint **2,000.00**
Davison Hawthorne, orig paint, sgd
on bottom **250.00**
George Boyd, New Hampshire,
carved, orig paint **8,000.00**
George Huey, head turned to left,
carved wing tips and eyes, inlet
neck, inset leather comb, sgd "G.R.
Huey" on bottom **800.00**

Unknown Maker, slender and graceful
carving, worn old paint **1,650.00**
Red Breasted Merganser, mated pair
Hurley Conklin, hollow carved, carved
wing tips, turned heads, branded
"H Conklin" on bottom **600.00**
Norman Hudson, Virginia, carved
crests, bills, and tails, c1949 . . . . **900.00**
Oscar Bibber, hollow carved, turned
head, orig horsehair combs, orig
paint **4,000.00**
Willie Ross, Maine, graceful body, in-
let necks, ostrich feather crests,
orig paint **3,700.00**
Redhead Hen, A. E. Crowell, carved tail
feathers, raised crossed wing tips . . **4,000.00**
Robin Snipe
Obediah Verity, carved wings and
eyes, orig paint **4,250.00**
Unknown maker, carved wings, split
tail, one painted eye, other is seal-
ing wax, orig paint **4,200.00**
Ruddy Turnstone, unknown maker, orig
paint **600.00**
Squaw, mated pair, Gus Wilson, carved
wings and eyes, swivel heads, pr . . **3,250.00**
Surf Scoter, unknown maker, inlet neck,
old paint **950.00**
White Wing Scoter, unknown maker,
Maine, deep inlet neck, graceful form,
old paint **150.00**
Widgeon, mated pair, Charlie Joiner,
Maryland, sgd on bottom **775.00**
Widgeon Drake, Ward Brothers, balsa
body, orig paint, sgd "Lem and Steve"
on bottom, dated "1953" **1,200.00**
Widgeon Hen, Gilbert St. Ours, Rhode
Island, orig paint **120.00**
Yellowlegs
A. E. Crowell, carved split tail, mellow
dry paint, brass tack **5,500.00**
Joe Lincoln, carved wings, split tail,
stippled paint on sides, branded
"S" on bottom **1,700.00**
Unknown Maker, feeding position, in-
cised wings, split tail, orig paint . . **1,000.00**
William Mathews, carved "V" tail,
head turned slightly to left **800.00**

DEDHAM POTTERY

History: Alexander W. Robertson established
the Chelsea Pottery in Chelsea, Massachusetts,

in 1860. In 1872 it was known as the Chelsea Keramic Art Works.

In 1895 the pottery moved to Dedham, and the name was changed to Dedham Pottery. Their principal product was gray crackleware dinnerware with a blue decoration, the rabbit pattern being the most popular. The factory closed in 1943.

The following marks help determine the approximate age of items: (1) Chelsea Keramic Art Works, "Robertson" impressed, 1876–1889; (2) C.P.U.S. impressed in a cloverleaf, 1891–1895; (3) Foreshortened rabbit, 1895–1896; (4) Conventional rabbit with "Dedham Pottery" stamped in blue, 1897; (5) Rabbit mark with "Registered", 1929–1943.

Reference: Lloyd E. Hawes, *The Dedham Pottery And The Earlier Robertson's Chelsea Potteries*, Dedham Historical Society, 1968.

Reproduction Alert: Several rabbit pattern pieces have been reproduced.

Plate, Lobster pattern, pre–1929, blue rabbit mark and impressed rabbit under glaze mark, 8⅞″ d, $550.00.

Bowl
 7½″, Turtle
  10″, Magnolia, oval 225.00
Butter Dish, Rabbit 200.00
Celery Dish, Rabbit 200.00
Chocolate Pot, Rabbit 300.00
Creamer
 3″, Magnolia 150.00
 4″, Rabbit 125.00
Cup and Saucer
 Duck 135.00
 Elephant 150.00
 Pond Lily 125.00
Egg cup, 4″, double, Rabbit 150.00
Mug, Rabbit 148.00
Pitcher, 8″, Rabbit 275.00
Planter
 6 x 3¼ x 3¼″, green, circular mirror
  dec, marked "JHR, HCR" 250.00
 8¼ x 5¾ x 3¾″, green, zig zag dec,
  marked 450.00

 8¹¹⁄₁₆ x 4¾ x 4½″, pedestal, leaf design, ruffled top, short rabbit mark 300.00
 8¾ x 5¼ x 3¾″, green, blocked mirror, ruffled top, marked "Capt." DPCO in hexagon 350.00
Plate
 6″
  Grape border, imp rabbit ears mark 100.00
  Iris 100.00
  Polar Bear 200.00
  Pond Lily, imp rabbit ears 100.00
  Rabbits 75.00
 6¼″, crab and waves, post 1929 mark 325.00
 7½″
  Azalea 100.00
  Grape 100.00
 8½″
  Fish in center, blue waves, Crackleware, pre 1929 mark 1,100.00
  Horse Chestnut, cipher mark of Maude Davenport 250.00
  Pond Lily 175.00
  Poppy, pre 1929 mark 500.00
  Rabbit, 2 ears, pre 1929 mark . . . 90.00
  Snowtree, pre 1929 mark 125.00
  Turkey 150.00
 8⅜″, Woodcock in flight, pre 1929 mark 1,450.00
 10″
  Butterfly 300.00
  Mushroom, blue mark, imp rabbit ears 125.00
Platter, 12½″, Rabbit 225.00
Salt Shaker, Rabbit, light blue, Crackleware 135.00
Sugar, cov, Rabbit 150.00
Tea Cup, 2¼″ h, 4″ d, Snowtree 100.00
Tile
 Horse Chestnut 125.00
 Magnolia 110.00
 Rabbit 120.00
Vase
 7¼″, Volcanic, orange peel texture, red dragon's blood glaze, white finger-like runs, marked "Hugh Robertson" 800.00
 8″, Crackleware, blue dogwood, emb, rabbit mark 450.00

DELFTWARE

History: Delftware is pottery of a soft red clay body with tin enamel glaze. The white, dense, opaque color came from adding tin ash to lead glaze. The first examples had blue designs on a white ground. Polychrome examples followed.

The name originally applied to pottery made in

the region around Delft, Holland, beginning in the 16th century and ending in the late 18th century. Tin came from the Cornish mines in England. By the 17th and 18th centuries English potters in London, Bristol, and Liverpool were copying the glaze and designs. Some designs unique to English potters also developed.

In Germany and France, the ware is known as Faience and in Italy as Majolica.

Reference: Susan and Al Bagdade, *Warman's English & Continental Pottery & Porcelain, 1st Edition,* Warman Publishing Co., Inc., 1987.

Reproduction Alert: Much souvenir Delft-type material has been produced in the late 19th and 20th centuries to appeal to the foreign traveler. Don't confuse these modern pieces with the older examples.

Miniature Lamp, 6⅛″ h, $100.00.

Bird Feeder, 14½″, cylindrical, five pierced arches, blue and white swags and florals, line and trellis borders, Bristol, c1760 .... 715.00
Bottle, 10″, globular, flared garlick neck, blue and white, stylized baskets of flowers and trailing branches, Liverpool, c1770 .... 500.00
Bowl, 12″, blue and white, bird on flowering foliage and insert, in. with flower spray, yellow rim, band of stylized flowerheads, Liverpool, c1740 ..... 275.00
Charger
  13⅝″, broad cavetto with flowers and geometric dec, bird and flowers in center, late 17th C, one faint age crack 600.00
  21″, broad cavetto, plain center,

scenes of Chinese at tea, shades of blue, mid 18th C 850.00
Dish, 13½″ d, deep, yellow and lavender flowers, green leaves, Lambeth 700.00
Ewer, 8½″, floral dec, zigzag band, blue, purple, and yellow ochre 250.00
Figure, 4½″ h, cows, polychrome, glazed, Dutch, pr 400.00
Flower Brick, 5″ l, rect, blue and white scene, buildings in landscape on long side, figure in boat on short sides, pierced top with blue dot pattern, four ogee feet, English, c1750 .... 375.00
Ink Well
  4 x 4 x 2″, polychrome flowers, white ground 250.00
  4¼″, handle, stylized floral dec, multicolored, Lambeth, English, c1700 350.00
Jar, cov
  15½ h, lobed baluster, blue and white, four cartouches of seascapes, diapered ground with flowerheads, foliage, and scrolls, lion shaped knob, inscribed "AL" in underglaze blue, Dutch, pr 1,320.00
  15¾″ h, octagonal baluster, four peacocks on densely dec floral ground, border and cov with lappet band, blue fu dog finial, blue inscribed claw mark, Dutch 400.00
  17¼″ h, ribbed octagonal baluster, blue and white, four cartouches with seashore landscapes, two panels with amorous couples, upper border of flowerheads and scrollwork, densely painted ground, lion form knob, inscribed "AL" ... 550.00
  24″ h, octagonal baluster, blue and white, sailboats in molded and painted scrollwork border, reverse with floral spray, foliate strays and scrolls ground, bird shaped knob, minor restoration, Dutch 1,000.00
Plaque, 16½″, portrait of lady, flow blue, urn and letters mark, pierced for hanging 400.00
Plate, 9″, blue and white, floral design, late 18th C 185.00
Shoe, 6¾″, blue and white, high heel, pointed toe, molded buckle, band of trellis pattern ribbon, Bristol, c1760 . 600.00
Soup Plate, 8¾″, blue and white, fisherman on pier, boat, buildings, and trees in background, pine cones and foliage border, Bristol, c1760, pr ... 375.00
Stein, 7½″, blue and white florals, sponged purple dec, pewter lid and base, marked "BP" 450.00
Tile, manganese, roundels of boats, buildings, and windmills in river scene, stylized floral sprays in corners, Dutch, 18th C, set of 15 ..... 550.00

DEPRESSION GLASS

History: Depression glass is a glassware made during the period of 1920–40. It was an inexpensive machine-made glass, produced by several companies in various patterns and colors. The number of pieces within a pattern also varied.

Depression glass was sold through variety stores, given as premiums, or packaged with certain products. Movie houses gave it away from 1935 until well into the 1940s.

Like pattern glass, knowing the proper name of a pattern is the key to collecting. Collectors should be prepared to do research.

References: Gene Florence, *The Collector's Encyclopedia of Depression Glass, Ninth Edition*, Collector Books, 1990; Gene Florence, *Elegant Glassware of the Depression Era, Third Edition*, Collector Books, 1988; Gene Florence, *Very Rare Glassware Of The Depression Years*, Collector Books, 1987; Carl F. Luckey and Mary Burris, *An Identification & Value Guide to Depression Era Glassware, Second Edition*, Books Americana, 1986; Mark Schliesmann, *Price Survey, Second Edition*, Park Avenue Publications, Ltd, 1984; Hazel Marie Weatherman, *1984 Supplement & Price Trends for Colored Glassware Of The Depression Era, Book 1*, published by author, 1984.

Periodical: The Daze, Box 57, Otisville, MI 48463.

Collectors' Club: National Depression Glass Association, Inc., Box 69843, Odessa, TX 79769.

Reproduction Alert: Send a self addressed stamped business envelope to *The Daze* and request a copy of their glass reproduction list. It is one of the best bargains in the antiques business.

Additional Listings: See *Warman's Americana & Collectibles* for more examples.

AMERICAN PIONEER, Liberty Works, 1931–34. Made in crystal, green, and pink; limited production in amber.

	Crystal	Green	Pink
Bowl			
5½", handled	9.50	12.00	9.50
8¾", cov	75.00	100.00	75.00
9", handled	10.00	15.00	12.00
9¼", cov	75.00	100.00	75.00
10¾", console	35.00	45.00	35.00
Candlesticks, 6½", pr.	50.00	70.00	50.00
Candy Dish, cov, 1 lb.	65.00	80.00	65.00
Cheese & Comport	35.00	50.00	35.00
Coaster, 3½"	13.00	15.00	12.50
Creamer, 3½"	10.00	18.00	12.00
Cup & Saucer	8.75	15.00	9.00
Goblet			
4", 3 oz, wine	15.00	25.00	18.00
6", ftd, 8 oz, water	15.00	25.00	18.00
Ice Bucket, 6"	30.00	40.00	30.00
Lamp, 8½" h	55.00	70.00	65.00
Pitcher			
5", cov, urn	110.00	160.00	110.00
7", cov	135.00	175.00	135.00
Plates			
8", luncheon	9.00	12.00	8.00
11", handled	12.00	15.00	12.00
Rose Bowl, ftd, flared	—	60.00	—
Sherbert			
3½"	10.00	15.00	10.00
4¾"	18.00	24.00	18.00
Sugar, 3½"	15.00	18.00	15.00
Tumbler			
5 oz, juice	18.00	24.00	18.00
8 oz, 4"	20.00	25.00	22.00
12 oz, 5"	28.00	40.00	30.00
Vase, 7"	55.00	65.00	60.00

 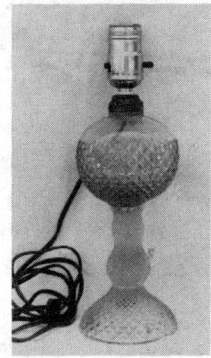

Left: Dogwood, plate, dinner, grill, pink, $14.00. Right: English Hobnail, lamp, pink, 9″, $115.00.

CORONATION, "Banded Rib," "Saxon," Hocking Glass Company, 1936–48. Made in green, pink, and royal ruby.

	Green	Pink	Royal Ruby
Bowl			
4¼″, berry	—	3.00	4.50
6½″, nappy	—	3.50	8.00
8″, berry, handled	—	7.00	9.00
8″, no handles	20.00	—	—
Cup	—	3.50	4.50
Pitcher, 7¾″, 68 oz	—	150.00	—
Plate			
6″, sherbet	—	1.50	—
8½″, luncheon	18.00	3.50	5.00
Saucer	—	1.50	—
Sherbet	35.00	3.50	—
Tumbler, 5″, 10 oz, ftd	40.00	15.00	—

DOGWOOD, "Apple Blossom, Wild Rose," Macbeth-Evans Glass Co., 1929–1932. Made in cremax, crystal, green, monax, pink, yellow. Limited production in crystal, monax, yellow.

	Cremax	Green	Pink
Ashtray	—	—	12.00
Bowl			
5½″, cereal	16.00	18.50	12.50
8½″, berry	42.50	60.00	35.00
10¼″, fruit	65.00	120.00	200.00
Cake Plate, ftd, 13″	145.00	60.00	75.00
Cup and Saucer	18.75	18.75	15.00
Pitcher, 8″, decorated	—	—	125.00
Plate			
6″, bread & butter	20.00	6.75	4.50
8″, luncheon	—	3.85	4.50
9¼″, dinner	—	—	18.00
10½″, grill, all over pattern	—	12.00	14.00

	Cremax	Green	Pink
Saucer	18.00	6.50	2.00
Sherbet, low, ftd	—	40.00	17.50
Sugar, 2½"	—	25.75	8.00
Tumbler			
4", 10 oz, decor	—	50.00	20.00
4¾", 10 oz, decor	—	75.00	30.00
5", 12 oz decor	—	80.00	35.00

ENGLISH HOBNAIL, Westmoreland Glass Company, 1920–70s. Made in amber, cobalt blue, crystal, green, pink, and turquoise.

	Amber	Cobalt Blue	Crystal	Green	Pink	Turquoise
Ashtray, sq	20.00	40.00	5.00	20.00	20.00	40.00
Basket	—	—	10.00	—	—	—
Bowl						
4½"	9.50	9.50	4.50	10.00	10.00	20.00
5"	10.00	9.50	5.00	10.00	10.00	20.00
6"	10.00	10.00	5.00	10.00	10.00	22.75
8"						
Ftd	25.00	40.00	14.50	18.00	18.00	35.00
Handles	25.00	40.00	12.50	25.00	25.00	40.00
11", rolled edge	15.00	15.00	10.00	15.00	15.00	75.00
12", nappy	35.00	70.00	18.00	30.00	30.00	70.00
Candlesticks						
3½"	35.00	35.00	30.00	35.00	35.00	68.00
8½"	45.00	45.00	35.00	45.00	40.00	90.00
Candy Dish, 3 feet	60.00	60.00	45.00	60.00	60.00	85.00
Celery, 12"	20.00	20.00	15.00	18.00	18.00	25.00
Cigarette Box	25.00	45.00	15.00	25.00	25.00	45.00
Cologne Bottle	35.00	50.00	30.00	32.00	32.00	50.00
Creamer						
Flat	20.00	20.00	8.00	20.00	20.00	35.00
Ftd	20.00	20.00	8.00	20.00	20.00	35.00
Cup	12.00	15.00	6.00	12.00	12.00	18.00
Decanter	75.00	75.00	30.00	75.00	75.00	85.00
Demitasse Cup and Saucer	25.00	30.00	15.00	20.00	20.00	45.00
Egg Cup	25.00	28.00	18.50	25.00	25.00	40.00
Goblet						
1 oz, cordial	16.00	16.00	8.00	16.00	16.00	32.00
2 oz, wine	14.00	14.00	7.00	14.00	14.00	28.00
3 oz, cocktail	15.00	15.00	7.00	15.00	15.00	30.00
5 oz, claret	14.00	14.00	7.50	14.00	14.00	28.00
8 oz, 6¼", water	18.00	32.00	9.00	25.00	25.00	45.00
Ice Tea Stirrers	—	—	8.00	—	—	—
Lamp						
6¼", electric	75.00	75.00	65.00	75.00	75.00	150.00
9¼", oil	120.00	200.00	95.00	125.00	115.00	200.00
Marmalade, cov	35.00	40.00	25.00	35.00	35.00	70.00
Pitcher						
23 oz	120.00	120.00	60.00	120.00	125.00	175.00
39 oz	125.00	125.00	75.00	125.00	125.00	180.00
60 oz	135.00	135.00	80.00	135.00	135.00	185.00
64 oz	155.00	155.00	85.00	150.00	150.00	200.00
Place Card Holder	—	—	10.00	—	—	—

	Amber	Cobalt Blue	Crystal	Green	Pink	Turquoise
Plate						
5½"................	3.50	7.00	3.00	4.00	4.00	8.00
6½"................	4.50	7.00	3.50	5.00	5.00	10.00
7½"................	5.00	6.00	4.00	6.50	6.50	12.00
8"..................	10.00	20.00	6.50	10.00	10.00	15.00
10".................	18.00	20.00	15.00	20.00	20.00	16.25
Salt and Pepper	70.00	75.00	20.00	65.00	70.00	150.00
Salt Dip and Place Card						
Holder, ftd...........	20.00	20.00	10.00	20.00	20.00	32.50
Saucer...............	3.50	4.00	2.00	3.50	3.75	6.00
Sherbet..............	12.50	24.00	5.00	12.00	12.00	25.00
Sugar						
Flat................	20.00	20.00	8.00	20.00	20.00	35.00
Ftd.................	20.00	20.00	8.00	20.00	20.00	35.00
Tidbit, 2 tier...........	—	—	15.00	—	—	—
Tumbler						
3¾"...............	15.00	15.00	10.00	15.00	15.00	25.00
4"..................	16.00	16.00	12.00	16.00	16.00	30.00
5"..................	17.50	18.00	8.50	18.00	18.00	30.00
Vase, 7¼"............	—	—	—	20.00	—	—
Whiskey..............	18.00	18.00	15.00	18.00	18.00	18.00

FLORENTINE NO. 1, "Old Florentine, Poppy No. 1," Hazel Atlas Co., 1932–1935. Made in cobalt blue, crystal, green, pink, yellow. Limited production in cobalt blue.

	Crystal	Green	Pink	Yellow
Ashtray, 5½"............	20.00	20.00	25.00	35.00
Bowl				
5", berry.............	6.50	12.00	12.50	7.00
6", cereal............	8.00	8.00	12.00	10.00
8½", master berry......	14.00	15.50	22.00	18.00
9½", oval, veg. cov.....	28.00	27.75	36.00	35.00
Coaster, 3¾"...........	13.00	12.50	21.00	14.00

Left: Miss America, plate, grill, clear 10¼", $15.00. Right: Queen Mary, tumbler, pink, 5", $20.00.

	Crystal	Green	Pink	Yellow
Creamer				
Plain edge............	7.50	7.50	10.00	8.75
Ruffled edge	17.00	17.50	24.00	23.00
Cup	4.00	6.00	8.00	6.50
Pitcher, 6½″, 36 oz, ftd	36.00	35.00	55.00	39.75
Plate				
6″, sherbet............	5.25	5.00	4.75	4.00
8½″, salad............	6.00	6.25	8.25	9.00
10″, dinner............	8.50	9.25	12.00	13.00
10″, grill.............	8.25	8.00	9.25	10.00
Platter, 10½″, oval	15.00	15.00	18.50	18.00
Saucer................	2.00	2.00	3.00	3.00
Salt and Pepper Shakers, pr	25.00	24.75	42.50	40.00
Sherbet	8.00	8.50	7.75	8.50
Sugar				
Plain edge............	8.00	4.75	9.00	7.00
Ruffled edge	13.50	14.00	18.00	21.00
Sugar Ltd	12.00	12.00	15.00	15.00
Tumbler				
3¼″, 5 oz, ftd.........	20.00	20.00	—	—
3¾″, 5 oz, ftd, juice	12.00	12.00	14.00	12.00
4¾″, 10 oz, ftd, water....	12.00	12.00	18.00	15.00
5¼″, 12 oz, ftd, iced tea ..	14.00	14.00	22.00	20.00

HEX OPTIC, "Honeycomb," Jeannette Glass Company, 1928–32. Made in green and pink.

	Green	Pink		Green	Pink
Bowl			Platter, 11″	8.50	8.50
4¼″, berry, small	4.00	4.50	Refrigerator Dish, 4 × 4″...	8.00	8.00
7¼″, mixing	10.00	10.00	Refrigerator Stack Set, 3		
7½″, berry, master	5.00	5.00	pcs	30.00	32.00
8¼″, mixing	14.00	14.00	Salt and Pepper	18.00	18.00
9″, mixing	15.00	15.00	Sherbet	4.00	4.00
10″, mixing	18.00	18.00	Sugar.................	4.00	5.00
Butter Dish	50.00	55.00	Sugar Shaker	75.00	75.00
Creamer...............	4.00	4.25	Tumbler		
Cup	2.50	2.50	3¾″, 9 oz, flat	4.00	4.00
Ice Bucket, metal handle ...	12.50	12.50	5″, 10 oz	5.00	5.00
Pitcher			7″, ftd	5.50	5.50
5″, 32 oz	14.00	14.00	Whiskey, 2″, 1 oz	5.00	5.00
9″, 48 oz, ftd	30.00	30.00			
Plate					
6″, sherbet............	1.75	1.75			
8″, luncheon	4.50	4.50			

LACE EDGE, "Open Lace," Hocking Glass Co., 1935–1938. Made in pink, limited pieces in crystal.

	Pink		Pink
Bowl		9½″	
6½″, cereal	12.50	Plain	11.25
6⅝″, cream soup	8.50	Ribbed.............	14.50
7¾″, salad............	20.00	Butter Dish, cov	45.00

	Pink		Pink
Candlesticks, pr	150.00	Platter	
Candy Dish, ribbed	32.00	3 part, 10½"	12.00
Compote, cov, ftd	27.50	5 part, 12¾"	15.50
Cookie Jar	48.50	Relish, 10½", divided	9.00
Creamer	12.00	Saucer	6.50
Cup and Saucer	22.00	Sherbet	40.00
Flower Frog	18.00	Sugar	15.00
Plate		Tumbler	
7¼", salad	10.00	4¼", 9 oz	10.00
8½", luncheon	12.50	5", 10½ oz, ftd	32.50
10½", dinner	15.00	Vase, 7"	260.00
10½", grill	12.50		

MISS AMERICA, "Diamond Pattern," Hocking Glass Co., 1935–37. Made in crystal and pink, limited production in green, ice blue, and red.

	Crystal	Green	Pink	Red
Bowl				
4½", berry	—	7.50	12.00	—
6¼", cereal	6.00	10.00	14.00	—
8", vegetable	30.00	—	45.00	300.00
8¾", fruit	24.00	—	40.00	—
10", vegetable, oval	10.00	—	14.50	—
Butter Dish, cov	175.00	—	375.00	—
Cake Plate, ftd, 12"	20.00	—	32.00	—
Candy Dish, cov, 11½"	50.00	—	100.00	—
Celery, 10½"	10.00	—	17.50	—
Coaster	14.00	—	20.00	—
Compote, 5"	12.00	—	18.00	—
Creamer, ftd	6.50	—	14.00	135.00
Cup	7.50	10.00	12.00	—
Goblet				
3¾", 3 oz, wine	18.00	—	50.00	150.00
4¾", 5 oz, juice	16.00	—	50.00	—
5½", 10 oz, water	18.00	—	40.00	150.00
Pitcher				
8", 65 oz	50.00	—	85.00	—
8½", 65 oz, ice lip	55.00	—	90.00	—
Plate				
5¾", sherbet	3.00	5.00	4.00	—
6¾", bread & butter	—	6.00	9.50	—
8½", luncheon	5.00	8.00	13.00	60.00
10", dinner	9.00	—	17.00	—
10¼", grill	15.00	—	18.00	—
Platter, 12½"	14.00	—	15.00	—
Relish				
8¾", 4 part	8.00	—	16.50	—
11¾", round	20.00	—	125.00	—
Salt and Pepper	20.00	175.00	40.00	—
Saucer	2.50	—	4.50	—
Sherbet	7.00	—	15.00	—
Sugar	6.00	—	12.00	125.00
Tumbler				
4", 5 oz, juice	16.00	—	32.00	—
4½", 10 oz, water	18.00	15.00	25.00	—
6¾", 14 oz, iced tea	20.00	—	42.50	—

OYSTER & PEARL, Anchor Hocking Corp., 1938–1940. Made in crystal, pink, ruby red, white fired on pink or green interior.

	Crystal	Pink	Red	White with Green	White with Pink
Bowl					
5¼"					
Handled	5.00	5.00	6.00	5.50	5.50
Heart shaped	5.00	5.00	—	6.00	6.00
Round	5.00	5.00	8.70	6.00	6.00
6½", deep handled	8.00	8.00	12.00	—	—
10½", deep, fruit.	14.00	14.00	25.00	10.00	10.00
Candleholder, 3½", pr	15.00	15.00	30.00	12.00	12.00
Plate, 13½", sandwich	15.00	15.00	25.00	—	—
Relish, 10¼", oblong	6.50	6.50	—	7.00	7.50

QUEEN MARY, "Vertical Ribbed," Hocking Glass Company, 1936–40. Made in crystal and pink.

	Crystal	Pink		Crystal	Pink
Ashtray			Plate		
2 × 3¾", oval	2.00	3.00	6", sherbet.	2.50	3.00
3½", round	2.75	—	6⅝", bread and butter . . .	3.00	5.50
Bowl			8½" salad	5.00	8.00
4", nappy.	2.75	3.00	9¾", dinner	15.00	25.00
5", berry	2.00	2.50	12", sandwich	15.50	18.00
5½", two handles	3.50	4.50	14", serving	18.00	20.00
6", cereal.	4.50	6.00	Relish		
7", ice, metal holder, tongs	10.00	15.00	12", 3 pt	6.00	24.50
8¾", berry	6.00	8.00	14" 4 pt.	7.50	26.00
Butter Dish, cov	20.00	25.00	Salt and Pepper	18.00	85.00
Candlestick, 4½"	12.00	—	Saucer	1.50	2.00
Candy Dish.	12.00	15.00	Sherbet	4.00	5.00
Celery	5.00	6.00	Sugar.	4.00	6.00
Cigarette Jar	4.00	5.00	Tumbler		
			3½", 5 oz, juice	3.75	4.00
Coaster			4", 9 oz, water	5.00	8.00
3½".	2.00	2.50	5", 10 oz, ftd	12.00	30.00
4¼", sq	4.50	4.50			
Compote, 5¾".	4.50	5.00			
Creamer.	4.00	5.00			
Cup					
Large	3.25	3.75			
Small	3.00	3.50			

ROXANA, Hazel Atlas Glass Company, 1932. Made in crystal and yellow.

	Crystal	Yellow		Crystal	Yellow
Bowl			Plate, 6", sherbet.	2.50	2.75
4½", fruit	5.50	5.75	Saucer	2.50	2.75
5", berry, small.	3.75	4.00	Sherbet	3.50	4.00
6", cereal.	6.00	7.50	Tumbler, 4", 9 oz.	9.00	10.00

SIERRA, "Pinwheel," Jeanette Glass Co., 1931–1933. Made in green and pink.

	Green	Pink		Green	Pink
Bowl			Plate		
5½", cereal	9.00	8.00	8", luncheon	—	8.50
8½", master berry	10.00	8.00	9", dinner	8.50	7.50
9¼", oval	26.00	20.00	11", salver	16.00	12.00
Butter Dish, cov	45.00	50.00	Platter, 11"	30.00	28.00
Creamer	15.00	12.00	Salt and Pepper Shakers, pr	25.00	25.00
Cup	10.00	8.00	Saucer, 6"	4.00	3.50
Pitcher, 6½", 32 oz	62.50	36.50	Sugar	15.00	12.00
			Sugar Lid	10.00	10.00

TEAROOM, Indiana Glass Co., 1926–31. Made in pink and green; limited production in amber and crystal.

	Crystal	Green	Pink
Banana Split, 7½", ftd	—	60.00	70.00
Bowl			
8¾", master berry	—	50.00	60.00
Vegetable, oval	—	45.00	50.00
Candlesticks, pr	—	30.00	45.00
Ceiling Fixture	100.00	—	—
Celery, 8½"	14.00	16.50	17.00
Center Handle Plate	—	55.00	70.00
Creamer			
3½"	—	12.00	15.00
5½", ftd	12.00	10.00	10.00
Cup	—	27.00	23.50
Finger Bowl	—	40.00	30.00
Goblet	—	49.00	45.00
Ice Bucket	—	70.00	60.00
Lamp	165.00	45.00	40.00
Marmalade, cov	—	165.00	125.00
Mustard	37.50	48.00	48.00
Pitcher	—	95.00	85.00
Plate			
6½", sherbet	—	22.50	20.00
8½", luncheon	—	25.00	22.50
10½", 2 handles	—	42.50	35.00
Relish, 2 parts	15.00	13.50	15.00
Salt and Pepper Shakers, pr	50.00	35.00	40.00
Saucer	—	15.00	16.00
Sherbet			
Low	18.00	20.00	17.50
Tall	—	30.00	25.00
Sugar			
3½"	—	12.00	14.00
4½"	12.00	10.00	10.00
Sundae	—	75.00	60.00
Tray for 3½" creamer and sugar	—	35.00	30.00
Tumbler			
6 oz ftd	—	16.50	20.00
9 oz	—	18.00	20.00
12 oz, ftd	—	12.50	30.00
Vase			
6", ruffled	20.00	90.00	75.00
9", ruffled	—	80.00	65.00
11", ruffled	50.00	150.00	175.00

DISNEYANA

History: Walt Disney and the creations of the famous Disney Studios hold a place of fondness and enchantment in the hearts of people throughout the world. The release of "Steamboat Willie" featuring Mickey Mouse in 1928 heralded an entertainment empire.

Walt and his brother, Roy, showed shrewd business acumen. From the beginning they licensed the reproduction of Disney characters in products ranging from wristwatches to clothing. In 1984 Donald Duck celebrated his 50th birthday, and collectors took a renewed interest in material related to him.

The market in Disneyana has been established by a few determined dealers and auction houses. Hake's Americana and Collectibles of York, PA, offers several hundred Disneyana items in each of their bimonthly mail and phone bid auctions. Sotheby's collector carousel auctions often include Disney cels, and Lloyd Ralston Toys auctions include Disney toys.

References: Robert Heide & John Gilman, *Cartoon Collectibles*, 1984 (only covers Disney material); Richard Schickel, *The Disney Version: The Life, Times, Art and Commerce of Walt Disney*, Avon Books, 1968; Michael Stern, *Stern's Guide to Disney Collectibles*, Collector Books, 1989; Tom Tumbusch, *Tomart's Illustrated Disneyana Catalog and Price Guide*, Vols. 1, 2, and 3, Tomart Publications, 1985.

Archives: Walt Disney Archives, 500 South Buena Vista Street, Burbank, CA 91521

Collectors' Club: Mouse Club, 2056 Cirone Way, San Jose, CA 95124

Additional Listings: See *Warman's Americana & Collectibles* for more examples.

Advisor: Ted Hake

Alice in Wonderland
  Fan card, full color, caption "Walt Disney's All Cartoon Feature—Alice in Wonderland," 8 x 10" **40.00**
  Marionette, composition, blue dress, white apron, yellow hair, black felt hair bow, 14", by Peter Puppet Playthings, 1950s **75.00**
Bambi
  Alarm Clock, animated, Flower and Thumper on dial, second hand is butterfly on Bambi's tail, light blue metal case, 2½ x 4½ x 5", orig box, Bayard of France, 1972 . . . . **125.00**
  Bowl, cereal, 5" d, Bambi on bottom, butterfly on tail, flowers, Walt Disney Productions, c1940 . . . . **20.00**
  Figure, glazed ceramic, turned head looking at butterfly on tail, copyright marked "Walt Disney Productions/Japan, 2½ x 7 x 6½", c1960 . . . . **30.00**
  Picture, framed, "Bambi and Mother,"

c1940, Courvoisier Galleries sticker, c1940 . . . . **250.00**
Davy Crockett, Toy, "Walt Disney's Official Davy Crockett Western Prairie Wagon," red litho tin, full color scene, Mouseketeer symbol on side, orig brown cartoon with red illus, Adco-Liberty Mfg Co, c1950 . . . . **65.00**

Donald Duck Acrobat Gym Toy, Linemar Toys, 9 x 7" orig box, $210.00.

Donald Duck
  Celluloid, Donald Duck as musketeer on the defense, 9¼ x 6¼" **150.00**
  Comic Book Art, orig 8 panel strip, pen and ink by Al Taliaferro, Walt Disney Comics #55, page 29, 19 x 13" **600.00**
  Doll, 16", leatherette, angry Donald, by Richard G. Krueger, c1935 . . . **400.00**
  Planter, figural, sitting on top of ABC blocks, 5½", Leeds, c1940 . . . . . **25.00**
  Toy, wooden, Donald playing xylophone, paper labels, Fisher Price #177, 6 x 11 x 13", c1940 . . . . . . **75.00**
Dumbo
  Figure, 5½" h, Baby Weems, seated, baby bonnet, incised No 41 American Pottery, c1940 . . . . **75.00**
  Sketchpad, 24 ink drawings in sequence, stamped Disney Studios, c1940, 13 x 17" **300.00**
Fantasia
  Celluloid, satyrs and unicorns dancing in pasture, applied to airbrushed ground, Courvoisier Galleries label, sgd "Walt Disney" in pencil on mat, 1940, 11½ x 8" . . . **1,450.00**
  Planter, ceramic, dancing mushrooms, turquoise, high relief on both sides, 12" l x 7" w x 2" d, Vernon Kilns, c1940 . . . . **100.00**
  Toy, carousel, unicorns, 25", 1940 . . **225.00**
Goofy
  Plate, china, Goofy seated on a crate, brick wall and flowers in back, cameos of Bambi, Thumper, Flower,

two butterflies, and bluebird around
edge, marked "Beswick, England,
7" **35.00**
Wristwatch, "Backwards," 17 jewels,
leather band, MIB **350.00**

Mickey Mouse
Bank, treasure chest, red leatherette,
brass trim, emb Mickey and Minnie
on top, marked "Zell Products" .. **175.00**
Button, 1¼" celluloid, red, black,
white, Good Teeth, Mickey brushing Big Bad Wolf's teeth **65.00**
Game, Mickey Mouse Coming Home
Game, Marks Brothers, 2 x 9 x 20"
cardboard box, 16 x 16" board,
multicolored **75.00**
Guitar, plastic, 6½ x 21", yellow front,
large paper label, six plastic
strings, Walt Disney copyright,
c1970 .... **15.00**
Handkerchief, 7½" sq, small black figure of Mickey in one corner, 1930s **20.00**
Hot Pad, fabric, beige, 6 x 6", 3" center stripe depicts Mickey images in
black, white, and red, c1930 .... **25.00**
Painting, Mickey and Minnie on country lane, Mickey pointing to moon,
tempera on card, sgd "Walt Dis-
ney," c1935, 15½ x 10½" **2,500.00**

**Mickey Mouse Sand Pail, tin, multico-
lored, marked "J Chein & Co, Made In
U. S. A.," 5⅜" h, 8" w, $25.00.**

Umbrella, two silk screen poses of
Mickey, Minnie on satin-like cloth,
20" l, Walt Disney Enterprises,
c1930 .... **150.00**

Minnie Mouse
Book, *Minnie Mouse And The An-
tique Chair*, Whitman, No 845,
hardcover, 5 x 5½", 1948 ...... **20.00**
Mug, Minnie brushing hair, marked
"Salem China" **45.00**

Figure
3½" bisque, playing accordion, orig
label, c1930 .... **65.00**
3½" bisque, carrying first aid kit,
c1930 .... **50.00**

Pinocchio
Celluloid, Jiminy Crickett standing behind the eight ball with fists raised,
titled "I'll Teach You," applied to airbrushed ground, 1939, 10½ x 8" . **1,400.00**
Plaque, wood, Jiminy Crickett and
Pinocchio seated on Gepetto's sideboard, Blue Fairy holding wand,
brown finish, blue dress, yellow
hair, white wings, and yellow hat, 4
x 5", c1940 .... **75.00**

Pluto
Celluloid, Sheep Dog, Pluto walking
across desert with bone in mouth,
1949, 9 x 27" **250.00**
Mug, glazed china, Pluto on one side,
seated Mickey Mouse on other, 3",
c1930 .... **30.00**
Planter, glazed china, multicolored, 4
x 8 x 6½", c1940 .... **30.00**
Salt Shaker, glazed china, Disney
copyright on base, 4" h, c1960 .. **10.00**

Snow White
Drinking Glasses, 4½" h, full figures,
poems on each, set of eight, Libbey, c1930 .... **125.00**
Handkerchief, small image of Snow
White, deer, rabbits, and birds, red,
white, blue, and brown, 8½" sq,
c1938 .... **15.00**
Pin, molded celluloid, multicolored,
Snow White surrounded by dwarfs
with musical instruments, orig 3½ x
4" white, blue, and yellow card, pin
1¾ x 2" **25.00**
Pitcher, glazed china, raised figures,
multicolored, large handle with two
bluebirds and squirrel, music box
base plays "Whistle While You
Work," Wade Heath, England, 7½"
h, 6" d, c1938 .... **250.00**

Three Little Pigs
Bisque Set, litho box, 2 x 3½ x 5", top
shows wolf puffing at brick house,
3½" figures, c1930 .... **175.00**
Plate, glazed white china, color center scene, Patriot China (Syracuse
China Co), 7" **35.00**
Toothbrush Holder, bisque, pigs
shown with fife, fiddle, and orange
bricks, 2 x 3½ x 4" **75.00**

Zorro
Dominoes, Zorro on horseback on
back, 1 4½ x 7½", Halsman, 1950s **35.00**
Lunch Box, litho tin, raised figures,
thermos, c1950 .... **40.00**

DOLL HOUSES

History: Doll houses date from the 18th century to modern times. Early doll houses often were handmade, som~times with only one room. The most common ty~ was made for a young girl to fill with replicas of ~rniture scaled especially to fit into a doll house. ~pecial sized dolls also were made for doll houses. All types of accessories and styles allowed a doll house to portray any historical period.

References: Flora Bill Jacobs, *Dolls' Houses in America: Historic Preservation in Miniature*, Charles Scribner's Sons, 1974; Donald and He- lene Mitchell, *Dollhouses, Past and Present*, Col- lector Books, 1980; Stille, Eva, *Doll Kitchens 1800–1980*, Schiffer Publishing, 1988; Blair Whit- ton (ed.), *Bliss Toys And Dollhouses*, Dover, 1979.

Museums: Margaret Woodbury Strong Mu- seum, Rochester, NY; Washington Dolls' House and Toy Museum, Washington, D.C.

Bliss
  House, 2 story, wood, front door
    opens, litho paper designs, four ei-
    senglass windows, lace curtains,
    metal porch rain, two chimneys,
    ext. stair, 20 x 13 x 9" **2,100.00**
  Victorian, 2 rooms, 2 story, litho on
    wood, high steepled roof, dormer
    windows, spindled porch railing,
    second floor balcony, 27 x 18 x 11" **900.00**
Converse
  Cottage, red and green litho on red-
    wood, printed bay window, stone
    base, roof dormer, 15 x 17" **400.00**
  Red Robin Farm, double barn doors,
    six stalls, nine orig animals, cupola
    on roof, 1912, 19½ x 17" **425.00**
German
  English Tudor, 3 rooms, cream,
    brown trim, yellow recessed sec-
    tion, olive green door, red roof, orig
    wallpaper, front opens in two sec-
    tions, c1880, 21 x 12 x 17" **650.00**
  Victorian style, 1 room, cardboard,
    litho, three sided, hinged, wood fur-
    niture, marked "Made in Germany,"
    c1880 . . . . **250.00**
Nita Gearhart, house, 7 rooms, wallpa-
    per covered walls, handmade wood
    furniture, ten handmade bisque dolls,
    10 x 25", c1976 . . . . **500.00**
McLoughlin, house with garden, 2 story,
    2 rooms, c1911, orig box **750.00**
Schoenhut
  Bungalow, 1 story, attic, yellow and
    green, red roof, orig decal, 12¾ x
    11 x 9" **350.00**
  Mansion, 2 story, 8 rooms, attic, tan
    brick design, red roof, large dormer,

    20 glass windows, orig decal, 1923,
    29 x 26 x 30" **1,500.00**
Unknown Maker, 2 story, ornate, wood,
    litho brick, hinged side and attic, 2 car
    garage, porch with railings and
    benches, windows with shutters and
    flower boxes, removable steps, c1920 **100.00**

DOLLS

History: Dolls have been children's play toys for centuries. Dolls also have served other functions. During the 14th through 18th century doll making was centered in Europe, mainly in Germany and France. The French dolls produced in this era rep- resented adults and were dressed in the latest couturier designs. They were not children's toys.

During the mid-19th century, child and baby dolls, made in wax, cloth, bisque, and porcelain, were introduced. Facial features were hand painted; wigs were made of mohair and human hair. They were dressed in baby or children's fash- ions.

Marks from the various manufacturers are found on the back of the head, neck, or back area. These marks are very important in identifying the doll and date of manufacture.

Doll making in the United States began to flour- ish in the 1900s with names like Effanbee, Mad- ame Alexander, Ideal, and others.

References: Johana Gast Anderton, *More Twentieth Century Dolls From Bisque to Vinyl, Vol- ume A-H, Volume I-Z, Revised Edition,* Wallace- Homestead, 1974; John Axe, *The Encyclopedia of Celebrity Dolls,* Hobby House Press Inc., 1983; Jean Bach, *Collecting German Dolls*, Main Street Press, 1983; Jan Foulke, *9th Blue Book Dolls and Values*, Hobby House Press Inc. 1989; R. Lane Herron, *Herron's Price Guide To Dolls,* Wallace- Homestead, 1990; Wendy Lavitt, *American Folk Dolls*, Alfred Knopf, Inc., 1982; Wendy Lavitt, *Dolls*, Alfred A. Knopf, 1983; Robert W. Miller, *Wallace- Homestead Price Guide For Dolls, 1986–87*, Wal- lace-Homestead, 1986; Patricia R. Smith, *Modern Collector's Dolls, Editions 1, 2, 3, 4, 5*, Collector Books, 1973, 1975, 1976, 1979, 1984; Patricia R. Smith, *The World of Alexander-kins,* Collector Books, 1985; Marjorie Victoria Sturges Uhl, *Mad- ame Alexander, Ladies of Fashion,* Collector Books, 1982.

Periodicals: *Doll Reader*, Hobby House Press, Inc., 900 Frederick Street, Cumberland, MD 21502; *Dolls The Collector's Magazine*, P.O. Box 1972, Marion, OH 43305.

Collector's Clubs: Madame Alexander Fan Club, P. O. Box 146, New Lenox, IL 60451; United Federation of Doll Clubs, P.O. Box 14146, Park- ville, MO 64152.

Museums: Margaret Woodbury Strong Mu- seum, Rochester, NY; Yesteryears Museum, Sandwich, MA.

Additional Listings: See *Warman's Americana & Collectibles* for more examples.

Left: Early Bru bisque head bebe, 16″ h, $2,600.00; center: A. T. bisque head bebe, 18″ h, $10,000.00; right: French bisque head bebe, 18″ h, $3,200.00.

Alt, Beck, and Gottschalck
 22″, solid domed bisque shoulderhead, kid pin jointed body, bisque forearms, blonde human hair, blue glass inset eyes, closed mouth, well costumed, c1885, marks: 639 Made in Germany **900.00**
 26″, bisque socket head, composition, wood ball jointed body, gray glass sleep eyes, real lashes, painted features, open mouth, four porcelain teeth, brunette human hair, antique dress, c1910, marks: ABG 1362 Made in Germany **360.00**
Averill, Georgene, 15″, solid domed bisque head, flanged neck, muslin torso, composition lower arms and legs, tinted light brown baby hair and brows, half moon shape blue glass sleep eyes, open mouth, crooked smile, two porcelain lower teeth, well costumed, c1920, marks: Copyright by Georgene Averill/Made in Germany **1,000.00**
Bahr & Proschild
 11″, bisque socket head, composition bent limb baby body, blue glass sleep eyes, open mouth, two upper teeth, well costumed, c1915, marks: BP 585 2.0 . . . . **400.00**
 20″, bisque socket head, composition bent limb baby body, brunette human hair, brown glass sleep eyes, open mouth, two porcelain upper teeth, c1915, marks: BP 585 6 . . **700.00**
Belton, 14″ h, German bisque shoulderhead, cloth body, composition arms, blue eyes, closed mouth orig dress marks: incised 3094 . . . . **600.00**
Bergmann, C. M.
 15″, bisque socket head, composition bent limb baby body, brunette mohair wig, almond shape small gray glass sleep eyes, open mouth, two porcelain upper teeth, well costumed, c1910, marks: Simon and Halbig, C.M. Bergmann 612 6 . . . **900.00**
Borgfeldt, George
 12½″, Hug Me Kiddy, composition face mask, pink felt body, fleecy brunette hair, inset large round glass side glancing googly eyes, pug nose, closed mouth, c1910 . . **425.00**
 26″, bisque socket head, composition bent limb baby body, blonde human hair, brown glass inset eyes, open mouth, two porcelain upper teeth, tongue, well costumed, c1915, marks: G.B. 15 . . . . **1,200.00**
Bru, Casimir, 13″, bisque swivel head, kid-lined bisque shoulderplate, kid gusset jointed body, carved wooden lower legs, bisque forearms, blonde karakul wig, brown glass paperweight inset, accented and shaded lips with small hole in center, c1885, marks: Bru Jne 4 . . . . **3,000.00**
Chase, Martha, 18½″, cloth, painted features, blue eyes, short blonde hair, marks: Martha Chase, Pawtucket, Rhode Island **320.00**
Danel et Cie, 26″, bisque socket head, French composition and wooden jointed body, blonde human hair, amber brown glass paperweight inset eyes, closed mouth, pierced ears, well costumed, c1885, marks: Paris Bebe Depose 11 Eiffel Tower symbol on torso **2,500.00**
Dressel, Cuno and Otto, 7″, bisque socket head, five piece toddler body, almond shape blue glass sleep eyes, open mouth, painted shoes and socks, c1915, marks: 18/0 Jutta 1914 **500.00**
Effanbee
 19″, composition socket head, five piece composition body, molded bent right arm, painted short brown bobbed hair, green sleep eyes, closed mouth, c1935, marks: Effanbee Patsy Ann, Pat. 1285558 . . . **200.00**
 27″, composition socket head, 5 pc composition body, blue sleep eyes, real lashes, closed mouth, strawberry blonde human hair, orig pink organdy ball gown, gold heart bracelet, c1940, marks: Little Lady **275.00**
Falk, Giebeler, 21″, aluminum socket

head, composition and wooden ball jointed body, brunette human hair, brown metal sleep eyes, open mouth, four beaded teeth, marks: 20 G, US Pat, six pointed star **275.00**

Fulper, 17", bisque socket head, composition five piece toddler body, molded short brown curly tousled hair, blue intaglio eyes, closed mouth in "O" expression, two beaded upper teeth, well costumed, c1917, marks: Fulper in scroll, CMU in triangle . . . **2,500.00**

Gaultier, F., 11", bisque swivel head, kid lined bisque shoulderplate, kid fashion body with gusset jointing at hips, brunette human hair, blue glass paperweight inset eyes, closed mouth, pierced ears, well costumed, blue straw bonnet, c1880, marks: 3/0 (head and shoulderplate) F.G. (shoulderplate) **1,500.00**

Gaultier and Gesland, 33", bisque socket head, composition shoulderplate, stockinette cov armature body, composition forearms and legs, blonde human hair over cork pate, dark brown glass paperweight inset eyes, closed mouth, imp dimpled chin, pierced ears, maroon taffeta, brown knit stockings, black leather shoes, c1875, marks: F,14 G, Gesland Bte S.G.D.G. stamp on torso . . **6,250.00**

Greiner, Ludwig, 25", papier mache shoulderhead, muslin body, brown leather arms, stitched fingers, painted hair, painted blue upper glancing eyes, closed mouth, partially exposed ears, well costumed, c1860, marks: Greiner Improved Patent heads, Pat. March 30, '58 . . . . **600.00**

Handwerck, Heinrich
20", bisque socket head, composition and wooden ball jointed body, brunette human hair, brown glass sleep eyes, open mouth, four porcelain teeth, pierced ears, well costumed, c1900, marks: 109-11 H 2 1/1 . . . . **500.00**

22", bisque socket head, fully jointed composition body, brown glass sleep flirty eyes, open mouth, four teeth, pierced ears, blonde wig, old red dress, lace trim overcoat, marks: Germany/Heinrich/Handwerck/Simon & Halbig/3 . . . . **425.00**

Hertel, Schwab, and Co, 12", bisque socket head, composition bent limb baby body, blonde mohair wig, blue glass side glancing googly eyes, closed mouth, watermelon smile, well costumed, c1910, marks: 165 2/0 . . **1,800.00**

Heubach, Gebruder
10", bisque shoulderhead of young baby, muslin body, composition lower arms and legs, blonde forehead curls, blue intaglio eyes, closed mouth, two white beaded teeth, well costumed, c1915 . . . . **400.00**

19", pint tinted bisque shoulderhead, muslin body, composition lower arms and legs, painted light blonde boyish hair, blue intaglio eyes, painted facial features, closed mouth, two beaded upper teeth, well costumed, c1910, marks: 6 Germany 7654, Holz-masse black stamp on leg **900.00**

22½", bisque socket head, fully jointed composition body, brown glass sleep eyes, open mouth, four teeth, brown wig, marks: Heubach/250-4/Koppelsdorf/Germany **225.00**

Horsman, E. I. and Co, 10", solid domed bisque head, flanged neck, muslin body, composition hands, brown painted baby hair, slightly modeled curls, blue glass sleep eyes, closed mouth pouty lips, well costumed, c1925, marks: E.I. Horsman and Co **800.00**

Jumeau, Emile
14", bisque socket head, French composition and wooden jointed body, brunette human hair over cork plate, blue glass paperweight inset eyes, closed mouth, pierced ears, well costumed, c1880, marks: Bte S.G.D.G.4 Depose Tete Jumeau, artist's checkmarks, Jumeau Medaille d'or Paris, blue stamp on torso **2,500.00**

15", bisque socket head, composition, wood ball jointed body, blue glass sleep eyes, painted features, open mouth two porcelain teeth, dimple blonde human hair, c1915, marks: D Made in Germany 143 8 . . . . . **500.00**

18", bisque socket head, French eight ball jointed composition and wooden body, straight wrists, blonde mohair wig, blue glass paperweight inset eyes, closed mouth, pierced ears, well costumed, c1870, marks: 1 . . . . **4,500.00**

Kammer & Reinhardt
12", bisque socket head, composition bent limb baby body, brunette mohair wig, brown glass sleep eyes, open mouth, two porcelain teeth, well costumed, c1915, marks: K*R Simon and Halbig 122 28 . . . . . . **600.00**

14", Peter, bisque socket head, composition, wood ball jointed body, painted features, narrow painted blue eyes, closed mouth, pouty expression, blonde mohair wig, well costumed, c1915, marks: D * R 101 34 .... **1,900.00**

17″, bisque socket head, composition bent limb baby body, brunette mohair wig, dark blue glass sleep eyes, open mouth, two porcelain upper teeth, well costumed, c1915, marks: K*R Simon and Halbig 122 62 .... **500.00**

Kestner

11″, Hilda, solid domed bisque socket head, composition bent limb baby body, narrow almond shaped gray glass sleep eyes, painted features, open mouth, two porcelain teeth, white baby gown, repainted body, c1915, marks: Hilda c J.D.K. jr. 1070 Ges Gesch Made in Germany **750.00**

16″, bisque socket head, composition and wooden ball jointed body, one piece composition legs hinged at thighs for walking mechanism, brunette human hair, blue glass sleep eyes, open mouth, six porcelain teeth, c1895, marks: 289 dep S (head) D.R.P. Germany Linon 66543 (foot) **00.00**

21″, bisque socket head, composition and wooden ball jointed bod⁻ blonde mohair wig, blue ⨯⸍ sleep eyes, open mouth, four porcelain teeth, pierced ears, well costumed, c1910, marks: F½ made in Germany 10½ 167 .... **800.00**

Kley and Hahn, 15″, bisque socket head, composition bent limb baby body, brunette mohair wig, almond shape gray glass sleep eyes, open mouth, two beaded upper teeth, tongue, well costumed, c1910, marks: K&H germany 167-6 .... **500.00**

Koppelsdorf, Heubach, 14″, bisque socket head, composition bent limb baby body, blonde human hair, blue glass sleep eyes, open mouth, two upper teeth, well costumed, c1925, marks: Heubach Koppelsdorf 300.4 . **400.00**

Kruse, Kathe, 15″, celluloid socket head, celluloid jointed body, blonde human hair, blue inset eyes, closed mouth, well costumed, c1958, marks: (turtle mark) Modell Kathe Kruse T40 (head and torso) **400.00**

Kuhnlenz, Gebruder, 20″, bisque socket head, French type composition and wooden jointed body, straight wrists, blonde human hair, blue glass paperweight inset eyes, open mouth, four porcelain teeth, pierced ears, well

costumed, c1895, marks: Bgr. K in sunburst 44.30 dep **1,000.00**

Lanternier & Cie, 23″, bisque socket head, French composition and wooden jointed body, brunette human hair, almond shape brown glass inset eyes, open mouth, row of molded teeth, well costumed, c1900, marks: depose Fabrication Francaise Favorite No 8 Ed Tasson **650.00**

Lenci, 20″, felt swivel head, masked pressed and painted features, muslin torso, felt jointed arms and legs, blonde mohair wig, brown glass "O" shape googly eyes, "O" shape mouth, c1925 .... **1,500.00**

Madame Alexander, plastic, jointed arms and legs, blonde hair, blue net over satin dress, lace trim, marked on back, $60.00.

Madame Alexander

14″, Snow White, hard plastic socket head, 5 pc plastic body, green sleep eyes, real lashes, painted features, closed mouth, black saran wig, orig ivory satin gown, gold leaf pattern, gilt brocade vest, c1952, marks: Alex on head, Walt Disney Snow White Madame Alexander U.S.A. on tag **450.00**

16″, composition socket head, five piece composition body, black human hair, brown sleep eyes, real lashes, closed mouth, c1940, marks: Princess Elizabeth Madame Alexander (doll), Snow White, Madame Alexander (cloth tag on costume) **600.00**

16″, mask felt face, muslin body, painted facial features, blonde human hair wig, brown side glancing eyes, closed mouth, mitten hands, orig blue flannel trousers, black felt jacket and top hat, white shirt and bowtie, c1933, marks: David Cooperfield **525.00**

Marseille, Armand, 20″, bisque socket head, composition and wooden ball jointed body, blonde mohair wig, brown glass sleep eyes, open mouth, well costumed, c1900, marks: made in Germany 390 A5M **400.00**

Mason and Taylor, 12″, wooden, dowel jointed body, sculpted and painted short blonde hair, blue eyes, painted facial features, orig paper band at waist, c1880 .... **300.00**

Ohlhaver, Gebruder, 20″, bisque socket head, composition bent limb baby body, auburn human hair, blue glass sleep eyes, real lashes, open mouth, two molded upper teeth, well costumed in antique christening gown, c1915, marks: Germany Revalo 22-12 .... **600.00**

Putnam, Grace, 11″, Bye-Lo Baby, composition head, flanged neck, muslin body, celluloid hands, painted tan hair, blue glass eyes in half moon shape, closed mouth, c1925, marks: Copyright by Grace S. Putnam Made in USA **1,800.00**

Rabery and Delphieu, 17″, bisque socket head, French composition and wooden jointed body, brunette human hair, amber brown glass paperweight inset eyes, closed mouth, pierced ears, well costumed, c1885, marks: 2/0 R.L.D. **2,000.00**

Recknagel, 13″, bisque socket head, five piece papier mache body, brunette mohair wig, gray glass sleep eyes, open mouth, four teeth, c1920, marks: Dep R 7/0 A **400.00**

Revalo, 12″, bisque socket head, composition and wooden ball jointed body, modeled short brown curly hair, molded blue ribbon and rosette trim, gray eyes, painted facial features, closed mouth, c1915, marks: Revalo dep **450.00**

Schoenau and Hoffmeister, 21″, bisque socket head, composition and wooden ball jointed body, brunette hair, brown glass sleep eyes, real lashes, open mouth, four porcelain teeth, c1920, marks: S*H 1909 Germany **525.00**

Schoenhut, 14″, carved wooden socket head, all wooden spring jointed body, auburn mohair wig, blue intaglio eyes, closed mouth, holes in feet for positioning, c1912, marks: Schoenhut

Simon and Halbig, orig gown, turquoise beads and gold trim, sapphire and gold topped walking stick, $5,000.00.

Doll Pat. Jan 17, 1911 USA and Foreign Countries **500.00**

Simon & Halbig

27″, bisque socket head, composition and wooden ball jointed body, brunette mohair wig, blue glass sleep eyes, open mouth, four porcelain teeth, pierced ears, well costumed, c1910, marks: Simon and Halbig K*R 66 .... **500.00**

37″, bisque socket head, composition and wooden ball jointed body, brunette human hair, brown glass sleep eyes, open mouth, four porcelain teeth, pierced ears, c1900, marks: Simon and Halbig 1249 dep Germany 17 .... **2,000.00**

Smith, Ella, 19″, stockinette hardpressed head, muslin body, oil painted arms and legs, painted short brown hair, painted brown eyes, stitched ears, well costumed, c1910, marks: Pat. April, No. 1 Ella Smith's Indestructible Dolls, Roanoke, Alabama **1,700.00**

Societe Francaise de Bebes et Jouets

18″, bisque socket head, French composition and wooden toddler body, side hip jointing, blonde human hair, blue glass sleep eyes, real lashes, closed mouth, pouty downcast expression, well costumed, c1915: S.F.B.J. 252 Paris 8 **2,500.00**

26″, bisque socket head, composition and wooden jointed toddler body,

side hip jointing, brunette human hair, blue glass sleep eyes in half moon shape, open mouth, beaded upper teeth, tremble tongue, well costumed, c1910, marks: 21 S.F.B.J. 251 Paris 12, orig paper label on body **3,000.00**
Steiner, Edmund, 13", bisque socket head, composition and wooden ball jointed body, blonde mohair wig, brown glass inset eyes, open mouth, four teeth, well costumed, c1900, marks: E.U.St. **400.00**
Steiner, Jules Nicholas, 15", Le Petit Parisien Bebe, bisque socket head, French composition and wooden jointed body, straight wrists, blonde human hair, blue glass paperweight eyes, closed mouth, pierced ears, well costumed, c1885, marks: Steiner Paris Fre A 7 (head) Le Petit Parisien Bebe Steiner (stamp on torso) **3,500.00**
Swaine and Company, 14", solid domed bisque socket head, composition bent limb baby body, lightly tinted blonde baby hair, almond shape blue glass sleep eyes, closed mouth, well costumed, c1915 . . . .   **800.00**
Unknown Maker
18", French Fashion, bisque swivel head, kid lined shoulderplate, kid over wood body, dowel jointed at shoulders, hips, and knees, bisque arms, plumply molded, almond shape blue threaded inset eyes, delicately painted features, pale blonde mohair wig, elaborate costume, c1870 . . . .   **2,600.00**
21", American bleached muslin, mask face, curly brown hair at edge of face, blue eyes, orig calico costume, white ruffled apron, 19th C .   **60.00**

DOOR KNOCKERS

History: Before the advent of the mechanical bell or electrical buzzer and chime, a door knocker was considered an essential door ornament to announce the arrival of visitors. Metal was used to cast or forge the various forms; many cast iron examples were painted. Collectors like to find knockers with English registry marks.

BRASS

Anchor	**55.00**
Atlantis, head, dolphin, and seashells .	**75.00**
Bust of William Shakespeare, 4"	**75.00**
Devil, head, serpent striker ring	**40.00**
Lady's hand holding mirror	**32.00**
Oval, ring knocker, monogrammed . . .	**25.00**

Cast iron, owl, yellow eyes, green ribbon, orig paint, $75.00.

Pheasants	**45.00**
Turtle, marked "China"	**40.00**

BRONZE

Fu Dog, large	**100.00**
Grecian head, 4½"	**80.00**
Hand, ruffled sleeve, 5"	**75.00**
Shakespeare	**70.00**

CAST IRON

Basket of flowers, openwork patterned back plate, painted	**45.00**
Fox, head, knocking ring in mouth, 5½"	**75.00**
Lady's Hand	**20.00**
Parrot	**45.00**
Quaker, head, man wearing wide brimmed hat	**50.00**

DOORSTOPS

History: Doorstops became popular in the late 19th century. They can be found flat or three dimensional and were made in cast iron, bronze, wood, and other material. Hubley, a leading toy manufacturer, made many examples.

References: Jeanne Bertoia, *Doorstops: Identification And Values*, Collector Books, 1985; Marilyn Hamburger and Beverly Lloyd, *Collecting Figural Doorstops*, A.S. Barnes and Company, 1978.

Reproduction Alert: Reproductions are proliferating as prices on genuine doorstops continue to rise. There is usually a slight reduction in size in a reproduced piece unless an original mold is used at which time size remains the same. Reproductions have less detail, lack of smoothness to the overall casting, and lack of detail in the paint.

If there is any bright orange rusting, this is strongly indicative of a new piece. Beware. If it looks too good to be true, it usually is.

Notes: Pieces described below contain at least 80% or more of the original paint and are in very good condition. Repainting drastically reduces price and desirability. Poor original paint is preferred over repaint.

All listings are cast iron and flatback castings unless otherwise noted.

Doorstops marked with an asterick are currently being reproduced.

B + H = Bradley and Hubbard.
Advisor: Craig Dinner.

Basket of flowers, yellow basket, blue, yellow, and red tulips, green stems and leaves, painted cast iron, 8½″ h, $95.00.

Bear, 15″ h, standing, holding honey pot in both hands, full figure, brown, red lips, some darker coloration	525.00
Bull	40.00
Butler, 12½″ h, red vest and bowtie, black tuxedo, white gloves, mustache, short black hair	325.00
Camel, 7″ h, brown, two humps, standing on four feet	245.00
Cat, 10¾″ h, white, black patches, seated, licking front paw, red tongue, sgd "Sculptured Metal Studios"	225.00
Church, 8½″ h, white, steeple, gray roof, blue sky, green grass, three red doors	165.00
Cornucopia and roses, 10¼″ h, cast iron, orig polychrome paint	85.00
Cottage, 5¾″ h, brown roof, red chimney, Dutch dormer, blue shutters, flowers on sides, sgd "Hubley #211"	100.00
Dog	
Dachshund, 8″ h, 12″ l, full figure, sit-	

ting on hind legs, leaning against door, front legs erect	315.00
Doberman Pinscher, 8½″ l, 8″ h, black, brown markings, Hubley	255.00
Setter, brass	225.00
St. Bernard, 10½″ l, 3½″ h, full figure, white, brown markings, laying, head on front paws, Hubley	285.00
Terrier, running, white, black spots, sgd "Spencer, Guilford, CT"	125.00
Duck, 7½″ h, figure, 2 sided, yellow, black top hat, white beak, blue pants, black shoes and base	285.00
Flower	
Daisies, 17¾″ h, pink and blue flowers, green two tone leaves, cream cosmos vase, sgd "Hubley #455"	300.00
Gladiolus, 10″ h, yellow, pink, and cream flowers, green two tone leaves, white vase, sgd "Hubley #489"	110.00
Iris, 10⅝″ h, purple and white flowers, green stems, sgd "Hubley # 469"	185.00
Marigold, 7½″ h, cream, blue, and yellow flowers, cream vase with horizontal blue stripes, sgd "Hubley #315"	115.00
Primrose, 7⅜″ h, cream flowers with red dots, green leaves, white flower pot and base, sgd "Hubley #488"	135.00
Tulips, 10½″ h, orange and yellow flowers, green leaves, green and mustard pot and base, sgd "LACS770"	165.00
Footmen, 12⅛″ h, two men side by side, red coats, black pants, and shoes, sgd "C Fish, Hubley"	425.00
Giraffe, 12½″, yellow, mustard skin, standing, Hubley	485.00
Girl, 9⅞″ h, holding yellow floppy hat on head, blue dress, yellow shoes, green base	300.00
Gnome	
9½″ h, with shovel, figure, red hat, brown apron, blue shirt	245.00
14½″ h, holding barrel on shoulder, figure, pouring grog into cup, red hat and shirt, green pants, black shoes	355.00
Golfer, 10″ h, red jacket, gray pants, socks, and hat, white ball on grass, sgd "Hubley #238"	410.00
House	
7½ x 6⅛″, yellow and red, brown roof, open door, two chimneys, sgd "AM Greenblatt, copyright 1927 #114"	165.00
8¾ x 15⅜″, two story, gray siding, two red chimneys, tree on right	145.00
Huckleberry Finn, 12½″ h, blue overalls with red trim, yellow floppy hat, brown, staff in right hand, Littco Products label	475.00

Jungle Boy, 12¾" h, turban, leopard skin, one hand extended **435.00**

Koala, 7¼" h, yellow and black, standing on orange tree stump, orange and black ears, sgd "N 5 copyright 1930 Taylor Cook" **445.00**

Lighthouse, 11½" h, Gloucester, MA, two houses, green and blue waves, sgd "Greenblatt Studios, Boston, MA #8, 1925" **265.00**

Little Red Riding Hood and Wolf, 7½", red cape, basket, yellow hair, green grass, storybook, tan wolf looking sideways with red tongue hanging out, sgd "Nuydea" **340.00**

Maid of Honor, 8¼" h, cream dress, black hat, yellow hair, holding bouquet in right hand, left hand holding dress out, Hubley **245.00**

Man, 9½" h, holding yellow and red wine bottles, blue apron, green coat and abase **500.00**

Mary Quite Contrary, 15" h, yellow dress, dark green bonnet, holding flower bouquet in right hand, watering can and rake in left **265.00**

Mayflower, 8¼" h, sails, three masts, green and white waves, sgd "Mayflower Eastern Spec Mfg Co" **40.00**

Monkey on barrel, 8⅜" h, yellow and green, yellow drum with two black stripes, 1930, sgd "Taylor Cook #3" **345.00**

Oxen and wagon, 6¼" h, 10¼" l, tan and white oxen, two people riding covered wagon, red spoke wheels . **75.00**

Pelican, 14⅜" h, 2 sided figure, white, yellow beak and feet, green base, sgd "Spencer, Guilford, CT" on foot **385.00**

Penguin, 9½" h, black, yellow chest, red and yellow beak, sgd "#1 1930 Taylor Cook" **575.00**

Pine Trees, 6¾" h, green with white and brown **155.00**

Pirate, 12" h, silver sword, gun in green waistband, red shirt, gray kerchief with red dots, black beard **275.00**

Puppy, 7 x 5", figure, yawning, gray and tan, red tongue **215.00**

Rabbit
  8" h, white, red sweater, cream pants, holding flowers to nose **300.00**
  8⅝" h, grandpa, brown, sitting, red and black tuxedo jacket, white vest, green bowtie **435.00**

Rooster, 13¼" h, 2 sided, white feathers, red comb, yellow beak and feet, green base, sgd "Spencer" on leg . **400.00**

Salt, 14½" h, figure, yellow pants and coat, black hat and boots, hands in pocket, sgd "Eastern Spec Co" **245.00**

Senorita, 11¼" h, yellow dress, blue-

green shawl, flower in hair, holding basket of flowers in right hand **145.00**

Ship, cast iron **50.00**

Shoe, high heel **75.00**

Southern Belle, 4½" h, cast iron, full figure, worn polychrome paint **10.00**

The Patrol, fisherman style figure, kerosene lamp in right hand, black boots and hat, yellow jacket and pants, sgd on front **185.00**

Turkey, 13" h, blue-gray, yellow, and tan feathers, red head, mustard feet, green grass **435.00**

DRESDEN/MEISSEN

History: Augustus II, Elector of Saxony and King of Poland, founded the Royal Saxon Porcelain Manufactory in the Albrechtsburg, Meissen, in 1710. Johann Frederick Boettger, an alchemist, and Tschirnhaus, a nobleman, experimented with kaolin clay from the Dresden area to produce porcelain. By 1720 the factory produced a whiter hard paste porcelain than that from the Far East. The factory experienced its golden age in the 1730–50s period under the leadership of Samuel Stolzel, kiln master, and Johann Gregor Herold, enameler.

Many marks were used by the Meissen factory. The first was a pseudo-oriental mark in a square. The famous crossed swords mark was adopted in 1724. A small dot between the hilts was used from 1763–74 and a star between the hilts from 1774 to 1814. Two modern marks are swords with a hammer and sickle and swords with a crown.

The Meissen factory was destroyed and looted by forces of Frederick the Great during the Seven Years' War (1756–1763). It was reopened, but never achieved its former greatness.

In the 19th century, the factory reissued some

of its earlier forms. These later wares are called "Dresden" to differentiate them from the earlier examples. Further, there were several other porcelain factories in the Dresden region, and their products also are grouped under the "Dresden" designation of collectors.

Reference: Susan and Al Bagdade, *Warman's English & Continental Pottery & Porcelain, 1st Edition,* Warman Publishing Co., Inc., 1987.

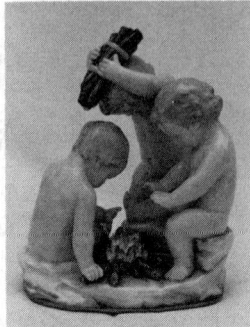

Dresden, figurine, three putti around campfire, crossed swords mark, 5⅞" l, $750.00.

DRESDEN

Charger, 14½", stormy sailing ship scene, gilt floral border, puce, pink, purple and iron-red panels, c1900 . .   **725.00**
Cup, 3½", white, relief prunus dec, two handles, attributed to Boettger, unmarked, 1715 . . . .   **250.00**
Demitasse Cup and Saucer, floral reserves, blue ground **250.00**
Dessert Plate, 9", central female portrait, heavily gilt, green ground, marked, c1910, set of 12 . . . .   **1,000.00**
Ewer, 5½" d, 12" h, flattened oval, maroon bands top and bottom, heavy gold trim, center scene of two ladies and cupid in garden, obverse with four children playing blind man's bluff, ornate gold handle, Wissmann mark, c1890 . . . .   **800.00**
Figure
   4", boy and girl, multicolored period dress, carrying baskets of flowers, pr **225.00**
   10¾", man with basket of fruit, dog at feet, women with fruit in apron, multicolored period dress, blue crossed swords mark, pr **500.00**

11", maiden, blindfolding cupid, multicolored, c1900 . . . .   **175.00**
Tea Caddy, 5¼ x 3½", sq, lacy gold flowers on two panels, scene of courting boy and girl, crossed swords mark, "H" and "Dresden" **175.00**
Vase
   8½", portrait scene, cobalt blue ground, raised gold dec, artist sgd   **375.00**
   13½", three panels, each with fill figure portrait of young lady, marked "Dresden" **525.00**

MEISSEN

Bowl, 10", gold and pink, raised leaf dec, c1920 . . . .   **165.00**
Candelabra, five light, shaped sq base, waisted plinth, applied cartouches with arms of Saxony and Poland, putti, seated maiden, floral dec tunic, purple drape, foliate stem spreading as light branch, foliate molded drip pan and nozzle, pink, turquoise, and gilt highlights, underglaze blue crossed swords mark, late 19th C, minor restoration, pr **4,675.00**
Coffee Service, cov 10½" coffeepot, creamer, cov sugar, twelve 6½" d cups and saucers, white ground, foliage gilt highlights, orig fitted case, underglaze blue crossed swords mark, early 20th C **2,750.00**
Figure
   3" h, boy and girl, flower garland, underglaze blue crossed swords mark   **475.00**
   5½" h, Flower Girl, flowered white apron, yellow skirt, laced lavender bodice, offering basket of flowers, scroll molded circular mound base, underglaze blue crossed swords mark with small crescent, imp and incised numbers **175.00**

   7½" h, Pluto with pink drape and gilt crown, carrying struggling Proserpine, oval base with molded and applied gilt scrolls, underglaze blue crossed swords, incised and imp numbers, after model by J J Kaendler, c1900 . . . .   **600.00**

   7¾" h, kissing couple, lady in white dress with scattered polychrome floral sprays, white cap, gentleman in gilted purple overcoat, black breeches, shaped oval base with applied flowerheads and leaves, underglaze blue crossed swords mark, iron–red inscribed numerals, imp numerals, after model by J J Kaendler, c1900 . . . .   **775.00**

8¼" h, cavalier and lady, standing side by side, lady in black dress dec with iron–red, purple, and blue floral sprays, white ruffled neckline and cap, holding fan, gentleman in orange and pale blue coat, dark puce breeches, oval base with applied flowerheads, underglaze blue crossed swords, incised and imp numbers, after model by J J Kaendler, c1900 . . . . **900.00**

10½", Arabian stallion, rearing on hind legs, attendant by side wearing plumed turban, yellow and green sashed tunic, blue pantaloons, shaped oval base, polychrome floral vines, underglaze blue crossed swords mark with cancellation marks, minor losses . **715.00**

12" h, Diana, seated on sq socle, quiver at side, white, clear glaze, blue underglaze mark **875.00**

13½" h, gardeners, 18th C costumes, woman holding hem of skirt with small bouquet in other hand, gilt rimmed pink hat, floral dec bodice and skirt, striped shawl, flower urn with applied flowers at base, boy standing next to tree stump, spade in left hand, bouquet of posies in right hand, black hat, pale turquoise coat, gray breeches with puce tassels, grassy mound base, shell and scroll molded border, underglaze blue crossed swords mark **2,000.00**

Garniture, 12" h centerpiece, Baroque style basket, three applied cherubs with rose blossoms, matching pair of four light candelabra formed as seated women holding infants, similar rose dec, blue underglaze mark . . . **700.00**

Plate, 9¾" d, molded scrolls and flowers, white ground, blue enameled deutsche Blumen, underglaze blue factory mark **100.00**

Soup Plate, floral dec, canceled underglaze factory mark, set of 12 . . . . . . **650.00**

Sugar Box, cov, 4½ x 3¼ x 3", oval, yellow tiger, brown rim, rabbit finial, crossed swords mark, c1730 . . . . . **185.00**

Teacup and Saucer, Kakiemon style birds and flowers, brown ground on cup, white ground saucer, underglaze blue crossed swords mark, pr **275.00**

Wine Bottle Stand, 9 x 6¾", flattened ovoid form, scalloped rim, pierced flowerhead and C scroll frieze, molded and painted pink grisaille body, storks and swans, raised shell molded foot, oval base, underglaze blue crossed swords mark, pr **2,750.00**

DUNCAN AND MILLER

History: George Duncan, Harry B. and James B., his sons, and Augustus Heisey, his son-in-law, formed George Duncan & Sons in Pittsburgh, Pennsylvania, in 1865. The factory was located just two blocks from the Monongahela River, providing easy and cheap access by barge for materials needed to produce glass. The men, from Pittsburgh's southside, were descendants of generations of skilled glass makers.

The plant burned to the ground in 1892. James E. Duncan, Sr., selected a site for a new factory in Washington, Pennsylvania, where operations began on February 9, 1893. The plant prospered, producing fine glassware and table services for many years.

John E. Miller, one of the stockholders, was responsible for designing many fine patterns, the most famous being "Three Face." The firm incorporated, using the name The Duncan and Miller Glass Company until its plant closed in 1955. The company's slogan was "The Loveliest Glassware in America." The U. S. Glass Co. purchased the molds, equipment, and machinery in 1956.

References: Gail Krause, *The Encyclopedia Of Duncan Glass*, published by author, 1984; Gail Krause, *A Pictorial History Of Duncan & Miller Glass*, published by author, 1976; Gail Krause, *The Years Of Duncan*, published by author, 1980.

Collectors' Club: National Duncan Glass Society, P. O. Box 965, Washington, PA 15301. *National Duncan Glass Journal* (quarterly).

Additional Listings: Pattern Glass.

Centerpiece Bowl, Sanibel, pink opalescent, 13½" l, $40.00.

Ashtray
Duck, 4" **22.00**
Teardrop, 3", round **4.50**
Bookends, pr, anchor, blue **100.00**
Bowl
Caribbean, blue, 8½" **36.00**
First Love, 5½", handle **36.00**
Hobnail, blue opal, 12", crimped . . . **68.00**
Passion Flower, 12½" **28.50**
Puritan, green, 4¾", ftd **8.00**
Sandwich, crystal, 11", flared **40.00**

Spiral Flutes, green, 6¾", flange . . .   6.00
Viking Boat 150.00
Cake Plate, Sandwich, crystal, 13", ftd   70.00
Candlesticks, pr
   American Way, blue opal, 2" 28.00
   First Love, two lite 100.00
   Hobnail, blue opal, 4" 55.00
Candy Box, Canterbury, cov, flat 40.00
Celery
   Sandwich, crystal, 10" 27.00
   Sanibel, pink opal, 13", three part . .   42.00
Champagne
   Canterbury, blue 15.00
   Remembrance 15.00
Cheese Compote, Canterbury, crystal .   18.00
Cigarette Box, crystal
   Duck 50.00
   Sandwich 36.00
Claret, Canterbury, blue, 5" 15.00
Cocktail, Caribbean, blue, ftd 35.00
Cologne, Hobnail, pink opalescent . . .   35.00
Compote
   Charmaine, rose etching, 7" 35.00
   Spiral Flutes, amber, 6" 15.00
Creamer and Sugar, Canterbury, crystal   20.00
Cruet, orig stopper, Sandwich, crystal,
   3 oz 25.00
Cup, Sandwich, crystal 6.00
Cup and Saucer
   Hobnail 18.00
   Teardrop, crystal 10.00
Demitasse Set, Spiral Flutes, amber . .   20.00
Deviled Egg Plate, Sandwich, 12" 60.00
Flower Frog, crystal, 5" 16.00
Goblet
   Canterbury, crystal, 6", 9 oz 15.00
   First Love 16.50
   Sandwich, 5¾", 9 oz 8.00
   Terrace, crystal, three ball stem, 10
     oz 15.00
Hat, Hobnail, blue opal, 2½" 25.00
Iced Tea Tumbler, Remembrance 16.00
Juice Tumbler, Teardrop 5.00
Mayonnaise, liner, Teardrop 15.00
Mint Tray, Sanibel, blue opal, 7" 24.00
Mustard, cov, Caribbean 28.00
Parfait, Spiral Flutes, green 18.00
Pickle
   Sandwich, crystal, 7" 20.00
   Spiral Flutes, green, 8⅝", oval 16.00
Plate
   Indian Tree, etched, 6" 5.00
   Nautical, blue, 12" 30.00
   Passion Flower, 14½", salad 28.50
   Sandwich, crystal, 16" 55.00
   Sanibel, pink opal, 8½", salad 27.00
Punch Bowl Set, Caribbean, ruby han-
   dles, 15 pcs 225.00
Punch Cup
   Caribbean 6.00
   Colonial 5.75

Relish, three part
   First Love, 8½" 24.00
   Sandwich, crystal, 10" 22.00
   Teardrop, 11" 22.00
Salt and Pepper Shakers, Sandwich,
   2½", pr 18.00
Sherbet
   Sandwich, crystal 5.00
   Spiral Flutes, green, 4¾" 10.00
   Teardrop 4.50
Swan
   3", solid 30.00
   5", solid 40.00
   7" 20.00
Tumbler
   Canterbury, crystal, 6¼" 10.00
   Sandwich, ftd, 3¾", 5 oz 7.00
   Spiral Flutes, 5", green, ftd 20.00
Urn, 7", sq handles 65.00
Vase, Canterbury, 7¼", inverted candle   110.00

DURAND

History: Victor Durand (1870–1931), born in Baccarat, France, apprenticed at the Baccarat glass works where several generations of his family worked. In 1884 Victor came to America to join his father at the Whitall-Tatum & Co. in New Jersey. In 1897 father and son leased the Vineland Glass Manufacturing Company in Vineland, New Jersey. Products included inexpensive bottles, jars, and glass for scientific and medical purposes. By 1920 four separate companies existed.

When Quezal Art Glass and Decorating Company failed, Victor Durand recruited Martin Bach, Jr., Emil J. Larsen, William Wiedebine, and other Quezal men and opened an art glass shop at Vineland in December, 1924. Quezal style iridescent pieces were made. New innovations included cameo and intaglio designs, geometric Art Deco shapes, Venetian Lace, and oriental style pieces. In 1928 crackled glass, called Moorish Crackle and Egyptian Crackle, was made.

Much of Durand glass is not marked. Some bears a sticker labeled "Durand Art Glass," some has the name "Durand" scratched on the pontil, or "Durand" inside a large "V". Etched numbers may be part of the marking.

Durand died in 1931. The Vineland Flint Glass Works was merged with Kimble Glass Company a year later, and the art glass line discontinued.

Box, 3½" d, cov, green luster glass, gold
   luster King Tut dec 950.00
Candlesticks, pr, 10", blue, sgd 425.00
Compote,
   5½" d, 4½" h, irid gold and opal, King
     Tut, sgd 250.00
   6", gold, blue, King Tut int., gold stem,
     blue highlighted foot 750.00

Durand, vase, King Tut, gold iridescent interior, 7¼" h, $650.00.

Ginger Jar, 10½" cov, gold and green, King Tut dec	1,850.00
Goblet, 5½", irid ruby, pale yellow stem and base, sgd	450.00
Jar, cov	
7" d, 9" h, ruby and amber, opal pull, feather, sgd	850.00
8¾" d, 10¼" h, irid gold, green, and blue, King Tut dec, sgd	1,250.00
Lamp	
Boudoir, 17" h, overall threading, butterscotch ground, matching petal leaf dec shade	1,100.00
Table, 17" h base, 31" h overall, irid gold and ivory, King Tut dec, sgd	600.00
Plate	
7¾", cobalt blue, opal pulled feather, crosshatch pontil, sgd	500.00
8½", ruby, paneled, 10 sided, hand blown, sgd	150.00
14", gold scalloped edge, clear green glass trim	250.00
Rose Bowl, 5½", blue, gold threads, gold foot, sgd	375.00
Sherbet, 3⅜", ruby and opal, feather pattern	150.00
Vase	
8¼", baluster, everted lip, heart and vine pattern, orange body, blue foot, sgd	800.00
12¼", conical, circular foot, silvery salmon irid, applied glass threading, numbered and inscribed "Durand"	600.00

ENGLISH CHINA AND PORCELAIN (GENERAL)

History: The manufacture of china and porcelain was scattered throughout England, with the majority of the factories located in the Staffordshire district. The number of potteries was over one thousand.

By the 19th century English china and porcelain had achieved a world wide reputation for excellence. American stores imported large amounts for their customers. The special production English pieces of the 18th and early 19th centuries held a position of great importance among early American antiques collectors.

References: Susan and Al Bagdade, *Warman's English & Continental Pottery & Porcelain, 1st Edition,* Warman Publishing, 1987; David Battie and Michael Turner, *The Price guide to 19th and 20th Century British Porcelain,* Antique Collectors' Club; Peter Bradshaw, *18th Century English Porcelain Figures, 1745–1795,* Antiques Collectors' Club; Geoffrey A. Godden, *Godden's Guide To Mason's China And The Ironstone Wares,* Antique Collectors' Club; Geoffrey A. Godden, *Lowestoft Porcelain,* Antique Collectors' Club; R. K. Henrywood, *Relief Molded Jugs, 1820–1900,* Antique Collectors' Club; Rachael Feild, *Macdonald Guide To Buying Antique Pottery & Porcelain,* Macdonald & Co., Ltd., 1987; Griselda Lewis, *A Collector's History Of English Pottery,* Antique Collectors' Club; Simon Spero, *The Price Guide To 18th Century English Porcelain,* Antique Collectors' Club.

Additional Listings: Castleford, Chelsea, Coalport, Copeland and Spode, Liverpool, Royal Crown Derby, Royal Doulton, Royal Worcester, Historical Staffordshire, Romantic Staffordshire, Wedgwood, and Whieldon.

BOW

Bowl, 4½", blue trailing vine, white ground, c1770	170.00
Candlesticks, pr, two birds on flowering branches, dog and sheep on grassy base, wood stand, c1755	1,200.00
Cup and Saucer, three molded prunus branches, c1735	175.00
Egg Cup, 2½" h, two half flower panels, powder blue ground, pseudo Oriental mark, c1760	850.00
Figure	
5½", sportsman, seated, gun on arm, tricorn hat, white sq mound base, c1752	310.00
9½", gardener, puce jacket, underglaze blue hat, turquoise breeches, black shoes, blue, puce, and gilt base, c1765	750.00
Pickle Dish, 4", leaf shape, painted flowers and grapes, molded veins, serrated edge, c1760	140.00
Plate	
7⅛", octagonal, center reserve Oriental island scene panel, circular and fan shape panels of landscapes and flowers border, pseudo Oriental mark, c1765	440.00

9″, Turk's Cap Lily, dragonfly and
moths, c1755 . . . . **850.00**

COALBROOKDALE

Cologne Bottle, pr, 7½″, raised floral
dec, c1820 . . . . **750.00**
Inkstand, 10″ l, floral encrusted, molded
asters, leafy ground, scrolling handle,
early 19th C **200.00**
Vase, cov, pr, 15″, pear shape, raised
floral dec, gilt rim and cov, flower
spray finial, c1840 . . . . **800.00**

CAUGHLEY

Creamer, 5¼″, milkmaid and cow
scene, marked "Salopian" **180.00**
Custard Cup, cov, 3⅛″, Oriental river
scene, blue printed buildings **25.00**
Jug, 7¼″, cabbage leaf mold, gilt entwined "JPM" in oval gilt and blue
cartouche, gilt and blue flowers from
pink ribbon swags, mask spout,
c1795 . . . . **290.00**
Tea Caddy, 5¼″, blue printed bouquets
and butterflies, c1770 . . . . **70.00**

DERBY

Butter Dish, cov, pr, stand, 7″, blue, iron-
red, and gilt, flowering scrolling foli-
age bands, c1800 . . . . **250.00**
Figure, pr, 8 and 8½″, pastoral, boy resting against tree stump playing bagpipe, black hat, bleu–du–roi jacket,
gilt trim, butter yellow breeches, girl
with green hat, bleu–du–roi bodice,
pink skirt, white apron with iron–red
flowerheads, gilt centers, leaves,
scroll molded mound base, crown
and incised iron–red D mark **2,000.00**
Jar, cov, pr, 22″ h, octagonal, iron red,
bottle green, and leaf green, alternating cobalt blue and white grounds,
gilding, grotesque sea serpent handles, now fitted as lamp with carved
base, 19th C **10,000.00**
Plaque, pr, cluster of fruit, carved gilt-
wood frame, c1830 . . . . **2,000.00**

FLIGHT, BARR, & BARR

Crocus Pot, 9″ w, 4″ d, 6¼″ h, D form,
molded columns and architrave,
peach ground panels, ruined abbey
landscape reserve, gilding **2,200.00**
Pastille Burner, 3½″, cottage, four open
chimneys, marked, c1815 . . . . **400.00**
Plate, 8″ d, armorial, iron-red, gold,
blue, and black arms and crest, Abbot
quartering Bryan impaling Harris

quartering another, iron-red and gray
mantling, pink banderole, motto "Tou-
jours Prest," gilt edged rim and
salmon ground border, incised letter
mark, crowned and plumed brown
"Barr Flight & Barr Royal Porcelain
Works, Worcester" oval mark, c1804–
09 . . . . **975.00**

HICKS, MEIGH & JOHNSON

Sugar, cov, pr, 8¼″ d, printed and
painted transfer, famille rose type
dec, gilted, molded rim, handles, and
finial, stand, c1860 . . . . **425.00**
Tureen, 11″ l, octagonal, flaring rim, applied acanthus tip handle, underglaze
blue and white, gilt, iron–red, dark
red, and underglaze blue flowerheads, scrolling foliage, and vases,
c1813–30 . . . . **350.00**

JACKFIELD

Creamer, 4¼″, bulbous, emb grapes design, leaves, and tendrils, gilt highlights, three paw feet, ear shape han-
dle **150.00**
Sugar, 4½ x 3¾″, scalloped SS rims,
SS mounted cov and ornate pierced
finial **225.00**
Teabowl and Saucer, plain **100.00**

LOWESTOFT

Coffeepot, cov, 9″, dark blue, underglaze river scene, Chinese man fish-
ing, trellis diaper border, c1770–75 . **910.00**
Demitasse Cup and Saucer, blue un-
derglaze **120.00**
Milk Jug, 3¼″, dark blue underglaze,
Chinese river scene, diaper border,
brown rim, c1775 . . . . **200.00**

MASON'S

Creamer, 4″, Oriental style shape,
marked "Mason's Patent Ironstone" **75.00**
Dessert Dish, Oriental floral dec, c1830 **50.00**
Ice Cooler, 14½″ h, straight sides, two
applied molded twig form handles,
liner with dished gilt rimmed border,
fluted high domed cov, inverted pear
shaped knob, underglaze blue and
enamel iron–red and gold florals, foliage, and vase shapes, imp "Ma-
son's Patent Ironstone China," pr . . **2,750.00**
Jug, 8″ h, octagonal, Hydra pattern, waisted straight neck, green enameled
handle, lion head terminal, underglaze blue and iron–red flowers and

vase, two imp marks and printed
rounded crown mark, c1813–30 ... **300.00**
Platter, 13½ x 10¾", Double Landscape
pattern, Oriental motif, deep green
and brick red, c1883 .... **250.00**
Potpourri Vase, cov, pr, 25¼", hexagonal body, cobalt blue, large gold stylized peony blossom, chrysanthemums, prunus, and butterflies, gold
and blue dragon handles and knobs,
trellis diaper rim border, c1820–25 .. **1,650.00**
Punch Bowl, 14⅛", ironstone, famille
rose type dec, c1825 .... **825.00**

**New Hall, teapot, bulbous body, helmet
top, oval finial, red and blue floral dec,
gold trim, Pattern 422, 1790–1805,
$350.00.**

NEW HALL

Creamer, Chinese figure on terrace,
c1790 .... **170.00**
Dessert Set, two oval dishes, eight
plates, bat printed and colored named
views, lavender-blue borders, light
blue ground, c1815 .... **425.00**
Dish, deep blue underglaze, orange
flowers and leaves dec, gilt, c1825 . **120.00**
Sugar, cov, multicolored bands of flowering foliage, puce rims, two handles,
c1790 .... **125.00**
Tea Set, 44 pcs, interwoven ribbon and
leaf trails, blue and gilt oval medallions border, minor repairs, c1790 .. **1,450.00**

ENGLISH SOFTPASTE

History: Between 1820 and 1860 a large number of potteries in England's Staffordshire district
produced decorative wares with a soft earthen-

ware (creamware) base and a plain white or yellow
glazed ground.

Design or "stick" spatterware was created by a
cut-sponge (stamp), hand painting, or transfer.
Blue was the dominant color. The earliest patterns
were carefully arranged geometrics and generally
covered the entire piece. Later pieces had a decorative border with a center motif, usually a tulip.
In the 1850s Elsmore and Foster developed the
Holly Leaf pattern.

King's Rose features a large, cabbage-type rose
in red, pale red, or pink. The pink rose often is
called "Queen's Rose." Secondary colors are pastels of yellow, pink, and occasionally green. The
borders vary: a solid band, vined, lined, or sec-
tional. The King's Rose exists in an oyster motif.

Strawberry China ware comes in three types:
strawberries and strawberry leaves (often called
strawberry luster), green feather-like leaves with
pink flowers (often called cut-strawberry, primrose,
or old strawberry), and a third type with the decoration in relief. The first two types are characterized by rust red moldings. Most pieces have a
creamware ground. Davenport was one of the
many potteries who made this ware.

Yellow-glazed earthenware (canary luster) has
a canary yellow ground, transfer design which is
usually in black, and occasional luster decoration.
The earliest pieces date from the 1780s and have
a fine creamware base. A few hand painted pieces
are known. Not every piece has luster decoration.
Marked pieces are uncommon. Because the
ground is softpaste, the ware is subject to cracking
and chipping. Enamel colors and other types of
decoration do not hold well. It is not unusual to
see a piece with the decoration worn off.

Reference: Susan and Al Bagdade, *Warman's
English & Continental Pottery & Porcelain, 1st Edition,* Warman Publishing Co., Inc., 1987.

Additional Listings: Adams Rose, Gaudy
Dutch, Salopian Ware, Staffordshire Items.

DESIGN SPATTERWARE

Creamer, 4", blue and red flower, blue
stick spatter, green stripe on base .. **65.00**
Cup and Saucer
Floral pattern, red, blue, green, and
black **25.00**
Peony, red and green **175.00**
Jug
5½", Holly Leaf, red and green **120.00**
7", barrel shape, blue, rosettes and
fern prongs **150.00**
Pitcher, 10¾", red, green, and purple
floral wreaths, red borders **100.00**
Plate
8½", red and blue flower center,
green leaves, black stick spatter
border **175.00**
8⅞", brown and purple stick spatter,
green stripes **25.00**

Platter, 15⅝", Rosebud and Thistle pattern, red stripe and columbine, green spatter 235.00
Sugar, cov, 5", white, blue, and red flowers, green leaves, closed ring and shell handles 100.00
Teapot, cov, rose dec, pink and blue . 200.00

KING'S ROSE

Coffeepot, pink, green, yellow, and red dec 800.00
Creamer, helmet shape, brick red rose 225.00
Cup and Saucer, handleless
Applied yellow, red, pink, and green enamel dec 75.00
Line border, minor enamel wear ... 100.00
Gravy Tureen, cov, 7⅛ x 4½", pearlware, deep purple enamel dec, shell like handles, 3" meandering crack on cov 70.00
Plate
6½", yellow puff balls, vine border .. 140.00
7½", blue rim, border design of pink and red scrolls joined by tiny red King's roses, green leaves, gray stems, stained 25.00
8⅜", emb feather edge border, red, green, brick-red, and yellow center flower dec, imp "Rogers" 75.00
Soup Plate, 9¼", broken band border, puff balls 145.00
Sugar, scalloped rim, ribbed, vine border, pink rose 165.00
Teapot Caddy, 8¼", enameled red, green, blue, and purple flowers, rust line border 50.00
Teapot, Queen Anne shape, minor chips on cov 450.00

STRAWBERRY CHINA

Bowl, 4" 150.00
Cup and Saucer, pink border, scalloped edge 220.00
Plate
5¾", strawberry center, strawberry and vine border, chipped 40.00
7¼", leaf and strawberry center, strawberry and vine border 400.00
8¼", Cut Strawberry 190.00
Relish Dish, 8¾", shell shape 120.00
Sugar, cov, raised strawberries, strawberry knob 130.00
Teabowl and Saucer, vine border 225.00
Vegetable Dish, cov, octagonal 375.00

YELLOW GLAZED EARTHENWARE

Creamer, 4½" h, canary band, white reserves, rust transfers of woman and child playing badminton and writing,

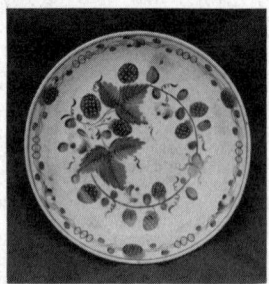

Strawberry, saucer, 5⅝" d, $175.00.

green and blue enamels, copper luster body 45.00
Jug
4½", silver luster, round medallion of Peace as young girl 360.00
5½", black transfer, canary ground, silver luster banding and roundels with Hope and Charity, c1810 ... 250.00
Mug, 2½", red transfer, children and beehive, purple luster band, canary ground 95.00
Pitcher
5½" h, black transfer, Sir Francis Burdett, silver luster roundel, canary ground, c1835 .... 950.00
6¾", russet transfer of mother and child in garden, "Token of Love," border molded with animals, early 19th C 300.00
Plate, 8½", red center transfer scene, molded acanthus border, imp "Wood" 275.00
Waste Bowl, 5⅜ x 2⅞", red and green floral dec, emb floral rim 250.00

FAIRINGS, MATCH-STRIKERS, AND TRINKET BOXES

History: Fairings are small, charming china objects which were purchased or given away as prizes at English fairs in the 19th century. Although fairings are generally identified with England, they actually were manufactured in Germany by Conte and Boehme of Possneck.

Fairings depicted an amusing scene either of courtship and marriage, politics, war, children, and animals behaving as children. Over four hundred varieties have been identified. Most fairings bore a caption. Early examples, 1860–70, were of better quality than later ones. After 1890 the colors became more garish, and gilding was introduced.

The manufacturers of fairings also made matchstrikers and trinket boxes. Some were captioned.

The figures on the lids were identical to those of the fairings. The market for the match-strikers and trinket boxes was identical to that for the fairings.

Reference: Susan and Al Bagdade, *Warman's English & Continental Pottery & Porcelain, 1st Edition,* Warman Publishing Co., Inc., 1987.

Advisors: Barbara and Melvin Alpren.

Fairing, "Three O'Clock in the Morning," woman in bed, husband sitting on edge holding baby, 3⅝ x 2 x 3″, $235.00.

FAIRINGS

A Long Pull and a Strong Pull, three figures, one having tooth pulled	100.00
Between Two Stools You Fall to the Ground, two gentlemen assisting lady to a chair	175.00
God Save the Queen	170.00
Kiss Me Quick	175.00
Landlord In Love, gentleman in dressing gown peeking through keyhole	250.00
O Do Leave Me A Drop, two cats drinking out of same bowl	250.00
Our Best Wishes, hearts dec	150.00
Out By Jingo, three figures	275.00
The Murderer	75.00

MATCH-STRIKERS

Boy, with pig and basket	200.00
Dog in doghouse, colorful, striker at back	200.00
Elephant and rider, howdah striker	275.00
Girl, picking flowers, holding them in apron, standing in front of match holder, corrugated scratch panel	150.00

TRINKET BOXES

Basket, oval, two cats on cov	200.00

Benjamin Franklin, bust on dresser, American eagle at bottom	250.00
Cabbage Rose, flower and leaf on dresser	150.00
Cavalier, reclining, full color	150.00
Child's Prayer, young girl in bed	200.00
Musical Group, two ladies and man, playing instruments	200.00
Punch, sitting on chair	250.00
Returning At One In The Morning, woman hitting man on head with shoe, fancy bed	60.00

FAIRY LAMPS

History: Fairy lamps, originating in England in the 1840s, are candle burning night lamps. They were used in nurseries, hallways, and dim corners of the home.

Two leading candle manufacturers, the Price Candle Company and the Samuel Clarke Company, promoted fairy lamps as a means to sell candles. Both contracted with other manufacturers of glass, porcelain, and metal to produce the needed shades and cups. For example, Clarke used Worcester Royal Porcelain Company, Stuart & Sons, and Red House Glass Works in England, plus firms in France and Germany. Clarke's trademark was a small fairy with a wand surrounded by the words "Clarke Fairy Pyramid, Trade Mark."

Fittings were produced in a wide variety of styles. Shades ranged from pressed to cut glass, from Burmese to Nailsea. Cups are found in glass, porcelain, brass, nickel, and silver plate.

American firms selling fairy lamps included Diamond Candle Company of Brooklyn, Blue Cross Safety Candle Co., and Hobbs-Brockunier of Wheeling, West Virginia.

Fairy lamps are found in two pieces (cup and shade) and three pieces (cup with matching shade and saucer). Married pieces are common.

References: John F. Solverson, *Those Fascinating Little Lamps,* Antique Publications, 1988; John F. Solverson (comp.), *Those Fascinating Little Lamps, Miniature Lamps Value Guide,* Antique Publications, 1988.

Reproduction Alert: Reproductions abound.

Amber, 4″ h, diamond point shade, matching base marked "Clarke Pyramid"	185.00
Bisque, figural	
3″ d, 4¼″ h, gray owl head, blue bow around neck, amber and black glass eyes	200.00
4″ d, 4″ h, owl, cat, and dog, glass eyes, clear marked "Clarke" glass candle cup	250.00
Burmese	
4″ h, salmon pink to yellow acid finish,	

Clarke Floral Pyramid, clear and rose pink petal shade, cranberry inner shade, sgd twice, $175.00.

matching base marked "Clarke
Pyramid" **500.00**
7" d, 7" h, salmon pink shaded to yel-
low, acid finish, matching ruffled
base, marked "Clarke's Patent
Fairy Lamps," clear marked
"Clarke" glass candle cup, brass
frame with two scrolling arms,
hooks for attaching hanging chains **750.00**
Cranberry, 6½" d, 5½" h, frosted cranberry verre moire dome shade,
matching ruffled base, clear marked
"Clarke" insert, clear candle cup . . . **500.00**
Nailsea
5½" d, 4" h, red verre moire dome
shade, red base, clear glass candle
cup holder marked "S Clarke's Pyramid Trade Mark" and "C. W. S.
Night Light" **485.00**
5½" d, 5" h, frosted cranberry opaque
white loopings, clear marked
"Clarke" glass candle cup **425.00**
Opalescent, 2⅞" d, 3⅞" h, pyramid,
blue, emb ribbed shade, clear marked
"Clarke" base **100.00**
Overshot, 2⅞" d, 3½" h, yellow swirl,
cased, clear marked "Clarke" glass
base **115.00**
Pairpoint, 10" h, puffy shade with
grapes and butterflies, turned mahog-
any base **500.00**
Peach Blow, 3¾" h, green leaves dec,
Thomas Webb & Sons, marked
"Clarke" clear glass base **400.00**
Porcelain, 3¼" d, 7¾" h, lighthouse,
green roof, pink, white, and gold trim **185.00**
Sapphire Blue, 3⅞" d, 4⅝" h, DQ, melon
ribbed, clear marked "Clarke" clear
base **165.00**
Satin
2⅞" d, 3½" h, rose, DQ, MOP, white
lining, clear marked "Clarke" glass
base **165.00**
3⅞" d, 4⅝" h, chartreuse green,

melon ribbed overlay, white lining,
clear marked "Clarke" glass base **200.00**
Stevens and Williams, 5¼" d, 6" h,
matching ruffled base, turned down
edge, blue, white, and crystal stripes,
applied clear base, clear marked
"Clarke" glass candle cup **815.00**

FAMILLE ROSE

History: Famille Rose is Chinese export enameled porcelain in which the pink color predomi-
nates. It was made primarily in the 18th and 19th
centuries. Other porcelains in the same group are
Famille Jaune (yellow), Famille Noire (black), and
Famille Verte (green).

Decorations include courtyard and home
scenes, birds, and insects. Secondary colors are
yellow, green, blue, aubergine, and black.

Mid to late 19th century Chinese export wares
similar to Famille Rose are identified as Rose Canton, Rose Mandarin, and Rose Medallion.

Reference: Sandra Andacht, *Oriental Antiques
& Art: An Identification And Value Guide,* Wallace-
Homestead, 1987.

Snuff Bottle, 2½ x 2", $135.00.

Bowl
7½" d, flaring rim, int. dec of single
group of objects, auspicious symbols border, ext. with multicolored
scholar's objects, lingzhih mark,
early 18th C **2,200.00**
10" d, int. citron medallion, ext. with
elaborate cartouches of figural
scenes, diapered and gilt scroll
ground, mid 18th C **750.00**
10" d, int. floral and scrolled border,
figural cartouche on scrolled gilt
ground ext., 19th C **600.00**
11½" d
Int. with bouquet of flowers, floral

chain, elaborate rim borders, floral trellis ext. band and border, late 18th C **1,000.00**
Int. with central floral cluster, ornate and diaper border, ext. with alternating large and small flower clusters suspended from green garland, broad rose diapering border, late 18th C **1,300.00**
13″ d, int. dec with arms of Dailing, Foster in pretense, underglaze blue Fitzhugh border, later gilding, rolled lip, arms repeated on each side of ext., small blue enamel floral sprays, c1785 . . . . **2,700.00**
Brush Washer, 7½″ l, lotus pad shape, int. with ducks, lotus blossoms, and pads, 19th C **625.00**
Charger, 17″ d, center arms of city of Utrecht, flowers, and birds, blue diaper cavetto and wide rim with reserve cartouches of sea creatures, Chinese figures, and flowers, first quarter 18th C, for Dutch market **2,600.00**
Dish, 8½″ l, oval, central figural gardenscape, foliated piercework basketry rim, multicolored flowers **700.00**
Figure, 22¾″ h, peacock, perched on gnarled pine trunk beside bamboo reeds, enameled plumage, black penciled details, restored necks, 19th C, pr **2,700.00**
Garden Seat, 18¾″, hexagonal, animals and cranes beneath ruyi borders with bats and fruit, pierced top and sides **1,800.00**
Jar, cov
8½″ h, ovoid, ogee and leaf form reserve panels, multicolored flowers, bronze ground, pierced wood lid, 18th C **800.00**
11½″ h, ribbed ovoid, twin ogee panels of bright floral sprays, green vines, polychrome flowers, black ground, conforming lid, lotus knop, mid 18th C, pr **4,750.00**
18½″ h, ovoid, scattered peony sprays and flowers, peacocks and exotic birds on rockwork, cloud collar band, domed lid, c1900, pr . . . **2,475.00**
Teapot, 6¾″, couple viewing harbor through spy glass, gilt handles and spout, late 18th C **465.00**
Tray, 8″ l, oval, reticulated rim, multicolored center armorial arms, underglaze blue diaper and trefoil borders, late 18th C, pr **1,000.00**
Tureen, 15″ l, goose form, relief feathers, detailed feet, neck, and iron red beak, pr **1,500.00**
Umbrella Stand, 24″, turquoise, ducks in lotus pond, ornate ruyi lappet border, pr **1,200.00**

Vase
17½″ h, sq sectioned bottle, each face dec with seasonal flower, brilliant enamels, shiny black ground, 19th C **1,300.00**
35″ h, baluster, gilt relief dragons, foo dog handles, figural panels, scattered clusters of flowers, objects, and insects, celadon ground, 19th C **1,800.00**
Wine Cup, 3⅛″ d, Chinese child watching rooster, hen, and chicks in garden, 1776 dated Zianlong mark, pr **375.00**

FENTON GLASS

History: The Fenton Art Glass Company began as a cutting shop in Martins Ferry, Ohio, in 1905. In 1906 Frank L. Fenton started to build a plant in Williamstown, West Virginia, and produced the first piece of glass in 1907. Early production included carnival, chocolate, custard, and pressed plus mold blown opalescent glass. In the 1920s stretch glass, Fenton dolphins, jade green, ruby, and art glass were added.

In the 1930s boudoir lamps, "Dancing Ladies," and various slags were produced. The 1940s saw crests of different colors being added to each piece by hand. Hobnail, opalescent, and two-color overlay pieces were popular items. Handles were added to different shapes, making the baskets they created as popular today as then.

Through the years Fenton has added beauty to their glass by decorating it with hand painting, acid etching, color staining, and copper wheel cutting. Several different paper labels have been used. In 1970 an oval raised trademark also was adopted.

References: Shirley Griffith, *A Pictorial Review Of Fenton White Hobnail Milk Glass,* published by author, 1984; William Heacock, *Fenton Glass: The First Twenty-Five Years,* O-Val Advertising Corp, 1978; William Heacock, *Fenton Glass: The Second Twenty-Five Years,* O-Val Advertising Corp, 1980.

Collectors' Club: Fenton Art Glass Collectors Of America, Inc, P. O. Box 384, Williamstown, WV 26187. **Additional Listings:** Carnival Glass.
Advisor: Ferill J. Rice

Basket
Amethyst opal, Waterlily & Cattails, berry, 4″ **25.00**
Burmese, Maple Leaf **35.00**
Bowl, Crystal, Viking, 13″ l **160.00**
Dot Optic, cranberry opalescent, 7″ d, 3″ h **45.00**
Hobnail, opalescent
Cranberry, mayonnaise, 3 pc set . **85.00**
Turquoise, bowl, 9″ **40.00**
Silver turquoise, 10″ **45.00**
#601, shallow, Pekin blue bowl **95.00**

#847, Lilac Petal bowl 77.00
#1562, Lilac, banana boat bowl . . . 65.00
Bowl, 11″, jade, flared 40.00
Cake Plate
  Milk Glass, black crest 50.00
  Spanish Lace, green pastel 40.00
Candlesticks, pr
  Ivory Crest, cornucopia 65.00
  Silver Crest, cornucopia 45.00
  Silver Turquoise, short 45.00
Candy Dish
  Colonial green, Valencia 15.00
  Rosalene, Ogee, 3 pc 85.00
  Ruby, irid butterfly, (FAGCA) 65.00
Compote
  Ebony, Mikado 125.00
  Orange, Roses pattern 8.00
  Plum opalescent, hobnail, large,
    c1962 . . . . 85.00
  Persian Medallion, Rosaline 200.00
  Spanish Lace, Violets in Snow, milk-
    glass 17.50
Creamer and Sugar
  Colonial blue, thumbprint 25.00
  Diamond Optic, #1502
    Orchid 40.00
    Ruby 60.00
  French opalescent, hobnail, mini . . . 15.00

Bell, Rosaline, orig paper label, c1967–1971, 7″ h, $30.00.

Cruet
  Cranberry opalescent
    Coin Dot, 6″ 75.00
    Polka Dot 125.00
    Jamestown Blue 32.00
  Decanter, hobnail, mulberry, crystal
    stopper, jug type 250.00
  Decanter Service, decanter, tray, six
    glasses
    Georgian, ruby, 8 pc set 125.00
    Hobnail, plum opalescent, 8 pc set 125.00

Egg, pedestal
  Custard, blue roses 25.00
  Ebony, white flowers 50.00
  White satin, flowers and butterfly . . . 40.00
Goblet
  Colonial
    Amber, Empress, sticker 7.50
    Pink, thumbprint 11.00
Hat
  Black Crest, #1923 . . . . 55.00
  Daisy and Button, topaz opalescent,
    4½″ 25.00
  Peach Crest, 4″, 1924 . . . . 37.50
  Rib Optic, French opalescent, #1922 125.00
  Rose Overlay, #1924 . . . . 35.00
  Silver Crest, violets, #1923 . . . . . . 65.00
  Spiral Optic, cranberry opalescent,
    10″, #1927 . . . . 140.00
Lamp
  Boudoir, Coin Dot, blue opalescent . 40.00
  Courting, Diamond Optic, colonial
    blue, #7343 . . . . 70.00
  Hurricane, Spiral Optic, snow crest,
    amber 70.00
  Wrisley bottle, Hobnail, cameo opa-
    lescent 40.00
Kettle, hobnail
  #3979, mustard, blue paste 25.00
  #3990, milk glass 7.00
Miscellaneous
  Candleholder, three hole, Butterfly,
    purple carnival 150.00
  Decanter, stopper, elephant, crystal . 80.00
  Jam and Jelly Set, Block and Star,
    #5603 . . . . 65.00
  Lavabo, Wild Rose, hobnail 300.00
Perfume
  Lilac, stopper, #53 . . . . 45.00
  Rose Overlay, melon rib 20.00
  Silver Crest, melon rib 10.00
Pitcher
  Coin Spot, green opalescent, green
    handle 95.00
  Ebony, #1639 . . . . 60.00
  Jacqueline, milk glass, 5″ 20.00
  Ruby, #1639 . . . . 80.00
Rose Bowl
  Heart Optic, cranberry opalescent . . 60.00
  Melon ribbed, yellow overlay 30.00
  Persian Medallion, Persian blue . . . 27.50
Salt and Pepper, hobnail
  Cranberry opalescent, #3806, pr . . 60.00
  Topaz opalescent, ftd, pr 30.00
Tumbler
  Colonial blue, thumbprint, ice tea . . 15.00
  Ruby, #9133 . . . . 7.50
Vase
  Bubble Optic, honey amber, 11″ . . . 150.00
  Dolphin, jade, 6″ 18.00
  Green overlay, beaded, melon, 9″ . . 45.00
  Ivory Dot Optic, cranberry opalescent,
    5″ 52.00

Plated, amberina, 9″	**65.00**
Spiral Optic, emerald snow crest, 8¾″	**90.00**
Wild Rose and Bow Knot, apple green	**45.00**
Water Set, pitcher, six tumblers	
Jade green, 6 ring, 7 pc set	**200.00**
Rose, 7 pc set, Ming, Fenton	**200.00**

FIESTA

MADE IN USA

History: The Homer Laughlin China Company introduced Fiesta dinnerware in January, 1936, at the Pottery and Glass Show in Pittsburgh, Pennsylvania. Fredrick Rhead designed the pattern; Arthur Kraft and Bill Bensford molded it. Dr. A. V. Blenininiger and H. W. Thiemecke developed the glazes.

The original five colors were red, dark blue, light green (with a trace of blue), brilliant yellow, and ivory. A vigorous marketing campaign took place between 1939 and 1943. In 1938 turquoise was added; red was removed in 1943 because of the war effort and did not reappear until 1959. In 1951 light green, dark blue, and ivory were retired and forest green, rose, chartreuse, and gray added to the line. Other color changes took place in the late 1950s, including the addition of a medium green.

Fiesta ware was redesigned in 1969 and discontinued in 1972–73. In 1986 Fiesta was reintroduced by Homer Laughlin China Company. The new china body shrinks more than the old semi-vitreous and ironstone pieces, thus making the new pieces slightly smaller than the earlier pieces. The modern colors are also different in tone or hue. The cobalt blue is darker than the old blue. Other modern colors are black, white, apricot, and rose.

References: Linda D. Farmer, *The Farmer's Wife Fiesta Inventory and Price Guide,* published by author, 1984; Sharon and Bob Huxford, *The Collectors Encyclopedia of Fiesta, Sixth Edition,* Collector Books, 1987.

Reproduction Alert.

Additional Listings: See *Warman's Americana & Collectibles* for more examples.

Ashtray	
Medium green	**175.00**
Rose	**40.00**
Turquoise	**25.00**
Bowl	
4¾″, fruit, medium green	**40.00**
5½″, fruit, turquoise	**11.00**

Syrup Pitcher, cobalt blue, $120.00.

6″, dessert, rose	**18.00**
7⅜″, salad, ivory	**35.00**
8½″, fruit, red	**28.00**
9½″, salad, yellow	**55.00**
Butter Dish, cov, green opal, Honeycomb and Clover	**275.00**
Candleholders, pr	
Bulb, cobalt	**40.00**
Tripod, yellow	**100.00**
Carafe, three pint, red	**100.00**
Casserole, cov, yellow	**50.00**
Coffeepot, yellow	**85.00**
Compote, 12″, red	**70.00**
Creamer, ring handle, rose	**15.00**
Cup and Saucer	
Cobalt	**18.00**
Turquoise	**15.00**
Demitasse Cup and Saucer, red	**35.00**
Egg Cup	
Light green	**20.00**
Red	**55.00**
Gravy Boat, medium green	**95.00**
Jug, two pint, chartreuse	**48.00**
Marmalade	
Light Green	**135.00**
Turquoise	**35.00**
Yellow, cov	**125.00**
Mixing Bowls, nested, set of 3, yellow .	**100.00**
Mustard, cov, yellow	**95.00**
Nappy, 8½″, medium green	**75.00**
Pie Plate, 8¾″, rose	**20.00**
Pitcher	
Juice, red	**275.00**
Water, yellow, ice lip	**35.00**
Plate	
6″, dessert, yellow	**3.50**
7″, bread and butter, gray	**6.50**
9″, luncheon, light green	**8.00**
10″, dinner, cobalt	**10.00**
10½″, grill, cobalt	**6.00**
13″, chop, ivory	**18.00**
Platter, 12″, oval, turquoise	**15.00**
Relish Tray	
Cobalt, round	**10.00**
Red, five parts	**60.00**

Salt and Pepper Shakers, chartreuse,
pr 16.00
Soup Plate, 6", cream, gray 30.00
Sugar, cov, ivory 20.00
Syrup Pitcher, yellow 145.00
Teapot, six cups, ivory 48.00
Tumbler, water, 10 oz, turquoise 22.00
Vase
  8", light green 295.00
  10", red 650.00
  12", yellow 425.00
Water Set, 5 pcs, pitcher and four tum-
blers, green opal, Honeycomb and
Clover 650.00

FIGURAL BOTTLES

History: Figural Bottles, made of porcelain either in glaze or bisque form, achieved popularity in the late 1800s and remained popular to the 1930s. The majority of figural bottles were made in Germany, with Austria and Japan accounting for the balance. They averaged in size from three to eight inches.

Figural bottles were shipped to the United States empty and filled upon arrival. They were then given away to customers by brothels, dance halls, hotels, liquor stores, and taverns. Some were lettered with the names and addresses of the establishment; others had paper labels. Many were used for holidays, e.g., Christmas and New Year.

Figural bottles also were made in glass and other materials. The glass bottles held perfumes, foods, or beverages.

References: Ralph & Terry Kovel, *The Kovels' Bottle Price List, 8th Edition,*, Crown Publishers, 1987; Otha D. Wearin, *Statues That Pour*, Wallace-Homestead, 1965.

Periodical: *Antique Bottle And Glass Collector,* P.O. Box 187, East Greenville, PA 18041.

Additional Listings: See *Warman's Americana & Collectibles* for more examples.

BISQUE

Goat, carrying briefcase and walking
stick, emb "You Get My Goat" 40.00
Jolly Man, 4½" h, toasting "Your
Health," flask style, tree bark back . 75.00
Sailor, 6½" h, cartoon type, white pants,
blue blouse, hat, high gloss front,
marked "Made in Germany" 100.00
Turkey Trot, 6⅜" h, tree trunk back,
made in Germany 135.00

GLASS

Birdcage, 3½", aqua, c1860 .... 80.00
Book, 5" h, blue glaze, "Coming Thro/
The Rye" 110.00
Cabin, "E. G. Booz's Old Cabin Whis-

Sailor, high gloss, white pants, blue blouse and hat, image back, marked "Made in Germany," $15.00.

key," golden amber, sloping collared
mouth 260.00
Dutchman, 10", milk glass, c1870 .... 85.00
Grover Cleveland, 9½" h, bust, clear an
frosted, tooled mouth, pontil 70.00
Indian Warrior, 12¼" h, yellow amber,
rolled mouth, H. Pharazyn 500.00
Owl, 8", orange, painted face and feet 65.00
Pipe, amber, orig stopper mouthpiece . 110.00
Skull, 4¼" h, cobalt blue, tooled mouth,
emb "Poison" 2,900.00

PORCELAIN

Book
  5¾" h, brown, cream, and yellow
  glazes 375.00
  10½" h, brown, tan, cream, and green
  flint enamel, "Bennington Battle" . 1,000.00
Coachman, 10½" h, tan and brown mottled glaze, Bennington mark 275.00
Pig, 9½" l, standing, brown and tan
glazes, Bieler's/Ronny Club 375.00

FINDLAY ONYX GLASS

History: Findlay onyx glass, produced by Dalzell, Gilmore & Leighton Company, Findlay, Ohio, was patented in 1889 for the firm by George W. Leighton. Due to high production costs resulting from a complex manufacturing process, the glass was made only for a short time.

Layers of glass were plated to a bulb of opalescent glass through repeated dippings into a glass pot. Each layer was cooled and reheated to develop opalescent qualities. A pattern mold then was used to produce raised decorations of flowers and leaves. A second mold gave the glass bulb its full shape and form.

A platinum luster paint, producing pieces identified as silver or platinum onyx, was applied to the raised decorations. The color was fixed in a muffle kiln. Other colors such as cinnamon, cranberry, cream, raspberry, and rose were achieved by using an outer glass plating which reacted strongly to reheating. For example, a purple or orchid color came from the addition of manganese and cobalt to the glass mixture.

Reference: James Measell and Don E. Smith, *Findlay Glass: The Glass Tableware Manufacturers, 1886-1902,* Antique Publications, 1986.

Sugar Shaker, silver dec, white opalescent ground, 6″ h, $300.00.

Bowl, 7″ d, 2¾″ h, silver	**300.00**
Butter Dish, cov, 5½″ d, silver	**800.00**
Celery, 6¼″ h, cream	**250.00**
Creamer, 4½″ h, raspberry	**925.00**
Mustard, 3″ h, cream	**375.00**
Pitcher, 8″ h, cream, applied opalescent handle	**750.00**
Salt and Pepper Shakers, pr, 3″ h, platinum	**550.00**
Spooner, 4¼″ h, raspberry	**600.00**
Sugar, cov, 5½″ h, cream	**325.00**
Sugar Shaker, 6″ h, silver	**300.00**
Syrup, 7″ h, SP lid marked "Pat. March 28, 82", lid finial missing, silver	**400.00**
Toothpick, 2½″ h, cream	**375.00**
Tumbler, raspberry, Floradine pattern	**785.00**

FIREARM ACCESSORIES

History: Muzzle loading weapons of the eighteenth and early nineteenth centuries varied in caliber and required the owner to carry a variety of equipment with him, including a powder horn or flask, patches, flints or percussion caps, bullets, and bullet molds. In addition, military personnel were responsible for bayonets, slings, and miscellaneous cleaning equipment and spare parts.

In the mid-19th century, cartridge weapons replaced their black powder ancestors. Collectors seek anything associated with early ammunition from the cartridges themselves to advertising material. Handling old ammunition can be extremely dangerous due to decomposition of compounds. Seek advice from an experienced collector before becoming involved in this area.

Military related firearm accessories generally are worth more than their civilian counterparts. See "Militaria" for additional listings.

Reproduction Alert: The amount of reproduction and fake powder horns is large. Be very cautious!

Bayonet, 21⅛″, 17″ triangular blade stamped "H" with large "US" surcharge, surface with deep age patina, some scaling encrusted rust	**100.00**
Bullet Mold	
Colt, .56 caliber Root rifle or carbine, sprue cutter deeply stamped "COLTS/PATENT," iron body with wooden handles and brass ferrules, 30 to 40% orig blue	**225.00**
Colt, Conversion Mold A steel, .36 caliber marking stamped out and remarked "41 CAL," a fitting for seating the primer added to one arm and the cavities enlarged, usual "COLT'S/PATENT" stamping on sprue cutter, 95% orig blue	**450.00**
Military .44 Caliber Gang, 12½″, wooden handles with brass ferrules, each side stamped with letter "S," right side stamped "44.H,", casting 6 conical bullets	**160.00**
Sharps Rifle Co. Military Gang, iron, 13½″, wooden handles with iron ferrules, casting 6 bullets for the rifle or carbine, one side stamped "SHARP'S RIFLE/MANUFG. CO./ HARTFORD CONN./U.S.," other side with "W.A.T." inspection mark, sprue cutter moves back and forth in a groove along top of mold	**950.00**
Smith & Wesson Bullet, 7″, casting both a round and conical .44 or .45 bullet, blued steel body, walnut handles, provision for capping shells, over 95% orig blue	**175.00**
Carbine Sling, black leather, 2½″ wide strap, unmarked, brass fittings and steel swivel and hook	**300.00**
Cartridge Belt, Western, approx 28-30 waist, made of doubled over brown leather 3″ wide with single sewn seam and loops for twenty-five .44-.45 cartridges, heavy nickel plated steel buckle, c1900	**160.00**

Cartridge Board, Union Metallic Cartridge Co., 44 x 31", printed display with attached cartridges, orig oak frame, 55 x 41½", board of frame with applied raised cast panel "TRADE/ U.M.C./MARK" on top and "THE UNION METALLIC CARTRIDGE CO." on bottom, cartridges range from 22 BB cap to one inch Gatling, plus a selection of shotgun shells and a display of various primers in little glazed frame, repainted frame, orig glass cov missing 3,600.00

Powder Flask, tin, marked "Indian Rifle Gun Powder, Made By Hazard Powder Co, Hazardville, CT," 6½" l, 4" w, $50.00.

Flask, Powder
Brass
8¼", body emb on one side "RIFLE HORN" within a curved panel surrounded with a toothed design, complete with the original faded green carrying cord, orig lacquer finish 150.00
8¼", fluted pattern emb on both sides, top stamped "A.M. FLASK & CAP Co.," fitted with orig bright green woven carrying cord, 97% orig gold lacquer finish 125.00
Copper
6½", Colt Type Navy, emb on both sides with crossed pistols, stars, spread winged eagle clutching a shield and flags over a cannon, with naval anchor, bugle, etc., below, 95% orig lacquer finish, bright blued spring, perfect seams 900.00
7¾", pear shape, emb on both sides with group of hounds fighting with bear in woods, script initials below, brass top 90.00
10", Batty Peace Flask, emb pattern on both sides, inspected

"A.D.K." at the neck, the top stamped "BATTY" and dated 1853, body retaining over 90% of orig lacquer finish, orig brass carrying rings 350.00
Horn, German, 13¾", flattened horn body engraved on both sides, back with a series of concentric circles, front with 2 mythological scenes, one with the date 1596, steel mounts with a long belt hook, minor worm damage to body, base loose 500.00
Iron, military, 10¼" overall, turned wooden plug for spout, body made of molded or stamped sheet iron with rolled over seam and two steel carrying rings on each side, orig black paint, complete with orig carrying cord, early 19th C 75.00
Flask, Shot, leather
7", black pigskin body stamped "SYKES/EXTRA/lb/1," fitted with carrying ring, 2" German silver top with bright steel dispenser stamped "SYKES EXTRA" 70.00
8½", emb on both sides with a Highland scene showing a Scottish hunter alongside a fallen stag with 2 hounds, brass top 50.00
Grease Pump, brass, 6", for use with an approx .32 caliber bullet, designed for hand use with no provision for attaching to a bench, the grease fitting is not changeable, appears to be simplified version of Pope grease pump 60.00
Holster, Western
Colt New Service revolver with 7½" barrel, emb or tooled overall with floral and leaf patterns plus a large scene showing a cowboy on horseback, brown leather, 12½" overall, early 20th C 225.00
Colt Single Action Holster, tooled decoration along borders on both sides, brown leather 110.00
Horn, Powder
10½", orig oak spout plug carved in the shape of an eagle's head, plain wood base fitted with a large brass stud, body with raised carving of a large eagle, an Indian Head, grape vines, a flying pheasant, the American shield, flowers, and the name "Paul/Bohret," late 19th C 300.00
11", spout carved with a faceted pattern ending in scallops, scalloped pattern repeated about ⅓ down towards pine base, body engraved with 2 pecking chickens and a large marine scene showing a 3 masted warship flying the English flag plus 2 smaller large boats and 2 row-

boats with a man in each, the carving primitive but well done, base with a brass button for carrying cord, c1800 with nice age patination **400.00**

12″, Texas hunting, steer, tip carved with an open mouthpiece and then with a raised ring fitted with a silver wire bent to form a ring for carrying strap, open end of the horn fitted with a half inch silver band with raised ring at edge, the band with orig period script engraving "From Barbee to Louis Flatau Sr. to Louis Flatau Jr.," horn body with a large finely engraved script presentation "John T. Patterson/to/Dr. James Barbee/of Texas/May 13th 1834/James K. Polk/ and/Geo. M. Dullas" **1,300.00**

15¾″, US unmarked, turned wooden base and combination screw-off wooden filling plug and post for the carrying strap, 3″ brass tip with spring loaded dispenser stamped "US" and large brass carrying ring, c1814–20 .... **1,450.00**

Lithophane, oval, 7 x 5¾″, depicts Samuel Colt seated holding a Texas Paterson with loading lever in his right hand, his left arm resting on a desk with papers and loading dividers, marked "KPM/460/Z" **2,400.00**

Medal
1⅛″ d, gold, obv: "SOUTH AFRICA 1900–1" with a lion seated on a crown over thistles and "Q.O.R.G.I.Y.," rev engraved: "1905/C. Squadron/Troop Shooting/Cup/Won by 4th Troop/Sergt. J. D. Eadie" and hallmarks, suspension ring also hallmarked **450.00**

2¾″ d, bronze, obv: portrait of Franz Joseph I with titles, rev: 3 figures and "WELTAUSSTELLUNG 1873 WIEN./DEM/MITARBEITER," original maroon leather covered case with green lining **40.00**

Nipple Display Board, cast brass, 4½ x 2″, cast lettering and numbers "W & C ELEY LONDON/MANUFACTURERS OF/PERCUSSION CAPS," mounted with 11 dummy steel nipples, each marked with a number or "MILITARY" designating what size cap should be used with each size nipple, late 19th C **250.00**

Powder Measure, 9¾″, Ideal Universal No. 6, cast address and model number in iron body, complete with original 14 x 8½″ instruction sheet printed on both sides, 75% orig black paint,

missing screw that hold dispensing tube **175.00**

Rifle Bag, Kentucky, 9 x 7″, leather bag, tarred fabric cover, containing some old flints and lead balls, leather carrying strap with hand made 6″ wooden leather covered knife scabbard containing old home made 6½″ knife with 3½″ blade **175.00**

FIREARMS

History: The 15th century arquebus was the forerunner of the modern firearm. The Germans refined the wheelock firing mechanism during the 16th and 17th centuries. English settlers arrived in America with the smoothbore musket; German settlers had rifled arms. Both used the new flintlock firing mechanism.

A major advance was achieved when Whitney introduced interchangeable parts into the manufacturing of rifles. The warfare of the 19th century brought continued refinements in firearms. The percussion ignition system was developed by the 1840s. Minie, a French military officer, produced a viable projectile. By the end of the 19th century cartridge weapons dominated the field.

Two factors control pricing firearms–condition and rarity. The value of any particular antique firearm covers a very wide range. For instance, a Colt 1849 pocket model revolver with a 5″ barrel can be priced from $100.00 to $700.00 depending on whether or not all the component parts are original, whether some are missing, how much of the original finish (bluing) remains on the barrel and frame, how much silver plating remains on the brass trigger guard and back strap, and the condition and finish of the walnut grips. Be careful to note any weapons' negative qualities. A Colt Paterson belt revolver in fair condition will command a much higher price than the Colt pocket model in very fine condition. Know the production run of a firearm before buying it.

References: Norman Flayderman, *Flayderman's Guide To Antique American Firearms...And Their Values*, 4th ed., DBI Books, 1987; Joseph Kindig, Jr., *Thoughts On The Kentucky Rifle In Its Golden Age*, 1960, available in reprint; Russell and Steve Quetermous, *Modern Guns: Identification & Values, Revised 7th Edition*, Collector Books, 1989.

Periodical: *Gun List,* 700 East State Street, Iola, WI 54990.

FLINTLOCK PISTOLS — SINGLE SHOT

English, officer's, 7″ round steel barrel marked "London," lockplate marked "Sharpe, full oak stock with brass trigger guard and ramrod pipes **500.00**

Pistol, 38 cal. with factory MOP grips, ser. #181, Iver Johnson's Arms & Cycle Works, 1895 Mfg, Fitchburg, MA, $225.00.

Kentucky, T. P. Cherington, 12½″ octagonal smoothbore barrel, stamped "T. P. CHERINGTON" on barrel and lockplate, 45 caliber, brightly polished iron parts, walnut stock **2,500.00**

Kentucky, Daniel Sweltzer & Co, Lancaster, 1807–08, 10½″ round barrel, smoothbore, 54 caliber, walnut stock, only lock may be by Sweitzer with barrel from Guest **6,500.00**

U. S. Model 1805 (Harper's Ferry), 10″ round iron barrel with iron rib underneath holding ramrod pipe, lockplate marked with spread eagle and shield over "US" and vertically at rear "HARPER'S/FERRY" over "1808," 54 caliber, walnut half stock with brass butt plate and trigger guard (Flayderman 6A-008) **2,750.00**

U.S. Model 1836, Asa Waters, Millbury, MA, 54 caliber, smoothbore, 8½″ round barrel, brass blade front sight, oval shaped rear sight on barrel tang, overall length 14″, swivel type ramrod with button shaped head, all mounting of iron, lockplate marked "A. H. WATERS & Co/MILLBURY, MASS/1844" **1,000.00**

PERCUSSION PISTOLS — SINGLE SHOT

Note: Conversion of flintlock pistols to percussion was common practice. Most English and U.S. military flintlock listed above can be found in percussion. Values for these percussion converted pistols are from 40 to 60% of the flintlock values as given.

Dueling, pair, cased, J. E. Evans, 10″ octagonal barrel, smoothbore barrel, patent breeches stamped "J. E. EVANS/PHILADE," scroll and border engraved patent breeches, trigger guards, and trigger plates, set triggers, 50 caliber, French style brass bound mahogany casing lined in purple velvet containing a powder flask, a can of Eley percussion caps, a screwdriver, a nipple wrench with a screw top containing a nipple-prick, cleaning rod, rammer, mallet head and handle, quantity of bullets, brass plaque on lid inscribed "Mr. Charlos Cambos Jr Philadelphia, Pa" **6,000.00**

English, belt, 14½″ overall, 9″ round brass barrel sgd "LONDON" and stamped with Birmingham proofs and a maker's mark, fitted with a round drum for the percussion nipple, "LONDON WARRANTED" lock originally flintlock and converted to percussion with light engraving at rear of the plate and fitted with a plain flat hammer, both tangs of trigger guard shortened, 2 brass ramrod caps but no buttcap, left side fitted with 3″ steel belt hook **300.00**

Tyron, Merrick & Co (partnership between George Tyron and Samuel Merrick, Phila. from 1832–38), 12¾″ overall, 8″ octagonal barrel, smoothbore, 64 caliber, top flat inlaid in gold letters "TYRON, MERRICK & Co," bottom flat stamped with English proofs, walnut half stock with checkered wrist, German silver patch box in butt, barrel keys, and forend tip, steel tailpipe and engraved trigger guard, unsgd back action lock, missing ramrod, break in stock at wrist repaired **400.00**

U.S. Model 1842 Navy, 54 caliber, smoothbore, 11⅝″ overall length, swivel type ramrod with button shaped head, trigger guard and trigger plate are integral:

"N. P. AMES/SPRINGIELD/MASS." marked centrally on lock, "USN/1845" stamped vertically at rear of lock (Flayderman 6A-046) **650.00**

"US/DERINGER/PHILADELA" marked centrally on lock, "USN/1847" also on lock, barrel stamped "DERINGER/PHILADELPA" and "RC" (Flayderman 6A-049) **1,250.00**

PERCUSSION PISTOLS — MULTI-SHOT

Colt

1860 Army Model, 8″ round barrel, marked "ADDRESS COL. SAML COLT, NEW YORK U.S. AMERICA," 44 caliber, 6 shot, cylinder engraved with naval battle scene, walnut grips (Flayderman 5B-092) **850.00**

Dragoon, Baby Model, 1848, 5″ barrel, marked "ADDRESS SAML COLT, NEW-YORK CITY," 31 cali-

ber, 5 shot, octagonal barrel, stagecoach holdup cylinder, oval stop
slots, varnished walnut one piece
grips (Flayderman 5B-039) **1,600.00**

Dragoon, First Model, c1849, 7½″
part round, part octagonal barrel,
marked "ADDRESS SAML COLT,
NEW-YORK CITY -, COLT'S/PAT-
ENT," 44 caliber, 6 shot, cylinder
engraved with Indian fight scene,
square backed trigger guard, wal-
nut grips (Flayderman 5B-023) .. **4,500.00**

Navy, 1851 Model, 7½″ octagonal
barrel, marked "ADDRESS SAML
COLT NEW YORK U.S. AMERI-
CAN," 36 caliber, 6 shot, cylinder
engraved with naval battle scene,
round trigger guard, walnut grips
(Flayderman 5B-124) **750.00**

Paterson Revolver, No. 5, Holster
Model, c1838–40, 9″ octagonal
barrel, marked "Patent Arms M'g
Co., Paterson N:J-Colt's Pt.," 36
caliber, 5 shot, cylinder roll scene
of stagecoach holdup, hidden trigger, varnished polished walnut grip
(Flayderman 5B-007) **10,000.00**

Sidehammer (Root) Model 1855, 3½″
octagonal barrel marked "AD-
DRESS SMAL COLT, HARTFOR,
CT," 18 caliber, cylinder engraved
with Indian fight scene, hammer
mounted on right side of frame,
walnut grips (Flayderman 5B-065) **750.00**

Remington
Army Model, 1861, 8″ octagonal barrel, marked "PATENTED DEC. 17,
1861 - MANUFACTURED BY
REMINGTON'S ILION, NY," 44 caliber, 6 shot, walnut grips (Flayderman 5E-011) **550.00**

New Model Police Revolver, 1863–
73, 5½″ octagonal barrel, marked
"PATENTED SEPT. 14, 1858,
MARCH 17, 1863/E. REMINGTON
& SONS, ILION, NEW YORK,
U.S.A./NEW MODEL," 36 caliber, 5
shot, walnut grips (Flayderman 5E-
028) **500.00**

Remington-Beals, 1st Model, 3″ octagonal barrel marked "F. BEAL'S
PATENT" and date, frame marked
"REMINGTONS, ILION, NY," 31 caliber, 5 shot, gutta percha grips,
round trigger guard (Flayderman
5E-001) **400.00**

Other
Deringer and Deringer Type
F. H. Clark & Co., Memphis, TN,
c1850s–60s, 41 caliber, 3½″ bar-
rel, marked "F. H. CLARK & CO./
MEMPHIS," German silver cap

on forend, plain unengraved silver mounts, oval shaped barrel
wedge escutcheons, wooden
ramrod (Flayderman 7D-012) .. **800.00**

Slotter & Co., Philadelphia, c1860–
1869, 41 caliber, 3″ barrel, engraved German silver mountings, varnished walnut stock,
checkered handle (Flayderman
7D-026) **575.00**

Pepperbox
Thomas K Bacon, Norwich, CT,
c1852–58, single action, under-
hammer, 31 caliber, 6 shot, 4″
ribbed barrel, large curved finger
spur for cocking, engraved nipple
shield, walnut grips (Flayderman
7B-00a) **375.00**

Sharps & Hankins, Philadelphia,
PA, c1859–74, Model 3A, Serial
No. 1759, 32 caliber short rimfire,
4 shot, marked "ADDRESS
SHARPS & HANKINS, PHILA-
DELPHIA, PENN." on top of barrel and "SHARPS PATENT/
JAN. 25, 1859" on right side of
frame, circular sideplate and button barrel release on left side of
frame, gutta percha grips, complete and orig throughout, barrels
with 20-30% blue mixed with age
brown, frame with dulled aged
silver color (Flayderman 5F-083) **275.00**

Swedish, "Darling," 30 caliber, 4 shot,
7¾″ overall, 3½″ barrel, bottom of butt
carved with initials "JM," nipple protection shield loose and marred all the
way around with deep scuff marks,
otherwise complete and orig **250.00**

Revolvers
Hopkins & Allen, Norwich, CT, Dic-
tator Model, late 1860s through
early 1870s, 36 caliber, 5 shot
round cylinder, roll engraved
scene of panel motif, walnut
grips (Flayderman 7A-034) **225.00**

C. S. Pettengill, New Haven, CT,
Army Model, early 1860s, 44 caliber, 6 shot round cylinder, 7½″
octagonal barrel, loading lever
assembly standard, double action hammerless type frame, two
piece walnut grips, no gov inspector markings (Flayderman
7A-079) **600.00**

REVOLVERS (CARTRIDGE)

Browning, Nomad, Serial No. 45PI, 22
caliber, 4½″ barrel, orig carton **225.00**
Charter Arms, Pathfinder 22, Serial No.

119194, 22 caliber, 3″ barrel, orig carton and papers **950.00**

Colt, Model 1903, Pocket Auto, Serial No. 32955, 38 caliber, spur hammer, hard rubber "COLT" grips, complete and orig, 95% plus bright blue finish, right side of slide with some spotty surface rust (Flayderman 5B-226) . . **500.00**

Hawes Firearms Co., Favorite Target, Serial No. 16937, 22 caliber, 8″ barrel, barrel with some spotty rust or acid spots from careless storage **100.00**

J. C. Higgins, Model 88, Serial No. 2951, 22 caliber, 6″ barrel, orig carton **60.00**

High Standard, Sentinel Mark III, Serial No. H4402, 357 Magnum caliber, 3¾″ barrel, orig carton **150.00**

Intercontinental Arms, Dakota, Serial No. 2391, 357 Magnum caliber, 5½″ barrel, orig carton **150.00**

Japanese Nambu, Serial No. 80712, 8mm caliber, production code 18.6, mis-matched magazine **250.00**

Miroku, Liberty Chief, Serial No. 3040, 38 Special caliber, 3″ barrel, orig cardboard carton with yellow satin lining **75.00**

Remington, Model 51, Serial No. PA30819, 380 caliber, 97-98% orig blue **380.00**

Russian Nagant, Serial No. 7271, 7.62mm caliber, left side of frame with Russian markings and "1906," about 50% blue **130.00**

Smith & Wesson, 38 Double Action, Third Model, Serial No. 417855, 38 caliber, 6″ barrel, hard rubber checkered "S & W" grips, complete and orig, 95% plus orig bright blue finish, but with some scattered areas of storage pitting on top of the barrel and right side (Flayderman 5G-076) **225.00**

Star, Model PD, presentation, Serial No. 1363196, 45 caliber, plain wood grips with special Toledo work gold damascened medallions, the right the American eagle and shield, the left "John Amber/FROM/YOUR FRIENDS AND STAR" **950.00**

Walther, Manurhin PP, Serial No. 10073A, 9mm caliber, orig carton, missing magazine, bright finished barrel with some slight surface rust discoloration **275.00**

Walther, PP22, Serial No. 302362P, 22 caliber, extended checkered wood grips and magazine extension, Nazi proofs, 95% orig dull blue War time finish **625.00**

Dan Wesson, Model 15, Serial No. 10245, 357 Magnum caliber, 5¾″ barrel, orig carton with spare 5¾″ barrel and a pair of finger groove grips . . . **175.00**

FLINTLOCK LONG ARMS

French Model, 1763 Musket, 75 caliber, 44½″ round barrel, lockplate marked "St. Etienne," full length walnut stock with three iron barrel bands, iron trigger guard and butt plate, the major weapon of French infantry troops during the Revolutionary War **1,250.00**

Kentucky, H. Deringer, Philadelphia, 60 caliber, 59⅜″ overall, 43⅜″ octagonal barrel, brass furniture, patchbox with scalloped edges and stylized eagle head finial, tiger stripped stock **3,000.00**

U.S. Model 1816 Musket, Type II, made at Springfield Armory, 69 caliber, single shot, muzzleloader, 42″ round barrel, walnut stock, lockplate marked "SPRING/FIELD/1829," complete with orig issue bayonet in black leather scabbard, throat mount marked "R DINGEE/N-YORK" (Flayderman 9A-197 . . . . **3,000.00**

PERCUSSION LONG ARMS

Note: Conversion of flintlock long arms to percussion was common practice. Most English, French, and U.S. Military flintlock model long arms listed in the previous section can be found in percussion. Values for these percussion converted long arms are from 40 to 60% of the flintlock values previously noted.

English Infantry Rifle, 577 caliber, 48½″ overall, 33″ round barrel, stud for a saber bayonet, 900 yard folding sight, lock stamped with a large crown and engraved "John O. Evans 1860," all iron furniture, two clamping barrel ends, lock still retains orig nipple protector and chain **850.00**

Kentucky, 52¼″ overall, 36¾″ heavy octagonal barrel, top flat engraved with a rope pattern and "L. Biddle" in script (Levi Biddle, Shanesville, OH, c1834–45), lightly engraved percussion lock with indistinct maker's mark, tiger stripped bull stock with brass forend cap, 3 ramrod pipes, trigger guard and butt plate, fancy engraved German silver openwork patch box, long toe plate and stripe along comb, fitted with 15 German silver inlays, missing one inlay, stock with old refinish **1,700.00**

Kentucky, 56″ overall, 40½″ octagonal barrel, 38 caliber, signed on top flat "FRANCOIS GOME" (No record maker, possibly owner), lightly engraved "JOSH GOLCHER" lock secured with a large pin with hammered head rather than usual screw, tiger stripped full stock with all German silver mounts including open work patch box with light engraving and 15 inlays including the large oval on the check rest which is engraved with a classic primitive American eagle, old partial break in stock at rear of barrel, otherwise complete and orig 1,200.00

Kentucky, 56¼″ overall, 41″ octagonal barrel, 41 caliber, simple scroll engraving on 3 upper flats at the breech, top flat stamped "N. SHENNENFELT" (Nicholas Shennenfelt, working in PA between 1823 and 1871), engraved percussion lock stamped "J. STEATHAM," elaborate brass furniture including trigger guard and butt plate, engraved open work patchbox, engraved toe plate and rib along the comb, openwork sideplate and forend wear plate, 3 ramrod pipes and forend cap, stock with 46 engraved German silver inlays of varied shapes and designs, bad break in stock in front of lock, repair on barrel tang, could use professional restoration . . 2,500.00

Remington Model 1863 (Zouave Rifle), Contract Rifle, c1862–65, 58 caliber, single shot, muzzleloader, 33″ round barrel, walnut stock, brass patchbox on right side of butt which still retains orig spare nipple and worm, screw fitting for ramrod, 7 groove rifle, lockplate marked ahead of hammer, American eagle over small "U.S.," two lines under bolster "REMINGTON'S/ILION, N.Y.," horizontally dated at rear "1863" (Flayderman 5E-076) 2,250.00

U. S. Model 1855, Rifled Musket, made at Harper's Ferry Armory, c1857–61, 58 caliber, single shot, muzzleloader, 33″ round barrel, two barrel bands, walnut stock, patchbox on right side of butt, lockplate marked "U.S./HARPERS FERRY," dated "1858," barrel with same date, complete with orig "U.S." marked bayonet in black leather brass mounted scabbard (Flayderman 9A-308) 2,750.00

RIFLES

C. D. Bartley Patent Sporting, Serial No. 3, 38 caliber, 49″ overall, 32¼″ full octagonal barrel, fitted with Beach's combination front sight and open rear sight, barrel and left side of frame both stamped "THE C.D. BARTLEY'S/PATENT OCT. 5, 1880," checkered walnut butt stock with Ger-

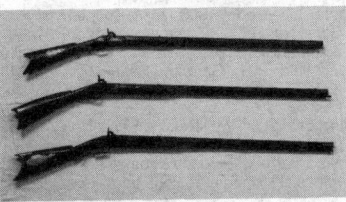

Pennsylvania Long Rifles, top: Leman, Lancaster, PA, $375.00; center: Unknown maker, $300.00; bottom: S. C. Johnston, Allegheny, $400.00.

man silver butt plate, burl walnut forend with pewter nose cap, odd action (when hammer is cocked the breech block moves straight down and stays locked open till the gun is fired; as the hammer drops the breech block moves up) 700.00

Colt, Model 1855, Military, Serial No. 1396, 56 caliber, 31½″ barrel fitted for socket bayonet, full stocked with sling swivels, trap in butt contains brass cleaning rod extension for ramrod, oil finished walnut stock, complete and orig, barrel with 98% blue (Flayderman 5B-079) 5,000.00

French, Model 1874, bolt action, Serial No. 53912, manufactured at the St. Etienne Arsenal in 1877, barrel and action with 97-98% orig blue 250.00

German, Model 71/84, bolt action, Serial No. 70430, made at the Amberg Arsenal, 1877, 98% orig blue 350.00

Phoenix Target Rifle, Serial No. 238, 44 caliber, 30″ full octagonal barrel, top flat stamped "PHOENIX.CAL44," fitted with orig windgauge front sight, a two leaf folding rear barrel sight, 5″ tang peep sight, heel of checkered pistol grip butt fitted with orig sight base and plain steel butt plate, 50-60% orig blue (Flayderman 5J-055) 1,100.00

Sharps, Model 1878, Express, Serial No. 16815, 45 caliber, 27/8″ case, straight 30″ full octagonal barrel, matted top flat fitted with blade front and folding open rear sights, bottom of barrel slotted for a sling swivel, hole now filled with a key, tang tapped for a sight, holes now filled with tap screws, grained burl walnut checkered forend and buttstock, hard rubber pistol grip cap and butt plate, but with a silver oval plate script engraved "WLE," 95% of orig blue finish, only 31 produced (Flayderman 5F-066) 5,500.00

Springfield, Model 1903, NRA Sporter, Serial No. 1277238, same number on bolt and Star Gauge barrel **2,300.00**

Springfield, M1 Garand, Serial No. 433182, some slight cuff marks near muzzle **775.00**

Winchester, Low Wall Deluxe, Serial No. 9184, 32 caliber, WCF, 28″ half round No. 2 barrel with Beach's combination front sight, open rear sight, tang fitted with orig Winchester peep sight, deluxe pistol grip walnut stocks checkered at the wrist and forend, raised cheek piece on left side, fitted with rifle butt plate, fine to very good cond (Flayderman 5K-116) **2,250.00**

Winchester, Model 1873, Serial No. 72056, 44-40 half round 24″ barrel with half magazine, steel shotgun butt plate, fitted with sling swivels, varnished forend and butt stock burl walnut which is usually found only on guns with checkered stocks, barrel with 97-98% blue (Flayderman 5K-041) **1,800.00**

SHOTGUNS

AYA Model 1 Double Barrel, Serial No. 543042, 28 gauge 26″ barrels, double triggers, auto ejectors, detachable side lock action fully scroll engraved in English manner, oil finished deluxe walnut stocks with checkered wood butt, orig leather trunk casing with label in lid **3,250.00**

Colt, Model 1878, Serial No. 12346, 10 gauge, 34″ barrels, action with border scroll engraving, grained deluxe varnish stock with hard rubber Rampant Colt butt plate, complete and orig, 97–98% orig Damascus twist finish on barrels (Flayderman 5B-261) ... **4,100.00**

Darne Double Shotgun, Serial No. 5T693, 12 gauge, 27½″ barrels, very near new **900.00**

Ferlack Double, Serial No. 1150, 20 gauge, 28″ vent rib barrels with beaver tail forend, engraved box lock action with single trigger, built by Bereinigle, butt with a check rest on right side, 13½″ pull, slight wear of blue at breech **950.00**

German, Pinfire, 8 gauge 30″ double barrels engraved on the rib "Ph. Bartholomae, Chicago, Ill.," the action profusely scroll engraved with woodland scenes on each side, the left with two gold inlaid foxes, the right with two gold inlaid deer, the trigger guard with similar scroll engraving and a gold inlaid hound and flying bird, the back action locks scroll engraved and with gold inlaid scenes; the right lock with a gold bird dog and flying pheasant plus "F. Baurenfeind," the left with a gold fox and flying snipe plus "Heidelburg," the engraved tan with a gold rabbit, checkered walnut forend and butt stock, missing the horn forend cap, barrel with 60-70% orig twist brown finish **750.00**

Stephen Grant & Sons, Serial No. 17784, 28″ barrels with some tight scroll engraving at the breech, gold inlaid with the number "1," the sidelock action fully English scroll engraved and sgd "Stephen Grant & Sons," the opening lever gold inlaid "1," gold inlaid "SAFE," double triggers, auto ejectors, straight English walnut stock with rubber butt pad, 15″ pull, orig labeled trunk casing for 2 shotguns with oil bottle, cleaning kit, 2 snap caps and 2 screw drivers ... **7,400.00**

Griffin & Howe Double Barrel, Serial No. 88761, 12 gauge, 29¼″ auto ejector barrels sgd "engraved by Josef Fugger" in very small letters, side lock action with scroll engraving and large panels with hunting scenes, left side shooting ruffled grouse in woods, right side shooting quail in fields, bottom shooting ducks in marsh, superbly grained walnut stock with 14¾″ pull, double triggers, checkered wood butt plate, belly inlaid with a gold oval engraved "WGR," leg of mutton leather case **4,250.00**

Remington, Model 1100, 150th Anniversary, Serial No. 233790V, 12 gauge, 30″ full coke vent rib barrel, spare 26″ Custom coke barrel and 22″ vent rib barrel with Jetway Choke, scroll engraved silver oval escutcheon on the butt stock with "JTA" initials, about new **600.00**

Stevens Model 5100, Serial No. XQ, 20 gauge 28″ barrels, Tenite stocks ... **200.00**

FIREHOUSE COLLECTIBLES

History: The volunteer fire company has played a vital role in the protection and social growth of many towns and rural areas. Paid professional firemen usually are found only in large metropolitan areas. Each fire company prided itself on equipment and uniforms. Conventions and parades gave the fire companies a chance to show off their equipment. These events produced a wealth of firehouse related memorabilia.

Reference: Mary Jane and James Piatti, *Firehouse Collectibles,* The Engine House, 1979.

Museums: Insurance Company of North America (INA) Museum, Philadelphia, PA; Oklahoma State Fireman's Association Museum, Oklahoma City, OK; San Francisco Fire Dept. Memorial Museum, San Francisco, CA.

Additional Listings: See *Warman's Americana & Collectibles* for more examples.

Advertising
Paperweight, bronze, "The Charter Oak Fire Insurance Co, Ltd Edit. No 301" **75.00**
Ruler, tin, Hartford Fire Insurance, 1885 . . . . **50.00**
Alarm Box, marked "Gamewell" and "Telegraph Station," 1880s **75.00**
Badge
Kearny & Trecker District 7, 2¾" d, celluloid, red helmet **20.00**
Tri-County Firemen's Convention, 1½ x 2¼", brass, diecut pendant with fire symbols, hanger bar with lantern and "July 2-3, 1897" **25.00**
Bell, 11", brass, iron back **100.00**
Belt, 3" w, leather, black, aluminum loops and hook **40.00**
Book, *The Fire Chief's Handbook,* Shepperd, 1932, illustrated **20.00**
Bucket
Leather
11½" h, set of four, gilt painted sides, bail handle, numbered 1 through 4, marked "J. Wendell, F.F.S." **26,500.00**
12" h, polychrome dec, inscribed "Harnden & Co," 19th C **275.00**
12½" h, hand painted, blazing fire scene, blue-green ground, tooled rim, swing handle, foliate scroll inscribed "Joshua Swan," "Lowell U. F. Society" above, c1840 . **16,500.00**
Metal, hand forged, red paint, brass finial **90.00**
Cabinet Card, 4½ x 6½", fireman in shirt and badge, foreman's cap **25.00**
Catalog, Ahrens Fox Fire Engines, 32 pgs, 1927, 8½ x 11" **70.00**
Ceremonial Parade Hat
Leather, hand painted
6¾" h, blacksmith at forge and romantic scene, inscribed "Mechanic Fire company" above initials "CHL," reverse with initials "FA" with water keg, red ground, painted dark green under brim, int. lined with period newspaper, c1840 . . . . **27,500.00**
7½" h, American bald eagle perched on United States shield, inscribed scroll "United States

Fire Co," reverse with deep diamond point sawtooths with "U.S." initials, script initials "JST" on top, black ground, c1840 . . . **12,100.00**
Pressed Felt, 7½" h, painted, winged figure in white gown with flowing green sash blowing trumpet, rising sun with beams and white cloud background, inscribed "Fame, Hose Compy" in gilt lettering, painted fire scene on top, initials "MC" on back, gray painted ground, 7½" h, c1840 . . . . **10,450.00**
Extinguisher, 6¼", Hayward's Hand Fire Grenade, yellow, ground mouth, smooth base, c1870 . . . . **75.00**
Hat, 13½" l, leather, brass eagle head and shield "F.C.F.D. 1," black paint with red and white **115.00**

Helmet, marked "N. F. D., 1st Asst," tin, painted white, gold and red trim, marked "Pat'd '87," $165.00.

Helmet
Brass, eagle finial, Barnicoat, Boston **375.00**
Leather, Chapman Steamer, Cairns & Bro **175.00**
Lantern, Dietz, King Fire Dept, copper bottom **130.00**
Nozzle, hose, 16" l, brass, removable, double handle, marked "Akron Brass Mfg Co, Inc" **135.00**
Pinback Button
Newark Fire Department, 1¼", red and white, attached fabric ribbons inscribed "June 27-28, 1928" and "Newark, NY" **20.00**
Weccacoe Fire Co, 1¼", black and white, horsedrawn pumper photo . **12.00**
Sign, 10 x 14", tin, painted, ribbon banner reads "Rainbow Fire Company," eagle on shield, black edge background, red and yellow foliate designs **800.00**
Stereograph, Chicago Fire, court house scene after fire **10.00**
Stickpin, ⅞", multi illus, white ground, c1900 . . . . **15.00**
Trophy, 11 x 34", axe, red painted handle and head, silver trumpets and

edge, yellow trim, Concord, NH, Fire Dept, marked "Captured by J. J. McNulty, at London, NH, March 13, 1896 .... **250.00**

Trumpet, presentation

16¼" h, coin silver, derby style bell, inscribed "Presented by the City of Lowell to Mazeppa Engine Company No 10 for the Third Best Horizontal Playing July 4, 1856" **1,430.00**

17¾" h, silver plated, chased floral design, steamer, helmet, crossed trumpets, and ladder dec, inscribed "Presented to Captain Joseph Frye by the members of the Bradlee Hose Co No 10, March 11, 1870" **1,650.00**

FIREPLACE EQUIPMENT

History: The fireplace was a gathering point in the colonial home for heat, meals, and social interaction. It maintained its dominant position until the introduction of central heating in the mid-19th century.

Because of the continued popularity of the fireplace, accessories still are manufactured, usually in an early American motif.

Reproduction Alert: Modern blacksmiths are reproducing many old iron implements.

Additional Listings: Brass and Iron.

Andirons, brass, Connecticut, late 18th C, 17½" h, $265.00.

Andirons, pr

14½" h, wrought iron, tooled stems, penny feet, gooseneck tops with faceted finials **175.00**

17" h, cast iron, sitting cat form, yellow glass eyes **120.00**

25" h, brass, tapered, spurred arch

supports with claw and ball feet, lemon form finial, c1790 .... **3,575.00**

26" h, brass and wrought iron, faceted, spurred arch supports with claw and ball feet, lantern form finial, c1810 .... **5,775.00**

Bellows

16½" l, leather, red, green, and black stenciled and free hand fruit and foliage, orig white smoked ground **265.00**

17" l, turtle back, orig yellow paint, red, green, black, and gold striping and stenciled and freehand fruit and foliage dec, brass nozzle, releathered **550.00**

18" l, leather, turtle back, gold and bronze stenciled floral dec, brass nozzle, orig dark green paint **55.00**

20" l, walnut, carved roses, basket of flowers, fruit, and tassels, punchwork ground, brass nozzle, c1800 **19,800.00**

Chestnut Roaster, 23" l, brass, reticulated detail, England **150.00**

Coal Box, 19 x 20", cast iron, green, floral dec, gold trim, English **175.00**

Fender

20¾ x 12 x 20", iron, wire grill, brass top rail **275.00**

43¼" l, brass, three engraved Eagles, geometrically pierced, early 19th C **8,250.00**

57" l, 8" h, brass, double rail **90.00**

67" l, 6¾" h, brass, double rail, six posts **55.00**

Fire Back

22½ x 27", cast, high relief design, anchors and fleur–de–lis, arched crest, date "1788, IFC" **950.00**

34¼ x 31⅝", cast iron, coat-of-arms design, arched crest, bead and reel edge, ribbon with "FARE FAC," "ZANE and MARLBORO" below, c1770 .... **42,900.00**

Fire Mark, 7¼ x 10½", cast iron, relief cast of four clasped hands design and No 906 .... **300.00**

Grate, 9 x 17½", cast iron, mid 19th C **75.00**

Hearth Brush, 15", gilted leaf design highlighted in red and black, turned wood handle, orig green paint **700.00**

Heat Reflector, 8" w, 6½" h, tin, semi–circular form, pierced heart, diamonds, dots, and stars design, loop handle **500.00**

Mantle

51 x 46½", poplar, brown stain finish, 28 x 30¾" opening **160.00**

69¼ x 56½", Federal, poplar, applied moldings, stop and dec fluting, pine repairs **600.00**

Mantle Clock, 16¼" h, cast metal, blue and white enameled face, white alabaster and gold repaint **125.00**

Mantle Set, 3 pcs
Bronze, 18″ h clock, pair 22″ h candelabras, marked "Made in France" **1,000.00**
Marble and cast metal, clock, pair candleholders, variegated red marble, clock face labeled "Paris" ... **100.00**
Screen
34¼″ h, brass, three panels, folding, c1930 .... **70.00**
34½″ h, cherry, adjustable pleated green silk screen, tripod base with spider legs, turned base and pole, urn finial, folding shelf with "Polly Pomeroy Starr" and "1781" **11,000.00**
51″ h, mahogany, circular frame with young boy in needlework, tripod base, New England, 19th C **3,300.00**
56″ h, mahogany, rosewood frame, crewel embroidered screen, tripod base with snake feet and turned post **240.00**
Tool Set, four pcs, brass, matching stand **120.00**
Trammel, 20″ l, wrought iron, sawtooth type, adjustable **65.00**

FISCHER J. BUDAPEST.

FISCHER CHINA

History: In 1893 Moritz Fischer founded his factory in Herend, Hungary, a center of porcelain production from the 1790s.

Confusion exists about Fischer china because of its resemblance to the wares of Meissen, Sevres, and Oriental export. It often was bought and sold as the product of these firms. Forged marks of other potteries are found on Herend pieces. The mark "MF," often joined, is the mark of Moritz Fischer's pottery.

Fischer's Herend is hard paste ware with luminosity and exquisite decoration. Pieces are designated by pattern names, the best known being Chantilly Fruit, Rothschild Bird, Chinese Bouquet, Victoria Butterfly, and Parsley.

Fischer also made figural birds and animal groups, Magyar figures (individually and in groups), and Herend eagles poised for flight.

Reference: Susan and Al Bagdade, *Warman's English & Continental Pottery & Porcelain, 1st Edition,* Warman Publishing Co., Inc., 1987.

Bowl, 6¾″, reticulated edge, birds, butterflies, and flowers, multicolored, late, marked **50.00**
Cache Pot, 5″, handled, Rothchild Bird pattern **160.00**

Jar, cov, white ground, multicolored floral motif, raised relief medallions with reticulated fleur–de–lis, matching oval reticulated finial, 7¼″ h, $250.00.

Charger, 13″, multicolored enamel floral dec, gold trim **325.00**
Ewer
7½″, enameled floral dec **200.00**
16½″, reticulated body, rose, blue, green, and gold enamel floral dec **275.00**
Nappy, 4½″, triangular, Victoria Butterfly pattern, gold trim **125.00**
Pitcher, 12″, reticulated, multicolored floral dec **285.00**
Plate, 7½″, luncheon, Chantilly Fruit pattern **90.00**
Sauce Boat, underplate, and matching china ladle
Parsley pattern **225.00**
Victoria Butterfly pattern **250.00**
Tureen, cov, 8½″, handled, Chantilly Fruit pattern, natural molded fruit finial **300.00**
Urn, 12″, blue floral dec, reticulated, shield mark **325.00**
Vase
8″, gold handles, blue flowers and green leaves, reticulated, shield mark **230.00**
10½″, reticulated, flowers, pink, blue, green, and white **200.00**
12″, bulbous, extended neck, cobalt blue reticulated handle, ochre, multicolored flowers, gold accents, deep rose sides **375.00**

FITZHUGH

History: Fitzhugh, one of the most recognized Chinese Export porcelain patterns, was named for the Fitzhugh family for whom the first dinner service was made. The peak period of production was from 1780 to 1850.

Fitzhugh features an oval center medallion or

monogram surrounded by four groups of flowers or emblems. The border is similar to that on Nanking china. Occasional border variations are found. Butterfly and honeycomb are among the rarest.

Blue is the common color. Color is a key factor in pricing with rarity in ascending order of orange, green, sepia, mulberry, yellow, black, and gold. Combinations of colors are scarce.

Reference: Sandra Andacht, *Oriental Antiques & Art: An Identification And Value Guide,* Wallace-Homestead, 1987.

Reproduction Alert: Spode Porcelain Company, England, and Vista Alegre, Portugal, currently are producing copies of the Fitzhugh pattern. Oriental copies also are available.

Plate, orange dec, white ground, 9⅝" d, $300.00.

Basket, 7⅝" l, oval 9¼" stand, shades of orange, gilding in center, floral sprig in trellis diaper, beast medallion edged in spearheads and dumbbells, surrounded by four clusters of flowers and precious objects, pierced rim, gilt edge, metal grape cluster and loop replacement handles, c1820 ...... **2,325.00**

Hot Water Dish, 10⅝" d, underglaze blue, center pine cone and beast medallion, four clusters of flowers and precious objects in trellis diaper border, spearhead and dumbbell border, blue spouts, c1840 .... **400.00**

Plate
  7⅞", dessert, orange, center floral sprig medallion, border of butterflies, diaper, and scalework panels, key fret and floral springs on gilt edged rim, c1820, pr **350.00**
  9¾", dinner, orange, floral sprig in medallion of beasts and trellis diaperwork, edged in spearheads and dumbbells, four clusters of flowers

and precious objects, set of six, minor chips and restoration, c1810 . **2,475.00**

Platter and Strainer, 15⅞" l, oval, orange, deep platter, pierced strainer, gilt edged central aperture, three rows of smaller holes, floral sprig in medallion of beasts and trellis diaperwork, edged in spearheads and dumbbells, four clusters of flowers and precious objects, c1810 ...... **2,750.00**

Salt, 4" l, oval, underglaze blue, center pine cone and beast medallion, spearhead and dumbbell border, ruffled rim, Mared pattern border, feathered edge, fluted sides, four clusters of flowers and precious objects, c1820, pr **1,430.00**

Soup Tureen, 13⅞" l, cov, 16⅛" platter, oval, orange, floral sprig in medallion of beasts and trellis diaperwork, edged in spearheads and dumbbells, four clusters of flowers and precious objects, foot and cavetto of platter with cell diaper border, border of diaper and scalework panels, butterflies, floral sprigs, and fret motifs on gilt-edged rims, re-gilt entwined strap handles, re-gilt flowerhead knob, c1810 .... **5,000.00**

FLASKS

History: A flask is a container for liquids, usually having a narrow neck. Early American glass companies frequently formed them in molds which left a relief design on the front and/or back. Historical flasks with a portrait, building, scene, or name are the most desired.

A chestnut is hand blown, small, and has a flattened bulbous body. The pitkin has a blown globular body with vertical ribs with a spiral rib overlay. Teardrop flasks are generally fiddle shaped and have a scroll or geometric design.

Dimensions can differ for the same flask because of variations in the molding process. Color is important, with scarcer colors demanding more money. Aqua and amber are the most common colors. Bottles with "sickness," an opalescent scaling which eliminates clarity, are worth much less.

Reference: George L. and Helen McKearin, *American Glass,* Crown Publishers, 1941 and 1948.

Collectors' Club: The National Early American Glass Club, B0x 57, Fishers Hill, VA 22626.

Art Glass, 6½" h, oval, canary, fiery opalescent highlights, raised flower motif **140.00**
Chestnut
  4¾" h, yellow amber, vertically ribbed, pontil **200.00**

Historical, emb "Geo. Wash., Father of his Country, Gen Taylor Never Surrenders," Dyottville Glassworks, Phila, 6¾" h, $75.00.

5¼" h, red amber, freeblown, sheared
mouth, pontil 140.00
Gemel, 9¾" h, clear, amethyst and
white loopings, tooled mouths 100.00
Historical
Agriculture, sheaf of wheat and eagle,
greenish aquamarine, sheared
mouth pontil, pt, GII-10 . . . . 500.00
Benjamin Franklin and T. W. Dyott
M.D., clear, amethyst tint, pontil, qt,
GI-96 . . . . 310.00
Columbia and Eagle, aquamarine,
sheared mouth, pontil, pt, GI-117 . 450.00
Eagle, double, yellow green, olive
tone, applied mouth, pint, ... 250.00
"For Pike's Peak," aquamarine, applied mouth, 1½ pt, GIX-47a 300.00
General Washington and eagle,
greenish aquamarine, sheared
mouth, pontil, pt, GI-2 . . . . 160.00
Horse and Cart Railroad, dark olive
green, pt, GV-7 . . . . 310.00
Jenny Lind, factory portrait, blue green,
round collared mouth, iron pontil,
qt, GI-104 . . . . 425.00
Masonic, eagle, blue green, tooled
mouth, pt, GIV-7 . . . . 120.00
Roosevelt, aquamarine, sloping col-
lared mouth, qt, GI-129 . . . . 30.00
Success To The Railroad, olive am-
ber, sheared mouth, pontil, pt,
GV-3 . . . . 185.00
Washington & Taylor, golden yellow,
double collared mouth, pontil, pt,
GI-40a 700.00
Washington Monument, "Corn For
The World," apricot, qt, GVI-32 . . 525.00
Pitkin
Light green, ribbed and swirled,
7¼" h 160.00

Light olive amber, sheared mouth,
pontil, 6" h 360.00
Sea green, sheared mouth, pontil,
6½" h 410.00
Scroll
Sapphire blue, double collared
mouth, iron pontil mark, pint, Amer-
ica, 1845–60 . . . . 2,600.00
Yellow green, olive tone, sheared
mouth, pontil,½ pt, GIX-36 . . . . . 475.00
Teardrop, Nailsea type
Cobalt Blue, vertical ribbed, flared
mouth, 7¾" h 130.00
Cranberry, sheared mouth 7½" h . . . 85.00

FLOW BLUE

History: Flow blue or flowing blue is the name
applied to china of cobalt and white whose color,
when fired in a kiln, produced a flowing or
smudged effect. The blue varies in color from dark
cobalt to a grayish or steel blue. The flow varies
from very slight to a heavy blur where the pattern
cannot be easily recognized. The blue color does
not permeate through the china.

Flow blue was first produced around 1835 in the
Staffordshire district of England by a large number
of potters including Alcock, Davenport, J. Wedgwood, Grindley, New Wharf, Johnson Brothers,
and many others. The early flow blue, 1830s to
1870s, was usually of the ironstone variety. The
late patterns, 1880s to 1910s, and modern patterns, after 1910, usually were made of the more
delicate semi-porcelain variety. Approximately
95% of the flow blue was made in England, with
the remaining 5% made in Germany, Holland,
France, and Belgium. A few patterns also were
made in the United States by Mercer, Warwick,
and Wheeling Pottery companies.

References: Mary F. Gaston, *The Collector's
Encyclopedia Of Flow Blue China,* Collector
Books, 1983, 1989 value update; Petra Williams,
*Flow Blue China—An Aid To Identification, Re-
vised Edition,* Fountain House East, 1981; Petra
Williams, *Flow Blue China II, Revised Edition,*
Fountain House East, 1981; Petra Williams, *Flow
Blue China and Mulberry Ware—Similarity and
Value Guide, Revised Edition,* Fountain House
East, 1981.

Collectors' Club: Flow Blue International Collectors' Club, P.O. Box 205, Rockford, IL 61105.

EARLY PATTERNS: c1825–1850

Bowl, Kin-Shan, Philips & Sons, c1840,
8½" 110.00
Butter Dish, cov
Amoy, Davenport, c1844 . . . . 125.00
Chusan, Podmore Walker & Co,
c1845 . . . . 120.00

Pelew, E Challinor, c1840 . . . . **125.00**

Creamer
Amoy, Davenport, c1844 . . . . **225.00**
Cashmere, Ridgway & Morley, c1840 **275.00**
Hong Kong, Charles Meigh, c1845 . **100.00**
Indian Jar, Thomas Ford, c1840 . . . **175.00**
Sabraon, unknown English maker,
c1845 . . . . **200.00**
Scinde, J & G Alcock, c1840 . . . . . **200.00**
Tonquin, W Adams & Son, c1845 . . **100.00**

Cup and Saucer, handleless
Amoy, Davenport, c1844 . . . . **85.00**
Chapoo, Wedgwood, c1850 . . . . . . **125.00**
Jeddo, Adams & Co, c1840 . . . . . . **90.00**
Kyber, Adams & Co, c1850 . . . . **85.00**
Scinde, J & G Alcock, c1840 . . . . . **125.00**

Cup Plate
Oregon, T J & J Mayer, c1845, 4″ d **125.00**
Rhine, Thomas Dimmock, c1844 . . . **50.00**
Scinde, J & G Alcock, c1840 . . . . . **65.00**

Gravy Boat
Daliah, E Challinor, c1850 . . . . **100.00**
Sabraon, unknown English maker,
c1845 . . . . **150.00**

Pitcher, Cashmere, Ridgway & Morley,
c1840, 7″ h, octagonal **325.00**

**Early Pattern, Chen–Si sugar bowl, 7½
x 7″, $200.00.**

Plate
Amoy, Davenport, c1844, 8¼″ **50.00**
California, Podmore Walker & Co,
c1849, 7¾″ **48.00**
Chapoo, Wedgwod, c1850, 8½″ . . . **60.00**
Chen–Si, John Meir, c1835, 8½″ . . . **80.00**
Indian Jar, Jacob & Thos Furnival,
c1843, 10½″ **115.00**
Jeddo, Adams & Co, c1840, 9″ **65.00**
Manilla, Podmore, Walker & Co,
c1845, 9½″ **100.00**
Oregon, T J & J Mayer, c1845, 10″ . **115.00**
Scinde, J & G Alcock, c1840, 7″ . . . **60.00**
Tonquin, W Adams & Son, c1845,
7½″ **65.00**

Platter
Chen–Si, John Meir, c1835, 14 x 17″ **250.00**
Indian Jar, Jacob & Thos Furnival,
c1843, 9¾ x 12⅜″ **285.00**
Kyber, Adams & Co, c1850, 17″ . . . **300.00**
Manilla, Podmore, Walker & Co,
c1845, 16″ **400.00**
Oregon, T J & J Mayer, c1845, 13½″ **250.00**

Sauce Dish
Amoy, Davenport, c1844, 5″ **60.00**
Indian Jar, Jacob & Thos Furnival,
c1843 . . . . **50.00**
Oregon, T J & J Mayer, c1845, 5″ . . **65.00**
Scinde, Thomas Walker, c1847, 5″ . **60.00**
Shell, Wood & Challinor, c1840 . . . . **42.00**
Tulip & Sprig, Thomas Walker, c1845 **38.00**

Soup Plate
Arabesque, T J & J Mayer, c1845 . . **75.00**
Oregon, T J & J Mayer, c1845, 9½″
d, flange rim **115.00**
Sabraon, unknown English maker,
c1845, 9″, flange rim **100.00**

Soup Tureen
Chusan, Podmore Walker & Co,
c1845 . . . . **175.00**
Scinde, J G Alcock, c1840, cov **600.00**

Sugar, cov
Oregon, T J & J Mayer, c1845 . . . . **225.00**
Scinde, J & G Alcock, c1840 . . . . . **350.00**

Tea Set, cov teapot, creamer, and cov
sugar
California, Podmore Walker & Co,
c1849 . . . . **300.00**
Oregon, T J & J Mayer, c1845 . . . . **900.00**

Toddy Plate, Tonquin, W Adams & Son,
c1845 . . . . **75.00**

Vegetable Dish, cov
Cashmere, Ridgway & Morley, c1840 **775.00**
Manilla, Podmore, Walker & Co,
c1845, octagonal **445.00**

Vegetable Dish, open, Amoy, Daven-
port, c1844, 6 x 8″ **175.00**

Waste Bowl
Chen–Si, John Meir, c1835, 8½″ . . . **120.00**
Kyber, Adams & Co, c1850 . . . . **85.00**

MIDDLE PATTERNS: c1850–1870

Coffeepot, Simila, Elsmore & Forster,
c1860 . . . . **165.00**

Creamer
Genevese, Edge Malkin, c1873 . . . . **100.00**
Honc, Petrus Regout, c1858 . . . . . . **148.00**

Dish, Blossom, G L Ashworth & Bros,
c1865, 9½″ d **30.00**

Pitcher, Temple, Podmore Walker & Co,
c1850, 8″ h **300.00**

Plate
Carlton, Samuel Alcock, c1850, 9½″ **60.00**
Gothic, Jacob Furnival, c1850, 8¼″ . **80.00**
Honc, Petrus Regout, c1858, 8″ . . . **75.00**

Temple, Podmore Walker & Co, c1850, 10″ **115.00**
Platter
Hindustan, 12 x 16″ **220.00**
Shanghae, J Furnival, c1860, 13½″ . **165.00**
Soup Plate
Blossom, G L Ashworth & Bros, 9″, flange rim **20.00**
Carlton, Samuel Alcock, c1850, 10½″, flange rim **80.00**
Gothic, Jacob Furnival, c1850, flange rim **65.00**
Sugar, cov, Temple, Podmore Walker & Co, c1850 .... **250.00**
Syllaub Cup, Blossom, G L Ashworth & Bros **50.00**
Teapot, cov, Gothic, Jacob Furnival, c1850, 7″ h **525.00**
Vegetable Dish, cov
Asiatic Pheasants, John Meir & Son, c1865 .... **110.00**
Victor, J Maddock & Sons, c1850 .. **115.00**
Vegetable Dish, open, Gothic, Jacob Furnival, c1850 .... **90.00**
Waste Bowl, Temple, Podmore Walker & Co, c1850 .... **175.00**

LATE PATTERNS: c1880–1900s

Bone Dish
Argyle, W H Grindley, c1896 ...... **48.00**
Duchess, W H Grindley, c1891 .... **35.00**
Irdis, W H Grindley, c1910 .... **50.00**
Bouillon Cup, underplate, Irdis, W H Grindley, c1910, two handles **48.00**
Bowl
Keswick, Wood & Sons, c1891, 9½″ d **40.00**
Raleigh, Burgess & Leigh, c1906 .. **25.00**
Butter Dish, cov
Colonial, J & G Meakin, c1891, orig insert **110.00**
Kenworth, Johnson Bros, c1900 ... **150.00**
Linda, John Maddock & Sons, Ltd, c1896 .... **75.00**
Oriental, Ridgways, c1891, orig patterned insert **150.00**
Butter Pat
Argyle, W H Grindley, c1896 ...... **32.00**
Blue Danube, Johnson Bros, c1900 **25.00**
Lugano, Ridgways, c1910 .... **22.00**
Creamer, Richmond, Johnson Bros, c1900 .... **75.00**
Cup and Saucer
Duchess, W H Grindley, c1891 .... **40.00**
Lancaster, New Wharf Pottery, c1891 **60.00**
Lugano, Ridgways, c1910 .... **70.00**
Oriental, Ridgways, c1891 .... **42.00**
Fruit Bowl, Jenny Lind, Arthur Wilkinson Ltd, Royal Staffordshire Pottery, c1895, 7½″ d **125.00**

Gravy Boat, attached underplate
Kenworth, Johnson Bros, c1900 ... **75.00**
Richmond, Johnson Bros, c1900 ... **85.00**
Ladle, Vermont, Burgess & Leigh, c1895 .... **85.00**
Pitcher, Colonial, J & G Meakin, c1891, 6″ **125.00**
Plate
Bentick, Cauldon, c1905, 8″ **35.00**
Hamilton, John Maddock & Sons, c1896, 10½″ **75.00**
Holland, Johnson Bros, c1891, 8″ .. **55.00**
Kenworth, Johnson Bros, c1900, 10″ **48.00**
Lancaster, New Wharf Pottery, c1891, 9″ **50.00**
Linda, John Maddock & Sons, Ltd, c1896, small **20.00**
Lorne, W H Grindley, c1900, 8″ **48.00**
Lugano, Ridgways, c1910
8″ **65.00**
10″ **85.00**
Platter
Argyle, W H Grindley, c1896, 15″ .. **175.00**
Kenworth, Johnson Bros, c1900, 12″ **75.00**
Keswick, Wood & Sons, c1891 .... **75.00**
La Belle, Wheeling Pottery, c1900, 12″ **85.00**
Lancaster, New Wharf Pottery, c1891, 9½″ **90.00**
Soup Plate
Lancaster, New Wharf Pottery, c1891, 9″, flange rim **48.00**
Lugano, Ridgways, c1910, 9″ **65.00**
Rose, Ridgways, c1910, 9″, flange rim **20.00**
Tulip, Johnson Bros, c1900, 9″, gilt . **65.00**
Sauce Dish, Richmond, Johnson Bros, c1900 .... **20.00**
Saucer, Lancaster, New Wharf Pottery, c1891 .... **15.00**
Teapot, cov, Oriental, Ridgways, c1891 **245.00**
Tureen, cov
Linda, John Maddock & Sons, Ltd, c1896 .... **130.00**
Lugano, Ridgways, c1910, 11½″ ... **275.00**
Vegetable Dish, cov
Bentick, Cauldon, c1905, oblong ... **150.00**
Oriental, Ridgways, c1891 .... **145.00**
Peach, Johnson Bros, c1891, 6 x 8″ **50.00**
Vermont, Burgess & Leigh, c1895 .. **175.00**
Vegetable Dish, open
Irdis, W H Grindley, c1910 .... **110.00**
Jenny Lind, Arthur Wilkinson Ltd, Royal Staffordshire Pottery, c1895, 7½″ d **125.00**
Keswick, Wood & Sons, c1891, 9″ .. **60.00**

FOOD BOTTLES

History: Food bottles were made in many sizes, shapes, and colors. Manufacturers tried to make an attractive bottle that would ship well and allow the purchaser to see the product, thus assuring him that the product was as good and as well made as home preserves.

Reference: Ralph & Terry Kovel, *The Kovels' Bottle Price List, 8th Edition* Crown Publishers, Inc, 1987.

Periodical: *Antique Bottle and Glass Collector,* P. O. Box 187, East Greenville, PA 18041.

Additional Listings: See *Warman's Americana & Collectibles* for more milk bottle listings.

Milk Bottle, clear glass, emb "RM Deger, Phoenixville, PA, Pure Milk," 9½" h, $5.00.

Banana Flavor, Herberlings, 8", paper label	8.00
Catsup	
Curtis Brothers, clear, blue label	10.00
Quickshank, paper label	4.00
Coffee, Sunshine, oval shape, zinc lid	5.00
Ginger, Sanford's, label	10.00
Grape Juice, Bass Islands, 5"	5.00
Honey, Land of Lakes, honeycomb, metal cap	8.00
Horseradish	
As You Like It, pottery, clamp	25.00
E. T. Caldren, aqua, paper label	8.00
Lemon Extract, Louis & Company	10.00
Milk	
Alden Bros, round, emb, applied top, qt	25.00
Bayonne City Dairy, clear, qt	125.00
Farm Dairy Quality Products, yellow	18.00
Gold Spot, rect, green, ½ gal.	40.00
Hebrew Dairy, three emb flags, qt	30.00
Palmer Dairy, dripless, qt	25.00
Ridgeview Farms, sq, pyro, pt	45.00
Turner Centre System, round, tin tip, qt	45.00
Wanger's, dark amber, ½ pt	80.00
Olive, Chef, 5"	5.00
Peanut	
Nut House, emb house, bulb shape	170.00

Squirrel Brand Salted Nuts, 13", emb squirrel	110.00
Peanut Butter, Bennett Hubba, 5"	12.00
Pepper Sauce, 8", aqua	35.00
Pickle	
Shaker Brand, olive yellow	325.00
Skilton Foote & Co, 11⅜", yellow amber, lighthouse shape	130.00
Vinegar, Weso Biko Company Cider Vinegar, jug shape	40.00
Yogurt, Yami, Pellissier Dairy Farms, round, red, metal foil lid, 8 oz	5.00

FOOD MOLDS

History: Food molds were used both commercially and in the home. For the most part, pewter ice cream molds and candy molds were used on a commercial basis; pottery and copper molds were used in homes. Today, both types are collected largely for decorative purposes.

Pewter ice cream molds were made primarily by two American companies: Eppelsheimer & Co. [molds marked E & Co., N.Y.] and Schall & Co. [molds marked S & Co.]. Both companies used a numbering system for their molds. The Krauss Co. bought out Schall & Co., removed the S & Co. from some, but not all the molds, and added more designs [marked K or Krauss].

The majority of pewter ice cream molds are individual serving molds. When used, one quart of ice cream would make eight to ten pieces. Scarcer, but still available, are banquet molds which used two to four pints of ice cream per example. European pewter molds [CC is a French mold mark] are available.

Chocolate mold makers are more difficult to determine. Unlike the pewter ice cream molds, maker's marks were not always on the mold or were covered by frames. Eppelsheimer & Co. of New York marked many of their molds, either with their name or with a design resembling a child's toy top with "Trade Mark" and "NY." Many chocolate molds were imported from Germany and Holland and were marked with the country of origin and, in some cases, the mold maker's name.

Reference: Judene Divone, *Chocolate Moulds: A History & Encyclopedia,* Oakton Hills Publications, 1987.

Additional Listings: Butter Prints.

CHOCOLATE MOLDS

Clamp Type, no hinge, two piece	
Basket, 3 x 9", marked "Made in USA 6068"	55.00
Hen on basket, marked "E & Co/Toy"	45.00
Jack O'Lantern, wire clamp	30.00
Rabbit, 6"	45.00
Teddy Bear, marked "Reiche"	275.00

Frame or Book Type, (Measurements based on single cavity size)

Basket, 3½ x 6", 1 cavity	**45.00**
Elephants, tin, 3 cavities	**75.00**
Hearts, 6½ x 6", 2 cavities	**65.00**
Mother Hen, bonnet, 5 x 4½"	**45.00**
Poodle, 3½ x 3½"	**40.00**
Rabbit, 13 x 6", 1 cavity	**65.00**
Witch, 4½ x 2", four cavities	**55.00**

Tray Type (Measurement is overall tray size)

Circus Peanuts, 28 x 13", 105 cavities	**50.00**
Rabbit, with pack, 12 x 10", 4 cavities	**48.00**
Rabbit, playing saxophone, 14 x 10", six cavities	**40.00**
Silverware Set, knife, fork, and spoon, 3 pcs, marked "Reiche"	**200.00**
Turkey, 14 x 10", 8 cavities	**45.00**

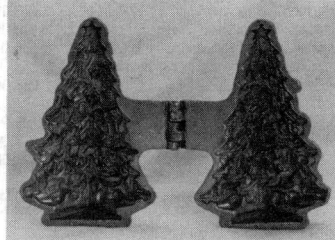

**Ice cream mold, Christmas tree, pewter, marked "E & Co, 1154, 8 to Qt,"
$60.00.**

ICE CREAM MOLDS

Banquet Size

Lamp, marked "S & Co, #41"	**475.00**
Owl, 4 pts, marked "S & Co/7"	**550.00**
Pear, marked "S & Co, #17"	**250.00**
Ship, 2 qt	**225.00**
Shell, marked "Krauss 36B"	**250.00**

Individual Size

Airplane, 5¼" l, pewter	**55.00**
Bunch of asparagus, 3⅝" h, pewter	**20.00**
Cabbage with bunny, 3⅝" l, pewter	**25.00**
Cherub riding Easter bunny, 4" h, pewter	**20.00**
Envelope, heart pierced with arrow and "Valentine," 4¼" l, pewter	**15.00**
Flag, thirteen stars, pewter	**50.00**
Flower, No 548	**40.00**
Kewpie, pewter, dated 1913	**140.00**
Lily, three part, pewter, marked "E & Co"	**45.00**
Man in the moon, 5½" h, pewter marked "E & Co, copyright 1888"	**70.00**
Mushroom, pewter, marked "CC814BIS"	**20.00**

Pear, pewter, marked "CC849 Brevete"	**22.00**
Pineapple, pewter, marked "CC815 Brevete"	**20.00**
Steamboat, pewter	**90.00**
Tulip, 4⅛" h, pewter, marked "E & Co, NY"	**30.00**
Uncle Sam, 5¾", tin	**90.00**

MISCELLANEOUS

Butter, 3¾ x 3¾ x 4", wood, five sided, relief carved scenes of farmer's arms, flowers, cow, farmer and wife, and house, staple hinges, bentwood band	**400.00**
Cheese, 5 x 13", wood, pinned, relief carved design and "Bid," branded "Los," scratch carved date 1893	**45.00**
Cookie, 3½ x 6¼", six classical head, pewter, wood back	**45.00**
Maple Sugar, 6¼ x 15", wood, carved, crowing roaster, patina	**325.00**
Pudding	
3 x 6", round, flared fluted sides, tin	**10.00**
5 x 5 x 6½", oval, pineapple, tin and copper	**65.00**

POTTERY (Center design indicated)

Bunch of grapes and leaf, 3 x 5 x 7", oval, collar ftd, Wedgwood Creamware	**110.00**
Ear of corn, 6" l, yellowware, oval	**35.00**
Fish, 10⅜" l, redware, green glaze, Shenandoah	**145.00**
Lion, ironstone	**90.00**
Rose, ironstone, marked "Alcock"	**50.00**
Strawberries, 4"	**55.00**

FOSTORIA GLASS   FOSTORIA

History: Fostoria Glass Co. began operations at Fostoria, Ohio, in 1887, and moved to Moundsville, West Virginia, its present location, in 1891. By 1925 Fostoria had five furnaces and a variety of special shops. In 1924 a line of colored tableware was introduced. Fostoria was purchased by Lancaster Colony in 1983, and continues to operate under the Fostoria name.

Reference: Hazel M. Weatherman, *Fostoria, Its First Fifty Years*, published by author, c1972.

Collectors' Club: Fostoria Glass Society of America, P.O. Box 826, Moundsville, WV 26041.

Museum: Huntington Galleries, Huntington, WV.

Ashtray, Mayfair, red	**20.00**
Basket, Bouquet, #342 etching, 10¼", reed handle	**60.00**
Bell, American	**75.00**

Bonbon, Colony	18.00
Bookends, pr	
Owls, clear	275.00
Plumes, clear	60.00
Bowl	
Fairfax, 10¾" d, green, flared	24.00
Meadow Rose, 12" d	35.00
Versailles, 12" oval, rose	58.00
Butter Dish, cov	
American	100.00
Colony	48.00
Candlesticks, pr	
Coin, 8" h, red	125.00
Heirloom, 10", white opal	50.00

Candy Dish, Baroque pattern, marigold, 4¾" h, 5½" d, $24.00.

Candy Dish, cov, Bouquet, #342 etching, 7" d	50.00
Celery Tray	
June, 11¼" l, yellow	30.00
Versailles, 11½", green	30.00
Champagne, Heather	15.00
Claret, Holly	30.00
Cocktail, Navarre	20.00
Compote, Versailles, pink, high standard	48.00
Cordial	
Buttercup	20.00
Romance, clear	40.00
Versailles, green	65.00
Cream Soup, Trojan, topaz	18.00
Creamer and Sugar, cov	
Baroque, topaz	24.00
Fairfax, rose	50.00
Navarre	35.00
Cup and Saucer	
Arcady, #326 etching	18.00
Navarre	20.00
Demitasse Cup and Saucer	
Beverly, green	30.00
Mayfair, yellow	20.00
Figure	
Deer, 4½" h, standing, blue	35.00
Mermaid, 10" h, clear	90.00

Goblet	
Colony	13.75
Corsage, #325 etching	24.00
June, topaz bowl, clear stem	25.00
Navarre	20.00
Ice Bucket, orig tongs	
Century	40.00
Fairfax, green	35.00
Lemon Dish, cov, American	40.00
Marmalade, cov, Chintz, clear	50.00
Nappy	
Baroque, 3", Azure blue	20.00
Coin, red	25.00
Olive Tray, Morning Glory	12.00
Pitcher	
June, Azure blue	300.00
Seville, amber	135.00
Plate	
Arcady, #326 etching, 7½"	10.00
Chintz, 9"	20.00
Fairfax, 10¼", blue	40.00
Mystic, 7½" d, green	5.00
Punch Bowl, American, 14" d, matching pedestal base, 2 pcs	135.00
Relish	
Romance, 10", three part	25.00
Versailles, 8½", green	32.00
Rose Bowl, American, 5"	35.00
Sandwich Server, center handle	
Holly	50.00
Trojan, yellow	40.00
Sherbet	
Chintz	10.00
Dolly Madison	10.00
Trojan, topaz	15.00
Shrimp Bowl, American, 12¼" d	245.00
Straw Jar, cov, American, 12" h	235.00
Torte Plate, American	90.00
Tumbler	
Dolly Madison	10.00
Fairfax, blue	18.00
Navarre	20.00
Rogene	17.50
Vase, Century, 6½"	35.00
Wine	
Fascination	8.00
Lotus	15.00
Meadow Rose, #328 etching	25.00

FRAKTUR

History: Fraktur, the calligraphy associated with the Pennsylvania Germans, is named for the elaborate first letter found in many of the hand drawn examples. Throughout its history printed, partially printed-hand drawn, and fully hand drawn works existed side by side. Frakturs often were made by the school teachers or ministers living in rural areas of Pennsylvania, Maryland, and Virginia. Many artists are unknown.

Fraktur exists in several forms—geburts and

taufschein (birth and baptismal certificates), vorschrift (writing example, often with alphabet), haus sagen (house blessing), bookplates and marks, rewards of merit, illuminated religious text, valentines, and drawings. Although collected for decoration, the key element in fraktur is the text.

Fraktur prices rise and fall along with the American folk art market. The key market place is Pennsylvania and the Middle Atlantic states.

References: Donald A. Shelley, *The Fraktur-Writings Or Illuminated Manuscripts Of The Pennsylvania Germans,* Pennsylvania German Society, 1961; Frederick S. Weiser and Howell J. Heaney (compilers), *The Pennsylvania German Fraktur Of The Free Library Of Philadelphia,* Pennsylvania German Society, 1976, two volumes.

Museum: The Free Library of Philadelphia, Philadelphia, PA.

Hand drawn, Copy Book cover, $225.00.

HAND DRAWN

Jacob Brenholtz, copy of "Way To Heaven And Hell" broadside, 13 x 16", watercolor on wove paper, dated "August 19th, 1828" **5,000.00**
Blowsy (Flying) Angel Artist, birth and baptismal certificate, Northampton County, dated 1800, 9½" x 13½", watercolor, pen, and ink on paper, center text block consumes lower two-thirds of paper, flanked by flowers above which are blowsy angels extending into center above text block, birth of Magdelena Gunziger **2,000.00**
Crossed Legged Angel Artist, birth and baptismal certificate, Lancaster Country, dated 1812, 14 x 17¼", watercolor, pen, and ink on laid paper, block format, floral motif on side borders, crossed legged angel in center

of top panel, star burst in center of bottom panel, birth of Michael Klop . **2,500.00**
Heydrich, Baltzer, drawing, Montgomery County, 1845, pen, ink, and watercolor drawing on wove paper, checkerboard border, center with wall (altar) flanked by stylized flowers in a semicircular motif, bird on branch of two of flowers, PA German inscription, "Baltzer Heydrich...1845...in his 83rd year," tones of red, black, green, blue, and yellow, minor stains, tears and damage at fold line, beveled frame with red graining, 16¼ x 20¼" **7,600.00**
Daniel Otto (The Flat Tulip Artist), birth and baptismal certificate, Northumberland County, dated 1788, 11½ x 14¾", watercolor, pen, and ink on paper, central heart text, flanked at bottom by two large parrots with checkered wings facing outward and at top by two smaller parrots with plain wings facing inward, heart with border of attached flowers, red and yellow tones, birth of Catharina Lotz **13,250.00**
Seller, H., birth certificate, Dauphin County, PA, 1807, 16¼ x 19¼", pen, ink, and watercolor on laid paper, central heart flanked at base by large parrots above which is a tulip and peacock, tulip flanked by starburst across top, geometric circles along bottom with "H./Seiler", shades of red, green, blue, brown, yellow, and black, text is primarily in red ink, minor stains, short tears, large tulips have some holes caused by acid ink, bottom edge a bit ragged **12,000.00**
Spanenberg, John, double bookplate for Catharina Haupt, 5¾ x 6¼", pen, ink, and watercolor on laid paper, stylized horizontal floral bands across top and bottom, tones of red, blue, green, yellow, and brown, some stains, fading, and damage on fold line, gilt frame 8½ x 10½" **3,500.00**
Unknown
Bookplate
Southeastern PA, c1820s, 3¾ x 5¾", fly leaf of Martin Luther's *Book of Catechisms,* published by Johann Bar, block motif, central block with heart from which flower radiates, starbursts in corner blocks, stemmed floral motifs in remaining blocks, shades of red, blue, yellow, and green, heart marked "Salome Beinhauer/1828," worn marbleized paper, leather binding for book . **2,350.00**
Southeastern PA, c1820–40, 5 x 5⅝", laid paper, central heart with

text, face from which radiates two stemmed tulips at top, bottom of heart decorated with fern-like leaves with two star floral motifs, heart contains name "Elizabeth Richter," dark shades of brown, olive, and reddish brown, minor stains, small edge damage, glued to lined paper, frame 10¾ x 11½" **1,650.00**

Southeastern PA, c1840s, 3 x 4¾", watercolor, pen, and ink on paper lining of cardboard book cover, heart with text from which radiates tulips and stems, bird sits on two of lesser tulips, shades of orange, yellow, lavender, and black, for "Georg Reiff," dated 1844, stains, frame 5 x 6¾" ... **425.00**

Drawing, southeastern PA, c1820–40, laid paper, horizontal dec bands, top with two facing birds surrounded by flowers, block letters "REBECCA SNYDER," birds and flowers, bottom with man and dog flanking central flower, red, yellow, blue, pale green, and brown, stains and small tears, old black frame 8½ x 9¾" **3,700.00**

Reward of Merit, southeastern, PA, c1820–40, wove paper, 8 x 12¾", stylized vining plant with flowers and birds, initials "F/Z," green, brown, blue, and faded red, old damage and repairs, frame 12¾ x 16⅞" **1,600.00**

Song Book, southeastern PA, c1800–10, possibly Bucks County, dated 1804, 6⅜ x 3¾", bookplate has circular text flanked by vertical flower with multi-leaf stem, checkered border, belongs to "Abraham Landes," cover pulled loose from string binding but is not damaged **3,000.00**

HAND DRAWN-PRINTED

Brechall, Martin, birth and baptismal, printed form by Hütter, Easton, 1821, 13 x 16", central heart, borders hand painted with filigrees and flowers in red, yellow, blue, and green, for Lea Schull **950.00**

Dulheur, Henrich, birth and baptismal, 13 x 15¾" **950.00**

Otto, Heinrich, The Great Comet Of 1769, decorated with parrots and shooting stars **2,500.00**

Unknown Artist, birth certificate, Northampton County, 1821, 7¾" x 12", German calligraphy, inscription within a keystone device, hand painted

paired birds and large flowering tulip plants, birth of Maria Margaretha Scherner **750.00**

PRINTED

Adam and Eve
  Bruckman, C. A., Reading **300.00**
  Dahlem, S., Philadelphia **400.00**
Birth and Baptismal
  Baumann and Ruth, Ephrata **350.00**
  Baumann, S., Ephrata **400.00**
  Blumer, A. & W., Allentown **175.00**
  Hartman, Joseph, Lebanon **250.00**
  Hanesche, J. G., Baltimore **150.00**
  Herschberger, Johann, Chambersburg **325.00**
  Hütter, C. J., Easton **350.00**
  Lepper, Wilhelm, Hannover **300.00**
  Lippe, G. Ph., Pottsville **150.00**
  Puwelle, A., Reading **125.00**
  Saeger and Leisenring, Allentown, early form **150.00**
  Sage, G. A., Allentown **175.00**
  Scheffer, Theo. F., Harrisburg **75.00**
  Wiestling, Johann S., Harrisburg ... **200.00**
  Note: If signed by a scrivener, increase value by 25% to 40%
Haus Sagen
  Gräter and Blummer, Allentown **175.00**
  Palm, Issac, Brecknock Township, Lancaster Country **500.00**

FRANKART

History: Arthur Von Frankenberg, artist and sculptor, founded Frankart, Inc., in New York City in the mid-1920s. Frankart, Inc., mass produced practical "art objects" in the Art Deco style into the 1930s. Pieces include aquariums, ashtrays, bookends, flower vases, lamps, etc. Although Von Frankenberg used live female models as his subjects, his figures are characterized by their form and style rather than specific features. Nudes are the most collectible; caricatured animals and other human figures were also produced, no doubt, to increase sales.

With few exceptions, pieces were marked Frankart, Inc., with a patent number or "pat. appl. for."

Pieces were cast in a white metal composition in the following finishes: cream–a pale iridescent white; bronzoid–oxidized copper, silver, or gold; french–a medium brown with green in the crevices; gun metal–art iridescent gray; jap–a very dark brown, almost black, with green in the crevices; pearl green–pale iridescent green; and verde–a dull light green. Cream and bronzoid were used primarily in the 1930s.

Note: All pieces listed are all original in very good condition unless otherwise indicated.

Advisor: Walter Glenn.

Figurine, elk, bronze patinated finish, 6¼″ l, $115.00.

Ashtray

Horse, standing, orig paint, label . . .	100.00
Nude, marked "No. T301"	125.00

Bookends, pr

5½″ h, angle fish, exaggerated fins, stylized	90.00
6″ h, nudes, seated, legs extended, hands outstretched to knees, backs support books	175.00
6½ x 5½″, metal, nude woman, seated, painted white	290.00

Candlesticks, pr, 12″, nudes, orig paint	275.00

Figurine

6¼″ h, elk, bronze patina finish	120.00
12″, nude, bronze patina finish	150.00

Lamp

9″ h, nude

Sitting atop ribbed column, arms support 3″ crackle glass globe on lap	370.00
Two back to back, kneeling, arms support 8″ crackle glass globe .	575.00

11″ h, nude

Coy, stands on geometric base, 3″ crackle glass globe at feet	390.00
Standing, embraces orig 8″ candle-light bulb	310.00
Night Light, 11″, sailor leaning against lamp post, bronze patina, orig shade	250.00
Smoker's Set, 12″ h, nude, standing, arched back, arms outstretched to hold green glass cigarette box, 3½″ round green glass ashtray on base .	410.00

FRANKOMA POTTERY

History: John N. Frank founded a ceramic art department at Oklahoma University in Norman and taught there for several years. In 1933 he established his own business and began making Oklahoma's first commercial pottery. Frankoma moved from Norman to Sapulpa, Oklahoma, in 1938.

A fire completely destroyed the new plant later the same year, but rebuilding began almost immediately. The company remained in Sapulpa and continued to grow. Frankoma is the only American pottery to be permanently exhibited at the International Ceramic Museum of Italy.

In September 1983 a disastrous fire struck once again, destroying 97% of Frankoma's facilities. The rebuilt Frankoma Pottery reopened on July 2, 1984. Production has been limited to 1983 production molds only. All other molds were lost in the fire.

Prior to 1954 all Frankoma pottery was made with a honey-tan colored clay from Ada, Oklahoma. Since 1954 Frankoma has used a brick red clay from Sapulpa. During the early 1970s the clay became lighter and is now pink in color.

There were a number of early marks. One most eagerly sought is the leopard pacing on the FRANKOMA name. Since the 1938 fire, all pieces have carried only the name FRANKOMA.

References: Phyllis and Tom Bess, *Frankoma Treasures,* published by authors, 1983; Susan N. Cox, *Collectors Guide To Frankoma Pottery,* Book I, published by author, 1979, and Book II, published by author, 1982.

Additional Listings: See *Warman's Americana & Collectibles* for more examples.

Advisor: Phyllis Bess.

Bookends, 5¾″ h, Mountain Girl	60.00

Bottle Vase

V-2, 1970, sgd "John Frank"	50.00
V-5, 1973, sgd "Grace Lee Frank" .	70.00
V-6, 1974, Grace Lee Frank	70.00
V-8, 1976, Joniece Frank	65.00
V-12, 1980, Joniece Frank	45.00

Cider Set, pitcher and six mugs, green and brown, $50.00.

Bowl, 10″, Cactus, carved	40.00
Candleholder, Christ the Light of the World	12.00

Christmas Card

1952, Donna Frank	45.00
1960, Gracetone	75.00
1960, The Franks	55.00
1975, Grace Lee & Milton Smith . . .	85.00
Coin, 1¾″, Elect John Frank	15.00
Cornucopia, 15″ #215	35.00
Decanter, Fingerprint, stopper, 2 qt . . .	25.00
Dish, leaf shape, Gracetone	15.00

Jar, carved, #70	25.00
Jewelry, earrings, clip, pr	20.00
Match Holder, 1¾" h, #89A	15.00

Mask
Comedy	5.00
Tragedy	5.00

Mug
American Airlines Eagle	35.00
Donkey, red and white, 1976	18.00
Elephant, Nixon-Agnew, desert gold and white, 1973	50.00

Pitcher
Thunderbird, 5"	50.00
Wagon wheel, 2 qt	20.00

Plate
Christmas
1972	20.00
1986	12.00
Conestoga wagon, 1971	30.00
Jesus The Carpenter, 1971	20.00
Liberty, 1986	15.00
Madonna of Love, 1978	15.00

Salt and Pepper Shakers, pr
Monogrammed	25.00
Wagon wheels	10.00

Sculpture
Amazon Woman, 6¼"	225.00
Buffalo, 3½" h	225.00
Clydesdale, 6¾", rearing position	55.00
Colt, prancing, 8"	250.00
Fan Dancer, red clay	150.00
Gannet, 9"	225.00
Greyhound, 14" l, peach glow	125.00
Indian, maiden, 12"	10.00
Irish, setter, head	55.00
Mare and Colt, W. Stone	10.00
Ocelot, 7", walking	175.00
Terrier, 5¼"	60.00

Toby Mug
Cowboy, 4½"	8.00
Uncle Sam, 4½"	8.00

Trivet
Cattle Brands	10.00
Lazybone	30.00

Vase
3½", Hobby Horse	75.00
9", Chinese Bottle, Chinese red glaze	90.00
11½", Flowerabrum, #58	70.00
17", Fireside	30.00

Wall Pocket
Boot	15.00
Leaf, 8½"	35.00
Ram's Head	50.00
Wreath, "With Our Love, Frankoma" on back	40.00

FRATERNAL ORGANIZATIONS

History: Benevolent and secret societies played an important part in American society from the late 18th to the mid-20th centuries. Initially the societies were organized to aid members and their families in times of distress or death. They evolved from this purpose into important social clubs by the late 19th century.

In the 1950s, with the arrival of civil rights, an attack occurred on the secretiveness and often discriminatory practices of these societies. The fraternal movement, with the exception of the Masonic organizations, suffered serious membership loss. Many local chapters closed and sold their lodge halls. This resulted in many fraternal items arriving in the antiques market.

Additional Listings: See *Warman's Americana & Collectibles* for more examples.

MASONIC

Anvil, 12" l, wood, symbols, "Q.U.A.M. No 74"	150.00

Apron
14 x 12", leather, white, blue silk trim, white embroidery, silver fringe	25.00
15¼ x 15¼", leather, gilt painted designs	185.00
16 x 17", cotton, blue printed design	10.00
18 x 17", satin, ivory, red fringe, polychrome painted insignia	45.00
Ashtray, brass, dated 1934	25.00
Book, *Freemasonry in Indiana, 1806–98,* Daniel McDonald	25.00
Creamer, pressed, Ruby Thumbprint pattern, engraved "Masonic Temple 1893"	30.00

Masonic, fan, Syrian Temple, A.A.O.N.M.S., marked "Drawn by Freddy, Manufactured by Achart & Hanckel, Ohio," orig booklet and box, $20.00.

Flask
Blue-green, ½ pt	200.00
Gold amber, eagle, pt	150.00
Gavel, ivory and silver, leather case	175.00
Lamp, 7½" h, light bulb with Masonic symbol	45.00
Match Holder, 11", wall type, walnut, pierce carved symbols	70.00

Shaving Mug, gold and blue symbol, red "C. A. Beck," and incised "Austria" . **35.00**

Sign, 29″ d, wrought iron, hammered wreath mounted with ribbon, encircling calipers and triangle, three hanging bells, 19th C **440.00**

Toasting Glass, 4¾″ h, tapered, flared fluted foot, engraved wheel with leaf border and symbols, inscribed "B. Arnold," 19th C **1,760.00**

OTHERS

Benevolent & Protective Order of the Elks, B.P.O.E.

Beaker, 5″ h, cream, black elk head, marked "Mettlach, Velleroy & Boch" **100.00**

Book, *Elk's Authentic History of Elks,* Charles Eillis, 1910, purple cover, includes history of Chicago Lodge No. 4 . . . . **35.00**

Pitcher, 10½″ h, elk's head, clock emblem, and "B.P.O.E.," shaded brown ground, Warwick China . . . **200.00**

Plaque, 10½″ d, hp, elk head, BPOE, Sioux City Lodge #112, c1895 . . **110.00**

Shaving Mug, pink and white, gold elk head, crossed American flags and floral dec, marked "Germany" on bottom **70.00**

Watch Fob, 14k gold mounted elk's tooth **50.00**

Eastern Star

Pendant, SP, rhinestones and rubies **40.00**

Ring, 14k white gold filigree, seven point diamond emblem **225.00**

Independent Order of Odd Fellows, I.O.O.F.

Creamer, 4½″ h, earthenware, ovoid, pink luster band, applied handle, inscribed "Independent Order of Odd Fellows" & "Armor, Honor, Justitiad," reverse "Odd Fellows Honor/ How grand in age/How fair in youth/ Is holy friendship/Love and Truth," England, c1825 . . . . **440.00**

Sign, 29½ h, 100″ l, carved, painted, gilt lettering, three interlacing ropes, marked "Phillipstown Lodge 815, c1830" **2,640.00**

Table, 35½″ d, 29″ h, parlor type, inlaid wood, octagonal top, tri-color marquetry and gallery, eight leg inlaid pedestal above round base, symbols and "Forget me not, Friendship forever," eight shaped marquetry legs, 19th C **2,530.00**

Knights of Columbus, sword, dress, scabbard, detailed blade, Marked "The McLilley Co., Columbus, OH" . **50.00**

Knights Templar, mug, 4″, amethyst flashed design, insignia, gold trim . . **90.00**

Shrine

Cup and Saucer, glass, painted, "Los Angeles, May 1908" **145.00**

Goblet, ruby stained, pedestal foot, "St. Paul 1908" **50.00**

Mug, sword handle, Indian chief, "Saratoga 1903" **110.00**

Pendant, tiger claw and emblem, Victorian **100.00**

Woodsmen of the World, belt, red leather, cast buckle, "WOW" and crossed arc and sledge hammer . . . **25.00**

FRUIT JARS

History: Fruit jars are canning jars used to preserve food. Thomas W. Dyott, one of Philadelphia's earliest and most innovative glass makers, was promoting his glass canning jars in 1829. John Landis Mason patented his screw-type canning jar on November 30, 1858. This date refers to the patent date, not the age of the jar. There are thousands of types of jars in many colors, types of closures, sizes, and embossings.

References: Alice M. Creswick, *The Red Book of Fruit Jars No. 5,* published by author, 1987; Bill Schroeder, *1000 Fruit Jars: Priced And Illustrated, Revised 5th Edition,* Collector Books, 1987.

Atlas E-Z Seal, quart, blue glass, $5.00.

ABGA Mason Perfect, aqua, qt	**28.00**
Acme, pt, shield with stars and stripes	**4.00**
Allen's, aqua, pat June 1871	**130.00**
Atlas E-Z Seal, cornflower blue, pt . . .	**10.00**
Ball	
Ideal, aqua, qt, reverse, July 14, 1908	**30.00**
Mason's Patent 1858, green, qt, handmade, zinc lid, ground lip . . .	**5.00**
Standard, yellow green, qt	**70.00**

Baltimore Glass Works, aqua, qt, handmade, applied lid 175.00
Beehive, qt, emb bees and hive 125.00
Boldt Mason Jar, blue, pt, zinc lid 15.00
Bosco Double Seal, clear, qt, glass lid . . 5.00
Brockway Clear-Vu M, pt 10.00
Buckeye No 1, aqua, ½ gal, metal yoke 140.00
Champion Syrup and Refining Co, aqua, qt 25.00
Clyde Improved Mason, green, qt, glass lid, metal band 15.00
Columbia, aqua, pt, handmade, glass lid, wire clip 25.00
Crystal Jar, amethyst, qt, handmade, glass lid 35.00
Double Safety, widemouth, pt 5.00
Drey Ever Seal, clear, ½ pt, glass lid, wire bail 4.00
E I, Newark, Ohio, yellow green, ½ gal, c1860 . . . . 85.00
Eagle, green, qt, handmade wax seal . 75.00
Eureka, script, aqua, pt 10.00
Faxon, blue, qt, handmade, zinc lid . . 8.00
Garden Queen, qt 4.00
Gem, Wallaceburg, clear, qt, glass lid, screw band 8.00
Green Mountain Co, aqua, pt, slug plate 10.00
Halle, green, qt, handmade, wax seal . 50.00
Harvest Mason, ½ gal, beaded neck . . 10.00
Howe, Scranton, ½ gal 75.00
Inker, qt, Mason patent 30.00
Ivanhoe, clear, qt, metal lid, name on bottom 5.00
King, Kant Krack Lid, pt, side clips . . . 10.00
Knowlton Vacuum, Star, aqua, qt 20.00
L'Ideale, green, pt, glass lid, wire clip . 18.00
Mallinger, clear, qt, machine made, zinc lid 4.00
Marion Jar, aqua, pt, Mason's Pat Nov 30th, 1858 . . . . 35.00
Mason's
    Fruit Jar, qt, three lines 8.00
    Improved, Cross, light green, qt . . . 15.00
    Patent, 1868, green yellow 110.00
Mission, bell, trademark, clear, qt, zinc lid 15.00
My Choice, amber, ½ gal 200.00
Penn, The, green, qt, handmade glass lid, zinc band 25.00
Potter & Bodine, Philadelphia, aqua, qt, name emb in script 85.00
Protector, aqua, qt, recessed panel . . . 40.00
Rau's Improved Grove Ring Jar, aqua, pt, handmade, wax seal 25.00
Reverse Ball, script, aqua, qt 5.00
Royal, deep aqua, qt, emb "Royal of 1876" 60.00
Schram Automatic Sealer, aqua, qt, flag 5.00
Sealtite, aqua, qt, glass lid, wire bail . . 3.00
Selco Surety Seal, blue, pt 4.00
Smalley's Royal Trademark Nu-Seal, pt, double helix 10.00

Stevens, aqua, ½ gal, handmade, wax seal 75.00
Sun, aqua, ½ gal, circle with radiating rays 50.00
Texas Mason, clear, qt, zinc lid 15.00
Tropical Canners, pt 5.00
Valve Jar Co, Philadelphia, aqua, qt, 8" h 125.00
Victory, qt, milk glass lid with shield . . 10.00
Universal, aqua, qt, zinc lid, name emb upside down 10.00
Weideman Boy Brand, Cleveland, qt . . 6.00
White Crown Mason, milk glass, aqua, pt 10.00
Woodbury Improved, aqua, pt, handmade, glass lid, metal clip 25.00
Yeoman's Fruit bottle, aqua, ½ gal . . . 20.00

FRY GLASS

History: The H. C. Fry Glass Co. of Rochester, Pennsylvania, began operating in 1901 and continued until 1933. Their first products were brilliant period cut glass. They later produced depression tablewares. In 1922 they patented heat resisting ovenware in an opalescent color. This "Pearl Oven Glass" was produced in a variety of oven and table pieces including casseroles, meat trays, pie and cake pans, etc. Most of these pieces are marked "Fry" with model numbers and sizes.

Fry's beautiful art line, Foval, was produced only in 1926-27. It is pearly opalescent, with jade green or delft blue trim. It is rarely signed, except for occasional silver overlay pieces marked "Rockwell." Foval is always evenly opalescent, never striped like Fenton's opalescent line.

Reference: Fry Glass Society, *Collector's Encyclopedia of Fry Glass,* Collector Books, 1989.

Collectors' Club: H. C. Fry Glass Society, P.O. Box 41, Beaver, PA 15009.

Reproduction Alert: In the 1970s, reproductions of Foval were made in abundance in Murano, Italy. These pieces, including candlesticks, toothpicks, etc., have teal blue transparent trim.

Bowl, 8", cut glass, pineapple design, wheel cutting, sgd 100.00
Butter Dish, cov, Pearl Oven Ware . . . 65.00
Canape Plate, 6¼" d, 4" h cobalt blue center handle, Foval 160.00
Casserole, cov, Pearl Oven Ware 25.00
Compote, 6¾", Foval, jade green stem 115.00
Creamer, Foval, blue tinted loopings, applied Delft blue handle 150.00
Cruet, Foval, cobalt blue handle, orig stopper 115.00
Cup and Saucer, Foval, cobalt blue stripe, pale blue opaline ground . . . 60.00
Decanter, 9", ftd, Foval, applied Delft blue handle 165.00
Ice Cream Tray, 14 x 7", cut glass, Nel-

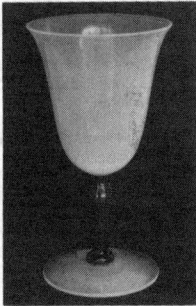

Goblet, Foval, cobalt blue stem, 5¾" h, $70.00.

son pattern variation, all over cutting,
sgd "Fry" **270.00**
Pitcher, cov, Crackle, clear, applied jade
green handle and finial **100.00**
Plate, 9½", Foval, Delft blue rim **72.00**
Platter, Pearl Oven Ware, etched rim . **20.00**
Punch Cup, Crackle, clear, cobalt blue
ring handle **42.00**
Sherbet, cut glass, Chicago pattern,
4" h **72.00**
Teapot, Foval, cobalt blue spout, handle
and knob **215.00**
Tumbler, 5¼" h, Crackle, green handle **65.00**
Vase
7½", Foval, jade green, rolled rim and
foot **200.00**
10", Foval, bud, cobalt blue foot ... **125.00**

FULPER POTTERY

History: The American Pottery Company of Flemington, New Jersey, made pottery jugs and hou-
sewares from the early 1800s. They made Fulper
Art Pottery from approximately 1910 to 1930.

Their first line of art pottery was called Vasekraft.
The shapes were primarily either rigid and controlled, being influenced by the arts and crafts
movement, or of Chinese influence. Equal concern
was given to the glazes which showed an incre-
dible diversity.

Pieces made between 1910 and 1920 were of
the best quality, because less emphasis was put
on production output. Almost all pieces are
molded.

Reference: Robert Blassberg, *Fulper Art Pottery: An Aesthetic Appreciation,* Art Lithographers,
1979.

Bowl
3 x 6", boat shape, green matte ... **40.00**
4 x 6", leopard skin glaze, two handles, underglaze mark **115.00**
11", dark blue drip, rose ground ... **95.00**
Candlesticks, 11", yellow and brown
shading to blue flambe, pr **275.00**
Decanter
9", musical, gun metal shading to
green, beige ground, orig stopper **45.00**
9¾", green glossy glaze, silver highlights, orig stopper **120.00**
Flower Frog
Mushroom **40.00**
Nude, white, gray, and yellow **75.00**
Jar, 8 x 9", pedestal, blue to green ... **400.00**
Jug and Bowl, mottled brown, hand
thrown, horizontal ribs, vertical ink
stamp **180.00**
Lamp, ballerina, bisque **185.00**
Pitcher, 7 x 4¾", crystallized blue glaze
over mustard, marked "830M" **100.00**
Planter, V shape, oval top, crystallized
blue glaze over mustard **45.00**
Tobacco Jar, cov, 6½", mirror black .. **235.00**

**Vase, brown over pumpkin ground, oil
and high glaze, stamped mark under
glaze, 5⅞" h, $85.00.**

Vase
7", raspberry, three handles, 125th
Anniversary sticker **100.00**
7½", round body, pink and red, two
handles **110.00**
7¾", green, cucumber textured, orig
paper label **200.00**

8", rose flambe shaded to green at top, flat shape, handles at base, sgd	**200.00**
8½ x 7½", two handles, green matte	**350.00**
10", two handles, cucumber green .	**225.00**
10½", green-brown shading to sky blue flambe, ink stamp mark	**250.00**
12", round base, blue crystalline . . .	**260.00**
Wall Pocket, Pipes of Pan, matte green	**185.00**

FURNITURE

History: Two major currents dominate the American furniture marketplace–furniture made in Great Britain and furniture made in the United States. American buyers continue to show a strong prejudice for objects manufactured in the United States. They will pay a premium for such pieces and accept them about as technically superior and more aesthetic English examples.

Until the last half of the 19th century formal American styles were dictated by English examples and design books. Regional furniture, such as the Hudson River Valley [Dutch] and the Pennsylvania German styles, did develop. A less formal furniture, often designated as the "country" or vernacular style, developed throughout the 19th and early 20th centuries. These country pieces deviated from the accepted formal styles and have a genre charm that many collectors find irresistible.

America did contribute a number of unique decorative elements to English styles. The American Federal period is a reaction to the English Hepplewhite period. American designers created furniture which influenced, rather than reacted, to world taste in the Gothic Revival style, Arts and Craft Furniture, Art Deco, and Modern International movement.

FURNITURE STYLES (APPROX. DATES)

William and Mary	**1690–1730**
Queen Anne.	**1720–1760**
Chippendale.	**1755–1790**
Federal [Hepplewhite]	**1790–1815**
Sheraton	**1790–1810**
Empire [Classical]	**1805–1830**
Victorian	
French Restoration	**1830–1850**
Gothic Revival.	**1840–1860**
Rococo Revival	**1845–1870**
Elizabethan.	**1850–1915**
Louis XIV	**1850–1914**
Naturalistic	**1850–1914**
Renaissance Revival	**1850–1880**
Neo-Greek	**1855–1885**
Eastlake	**1870–1890**
Art Furniture	**1880–1914**
Arts and Crafts	**1895–1915**
Art Nouveau.	**1896–1914**
Art Deco.	**1920–1945**
International Movement	**1940–Present**

In the 1988 auction season, a Newport, Rhode Island, Chippendale desk–bookcase sold for 12.1 million dollars. Many other pieces broke the half million dollar barrier.

Country pieces, with the exception of Windsor chairs, seem to have stabilized and even dropped off slightly in value. The country-designer-look no longer enjoys the popularity it did during the American Bicentennial period.

Furniture is one of the few antiques fields where regional preferences are a factor in pricing. Victorian furniture is popular in New Orleans, and unpopular in New England. Oak is in demand in the Northwest, not so much in the Middle Atlantic states.

Prices vary considerably on furniture. Shop around. Furniture is plentiful unless you are after a truly rare example. Examine all pieces thoroughly. Too many furniture pieces are bought on impulse. Turn furniture upside down; take it apart. The amount of repairs and restoration to a piece has a strong influence on price. Make certain you know about all repairs and changes before buying.

Beware of the large number of reproductions. During the twenty-five years following the American Centennial of 1876, there was a great revival in copying furniture styles and manufacturing techniques of earlier eras. These centennial pieces now are over one hundred years old. They confuse many dealers and collectors.

The prices listed below are "average" prices. They are only a guide. High and low prices are given to show market range.

References: Joseph T. Butler, *Field Guide To American Furniture,* Facts on File Publications, 1985; E & R Dubrow *Furniture, Made In America, 1875–1905,* Schiffer Publishing, Ltd., 1982; Eileen and Richard Dubrow, *American Furniture of the 19th Century, 1840–1880,* Schiffer Publishing, Ltd., 1983; Rachael Feild, *Macdonald Guide To Buying Antique Furniture,* Wallace-Homestead, 1989; Benno M. Forman, *American Seating Furniture, 1630–1730,* Winterthur Museum, W. W. Norton & Company, 1988; Don Fredgant, *American Manufactured Furniture,* Schiffer Publishing, Ltd., 1988; *Furniture Dealers' Reference Book, Zone 3, 1928–29,* reprint by Schiffer Publishing, Ltd., 1988; Phillipe Garner, *Twentieth-Century Furniture,* Van Nostrand Reinhold, 1980; Myrna Kaye, *Fake, Fraud, Or Genuine, Identifying Authentic American Antique Furniture,* New York Graphic Society Book, 1987; William C. Ketchum, Jr., *Furniture, Volume 2: Chests, Cupboards, Desks, & Other Pieces,* Knopf Collectors' Guides To American Antiques, Alfred A. Knopf, 1982; Kathryn McNerney, *Pine Furniture, Our American Heritage,* Collector Books, 1989; Kathryn McNerney, *Victorian Furniture,* Collector Books, 1981, values updated 1988; Milo M. Naeve, *Identifying Ameri-*

can *Furniture: A Pictorial Guide To Styles and Terms, Colonial to Contemporary,* American Association for State and Local History, 1988; Don & Carol Raycraft, *Collector's Guide To Country Furniture, Book II,* Collector Books, 1988; Charles Santore, *The Windsor Style in America, Volume II,* Running Press Book Publishers, 1987; Marvin D. Schwartz, *Furniture: Volume 1: Chairs, Tables, Sofas & Beds,* Knopf Collector's Guides To American Antiques, Alfred A. Knopf, 1982; Robert W. and Harriett Swedberg, *American Oak Furniture, Style and Prices, Book II,* Wallace-Homestead, 1984; — *Country Furniture and Accessories with Prices, Book 1,* 1983, *Book II,* 1984, Wallace-Homestead; — *Country Pine Furniture,* Wallace-Homestead, 1983; —*Furniture of the Depression Era,* Collector Books, 1987; —*Victorian Furniture, Book I,* 1976, *Book II,* 1983, *Book III,* 1985, Wallace-Homestead; —*Wicker Furniture,* Wallace-Homestead, 1983; Gerald W. R. Ward, *American Case Furniture,* Yale University Art Museum, 1988; Derita Coleman Williams and Nathan Harsh, *The Art and Mystery of Tennessee Furniture,* Tennessee Historical Society, 1988; Lyndon C. Viel, *Antique Ethnic Furniture,* Wallace-Homestead, 1983.

There are hundreds of specialized books on individual furniture forms and styles. Two examples of note are: Monroe H. Fabian, *The Pennsylvania-German Decorated Chest,* Universe Books, 1978, and Charles Santore, *The Windsor Style In America, 1730–1830,* Running Press, 1981.

Additional Listings: Arts and Craft Movement, Art Deco, Art Nouveau, Children's Nursery Items, Orientalia, Shaker Items, and Stickley.

BEDS

Amish, child's, decorated, pine, orig brown flame graining, light colored

Bed, Sheraton, tester, mahogany, turned and fluted posts, $5,000.00.

ground, sq tapered legs, inset rockers (cut flat), mortised sides, removable round tapering posts, replaced tester frame, 24″ w, 54 ″ l, 55″ h **600.00**
Colonial Revival, Regency style, inlaid rosewood, upholstered head and footboard, shaped framework, brass inlay and mounts, double, 56″ h . . . **600.00**
Day, country
  Curly maple, turned posts and rails, refinished, minor insect damage, white cotton duck cov and matching cushion, 77″ l **1,600.00**
  Maple, Texas, mid 19th C, slat back, molded crest ends, nine slats, painted red, 77″ l **1,750.00**
Eastlake, American, c1870, suite, tall half tester bed, mirrored armoire, marble top dresser, and washstand, foliate carving, spiral carved half columns **7,000.00**
Empire
  American, c1820, tester, tiger maple posts, bird's eye maple headboard, refinished, replacement tester, 83″ h **2,000.00**
  American, c1820–30, maple, carved bell and ball posts, pine headboard, restored and refinished, 47½″ h . . **250.00**
  American, c1830, rope, cherry, bold turnings, pineapple carving, cannon ball finials, paneled headboard with scalloped detail, orig rails, 56 x 71¾″ **700.00**
  American, c1840, sleigh, mahogany, scrolled head and foot boards, 5′ 11″ l **1,300.00**
  New York, c1820–25, carved maple, baluster and ring turned headposts, carved acanthus, leaves, and swag drapery, double paneled headboard surmounted by carved bowl of fruit, bow shaped scrolled footboard, carved paw feet, 55 x 77″ . **2,000.00**
Federal
  Country, c1830, high post, bird's eye maple, highly figured and paneled headboard, scrolling crest flanked by turned urn form posts, 6′ 8″ l, 4′ 6″ w, 6′ 4″ h **2,900.00**
  Country, mid 19th C, tall post, cherry, scrolled and paneled headboard, acorn finialed posts, later molded tester, 6′ 3″ l, 46″ w, 7′ 3″ h **1,800.00**
  New York, c1810, tester, mahogany, reeded posts, turned swag carved urns, reeded legs, turned spade feet, 5′10″ l, 4′5″ w, 8′10″ h **4,250.00**
  Philadelphia, c1830, youth, tiger maple, four tapering sq posts, slender ring turned sides, old fitted mattress **1,600.00**
Georgian, English, c1770–80, four pos-

ter, flat tester, mahogany, claw and
ball feet, 82″ **1,500.00**
Hired Man's, folding, maple, pine head-
board, pinned sides to facilitate folding, orig first coat of red paint, 70⅛ x
45¾ x 27⅜″ **700.00**
International Movement, American,
c1950, mahogany, cane inserts, dou-
ble, 57″ w **150.00**
Renaissance Revival, New Orleans,
c1850, half tester, carved rosewood **10,000.00**
Rococo Revival, NY, c1850–60
  Belter, John Henry, attributed to,
  carved rosewood and laminated,
  pair of classical carved putti atop
  headboard, 63½″ w, 81″ l, 71″ h . . **34,000.00**
  Unknown Maker, carved rosewood,
  floral carving, rocaille shell head
  and footboards, minor losses to
  carving **3,250.00**
Sheraton, American, c1800, tester
  Birch, plain turned headposts, fluted
  footposts, 65″ **1,200.00**
  Maple, fluted posts, urn finials, re-
  stored and refinished, 73″ h **1,500.00**
Victorian
  American, c1850, walnut, veneer
  panels, roundels, applied dec,
  headboard surmounted by carved
  head of Columbia, urn finials, 60 x
  81 x 92″ **2,500.00**
  American, late 19th C, brass, straight
  upright posts with ball finials, cylindrical posts, ball finials, cylindrical
  support rails for side curtains, vertical and horizontal bars joined with
  ball details, 87″ w **2,000.00**
Windsor, American, mid 19th C, maple
and bird's eye maple, bamboo turn-
ings, pr **5,250.00**

BENCHES

Bin, country, pine, wide single board
construction, lid seat, two part bin int.,
cut out feet, scrolled ends, old dark
finish, 62″ l, 19″ d, 32″ h **450.00**
Cobbler, country, pine, top divided shelf,
drawers, old nut brown patina, work,
old repairs, 44″ l **450.00**
Fireside, pine, high back, scalloped top
and base, 59″ h **750.00**
Garden, Gothic Revival, American, Philadelphia, mid 19th C, cast iron,
scrolled back and arms, slat seat,
marked "Wood & Perot, Makers Phi-
lad..." **2,100.00**
Kneeling, walnut, old dark finish, 39″ l . . **45.00**
Low, Louis XV, mid 18th C, oak, oblong
padded top, later verdure tapestry
cov, shaped skirt with carved summer
flowers, cabriole legs, pr **1,300.00**

**Bench, single board top, 36″ l, 11½″ w,
18″ h, $75.00.**

Mammy, Sheraton, decorated, worn orig
red and black graining, yellow and
green striping, gold stenciled floral
dec, plank seat, removable baby
guard, good turnings, age crack in
crest, 60″ l **1,500.00**
Settle
  87″ l, plank seat, turned detail, green
  repaint **175.00**
  90″ l, plank seat, arrow back, simple
  turnings, curved arms, refinished
  brown **600.00**
Water
  American, early 19th C, pine, two
  shelves, back stretchers, shaped
  ends, 48″ l **400.00**
  Country, poplar, one board bootjack
  ends, two shelves, sq nail construction, 36¼ x 17⅜ x 33½″ **350.00**
Window, Regency style, stained wood,
carved sides, needlepoint upholstered seat, circular turned legs, 52 x
16 x 30″ **200.00**

**Bentwood, bride's box, oval, 22″ l, 14¾″
w, $200.00.**

BENTWOOD

In 1856, Michael Thonet of Vienna perfected the
process of bending wood using steam. Shortly after, Bentwood furniture became popular. Other
manufacturers of Bentwood furniture were Jacob
and Joseph Kohn; Philip Strobel and Son; She-
boygan Chair Co.; and Tidoute Chair Co. Bent-

wood furniture is still being produced today by the Thonet firm and others.

Bed, c1900, double, scrolled and carved headboard, conforming footboard, 60" h **750.00**

Chair
Arm, Thonet, c1900, scrolled back and arms, cane seat, splayed legs, orig label and stamp **300.00**
Side, Thonet, c1900, scrolled back, cane seat, orig label **245.00**

Cradle, c1900, oval bentwood basket, shaped cradle, extended ornate scrolled support, 52 x 36" **750.00**

Easel, artist's **85.00**

Rocker, sleigh type, sgd Thonet **850.00**

Screen, Thonet, c1904, three folds, inset with green glass above laminated panels cut with geometric devices, "Spanish Wand" model **3,000.00**

Settee, Kohn, three part scrolled back and arms, cane back and seat, splayed legs, 47" l **675.00**

Shaving Stand and Mirror, designed by J Hoffman, made by Thonet, c1906, 54" **2,250.00**

Table
Center, Austria, c1900, white marble top, shaped oblong top, narrow frieze on elaborate bentwood cruciform base with interlocking and overlapping scrolls centering on turned standard, 45½ x 28½" ... **200.00**
Writing, Kohn, c1900, rect top, scrolled supports and stretchers, imp mark "J J Kohn," 37 x 21 x 30" **300.00**

BLANKET CHESTS

Chippendale, New England, c1780, country, maple, molded lift top, case with two simulated and two real thumb molded drawers, bracket feet, old oval brass pulls, refinished, 40½" w, 18" d, 41½" h **525.00**

Country
Beech, European, corner posts, paneled sides and ends, peaked lid, wood hinge, brown paint, 40¼" w, 28" h **35.00**
Cherry, curly maple panels, turned feet and till, refinished, 38¼" w, 20" h **325.00**
Pine, six board, scalloped feet, 44" w, 25" h **400.00**
Poplar, 46 x 21 x 25½", dovetailed case, turned feet, moldings and till base and lid, flamboyant stripes, orig brown graining **1,200.00**

Walnut
Ohio, dovetailed case, two dovetailed drawers, beaded edges, orig brasses, int. till with secret compartment and dovetailed drawer, orig lock and wrought iron strap hinge, feet and till lid replaced, old refinishing, 46¼" w, 19" d, 26¼" h **1,200.00**
Pennsylvania, c1800, two drawers, inlaid line dec, ogee bracket feet, 50½" w, 23¼" d, 30¾" h **1,750.00**

Decorated
Pine, attributed to Pennsylvania, Rank or Selzer, orig dark blue paint, two painted arched panels with pots of stylized flowers in red, blue, green, black, and brown on white ground, two white and brown stars on lid, detailed case, till and bracket feet, wrought iron strap hinges and bear trap lock with escutcheon and key, professional molding replacement, 50" w, 21¾" d, 21" h **2,800.00**
Poplar, Soap Hollow, PA, orig red paint, black trim, yellow striping, gold stenciled initials and date "J. B. 1878," colored floral decals, dovetailed case and bracket feet, reeded trim, two dovetailed drawers, white porcelain pulls, till with lid, 48" w, 21" d, 26½" h **3,400.00**

Hepplewhite, PA, Lehigh County, country, pine, orig red paint, traces of graining, three dovetailed overlapping drawers, dovetailed case, till with lid, French feet, orig locks, wrought iron strap hinges, and brass escutcheons, minor repairs, lid int. stenciled "W. H. G.," 50" w, 23" d, 29¼" h **2,250.00**

Queen Anne, New England, mid 18th C, Marriage Chest, pine, upper half faced with false drawer fronts, hinged top, blanket storage chest, orig brown paint and hardware, 35" w **3,300.00**

BOOK CASES

Art Deco, American, early 1900s, polished aluminum, tin plate, pair of leaded glass doors, bird's eye maple back panels, 58" w, 17" d, 65" h ... **7,000.00**

Art Nouveau, Majorelle, c1900, carved walnut, molded crest, carved splayed leaves, glazed door mounted with central textured purple glass panel, silvered bronze branch form spandrels, pair of narrow cupboards, molded base, carved feet, 64¼" w, 79" h **3,350.00**

Eastlake, American, c1870, carved walnut and burl walnut, three sections, broken pediment with architectural center ornament, plinth base with drawers **1,600.00**

Empire, mahogany, three sections, each with pair doors with Winthrop style glass division, rope twisted columns, paw feet, reeding at top molding **2,750.00**

George III, early 19th C, inlaid mahogany, broken pediment centered by lobed urn form finial, pair of glazed doors, shelves, lower section with fitted secretary drawer over three long drawers, inlaid with scrolling foliage, bracket feet, 37¼" w, 98¼" h **2,750.00**

Gothic Revival, American, possibly Baltimore, c1830, carved rosewood, architectural pediment, two glass doors, 45¾" w, 13¾" d, 86" h **3,200.00**

Queen Anne, walnut and burl walnut veneer, double arch molded cornice dome top, later finials, arched side cornices, pair of glazed doors, three shelves, two candle slides, lower section in two parts, cross banded fall front with fitted interior, base with three long graduated drawers, later bun feet, restorations, 40" w, 85" h . **14,500.00**

Renaissance Revival, American, c1865, walnut, highly carved, three glass doors enclosing shelves, three cupboards below, 90" w, 17½" d, 118½" h **3,750.00**

BOXES

Ballot

Maple, dovetailed, sliding top, 8" w, 6" d, 12" h **175.00**

Pine, dovetailed, carved wooden handles, c1850, 7½" w, 7" d, 18¼" h . **100.00**

Walnut, wide dovetails, brass hardware, 11" w, 8½" d, 16" h **175.00**

Band

New England, printed paper, rural country scene, 10½" w, 15" h . . . **375.00**

Pennsylvania, white floral pattern on rainbow ground, black beaver hat by C Hickerson, 8" h **150.00**

Bible, late 17th C, oak chip work, rect molded top slanting above deep well having floral carved dec, 25" w, 16" d, 10" h **200.00**

Blanket Box, American, early 19th C, painted and decorated imitation rosewood, hinged top, red and black painted graining, 43" w, 19½" d, 23" h **200.00**

Bonnet Box, PA, late 18th C, bentwood, fitted lid, dower chest type dec, green ground, large central stellate device in red, yellow, black, and white, two large sprouting dark green feathered

leaf forms, foliage and vines on lid, 21" oval, 11¾" h **5,775.00**

Bride's, oval

Bentwood, fitted lid, painted Biblical scene, sides painted with large red and white tulip buds, black ground, Continental, 18th C **850.00**

Decorated, pine, laced seams, orig red paint, polychrome floral dec on sides, lid scene of two couples, trees and verse, branded mark, 18" l **2,000.00**

Sponged dec, c1840, 27" l **375.00**

Candle

Decorated, sliding lid, pine, old red paint, faded floral dec **250.00**

Hanging, pine, one drawer, rounded back, scalloped front panel, natural weathered wood finish, 15¾" h . . **400.00**

Poplar, sliding lid, sq nail construction, old brown patina, 13¼" l . . . **95.00**

Walnut, sliding lid, dovetailed, 11" sq, 3½" h **90.00**

Cigar, mahogany, stripe inlay on lid and base, zinc lined, nickel plated hardware, 7½" w, 4" d, 12" h **125.00**

Decorated

Pine, orig red graining, black edge stripe, lined with 1841 New Hampshire newspaper, 12" l **250.00**

Pine, orig salmon paint, black, yellow, red, and green border designs, central flower on each side and top, 13½" l **125.00**

Desk, table top, poplar, dovetailed case, nailed drawer, lift top lid, dovetailed gallery, int. fitted with pigeonholes, old red paint, repairs, 26" sq, 15¾" h . . **100.00**

Document

American, flame mahogany veneer, poplar secondary wood, bevel edge lid, divided two part int., orig brass ball handle, 13½" l **200.00**

Pennsylvania, western, dec, dome top, poplar, orig black paint, yellow striping, well detailed polychrome floral design, 13½" l **125.00**

Hat

Cardboard, c1880, floral paper cov, 12" h **60.00**

Pine, domed top, strap handle, 16" sq **185.00**

Knife

Chestnut, scrolled sides, high curved divided, cutout heart shaped handle, 10½" w, 10" d, 6½" h **175.00**

Inlaid Mahogany, George III, late 18th C, serpentine front, sloping hinged top, central shell in oval reserve, int. lid with six pointed star, fitted int., pr, 9 x 14⅜" **3,000.00**

Pantry, American

Decorated, mid 19th C, blue and

green painted dec, compass star
on cov in yellow, black, and putty,
9¼″ d **240.00**
Splint Wood, orig dark stain, 14½″ l . **85.00**
Pipe, cherry, well scalloped top edge
with heart cutout in front, circular crest
for hanging, dovetailed overlapping
drawer, dovetailed base, applied
edge molding, refinished, 22¼″ h . . **4,000.00**
Salt, hanging, oak, dovetailed, cut out
opening, 6½″ w, 7½″ d, x 15″ h **125.00**
Spice
   Grained, American, 19th C, round,
   locking top, 9¾″ **185.00**
   Oak, four drawers, brass pulls **125.00**
   Pine
      Eight drawers, orig green paint . . **225.00**
      Nine drawers, wall type, old repaint **150.00**
Trinket, New England, rect, coffered lid
   Decorated, red and yellow splotches,
   dark ground, fitted int., 6¾″ h **365.00**
   Smoke grained, basket of floral motif
   on lid, brass feet, 4½″ h **600.00**

**Cabinet, spool or yarn, oak, 18¾ x 17⅛
x 16″, $650.00.**

CABINETS

China
  Colonial Revival
    Chippendale Style, c1940, walnut
    veneer, breakfront, scrolled bro-
    ken pediment, center urn finial,
    pair of glazed doors and panels,
    long drawer over two cupboard
    doors, 44″ w, 15″ d, 76″ h **600.00**
    Victorian Style, mahogany, rect top,
    veneer band at top and back-
    board, carved columns, adjusta-
    ble shelves, hairy paw feet, 48¾″
    w, 17″ d, 65¼″ h **325.00**
  Hepplewhite, inlaid mahogany,
  leaded glass and velvet lined int.,
  63″ w, 21″ d, 75½″ h **650.00**
  Victorian
    Oak
      Bow Front, leaded glass, amber

glass diamonds in top panels,
37½″ w, 14½″ d, 61¾″ **400.00**
      Serpentine Front, carved details,
      glass front and sides, 38½″ w,
      16″ d, 62″ h **600.00**
Display, Art Nouveau, French, c1900,
  carved mahogany, arched crest with
  carved tendrils and lunettes, open
  platform with pierced undulating foliage framework, poppy carved stiles,
  rect beveled and mirrored glass door,
  shelves int., short cabriole legs with
  tendril pierced spandrels, wired for
  int. lighting, 35¼″ w, 98″ h **3,125.00**
Dye, Diamond Dye Co, oak, litho tin
  scene of children playing, 29¾″ **300.00**
Etagere, Art Nouveau, Galle, c1900,
  marquetry, molded rect top, arched
  back panel inlaid with flowerheads
  and leaves, narrow central cabinet
  with glazed door, two flanking open
  shelves, each shelf inlaid at back with
  flowerheads and leaves, carved gallery of pendant fuchsias and leaves,
  shallow drawer inlaid with butterflies,
  large cupboard door inlaid with fuchsias, leaves, and three butterflies,
  sides inlaid with large fuchsias,
  slightly cabriole feet, signed "Galle"
  in marquetry, 25¼″ w, 15″ d, 4′ 8½″ h **9,350.00**
Hardware, hexagonal, rotating base,
  eight drawers, two open shelves per
  side, porcelain pulls **650.00**
Kitchen, Hoosier, oak, glass doors, porcelain work surface, flour bin, etc. . . **475.00**
Parlor, Aesthetic Movement, American,
  attributed to Herter Brothers, NY,
  c1875–80, ebonized and parcel gilt
  cherry, lighter wood marquetry, beveled glass, mirrored and gilt bronze,
  two int. shelves **9,250.00**
Side, Art Nouveau, Majorelle, c1900,
  carved walnut, rect top, molded edge,
  two drawers, gilt bronze tendril pulls,
  center carved splayed foliage,
  molded base, bracket feet, 42″ l,
  39½″ h **1,850.00**
Smoker's, Arts and Crafts, Limbert,
  c1908–12, oak, sq top, single door,
  copper hinges and pull, int. rack and
  shaped shelf, arched aprons, straight
  rect stiles continue to form legs, platform shelf, underside with burned
  shopmark "Limbert's Arts Crafts/Fur-
  niture/Trademark/Made In Grand
  Rapids/And Holland," stamped 753,
  int. with oval stamp "Checked/OK/
  Paul Brown," 11¾″ w, 36¼″ h **800.00**
Vitrine
  Art Nouveau
    Galle, c1900, marquetry, shaped
    rect top, chamfered corners,

molded edge, rect cabinet, glazed door and sides, back inlaid with tall stalks of cow parsley, door inlaid with cow parsley and butterfly, reeded legs, 25¾" w, 18" d, 47¾" h **5,225.00**

Jugendstil, c1900, carved mahogany, central section with shaped rect beveled glass door, two int. shelves, flanked by rect platforms with outset rounded corners, leafy tendril supports, over glazed cupboard doors, inverted floriform feet, 42" w, 63" h **6,600.00**

CANDLE SHIELDS

Country, cherry, snake feet, turned column, replaced maple scrolled top, refinished, minor repairs, 15½" w, 15" d, 26½" h **280.00**

George III, mahogany, walnut and satinwood, shield form screen fitted with later embroidered and painted satin panel, adjusting on rect standard, entwined C scroll base with ball feet, pr **8,500.00**

Hepplewhite, mahogany, embroidered floral motif, 53" h **560.00**

Candlestand, Queen Anne, American, mahogany, serpent feet, 18" d, top, 27½" h, $750.00.

CANDLESTANDS

Chippendale, walnut, tilt top, tripod base with snake feet, turned column, bird cage with turned posts, dish turned top, 35" d, 28½" h **900.00**

Classical, American, NY, c1815–25, carved mahogany, rect top, canted corners, turned baluster standard, paw feet, ... **450.00**

Empire Style, country, curly maple, tilt

top, scrolled legs, turned column, two board top, refinished, repairs, 19" d, 26¾" h **550.00**

Federal

American, Cherry, c1820, rect top, canted corners, spiral carved baluster standard, three arched legs, 18½" w, 29½" h **625.00**

Massachusetts, 1800–15, inlaid mahogany, elongated octagonal tilt top, inlaid diamond and banding, ring turned baluster support, stringing, three arched sq tapering legs, 23" w, 30¾" h **2,500.00**

Pennsylvania, walnut, oval top, shaped and ring turned round standard, cabriole legs, 26" w, 28¾" h **275.00**

George III, mahogany, polychrome grapevine dec, pale blue painted ground, spiral fluted pedestal, sq tripod legs, 15¾" w, pr **3,600.00**

Hepplewhite, American, country, cherry, inlay on top, dovetailed drawer, slender snake feet with chip carving at base of turned column, refinished, small patches in base, 16¾" w, 26¾" h **2,500.00**

Hepplewhite Style, country

Birch, tilt top, spider legs, turned column, 16 x 17", 28½" h, repairs .. **450.00**

Cherry, tilt top, tripod base with curved molded legs, turned column and octagonal top, refinished, 16¼ x 20", 28½" h **300.00**

Queen Anne, American

Cherry, sq top, chamfered corners, snake feet **600.00**

Mahogany, dish top, delicate base, toe carved snake feet **350.00**

Walnut, circular top, vasiform stem, snake feet, 27¾" h **450.00**

CHAIRS

Art Deco

Arm, tiger's eye maple, brown leather inserts, red lacquered fretwork ... **500.00**

Side, walnut, black stain, shaped back, scrolled side rails, upholstered seat, Viennese **350.00**

Art Nouveau, side, carved walnut, rounded crestrail over solid vertical rect splat with carved poppy sprigs, nail studded simulated light brown bow front seat, channeled cabriole legs, pointed toes, pr **725.00**

Arts and Crafts, Frank Lloyd Wright, 1908, dining, created for Ray Evans Chicago house **27,500.00**

Chippendale

Arm

American, country, hardwood, gold

striking, sq legs, mortised and pinned construction, short scrolled arms, pierced splat, shaped crest, rush seat, black repaint **250.00**

Philadelphia, c1770, mahogany, pierced splat, knuckle arms . . . **1,750.00**

Corner, CT, c1770, cherrywood, shaped crest, carved stylized fan, shaped handholds, pierced vase form splats, turned colonettes, molded seat rail enclosing slip seat, shaped skirt, C scroll carved frontal cabriole leg, claw and ball foot, two paper labels on underside of seat **20,350.00**

Lolling, Martha Washington, mahogany, open tapered and molded arms, sq molded legs, "H" stretcher, reupholstered in rose and ecru damask, refinished **4,250.00**

Side

American, ribbon back, cherry, pierced slats, molded edge seat frame, rushed slip seat, sq legs, molded corners, inside chamfer, orig finish **500.00**

Country, cherry, carved crest and ears, pierced splat, upholstered seat, sq legs, molded corners, "H" stretcher, old refinishing . . . **750.00**

Philadelphia, c1765, carved walnut, shaped crest, center carved shell, volute and acanthus carved pierced vase form splat, slip seat, cabriole legs with shell and acanthus carved motifs, claw and ball feet **8,525.00**

Classical, arm, mahogany, turned and reeded legs, reeded seat frame, scrolled arms, carved eagle slat and crest, green leather upholstery **600.00**

Colonial Revival, country, Indiana, c1900, dining, spindle back, woven seat, thick legs, marked "Old Hickory, Indiana," set of 8 . . . . **850.00**

Decorated, American, painted, stenciled, three graduated splats, rabbit ear stiles, shaped seat, turned legs, box stretcher, set of six, labeled "Stenciled by W Smith, Catskill, NY" **800.00**

Eastlake, Victorian

Arm, NY, c1876, George Hunzinger, arched crest with spindles, inlay cloth cov woven metal back and seat, marked "Hunzinger NY Pat March 20, 1869, Pat April 18, 1876," 18 x 17½ x 38" **1,200.00**

Side, walnut, small arms, cane seat **225.00**

Empire

Arm chair, barrel back, green water-silk upholstery **675.00**

Side, mahogany and mahogany veneer, fiddleback, serpentine seat, saber leg **200.00**

Federal

Lolling, MA, c1790, carved mahogany, upholstered back, serpentine crest above shaped arms, molded terminals, down curved supports, flared seat, molded tapering sq legs joined by stretchers, minor repairs **2,000.00**

Side, Samuel Gragg, Boston, early 19th C, side, painted, bentwood back, peacock feather polychrome dec **1,400.00**

Side, Haines-Connelly School, Philadelphia, c1810, carved mahogany, sq back, molded crest rail, three reeded and leaf carved uprights, ring turned and reeded stiles, leaf carved seat support, reeded front legs, ring turned and out flaring rear legs, paper label on seat rail inscribed "Charles H Satterthwaite" **2,250.00**

George II, arm, mahogany, shield form back, scrolling arms, whorled terminals, padded seat, floral needlework, cabriole legs, trefid feet **20,000.00**

George III

Arm, tan leather upholstery, tufted seat and back, sq tapering legs . . **1,250.00**

Child's, mahogany, serpentine crest rail, pierced interlaced vertical splat, scrolled arms, flared drop in seat, molded sq legs joined by stretchers **400.00**

Corner, walnut, two strapwork splats, rush seat, sq legs, beaded edge, X stretcher **1,300.00**

Hall, c1800, inlaid mahogany, shield back, inlaid brass and ebony diamond above shaped seat, turned tapered legs, pr **750.00**

Library, late 18th C, carved mahogany, rect upholstered back, padded arms, down-swept supports carved with flowerheads and foliage, rect seat, sq legs joined by stretchers . **3,150.00**

Side, early 19th C, carved mahogany

Central urn form splat carved with beaded pendant, flanked by columnar splats with foliage, flared seat, sq legs joined by stretchers, pr **825.00**

Serpentine crest rail carved with swags, pierced interlaced splat, rect needlepoint upholstered drop in seat, molded sq legs, stretchers, set of 6 . . . . **3,300.00**

Gothic Revival, American, mid 19th C

Arm, carved walnut, upholstered seat and arms **5,250.00**

Side, child's, embroidered uphol-
stered seat **1,000.00**

Hepplewhite
American, side, cherry, curved crest,
pierced splat with urn detail, slip
seat, sq tapering legs, "H"
stretcher, refinished, pr **1,150.00**

Chair, Hepplewhite, Martha Washington, arm, string inlay, $3,600.00.

CT, c1780, side, mahogany, pierced
vase splat, urn finial, upholstered
seat, straight tapering legs, re-
placed rear corner braces **650.00**
Hitchcock, American, 2nd quarter 19th
C, bar back, rush seat, turned legs
and stretchers, black painted ground,
stenciled fruit dec, three side chairs,
matching arm chair **500.00**
International Movement, Heywood-
Wakefield, MA, Lloyd Manufacturing,
tubular metal, backrest and seat upholstered in brown vinyl, c1935 . . . . **125.00**
Ladder Back, side, three curved slats,
turned finials, red paint, replaced seat **225.00**
Mission
Arm, Gustav Stickley, c1910, oak, V
back **450.00**
Side, Charles Rohlf, 1900, octagonal
style, butterfly pierced single back
splat, shaped skirt, 37½" **1,500.00**
Wing, L & G Stickley, c1910, oak,
clamp decal mark **900.00**
Morris, oak
Gustav Stickley, c1905, red decal
mark **1,900.00**
Limbert, c1910, pierced wide stretch-
ers, orig paper label **575.00**
Moravian, side, well carved back with
scrolls, stylized flowers, shell crest,
inlaid initials, relief carved "1830,"

plank seat, splayed tapered legs, old
natural finish **115.00**
Queen Anne
Arm, northern New England, early
18th C, deep frontal skirt, scroll
arms, Spanish feet, worn rush seat **3,250.00**
Side
Boston, MA, c1740, turned maple,
urn form finials above orig
leather upholstered back and
seat, vase and block turned legs,
frontal turned stretcher **12,650.00**
Hudson River Valley, late 19th C,
painted and dec, yoke form crest,
vasiform splat, turned stiles, rush
seat, turned legs, pad feet, bul-
bous turned stretcher **600.00**
Philadelphia, c1750, walnut,
shaped crest, vase form splat,
slip seat, lambrequin carved cabriole legs, shaped stretchers,
stockinged pad feet, repair to left
foot and crest **5,500.00**
Rhode Island, c1760, walnut,
shaped crest, vase form splat,
slip balloon seat, cabriole legs,
stretchers, pad feet, pr **9,500.00**
Queen Anne Style, maple, cherry finish,
turned legs, bulbous turned front
stretcher, vase splat back and shaped
crest, Spanish feet **750.00**
Regency, c1815
Arm
Mahogany, inlaid, curved rect top
rail inlaid with arrow medallion,
scrolled arms, flared drop in seat,
saber legs, pr **2,250.00**
Painted black, sq back, seven
shaped spindles, matching arms,
oval caned seat, turned legs, box
stretchers, pr **1,300.00**
Desk, fruitwood, swivel, brown
leather, splayed legs, brass casters **375.00**
Rococo Revival
New York, attributed to J. and J. W.
Meeks, c1850, arm, carved rose-
wood, laminated, Stanton Hall pat-
tern, pr **8,000.00**
New York, attributed to John Henry
Belter, c1850–60, carved rose-
wood, laminated, floral upholstery **4,250.00**
Sheraton
Arm, turned detail, well shaped arms,
gold striping, orig dark paint **200.00**
Side, curly maple, scrolled slat, re-
placed rush seat, detailed turnings,
refinished **625.00**
Victorian
Arm
Bobbin turned frame, c1840, loung-
ing type, reupholstered **600.00**
Upholstered, tufted back, mahog-

any open arms, scroll feet, shaped stretcher **150.00**
Corner, carved walnut, lion mask head carved crest rail, hawk carved twin back splat, needlework seat, shaped legs **325.00**
Side, balloon back, shell carved crest rail, ivory floral fabric cov seat, serpentine legs, set of 6 . . . . **1,225.00**
William and Mary, English, early 18th C, arm, walnut, pierced leaf crest, molded caned back, acanthus carved rolled arms, block and ring turned legs, 51″ **1,150.00**

Chair, Windsor, bow back, arm, maple, New England, c1800, $2,000.00.

Windsor
Brace Back, side, splayed base, bulbous turnings and "H" stretcher, saddle seat, turned back posts, shaped crest, black repaint **400.00**
Bow Back
American, early 19th C, side, nine spindle, "Sanborn" branded on bottom, old refinishing, pr **650.00**
Philadelphia, John Brientnall Ackley, c1800, side, bamboo turned spindles, shaped seat, bamboo turned legs, pr **900.00**
Cage Back, American, early 19th C, side, old black paint over orig mustard yellow **250.00**
Comb Back, splayed base, bamboo turnings and "H" stretcher, oval seat, spindle back, shaped crest, refinished, repairs **450.00**
Fan Back, splayed base, turned legs and "H" stretcher, saddle seat, spindle back, turned posts and

yoke crest, branded monogram "L.B.," refinished, pr **1,200.00**
Step Down, American, early 19th C, set of six matched side chairs, orig black paint, floral dec crests, set . **5,700.00**

Chests of Drawers, Hepplewhite, cherry, four graduated drawers, bracket feet, 36½″, $4,000.00.

CHESTS OF DRAWERS

Chippendale
American, late 18th C, cherry, molded top, conforming case, four thumb molded and graduated long drawers, ogee bracket feet, 37″ w, 19″ d, 35″ h **6,000.00**
Connecticut, late 18th C, ox bow, birch, molded top, conforming case, four graduated long drawers, cockbeaded surrounds, molded base, later short cabriole legs, ball and claw feet, 42″ w, 29″ d, 40″ h . **15,000.00**
Connecticut, late 18th C, ox bow, mahogany, molded top, conforming case, four graduated long drawers, cockbeaded surrounds, molded base, later short cabriole legs, ball and claw feet, 44″ w, 29″ d, 40″ h . **7,250.00**
Pennsylvania, c1780, cherry, rect molded top, conforming case, four thumb molded and graduated long drawers, flanked by fluted quarter columns, molded base, ogee bracket feet, 39″ w, 21″ d, 37″ h . . **2,500.00**
Colonial Revival
Hepplewhite Style, c1920, solid mahogany, inlay on drawers and back rail, two small drawers over two long drawers, eagle brasses, 42″ w, 19″ d, 38″ h **350.00**
William and Mary Style, American, maple, rect molded top, conforming case, two thumb molded short drawers, four graduated long drawers, molded base, turned bun feet, 27″ w, 19″ d, 41″ h **1,000.00**

Empire, American, c1820–40
  Mahogany, rope carved front posts, acanthus carved bells, crosshatched cut panels, two door center cupboard, center heart inlay on back splash, claw and ball feet (may be later additions), orig finish, orig hardware, 43″ w **1,500.00**
  Tiger Maple, bird's eye maple drawer facings, finely made columns, cherry sides and top, four graduated drawers, glass pulls, 42½ x 21¾ x 47½″ **1,350.00**
Empire Style, country, cherry, walnut and curly maple inlay, paneled ends, turned feet, turned and rope carved pilasters, scrolled apron, carved reeded detail on top edge, six dovetailed drawers with applied edge bead, turned wood pulls, refinished, 38¼″ w, 47″ h **2,250.00**
Federal
  American, c1790, bow front, mahogany, oblong top, conforming top, six cockbeaded long drawers, shaped apron, French bracket feet, 43″ w, 22″ d, 39″ h **2,300.00**
  American, c1800, bow front, mahogany, oblong top with reeded edge, conforming case, four graduated cockbeaded drawers, shaped skirt, French bracket feet, 42″ w, 24″ d, 36″ h **3,500.00**
  American, c1800, box front, birch, oblong top, conforming case, four cockbeaded and graduated long drawers, molded base, bracket feet, 39″ w, 22″ d, 33″ h **2,500.00**
  New York, c1800, bow front, mahogany, oblong top, conforming case, four cockbeaded long drawers, shaped apron continuing to French bracket feet, 42″ w, 23″ d, 38″ h . . **1,900.00**
George III, mahogany, straight front, two small over three wide graduated drawers, brass ring pulls, French bracket feet, 41″ w, 20″ d, 40½″ h . . **950.00**
Georgian, English, c1850, mahogany, pair of small drawers at top, three graduated drawers, restored, refinished, replaced base and hardware, 33″ w, 19¾″ d, 35½″ h **600.00**
Hepplewhite, American, late 18th C, swell front
  Mahogany veneer, banded inlay around base and top edge, ivory inlaid escutcheons, French feet, scalloped apron, four dovetailed drawers, applied beaded edge, wood pulls, 39¼″ w, 36⅝″ h . . **3,500.00**
  Tiger maple facings, maple sides, birch top, four drawers, scalloped skirt, orig emb hardware of shepherd fighting a wolf, minor repairs to veneer of skirt, old refinishing, 38″ w **1,600.00**
Hepplewhite Style, country, walnut, simple inlay, French feet, dovetailed case, four dovetailed cock beaded drawers, refinished, 40″ w, 37¾″ h . **875.00**
Renaissance Revival, American, NY, c1850–60, carved rosewood, marble top, three graduated long drawers, arched mirror back with carved pediment and finials, stenciled mark "From A. Roux French Cabinet Maker Nos. 479 & 481, Broadway, New York" **4,800.00**
Sheraton
  American, c1810, birch, four graduated drawers, orig red finish, orig hardware, later casters, 41″ w . . . **1,300.00**
  American, c1800, swell front, mahogany, band inlay, orig hardware, 39½″ w **2,900.00**
  American, c1820, country, cherry, inlaid walnut posts, inlaid escutcheons, line inlay top edge, turned feet, four dovetailed cock beaded drawers, orig brasses, refinished, 40¾″ w, 41¾″ h **1,300.00**
William and Mary, American, maple, molded rect top, conforming case, four graduated long drawers, molded base, turned bun feet, 38″ w, 19″ d, 36″ h **800.00**

CHESTS, OTHER

See also Blanket Chests and Chests of Drawers

Apothecary
  Desk, 32 small drawers, two large drawers at bottom, fall front desk in center top, hinged fold out top working surface, restored and refinished, 56¾″ w, 15″ d, 41″ w **1,000.00**
  Traveling, Victorian, rect, hinged lid, brass carrying handle, fitted int., ten compartments, rect glass bottles with stoppers, paper label inscribed "Savory, Moore & Co, Chemists to the Royal Family, 136 New Bond Street, & 220 Regent Street, London," drawer below with brass handle, 9⅞″ w, 7⅛″ l **715.00**
Campaign Chest, English, early to mid 19th C, mahogany, two small drawers over three full width drawers, ball feet and casters, recessed brass handles, 35¾″ w, 19½″ d, 41″ h **850.00**
Chest on Chest
  Chippendale, Massachusetts or New

Chests, Other, highboy, Queen Anne, tiger maple, orig hardware, $16,000.00.

Hampshire, c1780–90, curly maple, bonnet top, mahogany plinths, three small drawers top, four graduated drawers over four graduated base drawers, flame finials, refinished, minor repairs, orig hardware, finials and plinths, 39″ w, 19″ d, 87½″ h **18,000.00**

Federal, PA, cherry upper section with molded cornice, three small drawers, four long graduated drawers, base with three long drawers, shaped skirt, flaring bracket feet, 41¾″ w, 21½″ d, 75½″ h **3,650.00**

Georgian, English, 19th C, mahogany, flat top, dentil molding, upper section with two small drawers over three graduated beaded drawers, lower section with three graduated beaded drawers, bracket feet, 40″ w, 19″ d, 69⅜″ h **2,250.00**

Queen Anne, Philadelphia, c1730, walnut, flat top, two sections, upper with molded cornice above three short and three long graduated drawers, fluted canter corners, projecting mid molding above lower section of three graduated long drawers, bracket feet, orig bright cut brasses, 42¾″ w, 24¾″ d, 71½″ h **18,700.00**

Chest on Frame
Chippendale, PA, c1770, walnut, three parts, removable cornice with scroll carved tympanum, middle section of five short and four long graduated molded drawers, lower

section shaped skirt continuing to cabriole legs, claw and ball feet, orig brasses, 41½″ w, 22¾″ d, 73½″ h **7,500.00**

Queen Anne, American, maple, rect molded top, conforming case, five thumb molded graduated long drawers (appearing as six drawers), molded base, shaped skirt, short cabriole legs, pad feet, 39″ w, 20″ d, 62″ h **3,750.00**

Commode
George III, mahogany, serpentine, four long graduated drawers, inlaid, paneled sides, 58″ w, 22″ d, 35½″ h **6,000.00**

Regency, 20th C, gilt bronze, rouge royal marble top, kingwood, two small drawers, two long drawers, channeled sides, 51″ w, 34″ h . . . **3,000.00**

Highboy
Chippendale, Salem, MA, c1770, carved walnut, two parts, bonnet top with molded swan's neck pediment centering three spirally turned finials, three short and four long graduated, molded drawers, center drawer fan carved, lower section of three short and one long graduated, molded drawers, center drawer fan carved, volute carved and diamond pierced skirt, angular cabriole legs, claw and ball feet, restoration to base and top of crest, 40″ w, 21″ d, 89¼″ h **22,000.00**

Queen Anne
American, country, maple, top with cove molded cornice and six drawers, bottom with scrolled apron with turned acorn drops and dovetailed drawers, cabriole legs with duck feet, 36″ w, 70¾″ h **5,250.00**

Connecticut, maple, two parts, upper section with cavetto molded cornice, conforming case, two thumb molded short drawers, four graduated long drawers, lower section with two long drawers, second appearing as two drawers centering fan carved drawer, shaped apron, cabriole legs, pad feet, 39″ w, 20″ d, 73″ h **19,000.00**

New England, c1765, maple, flat top, two sections, upper with molded cornice, four molded graduated drawers, lower with one long and three short drawers, center drawer fan carved, shaped skirt, cabriole legs, pad feet, 37¾″ w, 20″ d, 70¾″ h . . . **30,000.00**

Lowboy
Queen Anne
    Connecticut, c1750, cherry, poplar secondary wood, boldly scalloped top with good overhang, four dovetailed overlapping drawers, carved center fan, scalloped aprons, cabriole legs, slender ankles, well shaped duck feet with pads, orig deep reddish brown finish, excellent patina, pieced repair on front foot, replaced engraved brasses, 20½" w, 38" d, 32⅛" h **145,000.00**
    Connecticut, c1760, carved cherry, rect top, molded edge, long drawer above central shell carved deep drawer flanked by deep drawers, blocked and arched apron, cabriole legs, pad feet, chalk inscription on int. backboard "B.S. Snow," frame slightly reduced, repair to front left leg, 31½" w, 30½" h **4,000.00**
    Massachusetts, mid 18th C, pine, rect molded top, recessed case, single long drawer, three short drawers, shaped apron, cabriole legs, pad feet, 36" h, 22" d, 30" h **3,800.00**
Mule, Chippendale, country, pine, wide single board construction, rect lift lid, blanket chest top with two fake drawers, two dovetailed overlapping drawers, scrolled feet, turned wood pulls, orig red paint, 38⅜" w, 19½" d, 41½" h **1,800.00**
Tea, Federal, American, 1815–25, mahogany, paw feet, eagle carved brackets, inlaid escutcheon, 12" w, 7¼" d, 8¾" h **850.00**

CRADLES

Birch, hooded, dovetailed, cut out rockers, scalloped ends, 41" l **500.00**
Carved hardwoods, four columnar finials and tapering sides, 36" l, 27" h . **175.00**
Mahogany, dovetailed, scrolled sides and ends, old dark finish, 49½" l . . . **500.00**
Pine, American, late 18th or early 19th C, pine, hooded, scalloped hood sides, plain bonnet top, orig finish, 45" l **300.00**
Poplar, open, central cut out sides and ends, hand holds, trestle rockers, old dark finish, 41" l **200.00**
Walnut
    Dovetailed, scalloped sides, hand holds, brass knobs, heart cut out in headboard, large rockers, 43½" . . **350.00**
    Self rocking, patent by Aaron Dodd

Crane, Feb 28, 1852, wind–up clockwork mechanism, flat spindles, scroll feet, 44" l **675.00**

Cupboard, corner, Country, pine, 38 x 25 x 61", $3,600.00.

CUPBOARDS

Armoire
    Art Nouveau, French, Majorelle, c1900, carved walnut, arched top, coved frieze, deeply carved poppies, scrolling leaves and stems, two beveled glass doors, poppy inlaid spandrels, two drawers, gilt bronze foliate pulls, flared feet, 52" w, 80½" h **6,600.00**
    Empire, American, mid Atlantic states, c1830, mahogany, rect projecting cornice, arched frieze, paneled doors, flattened half columns continuing to acanthus carved paw feet, 5'7" w, 21" d, 7'7" h **1,300.00**
    Federal, Louisiana, late 18th C, cherry, string inlay, center swirled acanthus leaf inlay, cornice of later date, fitted int., cabriole legs, some replaced drawers and shelves . . . **5,250.00**
    Louis-Phillipe, mid 19th C, inlaid rosewood, arched top, conforming mirrored door, brass molded cross banded frame, base with one long drawer, cabriole legs, ornate brass mounts, 43" w, 89" h **1,500.00**
Chimney, pine, full length overlapping door, seven mortised shelves, wrought iron hinges and slide bolt latch, 12" w, 10½" d, 91" h **2,250.00**
Corner
    Architectural, pine and poplar, two pcs, molded arch and keystone,

molded cornice and pilasters, turned blocks, raised panel doors, simple feet, cleaned down to old transparent yellow stain, 47½" w, 95" h **3,500.00**

Chippendale, PA, c1795, carved pine, molded projecting cornice, carved frieze, pair of arched glazed doors, red painted shelved int., pair of cupboard doors below, flanking fluted pilasters, restorations to cornice and other minor repairs, 60" w, 28½" d, 109½" h **10,000.00**

Colonial Revival, Chippendale style, pine, arched, glazed upper door, two paneled doors below, 29½" w, 12" d, 70" h **375.00**

Country

Butternut, beaded edge, paneled doors, applied molding waist and cornice, carved inscription "May the 31, 1856, Made by Jo Younker," 41" w, 79" h **1,200.00**

Decorated, PA, attributed to John Rupp, York County, two parts, pine, orig red flame graining, top with molded cornice, double doors, each with eight panes of old glass, base with three drawers, paneled doors, turned feet, orig hardware, white porcelain pulls, top section int. with orig light blue paint **7,200.00**

Pine and poplar, red, dark green trim, light green int., raised paneled bottom doors, twelve pane glass top door, picture frame molding, cove molded cornice with reeded frieze, bracket feet, 44" w, 88½" h ... **8,250.00**

Walnut, well developed cornice with dentil molding, raised panel doors, beaded frames, applied corner molding, replaced bracket feet, old varnish finish, replaced hinges and hardware, 49" w, 90¼" h **4,000.00**

Federal Style, country, cherry, molded cornice above conforming case, pair of glazed doors, short drawer, two paneled cupboard doors, block feet, 50" w, 20" d, 79" h **1,300.00**

Victorian, late, cherry, open, fluted vertical members, floral motifs on drawers, carved rosettes on two lower doors, natural finial, 59" w, 31" d, 88" h **2,000.00**

Hanging

Federal, country, mid 19th C, cherry, two paneled doors, painted shelves, 25" w, 11" d, 26" h **450.00**

Pine, worn orig blue paint, raised panel door, bat wing brass, beaded frame, perimeter molding, int. shelf dated "1835," 23" w, 8¼" d, 25" h **600.00**

Pine and poplar, orig rosewood graining, paneled doors, step back shelves, 34½" w, 33" h **200.00**

Walnut, base and cornice molding, reeded stiles, relief carved star flower designs, stamped sunbursts, flush panel door with relief carved design, shelf and two dovetailed drawers int., worn finish, 25" w, 34¾" h **525.00**

Jelly

Pine, c1850, two doors, four shelves, gallery top, orig red paint, 15" w, 33" d, 57½" h **750.00**

Poplar, two paneled doors, two overhanging drawers, shaped skirt, red and black graining, orig hardware, 41½" w, 21½" d, 46" h **650.00**

Linen Press

Chippendale, American, late 18th C, walnut, two parts, molded and dentil cornice, two paneled doors, lower section with three graduated thumb molded long drawers, molded base, bracket feet, 50" w, 20" d, 78" h **3,200.00**

Hepplewhite, two parts, broken arch crest with turned finial, frieze with inlaid geometrics and rosettes, top with double doors, inlay banding with spiral corners, stringing on doors conforms to scalloped rails and stiles, base with four dovetailed drawers with line inlay and invected corners, applied edge beading, scalloped apron, French feet, restored broken arch crest, refinished, 41" w, 95" h **5,250.00**

Pewter, American, late 18th C, pine, bent back, four shelves, single cupboard door base, refinished, 41¼" w, 18¾" d, 79⅝" h **850.00**

Pie Safe, American, mid 19th C

Maple, refinished, 39¼" w, 16" d, 43½" h **375.00**

Walnut, Southern, two cupboard doors each with three punched tin panels, punched tin paneled sides, two drawers, pair of cupboard doors **550.00**

Wall

American, poplar, 2 pcs, scrolled base, paneled doors, dovetailed drawers, pie shelf, cove molded cornice, cast iron latches, refinished, 55¼" w, 85" h **2,600.00**

Pennsylvania, early 19th C, pine, closed face, paneled doors and sides, molded flaring cornice, pair of two paneled top drawers, shelved int., three small mid–section drawers, molded waist, pair of paneled cupboard base doors, old refinishing, traces of old red paint, molding loss, 51½" w, 20" d, 83" h **3,000.00**

Shaker, 1 pc, walnut, cut out feet, raised panel doors, molded cornice, top door int. stamped "Congregational Church," 49½" w, 89½" h **1,900.00**

Desk, Eastlake, oak, cylinder roll top, $1,000.00.

DESKS

Art Nouveau
Austrian, gilt metal, repousse panels of country scenes, glass top, brocade lining, matching arm chair **1,200.00**
French, c1900, carved walnut, three–quarter shelf gallery mounted with small semi–circular platform, brown leather inset writing surface, three frieze drawers with gilt bronze pulls, pierced and arched spandrels continuing to form legs, spade feet, minor restoration to feet, 58½" l, 37½" h . . **4,675.00**

Arts and Crafts, Limbert, c 1908–12, oak, molded edge rect top above two drawers, straight rect supports with corbels, joined by H form stretcher, one drawer with branded shopmark inscribed "Limbert's/Arts Crafts/Furniture/Trademark/Made in Grand Rapids/and Holland," 48" l, 29" h . . . **660.00**

Chippendale
American
Massachusetts, c1789, mahogany, slant front, oxbow front, rect hinged lid, fitted int. of valanced pigeonholes, small drawers, center prospect section of small

drawers, upper fan carved, four reverse serpentine front graduated drawers, cockbeaded surrounds, claw and ball feet, incised "EM 1789" on bottom, 42" w, 22" d, 44" h **12,000.00**

New England, late 18th C, slant front, tiger maple, four thumb molded and graduated long drawers, molded base, bracket feet, 38" w, 20" d, 41" h **13,500.00**

English, mahogany, slant front, dovetailed bracket feet, four overlapping dovetailed drawers, fitted int., replaced hardware, refinished, 42" w, 40¼" h **3,000.00**

Colonial Revival
Chippendale Style, c1930, solid walnut case, walnut veneered slant front lid, block front, fitted int. with secret drawer, paw feet, 32" w, 18" d, 42" h **425.00**

Governor Winthrop Style, c1920, mahogany veneer, solid mahogany slant front, serpentine front, fitted int. with two document drawers, shell carved center door, four long drawers, brass pulls and escutcheons **400.00**

Queen Anne Style, c1940, walnut veneer top, sides, and front, crotch walnut veneer on two side drawers, shell carved cabriole legs, 44" w, 20" d, 31" h **450.00**

Federal
Butler's, mid Atlantic states, c1800, mahogany, rect top, conforming case, secretary drawer, satinwood fitted int., three graduated long drawers, shaped skirt, French bracket feet, 46" w, 23" d, 44" h . . **2,200.00**

Campaign, mahogany, rect case, opening to baize lined writing surface, three small drawers over cockbeaded long drawer, reeded legs, turned feet, 36" w, 21" d, 36" h **1,400.00**

Cylinder, mid Atlantic States, c1820, curly maple, three short drawers above retracting cylinder lid opening to short drawers over valanced pigeonholes, center tambour slide, retractable baize lined writing surface, two short drawers and long drawers, turned feet, 40½" w, 22" d, 50" h **5,000.00**

Lady's, writing, Boston, MA, c1800, inlaid mahogany, two parts, upper with molded cornice above two hinged drawers inlaid with satinwood columns, int. with small drawers centering valanced pigeonholes, lower section with hinged baize lined writing flap above two cockbeaded drawers, rect inlaid dies, sq tapering legs ending in shaped angular vase form feet, 39" w, 20¼" d, 44" h **9,000.00**

Federal Style, country, schoolmaster's, pine, lectern top hinged above simple fitted int., straight tapered legs, 31" w, 20" d, 40" h **350.00**

George I, early 18th C, slant front, walnut, rect cross banded top, canted lid, shaped and stepped int. of small drawers and conforming cubbyholes, center prospect door, rect case with three short, two short and two full cockbeaded and cross banded drawers, bracket feet, 37" w, 21" d, 40" h **6,500.00**

George III, partners, mahogany, rect top, green tooled inset leather top, each side fitted with single drawer over kneehole section flanked by four drawers, brass bail handles, platform base, 60" w, 48" d, 31" h **5,275.00**

Hepplewhite, American, late 18th C

Mahogany, inlay, cylinder front, four graduated drawers, orig eagle brasses, round condition, some loss of veneer to base, 44" w . . . **2,400.00**

Walnut, figured walnut with inlay, scalloped apron, dovetailed case, fitted int. with ten dovetailed drawers, four drawers, French feet, refinished, 40" w, 43½" h **2,500.00**

Queen Anne, New England, c1760, slant front

Maple, rect hinged lid, stepped int. with valanced pigeonholes, serpentine drawers and center paneled prospect door, arched small drawer, four graduated long drawers, bracket feet, repairs, 37" w, 18½" d, 43" h **2,750.00**

Walnut, shaped top above slant front with central cupboard door flanked by pigeonholes and small drawers, over long drawer, stand with three short drawers, later cabriole legs carved at the knees with shells, 37¼" h **6,000.00**

Regency, c1815, Davenport, rosewood, sliding sq writing surface, tooled brown leather inset, rect three quarter brass gallery, pull out writing slide on either side fitted with pen and ink drawer, four long drawers, false drawers on other side, turned cylindrical feet, minor losses to molding, 30" h . **3,500.00**

Restoration, America, c1835–40, carved rosewood, fall front, well fitted line inlaid int., 30½" w, 57" h **2,100.00**

Sheraton, American, c1820, slant front,

maple, bird's eye and tiger maple int., fourteen drawers, rope carved columns, refinished, glass knobs, 41" w, 20¼" d, 53¼" h **2,000.00**

Wooton, 1875–80, walnut and burl walnut, standard grade, pierced and carved gallery over double panel lifting frieze, maple veneer fitted int., trestle feet, 41" closed, 69½" h **7,500.00**

DOUGH TROUGHS

Cherry, dovetailed, turned feet, white porcelain knobs, name "Hardin" scratched on base **250.00**

Decorated, pine, orig blue paint, early train painted on one side in black, white, and faded red, sq nail construction, curved tin bottom, unpainted inner lid, worn leather hinges, 21 x 31" breadboard top, 15¼ x 25¾ x 28½" **600.00**

Maple, dovetailed, old replacement lid, traces of old red paint, 38 x 19¼ x 28¾" **400.00**

Pine, American, late 18th C, orig red paint, stretcher base, 46½ x 23 x 27⅜" **750.00**

Poplar, turned cherry legs, chestnut apron and hinged lid, refinished, 19 x 41 x 29½" **300.00**

Walnut, dovetailed, splayed legs, 20 x 27 x 39" **450.00**

Dry Sink, ash, single small drawer, two cupboard doors, wooden pulls, 46 x 17 x 45½", $500.00.

DRYSINKS

Cherry, Chippendale, two sections, two paneled doors on top, rect sink over two paneled base doors, 46" w, 23½" d, 77" h **1,000.00**

Curly Maple, poplar door panels, hard wood edge strips, drawer front replaced, top edge of well re–cut, refinished, 55" w, 20¼" d, x 34½" h **2,250.00**

Pine, country, 19th C, shallow well top over recessed pair of paneled cupboard doors, bracket feet, 45″ w, 22″ d, 29″ h **950.00**

Pine and Poplar

American, crest, paneled doors, one small nailed drawer, refinished, 62½″ w, 19¾″ d, 34″ h **900.00**

Attributed to PA, c1825, shelf back with two small drawers, pair of base cupboard doors, refinished, minor restoration, 52″ w, 22½″ d, 50⅜″ h **850.00**

Poplar, country, paneled doors, dovetailed drawer, cut out sides, shelf top, simple cut out feet, old worn refinishing, 48″ w, 19¾″ d, 48¾″ h **1,125.00**

FRAMES

Brass, Art Nouveau style, two oval openings, easel back, 7″ w, 12″ h . . **125.00**

Curly Maple, refinished, 16¾″ w, 2″ d, 20½″ h **85.00**

Decorated, poplar, orig black paint, gold stenciled dec, 9¾″ w, 1¼″ d, 11¾″ h **250.00**

Mahogany, pine secondary wood, laminated, folk art pyramid dec, old varnish finish, 9″ w, 12¾″ h **35.00**

Parcel Gilt, Art Nouveau, c1900, painted gesso, and wood, high relief carving, red and green floral sprigs, incised gold ground, 22″ w, 33″ h . . **675.00**

Pine, beveled, worn red flame graining, varnished, 9⅜″ w, 1½″ d, 11⅜″ h . . **75.00**

Veneer

Mahogany

Beveled, varnished, 11¼″ w, 1½″ d, 20″ h **45.00**

Empire, wide molding, 20″ w, 26″ h **65.00**

Maple, bird's eye, ogee, flat liner, 25″ w, 3⅝″ d, 28½″ h **100.00**

Rosewood, beveled, 7⅝″ w, 1⅞″ d, 8¾″ h **50.00**

Walnut

Chip carved edge, applied hearts at corners, 16″ w, 19½″ h **85.00**

Cross bar corners, 8″ w, 12″ h **50.00**

Wood Inlay, intricate design, back labeled "This frame was carved and glued together by hand 1730, Wm Hall, N.Y. State," worn finish **250.00**

HAT RACKS AND HALL TREES

Art Nouveau

French, c1900, carved walnut, thumb molded cornice over shaped mirror plate, molded tendril border, serpentine projecting shelf, panel carved at sides with tendrils and leafy sprays, shaped feet, 50″ w, 85″ h **1,325.00**

Galle, c1900, oak, arched superstructure inlaid with three divided panels, sheep grazing scene, buildings, and rolling hills, paneled back with relief carving of branch, leaf, and pod motifs, flanked by glazed cupboard doors, int. shelves, rect seat above panels inlaid with floral sprigs, insects, and water lilies, molded base, block feet, 77½″ w, 79½″ h **5,000.00**

Arts and Crafts

American, c1911, open rect back, horizontal X form splat flanked by vertical slats, joined by slightly flared drop arms, exposed tenons, rect supports, horizontal members, hinged rect seat opens to storage area, decal affixed "Lifetime Furniture/Grand Rapids Bookcase & Chair Co," 42″ l **600.00**

English, c1910, oak, rect top, central door mounted with leaded slag and textured glass panel, polychrome red, blue, and white stylized floral sprigs, over elongated rect panel with pewter inlay, flanked by small shelves, wrigglework side supports, beveled glass panels, small drawers, open platforms, stiles continuing form stylized spade feet, 48″ w, 84″ h **1,870.00**

Gothic, Victorian, American, c1855, oak, ornate arched open cut upper frame, hooks at side, white marble shelf, ornate open cut base flanked by umbrella racks **10,000.00**

Hall Tree, Renaissance, Victorian, walnut, beveled mirror, brown marble insert, 80″, $900.00.

Renaissance Revival, Victorian, American, c1870, walnut, ornate carved cresting, shaped mirror within molded framework, drop columns at each side, candle sockets, candle shelves, and sockets at lower sides, white marble shelf, single drawer flanked by umbrella racks, orig brass pans ... **1,450.00**

Rococo Revival, American, mid 19th C, cast iron, flower urn at top, center rococo framed mirror, six scrolling arms **950.00**

ICE CREAM PARLOR FURNITURE

Chair
Arm, wood seat	125.00
Heart back, refinished	75.00
Spectacle, refinished	85.00

Child's, table and two chairs, 18″ d table, 9½″ d seat, set **200.00**

Stool
26½″ h, refinished	50.00
30″ h, 12″ d seat, refinished	60.00

Table
25″ sq, claw and ball feet	225.00
30″ d, oak top	250.00

Table and four chairs, 30″ d table, wood top, 14″ d chairs, replaced seats, refinished, set **650.00**

LOVE SEATS

Adams, c1770, triple oval back, bellflower painted satinwood **4,000.00**

Art Nouveau, Majorelle, c1900, suite, carved walnut, 60″ l settee, two arm chairs, two side chairs, arched crestrail, pierced and carved with cow parsley flowers and leafy sprig, rounded crestrail terminals with matching leafage, molded undulating arms, flared rect seat, cow parsley tendril carved seat rail, floral legs, orig silk velvet Japanned embroidered upholstery, 5 pcs **38,500.00**

Chippendale, English, arched upholstered back, rolled arms, two cushion seat, carved foliate apron, 28 x 35 x 30″ **900.00**

Colonial Revival, William and Mary style, loose cushion, turned baluster legs, stretcher, 48″ **650.00**

Empire Style, American, mahogany, scrolling crest, cylindrical arms, fixed bolster, wing carved paw feet, 66″ l . **700.00**

Rococo, walnut frame, triple crest, rose carving, refinished and reupholstered **750.00**

Victorian, American, walnut, center crest with carved woman's head, finely carved arms form two busts of women, upholstery worn **375.00**

Magazine Rack, Canterbury, American, walnut, single drawer, brass pull, acorn finials, 17¼ x 22¾ x 23¼″, $600.00.

MAGAZINE RACKS

Arts and Crafts, Limbert, c1908–12, oak, four graduated shelves joined by canted spreading sides, divided oval cut outs, wooden buttons, branched shopmark inscribed "Limbert's/Arts Crafts/Furniture/Trademark/Made In/ Grand Rapids/And Holland," oval stamped "Checked/OK/Paul Brown," 16⅜″ w, 37″ h **885.00**

George III, late 18th C, upper portion divided into three sections, full frieze drawer, turned legs, 18″ w, 13½″ d, 19″ h **1,500.00**

Victorian
American, c1850, rosewood, single short drawer, turned feet, brass caps and casters, 18″ w, 16″ d, 19″ h **1,250.00**

English, first half 19th C
Rosewood, upper portion divided into four sections, turned supports at corners, apron with full drawer, ring turned legs, 20″ w, 15″ d, 21″ h **2,300.00**

Walnut, carved, three quarter gallery, shaped sides, molded base, turned feet **3,200.00**

William IV, c1835, rosewood, X form dividers, baluster turned rails, bellflower wreaths above single long drawer, baluster turned legs, casters, 20″ l, 19¾″ h **1,760.00**

MIRRORS

Adam, English, c1780, giltwood, vase and leaf finial, openwork scroll and leaf dec, oblong mirror plate in upright frame, 28″ w, 64″ h **900.00**

Art Nouveau, Majorelle, c1900, cheval, three parts, carved walnut, clematis pattern, arched rect beveled mirror plate in molded relief carved frame, surmounted by pierced intersecting framework, molded flared feet, 60″ w, 6′9″ h **16,500.00**

Centennial, Chippendale Style, mahogany, inner frame and back are 18th C, later replacements, 18″ w, 38¼″ h **400.00**

Chippendale, scroll, molded frame, gold over painted gilt liner, raised gilded feather ornament on crest, old repairs, 14¾″ w, 27″ h **450.00**

Eastlake, walnut, incised carving, 25¼″ w, 56½″ h **475.00**

Empire
   Architectural, two parts, mahogany, orig reverse painting with mill, boat, blue border with silvered flowers and red dec, minor paint flaking, 21¼″ w, 40″ h **200.00**
   Bull's Eye, American, attributed to Albany, c1830, gilt wood, circular glass surrounded by ebonized slip and spherule hung frame, surmounted by elaborate carved fruit filled basket flanked by overflowing cornucopia, acanthus carved pendant below, 32″ w, 47″ h, pr **20,000.00**

Federal
   American, c1800, rect glass, gilt slip, inlaid frame, pierced crest, gilt Phoenix, matching pendant below, 23″ w, 44″ h **2,200.00**
   American, c1825, shaving, mahogany, bowfront, rect tilting glass, turned supports, oblong case, three short drawers, ball feet, 22″ w, 8″ d, 22″ h **750.00**
   American, early 19th C, tabernacle, gilt wood, rect glass flanked by two pair of fluted colonnettes, surmounted by eagle and swag dec eglomise panel, spherule hung broken cornice with center floral basket, 24″ w, 45″ h **3,000.00**

George II
   Giltwood, late 19th C, chinaman standing within portico, mirror flanked and separated by frame elaborately carved with pagoda, cresting, C scroll, foliate, icicle, and columnar borders, carved figure of dog with up turned head on base, 58½″ w, 86″ h **8,250.00**
   Walnut veneer, parcel gilt, scrolled crest centered by pierced gilt foliage, shaped mirror plate flanked by fruit and floral sprig medallions, scrolled pendant below, 21¼″ w, 39¼″ h **1,875.00**

George III, third quarter 18th C, oval plate, beaded slip and carved fluted frame, egg and dart border, painted white, parcel gilt, 37¼″ w, 45″ h ... **2,500.00**

Hepplewhite, scroll, mahogany veneer, inlaid banding, repairs, one ear replaced, 19½″ w, 38¾″ h **550.00**

Mosaic, c1885, micro, lavender blossoms on one side, gold mosaic ground, detailed scenes of Venice on other side, three flying sparrows, crowned by Lion of Venice, 29″ w, 54″ h **3,000.00**

Queen Anne, 18th C, walnut
   Pier, parcel gilt and verre eglomise, shaped upper section, border of gilt arabesque work with two figures, green ground, triple glass plates, 27½″ w, 64″ h **4,500.00**
   Wall, figured veneer, pine secondary wood, applied gilded ornaments on crests and gilded liner, old veneer repairs, discolored mirror, 14¾″ w, 37″ h **1,600.00**

Regency
   Girandole, early 19th C, circular convex plate, ebonized slip and molded spherule hung frame, surmounted by sea horse and flowering cornucopia, two scrolling branches above acanthus skirt, 33″ w, 50″ h **7,000.00**
   Wall, c1815, parcel gilt, cornice with outset corners, ebonized Greek key frieze beneath spheres, rect mirror plate flanked by fluted stiles and ebonized classical busts, 35¼″ w, 50½″ h **2,500.00**

Mirror, Sheraton, c1810, mahogany, architectural, reverse painting on glass tablet, 10 x 22″, $400.00.

Sheraton, architectural, American or English, early 19th C, fluted half columns, classic figures relief panel at top, minor loss of gilding, 49⅞″ h .. **600.00**

Victorian
   Cheval, English, c1890, bird's eye maple frame, bamboo style, 71″ h **1,320.00**

Pier, mahogany, grape leaf carved molded cornice over rect beveled mirror, spiral column supports with paw feet, 61″ w, 102½″ h **650.00**

ROCKERS

Adirondack, American, early 20th C, bent rustic twigs and branches, interwoven latticework back and down swept arms, round seat, curlicue skirt   **200.00**

Arrowback, bamboo turnings, scrolled arms, three slat backs, red and black graining, stenciled floral designs on slats **125.00**

Boston, mid 19th C, grain painted, gilt stencil dec, scenic dec crest, rosewood grained seat **500.00**

Child's, oak, chicken head and gallery with turned spindles, worn white paint, red and yellow dec, 36″ h . . .   **200.00**

Eastlake, late 19th C, mahogany platform, incised and pierced cresting over sq panel back, center, pad arms, seat upholstered in pink velvet, reeded arms and supports **200.00**

Ladder Back, country, turned arms and arm supports, four slats, rabbit ear posts, replaced woven splint seat . .   **225.00**

Mission, L & J G Stickley, arm, c1910, vertical back and side slats, clamp decal mark **625.00**

Shaker, Mt Lebanon, NY, c1900, #7, arms, old brown wash, rush seat, 41½″ h **400.00**

Victorian, Grecian influence, c1860, walnut, caned back and seat, scroll cut arms, turned legs, refinished and recaned **350.00**

Wicker, loom woven fiber, padded back, flattened down swept arms, seat with loose cushion, turned and fiber wrapped legs, painted white **150.00**

Windsor

Bow Back, shaped arms, oblong seat, bamboo turnings, comb back crest, splayed base, "H" stretcher, added rockers, old refinishing, minor damage **450.00**

Comb Back, New England, c1800, turned, shaped crest, seven spindles back, shaped arms, elliptical seat, turned legs, grain painted, floral dec **625.00**

SECRETARIES

Colonial Revival, Governor Winthrop, c1928, mahogany veneer, two sections, broken pediment, center urn finial, molded cornice, pair of glazed doors, shelves, slant front, fitted int.,

Secretary, Victorian, country, c1860, pine, brass hardware, 24¼ x 45¼ x 87″, $2,000.00.

three long drawers, oval brasses, ball feet, 33″ w, 80″ h **500.00**

Eastlake, American, c1870, carved walnut and burl walnut, cylinder front, well fitted int., two drawers, two cupboard doors **2,400.00**

Federal

Eastern MA, c1810, mahogany, two parts, upper section with shaped pediment, turned urn form finials, pair of glazed hinged doors, two shelves, lower section with hinged baize lined writing flag, three cockbeaded graduated drawers, reeded legs, C scroll carved brackets, vase form feet, 36″ w, 21″ d, 81½″ h . . **19,800.00**

Massachusetts, Salem, c1800, attributed to William Appleton, inlaid mahogany, two parts, upper with molded swan's neck crest ending in carved pomegranates, center orig giltwood spread wing eagle finial above tympanum inlaid with intersection lines and diamond, pair of glazed hinged doors, two shelves, lower projecting section with line inlaid hinged lid opening to baize lined writing surface, small drawers over pigeonholes, three graduated cockbeaded drawers, line inlaid bracket feet, orig eagle, glass, baize and brasses, 43½″ w, 22″ d, 96″ h **36,000.00**

New York, c1805, lady's, mahogany, two parts, upper with shaped pediment centering eagle brass finial and two urn finials, pair of glazed hinged doors, adjustable shelves, lower section with hinged writing flap opening to divided well, lidded secret well with two drawers, line inlaid frieze, reeded circular legs, brass ball caps, int. drawers restored, 33″ w, 20″ d, 77″ h **13,200.00**

George III, c1760, mahogany, dental carved molded cornice, twin glazed lattice doors, lower section fitted with pull out drawer, fitted int. and writing surface over three graduated drawers, brass bail handles, bracket feet, 37″ w, 21″ d, 80″ h **2,750.00**

Gothic Revival

American, c1840–50, carved rosewood and burl, fall front flanked by maple columns, gilded Ionic capitals, arcaded int., mirrored, inlaid, 44″ w, 21½″ d, 77″ h **4,500.00**

American, NY, c1840–50, carved rosewood, two pcs, upper section with two glazed doors, bird's eye maple int., three fitted shelves in upper case, lower section with closed carved cupboard doors, restored feet, stenciled "J. and J. W. Meeks Makers, No. 14, Vesey St., New York," 91″ h **16,000.00**

Hepplewhite, American, c1790, butler's, inlaid cherry and mahogany, upper section of molded cornice, pair of cupboard doors with oval string inlay, lower section with slant front, fitted int., 8 small drawers, center prospect door, three graduated long drawers, French bracket feet, slight repair to banding around drawers, period hardware, 40½″ w, 20½″ d, 86″ h **4,500.00**

Sheraton, mahogany, two piece, flame veneer facade, upper section with scrolled crest, reeded blocks, and brass rosettes, double doors, three dovetailed int. drawers, fold down writing surface, four dovetailed drawers, applied edge beading, turned feet, refinished, replaced eagle brasses, minor veneer damage, 39″ w, 17½″ d, 64″ h **1,300.00**

SETTEES

Biedermeier, 2nd quarter 19th C, walnut, chairback, shaped arms, turned supports, sq tapered legs, 64″ l **1,200.00**

Classical Style, well shaped crest, plank seat, scrolled arms, turned spindles and legs, refinished, repairs, 80″ l . . **450.00**

Decorated

American, c1825, country, painted, three chair back, shaped crest, horizontal splats and spindles, rect seat, turned legs, box stretchers, 72″ l **1,400.00**

American, c1830, painted green, polychrome dec, shaped and foliated painted crest, two horizontal splats,

turned spindles, turned legs, box stretchers, 72″ l **400.00**

American, c1850, triple chair back, spindle back, scrolling arms, ring turned legs, box stretchers, 75″ h . **5,500.00**

Federal, country, c1835, polychrome rose painted crest, spindle back, scrolling arms, turned legs, box stretcher, 72″ l **2,000.00**

George III, provincial, early 19th C, oak, rect top rail, triple chairback, stylized baluster splats, drop in seat, sq legs joined by stretchers, 50″ l **2,125.00**

Gothic Revival, American, mid 19th C, carved and ebonized walnut, upholstered arms, seat, and three paneled back **1,400.00**

Settee, Hepplewhite, shield back, $1,500.00.

Victorian, American, c1860, floral dec, triple chair back, shaped crest, scrolling arms, caned back and seat, turned legs, 72″ l **1,600.00**

Windsor, American, early 18th C, decorated

Bow back, worn orig brown graining in imitation of curly maple, bamboo turnings, plank seat, three section back with open crests and butterfly medallions, minor repairs, 75½″ l, 17½″ h seat **3,500.00**

Rod back, bamboo turnings, orig gray paint, orig striping, 77¾″ l **2,000.00**

SIDEBOARDS

Arts and Crafts, English, c1910, oak, molded crest, open shelf over cupboard door flanked by vertical cupboard doors, central elliptical purple, green, and white striated and leaded slag glass floral medallions against purple and green enameled textured glass cruciform design, lower section with two drawers over two cupboard

Sideboard, Renaissance, Victorian, walnut, marble top, carved with game birds and fish, $1,200.00.

doors relief carved with fruiting sprays, stiles continuing to form spade feet, 47″ w, 82½″ h **1,000.00**

Classical, NY, c1820, mahogany, rect top, frieze with three inlaid drawers, three hinged cupboard doors, shelves, carved flanking columns, carved animal paw feet, brass casters, 66½″ w, 24″ d, 43½″ h **5,000.00**

Colonial Revival, Queen Anne style, c1920, striped mahogany veneer, two long drawers over pair of drawers flanked by cupboard doors, fiddle back veneer on drawers and doors, burl veneer on oval panels, solid cabriole legs **200.00**

Empire, American, c1820–30, mahogany, partially carved front posts, orig finish, orig brass hardware, 48″ w, 21″ d, 44¾″ h **500.00**

Federal, mid Atlantic states, c1800, serpentine, mahogany, oblong top, ovule corners, conforming case, long drawer, pair of cupboard doors flanked by candle drawers, bottle drawers, quarter round short drawers, conforming cupboard doors, straight tapered legs, banded cuffs, string inlay dec, 6'6″ w, 25″ d, 43″ h **27,000.00**

Federal Style, bow front, mahogany, oblong top, conforming frieze, two banded deep drawers, shallow drawer, knee hole cut, string inlaid straight tapered legs, spade feet, 37″ w, 20″ d, 34″ h **2,600.00**

George III, early 19th C, mahogany, bow front, conforming case, cock-beaded short drawer flanked by two deep drawers, straight tapered legs, 48″ w, 21″ d, 32″ h **1,000.00**

George IV, second quarter 19th C, inlaid mahogany, serpentine front, shaped top, central frieze drawer, flanked by one deep drawer and cupboard door, tapering sq legs, spade feet, 57½″ l, 36¼″ h **1,500.00**

Hepplewhite, American, 18th C, cherry, poplar secondary wood, checkerboard banded top, case with dovetailed edge beaded drawers flanked by serpentine doors and drawers, stringing inlay, mahogany cross banding around bottom edge of case, drawers, and doors, inlaid elongated diamonds, almond and circular bead like segments between strings at tops of sq tapered legs, top of posts have inlaid flutes (books), oval emb eagle brasses (two replaced copies), minor age cracks and veneer repairs, old refinishing, 72″ w, 24⅜″ d, 39¼″ h . . **11,750.00**

Regency, early 19th C, mahogany, D shaped top, single drawer over secret drawer, flanked by deep drawer and bottle drawer, ring turned tapering cylindrical legs, 42½″ l, 36″ h **1,600.00**

Victorian, mid 19th C, oak, highly carved, paneled suprastructure with griffins, broken arched pediment with center antlered deer head ornament, two shelves, two drawers, two cupboard doors with carved oval reserves of fish and game **2,000.00**

SOFAS

Chippendale, NY, c1770, mahogany, camel back, shaped crest, outward scrolling arm supports and seat, sq molded legs, flat stretchers, 80″ l . . **10,000.00**

Classical

American, NY, c1815–20, box style, carved mahogany and rosewood, carved eagle brackets, brass inlay, paw feet, cherry and pine secondary woods, slightly reduced, orig damaged brocade upholstery **1,800.00**

Philadelphia, 19th C, carved mahogany, scroll reticulated crest rail, out scrolled dolphin arms, carved sabre feet, orig upholstery removed **900.00**

Empire

American, c1820–40, eagle carved legs, modern tapestry upholstery . **700.00**

American, c1830, mahogany, carved cornucopias, acorns, oak leaves, and acanthus leaves, basket of flowers finial, refinished, gold brocade reupholstery, 83″ l **1,500.00**

New York, c1835, mahogany, acanthus carved shaped crest continuing to carved scrolled arms,

rounded base, acanthus carved
hairy paw feet, gilt feather returns,
6'6" l **1,400.00**
Federal, New York, c1815, mahogany,
sq back continuing to closed arms,
reeded vasiform arm supports,
reeded legs, brass caster guards and
casters, 6' 6" l **3,400.00**
Mission, L & J G Stickley, c1910, oak,
decal clamp mark, 72" l **1,350.00**
Restauration
  American, c1800, carved mahogany,
carved scroll crestrail, cornucopia
cut scrolled arms, carved legs, paw
feet, bolster pillows, later velvet upholstery **1,200.00**
  American, NY, c1835–40, carved mahogany, scrolling back extends to
form arms, orig upholstery removed **950.00**
Victorian, American, mid 19th C, carved
mahogany, shaped crestrail, arched
pediment, acanthus carved arm supports, velvet upholstery **950.00**

SPINNING WHEELS

Flax Wheels (Saxony)
  Maple, NE, c1830 .... **275.00**
  Mixed woods, PA, c1810, nice turn-
ings, incised heart dec **450.00**
  Mixed woods, PA, c1840, turned ... **300.00**
Oak, turned legs, chip carved back
marked "A. Knox," 36" h **200.00**
Wool Wheels (Walking)
  Oak, cast iron parts, 30" d wheel,
45" h **325.00**
  Walnut, PA, mid 19th C **450.00**

STANDS

Corner, Sheraton, American, early 19th
C, cherry, drawer and back splash . **525.00**
Dictionary, George III, English, walnut . **100.00**
Easel, Art Nouveau, brass, tubular,
scrolled and cast dec, 64" **250.00**
Gueridon, Art Nouveau, Schumann,
c1900, marquetry, slightly bowed triangular top, fruitwood inlay of intertwined flowering leafy vine, channeled hipped cabriole legs, shaped
triangular stretcher inlaid with overlapping leaves, sgd in marquetry
"Schumann/Nancy," 21¼" w, 31½" h **1,500.00**
Music, George III, English, c1760–70,
mahogany, fluted standard, tripod
base, adjustable brass candle arms,
26 x 44" **1,000.00**
Night, Queen Anne, walnut, rect top,
open shelf, single drawer, brass bail

handle and escutcheons, cabriole
legs, pad feet, 20" w, 13" d, 26" h .. **450.00**
Plant, Gothic Revival, American, c1880,
cast iron, painted and glazed earthenware, four sharply angled legs,
pierced openwork dec, two inset tiles
attributed to Longwy, oversized sq
top, 31½" h **1,600.00**
Sewing
  Empire, late, American, mid 19th C,
rosewood, molded hinged top, fitted int., two rounded full drawers,
scrolled supports, carved anthemion, scrolled feet, 21" w, 16" d,
31" h **1,000.00**
  Colonial Revival, Martha Washington,
c1920, solid mahogany, three
drawers, shaped ends, ring turned
legs, 28 x 14 x 29" **100.00**

**Stand, shaving, Queen Anne, mahog-
any, snake tripod feet, $450.00.**

Shaving, Victorian, American, c1840–
50, spool, walnut, 17" w, 25" h **150.00**
Sheet Music, Eastlake, American,
c1875, walnut, carved leaf form crest,
warrior head medallion, two hinged
holders, scrolled legs, 23" w, 42" h . **275.00**
Urn, George III, English, late 18th C,
inlaid mahogany, oval top, scalloped
gallery above candle slide, tapering
sq legs, 16 x 27" **800.00**
Wash
  Empire
    Cherry, mahogany and curly maple
veneer, turned and rope carved
legs with biscuit corners, two
dovetailed drawers, refinished,
20¾" w, 29" h **625.00**
    Hardwood and mahogany veneer,

turned and rope carved legs, two dovetailed drawers with curved fronts, clear blown drawer pulls, dark varnish finish, 15¾ x 19¾" 30" h **225.00**

Hepplewhite, country
Mahogany, sq tapered legs, one dovetailed drawer, refinished, 14 12 x 17¾", 28¼" h **450.00**

Poplar, red paint, stenciled black tulip and heart design on top, splayed base, sq tapered legs, one dovetailed drawer with overlapping edge dec, chip carving and molded edge, 17½ x 17½", 26½" h **425.00**

Sheraton, country
Cherry, sq tapered fluted legs, turned feet, ring turned ankles, dovetailed drawer, refinished, 19½ x 20", 28¾" h **475.00**

Walnut, black painted compass star on top, sq tapered legs, outward curve feet, mortised and pinned apron, one drawer, 22½" w, 23¼" d, 30½" h, ... **350.00**

Sheraton style, curly maple, splayed base, turned legs, one dovetailed drawer, drawer sgd and dated "1840," 17½ x 18½", 27⅝" h **600.00**

Victorian
American, mid 19th C, pine, stained, three quarter gallery, conforming frieze, molded drawer, ring turned legs joined by platform stretcher, 22" w, 18" d, 36" h **275.00**

American, late 19th, pine, basin hole shelf, medial platform with single drawer, turned legs, peg feet, 18" w, 15" d, 37" h **225.00**

American, c1860, walnut, carved, marble top **850.00**

Wig, Victorian, mahogany and fruitwood, domical top, baluster turned standard, turned circular base, 21½" h **100.00**

Writing, Sheraton, American, early 19th C, mahogany, poplar secondary wood, lift lid, tilt up writing surface, fitted compartments for pens and ink, two dovetailed drawers with applied beading, fitted dividers in top drawer, pull out shelf on left side, turned legs, ivory escutcheons, ivory pulls, orig finish, 15 x 21 x 30¼" **3,550.00**

Work, Federal, Massachusetts, c1810, tiger maple, lozenge form top, outset corners, conforming frieze, two cockbeaded short drawers, turned stiles continuing to reeded legs, peg feet, 17" w, 16" d, 28" h **2,800.00**

STEPS

Bed
George III, early 19th C, mahogany, three treads, later green leather treads, paneled risers, 21" w, 27" d, 27" h **1,000.00**

Regency, first quarter 19th C, mahogany, three treads, inset tooled morocco leather surfaces, paneled risers, drawer, turned tapering fluted legs, 20½" w, 29" d, 28" h **2,400.00**

Library
Georgian, mahogany, leather inserts, 30½" w, 16" d, 27" h **420.00**

Regency, mahogany, three reeded D form tiers, two lower cov in later tooled green leather, lined panels on risers, turned legs, 18½" w, 33" d, 26" h **3,750.00**

Victorian, four steps, arm rail support, 76" h **475.00**

STOOLS

Foot
George III, mahogany, oblong padded top, ivory cut velvet cov, cabriole legs, ball and claw feet **1,600.00**

Gothic Revival, Victorian, English, mid 19th C, carved oak, leather seat, 29" w, 16½" h **3,750.00**

Victorian, American, c1850
Mahogany, floral gros point cushion, sq molded base, bracket feet, 15" l, pr **800.00**

Mahogany, upholstered cushion, scrolled supports, 21" l **650.00**

Rosewood, upholstered cushion, serpentine frieze, 18" l, pr **650.00**

William IV, c1835–40, carved rosewood, X frame, upholstered seat . **850.00**

Windsor, early 19th C, circular, bamboo turned legs and cross stretcher, branded twice "M S Marsh," refinished, faint age split in seat, 10½ to 11" d, 6¾" h **300.00**

Gout
American, c1880, walnut, upholstered, rocking type, 12 x 19 x 21" **175.00**

English, c1890, 12 x 13 x 19" **275.00**

Milking, country, primitive, three legs, heart cut out handle, relief carving of cow, old dark finish **275.00**

Organ, Victorian, circular, three fancy metal legs, ebonized stem, upholstered top **125.00**

Pianoforte, Sheraton, adjustable, mahogany, four splayed fluted legs, screw type mechanism, upholstered seat **250.00**

Table, breakfast, drop leaf, Queen Anne, walnut, cabriole legs, pad feet, scalloped apron, 18th C, $4,750.00.

TABLES

Banquet, Hepplewhite, American, late 18th C, mahogany, later eagle inlay, three part, 47" w, 99" l, 28¾" h **3,500.00**

Billiards, B A Stevens, Co, Toledo, OH, 1850–75, inlaid walnut and cast iron, oblong top, geometrically inlaid edge and frieze, joined lions forming X stretcher, twelve cue sticks, orig triangles and cue rack, 110" l **8,000.00**

Breakfast, Regency, c1820, mahogany and satinwood, banded rect top, shallow drop leaves, conforming frieze, cockbeaded full drawer, sq pedestal with canted corners, incurvate platform, scroll feet, 22" w, 41" d, 29" h . **3,000.00**

Card
  Chippendale
    American, c1770, carved mahogany, hinged rect top, case with frieze drawer, bracketed and reeded sq tapering legs, minor restoration, 38½" w, 19¼" d, 28¼" h **2,000.00**
  Empire, birch and inlaid burlwood, "D" shape, trestle shaped feet, 35" h **400.00**
  Federal, late, Salem, MA, early 19th C, mahogany, serpentine top, outset corners, hinged over conforming frieze, star punched, carved, and reeded legs, ball feet, 36" w, 18" d, 30" h **1,300.00**
  Hepplewhite, cherry, inlay, shaped apron, conforming top, ovule corners, flame grain and curly maple veneers, light and dark wood banding, central four petal flower, sq tapering legs with stringing and tulips in light wood, teardrop in dark wood inlay, refinished, 36" w, 18" d, 28¾" h **3,250.00**

Queen Anne, English, rect overhanging top, cabriole legs, pad feet, 33" w, 17 " d, 28" h **1,000.00**

Regency, English, c1815, satinwood and rosewood, inlaid, 26" w, 36" h **1,600.00**

Center
  Art Deco, French, attributed to Jules Leleu, c1925, hexagonal brown and white marble top, broad apron, three scrolling supports of silvered wood, central shaped tripartite stretcher, 54½" w, 29¼" h **2,750.00**
  Empire, American
    Mahogany, rect top, gadrooned edge, conforming frieze, turned acanthus carved standard, circular medial platform, molded swept legs, acanthus carved returns, paw feet, casters, 45" w, 37" d, 30" h **800.00**
    Marble, sq molded green variegated marble top, rounded corners, conforming mahogany frieze, marble pedestal and tripod foot, 37" w, 37" d, 32" h ... **2,000.00**
  Restoration, American, c1850, mahogany, variegated marble top, scrolled supports, conforming platform stretcher, shaped feet, 39" w, 30" d, 31" h **1,200.00**
  Rococo Revival, American
    Belter, John Henry, attributed to, carved rosewood and laminated, shaped orig marble top, old rich dark finish, 40¼" l, 31" w, 28½" h **37,000.00**
    Meeks, J and J W, NY, c1850–60, attributed to, carved rosewood, laminated, orig marble top, Stanton Hall pattern **16,000.00**

Conference, Art Deco, Comm Fixture Company for Los Angeles Pacific Stock Exchange Building, c1930, walnut, massive rect top, wide canted corners, inlaid ebony border with walnut cartouche banding within narrow satinwood borders, edge carved with spaced stylized lobed panels, two octagonal pedestals ending in lobed bronze quatrapartite rect feet, inscribed "Made by Comm Fixture Co, Los Angeles, 1930," 62" w, 15' l, 30" h **11,000.00**

Console, Biedermeier, German, 19th C, fruitwood, rect deep apron, drawer, scroll supports, center wooden backboard and canted base, 21" w, 12½" d, 33" h **600.00**

Dining
  Art Deco, maple and ebony, blue rect mirror top, apron, three supports, plinth bases **1,500.00**

Arts and Crafts, Frank Lloyd Wright, 1955, designed for Hendron, orig inset copper edge **2,520.00**

Colonial Revival, c1925, extension, rect, walnut veneer top, molded apron, hardwood base, six heavy carved legs, pair of "U" shaped stretchers, 60″ w, 42″ d, 31″ h . . . **125.00**

Empire, mahogany, drop leaf, single drawer, paw feet, 28″ w, 51″ h . . . **400.00**

Federal, eastern MA, c1805, inlaid mahogany, two part, rect top, hinged rect leaf, molded edge, frieze centering rect inlaid dies, ring turned and tapering legs, 78″ w, 35¾′ d, 29″ h **23,000.00**

George III, late 18th C, inlaid mahogany, rect top, rounded corners, frieze with diamond inlaid edge, tapering sq legs, brass casters, 47½″ w, 29″ h **3,500.00**

George IV, early 19th C, mahogany, rect top, rounded corners, two baluster turned standards, each with four down swept reeded legs, brass casters, 73″ w, 27¾″ h **3,750.00**

Mission, Limbert, c1910, oak, oval top, branded mark, 44¼″ l **800.00**

Queen Anne, New England, c1765, maple, drop leaf, oblong top, two D shaped leaves, plain skirt, tapered circular legs, pad feet, minor repair to one foot, 56½″ w, 27″ h **5,500.00**

Regency, English, mahogany, extension, circular top with four semi–circular leaves, four down swept legs joined by platform stretcher, brass animal paw feet and casters, 101½″ l, 29″ h **5,575.00**

Shaker, early 19th C, stained maple, drop leaf, rect top, two hinged rect leaves, single drawer frieze, sq tapering legs, 34¾″ w, 35½″ d, 28″ h **6,600.00**

Victorian, oak, pedestal base, paw feet, 48″ d **850.00**

Dressing

Classical, American, NY, early 19th C, carved mahogany, center top drawer flanked by two small drawers, over long drawer, pressed glass pulls, turned stretcher, orig suprastructure missing **4,000.00**

George III, c1815, inlaid mahogany, bow front, single drawer over kneehole section, two drawers, circular ring brass pulls and escutcheons, sq tapering legs, 39″ w, 21½″ d, 31″ h **1,350.00**

Sheraton, selected grain mahogany, single full width drawer, four fluted legs, 31″ w, 18½″ d, 30″ h **625.00**

Restoration, American, NY, c1840, carved rosewood, gondole mirror frame, orig white marble top, drawer, scroll supports with center urn, turned and blocked stretcher . **1,900.00**

Drop Leaf

Chippendale, Massachusetts, c1770, mahogany, rect top, two drop leaves, recessed frieze, cabriole legs, ball and claw feet, 18″ w (closed), 48″ d, 30″ h **4,000.00**

Colonial Revival, pine, sq tapered legs, nailed apron, mellow refinishing, 25½″ w, 39″ d, 29¼″ h **125.00**

Federal

Country, early 19th C, cherry, rect top, deep drop leaves, conforming frieze, straight tapered legs, 19″ w (closed), 42″ d, 28″ h . . . **850.00**

Late, c1830, mahogany, rect, two deep rounded drop leaves, conforming frieze, six spirally turned legs, brass caps and casters, 21″ w, 47″ d, 29″ h **800.00**

George IV, c1825, mahogany, pedestal base **600.00**

Queen Anne, American, late 18th C, maple, rect top, two drop leaves, recessed frieze, shaped apron, cabriole legs, pad feet, 15″ w (closed), 32″ d, 28″ h **1,000.00**

Victorian, American, c1840, mahogany, rect top, molded frieze, ring turned legs, peg feet, 21″ w (closed), 39″ d, 28″ h **450.00**

Game

Colonial Revival, Chippendale style, c1936, figure mahogany veneer top and apron, hardwood pedestal base, three splayed legs, brass paw feet, 32″ w, 15″ d, 29″ h **175.00**

Empire, NY, c1815, flip top, stenciled, acanthus carved legs, caster feet, veneer loss, 35½″ w, 18″ d, 28¾″ h **1,800.00**

George I, early 18th C, carved mahogany, hinged rect top, outset rounded corners, brown leather lined playing surface surrounded by wells and candle recesses, frieze drawer, lappet carved cabriole legs, pad feet, 39″ w, 29″ h . **3,100.00**

Handkerchief, Queen Anne, mahogany, 38¾″ w, 21″ d, 28″ h **350.00**

Harvest, Sheraton, country, birch, oblong top, oblong drop leaves, turned legs, 85″ l **3,000.00**

Hutch

American, country, first quarter 19th C, pine, circular tilt top, sq seat, turned legs, 41″ d, 28″ h **850.00**

American, painted, late 18th C, pine, red paint, circular tile top, sq seat, sq molded legs, box stretcher, 44″ d, 26″ h **1,300.00**

English, 19th C, pine, rect tilt top, lidded till bench seat, 5'11″ w, 33″ d, 30″ h **1,100.00**

Kitchen

Hepplewhite, country, c1790–1800, southern pine, three plank top, six sq tapering legs, refinished, 34½″ w, 108″ l, 29″ h **1,500.00**

Pilgrim Century, late 17th or early 18th C, trestle, white pine, hinged top, large compartment beneath, double removable stretchers, hanging drawer or shelf under compartment, shown in Wallace Nutting's *Furniture of the Pilgrim Century*, 49″ w, 37½″ d, 30½″ h **3,000.00**

Library

Arts and Crafts

Gustav Stickley, c1910, oak, oblong top, apron with two short drawers, hammered cooper pulls, sq legs joined by medial shelf, branded mark, 42″ l, 30¾″ h **1,870.00**

Tobey Furniture Co, oak, cross lapped stretchers, key and tenon construction, 17¼″ w, 23½″ h .. **200.00**

Colonial Revival, Empire style, c1920, oak, pillar base, scrolled feet, 48″ w, 28″ d, 28″ h **400.00**

Federal, late, attributed to Duncan Phyfe NY, c1815, carved and brass inlaid mahogany, rect top, two shaped hinged leaves, single drawer frieze hung with turned pendants, hexagonal supports joined by ring turned and faceted medial stretcher, acanthus carved and reeded down curving feet, animal paw feet, brass casters, 48½″ w, 42″ d, 29½″ h **12,000.00**

George III, 19th C, carved mahogany, rect top, gilt dec brown leather writing surface, matching D shaped flaps, central frieze drawer flanked by banks of double drawers, fluted stiles, tapering sq legs, brass casters, 75″ l, 30¾″ h **4,500.00**

Louis XVI, carved and gilt walnut, shaped top inset with white leather, leaf carved corner blocks, single drawer, reeded tapering legs, stretcher, 53″ w, 30″ d, 30″ h **400.00**

Regency, c1820, attributed to George Bullock, Pollard oak, rect top, rounded corners, gilt tooled green leather inset writing surface, gadrooned edge, three frieze drawers on either side, lotus and berried sprig carved trestle supports with flowerhead carved terminals, leaf-tip carved feet on casters, 65″ l, 29½″ h **85,000.00**

Pembroke

Colonial Revival, Hepplewhite style, Grand Rapids, c1940, plain cut mahogany veneer top and drop leaves, figured mahogany drawer front, solid base, medallion inlay, sq tapering legs, 15″ w, 22″ d, 17″ h . **75.00**

Table, marble top, Renaissance, Victorian, walnut base, white marble, 34″ x 22½ x 30½″, $600.00.

Federal, late 18th–early 19th C, mahogany, rect top, two shallow drop leaves, conforming frieze, cockbeaded drawer, straight tapered legs, 20″ w, 30″ d, 28″ h **1,200.00**

George III, late 18th C, mahogany, oblong cross banded top, conforming recessed frieze, full end drawer, straight tapered line inlaid legs, brass caster feet, 32″ w, 19½″ d, 28½″ **2,300.00**

Pier

Classical, American, NY, c1820, mahogany, carved and stenciled, white marble top, minor restoration to surface **3,750.00**

Empire, American, mid 19th C, rosewood, rect top, conforming frieze, full drawer, gilt acanthus carved scroll supports, mirrored back flanked by pilasters over incurvate platform, acanthus carved and melon gadrooned feet, 38″ w, 20″ d, 38″ h **1,600.00**

Restoration, American, c1850, mahogany, serpentine molded black variegated marble top, conforming frieze, scrolled supports, conforming platform stretcher, shaped feet, mirrored back, 42″ w, 18″ d, 36″ h, pr **3,500.00**

Sewing

Empire, Baltimore, first quarter 19th C, bird's eye maple, walnut pedestal base, two drawers, pull out slide, carved foliate scrolls with floral band around stem, 22″ w, 17″ d, 33″ h **4,200.00**

Sheraton, American, c1800, mahogany, drop leaves, two drawers, orig finish **475.00**

Tramp Art, American, late 19th C, "Mother" inscribed on hinged lid, bowlegs, shelf **850.00**

Side, Eastlake, third quarter 19th C, walnut, oval marble top, scrolled pedestal and legs, 19″ w, 26″ l, 30″ h .. **250.00**

Tavern

Chippendale

Connecticut Valley, mid 18th C, attributed to Eliphalet Chapin, cherry, birdcage supports shaped as miniatures of standard, orig oiled finished, slight restoration to one leg and base of standard, 36½″ d, 29½″h **2,750.00**

Philadelphia, c1770, mahogany, tilt top, circular dished top, tilts and revolves above birdcage support, compressed ball standard, cabriole legs, claw and ball feet, 34″ d, 29″ h **19,800.00**

Georgian, English, mid 19th C

Mahogany, oval tilt top, ring and baluster turned standard, down swept tripod feet, brass casters, 38″ w, 29″ d, 26¼″ h **1,175.00**

Walnut, well formed, single drawer, 30¾″ w, 18¾″ d, 28½″ h **2,400.00**

Queen Anne

New England, 18th C, porringer corners, splay leg, refinished, 30″ w, 21½″ d, 26″ h **1,500.00**

Rhode Island, early to mid 18th C, maple, pine top, single large drawer, turned legs, molded stretchers, old refinishing, 34⅞″ w, 22½″ d, 26½″ h **2,700.00**

Victorian, tilt top, papier mache, black lacquer, gilt dec, center MOP inlay floral dec, 28″ h **400.00**

William and Mary, country, 19th C, pine and maple, rect top, breadboard ends, recessed frieze, turned legs, box stretcher, 33″ w, 22″ d, 25″ h **1,100.00**

Tea

Art Nouveau, Galle, c1895, marquetry, asymmetrical scalloped circular top, burled walnut, rosewood, sycamore, and fruitwood inlay of lakeside scene, hipped cabriole legs pierced and carved with trailing leafy branches, shaped triangular platform stretcher inlaid with autumn leaves, signed "Galle" in marquetry, 28″ d, 31¾″ h **9,350.00**

Tilt Top, Empire, American, c1835, mahogany, oblong top, rounded corners, acanthus carved standard, waterleaf carved arched supports, 17″ w, 22″ d, 29″ h **450.00**

Work

Biedermeier, 19th C, mahogany, three drawers **265.00**

Classical, mahogany, turned and reeded legs and posts, biscuit corners, two dovetailed drawers with beaded edge, pull out bag, 19″ w, 17¼″ d, 28¾″ h **500.00**

Empire, American, mid 19th C, rosewood, sq top, drop leaves, conforming frieze with two short rounded drawers, sq plinth, platform base, bun feet, 17″ w, 17″ d, 29″ h **450.00**

Federal, Philadelphia, early 19th C, mahogany, reeded top, conforming frieze with cockbeaded full drawer, reeded legs, peg feet, 20″ w, 22″ d, 29″ h **2,000.00**

Federal, late, second quarter 19th C, cherry and bird's eye maple, rect top, conforming frieze, two short drawers, spiral turned legs, brass cap feet, 22½″ w, 17½″ d, 28½″ h **450.00**

Hepplewhite

Butternut, removable top, two dovetailed overlapping drawers with int. dividers, mortised and pinned apron, sq tapered legs, old refinishing and repairs, 34″ w, 36″ l, 30″ h **625.00**

Pine, two board scrubbed top, base with old dark paint, sq tapered legs 26½″ w, 48″ l, 28¾″ h **300.00**

Rococo Revival, NY, c1850, carved rosewood, lift top sarcophagus fitted work box, cabriole legs **1,100.00**

Shaker, New Lebanon Community, early 19th C, painted birchwood and pine, rect top, rect splash board, single molded drawer, circular tapering legs, orig red paint, 37½″ w, 23″ d, 25½″ h **9,000.00**

Sheraton, country, American, second quarter 19th C, single drawer, solid 1½″ thick cherry top, tiger maple legs and drawer fronts, glass drawer pull **300.00**

Victorian

American, mid 19th C, walnut, rect top, conforming frieze with two graduated full drawers, turned legs, 23″ w, 17″ d, 28½″ h **400.00**

New York, c1845–50, carved rosewood, fitted maple int., dividers,
turned legs 450.00

TEA WAGONS

Black lacquer finish, raised Chinese figures, landscape, "D" shaped drop
leaves, turned legs, support, two
wheels 200.00
Victorian, brass, glass top and shelf .. 700.00
Wicker, serpentine edge, scrolled handle, removable glass serving tray top 325.00

WAGON SEATS

Wagon seats cannot be classified with seats
from a wagon. Early wagon seats were usually
constructed with a double frame and a basketry–
type seat. They served a dual purpose: in the
house and in the family wagon for additional seating.

Hickory, spindle back and arms, leather
basketweave seat, six legs, 18th C . 750.00
Maple and oak, double chair back,
flame turned finials, scrolled arms,
rush seat, turned supports, box
stretchers, 33" l 1,200.00
Painted
  Ladder Back, two slat back, turned
  stiles, splint seat, red paint, 35" l . 575.00
  Spindle, two seater, turned arms,
  open back, five vertical turned spindles, double stretchers, red and
  green paint, 36" l 800.00
Pine, Windsor, primitive, shoe feet,
30¾" l 500.00
Walnut, Windsor, one board seat, trestle
feet, natural finish, 33 x 28½" 225.00

WICKER

Bookcase, four oak shelves, turned
wood frame, reed and wood fancy
sunburst back, natural finish, c1890 . 500.00
Carriage, serpentine edges, natural finish, orig velvet upholstery, c1890 ... 450.00
Chair
  Arm, Edwardian style, gentleman's
  chair, spiderweb caned circular top
  panel, curved lower back, natural
  finish, c1880 .... 575.00
  Arm, serpentine arms and back
    Inverted triangle design woven in
    back, Heywood Brothers,
    painted, c1890 .... 400.00
    Mushroom shaped back splat,
    painted, c1890 .... 425.00
  Corner, elaborate scrolling, birdcage
  arms and supports, natural finish . 650.00
  High, shell design back, set in cane

seat, wooden footrest, turned
wooden legs, natural finish, c1880 275.00
Side
  Closely woven back panel with
  center scalloped design, closely
  woven shields over legs, Hey-
  wood Brothers and Wakefield
  Co, natural finish, c1890 ..... 350.00
High back, cane wrapped squares, birdcage design on back and legs, hori-
zontally woven reed seat 200.00
Foot Stool, upholstered seat, painted . 150.00
Rocker, serpentine edges with braid-
work, wooden rockers, painted white,
Wakefield Rattan Co 225.00
Settee, rect back, upholstered section
on back and seat, woven arms, scal-
loped skirt 425.00
Stand
  Lamp, scrolled supports, circular
  wooden top and mid shelf, 16" d,
  30½" h 200.00
  Music, three oak shelves, Wakefield
  Rattan Co paper label, c1883 ... 250.00
  Sewing Basket
    Bentwood handle, reed braidwork
    edges, two baskets, flared legs,
    natural finish, Wakefield Rattan
    Co, c1890 .... 250.00
    Hinged circular cov, spiderweb
    caned top basket, lower shelf
    open basket, three legs, natural
    finish, c1870 .... 300.00
Table
  Dining, round, repainted, 20" w,
  27¼" h 150.00
  Library, oval, Karpen Guaranteed
  Construction Furniture paper label 300.00

Yarn Winder, six spokes, pine, $175.00.

YARN WINDERS

Floor Type, primitive, oak, mortised frame, two reels, one stationery, other adjustable, 51″ h **100.00**

Niddy Noddy, hickory, turned, mortised and pinned joints, 18″ **85.00**

Spoke Type

Four Spoke

Primitive, counter snap mechanism, 27″ reel, 41″ h **100.00**

Shaker, Sabbathday Lake, combination of hard and soft woods, sq nail construction, geared side counter needle, 26″ reel, 32″ h . **375.00**

Table model, chip carved base, turned standard, geared counter, one spoke folds back, old red paint, 24″ reel **75.00**

Six Spoke

Pine, maple, and bird's eye maple, counter bell, 16″ reel, 40″ h . . . **175.00**

Pine, primitive counter device, old finish, 26″ reel, 37″ h **250.00**

Twelve Spoke, pine, turned, wooden gear, 45″ h **175.00**

GAME PLATES

History: Game plates, popular between 1870 and 1915, are specially decorated plates used to serve fish and game. Sets originally included a platter, serving plates, and a sauce or gravy boat. Many sets have been divided. Today, individual plates are used for wall hangings.

Reference: Susan and Al Bagdade, *Warman's English & Continental Pottery & Porcelain, 1st Edition,* Warman Publishing Co., Inc., 1987.

Bird, scalloped edge, mauve ground, heavy gold trim, sgd "Vitet Limoges," 9½″ d, $125.00.

BIRDS

Plate

9″, grouse, gold trim, Limoges, artist sgd "Comte de Artois" **50.00**

9¼″, wild geese, buffalo Pottery, 1908 **60.00**

10″, pheasant, Limoge, sgd "Max" . **90.00**

10½″, game bird and two water spaniels, crimped gold rim, sgd "RK Beck" **75.00**

12½″, flying game, hp, heavy gold, rococo border, Limoges, artist sgd "Rogin" **210.00**

13¼″, game bird and pheasant, heavy gold scalloped, emb rococo border, Coronet Limoges, sgd "Brussillon" **245.00**

Platter

16″, quail, two handles, hp gold trim, Limoges, France **125.00**

18 x 14¼″, harvest scene, turkey center, floral border, brown dec, Royal Staffordshire **55.00**

Set

7 pcs, wild game birds, pastoral scene background, molded edges, shell dec, Fazent Mehlem, Bonn, Germany **220.00**

9 pcs, 9¼″ plates, hp, various birds, gold scalloped edge, Haviland and Co **350.00**

DEER

Plate, 9″, buck and doe, forest scene . **50.00**

Set

5 pcs, Buffalo Pottery, artist sgd "Beck" **275.00**

13 pcs, platter, 12 plates, deer, bear, and game birds, yellow ground, scalloped border, Haviland China, sgd "MC Haywood" **3,000.00**

ELK

Plate, 9″, two elk in natural setting, Buffalo Pottery **45.00**

FISH

Plate

8″, bass, scalloped edge, gray-green trim, fern on side of fish, Limoges **50.00**

8½″, hanging type, colorful fish swimming on green shaded background, scalloped border, gold trim, sgd "Lancy," "Biarritz, W. S. or S. W. Co., Limoges, France" **35.00**

9″, bass, Lenox, sgd "Morley" **70.00**

Platter

14″, bass on lure, sgd "RK Beck" . . **90.00**

23″, hp, Charoone, Haviland **200.00**

Set

8 pcs, four plates, 24″ platter, sauce boat with attached plate, cov tureen, Rosenthal **350.00**

10 plates, artist sgd "Hammersley" . **175.00**

11 pcs, 10 plates, serving platter, sgd "Limoges"	**350.00**
14 pcs, platter, 12 plates, gravy boat, bass, blue beehive mark	**250.00**
15 pcs, twelve 9″ plates, 24″ platter, sauce boat with attached plate, cov tureen, hp, raised gold design edge, artist sgd, Limoges	**750.00**

FOX

Plate, 13″, stalking quail, gold scalloped border, Limoges, artist sgd	**350.00**

GAMES, 1840-1940

History: Mass production of board games did not take place until after the Civil War. Firms like McLoughlin Brothers, Milton Bradley, and Selchow and Righter were active in the 1860s, followed by Parker Brothers, who began in 1883. Parker Brothers bought out the rights to the W. & S. B. Ives Co., who had produced some very early games in the 1840s, including the "first" American board game, The Mansion of Happiness. All except McLoughlin Brothers are giants in the game industry today.

McLoughlin Brothers's games are a challenge to find. Not only does the company no longer exist [Milton Bradley bought them out in 1920], but the lithography on their games was the best of its era. Most board games are collected because of the bright, colorful lithography on their box covers. In addition to spectacular covers, the large McLoughlin games often had lead playing pieces and fancy block spinners, thus making them even more desirable.

Common games like Anagrams, Authors, Jackstraws, Lotto, Tiddledy Winks, and Peter Coddles do not command high prices, nor do the games of Flinch, Pit, and Rook, which still are being produced.

Games, with the exception of the common ones stated above, generally are rising in price. However, interesting to note is the fact that certain games dealing with good graphics on popular subject matter, e.g. trains, planes, baseball, Christmas and others, often bring higher prices because they are also sought by collectors in those particular fields.

Condition is everything when buying. Do not buy games that have been taped or that have price tags stickered on the face of their covers. Also, beware of buying games at outdoor flea markets where weather elements can cause fading and warping.

On September 17, 1988, Robert W. Skinner, Inc., auctioned the Game Preserve Museum collection, assembled by Lee and Rally Dennis. A record $4,600 was paid for McLoughlin Bros. "The

Game of The Man In The Moon." A Charles B. Darrow "Monopoly," c1934, sold for $2,400.

References: R. C. Bell, *The Board Game Book*, The Knapp Press, 1979; Lee Dennis, *Warman's Antique American Games, 1840-1940*, Warman Publishing Co., 1986; Brian Love, *Great Board Games, 1895–1935*, Macmillan Publishing Co., 1979; Brian Love, *Play The Game: Over 40 Games From The Golden Age Of Board Games*, Reed Books, 1978.

Collectors' Club: American Game Collectors Association, 4628 Barlow Dr., Bartlesville, OK 74006.

Museum: Washington Dolls' House and Toy Museum, Washington, D.C.

Additional Listings: See *Warman's Americana & Collectibles* for games from the post 1940 period.

A Visit To The Old Homestead, McLoughlin Bros, boxed board game, 1903, wooden box measuring 21½ x 13″, instructions on back of box cover, 19 pcs (spinner, 4 colored wooden tokens, 14 flat round wooden counters), multicolored lithographed board showing beautiful children's figures, track game	**300.00**
An Exciting Motor Boat Race, No. 112, American Toy Manf'g Co, boxed board game, 1925, 11½ x 9¼″, instructions on back of box cover, 4 colored wooden counters, multicolored lithographed board has spinner superimposed, track game	**75.00**
Battles, McLoughlin Bros, 1895, large, cardboard soldiers	**225.00**
Bottoms Up, The Embossing Company, © 1934, 6½ x 3″, instructions on back of box cover, pair of dice and 9 round domino-type counters with pigs' bottoms on their backs	**15.00**
Cats and Mice, Gantlope, and Lost Diamond, McLoughlin Bros, c1890, 7½ x 14″, wooden "book" board game with slipcase, 3 different multicolored lithographed boards, instruction book, box of playing pieces including block spinner, 32 wooden counters of assorted shapes	**120.00**
Colors, Game Of, McLoughlin Bros, boxed board game, c1888, 8 x 15½″, Gem Series, instructions on back of box cover, 23 pcs (spinner, red token, white token, 10 red counters, 10 white counters), multicolored lithographed board, pooling game	**95.00**
Columbia, E. I. Horsman, card game, 1885, 5¼ x 7¼″, 52 cards, instruction sheet	**35.00**
Comic Conversation Cards, J. Ottmann Lith Co, card game, c1905, 5 x 7″,	

instruction sheet, numerous question and answer cards **40.00**

Glider Racing Game, Milton Bradley, boxed board game, 1930s, 14½ x 8¼", instructions printed on center of board, multicolored lithographed board pasted on box bottom, spinner, 4 round wooden colored counters, track game **40.00**

Glydor, #423, All-Fair, 1931, 15½ x 12½", instructions on back of box cover, multicolored lithographed board with attached spinner and 4 gliders, track game **45.00**

Jack Straws, Crandall (of Montrose, PA), skill game, c1869, covered wooden cylinder 6¼" h, 39 wooden paddle letters, 2 hooks, Anagram game as well **95.00**

Jolly Darkie Target Game, Milton Bradley, skill game, c1905, 8 x 15½", instructions on back of box cover, multicolored lithographed board on platformed box, 3 wooden balls, same picture on board, Black theme **200.00**

Leap For Life Game, Milton Bradley, boxed board game, 1930s, 8¼ x 14", instructions printed in center of board, 4 wooden counters and spinner, multicolored lithographed board **25.00**

Limited Mail And Express Game, Parker Brothers, boxed board game, © 1894, 21 x 14", wooden box, instructions on back of box cover, pack of route cards, 4 wooden colored counters, 4 colored flat metal train tokens, board is multicolored lithographed map of U.S. pasted on box bottom . **300.00**

Merry Goblins, The, Parker Brothers, card game, c1900, 3½ x 4½", instructions on back of box cover, 20 multicolored lithographed cards, played like "Old Maid" **15.00**

Militac, Parker Brothers, card game, 1910, 5½ x 4", 52 cards, instruction card, and advertising card, cards show photographs of pre-WWI NCOs, Officers, and weaponry, red backs state "Tactics-The Military Game" . . **35.00**

Neutral Game of War, Peace And Indemnity, The, Biddle Corp, card game, 1916, 7¼ x 4", 104 cards, instruction card, light green backs depicting swords and cannon **35.00**

New Game Of Red Riding Hood, The, McLoughlin Bros, card game, c1888, 6¼ x 4½", 42 multicolored lithographed cards, instruction booklet . . **25.00**

New Premium Game of Logomachy, The, McLoughlin Bros, card game, 1887, 8½ x 6", wooden box, 56 multicolored lithographed alphabet cards

with bird on backs, instruction booklet, invented by F. A. Wright in 1874 **25.00**

Ocean To Ocean Flight Game, Wilder Mfg Co, boxed board game, c1927, 7½ x 12¼", spinner and 6 counters, multicolored lithographed board of U.S. map, directions in lower left corner of board **65.00**

Owl And The Pussy Cat, The, E. O. Clark, Tokalon Series, boxed board game, c1890, 19¼ x 10½", wooden box, instructions on back of box cover, spinner with 4 wooden counters, multicolored lithographed board with turkey and pig **85.00**

Palmistry, manufacturer unknown, card game, c1910, 6 x 5", numerous pcs including 4 diagrams of human hand, instruction sheet, key sheet **40.00**

Parker Brothers, Geography Up To Date, early 1900s, $20.00.

Parker Brothers Post Office Game, educational play acting game, c1910, 9 x 12", contains postman's mask, cancel stamp, sheets of stationery, envelopes, postcards, etc. **125.00**

Quartette Union War Game, E. G. Selchow, Civil War card game, 1874, 2½ x 3½", 48 cards, instruction card, cards black on white, involves battles and Union generals **45.00**

Round The World, Milton Bradley, boxed board game, c1912, 21¼ x 14¼", spinner with 4 round wooden counters, multicolored lithographed board with instructions printed on it, track game **195.00**

Rummy, manufacturer unknown, card game, c1910, 5½ x 7½", 48 cards, instruction sheet **12.00**

Setto, Game Of Syllables, Selchow and Righter, © 1882, 6 x 4", 51 black and white cards, 5 illustrated "prize" cards, instruction booklet, invented by Charles P. Goldey **25.00**

Ski-Hi New York To Paris, Cutler & Saleeby Co., #2117, boxed board game, c1927, 12½ x 7½", one die with 4 metal planes, multicolored lithographed board showing ocean, NYC, and Eiffel Tower, track game based on Lindbergh's crossing of the Atlantic **85.00**

Snake Eyes, Selchow & Righter, card game, c1930s, 11 x 7½", 185 pcs (120 cards, dice cup, 2 wooden dice, 62 chips), instructions on back of box cover, multicolored lithographed cards with "craps" expressions printed on them **55.00**

Teddy Bear's Trip, J. Ottmann Lith Co, card game, c1910, 7¼ x 11¼", storybook, instructions on bottom of box cover together with legend of the storybook, numerous printed cards, played like Peter Coddles **28.00**

Telephone Game, The, J. H. Singer, card game, © 1898, 7½ x 6", numerous question and answer cards, 2 black wooden "receivers" connected to each other by a string **55.00**

Tiny Town Bank, The, Spear, boxed play acting game, c1910, 10½ x 7½", instructions on back of box cover, cardboard bank teller's front, 2 bank books, deposit slips, withdrawal slips, fake paper money and change **85.00**

Uncle Wiggily's New Airplane Game, Milton Bradley, board game with matching box of playing pieces, 1920s, instructions on back of box cover, numerous playing cards and counters, multicolored lithographed board opens to 16" sq, track game .   **45.00**

Ups And Downs Of School Life, Spear, boxed board game, c1910, 12½ x 6½", instructions on back of box cover, 10 pcs (folding board, dice cup, 2 dice, 6 wooden counters), multicolored lithographed board featuring amusing pictures of school life **45.00**

When My Ship Comes In, Parker Brothers, card game, © 1888, 5¼ x 4", 84 non-illustrated cards, instruction sheet **25.00**

Wings, Parker Brothers, card game, © 1928, 5½ x 4", 99 cards, instruction booklet, card backs are pink and white picturing air mail planes **20.00**

Witch-ee, Selchow & Righter, boxed board game, c1930s, 6½" sq, instructions on back of box cover, chamois rubbing cloth and Witch-ee fortunes sheet, Halloween decor, multicolored lithographed deck of cards on box bottom with black witch tissue figure, game based on scientific principle of friction by rubbing **60.00**

Wonderful Game of Oz, Parker Bros, 1921, pewter playing pcs **70.00**

Wyhoo, Milton Bradley, card game . . .   **15.00**

X-Plor US, All-Fair, board game with matching box of pieces, c1922, 17½" sq, 4 metal airplanes and score pad, orange board has multicolored lithographed map of U.S. with instructions on bottom, track game **45.00**

GAUDY DUTCH

History: Gaudy Dutch is an opaque, soft-paste ware made between 1790 and 1825 in England's Staffordshire district. Most pieces are unmarked; marks of various potters, including the impressed marks of Riley and Wood, have been found on pieces.

The pieces first were hand decorated in an underglaze blue, fired, and then received additional decoration over the glaze. Many pieces today have the over glaze decoration extensively worn. Gaudy Dutch found a ready market within the Pennsylvania German community because it was inexpensive and intense with color. It had little appeal in England.

Reference: Eleanor and Edward Fox, *Gaudy Dutch,* published by author, 1970, out-of-print; John A. Shuman, III, *The Collector's Encyclopedia of Gaudy Dutch & Welsh,* Collector Books, 1990.

Reproduction Alert: Cup plates, bearing the impressed mark "CYBRIS," have been reproduced and are collectible in their own right. The Henry Ford Museum has issued pieces in the single rose pattern, although they are of porcelain and not soft-paste.

Advisor: John D. Querry.

Butterfly
Creamer	**875.00**
Cup Plate	**775.00**
Plate, 7¼"	**750.00**
Platter, 14", oval	**1,500.00**
Tea Bowl and Saucer, butterfly center position	**875.00**

Carnation
Coffeepot, high domed	**1,850.00**
Cup Plate	**625.00**
Creamer	**750.00**
Plate, 9¾"	**675.00**
Soup Plate	**725.00**
Sugar Bowl	**775.00**
Tea Bowl and Saucer	**575.00**
Teapot, repaired spout	**575.00**

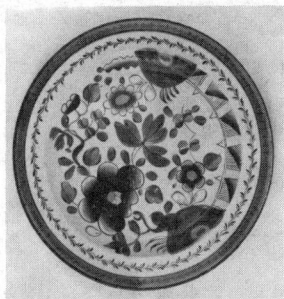

Plate, Single Rose pattern, 8¼″ d, $325.00.

Dahlia
 Creamer 850.00
 Plate, 8⅜″ d, double border 1,075.00
 Sugar Bowl 950.00
 Tea Bowl & Saucer 975.00
Double Rose
 Creamer, restored spout 400.00
 Cup Plate 675.00
 Plate, 8¾″ 750.00
 Tea Bowl and Saucer 525.00
 Toddy Plate 625.00
 Waste Bowl 675.00
Dove
 Creamer 675.00
 Plate, 8¼″ 675.00
 Sugar Bowl 750.00
 Tea Bowl & Saucer 650.00
 Teapot, restored knop on lid 625.00
 Toddy Plate 675.00
Grape
 Creamer 450.00
 Cup Plate 650.00
 Plate, 9¾″ 525.00
 Soup, 8¾″ 425.00
 Teapot 650.00
 Toddy Plate 450.00
Leaf
 Bowl, 8¾″, unusual shape 975.00
 Tea Bowl and Saucer 775.00
Oyster
 Creamer 375.00
 Plate
  6½″ 450.00
  8½″ 525.00
  10″ 650.00
 Tea Bowl and Saucer 375.00
 Teapot 475.00
 Toddy Plate 625.00
 Waste Bowl, rim chips 350.00
Primrose
 Plate, 8¾″, imp "Riley" 650.00
 Sugar Bowl 850.00

 Tea Bowl and Saucer 675.00
Single Rose
 Coffeepot, high domed 1,500.00
 Creamer 450.00
 Cup Plate 1,075.00
 Plate
  7½″, impressed mark 325.00
  9½″ 425.00
 Sugar Bowl 650.00
 Tea Bowl and Saucer 325.00
 Waste Bowl 300.00
Strawflower
 Plate, 9¼″ 750.00
 Soup Plate 975.00
Sunflower
 Plate, 6½″ 675.00
 Tea Bowl & Saucer 775.00
Urn
 Creamer 375.00
 Cup Plate 950.00
 Plate, 5½″ 775.00
 Soup Plate 450.00
 Tea Bowl and Saucer 350.00
 Teapot 600.00
 Waste Bowl 350.00
War Bonnet
 Creamer 575.00
 Cup Plate 950.00
 Plate
  6⅜″ 575.00
  8¼″ 675.00
 Soup Plate 775.00
 Tea Bowl and Saucer 550.00
Water Lily, tea bowl and saucer, pink
 luster border 1,075.00
Zinnia
 Plate
  6⅜″ 550.00
  8½″ 575.00
No Name, plate, 8½″ 375.00

GAUDY IRONSTONE

History: Gaudy Ironstone was made in England around 1850. Most pieces are impressed "Ironstone" and bear a registry mark. Ironstone is an opaque, heavy body earthenware which contains large proportions of flint and slag. Gaudy Ironstone is decorated in patterns and colors similar to Gaudy Welsh.

Butter Dish, 3¼″, octagonal, Seaweed
 pattern, three color, luster dec, orig
 insert 85.00
Creamer, 5″, Morning Glory pattern, underglaze blue and luster 65.00
Cup and Saucer, handleless
 Seaweed, underglaze blue and luster,
  red and green enamel 48.00
 Strawberry, four color, luster dec ... 65.00

Cup and Saucer, 3½″ d handleless cup, 5¾″ d saucer, $75.00.

Mug, 3″, underglaze blue stripes, luster, and red wavy lines	25.00
Pitcher, 9⅝″, Vintage pattern	175.00
Plate	
8¾″ d, pr, urn pattern	300.00
9⅝″, Strawberry, minor stains	35.00
Platter	
13¼″ l, rose design, red, blue, green, and black, marked "England"	75.00
14¼″, Berry pattern, Niagara shape, marked "E Walley"	75.00
15″, columbine, rosebud, and thistle dec, stick spatter rim	235.00
Soup Bowl, 7⅝″, three chrysanthemums, copper luster dec, blue, wide rim	95.00
Sugar, cov, 4⅞″, Urn of Flowers pattern, underglaze blue and luster, red and green enamel, emb lion head handles	75.00
Tea Set, Morning Glory, 9¼″ cov teapot, 6¼″ creamer, 8¼″ cov sugar, minor wear	350.00
Vegetable Dish, 12″, Indiana, blue, red rim	50.00

GAUDY WELSH

History: Gaudy Welsh is a translucent porcelain that was originally made in the Swansea area of England from 1830 to 1845. Although the designs resemble Gaudy Dutch, the body texture and weight differ. One of the characteristics is the gold luster on top of the glaze.

In 1890, Allerton made a similar ware. These wares are heavier opaque porcelain and usually bear the export mark.

References: John A. Shuman, III, *The Collector's Encyclopedia of Gaudy Dutch and Welsh*, Collector Books, 1990; Howard Y. Williams, *Gaudy Welsh China*, Wallace-Homestead, out-of-print.

Daisy and Chain	
Creamer	75.00
Sugar, cov	125.00
Teapot, cov	165.00

Feather	
Cake Plate	45.00
Cup and Saucer	40.00
Plate, 5½″	25.00
Flower Basket (also known as Urn or Vase)	
Bowl, 10½″	175.00
Creamer	75.00
Cup and Saucer, handleless	65.00
Dinner Service, 16 dinner plates, 28 luncheon plates, 8 ovoid salad plates, 4 graduated platters, 56 pcs	1,500.00
Plate, 8½″	45.00
Sugar, cov	90.00
Grape	
Bowl, 6⅜″, pink luster rim	185.00
Creamer, 4″	35.00
Morning Glory	
Creamer	85.00
Cup and Saucer	50.00
Pitcher, 6½″, Allerton, c1890	75.00
Plate, 8″	70.00
Platter, 14½″	135.00
Tea Set, teapot, creamer, sugar, six cups and saucers	750.00
Oyster	
Bowl, 6¼″	50.00
Creamer, 3½″	45.00
Cup and Saucer	65.00
Jug, 4½″	70.00
Pitcher, 5½″	95.00
Plate	
6″	40.00
9½″	100.00

Pitcher, 7⅜″ h, $75.00.

Shanghai	
Plate, 5½″	75.00
Sugar, cov, ftd	100.00
Strawberry	
Creamer	90.00
Mug, 4⅛″	125.00
Plate, 8½″	75.00
Spill Holder, pr, 4⅜″ h	200.00
Teapot, cov	165.00
Tulip	
Cup and Saucer	50.00

Creamer, 5¼"	**75.00**
Pitcher, milk	**110.00**
Plate	
6"	**30.00**
9"	**45.00**
Serving Dish, 9"	**40.00**
Teapot, 8½"	**135.00**
Waste Bowl, 6¾" d	**50.00**
Wagon Wheel	
Bowl, 7½" d	**50.00**
Cup and Saucer	**65.00**
Pitcher, 8"	**175.00**
Plate	
5½"	**35.00**
7½"	**50.00**
Platter	**100.00**

GEISHA GIRL PORCELAIN

History: Geisha Girl porcelain is a Japanese export ware whose production commenced during the last quarter of the 19th century and continued heavily until WWII. The ware features kimono-clad Japanese ladies and children amidst Japanese gardens and temples. There are over 125 brightly colored scenes depicting the pre-modern Japanese lifestyle. Over 140 marks and almost 200 patterns and variations have been identified on pieces.

Geisha Girl ware may be totally hand painted, hand painted over a stenciled design, or occasionally decaled. The stenciled underlying design is usually red-orange, but also is found in brown, black, and green (rare).

All Geisha Girl items are bordered by one or a combination of blues, reds, greens, rhubarb, yellow, black, browns, or gold. The most common is red-orange. Borders may be wavy, scalloped, or banded and range from ¹⁄₁₆" to ¼". The borders themselves often are further decorated with gold, white or yellow lacings, flowers, dots, or stripes. Some examples even display interior frames of butterflies or flowers.

Geisha Girl is found in many forms including tea, cocoa, lunch, and children's sets, dresser items, vases, serving dishes, etc. Large plates or platters, candlesticks, miniatures, and mugs are hardest to locate. Geisha Girl advertising items add to a collection.

Reference: Elyce Litts, *The Collectors Encyclopedia Of Geisha Girl Porcelain,* Collector Books, 1988.

Periodical: The Geisha Girl Porcelain Newsletter, P.O. Box 394, Morris Plains, NJ 07950.

Additional Listings: See *Warman's Americana & Collectibles* for more examples.

Reproduction Alert: Geisha Girl porcelain's popularity continued after WWII and it is being reproduced today. Chief reproduction characteristics are a red-orange border, very white and smooth porcelain, and sparse coloring and detail.

Reproduced items include dresser, tea and sake sets, toothpick holders, small vases, table plates, and salt and pepper shakers.

Advisor: Elyce D. Litts.

Biscuit Jar, 6½", Flower Gathering B, red and gold	**45.00**
Bouillon Cup and Saucer, lid, brown and gold, Rivers Edge	**38.00**
Bowl	
6", nut, nine lobed, three feet, Basket A, dark apple green	**30.00**
6½", lobed, red, gold lacing, Flag	**23.00**
9½", octagon shape, Geisha in Sampan E, red-orange, gold buds, Nippon	**43.00**
Celery Set, child's, 6 pc, master, 5 salts, Flower Gathering A, pine green, Made in Japan	**40.00**
Chocolate Pot, Parasol & Lesson, blue and gold, floral and butterfly ground	**100.00**

Creamer, cov, Garden Bench, black, beige, and red–orange geometric border with gold diaper patterns, red–orange lid and spout with stylized chrysanthemums and gold lacings, hp, marked "Ozan," $25.00.

Cup and Saucer	
After dinner, Parasol B, red-orange, gold buds, celadon ground, Japan	**25.00**
Tea, Kite A, brown and gold	**12.00**
Dresser tray, Flower Gathering A, pine green, Made in Japan	**35.00**
Hair Receiver	
Round, fluted rim, Spider Puppet, blue and gold, marked	**40.00**
Square, Geisha in Sampan, red, marked "t't' Japan"	**18.00**
Nut Cup, pedestal, fluted, Parasol, red, Made in Japan	**11.00**
Olive Dish, 7", oval, Mother and Son C, red-orange, Kutani	**25.00**
Pitcher, toy, 3⅝ x 1¾", cylindrical slenderizing towards top, almost indistinguishable pouring lip, Parasol B, red, Japan	**15.00**

Plate

6", Chinese Coin	15.00
8½", Geisha in Sampan A, brown and gold	25.00

Rice Bowl, Samurai Dance, red and gold **20.00**

Sake Cup, Garden Bench B, red rim . **6.00**

Salt and Pepper Shaker
Pointing, sq, pine green **18.00**
Visiting with Baby, individual, bulbous, blue and gold **20.00**

Salt
Temple A, floral and turquoise border, pedestal, marked **25.00**
To the Teahouse, red, fluted, handled, Kutani **20.00**

Stein, 7½", Chrysanthemum Garden, red, gold buds, marked "Japan" . . . **100.00**

Sugar Bowl, Flower Gathering B, green, gold lacing **15.00**

Teapot, Butterfly, apple green and gold, ftd, hairline on bottom **30.00**

Tea Tile, Feather Fan, gray and gold, marked "Royal Kaga Nippon" **50.00**

GIRANDOLES AND MANTEL LUSTRES

History: A girandole is a highly elaborate branched candleholder, often featuring cut glass prisms surrounding the mountings. A mantel lustre is a glass vase with attached cut glass prisms.

Girandoles and mantel lustres usually are found in pairs. It is not uncommon for girandoles to be part of a large garniture set. Girandoles and mantel lustres achieved their greatest popularity in the last half of the 19th century both in the United States and Europe.

GIRANDOLES, PR

11¾", gilt bronze, French, 19th C **630.00**

13", tulip shape, cranberry, rect prisms, gilt dec, circular foot, Bohemian, c1875 . . . . **310.00**

15", Victorian, pink, enameled and colored wild flowers, notched prisms . . **275.00**

16", two branch, cut glass, regency ormolu, bell shaped sockets, bobeches hung with beads, stepped oval base **1,000.00**

18", oval base, ormolu mounted, gilt brass foliage, porcelain flowers, maroon parrots, oriental birds as girandoles, electrified **350.00**

27", gilt bronze and cut glass, scrolling candle arms, faceted glass beads and pendant ropes electrified, French, early 20th C **850.00**

Mantel Lustres, ruby glass, enameled floral dec, 14" h, pr, $425.00.

MANTEL LUSTRES

9", pr, blue, enameled florals, gold trim, white beading, Waterford crystal prisms **225.00**

10½", green, cut to crystal, ten cut glass prisms **285.00**

12", opalene, green fold over top, white satin glass bodies, gold trim **225.00**

13", pr, white cut to cranberry, scalloped flaring bowl, facet cut prisms **575.00**

14", double cut overlay, white to emerald green, prisms of alternating lengths **250.00**

15¾", Bohemian, cobalt blue, gilt scrollwork dec, colored floral sprigs, two rows of clear prisms, late 19th C . . . **325.00**

GLASS, EARLY AMERICAN

History: Early American glass covers glass made in America from the colonial period through the mid-19th century. As such it includes the early pressed glass and lacy glass made between 1827 and 1840.

Major glass producing centers prior to 1850 were Massachusetts with the New England Glass Company and the Boston and Sandwich Glass Company, South Jersey, Pennsylvania with Stiegel's Manheim factory and Pittsburgh, and Ohio with Kent, Mantua, and Zanesville.

Early American glass was collected heavily during the 1920 to 1950 period. It now is regaining some of its earlier popularity. In April, 1984, Garth's sold the Jim and Eileen Courtney Early American Glass Collection, a major landmark sale. The trend continued with Bourne's three part William J. Elsholz collection in 1987. Leading sources for the sale of early American glass are the mail auctions of David and Linda Arman and the sales of Richard A. Bourne, Early Auction Company, Garth's, and Skinners.

References: William E. Covill, *Ink Bottles and Inkwells*, 1971; Lowell Inness, *Pittsburgh Glass: 1797–1891*, Houghton Mifflin Company, 1976, George and Helen McKearin, *American Glass*, Crown, 1975; George and Helen McKearin, *Two Hundred Years of American Blown Glass*, Doubleday and Company, 1950; Helen McKearin and Kenneth Wilson, *American Bottles And Flasks*, Crown, 1978; Adeline Pepper, *Glass Gaffers Of New Jersey*, Scribners, 1971; Jane S. Spillman, *American And European Pressed Glass*, Corning Museum of Glass, 1981; Kenneth Wilson, *New England Glass And Glassmaking*, Crowell, 1972.

Additional Listings: Blown Three Mold, Cup Plates, Flasks, Sandwich Glass, and Stiegel Type Glass.

Boston and Sandwich, whale oil lamp, Loop pattern, peacock blue, sq base, 8½″ h, $750.00.

Amelung (New Bremen Glass), flask, 4¼″, clear, ⅜ pint, checkered diamond, pattern blown molded, ex-William J Elsholz collection **1,450.00**

Bakewell

- Lamp, pr, fluid, 11¾″ h, clear, blown pear shaped font cut in typical Pittsburgh pattern, large bulbous knops, heavy pressed ftd base, pewter collar, ex-William J Elsholz collection **900.00**
- Windowpane, 6⁸⁄₇ x 4⅞″, clear, church, gothic arch design, sgd "Bakewell" on reverse, Innes Fig 303-2, ex-William J Elsholz collection **2,000.00**

Boston and Sandwich Glass Co., goblet, presentation piece, crystal, engraved hunting scene and monogram "JW" **125.00**

Engraved

- Celery Vase, 5⅛″ d, 8½″ h, clear, elaborate pattern of festoons, small flowers, and leaf band, twenty gadrooned ribs, applied foot with knob stem, early 19th C, slight crazing . **225.00**
- Mug, 3¾″, clear, 24 wide ribs, applied strap handle with curl, copper wheel engraved tendrils, letter "P" **125.00**
- Wine, 5⅛″ h, clear, blown, Pittsburgh type engraved foliage, tapered stem and bowl, applied foot, ex-Trier collection **50.00**

Keene (Marlboro Street) Glass Works

- Flask, historical, Masonic, amber, eagle, sheared mouth, pontil, McKearin, CIV-18 . . . . **100.00**
- Inkwell, 2½″ d, olive-amber, blown three mold, McKearin GIII-29, ex-Corning Museum of Glass collection **125.00**

Lockport

- Creamer, 4⅞″ h, blue, free blown, solid applied handle and foot, folded rim, wide flaring mouth, pontil **600.00**
- Vase, 3½″ d, 7⅛″ h, blue, free blown, three part vase, flared mouth, round base set onto solid baluster stem, thick solid circular foot, 5¼″ d witch ball cov **600.00**

Mantua

- Flask, 4⅛″, chestnut, amber, 16 vertical ribs, terminal ring, attributed to Mantua or Kent, ex-Jim and Eileen Courtney collection **300.00**
- Pan, 5½″ d, 1½″ h, brilliant aqua, blown, 15 diamond, folded in rim, ex-Jim and Eileen Courtney collection, minor flakes at pontil **3,850.00**

Midwestern

- Bowl, 5⅝″ d, 3⅞″ h, cobalt blue, lacy period, ftd, c1830, one moderate chip under rim, small rim chips and roughage, ex-William J Elsholz and James H Rose collections **900.00**
- Candlestick, pr, 7⅛″, clear, free blown sockets, lacy hairpin pattern base, ex-William J Elsholz collection . . . **5,250.00**
- Sugar, cov, clear, lacy, Peacock Feather pattern, one foot scallop chipped **500.00**

Mt Vernon Glass Co

- Lamp, fluid, 6⁷⁄₁₆″, clear, blown three mold, cylindrical font, patterned from half pint decanter mold, mounted with wafer to heavy pressed base of two lion's paws on stepped and scalloped flat oval base, ex-William J Elsholz and George S McKearin collections . . **1,200.00**
- Pitcher, 7¼″, light aquamarine, blown

three mold, quart, McKearin GIII-2, Type 1, ex-William J Elsholz, George S McKearin, and Crawford Wettlaufer collections **7,500.00**

New Jersey, South

Creamer, 5⅞" h, cobalt blue, applied crimped foot and solid curled handle, tooled rim, ex-Gest, Rolfing, and Gotjen collections, int. spall on side of spout **650.00**

Miniature

Compote, 2" d, 1⅞" h, brilliant green, circular, straight sides, hollow knop stem, applied circular foot, McKearin Plate 75, No 20, ex-William J Elsholz and George S McKearin collections . **400.00**

Creamer, 1⅜", aquamarine, free blown, baluster shaped bowl, applied circular flat foot, applied solid ear shaped handle, lower end turned back, ex-William J Elsholz collection **500.00**

Demijohn, 2³⁄₁₆", aqua, blown, globular body, narrow neck, folded rim, applied ear shaped handle, crimped circular applied foot, folded rim ground flat above handle, ex-William J Elsholz and George S McKearin collections . **300.00**

Pitcher, 2⅝", pale aquamarine, threaded neck, applied circular foot, applied handle crimped at base, blown ball cover, McKearin Plate 75, No 10, ex-William J Elsholz and George S McKearin collections **1,000.00**

Pitcher, 7⅝", aquamarine, opaque white loopings, double ribbed applied handle crimped at base, tooled lip, heavy circular applied foot **650.00**

New York

Compote, 8¼" d, tilted 4 to 4¾" h, bluish-aqua, applied lily pad dec, wide folded rim, heavy applied base, ex-McKearin, Wiedeman and Gotjen collections **1,200.00**

Plate, 6⅝" d, ¾" h, cobalt blue, blown, attributed to Lancaster, flake at pontil, ex-Jim and Eileen Courtney collection **65.00**

Pittsburgh

Candlestick, pr, 9", olive green, blown socket with bulbous base, ex-William J Elsholz and James H Rose collections **1,700.00**

Compote, cov, 6½" d, 7" h, lacy, Hairpin pattern, two large rim chips, two bull's eyes on foot chipped, ex-William J Elsholz collection **2,400.00**

Creamer

4½", deep sapphire blue, applied solid handle, heavy crimped end, McKearin Plate 52, No 3, ex-William J Elsholz collection **1,300.00**

5⅛", opalescent blue, 8 rib pillar molded, short circular stem, circular foot, applied handle, ex-William J Elsholz and Crawford Wettlaufer collections **4,500.00**

Inkwell, 5½", clear, free blown, egg shaped body, two reservoirs, applied rounded well, small cup for seals, short knop stem, circular foot, nine applied rosettes, ex-William J Elsholz and George S McKearin collections **1,000.00**

Pitcher, 8" h, eight pillar molded, blown, applied handle **350.00**

Plate

5¹⁵⁄₁₆" d, octagonal, clear, lacy, steamboat, Lee 170-3, minute roughage on upper rim, ex-William J Elsholz and James H Rose collections **1,800.00**

6⅛" d, octagonal, clear, lacy, Constitution "Union," Lee 170-4, small rim flakes, light roughage, ex-William J Elsholz and James H Rose collections **1,300.00**

Sugar, cov, 7¼", deep sapphire blue, patterned in 12 rib mold and expanded, foot not pattern molded, McKearin Plate 52, No 2, ex-William J Elsholz collection **2,500.00**

Redwood or Redford Glass Works, NY

Bowl, 14" d, 5⁷⁄₁₆ to 5⅞" h, brilliant aquamarine, wide flaring rim, heavy out folded edge, applied circular foot, superimposed lily pad dec, similar to McKearin Plate 15, c1831–50, ex-William J Elsholz and Crawford Wettlaufer collections **4,000.00**

Compote, 9" d, 4½" h, brilliant aquamarine, blown, circular bowl flaring to wide out folding rim, short cylindrical stem, circular stepped foot, superimposed gather of lily pad dec, ex-William J Elsholz and Crawford Wettlaufer collections . . **9,000.00**

Pitcher, 10¼", light aquamarine, free blown, globular body, broad cylindrical neck with fine wide spaced applied threading extending to slightly flaring rim, tiny pinched lip, applied ear shaped aquamarine handle, applied circular foot, superimposed gather tooled swooping lily pad dec, McKearin Plate 20, No 8, ex-William J Elsholz and Crawford Wettlaufer collections **19,000.00**

Vase, 4¾", free blown, brilliant aquamarine, urn form, two applied miniature like handles, ex-William J Elsholz and Crawford Wettlaufer
collections **700.00**

Saratoga, NY
Creamer, 4" h, olive-green, yellow
tones, applied solid handle and
foot, attributed to Morris Holmes . **575.00**
Miniature, pitcher, 1¹³⁄₁₆", deep green,
blown, applied handle crimped at
base, McKearin Plate 69, No 3, ex-
William J Elsholz and George S
McKearin collections **700.00**
Sugar, cov, 4½" d, 3⅛" h, olive-green,
yellow tones, wide folded rim, applied solid foot, attributed to Morris
Holmes **550.00**

South Boston
Decanter, 9", pr, clear, free blown, two
bands of chain dec around bodies
and two around necks, period stoppers, ex-William J Elsholz collection **700.00**
Sugar, cov, 5⅞" h, clear, free blown,
galleried rim, one band of applied
chain dec on base and one on
cover, ex-William J Elsholz collection **3,250.00**

Stourbridge Flint Glass Works, salt,
dark blue, lacy, Innes Color Plate 6,
tiny flakes, ex-William J Elsholz collection **900.00**

Union Glass Works
Cup Plate
Lee-Rose 227-B, deep green, dark
triangular spot on shoulder, uneven narrow smoky stream
around shoulder, small rim nick,
light roughage **1,700.00**
Lee-Rose 227-C, deep green, one
small rim chip **1,900.00**

Wheeling
Compote, 7¼" d, 4¼" h, octagonal,
Oak Leaf pattern, bull's eye rim,
Roman Rosette pattern base, two
shallow rim flakes, ex-William J Elsholz collection **1,000.00**
Windowpane, 7 x 5", clear, portrait of
steamboat in center with name "J
& C Ritchie" above, c1833, ex-William J Elsholz and James H Rose
collections **5,000.00**

Whitney Works, Glassboro, NJ, pitcher,
6¹⁵⁄₁₆", medium sapphire blue, free
flown, horizontal threading around
neck, folded rim, small pinched lip,
heavy circular applied foot, solid applied handle crimped at lower end,
Joel Duffield, South Jersey c1835–
40, McKearin Plate 60, No 6, ex-William J Elsholz collection **1,300.00**

Zanesville, OH
Bottle, blown
6", chestnut, aqua, 24 ribs, broken
swirl, pint, ex-Jim and Eileen
Courtney collection **125.00**
9", globular, amber, 24 swirled ribs,
ex-Jim and Eileen Courtney collection **600.00**
Bowl, 8½" d, 3¾" h, amber, blown,
folded rim, minor broken blisters,
ex-Jim and Eileen Courtney collection **450.00**
Flip, 4⅛" d, 4⅝" h, blue-green, 24
ribs, broken swirl to left **350.00**
Pan, 6⅝" d, light green, blown, faint
impression of 24 ribs, folded rim,
ex-George S McKearin and Jim
and Eileen Courtney collections .. **250.00**

GONDER POTTERY

History: Lawton Gonder established Gonder
Ceramic Arts, Inc., at Zanesville, Ohio, in 1941.
He gained experience while working for other factories in the area. Gonder experimented with
glazes, including Chinese crackle, gold crackle,
and flambe. Lamp bases were manufactured under the name Eglee at a second plant location.

Gonder pieces are clearly marked. The company ceased operation in 1957.

**Ewer, light green, matte finish, marked
"Gonder, U. S. A. H34," 9", $25.00.**

Bowl
6½", ribbed, yellow **8.50**
7¾ x 7", flower frog, swirl pattern,
blue and brown glossy glaze **18.00**
Candlestick, pr, 4¾", ext. turquoise, int.
pink coral, marked "E-14, Gonder .. **18.00**
Creamer and Sugar, dark brown drip
and brown spatter **24.00**
Ewer
6", mottled blue, pink int. **20.00**
13", Shell and Star, green **50.00**

Figure

7", swan, shaded blue 12.00
10½", elephant with raised trunk, rose and gray 40.00

Vase

7½", flower shape, pink and mottled blue glaze 15.00
8", beaded, petal and scroll dec, pink 18.00

GOOFUS GLASS

History: Goofus glass, also known as Mexican Ware, Hooligan glass, and Pickle glass, is a pressed glass with relief designs. The back or front was painted. The designs are usually in red and green with a metallic gold ground. It was popular from 1890 to 1920 and was used as a premium at carnivals.

It was produced by several companies: Cresent Glass Company, Wellsburg, West Virginia; Imperial Glass Corporation, Bellaire, Ohio; LaBelle Glass Works, Bridgeport, Ohio; and Northwood Glass Co., Indiana, Pennsylvania, Wheeling, West Virginia, and Bridgeport, Ohio. Northwood marks include "N," "N" in one circle, "N" in two circles, and one or two circles without the "N."

Goofus glass lost its popularity when people found the paint tarnished or scaled off after repeated washings and wear. No record of its manufacture has been found after 1920.

Reference: Carolyn McKinley, *Goofus Glass*, Collector Books, 1984.

Additional Listings: See *Warman's Americana & Collectibles* for more examples.

Vase, bulbous, gold ground, green and red flowers, 5¾" h, $30.00.

Bowl

4½", red roses, gold trim 15.00
9", carnations 25.00
10½", strawberries 25.00

Bread Tray, Last Supper 50.00
Cake Plate, 11", Dahlia and Fan, red dec, gold ground 32.00
Candle Holder, red and gold 18.00
Compote, 9½", strawberries and leaves,

red and green dec, gold ground, ruffled 45.00
Dish, 11", chrysanthemum sprays, red and gold, scalloped rim 70.00
Jar, butterflies, red and gold 20.00
Pickle Jar, aqua, molded, gold, blue, and red painted floral design 25.00
Pitcher, red rose bud, gold leaves ... 45.00

Plate

6", red and gold 8.00
7½", apples, red dec, gold ground .. 18.00
11", roses, red and gold, scalloped rim 25.00

Salt and Pepper Shakers, pr, 3", Poppy 35.00
Syrup, Strawberry 32.50

Vase

7½", brown, red bird 18.00
10", milk glass, painted roses, and leaves 30.00

MARK

GOSS CHINA AND CRESTED WARE

History: In 1858 William H. Goss opened his Henley factory and produced terra cotta ware. A year later he moved to Stoke-on-Trent and added Parian ware to his line. In 1883 Adolphus, William's son, expanded on his father's idea of decorating small ivory pots and vases, with the coat of arms of schools, hospitals, colleges [especially Oxford and Cambridge], and other motifs to appeal to the souvenir seeking English "day-tripper." The forms used were copied from ancient artifacts in museums.

William died in 1906, his son in 1913. Following business setbacks, the firm was sold in 1929 to Geo. Jones & Sons Ltd., who had previously acquired Arcadian, Swan, and other firms that made crested wares. As late as 1931 the Goss name was still being used. In 1936–37 Cauldon Potteries purchased the Goss assets. Production ceased in 1940. In 1954 Ridgeway and Adderley acquired all Goss assets [molds, patterns, designs, and right to use the Goss name and trademark].

From 1883 to 1931 pieces carry the mark of GOSHAWK, with W. H. Goss beneath, and "England" on later pieces. Many early examples carry an impressed "W. H. Goss," either with or without the printed mark.

Other manufacturers of crested ware in England were: Arcadian, Carlton China, Grafton China, Savoy China, Shelley, and Willow Art. Gemma in Germany also made crested wares.

Crests are of little value unless they match, e.g., Shakespeare's jug with Shakespeare's crest. Collectors tend to collect one form (vase, ewer, jug, etc.), one particular crest, or one type of object (boat, cat, dog, etc.). Price is determined not by crest, but size, condition, and bottom mark.

References: Sandy Andrews, *Crested China: The History of Heraldic Souvenir Ware,* Milestone Publications [England]; John Galpin, *A Handbook Of Goss China,* Milestone Publications; Nicholas Pine, *The 1984 Price Guide To Goss China,* Milestone Publications, 1984; Nicholas Pine and Sandy Andrews, *The 1984 Price Guide To Crested China* (including revisions to *Crested China*), Milestone Publications; Roland Ward, *The Price Guide To The Models Of W. H. Goss,* Antiques Collectors' Club.

Collectors' Clubs: The Goss Collectors Club, 3 Carr Hill Gardens, Barrowford, Nelson, Lancashire BB9 6PU; The Crested Circle, 26 Urswick Road, Dagenhem, Essex RM9 6EA.

Advisor: Mildred Fishman.

Vase, model of Roman vase found at Walmar Lodge, 2⅝" h, $25.00.

GOSS

Beer Bowl, dragon	25.00
Bottle	
Canterbury, leather	20.00
Sunderland	25.00
Waterlooville Army Water	45.00
Bucket, Norwegian, Maldon	25.00
Building	
First and Last House	145.00
Huers House	200.00
Look Out House	150.00
St Nicholas Chapel	200.00
Bust, parian, Dickens, 8"	150.00
Creamer, Yarmouth	25.00
Can, Welsh Mills	20.00
Carafe, Goodwin Sands	19.00
Ewer	
Arundel, 4½"	20.00
Chichester, Roman, Beaulieu Abbey	20.00
Japan, Windsor	35.00

Jug, Spanish, Eddyston	30.00
Lamp, Hamworthy, Reigate Poole	30.00
Night Light, Manx Cottage	200.00
Nogen, Irish, wood	22.00
Pitcher	
Cambridge	18.00
Leiston, Abbey	22.00
Pot, Roman, Painswick	20.00
Salt, Glastonbury, Wickford	30.00
Urn	
Laxey, Huntington	28.00
Tewkesbury Saxon, Lizard	24.00
Vase, pineapple	25.00

OTHER CRESTED WARE MANUFACTURERS

Arcadian	
Baby Chick, Cowes	18.00
Bathing Wagon, Stockbridge	30.00
Ewer, Wembley, handled	20.00
Statue, Cinotaph, small	25.00
Toby Jug, Wantage	30.00
Warming Pan, Tesbury	30.00
Carlton	
Bank, bell shape	20.00
Pot, handled, lid	25.00
Urn, Bourne	25.00
Coronet	
Cottage, Tony Panda	25.00
Pot, Arms of Weymouth, two handles, three legs	15.00
Gemma	
Cup, Aberystwyth	18.00
Helmet	30.00
Shelley	
Common market Harbarcuth	30.00
Fish Basket, Fleetwood	30.00
Luggage, Portugal, #53	30.00
Olive Jar, Sussex	25.00
Rose Bowl, Stafford, silver, #147	35.00
Tea Caddy, Abbey of Glastonbury	25.00
Urn, #118, Roman, Chester	25.00
Victoria, Cheshire Cat, matching crest	25.00
Willow Art	
Anvil, Saltash	25.00
Shakespeare Cottage	150.00
Tewkesbury, urn	15.00

GOUDA POTTERY

History: Gouda and the surrounding areas of Holland have been one of the principal Dutch pottery centers for centuries. Originally the potteries produced a simple utilitarian Delft type earthenware with a tin glaze and the famous clay smokers' pipes.

When the pipe making portion declined in the early 1900s, the Gouda potteries turned to art pottery. Influenced by the Art Nouveau and Art Deco movements, artists expressed themselves with free form and stylized designs in bold colors.

Reference: Susan and Al Bagdade, *Warman's English & Continental Pottery & Porcelain, 1st Edition,* Warman Publishing Co., Inc., 1987.

Reproduction Alert: With the Art Nouveau and Art Deco revivals of recent years, modern reproductions of Gouda pottery currently are on the market. They are difficult to distinguish from the originals.

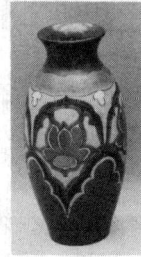

Vase, Hollandia pattern, 10″ h. $80.00.

Bowl
  6½″, multicolored floral dec, two handles, Pelta mark **75.00**
  8½″, floral dec, multicolored, two handles, Pelta mark **75.00**
Box, 4¼″, carved, black, gold, and white, glazed, Regina **150.00**
Candlestick, pr
  4⅛ x 7⅛″, Art Deco, Spino pattern, yellow flowers and green leaves, black ground, satin finish, house mark **165.00**
  12″, unusual shape **175.00**
  13″, blue, gold, and black, c1910 . . **150.00**
Creamer, Vernona pattern **35.00**
Decanter, 11″, matching stopper, 13 x 10″ underplate, Art Deco dec, black, matte finish, sgd "Emanuel" **275.00**
Ewer
  4½″, bulbous, handle, black ground, multicolored floral dec **75.00**
  6″, Art Deco, multicolored, Arnhem . **75.00**
  6½″, cobalt, rust, bright yellow design, marked "2960" **115.00**
Inkwell, attached undertray, Kelat house mark **150.00**

Jar
  3¼″ x 4½″, cov, scenic windmills, houses, and boats, multicolored, glossy finish **65.00**
  5¼″, black ground, blue handles, red and light green bands, marked . . **90.00**
Jardiniere, Art Nouveau dec, russet, royal blue, and mustard yellow, black ground **90.00**
Lantern, 6″, Art Nouveau dec, Plazuid House mark **115.00**
Match Holder, 2¼ x 2⅛″, red, blue, gold and black Art Deco designs, satin finish, striker on base **50.00**
Pitcher
  5″, multicolored, Metz Royal mark . . **48.00**
  6½″, Irene pattern, tulip dec **60.00**
Planter, 5 x 7″, Art Nouveau, Royal Zuid mark, 1917 . . . . **90.00**
Potpourri Jar, 4″, multicolored flowers . **75.00**
Tobacco Jar, cov, 5″, Verona pattern . . **80.00**
Toothpick Holder, sgd "Regina" **45.00**
Trivet, 4″, Damascus, c1895 . . . . **175.00**
Vase
  4½″, Art Nouveau, rust and cobalt . . **60.00**
  6″, multicolored pansies dec, Plazuid house mark **65.00**
  8 x 7¼″, Massa RR, green, cobalt blue, light blue, orange, house mark **135.00**
  10″, Art Deco, multicolored, Isolde . . **165.00**

GRANITEWARE

History: Graniteware is the name commonly given to iron or steel kitchenware covered with enamel coating.

The first graniteware was made in Germany in the 1830s. Graniteware was not produced in the United States until the 1860s. At the start of World War I, when European manufacturers turned to the making of war weapons, American producers took over the market.

Colors commonly marketed were white and gray. Each company made their own special color, including shades of blue, green, brown, violet, cream, and red.

Older graniteware is heavier than new graniteware. Pieces with cast iron handles date from 1870 to 1890; wood handles date from 1900 to 1910. Other dating clues are seams, wood knobs, and tin lids.

References: Vernagene Vogelzang and Evelyn Welch, *Granite Ware, Collector's Guide With Prices,* Wallace-Homestead, 1981; Vernagene Vogelzang and Evelyn Welch, *Granite Ware, Book II,* Wallace-Homestead, 1987.

Collectors' Club: National Graniteware Society, 4818 Reamer Road, Center Point, IN 52213.

Reproduction Alert: Graniteware still is manufactured in many of the traditional forms and colors.

Additional Listings: See *Warman's Americana & Collectibles* for more examples.

Chamberstick, round base, marbelized pink and green, 6″ h, $70.00.

Berry Bucket, cov, medium blue	48.00
Bucket, 9 x 11, gray, iron bail, wood handle	28.00
Candlestick, turquoise	90.00
Canister Set, 4 pcs, robin egg, blue	130.00
Coffee Boiler, variegated blue	210.00
Coffeepot, white, large	30.00
Cup and Saucer, white, blue trim	15.00
Desk Phone, 1940s	15.00
Flask, gray, no lid	70.00
Funnel, 2½″, white, black trim	30.00
Handkerchief Box, pretty lady on top	8.00
Kettle, 12½″ w, gray, iron bail, wood handle	22.00
Ladle, strainer, light blue	12.00
Lunch Pail, 3 pc, dark blue, white specks, wood bail handle	40.00
Measure	
Pint, gray	25.00
Quart, gray, emb "For Household Use Only"	38.00
Milk Pan	
Crystolite green, swirl	
Large	25.00
Medium	32.00
Small	32.00
Turquoise, swirl	25.00
Miniature Egg Poacher, cov, gray, speckled	90.00
Mold, gray, scalloped	20.00
Muffin Pan, gray, six section	12.00
Mustard Pot, 3½″ h, white, cov, matching 4½″ l ladle	80.00
Percolator, white, Foval glass dome, ftd	35.00
Pie Pan, Crystolite green, swirl	16.00
Plate	
8½″, gray, Mottled	12.00
9″, cobalt and white	15.00
Pot, blue and white	40.00

Roaster	
Cobalt blue, swirl	68.00
Iris blue	90.00
Salt, hanging, white, navy trim	125.00
Soap Dish, blue swirl	55.00
Sugar Shaker, brown, mottled	100.00
Teapot, bulbous, blue speckled, ornate pewter lid, collar, and spout, marked "Manning-Bowman"	175.00
Wash Basin, cobalt swirl	40.00

GREENAWAY, KATE K.G.

History: Kate Greenaway, or "K.G." as she initialed her famous drawings, was born in 1846 in London. Her father was a prominent wood engraver. Kate's natural talent for drawing soon was evident, and she began art classes at the age of 12. In 1868 she had her first public exhibition.

Her talents were used primarily in illustrating. She did cards for Marcus Ward, which are largely unsigned. China and pottery companies soon had her drawings of children appearing on many of their wares. By the 1880s she was one of the foremost children's book illustrators in England.

Reproduction Alert: Some Greenaway buttons have been reproduced in Europe and sold in the United States.

Book, *Birthday Book for Children,* 1st Edition, 1880, George Routledge & Sons, $100.00.

Book	
Alphabet, 1885, London	90.00
Little Ann, Kate Greenaway, 1883	75.00
Marigold Garden, illus and rhymes by Kate Greenaway, Frederick Warne & Co, 56 pgs	30.00
Toyland	100.00
Butter Pat, boy and girl	35.00
Button, ¾″, girl with kitten on fence	10.00
Coffeepot, figures, Kate Greenaway	170.00

Cup and Saucer, girl doing laundry in wooden tub	35.00
Dish, 11", oval, Jack Sprat and Sunbonnet girl dec	50.00
Figure	
4 x 8½", boy with basket, satin, gold, pink, and blue trim, marked "1893"	525.00
9", girl with tambourine beside tree, marked "Royal Worcester"	400.00
Hat, bisque, three girls sitting on brim, flowers	90.00
Inkwell, bronze, two children, emb . . .	200.00
Jewelry Box, wooden, stenciled children on front	45.00
Match Safe, pocket, SP, children, emb	50.00
Mug, 2½", pink, children playing	60.00
Napkin Ring, SS	
Boy holding books	165.00
Girl feeding yearling	150.00
Pencil Holder, porcelain	18.00
Perfume Bottle, 2" l, SS, girls in low relief, orig stopper	200.00
Pin Tray, children playing seesaw	65.00
Plate	
5", two girls playing ball	60.00
7", boy chasing rabbits	65.00
Salt and Pepper Shakers, pr, 4½" h, figural, girl and boy.	
Stickpin, figural, bronze, children playing ring around the rosy, c1900	25.00
Tape Measure, figural, girl holding muff	45.00
Tapestry, 14½ x 56", children playing outdoors	265.00
Teaspoon, SS, figural, girl handle, bowl engraved with Lucy Locket verse . .	50.00
Toothpick Holder	
Boy beside tree stump, bisque, 4" . .	60.00
Girl, seated, emb holder	145.00
Tray, girls playing, boy with hoop, silver frame	140.00

GREENTOWN GLASS

History: The Indiana Tumbler and Goblet Co., Greentown, Indiana, produced its first clear, pressed glass table and bar wares in late 1894. Initial success led to a doubling of plant size in 1895 and other subsequent expansions, one in 1897 to allow for the manufacture of colored glass. In 1899 the firm joined the combine known as the National Glass Company.

In 1900, just before arriving in Greentown, Jacob Rosenthal developed an opaque brown glass, called "chocolate," which ranged in color from a dark, rich chocolate to a lighter "cream" coffee hue. Production of chocolate glass saved the financially pressed Indiana Tumbler and Goblet Works. The Cactus and Leaf Bracket patterns were made almost exclusively in chocolate glass. Other popular chocolate patterns are Austrian, Dewey, Shuttle, and Teardrop and Tassel. In 1902

National Glass Company bought Rosenthal's chocolate glass formula so other plants in the combine could use the color.

In 1902 Rosenthal developed the Golden Agate and Rose Agate colors. All work ceased on June 13, 1903, when a fire of suspicious origin destroyed the Indiana Tumbler and Goblet Company Works.

After the fire, other companies, e.g., McKee and Brothers, produced chocolate glass in the same pattern design used in Greentown. Later reproductions also have taken place, with Cactus among the most heavily copied pattern.

References: Brenda Measell and James Measell, *A Guide To Reproductions of Greentown Glass,* 2nd ed., The Printing Press, 1974; James Measell, *Greentown Glass, The Indiana Tumbler & Goblet Co.,* Grand Rapids Public Museum, 1979.

Collectors' Club: National Greentown Glass Association, 1807 West Madison, Kokomo, IN 46901.

Museums: Greentown Glass Museum, Greentown, IN; Grand Rapids Public Museum [Ruth Herrick Greentown Glass Collection], MI.

Additional Listings: Holly Amber and Pattern Glass.

Tumbler, Cactus pattern, chocolate, 4" h, $55.00.

Berry Bowl, individual, Cactus, chocolate, ftd	45.00
Bowl	
Herringbone Buttress, green, 7¼" . .	130.00
Six Fluted, chocolate	160.00
Butter, cov	
Cactus, chocolate	175.00
Cupid, chocolate	575.00
Herringbone Buttress, green	200.00
Celery Vase, Beaded Panel, clear . . .	90.00
Compote	
Geneva, 4½" d, 3½" h, chocolate . .	145.00
Robin on Nest, milk glass	200.00
Cookie Jar, Cactus, chocolate	250.00
Cordial, Austrian, canary	125.00
Creamer	
Cactus, chocolate	70.00

Cupid, Nile green	400.00
Indian Head, opaque white	450.00
Shuttle, tankard, clear	35.00

Cruet, orig stopper, Dewey
Amber	125.00
Vaseline	165.00

Goblet
Overall Lattice	36.00
Shuttle, chocolate	500.00

Mug
Elf, green	75.00
Herringbone Buttress	65.00
Overall Lattice	40.00
Mustard, cov, Daisy, opaque white . . .	75.00
Nappy, Masonic, chocolate	85.00
Novelty, hairbrush, clear	55.00
Paperweight, buffalo, Nile green	600.00

Pitcher, water
Fleur-De-Lis, clear	80.00
Teardrop and Tassel, cobalt blue . .	175.00
Plate, Serenade, chocolate	85.00

Punch Cup
Cord Drapery	18.00
Shuttle, chocolate	75.00
Relish, Leaf Bracket, 8 x 5", oval, chocolate	75.00

Salt and Pepper Shakers, pr, Cactus,
chocolate, old lids, pr	135.00
Sauce, Cactus, chocolate, ftd	48.00

Stein, 4⅜" h, outdoor drinking scene,
Nile green	135.00

Sugar, cov
Cupid, opaque white	100.00
Dewey, cobalt blue	125.00

Syrup
Cactus, chocolate	125.00
Indian Feather, green	165.00

Toothpick
Cactus, chocolate	65.00
Indian Head, chocolate	140.00

Tumbler
Cactus, chocolate	55.00
Dewey, canary	60.00
Leaf Bracket, chocolate	125.00
Shuttle	65.00

GRUEBY POTTERY

History: William Grueby was active in the ceramic industry for several years before he developed his own method of producing matte glazed pottery and founded the Grueby Faience Company in Boston, Massachusetts, in 1897.

The art pottery was hand thrown in natural shapes, hand molded, and hand tooled. A variety of colored glazes, singly or in combinations, were produced with green being the most prominent. In 1908 the firm was divided into the Grueby Pottery Company and the Grueby Faience and Tile Co., the latter making art pottery until bankruptcy forced closure shortly after 1908.

References: Paul Evans, *Art Pottery of the United States, 2nd Edition*, Feingold & Lewis Publishing Corp., 1987; Ralph and Terry Kovel, *The Kovels' Collector's Guide to American Art Pottery*, Crown Publishers, Inc., 1974.

Bowl
7" d, throwing swirls center, curdled green matte glaze, flat sides	100.00
8" d, 5" h, closed, carved water lily design	1,500.00
Paperweight, 4½ x 3½", yellow, traditional scarab	175.00
Pot, 10" h, matte green, yellow dec flower buds	4,400.00

Tiles, water lily dec, white flowers, green pads, blue ground, 6 x 6" each, pr, $650.00.

Tile
3¾", hexagonal, deer and tree, four colors	125.00
6", cellist, mustard dec, red ground .	175.00
6", grape cluster, four colors	175.00

Vase
5", stick neck, bulbous base, mauve, die mark	275.00
7", teardrop shape, green, imp mark, orig label	175.00
10⅛" h, tapering cylindrical molded body, waisted at base and neck, sides paneled from top to bottom, shaped ogee form arches narrow at neck, avocado glaze, imp circular mark "Grueby Pottery Boston USA"	825.00

HAIR ORNAMENTS

History: Hair ornaments, one of the first accessories developed by primitive man, were used to remove tangles and keep hair out of one's face. Remnants of early combs have been found in many archaeological excavations.

As fashion styles changed through the centuries, hair ornaments kept pace through design and use changes. Hair combs and other hair ornaments are made in a wide variety of materials, e.g., precious metals, ivory, tortoise shell, plastics, and wood.

Combs were first made in America during the Revolution when imports from England were restricted. Early American combs were made of horn and treasured as valued toiletry articles.

Reference: Evelyn Haetig, *Antique Combs and Purses*, Gallery Graphics Press, 1983.

Comb, bakelite, two layers, red top layer, yellow bottom layer, lunette parrots in flight, c1900, 7 x 7″, $75.00.

Back Comb, tortoise shell, gilt brass and turquoise glass accents, Art Nouveau	**125.00**
Barrette, 4″, bar type, tortoise shell type, rhinestones	**10.00**
Bodkin, celluloid, imitation tortoise shell, sinuous contours, pique, rhinestones, Art Nouveau	**7.50**
Comb, ivory	
French, paste stones, Art Nouveau, c1910	**45.00**
Oriental, Victorian, c1860	**145.00**
Hairpin, tortoise shell, 14K gold piercework, Victorian, c1870	**125.00**
Ornament	
4½″, plastic, simulated stones, c1935	**65.00**
4¾″, rhinestones, simulated pearls, c1925	**45.00**
Ornamental Comb, 7¼ x 6″, plastic piercework, imitation blue stones, Art Nouveau	**75.00**
Pompadour Comb, faux tortoise shell, gilt brass and turquoise glass accents, Art Nouveau, pr	**75.00**

HALL CHINA COMPANY

History: Robert Hall founded the Hall China Company in 1903 in East Liverpool, Ohio. He died in 1904 and was succeeded by his son, Robert Taggart Hall. After years of experimentation, Robert T. Hall developed a leadless glaze in 1911, opening the way for production of glazed household products.

The Hall China Company made many types of kitchenware, refrigerator sets, and dinnerware in a wide variety of patterns. Some patterns were exclusive, such as Heather Rose for Sears.

One of the most popular patterns was Autumn Leaf, an exclusive premium designed in 1933 for the Jewel Tea Company by Arden Richards. Still a Jewel Tea property, Autumn Leaf has not been listed in catalogs since 1978 but, is produced on a replacement basis with the date stamped on the back.

References: Harvey Duke, *Superior Quality Hall China*, ELO Books, 1977; Harvey Duke, *Hall 2*, ELO Books, 1985; Harvey Duke, *The Official Price Guide To Pottery And Porcelain*, Collector Books, 1989; Margaret and Kenn Whitmyer, *The Collector's Encyclopedia of Hall China*, Collector Books, 1989.

Additional Listings: See *Warman's Americana & Collectibles* for more examples plus a separate section on Autumn Leaf.

Advisor: Harvey Duke.

MISCELLANEOUS

Bowl, cov, 7″ d, blue, Westinghouse	**25.00**
Pitcher, large, lip, red	**30.00**
Roaster, cov, canary, Westinghouse	**20.00**
Water Server, cov, blue, Westinghouse	**45.00**

PATTERNS

Autumn Leaf. Premium for Jewel Tea Co. Produced from 1933 until 1978.

Bean Pot	**90.00**
Cake Plate	**14.00**
Clock, electric	**345.00**
Coffeepot, electrical	**240.00**
Jug, ball	**25.00**
Mixing Bowl, 3 pc	**40.00**
Pitcher, ear shaped handle	**14.00**
Plate	
7¼″	**4.00**
9″	**7.50**
Platter, 13½″	**15.00**
Range Shakers and dripping jar, set	**30.00**
Sifter, metal	**140.00**
Vegetable, oval, cov	**36.00**

Cup and Saucer, Autumn Leaf pattern, 3½″ d cup, 6¼″ d saucer, $12.00.

Heather Rose. Produced during the 1940s.

Bowl, oval	8.00
Coffeepot, "Terrace"	30.00
Fruit Dish, 5¼″	3.00
Platter, 15½″	14.00
Pitcher	12.00

Orange Poppy. Premium for Great American Tea Co. Produced from 1933 through 1950s.

Bean Pot	55.00
Drip Jar, cov	17.00
Jug, ball	32.00
Salad Bowl	13.00
Teapot, Boston	55.00

Rose Parade. Kitchenware line introduced in the 1940s.

Baker, french	15.00
Bean Pot, tab handle	35.00
Bowl, 7½″, straight-sided #4	14.00
Drip Jar, tab handle	16.00
Jug, 7½″, "Pert"	25.00

Springtime. Premium for Standard Tea Co. Limited production.

Ball jug, #3	27.00
Batter Bowl, Chinese red	47.00
Bowl	
6″, cereal	6.00
9″, round	14.00
Casserole, thick rim	25.00
Drip Coffee	75.00
Gravy Boat	18.00
Jug, Radiance, #6	25.00
Plate, 8¼″	4.00
Platter, 14″	9.00
Soup, flat	9.00

TEAPOTS

Aladdin, black and gold	40.00

Birdcage, maroon	40.00
Doughnut, ivory	125.00
Globe, dripless, cadet and gold	175.00
Los Angeles, brown and gold	35.00
Nautilus, yellow, 6 cup	65.00
Philadelphia, pink, gold label	35.00
Plume, pink	20.00
Windcrest, yellow	55.00

HAMPSHIRE POTTERY

History: In 1871 James S. Taft founded the Hampshire Pottery Company in Keene, New Hampshire. Production began with redwares and stonewares, followed by majolica decorated wares in 1879. A semi-porcelain, with the recognizable matte glazes plus the Royal Worcester glaze, was introduced in 1883.

Until World War I the factory made an extensive line of utilitarian and art wares including souvenir items. After the war the firm resumed operations, but only made hotel dinnerware and tiles. The company dissolved in 1923.

Reference: Joan Pappas and A. Harold Kendall, *Hampshire Pottery Manufactured by J. S. Taft & Company, Keene, New Hampshire,* published by author, 1971.

Tankard, cylindrical, impressed abstract floral design, green, matte, impressed "Hampshire," 8¼″ h, $140.00.

Bowl	
5½ x 2½″, green, molded floral dec, matte finish	75.00
6½ x 2½″, blue, molded cattails	50.00
Chamberstick, 7″, hood, handle	60.00
Chocolate Pot, 11″, emb floral dec, cobalt glaze, matte finish, marked	135.00
Compote, 13¼″, ftd, two handles, Ivy pattern, cream ground, light green highlights, red decal mark	140.00
Inkwell, 4⅛ x 2¾″, round, large center	

hole for ink, three holes for pens,
marked **75.00**
Lamp, fluid, 6½", green, marked **60.00**
Mug, East Hampton Library, scenic . . . **50.00**
Nappy, 9", violets dec, ivory ground, art-
ist sgd **65.00**
Shaving Mug, scuttle, blue glazed,
molded ferns, gold dec **65.00**
Tankard, 8¼", imp abstract floral dec,
green, matte finish, imp "Hampshire" **140.00**
Vase
6", opalescent green glaze, raised
petal motif, marked "M" in circle . **80.00**
6⅞", shouldered ovoid, relief molded
alternating leaftips and stylized
buds, avocado green glaze, designed by Cadmon Robertson, incised "Hampshire Pottery," "M"
within a circle, raised "33," c1904 **275.00**
7", tulip buds and broad leaves, green
glaze **75.00**
8½", high relief crocus dec, green,
matte finish, marked **150.00**

HAND PAINTED CHINA

History: Hand painting on china began in the
Victorian era and remained popular through the
1920s. It was considered an accomplished art form
for women in the upper and upper middle class
households. It developed first in England, but
spread rapidly to the Continent and America.

China factories in Europe, America, and the Orient made the blanks. Belleek, Haviland, Limoges,
and Rosenthal are among the European firms.
American firms include A. H. Hews Co., Cambridge, Massachusetts; Willetts Mfg. Co., Trenton,
New Jersey; and Knowles, Taylor and Knowles,
East Liverpool, Ohio. Nippon blanks from Japan
were used heavily during the early 20th century.

The quality and design of the blank is a key
factor in pricing. Some blanks were very elaborate.
Many pieces were signed and dated by the artist.

Aesthetics is critical. Value is added to a piece
when a decorator goes beyond the standard forms
and creates a unique and pleasing design.

Bowl, 8", yellow roses, marked "Havi-
land" **35.00**
Bread Tray, 12", oval, open handles,
roses, artist sgd **50.00**
Compote, 8⅞" d, 5½" h, shallow, pink
roses, green leaves, artist sgd, dated
1907 . . . . **125.00**
Cup and Saucer, floral, marked "Clai-
ron" Ohme, Silesia, c1870 . . . . **35.00**
Demitasse Cup and Saucer, white,
roses and gold, artist sgd "Ahren-
feldt," marked "Limoges" **30.00**
Hair Receiver, violets dec, blue and
white, Limoges blank **50.00**

**Tobacco Jar, multicolored Indian bust,
gold trim and finial, initials on final, artist signed "Florence Weaver, 1925,"
blank marked "Favorite, Bavaria," 7¼"
h, $200.00.**

Ink Blotter, violets and foliage dec,
marked "Haviland" **35.00**
Jug, 5¾", green and purple grapes,
green leaves, gold trim **90.00**
Milk Pitcher, 7" h, white, porcelain, basketweave, yellow flowers, green leaf
handle **17.50**
Plate
8¼", red roses, artist sgd "Geor-
gianna, France" **15.00**
9⅜" d, cavalier and lady scene, artist
sgd "D.L.R.L.," marked "Limoges,
France" **100.00**
10", light green, peaches, gold border,
artist sgd "Ginori" **40.00**
Platter, 23½", yellow roses, green
leaves, gold trim, artist sgd, marked
"Haviland" **240.00**
Sugar Shaker, 3½" d, 4½" h, blue and
white, pink roses, green leaves, gold
top and feet **45.00**
Tankard, 14½", green and purple
grapes, green leaves, Lenox blank . **175.00**
Teapot, 5", purple violets, green leaves,
gold trim, Lenox blank **125.00**
Tray, 8⅝" l, floral dec, two handles, artist
sgd, marked "L. Haviland, France" . **55.00**
Trinket Box, 4½ x 3½ x 1½", yellow,
porcelain, couple and woodland setting, marked "JBH #121815, France" **75.00**
Vase
5", black ground, white orchids, artist
sgd, marked "Rosenthal" **100.00**
14", gold handles, green, pink, and
red roses, Belleek blank **175.00**

HATPINS AND HATPIN HOLDERS

History: When the vogue for oversized hats developed around 1850, hatpins became popular.

Designers used a variety of materials to decorate the pin ends, including china, crystal, enamel, gem stones, precious metals, and shells. Decorative subjects ranged from commemorative designs to insects.

Hatpin holders are porcelain containers which set on a dresser to hold these pins. The holders were produced by major manufacturers, among which were Meissen, Nippon, R. S. Germany, R. S. Prussia, and Wedgwood.

Reference: Lillian Baker, *Handbook for Hatpins & Hatpin Holders*, Collector Books, 1983.

Collectors' Club: International Club for Collectors of Hatpins and Hatpin Holders, 15237 Chanera Avenue, Gardena, CA, 90249.

Museum: Los Angeles Art Museum, Costume Dept., Los Angeles, CA.

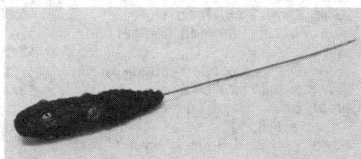

Hatpin, fabric and braid, brown, brass sequins, 8″ l, $10.00.

HATPINS

Art Deco, enameled mercury glass sliding shank	75.00
Art Nouveau, SS, plique-a-jour, two baroque pearls	385.00
Carnival Glass	
Butterfly, green irid	75.00
Zig Zag, purple	50.00
China, hand painted, violets, gold trim	25.00
Crystal, prism shape, 8″ steel pin	15.00
Enameled, turtle, green body, red eyes	30.00
Egyptian Revival, brass, scarab	30.00
Elk's Tooth, gold findings	75.00
Garnet, Etruscean granulation, round, c1860	85.00
Gold Filled, reticulated sides, engraved applied top, 9⅛″	18.00
Mercury Glass, cased elongated teardrop	70.00
Mosaic, 1″ d, multicolored flowers on brass button mount	60.00
Pearls, seed, cabochon, turquoise center, 14K gold, c1896	75.00
Quartz, rose, teardrop shape, gold fitting	35.00
Rhinestone studded, 1½″ d	25.00
Satsuma, flower, gold trim	60.00
Silver	
Plated, tennis racquet	25.00
Sterling, thistle, hallmarked	85.00
Tortoise Shell, butterfly	90.00

HATPIN HOLDERS

Bisque	
Nippon	
Lavender flowers, green leaves, gold beaded edges	35.00
Scenic, large sailing ship	85.00
Schafer & Vater, floral dec, Art Nouveau	225.00

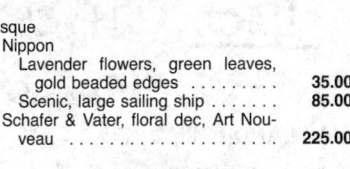

Hatpin Holder, white china ground, red roses, green leaves, gilt circles, 4″ h, $35.00.

China	
Austrian, 5″, hp blue forget-me-nots, marked	35.00
Bavarian, portrait of two boys eating fruit, gold ground, marked	50.00
Belleek, gold leaves, tiny blue flowers, red Willets mark	100.00
Germany, pink flowers, green luster, marked	20.00
Hand Painted	
4″, violets, gold trim and beading	75.00
4½″, figure "8″ tray, attached hatpin holder, ring tree, purple violets on white ground	50.00
Limoges, grapes, pink roses, matte finish, artist sgd	60.00
Jasperware, 5¼″ h, lilac, Art Nouveau blown out woman's face, elaborate hair style, gold trim	125.00
Royal Bayreuth, rose tapestry, three colored roses, blue mark	350.00
Schlegelmilch, 4¾″, scalloped base, roses, luster finish, red mark "R. S. Prussia"	215.00
Teplitz, cameo, ram handles	85.00
Glass	
Bristol, 6½″, ftd, multicolored jewels, blue ground, brass fittings	100.00

Carnival, Grape and Cable pattern,
marigold, 7" h **200.00**

H&C°   H&C°
L   L
        FRANCE

HAVILAND CHINA

History: In 1842, American china importer
David Haviland moved to Limoges, France, where
he began manufacturing and decorating china
specifically for the US market. Haviland is synonymous with fine, white, translucent porcelain although early hand painted patterns were generally
larger and darker colored on heavier whiteware
blanks than are later ones.

David revolutionized French china factories by
both manufacturing the whiteware blank and decorating it at the same site. In addition, Haviland
and Company pioneered the use of decals in decorating china.

David's sons, Charles Edward and Theodore
split the company in 1892. Theodore opened an
American division in 1936 which continues until
today. In 1941 Theodore bought out Charles Edward's heirs and recombined both companies under the original name of H and Co. The Haviland
family sold its interests in 1981.

Charles Field Haviland, cousin of Charles Edward and Theodore, worked for, and then ran, the
Casseaux Works after his marriage in 1857 until
1882. Items continued to carry his name as decorator until 1941.

Haviland patterns were not consistently named
until after 1926. Pattern identification is difficult
because of the similarity found in the over 66,000
patterns that have been made. Numbers assigned
by Arlene Schleiger and illustrated in her books
have become the identification standard for matching.

References: Mary Frank Gaston, *Haviland Collectibles & Art Objects*, Collector Books, 1984;
Arlene Schleiger, *Two Hundred Patterns of Haviland China, Books I–V*, published by author, 1950–
1977.

Asparagus Dish, scalloped edge, deep
  pink to purple flowers **65.00**
Bone Dish, Pansy, Ragged Robin, gray
  and pink, 1885 mark **25.00**
Bouillon, matching saucer, Rajah pat-
  tern, marked "Theo Haviland" **20.00**
Bowl
  5", fruit, "Ranson," white, H and Co . **10.00**
  6", oatmeal, scalloped edge with gold **18.00**
  7½", soup, "Troy," blue scroll, pink
    flower border **16.00**

Gravy Boat, attached underplate, conventional border, No. 278, 7" w, $50.00.

Butter Dish
  Silver Anniversary pattern, 3 pc, H
    and Co **60.00**
  Gold Band, 2 pc, Theo. Hav. **45.00**
Butter Pat, sq, rounded corners, gold
  trim **10.00**
Celery Dish, scalloped edge, green
  flowers, pale pink scroll **45.00**
Cereal Bowl, Rajah pattern, marked
  "Theo Haviland" **8.00**
Cream Soup and Saucer, scroll border
  in cranberry and blue **30.00**
Creamer and Sugar
  Gold Band, 1930s, Theo. Hav. **45.00**
  Rajah pattern, marked "Theo Havi-
    land" **20.00**
  Scalloped, small pink flowers, gold
    trim **65.00**
Cup and Saucer
  Coffee, scalloped gold edge, deep
    pink flowers **30.00**
  Tea, small blue flowers, green leaves **25.00**
Demitasse Cup and Saucer, 1885 . . . **30.00**
Dinner Set
  Gold Band, 77 pcs, service for 12,
    Theo. Hav. **1,195.00**
  Pink flowered, 55 pcs, service for 8,
    H and Co **895.00**
Gravy Boat
  Oval, pink flowers, blue ribbon, H and
    Co **45.00**
  Round, tray, double handles and lips,
    navy and rust, Theo. Hav. **35.00**
Oyster Plate, 9", blue and pink flowers,
  marked "Haviland & Co" **80.00**
Plate
  6", bread and butter, Rajah pattern,
    marked "Theo Haviland" **5.00**
  7", salad, Rajah pattern, marked
    "Theo Haviland" **9.00**
  7½", bread and butter, gold scalloped
    edge, pink flowers **16.00**
  8½", gold, pink clover, ornate border,
    1905 . . . . **40.00**
  9", luncheon
    Frontenac **18.00**

Whiteware, hp, pink rose, sgd H
and Co **22.00**
9½", dinner, "Princess," H and Co . . **22.00**
9¾", dinner, white, scalloped edge . **20.00**
10", cake
   Gold handles and border **35.00**
Platter
12", turquoise morning glories, gold
scalloped edge **35.00**
16", gold band, scalloped end han-
dles, Theo. Hav. **55.00**
22", deep pink flowers, two wells,
fancy gold edges **75.00**
Relish Dish, blue and pink flowers . . . **25.00**
Soup Plate
7½", Eden pattern, marked "Theo
Haviland" **15.00**
9½", olive and rust flowers, 1885
mark **22.00**
Vegetable Dish
Gold edges, small pink roses, cov . . **65.00**
Moss Rose, blue edges, rope han-
dles, 1885, cov **65.00**

HEISEY GLASS

History: The A. H. Heisey Glass Co. began producing glasswares in April, 1896, in Newark, Ohio. Heisey was not a newcomer to the field, having been associated with the craft since his youth.

Many blown and molded patterns were produced in crystal, colored, milk (opalescent), and Ivorina Verde (custard) glass. Decorative techniques of cutting, etching, and silver deposit were employed. Glass figurines were introduced in 1933 and continued until 1957 when the factory ceased production. All Heisey glass is notable for its clarity. Not all Heisey glassware is marked with the familiar "H" within a diamond.

References: Neila Bredehoft, *The Collector's Encyclopedia of Heisey Glass, 1925–1938,* Collector Books, 1986; Mary Louise Burns, *Heisey's Glassware of Distinction,* 2nd edition, published by author, 1983; Lyle Conder, *Collector's Guide To Heisey's Glassware for Your Table,* L-W Books, 1984; Tom Felt and Bob O'Grady, *Heisey Candlesticks, Candelabra, and Lamps,* Heisey Collectors of America, Inc, 1984; Sandra Stoudt, *Heisey On Parade,* Wallace-Homestead, 1985.

Collectors' Club: Heisey Collectors of America, P. O. Box 4367, Newark, OH, 43055.

Museum: National Heisey Glass Museum, Newark, OH.

Reproduction Alert: Some Heisey molds were sold to Imperial Glass of Bellaire, Ohio, and certain items were reissued. These pieces may be mistaken for the original Heisey. Some of the reproductions were produced in colors which were never made by Heisey and have become collectible in their own right.

Examples include: the Colt family in Crystal, Carmel Slag, Ultra Blue, and Horizon Blue; the mallard with wings up in Carmel Slag; Whirlpool (Provincial) in crystal and colors; and, Waverly, 7" oval footed compote in Carmel Slag.

Almond Dish, Greek Key, crystal, indi-
vidual size **35.00**
Animal
Asiatic Pheasant **250.00**
Cygnet **125.00**
Giraffe, head back **125.00**
Goose, wings down **285.00**
Mallard **150.00**
Pony, standing **50.00**
Rooster, fighting **125.00**
Scottie **95.00**
Sparrow **65.00**
Tropical Fish, frosted **850.00**
Ashtray
Crystolite, Zircon, sgd **60.00**
Grape Leaf, Moongleam **65.00**
Horsehead **45.00**
Kohinoor, Zircon **85.00**
Orchid, sq **30.00**
Puritan, sgd **20.00**
Banana Split Dish, Yeoman, Moon-
gleam, ftd **35.00**
Basket
Crystolite, 6" **165.00**
Daisy cutting, 7", sgd **175.00**
Bitters Bottle, Puritan, paper label . . . **45.00**
Bonbon
Fern, 6", handle, Zircon **60.00**
Lariat **25.00**
Lodestar, 11", Dawn, crimped **250.00**
Yeoman, 6½", Flamingo **30.00**
Bookends, pr, fish **150.00**
Bowl
Crystal, rolled rim, black and gold
trim, star base, 9" **30.00**
Empress, Moongleam (green,) 6",
dolphin ftd **40.00**
Horn of Plenty, 11", centerpiece, co-
balt blue **350.00**
Orchid, oval, dressing, 2 pt **45.00**
Pineapple and Fan, 8" **35.00**
Queen Anne, 9" **65.00**
Waverly, 10", crimped **75.00**
Butter Dish, cov
Cabachon, orchid, etched,¼ lb, sgd **225.00**
Rose, crystal **160.00**
Candelabra
Ridgeleigh, clear, Moongleam base,
3-light, pr **275.00**
Trident, 2-light, Sahara, 5" **90.00**
Candleblock, Crystolite, sq **8.00**
Candlesticks, pr
Cathedral, Moongleam, 9" **125.00**
Orchid, 5", two light, trident **110.00**

Queen Anne, crystal, bobeches and
prisms 150.00
Candy Dish, cov
  Empress, Flamingo, dolphin base, ftd   27.50
  Pleat and Panel, Flamingo, ftd, sgd .   50.00
  Rose, crystal, 5¼", flat, round 150.00
Celery
  Orchid, 11" 45.00
  Twist pattern, Moongleam 35.00
Champagne
  Galaxy, green, 5" 22.00
  Lariat, crystal 15.00
  Orchid 30.00
  Rose, crystal 32.00
Cigarette Holder
  Carcassone, crystal 12.75
  Kohinoor, sgd 20.00
Claret, Victorian, crystal, 4 oz, two ball
  stem 15.00
Coaster
  Maple, Flamingo 18.00
  Oak Leaf 25.00
Cocktail
  Aqua Caliente, Tally Ho etch, crystal
  stem 35.00
  Creole, Alexandrite, crystal stem ...   120.00
  Orchid 40.00
  Rooster stem 45.00
  Rosalie, crystal, 3 oz 18.00
  Seahorse stem 140.00
Cocktail Shaker, Fox Chase etching,
  clear 150.00
Cologne Bottle, Victorian, crystal, orig
  stopper 32.50
Compote
  Pleat and Panel, Flamingo, gold trim,
  cov, 7" 65.00
  Waverly, orchid etching, 6¼", low
  standard 50.00
Condiment Bottle, Orchid 250.00
Cookie Plate, Lariat 20.00
Cordial
  Jamestown, Rosalie etching 75.00
  Kenilworth 100.00
  Oxford, sgd 24.00
Cream Soup, Yeoman, green 15.00

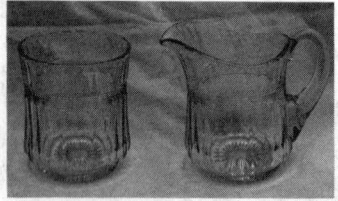

**Creamer and Sugar, Beaded Flute,
clear, marked, $45.00.**

Creamer and Sugar
  Lariat, crystal 16.75
  Old Colony, crystal, dolphin ftd 50.00
  Orchid, individual size 50.00
  Prince of Wales, ruby stained 100.00
  Victorian, crystal 21.00
Cruet
  Colonial, Flamingo, octagonal stop-
  per 600.00
  Pleat and Panel, Moongleam 95.00
  Priscilla 20.00
  Saturn 36.00
  Yeoman, Flamingo 45.00
Cup and Saucer, Orchid pattern 55.00
Custard Cup, Lariat 10.00
Goblet
  Carcassone, Sahara, 11 oz 12.00
  Duquesne, clear, 9 oz 10.00
  Minuet, crystal 35.00
  Narrow Flute, clear 25.00
  Orchid pattern 45.00
  Renaissance, crystal 35.00
  Sussex pattern, Stiegel cobalt blue .   100.00
  Trojan, Flamingo, 8 oz 20.00
Humidor, patent 7/7/08 ....   115.00
Ice Bucket
  Empress, crystal 55.00
  Twist, Moongleam 75.00
Iced Tea Tumbler
  Orchid pattern 45.00
  Rose 38.00
Ladle, crystal 28.00
Lemon Dish, cov, Empress, 6½", dol-
  phin handles 60.00
Madonna, Zircon, frosted, sgd 1,800.00
Mayonnaise
  Octagon, Moongleam, ftd 50.00
  Plantation, liner, spoon 65.00
Mint Dish, Bowtie, green, 4", handles .   40.00
Mustard, cov
  Coarse Rib, ruby stained 55.00
  Narrow Flute 35.00
  Priscilla 25.00
  Whirlpool 40.00
Nut Dish, Empress, Moongleam, indi-
  vidual size, dolphin ftd 32.00
Pitcher, Rose, crystal, ice lip 550.00
Plate
  Old Colony, Sahara, 8½", sq 22.00
  Rosalie, crystal, 16" 58.00
  Rose, 8" 20.00
Relish, three sections
  Lariat 45.00
  Yeoman, Moongleam, handle 55.00
Rose Bowl, Diamond Optic, Moongleam   48.00
Sauce, Prince of Wales, 5" d, clear ...   15.00
Sherbet
  Etching #415 ....   15.00
  Orchid 25.00
  Plantation Ivy, crystal 16.00
  Rose, crystal 28.00
Sherry, goose stem 160.00

Sugar Shaker, Plantation, clear	**115.00**
Toothpick	
Prince of Wales, clear, gold trim	**135.00**
Priscilla, clear	**65.00**
Punty Band, ruby stained	**55.00**
Torte Plate, 14″, Orchid, rolled edge	**40.00**
Tumbler	
Ambassador, crystal, 8 oz	**15.00**
Old Colony, Sahara, 5¾″, ftd	**25.00**
Provencial, Zircon, 9 oz, ftd	**55.00**
Vase	
Ridgeleigh, triangle	**40.00**
Warwick, cornucopia, 9½″, pr	**75.00**
Wine	
Locket on Chain	**100.00**
Old Dominion, Alexandrite	**115.00**
Orchid	**48.00**
Victorian	**20.00**
Wabash	**15.00**

HOLLY AMBER

History: Holly Amber, originally called Golden Agate, was produced by the Indiana Tumbler and Goblet Works of the National Glass Co., Greentown, Indiana. Jacob Rosenthal created the color in 1902. Holly Amber is a gold colored glass with a marbleized onyx color on raised parts.

A new pattern, Holly [No. 450], was designed by Frank Jackson for Golden Agate. Between January 1903 and June 1903, more than 35 items were made in this pattern; the factory was destroyed by fire in June.

References: Brenda Measell and James Measell, *A Guide To Reproductions of Greentown Glass, 2nd Edition*, The Printing Press, 1974; James Measell, *Greentown Glass, The Indiana Tumbler & Goblet Co.*, Grand Rapids Public Museum, 1979.

Collectors' Club: National Greentown Glass Association, 1807 West Madison Street, Kokomo, IN 46901.**Museums:** Greentown Glass Museum, Greentown, IN; Grand Rapids Public Museum [Ruth Herrick Greentown Glass Collection], MI.

Additional Listing: Greentown Glass.

Tumbler, 3⅞″ h, $350.00.

Bowl	
7½ x 4½ x 2″, oval	**360.00**
8½″, berry	**375.00**
Butter, cov, 7¼ x 6¼″	**1,200.00**
Cake Stand	**2,000.00**
Compote	
4¾″ d, jelly, open	**450.00**
8½ x 12″, cov	**1,800.00**
Creamer, 4½″ h	**425.00**
Cruet, 6½″ h, orig stopper	**2,100.00**
Honey, cov	**750.00**
Match Holder	**400.00**
Mug, 4½″ h, handle	**525.00**
Nappy	**375.00**
Parfait	**575.00**
Relish, oval	**275.00**
Salt and Pepper Shakers, pr	**500.00**
Sauce	**225.00**
Spooner	**425.00**
Sugar, open	**425.00**
Syrup, 5¾″ h, silverplated hinged lid	**2,000.00**
Toothpick, 2½″ h	**475.00**
Tumbler	**350.00**

HORN

History: For centuries horns from animals have been used for various items, e.g., drinking cups, spoons, powder horns, and small dishes. Some pieces of horn have designs scratched in them. Around 1880 furniture made from the horns of Texas longhorn steers was popular in Texas and the southwestern United States.

Additional Listings: Firearm Accessories.

Tumbler, 2½″ h, $25.00.

Beaker, 5¼″ h, George III, SS lined, London maker's mark, 1815, ext. SS rim bordered with rolled band of oak leaves and acorns, contemporary monogram	**800.00**
Calling Card Case, horn and ivory, floral design	**40.00**
Comb Case, 7½ x 9″, diamond shape mirror, pocket	**35.00**
Furniture	
Chair, arched back, brass acorn finial, splayed legs, upholstered seat	

missing, American or German, late 19th C, pr	**2,000.00**
Stand, Victorian, four horns form legs, American Southwest, 19th C	**275.00**
Shoehorn, scratched carved, 1756 ...	**65.00**
Spoon, 5½", monogrammed "MBL, 1907," thistle, hallmarked	**45.00**
Tea Caddy, 12¼ x 9¼ x 7½", sarcophagus shape, dark stain, tapering ribbed sides and cov, wide plain border, claw and ball feet, lobed domical flowerhead knop, Anglo–Indian, c1815 ...	**900.00**

HULL POTTERY

History: In 1905 Addis E. Hull purchased the Acme Pottery Company, Crooksville, Ohio. In 1917 the A. E. Hull Pottery Company began making a line of art pottery, novelties, stoneware, and kitchenware, later including the famous Little Red Riding Hood line. Most items had a matte finish with shades of pink and blue or brown predominating.

After a disastrous flood and fire in 1950, J. Brandon Hull reopened the factory in 1952 as the Hull Pottery Company. New, more modern style molds, mostly with glossy finish, were produced. The company currently produces pieces, e.g. the Regal and Floraline lines, for sale to florists.

Hull pottery molds and patterns are easily identified. Pre-1950 vases are marked "Hull USA" or "Hull Art USA" on the bottom. Many also retain their paper labels. Post-1950 pieces are marked "Hull" in large script or "HULL" in block letters.

Each pattern has a distinctive number, e.g., Wildflower with a "W" and number, Waterlily with an "L" and number, Poppy with 600 numbers, Orchid with 300 numbers, etc. Early stone pieces have an H.

References: Brenda Roberts, *The Collectors Encyclopedia Of Hull Pottery,* Collector Books, 1980; Mark E. Supnick, Collecting Hull Pottery's "Little Red Riding Hood": A Pictorial Reference and Price Guide, L-W Book Sales, 1989.

Additional Listings: See *Warman's Americana & Collectibles* for more examples.

Advisor: Joan Hull.

PRE-1950 (MATTE)

Bowknot	
Ewer, B1, 5½", green to blue	**45.00**
Vase, B4, 6½"	**40.00**
Calla Lily	
Bowl, 500-33, 10"	**65.00**
Vase	
520-33, 10½"	**75.00**
530-33, 5"	**30.00**

Camelia	
Ewer, 106, 13½"	**175.00**
Vase	
123, 6½"	**35.00**
138, 6¼"	**35.00**
Dogwood	
Basket, 501, 7½"	**65.00**
Ewer, 516, 11½"	**75.00**
Vase, 517, 4¾"	**25.00**
Little Red Riding Hood	
Batter Pitcher, side pour, 7"	**175.00**
Grease Jar, wolf	**350.00**
Spice, set of 6	**2,100.00**
Magnolia	
Cornucopia, double, 6, 12"	**65.00**
Ewer, 14, 4¾"	**30.00**
Vase, 21, 12½", tassel handle	**85.00**

Ebbtide, figurine, E-6, script mark "Hull, USA," $45.00.

Magnolia, pink glossy	
Cornucopia, H10, 8½"	**45.00**
Ewer, H16, 12½", winged handle ...	**75.00**
Vase, H1, 5½"	**25.00**
Orchid	
Bowl, 312, 7"	**40.00**
Vase	
304, 10¼"	**85.00**
306, 6¾"	**40.00**
Poppy	
Planter, 602, 6½"	**45.00**
Vase, 606, 10½"	**65.00**
Rosella, pink glossy	
Cornucopia, R13, 8½"	**45.00**
Ewer, R9, 6½"	**35.00**
Heart shape, R8, 6½"	**35.00**
Stoneware	
Stein, H499, 6½"	**30.00**
Tankard, H492, 8½"	**100.00**

Vase, H32, 8″	40.00
Thistle, 53	40.00
Tulip	
Jardiniere, 115-33, 7″	65.00
Vase	
104-33, 6″	40.00
107-33, 6″	335.00
Waterlily	
Ewer, L17, 13½″	175.00
Tea Set, L18, 19, 20	150.00
Vase, L15, 12½″	75.00
Wildflower	
Basket, W16, 10½″	150.00
Vase	
W1, 5½″	25.00
W18, 12½″	65.00
Woodland	
Bud Vase, W15, 8½″	50.00
Jardiniere, W7, 5½″	30.00
Wall Pocket, W13, 7½″, shell	45.00

POST 1950 (GLOSSY)

Blossom Flite	
Basket, T4, 8½″	50.00
Honey Jug, T1, 6″	30.00
Pitcher, T3, 8½″	50.00
Butterfly	
Lavabo Set, B25, 16″	80.00
Vase, B10, 7″	35.00
Capri	
Dish, C63, leaf	50.00
Planter, C81, swan, double	50.00
Ebb Tide	
Angel Fish, E6, 7¾″	45.00
Planter, E3, mermaid	65.00
Imperial	
Madonna, 7″	35.00
Swan, 69, 8½″	30.00
Urn, F88	20.00
Parchment & Pine	
Cornucopia, S6	55.00
Planter, S5, scroll	45.00
Serenade	
Candlestick, S16, pr	50.00
Fruit bowl, S15, ftd	75.00
Tea Set, S17, 18, 19	100.00
Sunglow	
Basket, 84, 6½″	35.00
Grease Jar, 53, 5¼″	25.00
Salt and Pepper Shaker, 54, 2¾″, pr	15.00
Tokay, Tuscany	
Basket, 15, 12″	65.00
Vase, 2, 6″	30.00
Tropicana	
Pitcher, T56, 12½″	65.00
Vase, T53, 8½″	45.00
Woodland, glossy	
Cornucopia, W2	25.00
Pitcher, W3	30.00
Vase, W18	45.00

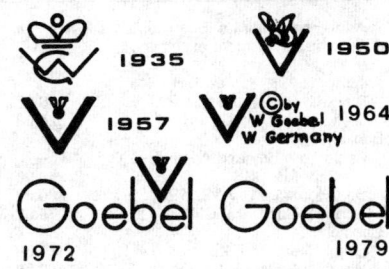

HUMMEL ITEMS

History: Hummel items are the original creations of Berta Hummel, born in 1909 in Massing, Bavaria, Germany. At age 18, she was enrolled in the Academy of Fine Arts in Munich to further her mastery of drawing and the palette. Berta entered the Convent of Siessen and became Sister Maria Inconnentia in 1934. In this Franciscan cloister, she continued drawing and painting images of her childhood friends.

In 1935 W. Goebel Co. in Rodental, Germany, began reproducing Sister Berta's sketches into 3 dimensional bisque figurines. The Schmid Brothers of Randolph, Massachusetts, introduced the figurines to America and became Goebel's U.S. distributor.

In 1967 Goebel began distributing Hummel items in the U.S. A controversy developed between the two companies involving the Hummel family and the convent. Law suits and countersuits ensued. The German courts finally effected a compromise. The convent held legal rights to all works produced by Sister Berta from 1934 until her death in 1946 and licensed Goebel to reproduce these works. Schmid was to deal directly with the Hummel family for permission to reproduce any preconvent art.

All authentic Hummels bear both the signature, M.I. Hummel, and a Goebel trademark. Various trademarks were used to identify the year of production. The Crown Mark (CM) was used in 1935, Full Bee (FB) 1940–1959; Small Stylized Bee (SSB) 1960–1972; Large Stylized Bee (LSB) 1960–1963; Three Line Mark (3L) 1964–1972; Last Bee Mark (LB) 1972–1980, Missing Bee Mark (MB) 1979–Present.

References: John F. Hotchkiss, *Hummel Art II,* Wallace-Homestead, 1981; Carl F. Luckey, *Hummel Figurines and Plates, 7th Edition,* Books Americana, 1984; Lawrence L. Wonsch, *Hummel Copycats With Values,* Wallace-Homestead, 1987.

Collectors' Clubs: Goebel Collectors' Club, 105 White Plains Road, Tarrytown, NY 10591; Hummel Collectors Club, P.O. Box 257, Yardley, PA 19067.

Additional Listings: See *Warman's Americana & Collectibles* for more examples.

Ashtray
Boy with Bird, #166 . . . . 80.00
Joyful, #33, CM, 3½ x 6" 325.00
Bookends, pr
Apple Tree Boy and Apple Tree Girl,
#252A&B, SSB 250.00
Bookworms, #14/A&B, SSB 300.00
Strolling Along, #5, CM 275.00
Candleholder
Silent Night, #54, LB 175.00
Watchful Angel, #194, FB 400.00
Candy Box
Happy Pastime, #III/69, 3L 125.00
Joyful, #III/53, 3L 115.00
Figurine
A Stitch In Time, I#255, LB 130.00
Adoration, #23/II, CM 750.00
Auf Wiedersehen, #153/0, LB 130.00
Baker, #128, SSB 85.00
Band Leader, #129, LB 120.00
Be Patient, #197/2/0, FB 125.00
Bird Duet, #169, 3L 90.00
Boy With Toothache, #217, 3L 110.00
Celestial Musician, #188 . . . . 80.00
Chick Girl, #57/0, FB 100.00
Chicken Licken, #385, 3L 100.00
Chimney Sweep, 122/0, LB 70.00
Close Harmony, #336 . . . . 100.00
Congratulations, #17/0 (no socks),
FB 225.00
Doll Bath, #319, 3L 130.00
Easter Time, #384, LB 85.00
Farewell, #65, LB 80.00
Feathered Friends, #344 . . . . 80.00
Going To Grandma's, #51/0, FB . . . 175.00
Heavenly Angel, #21/0, SSB 75.00

Heavenly Lullaby, #262, LB 110.00
Joyful, #52/0, 3L 135.00
Just Resting, #112/3/0, LB 85.00
Kiss Me, #311, 3L 145.00
Knitting Lessons, #256, 3L 350.00
Little Goat Herder, #200/0, SSB . . . 120.00
Little Hiker, I#16/2/0, FB 80.00
Little Pharmacist, #322, FB 2,500.00
March Winds, #43, LB 75.00
Mother's Darling, #175, FB 225.00
Not For You, #317, LB 130.00
Playmates, #58/I, SSB 150.00
Postman, #119, FB 145.00
Puppy Love, #1, CM 425.00
School Girls, 177/I, LB 900.00
She Loves Me, She Loves Me Not,
#174, FB 175.00
Smart Little Sister, #346, 3L 100.00
Stargazer, #132, 3L 50.00
Surprise, #94/3/0, FB 165.00
The Artist, #304, 3L 350.00
The Builder, #305, 3L 140.00
The Photographer, #178, SSB 140.00
To Market, #49/3/0, FB 195.00
Umbrella Boy, 152/A/II, CM 2,000.00
Village Boy, #51/3/0, CM 115.00
Wayside Devotion, #28/III, CM 1,300.00
Which Hand?, #258, SSB 350.00
Font
Angel Cloud, #206, LB, 2¼ x 4¾" . . 40.00
Child With Flowers, #36/I, SSB . . . 100.00
Child Jesus, #26/0, 3L 30.00
Guardian Angel, #248, 3L, 2¼ x 5½" 50.00
Holy Family, #246, SB, 3 x 4" 65.00
Seated Angel, #167, FB, 3¼ x 4¼" . 75.00
Music Box, Little Band, #388M, 3L . . . 250.00
Plaque
Ba-Bee Rings, #30/OA&B, FB 250.00
Madonna, #48/0, CM, 3 x 4" 250.00
Mail Coach, #140, LB, 4½ x 6¼" . . 135.00
Merry Wanderer, #92, FB, 4¾ x 5⅛" 185.00
Table Lamp
Culprits, #44/A, FB 350.00
Happy Days, #235, LB 280.00
Just Resting, #225/II, 3L 275.00

IMARI

History: Imari derives its name from a Japanese port city. Although Imari ware was manufactured in the 17th century, the wares most commonly encountered are those made between 1770 and 1900.

Early Imari was decorated simply, quite unlike the later heavily decorated brocade pattern commonly associated with Imari. Most of the decorative patterns are an underglaze blue and overglaze "seal wax" red supported by turquoise and yellow.

The Chinese copied Imari ware. Important differences of the Japanese type include grayer clay,

Figurine, Singing Lesson, #63, stylized bee mark, 2⅞" h, $85.00.

thicker glaze, runny and darker blue, and deep red opaque hues.

The pattern and colors of Imari inspired many English and European potteries, such as Derby and Meissen, to adopt a similar style of decoration for their wares.

Reference: Sandra Andacht, *Oriental Antiques & Art: An Identification And Value Guide,* Wallace-Homestead, 1987.

Reproduction Alert: Reproductions abound, and many manufacturers continue to produce pieces in the traditional style.

Platter, iron-red and cobalt blue border, c1875, 12⅜″ l, $125.00.

Beaker, 21¾″ h, inky blue, red and gilt, ho–o birds, flowers, and brocades, elaborate gilt bronze base, mounted as lamps, Japanese, late 18th C ... 1,900.00
Bowl, 10⅛″, polychrome dec, landscape medallion encircled by shaped floral reserves, irregular brocade ground . 325.00
Charger
   15½″, polychrome and gilt dec, ho-o and kiri medallion, shaped reserves of dragon and birds on branches, brocade ground, imp cartouche "Hizen Yamatoku," pr 800.00
   17¼″ d, shallow cavetto and broad rim with bold floral scrolls, arms of Tyssen in sepia rim roundel, Chinese, first quarter 18th C 3,500.00
Creamer and Sugar, 5½″ creamer, 5⅞″ cov sugar, ovoid, dragon form handles, gilt and bright enamels, shaped reserves, dragon-like beasts, stylized animal medallions, brocade ground, high dome lid, knob, cipher mark of Mount Fuji and Fukagama Studio marks, Meiji period 500.00
Jar, 27½″, cov, ovoid, narrow foot, continuous scene of blossoming sakura shrouding pavilion complex, narrow neck band of interlocking foliage spirals, domed lid, shishi finial 715.00

Jardiniere, 10″, hexagonal, bulbous, short flared foot, alternating bijin figures and immortal symbols, stylized ground 250.00
Plate
   5⅜″, central kiri medallion, nine Chinese sages, scrolling foliate rim band, four character inscription, set of 4 .... 250.00
   9″, wide everted rim, central medallion of Chinese scholars seated on garden terrace, blossoming plum tree, gilt highlights, Chinese, early 19th C 300.00
   9⅝″, gilt, multicolored enamels, and underglaze blue, irregular ho-o and floral reserves, blue ground, foliate and cloud design, foliate edge, set of 6 .... 500.00
Platter, 14″, hexagonal, central reserve of flowers in vase, cavetto with floral reserves, scrolling branches, narrow blue band, Meiji period, pr 1,000.00
Urn, 21″ h, gilt bronze mounts, deep bowl, red, blue, and gilt floral dec, everted pierced collar, S scroll arms of leaves and cattails, mid band of plaited reeds, flaring porcelain base banded in bronze, pierced skirt interspersing four foliate clasps, pr 14,000.00
Vase
   9″ h, octagonal gourd shape, relief dec, enameled multicolored chrysanthemum sprays, Japanese, 19th C, pr 1,100.00
   14½″ h, lake and phoenix bird reserves, overall patterned ground, gilt highlights, Japanese, c1900 .. 300.00
   24″ h, baluster form, pomegranate handles, Chinese 200.00

IMPERIAL GLASS

History: Imperial Glass Co., Bellaire, Ohio, was organized in 1901. Its primary product was pattern (pressed) glass. Soon other lines were added including carnival glass, NUART, NUCUT, and NEAR CUT. In 1916 the company introduced "Free-Hand," a lustered art glass line, and "Imperial Jewels," an iridescent stretch glass that carried the Imperial cross trademark. In the 1930s the company was reorganized into the Imperial Glass Corporation and continues to produce a great variety of wares.

Imperial recently has acquired the molds and equipment of several other glass companies–Central, Cambridge and Heisey. Many of the "retired" molds of these companies are once again in use. The resulting reissues are marked to distinguish them from the originals.

Reference: Margaret and Douglas Archer, *Imperial Glass*, Collector Books, 1978.

Collectors' Club: National Imperial Glass Collectors Society, Box 534, Bellaire, OH 43906.

Additional Listings: See Carnival Glass, Pattern Glass, and *Warman's Americana & Collectibles* for more examples of Candlewick.

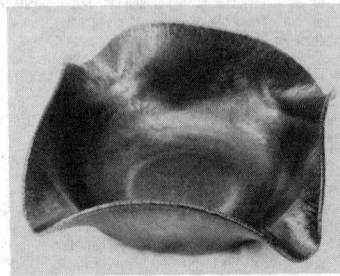

Lustered, bowl, stretch glass, peacock iridescent, scalloped corners, 2″ h, 6½″ w, $125.00.

ENGRAVED OR HAND CUT

Bowl
6½″, flower and leaf, molded star base	20.00
9″, berry, Design No. 114, five hand cut daisy like flowers	18.00
Candlesticks, 7″, Amelia, pr	32.00
Celery Vase, three side stars, cut star base	25.00
Nut Dish, 5½″, Design No. 112	15.00
Pitcher, tankard, Design No. 110, flowers, foliage, and butterfly cutting	50.00
Plate, 5½″, Design No. 12	12.00
Sherbet, ftd, Design No. 300, engraved stars	10.00
Syrup, Design No. 112, SP top	32.00

JEWELS

Bowl, 9 x 4″, irid amber	75.00
Candy Dish, cov, pink	35.00
Compote, 7½″, irid teal blue	60.00
Rose Bowl, amethyst, green irid	75.00

Vase, 6″, irid pearl green and purple luster	135.00

LUSTERED (FREE HAND)

Candlesticks, pr, 10¾″ h, cobalt blue, white vine and leaf dec	325.00
Hat, 9″ w, ruffled rim, cobalt blue, embedded irid white vines and leaves	100.00
Pitcher, 10″ h, applied clear handle, pale yellow luster, white pulled loops	225.00
Rose Bowl, 6″ d, irid orange, white floral cutting	75.00

Vase
6″, oyster white, embedded green hearts and vines, deep orange luster lining	250.00
8¼″, King Tut, deep irid blue, white loops	315.00
11¼″, baluster, triangular pull-ups at mouth, opal opaque white ground, embedded irid blue trailing vines, orig paper label	325.00

NUART

Ashtray	18.00
Lamp Shade, marigold	50.00
Vase, 7″, bulbous, irid green	125.00

NUCUT

Bowl, 4½″, berry, handles	15.00
Celery Tray, 11″	15.00
Creamer	15.00
Fern Dish, 8″ brass lining, ftd	32.00
Orange Bowl, 12″, Rose Marie	48.00
Punch Set, 13″ bowl, base, six cups, Rose Marie	175.00
Tumbler, flared rim, molded star	5.00

PRESSED

Animal Dish, cov, milk glass, rabbit on nest, 4½″	25.00
Basket, 10½″	30.00
Bonbon, 5¼″, D'Angelo, green, handle	15.00
Bowl, 9″, satin irid, handles	20.00
Butter Dish, cov, Colonial, rose	50.00
Cheese Dish, cov, Monticello	35.00
Cordial, Wakefield, amber	10.00

Creamer and Sugar
Cape Cod, clear	20.00
Flora, rose	15.00
Figure, Terrier, caramel slag	125.00
Goblet, Cape Cod, red	15.00
Mayonnaise, underplate, Monaco, amber, orig spoon	20.00
Salt and Pepper Shakers, pr, Huckabee, aluminum tops	25.00
Sandwich Tray, black handle	25.00
Sweet Pea Vase, 4″	12.00
Toothpick, ivory, orig label	15.00

INDIAN ARTIFACTS, AMERICAN

History: During the historic period there were approximately 350 tribes of Indians, grouped into the following regions: Eskimo, Northeast and Woodland, Northwest Coast, Plains, and West and Southwest.

American Indian artifacts are quite popular. Currently the market is in a period of stability following a rapid increase of prices during the 1970s.

References: John W. Barry, *American Indian Pottery, 2nd Edition,* Books Americana, 1984; Robert Edler, *Early Archaic Indian Points & Knives,* Collector Books, 1990; Lar Hothem, *Arrowheads & Projectile Points,* Collector Books, 1983; Lar Hothem, *North American Indian Artifacts, 3rd Edition,* Books Americana, 1984; *North American Indian Points,* Books Americana, 1984; Noel D. Justice, *Stone Age Spear And Arrow Points Of the Midcontinental and Eastern United States,* Indiana University Press, 1987; Sarah and William Turnbaugh, *Indian Baskets,* Schiffer Publishing, 1986.

Periodical: American Indian Basketry Magazine, P.O. Box 66124, Portland, OR 97266.

Note: American Indian artifacts listed below are objects made on the North American continent during the pre-historic and historic periods.

ESKIMO

Basket, 5½" d, baleen and ivory	800.00
Effigy, 4⅛" l, bone, carved, fish	30.00
Figure, 12" l, green stone, carved, three seals, sgd "Thomassie Toak '71"	325.00
Lamp, 5½" l, stone, finial, handle	45.00
Mittens, pr, 9¾" l, fur and leather	15.00
Sled, toy, 12½" l, jaw bone, baleen strips	40.00

NORTHEAST AND WOODLANDS

Bandolier Bag, 13 x 39", beaded, polychrome floral design, black velvet, blue cloth binding, bead fringe, Chippewa	700.00
Basket, 8 x 11½", woven splint, oval, brown and natural design handle	30.00
Moccasins, pr, 9½" l, beaded, Iroquois	45.00
Pouch, velvet, beaded, worn	10.00
Vessel, 5" h, round, gray-white, incised line dec on rim, Iroquois	175.00

NORTHWEST COAST

Apron, dance type, Nez Perce	100.00
Bag, 11 x 12", beaded woman design, blue background, Nez Perce	180.00
Basket, 6" d, geometric design, Tlingit	410.00
Bottle, 3" h, basketry, carved wooden totem stopper, Tlingit, c1910	130.00
Gauntlet, 7" l, moose hide, cut glass	

beads dec, beaded floral design panels on back, Nez Perce, c1930	180.00
Hat, 9" h, 13½" d rim, basketry, tight weave	400.00
Paddle, 15½" l, carved, painted killer whale design, sgd "John Bennall," Haida	70.00
Pipe, 2⅞" l,⅞" d, tubular, wineglass type	260.00
Tray, 5¾" d, basketry, Tlingit	45.00

Plains, Jicarella Apache, coiled food basket with handles, red and brown faded dec, 19¼" d, $150.00.

PLAINS

Doll Dress, 14" h, homespun, beaded, rawhide tassels, stenciled feed sack label "S Indian Ag" int., Sioux	475.00
Necklace, 64" l, rope, beaded, blue, glass bead ends	10.00
Pouch	
4½" l, leather, beaded, polychrome, cross on one side, lizard on other	55.00
7 x 11", leather, polychrome beading, tin cones and horsehair dec	350.00
Vessel, 8" h, leather over birch bark, beaded, polychrome designs, cotton duck lining, Sioux	125.00

WEST AND SOUTHWEST

Basket	
1½" h, miniature, yucca and devil's claw, made by Mary Thomas, Papago	155.00
1⅝" d, miniature, horsehair, white and black, Pima	125.00
7 x 7¾", figures and animals, Papago	215.00
7 x 9", oval, geometric design, Papago	30.00
8½" d, step design, Papago	45.00
9¼" d, 5¼" h, key-like design, Papago	65.00
12¼" d, coiled, brown geometric design	115.00

16" d, 10" h, geometric design and
lizards **275.00**
Bowl
  4¾" d, pink slip with black and white,
    sgd "E.M. Lalo," Hopi **30.00**
  5½" d, white slip with red and black,
    Hopi **475.00**
  6" d, smoked white slip with red and
    black, Hopi **250.00**
  6¾" d, white slip with red and black,
    Hopi **65.00**
Canteen, 3" h, miniature, white slip with
  red and black, "Moki Is," Hopi **255.00**
Concho Belt, 45" l, tooled silver, turquoise nuggets, six conchos and butterflies, sand cast silver buckle with
  four turquoise nuggets, Navaho ... **375.00**
Jar
  Acoma
    5" h, white slip with red and black **125.00**
    5¾" h, white slip with red and black,
      sgd "I Coucho, Acoma, NM" .. **150.00**
    6¼" h, white slip with red and black **115.00**
  Apache, 10½" h, basketry, geometric
    design **375.00**
  Casas Grande, 8¾" h, polychrome,
    sgd "Collo Silveird" **140.00**
  Rio Grande Pueblo, 4½" h, white slip
    with red and black **45.00**
Jewelry
  Bracelet, silver, five turquoise pcs,
    tooled, applied floral design **110.00**
  Necklace, silver, squash blossom,
    tooled, turquoise, 19th C **375.00**
Jug, 6¼" h, white slip with red and
  black, sgd "L Coucho, Sky City, NM,"
  Acoma **90.00**
Kachina
  9¼" h, wood, carved, polychrome
    paint, feather trim, sgd "L Long-
    haia," Hopi **185.00**
  14½" h, wood, carved, polychrome
    paint, leather, shell, bell, and fur
    trim, base marked "Koshari by
    Raymond Parkett," Hopi **175.00**
Mat, 18½ x 19", brown, gray, red, and
  orange central medallion, white
  ground **30.00**
Olla, 1⅜" h, miniature, fret pattern,
  made by Mary Thomas, Papago ... **115.00**
Pot, blackware, two tone design, Santa
  Clara **45.00**
Rug
  Chimayo, 51 x 90", gray with black,
    white, and green **425.00**
  Navaho
    35 x 62", gray, black, red, and tan,
      natural white ground **250.00**
    37 x 68", black, red, blue, and nat-
      ural white stripes, gray bands
      with black and white designs .. **450.00**

61 x 87", Germantown red, black,
  and white **1,250.00**
Saddle Blanket, Navaho
  29 x 30½", red, orange, gray, brown,
    and natural white **150.00**
  29 x 32", gray, red, black, tan, and
    white **35.00**
  32½ x 35", gray with gold, black, and
    white **30.00**
Tray
  14" d, basketry, coiled, brown geo-
    metric design, Pima **175.00**
  16" d, Pima **320.00**

INDIAN TREE PATTERN

History: The Indian Tree pattern is a popular
pattern of porcelain made from the last half of the
19th century until the present. The pattern consisting of an Oriental crooked tree branch, landscape, exotic flowers, and foliage is found in pre-
dominantly greens, pinks, blues, and oranges on
a white ground. Several English potteries, including Burgess and Leigh, Coalport, and Maddock,
made wares with the Indian Tree pattern.

Reference: Susan and Al Bagdade, *Warman's
English & Continental Pottery & Porcelain, 1st Edition,* Warman Publishing Co., Inc., 1987.

**Platter, marked "Maddock, England,"
11 x 14¼", $65.00.**

Berry Set, 10" master bowl, six 5"
  sauces, Maddox **150.00**
Bouillon Cup and Underplate, handles **15.00**
Bowl
  5⅜", KPM **7.50**
  8½ x 11", ftd, Minton **45.00**
Butter, cov, Johnson Bros **40.00**
Cake Plate, 10½", Coalport **35.00**
Chocolate Set, chocolate pot, six cups
  and saucers, Copeland and Spode . **185.00**
Creamer, Coalport **25.00**
Cup and Saucer, scalloped, Copeland **20.00**
Demitasse, Coalport **25.00**

Egg Cup, 4", Maddock	20.00
Fruit Bowl, 10 x 5½", ftd, scalloped, Copeland and Spode	135.00
Gravy Boat, Brownfield & Son, c1856	30.00
Pitcher, 6", Maddock & Sons	45.00

Plate

6", KPM	5.00
8", Cauldon	12.00
9½", KPM	15.00
10", Burgess & Leigh	18.50

Platter

8 x 11", KPM	25.00
18½", Spode	95.00
Salt and Pepper, Coalport	50.00
Sauce, 5", Johnson Bros	8.00
Soup Plate, 7½", Coalport	15.00
Soup Tureen, 10", matching cov and ladle, Maddock & Sons	130.00
Sugar, Coalport	25.00
Teapot, Burgess & Leigh	50.00
Vegetable Dish, 10", oval, Davison & Son	35.00

INK BOTTLES

History: Ink was sold in glass or pottery bottles in the early 1700s in England. Retailers mixed their own formula and bottled it. The commercial production of ink did not begin in England until the late 18th century and in America until the early 19th century.

Initially, ink was supplied in pint or quart bottles, often of poor manufacture, from which smaller bottles could be filled. By the mid-19th century when writing implements were improved, emphasis was placed on making an "untippable" bottle. Shapes ranging from umbrella style to turtles were tried. Since ink bottles were displayed, shaped or molded bottles became popular.

The advent of the fountain pen relegated the ink bottle to the back drawer. Bottles lost their decorative design and became merely functionable items.

References: Ralph & Terry Kovel, *The Kovels' Bottle Price List,* 8th edition, Crown Publishers, 1987; Carlo & Dot Sellari, *The Standard Old Bottle Price Guide,* Collector Books, 1989.

Periodicals: *Antique Bottle and Glass Collector,* P. O. Box 187, East Greenville, PA 18041.

Additional Listings: See *Warman's Americana & Collectibles* for more examples.

Billing & Co, Banker's Writing Ink, aqua, "B" in center, 2 x 1½"	15.00

Carter's

Blak Writing Fluid, yellow amber, wide beveled corner, double collared mouth, label, 9¼" h	190.00
Cathedral, cobalt blue, hexagonal, 9¾" h	55.00

Glass, umbrella style, light teal, octagonal base, open pontil, 2½" h, $35.00.

E. Waters/Troy, NY, aquamarine, cylindrical, applied flared mouth 2¼ h	275.00
Farley's, yellowish amber, octagonal, sheared mouth, 1¾" h	550.00
Harrison's Columbian Ink, aquamarine, twelve sided, applied flared mouth, 5⅞" h	120.00
Hover, Philadelphia, medium green, cylindrical, applied mouth with spout, 9¼" h	130.00
J. A. Williamson Chemist, bluish green, cylindrical, applied mouth with spout, 9⅝" h	120.00
J. K. Palmer/Chemist/Boston, olive amber, cylindrical, applied mouth with spout, 9¼" h	270.00
Lake's, aqua, cone, 2½"	15.00
Maynard & Noyes, olive amber, three part mold, sloping collared mouth with spout, label, 8" h	100.00
Pitkin Ink, Keene, dark aqua, open pontil, 1¾"	150.00
S M Bixby & Co NY, aquamarine, fluted dome, nine sided, tooled mouth, 1⅞" h	100.00
S. O. Dunbar Taunton, aquamarine, eight sided umbrella shape, rolled mouth, 2⅜" h	70.00
Shepard & Allen's Writing Fluid, golden amber, cylindrical, red label, 6⅜" h	85.00
Wood's Black Ink, Portland, ME, aqua, tapered, ring top, 2½"	25.00

INKWELLS

History: The majority of the commonly found inkwells were produced in the United States and Europe from the early 1800s to the 1930s. The most popular materials were glass and pottery because these substances resisted the corrosive effects of ink.

Inkwells were a sign of the office or a wealthy individual. The common man tended to dip his ink directly from the bottle. The period from 1870 to 1920 represented a "golden age," when inkwells in elaborate designs were produced.

References: William E. Covill, Jr., *Inkbottles and Inkwells*, William S. Sullwold Publishing, 1971; Betty and Ted Rivera, *Inkstands and Inkwells: A Collector's Guide*, 2nd edition, Crown Publishers, Inc., 1973.

Collectors' Club: Society of Inkwell Collectors, 5136 Thomas Avenue, Minneapolis, MN 55410.

Additional Listings: See *Warman's Americana & Collectibles* for more examples.

Marble, pink and gray, two attached 2½″ cube inkwells, 6¼ x 11½″ base, $85.00.

CERAMIC

Basalt, round, marked "Wedgwood Only," c1800, 4 x 2¾″	310.00
Flow Blue, floral, hinged, ornate brass stand, 6 x 8 x 5¾″	200.00
Hand Painted, sq, pink, hinged lid, underplate, thermometer on front	140.00
Nippon, sq, beige, gold, black flowers, 4″	130.00
Porcelain, domed cylinder, white glaze, multicolored floral dec, metal cap, 2⅜″ h, 3⅜″ d	30.00
Pottery, sq, wide beveled corners, white ground, multicolored leaf and berry dec, 3⅛″ h, 3¾″ l	130.00
Quimper, round, scalloped edge, marked "Henriot Quimper France," 5″	55.00

GLASS

Art Glass, fountain type, clear ground, straight blue, white, and green stripes on stem, swirled striped finial, marble base, metal cap, 4⅝″ h, 2⅜″ d, France	400.00
Art Nouveau, Tiffany type pattern, iridescent green, clear glass insert, brass closure, 2″ h, 5¼″ d	240.00
Blown Three Mold	
Amber, cylindrical, disc mouth, 1½″ h, 2½″ d	145.00
Olive amber, blown three mold, cylindrical, disc mouth, 1½″ h, 2¼″ d	40.00
Cobalt blue, teakettle shape, eight sided, ground mouth, 2⅛″ h, 3¾″ l	425.00
Cranberry, blown hemisphere, gold dec, brass hinged lid, 4½″ d	500.00

Figural	
Benjamin Franklin, greenish aquamarine, crude sheared mouth, 2¾″ h, 4″ l	360.00
Snail, clear, ground mouth, 1⅝″ h, 2⅝″ l	330.00
Paperweight, bulbous shape, clear, rose and green floral dec int., tooled mouth, matching stopper, 5¼″ h, 4⅛″ d	140.00
Pitkin type	
Golden amber, ribbed and swirled, disc mouth, 1½″ h, 2⅛″ d, New England	375.00
Yellow olive, conical cylinder, funnel shaped mouth, 1⅜″ h, 2″ d	725.00
Pressed, Daisy & button pattern, cat sitting on cover, orig insert	245.00
Ruby overlay, cut to clear cube, matching cut hinged lid, 3½″ h	400.00
Vaseline, cylinder, eight concave vertical flutes, matching hinged lid, 3″ h	775.00

METAL

Brass, cast, ornate Art Nouveau stand, hinged lid, glass insert, 5″ l	80.00
Bronze, three nude men, retrieve chest from sea, 11″ l, c1920	1,210.00
Iron, wheelbarrow shape, black, revolving, snail type milk glass insert, 3″ h, 8″ l	325.00
Pot Metal, cat's head on tray, green eyes, hinged, glass insert	70.00
Silver, circular form, circular foot, reeded band edge and hinged lid, marked "H M," Birmingham, England, 1906, 5″ d	165.00

IRONS

History: Ironing devices have been used for many centuries, with the earliest references dating from 1100. Irons from the Medieval, Renaissance, and early industrial era can be found in Europe, but are rare. Fine brass engraved irons and hand wrought irons dominated the period prior to 1850. After 1850 irons began a series of rapid evolutionary changes.

Between 1850 and 1910 irons were heated in four ways: 1) a hot metal slug was inserted into the body, 2) a burning solid, e.g., coal or charcoal, was placed in the body, 3) a liquid or gas, e.g., alcohol, gasoline, or natural gas, was fed from an external tank and burned in the body, and 4) conduction heating, usually drawing heat from a stove top.

Electric irons are just beginning to find favor among iron collectors.

References: Esther S. Berney, *A Collectors Guide To Pressing Irons And Trivets*, Crown Publishers, Inc., 1977; A. H. Glissman, *The Evolution Of The Sad Iron,* published by author, 1970; Brian Jewell, *Smoothing Irons, A History And Collector's Guide,* Wallace-Homestead, 1977.

Collectors' Clubs: Friends of Ancient Smoothing Irons, Box 215, Carlsbad, CA 92008; Midwest Sad Iron Collectors Club, 500 Adventureland Drive, Altoona, IA 50009. **Museums:** Henry Ford Museum, Dearborn, MI; Shelburne Museum, Shelburne, VT; Sturbridge Village, Sturbridge, MA.

Additional Listings: See *Warman's Americana & Collectibles* for more examples.

Advisors: David and Sue Irons.

Natural Gas, marked "Household Gas Iron Co, Phila & NY," $30.00.

Box, wrought iron, wooden handle, primitive	**115.00**
Charcoal, double spout, "Ne Plus Ultra," side vent, hand heat shield, removable top, 1902	**85.00**
Fluter, machine type, brass rolls, circular cone base, paint dec, Tucker-New Jersey	**130.00**
Goffering, iron, round base, S center post, 4" barrel, Kenrick	**85.00**
Liquid Fuel	
Alcohol, iron body, saw grip handle, cylindrical tank, German, c1900 . .	**110.00**
Natural Gas, "I Want For Comfort Gas Iron," pie shape, wood handle, extension pipe c1910	**35.00**
Miniature	
Flat, iron, strap handle, number on top, 2–3"	**30.00**
Swan, iron, paint dec more desirable, various sizes 1¾–5", c1870	**150.00**
Sad	
Belgium Tear Drop, iron, rect handle, raised numbers and letters, various sizes and styles, c1850	**20.00**
Enterprise, two pointed or straight back edge, removable C handle .	**15.00**
Ober, flat, ribbing on arched handle, weight number	**18.00**
Slug, brass, wood handle, lift trap door,	

turned posts, various sizes, c1850–1900, English	**120.00**
Speciality	
Hat, flat wood tolliker for crown pressing, Cross, c1900	**45.00**
Polisher, iron, round bottom, Sidons, England, c1900	**50.00**
Sleeve, Grand Union Tea Co, removable bentwood handle	**45.00**
Tailor, cast, narrow, raised weight number, c1890	**25.00**

IRONWARE

History: Iron, a metallic element that occurs abundantly in combined forms, has been known for centuries. Items made from iron range from the utilitarian to the decorative. Early hand-forged ironwares are of considerable interest to Americana collectors.

Reference: Kathryn McNerney, *Antique Iron,* Collector Books, 1984; Herbert, Peter, and Nancy Schiffer, *Antique Iron,* Schiffer Publishing Ltd., 1979.

Additional Listings: Banks, Boot Jacks, Doorstops, Fireplace Equipment, Food Molds, Irons, Kitchen Collectibles, Lamps, and Tools.

Andirons, pr	
25" h, Baroque style, twist and rect column, basket top, scrolled plaque and arched feet	**30.00**
28" h, basket top, spit holders, arched feet, c1700	**225.00**
Bootjack, 10¾" l, cricket	**20.00**
Bottle Opener, cast	
3½" h, pelican, polychrome	**100.00**
3⅝" h, donkey, polychrome traces . .	**65.00**
3⅞" h, drunk at sign post, "Sequoia Nat'l Park"	**25.00**
4⅛" h, drunk at lamp post	**25.00**
Candle Holder, 9¾" h, adjustable, spiral, wood base	**100.00**
Candlestick, 7" h, hog scraper, pushup, marked "Shaw's Birmg"	**75.00**
Cherry Pitter, 8½" h, hand crank, marked "Pat'd Nov 17, 1863"	**55.00**
Cigarette Dispenser, 8½" l, cast, elephant, bronze repaint	**30.00**
Cruisie, 6½" h, wrought, double, ram's horn finial	**110.00**
Door Handle, 13" l, wrought, thumb latch	**45.00**
Door Knocker, cast, orig polychrome paint	
3¾" l, basket of flowers	**30.00**
4¼" l, Amish man	**40.00**
Fence, 43 x 70", cast, four section, old green paint	**240.00**
Figure	
Frog, 5¼" l, green paint	**35.00**

Dough Scraper, wrought iron, triangular scrapper, 4¾″ base, 4½″ handle, $25.00.

Pig, 3″ l, gold paint traces **10.00**

Fireplace Equipment
 Fire Back, 22″ h, 16″ w, cast, arched, Tudor style, rose and portcullis dec **150.00**
 Fire Mark, 9 x 11½″, oval, pumper and "U. F.," pitted, black paint . . . **135.00**
 Shovel, 28″ l, wrought, scrolled detail, pitted blade **25.00**
 Tongs, 23½″ l, wrought, brass handle **25.00**

Floor Lamp, 63″ h, iron wrapped circular column, scroll trifid base, flame finial over carriage lamp **100.00**

Frame, 19 x 11½″, reticulated scroll crest, Cluette Peabody and Co **40.00**

Furniture
 Bench, 41″ l, kidney form, ornate trestle base joined by twist stretcher, upholstered top **170.00**
 Garden Bench, pr, 45″ l, overall open-work grape, leaf and vine motif, leaf form feet, painted white **275.00**
 Settee, 45″ l, linked oval and rosette back, shaped crest rail, acanthus cast cabriole legs, painted white . **300.00**
 Side Chair, openwork back, circular seat, down curving legs, painted white **120.00**
 Table
  24″ h, 30″ d, reticulated circular top, griffin and scroll legs, medial shelf, shaped feet, painted white **190.00**
  25″ l, 20″ w, 31″ h, wrought, rect top, twelve duck head legs, webbed feet, lily pad base **850.00**
 Window Bench, 25″ l, arrow head trestle base, twist stretcher, upholstered arms and seat **70.00**

Garden Urn, cast, pr
 27″ h, foliage scroll detail, open work handles, labeled "The Kramer Bros, Dayton, O" **600.00**
 38½″ h, swan base, white repaint . . **900.00**

Hitching Post, 62½″ h, cast, tree form, branch stubs, marked "Patent" **100.00**

Lawn Ornament, cast, jockey, polychrome repaint **100.00**

Lighting Stand, 41″ h, wrought, tripod base, adjustable arm, candle socket, three prong pricket **650.00**

Mortar and Pestle, 5½″ h, cast **20.00**

Nut Cracker, 11″ l, cast, figural, dog, nickel finish, marked "The L.A. Althoff Mfg Co, Chicago" **40.00**

Peel, 28″ l, wrought, ram's horn finial . **110.00**

Plant Stand, 38″ h, three twist legs joined at base surrounded by floral finial, three acanthus leaf rings support copper planter **60.00**

Porringer, 5″ d, imp "Bellevue" on handle, marked "E. & T. Clark/1 Pint" . . **60.00**

Skillet, 9¾″ d, cast, three short feet, 9¼″ handle **35.00**

Sconce, wrought, 19th C
 41″ h, three scrolling arms, open work shield form body with scroll, reticulated flower form boboeches, ball and acanthus leaf motifs **300.00**
 58″ h, pr, scrolling floral form, spear shaped leaves and flower form light sockets, electrified **100.00**

Skewer Holder, 16″ l, four skewers, pitted **300.00**

Spatula, 18½″ l, wrought **45.00**

Sugar Nippers, 5″ l, marked "R Timmons & Sons" **145.00**

Tea Kettle, 8″ h, cast, brass lid, decorative finial, wrought handle **45.00**

Toaster, 21″ l, wrought, revolving, baluster form handle, Queen Anne style, 18th C **200.00**

Trammel, 28″ l, diamond tooling, marked "A S" and "A H," dated "1785" **350.00**

Trivet, 7¼″ l, heart shape, wrought . . . **150.00**

Waffle Iron, 24″ l, cast, wrought handles, pitted **65.00**

IVORY

History: Ivory, a yellowish-white organic material, comes from the teeth or tusks of animals and lends itself well to carving. It has been used for centuries by many cultures for artistic and utilitarian items.

Ivory from elephants shows a reticulated crisscross pattern in a cross section. Hippopotamus teeth, walrus tusks, whale teeth, narwhal tusks, and boars tusks also are ivory sources. Vegetable ivory, bone, stag horn, and plastic are ivory substitutes which often confuse collectors.

Note: Dealers and collectors should be familiar with The Endangered Species Act of 1973, amended in 1978, which limits the importation and sale of antique ivory and tortoise shell items.

Box, 9 x 7 x 6¼", carved, judgment
scene on lift top, panel sides, gadroon
base border, c1900 . . . . **1,000.00**
Brush Pot, 4" h, carved, figures and pa-
vilions, Chinese, c1885 . . . . **1,000.00**
Cane, 36½" l, bamboo form, horse for-
eleg shape handle, 19th C **250.00**
Card Case, 4⅛" l, carved, figures and
pavilions, Chinese, 19th C **500.00**
Cane Handle, 4½, carved, monkey on
branch, holding egg away from bird,
c1900 . . . . **90.00**
Chess Set, carved, figural, 32 pcs,
Chinese **225.00**
Cigarette Holder, carved **25.00**
Cribbage Board, 5¼" l, engraved foliage
and two seals, three pegs **100.00**
Crochet Hook, 6¼", hand shaped finial **40.00**

**Diptych dial, German, 17th C, marked
"WELSGH VR" on left side, "NIREN-
PERGER/VHR" on right, orig string
gnomen present, but broken, 4¾ x 2¹⁵⁄₁₆
x¾", $5,100.00.**

Figure
Bear, fiercely attacking walrus, raised
head, inlaid eyes, sgd Tominuke" **140.00**
Elephant, 11" l, five in ascending size
on curved bridge, trunks up, carved
base, sgd "Yoneyama" **190.00**
Mother and daughter, 12½" h, carved,
Japanese, 19th C **375.00**
Penguin, 2¾" h, carved **100.00**
Scholar, 2", bearded man, scroll on
staff, brocade robes **120.00**
Frame, 5¼", blossoming plum trees on
double doors, peony border int.,
hinged stand **155.00**
Game, spelling, globular, 25 facets, incised and red wax inlaid with alphabet
letter, mid 19th C **900.00**

Gavel, 8¼", engraved scribe lines . . . **250.00**
Incense burner, animal masks, paw feet
domed cov, fu lion knop, ring handles **390.00**
Jagging Wheel, 4¾" l, carved, heart
shaped handle, mid 19th C **1,700.00**
Jewelry
Beads, 24", graduated, ivory clasp . **45.00**
Pendant, 1 x 1½ x 2¼", double
dragon design, orig silk chord . . . **150.00**
Ring, carved, nude lady form, back
arched forming ring, 19th C **1,150.00**
Kayak, 6½" l, carved, Eskimo and seal,
sgd "Paul Nattanguk," missing spears **150.00**
Ladle, 7⅛", African **100.00**
Lamp, 10⅛", Geisha holding closed um-
brella in right hand, skirt up with left
hand, gilt metal base, electrified . . . **825.00**
Memo Pad, 1½ x 2¾", silver fittings . . **25.00**
Napkin Ring, 2" h, relief carved bird . . **10.00**
Needle Case, 6½" l, carved, dragons
and clouds, Chinese, 19th C **150.00**
Plaque, painted, Kuan Yin holding
flower, famille rose details, 10 x 6"
wood panel, Chinese, 18th C **700.00**
Shoehorn, 8½", maiden and child **150.00**
Stand, 7", pierced relief, pink and cream
flowers, peony and lotus flowers,
green stones **425.00**
Table Decoration
Cabbage, cricket on leaves, poly-
chrome details, 13" **475.00**
Flowers, realistic pansies, daffodils,
lilies, and morning glories, 5½" . . **330.00**
Tusk, carved, African
17½" l, male and children **325.00**
37" l, reticulated, seated native and
hut motifs, 19th C **350.00**
Vase
4" h, carved, four vertical ribs,
Chinese, 18th C **500.00**
10", ovoid, carved court ladies in musical pursuits, domed cov with landscape pines and figures, two ring
handles **470.00**
Wrist Rest, pr, 7", maiden holding
branch on one, fly whisk beside at-
tendant on other **330.00**

JACK-IN-THE-PULPIT VASES

History: Jack-in-the-Pulpit glass vases, made
in the trumpet form, were in vogue during the late
19th and early 20th centuries. The vases were
made in a wide variety of patterns, colors, and
sizes.
Additional Listings: See specific glass categories.

Amberina, 13¼", IVT **300.00**
Burmese, 3½ x 6¾", ruffled, yellow, pas-
tel rust and tan ground, autumn

Spatter Glass, predominately yellow, strips of white, orange, green, and blue, 7″ h, $50.00.

leaves, blue berries, and tendrils dec, Mt Washington	485.00
Cased	
4 x 7¼″, creamy opaque ext., white and yellow flowers, green leaves, gold trim, deep rose pink int., amber edge, ormolu leaf feet	125.00
6½ x 6½″, white ext., shaded maroon int., ruffled	115.00
7 x 15¾″, blue ext., white int., applied clear shell trim and foot	175.00
Cranberry, 4¼ x 6⅜″, DQ, ruffled, applied clear wishbone feet	125.00
Green Overlay, 5¾ x 6¼″, white ext., soft green int., applied clear feet	100.00
Iridescent amethyst and gold luster, feather veining	200.00
Loetz, 12″, green, silver-blue irid spots, unsigned, c1900	450.00
Nailsea, 3¾ x 7½″, frosted chartreuse green, white loopings, applied frosted feet	135.00
Opalescent	
5⅜″, flower petal top, pink and yellow stripes	85.00
7½″, ruffled, chartreuse green	75.00
Spatter	
3¼ x 5″, gold overlay, ruffled pink top	115.00
5 x 8½″, white, green, and cranberry	100.00
Stevens and Williams, 9⅜″, ruffled, chartreuse and white stripes	120.00

JADE

History: Jade is the generic name for two distinct minerals, nephrite and jadeite. Nephrite, an amphibole mineral from Central Asia and used in pre-18th century pieces, has a waxy surface and ranges in hues from white to almost a black green.

Jadeite, a pyroxene mineral found in Burma and used from 1700 to the present, has a glassy appearance and comes in various shades of white, green, yellow-brown, and violet.

Jade cannot be carved because of its hardness. Shapes are achieved through sawing and grinding with wet abrasives, such as quartz, crushed garnets, and carborundum.

Prior to 1800 few pieces are signed or dated. Stylistic considerations are used for dating. The Ch'ien Lung period (1736–95) is considered the "golden age" of Jade.

Reference: Sandra Andacht, *Oriental Antiques & Art: An Identification And Value Guide,* Wallace-Homestead, 1987.

Museum: Avery Brundage Collection, de Young Museum, San Francisco, CA.

Floral centerpiece, 21½ x 12½″, $325.00.

Belt Hook, 4″, mottled icy green, dragon shape	125.00
Box, cov, 5″ l, octagonal, translucent white, incised lotus blossoms, medallions, and four gui dragons	1,200.00
Brush Pot, 4¼″, scrolling cloud pattern dec, Chinese, 19th C	310.00
Brush Washer, 4⅜″ l, translucent olive green, carved, irregular lotus leaf shape, incised vein details, russet inclusions, black mottling	200.00
Cup, 4½″, white, boat shape, dragon handles, curved spout, Chinese	350.00
Dish, 5½″, octagonal, green spinach	135.00
Figure	
Boat, 6¾″ h, pale gray, setting sail, man pulling on three ropes, standing celestial maiden holding bamboo pole, yellow tones	800.00
Female Immortal, 6″ h, carved, mirror image, astride prancing steed, playing lute, lavender highlights, pr	5,500.00
Maiden, 6″ h, carved, tiered robes encircled by billowing scarves, holding chrysanthemum in left hand	250.00
Inkstand, 7″ with coral and SS, marked "Edward I, Farmer, New York"	200.00
Inkstone, 3⅝″ l, oval form, incised rim	

band, oval depression to one side, black and white mottling	**175.00**
Lamp, 29" h, Goddess, Kuan Yin, standing, flowing cowl, robes and jewels, child on one upraised arm, rosary and fly whisk in other	**1,600.00**
Pendant, hand cut, floral, engraved sterling and gold frame	**60.00**
Pitcher, 5⅜" h, band of spirals and whirl circles, rope borders, angular strap handle	**520.00**
Plaque, 8¾", carved, archaic bronze vessels, taotie masks, open work handles, Chinese, 18th C, pr	**650.00**
Saucer, 4¼", slightly flared rim, short ring foot, deep green, brown mottling	**200.00**
Snuff Bottle, greenish-white tone, flattened ovoid shape, sloping shoulders, oval foot, 1800–80, pr	**600.00**
Stemcup, 2" h, pale mottled green, two finely carved taotie masks on bowl, hollow foot carved with ring, 18th C .	**1,150.00**
Urn, 8" h, flattened ovoid form, incised taotie mask dec, narrow neck, flanking handles, suspending carved chains attached to dome lid, yoke shape hanger	**700.00**
Vase, 7", ovoid, nephrite, animal headed ring handles, stork and lotus scroll on cov	**500.00**

JAPANESE AND CHINESE CERAMICS

History: The Chinese pottery tradition has existed for thousands of years. By the sixteenth century, Chinese ceramic wares were being exported to India, Persia, and Egypt. The Ming dynasty (1368-1643) saw the strong development of glazed earthenwares and shapes. During the Ch'ing dynasty, the Ch'ien Lung period (1736-95) marked the golden age of interchange with the west.

Trade between China and the west began in the sixteenth century when the Portuguese established Macao. The Dutch entered the trade early in the seventeenth century. With the establishment of the English East India Company, all of Europe was seeking Chinese-made pottery and porcelain. Styles, shapes, and colors were developed to suit Western tastes. The tradition continued until the late nineteenth century.

Like the Chinese, the Japanese spent centuries developing their ceramic arts. Each region established its own forms, designs, and glazes. Individual artists added to the uniqueness.

Japanese ceramics began to be exported to the west in the mid-19th century. Their beauty quickly made them a favorite of the patrician class.

The ceramic tradition continues into the 20th century. Modern artists enjoy equal fame with older counterparts.

Reference: Sandra Andacht, *Oriental Antiques & Art: An Identification And Value Guide,* Wallace-Homestead, 1987.

Periodical: *The Orientalia Journal*, P. O. Box 94P, Little Neck, NY 11363.

Additional Listings: Canton, Fitzhugh, Imari, Kutani, Nanking, Rose Medallion, and Satsuma.

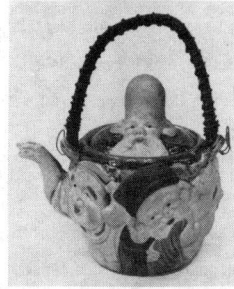

Teapot, Banko, Seven Gods of Wisdom, glazed and unglazed clay, polychrome, 5" h, 5½" w, $450.00.

CHINESE

Brush Pot, 4¼", scrolling cloud pattern, 19th C	**325.00.**
Charger, 14½", polychrome, flowering peach branch, laden with fruit, two diminutive flying wufu	**300.00**
Garden Seat, 18½", barrel form, two water scenes, pink and orange water plants, suspended interlocking pierced 'Cash' emblems, diaper and floral bands, keyfret border	**715.00**
Jar, cov, 25" h, two reserves of mythical phoenix, fanciful landscape, large pink peony blossoms, two crest shaped reserves of cranes in flight, lemon yellow ground, fronted pink lotus, lime green tendrils, ruyi shoulder band, floral swags, four coral-red applied mock lion mask handles, domed lid, fu dog finial, 19th C, pr	**3,575.00**
Jardiniere	
12¼", slender ovoid, everted rim, finely painted, court women engaging in leisurely pursuits, garden scene, ruyi head band, flower sprays, poetic dedication, pr	**550.00**
13¾", cylindrical, everted rim, narrow foot, four horizontal rows of multicolored shou characters, stylized	

pale pink and blue lappet bands, yellow ground, pr **825.00**
Tile, 16¼ x 23″, ochre colored rect plaque, fan shaped waterway scene, blue and white alternating borders of confronting dragons and scrolling tendrils, framed **385.00**

CHINESE EXPORT

Candleholder, 5″, animal form, crouching lap dog, whimsical face, iron–red glaze, gilt textured fur, ears, and tail, bell form urn, 19th C, pr **2,750.00**
Cup and Saucer, handleless, nude lady bathing, male attendant pouring water for her, Ch'ien Lung, c1790 . . **250.00**
Dish
  8″, carp shape, underglaze blue dec of scales, find, and eye on both sides, three low feet, c1625–50 . . **2,750.00**
  11⅝″, octafoil, Pseudo Tobacco Leaf pattern, stylized leaves, cut pomegranates and brocade rings, pink, deep blue, iron–red and chartreuse, gold highlights, late 18th C, pr **4,675.00**
Figure
  5″, Blanc-de-Chine, bearded man wearing visor cap with tassels, jacket, voluminous breeches, smoking pipe, seated astride scaly beast with bushy tail, mane, and beard, late 17th of early 18th C . . **1,650.00**
  6⅝ and 9½″h, cats grinning, ribbon collars, black painted eyes, one with turquoise glaze, other with coral, pr **425.00**
  9¼″, parrot, green glaze, coral-red beak and feet, standing on blue glazed rockwork, pr **1,100.00**
Ginger jar, 9½″, ovoid body, continuous scene of small boats, figures, and pavilions, ruyi head border, cov with scenes of man and small pagoda, underglaze blue, 19th C **475.00**
Mug, 4½″, British Marine dec, iron–red and black ship flying Union Jacks, rose and green floral spring on sides, black edged iron–red chain border, c1780–90 . . . . **425.00**
Planter, 4⅜″ h, elephant form, pr **750.00**
Plate
  7¾″, American ship of war, armed . . **1,200.00**
  9½″, American eagle center, gilt highlights on brown eagle, shield initialed "EHF," salmon rim and gilt border, gilt scallops and blue dots edge, c1795 . . . . **500.00**
Platter
  6¾″, oval, scattered pink flowers, gilt spear head band at cavetto, slightly

flaring rim with pink and pale turquoise brocade design, ribbon tied 'Cash' emblems, 19th C **1,760.00**
  11¾″, Pseudo Tobacco Leaf pattern, stylized leaves, cut pomegranates and brocade rings, pink, deep blue, iron–red and chartreuse, gold highlights, late 18th C **3,575.00**
  16⅝″, octagonal, armorial, arms of Nassau, Earl of Rochfort, motto, Qianlong, c1760, pr **3,850.00**
Punch Bowl, 11½″, overall dec of Masonic symbols **900.00**
Sauce Tureen, 12″, diamond shape, scalloped edge, Pseudo Tobacco Leaf pattern, stylized leaves, cut pomegranates and brocade rings, pink, deep blue, iron–red and chartreuse, blue and green glazed loop handles, two applied coral–red and yellow floral bloom finial, gold highlights, late 18th C **3,025.00**
Saucer, 6¼″ d, iron–red borders, stylized anthemion motif, c1815 . . . . . . **50.00**
Teapot, cov, Yixing stoneware, 27⅞″ h, squat spherical body, loop handle (repaired), straight spout, rims of pot, spout, cov, knob overlaid with thin layer of brass, incised mengchen mark for Hui Mengchen **400.00**
Vase, 6⅞″, cylinder, painted figures and flower vases **180.00**

JAPANESE

Basket, 5″, abstract figures related to tea ceremony, greens, bail handle, Oribe **85.00**
Bowl, 6¾″, int. painted in shades of iron–red, green, deep turquoise, black, gray, and gold, spray of chrysanthemums tied with tasseled gilt ribbon, ext. molded around base with border of incised petals, gold highlights, rim highlighted in worn gilting, Arita, 18th C **1,150.00**
Charger, 13¼″, two large iron oxide carp, underglaze blue ground, peonies, stylized waves, and flowering branches, Meiji period **165.00**
Ewer, 10½″, red and gilt motif, riverscapes and figures, loop handle, dragon finial, Kaga, late 19th C **525.00**
Figure, 3″, seated Sumo wrestler, left hand on ground, right raised, Sumida **1,000.00**
Incense Burner, 12″, Bijin leaning against lantern, pierced openwork, underglaze blue and white, Hirado, Mikawachi, 19th C **700.00**
Nodder, 5½″, Fukujurojin, seated figure, robe with knotted tie cord on chest,

extended cylindrical forehead, polychrome dec, Banko 450.00
Plate, 11¼", hexagonal, kakiemon palette, bird and flowering tree, wide rim of floral reserves on coral diaper ground 145.00
Sake Bottle, 7¼", rect body, underglaze blue, two pine trees and three pavilions, stylized landscape, sq top with leaf and cloud device, one corner with sq spout, opposite corner pierced with small hole, Arita, late 17th C . . 675.00
Vase, 12", ovoid, cylindrical neck, trumpet mouth, slightly flared foot, two circular painted reserves of hooo-o, varying brocade ground, overlaid dragon crawling up the body and around neck, iron–red Fukagama-Sei, Meiji marks 475.00

Clock, white classical figures and acanthus dec, blue ground, clock marked "Swiss Made," 6" h, $550.00.

JASPERWARE

History: Jasperware is a hard, unglazed porcelain with a colored ground, varying from the most common blues and greens to lavender, yellow, red, or black. The white designs are applied in relief and often reflect a classical motif. Jasperware was first produced at Wedgwood's Etruria Works in 1775. Josiah Wedgwood described it as "a fine Terra Cotta of great beauty and delicacy proper for cameos."

Many other English potters, in addition to Wedgwood, produced jasperware. Two of the leaders were Adams and Copeland and Spode. Several continental potters, e.g., Heubach, also produced the ware.

Reference: Susan and Al Bagdade, *Warman's English & Continental Pottery & Porcelain, 1st Edition*, Warman Publishing Co., Inc., 1987.

Reproduction Alert: Jasperware still is made today, especially by Wedgwood.

Note: This category includes all pieces of jasperware which were made by companies other than Wedgwood. Wedgwood jasperware is found in the Wedgwood listing.

Biscuit Jar, 7" h, light blue band on dark blue ground, white classical figures and acanthus leaf border, sterling silver top and handle 750.00
Box, 6" d, white cameos of cherubs and lovebirds on cov, gray–green ground, ftd 175.00
Creamer, 2½" h, pale pink frolicking Kewpies, sage green ground, sgd "O'Neill" 175.00
Cruet, 6¾", white relief man and woman toasting each other, small cupid and word "Prosit," sage green ground, matching orig stopper, Germany . . . 100.00

Cup and Saucer, dark blue, white classical figures 100.00
Dish, 4¼" d, white relief Indian with shield and hatchet, sheaf of wheat border, green ground, sgd "Heubach" . . 60.00
Hatpin Holder, 4¼", deep blue, white figures, band of flowers at top, marked "Adams" 50.00
Jar, 3½" h, white classical cameos, blue ground, SP lid and handle, marked "Adams, Tunstall, England" 110.00
Jug, 7", blue, classical figures representing the four seasons, angular handles with foliage motif, silver rim, marked "Adams," late 18th C 225.00
Pitcher
5", white cameos of cherubs in roses, green ground 125.00
8", blue, white classical figures, marked "Copeland, England," c1885 . . . . 225.00
Planter, large, blue, white relief Apollo and four muses, c1850 . . . . 225.00
Plaque
7½", white raised semi-nude female figure, green ground, marked "Germany" 110.00
11¼", white raised figures of children at play, soft green ground, marked "Germany" 125.00
11½", white raised figures of putti, blue ground, marked "Germany" . 175.00
Spill Vase, deep blue, white relief florals, trees, and muses representing poetry and drama 110.00
Teapot, 6½", blue, white relief birds and bamboo, pewter top and finial, marked "Copeland-Spode" 150.00
Tumbler, 4", white classical cameos, brown ground 65.00

Tureen, cov, 7½" d, blue, white relief bridge scene, floral dec, matching stand, marked "Copeland-Spode," c1820 . . . .   **160.00**

Vase

4", white cameos of man with spade, woman under tree, blue ground . .   **25.00**

7", white cameo of classic woman, carrying torch, light green ground .   **50.00**

8", white relief classical figure, blue ground, SP rim, c1850 . . . .   **50.00**

JEWEL BOXES

History: The evolution of jewelry was paralleled by the development of boxes in which to store it. Jewel box design followed the fashion trends dictated by furniture styles. Many jewel boxes are lined.

Silver plated, ftd, floral trellis like bail, bird finial, marked "Mermod Jaccard & Co, St Louis," c1870, resilvered, $275.00.

Amethyst Glass, 6 x 4⅞", enameled floral dec, SP rim and base **125.00**

Art Nouveau, 10 x 8 x 7", ormolu, raised figural and floral dec, plaque dated 1903 . . . .   **225.00**

Cranberry Glass, 4½ x 2¾", enameled floral dec, SP rim **150.00**

German Silver, 6½" l, 13 oz, rect, heavily molded and bellied sides, winged dolphin form feet, early 19th C **850.00**

Gilt Bronze, 16" w, 9½" h, elaborate Moorish design, semi precious stones, enamel dec **900.00**

Ivory, 8¾ x 5½ x 4¾", rect, hinged lid, delicate engraved and repousse mounts **200.00**

Malachite, 4½ x 2½", veneer, rect,

raised feet, satin lining, Russian, 19th C **225.00**

Pewter, 5½ x 9½", engraved brass frame like ornament on top, oval mosaic work, purple velvet lining, marked "Marshall & Sons, Edinburgh, Scotland" **250.00**

Silver

Plated, 8 x 5 x 3", oval, hinged lid, ftd emb cupids, daisy chain and roses, velvet lining, marked "Wilcox" . . .   **75.00**

Sterling, 13 x 5 x 4", repousse sides, small petal-like beaded edges, fancy feet, red velvet lining, marked "Meridan" **150.00**

Wave Crest

5¼ x 3", oval, hinged cov, gold emb scroll around edge, blue and white center florals, pink sprays, green leaves, marked **265.00**

6 x 3", pale blue painted flowers, red banner mark **570.00**

JEWELRY

History: Jewelry has been a part of every culture. It was a way of displaying wealth, power, or love of beauty. In the current antique marketplace, it is easiest to find jewelry dating between 1800 to 1950.

Jewelry items were treasured and handed down as heirlooms from generation to generation. In the United States, antique jewelry is any jewelry one hundred or more years old, a definition linked to U.S. Customs law. "Heirloom/estate" jewelry, i.e., jewelry at least twenty-five years old and acquired new, used, or through inheritance, is used for old jewelry that does not meet the "antique" definition.

The jewelry found in this listing fits either the antique or "heirloom/estate" definition. The list contains no new reproduction pieces. The jewelry is made of metals and gemstones proven to endure over time. Inexpensive and mass produced costume jewelry is covered in *Warman's Americana & Collectibles.*

Several major auction houses, especially Christie's, Doyle's, and Sotheby's in New York City, hold specialized jewelry auctions several times each year.

Note: The first step in determining the value of a piece of old jewelry is to correctly identify the metal and gemstones. Take into account the current value of the metal and gemstones plus the piece's age, identifying marks, quality, condition, construction, etc.

References: Lillian Baker, *Fifty Years of Collectible Fashion Jewelry, 1925–1975,* Collector Books, 1986, 1989 value update; Vivienne Becker, *Antique and 20th Century Jewelry,* Van Nostrand Reinhold; Rose L. Goldemberg, *Antique Jewelry:*

A Practical And Passionate Guide, Crown Publishers, Inc., 1976; Arthur Guy Kaplan, *The Official Price Guide To Antique Jewelry, Fifth Edition,* House of Collectibles, 1985; Dorothy T. Rainwater, *American Jewelry Manufacturers,* Schiffer Publishing Ltd., 1988.

Advisor: Elaine J. Luartes.

Dates:

Georgian	**1714–1837**
Victorian	**1837–1865**
Edwardian	**1885–1910**
Art Nouveau	**1880–1920**
Arts and Crafts	**1895–1915**
Art Deco	**1920–1930**
Art Retro	**1940–1950**

Bar Pin
  Art Deco, platinum, onyx center set
    with diamonds **1,000.00**
  Edwardian, platinum
    Lacy, round diamonds, pierced
      mounting, 14K gold stem **2,750.00**
    Tapered form, center pearl flanked
      by pierced floral motifs alternat-
      ing with twelve old mine dia-
      monds, approx 1.00 ct, sgd
      "Dreicer & Co" **2,200.00**
  Victorian
    Mosaic, bead and wire twist dec,
      micro–mosaic plaque **250.00**
    Rose and yellow 15K gold, double
      stalk of wheat and single blos-
      som **225.00**
    SS, "MIZPAH" and ribbon motif,
      English hallmarks **45.00**
    YG, 15K, set with three cabochon
      garnets **200.00**
Barrette, Edwardian, engraved 14K yg,
  lattice motif set with seed pearls . . . **500.00**
Beads
  Art Deco
    Carved ivory, lotus motif, 32" l . . . **450.00**
    Crystal rondelles alternating with
      faceted red beads, 44" l **85.00**
  Edwardian, seed pearl choker, four-
    teen strands, three gold bars set
    with half pearls **1,900.00**
  Victorian
    Coral, graduated beads, 14K yg or-
      nate clasp **225.00**
    Millefiori, graduated lampwork,
      29" l **150.00**
    Opals, forty-three opals alternating
      with faceted crystal rondelles,
      opal bead clasp **1,800.00**
Bracelet
  Art Nouveau
    Gold, 14K yg, pierced scrolls, three
      sapphires **575.00**
    Gold, 14K yg, relief chrysanthe-
      mum motif alternating with oval
      reserves **500.00**

Gold, 18K yg, enameled blue and
  green dec, Tiffany **285.00**
Pearls, nine Baroque pearls, each
  set in foliate link, 15K yg mount-
  ing **775.00**
Arts and Crafts, semi-circular, two in-
  dented copper bands on sterling
  silver band, stamped "Dirk Van Erp,
  Harry Dixon, San Francisco, Ster-
  ling," c1910 . . . . **330.00**
Edwardian, 10K yg, knife edge style,
  two hearts, bow and cluster motif,
  set with seed pearls and diamonds **700.00**
Victorian
  Baby, yg, hinged, black enamel
    dec, pr **450.00**
  Bangle, gold filled
    Etched band dec **75.00**
    Set with ruby and diamond cres-
      cent and star **660.00**
  Link, 14K rose gold, graduated oval
    cabochon moonstone links **900.00**
  Lion head motif, 10K yg, set with
    three diamonds and two garnets **800.00**
  Mesh style, 14K yg, clasp set with
    half pearls **1,200.00**
  Mogul style, over one hundred ta-
    ble cut diamonds, 22K gold and
    cloisonne enamel setting, c1875 **3,630.00**
Brooch
  Art Deco
    Carnelian, 14K yg, oval carved car-
      nelian, bands of green and black
      enamel and seed pearls **450.00**
    Platinum, pair of bleeding hearts
      set with calibre rubies, old mine
      and rose diamonds, polished
      platinum stems with diamond ter-
      minals **1,500.00**
  Art Nouveau
    SS, woman's head, Unger Bros
      trademark **350.00**
    YG, 18K, bird in flight, French and
      round cut diamonds, hallmarked,
      c1900 . . . . **1,650.00**
  Art Retro
    14K rose gold, floral spray motif set
      with rubies and diamonds **600.00**
    18K yellow and red gold, stylized
      floral scroll, center triangular cut
      aquamarine and diamond floral
      motif flanked by bands of rubies,
      pave diamond terminal **9,000.00**
  Edwardian, platinum, modified filigree
    style, oval shape, pave set dia-
    monds (approx 3.50 cts TW) and
    one 40 ct sapphire **18,000.00**
  Victorian
    Beaded dome, 14K yg, suspending
      two beads from foxtail link chain **385.00**
    Cameo, shell, oval yg frame, wom-
      an's head in profile **400.00**

Crescent, yg, tapered crescent set with nine sapphires alternating with ten old mine diamonds, sgd "Tiffany & Co" 3,200.00

Coral, yg, carved coral female head surrounded by grape vines, suspending three grape vine tassels 650.00

Eagle motif, 14K yg, mine-cut diamond suspended from beak ... 800.00

Floral motif, seed pearls, 14k rose and yg mounting 330.00

Handpainted portrait on porcelain, gold filled frame 250.00

Snake motif, 15K yg, coiled snake, sapphire and diamond highlights 600.00

Chain

Art Deco, platinum, fancy links spaced with diamonds, (2.5 cts TW), 32" l 5,800.00

Victorian

Slide Style, 14K yg, curb links, fancy shape engraved slide, 52" l 500.00

Watch-Vest style, 14K yg, fetter and five link style, 12" 350.00

Woven Hair, repousse gold clasp, 60" 170.00

Chatelaine, Victorian, belt style, silver, pierced, sculptured and engraved, orig memo case, scissors, sheath, and thimble receptacle, English hallmarks 800.00

Cuff Links

Art Deco, platinum, set with mother of pearl and half pearls 190.00

Victorian

Fancy shamrock motif, SS 80.00

Plain ball motif, 14K yg 90.00

Necklace Set, Art Nouveau, sterling silver, putti motif, matching necklace, clasp, and belt buckle, marked "Kerr," $950.00.

Earrings

Art Retro

Gold, 14K yg, tapered hoops centered by bands of rubies 800.00

Yellow and white gold, 14K, ribbon bows, rect cut aquamarine center flanked by bands of diamonds and rubies 500.00

Victorian

Dangle

Ram's head motif, ornate, 14k yg 750.00

Teardrop circle, 15K yg 475.00

Urn motif, high carat yellow gold 675.00

Diamond Drop style, silver and gold circular framed mounts set with mine-cut diamonds (approx 1.25 cts TW) 1,050.00

Hoop, small, 14K yg 130.00

Jabot, Art Deco, platinum, single cut diamond and jade arrow motif, jade ring terminal with rose diamond bail, sgd "Cartier" 4,000.00

Lavaliere

Art Nouveau

Gold, 14K yg, center openwork scrolling chandelier motif with collet set circular, kite, and pear shaped peridots and freshwater pearls suspended by triple strand freshwater pearl and gold chain from smaller peridot tassel motifs 2,800.00

Pansy, seed pearl, free form frame, turquoise beads, fine gold link chain, English hallmarks, c1900 330.00

Edwardian, 14K yg, delicate ring-line design set with half pearls 190.00

Victorian, 14K yg, bell shape, set with diamond and seed pearls 160.00

Locket

Art Deco, 14K white gold, geometric design 375.00

Art Nouveau, 14K yg, round swirl motif, set with one diamond 500.00

Victorian

Gold, yellow, oval painted miniature, half pearl floral frame 225.00

Silver, black onyx shield centered by turquoise and half pearl floral basket 200.00

Lorgnette, Victorian, silver gilt, oval retractable lenses in ornate cherub motif case 900.00

Necklace

Art Deco, enamel dec SS links, set with lapis color glass 165.00

Art Nouveau, gold chain, fresh water pearl spacers, six collet set sapphires, single center diamond, c1900 .... 3,410.00

Arts and Crafts, hand made, heavy-link silver chain, mounted with baroque pearl dec with large rect

shaped frame set with one polished
black opal, two suspended irregular
shaped polished black opals **4,500.00**
Victorian, gold chain, set with garnets **500.00**
Pendant
Art Nouveau
Cross, 18K yg, hand made, set with
one diamond **750.00**
Dragonfly motif, silver gilt, plique
a'jour enamel, set with cabochon
opals, baroque pearl, and diamonds **2,000.00**
Glass, bright blue oval, stylized floral design, orig silk tassel and
cord, sgd "R Lalique" **1,100.00**
Edwardian, platinum
Center oval sapphire in old mine
diamond frame suspended from
flexible graduated row of circular
old mine diamond links, platinum
chain with diamond barrel clasp **2,200.00**
Pear shaped fresh water pearl with
diamond cap suspended from
flexible collet set with row of rose
diamonds terminating in old mine
diamond, white gold chain **800.00**
Victorian
Figural, carved lava, gold fittings . **250.00**
Heart, yg, pave seed pearls **300.00**

**Pin, Art Nouveau, Lalique, jet center,
marquisite stones, sterling mountings,
$300.00.**

Pin
Art Deco
Antelope motif, SS **55.00**
Geometric design, platinum, set
with square-cut rubies and
round-cut diamonds **2,200.00**
Art Nouveau
Gold, sculpture, miniature face set
with baroque pearls and cabochon rubies **800.00**
Gold and opal, circular, head of
snarling creature, mosaic opal
ground, scaly body forming bor-
der, imp "Lalique," c1900, 1¼" d **8,250.00**
Arts and Crafts, SS, round orange
petaled flowers, star points, hall-

marked and stamped "JF," 1½" d,
pr **140.00**
Edwardian
Bow, pear shaped green tourmaline
surmounted by diamond set bow,
18K white gold **2,200.00**
Foliate, full cut diamonds, rect
pierced foliate platinum mounting **550.00**
Victorian
Crescent shape, 14 K yg, set with
half pearls **100.00**
Floral carved ivory **35.00**
Scroll motif, 14K yg, set with diamond and seed pearls **400.00**
Starburst motif, pin/pendant combination, 14K yg, set with ruby
and seed pearls **185.00**
Ring
Art Deco, platinum
Oval cabochon emerald carved
with foliate motifs, diamond border, flanked by bands of tapered
baguette and triangular cut diamonds **3,500.00**
Oval cabochon star sapphire, diamond geometric motifs **1,500.00**
Art Nouveau, oval black opal and two
small diamonds, 14K yg foliate
mounting **990.00**
Edwardian, platinum, filigree style,
three diamonds, straight row setting **2,000.00**
Victorian
9K yg, snakes motif, set with cabochon opal and amethyst, English hallmarks **450.00**
10K yg, cabochon opal surrounded
by six rose-cut diamonds **285.00**
10K yg, set with two mine-cut diamonds, ruby, and emerald **350.00**
14K yg, cabochon moss agate
flanked by two dogs **335.00**
14K yg, set with hardstone cameo **500.00**
Scarf Pin, Victorian, gold, Etruscan
bead work, pietra dura center **175.00**
Seal, Victorian, gold, flower motif, amethyst intaglio **850.00**
Stick Pin, tie
Art Deco, platinum, sugarloaf cabochon .50 ct sapphire, diamond ba-
guettes, sgd "Cartier, New York,"
orig fitted box **2,600.00**
Art Nouveau, 18K yg, miniature Gibson girl enameled portrait, set with
diamonds **750.00**
Victorian, 14K yg, gargoyle motif, set
with ruby **125.00**
Watch
Art Deco, open face, lapel, SS and
marcasite, marked "925" **220.00**
Art Nouveau, open face, lapel, 14K
yg, angel and floral motif **1,200.00**

Art Retro, wristwatch, lady's, 14K yg,
    dec with diamonds and sapphires   **775.00**
Victorian
    Hunting Case, gold filled, Waltham,
        three colored gold **400.00**
    Pocket, open face, 18 K yg, Ham-
        ilton, Arabic numerals **275.00**
Watch Chain, lady's, 14K yg, ornate
    gold tassel at end, black enameled
    slide set with 3mm pearl **400.00**
Watch Fob, Victorian, 14K yg and
    mother of pearl, horn motif **80.00**

JUDAICA

History: Throughout history, Jews have expressed themselves artistically in both the religious
and secular spheres. Most Jewish art objects were
created as part of the concept of "Hiddur Mitzva,"
i.e., adornment of implements involved in performing rituals both in the synagogue and home.

For almost 2,000 years, since the destruction of
the Jerusalem Temple in 70 A.D., Jews have lived
in many lands. The widely differing environments
gave traditional Jewish life and art a multifaceted
character. Unlike Greek, Byzantine, or Roman art
which have definite territorial and historical boundaries, Jewish art is found throughout Europe, the
Middle East, North Africa, and other areas.

Ceremonial objects incorporated not only liturg-
ical appurtenances, but also ethnographic artifacts
such as amulets and ritual costumes. The style of
each ceremonial object responded to the artistic
and cultural milieu in which it was created. Although diverse stylistically, ceremonial objects,
whether for Sabbath, holidays, or the life cycle,
still possess a unity of purpose.

Judaica has been crafted in all media, though
silver is the most collectible. Sotheby's, Christie's,
and Swann's hold several Judaica auctions in the
United States, England, Amsterdam, and Israel.

References: Abraham Kanof, *Jewish Ceremonial Art*, Harry N. Abrams, n.d.; Cecil Roth, *Jewish
Art—An Illustrated History*, Graphic Society of New
York, 1971; Geoffrey Wigoder, (ed.), *Jewish Art
and Civilization*, Chartwell Books, 1972.

Museums: B'nai B'rith Klutznick Museum,
Washington, DC; H.U.C., Skirball Museum, Los
Angeles, CA; Jewish Museum, New York, NY; Ju-
dah L. Magnes Museum, Berkeley, CA; Maurice
Spertus Museum of Judaica, Chicago, IL; National
Museum of American Jewish History, Philadelphia,
PA; Yeshiva University Museum, New York, NY.

Advisor: Arthur M. Feldman.

Amulet Case, 5½", Italian silver, Turin,
    master or assayer's mark GB, mid
    18th C **5,225.00**
Chalice, 13" h, Continental silver, Her-
    man Lang, Augsburg, 17th C, 29 oz   **2,325.00**

Charger, 23" d, Continental silver, re-
    pousse floral and figural dec, c1780,
    48 oz **1,650.00**
Circumcision Cup
    3½", SS, English, marked "Urquart
        and Hart, London, 1792" **950.00**
    5", German, double, silver gilt,
        marked "Johanna Becker, Augs-
        burg," c1755–57 . . . .   **13,200.00**
Circumcision Knife, 7", tortoise shell,
    SS, and steel, Continental, late
    18th C **1,650.00**
Comb, Burial Society, 6" w, brass, Hun-
    garian, 1881 . . . .   **5,775.00**
Esther Scroll, 10½", cased, Austro–
    Hungarian silver, Vienna, 1846 . . . .   **1,650.00**
Goblet, 4", presentation, German silver,
    c1850 . . . .   **660.00**
Hanukah Lamp, 9¾", Austrian 800 fine
    silver, scroll edge backplate sur-
    mounted by crown, facing emb with
    pair of unengraved tablets flanked by
    pair of griffins, cartouche of the Star
    of David, rect platform, contiguous
    row of eight urn form lamps on wire
    frame, four scrolled supports, lacking
    servant's lamp, late 19th C, 22 oz 10
    dwt **1,800.00**
Kiddush Cup, 5¼", silver gilt, Polish,
    mid 18th C **3,850.00**
Mezuzah Case, 4½", American silver,
    Ludwig Wolpert, NY, stamped "Toby
    Pascher Workshop, The Jewish Mu-
    seum, NY" **650.00**
Minora Wall Sconce, 10½" l, Continental
    silver, heraldic repousse back shield,
    c1858, 18 oz **2,860.00**
Passover Dish, 15¼", pewter, German,
    maker's initials "D.V.D.," c1768 . . . .   **3,750.00**
Passover Plate, 8¾", ceramic, Conti-
    nental, 18th C **500.00**
Plaque, 2¾ x 2", SS, rabbi, inscribed,
    after engraving by Boris Schatz,
    framed **500.00**
Sabbath Beaker, 3", silver gilt, German,
    Johann Friedrich Schutteler, Lipps-
    tadt, c1825 . . . .   **1,300.00**
Sabbath Candlesticks, pr, 16¼", Aaron
    Katz, London, 1894, Polish style . . .   **1,000.00**
Spice Box
    4¾", SS, Scandinavian, fish form,
        blurred marks on tail, articulated
        body, hinged head, green jeweled
        eyes, 19th C, 1 oz 10 dwt **385.00**
    5¼", SS, filigree, Bohemian, sgd "R.
        G., Prague, 1815" **1,200.00**
    10", tower shape, SS, filigree, Polish,
        18th C **7,500.00**
Torah Ark Key, 4", Italian silver, 18th C   **4,125.00**
Torah Pointer, 10½", Polish silver, worn
    on index finger, 18th C **825.00**

Urn, 6½", Bezalel, silver inlaid brass,
  c1910 . . . . **1,320.00**

JUGTOWN POTTERY

History: In 1920 Jacques and Julianna Busbee
left their cosmopolitan environs and returned to
North Carolina to revive the state's dying craft of
pottery making. Jugtown Pottery, a colorful and
somewhat off-beat operation, was located in
Moore County, miles away from any large city and
accessible only "if mud permits."

Ben Owens, a talented young potter, turned the
wares. Jacques Busbee did most of the designing
and glazing. Julianna handled promotion.

Utilitarian and decorative items were produced.
Although many colorful glazes were used, orange
predominated. A Chinese blue glaze that ranged
from light blue to deep turquoise was a prized
glaze reserved for the very finest pieces.

Jacques Busbee died in 1947. Julianna, with the
help of Owens, ran the pottery until 1958 when it
was closed. After long legal battles, the pottery
was reopened in 1960. It now is owned by Country
Roads, Inc., a non-profit organization. The pottery
still is operating and using the old mark.

**Bowl, pedestal, turquoise and maroon,
Oriental style, 6½" d, 4" h, $150.00.**

Bowl
  5 x 3", frogskin glaze 50.00
  6 x 2", crimped, Chinese blue and red
    glaze 75.00
Candlesticks, 3" h, Chinese Translation,
  Chinese blue and deep red, marked,
  pr 70.00

Cookie Jar, cov, 12" h, ovoid, strap han-
  dles 75.00
Creamer, cov, 4¾", yellow, marked . . .   45.00
Finger Bowl, Chinese Translation 100.00
Jar
  6¼", yellowware, marked 45.00
  6¾", cov, bulbous, flaring rim, eared
    handles, redware, bright orange
    glaze, minor edge chips 48.00
Mug, brown glaze 25.00
Pie Plate, 9½" d, orange, black concen-
  tric circles 65.00
Pitcher, 5", gray and cobalt blue salt
  glaze 75.00
Rose Jar, cov, 4½" h, blended olive
  green glaze 48.00
Sugar, cov, 3¾", Tobacco Spit glaze,
  marked 35.00
Teapot, 5¼", Tobacco Spit glaze, sgd,
  c1930 . . . .   40.00
Vase
  3¾", Chinese Translation, Chinese
    blue, marked 100.00
  7", four small handles, salt glaze . . .   85.00
  13", stovepipe neck, Chinese blue . .   250.00

KPM

$\mathcal{K.P.M}$

History: The mark, KPM, has been used separately and in conjunction with other symbols by
many German porcelain manufacturers, among
whom are the Königliche Porzellan Manufactur in
Meissen, 1720s; Königliche Porzellan Manufactur
in Berlin, 1832–1847; and Krister Porzellan Manufactur in Waldenburg, mid-19th century.

Collectors now use the term "KPM" to refer to
the high quality porcelain produced in the Berlin
area in the 18th and 19th centuries.

Reference: Susan and Al Bagdade, *Warman's
English & Continental Pottery & Porcelain, 1st Edition,* Warman Publishing Co., Inc., 1987.

Basket, 16¼" d, oval, two sq handles,
  pierced border, pale green ground,
  flowers and butterflies, blue scepter,
  iron red KPM mark, c1840 . . . .   325.00
Cheese Board, rose and leaf garland
  border, hole to hang, marked 45.00
Cream Jug, 4¼", cavorting cherubs, orb
  and scepter mark, c1870 . . . .   300.00
Cup and Saucer, hunting scene, filigree,
  18th C 50.00
Dinner Service, Art Deco style, gilt and
  jeweled in turquoise and pink, flowering plants on speckled gilt and iron
  red ground, sea green borders with
  molded gilt swags, blue scepter, iron
  red orb, KPM mark, c1880 . . . .   8,000.00

Dish, leaf shape, 9½", painted, birds on flowering branch, burgundy border, gilt drapery, blue scepter, iron red KPM and orb mark, c1860 . . . . **250.00**

Fruit Plate, 9", hp, gold dec, wide scroll reticulated rims, orb mark, set of 4 . **125.00**

Plaque

9¼ x 6⅜", Egyptian scene, incised mark on reverse, framed **2,700.00**

17¼ x 12½", oval, painted boat carrying Cupid and maidens playing musical instruments, sailing past forlorn looking man, imp "KPM" and scepter marks, late 19th C . . **2,475.00**

Scent Bottle, molded scrolls, multicolored painted bouquets of flowers, gilt trim, gilt metal C-scroll stopper, marked, mid 19th C **150.00**

Statue, male and female on pedestal, highly decorated, round base, 24" h, $3,500.00.

Urn, cov, cobalt blue and gilt, floral and cherub dec, pr **300.00**

Vase, cov, two loop handles, blue, painted floral bouquets with gilt foliage, flared foot, blue scepter and KPM mark, c1860 . . . . **1,150.00**

Wall Pocket, 15", ornate multicolored floral dec **275.00**

KAUFFMANN, ANGELICA

History: Marie Angelique Catherine Kauffmann was a Swiss artist who lived from 1741 until 1807. Her paintings were copied by many artists who hand decorated porcelain during the 19th century.

The majority of the paintings are neo-classical in style.

Reference: Susan and Al Bagdade, *Warman's English & Continental Pottery & Porcelain, 1st Edition,* Warman Publishing Co., Inc., 1987.

Plate, scalloped rim, cranberry, gold dec, three classical women in center, sgd "Kaufmann," Austria beehive mark, 8½" d, $85.00.

Bowl, 10½", blue, gold dec, two ladies **255.00**

Box, 2¾ x 4½", lilac, two maidens and child in woods on cov, brass hinges **85.00**

Cake Plate, 10", ftd, classical scene, two maidens and cupid, beehive mark **85.00**

Compote, 8", classical scene, beehive mark, sgd **80.00**

Cup and Saucer, classical scene, heavy gold trim, ftd **90.00**

Inkwell, pink luster, classical lady **75.00**

Pitcher, 8½", garden scene, ladies, children, and flowers sgd **100.00**

Plaque, 8¾", classical scene, three maidens dancing **75.00**

Plate

8", cobalt blue border, reticulated rim, classical scene with two figures . . **55.00**

8¾", classical scene, three maidens dancing **60.00**

Tobacco Humidor, SP top, pipe on top, green ground, ladies and cupid **400.00**

Tray, 16½" d, round, classical figures in reserve, sgd, beehive mark **175.00**

Vase, 9¼", two ornate handles, classical scene, pearlized ground, lacy, gold dec **120.00**

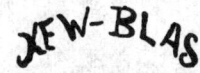

KEW BLAS

History: Amory and Francis Houghton established the Union Glass Company, Somerville, Massachusetts, in 1851. The company went bankrupt in 1860, but was reorganized. Between 1870 and 1885 the Union Glass Company made pressed glass and blanks for cut glass.

Art glass production began in 1893 under the direction of William S. Blake and Julian de Cordova. Two styles were introduced. A Venetian style consisted of graceful shapes in colored glass, often flecked with gold. An iridescent glass, labeled Kew Blas, was made in plain and decorated forms. The pieces are close in design and form to Quezel products, but lack the subtlety of Tiffany items.

The company ceased production in 1924.

Vase, urn shape, squatty bulbous top, pulled feather dec, dark glazed int., sgd, 7″ h, $1,200.00.

Bowl, 14 x 5″, pulled feather, red ground, sgd	1,200.00
Candlesticks, 8½″, irid gold, twisted stems, pr	725.00
Compote, 7″ h, twisted stem, ribbed bowl, irid gold, pink highlights	375.00
Creamer, 3¼″, irid gold, applied handle	225.00
Finger Bowl and Underplate, 5″ bowl, 6″ plate, ribbed, scalloped border, metallic luster, gold and platinum highlights	465.00
Rose Bowl, 3½″, green and gold hooked dec, butterscotch ground, gold int.	525.00
Salt, irid gold	200.00
Sherbet, 5″, irid gold	200.00
Tumbler, 4″, pinched sides, irid gold, sgd	185.00
Vase	
5″, spherical, rolled gold rim, green and gold pulled feather, white ground, early 20th C, sgd	475.00
6″, dark blue, light blue pulled loops, sgd	810.00
6¼″, cylinder, rolled rim, gold and green swags, pale orange, ground, early 20th C, sgd, orig paper label	600.00
7″, bulbous, flared, pulled feather, sgd	1,500.00
7¾″, Zipper, green and gold, sgd	850.00
Wine Glass, 4¾″, curving stem, irid gold	185.00

KITCHEN COLLECTIBLES

History: The kitchen was a central focal point in a family's environment until the 1960s. Many early kitchen utensils were handmade and prized by their owners. Next came a period of utilitarian products made of tin and other metals. When the housewife no longer wished to work in a sterile environment, color was added through enamel and plastic and design served both an aesthetic and functional purpose.

The advent of home electricity changed the type and style of kitchen products. Many items went through fads. The high technology field already has made inroads into the kitchen, and another revolution seems at hand.

References: Jane H. Celehar, *Kitchens and Gadgets, 1920 to 1950*, Wallace-Homestead, 1982; Linda Campbell Franklin, *300 Hundred Years of Kitchen Collectibles, Second Edition,*, Books Americana, 1982; Glydon Shirley, *The Miracle in Grandmother's Kitchen*, published by author, 1983.

Periodical: Kitchen Collectibles News, Box 383, Murray Hill Station, New York, NY 10016.

Additional Listings: Baskets, Brass, Butter Prints, Copper, Fruit Jars, Food Molds, Graniteware, Ironware, Tinware, and Woodenware. See *Warman's Americana & Collectibles* for more examples including electrical appliances.

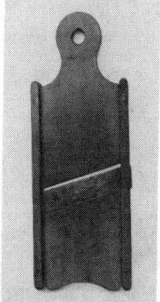

Cutting Board, wood, round top, shaped base, metal blade, 6⅝ x 18″, $85.00.

Bowl, 15¾ x 24″, almond shape, wood, natural patina	200.00
Butter Churn, 12½″ h, wood, stave constructed, lid and dasher, old varnish finish	325.00
Butter Paddle, 9″ l, burl bowl, scrubbed white, black stains, hook handle	75.00
Cheese Sieve, 8″ d, 7½″ h, wood stave construction, iron band	20.00

Colander, 10¾″ d, 3″ h, copper, punched star design **65.00**

Cookie Board
6¾ x 11″, oak, relief carved man and woman figures, brown patina **250.00**
9¾ x 16″, beech, carved basket of flowers one side, other bunch of grapes, scrubbed finish **300.00**
11 x 12″, pine, friesian and chip carved designs, dark brown finish on one side, other natural dark patina **200.00**
18″ d, poplar, worn finish **100.00**

Corn Husker, 4½″ l, bone **10.00**
Cranberry Scoop, 11½ x 17½″, wood and tin, sheet metal teeth, refinished **85.00**
Cutting Board, 11 x 17⅝″, wood, crest dec, drilled holes on sides, dark worn patina **65.00**
Egg Beater, Dover, 1873–91 . . . . **25.00**
Food Chopper, 7″ w, wrought iron, scalloped edge blade, turned wood handle **275.00**
Food Mold, 5½ x 12″, baby wrapped in floral blanket shape, reddish clay, amber int. glaze, green rim **155.00**
Fork, 11⅜″ d, wrought iron **55.00**

Kraut Cutter
8 x 21″, walnut, tombstone crest, dark worn patina **40.00**
26½″ l, poplar and oak, scrubbed finish, octagon hopper **100.00**

Ladle
10½″ l, wrought iron, turned wood handle **135.00**
15″ l, wood, pot hook handle **45.00**

Lemon Squeezer, wood **30.00**
Nutmeg Grater, Edgar **75.00**
Pastry Board, wood, three sided **30.00**
Pantry Box, 11½″ d, 6½″ h, wood, oak, bail handle, lid **165.00**
Rolling Pin, 23½″ l, curly maple **75.00**

Saucepan, 9″ d, 7″ h, copper, dovetailed, iron handle, marked "Carmichael Wilks Range Co" **70.00**

Skillet, copper
10½″d, wrought steel handle, stamped "Colony R.I." **85.00**
11½″ d, wrought iron handle, dovetailed construction, stamped "Smith & Anthony Co, Boston, Mass," handle marked "S & A Co" **110.00**

Spatula, 14½″ l, wrought iron, inlaid brass blade, initials "P. M." **255.00**

Spice Box
7¾ x 12 x 14½″, cherry, dovetailed, nine drawers, turned pulls, natural finish, label traces **550.00**
15 x 9 x 11½″, poplar, dovetailed case, slant top lid, divided drawer and int., worn brown finish **325.00**

Strainer, 9″ d, copper, wrought iron fittings, turned wood handle, European **100.00**
Toaster, 7½″ l, one slice size, wrought iron **350.00**

Trivet
7½″ l, cast iron, heart designs **125.00**
12″ l, lyre form, wrought iron frame and turned handle, brass top, replaced foot, stamped marker's mark **30.00**

Utensil Rack, 25½″ l, wrought iron, two tiers, seven hooks, stylized floral detail **300.00**

KUTANI

History: In the mid 1600s Kutani originated in the Kaga province of Japan. Kutani comes in a variety of color patterns, one of the most popular being Ao Kutani, a green glaze with colors such as green, yellow, and purple enclosed in a black outline. Wares made since the 1870s for export are enameled in a wide variety of colors and styles.

Reference: Sandra Andacht, *Oriental Antiques & Art: An Identification And Value Guide,* Wallace-Homestead, 1987.

Plate, 8½″ d, $40.00.

Beaker, 4½″ h, hp florals and birds, red, orange, and gold, white ground, marked "Ao-Kutani" **85.00**
Bowl, 6⅝″, gilt and bright enamel design, figural, animal, and floral reserves, kinrande ground, base inscribed "Kutani-sei", set of 10 . . . . . **385.00**
Charger, 18⅜″, pomegranate tree, chrysanthemums, and two birds on int., birds and flowers between scrolling foliate bands, irregular floral and brocade border, 11 character inscription **525.00**
Dish, 10½″, central scene, magpies in bamboo forest **250.00**

Figure
Bodhidharma, 12", standing, long red
   robe, flywisk in right hand **175.00**
Chinese Sage, 14¼", seated, hands
   on lamp, overglazed enameled brocade and floral robe **400.00**
Kannon, 14¼", polychrome and gilt
   dec, standing, dragon mount, high
   coiffure, wind-swept robe, inscribed
   "Kutani-sei" **500.00**
Garden Seat, 19" h, barrel shape, two
   large circular reserves of courtly figures in garden, small reserves with
   florals and landscape scenes, spiral-
   ing brocade ground, top pierced with
   circular florettes, pr **2,000.00**
Jar, 20½", ovoid, fan shaped reserves
   of warriors, molded ribbon tied tasseled ring handles, shippo-tsunagi
   ground, multicolored brocade patterned dome lid, pr **1,350.00**
Mustard Pot, attached saucer, Nishikide
   diapering, figural raised gold reserves, marked **65.00**
Tea Caddy, 6" h, bulbous, hexagonal,
   Nishikide diapering, figural raised
   gold reserves of children, red script
   mark **75.00**
Teapot, 4¼ x 6", cov, bulbous, One
   Thousand Faces **225.00**
Tray, 14", polychrome and gilt, figural
   scene, red, orange, and gold border **325.00**
Vase
   9¾", ovoid, waisted neck, recessed
   ring foot, upper portion with enameled reddish-brown wave pattern,
   underglaze blue wide band of ar-
   chaistic keyfret design, raised borders, lower section with gilt painted
   stylized lotus blossoms, green
   enamel scrolling leafy tendrils,
   bluish-black ground **360.00**
   10¾", trumpet, shaped figural and floral reserves, kinrande patterned
   ground, base inscribed "Kutani 3
   Kuma zukuri" **250.00**

LALIQUE

R.LALIQUE

LALIQUE

History: Rene Lalique (1860–1945) first gained
prominence as a jewelry designer. Around 1900
he began experimenting with molded glass
brooches and pendants, often embellishing them
with semiprecious stones. By 1905 he was devot-

ing himself exclusively to the manufacture of glass
articles.

In 1908 Lalique began designing packaging for
the French cosmetic houses. He also produced
many objects, especially vases, bowls, and figurines, in the Art Noveau style in the 1910s. The
full scope of Lalique's genius was seen at the 1925
Paris International Exhibition of Decorative Arts.
He later moved to the Art Deco form.

The mark "R. LALIQUE FRANCE" in block letters is found on pressed articles, tableware, vases,
paperweights, and mascots. The script signature,
with or without "France," is found on hand blown
objects. Occasionally a design number is included.
The word "France" in any form indicates a piece
made after 1926.

The post–1945 mark is "Lalique France" without
the "R"; there are exceptions to this rule.

References: Katherine Morrison McClinton, *Introduction to Lalique Glass*, Wallace-Homestead,
1978; Tony L. Mortimer, *Lalique,* Chartwell Books,
1989.

Reproduction Alert: Much faking of the Lalique
signature occurs, the most common being the addition of an "R" to the post–1945 mark.

Ashtray, 8", frosted cherubs, paper label **100.00**
Atomizer, clear and frosted, faceted and
   molded, circular frieze of tiny birds,
   etched "Lalique France" **175.00**
Bookends, pr
   6¼" h, figural, birds, sgd **475.00**
   7⅛" h, frosted, three molded putti
   bearing garlands, stenciled "Lalique France" **600.00**
Bowl
   8" d, Ondine Ouverte, opal, molded
   swimming mermaids among bub-
   bles, molded "F. Lalique" **1,000.00**
   9" d, Actina, blue opal **400.00**
   10" d, clear and frosted, molded rim
   frieze of tiny sparrows, inscribed
   "Lalique France" **700.00**
Box, cov, round
   3" d, female masks hiding among
   bunches of roses, turquoise stain,
   sgd "R Lalique" **345.00**
   4¾" d, molded antelope, black
   enamel, c1925 .... **500.00**
Carafe, 7¾" h, clear, indented and
   molded large blossoms, brown patina
   in recesses, inscribed "R. Lalique" . **400.00**
Centerpiece, opal, molded stylized fish
   around rim, glass nodules on body,
   stenciled "R. Lalique France" **1,000.00**
Charger, 14½" d, Martigues, opal,
   deeply molded swimming fish,
   molded "R. Lalique" **2,700.00**
Jar, cov, 3" h, 4" d, molded nude maidens on horseback, frosted **200.00**
Liqueur Service, 8¼" h decanter, five
   tumblers, 12" d tray, relief molded

grape bunches and stylized scrolling vines, frosted recesses, relief molded "R Lalique," inscribed France, c1925 **1,220.00**

Luminiere, 11⅛", Thais, clear and frosted, nude female holding drapery, cast bronze electrified base, inscribed "R. Lalique" **5,750.00**

Mascot, 8", Cockeral, smoked glass, c1920 . . . . **700.00**

Plate
9¼" d, Coquilles, four stylized shells, molded cameo mark, set of 6 . . . **650.00**
11¾", Assiette Plate Ondine, opal, mermaids among bubbles, inscribed "R. Lalique France" **1,400.00**
13½", Felix, clear and frosted, stylized petals, stenciled "R. Lalique, France" **200.00**

Powder Box, 4", Emiliane, #70 . . . . . **265.00**

Scent Bottle, 3", Dans La Nuit, for Worth Fragrances, blue spherical body, molded tiny stars **650.00**

Tray, 10½" d, opal pale blue, all over shell pattern, sgd "R Lalique" **225.00**

Vase, clear frosted thistle flowers and leaves, acid etched script signature "R Lalique, France," 8¼" h, $850.00.

Vase
6¼", Bleuets, conical, clear and frosted, cornflowers, inscribed "R. Lalique France" **450.00**
7", rows of vertical birds, sgd "Lalique, France" **475.00**
7⅛", Amiens, diamond shaped, gray, thick handles molded as ribbed scrolls, stenciled "R. Lalique" . . . **650.00**
7¼", Oursin, spherical, molded, stenciled "R. Lalique" **600.00**
8¼"
Grimpereaux, wide conical, six raised feet, tiny birds perched on leafy branches, blue patina in recesses, inscribed "R. Lalique" . **1,600.00**
Marguerites, ovoid, waisted neck,

molded myriad tiny blossoms, stenciled "F. Lalique France" . . **600.00**

9⅛", Monnaie du Pape, oviform, frosted, molded low and medium relief, blossoms, stems, and leaves, blue wash in recesses, molded "R. Lalique" **1,200.00**

9½", Six Figurines et Masques, frosted, deeply molded classical nude figures, masks, and thorny branches, brown wash in recesses, inscribed "R. Lalique" **2,500.00**

LAMP SHADES

History: Lamp shades were made to diffuse the harsh light produced by early gas lighting fixtures. These early shades were made by popular Art Nouveau manufacturers including Durand, Quezal, Steuben, Tiffany, and others. Many shades are not marked.

References: Dr. Larry Freeman, *New Lights on Old Lamps*, American Life Foundation, 1984; Jo Ann Thomas, *Early Twentieth Century Lighting Fixtures*, Collector Books, 1980.

Luster Art, blue pulled double hooked feather, gold border, opal glass, gold iridescent interior, acid etched signature, 5" h, 2¼" d fitter, $385.00.

Bradley and Hubbard, leaded glass, geometric mottled green pattern, 18" d **350.00**

Burmese, birds, butterflies, and flowers dec, gas fitting, 8¾" **275.00**

Cameo Glass, white leaves, yellow ground, 8⅜" d, 5" h, 3⅞" fitter **225.00**

Cased Glass, shaded rose to pink, mushroom shape, emb swirl design, ruffled top, 6⅞" d, 6⅜" h **225.00**

Custard Glass, brown nutmeg stain, 2" d fitter ring **35.00**

Durand
   Gold Egyptian Crackle, blue and
     white overlay, bulbous, ruffled rim,
     9½", sgd **175.00**
   Opal ground, irid threads, lily, 8" d,
     sgd **250.00**
Fenton, blue ground, white opal hob-
   nails, 4" **85.00**
Fostoria
   White luster ground, gold, green
     leaves, and vines, 5" d **150.00**
   Zipper pattern, green pulled dec, opal
     ground, gold lining, 5½" d **175.00**
Galle, cameo glass, milky sides overlaid
   with orange and olive, fire polished,
   floriform, 6½", sgd **475.00**
Lalique
   Amber, molded shells, 12", sgd **560.00**
   Crystal, molded ivy, green stain, 13",
     sgd **750.00**
Leaded Glass, unmarked
   Mottled green slag, hexagonal, 18" . **300.00**
   Purple and green grapes, green
     leaves, greenish amber ground,
     22" **850.00**
Loetz, irid, green oil spotting, ribbon
   work over white glass int., 8½" d,
   c1900 .... **225.00**
Luster Art
   Irid gold, pulled opal feathering,
     4¾" h **100.00**
   Opalescent ground
     Band of gold waves, 5" h, pr **350.00**
     Blue short hooked feathering, gold
      borders, gold lining **275.00**
Lutz, 7½ to 8" sq, 6¼" h, 2½" fitter,
   opaque white looping, applied cran-
   berry threading, ribbon edge, sq top **150.00**
Muller Freres, satin frosted white top,
   cobalt blue base, yellow highlights, 6"
   h, set of 3 .... **225.00**
NuArt, irid, Carnival glass, marigold, pr **125.00**
Pairpoint, 7" h, puffy, flower basket, re-
   verse painted pink and yellow pop-
   pies and roses **400.00**
Quezal
   Dark Green, platinum feathering, gold
     lining, 5½" **650.00**
   Iridescent gold ground
     King Tut, white pattern, gold lining **165.00**
     Opal fishnet design **175.00**
     Opal snakeskin top, irid gold and
      green snakeskin base, corset
      shape, pr **275.00**
   Opalescent Ground
     Irid gold trellis design, gold lining,
      ruffled rim, 6⅞" d **765.00**
     Pulled green feathering outlined in
      gold, irid gold lining, 6½" h **190.00**
Rubena, cranberry shading to clear,
   frosted and clear etched flowers and

leaves, ruffled, 7¼" d, 7⅝" h, 3⅞" fit-
   ter **175.00**
Steuben
   Aurene
     Irid blue, platinum leaf and vine mo-
     tif **850.00**
     Irid brown, platinum applied border **425.00**
     Irid gold, tulip shape, 4½" h **175.00**
   Calcite, etched dec, acorn shape .. **225.00**
Tiffany
   Iridescent blue ground, soft blue, yel-
     low pulled feather dec, scalloped
     rim, 1⅝" top d, 1½" base d, 3" h . **250.00**
   Iridescent gold ground
     Bell shape, 5¼", set of 4 ..... **1,000.00**
     Hexagonal, 4⅞" h, set of 6 ..... **1,500.00**
     Lily shape, set of 3 .... **1,450.00**
Verlys, raised birds and fish dec, 3⅝" d,
   1⅝" fitter, 5¾" h **275.00**
Williamson & Co
   Ball, white ground, yellow spots, red
     pulled feathers, 9" **175.00**
   Stalacite, blue and green ground,
     blue loops, 7" **135.00**

LAMPS AND LIGHTING

History: Lighting devices have evolved from
simple stone age oil lamps to the popular electrified models of today. Aimé Argand patented the
first oil lamp in 1784. Around 1850 kerosene became a popular lamp burning fluid, replacing
whale oil and other fluids. In 1879 Thomas A.
Edison invented the electric light bulb, causing
fluid lamps to lose favor and creating a new field
for lamp manufacturers to develop. Companies
like Tiffany and Handel developed skills in the
manufacture of electric lamps, having their decorators produce beautiful aesthetic bases and
shades.

References: J. W. Courter, *Aladdin, The Magic
Name in Lamps*, Wallace-Homestead, 1980; J. W.
Courter, *Collectors Manual & Price Guide Nine,
1983*, published by author, 1982; Robert De Falco,
Carole Goldman Hibel, John Hibel, *Handel Lamps*,
H & D Press, Inc., 1986; Dr. Larry Freeman, *New
Light on Old Lamps*, American Life Foundation,
1984; Nadja Maril, *American Lighting: 1840–1940*,
Schiffer Publishing, 1989; Leland & Crystal Pay-
ton, *Turned ON: Decorative Lamps of the 'Fifties*,
Abbeville Press, 1989; Jo Ann Thomas, *Early
Twentieth Century Lighting Fixtures*, Collector
Books, 1980; Catherine M. V. Thuro, *Oil Lamps*,
Wallace-Homestead, 1976; Catherine M. V. Thuro,
Oil Lamps II, Thorncliffe House, Inc., 1983.

Collectors' Club: The Mystic Light of the Aladdin Knights, R.D. #1, Simpson, IL 62985; Historical Lighting Society of Canada, P.O. Box 561,
Postal Station R, Toronto, ON M4G 4E1; Rushlight

Club, Old Academy Library, 150 Main Street, Wethersfield, CT 06109.

Museum: Winchester Center Kerosene Lamp Museum, Winchester Center, CT.

Additional Listings: See specific makers and Pattern Glass.

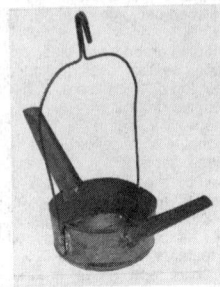

American, early, tin, lard, two handles, skillet type, $75.00.

AMERICAN, EARLY

Betty Lamp
    4", wrought iron, iron pick wick, rooster figure **130.00**
    5", wrought iron, wire pick, and hanger, swan figure, Pittsburgh, PA area **325.00**
Crusie, 6⅜" l, 6" h, 5¾" l hook, wrought iron, single **125.00**
Fat, 3¾" x 5 x 2", pottery, boat shaped, wick holes in end and center, PA . . . **250.00**
Hanging, 15", aqua, blown bell shaped globe, flared rim, applied knobs in tin crown frame, tooling, cut scallops, punching, traces of red paint **675.00**
Kettle, 10½", wrought iron, brass feet, spherical font, whale oil burner, twisted stem and pick on chain **190.00**
Lacemaker's, 16", cranberry overshot shade, polished brass base **375.00**
Peg, 5½", brass, acorn shaped, wooden base **100.00**
Rushlight and Candle Holder, iron, orig wooden base, 8½" h **150.00**
Rushlight Holder, iron, orig wooden base, 9⅞" h **100.00**
Tole, 7", saucer base, conical font, single spout burner, orig blue japanning **100.00**
Whale Oil
    6¼", tin, saucer base, burner, dark brown japanning **150.00**
    7⅜", pewter, double drop burner, Boston, c1840 . . . . **225.00**

Boudoir, Pairpoint, medium blue ground, blossom dec, wood base, sgd, 12" h, $750.00.

BOUDOIR

Handel, 14" h, Venetian scenic 7" shade, ornate base, sgd, #592S . . . **600.00**
Loetz, 12¼", white metal base, adjustable irid amber spotted and purple lined shades, pr **1,350.00**

CHANDELIERS

Brass, 19", six lights, baluster form standard above scrolled support, molded drip plates, candlecups, faceted pendant, 18th C **2,400.00**
Cameo, 23", etched glass, intaglio sgd "Daum Nancy," c1925 . . . . **900.00**
Gilt Bronze, 26 x 34", eight lights, scrolling branches, four rams heads above, pendant from ceiling cap, short chain, French, late 19th C **2,500.00**
Muller Freres, black painted wrought iron frame with scrolling floral vines, pierced ceiling plate, sq frame, inset mottled purple, pink, green, and orange circular bowl acid etched "Muller Freres, Luneville," four candle arms with ovoid mottled glass shades, electrified, 24" h, 24" d, c1925 . . . . **1,650.00**
Stickley, 20¼", hammered copper and glass dome, chain, c1910 . . . . **6,875.00**
Wrought Iron, 24", wood, six lights, green painted, cylindrical stem, hexagonal swellings joined by six candle arms, crenelated drip pans, Continental **275.00**

DESK

Handel, 6½" d, leaded glass green shade, bronze base, overhanging style, sgd **2,000.00**

Louis XVI, 33″, silverplated, four light, bouillotte, circular dished stand, ribbed border, hexagonal molded and coved standard, ribbed central knob, sq shaft, four S scroll arms, hexagonal nozzles and drip pans, beaded edges, black tole painted shade ... **3,500.00**

Tiffany Studios, NY, 15″, oval frame, two purple-green irid turtleback medallions, sixteen purple irid semiprecious stones embedded in circular bronze base, imp mark **4,500.00**

FLOOR

Aladdin, 60″ h, 18″ d shade, No. 1250 **325.00**

Handel, 61″ h, 20″ d, shade, leaded glass, double standard base **3,600.00**

J Kuyken, 69″, chromed metal, red glass, c1930 .... **5,775.00**

Michael Taylor, 78″, cast plaster, palm tree, painted white, rising leaf molded stem, wide fluted shallow cup, domical base **2,750.00**

Victorian, 68¼″, brass, ceramic ornaments, piano type, electrified **425.00**

FLUID

Boston and Sandwich, 8″, Blackberry pattern **225.00**

New England Glass Co, 9½″, Acorn and Drapery pattern, stepped pressed base, three ring knob, free blown font, cut and frosted, pewter collar **250.00**

Ripley
13¾″, candle, baptismal font, medium blue with cross and "I.H.S.," marked "Ripley & Co. Pat Pending," pewter connector and sockets, no lid, minor dents **300.00**
14½″, marriage, opaque white and blue, double fonts **475.00**

Satin, 9½″ d shade, 16½″ h, gold MOP satin base, shade with brass inset and feet, diamonds pattern, stylized flower in each diamond **750.00**

Sandwich Glass
11″, Acanthus Leaf pattern, opaque blue and white, whale oil burner, sandy finish **700.00**
13″, Onion pattern, opaque white, c1840 .... **650.00**

South Jersey, 10¾″, blown glass, large pear shaped amethyst font, mounted on clear standard and base, late ... **125.00**

HANGING

Brass, 11½″, pierced globular vessel suspended by three chains, 17th C . **365.00**

Handel, 16¼″ d, 19″ h, gold bronze tas-

sel and foliage emb fixture, satin finished dec shade with foliage dec .. **225.00**

Mount Washington, 15″, peachblow, hobnail shade, prisms, brass font and fittings **1,000.00**

Perzel, 40¼″, chrome metal and glass **1,225.00**

Victorian, 14½″, reticulated brass, umbrella style, jeweled **125.00**

STUDENT

20″, brass, double, peachblow shades, rope twist brass wire coil dec, electrified **500.00**

21½″, brass, green cased shade, electrified and polished **425.00**

24″, tin plated brass, milk glass shade **400.00**

40″ l, hanging, double, 10″ d green cased glass shades, burnished brass, electrified **1,250.00**

Table, cameo glass, Galle, conical shade, trumpet shaped base of translucent yellow glass overlaid in yellow–orange, lime green, and brown, etched with oranges, branches, and leaves, cameo sgd, 31″ h, $24,500.00.

TABLE

Argand, 31½″, brass, stepped scalloped base, reeded column and flat spherical font, clear cut and frosted shade, prisms **275.00**

Art Deco, bronze, girl sitting, green art glass shade **165.00**

Astral, gold ormolu stem, cut glass globe, marble base, dated 1870 ... **425.00**

Bradley & Hubbard, 23½″ h, 18¼″ d flattened domical shade, cylindrical border, eight radiating panels of light yellow etched glass, blue border, mounted in gilt metal ribbed frame, pierced paneled border of foliate and scrollwork, red and green enameled center quatrefoil, fluted column gilt metal standard, circular base with fluting, beading, and relief quatrefoils, early 20th C **1,875.00**

Cameo, Daum Nancy, 14″ h, 5″ d conical shade, trumpet base of translucent white mottled glass with blue, green–brown overlay, ten opal wheel carved flower heads, lighted base and shade, wrought iron shade supports, sgd **3,750.00**

Durand, 29½″, brass, blue glass standard, opaque white and clear feather pattern **250.00**

Handel, 21½″ h, reverse painted hemispherical shade, serene lake and swan scene, stylized stems and leaves on cast base **1,300.00**

Jefferson, 21″, reverse painted 16⅛″ shade with florals and leaves, apricot ground, black finished metal base, sgd **650.00**

Jensen, Georg, 27½″, silver, numbered "79" **3,575.00**

Pairpoint
17¾″ h, 13¾″ d puffy border shade, shaped circular shade with ribbed horizontal top, outwardly tapering sides, relief molded flowerheads and two hummingbirds, int. purple, blue, and yellow enameling, sponged purple ground, green and yellow birds, silvered metal knopped baluster form standard, molded lozenge mark, impressed "Pairpoint/E3032 . . . . **9,500.00**

22″ h, reverse painted conical shade with six painted glass panels of Grecian ruin in forest, patinated base stamped "Pairpoint Made in USA" **1,200.00**

Pittsburgh, 23¼″ h, 16″ d int. painted domical shade, continuous mountain lake and landscape, green, brown, and red highlights, deep blue water shading to violet, brown patinated metal standard cast with two loop handles and pendant rose garlands, spreading circular base with foliate bands, early 20th C **1,325.00**

Tiffany
18¼″, acorn, hemispherical shade, band of stylized mottled green and white glass acorns, geometric translucent green ground, bronze standard, stamped "Tiffany Studios New York" **4,750.00**

20″ h, lily, six slender cylindrical stems, pendant calyx form sockets, six irid purple and amber ribbed lily form shades, signed "L. C. T. Favrile," gilt bronze circular base, overlapping lily pads, etched finish, imp "Tiffany Studios/New York," c1898–1928 . . . . **5,750.00**

Wilkenson, 23″ h, 18″ d stained glass tulip border shade, twenty four narrow radiating amber and white striated and mottled slag glass panels, three narrow bands of rect blue and amber tiles, meandering vine with yellow shaded red tulips, green leaves, scalloped rim, gilt and turquoise patinated metal baluster form standard, foliate cast forms, spreading circular base with egg and dart band, early 20th C **1,325.00**

LANTERNS

History: A lantern is an enclosed, portable light source, hand carried or attached to a bracket or pole to illuminate an area. Many lanterns can be used both indoors and outdoors and have a protected flame. Fuels used in early lanterns included candles, kerosene, whale oil, coal oil, and later gasoline, natural gas, and batteries.

Dietz No. 30, $50.00.

Barn, tin, 13¼″, kerosene type, clear globe marked "Dietz D–Lite, No. 2" . . **48.00**

Wood, 11″ h, glass on four sides, hinged door **145.00**

Bicycle, nickel plated brass, carbide type, clear bull's eyes lens, red and green faceted glass insert sides, marked "C M Hall Lamp Co., Solar Model, Kenosha, Wis, USA" **50.00**

Candle
Pine, sliding panel, diamond shaped glass panes on sides, pierced,

three openings, low strap handle,
10 x 9 x 14¼" **375.00**

Tin

9" h, attributed to New England
Glass Co, orig black paint **275.00**

12", emb numeral "2" on three
sides, good, rusted surface . . . **75.00**

Walnut, sq, four glass sides, conical
pierced tin top and ring handle,
crimped pan and socket, 16" **625.00**

Dark room, 17" h, orig black paint, white
striping, tin kerosene font and burner,
"Carbutt's Dry Plate Lantern, Pa April
25th 1882" label **55.00**

Deck, 54½" h, copper, mounted on
ebonized base, from Hudson River
paddle wheel steamer **500.00**

Folding, tin, isinglass sides, emb "Sto-
nebridge 1908," 10" **65.00**

Japanese, adv for Patterson Brothers,
Lansing, MI, panels of General U. S.
Grant, puppies, young girl, and wil-
derness scene **175.00**

Kerosene

Brass, 9¾" h, curved lens replaced . **40.00**

Tin

12", pierced, brass burner, marked
"Vortex" **150.00**

15", pierced, orig tin kerosene
lamp, orig brass label "J. D.
Brown/Patent/May 29, 1860,"
rusted surface **150.00**

24½" h, orig black paint and kerosene burner, mercury reflector,
stenciled label "C.T. Ham Mfg
Co's New No 8 Tubular Square
Lamp, Label Registered 1886" . **175.00**

Miner's, tin, three part, leather fitting for
head, adapter with brass plate for
pole, two wire loop handles, adjustable reflector, hinged tin door, emb
"Ferguson, NY 1878" **150.00**

Nautical, masthead, 23" h, 11" d, copper
and brass, oil fired, orig burner, label
reads "Ellerman, Wilson Line, Hull,"
mid 19th C **250.00**

Political Rally, gilded wrought iron, flat
diamond shaped lantern, diamond
shaped windows outlined with gilding,
amber glass panels, "1842" in gilt,
acorn finials, pine carrying staff,
mounted on wooden base, 67" h . . . **1,800.00**

Railroad, 16", tin, wide reflector, kerosene burner, marked "Buhol No. 100" **75.00**

Skater's

Brass, clear bulbous globe, wire bail
handle, 11" **125.00**

Cast Iron, lacy base, bulbous clear
globe, pierced tin top and wire bail
handle, 13½" **225.00**

Wall, exterior, kerosene type, black
painted metal sq frame, glass sides,

pyramidal glass sided top, round
metal finial, orig burner and mercury
reflector, stenciled "C T Ham Mfg
Co's New No 8 Tubular Square
Lamp," c1886, 24½" **175.00**

Whale Oil, 12" h, pierced tin with brass
cap, orig tin whale oil lamp **160.00**

LEEDS CHINA

History: The Leeds Pottery in Yorkshire, England, began production about 1758. Among its
products was creamware that was competitive with
that of Wedgwood. The initial factory closed in
1820, but various subsequent owners continued
until 1880. They made exceptional cream colored
ware, either plain, salt-glazed, or painted with colored enamels, and glazed and unglazed redware.

Early wares are unmarked. Later pieces bear
marks of "Leeds Pottery," sometimes followed by
"Hartley-Green and Co." or the letters "LP". Reproductions also have these marks.

Reference: Susan and Al Bagdade, *Warman's
English & Continental Pottery & Porcelain, 1st Edition,* Warman Publishing Co., Inc., 1987.

**Chestnut Bowl, cream ware, 1790–
1800, $750.00.**

Asparagus Dish, 5½" l, creamware,
scrolled acanthus shape, England,
c1780 . . . . **100.00**

Candlestick, 10" h, spreading sq pedestal pierced shaft, stylized flowers,
balustrade nozzle, sq leaf sprig
molded bobeche, sq coved leaf sprig
molded and foliate reticulated base,
imp "Leeds Pottery" **225.00**

Charger, 15⅝", blue feather edge, five
color urn of flowers dec **450.00**

Creamer, 4½″, gaudy flowers and leaves, creamware 325.00
Cup and Saucer, handleless, multicolored floral design 200.00
Cup Plate, 3¾″, gaudy blue and white floral dec 250.00
Egg Cup, 2¾″, creamware, reticulated 145.00
Jar, cov, 4¼″ h, blue and yellow dec .. 175.00
Jug
5¾″ h, sponge dec in shades of gray and blue, entwined strap handle, flower head and foliage terminals . 400.00
8¾″, creamware, Mary and Elizabeth/William and Joseph, floral terminal on handle 3,500.00
Miniature
Cup and Saucer, handleless, enameled three color flowers 125.00
Pitcher, 2″ h, softpaste, three color dec, emb leaf handle 85.00
Mug, 5″, polychrome five color floral dec 240.00
Nut Dish, 4¾″, leaf shape, blue Oriental dec 140.00
Plate
6⅜″, five color scene of house, sponged trees, blue feather edge . 325.00
7½″, blue feather edge, five color strawberry dec 300.00
9¾″, blue feather edge, yellow ochre gaudy floral dec 250.00
Platter, 19¼″, blue flowers and leaves, blue feather edge, minor staining .. 235.00
Sugar, 4¾″ h, softpaste, fluted ribs, three color floral dec 200.00
Teapot
5½″ h, gold, blue, green, and brown garlands, spout repaired, discolored 75.00
10″ h, Queen Anne style, peafowl dec, extensively repaired top and lid 110.00
Vegetable Dish, 8¾ x 11″, blue feather edge, four color eagle and shield dec 400.00

LENOX CHINA

History: In 1889 Jonathan Cox and Walter Scott Lenox established The Ceramic Art Co. at Trenton, New Jersey. By 1906 Lenox formed his own company, Lenox, Inc. Using potters lured from Belleek, Lenox began making an American version of this famous ware.

Older Lenox china has two marks: a green wreath and a palette. The palette mark appears on blanks supplied to amateurs who hand painted

china as a hobby. The Lenox Company still exists and currently uses a gold stamped mark.

Reference: Mary Frank Gaston, *American Belleek*, Collector Books, 1984.

Additional Listings: Belleek.

Candlestick, scenic band, 8″ h, $75.00.

Basket, 6″ h, Thistle pattern, beige matte glaze, gold trim, rustic handle 850.00
Bouillon Cup and Saucer, gold band and handles, monogrammed 25.00
Bowl, ftd, sterling silver overlay, blue glazed ground, Art Deco 115.00
Chocolate Set, chocolate pot, cov, six cups and saucers, golden wheat dec, cobalt ground, 13 pcs 275.00
Cigarette Box, white apple blossoms, green ground, wreath mark 40.00
Cup and Saucer, Kingsley pattern ... 20.00
Honey Pot, 5″ h, 6¼″ underplate, ivory beehive, gold bee and trim 75.00
Jug, 4″, hp, grapes and leaves, shaded brown ground, sgd "G Morley" 240.00
Mug
4¾″, cobalt blue, SS overlay, marked "Ceramic Art Co" 100.00
5¼″, Harvard College dec, dated 1910 .... 85.00
6¼″, monk, smiling, holding up glass of wine, shaded brown ground, SS rim 150.00
Nappy, 5½ x 7″, ftd, shell shape, pink tinged beige 35.00
Perfume Lamp, 9″, figural, Marie Antoinette, bisque finish, dated 1929 ... 650.00
Pitcher, lemonade, silver overlay, marked "Lenox Belleek" 225.00
Plate, 10″, hp, orchids 250.00
Salt, 3 x 2 x 1″, creamy ivory ground, molded seashells and coral, green wreath mark 35.00
Salt and Pepper Shakers, hp, green and gold bird dec, pr 65.00

Tea Set, teapot, creamer, and sugar,
  Hawthorne pattern, silver overlay ..   **215.00**
Tea Strainer, hp, small roses dec **65.00**
Vase
  6″, roses dec, sgd "W Morley" **165.00**
  8″, tree stump, robin, glazed white .   **125.00**
  9¼″, hp, woodland scene, shaded
    brown ground, marked "Ceramic
    Art Co" **100.00**
  11″, corset shape, six leafy panels .   **85.00**

LIBBEY GLASS

History: In 1888 Edward Libbey established the Libbey Glass Company in Toledo, Ohio, after the closing of the New England Glass Works of W. L. Libbey and Son in East Cambridge, Massachusetts. The new Libbey company produced quality cut glass during the "Brilliant Period."

In 1930 Libbey's interest in art glass production was renewed. A. Douglas Nash was employed as a designer in 1931.

The factory continues production today as Libbey Glass Co.

Reference: Carl U. Fauster, *Libbey Glass Since 1818—Pictorial History & Collector's Guide,* Len Beach Press, 1979.

Additional Listings: Amberina Glass and Cut Glass.

Pitcher, crystal, paperweight base, sgd, c1925, 11″ h, $95.00.

Bowl, 8¼″, scalloped rim, turned over
  ruby border, amberina body, Wave
  pattern, three applied amber feet,
  acid stamped "Libbey" in circle,
  c1900 ....   **425.00**
Candlesticks, pr, Silhouette pattern,
  clear candle cup, opal figural camel
  stem **250.00**
Champagne, 6½″, twisted stem, thin
  green concentric circles, sgd **125.00**
Cordial, American Prestige pattern,
  c1930 ....   **45.00**

Plate, 7″, cut glass, border of strawberry
  diamonds and fans, sunburst center,
  sgd **50.00**
Punch Cup, Moravignian pattern, red
  pulled design, sgd **125.00**
Sugar Shaker, Maize pattern, amber,
  gold leaf **100.00**
Toothpick, 2½″, pink shading to white,
  blue flowers, green leaves, sgd **125.00**
Tumbler, Maize pattern, creamy opaque
  ground, yellow husks **125.00**
Vase
  9″, slightly flaring cylindrical, light ver-
    tical ribbing, blue threaded dec,
    opal ground, sgd, c1933 ....   **250.00**
  15″, floriform, amberina, c1917 ....   **950.00**

LIMITED EDITION COLLECTOR PLATES

History: Bing and Grondahl made the first collector plate in 1895. Royal Copenhagen issued their first Christmas plate in 1908.

In the late 1960s and early 1970s, several potteries, glass factories, mints, and artists began issuing plates commemorating people, animals, events, etc. Christmas plates were supplemented by Mother's Day plates, Easter plates, etc. A sense of speculation swept the field, fostered in part by flamboyant ads in newspapers and flashy direct mail promotions.

Collectors often favor the first plate issued in a series above all others. Condition is a prime factor. Having the original box also increases price.

Limited edition collector plates, more than any other object in this guide, should be collected for design and pleasure and only secondarily as an investment.

References: *The Bradford Book of Collector Plates, 12th Edition,* published by Bradford Exchange, 1987; Diane Carnevale, exec. ed., *Collectibles Market Guide & Price Index To Limited Edition Plates, Figurines, Bells, Graphics, Steins, and Dolls, Fifth Edition,* Schiffer Publishing, 1988; Gene Ehlert, *The Official Price Guide To Collector Plates, Fifth Edition,* House of Collectibles, 1988; Paul Stark, *Limited Edition Collectibles, Everything You May Ever Need To Know,* New Gallery Press, 1988.

Periodicals: Collector Editions, 170 Fifth Ave, New York, NY 10010; Collectors Mart, Inc. 15100 W. Kellogg, Wichita, KS 67235; Plate World Publication, 9200 N. Maryland Ave., Niles, IL 60648.

Collectors' Club: International Plate collectors Guild, P. O. Box 487, Artesia, CA 90701.

Museum: Bradford Museum, Niles, IL.

Additional Listings: See *Warman's Americana & Collectibles* for more examples of collector plates plus many other limited edition collectibles.

BAREUTHER (Germany)

Christmas Plates, Hans Mueller artist, 8″ d

1967 Stiftskirche, FE	100.00
1969 Christkindlemarkt	20.00
1971 Toys for Sale	20.00
1973 Christmas Sleigh Ride	20.00
1975 Snowman	25.00
1977 Story Time (Christmas Story)	30.00
1979 Winter Day	40.00
1981 Walk in the Forest	40.00
1983 The Night Before Christmas	45.00
1985 Winter Wonderland	42.50
1987 Decorating the Tree	46.50

Father's Day Series, Hans Mueller artist, 8″ d

1969 Castle Neuschwanstein	48.00
1971 Castle Heidelberg	24.00
1973 Castle Katz	30.00
1975 Castle Lichtenstein	35.00
1977 Castle Eltz	30.00
1979 Castle Rheinstein	30.00
1981 Castle Gutenfels	40.00
1983 Castle Lauenstein	40.00

Mother's Day

1969 Mother & Children	75.00
1971 Mother & Children	20.00
1973 Mother & Children	22.00
1975 Spring Outing	25.00
1977 Noon Feeding	28.00
1979 Mother's Love	38.00
1981 Playtime	40.00

Bing and Grondahl, Christmas plate, 1895, Behind The Frozen Window, first edition, $3,600.00.

BING AND GRONDAHL (Denmark)

Christmas Plates, various artists, 7″ d

1895 Behind The Frozen Window	3,600.00
1896 New Moon Over Snow Covered Trees	1,475.00
1897 Christmas Meal Of The Sparrows	1,100.00
1898 Christmas Roses And Christmas Star	600.00
1899 The Crows Enjoying Christmas	900.00
1900 Church Bells Chiming In Christmas	800.00
1901 The Three Wise Men From The East	485.00
1902 Interior Of A Gothic Church	285.00
1903 Happy Expectation of Children	150.00
1904 View of Copenhagen From Frederiksberg Hill	125.00
1905 Anxiety Of The Coming Christmas Night	130.00
1906 Sleighing To Church On Christmas Eve	100.00
1907 The Little Match Girl	125.00
1908 St. Petri Church of Copenhagen	85.00
1909 Happiness Over The Yule Tree	100.00
1910 The Old Organist	90.00
1911 First It Was Sung By Angels To Shepherds In The Fields	80.00
1912 Going To Church On Christmas Eve	80.00
1913 Bringing Home The Yule Tree	85.00
1914 Royal Castle of Amalienborg, Copenhagen	75.00
1915 Chained Dog Getting Double Meal On Christmas Eve	120.00
1916 Christmas Prayer of the Sparrows	80.00
1917 Arrival Of The Christmas Boat	75.00
1918 Fishing Boat Returning Home For Christmas	85.00
1919 Outside The Lighted Window	80.00
1920 Hare In The Snow	70.00
1921 Pigeons In The Castle Court	55.00
1922 Star Of Bethlehem	60.00
1923 Royal Hunting Castle, The Hermitage	55.00
1924 Lighthouse In Danish Waters	65.00
1925 The Child's Christmas	70.00
1926 Churchgoers On Christmas Day	65.00
1927 Skating Couple	115.00
1928 Eskimo Looking At Village Church In Greenland	60.00
1929 Fox Outside Farm On Christmas Eve	75.00
1930 Yule Tree In Town Hall Square Of Copenhagen	85.00
1931 Arrival Of The Christmas Train	75.00
1933 The Korsor-Nyborg Ferry	70.00
1935 Lillebelt Bridge Connecting Funen With Jutland	65.00
1937 Arrival Of Christmas Guests	75.00
1939 Ole Lock-Eye, The Sandman	150.00
1941 Horses Enjoying Christmas Meal In Stable	345.00
1943 The Ribe Cathedral	155.00

1945 The Old Water Mill	135.00
1947 Dybbol Mill	70.00
1949 Landsoldaten, 19th Century Danish Soldier	70.00
1951 Jens Bang, New Passenger Boat Running Between Copenhagen And Aalborg	115.00
1953 Royal Boat In Greenland Waters	95.00
1955 Kalundborg Church	115.00
1957 Christmas Candles	155.00
1959 Christmas Eve	120.00
1961 Winter Harmony	115.00
1963 The Christmas Elf	120.00
1965 Bringing Home The Christmas Tree	65.00
1967 Sharing The Joy Of Christmas	45.00
1969 Arrival Of Christmas Guests . .	30.00
1971 Christmas At Home	20.00
1973 Country Christmas	25.00
1975 The Old Water Mill	25.00
1977 Copenhagen Christmas	25.00
1979 White Christmas	30.00
1981 Christmas Peace	50.00
1983 Christmas in Old Town	55.00
1985 Christmas Eve at the Farmhouse	55.00
1987 The Snowman's Christmas Eve	60.00

Mother's Day Plates, Henry Thelander, artist, 6″ d

1969 Dog And Puppies	400.00
1971 Cat And Kitten	24.00
1973 Duck And Ducklings	20.00
1975 Doe And Fawns	20.00
1977 Squirrel And Young	25.00
1979 Fox And Cubs	30.00
1981 Hare And Young	40.00
1983 Raccoon And Young	45.00
1985 Bear and Cubs	40.00
1987 Sheep with Lambs	42.50

HAVILAND & PARLON (France)

Christmas Series, various artists, 10″ d

1972 Madonna And Child, Raphael, FE	80.00
1974 Cowper Madonna And Child, Raphael	55.00
1976 Madonna And Child, Botticelli .	50.00
1978 Madonna And Child, Fra Filippo Lippi	65.00

Lady And The Unicorn Series, artist unknown, 10″ d

1977 To My Only Desire, FE	60.00
1978 Sight	40.00
1980 Touch	110.00
1982 Taste	80.00

Tapestry Series, artist unknown, 10″ d

1971 The Unicorn In Captivity	145.00
1972 Start Of The Hunt	70.00
1974 End Of The Hunt	120.00

Haviland and Parlon, Tapestry series, 1971, Unicorn in Captivity, first edition, $145.00.

1976 The Unicorn Is Brought To The Castle	55.00

LALIQUE (France)

Annual Series, lead crystal, Marie-Claude Lalique, artist, 8½″ d

1965 Deux Oiseaux (Two Birds), FE	800.00
1966 Rose de Songerie (Dream Rose)	215.00
1968 Gazelle Fantaisie (Gazelle Fantasy)	70.00
1970 Paon (Peacock)	50.00
1972 Coquillage (Shell)	55.00
1974 Sous d'Argent (Silver Pennies)	65.00
1976 Aigle (Eagle)	100.00

LENOX (United States)

Boehm Bird Series, Edward Marshall Boehm, artist, 10½″ d

1970 Wood Thrush, FE	225.00
1972 Mountain Bluebird	65.00
1974 Rufous Hummingbird	60.00
1976 Cardinal	58.00
1978 Mockingbirds	60.00
1980 Black-Throated Blue Warblers .	75.00

Boehm Woodland Wildlife Series, Edward Marshall Boehm, artist, 10½″ d

1973 Raccoons, FE	80.00
1974 Red Foxes	50.00
1976 Eastern Chipmunks	60.00
1978 Whitetail Deer	60.00
1980 Bobcats	90.00
1982 Otters	100.00

LLARDO (Spain)

Christmas, 8″ d, undisclosed artists

1971 Caroling	30.00

1973 Boy & Girl	50.00
1975 Cherubs	60.00
1977 Nativity	70.00
1979 Snow Dance	80.00

Mother's Day, undisclosed artists

1971 Kiss of the Child	75.00
1973 Mother & Children	35.00
1975 Mother & Child	55.00
1977 Mother & Daughter	60.00
1979 Off to School	90.00

REED & BARTON (United States)

Christmas Series, Damascene silver, 11″ d through 1978, 8″ d 1979 to present

1970 A Partridge In A Pear Tree, FE	200.00
1971 We Three Kings Of Orient Are	65.00
1973 Adoration Of The Kings	75.00
1975 Adoration Of The Kings	65.00
1977 Decorating The Church	60.00
1979 Merry Old Santa Claus	65.00
1981 The Shopkeeper At Christmas	75.00

ROSENTHAL (Germany)

Christmas Plates, various artists, 8½″ d

1910 Winter Peace	550.00
1911 The Three Wise Men	325.00
1912 Shooting Stars	250.00
1913 Christmas Lights	235.00
1915 Walking To Church	180.00
1917 Angel Of Peace	210.00
1919 St. Christopher With The Christ Child	225.00
1921 Christmas In The Mountains	200.00
1923 Children In The Winter Wood	200.00
1925 The Three Wise Men	200.00
1927 Station On The Way	200.00
1929 Christmas In The Alps	225.00
1931 Path Of The Magi	225.00
1933 Through The Night To Light	190.00
1935 Christmas By The Sea	185.00
1937 Berchtesgaden	195.00
1939 Schneekoppe Mountain	195.00
1941 Strassburg Cathedral	250.00
1943 Winter Idyll	300.00
1945 Christmas Peace	400.00
1947 The Dillingen Madonna	975.00
1949 The Holy Family	185.00
1951 Star Of Bethlehem	450.00
1953 The Holy Light	185.00
1955 Christmas In A Village	190.00
1957 Christmas By The Sea	195.00
1959 Midnight Mass	195.00
1961 Solitary Christmas	225.00
1963 Silent Night	185.00
1965 Christmas In Munich	185.00
1967 Christmas In Regensburg	185.00
1969 Christmas In Rothenburg	220.00

1971 Christmas In Garmisch	100.00
1973 Christmas In Lubeck-Holstein	110.00

Royal Copenhagen, Mother's Day plate, 1980, An Outing With Mother, $35.00.

ROYAL COPENHAGEN (Denmark)

Christmas Plates, various artists, 6″ d 1908, 1909, 1910; 7″ 1911 to present

1908 Madonna And Child	1,750.00
1909 Danish Landscape	150.00
1910 The Magi	120.00
1911 Danish Landscape	135.00
1912 Elderly Couple By Christmas Tree	120.00
1913 Spire Of Frederik's Church, Copenhagen	125.00
1914 Sparrows In Tree At Church Of The Holy Spirit, Copenhagen	100.00
1915 Danish Landscape	150.00
1916 Shepherd In The Field On Christmas Night	85.00
1917 Tower Of Our Savior's Church, Copenhagen	90.00
1918 Sheep and Shepherds	80.00
1919 In The Park	80.00
1920 Mary With The Child Jesus	75.00
1921 Aabenraa Marketplace	75.00
1922 Three Singing Angels	70.00
1923 Danish Landscape	70.00
1924 Christmas Star Over The Sea And Sailing Ship	100.00
1925 Street Scene From Christianshavn, Copenhagen	85.00
1926 View of Christmas Canal, Copenhagen	75.00
1927 Ship's Boy At The Tiller On Christmas Night	140.00
1928 Vicar's Family On Way To Church	75.00
1929 Grundtvig Church, Copenhagen	100.00

1930 Fishing Boats On The Way To The Harbor	80.00
1931 Mother And Child	90.00
1932 Frederiksberg Gardens With Statue Of Frederik VI	90.00
1933 The Great Belt Ferry	110.00
1934 The Hermitage Castle	115.00
1935 Fishing Boat Off Kronborg Castle	145.00
1936 Roskilde Cathedral	130.00
1937 Christmas Scene In Main Street, Copenhagen	135.00
1938 Round Church In Osterlars On Bornholm	200.00
1939 Expeditionary Ship In Pack-Ice Of Greenland	180.00
1940 The Good Shepherd	300.00
1941 Danish Village Church	250.00
1943 Flight Of Holy Family To Egypt	425.00
1945 A Peaceful Motif	325.00
1947 The Good Shepherd	210.00
1949 Our Lady's Cathedral, Copenhagen	165.00
1951 Christmas Angel	300.00
1953 Frederiksborg Castle	120.00
1955 Fano Girl	185.00
1957 The Good Shepherd	115.00
1959 Christmas Night	120.00
1961 Training Ship Danmark	155.00
1963 Hojsager Mill	80.00
1965 Little Skaters	60.00
1967 The Royal Oak	45.00
1969 The Old Farmyard	35.00
1971 Hare In Winter	80.00
1973 Train Homeward Bound For Christmas	85.00
1975 Queen's Palace	85.00
1977 Immervad Bridge	75.00
1979 Choosing The Christmas Tree	60.00
1981 Admiring The Christmas Tree	55.00
1983 Merry Christmas	60.00
1985 Snowman	55.00

Mother's Day Plates, various artists, 6¼″ d

1971 American Mother	125.00
1973 Danish Mother	60.00
1975 Bird In Nest	50.00
1977 The Twins	50.00
1979 A Loving Mother	30.00
1981 Reunion	40.00

SCHIMD (Japan)

Disney Christmas Series, undisclosed artists, 7½″ d

1973 Sleigh Ride, FE	400.00
1975 Caroling	20.00
1977 Down The Chimney	25.00
1979 Santa's Surprise	20.00
1981 Happy Holidays	18.00

Disney Mother's Day Series

1974 Flowers For Mother, FE	80.00

1976 Minnie Mouse And Friends	20.00
1978 Flowers For Bambi	20.00
1980 Minnie's Surprise	20.00
1982 A Dream Come True	20.00

Peanuts Christmas Series, Charles Schulz, artist, 7½″ d

1972 Snoopy Guides The Sleigh, FE	90.00
1974 Christmas Eve At The Fireplace	75.00
1976 Woodstock's Christmas	30.00
1978 Filling The Stocking	20.00
1980 Waiting For Santa	50.00
1982 Perfect Performance	35.00

Peanuts Mother's Day Series, Charles Schulz, artist, 7½″ d

1972 Linus, FE	50.00
1974 Snoopy And Woodstock On Parade	40.00
1976 Linus And Snoopy	35.00
1978 Thoughts That Count	25.00
1980 A Tribute To Mom	20.00
1982 Which Way To Mother?	20.00

WEDGWOOD (Great Britain)

Christmas Series, jasper stoneware, 8″ d

1969 Windsor Castle, FE	225.00
1970 Christmas In Trafalgar Square	30.00
1972 St. Paul's Cathedral	40.00
1974 The Houses Of Parliament	40.00
1976 Hampton Court	45.00
1978 The Horse Guards	55.00
1980 St. James Palace	70.00
1982 Lambeth Palace	80.00
1984 Constitution Hill	80.00
1986 The Albert Memorial	80.00

Mothers Series, jasper stoneware, 6½″ d

1971 Sportive Love, FE	25.00
1972 The Sewing Lesson	20.00
1974 Domestic Employment	30.00
1976 The Spinner	35.00
1978 Swan and Cygnets	35.00
1980 Birds	48.00
1982 Cherubs With Swing	55.00
1984 Musical Cupids	55.00
1986 Anemones	55.00

Queen's Christmas, A. Price artist

1980 Windsor Castle	30.00
1981 Trafalgar Square	25.00
1982 Piccadilly Circus	35.00
1983 St. Pauls	32.50
1984 Tower of London	35.00
1985 Palace of Westminister	35.00
1986 Tower Bridge	35.00

LIMOGES

History: Limoges porcelain has been produced in Limoges, France, for over a century by numerous factories other than the famed Haviland. One of the most frequently encountered marks is ''T. &

V. Limoges" which is the ware made by Tressman and Vought. Other identifiable Limoges marks are A. L. (A. Lanternier), J. P. L (J. Pouyat, Limoges), M. R. (M. Reddon), Elite and Coronet.

References: Susan and Al Bagdade, *Warman's English & Continental Pottery & Porcelain, 1st Edition,* Warman Publishing Co., Inc., 1987; Mary Frank Gaston, *The Collector's Encyclopedia Of Limoges Porcelain,* Collector Books, 1980.

Additional Listings: Haviland China.

Berry Set, 9½" master bowl, eight 8" serving bowls, hp, purple berries on ext., white blossoms on int., marked "T & V" **250.00**

Bowl, 4½" h, ftd, hp, wild roses and leaves, sgd "J E Dodge, 1892" **75.00**

Box, 4¼" sq, cobalt and white ground, cupids on lid, pate–sur–pate dec ... **170.00**

Cache Pot, 7½" w, 9" h, male and female pheasants on front, mountain scene on obverse, gold handles and four ball feet **225.00**

Cake Plate, 11½" d, ivory ground, brushed gold scalloped rim, gold medallion, marked "Limoges T & V" **70.00**

Candlestick, 6", satin finish, blue forget-me-nots, cream ground, gold scalloped edges **60.00**

Chocolate Pot, 13" h, purple violets and green leaves, cream ground, gold handle, spout, and base, sgd "Kelly, JPL/France" **325.00**

Chocolate Set
  9½" h chocolate pot, four cups and saucers, light green, floral dec, gold trim **250.00**
  11" h chocolate pot, four cups and saucers, Coronet pattern **425.00**

Creamer, 3¼", purple flowers, white ground, gold handle and trim **40.00**

Cup and Saucer, hp, flowers and leaves, gold trim, artist sgd **75.00**

Mug, monk, brown flecked ground, 4¾" h, $35.00.

Dinner Service, twelve dinner plates, eleven salad plates, eight dessert plates, ten tea cups, eleven saucers, gilt geometric panels, white ground, stamped factory mark "J P, L France," incised numbers, 52 pcs **365.00**

Fish Service, twelve sq form plates, six different fishing scenes in center, gilt dec cobalt blue border, matching rect two handled sauce boat, underglaze green mark "CFH/GDM," Gerad Defraissein et Morel, late 19th C, 13 pcs **275.00**

Hair Receiver, blue flowers and white butterflies, ivory ground, gold trim, marked "JPL" **75.00**

Mug, hp, blackberries, pastel foliage, three small pink flowers highlighted with enameled petals, shaded pastel to dark green ground, gold handle and rim, barrel shape, 4" **50.00**

Nappy, 6" d, curved gold handle, gold scalloped edges, soft pink blossoms, blue-green ground **30.00**

Oyster Plate, 8", six wells, ribbed molded, gold tracery, cream and yellow ground **85.00**

Plaque, enamel on copper
  3¾ x 5", oval, bust portrait of Jacques Coevr, aubergine cap, shaded brown robe, gilt border lines, turned wood frame **600.00**
  4½ x 6", mythological, nude Venus with small cupid at her side, standing before seated figure of young man dressed as traveler, gray dog, forest setting in green, blue, violet, brown, and black, highlighted in red and iron–red foil, signed "Grandhomme Garmer" lower left, minor loss to enamel at border, early 19th C **300.00**
  5¾ x 9¾", rect convex surface painted en grisaille, archangel St Michael standing on back of Satan, rocky mountain peak, gilt spear and sky, ebonized wood frame **1,650.00**
  6 x 8½", mythological, Dionysius playing his flute for two dancing maidens, forest setting, cobalt blue, green, brown, and flesh tones, red, gold, and grisaille highlights, carved giltwood frame **1,210.00**

Perfume Tray, 9½" d, hp, apple blossoms, blue shaded to pink to gray ground, pierced handles **50.00**

Pitcher, 8 x 6½", hp, russet yellow apples, multicolored shaded ground, beaded handle, artist sgd "JPL" ... **115.00**

Plate
  8½", hp, pink roses, leaves, gold trim, scalloped rim **25.00**
  9", hp, pastel florals, Art Nouveau

enameled gold dec, ornate gold
scalloped rim **30.00**
13½", hp, scenic, natural ground,
hunter and dog on one, hunter and
fox on other, gold edges, artist sgd,
facing pr **650.00**
Presidential China, 8½" plate, cup, and
saucer, William Henry Harrison, made
for firm of M W Beveridge, Washington, DC, marked "Harrison 1892," 3
pcs **1,150.00**
Punch Bowl, 13" d, scalloped gold rim,
fruit blossom dec, gold band pedestal
base **225.00**
Snuff Box, hp, wildflowers and gold tracery, pink ground, artist sgd, dated
1800 .... **200.00**
Tankard Set, 14" tankard, four mugs,
hp, grape dec, gold and green
ground, 5 pcs **300.00**
Tray, 14⅛" d, scenic, thatched cottages,
bridge, and stream, two people on
path, emb leaf border, pink and gold
trim **225.00**
Vase, 6 x 20", floral dec, pale green
ground, 1½" gold collar **115.00**

LINENS

History: The term linen now has become a generic designation for household dressings for table, bed, or bath, whether made of linen, cotton, lace, or other fabrics.

Linen, as a table cover, is mentioned in the Bible and other writings of an early age. We see "borde cloths" in early drawings and paintings with their creases pressed in sharply. It was a sign of wealth and social standing to present such elegance.

During the period before the general use of forks when fingers were the accepted means of dining, napkins were important. They usually were rectangular and large in size. In the early 18th century, napkins lost their popularity. The fork had become the tool of the upper classes who apparently wished to show off their new found expertise in the use of the fork. After diners did much damage to tablecloths, finicky hostesses decided that the napkin was a necessity. It soon reappeared on the table.

The Victorian era gave us the greatest variety of household linens. The lady of the house had time to sit and sew a fine seam. Sewing became a social activity. Afternoon callers brought their handwork with them when they came to gossip and take tea. Every young girl was expected to fill her hope chest with fine examples of her prowess. In the late 19th century these ladies made some very beautiful "white work," using white embroidery of delicate stitchery, lace insertions, and ruffles on white fabrics. These pieces are highly sought after today.

The 20th century saw a decline in that type of fine stitchery. The social pace quickened. Household linens of that period show more bright colors in the embroidery, the designs become more lighthearted and frivolous, and inexpensive machine made lace was used. Kitchen towels were decorated with animals or pots and pans. Vanity sets dominated the bedroom; the Bridge craze put emphasis on tablecloths and napkin sets. To fill the desire for less expensive lace cloths and bedspreads, women of the Depression started crocheting. Many examples of this craft are available.

With the advent of World War II, more women went to work. The last remanence of fine stitchery quickly diminished. Technological advances in production and fibers lessened the interest in hand made linens.

Collecting And Use Tips: Most old linens are fragile, some are age stained from being stored improperly for years. Unless you have a secret for removing these stains without damaging the fabric, look for those items in very good or better condition.

Linens which are not used frequently are best stored unpressed, rolled Boy Scout style, and tucked away in an old pillowcase out of bright light. Be sure the linens and pillowcases have been rinsed several times to remove all residue of detergent.

For laundered pieces which are used often, wrap in acid free white tissue or muslin folders. If the tissue is not acid free, it will cause the folded edges to discolor. If possible, store on rollers to prevent creasing. Creased areas become weak and disintegrate in laundering. Acid-free wrapping material can be purchased from Talas, 104 Fifth Avenue, New York, NY 10011.

References: Virginia Churchill Bath, *Lace*, Henry Regnery Co., 1974; Lois Markrich and Heinz Edgar Kiewe, Victorian Fancywork, Henry Regnery Co., 1974; *McCall's Needlework Treasury*, Random House, 1963; Francis M. Montgomery, *Textiles In America, 1650–1870*, W. W. Norton & C. (A Winterthur/Barra Book); Patricia Esterbrook Roberts, *Table Settings. Entertaining And Etiquette. A History And Guide*, Viking Press, 1967.

Collectors' Club: International Old Lacers, Box 1029, West Minster, CO 80030.

Museums: Metropolitan Museum of Art, New York, NY; Museum of Early Southern Decorative Arts (MESDA) Winston-Salem, NC; Museum Of Fine Arts, Boston, MA; Rockwood Museum, Wilmington, DE; Shelburne Museum, Shelburne, VT; Smithsonian Institution, Washington, D.C.

Antimacassar Set, hand crocheted,
daisy chain motif, ecru, three pc set **20.00**
Bedspread
Crochet, double size, small medallion
motif, crocheted together with fine

webbing, pale green, green fringed, three sides **250.00**

Victorian, 104 x 112", white wool, bleached muslin, one third tucking and embroidered eyelet dec, eyelet edges, c1890 . . . . **225.00**

Bolster Case, white linen, ends open, embroidered garland of white flowers with script letter "P" in center, crocheted edging, c1920 . . . . **50.00**

Bridge Set

Irish Linen, double damask, over all floral and swirl pattern, wide hand hemstitched border, four matching napkins, set **35.00**

Madeira, white linen, drawn and embroidery work, embroidered flower basket corners, scalloped edges, four matching napkins, set **25.00**

Curtain Panel, appliqued linen and re-embroidered floral and scroll pattern, scalloped outer edge and bottom, net background, machine made, each panel 36 x 84", pr **75.00**

Doily, crochet, pansy border, 30 wt cotton, multicolored, 9½" d, $8.00.

Doily

Crochet, 10 x 13", rooster center, white **24.00**

Filet Net, 14" d, ecru, re-embroidered flowers and leaves **3.50**

Dresser Scarf

Madeira, cut work, hand embroidered satin stitch, pointe lace insets each end, filet lace borders on four sides, c1930 . . . . **30.00**

Victorian, 122 x 36", white linen, white work, floral design ends, heavy padded satin stitch, scalloped edges, c1890 . . . . **25.00**

Napkin

Cocktail, cotton, pale yellow, one corner elephant embroidered, fringed edges, c1930, set of eight **7.50**

Dinner, linen

20" sq, double damask,½" hand hemstitched border, wreath motif center, set of four **24.00**

22" sq, double damask, rose pattern, hand rolled hem, set of eight **36.00**

24" sq, double damask, satin stripe border, hand hemstitched, set of eight **40.00**

Luncheon, 14" sq, white Swiss linen, one corner flower basket embroidered, c1920, set of four **12.00**

Pillow Case

Cotton, embroidered girl with umbrella, bright colors, machine made lace edge, from stamped kit, c1935, pr **15.00**

Linen, cut work and embroidery, filet lace showing mythological marine theme in center and filet lace corner, edged in machine made lace, button back, 22 x 15" **65.00**

Madeira, linen, pointe lace surrounded by embroidered cut work, pale blue floral and swirl design, scalloped end opening, pr **45.00**

Percale, scalloped and eyelet border, 19 x 12" **15.00**

Pillow Sham

Double bed size, muslin, Victorian white work, narrow machine tucking on border, cut and embroidered edges, 50 x 35", c1890 . . . . **65.00**

Single bed size, white muslin, wide border of machine tucking, machine made lace edge, 48 x 34" . . **35.00**

Placemat Set, cotton, white, Battenberg, lavish corners and edging, napkins to match, c1940, set of eight . . **75.00**

Runner

Cotton, white, Chinese hand drawn work, 16 x 50", early 20th C **18.00**

Irish linen, white, double damask, all-over small flower design, hand rolled ends, 26 x 148", early 20th C **75.00**

Pointe de Venise, cartouche and circle design, hand made, 10½ x 105", early 20th C **275.00**

Sheet, linen, white

Floral and spray motif cut work top, scalloped sides down 24", machine hemmed bottom, 44 x 100" **95.00**

Madeira, bridal, 18" deep embroidered cut work, filet lace insets, 2" filet lace border top, narrow hemstitching bottom, 86 x 101", pr matching pillow cases, set **250.00**

Tablecloth

54 x 54", tea cloth, Chinese cotton, hand drawn central star motif, deep

drawn work borders sides, hand
hemstitched border **15.00**
60″ d, white linen, heavy padded satin
stitch, roses and open work, 4″ ma-
chine made lace border **50.00**
66 x 128″, banquet cloth, ecru, all-
over hand made Pointe de Venise
lace, central five medallions motif
with floral and foliate design set in
panel, bordered swirls of medallion
of flowers, interspersed flower vase
forms with flowers, floral design
outside border, scalloped edge,
twelve cream napkins with motif in
one corner and 1″ matching lace
edge, pre 1935, napkins unused . **3,500.00**
68 x 98″, Irish linen, double damask,
Queen Victoria Royal Jubilee 1887,
portrait of Queen circular motif center, surrounded by symbols of
countries of Realm interspersed
with thistles motif, Royal Jubilee
and 1887 ribbon motif, fleur-de-lis,
maltese crosses, and small bellflowers background border, 19th C **950.00**
68 x 100″, hemstitched, lavish blue
Madeira embroidery, twelve match-
ing napkins, 13 pcs **225.00**
72 x 58″, crochet, tobacco string, filet
lace sq motifs, c1930–40 . . . . **50.00**
76 x 116″, linen, cut work and filet
lace inserts, twelve large napkins,
13 pcs **325.00**
92 x 105″, cotton, cut work with blue
apenzell type cut work and embroidery design center, scalloped
edges **75.00**
Towel, hand
23 x 15″, linen huck, cut work and filet
lace inserts on both ends, late
19th C **7.50**
24 x 40″, white linen, double damask,
gold color woven border leaf pattern, satin stitch monogram "MW",
6″ hand tied fringe **18.00**
Tray Cover
Pale blue linen, embroidered small
pink flowers, "Good Morning" upper left corner, 2 matching napkins,
set **12.00**
Pale yellow organdy, appliqued pale
yellow linen floral motif, pocket with
matching napkin, set **15.00**

LITHOPHANES

History: Lithophanes are highly translucent porcelain panels with impressed designs. The design
is formed by the difference in thickness of the
plaque. Thin parts transmit an abundance of light
while thicker parts represent shadows.

Lithophanes were first made by the Royal Berlin
Porcelain Works in 1828. Other factories in Germany, France, and England later produced them.
The majority of lithophanes on the market today
were made between 1850 and 1900.

Collectors' Club: Lithophane Collectors Club,
P.O. Box 4557, Toledo, OH 43620.

Museum: Blair Museum of Lithophanes and
Carved Waxes, Toledo, OH.

**Fairy Lamp, figural, lady in tower, three
lithophane panels, two pcs, 9″ h,
$1,200.00.**

Candle Shield, 9″ h, panel with scene
of two country boys playing with goat,
castle in background **260.00**
Cup and Saucer, blue Oriental lady with
nude lady **150.00**
Fairy Lamp, 9″, three panels, lady lean-
ing out of tower, rural romantic scenes **1,200.00**
Lamp
Night, 5¼″, sq, four scenes, irid green
porcelain base, gold trim, electrified **600.00**
Table
8″ h, 8″ d five panel shade, 4½ x
6¼″ panels with scenes of children, lovers, emb floral brass
frame, panels sgd "PPM" **400.00**
20¾″ h, colored umbrella style
shade, four panels of outdoor
Victorian scenes, bronze and
slate standard, German **675.00**
Lamp Shade, five panels of children,
each 5½″ w, 5¼″ h, sgd "PPM" . . . **500.00**
Panel
KPM
2½ x 3¼″, view from West Point . **175.00**
3⅞ x 5¼″, lake setting, ship and
windmill **150.00**
4¾ x 6½″, man kneeling, mosque
type building **225.00**

PPM
   3¼ x 5¼", view of Paterson Falls . **175.00**
P.R. Sickle, 4¼ x 5"
   Cupid and girl fishing **150.00**
   Scene of two women in doorway,
      dog, and two pigeons, sgd,
      #1320 . . . . **115.00**
Unmarked
   6 x 7½", Madonna and Child **175.00**
   7¾ x 6", Paul and Virginia, scene
      of young man holding bird's nest
      and lemon, young woman, tropi-
      cal setting **100.00**
   8¼ x 6¾", Le Seaux du parc de
      Versailles, numbered **150.00**
Pitcher, puzzle type, Victorian scene,
   nude on bottom **165.00**
Stein, ½ liter
   Floral front, soldier bidding farewell
      on reverse **150.00**
   Negro Boy, 5" **175.00**
   Regimental **190.00**
Tea Warmer, 5⅞" h, 1 pc cylindrical
   panel, four seasonal landscapes with
   children, copper frame, finger grip
   and molded base **225.00**

LIVERPOOL CHINA

History: Liverpool is the name given to products made at several potteries in Liverpool, England, between 1750 and 1840. Among the early potters who made tin enameled earthenwares, were Seth and James Pennington and Richard Chaffers.

By the 1780s tin glazed earthenware gave way to cream colored wares decorated with cobalt, enamel colors, and blue or black transfers.

The Liverpool glaze is characterized by bubbles and most often there is clouding under the foot rims. By 1800 about 80 potteries were working in the town producing not only creamware, but soft paste, soapstone, and bone porcelain.

Reference: Susan and Al Bagdade, *Warman's English & Continental Pottery & Porcelain, 1st Edition,* Warman Publishing Co., Inc., 1987.

Bowl, 8¼", blue underglaze, iron-red overglaze, green gilting, scene of
   houses on wooded river islands,
   c1770 . . . . **450.00**
Jug
   5½" h, transfer of child holding bunch

Pitcher, American eagle on one side, poem "Oh Liberty thou Goddess" on obverse, fifteen states border, chip on base, $400.00.

   of grapes, verse relating to harvesting, old age crack, faded, minor
   discoloration **150.00**
   7½", black transfer of "The Farmers
      Arms" and rural scene, small base
      chips **300.00**
   9½" h, color transfer of American brig,
      The Three Sisters, "P. Delano" un-
      der spout with Masonic symbols,
      obverse with black transfer of Ma-
      sonic symbols and "Lodge No. 25,"
      tan toned ground, two small chips
      on pouring spout **1,400.00**
Mug, 3¾", dark brown transfer, Hope,
   all-over luster trim, c1820–30 . . . . . **125.00**
Pitcher
   5¼", creamware, brown transfer of
      two classical women in large oval,
      brown transfer of flowers on ext.
      rim, pseudo brown transfer Fitz-
      hugh border on int. rim, floral
      transfer on handle, highlighted with
      applied green, red, blue, and ma-
      genta, small base chip, minor res-
      toration to spout **100.00**
   6½", polychromed black transfer of
      Hope and man waving frantically at
      two ships, transfer verse "Hope as
      a Anchor firm and sure/Hold fast
      the Christian Vessel/And defies the
      blast," green, yellow, and red high-
      lights **350.00**
   8", creamware, black transfer
      Peace, Plenty, and Independence,
        American flag sailing vessel . . . **1,150.00**
      Washington, chain of fifteen states,
        banner beneath bust reads
        "Long Live the President of the
        United States," marked "F. Mor-
        ris, Shelton," tiny flake on spout **5,750.00**
      Washington Apotheosis, grieving
        Liberty and Indian seated in fore-

ground, Father Time raises Washington from his tomb towards rays emanating from heaven, words on tomb "Sacred to the Memory of Washington Ob 14 Dec. A.D., 1977 Ae 68," seal of the United States and ribbon under spout, another transfer of American flag frigate, three pinhead size flakes **3,500.00**

8⅞", black transfer oval of Washington, foot on prostrate lion, four soldiers at left, American frigate at right, military symbols, ribbon reads: "By Virtue and Valor, We Have Freed Our Country, Extended Our Commerce, And Laid The Foundation of a Great Empire," obverse with oval formed by chain bearing names of fifteen states enclosing a scene of Liberty and Justice, laurel wreath under spout with "Success to America," tiny flake on spout **3,650.00**

LOETZ

History: Loetz is a type of iridescent art glass made in Austria by J. Loetz Witwe in the late 1890s. Loetz was a contemporary of L. C. Tiffany and worked in the Tiffany factory before establishing his own operation; therefore, much of the wares are similar in appearance to Tiffany. Some pieces are signed "Loetz," "Loetz, Austria," or "Austria." The Loetz factory also produced ware with fine cameos on cased glass.

Bowl
10½ x 4", honeycomb, fluted rim, rainbow spotted irid, green glass, ground pontil **350.00**

Vase, amber iridescent stretch type glass, elongated bulbous body, shallow collar, flattened rim, sgd, $365.00.

12" d, ruffled rim, deep cranberry to mottled green to clear irid, sgd . . **400.00**

Bride's Basket, irid blue, silver threading, coin spots, brass holder **375.00**

Compote, 10⅝" d, 5¼" h, widely flaring circular rim, three ball feet, bright orange int., deep black ext., c1920 . . . **300.00**

Inkwell, 2¼" h, 5½" w, irid blue–purple and green, lava type dec, hinged bronze lid with leaf dec, clear glass insert **550.00**

Lamp, table, 17¾" h, hexagonal bronze base, irid mushroom glass shade, pinched and tooled dec **4,000.00**

Pendant, 1½", ovoid, irid turquoise, yellow glass **140.00**

Pitcher, 8⅝" h, pinched bulbous body, purple green irid, applied handle, gilt metal mount cast with tiny foliate motif **600.00**

Rose Bowl, 6½", ruffled, purple irid raindrop dec **200.00**

Sweetmeat Jar, cov
4¾ x 5¼", green base, maroon threading, SS top, sq handle, sgd "Loetz, Austria" **165.00**

5" h, irid silver spider web dec, green ground, sgd **400.00**

Urn, 9¼", ovoid, two handles, irid, three color, blue "oil spotting," inscribed "Loetz, Austria" **1,500.00**

Vase
5½", green, rust, orange, brown marquetry inlay, quatrefoil mouth **300.00**

8", tapering cylindrical swelling to bulbous base, mottled and striated deep blue, green, and copper tones, copper overlay strapwork, two inset semiprecious irid green cabochons **1,550.00**

8¼", flask, pinched and ribbed neck, applied glass snake, amber glass, peacock irid **700.00**

10¾", salmon colored ground, irid striation, oil spot dec, silver overlay, two chased blossoms **800.00**

13¼", translucent salmon ground, silver irid feather pulls, inscribed "Loetz Austria" **5,000.00**

14", baluster, blue glass ground, silver irid oil spots, silver overlay, pierced calla lily dec **3,000.00**

LOTUS WARE CHINA

History: Knowles, Taylor and Knowles Co., East Liverpool, Ohio, made a translucent, thinly potted china between 1891 and 1898. It compared favorably to Belleek. It first was marked "KTK." After being exhibited at the 1893 Columbian Exposition in Chicago, Col. John T. Taylor, company president, changed the marking to Lotus Ware, because the body resembled the petals of the lotus blossom.

Blanks also were sold to amateurs who hand painted them. Most artist-signed pieces fit this category.

Tea Set, pink blossoms in relief on white, gold trim, marked "KTK," $550.00.

Bowl
4", raised floral dec, filigree handles	**200.00**
7½", boat shape, pink and gold openwork, cherry blossoms, marked "KTK"	**500.00**
Creamer, 3¾", white ground, undecorated	**200.00**
Cup and Saucer, hp violets, white ground, marked "KTK"	**100.00**
Dish, shell shape, shell pink and pale green, small green florals, gilt coral feet, marked "KTK"	**400.00**
Ewer, 7½", pierced, jeweled, pastel panels, Lotus mark	**500.00**
Pitcher, 7", bulbous, fish net dec, gold, marked "KTK"	**450.00**
Sugar, 4", fish net dec, florals, white ground, handles	**350.00**
Teapot, emb flowers, gold trim, white ground, marked "KTK"	**350.00**
Vase	
8 x 5", cylinder, ball feet, green fish net pattern,orange flowers	**520.00**
10¼", applied white floral dec, dark green ground, Lotus mark	**1,000.00**
11", gold floral panels, white fish net over entire body, ftd, marked	**750.00**

LUSTER WARE

History: Lustering on a piece of pottery creates a metallic, sometimes iridescent, appearance. Josiah Wedgwood experimented with the technique in the 1790s. Between 1805 and 1840 luster earthenware pieces were created in England by makers such as Adams, Bailey and Batkin, Copeland and Garrett, Wedgwood, and Enoch Wood.

Luster decorations often were used in conjunction with enamels and transfers. Transfers used for luster decoration covered a wide range of public and domestic subjects. They frequently were accompanied by pious or sentimental doggerel as well as the humors of everyday life.

Copper luster was created by the addition of a copper compound to the glaze. It was very popular in America during the 19th century and experienced a collecting vogue from the 1920s to the 1950s. Today it has a limited market. The market stagnation can partially be attributed to the large number of reproductions, especially creamers and the "polka" jug, which fool many new buyers. Reproductions are heavier in appearance and weight than the earlier pieces.

Pink luster was made by using a gold mixture. Silver luster was first covered completely with a thin coating of a "steel luster" mixture, containing a small quantity of platinum oxide. An additional coating of platinum, worked in water, was applied before firing.

Sunderland is a coarse type of cream colored earthenware with a marbled or spotted pink luster decoration which shades from pink to purple. A solution of gold compound applied to the white body developed the many shades of pink.

The development of electroplating in 1840 created a sharp decline in the demands for metal-surfaced earthenware.

Reference: Susan and Al Bagdade, *Warman's English & Continental Pottery & Porcelain, 1st Edition,* Warman Publishing Co., Inc., 1987.

Additional Listings: English Softpaste.

Copper, mug, brown band, applied multicolored nymphs with bull dec, beaded bands top and bottom, floral base, 3¾" d, 3½" h, $100.00.

COPPER

Coffeepot, cov, pink luster scenes	**250.00**
Creamer	
3 1/8" h, two rect panels, Hope trans-	

fers, red, green, blue, and purple enamel highlights, pink luster dec handle and mouth int. **70.00**

3 3/8" h, three bands of copper luster alternating with two bands of mustard, round blue flowers **25.00**

4", pink and purple band at neck, house dec **50.00**

Figure, 8", spaniels, pr **110.00**

Goblet, 4 1/2" h, 3 1/2" d, pink luster band, floral resist dec, copper luster int. **45.00**

Jug, 8", three transfers of mother and child playing badminton and writing letters on canary yellow band **175.00**

Mug

3 5/8", horizontal ribbed base, white band with polychrome and luster floral design **60.00**

4", raised green and white flowers on tan luster band **50.00**

4 3/4", leaves and berries on orange luster band **60.00**

Pepper Shaker, 4 1/4", cream colored band **40.00**

Pitcher

6" h, two narrow white bands with pink luster house and trees dec, wide copper luster bands **50.00**

7", green and white flowers raised dec on broad blue band **90.00**

10", wide blue band around body, emb greyhound, bull, and urn of flowers in polychrome enamel, pink and purple luster **200.00**

Teapot, 6", emb ribs, polychrome enameled floral dec **125.00**

PINK

Bowl, 7 1/2", shallow, pink luster border, reddish transfer of grazing sheep . . **30.00**

Child's Mug, 2" h, pink luster band, reddish hunter and dogs transfer, green highlighted foliage transfer **50.00**

Creamer, 4 3/8" h, stylized flower band, pink luster highlights and rim, ftd . . . **52.00**

Cup and Saucer, magenta transfers, Faith, Hope, and Charity, applied green enamel highlights, pink luster line borders **45.00**

Dish, 12 5/8 x 7 1/2", shell shape, impressed "Wedgwood-DUF-I-R," black underglaze "R. PHOLAS EASTATUS" **85.00**

Jug

5 1/2" h, bulbous, gadrooned rim, molded berry vine border highlighted in purple–pink and lime green luster **75.00**

5 3/4", bulbous, applied scroll handle, green glazed ground, luster spotted

tracking dogs, lustered spout, rim, and handle **85.00**

8", church, white toned to tan **150.00**

Mug, 2 7/8", overall pink splash luster dec, handled **35.00**

Pitcher

5 1/2" h, ornate pink luster dec, single and double house **100.00**

5 5/8" h, hunting scenes, deep relief, pink luster, green enamel **55.00**

Plate

6 1/4", relief dogs running figures on rim, highlighted with green, red, and pink luster, red, green, and blue stylized floral dec in center . . **50.00**

7 5/8" d, King's Rose, red, green, and yellow, double pink luster band border **25.00**

Toddy Plate, 5 1/16", pink luster House pattern, emb sprigs of flowers border **40.00**

Toothpick Holder, 2 x 2 3/4", pink splash luster, white base **65.00**

Waste Bowl, 6", House pattern **125.00**

SILVER

Cake Set, 10" plate, eight 7" plates, wide luster border with pink and purple irises, marked "Bareuther, Bavaria" **125.00**

Creamer, 4 1/4" h, band of scrolling flowering foliage, iron-red and silver luster, Wedgwood, 19th C **85.00**

Jug, 4 1/2", ribbed, Staffordshire, 19th C **75.00**

Mustard Pot, 3 7/8", vertical ribbed design, emb body, matching cov, ftd . . **70.00**

Pepper Pot, 5" h, standing toby form, round hollow base, pouring holes . . **85.00**

Pitcher, 6 1/4", Sawtooth pattern in canary and silver luster, late 18th C . . **375.00**

Shaker, 3 5/8", ringed circumference, pedestal base **48.00**

Tea Set, pot, dome cov, sugar and creamer, oval, bulbous body, standard handles **135.00**

Vase, 5 1/4", flared top, painted red and silver luster nasturtium vine, c1810 . **110.00**

SUNDERLAND

Bowl

4", pink band **100.00**

10", House pattern **125.00**

Celery, couple courting, sgd "Bucher" . **120.00**

Cup and Saucer, handleless, black transfer, farm scene **85.00**

Dish, pink splash, black transfer, mother playing with son **22.00**

Gravy Boat, House pattern **150.00**

Jug

5 1/2", black and white transfer of

Sunderland, pitcher, stage coach and horses dec, marked "Made in England," 2¾" h, $40.00.

Mariners Arms on front, Cast Iron
Bridge on back **140.00**
9", black transfer, "A Frigate in Full
Sail," verse, sailor and maid,
French and English coat of arms
joined with "Cremea" **200.00**
17 1/4", heroic, pink luster inside and
out **850.00**
Mug, 5", transfer of The Foresters Arms
on front, The Mariner's Compass on
back **175.00**
Pitcher, 9 1/8", black transfer, farmer's
arms, "Cast Iron Bridge over the
River Wear at Sunderland...," poly-
chrome enameling, marked "Dixon
Austin & Co, Sunderland" **475.00**
Plate
  7", pink splash **15.00**
  8", floral center, luster border **50.00**
Salt, master **60.00**
Sugar, House pattern **75.00**
Syrup, cov, 5" **100.00**
Tumbler, 2 3/4" h **60.00**
Vase, 7", trumpet shape **100.00**
Wall Plaque, "Sailor's Farewell" **125.00**

LUTZ TYPE GLASS

History: Lutz type glass is an art glass attributed to Nicholas Lutz. He made this type of glass while at the Boston and Sandwich Glass Co. from 1869 until 1888. Since Lutz type glass was popular, copied by many capable glass makers, and unsigned, it is nearly impossible to distinguish genuine Lutz products.

Lutz is believed to have made two distinct types of glass, striped and threaded glass. This style often is confused with a similar style Venetian glass. The striped glass was made by using threaded glass rods in the Venetian manner. Threaded glass was blown and decorated by winding threads of glass around the piece.

Cake Stand, clear and white threads .   **115.00**

Compote, 8⅞ x 6½", threaded, DQ, am-
berina, clear hollow stem **500.00**
Epergne, three parts, pink threads . . .   **250.00**
Finger Bowl, 7" d, matching underplate,
ruffled, amber swirls, amethyst latti-
cino, gold metallic borders **150.00**
Lamp Shade, 8" sq, 6¼" h, 2½" fitter,
opaque white loopings, applied cranberry threading, ribbon edge, sq top   **175.00**
Punch Cup, 3 x 2⅝", cranberry thread-
ing on clear ground, circular foot, ap-
plied clear handle **85.00**

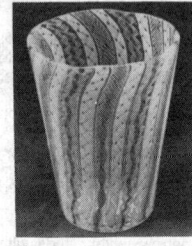

Tumbler, white, green, and orange latticino, 3½" h, $115.00.

Tumbler, 3¾", white and amethyst latti-
cino, goldstone highlights **75.00**
Whimsey, 6⅜" h, tiny "Frozen Char-
lotte" doll in clear glass tube, bulbous
finial, knob stem, and clear foot dec
with latticino rings **325.00**

MAASTRICHT WARE

History: Maastricht, Holland, is where Petrus Regout founded the De Sphinx pottery, in 1836. The firm specialized in transfer printed earthenwares. Other factories also were established in the area, many employing English workmen and their techniques. Maastricht china was exported to the United States in competition with English products.

Reference: Susan and Al Bagdade, *Warman's English & Continental Pottery & Porcelain, 1st Edition*, Warman Publishing Co., Inc., 1987.

Bowl
  6", Pompeia pattern **45.00**
  8", Oriental scene **40.00**

Chocolate Pot, transfer of children,
marked **75.00**
Cup and Saucer
  Blue Willow, handleless **25.00**
  Stick spatter and gaudy polychrome
  floral dec **35.00**
Mug, 3″ h, stick spatter and gaudy po-
lychrome floral dec, marked **65.00**
Pitcher, 4½″, Oriental scene **65.00**
Plaque, 10″, decal of realistic pears,
shaded rust border, back pierced for
hanging **35.00**

**Plate, marked "Made in Holland/Soci-
ety Ceramique Potiche," 7¾″ d, $18.00.**

Plate
  9″, gaudy stick spatter dec, polychrome floral enameling **25.00**
  11″, red and blue flower border, gold
  stick spatter flowers, marked
  "Maastricht, Holland" **65.00**
  14½″, children skating, windmill in
  background, blue transfer, sgd . . .   **65.00**
Platter, 11½″, gaudy polychrome florals
in red, yellow, and green, white
ground **50.00**
Waste Bowl, 5 x 3⅛″, multicolored mar-
bleized dec, minor stains **20.00**

MAJOLICA

History: Majolica, an opaque, tin glazed pottery,
has been produced by many countries for centuries. It originally took its name from the Spanish
Island of Majorca, where figuline (a potter's clay)
is found. Today majolica denotes a type of pottery
which was made during the last half of the 19th
century in Europe and America.

Majolica frequently depicted elements in nature:
leaves, flowers, birds, and fish. Human figures
were rare. Designs were painted on the soft clay
body using vitreous colors and fired under a clear
lead glaze to impart the rich color and brilliance
characteristic of majolica.

Among English majolica manufacturers who
marked their works were: Wedgwood, George
Jones, Holdcraft, and Minton. Most of their pieces
can be identified through the English Registry
mark and/or the potter-designer's mark. Sarreguemines in France and Villeroy and Boch in
Baden, Germany, produced majolica that compared favorably with the finer English majolica.
Most Continental pieces had an incised number
on the base.

Although 600 plus American potteries produced
majolica between 1850 and 1900, only a handful
chose to identify their wares. Among these manufacturers were George Morely, Edwin Bennett,
the Chesapeake Pottery Company, the New Mil-
ford-Wannoppee Pottery Company, and the firm of
Griffen, Smith, and Hill. The others hoped their
unmarked pieces would be taken for English examples.

References: Susan and Al Bagdade, *Warman's
English & Continental Pottery & Porcelain, 1st Edition,* Warman Publishing Co., Inc., 1987; Marilyn
G. Karmason with Joan B. Stacke, *Majolica: A
Complete History And Illustrated Survey,* Abrams,
1989; Mariann K. Marks, *Majolica Pottery: An
Identification And Value Guide,* Collector Books,
1983; M. Charles Rebert, *American Majolica
1850–1900,* Wallace-Homestead, 1981.

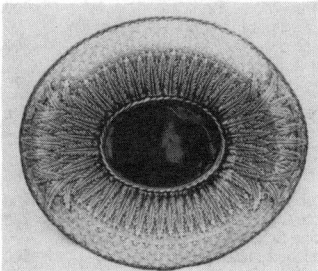

**Bread Tray, Pineapple pattern, gold
and brown center, green leaves, 12½″
l, 11″ w, $150.00.**

Basket, shells, lavender int., rope han-
dle **250.00**
Biscuit Jar, 8⅜ x 7⅝″, mottled green,
brown, and aqua int., attached SP ftd
base, hinged SP cov, sphinx finial,
c1875 . . . .   **250.00**
Bowl
  6″, Grape, oval, lavender int., George
  Jones **175.00**
  9″, Shell, figural, blue int., brown ext.,
  Holdcroft **150.00**

Bread Plate
    Oak Leaf, 13″, green and aqua, pink
      edge, Etruscan **140.00**
    Twin Shells on Wave, 14″ **185.00**
Butter Dish, cov, Bamboo, Etruscan . .   **225.00**
Cake Stand, Geranium, pedestal, Etrus-
    can **145.00**
Cheese Dish, Rope and Fern, 8″ **250.00**
Compote, Morning Glory, Etruscan . . .   **275.00**
Creamer
    Butterfly and Bamboo, 3″ **125.00**
    Coral, Etruscan **175.00**
Cup and Saucer, Shell and Seaweed,
    Etruscan **150.00**
Dish, Picket Fence and Morning Glory,
    brown mottled center **75.00**
Jardiniere, 33″ h, 16″ d, C scroll and
    foliage dec, shaped pedestal **275.00**
Match Holder, 2½ x 2¼″, drum shape,
    yellow and green, striker on base . .   **40.00**
Mustache Cup, Shell and Seaweed,
    Etruscan, pink and gray **265.00**
Oyster Plate, 9″, six multicolored shells,
    plain band rim, Etruscan **125.00**
Pitcher
    4¾″, Pineapple **75.00**
    6½″, Basketweave, turquoise and
      brown, lavender int. **50.00**
    7″, Pond Lily, yellow petal rim **165.00**
    8¼″, Rustic, molded leaves, tree
      trunk body, Etruscan **200.00**
    9½″, Stork in Marsh, eel figural han-
      dle **250.00**
Plate
    6¾″, rect, Lily of the Valley, leaf center
      8″   **70.00**
      Begonia Leaf **85.00**
      Fern and Floral **75.00**
    9″, Morning Glory, blue, yellow lobed
      edge **85.00**
Platter, 11¾″, Raspberry, mottled center   **100.00**
Relish, Onion and Pickle, cobalt ground   **185.00**
Sardine Box, 9½″, Pineapple, fish finial,
    attached underplate **300.00**
Sauce Dish
    Pineapple, 5″ **35.00**
    Wicker and Begonia Leaf, 5″ l, Etrus-
      can **60.00**
Spooner
    Bamboo **95.00**
    Bird and Fan **90.00**
    Shell and Seaweed, Etruscan, Albino,
      rust trim **75.00**
Strawberry Server, 10½ x 6¾″, pale
    green, lavender border, two brown
    baskets, yellow flowers, green leaves,
    English **425.00**
Sugar, cov
    Bird and Fan, marked "Wedgwood,
      England" **125.00**
    Shell and Seaweed, Etruscan **250.00**

Syrup
    Bamboo, Etruscan, pewter lid **285.00**
    Blackberry, metal lid **150.00**
    Sunflower, cobalt ground, Etruscan .   **300.00**
Teapot
    Basketweave and Flora, cream
      ground, pink and green, brown
      handle **150.00**
    Cauliflower, Etruscan **195.00**
    Holly and Berries, blue and green,
      bark handle and spout **160.00**
    Shell and Seaweed, Etruscan **350.00**
Toast Rack, 8½″ l, four slice, emb bas-
    ketweave, mottled green, brown, and
    blue **300.00**
Tray, 11½ x 14″, oval, shallow, cream
    weave, flowers, leaves, and birds in
    flight, green bamboo border, marked
    "Wedgwood" **350.00**
Umbrella Stand, 24¼″ h, cylindrical,
    band of carnations above stylized flo-
    ral dec, band of leaf tips **550.00**
Vase, 10½″ h, two panels of molded iris,
    brown and yellow ground **150.00**

MAPS

History: Maps provide one of the best ways to
study the growth of a country or region. From the
16th to the early 20th century, maps were both
informative and decorative. Engravers provided ornamental detailing which often took the form of
bird's eye views, city maps and ornate calligraphy
and scrolling. Many maps were hand colored to
enhance their beauty.

Maps generally were published in plate books.
Many of the maps available today result from these
books being cut apart and sheets sold separately.

In the last quarter of the 19th century, represen-
tatives from firms in Philadelphia, Chicago, and
elsewhere traveled the United States preparing
county atlases, often with a sheet for each township and a sheet for each major city or town. Although mass produced, they are eagerly sought
by collectors. Individual sheets sell for $25 to $75.
The atlases themselves can usually be purchased
in the $200 to $400 range. Individual sheets should
be viewed solely as decorative and not as investment material.

Canada
    "British America," Tallis, London/New
      York, 1851, 12¾ x 9½″, engraved,
      outline color **75.00**
    "Plan of City of Quebec," Andrews,
      c1771, engraved, vignettes, 33 x
      24 cm **125.00**
Mexico, "Hispaniae Novae," Ortelius,
    1579, uncolored, latin text, 53 x 42
    cm **350.00**

North America

"A New And Correct Map Of North America, With The West India Islands, Divided According To The Last Treaty Of Peace Concluded At Paris 10 February 1763...," Pownall, London, 1777, two sheets, 20½ x 46½" at platemarks, full margins, from Thomas Jeffreys *American Atlas* **750.00**

"British Possessions in North America," S. Lewis, 1794, 15 x 17" ... **50.00**

United States

"A General Atlas, Improved And Engraved Being A Collection Of Maps Of The World And Quarters, Their Principal Empires, Kingdoms, & c.," Mathew Carey, third edition, Philadelphia, 1814, Maryland, 12½ x 17¾" **375.00**

"Boston, Cape Cod, and New York Canal," wall chart, description info, maps, insect damage near top, 37¼" w, 24" h **300.00**

Florida, "A Map of Part of West Florida, from Pensacola to the Mouth of the Iberville River, with a View to show the Proper Spot for a Settlement on the Mississippi," London, J. Lodge, 1772, engraving, hand colored, inset of Plan for a New Settlement, 7½ x 13½" **250.00**

Idaho, "Railroad And County Map Of Idaho," Cram, Chicago, 1880, 19¾ x 16¾", lithograph, outline color .. **100.00**

Louisiana, "Plan of New Orleans the Capital of Louisiana," London, R. Benning, 1761, engraving, 7¼ x 9", $185.00

New Hampshire and Vermont, "A Map Of The States Of New Hampshire And Vermont," Denison, Boston, 1796, 7½ x 9" **185.00**

New York, "A Map of the Province of New York....," New Jersey added by topographical observation, Claude–Joseph Sauthier, London, 1776, engraved 29 x 25", framed **700.00**

New York and Brooklyn, ferry routes, hand colored, Mitchell, 1872, 16 x 24" **30.00**

San Diego River, survey to build levee–canal, 1853, 12 x 15" **50.00**

Santa Barbara, US Coast survey, 1857, 18 x 24" **40.00**

South Carolina, "State of South Carolina From The Best Authorities," Samuel Lewis, 15 x 18" **475.00**

"United States...," D Burr, New York, B Davenport, 1842, 17¾ x 21½", engraved, full color, city insets of Albany, Boston, New York, Cincin-

nati, Philadelphia, Baltimore, and Washington DC **150.00**

World

"A Chart Of The World According To Mercator's Projection Showing The Latest Discoveries Of Capt. Cook," Dilly and Robinson, 1785, 14½ x 19", colored borders and outlines . **100.00**

"A Map Of The World In Three Sections Describing The Polar Regions To The Tropics In Which Are Traced The Tracts Of Lord Mulgrave And Captain Cook ...," Bell, c1776, 9 x 16½", twin hemisphere, uncolored **125.00**

MARBLEHEAD POTTERY

History: This hand thrown pottery had its beginning in 1905 as a therapeutic program introduced by Dr. J. Hall for the patients confined to a sanitarium located in Marblehead, Massachusetts. In 1916 production was removed from the hospital to another site. The factory continued under the directorship of Arthur E. Baggs until it closed in 1936.

Most pieces found today are glazed with a smooth, porous, even finish in a single color. The most desirable pieces are decorated with conventionalized design in one or more subordinate colors.

Candlestick, rose matte glaze, impressed ship stamp, 4" h, $50.00.

Bowl, 8½" d, blue-gray int., green matte ext. **100.00**

Bookends, pr, sq tile form side, stylized cut back and incised panel of galleon on sea, dark blue glaze, incised mark and paper label, 5½ x 5¾" **150.00**

Bulb Bowl, 6" d, slate gray glaze, c1915   **80.00**
Honey Pot, 3½" h, light yellow-green ground, painted stylized grapevine with clusters of blue grapes, green leaves and vines, marked **465.00**
Pitcher, 6⅛" h, scenic band, brown bands, designed by Arthur Baggs, imp artist's marks, c1915 . . . .   **1,760.00**
Rose Bowl, 4⅛ x 3⅛", gray ground, leaf and fruit motif **550.00**
Teapot, 5¾" h, blue matte glaze, modified "C" handle **85.00**
Tile, 4¾" sq, high relief oyster white sailing ship, blue ground, marked **125.00**
Vase
  4½", inverted bell shape, red berries and green leaves on wide neck border, brown tree trunk dec, oatmeal yellow ground, c1915 . . . .   **1,000.00**
  6", ovoid tapering to flared rim, wide band of stylized hanging flowers in shades of blue, matte gray ground, imp mark, paper label, and artist's initials **935.00**
  8⅛", speckled light gray ground, darker gray branches, clusters of nuts and leaves **725.00**

MARY GREGORY TYPE GLASS

History: The use of enameled decoration on glass, an inexpensive imitation of cameo glass, developed in Bohemia in the late 19th century. The Boston and Sandwich Glass Co. copied this process in the late 1880s.

Mary Gregory (1856–1908) was employed for two years at the Boston and Sandwich Glass Co. factory when the enameled decorated glass was being manufactured. Some collectors argue that Gregory was inspired to paint her white enamel figures on glass by the work of Kate Greenaway and a desire to imitate pate-sur-pate. However, evidence for these assertions is very weak. Further, a question can be raised whether or not Mary Gregory even decorated glass as part of her job at Sandwich.

The result is that "Mary Gregory Type" is a better term to describe this glass. Collectors should recognize that most examples are either European or modern reproductions.

Box, hinged lid
  3⅛" d, 2¾" h, round, cranberry, white enameled girl and floral sprays . .   **265.00**
  5¼" d, 4¾" h, sapphire blue, white enameled young girl holding basket of flowers on lid, multicolored enamel dec on base, fancy wire legs **630.00**
Cruet, 8½" h, sapphire blue, sq, dimpled sides, white enameled two girls facing

Box, cov, dark amethyst ground, white enameled lady watering garden, floral band, 5½" d, $250.00.

each other, blue handle and orig stopper **485.00**
Decanter, 5" d, 10⅝" h, cranberry, white enameled young girl with hat by fence   **365.00**
Dresser Set, cranberry, tray, two perfume bottles, powder box, ring tree, and pin tray, 6 pcs **1,100.00**
Jewel Box, 3 x 3½", cranberry, hinged lid **400.00**
Liqueur Glass, stemmed, 3⅜" h, 1¼" d, lime green, white enameled girl **50.00**
Mug
  3" h, 2⅛" d, cranberry, white enameled boy, applied clear handle . . .   **80.00**
  3⅞" h, 2¼" d, amber, applied amber handles, white enameled boy on one, girl on other, pr **135.00**
Perfume Bottle, 4⅝" h, 2" d, cranberry, white enameled little girl dec, clear ball stopper **165.00**
Pitcher
  6⅝" h, 4¼" d, lime green, bulbous, optic effect, round mouth, white enameled boy, applied green handle **125.00**
  7½ x 9½", medium green, white enameled boy with bird and trees and girl with bowl and brush dec, pr **250.00**
Plate, 6¼" d, cobalt blue, white enameled girl with butterfly net **125.00**
Rose Bowl, 3" h, 3¼" d, 8 crimp top, cranberry, white enameled young girl   **225.00**
Salt Shaker, 5", blue, paneled, white enameled girl in garden, brass top .   **180.00**
Toothpick Holder, cranberry, white enameled girl and floral sprays **55.00**
Tumble–Up, cranberry, white enameled girl on carafe, boy on tumbler **400.00**
Tumbler, 1¾" d, 2½" h, cranberry, white enameled boy on one, girl on other, facing pr **100.00**

Vase

4¼" h, 1⅝" d, cranberry, clear pedestal foot, detailed white enameled girl **100.00**

8⅞" h, 4" d, cranberry, white enameled young girls carrying watering cans, facing pair **400.00**

9" h, 4" d, frosted emerald green, white enameled girl holds flowers in her apron and hand **150.00**

11¼" h, 3⅞" d, cranberry, white enameled young boy with tam holding sprig, cut scalloped top **325.00**

13" h, 6⅞" d, scalloped top, applied clear reeded snail handles, cranberry, white enameled girl with flowers in her apron **400.00**

14" h, 5¾" d, cobalt blue, white enameled boy with butterflies, pedestal base **225.00**

MATCH HOLDERS

History: After 1850 the friction match achieved popular usage. The early matches were packaged and sold in sliding cardboard boxes. To facilitate storage and to eliminate the clumsiness of using the box, match holders were developed.

The first examples were cast iron or tin, the latter often having advertising on them. A patent for a wall hanging match holder was issued in 1849. By 1880 match holders also were being made from glass and china. Match holders lost popularity in the late 1930s and 1940s with the advent of gas and electric heat and ranges.

Advertising

Apollinaris Soda Water **25.00**

New Process Gas Range, hanging, tin, gray ground, red ground **55.00**

Sharples Separator Co, tin, mother and daughter, farm scene **85.00**

Brass

Bear chained to post, 3" h, cast, orig fire gilt **225.00**

Fire Department, 2 x 2½", copper colored, hinged lid, Reading, PA Fire Hall cello insert in lid, early 1900s **40.00**

Owl, glass eyes, cast, 2¾" h **60.00**

Bronze, 3", shoe with mouse in toe, 19th C **120.00**

Cast Iron

Bird, figural **45.00**

Horseshoe shape, antlered stag crest, hanging, cov box at base with knob finial **35.00**

Shoe, 5½" h, high button, black paint, c1890 . . . . **40.00**

Glass, 4¼" h, cobalt blue, SP brass trim, cylindrical **40.00**

Metal, 2 x 2¼", black enamel paint,

Advertising, Ceresota Flour, tin, enamel, young boy cutting bread, figural barrel for matches, marked "Nell Sign & Poster Co., NY," 2¼" w, 5½" h, $125.00.

hinged lid, inside striking surface, "The Original Teddy" photo in lid, red inscription "Theodore Bear, 149 Market St., Chicago," c1910 . . . . **75.00**

Papier Mache, 2¾" h, black lacquer, Oriental dec **15.00**

Porcelain, girl, seated, feeding dog on table, sgd "Elbogen" **125.00**

Silver Plated, 3" h, devil's head, brass insert **40.00**

Sterling Silver, 1¾ x 2½", hinged lid, diecut striking area, cigar cutter on one corner, lid inscription "H. R." and diamond, inside lid inscription "Made For Tiffany & Co/Pat 12, 09/Sterling" **75.00**

Tin

Cigar, ¾ x 1½ x 2¼", wrap around red, white, and blue cello, Davenport Cigars **50.00**

Top Hat, 2⅜" h, hinged lid, orig green paint, black band **60.00**

Wood, 2½" h, dome shape, "Prince Charles," tartan decoupage **35.00**

MATCH SAFES

History: Match safes are small containers used to safely carry matches in one's pocket. They were first used in the 1850s. Match safes are often figural with a hinged lid and striking surface.

Reference: Audrey G. Sullivan, *A History of Match Safes In The United States,* published by author, 1978.

Note: While not all match safes have a striking surface, this is one test, besides size, to distinguish a match safe from a calling card case.

Brass, nickel plating, four cigars, center band reads "Havana," 1⅜ x 1⅝", $275.00.

Advertising
Colemans Mustard, SP, inlaid enamel, brass plaque of Bradfords Victory Over Manchester 100.00
Minnesota State Firemen's Association 1916 Tournament, silvered brass, wrap–around cello, winged nude lady angel illus on button, issued 1915 . . . . 100.00
National Supply Co, Boston, silvered brass, wrap–around cello, horse head illus, black and white design and text, early 1900 . . . . 45.00
San Felice Cigars, pocket, man and woman, "For Gentleman of Good Taste," dated 1912 . . . . 65.00
United Hatters Union, silvered brass, black and white cello insert panels, union text, 1½ x 2¾", 1900–01 . . 75.00
Vacuum Oil Co, Rochester, NY, silvered brass, lighthouse with beam and floating barrel of marine oil on one side, 1⅜ x 2¼" 50.00
Agate and brass, banded, brown, white, and gray, 2½ x⅞" 400.00
Art Nouveau stylized flowers, loop, 1⅜ x 1⅝", German (800 silver) 75.00
Brass
Billiken, watch chain loop, 1908 . . . 275.00
Dragon, Chinese 175.00
Metamorphic, skull changes to rooster 275.00
Milk Pail 185.00
Walnut 200.00
Copper and Brass, figural, baby in shirt 150.00
Gunmetal, three miniature rose diamond horseshoes, 27 diamonds, sapphire, gold button 325.00
Lapis with brass, cylindrical, hinged top, 2⅝ x⅞" 350.00
Nickel Plated, figural
Cigar 115.00
Shoe 125.00
Silver Plated, playing card dec, King of Hearts, two score keeping dials, marked "Gorham" 200.00

Silvered Pewter, figural, pig 175.00
Sterling Silver
Art Nouveau, repousse, lady, long flowing hair, flowers, marked "Sterling" 70.00
Wreath and Ribbon design, 2⅝ x 1¾" 100.00

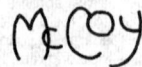

McCOY POTTERY

History: The J. W. McCoy Pottery Co. was established in Roseville, Ohio, in September, 1899. The early McCoy Co. produced both stoneware and some art pottery lines, including Rosewood. In October, 1911, three potteries merged creating the Brush-McCoy Pottery Co. This company continued to produce the original McCoy lines and added several new art lines. Much early pottery is not marked.

In 1910, Nelson McCoy and his father, J. W. McCoy, founded the Nelson McCoy Sanitary Stoneware Co. In 1925, the McCoy family sold their interest in the Brush-McCoy Pottery Co. and started to expand and improve the Nelson McCoy Co. The new company produced stoneware, earthenware specialities, and artware. Most of the pottery marked McCoy was made by the Nelson McCoy Co.

References: Sharon and Bob Huxford, *The Collectors Encyclopedia of McCoy Pottery,* Collector Books, 1980; Harold Nichols, *McCoy Cookie Jars: From The First To The Latest,* Nichols Publishing, 1987.

Additional Listings: *See Warman's Americana & Collectibles* for more examples.

Planter, Down By The Old Mill Stream, white seated figures, Bennington style brown glaze, well in back, 7¼ x 4⅛ x 6⅜", $15.00.

Bank, Woodsy Owl	35.00
Basket, Rustic, pine cone dec, 1945	25.00
Bowl, Mt. Pelee, lava type, charcoal irid, 1902	325.00
Clothes Sprinkler, turtle	15.00

Cookie Jar

Apple Basket	35.00
Cat	35.00
Clown	35.00
Cook Stove, black	40.00
Ducks, yellow	40.00
Frontier Family	30.00
Mammy	70.00
Penguins	27.50
Pineapple	30.00
Strawberry	30.00
Train Engine, yellow	35.00
Wish I Had A Cookie	25.00
Creamer and Sugar, Daisy, brown and green	17.50

Decanter

Apollo Missile, c1968	185.00
Pierce Arrow, Sport Phantom	35.00

Jardiniere

4", Blossomtime	20.00
9", Rosewood, brown glaze, orange streaks	65.00
Lamp, Arcanture, bird and foliage dec	275.00
Pitcher, W.C. Fields	25.00

Planter

Cat, green bow	8.75
Cradle	8.00
Dog, light green	12.00
Lamb, blue bow	8.00
Swan, white	7.50
Triple Lily, 1953	45.00
Spittoon, 4½", pansies, marked "Loy–Nel Art"	100.00
Tankard, corn, marked "J.W. McCoy"	80.00
Tea Set, English Ivy pattern, vine handles, 3 pcs	40.00

Vase

9", iris dec, marked "Loy–Nel–Art"	100.00
12", handles, Olympia	175.00
15", fan, glossy, browns and yellows	200.00

Wall Pocket

Clock	24.00
Orange	15.00
Violin	17.50
Watering Pitcher, 9½", turtle, green, twig handle	20.00

McKEE GLASS

History: The McKee Glass Co. was established in 1843 in Pittsburgh, Pennsylvania. In 1852 they opened a factory to produce pattern glass. In 1888 the factory was relocated to Jeannette, Pennsylvania, and began to produce many types of glass kitchenwares, including several patterns of glass

Depression Glass. The factory continued until 1951 when it was sold to the Thatcher Manufacturing Co.

McKee named its colors Chalaine Blue, Custard, Seville Yellow, and Skokie Green. McKee glass may also be found with painted patterns, e.g., dots and ships. A few items were decaled. Many of the canisters and shakers were lettered in black to show the purpose for which they were intended.

References: Gene Florence, *Kitchen Glassware of the Depression Years, 3rd edition*, Collector Books, 1988; Lowell Innes and Jane Shadel Spillman, *M'Kee Victorian Glass*, Dover Publications, 1981.

Additional Listings: See *Warman's Americana & Collectibles* for more examples.

Candy Dish, orange body, gold trim, gold finial, clear base, 7¾" h, $24.00.

Animal Dish, dove, round base, beaded rim, vaseline, sgd	350.00
Birdhouse	85.00
Berry Set, Hobnail with Fan pattern, blue, master berry and eight sauce dishes	150.00
Bowl, 9½", flower band, jade	12.00
Butter Dish, Wiltec pattern, Prescut ware, frosted	50.00
Candlesticks, 9", Rock Crystal, pr	130.00
Candy Dish, nude, lid	225.00
Cheese and Cracker Set, red, Rock Crystal	165.00
Clock, amber, tambour art	300.00
Cookie Jar, Patrician Crystal	80.00
Cruet, stopper, amber, Rock Crystal	185.00
Egg Cup, ivory, set of 4	6.00
Ice Bucket, cov, black	55.00
Lamp, nude, green	150.00
Measuring Pitcher, 2 cup, red ships dec	25.00
Pitcher, 8", Wild Rose and Bowknot, frosted, gilt dec	45.00
Punch Bowl Set, bowl, twelve mugs, Tom and Jerry, red scroll dec	35.00
Reamer, Jadite	20.00
Ring Box, cov, Jadite	15.00
Server, center handle, red, Rock Crystal	125.00
Toothbrush Holder, Jadite	15.00

Tumbler, Gladiator pattern, green, gold trim	**30.00**
Vase, 8½", nude, Chalaine	**165.00**
Water Cooler, 21" h, spigot, vaseline, 2 pc	**300.00**

MEDICAL AND PHARMACEUTICAL ITEMS

History: Medicine and medical instruments are well documented for the modern period. Some instruments are virtually unchanged since their invention. Others have changed drastically.

The concept of sterilization phased out decorative handles. Early handles of instruments were often carved and can be found in mother-of-pearl, ebony, and ivory. Today's sleekly designed instruments are not as desirable to collectors.

Pharmaceutical items include items commonly found in a drug store and pertain to the items used to store or prepare medications.

References: Bill Carter, Bernard Butterworth, Joseph Carter, and John Carter, *Dental Collectibles & Antiques,* Dental Folklore Books of K.C., 1984; Don Fredgant, *Medical, Dental & Pharmaceutical Collectibles,* Books Americana, 1981; Keith Wilbur, *Antique Medical Instruments,* Schiffer Publishing, 1987.

Museums: National Museum of History and Technology, Smithsonian Institution, Washington, DC; Waring Historical Library, Medical University of South Carolina, Charleston, SC.

APOTHECARY

Bottle, 5⅞" h, pressed, amber, tole lid .	**25.00**
Chest, 32 small drawers, two large drawers at bottom, fall front desk in center top, hinged fold out top working surface, restored and refinished, 56¾ x 15 x 41"	**1,000.00**
Jar, ointment, silver, lid inscribed "O Infirm"	**150.00**
Mortar and Pestle, 9", turned ash burl, wide turned foot, plain birch pestle .	**125.00**
Pill Roller, 2 pcs, 7 x 14", walnut and brass, makes 24 pills	**100.00**
Scale, counter top, wooden base, marble top, two brass pans, orig weights	**175.00**
Sign	
Metal, mortar and pestle, 26½" h, gold–bronze repaint, 19th C	**400.00**
Neon, Cosmos Medical Healer	**300.00**

DENTAL

Account Book and Ledger, 1886—90 .	**15.00**
Cabinet, oak, door, two rect windows, pull out shelves, ceramic drawer pulls	**1,500.00**

Catalog, Consolidated Dental Manufacturing Catalog & Price List, New York, 1915	**150.00**
Chair, mahogany, cast iron, mfg by George Archer, Rochester, NY, c1880	**550.00**
Instrument	
Cheek retractor, carved MOP handle	**75.00**
Extracting forceps, SP, design on handle, F. Arnold	**50.00**
Pliers, nerve canal	**15.00**
Sterilizer, formaldehyde, wall mounted	**50.00**

MEDICAL

Anesthesia Mask, brass, folding, c1870	**75.00**
Bleeder, spring loaded, brass, "POL 1842" etched on back, orig box	**75.00**
Book	
Diseases of the Skin, Crocker, 1905	**15.00**
Gunn's New Family Physician, 1884, illustrated, 1,230 pgs	**25.00**
Practical Home Physician, 1886, color litho illustrations, 1,142 pgs .	**40.00**
Catalog, Dugan Johnson Co. Standard Surgical Instruments, 1920	**30.00**

Flems, bleeding knife, three blades, brass case, $50.00.

Flems, tortoise shell, orig box	**325.00**
Hearing Aid, silk tubing	**85.00**
Lancet, brass, spring, orig case	**125.00**
Medicine Spoon, folding, sterling silver, teaspoon on one end, tablespoon on other, six graduated pierced holes, five point star and wing hallmarks, orig pigskin case	**100.00**
Phrenological Bust, 11" h, pottery, transfer decorated, marked "L N Fowler, London," late 19th C	**1,000.00**
Saw, amputation, bow blade, ebony handle	**120.00**
Scalpel, set of 3, ebony, c1860	**400.00**
Stethoscope, monaural, metal	**100.00**
Surgical Kit, pocket	**275.00**

OPTICAL

Book, *Optical Dictionary and Encyclopedia,* 1908	**25.00**
Eyelid Retractor, ivory handle, marked "Hills King St.," c1853	**125.00**
Ophthalmoscope, Morton, cased	**100.00**
Verometer, eyeglass tester, Bausch & Lomb, electric	**175.00**

MEDICINE BOTTLES

History: The local apothecary and his book of formulas played a major role in early America. In 1796 the first patent for a medicine was issued by the United States Patent Office. Anyone could apply for a patent. As long as the dosage was not poisonous, the patent was granted.

Patent medicines were advertised in newspapers and magazines and sold through the general store and by "medicine" shows. In 1907 the Pure Food and Drug Act, requiring an accurate description of contents of medicine on the label, put an end to the patent medicine industry. Not all medicines were patented.

Most medicines were sold in distinctive bottles, often with the name of the medicine and location in relief. Many early bottles were made in the glass manufacturing area of southern New Jersey. Later companies in western Pennsylvania and Ohio manufactured bottles.

References: Joseph K. Baldwin, *A Collector's Guide To Patent And Proprietary Medicine Bottles Of The Nineteenth Century,* Thomas Nelson, Inc., 1973; Ralph & Terry Kovel, *The Kovels' Bottle Price List, 8th Edition,* Crown Publishers, 1987; Carlo & Dot Sellari, *The Standard Old Bottle Price Guide,* Collector Books, 1989.

Periodicals: *Antique Bottle And Glass Collector,* P.O. Box 187, East Greenville, PA 18041.

American Drug Store N.O., tapered top, amber, 9¼"	**50.00**
Barber Medicine Co, Kansas City, MO, aqua, label, 7½"	**20.00**
Chlorate Potassique, pontil, clear, painted brown, 6½"	**20.00**
E. A. Burkhout's Dutch Liniment, Prepared At Mechanicville, Saratoga Co, NY, pontil, aqua, 5¼"	**150.00**
J. A. Gilka, two men with club and crown, black, 9"	**25.00**
Girolamo Pagliano, vertical letters, rect, beveled corners, apple green, 4⅜"	**25.00**
Gra Car Certosa of Pavia, aqua, 9½"	**20.00**
Granular Citrate of Magnesia, kite with letter inside, ring top, cobalt, 8"	**30.00**
G. W. House Clemens Indian Tonic, ring top, aqua, 5"	**100.00**
Kobole Tonic Med Co, Chicago, IL, milk glass, 8½"	**35.00**

Balsam De Malt, Chas. H. Texter, Mfg Chemist, Quakertown, PA, orig paper label, $10.00.

O.K. Plantation, triangular, amber, 11"	**200.00**
Phillips Emulsion, (N backwards), amber, 9½"	**30.00**
Pine Tree Tar Cordial, Phila, tree and patent 1859 on one panel, L.Q.G. Wisharts on other, blob top, green, 8"	**50.00**
Reed & Carnrick, NY, dark blue, 6¼"	**25.00**
Roshton & Aspinwall, New York, Compound Chlorine Tooth Wash on back, flared top, pontil, golden olive, 6"	**250.00**
Smith, John J, Louisville, KY, round, deep green, sloping collared mouth, scarred base, 5¾"	**175.00**
Teissier Prevos A Paris, graphite pontil, blue, 7½"	**70.00**
Whitwell's Liquid Improved Opodeloc, cylindrical, clear, emb, sloping flanged lip, pontil, two part mold, 4⅝"	**100.00**

MERCURY GLASS

History: Mercury glass is a light bodied, double walled glass that was "silvered" by applying a solution of silver nitrate to the inside of the object through a hole in the base of the formed object.

F. Hale Thomas, London, patented the method in 1849. In 1855 the New England Glass Co. filed a patent for the same type of process. Other American glass makers soon followed. The glass reached the height of its popularity in the early 20th century.

Atomizer, dec colored floral bud shaped glass stopper	**48.00**
Bowl, 4¾", enameled floral dec, gold int.	**50.00**
Cake Stand, 8" d, pedestal base, emb floral dec	**75.00**
Candlesticks, pr, 12¾", baluster, domed circular foot, amber, enameled floral sprigs, pr	**300.00**

Salt, master, silver ground, pedestal, 2¾" d, 2¾" h, $22.50.

Cologne Bottle, 4¼ x 7½", bulbous, flashed amber panel, cut neck, etched grapes and leaves, corked metal stopper, c1840 .... 150.00
Creamer, 6½" h, etched ferns, applied clear handle, Sandwich 125.00
Garniture, 14", baluster, raised circular molded foot, everted rim, enameled foliate motif 215.00
Goblet, 6⅞" h, silver, etched Vintage pattern, gold int. 50.00
Pitcher, 5½ x 9¾", bulbous, panel cut neck, engraved lacy florals and leaves, applied clear handle, c1840 . 200.00
Tiebacks
   3¼", etched grapes, vines, and leaves, pewter shanks, pr 65.00
   4", etched budding iris and scrolls, pr 90.00
Sugar, 4¼ x 6¼", cov, low foot, enameled white foliage dec, knob finial .. 35.00
Vase
   9¾", cylindrical, raised circular foot, everted rim, bright enameled yellow, orange, and blue floral sprays and insects, pr 225.00
   13", trumpet shape, enameled panel of orange, yellow, green, and blue floral clusters and butterflies 220.00

METTLACH

History: In 1809 Jean Francis Boch established a pottery at Mettlach in Germany's Moselle Valley. His father had started a pottery at Septfontaines

in 1767. Nicholas Villeroy began his pottery career at Wallerfanger in 1789.

In 1841 these three factories merged. They pioneered in underglaze printing on earthenware, using transfers from copper plates, and in using coal fired kilns. Other factories were developed at Dresden, Wadgassen, and Danischburg.

The castle and Mercury emblems are the two chief marks. Secondary marks are known. The base also contains a shape mark and usually a decor mark. Pieces are found in relief, etched, prints under the glaze, and cameo.

Prices are for print under glaze unless otherwise specified.

References: Susan and Al Bagdade, *Warman's English & Continental Pottery & Porcelain, 1st Edition,* Warman Publishing Co., Inc., 1987; Gary Kirsner, *The Mettlach Book, Second Edition,* published by author, 1987, R. H. Mohr, *Mettlach Steins, Ninth Edition,* published by author, 1982.
Additional Listings: Villeroy & Boch.
Advisor: Ron Fox.

Beaker
   2327,¼ L, serving girl 85.00
   2366,½ L, woman and child 150.00
   2781,¼ L, cameo, couple, man seated 230.00
Bowl, 2415, 8¼ x 10½ x 7¼", squatty oval body, short legs, scalloped rim, Art Nouveau style, etched gold and green leaves, blue highlights on gray ground, glossy gold trim, 1898 .... 675.00
Compote, 346, 5½", relief, grapes and leaves, flake on base 70.00
Creamer and Sugar, 3321, etched ... 150.00
Cup and Saucer, relief, cupids, blue gray, and silver 75.00
Jar, cov, 1324, 5", glazed mosaic 175.00
Mug, 3287,½ L, "Sons of the Revolution, Feb. 22, 1910" 65.00
Mustard, cov, 3¼", relief, floral 85.00
Pitcher, cov, 2085, 13", 3 L, cylindrical body tapering at shoulder to tall neck, tall circular foot, pottery inset domed cov, neck panels of relief molded shields, center dark blue relief band, white relief band of dancing peasants, scrolling dividers 450.00
Plaque
   1044/102B, 14", PUG, geese 100.00
   1044/147, 14", Liechtenstein castle . 375.00
   1044/165, 12" Meissen/Elbe 250.00
   1044/1205, 17", PUG, cavaliers ... 385.00
   2112, 16", etched, dwarf in nest holding wine bottles, sgd "H. Schlitt," rim flake 1,025.00
   2323, 14½", etched, wounded knight and maiden 900.00
   2625, 7½", etched, mandolin player . 300.00
   3181, 17", etched, Hohkonigsburg .. 1,245.00

Pokal, 454,½ L, relief, king fills walking
steins, line repair, pr **350.00**
Punch Bowl, 1888, 6 L, relief, Imperial
eagle with state shields **1,000.00**

**Stein, #2092II, matte finish, sgd "H
Schlitt," $595.00.**

Stein
228,½ L, relief, cavaliers **135.00**
1467,½ L, relief, harvest scene **225.00**
1508,½ L, etched, tavern scene, sgd,
"Gorig" **435.00**
1526/598, 1 L, man with rifle scene . **305.00**
1526/1108,½ L, ram and dancers
scene, sgd "Hein Schlitt" **265.00**
1909/726,½ L, comical scene, walk-
ing beer stein **360.00**
1909/1143,½ L, Schlitt scene, 4 men
in early dress drinking, exceptional
relief pewter lid **250.00**
1940, 3 L, etched, keeper of the wine,
sgd "Warth" **1,500.00**
2001,½ L **375.00**
2134,½ L, etched, dwarf in nest . . . **1,440.00**
2530,½ L, boar hunt **850.00**
2772,½ L, Brown University seal, owl
thumb piece **225.00**
2893/1197 2L, PUG, Hessen shield . **450.00**
2951,½ L, cameo, crest of Prussian
eagle **375.00**
Tile, 3¼ x 5¾", blue warrior **225.00**
Tray, 8 x 12", frame and handles, flying
geese and large flowers **275.00**
Vase
1836, 5½", brown blue floral relief . . **135.00**
2706, 13", Rookwood style **400.00**

MILITARIA

History: Wars always have been part of history.
Until the mid-19th century, soldiers often had to fill
their own needs, including weapons. Even in the

20th century a soldier's uniform and some of his
gear are viewed as his personal property, even
though issued by a military agency.

Conquering armed forces made a habit of ac-
quiring souvenirs from their vanquished foes. They
brought their own uniforms and accessories home
as badges of triumph and service.

Saving militaria may be one of the oldest collecting traditions. Militaria collectors tend to have
their own special shows and view themselves outside the normal antiques channels. However, they
haunt small indoor shows and flea markets in
hopes of finding additional materials.

References: Ray A. Bows, *Vietnam Military
Lore 1959–1973,* Bows & Sons, 1988; Robert
Fisch, *Field Equipment of the Infantry 1914–1945,*
Greenberg Publication, 1989; *North South Trad-
er's Civil War Price Guide, 4th Edition,* North South
Trader, 1988; *Official Price Guide To Military Col-
lectibles,* House of Collectibles, 1985; Jack H.
Smith, *Military Postcards 1870–1945,* Wallace-
Homestead, 1988; Sydney B. Vernon, *Vernon's
Collectors' Guide To Orders, Medals, and Deco-
rations,* published by author, 1986.

Periodicals: *Military Collectors' News,* P.O.
Box 702073, Tulsa, OK 74170; *North South
Trader,* 724 Caroline Street, Fredericksburg, VA
22401.

Collectors' Clubs: American Society of Military
Insignia Collectors, 1331 Bradley Avenue, Hummelstown, PA 17036; Association of American Military Uniform Collectors, 446 Berkshire Rd, Elyria,
OH 44035; Company of Military Historians, North
Main Street, Westbrook, CT 06498; Imperial German Military Collectors Association, Box 38, Key-
port, NJ 07735.

Reproduction Alert: Pay special attention to
Civil War and Nazi material.

Additional Listings: Firearms and Swords. See
World War I and World War II in *Warman's Americana & Collectibles* for more examples.

WAR OF 1812

Buttons, set of 15 buttons, coat and
vest, Army, General Service, pewter
1808–30, Infantry, pewter 1812–15,
Regiment of Artillerists 1811–13, Artillery 1813–14, Light Artillery 1808–
21, Artillery Corps 1814–21 . . . . . . **250.00**

CIVIL WAR

Belt, enlisted man's, black leather, brass
retaining clips, oval brass "US" buc-
kle **150.00**
Bullet Mold, Confederate, small brass
mold, picket pattern bullet **85.00**
Buttons, Confederate, lot of thirty-five
buttons, coat and vest, initials, states **925.00**

Canteen, 8″, tin, cloth cov, stopper and carrying strap, stamped "Wadden, Porter & Booth, Phila" on pewter spout **150.00**

Cartridge Box, leather, oval brass plate emb "US" outer flap, inner flap marked "H.H. Hartzell/US/Ord Dep'/ Sub Inspector," and "E. Metzger, Phila" **275.00**

Drum, 12″ h, 14¾″ d, body painted, 9″ gold and black spread wing eagle clutching red, white, and blue shield, orig label "Russell & Pater/61 Court Street, Boston/Mass," inscription . . . **650.00**

Epaulets, officer's, gilded brass, attaching bars with silver stars, emb eagle, shield, olive branches, and arrows button, pr **200.00**

Civil War, cartridge box belt plate, eagle, $65.00.

Flag, Grand National Confederate, 5 x 10′, used at the 4th Encampment . . **225.00**

Microscope, Army doctor's, mobile, brass tweezers, mahogany case, 6″ h **35.00**

Plate, 8½″, tin **35.00**

Slouch Hat, Confederate cavalry **650.00**

Sword, Confederate Cavalry, curved 36″ steel blade, black steel scabbard, brass basket handle, initialed and serial numbered, marked "R" & "S" . . **175.00**

Sword Belt Plate, Union, NY, sq, silver wreath **150.00**

INDIAN WARS

Belt Buckle, Naval officer, brass, stamped "Horstman, Phila" **100.00**

Broadside, Ohio massacre, Nov 4, 1791, printed in Boston, 1792, foxed, water stained, modern frame, 60¾″ w, 22″ h **900.00**

Hat Insignia, cavalry, brass, crossed sabers, 3″ w **50.00**

Sleeve Patch, medical, Army, dark blue wool backing, 4 x 4″ **8.00**

Trowel Bayonet, Model 1873, 3½″ w blade **75.00**

FRANCO-PRUSSIAN WARS

Badge, bronze, Emperor Josef under eagle with crown, maker's mark "Wien" **50.00**

Bayonet, black anodized scabbard, 22½″, curved blade, solid brass handle, marked "MRE d'Armes Je St. Etienne, 1873" **50.00**

Helmet, Prussian General Officer, spiked, silver grade star, enameled black Eagle Order on breast of Heraldic Eagle, gilt chinstrap and rosettes, silk lining **1,500.00**

Medal, "Order of the House of Hohenzollen Knight," badge with swords, silver gilt and enameled breast badge **350.00**

SPANISH AMERICAN WAR

Button, pinback, "Remember The Maine," battleship scene, patent 1896 **20.00**

Cartridge Box, US Army **125.00**

Hat Badge, infantry, brass, crossed krag rifles, 2″ l **50.00**

Spy Glass, pocket, Naval, brass, round holder, brown leather grip, 16″ **100.00**

WORLD WAR I

Bayonet, Erzatz style, Mauser, 12″ steel blade, green painted handle, scabbard, Serial #7979 . . . . **30.00**

Binoculars, French Officer's, leather carrying case, 8 x 32″, excellent optics **30.00**

Book, *History of the 79th Division,* A.E.F., 510 pgs, battle field photos, published 1919 . . . . **35.00**

Coat, officer's, wool, black scrolls on sleeves, belonged to Capt G. E. Shepherd **30.00**

Compass, British **90.00**

Parade Bar, 5 medal, includes EK 2nd Class, nine year service silver medal 3rd class, Hindenburg cross with swords, Leopold Bavarian 1905 medal, and Bavarian reserves medal **75.00**

Photo Album, Field Artillery Unit #27 under General Hindenburg, 34 photos, dated 1907 . . . . **135.00**

Propeller, US, wood, four blade **325.00**

Sword, officer's, German, brass lion head handle with ruby eyes, detailed mane and mouth holding oak leaf guard, helmeted women on back of handle, 33″ engraved blade, black scabbard with brass ring **275.00**

Tunic, observer's, US Air Service **50.00**

Wound Badge, silver, crossed silver swords stickpin **10.00**

WORLD WAR II

Badge Wings, Air Crew Member's, SS,
 snap on back, marked 22.00
Belt Buckle, German, DAK Luftwaffe
 Em, tan web belt, marked "#85" . . .   75.00
Boots, German, leather, felt wool tops,
 sewn leather reinforcement straps, pr   30.00
Bracelet, Air Crew Member, SS, curved
 wings 25.00
Coat, Navy, flier's, leather and wool,
 marked "BuAero-US Navy" 50.00
Combat Boots, light brown, unused . .   10.00
Desk Stand, prisoners, handmade,
 metal, 6½" h, iron cross, eagle top,
 dated 1940 & 1941, hand scratched
 Air Force Pilot in POW camp from 11/
 44 to 11/45 . . . .   15.00
Diver's Knife, deep sea demolition, solid
 brass scabbard, ribbed oak handle
 with brass guard, 8" steel blade . . . 120.00
Flying Cross, ribbons with attached
 bronze oak leaves, cased 50.00
Helmet, Tanker's, football style, leather
 liner, green, snaps for earphones,
 made by Wilson Ath Goods 65.00
Leggins, Japanese, straps, hooks,
 brought back from Guam 42.00
Medal, soldier's, parade ribbon, enameled lapel bar, black leather case . .   20.00
Recognition Book, Naval Forces Ship,
 70 pgs, some entries, marked "Restricted", separate wall chart 10.00
Swagger Stick, US, officer's, brass shell
 casings, copper bullet tip, 22" l 20.00
Window Flag, US Merchant Marine, 8½
 x 12" 20.00

VIETNAM

Ammo Box, steel, M5-20A1, dated . . .   10.00
Helmet, flight, South Vietnam Officer's,
 sun visor, white poly lining, attached
 black muffed earphones, marked
 "Maker Gentax Corp" 65.00
Medal, Air Force Commendation, pa-
 rade ribbon and lapel bar, case 20.00
Parachute, cargo, camouflage, nylon
 straps, hooks, etc, American manu-
 facturer 30.00
Tunic, US Army, Sgt, green gold stripes,
 5th Division red diamonds insignia .   20.00

MILK GLASS

History: Opaque white glass attained its greatest popularity at the end of the 19th century. American glass manufacturers made opaque white tablewares as a substitute for costly European china
and glass. Other opaque colors, e.g., blue and
green, were made. As the Edwardian era began,
milk glass expanded into the novelty field.

The surge of popularity in milk glass subsided
after World War I. However, milk glass continues
to be made in the 20th century. Some modern
products are reissues and reproductions of early
forms. This presents a significant problem for collectors, although it is partially obviated by patent
dates or company markings on the originals and
by the telltale signs of age.

Collectors favor milk glass from the pre-World
War I era, especially animal covered dishes. The
most prolific manufacturers of these animal covers
were Atterbury, Challinor-Taylor, Flaccus, and
McKee.

References: E. McCamley Belknap, *Milk Glass,*
Crown Publishers, 1949, out-of-print; Regis F. and
Mary F. Ferson, *Yesterday's Milk Glass Today,*
privately printed, 1981; Regis F. and Mary F. Ferson, *Today's Prices For Yesterday's Milk Glass,*
privately printed, 1985; S. T. Millard, *Opaque
Glass,* Wallace-Homestead, 1975, 4th edition.

Periodical: *Opaque News,* P. O. Box 402,
Northfield, MN 55057.

Collectors' Club: National Milk Glass Collectors Society, 1203 South 12th St, Springfield, IL
62703.

Museum: Houston Antique Museum, Chattanooga, TN.

Notes: There are many so-called McKee animal
covered dishes. Caution must be exercised in
evaluating pieces because some authentic covers
were not signed. Further, many factories have
made, and many still are making, split rib bases
with McKee-like animal covers or with different
animal covers. There also is disagreement among
collectors on the issue of flared vs. unflared bases.
The prices for McKee pieces as given are for authentic items with either the cover or base signed.

Pieces are cross referenced to the Ferson's and
Belknap's books by the (F —-) or (B —-) marking
at the end of a listing.

Advisors: Regis and Mary Ferson.

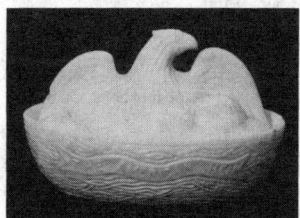

**Animal Dish, cov, eagle on nest, banner
embossed "The American Hen," eggs
embossed "Porto Rica, Cuba, and Phil-
ippines," white, $85.00.**

Animal Dish, cov
Fish, 8¾" l, walking, divided horizontally, five central fins support body, detailed scales, red glass eyes (B167b) **175.00**
Hen, 7½" l, marbleized, head turned to left, lacy base, white and deep blue, Atterbury (F8) **150.00**
Bottle, duck, figural, 11½" h, vertical bill, head, and neck form flanged opening, rimmed oval for label, no closure, Atterbury (F433) **350.00**
Bowl, 8¼" d, Daisy, allover leaves and flower pattern, repeated on inner base, open scalloped edge (F165) . **80.00**
Butter Dish, cov, 4⅞" l, sq, ftd base, curves outwards toward top, Roman Cross pattern, cube shape finial (F240) **50.00**
Calling Card Receiver, bird, back view, wings extended over fanned tail, head resting on leaf, detailed feather pattern (F669) **130.00**
Candlestick, 7¾" h, swirl, ribbing twists counter–clockwise form base, column, cup, and wax guard (F522) .. **35.00**
Celery, 6⅝" h, scalloped rim, plain band above vertical surface, Blackberry pattern, low stem rising from circular base, Hobbs Brockunier (F317) **95.00**
Compote, 11" h, pedestal, Chick and Eggs, chick emerging from heaped eggs, finial cov, mounted on curved tripod, central support, rounded lacy edge base, emb Atterbury patent date, Aug 6, 1889 inside cov (F362) **175.00**
Condiment Set, Forget-me-not pattern, salt and pepper, 5⅛" h cruet, trefoil tray, bulbous shape, six lobed, floral pattern, blue, Challinor, Taylor (F164) **190.00**
Creamer, 4⅜" h, row of paneled sunflowers above row of paneled lilies of the valley, long lip, heavy handle, purple slag, Atterbury (F288 a) **60.00**
Egg Cup, 4¼" h, bird, cov, round, fluted, Atterbury (F130) **130.00**
Jar, eagle, 6½" h, "Old Abe," rests upright, leafy base, "E Pluribus Unum" on encircled banner, gray (F568) ... **95.00**
Lamp, 11" h, Goddess of Liberty, bust, three stepped hexagonal base, clear and frosted font, brass screw connector, patent dated, Atterbury (F329) .. **200.00**
Match Safe, 4½" h, baby in hat, corrugated striker, black hat, match design (F534) **310.00**
Pickle Dish, 9⅝" l, fish, realistic detailed scales, head, and fins, tail handle, Atterbury patent dated June 4, 72 (F360 A) **25.00**
Plate, 6" d, two cats form upper edge, bracketed dog head, open work

swirled leaves, emb "He's all right" (B20d) **90.00**
Spooner, 5⅛" h, monkey, cylinder shape, scalloped top, seated monkeys molded around circumference (F275) **115.00**
Sugar, Ihmsen Glass Co, nine panel, flared bowl, factory product on low feet panel, cov fits inside base edge (F670) **400.00**
Syrup, 6" h, Bellflower pattern, single vine, dated, Collins & Wright (F155C0) **225.00**

MILLEFIORI

History: Millefiori (thousand flowers) is an ornamental glass composed of bundles of colored glass rods fused to become canes. The canes were pulled while still ductile to the desired length, sliced, arranged in a pattern and again fused together. The Egyptians developed this technique in the first century B. C.; it was revived in the 1880s.

Reproduction Alert: Millefiori items, such as paperweights, cruets, toothpicks, etc., are being made by many modern companies.

Vase, waisted, ruffled top, light blue, cobalt blue, medium blue, and white canes, four knob handles, 3½" h, $35.00.

Bowl
4", applied handles, blue and white canes **80.00**
8 x 2½", tricorn, scalloped, folded sides, amethyst and silver deposit **125.00**
Creamer, 3 x 4¼", white and cobalt blue canes, yellow centers, satin finish .. **100.00**
Cruet, bulbous, multicolored canes, applied camphor handle, matching stopper **100.00**
Cup and Saucer, white and cobalt blue canes, yellow centers, satin finish .. **85.00**
Door Knob, 2½", paperweight, center

cane dated 1852, New England Glass
Co **375.00**
Goblet, 7½" h, multicolored canes, clear
stem and base **150.00**
Pitcher, 6½", multicolored canes, applied candy cane handle **165.00**
Rose Bowl, 6", crimped top, cased,
white lining **145.00**
Slipper, 5", camphor ruffle and heel .. **135.00**
Sugar, cov, 4 x 3½", white canes, yellow
centers, satin finish **115.00**
Vase
3½", cabinet, waisted, ruffled top,
light blue, cobalt blue, medium
blue, and white canes, four applied
knob handles **35.00**
4", multicolored canes, applied double handles **100.00**

MINIATURE LAMPS

History: Miniature oil and kerosene lamps, often
called "night lamps," are diminutive replicas of
larger lamps. Simple and utilitarian in design, miniature lamps found a place in the parlor (as "courting" lamps), hallway, children's rooms, and sick-
rooms.

Miniature lamps are found in many glass types
from amberina to satin glass. Miniature lamps
measure 2½ to 12 inches in height with the principal parts being the base, collar, burner, chimney,
and shade. In 1877 both L. J. Atwood and L. H.
Olmsted patented burners for miniature lamps.
Their burners made the lamps into a popular
household accessory.

Study a lamp carefully to make certain all parts
are original; married pieces are common. Reproductions abound.

References: Ann Gilbert McDonald, *Evolution
of the Night Lamp*, Wallace-Homestead, 1979;
Frank R. & Ruth E. Smith, *Miniature Lamps*, Schif-
fer Publishing Ltd., 1981, 6th printing; Ruth E.
Smith, *Miniature Lamps - II*, Schiffer Publishing
Ltd., 1982; John F. Solverson, *Those Fascinating
Little Lamps*, Antique Publications, 1988; John F.
Solverson (comp.), *"Those Fascinating Little
Lamps"/Miniature Lamps*, (includes prices for
Smith numbers) *Value Guide*, Antique Publica-
tions, 1988.

Note: The numbers given below refer to the
figure numbers found in the Smith books.

#9-I, Fire Fly, opaque white, orig dated
burner **225.00**
#11-I, milk glass pedestal base and
shade, clear pressed font, Sandwich,
6¾" **245.00**
#25-II, cranberry, Berger Lamp **125.00**
#29-I, cobalt blue glass font, emb "Nut-
meg," narrow brass band forming

**Smith #284, satin, red, petal type
shade and base, embossed pattern,
$275.00.**

handle, nutmeg burner, clear glass
chimney, 2¾" base **100.00**
#59-II, clear, emb "Vienna" **125.00**
#68-I, pewter base, emb rococo design,
burner marked "Stellar, E M & Co,"
3½" **85.00**
#78-I, nickel plated, wall type, emb
"Comet," blue glass beehive chimney
shade, 7¼" **75.00**
#89-I, brass, double student lamp, orig
opaque white shades, 9¾" **500.00**
#98-II, clear, applied handle **100.00**
#100-II, dark blue, emb star **110.00**
#109-I, green, Beaded Heart pattern,
acorn burner, clear glass chimney,
5½" **190.00**
#112-I, amber, Bull's Eye pattern, nut-
meg burner, clear glass chimney, 5" **100.00**
#116-I, amber, Fishscale pattern, nut-
meg burner, clear glass chimney ... **135.00**
#118-I, amber, Buckle pattern, 8½" .. **125.00**
#125-I, red paint, ball shaped shade,
emb flowers and designs, acorn
burner, clear glass chimney, 7¼" ... **135.00**
#154-II, brass, pedestal, saucer base . **80.00**
#156-1, milk glass, emb flower and
scrolls, 8" **115.00**
#184-I, milk glass, beaded and emb de-
sign, blue painted highlights on base
and globe-chimney shade, hornet
burner **200.00**
#190-I, milk glass, Block and Dot pat-
tern, 7¾" **135.00**
#192-I, clear, Block pattern, hp blue and
green flowers, acorn burner, 6½" ... **60.00**
#204-II, blue, camphor shade **100.00**
#213-I, red, stain, Chrysanthemum and
Swirl pattern base and globe, hornet
burner, 9" **425.00**
#215-I, milk glass, emb beaded panels

and boats, windmill and lighthouse on base, vertical roses of beading on globe-chimney shade, hornet burner, 7¾" **325.00**

#230-I, milk glass, Acanthus pattern, fired on yellow dec, base marked "Buc. PA/1898," 8½" **175.00**

#231-I, green, satin, Drape pattern, globe shade, nutmeg burner, clear glass chimney, 8½" **315.00**

#267-II, Pairpoint, all orig, sgd "Dresden" on base **400.00**

#287-I, apricot shaded to clear, overshot glass, tulip molded base and shade, nutmeg burner, clear glass chimney, 8½" **650.00**

#289-II, brass, pedestal, handle **100.00**

#317-I, milk glass, pink and yellow flowers, shaded green ground **300.00**

#369-I, spatter, tortoiseshell, 8¼" **250.00**

#393-I, white, satin, emb ribbing, hp pink, yellow, and green florals, nutmeg burner, clear glass chimney ... **285.00**

#394-I, blue, satin, puffy DQ pattern base and umbrella shade, nutmeg burner, clear glass chimney, 8" **475.00**

#403-I, cranberry opal, Beaded Drape pattern, 9½" **350.00**

#409-II, cranberry, threaded base ... **125.00**

#460-I, cranberry, white enamel floral dec, 11⅝" **450.00**

#477-I, sapphire blue, hobnail, 7¼" .. **375.00**

#482-I, clear, Daisy and Cube pattern, nutmeg burner, 8" **225.00**

#538-I, amberina, paneled, amber feet, 9¼" **1,500.00**

#546-I, blue, Swirl pattern, 8½" **500.00**

#600-I, satin, MOP, Raindrop pattern, four petal feet, 8¾" **600.00**

MINIATURES

History: There are three sizes of miniatures: doll house scale (ranging from ½ to 1"), sample size, and child's size. Since most earlier material is in museums or extremely expensive, the most common examples are 20th century.

Many mediums were used for miniatures: silver, copper, tin, wood, glass, and ivory. Even books were printed in miniature. Prices are broad ranged, depending on scarcity and quality of workmanship.

The collecting of miniatures dates back to the 18th century. It remains one of the world's leading hobbies.

References: Lillian Baker, *Creative and Collectible Miniatures*, Collector Books, 1984; Flora Gill Jacobs, *Dolls Houses in America: Historic Preservation in Miniature*, Charles Scribner's Sons, 1974; Flora Gill Jacobs, *History of Dolls Houses*, Charles Scribner's Sons; Constance Eileen King,

Dolls and Dolls Houses, Hamlyn; Eva Stille, *Doll Kitchens, 1800–1980*, Schiffer Publishing, Ltd., 1988; Von Wilckens, *Mansions in Miniature*, Tuttle.

Periodicals: Miniature Collector, Collector Communications Corp., 170 Fifth Ave, New York, NY 10010; Nutshell News, Clifton House, Clifton, VA 22024.

Collectors' Clubs: International Guild Miniature Artisans, P.O. Box 842, Summit, NJ 07901. Newsletter (biannual); National Association of Miniature Enthusiasts, 123 N. Lemon St., Fullerton, CA 92632. *Miniature Gazette* (quarterly).

Museums: Kansas City Doll House Museum, Kansas City, MO; Margaret Woodbury Strong Museum, Rochester, NY; Mildred Mahoney Jubilee Doll House Museum, Fort Erie, Canada; Toy Museum of Atlanta, Atlanta, GA; Washington Dolls House and Toy Museum, Washington, DC.

Additional Listings: See Doll House Furnishings in *Warman's Americana & Collectibles* for more examples.

DOLL HOUSE SIZE

Armoire, tin litho, purple and black ... **20.00**
Bathroom
  Porcelain, toilet, sink, tub, cherry wood medicine cabinet, Collector's Miniature Masterpiece **70.00**
  Wood, painted white, Strombecker . **35.00**
Bedroom
  French Provincial style, antique white, includes dressing table and bench, bed, night stands **150.00**
  Stenciled, pair of canopy beds, dressing table with mirror, pair of night stands and three chest of drawers with faux marble tops, side chair, accessories, Biedermeier **1,000.00**
  Victorian style, metal, veneer finish, bed, night stand and commode with faux marble tops, armoire and mir-

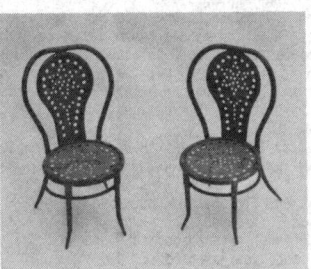

Chairs, tin, bentwood ice cream parlor style, pierced seat and back, 3½" h, pr, $75.00.

ror, cradle, Biedermeier clock, metal washstand **650.00**

Bench, wood, rush seat **20.00**

Breakfront, Renwal **15.00**

Buffet, stenciled, three shelves, columns supports, 6½ x 6", Biedermeier **400.00**

Chair

Golden Oak, center splat, upholstered seats, German, c1875, pr . **70.00**

Ivory, high pointed back, ornately pierced, 2" h, 19th C **175.00**

Ormolu, ornate, 3" h, c1900, pr **75.00**

Couch, wood frame, floral design seat, blue painted back, six legs, 6" h, Tynietoy stamp **70.00**

Curio Cabinet, maple, four graduated shelves, fancy carved sides, 7" **50.00**

Desk

Chippendale style, slant top, drawers open **50.00**

Roll top, oak, office chair, drawers open **75.00**

Dining Room

Edwardian style, dark red stain, extension table, chairs, marble top cupboard, grandfather clock, chandelier, candelabra, 5" bisque head and shoulder maid doll, table service for six, Gebruder Schneegrass, Waltershausen, Thuringia, c1915 . . . . **1,200.00**

French style, gilded wood, round pedestal table, six matching chairs, damask upholstered settee, pier mirror, fireplace, table with faux marble top **800.00**

Hall Rack, walnut, carved, fretwork, arched mirror back shelves, umbrella holder **450.00**

Kitchen Stove, Petite Princess **70.00**

Living Room

Empire style, sofa, fainting couch, two side chairs, upholstered tapestry, matching drapery **350.00**

Tudor style, settee, two chairs, footstool, upholstered, fringe trim, marble topped table, candle stand . . . **250.00**

Victorian style, upholstered red velvet, settee, two parlor chairs, footstool, two plant stands, two gilt filigree tables, three panel screen, Gone with the Wind style lamp . . **500.00**

Lounge, Victorian style, minor upholstery wear **100.00**

Parlor Set, 1¼ x 1¾" couch, four 1¼" h chairs, cut design, painted red, gold seats **40.00**

Piano

Grand, wood, eight keys, 5" h **30.00**

Spinet, wood, cabriole legs, handmade, 3½" h **25.00**

Upright, movable keys, bench, 4½" . **40.00**

Rocker

Cast Iron, green and red, 4" h **40.00**

Victorian style, faded upholstery . . . **50.00**

Sewing Table, wood, golden oak, drawer, c1880 . . . . **100.00**

Side Chairs, Victorian, pr **125.00**

Table

Ivory,¾", scale, c1870 . . . . **275.00**

Tin, painted brown, white top, floral design, 1½" l,¾" h, ornate **20.00**

Tea Cart, Petite Princess **20.00**

Trestle Table, golden oak, turned legs and stretcher, c1900 . . . . **30.00**

Vanity, Biedermeier **90.00**

Accessories, tea service, Britannia, $65.00.

ACCESSORIES

Ashtray, stand, c1910 . . . . **30.00**

Bird Cage, brass, bird, stand, 7" h . . . **60.00**

Bookends, wood, seated cats, pr **15.00**

Candelabra, Petite Princess **20.00**

Carpet Sweeper, gilt, Victorian **65.00**

Cash Register, German **150.00**

Christmas Tree, with accessories **40.00**

Cigar Cutter, metal, c1920 . . . . **25.00**

Clock, metal **25.00**

Coffeepot, brass **20.00**

Cradle, cast iron, painted green, 2" l, 2½" h **40.00**

Cup and Saucer, china, flower design, 1" scale, c1940 . . . . **8.00**

Decanter, two glasses, Venetian, c1920 **25.00**

Dust Pan and Broom, pewter, German, c1890 . . . . **30.00**

Fan, table, brass ormolu **350.00**

Fireplace, tin, Britannia metal fretwork, draped mantle, carved grate **75.00**

Fireplace Tools, metal, stand, c1930 . **50.00**

Floor Lamps, brown, ecru shade on one, blue shade on other, 2¾" h, Tootsie Toy, pr **25.00**

Grandfather Clock, rounded top, walnut stain door with black and blue, paper face, impressed Tynietoy on back . . **70.00**

Measuring Cup, Pyrex **10.00**

Mirror, wood, Tynietoy, c1930	**45.00**
Radio, Strombecker, c1930	**25.00**
Refrigerator, Petite Princess	**75.00**
Sewing Machine, copper, treadle	**50.00**
Silhouettes, Tynietoy, c1930, pr	**15.00**
Tea Set, teapot, cream and sugar, two cups and saucers, tray, green and white floral pattern, two handles repaired	**100.00**
Tea Wagon, gilt, German, c1910	**160.00**
Telephone, wall, oak, speaker and bell, German, c1890	**30.00**
Towel Stand, golden oak, turned post .	**45.00**
Typewriter, steel, black, AM., c1925 . .	**70.00**
Umbrella Stand, brass ormolu, sq, emb palm fronds	**50.00**
Urn, silver, handled, ornate	**100.00**

SAMPLE SIZE

Bed, mahogany, poster, canopy top, turned posts, arched headboard . . .	**275.00**
Blanket Chest, Victorian, country, pine, 19th C, 19″ w, 9½″ d, 26″ h	**300.00**
Bookcase Cabinet, Victorian, mid 19th C, mahogany, molded cornice, glazed door, adjustable shelves, lower section with two paneled cupboard doors, molded base, 14″ w, 6½″ d, 26″ h	**450.00**

Chest of Drawers

Empire, American

Birch, four dovetailed drawers, turned and carved half column pilasters, turned feet, worn old mahogany red finish, 28¾″ w, 14¼″ d, 28¾″ h	**2,600.00**
Mahogany, bowed top drawer over three drawers, shaped splash back, wooden knob handles, 8½″ w, 6¾″ d, 13″ h, c1825–40	**325.00**
Federal, mahogany, rect top, reeded edge, four graduated drawers, astragal moldings, ivory pulls, shaped aprons continue to form feet, 10″ l, 9″ h	**550.00**
Sheraton, mahogany, top with simple inlay, four dovetailed drawers with flame grain veneer facade, edge veneer, inlaid ivory escutcheons, rope carved corner columns with biscuit corners, turned front feet, old refinishing, 12¾″ w, 8¼″ d, 12¾″ h	**1,100.00**

Victorian

American, mid 19th C, mahogany, rect top, conforming case, two short and three long drawers, bracket feet, 23″ w, 11″ d, 23″ h	**700.00**
Country, 19th C, mahogany, rect top, conforming case, three molded long drawers, bracket feet, 22″ w, 13″ d, 23″ h	**450.00**
Cradle, pine, orig blue paint, 16″ l	**120.00**
Desk, Chippendale, country, pine, slant front, three long drawers, molded base, bracket feet, 22″ w, 13″ d, 21″ h	**2,600.00**
Plow, pine and steel, splayed handles, projecting plow support, gilt dec, red painted ground, inscribed "South Bend Chilled Plow Co, Pat May 25, 1886, No. 15 trademark," South Bend, IN, c1886, 23½″ l	**2,000.00**

CHILD SIZE

Blanket Chest, William and Mary, walnut, dovetailed, turnip feet, inset initials "EB" made with cut-off nails, green paper lining, 14¾ x 7¼ x 7½″	**275.00**
Chair, arrow back, arm, dec, worn dark repaint, yellow and orange striping, stenciled floral crest, 18½″ h, minor damage	**125.00**

Chest of Drawers

Chippendale, Centennial, mahogany, four drawers, bracket base, Victorian bail brass, 10⅝ x 6½ x 16¼″	**350.00**
Georgian, burl walnut, band inlay, 15½ x 8¼ x 16⅜″	**700.00**
Hepplewhite, English, late 19th C, select mahogany with some curl, pair of small drawers at top, three graduated full width drawers, French splayed bracket base, brass pulls with engraved flowers, 11⅞ x 7¾ x 15⅝″	**550.00**
Cupboard, country style, pine, two glazed doors, two drawers and doors in base, white porcelain knobs, 24½ x 23 x 13″	**400.00**
Desk, Chippendale, MA, c1770, painted and dec maple, slant front, rect hinged lid, int. of valanced pigeonholes, center two blocked and concave carved drawers, prospect drawers flanking, three graduated long drawers below, bracket feet, painted black on reddish-brown ground, 23 x 12½ x 28″	**30,000.00**
Dresser, Eastlake style, stenciled design, mirror panel, one drawer, two cabinets, 31″ h	**125.00**

Rocker

Eastlake style, folding, bamboo turnings, tapestry seat and back, 27″ h	**150.00**
Empire style, mahogany, vase shaped splat, rush seat, scrolled arms, 22″ h	**200.00**
Victorian, American, late 19th C, painted black, wooden arms, caned back and seat	**300.00**

Side Chair, country style, pine plank
seat, crest rail, turned legs, 22½" h . **150.00**
Table, country style, drop leaf, walnut,
turned legs. 24 x 28 x 21" **150.00**
Tea Service, 15 pcs, ridged, white, gold
sprayed on trim, blue flowers, En-
glish, c1900 . . . . **175.00**

MINTON CHINA

History: In 1793 Thomas Minton and others
formed a partnership and built a small pottery at
Stoke-on-Trent, Staffordshire, England. Production began in 1798 with blue printed earthenware,
mostly in the Willow pattern. In 1798 cream colored earthenware and bone china were introduced.

A wide range of styles and wares was produced.
Minton introduced porcelain figures in 1826, Parian wares in 1846, encaustic tiles in the late 1840s,
and Majolica wares in 1850. Many famous designers and artists in the English pottery industry
worked for Minton.

Many early pieces are unmarked or have a
Sevres type marking. The "ermine" mark was
used in the early 19th century. Date codes can be
found on tableware and Majolica. Between 1873
and 1911 a small globe signed Minton with a crown
on top was used.

In 1883 the modern company was formed and
called Mintons Limited. The "s" was dropped in
1968. Minton still produces bone china tablewares
and some ornamental pieces.

Reference: Susan and Al Bagdade, *Warman's
English & Continental Pottery & Porcelain, 1st Edition,* Warman Publishing Co., Inc., 1987.

Centerpiece, 16" l, elongated parian
vessel, molded scroll handles and
feet, pierced rim, two brown reserves,
white pate–sur–pate amorini, gilding,
dec attributed to Lawrence Birks,
marked "Minton," retailer's marks of
Thomas Goode & Co., Ltd., London,
c1889 . . . . **1,300.00**
Dessert Service, Pattern No. G3439,
fruits, twelve plates, three stands,
light wear, imp mark, 1880 date code **825.00**
Dresser Set, pin box, 5½" pitcher, and
11" d tray, pink roses dec, gold trim,

Oyster Plate, five scallop shells, fish
motif between scallops, white salt
glaze, stamp mark "18th Cent, Staffordshire Salt Glaze," 10⅝" d, $75.00.

incised maker and potter marks,
c1898 . . . . **250.00**
Dish, 10¾", earthenware, artist sgd "W
S Coleman," imp mark, 1869 . . . . . **685.00**
Ewer, 21¼", majolica, heron and fish,
after model by J Protat, imp mark,
1869 date code **2,300.00**
Figure, 12", parian, two nude girls . . . **400.00**
Garden Seat, majolica
18", "Aesthetic," dark ground, applied
scrolls and foliage, imp mark, 1881
date code **2,350.00**
20¾", streaky turquoise glaze, imp
"Minton, 1896" **550.00**
Jardiniere, 7" h, molded wooden planks,
white vines, lilac int., majolica, match-
ing stands, pr **425.00**
Jug
67½", majolica, green leaves, white
flowers, lilac rim, imp mark, 1869 . **600.00**
9⅞", majolica, bright yellow, green,
blues, aubergine, and white, imp
mark "437," and 1873 date code . **2,345.00**
Oyster Stand, 10", majolica, revolving
base, glazed green, brown, and
white, imp mark, 1869 . . . . **2,225.00**
Plaques, 7⅝ x 7", pate–sur–pate,
matching pr, one with maiden and
cupid spinning web, other with
maiden seated on bench with whip in
one hand, sunflowers stalked with humanistic snail in other, artist sgd
"Louis Solin," both marked on back,
framed **2,000.00**
Plate, 9", portrait panels, multicolored,
gilt tracery, reticulated border **70.00**
Soup Plate, 10⅜" d, printed and painted
famille rose style, Orientals, molded
floral band border, ironstone, c1825 . **50.00**
Sweetmeat Dish, 8", majolica, blue tit-

mouse on branch, leaf shaped dish,
imp mark, 1868 . . . . **665.00**
Tea Service, salt glazed, polychrome
dec, Botanical pattern, 15 pcs **450.00**
Vase, 11½" h, yellow glazed, leaf dec
narrow neck, pierced handles, tapering ovoid body, circular foot, imp
"Minton" **600.00**

MOCHA

History: Mocha decoration usually is found on
utilitarian creamware and stoneware pieces and is
produced through a simple chemical action. A
color pigment of brown, blue, green, or black is
made acidic by an infusion of tobacco or hops.
When the acidic colorant is applied in blobs to an
alkaline ground, it reacts by spreading in feathery,
seaplant-like designs. This type of decoration usually is supplemented with bands of light colored
slip.

Types of decoration vary greatly, from those
done in a combination of motifs, such as "Cat's
Eye" and "Earthworm," to a plain pink mug decorated with green ribbed bands. Most forms of
mocha are hollow, e.g., mugs, jugs, bowls, and
shakers.

English potters made the vast majority of the
pieces. Marked pieces are extremely rare. Collectors group the ware into three chronological
periods: 1780–1820, 1820–1840, and 1840–1880.

Reference: Susan and Al Bagdade, *Warman's
English & Continental Pottery & Porcelain, 1st Edition,* Warman Publishing Co., Inc., 1987.

**Mug, one half pint, tree design, wide
blue band, black ribbon bands,
$145.00.**

Bowl, 6½" d, 3⅜" h, broad band of deep
chocolate brown with six diamond
shaped groups of nine cat's eyes,
medium blue band around base, mi-
nor int. wear, two rim hairlines **350.00**
Cider Mug, 6⅛" d, 8" h, two wide baby
blue bands with flowing black dec,

two black lines flank pastel green
bands, minor damage **900.00**
Compote, 4⅞" d, 3½", broad purple–
gray band, marbleized blue, black,
white, and cream, white rim and base **300.00**
Creamer, 2⅛" h, bulbous, short foot,
leaf emb strap handle, brown seaw-
eed **350.00**
Cup and Saucer, ochre and brown cat's
eye dec, brown bands **200.00**
Cup Plate, 3½" d, pale yellow, black
seaweed dec **425.00**
Mug, ftd, bold marbled canary, beige,
coffee, brown and black earthworm
dec, broad shaded leather brown
band flanked by canary base and rim,
bright canary int. **3,875.00**
Mustard Pot
2¾ x 2¼", wide band of reddish
brown with four seaweed dec, design repeated on cov, dark brown
line borders, minor damage **175.00**
3¾", matching cov, orange–ochre
ground, dark brown seaweed dec,
chocolate brown band around
neck, plain white handle **1,150.00**
Pepper Pot, 4½", band of medium tan
flanked by parallel deep brown ¼"
bands, blue starburst design on top,
small chip under top flange **300.00**
Pitcher
5", Liverpool shape, three broad medium blue bands alternating with
two incised bands, brown and white
checkerboard pattern, handle with
leaf shaped ends, applied inverted
fleur–de–lis under emb spout **450.00**
6⅛", barrel shape, two parallel thin
bands of green arrows flanked by
series of wide brown bands which
contain white, brown, and baby
blue cat's eye and earthworm dec,
professional restoration to spout
and base of handle **900.00**
Plate, 8⅜" d, emb design of beads and
leaves on rim, highlighted in green,
center with swirled marbleized tan,
white, cream, and deep brown, bit
warped, 2" hairline off rim **225.00**
Porringer, 4⅛ x 2⅞", narrow band of
deep chocolate above brick–red wide
band with three palm shaped leaves,
deep brown, mocha, and white marbleized design, flared mouth, applied
handle **1,450.00**
Salt, 3¼" d, 2¼" h, master, ftd, earth-
worm dec, blue band, black and white
stripes **200.00**
Sugar Shaker, 4½", white, tan, and
black cat's eye dec, blue band with
tan, white, and black stripes **675.00**
Tankard, 3¼" d, 5" h, 4⅛" w band of

combed and marbleized browns, tan, white, cream, yellow–ochre, brick–red, chocolate brown, and pale green, between two parallel bands of four green incised lines, center medallion with relief bust of military officer, hanging from long ribbon with emb words "Success to Admiral Rodney and His Fleet" **3,150.00**

Teapot, 5¼″ h, squatty round body, wide white middle band with green seaweed, blue trim stripes, minor wear and stains **950.00**

Waste Bowl, 5⅝″ d, 3″ h, earthworm dec, green emb rim, orange band with pattern, minor wear and stains **350.00**

MONART GLASS

History: Monart glass is a heavy, simple shaped art glass in which colored enamels are suspended in the glass during the glass making process. This technique was originally develped by the Ysart family in Spain in 1923. John Moncrief, a Scottish glassmaker, discovered the glass while vacationing in Spain, recognized the beauty and potential market, and began production in his Perth glassworks in 1924.

The name "Monart" is derived from the surnames Moncrief and Ysart. Two types of Monart were manufactured: a "commercial" line which incorporated colored enamels and a touch of adventurine in crystal, and the "art" line in which the suspended enamels formed designs such as feathers or scrolls. Monart glass, in most instances, is not marked. The factory used paper labels.

Vase, round, wide doughnut base, flaring urn body, Scottish Cluthra, shading from goldstone to clear, $100.00.

Basket, brown to light tan opal vertical striations, Cluthra type **585.00**

Bowl, 11½″, mottled orange and green **135.00**

Candlestick, two shades of green, goldstone mica, paper label **75.00**

Lamp Shade, 6½″ d, white opal **85.00**

Vase
  6½″, mottled shades of red and blue, white lining **100.00**
  8 x 8½″, blue, silver, mica, orange streaks, small bubbles **150.00**
  16″, green, flecked neck, orange body, dark inclusions, gold Cluthra centers **450.00**

MONT JOYE GLASS

History: Mont Joye is a type of glass produced by Saint-Hilaire, Touvier, de Varreaux & Company at their glassworks in Pantin, France. Most pieces were lightly acid etched to give them a frosted appearance and decorated with enameled floral decorations. All pieces listed are frosted, unless otherwise noted.

Rose Bowl, acid etched, enameled purple violets, gold stems, gold dec, pinched sides, 3¾″ h, 4¼″ d, $145.00.

Jar, cov, 7″, cylindrical, clear, etched, enameled iris, gilt leaves, clear knop, gilt factory mark, c1900 . . . . **250.00**

Pitcher, 10″, amethyst, enameled flowers, aqua, blue, pink. and gold, sgd . **250.00**

Vase
  5¾″, green glitter body, gold leaf painted dec, applied opal glass spheres **375.00**
  6½″, green, cut poppies, enameled in crimson and gilt, sgd **250.00**
  8½″, cameo, enameled leaves, deep red poppies on icy ground, sgd . . **430.00**
  10″, bulbous, narrow neck, clear to opalescent green, thistle dec in natural colors, highlighted in gold . . . **275.00**
  13¾″, flattened ovoid shape, cameo, clear, etched, molded and enameled iris, gilt leaves, c1900 . . . . . **325.00**
  18″, green, enameled purple flowers, gold leaves, sgd **250.00**
  25¾″ h, flaring waisted bottle form, green metallic flaked ground, overlaid foliate dec, MOP beads, base stamped "Mont Joye," c1910 **1,200.00**

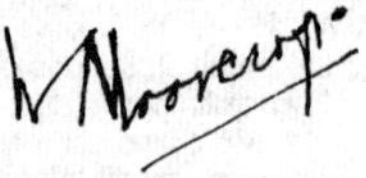

MOORCROFT

History: William Moorcroft was first employed as a potter by James Macintyre & Co., Ltd. of Burslem in 1897. He established the Moorcroft pottery in 1913. The company initially used an impressed mark, "Moorcroft, Burslem;" a signature mark, "W. Moorcroft," followed.

The majority of the art pottery wares were hand thrown, resulting in a great variation among similarly styled pieces. Color and marks are keys to determining age.

Walker, William's son, continued the business upon his father's death and made the same style wares. Modern pieces are marked simply "Moorcroft" with export pieces also marked "Made in England."

Reference: Susan and Al Bagdade, *Warman's English & Continental Pottery & Porcelain, 1st Edition,* Warman Publishing Co., Inc., 1987.

Vase, high glaze, pomegranate dec, cobalt blue ground, green script mark, imp "Moorcroft/Burslem/England/39," $325.00.

Ashtray, coral hibiscus, green ground .	**65.00**
Bowl	
6", pink magnolia, dark blue ground, initials	**125.00**
10", octagonal, grapes dec	**200.00**
11", wisteria	**185.00**
Box, cov, 4¾ x 3½ x 1½", orchids, green ground	**85.00**
Candlesticks, 10", tree dec, shades of yellow, cobalt blue ground, script sgd, pr	**150.00**
Coffeepot, cov, Sicilian pattern, sgd "Moorcroft–MacIntyre"	**250.00**
Compote, 7½", multicolored cornflowers dec, green ground, sgd "W Moorcroft"	**500.00**

Ginger Jar, cov, 11¼", pomegranate dec	**515.00**
Jardiniere, 12", Florian Ware, yellow, green, and white flowers, blue ground, sgd "Moorcroft–MacIntyre" .	**500.00**
Loving Cup, 4¼", three handles, tulips and cornflowers, green, blue, and red, printed and painted signature, c1900	**340.00**
Marmalade Jar, blue flowers, attached stand, sgd "MacIntyre"	**150.00**
Pitcher	
6", blue flowers, pewter lid, sgd	**185.00**
7", red poppies, pewter lid, sgd "MacIntyre"	**250.00**
Plate, 8½", Natural Ware, green and blue glaze, pr	**150.00**
Teapot, 8", orchids, cobalt blue ground	**200.00**
Trivet, 5½", mushrooms, c1922	**185.00**
Vase	
7"	
Blue Dragon	**135.00**
Red Tulip	**125.00**
10"	
Blue Hibiscus	**190.00**
Yellow Tulip	**200.00**
10¼", purple and blue wisteria, cream ground, sgd "Moorcroft–Macintyre"	**550.00**
11¾"	
Florian Ware, baluster, poppies and leaves, shades of blue, printed and painted signature, c1900 . .	**425.00**
Hazeldene, cylindrical, green, blue, and yellow trees, printed Liberty mark, c1912	**1,275.00**
12", Anemone	**275.00**
12½", baluster, white slip trail, dark glaze, imp "Burslem," green script sgd, c1920, pr	**1,325.00**

MORIAGE, JAPANESE

History: Moriage refers to applied clay (slip) relief motifs and decorations used on certain classes of Japanese pottery and porcelain.

This decorating was done by three methods: 1), handrolling and shaping, which was applied by hand to the biscuit in one or more layers; the design and effect required determined thickness and shape, 2), tubing, or slip trailing, which applied decoration from a tube, like decorating a cake, and 3), hakeme, which is reducing the slip to a liquid and decorating the object with a brush. Color was applied either before or after the process.

Bowl, 7", orange flowers and leaves, green wreath mark	**135.00**
Box, 4¾ x 3⅝ x 2¼", dragon ware, detailed dragon, blue jeweled eyes, scrolled footing, unmarked	**38.00**
Chocolate Pot, 9", green ground, four floral medallions, heavy moriage . . .	**225.00**

Salt and Pepper Shakers, top with white ground and gold dec, base with green ground and blue dots, $25.00.

Demitasse Set, pot, two ftd cups and saucers, white wisteria flowers, green trim	**400.00**
Manicure Set, three tools, buffer, and cov trinket box, heavy dec	**175.00**
Pitcher, 6 x 6½", squatty, panels of roses, slip-trail enamels, fancy handle	**250.00**
Powder Box, 5", light green, raised turquoise beading, hp flowers	**75.00**
Rose Bowl, 5¼ x 4", green, pink, and blue, brown band at base	**225.00**
Tea Set, teapot, creamer, cov sugar, five cups and saucers, mauve ground, red roses, delicate white slipwork, unmarked	**650.00**
Vase	
5½", green, tan, and lavender dec	**110.00**
9¼", pedestal base, green ground, white overall slipwork, floral medallions	**250.00**

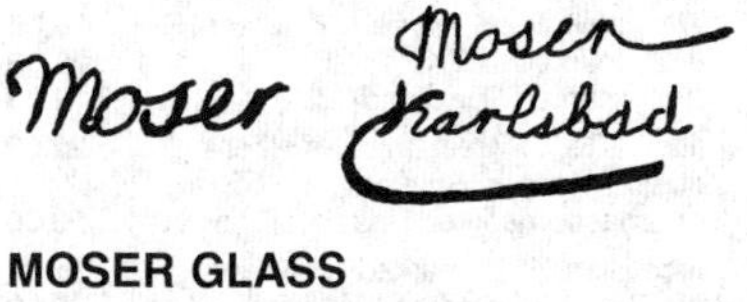

MOSER GLASS

History: Ludwig Moser (1833–1916) founded his polishing and engraving workshop in 1857 in Karlsbad (Karlovy Vary), Czechoslovakia. He employed many famous glass designers, e.g., Johann Hoffmann, Josef Urban, and Rudolf Miller. In 1900 Moser and his sons, Rudolf and Gustav, incorporated Ludwig Moser & Söhne.

Moser art glass included clear pieces with inserted blobs of colored glass, cut colored glass with classical scenes, cameo glass, and intaglio cut. Many inexpensive enamaled pieces also were made.

In 1922 Leo and Richard Moser bought Meyr's Neffe, their biggest Bohemian rival in art glass. Moser executed many pieces for the Wiener Workstátte in the 1920s. The Moser glass factory continues to produce new items.

Reference: Mural K. Charon and John Mareska, *Ludvik Moser, King of Glass: A Treasure Chest of Photographs And History,* published by author, 1984.

Vase, octagonal tapered body, flared top, faceted, yellow, "Moser" in circle mark, 7⅞" h, $350.00.

Box, cov	
3⅜" h, circular, deep purple, gold enameled fauns and maidens, fitted cov, four ball feet, etched "Made in Czechoslovakia Moser Karlsbad"	**1,200.00**
6 x 3¾", cranberry, white enamel dec of woman carrying cornucopia and grapes, enameled gold vine and berries	**650.00**
Calling Card Holder, cranberry, turquoise jewels, gold prunts, four scrolled feet	**350.00**
Centerpiece, 11", oval bowl, intaglio, emerald green shading to clear, sgd	**200.00**
Cologne Bottle, 10¾", cranberry, gold leaves outlined in white, gold and black dots, white dotted blossoms, neck, base, and orig stopper heavily gold encrusted	**400.00**
Compote, 4" h, 8¼" d, 4¼" d hollow base, pale amber, electric blue rigaree and four applied dec, int. dec of twelve painted leaves, brown branches, gold leaves, white cherries, matching branch on base	**645.00**
Decanter, 12½", amber, allover etching	**250.00**
Ewer, 10¾", cranberry, gold oak leaves, lacy gold foliage, small applied glass acorns, pedestal foot, ruffled top, applied clear handle, unsigned	**750.00**

Goblet, 5¾", deep amethyst, gold figures dec, pr **175.00**
Ice Cream Set, master bowl and four serving bowls, mermaid relief, clear and gold, gilt highlights **385.00**
Liqueur, 2½", cranberry, multicolored applied acorns and leaves, sgd **200.00**
Mug, 3¼", green, multicolored oak leaves and bee, applied acorns **300.00**
Perfume Bottle, 4¼ x 6½", malachite, molded bottle and stopper, slab polished sides and top **225.00**
Pitcher
  8½", amber, multicolored floral enamel **200.00**
  9½", sq top, blue and gold, sgd **200.00**
Plate, 7⅜", amberina, gold dec **125.00**
Scent Bottle
  3", purple, prism cutting, orig stopper **200.00**
  5", green, multicolored leaves and berries, ball stopper **165.00**
  11", cranberry, leaves, white and gold dec **400.00**
Sweetmeat Dish, round, cranberry, engraved, gold band **225.00**
Tumbler
  3½", octagonal, ruby cut to clear, gold dec **60.00**
  3⅞", thin, delicate crystal, hp, medallion of mischievous cupid teasing bashful maiden **485.00**
  4", lavender, vines, leaves, berries, and floral work, heavy gilting **175.00**
Vase
  4⅛", shaded apricot, opal, multicolored enameled oak leaves, applied lustered glass acorns, sgd **250.00**
  7¾", long green to clear neck, bulbous base, gold and platinum floral dec, diamond point signature **350.00**
  8", chocolate brown ground, jeweled, gold trim **225.00**
  8½", cranberry, lady playing harp, heavy gold dec, handles **250.00**
  9½", emerald green, multicolored florals, applied gold bees, sgd **475.00**
  11", green, intricately enameled fish, four applied pickerel, handles ... **900.00**
  15½", clear and frosted, deeply etched thistles, inscribed "Moser/Karlsbad" **400.00**

MOSS ROSE PATTERN CHINA

History: Several English potteries manufactured china with a Moss Rose pattern in the mid-1800s. Knowles, Taylor and Knowles, an American firm, began production of a Moss Rose pattern in the 1880s.

The moss rose was a common garden flower grown in English gardens. When American consumers tired of English china with oriental themes, they purchased the Moss Rose pattern as a substitute.

Bowl, 8½", openwork, gold trim, marked "Rosenthal" **40.00**
Box, cov, 6½", oval **24.00**
Butter Pat, sq, marked "Meakin" **15.00**
Coffee Mug and Saucer, marked "Meakin" **40.00**
Coffeepot, 9", marked "E. C. & Co" .. **75.00**
Cup and Saucer, marked "Edwards" .. **25.00**
Dessert Set, eight 7½" plates, eight cups and saucers, creamer and sugar, cake plate, 28 pcs, marked "Fr Haviland" **250.00**
Gravy Boat and Underplate, marked "Green & Co, England" **40.00**
Nappy, 4½", marked "Edwards" **10.00**

Plate, 8½" d, $20.00.

Plate
  7½", pink edge, marked "Haviland" . **16.00**
  8½", marked "KTK" **20.00**
  9½", marked "Haviland" **12.00**
Platter, 10 x 14", rect, marked "Meakin" **26.00**
Salt and Pepper Shakers, 5", SS top and base, marked "Rosenthal," pr .. **50.00**
Sauce Dish, 4½", marked "Haviland" . **15.00**
Soup Plate, 9", marked "Meakin" **16.00**
Sugar, cov **48.00**
Syrup, 8½", pewter top, marked "KTK," c1872 .... **165.00**
Tea Service, teapot, 5½" creamer, 6¼" sugar bowl, marked "Meakin," 3 pcs **200.00**
Teapot, 8½", bulbous, gooseneck spout, basketweave trim, marked "T & V" **40.00**
Tureen, cov, 12", gold trim **70.00**
Wash Bowl and Pitcher, 13½" twelve sided bowl, 11" pitcher **250.00**

MOUNT WASHINGTON GLASS COMPANY

History: In 1837 Deming Jarves, founder of the Boston and Sandwich Glass Company, established for George D. Jarves, his son, the Mount Washington Glass Company in Boston, Massachusetts. In the following years the leadership and the name of the company changed several times as George Jarves formed different associations.

In the 1860s the company was owned and operated by Timothy Howe and William L. Libbey. In 1869 Libbey bought a new factory in New Bedford, Massachusetts. The Mount Washington Glass Company began operating again there under its original name. Henry Libbey became associated with the company early in 1871. He resigned in 1874 during the general depression, and the glass works was closed. William Libbey had resigned in 1872 to work for the New England Glass Company.

The Mount Washington Glass Company opened again in the fall of 1874 under the presidency of A. H. Seabury and the management of Frederick S. Shirley. In 1894 the glass works became a part of the Pairpoint Manufacturing Company.

Throughout its history the Mount Washington Glass Company made a great variety of glass including: pressed glass, blown glass and art glass, lava glass, Napoli, cameo, cut glass, Albertine, and Verona.

References: George C. Avila, *The Pairpoint Glass Story,* Reynolds-DeWalt Printing, Inc., 1968; Leonard E. Padgett, *Pairpoint Glass,* Wallace-Homestead, 1979; John A. Shuman III, *The Collector's Encyclopedia of American Art Glass,* Collector Books, 1988.

Museum: The New Bedford Glass Museum, New Bedford, MA.

Additional Listings: Burmese, Crown Milano, Peachblow, and Royal Flemish.

Sugar Box, melon body, peachblow ground shading from white to light blue, painted and raised enamel floral motif, pewter top with relief leaf design, $375.00.

Biscuit Jar, cov, enameled pink and brown chrysanthemums, relief oak leaf on base, SP cov, rim, and bail handle, marked "M. W."	650.00
Box, 7", blown–out floral dec, pink roses, light to dark green ground . . .	525.00
Bride's Basket, 8¼", sq, cased, deep rose and white ext., white int., dragon, floral and leaf dec, ruffled edge	650.00
Candlestick, 12", pink and white, hp florals, ftd Pairpoint holder	200.00
Compote, 6¼" d, 10" h, Napoli, crystal clear body, pastel green chrysanthemum leaves on wafer base, stem forms pedestal, four golden yellow chrysanthemum blossoms on underside of flared bowl, flowers outlined in gold on int.	585.00
Creamer, 3", melon ribbed, enameled leaf and floral dec, SP handle and spout	185.00
Cruet, 5¾", amberina, IVT, applied amber handle, period amber stopper . .	325.00
Ewer, 7¾" h, conical lusterless white body, hp and enameled thistle blossoms and leaves, elongated pouring lip, applied reeded handle	175.00
Miniature Lamp, 8½" h, Delft blue windmill dec, white opaque base and shade, Smith #276–II, sgd on base	585.00
Perfume, 2¼ x 6", sq, satin, woman in 1890's dress, script on back "Hout's Milk White March 19, 1894–50th Performance Boston Theatre Boston," orig screw atomizer	135.00
Plate	
7", country scene of stone bridge, cottage, and lack, factory dec, orig paper label	100.00
12", twin cupids, leaf and floral border	115.00
Pitcher, 8", Verona, bulbous, maiden hair fern dec, gold highlights, applied clear reeded handle	225.00
Rose Bowl, 4", two cupids floating on cloud, white	185.00
Salt and Pepper Shakers, pr	
Fig, enameled pansy dec, satin, orig prong top	225.00
Melon, squatty, enameled daisy dec, satin, orig 2 pc top	115.00
Scent Bottle, white, reserve with couple, basket of flowers on reverse	100.00
Sugar Shaker	
3¼ x 4", egg shape, pastel pansies, pronged top	585.00
5½", IVT, lighthouse shape, bluerina, orig metal top	270.00
Toothpick Holder, satin glass, Brownie Policeman, billy club in hand, holding another Brownie by scruff of neck, sitting Brownie on back	550.00
Tumbler, peachblow, band of apple	

blossom pink shades to soft blue—
gray **1,450.00**
Vase
3¾", classic shape, Lava, shiny jet
black body, inlaid chips of blue,
green, and pink, two curl handles,
gold dec **1,750.00**
7⅞", lily shape, Burmese, shiny finish **350.00**
8¼", lily shape, peachblow, rich color,
satin finish **1,800.00**
9⅜", lily shape, Burmese, gilded
white metal figural holder **200.00**
9¾", lily shape, Burmese, shiny finish,
copper lily pad style holder **750.00**
10", Lava, black, reeded handles, orig
paper label **2,500.00**
10¾", cylindrical, ruffled everted rim,
white ext., enameled wildflowers
and leaves, blue int., three gilt
metal animal maskform feet, acid
etched mark **185.00**
16", court jester and blossom dec,
pink ground, sgd **750.00**
18⅜", Napoli, base sgd "Napoli/841" **1,400.00**

MULBERRY CHINA

History: Mulberry china, made primarily in the
Staffordshire district of England between 1830 and
1850, is porcelain whose transfer pattern is the
color of mulberry juice. The potters that manufactured flow blue also made Mulberry china; the ware
often has a flowing effect similar to flow blue.

References: Susan and Al Bagdade, *Warman's
English & Continental Pottery & Porcelain, 1st Edition,* Warman Publishing Co., Inc., 1987; Petra Williams, *Flow Blue China and Mulberry Ware-Simi-
larity and Value Guide,* Fountain House East,
Revised Edition, 1981.

Bowl, Vista, Mason, sq, 9" **45.00**
Coffeepot,
Corean, Podmore, Walker **350.00**
Jeddo, Adams **175.00**

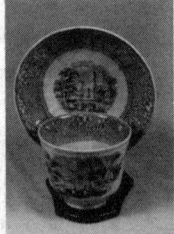

**Cup and Saucer, Bagshaw, Meir, 1802–
08, $45.00.**

Creamer
Beehives in Garden **140.00**
Foliage, Edward Walley **85.00**
Jeddo, Adams **100.00**
Marble, Wedgwood **65.00**
Tavoy **100.00**
Temple, Podmore, Walker **125.00**
Cup and Saucer, handled cup
Genoa, Davenport, 1852 .... **40.00**
Roselle, J M & Son, England **40.00**
Cup and Saucer, handleless cup
Castle Scenery, Jacob Furnival **50.00**
Pelew, Edward Challinor **60.00**
Temple, Podmore Walker **40.00**
Washington Vase, Podmore Walker . **60.00**
Cup Plate
Allegheny, Thomas Goodfellow **45.00**
Corean, Podmore Walker **45.00**
Gravy Boat
Jeddo, Adams **65.00**
Pelew **85.00**
Pitcher, Vincennes, J Alcock, 9½" **135.00**
Plate
7", Genoa **20.00**
8", Temple **25.00**
9½"
Corea, Clementson **65.00**
Ning Po **40.00**
10½"
Bochara, Edwards **35.00**
Cyprus, Davenport **60.00**
Vincennes **45.00**
Platter
Abbey, 12½ x 9½", Adams, c1900 .. **100.00**
Lucerne, 8 x 10", Parkhurst mark .. **35.00**
Peruvian, 16" **125.00**
Rhone Scenery, 15½" **150.00**
Washington Vase, Podmore Walker,
15¾ x 12¼" **135.00**
Relish, Percy, Morley, shell shape ... **35.00**
Sauce Dish, Corea, Clementson, 5" .. **18.00**
Sauce Tureen, cov, Bochara, Edwards **125.00**
Soup Bowl, Scinde, 10½" **30.00**
Sugar, cov, Jeddo, Adams **75.00**
Teapot, Strawberries **175.00**
Vegetable Bowl, cov, octagonal, ped-
estal base
Cyprus, Davenport **75.00**
Jeddo **100.00**
Wash Bowl and Pitcher, Jeddo, W Ad-
ams & Sons **525.00**

MUSIC BOXES

History: Music boxes were invented in Switzerland around 1825. They cover a broad field of
automatic musical instruments from a small box to
a huge circus calliope.

A cylinder box consists of a comb with teeth

which vibrate when stricking a pin in the cylinder and producing music from light tunes to opera and overtures.

The first disc music box was invented by Paul Lochmann of Leipzig, Germany, in 1886. It used an interchangeable steel disc with pierced holes bent to a point which hit the star-wheel as the disc revolved, and thus produced the tune. Discs were easily stamped out of metal, allowing a single music box to play an endless variety of tunes. It reached the height of its popularity from 1890 to 1910. The phonograph replaced it.

Music boxes also were put into many items, e.g., clocks, sewing and jewelry boxes, steins, plates, toys, perfume bottles, and furniture.

Reference: H. A. V. Bulleid, *Cylinder Musical Box Design and Repair,* Almar Press, 1987.

Collectors' Club: Musical Box Society, International, Rt. 3, Box 205, Morgantown, IN, 46160.

Museums: Bellms Cars and Music of Yesterday, Sarasota, FL; Lockwood Matthews Mansion, Norwalk, CT.

Additional Listings: See *Warman's Americana & Collectibles* for more examples.

Disc-Type, Mira, twenty discs, restored and cleaned, 19 x 25½ x 14″, $3,000.00.

CYLINDER-TYPE

3½″ cylinder, Bremond, 6 tune, inlaid rosewood veneer case, inner glass lid, single comb **300.00**

4½″ cylinder, J. H. Heller, 6 tune, walnut dec, floral motifs, inner glass lid, Bern, Switzerland **600.00**

5″ cylinder, L'Epee, France, 4 tune, simple case **350.00**

5⅛″ cylinder, Junod, 4 tune, inlaid rosewood case, tune indicator, 2 bells, dec figural tune card, inner glass lid . . . **1,000.00**

6″ cylinder, Ducommon Girod, 6 tune, case, tune sheet, c1880 . . . . **750.00**

7¾″ cylinder, 4 tune, key wind, simple case style **750.00**

8½″ cylinder, Imhof and Mukle, spring driven movement, rosewood and ebony case, marquetry dec, trade label, c1880 . . . . **400.00**

10¾″ cylinder, Paillard, 8 tune, lever wind, rosewood case, floral dec, c1860 . . . . **800.00**

12″ cylinder, 4 tune, keywind, 20½″ plain case **2,500.00**

13″ cylinder, 6 tune, interchangeable cylinders, piccolo attachment, walnut burled case, matching storage table **3,000.00**

15″ cylinder, 12 tune, lever wind, rosewood with floral dec **1,250.00**

17″ cylinder, Baker-Troll, 6 tune, interchangeable cylinders, six bells, bee strikes, walnut case, brass inlay dec, matching storage table **2,500.00**

DISC-TYPE

6½″ disc, Polyphone, 4 bells, spring driven, litho inside cov, wood case, decal **600.00**

7½″ disc, sq mahogany case, lid int. shows little girls at play, crank wound, single comb, Germany, c1900 . . . . . **275.00**

8¾″ disc, Criterion, table model, mahogany case, figural litho inside lid **750.00**

9″ disc, Britannia, simple case, table model, c1900 . . . . **900.00**

9¼″ disc, 6 bells, walnut case, floral inlay lid, figural litho inside cov **950.00**

10½″ disc, Perfection, table model, mahogany case, scenic litho inside lid, zinc discs **1,400.00**

15½″ disc, Regina, Style 15, No 23256, coin operated, double comb, side crank wound, printed instruction inside cov, 21″ walnut case, leaf tip carved base, 26 discs, American, c1897 . . . **2,300.00**

17¼″ disc, Stella Grand, carved front panel of base with drawer, oak **2,500.00**

27″ disc, Regina Orchestral Corona Style 33, #46968, automatic disc changer, mahogany case, spooled gallery and corner finials, glazed doors with copper gilt foliate open spandrels, glazed panel beneath, 35½ x 23½ x 66½″, 12 discs, c1905 **10,450.00**

MISCELLANEOUS

Album, photograph, 2″ cylinder, 2 tunes, Chicago Exposition pictured on cov with drawings on pages inside, emb brass clasp closing **250.00**

Bird in Cage, domed cage on sq base,

cast and enameled geometric dec,
9″ h 275.00
Roller Organ
  Automatic Melodia, Bates & Co, sliding tremolo stop, 11½ x 9½ x 8½″, gilt stencil dec case, 4 paper rolls **500.00**
  Barrel Organ, 6 air, paper roll, 20½ x 11 x 11¼″, lid stamped Archibald Campbell, impressed line border, scroll spandrels, German **950.00**
  Gem, 14¼ x 12 x 8″, gilt stenciled floral case, 23 cobs **425.00**
  Melodia, Mechanical Organette Co, 12¼ x 10½ x 11½″ case, gilt stencil dec, 4 rolls, late 19th C **520.00**
  Whistling Figure, heavily carved man, elaborate bow tie, bowler hat, hands in pockets, whistles "How Dry I Am," 13½″ h, c1920 .... **525.00**

MUSICAL INSTRUMENTS

History: From the first beat of the prehistoric drum to the very latest in electronic music makers, musical instruments have provided popular modes of communication and relaxation.

The most popular antique instruments are violins, flutes, oboes, and other instruments associated with the classical music period of 1650 to 1900. Many of the modern instruments, such as trumpets, guitars, drums, etc., have value on the "used," rather than antique market.

The collecting of musical instruments is in its infancy. The field is growing very rapidly. Investors and speculators play a role since the 1930s, especially in early string instruments. Sotheby's and Christie's hold annual auctions of fine musical instruments.

References: Tom and Mary Anne Evans, *Guitars: From the Renaissance To Rock; The Official Price Guide To Music Collectibles, Sixth Edition,* House of Collectibles, 1986.

Collectors' Club: Fretted Instrument Guild of America, 2344 South Oakley Avenue, Chicago, IL 60608.

Accordion, Concertone, 21 pearl keys, 12 basses, four sets of steel reeds, 18 fold bellows, leather cov, rosewood finish frames, marked "Made in Italy, Nicolo Salanti", early 1920s ... **300.00**
Bagpipe, Scottish, rosewood chanters, late 17th C **4,500.00**
Banjo
  American, trap door style, snakehead, straight neck, 1920s **250.00**
  Edgemere, nickel shell, wood lined, 17 nickel plated hexagon brackets, raised frets, birch neck finished in imitation mahogany, c1900 ..... **320.00**
Bugle, American, artillery, brass, c1900 **150.00**

Harmonica, Hohner, marked "The 64 Chronomica," orig box, 8¾″ l, 2″ h, 2½″ d, $50.00.

Castanets
  Argentinian, early 19th C **170.00**
  Spanish, late 18th C **250.00**
Cello, Fonclause, silver mounted, unbranded, round stick with ivory face, silver and ebony replacement frog, French silver and ebony adjuster .. **2,000.00**
Clarinet, Laube, 13 nickel silver keys, two rings, Grenadilla wood, trimming cork joints, graduated bore, A, low pitch, c1920 .... **325.00**
Cornet
  Artist B–Flat, nickel plated **275.00**
  Dupont C, triple SP, satin finish **160.00**
  Marceau E–Flat, brass, highly polished, c1905–10 .... **110.00**
Drum, parade, 16″ d, 13″ h, polychrome dec, inscribed "Virginia" above panel depicting Washington and Mt Vernon, mid 19th C **850.00**
Flute
  French, 22⅜″, ivory, one keyed, mid 18th C **6,500.00**
  Unmarked, carved, walnut, 16½″ l, c1780 .... **625.00**
French Horn, King, sgd "USMC," 1890s **200.00**
Guitar
  American, The Kenmore, c1900 ... **200.00**
  The Stanford, hardwood sides and back, imitation rosewood finish, spruce top, brass head, rosewood fingerboard, nickel plated tailpiece **85.00**
Harp, Lyon & Reily, Chicago, No. 701, parcel gilt satinwood, 68″ h, late 19th C **3,500.00**
Mandolin
  The Edgemere, English, early 18th C **6,100.00**
Oboe
  English, early 18th C **8,000.00**
  Italian, c1840 .... **700.00**
Piano
  Chickering, model 84, rosewood, bench **3,750.00**
  Kimball, Grand, 68″, walnut **4,800.00**

Steinway & Sons
 Model B, ebonized, orig bench . . **18,000.00**
 Model M, mahogany **3,000.00**
 Model O, mahogany, orig bench . **4,250.00**
Piccolo
 Italian, hardwood, silver trimming, dec
 walnut box lined with plush, c1742 **1,100.00**
 Meyer, grenadilla wood, ivory head,
 six keys, c1900 . . . . **275.00**
Saxophone
 Bantone, bell front, tree valves, lac-
 quer bore **1,200.00**
 Tourville & Co, tenor, silver, satin fin-
 ish **350.00**
Tambourine, Brazilian, second quarter
 19th C **180.00**
Trombone, Lamoreaux Freres Slide, or-
 namented bell, brass, polished,
 c1905 . . . . **275.00**
Trumpet, Holton, four valve **1,500.00**
Tuba, Tourville & Co, E–Flat Bass, SP,
 satin finish **525.00**
Ukulele, birch body, black rings around
 sound hole, white celluloid binding,
 c1920 . . . . **50.00**
Violin
 Abbati, Giambattista, Modena, 1755–
 95 . . . . **7,500.00**
 Arthur Bultitude, octagonal stick
 mounted with gold and tortoiseshell, tortoiseshell frog, gold flower ornaments **2,100.00**
 Filano, Donato, Naples, 1763–83 . . **3,600.00**
 Marcel Lapierre, round stick mounted
 with gold and ivory, ivory frog, pearl
 dots, gold rings, ivory adjuster . . . **1,200.00**
Zither, Columbia, 19½", maple, c1900 . **150.00**

MUSIC RELATED

Advertising, sign, Poole Pianos, 20 x
 13", tin, fancy black lettering **75.00**
Ashtray, 3¼ x 4", cast iron, figural,
 bearded black man playing banjo,
 c1920 . . . . **65.00**
Book
 Anecdotes of Music, Burgh, A, historical and biographical, letters series, 3 volumes, London, 1814 . . . **90.00**
 The Violin: How to Master It, Honney-
 man, William C, Boston, n.d.c.,
 1895 . . . . **65.00**
Mandolin Case, black leather, hand–
 sewn, flannel lined, leather carrying
 strap **65.00**
Music Stand, Duet Stand, rosewood,
 pierced lyres, brass candleholders,
 adjustable baluster support, raised
 trefoil base, ball shape feet **1,600.00**
Poster, Metropolitan Opera House, illus,
 1920s **125.00**

Violin Chin Rest, Becker's, ebonite and
 nickel, pre 1900 . . . . **25.00**

MUSTACHE CUPS AND SAUCERS

History: Mustache cups and saucers were popular in the late Victorian era, 1880–1900. They
were made by many companies in porcelain and
silver plate. The cups have a ledge across the top
of the bowl of the cup to protect a gentleman's
mustache from becoming soiled while drinking.

 Reference: Susan and Al Bagdade, *Warman's
English & Continental Pottery & Porcelain, 1st Edition,* Warman Publishing Co., Inc., 1987.

**Bone China, blue and pink floral de-
sign, white ground, gilded beaded
bands, twig handle, $65.00.**

PORCELAIN

Austrian, portrait medallion **75.00**
Carlsbad, floral dec, ring handle **35.00**
German, "Papa," florals, pink and
 green, gold trim **40.00**
Hand Painted, pink and white flowers,
 green leaves, pale green ground,
 gold trim **45.00**
Haviland, white, gold trim **90.00**
Limoges, hp pastel flowers, rococo
 molded scrolls, all-over gold **45.00**
Majolica, Bird and Fan pattern **135.00**
Onion Meissen, c1890 . . . . **85.00**
Pink Luster, gold leaves, beaded edges **65.00**
Royal Worcester, hp, flowers, peach
 ground **125.00**
White Patterned Ironstone, copper lus-
 ter dec, c1850 . . . . **250.00**

SILVER PLATED

Barbour Bros Co, bright cut floral design **60.00**
Derby Silver Co, crimped rim, engraved
 floral design **50.00**

Tufts, 1″ band of flowers, strawberries, leaves within border, matching design on saucer, marked **125.00**

NAILSEA TYPE GLASS

History: Nailsea type glass is characterized by swirls and loopings, usually white, on a clear or colored ground. One of the first areas where this glass was made was Nailsea, England, 1788–1873, hence the name. Several other glass houses, including American factories, made this type of glass.

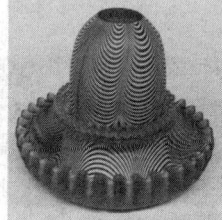

Fairy Lamp, pink and white, ruffled base, Clarke signed insert, $265.00.

Barber Bottle, red ground, white loopings, pewter top **125.00**
Bottle
  10″, gemel, clear, white looping, applied rigaree **130.00**
  10½″, bellows, white, rose loopings, applied rigaree, stand **250.00**
Candlestick, 10″, clear, white loopings, folded socket rim, hollow blown socket drawn out to a double knop, bulb shaped stem, and two additional knops, inverted cone shaped base, early 19th C **375.00**
Fairy Lamp, 4″ d, 4¼″ h, lime green, white loopings, pie crust crimped edge **385.00**
Finger Bowl, 4¼ x 2¼″, ftd, clear body, swirled streaks of deep blue and white, foot drawn from body, applied clear handles imp with cherub's face **60.00**
Flask, 8″ h, slightly flared, clear, white loopings, tooled mouth and pontil . . **90.00**
Mug, 6¾″, clear, white looping, attributed to Pittsburgh **250.00**
Perfume Bottle, chatelaine, 3″, gold wash stopper **85.00**
Pitcher
  4″ d, 6½″ h, clear, white loopings, ftd, solid applied base, triple ribbed solid handle with curled end, flaring

formed mouth, attributed to South Jersey, c1840–60 . . . . **1,125.00**
7¾″ d, 9¾″ h, clear, white and amethyst loopings, applied heavy solid clear handle with gauffered and curled end, applied clear base, flared mouth, attributed to Pittsburgh area **2,750.00**
Powder Horn, 13″, clear, white loopings and red stripes, stand **250.00**
Rolling Pin, 18″, clear, pink and white loopings **250.00**
Sugar, 4½″, opaque white, pink and red loopings, applied clear foot, attributed to Pittsburgh **125.00**
Tumbler, white, blue loopings **115.00**
Vase, 5″ d, 8″ h, cylindrical, flared mouth and base, clear, white loopings, plain sheared rim-pontil, attributed to South Jersey **175.00**
Witch Ball, 5¼″ d, clear, opaque white casing, red loopings, attributed to Pittsburgh **250.00**

NANKING

History: Nanking is a type of Chinese porcelain made in Canton, China, from the early 1800s into the 20th century for export to America and England. It often is confused with the Canton pattern.

Three elements help distinguish Nanking from Canton. Nanking has a spear and post border, as opposed to the scalloped line style of Canton. The blues may tend to be darker on the Nanking ware. Second, in the water's edge or Willow pattern, Canton usually has no figures. Nanking features a standing figure with open umbrella on the bridge. Finally, Nanking wares often are embellished with gold.

Green and orange variations of Nanking survive, although scarce.

Reference: Sandra Andacht, *Oriental Antiques & Art: An Identification And Value Guide,* Wallace-Homestead, 1987.

Reproduction Alert: Copies of Nanking ware currently are being produced in China. They are of inferior quality and decorated in lighter rather than the darker blues.

Cup and Saucer
  Handleless **75.00**
  Loop handle **50.00**
Dish, 7¾″, leaf shape, blue and white, c1795 . . . . **185.00**
Ewer, 11″, small spout, blue and white, mid 19th C **300.00**
Fruit Bowl, 9″, oval, reticulated, blue and white, matching underplate **700.00**
Jug, 9½″, blue and white, c1800 . . . . . **450.00**
Plate, 9½″, water's edge scene, c1780–1800 . . . . **85.00**

Plate, water's edge scene, 1780–1800, 9½″ d, $95.00.

Platter
11½ x 14½″, blue and white, pagoda in foreground **400.00**
14¾″, oval, blue and white, landscape, stylized dragons on cavetto, geometric patterned bands, base inscribed "Da Nihon Tatebayashisei," Meiji period **275.00**
Teapot, 5¾ x 4⅜″, scenic, gold dec, matching stand, 18th C **565.00**
Tureen, 14½ x 10½″, oval, dome cov, flower finial, ftd base, twisted strap handles, early 19th C **1,300.00**
Urn, 5½″, blue, lavender, and green floral, gold handles, pr **325.00**

NAPKIN RINGS, FIGURAL

History: Gracious home dining during the Victorian era meant each household member had their personal napkin ring. Figural napkin rings were first patented in 1869. The remainder of the 19th century saw most plating companies, e.g., Cromwell, Eureka, Meriden, Reed and Barton, etc., manufacturing figural rings, many copying with slight variations the designs of other companies.

Values are determined today by the subject matter of the ring, the quality of the workmanship, and the condition.

Reference: Victor K. Schnadig, *American Victorian Figural Napkin Rings*, Wallace-Homestead, 1971, out-of-print.

Reproduction Alert: Quality reproductions do exist.

Additional Listings: See *Warman's Americana & Collectibles* for a listing of non-figural napkin rings.

Baby in cradle, James W Tufts, Boston   **300.00**
Barrel, two cherubs holding dolls, Meriden Brittania Co **135.00**

Bird, wings spread over nest of eggs .   **145.00**
Boy
Holding baseball bat, hands clasped behind him **190.00**
Pulling wheeled cart **245.00**
Sitting on bench, holding drumstick .   **180.00**
Brownie, climbing up side of ring, Palmer Cox **175.00**
Butterfly, perched on pair of fans **100.00**

Silver Plated, chick and egg, engraved "Best Wishes," marked "Derby Silver, Birmingham, Conn," 3½″ w, 2¼″ h, $95.00.

Cat, glass eyes, ring on back **260.00**
Cherries, stems, leaf base, ball feet . .   **70.00**
Cherub, sitting cross legged on base, candleholder and ring combination .   **175.00**
Chicken, nesting beside ring **160.00**
Dachshund, supporting ring on back . .   **160.00**
Dog pulling sled, emb sides, engraved name, Meriden **165.00**
Deer, standing next to fence **175.00**
Eagle, one on each side of ring **110.00**
Fox, standing erect, dressed **225.00**
Frog, holding drumstick, pushing drum–like ring **300.00**
Goat, pulling wheeled flower cart **245.00**
Greenaway, Kate
Girl
Holding stick above begging dog .   **240.00**
Pulling wheeled cart **270.00**
Horse, standing next to elaborate ring   **175.00**
Man, walking uphill, ring on shoulders   **190.00**
Owl, sitting on leafy base, owls perched on upper limbs **250.00**
Parrot, on wheels, Simpson, Hall, Miller & Co **175.00**
Rabbit, sitting alertly next to ring **175.00**
Roman Centurion, stands next to ring, sword drawn **130.00**
Runner, male nude, holding torch, sq base **150.00**
Sailor Boy, anchor **210.00**
Schoolboy with books, feeding begging puppy **225.00**

Sheep, resting on base near ring	**165.00**
Squirrel, eating nut, log pile base	**125.00**
Swan, one each side of ring, separate bases	**110.00**
Turtle, crawling, ornate ring on back . .	**200.00**

NASH GLASS

History: Nash glass is a type of art glass attributed to Arthur John Nash and his sons, Leslie H. and A. Douglas. Arthur John Nash, originally employed by Webb in Stourbridge, England, came to America and was employed in 1889 by Tiffany Furnaces at its Corona, Long Island, plant.

While managing the plant for Tiffany, Nash designed and produced iridescent glass. In 1928 A. Douglas Nash purchased the physical facilities of Tiffany Furnaces. The A. Douglas Nash Corporation firm remained in operation until 1931.

Cologne Bottle, Chintz, wide pale green stripes separated by wide clear stripes with thin blue centers, clear stopper, marked "Nash/1008/JJ," 5" h, $485.00.

Bottle, 4½" h, squatty, pinched sides, amber irid, green and amber irid striated feather dec, inscribed "LCT B1," c1890	**1,150.00**
Bowl, 7¾ x 2½", Jewel pattern, gold phantom luster	**275.00**
Candlesticks, pr, 4", ball stem, Chintz pattern, blood red and silver, sgd . .	**450.00**
Cologne Bottle, Chintz pattern, paperweight stopper	**225.00**
Compote, 6 x 2", fold over rim, Chintz pattern, green–blue bowl, clear pedestal foot, sgd	**175.00**
Cordial, 5½" h, Chintz pattern, green and blue	**75.00**
Goblet, 6¾" h, feathered leaf motif, gilt dec, sgd	**275.00**

Plate, 8" d, Chintz pattern, green and blue	**175.00**
Tumbler, 5" h, conical, Chintz pattern, blue and silver, low pedestal foot, sgd	**115.00**
Vase	
6¼" h, sq top, irid gold, sgd	**275.00**
12" h, trumpet, orange and yellow vertical stripes, inscribed "Nash 62AA"	**450.00**

NAUTICAL ITEMS

History: The seas that surround us have fascinated man since time began. The artifacts of sailors have been collected and treasured for years. Because of their environment, merchant and naval items, whether factory or handmade, must be of quality construction and long lasting. Many of these items are aesthetically designed as well.

Richard Bourne, Hyannis, Massachusetts, and Chuck DeLuca, York, Maine, regularly hold auctions of marine items.

References: Alan P. Major, *Maritime Antiques,* A. S. Barnes & Co., 1981; Jean Randier, *Nautical Antiques,* Doubleday and Co., 1977.

Periodical: *Conklin's Guide: Maritime Auction Annual,* Leeward Shore Press, P.O. Box 838-20, Brisbane, CA 94005; *Nautical Brass etc.,* Box 744, Montrose, CA 91020.

Museums: Burgess Mariner's Museum, Newport News, VA; Museum of Science and Industry, Chicago, IL; Mystic Seaport Museum, Mystic, CT; National Maritime Museum, San Francisco, CA.

Alarm, 13" h, walnut, brass mounted, 19th C	**550.00**
Barometer, ebonized fluted sq wood case, orig dolphin and shell-form gimbal, Manzioli, Frieste	**1,950.00**
Bell, 16" d, ship's, 67 pounds, *Queen Anna Maria 1965* cast in side, brass	**250.00**
Bench, 46½" l, used for making ship's dead eyes, early to mid 19th C	**2,300.00**
Binnacle, 16½" h, compass, lights, circular mahogany base, orig lamps, marked "E. Miller & Co., Meriden, Conn," 19th C	**700.00**
Bow-Sprit, 44½" l, eagle's head at front, relief carved foliate work, traces blue and green paint, well preserved . . .	**850.00**
Candleholder, brass, spring loaded, used as a hanging or standing, weighted bottom, mid 19th C	**375.00**
Carpenter Chest, 36" l, tools, five sliding trays, "M. Jobin" on lid, "Eagle" on front	**1,000.00**
Chronometer	
Ship, E. Dent & Co., London, No. 49872, orig box and label, good working order, 7¼" sq, 7¾" h case	**1,800.00**

Yacht, Waltham, case and carrying case, 5 x 5 x 5⅛" 550.00
Clock, 7¼" d, navigation or engine use, Chelsea 250.00
Deck Seat, 57" l, 28" h, carved, polychrome, chest in bottom, originally on *Royal Dutch* yacht, well preserved, 18th C 1,200.00
Ditty Box, 6" d, 4" h, pine, pierced baleen, pinwheels, stars, and fretwork, paper backing, Nantucket, 19th C . . 500.00
Diver's Helmet, copper and brass, Galeazzi 600.00
Diving Suit, helmet, boots, weighted belt and hanger, A. J. Morse & Son, Boston, MA 1,300.00
Figurehead, 51" l, eagle, carved, early 19th C 4,000.00
Flensing Knife, 56¾" l, used to separate blanket piece from the carcass, well preserved 500.00
Fog Horn, 30" l, brass, 19th C 85.00
Gangway Boards, 44" h, mahogany, relief carved, brass fittings, 19th C, pr 1,700.00
Gradient Indicator, Moss Flower's, 9½", holly wood and brass, level set into top 250.00
Harpoon, 36" l, incised "B.Y.G." initials on one side, impressed "JD" initials on other, some orig wrapping around cone 475.00
Harpoon Gun, 34" l barrel, swivel, brass mount, engraved "S. S. Terra Nova. Dundee," well preserved 4,000.00

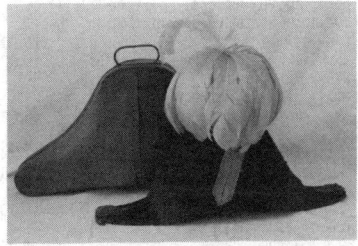

Hat, French officer's, black felt, silver thread and fabric, white feather plume, orig travel case with red paint, c1812, 17" l, 11" h, $265.00.

Jug, 9¼" h, map of Newburyport Harbour on one side, ship *Massachusetts* transfer on other, early 19th C, repair to spout 2,500.00
Lantern, 18" h, brass, orig whale oil burner and blown glass globe 550.00

Light, 15" h, masthead, Whaling Bark *Wanderer*, copper, electrified 150.00
Liquor Chest, 7¼" sq, 8" h, mahogany, four gold dec Bristol glass bottles, matching wine glass, early 19th C . . 300.00
Log Book
 Bark *Mignon*, Boston, kept by master, Capt M. E. Colcord, 1880s 300.00
 Bark *Morning Star,* New Bedford, Saturday, May 14, 1864, thru October 14, 1865, orig boards, back cover worn through at top, spine worn . . 5,200.00
Model, scale
 Bark *Morning Star*, 30" 600.00
 Brig, plank on hull frame mounted in case 900.00
 Warship, English Prisoner-of-war, bone and ebony, two deck, tortoiseshell mounted base and case, 19 x 9¾ x 18" case 9,000.00
 Whaleboat, cased, harpoons, oars, lines 700.00
Navigation Scale, B. Dodd, early 19th C, 24" l, boxwood 210.00
Octant, ebony, brass, inlaid ivory scale, James Whythe of Glasgow label . . . 350.00
Provision Cask, 13" h, oak, iron hoops 325.00
Quarter Board, 90" l, 8½" h, Ferryboat *Weehawken* 900.00
Rudder, 59" h, small vessel, well preserved, traces of orig white paint, 19th C 50.00
Sailing Card, *The A1 Extreme Clipper Barque Wm. H. Thorndike*, dated at Boston, February 17, 1874, voyage to Melbourne and Sydney Australia . . . 400.00
Sea Chest
 Dovetailed, 51 x 21 x 21½", beckets, lidded compartment inside, provisions for holding four decanters or bottles, orig blue-green paint, "William Bunnell" on front, mid 19th C 700.00
 Hardwood, 44 x 19 x 18", orig brown grain painting, dark brown borders, "Capt. F.C. Smith" on front panel . 600.00
Sewing Box, 9½" l, multiwood inlays, compass rose, stars, and diamonds, ivory ring handle and escutcheon, mid-19th C 600.00
Shaving Kit, 8½" l, mahogany case, hinged lid, mirror inset, two bone handled razors, toothbrush, shaving brush, drill sewing knife, and pewter container 625.00
Signal Horn, 15" l, foot operated, "E. A. Gill, Gloucester, MA," 19th C 110.00
Spyglass, single-draw
 Leather wrapped case, extends to 43¼", made for W. Desilva, Liverpool, early 19th C 200.00
 Mahogany tube, Spencer, Browning, and Rust, London, early 19th C . . 175.00

Steamship Whistle, triple, brass and iron, 19th C **450.00**

Stern Board, carved, polychrome, eagle, orig paint, 27¾" wingspread, late 19th C **1,500.00**

Strong Box, 27" l, iron, European-style chest, elaborate locking device, orig key, well preserved, 17th C **1,200.00**

Telegraph, 44" h, brass, Bendix, Brooklyn, NY **600.00**

Travel Box, 11¾ x 9½ x 4¼", mahogany, brass escutcheon, handles, and nameplate, engraved "From/Captn Baynes/To John Hunt," mid 19th C . **250.00**

Travel Desk

    17" l, ebony, three hidden drawers, roller, and pen tray, orig felt cov writing surface **400.00**

    18 x 14 x 28¾", camphor wood, drawer, fold-out writing lid, raised section containing pigeonholes and compartments, mounted on ebonized base, mid 19th C **1,200.00**

Valentine, sailor's, 8¾" d, octagon shape, anchor on left side, floral like design on right **1,600.00**

Water Keg, 18" h, pine, brass hoops and spout **75.00**

Wheel, 36" w, steering, wood, iron hub **300.00**

NAZI ITEMS

History: The National Socialist Party came to power in the 1920s during a period of severe economic depression in Germany. Under the leadership of Adolph Hitler, the party assumed first political control and then social control over Germany. National socialism dominated all aspects of German life. World War II was launched in 1939 to achieve a military conquest of Europe. The Nazi era ended in 1945 when Germany surrendered at the end of World War II.

References: John M. Kaduck, *World War II German Collectibles,* published by author, 1978, 1983 price update; *The Official Price Guide To Military Collectibles, Fifth Edition,* House of Collectibles, 1985; Sydney B. Vernon, *Vernon's Collectors' Guide To Orders, Medals, and Decorations (With Valuations),* published by author, 1986.

Periodicals: *Military Collectors News,* P.O. Box 702073, Tulsa, OK, 74170; *The MX Exchange,* P.O. Box 3, Torrington, CT 06790.

Armband, NSDAP, 17" l, printed type . **15.00**

Banner, 16 x 21", Artillery Regt #27, black embroidered eagle on wine red field, reverse side white embroidered FR 27 on blue field, three sided white fringe, tie ropes **275.00**

Bayonet, police, dress, 13" blade, stag handle, attached police insignia,

Badge, Luftwaffe, pilot's, white metal, silver wash finish, $100.00.

black leather scabbard, silvered fittings, orig black frog, guard marked "S. MG. 415" and matching numbers **165.00**

Belt Buckle

    Prison official's, round, eagle holding sword and bolts, swastika on breast **50.00**

    SA, rotated swastika, brass body, SP faceplate, 2 pcs **45.00**

Cap Badge, RAD, silver finish, enameled, wreath **25.00**

Car Pennant, 8½ x 11½", Teno, printed on both sides, white eagle on blue field, two tie strings **75.00**

Cigarette Case, presentation piece, steel, painted, brass plate, emb heads of Mussolini and Hitler, "Vincere," above heads, eagle embracing wreath of swastikas, wreath with Italy's emblem **175.00**

Collar Tabs, rank of Zollwachtmeister . **10.00**

Correspondence Card, 5 x 8", raised gold eagle and Adolf Hitler, Mujnchen, Den address, orig gilt stamped, 2 pcs **45.00**

Dagger, orange and yellow celluloid grip, SP fittings and scabbard, marked "E & F Horstaer" **110.00**

Document, 6 x 8", "Kriegsurlaubsschein," seal, unissued **10.00**

Emblem, 27 x 16", train engine, eagle with swastika **250.00**

Fez, SS **175.00**

Flag, sport, 58 x 31", double sided, sports eagle and swastika **50.00**

Flag Pole Top, 8½", nickel plated, swastika inside round gear **45.00**

Hat

    Panzer Officer, cloth, black, eagle and wreath, silver wire bullion, WWII . **15.00**

    Police Officer, back visor, bright eagle and wreath device, green–blue wool, silver cord, leather chin strap, pebbled side buttons **150.00**

Helmet, Luftwaffe pilot's, summer, throat mikes **250.00**
Holster, P-38, black leather, Nazi acceptance mark, pouch for extra clip . **50.00**
Invitation, 4½ x 7", gold gilt heading, black printed German script, Hitler engraved, orig **35.00**
Knife, paratrooper's **100.00**
Lamp, table, 16" h, figural, eagle, Munich party headquarters, plaster, gold leaf, marbleized stand **100.00**
Meat Fork, 10" l, SS, Runes engraved in handle **150.00**
Mess Kit, steel, large spoon, fork, knife, can opener, steel handle, hallmarked, standing eagle and swastika, 1942 . **75.00**
Passbook, D. R. Arbeitsbuch, Weimer eagle, dated 1936, some entries ... **15.00**
Patch, Air Force, 7" **15.00**
Postcard, celebrating 700 years of Berlin, seven city and state shields, gold letter inscription, dated 18.8.37, special anniversary cancellation, sent to London **20.00**
Shot Glass, SS, Pioneer Battalion ... **30.00**
Shooting Medal, silver finish, "Kreisschiessen Kofstein, 1942" **25.00**
Shoulder Boards, police, Wachtmeister Rank, black and silver cord, pink piping, removable style **10.00**
Stationery, 8½ x 11½", NSDAP eagle and Der Fuhrer in raised gold, orig singe sheet **40.00**
Stickpin, SS, NSDAP, swastika **20.00**
Street Sign, "Juden Gasse," enameled metal, historical piece, orig **650.00**
Sword
 Dress, eagle and Swastika, engraved brass handle, black wire wrapped plastic grip, black painted scabbard **100.00**
 Officer's, dove head, scabbard, NSDAP eagle on guard **65.00**
Tunic, police, green piping, removable shoulder boards, Bevo collar tabs, Bevo green Police Eagle Arm Shield left sleeve, silver pebbled buttons, tailored cuffs, dark brown trim **185.00**
Whistle, pewter, concentration camp .. **25.00**

NETSUKES

History: The traditional Japanese kimono has no pockets. Daily necessities such as money, tobacco supplies, etc., were carried in leather pouches or *inros* which hung from a cord with a netsuke toggle. Netsuke comes from "ne" (to root) and "tsuke" (to fasten).

Netsukes originated in the 14th century and initially were associated with the middle class. By the mid-18th century all levels of Japanese society

used them. Some of the most famous artists, e.g., Shuzan and Yamada Hojitsu, worked in the netsuke form.

Netsukes average 1 to 2 inches and are made from wood, ivory, bone, ceramics, metal, horn, nutshells, etc. The subject matter is broad based, but always portrayed in a lighthearted, humorous manner. A netsuke must have no sharp edges and balance so it hangs correctly on the sash.

Value depends on artist, region, material, and skill of craftsmanship. Western collectors favor *katabori*, pieces which represent an identifiable object.

Reference: Sandra Andacht, *Oriental Antiques & Art: An Identification And Value Guide,* Wallace-Homestead, 1987.

Collectors' Club: Netsuke Kenkyukai Society, Box 11248, Torrance, CA 90510.

Reproduction Alert: Recent reproductions are on the market. Many are carved from African ivory.

Ivory, carved, 19th C, $95.00.

Bat, resting on one wing, other outstretched, wood, soft metal inlaid eyes, sgd, Terumasa, 19th C **225.00**
Chrysanthemum, boxwood, carved, finely etched and curved petal, sgd Kosei, Hideyuki in rect gold plaque . **1,210.00**
Dancer, carved, circular shape, Shishiabori technique, Okina mask captured in middle of dance, unsigned, 19th C **385.00**
Dragon, carved openwork technique, captured amidst flaming clouds, unsigned, 19th C **880.00**
Duck, ivory, carved, sitting, Hakusen .. **150.00**
Folk Figure, puckered mouth drawn over to the right side of face, sgd Sangyoku, 19th C **275.00**
Man, crawling on bundle of cloth and fan, ivory, sgd **110.00**
Matchlock Gun, iron, movable hammer, lacquered case, brass ring for mounting, 19th C **330.00**
Monkey, boxwood, male, seated,

hunched body, fixed gaze to left arm being groomed by right hand, inlaid horn eyes, sgd Ikkan **1,000.00**
Quail in Millet, stained ivory, Tadomitsu **200.00**
Rabbit, boxwood, hunched, feeds on cluster of blossoms held in forepaws, inlaid eyes, sgd Tomokazu, 19th C . **1,200.00**
Shishi, captured crouching on all fours, gaping mouth, holding small tama, body and paws slightly worn, unsigned, late 18th C **600.00**
Snail, ivory, mollusk turned head, spiral form shell, overlaid lacquer and aogai beetle, 19th C **300.00**
Tiger, stained and white striped ivory, snarling showing teeth, Ikko **300.00**
Turtle, ivory, pouring water from gourd into bowl held by man, Mitsu Hide, late 18th C **275.00**
Whistle, pottery, bulbous shaft, band of phoenix birds, scrolling foliage, green, blue, and purple glaze, yellow glazed ground, deep green bowl and mouth piece, 19th C **470.00**
Wolf, holding monkey, ivory with inlaid eyes, script sgd Tomatoda, 19th C . **1,200.00**

NEWCOMB POTTERY

History: William and Ellsworth Woodward, two brothers, were the founders of a series of businesses which eventually merged into the Newcomb pottery effort. In 1885 Ellsworth Woodward, a proponent of vocational training for women, organized a school from which emerged the Ladies Decorative Art League. In 1886 the brothers founded the New Orleans Art Pottery Company with the ladies of the league serving as decorators. The first two potters were Joseph Meyer and George Ohr. The pottery closed in 1891.

William Woodward was on the faculty at Tulane. Ellsworth taught fine arts at the Sophie Newcomb College, a women's school which eventually merged with Tulane. In 1895 Newcomb College developed a pottery course in which the wares could be sold. Some of the equipment came from the old New Orleans Art Pottery.

Mary G. Sheerer joined the staff to teach decoration. In 1910 Paul E. Cox solved many of the technical problems connected with making pottery in a southern environment. Other leading figures were Sadie Irvine, Professor Lota Lee Troy, and

Kathrine Choi. Pottery was made until the early 1950s.

Students painted a quality art pottery with a distinctive high glaze. Designs have a decidedly southern flavor, e.g., myrtle, jasmine, sugar cane, moss, cypress, dogwood, and magnolia motifs. Later matte glazed pieces usually are decorated with carved back floral designs. Pieces depicting murky, bayou scenes are most desirable.

References: Suzanne Ormond and Mary E. Irvine, *Louisiana's Art Nouveau: The Crafts Of The Newcomb Style,* Pelican Publishing Company, 1976; Jessie Poesch, *Newcomb Pottery: An Enterprise for Southern Women,* Schiffer Publishing, Ltd, 1984.

Collectors' Club: American Art Pottery Association, 9825 Upton Circle, Bloomington, MN 55431.

Museum: Newcomb College, Tulane University, New Orleans, LA.

Vase, floral design, artist sgd "S Irvine," 4" h, $350.00.

Bowl, 7¾" d, 3⅞" h, waisted cylindrical flaring to straight rim, white flowering Cat's Claw vines, yellow stamens, powdered medium blue glaze, natural tan int., imp "NC 263 LE9," incised potter's initials of Joseph Fortune Meyer, decorator's ciphers of Anna Francis Simpson, 1921 . . . . **1,000.00**
Candlestick, 7⅜" tapering cylindrical form, bordered drip pan, loop handle, circular dished base, deep blue and butterscotch design of two whimsical masks, buff ground, faint blue shading, restoration to handle, base inscribed, orig paper label **1,450.00**
Pitcher, 4½" h, slightly swelling cylinder, everted spout, angled handle, relief molded, continuous panel of white Naked Ladies, yellow stamens, blue green stalks, blue ground, incised "N"

within a C, imp potter's monogram of Joseph Fortune Meyer, incised decorator's cipher of Anna Francis Simpson, 1921 .... **1,450.00**

Vase

2¾" h, ribbed ovoid, slightly everted circular rim, irid dark gray gun metal glaze, imp "N" within a C .. **175.00**

3½" h, slightly ribbed ovoid, slightly everted circular rim, finely crackled pumpkin glaze, imp "N" within a C **150.00**

6" h, shouldered ovoid, tapered cylindrical natural tan rim, relief molded, Spanish moss hanging from six large oak trees, blurred trees in distance, glazed in streaked and running blue to buff, imp "NC SB65 500," incised potter monogram of Jonathon Brown Hurt, decorator's cipher of Anna Francis Simpson, Newcomb College paper label, 1930 .... **1,225.00**

6⅛" h, shouldered ovoid, relief molded continuous landscape, Spanish moss hanging from large oak trees, streaked and running blue glaze, incised artist's monogram and R5, impressed cipher, designed by Julia Michel (Hoerner), c1917 .... **1,250.00**

NILOAK POTTERY, MISSION WARE

History: Niloak Pottery was made near Benton, Arkansas. Charles Dean Hyten experimented with native clay, trying to preserve its natural colors. By 1911 he perfected Mission Ware, a marbleized pottery in which the cream and brown colors predominate. The pieces were marked Niloak (kaolin spelled backwards).

After a devastating fire, the pottery was rebuilt and named Eagle Pottery. This factory included the space to add a novelty pottery line which was introduced in 1929. This line usually was marked Hywood-Niloak, until 1934 when the name Hywood was dropped from the mark. Mr. Hyten left the pottery in 1941. In 1946 operations ceased.

Additional Listings: See *Warman's Americana & Collectibles* for more examples, especially the novelty pieces.

Note: Prices listed below are for Mission Ware pieces.

Ashtray, marbleized swirls **25.00**
Bowl, 7½", marbleized swirls **65.00**

Candlesticks, pr, 8", marbleized swirls, blue, cream, terra cotta, and brown . **250.00**
Toothpick Holder, marbleized swirls, tans and blues **100.00**
Urn, 4½", marbleized swirls, brown and blue **35.00**

Vase, wide flat rim, Mission Ware, glazed interior, 3⅛" h, 5⅜" w, $65.00.

Vase

4½", marbleized swirls
Red and brown **55.00**
Tans and blue **45.00**
5½", bulbous, marbleized swirls, rust, blue, and cream **65.00**
6", marbleized swirls, cream, turquoise blue, rust, and brown **70.00**
Wall Pocket, marbleized swirls **250.00**

NIPPON CHINA, 1891-1921

History: Nippon, Japanese hand painted porcelain, was made for export between 1891 and 1921. In 1891, when the McKinley tariff act proclaimed that all items of foreign manufacture be stamped with their country of origin, Japan chose to use "Nippon." In 1921 the United States decided the word "Nippon" no longer was acceptable and required that all Japanese wares be marked with "Japan." The Nippon era ended.

There are over 220 recorded Nippon backstamps or marks. The three most popular are the wreath, maple leaf, and rising sun marks. Wares with variations of all three marks are being reproduced today. A knowledgeable collector can easily spot the reproductions by the mark variances.

The majority of the marks are found in three different colors: green, blue, and magenta. Colors indicate the quality of the porcelain used: green for first grade porcelain, blue for second grade, and magenta for third grade. Marks were applied by two methods, decal stickers under glaze and imprinting directly on the porcelain.

References: Gene Loendorf, *Nippon Hand Painted China*, McGrew Color Graphics, 1975; Joan Van Patten, *The Collector's Encyclopedia Of Nippon Porcelain, Series One*, Collector Books, 1979; Joan Van Patten, *The Collector's Encyclopedia Of Nippon Porcelain, Series Two*, Collector Books, 1982; Joan Van Patten, *The Collector's Encyclopedia Of Nippon Porcelain, Series Three*, Collector Books, 1986.

Collectors' Clubs: Great Lakes Nippon Collectors Club, Rt 2, Box 81, Peotone, IL 60468; International Nippon Collectors Club, P.O. Box 88, Jericho, NY 11753; Long Island Nippon Collectors Club, P. O. Box 88, Jericho, NY 11753; New England Nippon Collectors Club, 22 Mill Pond, North Andover, MA 01845.

Additional Listings: See *Warman's Americana & Collectibles.*

Advisor: Kathy Wojciechowski.

Plaque, hand painted, large white and yellow floral dec, shaded yellow ground, green maple leaf mark, pierced for hanging, 10″ d, $145.00.

Ashtray, triangular shape, dog's head medallion center, moriage trim, maple leaf mark **225.00**
Basket, 8¾″ h, pastoral tapestry scene, ducks and pond **790.00**
Berry Set, master, five matching smaller bowls, lavender and purple columbines, gold outlining, Wreath, six pcs **95.00**
Bowl
　7″, red and pink roses, green leaves, gold flowers on edge, gold trim, green M in Wreath mark **65.00**
　7½″, swans in flight, pond, raised gold beading, crimped top, artist sgd, Leaf **110.00**
　12″, bisque, scenic, Egyptian boat, palm trees, city in background, gold bead trim, scroll handles, Maple Leaf mark **200.00**

Bread Tray, gaudy, green and gold, pink asters **225.00**
Calling Card Tray, 7¾ x 6″, mythical dragon and bird, blue Maple Leaf mark **45.00**
Candle Lamp, bisque, sailing ships, pastel blue, Wreath, pr **3,200.00**
Candlestick
　6″ h, Wedgwood and rose nosegay design, Jasperware, Wreath mark, pr **235.00**
　10″ h, Galle scene, moriage trees, Maple Leaf mark, pr **400.00**
Candy Dish, scalloped edge, pink roses, gold trim, twisted handle **50.00**
Celery Set, 12″ l, master, six matching salts, Wreath mark **125.00**
Child's Dishes
　Mug, 3¾″ h, clowns and rabbit, white, Rising Sun mark **75.00**
　Tea Set, teapot, creamer and sugar, four cups, saucers, and plates, gold flowers and beading, white background, Rising Sun **235.00**
Chocolate Set, 9″ h pot, five matching cups and saucers, white background, bands of rosebuds and gold top and bottom, Maple Leaf mark **225.00**
Compote, 4¾″ h, 8½″ d, Wedgwood and rose nosegay dec, Wreath mark ... **200.00**
Cracker Jar, melon ribbed, bisque background, Indian in canoe shooting moose on river edge, ftd, Wreath mark **425.00**
Decanter, 8″ h, blue and pink background, pink and lavender roses, gold overlay designs and trim, Maple Leaf mark **180.00**
Doll
　11″, boy, bisque head, brown hair and eyes, teeth, composition body, FY mark **275.00**
　12″, bisque head, sleep eyes, dark brown hair, composition body, Christening gown, FY Nippon mark **175.00**
Dresser Set, woodland scene, tray, hatpin holder, powder box, and hair receiver, Maple Leaf mark **950.00**
Egg Warmer, holds four eggs, stopper, sailboat scene, Rising Sun mark ... **110.00**
Dutch Shoe, 3″ l
　Bisque scenic design, Wreath mark . **125.00**
　Forget-me-nots, multicolored foliage, Wreath mark **100.00**
Ewer, 6″ h, multicolored moriage design, enameling technique, floral bouquet medallions front and back, unmarked **90.00**
Ferner, 6″, floral dec, gold beading, four handles, green M in Wreath mark .. **125.00**
Hair Receiver, 5″, yellow and red roses, black ground, blue Maple Leaf mark **60.00**

Hatpin Holder, 5″, serpent in relief, mottled ground **165.00**

Humidor, 6½″, children sitting by tree, M-I-R, Wreath mark **1,750.00**

Inkwell, 4″, palm trees, boat on lake . . **125.00**

Jam Jar, floral dec, gold trim **45.00**

Jelly Dish, underplate, violet dec, gold design **45.00**

Lazy Susan, 10″, floral dec, pastel shades, heavy gold overlay, orig papier mache box **175.00**

Mayonnaise Dish, 4½″ d, ladle, multicolored floral dec, gold trim **60.00**

Mug, 5½″ h, gray bisque background, moriage dragon, blue enameled eyes, green M in Wreath mark **225.00**

Napkin Ring, 4″ h, figural, owl on tree stump, Wreath mark **375.00**

Nappy, 5″, scalloped, cobalt, red flowers, elaborate gold overall design . . **127.50**

Nut Set, 7″, master bowl, six cups, relief molded, nut shell shape **225.00**

Pitcher, 7″ h, slate gray ground, moriage sea gulls, Leaf mark **250.00**

Planter, 7″ d, Egyptian designs, gold outlining, supported by three columns forming Egyptian heads **225.00**

Plaque

10″, three dancing children, rim, animals, Wreath mark **350.00**

10½″, collie and terrier, molded in relief, Wreath mark **950.00**

12″, farmer sowing seeds, molded in relief, Wreath mark **2,100.00**

Plate

8½″, lake, house, and roses scene, cobalt and gold trim, Leaf mark . . **185.00**

10″ w, gold center, cobalt and gold trim, Maple Leaf mark **150.00**

Powder Box, cov

3½″, child's, green, "Happy Face" . . **65.00**

5¼″, portrait on cov, green and white base, heavy gold scrolling, gold feet, blue Maple Leaf mark **125.00**

Punch Bowl and Stand, 12½″ d, 6½″ h, bisque, bouquet of roses scene, wide rim decorated with gold and jewels, Wreath mark **295.00**

Ring Tree, gold, beading, green M in Wreath mark **40.00**

Salt and Pepper Shaker, cobalt and red roses, gold overlay, beads, Leaf mark **55.00**

Scent Bottle, 4¼″, cream, pink and red roses, green raised lattice with white dots **125.00**

Serving Tray, 11″ d, gold and burgundy medallions inside gold fluted rim, multicolored roses and leaves center, gold open pierced handles, Royal Kinran mark **195.00**

Shaving Mug, shaded green, floral dec, gold beading, gold handle **225.00**

Spittoon, lady's hand, violets, turquoise beading, green M in Wreath mark . . **150.00**

Stein, relief molded, dog heads, leash handle, green M in Wreath mark . . . **950.00**

Stick Pin Holder, 1½″ h, multicolored roses, gold trim, Wreath mark **100.00**

Sugar Shaker, 4¼″ h, cobalt, floral, Maple Leaf mark **145.00**

Tankard, 13¼″, cobalt, red roses, gold, sgd **250.00**

Tea Set, three pcs, melon ribbed shape, gold handles and trim, gold overlay design, pink roses, Leaf mark **250.00**

Tea Strainer, pink roses **50.00**

Tea Tile, scenic, cow, pasture **45.00**

Toothpick Holder, 2½″, fruit and floral dec, Rising Sun mark **65.00**

Trivet, octagonal, portrait, Egyptian lady, shaded red ground, blue trim . **140.00**

Urn

9½″ h, white flowers, gold outline, fancy handles, dome lid, pedestal base, Royal Kimran **425.00**

16″ h, medallion in center with cow drinking from pond, gold floral overlay, gold stand-up handles, bolted base, Wreath mark **575.00**

Vase

6″, scenic cartouche front, beaded overall, handled, sgd **100.00**

8¼″, abstract brown and pink pine cones and needles, olive green ground, gold leaf trim, matte glaze, double scroll handles **275.00**

8½″, red roses, moriage design, loop handles and rim, green M in Wreath mark, pr **400.00**

9¼″, woodland and water scene, shaded ground, gold handles, green M in Wreath mark **150.00**

11½″, scenic, trees, water, etc, lavender accents, neck and base mustard yellow, raised gold flowers, garlands and dots, gold handles, green Wreath mark **235.00**

12″, red flowers, gold neck and base, jeweling, blue Maple Leaf mark . . **275.00**

13″, mums in medallions, gold handles, blue Maple Leaf mark **225.00**

Wall Pocket, 6″, molded dog, floral dec **65.00**

Whiskey Jug, palm trees and lake scene, raised moriage trim **450.00**

NODDERS

History: Nodders are figurines with heads and/or arms attached to the body with wires to enable them to move. They are made in a variety of materials—bisque, celluloid, papier mache, porcelain, and wood.

Most nodders date from the late 19th century

with Germany being the principal source of supply. Among the American made nodders, those of Disney and cartoon characters are most eagerly sought.

African Couple, bisque, black man and woman, pr	575.00
Baby, 4½", bisque, pink and white gown, pulling off blue sock	175.00
Black, 5½", bisque, school boy, seated in chair, white shirt, blue, white, and tan plaid pants, holding slate	125.00

Bisque, man on chair, 7″ h, 4½″ d base, $85.00.

Brownie, 10″, cop, blue, Palmer Cox	275.00
Bulldog, 10 x 6½″, brown, sanded finish	60.00
Buttercup, bisque, German	175.00
Colonial Woman, 7½″, bisque	185.00
Daddy Warbucks, bisque	100.00
Donald Duck, plastic, Louis Marx & Co	25.00
Elephant, 8½ x 6½″, gray felt, canvas blanket, wood base	150.00
Happy Hooligan, 6″, papier mache, red jacket, blue pants	90.00
Indian Princess, 3¾″, bisque, seated, holding fan, pale blue, gold trim	115.00
Japanese Boy and Girl, 5½″, papier mache, pr	35.00
Kayo, bisque, marked "Germany"	125.00
Monk, 5¾″, bisque, standing, holding wine pitcher, German	140.00
Oriental Couple, 8¾″, bisque, pink robes, gilding, seated before keyboard and music book, Continental, 19th C, pr	500.00
Orphan Annie, bisque, German	100.00
Rabbit, 8″, papier mache, sitting, light brown	80.00

Santa Claus, 10″, papier mache, candy container, mica glitter trim, German	100.00
Turkish Girl, 6 x 6″, bisque, white beading	300.00
Uncle Walt, bisque, German	100.00

NORITAKE CHINA

History: Morimura Brothers founded Noritake China in 1904 in Nagoya, Japan. They made high quality chinaware for export to the United States and also produced a line of china blanks for hand painting. In 1910 the company perfected a technique for the production of high quality dinnerware and introduced streamlined production.

During the 1920s Larkin Company, Buffalo, New York, was a prime distributor of Noritake China. Larkin offered Azalea, Briarcliff, Linden, Modjeska, Savory, Sheridan, and Tree In The Meadow patterns as part of their premium line.

The factory was heavily damaged during World War II; production was reduced. Between 1946 and 1948 the company sold their china under the "Rose China" mark, since the quality of production did not match the earlier Noritake China. An 1948 expansion saw the resumption of quality production and the use of the Noritake name once again.

There are close to 100 different marks for Noritake, the careful study of which can determine the date of production. Most pieces are marked "Noritake" and have a wreath, "M," "N," or "Nippon." The use of the letter "N" was registered in 1953.

References: Aimee Neff Alden and Marian Kinney Richardson, *Early Noritake China: An Identification And Value Guide To Tableware Patterns*, Wallace-Homestead, 1987; Joan Van Patten, *Collector's Encyclopedia of Noritake*, Collector Books, 1984.

Additional Listings: See *Warman's Americana & Collectibles* for price listings of the Azalea pattern.

Ashtray

4¾″, triangular, figural pipe in center, shades of brown and tan, green mark	75.00
5″, circular, horses dec, green border, red cigarette rests, red mark	65.00
Basket, 7″, handles, multicolored florals	30.00
Bouillon Cup and Saucer, Azalea pattern	24.00
Bowl, 8½″, gold, wood scene border	65.00
Bread Plate, 14 x 6¼″, white, pale green and gold floral border, open handles	24.00
Candy Dish, 6½″, round, black luster, orange flowers, gold trim	135.00
Children's Dishes, white, gold trim, six cups and saucers, plates, teapot, creamer, sugar, cookie plate, platter, cov casserole, orig box, 1922	250.00

Bowl, light orange ground, white floral motif, green band on rim, gold edge, three oval openings for handles, red M in wreath mark, 8½″ d, 2″ h, $25.00.

Cigarette Holder, 5″ h, bell shaped, floral dec, bird finial, red mark 100.00

Condiment Set, salt and pepper shakers, mustard, and round tray, red ground, blue and yellow birds on perch 75.00

Cup and Saucer, 3″ d cup, 5″ d saucer, white, pink and blue flowers, gold trim 25.00

Demitasse Cup and Saucer, orange and blue florals 18.00

Dresser Doll, figural, gold luster 185.00

Ferner, 6″, triangular 75.00

Hatpin Holder, 4½″, gold luster, black band at top with multicolored flowers 45.00

Lemon Dish, 6″ d, relief molded, lemon, hp blossoms and leaves, M in wreath mark 50.00

Mustard Jar, underplate, orange luster finish, blueberries finial 45.00

Nut Set, figural, peanut shape, 7¼″ master bowl, six 3″ individual figural dishes 175.00

Perfume, orange luster bottle, blue flower stopper 85.00

Plaque
    8½″ d, silhouette of girl in bouffant dress, looking into hand mirror, green M in wreath mark 100.00
    10″, hp, cottage, trees, and pastel flowers, brown rim 65.00

Powder Box, desert scene, Arab on camel, cobalt blue ground, ornate gold beading 300.00

Punch Bowl Set, banquet size, eight matching cups, scenic, swans, cottage, island, and trees, heavy raised gold, green M in wreath mark 675.00

Shaving Mug, 3¾″, hp, scene of stalking tiger, green M in wreath mark 200.00

Tile, hp, scenic, water, willow tree, rushes, and man in boat 38.00

Tobacco Jar, 6½″ h, hp, golfer, red jacket and cap, black and white checkerboard knickers, green M in wreath mark 190.00

Tray, 8″ l, two handles, hp, blue violets, red M in wreath mark 40.00

Vase
    5¼″, relief molded, squirrel on berried leafy branch, multicolored, shaded brown ground 150.00
    7″, bulbous, figural red birds on rim, orange and pale blue luster, red and black floral dec 150.00
    11½″, cylindrical, two gold trimmed handles, hp, white and pink poppies, green leaves, gold foliate design on shoulder and base 150.00

Vegetable Bowl, Wild Ivy pattern 12.00

Wall Pocket
    6¾ x 5″, bulbous, blue luster, exotic bird dec 60.00
    8¼″, cylindrical, floral dec 48.00

NORITAKE: TREE IN THE MEADOW PATTERN

History: Tree In The Meadow is one of the most popular patterns of Noritake china. Since the design is hand painted, there are numerous variations of the scene. The basic scene features a large tree (usually in the foreground), a meandering stream or lake, and a peasant cottage in the distance. Principal colors are muted tones of brown and yellow.

The pattern is found with a variety of backstamps and appears to have been imported into the United States beginning in the early 1920s. The Larkin Company distributed this pattern through its catalog sales in the 1920–1930 period.

Reference: Joan Van Patten, *Collector's Encyclopedia of Noritake*, Collector Books, 1984.

Bowl, handles, 9″ d, $35.00.

Ashtray, 5¼", green mark	35.00
Berry Set, large bowl, pierced handles, six small bowls	68.00
Bowl, 6½", green mark	25.00
Cake plate, 10", pierced handles	30.00
Condiment Set, mustard pot, ladle, salt and pepper shakers, tray	40.00
Creamer	25.00
Dish, 6", pierced handles, blue luster border	40.00
Jam Jar, underplate, and spoon	65.00
Lemon Dish, 5½", center ring handle	15.00
Plate	
6½"	10.00
7½"	12.00
8½"	15.00
Platter	
12"	30.00
14"	35.00
Relish, divided	40.00
Salt and Pepper Shakers, marked "Made In Japan," pr	30.00
Sauce Dish, underplate, and spoon, green mark	50.00
Shaving Mug, 3¾", green mark	85.00
Sugar, cov	25.00
Tea Set, teapot, creamer, and cov sugar, six cups and saucers	135.00
Tea Tile, 5" w, chamfered corners, green mark	25.00
Toothpick Holder	55.00
Vase, 7", fan shape	120.00
Vegetable Dish, 9⅜", oval, Noritake mark	30.00
Waffle Set, sugar shaker and syrup jug	70.00
Wall Plaque, 8½", green mark	75.00

NORTH DAKOTA SCHOOL OF MINES

History: The North Dakota School of Mines was established in 1890. Earle J. Babcock, an instructor in chemistry, was impressed with the high purity of North Dakota potter's clay. In 1898 Babcock received funds to develop his finds. He tried to interest commercial potteries in North Dakota clay, but had limited success.

In 1910 Babcock persuaded the school to establish a Ceramics Department. Margaret Cable, who studied under Charles Binns and Frederick H. Rhead, was appointed head. She remained until her retirement in 1949.

Decorative emphasis was placed on native themes, e.g., flowers and animals. Art Nouveau, Art Deco, and fairly plain pieces were made.

The pottery is marked in cobalt blue underglaze with "University of North Dakota/Grand Forks, N.D./Made at School of Mines/N.D. Clay" in a circle. Some earlier pieces only are marked "U.N.D." or "U.N.D./Grand Forks, N.D." Most pieces are

numbered (they can be dated with University records) and signed by both the instructor and student. Cable signed pieces are most desirable.

Reference: *University Of North Dakota Pottery, The Cable Years,* Knight Publishing Company, 1977.

Bowl, 6″ d, blue matte, tulip motif, stamped mark, $400.00.

Ashtray, Flossie The Fish, sgd "M Cable"	165.00
Bowl	
3½ x 4", carved turkeys, green to brown, sgd "Mattson"	275.00
5", dark blue gloss, sgd "JIT"	60.00
5½", carved floral, gray green matte	100.00
Curtain Pull, Indian head, turquoise, marked "Homecoming 1939," orig box	100.00
Paperweight, 3½" d, "Parent's Day, 1938," deep blue	85.00
Tile, 3½", high relief dec, "R" for Rebekah Assemblies	100.00
Vase	
4¾", brown and cream glossy, line design	80.00
8½", bud, green semi–gloss, sgd "M Cable"	75.00
9 x 5¼", hand thrown, green metallic crystalline glaze, marked	175.00

OCCUPIED JAPAN

History: At the end of World War II, the Japanese economy was devastated. To secure needed hard currency, the Japanese pottery industry produced thousands of figurines and other knickknacks for export. From the beginning of the American occupation until April 28, 1952, these objects were marked "Japan," "Made in Japan," "Occupied Japan," and "Made in Occupied Japan." Only pieces marked with the last two designations are of strong interest to Occupied Japan collectors. The first two marks also were used at other time periods.

The variety of products is endless—ashtrays,

dinnerware, lamps, planters, souvenir items, toys, vases, etc. Initially it was the figurines which attracted the largest number of collectors; today many collectors focus on non-figurine material.

References: Gene Florence, *The Collector's Encyclopedia Of Occupied Japan Collectibles*, Collector Books, 1976, 1982 edition; Gene Florence, *The Collector's Encyclopedia Of Occupied Japan Collectibles, 2nd series*, Collector Books, 1979, 1982 revision.

Collectors' Clubs: Occupied Japan Collectors Club, 18309 Faysmith Avenue, Torrance, CA 90504; O.J. Club, 29 Freeborn Street, Newport, RI 02840.

Additional Listings: See *Warman's Americana & Collectibles* for more examples.

Bisque

Ashtray, 2¼", heart shape, hp, floral sprays, white ground	12.00
Creamer, figural cow	20.00
Figure	
3½", frog	15.00
6½", boy standing by fence	20.00
7 x 5", horse and colt	18.00
8", Victorian Man, playing instrument	40.00
Miniature, pitcher, multicolored applied floral spray, pink ground	8.00
Planter, 6", figural, peasant girl standing beside leaf covered planter	35.00
Shelf Sitter, 4¾", Oriental girl, green	12.00
Vase, 7", ftd, emb floral dec	18.00
Wall Pocket, 5", cuckoo clock, orange luster, pine cone weights	12.00

Celluloid

Doll Carriage, 2¾" h, pink and blue, movable hood, Acme	24.00
Figure, 6", Betty Boop, 6", blond hair, movable arms	24.00
Toy, wind-up	
Boy with tin suitcase	45.00
Lion	32.00

Metal

Ashtray, 6¾", chrome plated, pierced floral rim	10.00
Binoculars, Egyptian figures, emb	32.00
Candy Dish, pedestal base	10.00

Cigarette Lighter, miniature camera with tripod	40.00
Harmonica, butterfly shape	20.00
Nut Dish, 6", floral borders	10.00
Pincushion, figural, shoe, silver finish, red velvet cushion	15.00
Plate, 4½", pierced scalloped fancy rim, silvered metal	12.00
Vase, 6", SP, Art Deco style, stylized blossoms, ftd	25.00

Papier Mache

Nodder, rabbit, sitting	35.00
Tray, 10½", rect, floral dec	50.00

Porcelain

Child's Tea Set, 24 pcs, white, floral dec	100.00
Creamer and Sugar, rose, pink, and white	24.00
Dish, 5", triangular, handled, gold trim	20.00
Figure, 3", cherub, playing drum, pierced pedestal base	10.00
Honey Pot, 4½", black Mammy, head lifts off, spoon as tongue, holding spoon and frying pan	35.00
Humidor, cov with Foo Dog finial, 3 ftd, artist sgd	50.00
Incense Burner, cobalt blue, floral dec, gold trim	18.00
Lamp, figural, Colonial man and woman, pr	65.00
Planter, figural, shoe, floral dec	18.00
Plaque, ducks in flight	18.00
Plate, 7½", Ambassador pattern	8.00
Rice bowl, 6", emb dragon	25.00
Salt, master, figural, swan	18.00
Salt and Pepper Shakers, pr, negro chiefs, 3½" w	30.00
Tea Set, cov teapot, four cups and saucers, white, small pink roses, green leaves	65.00

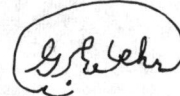

G.E. OHR, BILOXI.

OHR POTTERY

History: Ohr pottery was produced by George E. Ohr in Biloxi, Mississippi. There is some discrepancy as to when he actually established his pottery. Some suggest 1878, but Ohr's autobiography indicates 1883. In 1884 Ohr exhibited 600 pieces of his work, indicating that he had been working for some time.

Ohr's techniques included twisting, crushing, folding, denting, and crinkling thin walled clay into odd, grotesque, and sometimes graceful forms.

Miniature, tea set, $25.00.

Much of his early work is signed with an impressed stamp of his name and location in block letters. His later work, often marked with the flowing script designation "G E Ohr," was usually left unglazed.

In 1906, Ohr closed the pottery and stored over 6,000 pieces as his legacy to his family. He hoped it would be purchased by the U.S. Government, which never happened. The entire collection remained in storage until it was rediscovered in 1972.

Today Ohr is recognized as one of the leading potters in the American Art Pottery movement. Some greedy individuals have taken the later unglazed pieces and covered them with poor quality glazes, in hopes of making them more valuable. These pieces, usually with the flowing script mark, do not have "stilt marks" on the bottom.

Reference: Garth Clark, Robert Ellison, Jr., and Eugene Hecht, *The Mad Potter of Biloxi: The Art & Life of George Ohr*, Abbeville Press, 1989.

Bowl, 6½" d, 3½" h, squatty, closed folded rim, pink semi–gloss, green sponging, dappled textured dark blue, sgd 13,200.00
Candlestick
  3⅞", dark and light green mottled glaze, marked **175.00**
  4½", twisted body, handles, gunmetal black **425.00**
Creamer, 5" h, pinched cylinder, open handle, deep violet and mottled blue glaze, imp "G. E. OHR Biloxi, Miss" **5,000.00**

Dish, yellow orange ground, green streaking, impressed mark "Geo. E. Ohr, Biloxi, Miss," $200.00.

Jug, 5", bisque, tapered, script sgd ... **350.00**
Mug
  Single handle, gun-metal gray **350.00**
  Three handles, green, brown, and gray **700.00**
Novelty
  Log Cabin, 3¾ x 2¼", unglazed oyster white clay **100.00**
  Puzzle Mug, 3½", mottled green high glaze, pressed rope and leaf handle, screw under handle, script sgd "G E Ohr" **375.00**

Seashell, 4½ x 4", mustard yellow glaze, marked **85.00**
Pitcher
  5", bulbous, off center handle, brown irid, imp mark **415.00**
  8¼", black speckled dark mustard, handle, imp mark **600.00**
Teapot, 4⅛", unglazed bisque, shading orange to cream, marked **85.00**
Vase
  3", metallic black, leathery bottom, concave shoulder **165.00**
  3¾", raspberry and brown, wide cylinder, ftd, imp mark **300.00**
  4½", dark green speckles, yellow and light green ground, imp mark **250.00**
  5⅛", thin, unglazed bisque, taupe luster, marked **225.00**
  6", deep moss green, narrow vertical ridges on one side, metallic black smooth surface on other, three prong kiln stilt on base, marked .. **400.00**
  6¾", bottle shape, green gunmetal top to moss speckle **220.00**
  7", tall pedestal base, flaring bulbous top with twist at base, diagonal indentations, cobalt blue ext., gold, green, and gunmetal feathering, top glazed with raspberry, green, and gold flambe, die stamped "GEOHR–Biloxi, Miss" **3,500.00**

OLD IVORY
84

OLD IVORY CHINA

History: Old Ivory derives its name from the background color of the china. It was made in Silesia, Germany, during the second half of the 19th century. Marked pieces usually have a pattern number (pattern names are not common) and the crown Silesia mark.

Reference: Susan and Al Bagdade, *Warman's English & Continental Pottery & Porcelain, 1st Edition*, Warman Publishing Co., Inc., 1987.

Bowl
  6½", cereal, #15 .... **40.00**
  9½", #28 .... **95.00**
Buffet Tray, #200 .... **80.00**
Cake Plate, #84, open handles **85.00**
Celery Tray, #84 .... **80.00**

Plate, scalloped edge, autumn toned flowers, gold border, two handles, marked "Old Ivory, Germany," 9¼" d, $55.00.

Chocolate Pot, #11	350.00
Creamer, #8	65.00
Cup and Saucer, #10	48.00
Mustard Pot, #16	90.00
Nappy, 6½", #84	48.00
Plate	
7½", #11, Clarion	24.00
8", #16	35.00
9½", #6, Elysee	100.00
Platter, #84, 11½"	150.00
Relish Tray, #200	60.00
Salt and Pepper Shakers, pr	
#15	100.00
#28	110.00
Soup Plate, #84	45.00
Sugar, cov	
#15	50.00
#84	35.00
Teapot, #84	285.00
Toothpick, #10	135.00
Vegetable Dish, #84	60.00

OLD PARIS CHINA

History: Old Paris china is fine quality porcelain made by various French factories located in and about Paris during the 18th and 19th centuries. Some pieces were marked, but the majority was not. Characteristics of this type of china include fine porcelain, beautiful decorations and gilding. Favorite colors were dark maroon, deep cobalt blue, and a deep green.

Reference: Susan and Al Bagdade, *Warman's English & Continental Pottery & Porcelain, 1st Edition*, Warman Publishing Co., Inc., 1987.

Additional Listing: Continental China and Porcelain (General).

Bust, 14" h, man and woman, elaborate Empire dress, pr	600.00

Cachepot, 6" h, Neo–classical style, gilt ornaments, sepia bands, center polychrome summer flower spray, early 19th C, pr	1,150.00
Clock Case, 20", surmounted by group of lovers, richly dec clothes, minor damage, c1830	525.00
Dessert Set	
8 pcs, cov tureen, six plates, gilt leaves and devices on lilac banding, polychrome center panel of exotic and domestic animals, early 19th C	1,500.00
33 pcs, thirteen plates, two compotes, sauce tureen and stand, seven cups, eight saucers, pierced compote, specimen botanical center, cobalt border, gilt vermicelli ornament	3,800.00
Dinner Service, purple border with gilt bands, gilt center medallion, white ground, some gilt marked "Schoelcher," 81 pcs	900.00
Figure, 6" h, recumbent lion, faux lapis glaze, gilded base, pr	1,800.00
Jardiniere and Stand, portraits, green ground, small chips, gilding rubbed, mid 19th C, pr	1,650.00

Urns, courting scenes, gilded mask handles, c1840, 10½" h, pr, $1,500.00.

Inkwell, 4¾" h, fountain shape	1,200.00
Tray, 13½", sq, mythological, iron–red Duc d'Angouleme, factory mark, c1800	450.00
Urn	
9½" h, two sections, gilded bands of griffins and anthemions, mottled turquoise ground, shallow bowl socle, early 19th C	900.00
15½" h, European landscape on obverse, reverse with romantic figural scene, winged maiden figural handles, matte and burnished gilt ground, pr	5,000.00
Vase, 11", campana form, elongated bisque floral dec neck, everted rim,	

flower filled basket dec, gilt C–scroll and flowerhead borders, sq black slate plinth, c1850, pr **1,000.00**

OLD SLEEPY EYE

History: Sleepy Eye, a Sioux Indian chief who reportedly had a droopy eye, gave his name to Sleepy Eye, Minnesota, and one of its leading flour mills. In the early 1900s Old Sleepy Eye Flour offered four Flemish gray heavy stoneware premiums, decorated in cobalt blue: a straight-sided butter crock, curved salt bowl, stein, and vase. The premiums were made by Weir Pottery Company, later to become Monmouth Pottery Company, and finally to emerge as the present-day Western Stoneware Company of Monmouth, Illinois.

Additional pottery and stoneware pieces were issued. Forms included five sizes of pitchers (4, 5½, 6½, 8, and 9 inches), mugs, steins, sugar bowls, and tea tiles (hot plates). Most were cobalt blue on white, but other glaze hues, such as browns, golds, and greens, were used.

Old Sleepy Eye also issued many other items, including bakers' caps, lithographed barrel covers, beanies, fans, multicolored pillow tops, postcards, trade cards, etc. Production of Old Sleepy Eye stoneware ended in 1937.

In 1952 Western Stoneware Company made a 22 and 40 ounce stein in chestnut brown glaze with a redesigned Indianhead. From 1961 to 1972 gift editions, dated and signed with a Maple Leaf mark, were made for the Board of Directors and others within the company. Beginning in 1973, Western Stoneware Company issued an annual limited edition stein, marked and dated, for collectors.

Reference: Elinor Meugnoit, *Old Sleepy Eye*, published by author, 1979.

Collectors' Club: Old Sleepy Eye Collectors Club, Box 12, Monmouth, IL 61462.

Reproduction Alert: Blue and white pitchers, crazed, weighted, and often with a stamp or the word "Ironstone" are the most copied. The stein and salt bowl also have been made. Many reproductions come from Taiwan.

A line of fantasy items, new items which never existed, includes an advertising pocket mirror with miniature flour barrel label, small glass plates, fruit jars, toothpick holders, glass and pottery miniature pitchers, and salt and pepper shakers. One mill item has been made, a sack marked as though it were old but of a size that could not possibly hold the amount of flour indicated.

MILL ITEMS

Barrel Label, framed	315.00
Bread Board Scraper	625.00
Calendar, 1904	200.00
Cookbook, loaf of bread shape	120.00

Demitasse Spoon	130.00
Postcard	
Monument	45.00
Picture of mill	17.50
Stationery, envelope	65.00
Teaspoon, silverplate	90.00

Vase, cylindrical, stoneware, 8½″ h, $185.00.

POTTERY AND STONEWARE

Creamer, #1, all white, pottery	900.00
Mug	
Brush–McCoy, green and brown, cream ground	255.00
Stoneware	420.00
Pitcher, pottery	
#2, blue rim	580.00
#4, blue rim	425.00
#5, blue rim	420.00
Standing Indian, blue dec, gray ground	850.00
Salt Bowl, stoneware	465.00
Stein	
Blue dec, white ground	475.00
Brown dec, gold ground, marked on bottom	1,050.00
Directors, 1968	185.00
Stoneware	350.00
Sugar Bowl, blue dec, white ground ..	510.00
Vase	
Blue dec, stoneware	240.00
Brown dec, white ground, cattails ..	1,000.00

ONION MEISSEN

History: The blue onion or bulb pattern is of Chinese origin and depicts peaches and pomegranates, not onions. It was first made in the 18th century by Meissen, hence the name Onion Meissen.

Factories in Europe, Japan, and elsewhere copied the pattern. Many still have the pattern in production, including the Meissen factory now located in East Germany.

Note: Prices given are for pieces produced between 1870 and 1930. Many pieces are marked with a company's logo; after 1891 the country of origin is indicated on imported pieces. Early Meissen examples bring a high premium.

Bone Dish	60.00
Bouillon Cup and Underplate	42.00
Bowl	
6″	40.00
9″	135.00
Butter Dish, cov	40.00
Butter Pat	90.00
Candle Snuffer, 10¼″, SP handle	62.00
Cheese Board	45.00
Cheese Dish, cov	150.00
Coffeepot, 9½″	160.00
Compote, 9″ h, 9″ d, reticulated rim	350.00
Creamer, 3½″	50.00
Cup and Saucer	
Coffee	40.00
Tea	30.00
Darner, wooden handle	75.00
Dipper, wooden handle	100.00
Dish, 10½″, round, deep, imp mark	55.00
Egg Cup	225.00
Fish Plate, pierced drain insert	225.00
Fruit Knives, set of 6	85.00
Funnel, 4¾″	85.00
Knife Rest	30.00
Ladle, 4 x 2″, wood handle	135.00
Lemon Dish	35.00
Match Holder	35.00
Mustache Cup	85.00
Pastry Wheel	135.00
Pitcher, water, 7″, rococo molded, c1860	225.00
Plate	
6″	35.00
9″	48.00
10½″	70.00

Platter, Meissen crossed swords mark and imp mark, 12½ x 25″, $500.00.

Platter	
12″, oval, marked	160.00
17″	225.00
19″	250.00
Pot de Creme	50.00
Relish Dish	
6½ x 4¾″, oblong, octagonal	45.00
11¾ x 7¼″, scalloped edge	85.00
Rolling Pin	150.00
Salt Box	135.00
Salt Dip, crossed swords mark	48.00
Sauce Dish, 4¾″	30.00
Soup Bowl, 9″	60.00
Soup Tureen, cov, 10½ x 14″, rose finial	250.00
Spill Vase, 5½″, scroll feet	65.00
Stein, ½ L, matching conical lid, dwarf thumb lift	500.00
Sugar, cov, melon ribbed, late 19th C	100.00
Tea Strainer, 5″, l, handle	65.00
Teapot, 10″, rose finial, 19th C	200.00
Vegetable Dish, cov	
8½″	90.00
10″, sq	130.00
14″, divided	225.00
Vinegar Jar, stopper	225.00

OPALESCENT GLASS

History: Opalescent glass is a clear or colored glass with milky white decorations which shows a fiery or opalescent quality when held to light. The effect was achieved by applying bone ash chemicals to designated areas while a piece was still hot and then refiring it at tremendous heat.

There are three basic categories of opalescent glass: (1) Blown (or mold blown) patterns, e.g., Daisy & Fern and Spanish Lace; (2) Novelties, pressed glass patterns made in limited pieces which often included unusual shapes such as Corn or Trough; and (3) Pattern (pressed) glass.

Opalescent glass was produced in England in the 1870s. Northwood began the American production in 1897 at its Indiana, Pennsylvania, plant. Jefferson, National Glass, Hobbs, and Fenton soon followed.

References: William Heacock, *Encyclopedia of Victorian Colored Pattern Glass, Book II, Opalescent Glass from A to Z, Second Edition,* Antique Publications, 1977; William Heacock and William Gamble, *Encyclopedia of Victorian Colored Pattern Glass, Book 9, Cranberry Opalescent from A to Z,* Antique Publications, 1987.

Additional Listings: See Pattern Glass for pressed opalescent patterns.

BLOWN

Biscuit Jar, Spanish Lace, vaseline	275.00
Bottle, Bull's Eye, blue	115.00

**Sugar Shaker, Swirl, cranberry, white
metal top, 4¾" h, $90.00.**

Bowl

Consolidated Criss–Cross, cranberry,
8" d **150.00**
Roman Rosette, lacy, Sandwich, 6¾" **200.00**
Seaweed, white, 9" **60.00**
Butter Dish, cov, Spanish Lace, blue .. **250.00**

Celery Vase

Consolidated Criss–Cross, Rubena,
satin finish **250.00**
Daffodils, blue **75.00**
Ribbed Coin Spot, cranberry **150.00**
Creamer, Reverse Swirl, blue **75.00**
Cruet, Christmas Pearls **250.00**
Curtain Tie Back, 5¾", fiery, lacy, young
woman seated holding straw hat,
Boston & Sandwich Glass Co **150.00**

Finger Bowl

Hobb's Hobnail, cranberry **50.00**
Spanish lace, blue **48.00**

Lamp

Christmas Snowflake, cranberry ... **300.00**
Reverse Swirl, cranberry, satin base **425.00**
Snowflake, cranberry, hand type ... **500.00**

Miniature Lamp

Coin Spot, (Smith #510), 8¾" **625.00**
Spanish Lace, 4", blue **225.00**
Mustard, Reverse Swirl, vaseline **50.00**

Pitcher, water

Arabian Nights, cranberry **325.00**
Buttons and Braids, blue **80.00**
Christmas Snowflake, cranberry ... **375.00**
Daisy in Criss–Cross, cranberry ... **600.00**
Hobb's Hobnail, cranberry, heavy
opalescent, opal handle **200.00**
Poinsettia, blue, tankard, 13" **200.00**
Spanish lace, ruffled rim, blue **250.00**
Stripe and Swirl, sq top **285.00**
Rose Bowl, Daisy and Fern, blue **50.00**
Salt Shaker, Consolidated Criss–Cross,
cranberry, orig top **85.00**

Spooner

Consolidated Criss–Cross, cranberry **125.00**
Spanish Lace, cranberry **75.00**

Sugar, cov

Bubble Lattice, cranberry **125.00**
Reverse Swirl, blue **125.00**
Stripe, cranberry **80.00**

Sugar Shaker, orig top

Bubble Lattice, blue **135.00**
Poinsettia, blue **165.00**
Reverse Swirl, cranberry **150.00**

Syrup Pitcher, orig top

Bubble Lattice, canary yellow **150.00**
Coin Spot & Swirl, white **65.00**
Daisy in Criss–Cross, blue **250.00**
Poinsettia, blue **450.00**

Toothpick

Swirl, blue **100.00**
Windows, cranberry **115.00**

Tumbler

Arabian Nights, blue **60.00**
Consolidated Criss–Cross, white ... **50.00**
Herringbone, cranberry **75.00**
Poinsettia, green **35.00**
Spanish Lace, cranberry **45.00**
Water Set, water pitcher and six tum-
blers, 7 pcs
Arabian Nights, blue **400.00**
Button and Braids, blue **300.00**
Daffodils, blue **650.00**

NOVELTIES

Barber Bottle, Stars and Stripes, cranberry **150.00**
Basket, bushel, blue, Northwood **55.00**

Bowl

Beaded Stars, green, 8½" **40.00**
Jolly Bear, white **75.00**
Bushel Basket, blue **75.00**
Compote, Dolphin, vaseline **65.00**
Epergne, 9½ x 19½", four lilies, green,
ruffled base, applied glass spiral trim **325.00**

Rose Bowl

Fancy Fantails, cranberry, four clear
applied feet **650.00**
Leaf Chalice, green pedestal **50.00**

Vase

4", melon ribbed body, vaseline, applied clear leaf feet, flower petal top **65.00**
10", Piasa Bird, blue **50.00**

OPALINE GLASS

History: Opaline glass was a popular mid to
late 19th century European glass. The glass has
a certain amount of translucency and often is
found decorated in enamel designs and trimmed
in gold.

Basket, deep blue dec, gold enamel .. **150.00**
Biscuit Jar, hp, florals and bird dec,
brass lid and bail handle **150.00**
Box, 5½ x 3⅝ x 4¼", brass fittings ... **125.00**

Chalice, white, Diamond Point pattern . 25.00
Cheese Dish, cov, white ground, gold
  enamel dec 180.00
Cologne Bottle, 8¾", jade green, gold
  ring dec, orig stopper 85.00
Creamer, shaded yellow to white, pink
  roses and blue forget–me–nots, SP
  rim and handle 125.00
Dresser Jar, 7½ x 5½ x 5½", egg shape,
  blue, heavy gold dec 200.00
Ewer, 13¼", white, Diamond Point pat-
  tern 125.00
Finger Bowl, matching underplate, pow-
  der blue 125.00

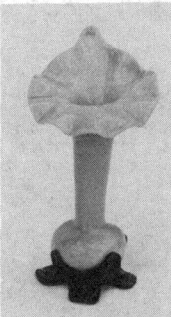

Jack In The Pulpit Vase, robin's egg blue body, applied amber feet, 5½" h, $75.00.

Perfume Bottle, 4", blue ground, gold,
  white, and yellow dec, matching stop-
  per 65.00
Pitcher, 4¼", pink ground, applied white
  handle 70.00
Posy Holder, 8", blue, figural hand hold-
  ing small vase, ruffled rim 75.00
Rose Bowl, 4", opaque green, gilt strawberries, flowers, and leaves dec . . . 50.00
Salt, 3¾", jade green, marked "Turn-
  bridge, England" 75.00
Sugar, cov, shaded yellow to white, pink
  roses and blue forget–me–nots, SP
  cover, rim, and handle 150.00
Toothpick, lavender, small ball feet . . . 75.00
Tumble–Up, carafe, tumbler, and underplate, pale green ground, gold
  beading, black and white jeweled
  dec, 3 pcs 300.00
Tumbler, enameled pink rose 25.00
Vase
  13", urn shape, flared rim, blue
    ground, enameled blue flowers, gilt
    trim, pr 335.00

16¾", oviform, circular cushioned
foot, parcel gilt, enameled, turquoise blue ground, gilt rimmed
molded border and handles, oval
panels with artists' portraits, one
with Raphel, other Van Dyke,
brown, caret, white, and flesh
tones, gilt borders with scrolling foliate edges, French, 19th C, pr . . . **2,475.00**

ORIENTAL RUGS

History: The history of oriental rugs or carpets dates back to 3,000 B.C.; but, it was in the 16th century that they became prevalent. The rugs originated in the regions of Central Asia, Iran (Persia), Caucasus, and Anatolia. Early rugs can be classified into basic categories: Iranian, Caucasian, Turkoman, Turkish, and Chinese. Later India, Pakistan, and Iraq produced rugs in the oriental style.

The pattern name is derived from the tribe which produced the rug, e.g., Iran is the source for Hamadan, Herez, Sarouk, Tabriz, and others.

When evaluating an oriental rug, age, design, color, weave, knots per square inch, and condition determine the final value. Silk rugs and prayer rugs bring higher prices.

References: Murray Eiland, *Oriental Rugs: A New Comprehensive Guide,* Little, Brown and Company, 1981; Linda Kline, *Beginner's Guide To Oriental Rugs,* Ross Books, 1980; Ivan C. Neff and Carol V. Maggs, *Dictionary of Oriental Rugs,* Van Nostrand Reinhold Company, 1979.

Periodical: *Oriental Rug Review,* Beech Hill Road, R.F.D. 2, Meredith, NH 03253.

Reproduction Alert: Beware! There are repainted rugs on the market.

Armenian, Caucasus, last quarter 19th
C, 6' 10" x 4' 11", indigo ground, large
diamond medallion flanked by diamond halves, cruciform lozenges,
scattered geometrics, madder reserves with similar devices and human figures, narrow checkered band,
reciprocal guards **2,475.00**
Azerbaijani, Persia/Caucasus, early
20th C, red ground, row of latchhook
medallions on central axis, small
hooked diamonds, ivory crab border,
three pairs of guards **1,100.00**
Bakhtiari, Persia
12' 9" x 6' 9", early 20th C, rows of
complimentary polychrome medallions, small center floral arrangement, wide madder border of birds
and flowering vines, three decora-
tive guards **2,475.00**
14' 9" x 8' 9", mid 20th C, rose field,
composite medallion of European

style floral motifs, similar frame, burgundy reserves, indigo and beige cartouche border, indigo flower secondary border, reciprocal guards **3,300.00**

Bidjar, Persia, early 20th C, 11' 10" x 7' 11", red ground, allover herati pattern, central indigo medallion, spandrels, indigo turtle border, four pairs of narrow guards **6,000.00**

Fachralo Kazak Prayer, Caucasus, last quarter 19th C, 4' 3" x 3' 5", red field, octagonal medallion, angular arch and re–entry niche, reciprocal borders and several narrow guards ... **2,000.00**

Isphahan, Persia, c1925
  6' 11" x 4' 6", meditation, flower filled ivory mihrab, burgundy spandrels, midnight primary border with birds and hands holding bouquets, three pairs of guards **4,125.00**
  7' 4" x 4' 10", prayer, mid–blue field, elaborate floral arrangement, red mihrab, red primary border of lozenges and vines, pair of ivory guards **6,600.00**
  18' 7" x 12' 4", red field of scrolling vines and flowers, ivory sixteen point medallion, pale blue and lilac spandrels, indigo flowerhead and leaf primary border, eight decorative guards **11,000.00**

Jajim, Caucasus, early 20th C, 8' 4" x 5' 8", indigo ground, compartment pattern brocade, large and small polychrome boxes, three reciprocal sawtooth borders, woven in two sections **2,750.00**

Kazak, Caucasus, early 20th C, prayer, 5' 9" x 3' 6", latchhook medallions, angular red prayer arch, indigo reserves with pair of supplicant hands, ivory border of stylized bird pairs, three twin guards **2,000.00**

Kerman, Persia
  4' 10" x 36", indigo field, four sided floral sprays converging towards center, wine red flowerhead border, twin ivory guards **1,320.00**
  18' 7" x 11' 7", sky–blue field, oval floral medallion, angular frame of pastel floriforms, primary rose cartouche, flowerhead border, complimentary guards **4,400.00**

Kuba, Caucasus, mid 20th C, 6' 1" x 4' 1", Seichour, deep indigo field, diamond lattice of cruciforms, octagons, and geometrics, ivory and indigo running dog border, indigo flowerhead outer guard **1,450.00**

Kurdish, runner, early 20th C, 13' 11" x 3' 1", camel ground, diagonal rows of

small flowers, ivory border of quartered polygons, five guards **1,210.00**

Lenkoran, Caucasus, early 20th C, 6' 7" x 4' 9", indigo field, detached flowerhead heads, two central medallions, primary border of birds and small flowers, five pairs of narrow guards . **3,300.00**

Mahal, Persia, early 20th C, 17' 10 x 13' 5", cream field, tiny cornflower blue spandrels, indigo primary border of stylized florals and geometrics, five pairs of narrow guards **5,500.00**

Qashaq'i, Persia, c1900, 10' 3" x 3' 1", runner, deep indigo field, aligning madder and ivory diamond latchhook medallions, madder reserves, ivory floral meander border, three pairs of guards **2,750.00**

Ravar Kerman, Persia, late 19th C, 7' 2" x 4' 5", prayer, ivory field, flower vase, black arch, plum arabesques, pair of olive–brown columns, ivory main border, three narrow guards .. **6,000.00**

Sarouk, Persia, c1925, 18' 11" x 10' 3", wine field, vases and floral sprays,

Sarouk, ivory field woven with directional floral motifs, midnight blue main border, 4' 2" x 6' 4", $725.00.

central foliate composite medallion, indigo palmette and blossom border, two pairs of guards **5,500.00**
Serab, Persia, early 20th C, 14' x 3' 4", runner, indigo field, poled diamond medallions, geometric lozenges, pair of human figures, yellow spandrels, polychrome double "S" border, two pairs of guards **1,215.00**
Shirvan, Caucasus, late 19th C
  5' 3" x 3' 6", mid–blue field, three connected stepped diamond medallions, animals and geometrics, ivory repeat border of stylized bird pairs, eight narrow guards **3,575.00**
  6' 4" x 3' 6", dark indigo field, three aligned polychrome latchhook medallions, diamond halves, ivory star and box border, three pairs of guards **2,750.00**
Zeigler Mahal, Persia, c1925, 13' 11" x 10' 4", madder foliate field, concentric cobalt blue and ivory petal form medallions, indigo primary border of large blossoms and flowering vines, six narrow guards **11,000.00**
Zejwa, Caucasus, late 19th C, 5' 8" x 2' 8", chocolate brown ground, three ivory and madder medallions, geometric filler devices, narrow medachyl border **2,200.00**

ORIENTALIA

History: Orientalia is a term used to apply to objects made in the Orient, which encompasses the Far East, Asia, China, and Japan. The diversity of cultures produced a variety of objects and styles.

References: Sandra Andacht, *Oriental Antiques & Art: An Identification And Value Guide,* Wallace-Homestead, 1987; Lea Baten, *Japanese Animal Art: Antique & Contemporary,* Charles Tuttle, 1989; John Esten (editor), *Blue and White China,* Little, Brown, and Company, 1987; Patricia Salmon, *Japanese Antiques With A Guide To Shops,* Art International Publishers, 1985 edition.

Periodical: *The Orientalia Journal, P. O. Box 94, Little Neck, NY 11363.*

Additional Listings: Canton, Celadon, Cloisonne, Fitzhugh, Nanking, Netsukes, Rose Medallion, Japanese Prints, and other categories.

Bowl
  Chinese, polychrome enamel, fish, flowers, butterflies, and family scenes, 16" d **150.00**
  Korean, Koryo, shallow rounded sides, int. inlaid with four concentric

Dish, Dingyao, carved single carp swimming among flowering lotus and water weeds, Northern Song Dynasty, $12,100.00.

bands, crackled gray-green glaze, 7" **200.00**
Box, Mongolian, sq, ftd, silver covered, fitted with flat corner russet skinned jade panels flanking principal sides with turquoise and coral inlay, white jade panels carved with sage reversed by inscription, alternating sides with high set loop handles, loose rings, orange skin nephrite qilong, cov with circular chased corner medallions of demons flanking central inscribed rust colored jade disk, green stone finial, 5⅞" h **2,000.00**
Brush Pot, Meiji Period, Shibayama style, ivory, curved tusk, scene of small birds, butterflies, and pair of cranes among flowering wisteria vines, leafy bamboo stalks, blossoming peony, wild pinks and flowers, reverse with long tailed bird beneath fruiting loquat tree, gold and silver hiramaki-e, takamaki-e, and gold gyobu, additional inlay of carved and incised coral, mother of pearl, aogai, tortoise shell, and semi-precious hardstone, 7⅝" h, pr **2,750.00**
Calligraphy Tablet, Chinese, Qing Dynasty, spinach green made, white mottling, black flecking, four rows of Manchurian script, rect, 11⅛ x 4" . . **1,200.00**
Charger, Chinese, porcelain, polychrome enameled floral and leaf dec, gold highlighting, sgd, 18" d **225.00**
Cup and Saucer, Japanese, silver, double walled 2¾" d cup, flared rim, high splayed ring foot, repousse design of blossoming chrysanthemum sprigs,

engraved ground of diamond patterned basketweave pattern, triangular faux bamboo handle, matching 4½″ d saucer **225.00**

Ewer, Korean, Koryo Dynasty, globular, short shaped spout, double loop handle, short cylindrical neck, brown slip under gray celadon glaze, scroll of stylized flowering branch below wide shoulder petal border **1,250.00**

Fan

Chinese, painted continuous court scene of figures with inlaid textile robes, 10½″ l, minor damage **200.00**

Japanese, Gyosai, Battling Frogs, painting of ink and colors on paper, wood fan sticks, sgd, 8½ x 14″ .. **400.00**

Figure

Bodhisattva, Edo Period, giltwood, elongated torso, gilt bronze ornaments, face with crystal urna, high chigon, gilt bronze jeweled crown, almond shaped mandorla with low relief carving of cloud scrolls, double lotus base, high galleried hexagonal pedestal, 13″ h **500.00**

Buddha, Chinese, 18th C, seated, legs crossed, holding cup, gilt, Chinese, 12″ h **550.00**

Dragon, Japanese, Meiji period, silver, writhing, scaly body with sharp jointed projections, flame like appendages, convoluted posture, raised head, large gold inset eyes, open mouth, long curving whiskers, underside incised "Kunitoko," 16¾″ l **6,125.00**

Maiden, Chinese, Tang Dynasty, straw glazed buff colored body, slender figure, high waisted court dress, high chigon, 8⅛″ h **250.00**

Furniture

Arm Chair, Chinese, walnut, relief carving, stylized dragons and elephants, floral carving on sides ... **200.00**

Cabinet, Chinese, rosewood, display type, rect, upper tier of staggered shelves next to single door, above two drawers over double doors, panels heavily carved with flowering lotus and bamboo branches, 72½ x 34½ x 13¼″ **300.00**

Chest

Japanese, Meiji Period, Noh costume type, lacquered, front panel dec with scene of lotus pods and waterlife in gold takamaki-e, hiramaki-e, and togidashi shading to silver and black, dense nashiji ground, hinged top fitted with shakudo mounts etched in floral motifs, concave top, back with

haga and blossoming iris, int. lined in Edo Period fabric, 24½ x 60 x 24½″ **3,350.00**

Korean, storage, 19th C, rect top, two hinged sections, banded with iron bamboo shaped brackets, central hinged lockplate on front, iron U shaped handles, 22¼ x 58½ x 24½″ **950.00**

Garden Seat, Chinese, porcelain, blue and white, birds amidst foliage dec, 19″ h **160.00**

Screen, Chinese

73″ h, 67½″ w, lacquer, pagoda style cornice, phoenix bird on diamond pattern ground, foo lion feet, 19th C **900.00**

76 x 27″, four panels, black silk, gilt embroidered, fighting hawks amidst trees, painted landscape scene on reverse **375.00**

Stand, Japanese, 20th C, pr, bronze, flaring form, applied dec, ring handles, 21″ h **800.00**

Table, Chinese, 19th C, mahogany, carved, ship at sea scene inlay, figural and dragon border, round base with bracket feet, 32″ h, 42″ w **3,400.00**

Ginger Jar, 9¾″ h, pr, enameled floral dec, dark blue ground **110.00**

Hand Warmer, 7½″ l, bronze, silver inlay **85.00**

Incense Burner, 19th C, enamel, globular form, scrolled floral dec, green ground, three foo lion feet, domed cover with foo lion finial, 45″ h **3,400.00**

Inro, 19th C

Four Case, Shunsho, Noh play rendition of the tale of Dojoji bell, red lacquer ground, bottom lacquered with dense gold nashiji, sgd "Shunsho saku," coral ojime, ivory figure of Noh dancer, sgd "Koma Bunsai" and "Jugyoku" on underside **9,350.00**

Five Case, elegant peacock on branch of blossoming sakura overlooking companion below, leaves overlaid in silver hiramaki-e, tortoise accents, gold highlights, reverse with group of chidori in flight, bright kinji surface **2,500.00**

Jar, 6⅜″ h, porcelain, inlaid lacquer covering **100.00**

Jardiniere, Chinese

9½″ h, 12¼″ d, porcelain, undertray **120.00**

14″ h, porcelain, coral dragon, black ground **110.00**

Lamps, table, pr, Chinese, bronze, pagoda form, flaming pearl finials, dolphin spouts, high relief dragon, bird and turtle dec, 19″ h **425.00**

Lantern, Japanese, cast bronze, diamond shaped body, roof form top, 9" ... **125.00**

Mirror, Chinese, 19th C, giltwood, rect, carved and pierced freize of flowers and scrolls, columns, flame finials, drawer, carved feet, 20" h, 15" w ... **160.00**

Plate, Meiji Period, Shibayama and silver mounts, scalloped edge cavetto with scene of two vases, blossoming peonies, chrysanthemums, fuji bakuma, kikyo, and chidori hovering, overlays of aogai, carnelian, horn, coral, and semi-precious hardstones on bright kinji ground, framed by nine petaled silver openwork border, each with sixteen petal chrysanthemum blossom, sgd "Kogyoku" on underside with gilt metal plaque on nashiji ground, 11" d ... **3,100.00**

Pot, 11½" h, 18" d, white craquelle glaze, green foliage design ... **30.00**

Print, Japanese, wood black, matted and framed, 15½" h, 20½" w ... **40.00**

Robe, Chinese, 20th C, silk, embroidered, gold ground ... **140.00**

Roof Tile, Chinese, Ming Dynasty, pottery, figural, lead green glaze with yellow and cream, modeled as demon riding fu lion, 22¼" ... **3,000.00**

Seal, Chinese, jade, pale green, sq, carved with dragons, horned beasts, pierced, 4¼" ... **1,600.00**

Teapot
Chinese, Famille Verte, fluted, baluster body, straight spout, yellow sq handle, rect panels of blossoming branches, 7" h ... **1,250.00**

Japanese, silver, compressed ovoid body, wide band of raised bosses, circular lid with pierced jewel finial bracket, loop handle, S shaped spout, base stamped "jungin (pure silver)," lid inscribed "Club Casbah, Kobe, Dec 14, 1948," 7¼" h ... **600.00**

Textile, Chinese
Panel, 20 x 48", silk batik, port scene ... **50.00**

Pillow, Qianlong, Imperial, yellow brocade, central metallic gold dragon, other striding drawings on floral ground, peach, blue, and green, 26½" ... **1,250.00**

Urn, Japanese, 19th C, bronze, ovoid, relief reserves of hawk and trees, domed cov with mounted hawk, hawk and tree handles, pedestal base, 39" h ... **2,300.00**

Vase
Chinese
10½" h, porcelain, bulbous form, painted figures in gilt cream reserves, navy ground, double scroll handles, Chinese ... **40.00**

14¼" h, pr, polychrome dec, flowers and butterflies, salmon ground ... **110.00**

Japanese, 19th C, 35" h, globular from, relief birds and flowering trees, bird handles, pedestal base, round foot ... **900.00**

Watercolor, handmade
28" h, 19¼" w, two women gathering plants, framed ... **135.00**

37" h, 30¾" w, peonies and birds ... **75.00**

OVERSHOT GLASS

History: Overshot glass was developed in the mid-1800s. A gather of molten glass was rolled over the marver upon which had been placed crushed glass to produce overshot glass. The piece then was blown into the desired shape. The finished effect was a glass that was frosted or iced in appearance.

Early pieces mainly were made in clear. As the demand for colored glass increased, color was added to the base piece and occasionally to the crushed glass.

Pieces of overshot generally are attributed to the Boston and Sandwich Glass Co., although many other companies also made it as it grew in popularity.

Compote, clear, flint glass, attributed to Sandwich, 7¾" d, 5⅞" h, $165.00.

Bowl, petal top, blue ... **150.00**

Compote
8½ x 12¾", rubena overshot bowl, white metal bronze finished figural standard ... **125.00**

9 x 8⅞", applied gold dec cranberry serpent around stem ... **100.00**

9 x 14", rubena overshot bowl, white metal bronze finished figural standard ... **150.00**

Custard Cup, pink, applied clear handle, Sandwich ... **50.00**

Dish, 6¼", crimped edge, canary yellow,
cranberry overshot **160.00**
Ewer, 13½", trefoil top, clear, twisted
rope handle, Sandwich **250.00**
Ice Bucket, silver rim and handle **75.00**
Mug, 3", clear, applied clear handle . . **20.00**
Pitcher
6", bulbous, cranberry **115.00**
7½", bulbous, clear **100.00**
8", heavy enamel dec of white roses,
blue forget–me–nots, and green
leaves **125.00**
Vase, two handles, metal collar in-
scribed "Joseph Barn, Gloucester" . **175.00**

**Vase, Utopia, three handles, mug
shape, brown glaze, grape and leaf
dec, artist sgd "J. B. Owens, Utopia,"
7" h, $165.00.**

OWENS POTTERY

History: J. B. Owens began making pottery in
1885 near Roseville, Ohio. In 1891 he built a plant
in Zanesville and in 1897 began producing art
pottery. Not much art pottery was produced by
Owens after 1907, when most of their production
centered on tiles.

Owens Pottery, employing many of the same
artists and designs of its two crosstown rivals,
Roseville and Weller, can appear very similar to
that of its competitors (i.e. Utopian—brown glaze;
Lotus—light glaze; Aqua Verde—green glaze,
etc.).

There were a few techniques used exclusively
at Owens. These included Red Flame ware (slip
decoration under a high red glaze) and Mission
(over-glaze, slip decorations in mineral colors) depicting Spanish Mission scenes. Other specialities
included Opalesce (semi-gloss designs in lustred
gold and orange) and Coralene (small beads affixed to the surface of the decorated vases).

References: Paul Evans, *Art Pottery of the
United States, 2nd Edition,* Feingold & Lewis Pub-
lishing Corp., 1987; Ralph and Terry Kovel, *The
Kovels' Collector's Guide to American Art Pottery,*
Crown Publishers, Inc., 1974.

Bowl, 3", Aborigine, brown Indian de-
signs, redware **60.00**
Creamer, 3½", Aqua Verdi, green matte,
imp mark **65.00**
Inkwell, 3¾", Light Weight, lime leaves,
brown ground, sgd **100.00**
Jardiniere, 9¼", orange and cream
swirls, green ground, marked "JB
Owens/Art Nouveau/1005" **175.00**

Jug, handled, tomato dec **175.00**
Mug, 4½", Utopian, cherries **75.00**
Pitcher, 12", tankard, Utopian, goose-
berries, artist sgd **275.00**
Tile, 6", relief foliage dec, matte green,
sgd **115.00**
Vase
5", Chinese Translation, thick white
flowing glaze, marked **100.00**
6¾", incised profile of woman's head,
chocolate brown ground, artist sgd
"Henri Deux" **200.00**
8", bud, Utopian, floral design, artist
sgd "Martha Gray" **100.00**
11", Lotus, morning glories dec, artist
sgd "Charles Fouts" **150.00**
14", two handles, Art Nouveau, frolicking nudes and flowers, green,
white, and orange, brown ground,
raised gold base **500.00**
Wall Pocket, green, sgd "Owensart" . . **125.00**

PAIRPOINT

History: The Pairpoint Manufacturing Co. was
organized in 1880 as a silverplating firm in New
Bedford, Massachusetts. The company merged
with Mount Washington Glass Co. in 1894 and
became the Pairpoint Corporation. The new company produced speciality glass items, often accented with metal frames.

Pairpoint Corp. was sold in 1938 and Robert
Gunderson became manager. He operated it as
the Gunderson Glass Works until his death in
1952. From 1952 until the plant closed in 1956,
operations were maintained under the name Gun-
derson-Pairpoint. Robert Bryden reopened the
glass manufacturing business in 1970, moving it
back to the New Bedford area.

References: Leonard E. Padgett, *Pairpoint
Glass,* Wallace-Homestead, 1979; John A. Shu-
mann III, *The Collector's Encyclopedia of American Art Glass,* Collector Books, 1988.

Biscuit Jar, 7 x 6", hp, daisy dec, apricot ground, molded bulbous base, SP rim, cov, and bail handle, sgd and numbered 300.00

Bowl

8 x 6½", cov, raised gold chrysanthemum blossoms and foliage, eggshell white ground, gold striped handles, fish finial, sgd and numbered 550.00

8½", peppermint stick, satin, clear, overlay rose rim cut to clear stripes, engraved 125.00

8½ x 3½", Ambero, heavy, textured ext., int. painted with trailing vines, three pink lotus blossoms, lush green leaves floating on pool of lime green water, sgd "Ambero L" 745.00

Bride's Basket, pink and white, ornate ruffled edge 325.00

Box, 7¼ x 6", hinged lid, enameled gold and silver iris and foliage, buff ground, sgd 450.00

Candlesticks, pr

4", amethyst, clear controlled bubble ball connector 100.00

6", Blue Swirl pattern, clear controlled bubble ball connector 185.00

Calling Card Receiver, 5" d, engraved floral dec, clear controlled bubble ball connector to saucer base 125.00

Champagne, 5⅛", Flambo pattern, crystal 50.00

Cologne Bottle, 8", applied vertical cranberry ribbing, elaborate flower form cranberry and clear stopper 100.00

Compote

6", amber, engraved florals 75.00

9¼", cov, ruby, clear controlled bubble ball connector, ruby base, steeple bubble finial 125.00

Decanter, 10", Old English pattern, quart, matching stopper 1,250.00

Hat, 4¼", deep red, white with controlled bubbles, orig paper label ... 75.00

Inkwell, 4" d, clear, all-over controlled bubbles, SS cap 200.00

Jewelry Box, 10", hinged, cut, Viscaria pattern, opal flowers, thumbprint base 225.00

Lamp, table, 23⅝" h, reverse painted dome shaped shade, autumn village scene, patinated metal baluster form base, sgd and numbered 1,600.00

Napkin Ring, 5¼", SP, figural, seated Cupid, posy holder, marked 325.00

Perfume Bottle, 5½", heavy crystal, controlled bubbles 60.00

Punch Cup, cylindrical, flaring rim and low foot, vaseline, engraved grapes 30.00

Rose Bowl, 6½", egg shape, enameled blue windmill scene, white opaline ground, c1890 .... 575.00

Urn, 14", cov, Vintage pattern, amethyst 225.00

Vase

5½", bud, amethyst, clear controlled bubble ball connector, orig label .. 100.00

7¾", jack in the pulpit, ruby, enameled bird on pine bough 165.00

8½" h, blood red, turned down collar, clear controlled bubbles in ball stem 200.00

9", Ambero, int. painted with scene of couple strolling down country lane, textured finish 750.00

15", winged cherub in flowing pink drape with tray of peonies, reverse with spray of multicolored poppies, gold borders, powder blue rim shading to cobalt blue ground, applied cobalt blue openwork handles 1,250.00

Wine, 5⅛", flambe, red bowl, black stem, Rockwell silver design 150.00

PAPERWEIGHTS

History: Although paperweights had their origin in ancient Egypt, it was in the mid-19th century that this art form reached its zenith. The classic period for paperweights was 1845–55 in France where the Clichy, Baccarat, and Saint Louis factories produced the finest examples of this art. Other weights made in England, Italy, and Bohemia during this period rarely matched the quality of the French weights.

In the early 1850s New England Glass Co. in Cambridge, Massachusetts, and the Boston and Sandwich Glass Co. in Sandwich, Massachusetts, became the first American factories to make paperweights.

Popularity peaked during the classic period and faded toward the end of the 19th century. Paperweights were rediscovered nearly a century later in the mid-1900s. Contemporary weights still are

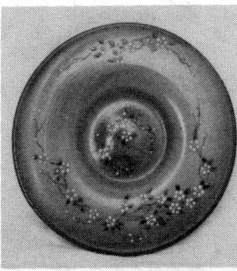

Plate, floral dec, artist signed "P Kulik," dated, 5⅛" d, $115.00.

made by Baccarat, Saint Louis, Perthshire, and by many studio craftsmen in the U.S. and Europe.

References: Paul Hollister, Jr., *The Encyclopedia of Glass Paperweights*, Paperweight Press, 1969; Leo Kaplan, *Paperweights*, published by author, 1985; George N. Kulles, *Identifying Antique Paperweights-Lampwork*, Paperweight Press, 1987; James Mackay, *Glass Paperweights*, Facts on File, 1973; Edith Mannoni, *Classic French Paperweights*, Paperweight Press, 1984; L. H. Selman Ltd, *Collector's Paperweights: Price Guide and Catalogue*, Paperweight Press, 1986.

Collectors' Club: Paperweight Collectors, P.O. Box 468, New Hyde Park, NY 11040.

Periodicals: *Paperweight Gaffer*, 35 Williamstown Circle, York, PA 17404; *Paperweight News*, 761 Chestnut Street, Santa Cruz, CA 95060.

Additional Listings: See *Warman's Americana & Collectibles* for examples of advertising paperweights.

ANTIQUE

Baccarat
Clematis, 2½", white center flower, single bud, five green leaves, encircled in ring of canes	600.00
Double Cut Overlay, 2¾", ruby cut to clear, interlaced strings of fine green and white canes encircling center group of circular set up canes, star cut base, minute edge nicks	900.00
Millefiori, 3¼", close millefiori mushroom, two silhouette canes of horse and monkey, blue and white torsade, star cut base	700.00
Primrose, 3¼", white flower, red center cane, petals outlined in blue, green leaves and stem, star cut base	600.00

Clichy
Millefiori, 2⅜", spaced millefiori, center rose cane, dark blue ground, minor scratches and wear	850.00
Pansy, 2⅝", soft purple upper and lower petals shaded lighter at edges, lower with purple-striped yellow centers, nodding bird, clear	1,400.00
Rose, 2⅛", green and white center cane encircled by eight roses which encircle fifteen blue and white canes, clear ground	400.00
Sodden Snow, 3", multicolored pastry mold canes, opaque white ground	950.00
Swirl, 2", miniature, turquoise and white, predominantly red central pastry mold cane	950.00

New England Glass Company
Apple, 3", molded, deep red shading to yellow, clear	750.00
Clematis, 2⅞", double pink flowers with striated petals, white center, five green leaves, swirling white latticinio	1,700.00
Floral, 2½", three yellow, red, and white flowers, air trap centers, three multicolored canes surrounding pink, blue, and white center cane, six green leaves, white latticinio ground	1,400.00
Fruit, 3", five pears, four cherries, three green leaves, white latticinio ground	475.00
Mushroom, concentric circle, 3³⁄₁₆", faceted with quatrefoils, multicolored, shamrocks, hearts, and millefiori canes, white torsade	325.00
Poinsettia, 3⅜", ten petals, five pale blue dots, and dew drops on petals, pebble ground	325.00

Pantin, Lilies of the Valley, 2⅝", pink spray, thin pale amber stems, green leaves, clear 6,000.00

Sandwich
Bouquet, 2½", red center flower, two flowers on either side, green leaves, clear ground, white torsade	900.00
Floral and Fruit, 3⅞", red, white, and blue flowers, three pears, and two cherries, twenty green leaves, white latticinio ground	13,000.00
Pansy, 3" d, clear, bull bloom, two pink, two cobalt, and one white and blue striped petal encircling a blue, pink, and white center cane, three green leaves, single stem	250.00
Poinsettia, 2½" d, blue, ten petal blossom, five jeweled green leaves, white latticinio ground	475.00
Wild Rose, 3" d, white, blue and pink striping, eight leaves on green stem	500.00

Saint Louis
Bouquet, 2⅞", three blue flowers with

Modern, Paul Ysart, Dahlia, purple flower, circle of red and white canes, cobalt carpet, sgd, orig paper label, $350.00.

yellow centers surrounded by garland of multicolored canes, clear ground **2,500.00**

Chrysanthemum, 2¾", pink with striped petals, four green leaves and stem, swirling white latticinio . **1,850.00**

Crown, 2⅞", center animal silhouette cane dated 1825, red, blue, green, and white **1,150.00**

Posy, 2⅝", five florets, pink, ochre, pale and dark blue, and white, five green leaves, strawberry cut base **490.00**

Whitefriars, millefiori, close concentric, pale blue, white, olive green, and pink, six facets around sides, one on top, clear **200.00**

MODERN

Ayotee, Rick
Cockatoo, yellow sulfur crest, deep blue translucent ground **350.00**
Snow Owl, perched on pine branch, moon on midnight ground, sgd .. **400.00**

Baccarat
John F. Kennedy, 2⅞" d, sulfide bust, black amethyst ground **90.00**
Mount Rushmore, 4⅛", sulfide, red over white overlay, clear blue base, dated 1976 .... **100.00**

Banford, Ray, 2½", iris, red, white, and blue, green foliage, faceted, sgd Ray Banford **600.00**

Charles Kaziun
Faceted, 2½" d, single pink and yellow flowers, star cut base, signature cane in center of three green leaves **1,950.00**
Millefiori, 2", seven multicolored millefiori canes with fish, turtle, duck, and heart silhouettes, white filigree with "K" initial, light green ground shot with gold, sgd "K" on base .. **500.00**

Miniature
1¼" d, 2" h, pedestal, single yellow and red flower, four green and white leaves, lavender ground shot with gold, sgd with gold "K" on base **250.00**
1⅞" d, set up canes in center, surrounded by pink and white spiral ring, cobalt ground shot with gold **800.00**

Overlay
2⅜" d, triple cut overlay, blood red to white to clear **4,500.00**
2¼", double cut overlay, plum cut to white cut to clear, six side windows, single window on top, multicolored center cane with "K" signature surrounded by two concentric circles of green, red,

and white canes, raised black ground **1,200.00**

Perthshire, penguin in hollow bubble, ice blue flash overlay **350.00**

St Louis
Faceted, 3" d, bust, Queen Elizabeth encircled in pink and white ring, green and white alternating setup canes, sgd, dated 2/6/53 .... **100.00**
Pansy, 3", faceted, white muslin ground, sgd S.L./1980 in red cane on back **250.00**

Stankard, Paul
Cactus, two yellow flowers and buds, stem, translucent dark blue ground **950.00**
Violets, wood, bouquet, purple and white flowers, green leaves and stem, clear ground **1,000.00**

Whittemore, F. D.
Rose, pedestal base
2¾", pink, four green leaves, yellow and black signature cane **150.00**
3⅛" h, powder blue, four green leaves, yellow and black signature cane **175.00**

Paul Ysart
Butterfly, 3", single blue flower with white center, long green stem, eight leaves, mottled pink and white ground **250.00**
Flower, 3", yellow and white, brown stem, three green leaves, setup pink and white canes, deep amethyst ground **450.00**

PAPIER MACHE

History: Papier Mache is made from a mixture of wood pulp, glue, resin, and fine sand which is subject to great pressure and then dried. The finished product is tough, durable, and heat resistant. Various finishing treatments are used, such as enameling, japanning, lacquering, mother-of-pearl inlaying, and painting.

During the Victorian era Papier Mache articles such as boxes, trays, and tables were in high fashion. Papier Mache also found use in the production of banks, candy containers, masks, toys, and other children's articles.

Bellows, 12½" h, spade shaped, floral spray dec, gilt stem, white, pink, and green abalone flowers and leaves, pierced obverse, studded leather sides **150.00**

Candy Container
Angel, 10", fur, wax face, German .. **575.00**
Rabbit, 9", glass eyes **45.00**

Crumber, 11" w, shell shaped, chinoiserie dec, black ground **125.00**

Desk, lap, slant front, hinged rect top,

black japanned ground, inlaid central abalone shell bouquet and corner foliate sprigs, int. pen tray, flanked by two wells, ink bottle, hinged red velvet lined writing surface, hidden compartment, sides painted in gilt scrolling foliate scrolls, red, blue, brown, and ivory highlights, Victorian, 12½" w (18¾" open), 3¼" h **420.00**

Hand Screen, 10" w, 15¼" h, cartouche shape, enameled chinoiserie figural group in garden, crest with lyre and foliate forms, black ground, turned black wood handles, pr **200.00**

Jack–O–Lantern, 7" h, orange, printed tissue paper screen, electric lamp, bracket for battery **55.00**

Mask, clown head, orig polychrome dec **110.00**

Pip Squeak
  Husky, 7" h, orig white paint with green trim, repaired and reglued bellow, silent **200.00**
  Lion, 4¼" h, orig yellow and tan paint, leather bellow, silent **75.00**
  Turkey, 3½" h, orig polychrome paint, bellow cov replaced, silent **275.00**

Plate, 12" d, primitive cat painting, marked "Patented August 8, 1880" . **35.00**

Powder Box, lady, bouffant skirt, French **45.00**

Roly Poly, clown, 4⅛" h, orig white and blue paint, polychrome trim, green ribbon around neck **60.00**

Bank, black ground, red and gold Oriental dec, 4¾ x 2 x 3", $60.00.

Snuff Box
  2¾" d, girl in dressing gown holding mirror painted on lid **150.00**
  3⅝" d, naval battle on lid, chipped . . **35.00**
Tobacco Jar, figural, Mandarin **75.00**
Toy, Santa, 6¾" h, spring, red felt coat and white rabbit fur beard **75.00**
Tray, 12½" l, shell shape, Victorian, japanned, red, inlaid with radiating

panels of abalone, gilt oriental figures, c1850 . . . . **100.00**

PARIAN WARE

History: Parian ware is a creamy white, translucent, marble-like porcelain. It originated in England in 1842 and was first known as "Statuary Porcelain." Minton and Copeland have been credited with its development. Wedgwood also made it. In America, parian ware was manufactured by Chistopher Fenton in Bennington, Vermont.

At first parian ware was used only for figures and figural groups. By the 1850's it became so popular a vast range of wares were manufactured.

Vase, child's face on both sides, 5⅜" h, $40.00.

Bowl, 8½" d, crimped edge, roses, high relief **40.00**

Box, 5¾ x 4¼", irregular oval, full figural sleeping child on lid, Bennington . . . **100.00**

Bust, 9½", Clytie, in process of metamorphosis, downcast head, wavy hair, drape falling to reveal left shoulder, sunflower petal border, raised socle base **500.00**

Creamer
  5"
    Tulip relief dec **75.00**
    Wildflower relief dec **70.00**

Ewer, 10¼", blue and white, applied grapes and leaves dec, Bennington, c1850 . . . . **200.00**

Figure
  Boy
    Colonial dress, sitting on rock, holding bird, dog seated at side, 9½" **145.00**
    Nude, leaning against tree stump, stroking bird, sgd "J & TB," c1865, 8 x 4¾" **140.00**
  Man, cloak and beret, 13½ x 4⅛" . . **115.00**

Woman
   Nude, standing, drapery over one
      arm and down side, round soap
      bar in hand, turtle at feet, circular
      base, Bennington, 16″ **165.00**
   Kneeling, hands in front of lamp,
      palms up, head on ground, 7″ .   **125.00**
Loving Cup, 8⅜ x 6⅝″, white relief figures of Bacchus and woman, grapes,
   and vines, Charles Meigh, c1840 .. **300.00**
Pastille Burner, 8¼″ sq, relief molded,
   bird and human figures, raised on
   turned columns, stepped sq base, pr **150.00**
Pin Box, oval, white relief cupid, blue
   ground **50.00**
Pitcher
   3½″, white grape relief dec, pink
      ground **90.00**
   6″, lilac bowl, 19th C **75.00**
   6½″, ivy relief dec **75.00**
   7″, lilac and white figural children
      sleeping dec, English, Victorian .. **175.00**
   7½″, iris relief dec **75.00**
   8″, Philosophers, cameo relief, En-
      glish **200.00**
   8½″, blue and white, figural relief of
      "Now I'm Grand Ma Ma and Now
      I'm Grand Pa Pa," English **175.00**
   10″, figural relief
      Jousting knights, English, 19th C . **150.00**
      Mother and daughter, English,
      19th C **175.00**
Toothpick, 3″, boy kneeling by boat ..   **30.00**
Vase, 10″, applied white monkey type
   creatures, grape clusters at shoul-
   ders, blue ground, c1850, pr **250.00**

PATE-DE-VERRE

History: Pate-de-Verre can be translated simply
as glass paste. It is manufactured by grinding lead
glass into a powder or crystal form, making it into
a paste by adding a 2 or 3% solution of sodium
silicate, molding, firing, and carving. The Egyptians
discovered the process as early as 1500 B.C.

In the late 19th century, the process was rediscovered by a group of French glassmakers. Amal-
ric Walter, Henri Cros, Georges Despret, and the
Daum brothers were leading manufacturers.

Contemporary sculptors are creating a second
renaissance, lead by the technical research of
Jacques Daum.

Ashtray
   3½″, sq, mottled turquoise and midnight blue, two rect compartments,
   molded bumblebee with black and
   orange body, green wings, deep
   brown head, sgd "A Walter/Nancy"
   and Berge/SC," c1925 . . . . **800.00**

**Vase, rosettes, red flowers with yellow
centers, purple tones throughout
ground, 10¼″ h, $6,000.00.**

5″, circular, brown beetle surmount,
   Almeric Walter **1,200.00**
6¼ x 3½″, center medallion with
   Egyptian head, reds and purples,
   small flower buds around edge,
   raised lattice work on bottom **1,600.00**
Atomizer, 5¾″, red berries, green
   leaves, sgd "H Berge" **1,000.00**
Bookend, 5¾″ h, yellow fox leaping from
   leaf molded green ground to trellis
   hung with green and purple grapes
   and foliage, sgd "A Walter Nancy,"
   c1925 . . . . **850.00**
Bowl
   2¾″, molded sprays of red berries,
   green–brown branches, body
   lightly streaked with purple, c1920   **850.00**
   10¼″, ftd, molded with concentric
   blossoms, long necked birds rim,
   gray sides streaked with lavender
   and rose **4,000.00**
Clock, 4½″, sq, stars within pentagon
   and tapered sheaves motif, orange
   and black, molded sgd "G Argy–
   Rousseau," clock by J E Caldwell .. **2,650.00**
Jewelry, pendant, circular, molded
   green mistletoe leaves encircling purple berried center, amethyst translucent ground trimmed in blue, green
   knotted silk cord and hanging tassel   **600.00**
Sculpture
   4″ h, baby blue jay, dark turquoise,
   molded sgd "A Walter, Nancy," designed by Henri Berge **1,250.00**
   12″ h, Loie Fuller, dancer, shades of
   blue, sgd "A Walter" **5,750.00**
Tray, 6 x 8″, apple green, figural green
   and yellow duck with orange beak at
   one end, sgd "Walter, Nancy" **750.00**
Vase
   7″, mottled gray sides molded in low
   relief with blue Australian bush ba-

bies hiding among grasses, molded
sgd "G Argy Rousseau–France" . **6,000.00**

9", tapered cylindrical, border of rose
faun, satyr, girl among amber
waves, framed by purple morning
glories, green ground **3,600.00**

9¾", baluster shape, aquamarine,
purple streaked translucent
ground, cobalt and sea–green geometric and stylized floral design,
molded sgd "G Argy–Rousseau–
France" **2,500.00**

PATE-SUR-PATE

History: Pate-sur-Pate, paste on paste, is a
19th century porcelain form featuring relief designs
achieved by painting successive layers of thin pottery paste one on top of the other.

About 1880 Marc Solon and other Sevres artists,
inspired by a Chinese celadon vase in the Ceramic
Museum at Sevres, experimented with this process of porcelain decoration. Solon migrated to
England at the outbreak of the Franco-Prussian
War and worked at Minton, where he perfected the
pate-sur-pate process.

**Plaque, man sowing seeds, Wedgwood
green ground, French marks, 4⅜ x 7½",
$300.00.**

Box, 4¼ x 4", blue and white, cupids,
artist sgd, marked "Limoges" **200.00**

Demitasse Cup and Saucer, roses, gold
trim, Coalport **350.00**

Dessert Plate, 8¾" d, alternating
paneled borders, three panels decorated with classical figures and cupids
in white on pale medium blue ground,
three larger panels with gilt scrolling
foliate dec, narrow bead borders,
gilded rims, inscribed "Mintons," gilt
painted factory and retailer's mark,
decorated by R Bradbury, retailed by
Tiffany & Co, New York, set of twelve **2,750.00**

Flask, 8⅞", sunrise, sunset, two white
figures floating above horizon, deep
olive green parian body, sgd "Frederick Schenk," mounted as table
lamps, pr **600.00**

Pitcher, 8", mythical figures, bearded
mask handle, white and pink **225.00**

Plaque
4", white relief pastoral scene with
couple courting beneath tree, blue
ground, wooden frame, marked
"F M Limoges, France" **300.00**

7⅝ x 7", pr, one with maiden and
cupid spinning web, other with
maiden seated on bench with whip
in one hand, sunflower stalk with
humanistic snail in other, artist sgd
"Louis Solin," marked "Mintons" on
back, framed **2,000.00**

Plate, 10⅝" d, alternating paneled borders, three panels decorated with
classical figures and cupids in white
on pale medium blue ground, three
larger panels with gilt scrolling foliate
dec, narrow bead borders, gilded
rims, inscribed "Mintons," gilt painted
factory and retailer's mark, decorated
by R Bradbury, set of twelve **3,575.00**

Sardine Dish, 2½ x 5½ x 4½", fish and
seaweed dec, deep brown ground,
SP cov, sgd "Jones" **500.00**

Vase
10", pilgrim bottle shape, white relief
cupids, one armed with large net,
other with arrow, frolicking in tall
weeds and flowers, chasing butterflies, gilding on neck, shoulder, and
handles, marked "Mintons," c1880 **900.00**

10⅝", flattened oviform, obverse dec
of classical maidens on swing suspended from leafy tree, enchanced
with gold, upper and lower frieze of
stylized blossoms and leaves, olive
green ground, clear overglaze, pr **1,500.00**

PATTERN GLASS

History: Pattern glass is clear or colored glass
pressed into one of hundreds of patterns. Deming
Jarves of the Boston and Sandwich Glass Co.
invented the first successful pressing machine in
1828. By the 1860s glass pressing machinery had
been improved, and mass production of good
quality matched tableware sets began. The idea
of a matched glassware table service (including
goblets, tumblers, creamers, sugars, compotes,
cruets, etc.) quickly caught on in America. Many
pattern glass table services had numerous accessory pieces among which were banana stands,
molasses cans, water bottles, etc.

Early pattern glass (flint) was made with a lead

formula, giving it a ringing quality. During the Civil War lead became too valuable to be used in glass manufacturing. In 1864 Hobbs, Bruckunier & Co., West Virginia, developed a soda lime (non–flint) formula. Pattern glass also was produced in colors, milk glass, opalescent glass, slag glass, and custard glass.

The hundreds of companies which produced pattern glass have involved histories of development, expansions, personnel problems, material and supply demands, fires, and mergers. In 1899 the National Glass Co. was formed as a combine of nineteen glass companies in Pennsylvania, Ohio, Indiana, West Virginia, and Maryland. U. S. Glass, another consortium, was founded in 1891. These combines resulted as attempts to save small companies by pooling talents, resources, and patterns. Because of this pooling, the same pattern can be attributed to several companies.

Sometimes the pattern name of a piece was changed from one company to the next to reflect current fashion trends. U. S. Glass created the States series by issuing patterns named for a particular state. Several of these patterns were new issues, others were former patterns renamed.

References: E. M. Belnap, *Milk Glass,* Crown Publishers, Inc., 1949; Regis F. and Mary F. Ferson, *Yesterday's Milk Glass Today,* privately printed, 1981; William Heacock, *Toothpick Holders from A to Z, Book 1, Encyclopedia of Victorian Colored Pattern Glass,* Antique Publications, 1981; William Heacock, *Opalescent Glass from A to Z, Book 2,* Antique Publications, 1981; William Heacock, *Syrups, Sugar Shakers & Cruets, Book 3,* Antique Publications, 1981; William Heacock, *Custard Glass From A to Z, Book 4,* Antique Publications, 1980; William Heacock, *U. S. Glass From A to Z, Book 5,* Antique Publications, Inc. 1980; William Heacock, *Oil Cruets From A to Z, Book 6,* Antique Publications, 1981; William Heacock, *Ruby Stained Glass From A To Z, Book 7* Antique Publications, Inc., 1986; William Heacock, *More Ruby Stained Glass, Book 8,* Antique Publications, 1987; William Heacock and William Gamble, *Cranberry Opalescent From A to Z, Book 9* Antique Publications, 1987; William Heacock, *Old Pattern Glass,* Antique Publications, 1981; William Heacock, *1000 Toothpick Holders: A Collector's Guide,* Antique Publications, 1977, William Heacock, *Rare and Unlisted Toothpick Holders,* Antique Publications, 1984.

Bill Jenks and Jerry Luna, *Early American Pattern Glass–1850 to 1910: Major Collectible Table Settings with Prices,* Wallace-Homestead Book Co. 1990; Minnie Watson Kamm, *Pattern Glass Pitchers, Books 1 through 8,* privately printed, 1970, 4th printing; Ruth Webb Lee, *Early American Pressed Glass,* Lee Publications, 1966, 36th edition; Ruth Webb Lee, *Victorian Glass,* Lee Publications, 1944, 13th edition; Bessie M. Lindsey, *American Historical Glass,* Charles E. Tuttle Co., 1967; Robert Irwin Lucas, *Tarentum Pattern Glass,*

privately printed, 1981; Mollie H. McCain, *Pattern Glass Primer,* Lamplighter Books, 1979; Mollie H. McCain, *The Collector's Encyclopedia of Pattern Glass,* Collector Books, 1982; George P. and Helen McKearin, *American Glass,* Grown Publishers, 1941; James Measell, *Greentown Glass,* Grand Rapids Public Museum Association, 1979; James Measell and Don E. Smith, *Findlay Glass: The Glass Tableware Manufacturers, 1886-1902,* Antique Publications, Inc, 1986; Alice Hulett Metz, *Early American Pattern Glass,* published by author, 1958; Alice Hulett Metz, *Much More Early American Pattern Glass,* published by author, 1965.

Robert W. Miller and Dori Miles, *Wallace-Homestead Price Guide To Pattern Glass, 11th Edition,* Wallace-Homestead, 1986; S. T. Millard, *Goblets I,* privately printed, 1938, reprinted Wallace-Homestead, 1975; S. T. Millard, *Goblets II,* privately printed, 1940, reprinted Wallace-Homestead, 1975; Arthur G. Peterson, *Glass Salt Shakers: 1,000 Patterns,* Wallace-Homestead, 1970; Jane Shadel Spillman, *American and European Pressed Glass in the Corning Museum of Glass,* Corning Museum of Glass, 1981; Jane Shadel Spillman, *The Knopf Collectors Guides to American Antiques, Glass Volumes 1 and 2,* Alfred A. Knopf, Inc., 1982, 1983; Doris and Peter Unitt, *American and Canadian Goblets,* Clock House, 1970; Doris and Peter Unitt, *Treasury of Canadian Glass,* Clock House, 1969, 2nd edition; Peter Unitt and Anne Worrall, *Canadian Handbook, Pressed Glass Tableware,* Clock House Productions, 1983; Dina von Zweck, *The Woman's Day Dictionary of Glass,* The Main Street Press, 1983.

Museums: Corning Museum of Glass, Corning, NY. National Museum of Man, Ottawa, Ontario, Canada.

Periodical: *Glass Collector's Digest,* Richardson Printing Corp., P. O. Box 663, Marietta, OH 45750.

Additional Listings: Bread Plates, Children's Toy Dishes, Cruets, Custard Glass, Milk Glass, Sugar Shakers, Toothpicks, and specific companies.

Abbreviations: ah—applied handle

GUTDOBD—Give Us This Day Our Daily Bread

hs—high standard

ls—low standard

os—original stopper

We continue to be fortunate in assembling a panel of prestigious pattern glass dealers to serve as advisors in reviewing the pattern glass listings found in this edition. Their dedication is symbolic of those dealers and collectors who view price guides as useful market tools and contribute their expertise and time to make them better.

Research in pattern glass is continuing. As in the past, we have tried to present patterns with correct names, histories, and pieces. Categories have been changed to reflect the most current thinking of all patterns alphabetically. Colored, opalescent, and clear patterns now are included in one listing, avoiding duplication of patterns and colors.

Pattern glass has been widely reproduced. We have listed reproductions with an *. These mark-

ings are given only as a guide and clue to the collector that some reproductions may exist in a given pattern.

Advisors: John and Alice Ahlfeld, Mike Anderton, William Jenks, and Darryl K. Reilly.

ACTRESS (Theatrical)

Made by LaBelle Glass Co., Bridgeport, Ohio, and Crystal Glass Co., c1870. All clear 20% less. Some items have been reproduced in clea and color by Imperial Glass Co.

	Clear and Frosted		Clear and Frosted
Bowl		Creamer	75.00
6", ftd	45.00	Dresser Tray	60.00
7", ftd	50.00	Goblet, Kate Claxton (2	
9½, ftd	85.00	portraits)	80.00
8", Miss Neilson	85.00	Marmalade Jar, cov	125.00
Bread Plate		Mug, HMS Pinafore	50.00
7 x 12", HMS Pinafore	90.00	Pickle Dish, Love's Request	
9 x 13", Miss Neilson,		is Pickles	45.00
motto	70.00	Pickle Relish, different ac-	
Butter, cov	90.00	tresses	
Cake Stand, 10"	145.00	4½ x 7"	35.00
Candlesticks, pr	250.00	5 x 8"	35.00
Celery Vase		5½ x 9"	35.00
Actress Head	130.00	Pitcher	
HMS Pinafore, pedestal	145.00	Milk, 6½", HMS Pinafore,	
Cheese Dish, cov, The Lone		Fanny Davenport and	
Fisherman on cov, Two		Miss Neilson	275.00
Dromios on base	250.00	Water, 9", Romeo & Juliet,	
Compote		balcony scene	250.00
Cov, hs, 8" d	225.00	Salt, master	70.00
Cov, hs, 10" d	250.00	Salt Shaker, orig pewter top	42.50
Cov, hs, 12" d	300.00	Sauce	
Open, hs, 10" d	90.00	Flat	15.00
Open, hs, 12" d	120.00	Footed	20.00
Open, ls, 5" d	45.00	Spooner	60.00
Open, ls, 6" d	50.00	Sugar, cov	100.00
Open, ls, 7" d	65.00		

ADONIS (Pleat and Tuck, Washboard)

Pattern made by McKee Bros. of Pittsburgh, Pennsylvania in 1897.

	Canary	Clear	Deep Blue
Bowl, 5", berry	15.00	10.00	20.00
Butter, cov	70.00	45.00	80.00
Cake Plate, 11"	25.00	18.00	32.00
Cake Stand, 10½"	45.00	30.00	50.00
Celery Vase	35.00	25.00	40.00
Compote,			
Cov, hs	65.00	40.00	75.00

	Canary	Clear	Deep Blue
Open, hs, 8″	45.00	30.00	50.00
Open, jelly, 4½″ . .	28.00	18.00	32.00
Creamer.	28.00	22.50	32.00
Pitcher, water	55.00	35.00	60.00
Plate, 10″	25.00	18.00	32.00
Relish.	18.00	15.00	20.00
Salt and Pepper pr .	40.00	35.00	45.00
Sauce, flat, 4″	10.00	8.50	12.00
Spooner	35.00	20.00	38.00
Sugar, cov	40.00	35.00	45.00
Syrup	150.00	50.00	150.00
Tumbler	20.00	16.00	20.00

AEGIS (Bead & Bar Medallion, Swiss)

Non-flint pattern made by McKee and Brothers of Pittsburgh, Pennsylvania, in the 1880's. Shards have also been found at the site of the Burlington Glass Works, Hamilton, Ontario.

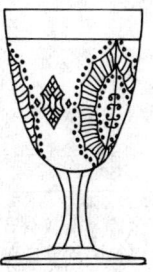

	Clear		Clear
Bowl, oval.	15.00	Pickle, 5 x 7″	15.00
Butter, cov	35.00	Pitcher, water	55.00
Compote		Salt	15.00
Cov, hs	50.00	Sauce	
Open, hs.	25.00	Flat.	7.50
Creamer.	25.00	Footed	10.00
Egg Cup.	25.00	Spooner	15.00
Goblet	30.00	Sugar, cov	35.00

ALABAMA (Beaded Bull's Eye and Drape)

Made by U. S. Glass Co., c1898. One of the States patterns. Also found in green (rare).

	Clear	Ruby Stained		Clear	Ruby Stained
Bowl, berry, master .	30.00	—	Nappy	25.00	—
Butter, cov	60.00	160.00	Pitcher, water	72.00	—
Cake Stand	55.00	—	Relish.	24.00	35.00
Castor Set, 4 bottles,			Salt & Pepper	65.00	—
glass frame	125.00	—	Sauce	18.00	—
Celery Vase	35.00	110.00	Spooner	30.00	—
Compote, open, 5″,			Sugar, cov	48.00	—
jelly.	65.00	—	Syrup	125.00	250.00
Creamer.	45.00	60.00	Toothpick	60.00	150.00
Cruet, os	65.00	—	Tray, water, 10½″ . .	50.00	—
Dish, rect	20.00	—	Tumbler	45.00	—
Honey Dish, cov . . .	60.00	—			

ALASKA (Lion's Leg)

Non-flint opalescent made by Northwood Glass Co. from 1897 to 1910. Forms are square except cruet, tumblers, salt and pepper shakers. Some pieces are found with enamel decoration. Sauces can be found in clear ($30.00); the creamer ($110.00) and spooner ($95.00) are known in clear blue.

	Clear Emerald Green	Blue Opal	Vaseline Opal	White Opal
Banana Boat.	85.00	250.00	250.00	75.00
Bowl, berry, ftd	65.00	100.00	95.00	45.00
Butter, cov	150.00	280.00	275.00	150.00
Celery Tray.	45.00	130.00	120.00	85.00
Creamer.	42.50	75.00	65.00	40.00
Cruet	225.00	250.00	230.00	135.00
Pitcher, water	75.00	385.00	375.00	175.00
Salt Shaker, dec . . .	—	60.00	55.00	45.00
Sauce	30.00	45.00	35.00	25.00
Spooner	55.00	65.00	55.00	50.00
Sugar, cov	65.00	150.00	130.00	100.00
Tumbler	45.00	75.00	65.00	55.00

ALL-OVER DIAMOND (Diamond Splendor, Diamond Block #3)

Made by George Duncan and Sons, Pittsburgh, Pennsylvania, c1891 and continued by U.S. Glass Co. It was occasionally trimmed with gold, and had at least 65 pieces in the pattern. Biscuit jars are found in three sizes; bowls are both crimped and non-crimped; and nappies are also found crimped and non-crimped in fifteen sizes. Also made in ruby stained.

	Clear		Clear
Biscuit Jar, cov	60.00	Ice Tub, handles	35.00
Bitters Bottle.	30.00	Lamp, Banquet, tall stem . . .	140.00
Bowl		Nappy	
7"	20.00	4"	15.00
11"	35.00	9"	35.00
Cake Stand	35.00	Plate	
Candelabrum, very ornate, 4		6"	15.00
arm with lusters	175.00	7"	15.00
Celery Tray, crimped or		Pickle Dish, long	15.00
straight	20.00	Pitcher, water, bulbous, 6	
Claret Jug.	50.00	sizes.	45–60.00
Compote, cov	40.00	Punch Bowl	50.00
Condensed Milk Jar, cov . . .	25.00	Salt Shaker.	15.00
Cordial	35.00	Spooner	20.00
Creamer.	20.00	Sugar	
Cruet, patterned stopper		Cov.	35.00
1 oz	50.00	Open	18.00
2 oz	45.00	Syrup.	55.00
4 oz	45.00	Tray	
6 oz	25.00	Ice Cream	30.00
Decanter		Water	30.00
Pint.	45.00	Wine.	30.00
Quart	45.00	Tumbler	15.00
Egg Cup.	20.00	Water Bottle	35.00
Goblet	25.00	Wine	15.00

ALMOND THUMBPRINT (Pointed Thumbprint, Finger Print)

An early flint glass pattern with variants in flint and non-flint. Pattern has been attributed to Bryce, Bakewell, and U. S. Glass. Sometimes found in milk glass.

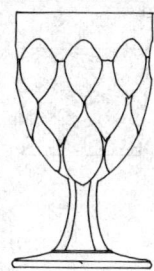

	Flint	Non-Flint		Flint	Non-Flint
Bowl, 4½″ d, ftd ...	—	20.00	Decanter	70.00	—
Butter, cov	80.00	40.00	Egg Cup.........	45.00	25.00
Celery Vase	50.00	25.00	Goblet	28.00	12.00
Champagne	60.00	35.00	Salt		
Compote			Flat, large	25.00	15.00
Cov, hs, 4¾″, jelly	60.00	40.00	Ftd, cov........	45.00	25.00
Cov, hs, 10″.....	80.00	45.00	Ftd, open	25.00	10.00
Cov, ls, 4¾″.....	55.00	30.00	Spooner.........	20.00	15.00
Cov, ls, 7″.....	45.00	25.00	Sugar, cov	60.00	40.00
Open, hs, 10½″ ..	65.00	—	Sweetmeat Jar, cov.	65.00	45.00
Cordial..........	40.00	30.00	Tumbler	45.00	20.00
Creamer.........	60.00	40.00	Wine	28.00	12.00
Cruet, ftd, os......	55.00	—			

AMAZON (Sawtooth Band)

Non-flint; made by Bryce Brothers, Pittsburgh, Pennsylvania, late 1870s–1880 and also by the U. S. Glass Co., c1890. Mostly found in clear, either etched or plain. Heacock notes pieces in amber, blue, vaseline, and ruby stained. Over 65 pieces made in this pattern, including a toy set. Add 200% for color, e.g., pedestalled amber cruet with maltese cross stopper ($165.00) and pedestalled blue cruet with hand and bar stopper ($200.00). An amethyst cruet with a hand-bar stopper ($275.00) also is known.

	Etched	Plain		Etched	Plain
Banana Stand.....	95.00	65.00	Cordial	40.00	25.00
Bowl			Creamer..........	30.00	28.00
4″, scalloped	—	10.00	Cruet, os	50.00	45.00
4½″, scalloped...	—	10.00	Egg Cup.........	—	14.00
5″, scalloped	—	15.00	Goblet		
6″, scalloped	—	25.00	4½″..........	30.00	—
6½″, cov, oval ...	—	50.00	5″............	25.00	—
7″, scalloped	—	20.00	6″............	30.00	—
8″, scalloped	—	25.00	Pitcher, water	60.00	55.00
9″, cov	30.00	25.00	Relish...........	28.00	25.00
Butter, cov	65.00	50.00	Salt & Pepper, pr...	50.00	40.00
Cake Stand			Salt		
Large	—	50.00	Individual........	—	15.00
Small	—	40.00	Master	—	18.00
Celery Vase	35.00	30.00	Sauce, ftd........	10.00	10.00
Champagne	—	35.00	Spooner	25.00	20.00
Claret...........	35.00	30.00	Sugar, cov	55.00	45.00
Compote			Syrup...........	50.00	42.50
Cov, hs. 7″.......	—	65.00	Tumbler	25.00	20.00
Open, 4½″, jelly..	45.00	35.00	Wine	25.00	20.00
Open, hs, 9½″, sawtooth edge .	—	45.00			

ANTHEMION (Albany)

Non-flint made by Model Flint Glass Co., Findlay, Ohio, c1890–1900, and by Albany Glass Co. Also found in amber and blue.

	Clear		Clear
Bowl, 7″, sq, turned-in edge .	20.00	Pitcher, water	50.00
Butter, cov	65.00	Plate, 10″	20.00
Cake Plate, 9½″	35.00	Sauce	10.00
Cake Stand	40.00	Spooner	25.00
Celery Vase	35.00	Sugar, cov	35.00
Creamer	30.00	Tumbler	25.00
Marmalade Jar, cov	45.00		

APOLLO

Non-flint, first made by Adams and Co., Pittsburgh, Pennsylvania, c1870, and later by U. S. Glass Co., c1891. Frosted increases price 20%. Also found in ruby stained and engraved.

	Clear		Clear
Bowl		Egg Cup	30.00
4″	10.00	Goblet	35.00
5″	10.00	Lamp, 10″	125.00
6″	12.00	Pickle Dish	15.00
7″	15.00	Pitcher, water	65.00
8″	22.50	Plate, 9½″, sq	28.00
Butter, cov	55.00	Salt	20.00
Cake Stand		Salt Shaker	25.00
8″	35.00	Sauce	
9″	40.00	Flat	10.00
10″	50.00	Ftd, 5″	12.00
Celery Tray, rect	22.50	Spooner	28.50
Celery Vase	35.00	Sugar, cov	45.00
Compote		Sugar Shaker	45.00
Cov, hs	65.00	Syrup	110.00
Open, hs	35.00	Tray, water	45.00
Open, ls, 7″	25.00	Tumbler	30.00
Creamer	35.00	Wine	35.00
Cruet	60.00		

ARCHED FLEUR-DE-LIS (Late Fleur-De-Lis)

Made by Bryce, Higbee and Co., in 1897–1898. Also gilded.

	Clear	Ruby Stained		Clear	Ruby Stained
Banana Stand	35.00	150.00	Olive, handled	15.00	—
Bowl, 9″, oval	18.00	—	Pitcher, water	125.00	300.00
Butter, cov	40.00	135.00	Plate, 7″, sq	12.00	45.00
Cake Stand	35.00	—	Relish, 8″	15.00	—
Compote, jelly, cov .	18.00	—	Salt Shaker	16.00	45.00
Creamer	30.00	60.00	Sauce	8.00	20.00
Dish, shallow, 7″ . . .	12.50	25.00	Spooner, double		
Mug, 3¼″	20.00	30.00	handled	20.00	65.00

	Clear	Ruby Stained		Clear	Ruby Stained
Sugar, cov, double handled	35.00	100.00	Tumbler	15.00	45.00
Toothpick	30.00	300.00	Vase, 10″	35.00	75.00
			Wine	25.00	65.00

ARCHED GRAPE

Flint and non-flint made by Boston and Sandwich Glass Co., c1880.

	Non-Flint		Non-Flint
Butter, cov	45.00	Pitcher, water, ah	60.00
Celery Vase	35.00	Sauce, flat	8.00
Champagne	35.00	Spooner	30.00
Compote, cov, hs	50.00	Sugar, cov	45.00
Creamer	40.00	Wine	35.00
Goblet	25.00		

ARCHED OVALS

Made by U. S. Glass Co., c1908. Found in gilt, ruby stained, green, and rarely in cobalt blue. Popular pattern for souvenir wares.

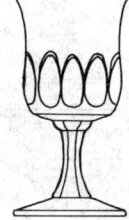

	Clear	Cobalt	Green	Ruby Stained
Bowl, berry	12.50	—	18.00	—
Bowl, cov, 7″	40.00	—	—	—
Butter, cov	45.00	—	50.00	80.00
Cake Stand	35.00	—	—	—
Celery Vase	15.00	40.00	20.00	—
Compote				
Cov, hs, 8″, belled	42.00	—	—	—
Open, hs, 8″	30.00	—	—	—
Open, hs, 9″	35.00	—	—	—
Creamer				
Ind	20.00	—	—	—
Regular	30.00	—	—	25.00
Cruet	35.00	—	45.00	—
Goblet	20.00	—	30.00	35.00
Mug	18.00	30.00	20.00	25.00
Pitcher, water	30.00	—	40.00	—
Plate, 9″	20.00	—	25.00	—
Punch Cup	8.00	—	—	—
Relish, oval, 9″	20.00	—	—	—
Salt & Pepper, pr	45.00	—	50.00	—
Sauce	7.50	—	—	—
Saucer	—	—	—	30.00
Syrup	35.00	—	—	—
Spooner	20.00	—	25.00	35.00
Sugar, cov	35.00	—	40.00	—
Toothpick	18.00	50.00	25.00	35.00
Tumbler	12.00	25.00	18.00	30.00
Wine	15.00	—	20.00	30.00

ARGONAUT SHELL (Nautilus)

Made by Northwood Glass Co., c1897. Also made in carnival glass. Heavily reproduced in blue and custard.

	Blue Opal	Custard	Vaseline Opal
Bon Bon.........	60.00	—	—
Bowls			
Berry, large	150.00	125.00	125.00
Small	45.00	50.00	45.00
Butter, cov	250.00	280.00	225.00
Compote, Jelly	150.00	135.00	250.00
Creamer.........	200.00	125.00	175.00
Cruet, os	250.00	350.00	175.00
Pitcher, water	300.00	350.00	375.00
Salt & Pepper Shakers, pr..........	100.00	350.00	100.00
Spooner.........	75.00	100.00	95.00
Sugar, cov	250.00	225.00	225.00
Toothpick	—	295.00	—
Tray............	60.00	—	45.00
Tumbler	185.00	75.00	175.00

ARGUS

Flint, thumbprint type pattern made by Bakewell Pears & Co. in Pittsburgh, Pennsylvania, in the early 1870s. Copiously reproduced, some by Fostoria with raised "HFM" trademark for Henry Ford Museum.

	Clear		Clear
Ale Glass	75.00	Goblet	40.00
Bitters Bottle...........	60.00	Lamp, ftd	75.00
Bowl, 5½"..............	50.00	Mug, ah	65.00
Butter, cov	85.00	Pitcher, water, ah	225.00
Celery Vase	90.00	Salt, master, open........	30.00
Champagne	65.00	Spooner...............	48.50
Compote, open, 6" d, 4½" h.	50.00	Sugar, cov	65.00
Creamer, applied handle ...	100.00	Tumbler, bar............	65.00
Decanter, qt	70.00	Whiskey, ah	75.00
Egg Cup..............	25.00	Wine	45.00

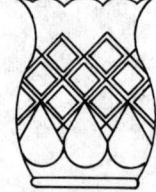

ART (Job's Tears)

Non-flint produced by Adams and Co., Pittsburgh, Pennsylvania, in the 1870s. Reissued by U. S. Glass Co. in the early 1890s. A milk glass covered compote is known.

	Clear	Ruby Stained		Clear	Ruby Stained
Banana Stand.....	95.00	195.00	7", low, collar base	30.00	—
Biscuit Jar	135.00	195.00	8", berry, one end pointed	50.00	55.00
Bowl					
6" d, 3¼" h, ftd ..	30.00	—			

	Clear	Ruby Stained		Clear	Ruby Stained
Butter, cov	60.00	100.00	Cruet, os	125.00	250.00
Cake Stand			Goblet	58.00	—
9"	55.00	—	Mug	35.00	50.00
10¼"	65.00	—	Pitcher		
Celery Vase	42.50	65.00	Milk	115.00	150.00
Compote			Water, 2½ qt	85.00	—
Cov, hs, 7"	55.00	185.00	Plate, 10"	40.00	—
Open, hs, 9", flared scalloped edge	50.00	—	Relish	20.00	65.00
			Sauce		
Open, hs, 9½" d, 9"h	60.00	—	Flat, round, 4"	15.00	—
			Pointed end	18.50	—
Open, hs, 10"	65.00	—	Spooner	25.00	55.00
Creamer			Sugar, cov	45.00	85.00
Hotel, large, round shape	45.00	55.00	Tumbler	45.00	—
Regular	55.00	60.00	Vinegar Jug, 3 pt.	75.00	—

ASHBURTON

A popular pattern produced by Boston and Sandwich Glass Co. and McKee Brothers from the 1850s to the late 1870s with many variations. Originally made in flint by New England Glass Co. and others and later in non-flint. Prices are for flint. Also reported is an amber handled whiskey mug and a scarce emerald green wine glass ($200.00). Some items known in fiery opalescent.

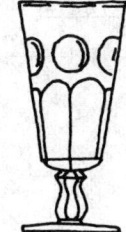

	Clear		Clear
Ale Glass, 5"	90.00	Honey Dish	15.00
Bar Bottle		* Jug, qt	90.00
Pint	55.00	Lamp	75.00
Quart	75.00	* Lemonade Glass	55.00
Bitters Bottle	55.00	Mug, 7"	100.00
Bowl, 6½"	75.00	Pitcher, water	450.00
Carafe	175.00	Plate, 6⅝"	75.00
Celery Vase, scalloped top	125.00	Sauce	15.00
Champagne, cut	75.00	Spooner	40.00
Claret, 5¼" h	50.00	* Sugar, cov	90.00
Compote, open, ls, 7½"	65.00	Toddy Jar, cov	375.00
Cordial, 4¼" h	75.00	Tumbler	
Creamer, ah	210.00	Bar	75.00
Decanter, qt, cut and pressed, os	250.00	Water	75.00
		Whiskey	60.00
Egg Cup		Whiskey, ah	125.00
Double	95.00	Water Bottle, tumble up	95.00
Single	30.00	* Wine	
Flip Glass, handled	140.00	Cut	65.00
* Goblet	40.00	Pressed	40.00

ASHMAN

Non-flint, c1880. Pieces are square in shape. There are frequent variations within pieces. Also made in blue.

	Amber	Clear		Amber	Clear
Bread Tray, motto . .	—	55.00	Creamer	45.00	35.00
Bowl	—	20.00	Goblet	—	35.00
Butter, cov			Pitcher, water	—	65.00
Conventional final	50.00	38.00	Relish	—	15.00
Large ball-type fi-			Spooner	—	40.00
nial, sometimes			Sugar, cov	—	45.00
with flowers			Tray, water	50.00	40.00
within the ball . .	—	50.00	Tumbler	—	25.00
Cake Stand, 9"	—	40.00	Wine	—	25.00
Compotes					
Cov, hs, 12"	—	95.00			
Open hs	—	37.50			

ATLANTA (Square Lion, Clear Lion Head)

Produced by Fostoria Glass Co., Moundsville, West Virginia, c1895. Pieces are usually square in shape. Also found in milk glass, ruby and amber stain.

	Clear	Frosted		Clear	Frosted
Bowl			Goblet	50.00	60.00
7", scallop rim . . .	60.00	75.00	Marmalade Jar	65.00	85.00
8", low collar			Pitcher, water	125.00	175.00
base	55.00	85.00	Relish, oval	35.00	40.00
Butter, cov	85.00	125.00	Salt & Pepper, pr. . .	100.00	125.00
Cake Stand, 10" . . .	95.00	110.00	Salt		
Celery Vase	45.00	75.00	Individual	30.00	40.00
Compote			Master	50.00	70.00
Cov, hs, 7"	90.00	125.00	Sauce, 4"	22.00	25.00
Cov, hs, 8" d,			Spooner	50.00	60.00
9½" h	110.00	150.00	Sugar, cov	85.00	100.00
Open, hs, 5", jelly .	55.00	65.00	Toothpick	55.00	60.00
Creamer	50.00	65.00	Tumbler	45.00	55.00
Cruet	125.00	150.00	Wine	40.00	65.00

ATLAS

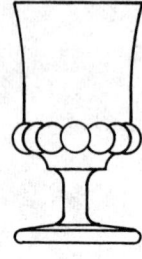

Non-flint glass pattern occasionally ruby stained and etched. Made by Adams and Co., U. S. Glass Co. in 1891, and Bryce Brothers, Mt. Pleasant, Pennsylvania, in 1889.

	Clear	Ruby Stained		Clear	Ruby Stained
Bowl, 9"	20.00	—	Creamer		
Butter, cov, regular .	45.00	75.00	Table, ah	30.00	55.00
Cake Stand			Tankard	25.00	—
8"	35.00	—	Goblet	38.00	52.00
9"	40.00	95.00	Marmalade Jar	45.00	—
Celery Vase	28.00	—	Pitcher, water	45.00	—
Champagne, 5½" h .	35.00	45.00	Salt		
Compote			Master	20.00	—
Cov, hs, 8"	65.00	—	Individual	15.00	—
Cov, hs, 5", jelly . .	50.00	65.00	Salt & Pepper, pr. . .	20.00	—
Open, ls, 7"	40.00	—	Sauce		
Cordial	35.00	—	Flat	10.00	—

	Clear	Ruby Stained		Clear	Ruby Stained
Footed	15.00	20.00	Toothpick	20.00	45.00
Spooner	30.00	35.00	Tray, water	75.00	—
Sugar			Tumbler	28.00	—
Cov.	38.00	65.00	Whiskey	20.00	45.00
Open	20.00	—	Wine	25.00	—
Syrup (molasses can)	65.00	—			

AURORA (Diamond Horseshoe)

Made in 1888 by the Brilliant Glass Works, which only existed for a short time. Taken over by the Greensburg Glass Co. who continued the pattern. Also found etched.

	Clear	Ruby Stained		Clear	Ruby Stained
Bread Plate, 10", round, large star in center	30.00	35.00	Relish Scoop, handle.	10.00	25.00
Butter, cov	45.00	90.00	Salt & Pepper, pr. ..	45.00	80.00
Cake Stand	35.00	85.00	Sauce, flat	8.00	18.00
Celery Vase	32.50	42.50	Spooner	25.00	48.00
Compote, cov, hs ..	65.00	110.00	Sugar, cov	45.00	65.00
Creamer.........	35.00	50.00	Tray, water	45.00	60.00
Goblet	30.00	45.00	Tray, wine........	35.00	60.00
Mug, handle	50.00	65.00	Tumbler	25.00	45.00
Olive, oval	18.00	35.00	Waste Bowl.......	30.00	45.00
Pitcher, water	40.00	100.00	Wine	25.00	35.00
			Wine Decanter, os..	75.00	150.00

AUSTRIAN (Finecut Medallion)

Made by Indiana Tumbler and Goblet Co., Greentown, Indiana, 1897. Experimental pieces were made in cobalt blue, nile green, and opaque colors.

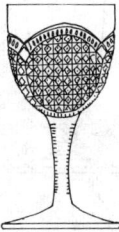

	Amber	Canary	Clear	Emerald Green
Bowl				
8", round	—	150.00	55.00	—
8¼", rect	—	145.00	50.00	—
Butter, cov	185.00	300.00	90.00	—
Compote, open, ls..	—	150.00	75.00	—
Cordial	145.00	150.00	50.00	150.00
Creamer.........	120.00	125.00	40.00	120.00
Goblet	—	150.00	40.00	—
Nappy, cov	—	135.00	55.00	—
Pitcher, water	—	350.00	100.00	—
Plate, 10"	—	—	40.00	—
Punch Cup	150.00	150.00	18.00	125.00
Rose Bowl	—	150.00	50.00	—
Sauce, 4⅝" d	—	50.00	20.00	—
Spooner.........	—	100.00	40.00	—
Sugar, cov	—	175.00	45.00	—
Tumbler	175.00	85.00	25.00	—
Wine	175.00	150.00	30.00	150.00

AZTEC

Made by McKee Glass Co., 1900 to 1910. Late imitation cut pattern, often marked "PRES-CUT" in circle in base; about 75 items in pattern.

	Clear		Clear
Bon Bon, ftd, 7″	15.00	Goblet	25.00
Bowl, berry	15.00	Pitcher, ah, ½ gal.	35.00
Butter, cov	40.00	Plate	20.00
Cake Plate, trilobed	20.00	Punch Bowl, stand, and 12	
Cake Stand	30.00	handled cups	125.00
Carafe, water	40.00	Punch Cup	5.00
Celery Tray.	15.00	Relish.	15.00
Celery Vase	18.00	Salt & Pepper, pr.	35.00
Champagne	25.00	Sauce	5.00
Compote, open	30.00	Soda Fountain Accessories	
Condensed Milk Jar.	20.00	Crushed Fruit Jar.	55.00
Cordial	20.00	Straw holder, glass lid . . .	65.00
Cracker Jar, cov	50.00	Spooner	15.00
Creamer		Sugar, cov	25.00
Individual.	15.00	Syrup	50.00
Regular	25.00	Toothpick	24.00
Cruet	35.00	Tumbler	
Crushed Fruit Bowl, cov,		Iced Tea	22.00
8½″	75.00	Water	20.00
Cup	8.00	Whiskey	12.00
Decanter, cut stopper	32.50	Wine	25.00
Finger Bowl, underplate	20.00		

BABY FACE

Non-flint made by George Duncan & Sons, c1870.

	Clear		Clear
Butter, cov	250.00	Goblet	100.00
Celery Vase	75.00	Pitcher, water	200.00
Compotes		Salt	50.00
Cov, hs, 5¼″	165.00	Spooner	95.00
Cov, hs, 8″.	250.00	Sugar, cov	195.00
Open, ls, 8″	85.00	Wine	160.00
Creamer	110.00		

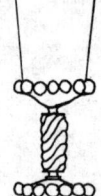

BALL AND SWIRL

Made by McKee Glass Co, Jeanette, PA, 1894.

	Clear		Clear
Butter, cov	35.00	Pitcher, water	40.00
Cake Stand	35.00	Sauce, ftd.	12.50
Compote, open, hs	30.00	Spooner	20.00
Creamer	20.00	Sugar, cov	20.00
Goblet	20.00	Syrup	40.00
Mug		Tumbler	15.00
Large	15.00	Wine	20.00
Small	10.00		

BALTIMORE PEAR (Gipsy)

Non-flint, originally made by Adams and Company, Pittsburgh, Pennsylvania, in 1874. Also made by U. S. Glass Company in 1890s. There are 18 different size compotes. Given as premiums by different manufacturers and organizations. Heavily reproduced. Reproduced in cobalt blue.

	Clear		Clear
Bowl		Pickle	20.00
6″	30.00	* Pitcher	
9″	35.00	Milk	80.00
Bread Plate, 12½″	70.00	Water	95.00
* Butter, cov	75.00	Plate	
* Cake Stand, 9″	65.00	8½″	30.00
* Celery Vase	50.00	10″	40.00
Compote		Relish	25.00
Cov, hs, 7″	80.00	* Sauce	
Cov, ls, 8½″	45.00	Flat	15.00
Open, hs	30.00	Footed	20.00
Open, jelly	28.50	Spooner	40.00
* Creamer	30.00	* Sugar, cov	50.00
* Goblet	35.00	Tray, 10½″	35.00

BANDED PORTLAND (Virginia #1, Maiden's Blush)

States pattern, originally named Virginia, by Portland Glass Co. Painted and fired green, yellow, blue, and possibly pink; ruby stained, and rose-flashed (which Lee notes is Maiden's Blush referring to the color, rather than the pattern, as Metz lists it). Double flashed refers to color above and below the band, single flashed refers to color above or below band only.

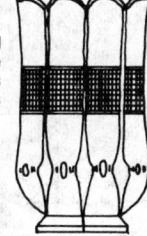

	Clear	Color Flashed	Maiden's Blush Pink
Bowl, 9″	30.00	—	40.00
Butter, cov	50.00	165.00	85.00
Cake Stand	55.00	—	90.00
Candlesticks, pr . . .	80.00	—	125.00
Carafe	80.00	—	90.00
Celery Tray	25.00	—	40.00
Celery Vase	35.00	—	45.00
Cologne Bottle	50.00	65.00	85.00
Compote			
Cov, hs, 7″	95.00	—	125.00
Cov, jelly, 6″	40.00	65.00	90.00
Creamer			
Individual, oval . . .	25.00	35.00	38.00
Regular, 6 oz. . . .	35.00	45.00	50.00
Cruet, os	60.00	90.00	125.00
Decanter, handled . .	50.00	—	100.00
Dresser Tray	50.00	—	65.00
Goblet	40.00	55.00	65.00
Lamp			
Flat	45.00	—	—
Tall	50.00	—	—
Nappy	15.00	55.00	65.00
Olive	18.00	—	35.00
Pin Tray	16.00	—	25.00

	Clear	Color Flashed	Maiden's Blush Pink
Pitcher,			
water, tankard . . .	75.00	90.00	250.00
Pomade Jar, cov . . .	35.00	45.00	65.00
Punch Bowl, hs. . . .	110.00	—	300.00
Punch Cup	20.00	—	30.00
Relish			
6½".	25.00	30.00	20.00
8¼".	20.00	35.00	40.00
Ring Holder, gold rim and post,			
scarce.	80.00	—	135.00
Salt & Pepper, pr. . .	45.00	75.00	75.00
Sardine Box	55.00	—	90.00
Sauce, round, flat,			
4 or 4½"	12.00	—	20.00
Spooner	28.00	—	45.00
Sugar			
Cov, large	45.00	75.00	75.00
Open, individual, oval.	20.00	—	35.00
Sugar Shaker, orig			
top	45.00	—	85.00
Syrup.	50.00	—	135.00
Toothpick	35.00	45.00	40.00
Tumbler	25.00	—	45.00
Vase			
6".	20.00	—	38.00
9".	35.00	—	50.00
Wine	35.00	—	75.00

BARBERRY (Berry)

Non-flint made by McKee Glass Co. and the Boston and Sandwich Glass Co. in the 1860s and 1880s. 6" plates are found in amber, canary, pale green, and pale blue; they are considered scarce. Also alleged to have been made at Iowa City. Pattern comes in "9 berry bunch" and "12 berry bunch" varieties.

	Clear			Clear
Bowl			Creamer.	30.00
6", oval	20.00		Cup Plate	15.00
7", oval	25.00		Egg Cup.	20.00
8", oval	28.00		Goblet	25.00
8", round, flat.	30.00		Pickle.	10.00
9", oval	32.00		Pitcher, water, ah	100.00
Butter			Plate, 6"	20.00
Cov.	50.00		Salt, master, ftd.	25.00
Cov, flange, pattern on			Sauce	
edge	100.00		Flat.	10.00
Cake Stand	150.00		Footed	15.00
Celery Vase	40.00		Spooner, ftd	30.00
Compote			Sugar, cov	45.00
Cov, hs, 8", shell finial . . .	85.00		Syrup.	150.00
Cov, ls, 8", shell finial	75.00		Tumbler, ftd	25.00
Open, hs, 8"	35.00		Wine	30.00

BARLEY

Non-flint, originally made by Campbell, Jones and Co., c1882, in clear; possibly by others in varied quality. Add 100% for color which is hard to find.

	Clear		Clear
Bowl		Pitcher, water	
8″, berry	15.00	Applied handle	95.00
10″, oval	20.00	Pressed handle	45.00
Bread Tray	30.00	Plate, 6″	35.00
Butter, cov	42.50	Platter, 13″ l, 8″ w	30.00
Cake Stand		Relish	
8″	28.00	Flat, 8″ l, 6″ w	18.00
10″	32.00	Wheelbarrow, 8″, pewter	
Celery Vase	25.00	wheels	75.00
Compote		Salt, master, wheelbarrow,	
Cov, hs, 6″	45.00	pewter wheels	75.00
Cov, hs, 8½″	60.00	Sauce	
Open, hs, 8½″	35.00	Flat	9.00
Cordial	50.00	Footed	12.00
Creamer	30.00	Spooner	21.50
Goblet	28.00	Sugar, cov	35.00
Honey, ftd, 3½″	8.00	Vegetable Dish, oval	15.00
Marmalade Jar	55.00	Wine	30.00
Pickle Castor, SP frame and			
tongs	85.00		

BASKETWEAVE

Non-flint, c1880. Some covered pieces have a stippled cat's head finial.

	Amber or Canary	Apple Green	Blue	Clear	Vaseline
Bowl	22.00	—	25.00	18.00	—
Bread Plate, handled, 11″	35.00	—	35.00	10.00	—
Butter, cov	35.00	60.00	40.00	30.00	40.00
Compote, cov, 7″	—	—	—	35.00	—
Cordial	25.00	40.00	28.00	20.00	30.00
Creamer	30.00	50.00	35.00	28.00	36.00
Cup & Saucer	35.00	60.00	35.00	30.00	38.00
Dish, oval	12.00	20.00	15.00	10.00	16.00
Egg Cup	18.00	30.00	20.00	15.00	25.00
* Goblet	28.00	50.00	35.00	20.00	30.00
Mug	25.00	40.00	25.00	15.00	30.00
Pickle	18.00	30.00	20.00	15.00	22.00
Pitcher					
Milk	40.00	60.00	45.00	35.00	50.00
* Water	60.00	75.00	80.00	45.00	65.00
Plate, 11″, handled	25.00	38.00	25.00	20.00	30.00
Sauce	10.00	10.00	12.00	8.00	12.00
Spooner	30.00	36.00	30.00	20.00	30.00
Sugar, cov	35.00	60.00	35.00	30.00	40.00
Syrup	50.00	75.00	50.00	45.00	55.00
* Tray, water, scenic center	35.00	45.00	40.00	30.00	55.00

	Amber or Canary	Apple Green	Blue	Clear	Vaseline
Tumbler, ftd	18.00	30.00	20.00	15.00	20.00
Waste Bowl.	20.00	36.00	25.00	18.00	25.00
Wine	30.00	50.00	30.00	25.00	30.00

BEADED ACORN MEDALLION (Beaded Acorn)

Made by the Boston Silver Glass Co., East Cambridge, Massachusetts, c1869.

	Clear		Clear
Butter, cov, acorn finial.	65.00	Plate, 6″	30.00
Champagne	65.00	Relish.	15.00
Compote, cov, hs	50.00	Salt, master	30.00
Creamer.	40.00	Sauce, flat	15.00
Egg Cup.	20.00	Spooner	25.00
Goblet	30.00	Sugar, cov	45.00
Pitcher, water	90.00	Wine	45.00

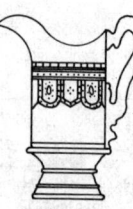

BEADED BAND

Attributed to Burlington Glass Co., Hamilton, Ontario, Canada, c1884. Limited production and scarce pattern. May have been made in light amber and other colors.

	Clear		Clear
Butter, cov	35.00	Relish	
Cake Stand, 7⅝″.	25.00	Double	30.00
Compote, cov		Single	15.00
hs, 8″	55.00	Sauce, ftd.	10.00
ls, 9″	50.00	Spooner	25.00
Creamer.	30.00	Sugar, cov	40.00
Goblet	25.00	Syrup	95.00
Pickle, cov	45.00	Wine	30.00
Pitcher, water, applied strap handle.	100.00		

BEADED GRAPE MEDALLION

Non-flint made by Boston Silver Glass Co., Cambridge, Massachusetts, c1868. Also found in flint; add 40%.

	Clear		Clear
Bowl, 7″	25.00	Cov, hs	75.00
Butter, cov, acorn finial.	45.00	Open, hs, 8″	35.00
Cake Stand, 11″	150.00	Creamer, ah	48.00
Celery Vase	50.00	Egg Cup.	30.00
Castor Set, 4 bottles	110.00	Goblet	
Compote		Buttermilk	30.00
Cov, collared base	80.00	Lady's.	30.00

	Clear		Clear
Honey Dish, 3½"	10.00	Salt	
Pitcher, water, ah	115.00	Individual, flat	20.00
Plate, 6"	30.00	Master, ftd	25.00
Relish		Spooner	30.00
Cov	140.00	Sugar, cov, acorn finial	60.00
Open, mkd "Mould Pat'd		Vegetable, cov, ftd	75.00
May 11, 1868	40.00	Wine	55.00

BEADED MIRROR (Beaded Medallion)

Flint pattern made by Boston Silver-Glass Co, Sandwich, Massachusetts, patented May 11, 1869. Finials are acorn shaped. Also found in non-flint. Values are about the same.

	Clear		Clear
Butter, cov	40.00	Goblet	25.00
Castor Bottle		Pitcher, water	85.00
Mustard	18.00	Plate, 6"	20.00
Oil	25.00	Relish	15.00
Set, 5 pcs, metal frame	100.00	Salt, ftd	15.00
Celery	35.00	Sauce, flat	8.00
Compote, cov, hs	50.00	Spooner	25.00
Creamer	40.00	Sugar, cov	45.00
Egg Cup	20.00		

BEADED SWIRL (Swirled Column)

Made by George Duncan & Sons, c1890. The dual names are for the two forms of the pattern. Beaded Swirl stands on flat bases and is solid in shape. Swirled Column stands on scrolled (sometimes gilded) feet, and the shape tapered towards the base. Some pieces trimmed in gold and also in milk white.

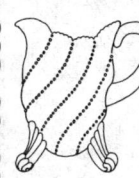

	Clear	Emerald Green		Clear	Emerald Green
Bowl			Goblet	35.00	40.00
Berry, 7"	10.00	20.00	Mug	10.00	12.00
Flat	15.00	25.00	Pitcher, water	40.00	85.00
Footed, oval	18.00	24.00	Sauce		
Footed, round	18.00	24.00	Flat	8.00	12.00
Butter, cov	35.00	45.00	Footed	10.00	14.00
Cake Stand	35.00	45.00	Spooner		
Celery Vase	30.00	55.00	Flat	25.00	40.00
Compote			Footed	30.00	45.00
Cov, hs	40.00	50.00	Sugar, cov		
Open, hs	35.00	45.00	Flat	35.00	45.00
Creamer			Footed	35.00	45.00
Flat	25.00	35.00	Sugar Shaker	35.00	60.00
Footed	30.00	40.00	Syrup	48.00	100.00
Dish	10.00	15.00	Tumbler	20.00	30.00
Egg Cup	14.00	15.00	Wine	25.00	35.00

BEADED TULIP (Andes)

Non-flint made by McKee Brothers, Pittsburgh, Pennsylvania, c1894.

	Clear	Emerald Green		Clear	Emerald Green
Bowl, 9½", oval....	20.00	—	Relish...........	20.00	—
Butter, cov	50.00	125.00	Sauce		
Cake Stand	50.00	—	Flat, leaf shape		
Compote, cov, hs ..	55.00	—	edges	10.00	—
Creamer.........	35.00	75.00	Footed	12.00	—
Goblet	35.00	—	Spooner........	30.00	—
Marmalade Jar	40.00	—	Sugar, cov	45.00	80.00
Pickle, oval.......	18.00	—	Tray		
Pitcher			Water	50.00	—
Milk...........	45.00	65.00	Wine...........	50.00	—
Water	65.00	—	Wine	30.00	—
Plate, 6".........	25.00				

BEATTY HONEYCOMB (Beatty Waffle)

Non-flint made by Beatty Glass Co., Tiffin, Ohio, c1888. Reproduced by Fenton Glass in green opalescent (basket, rose bowl, and vases) and milk glass.

	Blue Opal	White Opal		Blue Opal	White Opal
Bowl, berry	100.00	50.00	Pitcher, water	300.00	200.00
Butter, cov	120.00	100.00	Salt & Pepper, pr...	65.00	45.00
Celery Vase	85.00	45.00	Sauce	20.00	20.00
Creamer			Spooner.........	40.00	30.00
Individual........	35.00	20.00	Sugar, cov		
Regular.........	30.00	25.00	Individual.......	65.00	55.00
Cruet, os	235.00	175.00	Regular.........	70.00	65.00
Mug.............	35.00	25.00	Toothpick	50.00	45.00
Mustard	60.00	45.00	Tumbler	65.00	40.00

BEATTY SWIRLED OPALESCENT (Swirled Opal)

Made by Beatty and Sons Glass Co., Tiffin, Ohio, c1889.

	Blue Opal	Vaseline Opal	White Opal
Bowl, berry	80.00	85.00	70.00
Butter, cov	125.00	150.00	100.00
Celery Vase	50.00	55.00	45.00
Creamer.........	40.00	50.00	30.00
Cruet, os	120.00	—	—
Mug.............	35.00	40.00	30.00
Pitcher, water	150.00	165.00	125.00
Sauce	35.00	35.00	30.00
Spooner.........	50.00	55.00	40.00
Sugar, cov	55.00	100.00	50.00
Syrup...........	125.00	150.00	115.00
Toothpick	50.00	—	45.00
Tray, water	120.00	125.00	110.00
Tumbler	50.00	55.00	45.00

BEAUTIFUL LADY

Made by Bryce, Higbee and Co. in 1905.

	Clear		Clear
Banana stand, hs	30.00	Goblet	35.00
Bowl		Pitcher, water	45.00
8", low collared base	15.00	Plate	
9", flat	18.00	7", sq	15.00
Bread Plate	15.00	8"	18.00
Cake Plate, 9"	25.00	9"	25.00
Cake Stand, hs	35.00	11"	27.50
Compote		Salt and Pepper, pr	60.00
Cov, hs	35.00	Spooner	15.00
Open, hs	25.00	Sugar, cov	25.00
Open, jelly	15.00	Tumbler	15.00
Creamer	25.00	Vase, 6½"	15.00
Cruet	30.00	Wine	20.00

BELLFLOWER

A fine flint glass pattern first made in the 1830s and attributed to Boston and Sandwich. Later produced by McKee Glass Co. and other firms for many years. There are many variations of this pattern - single vine and double vine, fine and coarse rib, knob and plain stems, and rayed and plain bases. Type and quality must be considered when evaluating. Very rare in color. Prices are for high quality flint. Reproductions have been made by the Metropolitan Museum of Art. Abbreviations: DV - double vine; SV - single vine; FR - fine rib; CR - coarse rib.

	Clear		Clear
Bowl		Quart	
6" d, 1¾" h, SV	75.00	DV-FR, orig patterned	
8", all types	75.00	stopper	275.00
Butter, cov, SV-FR	100.00	SV-FR, bar top	185.00
Castor Set, 5 bottle, pewter		Dish, SV-FR, 8", round, flat,	
stand	225.00	scalloped top	65.00
Celery Vase, SV-FR	165.00	Egg Cup	
Champagne		CR	35.00
DV-FR, cut bellflowers	225.00	SV-FR	40.00
SV-FR, knob stem, rayed		Goblet	
base, barrel shape	100.00	DV-FR, cut bellflowers	230.00
Compote		SV-CR, barrel shape	45.00
Cov, hs, 8" d, SV-FR	375.00	SV-CR, straight sides	40.00
Cov, ls, 7" d, SV	200.00	SV-FR, knob stem, barrel	
Cov, ls, 8" d, SV	225.00	shape	55.00
Open, hs, 8", SV	225.00	* SV-FR, plain stem, rayed	
Open, ls, 7", DV-FR, scal-		base, barrel shape	30.00
loped top	100.00	Hat, SV-FR, made from tum-	
Open, ls, 7", SV	100.00	bler mold, rare	350.00
Open, ls, 8", SV	100.00	Honey Dish, SV-FR, 3"	35.00
Open, ls, 9", SV-CR	125.00	Lamp, whale oil, SV-FR,	
Cordial, SV-FR, knob stem,		brass stem, marble base	175.00
rayed base, barrel shape	115.00	Mug, SV-FR	250.00
Creamer, DV-FR	135.00	Pitcher	
Creamer, SV-FR	135.00	Milk, DV-FR	500.00
Decanter		Milk, DV, pint	175.00
Pint, DV-FR, bar top	225.00	Milk, SV-CR, quart	175.00

	Clear			Clear
Water, DV-CR	350.00	Syrup, ah		
* Water, SV-FR	250.00	Ftd, 10 sides		750.00
Plate, 6", SV-FR	125.00	SV-FR.		550.00
Salt, master		Tumbler		
SV-FR, ftd	75.00	DV-CR		95.00
DV-FR	35.00	SV-FR, ftd		90.00
Sauce, flat, SV-FR	15.00	* SV-FR, cut bellflowers		250.00
Spooner		Whiskey, 3½", SV-FR		135.00
DV	45.00	Wine		
SV-FR.	35.00	DV-FR, cut bellflowers,		
Sugar		barrel shape		250.00
Cov, DV	100.00	SV-FR, knob stem, rayed		
Cov, SV-CR.	95.00	base, barrel shape.		90.00
Open, DV-CR	45.00	SV-FR, plain stem, rayed		
Sweetmeat, cov, hs, 6", SV	300.00	base, straight sides		75.00

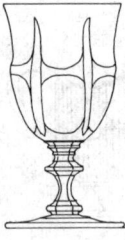

BIGLER

Flint, made by Boston and Sandwich Glass Co. and by other early factories. A scarce pattern in which goblets are most common and vary in height, shape and flare. Rare in color.

	Clear		Clear
Ale Glass	65.00	Goblet	
Bar Bottle, qt	80.00	Regular	45.00
Bowl, 10" d	40.00	Short Stem	50.00
Butter, cov	125.00	Lamp, whale oil, monument	
Celery Vase	100.00	base	155.00
Champagne	95.00	Mug, applied handle	60.00
Compote, 7"	40.00	Plate, 6"	32.00
Cordial	65.00	Salt, master	20.00
Creamer	75.00	Tumbler, water	65.00
Cup Plate	30.00	Whiskey, handled	100.00
Egg Cup, double	50.00	Wine	65.00

BIRD AND STRAWBERRY (Bluebird)

Non-flint, c1890. Made by Beatty and Indiana Glass Co., Dunkirk, IN. Pieces occasionally highlighted by the coloring of birds blue, strawberries pink, and leaves green, plus the addition of gilding.

	Clear	Colors		Clear	Colors
Bowl			Cup	25.00	35.00
5"	25.00	45.00	Goblet	200.00	350.00+
9½", ftd	50.00	85.00	Nappy	40.00	65.00
10½"	55.00	95.00	Pitcher, water	235.00	350.00
Butter, cov	100.00	200.00	Plate, 12"	125.00	175.00
Cake Stand	65.00	125.00	Punch Cup	25.00	35.00
Celery Vase	45.00	85.00	Relish	20.00	45.00
Compote			Spooner	50.00	120.00
Cov, hs	125.00	200.00	Sugar, cov	65.00	125.00
Open, ls, ruffled	65.00	125.00	Tumbler	45.00	75.00
Jelly, cov, hs	150.00	225.00	Wine	70.00	100.00
Creamer	55.00	135.00			

BLEEDING HEART

Non-flint, originally made by King & Son, Pittsburgh, PA, c1870, and by U. S. Glass Co., c1898. Also found in milk glass. Goblets are found in six variations. Note: A goblet with a tin lid, containing a condiment (mustard, jelly, or baking powder) was made. It is of inferior quality compared to the original goblet.

	Clear			Clear
Bowl		Dish, cov, 7″		55.00
7¼″, oval.	30.00	Egg Cup.		45.00
8″	35.00	Egg Rack, cov, 3 eggs.		350.00
9¼″, oval, cov	65.00	Goblet, knob stem.		35.00
Butter, cov	75.00	Honey Dish.		15.00
Cake Stand		Mug, 3¼″		40.00
9″	60.00	Pickle, 8¾″ l, 5″ w, pear		
10″	85.00	shape		35.00
11″	90.00	Pitcher, water, ah		150.00
Dessert slots	125.00	Plate		75.00
Compote		Platter, oval.		65.00
Cov, hs, 8″.	75.00	Relish, oval, 5½ x 3⅝″.		35.00
Cov, hs, 9″.	95.00	Salt, master, ftd.		60.00
Cov, ls, 7″	60.00	Salt, oval, flat		20.00
Cov, ls, 7½″.	60.00	Sauce, flat		15.00
Cov, ls, 8″	75.00	Spooner		30.00
Open, ls, 8½″	30.00	Sugar, cov		60.00
Creamer		Tumbler, ftd		80.00
Applied Handle	60.00	Wine		165.00
Molded Handle	35.00			

BLOCK AND FAN

Non-flint made by Richard and Hartley Glass Co., Tarentum, PA, late 1880s. Continued by U. S. Glass Co. after 1891.

	Clear	Ruby Stained		Clear	Ruby Stained
Biscuit Jar, cov	65.00	150.00	pepper & cruet on		
Bowl			tray.	75.00	—
4″, flat.	15.00	—	Creamer		
8″, flat.	25.00	—	Individual.	—	35.00
8″, ftd	20.00	—	Regular.	25.00	45.00
9½″.	30.00	—	Large	30.00	100.00
10 x 6″, rect.	50.00	—	Small	35.00	75.00
Butter, cov	50.00	85.00	Cruet, os	40.00	—
Cake Stand			Dish, large, rect. . . .	25.00	—
9″	35.00	—	Finger Bowl	55.00	—
10″	42.00	—	Goblet	48.00	120.00
Carafe	50.00	95.00	Ice Tub.	45.00	50.00
Celery Tray.	30.00	—	Orange Bowl.	50.00	—
Celery Vase	35.00	75.00	Pickle Dish	20.00	—
Compote			Pitcher		
Open, hs, 8″	40.00	165.00	Milk.	35.00	—
Open, ls, 4″.	10.00	—	Water	48.00	125.00
Open, ls, 7″.	25.00	—	Plate		
Open, ls, 8″.	30.00	—	6″	20.00	—
Condiment Set, salt,			10″	22.00	—

	Clear	Ruby Stained		Clear	Ruby Stained
Relish, rect	25.00	—	Sugar Shaker	40.00	—
Rose Bowl	25.00	—	Syrup	75.00	95.00
Salt & Pepper	30.00	—	Tray, Ice Cream, rect	75.00	—
Sauce			Tumbler	30.00	40.00
Flat, 5	8.00	—	Waste Bowl	30.00	—
Ftd, 3¾″	12.00	25.00	Wine	45.00	80.00
Spooner	25.00	—			
Sugar, cov	50.00	—			

BOSWORTH (Star Band)

Non-flint, Indiana Glass Co., c1907.

	Clear		Clear
Bowl, berry	12.00	Pitcher, water	35.00
Butter, cov	25.00	Relish	10.00
Celery Vase, handles	20.00	Spooner	15.00
Compote, jelly	15.00	Sugar, cov	30.00
Creamer	20.00	Tumbler	15.00
Goblet	25.00	Wine	20.00

BOUQUET

(Narcissus Spray) Made by Indiana Glass Company, c1918. Flowers and leaves are found with cranberry or amethyst flashing. Prices are for clear, flashed pieces would be approximately 20% higher.

	Clear		Clear
Bowl, berry		Nappy	15.00
6″, ind	12.00	Pitcher, water	40.00
8″, master	18.00	Sauce	5.00
Butter, cov	40.00	Spooner	20.00
Cake Plate	25.00	Sugar, cov	35.00
Creamer	25.00	Tumbler	15.00
Goblet	25.00	Water Tray	25.00

BOW TIE

Non-flint made by Thompson Glass Co., Uniontown, PA, c1889.

	Clear		Clear
Bowl		Compote, open	
7″	30.00	hs, 5½″	60.00
8″	40.00	hs, 9¼″	65.00
10¼ d, 5″ h	65.00	ls, 6½″	45.00
Butter, cov	72.50	ls, 8″	55.00
Butter Pat	30.00	Creamer	60.00
Cake Stand, large, 9″ d	60.00	Goblet	60.00

	Clear			Clear
Honey, cov	55.00		Relish, rect	25.00
Marmalade Jar	65.00		Salt	
Orange Bowl, ftd, hs, 10"	75.00		Individual	25.00
Pitcher			Master	40.00
Milk			Salt Shaker	65.00
5½"	45.00		Sauce, flat	18.00
8"	80.00		Spooner	35.00
9"	90.00		Sugar, cov	65.00
Water	75.00		Tumbler	50.00
Punch Bowl	100.00			

BROKEN COLUMN (Irish Column, Notched Rib, Rattan)

Made in Findlay, Ohio, c1891, by Columbia Glass Co., c1892, and later made by U. S. Glass Co. May also have been made at Portland, ME. Notches may be ruby stained. A cobalt blue cup is known. The square covered compote has been reproduced. Some items have been reproduced for the Metropolitan Museum of Art. Some items are reproduced by the Smithsonian Institution with a raised "SI" trademark.

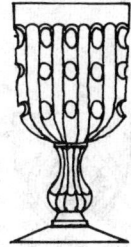

	Clear	Ruby Stained		Clear	Ruby Stained
Banana Stand	110.00	—	Creamer	42.50	125.00
Basket, applied han-			Cruet, os	85.00	150.00
dle, 12" h, 15" l	125.00	—	Decanter	85.00	—
Biscuit Jar	85.00	165.00	Finger Bowl	30.00	—
Bowl			* Goblet	50.00	100.00
4", berry	15.00	20.00	Marmalade Jar	85.00	—
6", berry	20.00	45.00	Pickle Castor, sp		
8"	35.00	—	frame	150.00	450.00
9"	40.00	—	Pitcher, water	90.00	230.00
Bread Plate	60.00	125.00	Plate		
Butter, cov	85.00	175.00	4"	25.00	40.00
Cake Stand			5"	35.00	—
9"	70.00	225.00	7½"	40.00	95.00
10"	80.00	245.00	Punch Cap	15.00	—
Carafe, water	75.00	150.00	Relish		
Celery Tray, oval	35.00	85.00	Oval, 7½ x 4"	20.00	—
Celery Vase	50.00	135.00	Oval, 11 x 5"	22.00	—
Champagne	100.00	—	Rect, 7½ x 5"	25.00	—
Claret	75.00	—	Salt Shaker	45.00	65.00
Compote			* Sauce, flat	15.00	32.00
Cov, hs, 5¼" d,			* Spooner	35.00	85.00
10¼" h	90.00	200.00	Sugar, cov	70.00	135.00
Cov, hs, 7" d,			Sugar Shaker	85.00	200.00
12"h	85.00	—	Syrup	130.00	400.00
Cov, hs, 10"	110.00	350.00	Tumbler	40.00	50.00
Open, hs, 7" d	—	150.00	Vegetable, cov	90.00	—
Open, hs, 8" d	75.00	175.00	Wine	80.00	125.00
Open, ls, 5" d, 6"					
h, flared	65.00	135.00			

BUCKLE

Flint and non-flint pattern. Sandwich Glass Co. in Massachusetts is attributed to the flint production. The non-flint production was made by Gillinder and Sons in Philadelphia, PA, in the late 1870s.

	Flint	Non-Flint		Flint	Non-Flint
Bowl			Creamer, ah	110.00	40.00
8", berry, orig had			Egg Cup	38.00	28.00
wire basket			Goblet	40.00	25.00
frame	60.00	50.00	Pickle	40.00	15.00
10"	60.00	50.00	Pitcher, water, ah	500.00	85.00
Butter, cov	65.00	60.00	Salt, flat, oval	30.00	15.00
Cake Stand, 9¾"	—	30.00	Salt, footed	20.00	18.00
Champagne	60.00	—	Sauce, flat	10.00	8.00
Compote			Spooner	35.00	27.50
Cov, hs, 6" d	95.00	40.00	Sugar, cov	75.00	55.00
Open, hs, 8½",			Tumbler	55.00	30.00
fluted	45.00	40.00	Wine	75.00	32.00
Open, ls	40.00	35.00			

BUCKLE WITH STAR (Orient)

Non-flint made by Bryce, Walker and Co. in 1875, U. S. Glass Co. in 1891. Finials are shaped like Maltese crosses.

	Clear		Clear
Bowl		Relish	15.00
6", cov	25.00	Salt, master, ftd	20.00
7", oval	15.00	Sauce	
8", oval	15.00	Flat	8.00
9", oval	15.00	Footed	10.00
10", oval	18.00	Spill holder	55.00
Butter, cov	40.00	Spooner	25.00
Cake Stand, 9"	35.00	Sugar	
Celery Vase	30.00	Cov	45.00
Compote		Open	25.00
Cov, hs, 7"	60.00	Syrup	
Open, hs, 9½"	30.00	Applied handle, pewter or	
Creamer	35.00	Brittania top, man's head	
Goblet	30.00	finial	80.00
Mug	60.00	Molded handle, plain tin	
Mustard, cov	75.00	top	60.00
Pickle	15.00	Tumbler	55.00
Pitcher, water, applied		Wine	35.00
handle	70.00		

BUDDED IVY

Non-flint, c1870. Contemporary of Stippled Ivy. Pieces have applied handles and ivy leaf finials.

	Clear		Clear
Butter, cov	45.00	Pitcher, water	50.00
Compote		Relish	15.00
Cov, hs	60.00	Salt, ftd	25.00
Cov, ls	45.00	Sauce, ftd	7.50
Open, hs	25.00	Spooner	24.00
Creamer	30.00	Sugar, cov	45.00
Egg Cup	25.00	Syrup	85.00
Goblet	30.00	Wine	35.00

BULLET EMBLEM (Shield In Red, White And Blue)

Made by U. S. Glass Co., c1898. Made to commemorate the Spanish-American War.

	Clear		Clear
Butter, cov	265.00	Spooner	125.00
Creamer	150.00	Sugar, cov	250.00
Goblet	125.00		

BULL'S EYE

Flint made by the New England Glass Co. in the 1850s. Also found in colors and milk glass, which doubles the price.

	Clear		Clear
Bitters Bottle	80.00	Lamp	100.00
Butter, cov	150.00	Mug, 3½", applied handle	110.00
Carafe	45.00	Pitcher, water	285.00
Castor Bottle	35.00	Relish, oval	25.00
Celery Vase	85.00	Salt	
Champagne	95.00	Individual	38.50
Cologne Bottle	85.00	Master, ftd	100.00
Cordial	75.00	Spill holder	85.00
Creamer, ah	125.00	Spooner	40.00
Cruet, os	125.00	Sugar, cov	125.00
Decanter, qt, bar lip	120.00	Tumbler	85.00
Egg Cup		Water Bottle, tumble up	125.00
Cov	165.00	Whiskey	70.00
Open	48.00	Wine	50.00
Goblet	65.00		

BULL'S EYE AND DAISY

Made by U. S. Glass Co., 1909. Also made with amethyst, blue, green, and pink stains in eyes.

	Clear	Emerald Green	Ruby Stained
Bowl	12.00	16.00	30.00
Butter, cov	25.00	28.00	90.00

	Clear	Emerald Green	Ruby Stained
Celery Vase	18.00	25.00	40.00
Creamer.	25.00	28.00	50.00
Decanter	—	110.00	—
Goblet	25.00	28.00	50.00
Pitcher, water	35.00	40.00	95.00
Salt Shaker.	20.00	20.00	35.00
Sauce	7.50	10.00	20.00
Spooner	20.00	25.00	40.00
Sugar, open	22.00	30.00	45.00
Tumbler	15.00	18.00	35.00
Wine	15.00	25.00	40.00

BULL'S EYE AND FAN (Daisies in Oval Panels)

Made by U.S. Glass, c1910. Also made in blue; prices same as emerald green.

	Amethyst Stain	Clear	Emerald Green	Pink Stain	Sapphire Blue Stain
Bowl					
5", pinched ends .	—	—	18.00	—	—
8", berry	—	15.00	20.00	—	30.00
Butter, cov	—	45.00	65.00	—	—
Cake Stand	—	25.00	—	—	—
Creamer					
Individual.	—	10.00	—	—	—
Regular.	—	25.00	30.00	—	35.00
Custard Cup	—	10.00	—	—	—
Goblet	25.00	22.50	45.00	25.00	45.00
Lemonade Mug. 5" .	—	20.00	—	—	—
Pitcher					
Lemonade, ftd . . .	—	55.00	—	—	—
Water, tankard . . .	55.00	40.00	100.00	50.00	100.00
Relish.	20.00	15.00	35.00	20.00	35.00
Sauce	25.00	10.00	20.00	25.00	30.00
Spooner	25.00	21.50	45.00	25.00	45.00
Sugar, cov	40.00	35.00	60.00	30.00	35.00
Toothpick	—	35.00	40.00	65.00	—
Tumbler	55.00	15.00	45.00	40.00	35.00
Wine	22.00	20.00	40.00	40.00	25.00

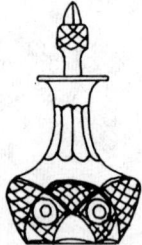

BULL'S EYE WITH DIAMOND POINT (Union)

Made in flint by New England Glass Co., c1869.

	Clear		Clear
Butter, cov	250.00	Egg Cup.	90.00
Celery Vase	150.00	Goblet	110.00
Champagne	145.00	Honey Dish, flat	25.00
Cologne Bottle, os.	90.00	Lamp, finger, ah	165.00
Creamer.	200.00	Pitcher, water, 10¼",	
Cruet, os	225.00	tankard	275.00
Decanter, qt, os.	200.00	Salt, master, cov	100.00

	Clear		Clear
Sauce	20.00	Tumbler	145.00
Spill	75.00	Tumble-Up	165.00
Spooner	125.00	Whiskey	150.00
Sugar, cov	175.00	Wine	135.00
Syrup	175.00		

BULL'S EYE WITH FLEUR-DE-LIS

Flint, c1850.

	Clear		Clear
Ale Glass	250.00	Lamp, marble base	175.00
Bar Bottle, qt	110.00	Mug, handle	100.00
Bowl, fruit	85.00	Pitcher, water	400.00
Butter, cov	175.00	Salt, master	55.00
Celery Vase	95.00	Spooner	50.00
Creamer	250.00	Sugar, cov	115.00
Egg Cup	50.00	Wine	90.00
Goblet	85.00		

BUTTERFLY & FAN (Grace, Japanese)

Non-flint pattern made by Duncan, Pittsburgh, PA, c1880.

	Clear		Clear
Bread Plate	80.00	Creamer, ftd	45.00
Butter, cov		Goblet	50.00
Flat	100.00	Marmalade Jar	75.00
Footed	75.00	Pitcher, water	115.00
Celery Vase	75.00	Sauce, ftd	15.00
Compote		Spooner	30.00
Cov, hs, 8" d	95.00	Sugar, ftd	
Cov, hs, 7" d	95.00	Covered	65.00
Open, hs	30.00	Open	30.00

BUTTON ARCHES

Non-flint, made by Duncan and Miller Glass Co. in 1885. Pieces have frosted band. Some pieces, known as "Koral," usually souvenir type, are also seen in clambroth, trimmed in gold. The toothpick holder comes in both a smooth scallop and beaded scallop variety. They have the same value. In the early 1970s souvenir ruby stained pieces, including a goblet and table set, were reproduced.

	Clambroth	Clear	Ruby Stained
Bowl, 8"	—	20.00	50.00
Butter, cov	—	48.00	100.00
Cake Stand, 9"	—	35.00	180.00
Compote, jelly	—	48.00	50.00
Creamer	25.00	20.00	45.00
Cruet, os	—	55.00	175.00

	Clambroth	Clear	Ruby Stained
* Goblet	40.00	25.00	40.00
Mug	30.00	25.00	30.00
Mustard, cov, underplate	—	—	100.00
Pitcher			
Milk	—	35.00	100.00
Water, tankard . . .	—	75.00	125.00
Plate, 7″	—	10.00	25.00
Punch Cup	—	15.00	25.00
Salt, ind	—	15.00	—
Salt Shaker, three types	—	15.00	30.00
Sauce, flat	—	8.00	22.00
Spooner	—	25.00	40.00
Sugar, cov	—	35.00	75.00
Syrup	—	75.00	175.00
Toothpick	30.00	20.00	35.00
Tumbler	20.00	24.00	35.00
Wine	25.00	15.00	35.00

BUTTON BAND (Umbilicated Hobnail, Wyandotte)

Non-flint made by Ripley and Co. in 1880s and U. S. Glass Co. in 1890s. Can often be found engraved, priced the same.

	Clear		Clear
Bowl, 10″	30.00	Goblet	40.00
Butter, cov	45.00	Pitcher	
Cake Stand, 10″	70.00	Milk	40.00
Castor Set, 5 bottles in glass stand	135.00	Water, tankard	50.00
Compote		Spooner	28.00
Cov, hs, 9″	120.00	Sugar, cov	35.00
Open, ls	65.00	Tray, water	40.00
Cordial	35.00	Tumbler	25.00
Creamer	30.00	Wine	35.00

CABBAGE ROSE

Non-flint made by Central Glass Co, Wheeling, WV, c1870. Reproduced in colors.

	Clear		Clear
Basket, handled, 12″	125.00	Cake Stand	
Bitters Bottle, 6½″ h	125.00	11″	40.00
Bowl, Oval		12½″	50.00
7½″	32.50	Celery Vase	48.00
8½″	38.00	Champagne	50.00
9½″	40.00	Compote	
Bowl, Round		Cov, hs, 7½″	110.00
6″	25.00	Cov, hs, 8½″	120.00
7½″, cov	65.00	Cov, ls, 6″	95.00
7½″, open	35.00	Cov, ls, 7½″	100.00
Butter, cov	60.00	Cov, ls, 8½″	110.00

	Clear
Open, hs, 7½"	75.00
Open, hs, 9½"	100.00
Creamer, applied handle	55.00
Egg Cup	45.00
* Goblet	42.50
Mug	60.00
Pitcher	
Milk	150.00
Water	125.00

	Clear
Relish, 8½" l, 5" w, rose-filled	
horn of plenty center	38.00
Salt, master, ftd	25.00
Sauces, six sizes	10–20.00
Spooner	25.00
Sugar, cov	55.00
Tumbler	40.00
Wine	40.00

CABLE

Flint, c1850. Made by Boston and Sandwich Glass Co. to commemorate the laying of Atlantic Cable. Also found with amber stained panels and in opaque colors (rare).

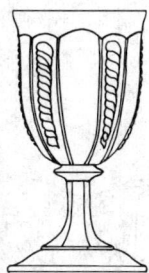

	Clear
Bowl	
8", ftd	45.00
9"	70.00
Butter, cov	100.00
Cake Stand, 9"	100.00
Celery Vase	75.00
Champagne	250.00
Compote, open	
hs, 5½"	65.00
ls, 7"	50.00
ls, 9"	55.00
ls, 11"	75.00
Creamer	400.00
Decanter, qt, ground stopper	295.00
Egg Cup	
Cov	225.00
Open	60.00

	Clear
Goblet	75.00
Honey Dish	15.00
Lamp, 8¾"	
Glass Base	135.00
Marble Base	100.00
Pitcher, water, rare	500.00
Plate, 6"	75.00
Salt, ind, flat	35.00
Sauce, flat	20.00
Spooner	40.00
Sugar, cov	120.00
Syrup	225.00
Tumbler, ftd	200.00
Wine	175.00

CADMUS

Non-flint made by Beaumont Glass Co., Grafton, WV, in mid-1880s.

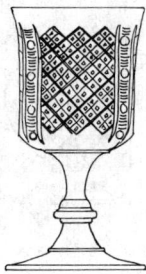

	Clear
Bowl	15.00
Butter, cov	35.00
Compote, open	
High std	25.00
Jelly	20.00
Creamer	25.00

	Clear
Goblet	20.00
Sauce	8.00
Spooner	15.00
Sugar, cov	25.00
Tumbler	20.00
Wine	18.00

CALIFORNIA (Beaded Grape)

Non-flint made by U. S. Glass Co., Pittsburgh, PA, c1890. Also with gold trim. Many pieces reproduced.

	Clear	Emerald Green		Clear	Emerald Green
Bowl			Cruet, orig swirled		
5½", sq	17.50	20.00	stopper	65.00	125.00
5½ x 8"	—	30.00	* Goblet	35.00	50.00
6" sq	—	25.00	Olive, handle	20.00	35.00
7½", sq	25.00	35.00	Pickle	20.00	30.00
8", round	28.00	35.00	Pitcher		
Bread Plate, 10¼ x			Milk	75.00	—
7¼"	25.00	45.00	Water	85.00	120.00
Butter, cov	65.00	85.00	* Plate, 8¼", sq	28.00	40.00
Cake Stand, 9"	65.00	85.00	Salt & Pepper	45.00	65.00
Celery Tray	30.00	45.00	* Sauce, 4"	15.00	18.00
Celery Vase	40.00	60.00	Spooner	35.00	45.00
Compote			Sugar, cov	45.00	55.00
Cov, hs, 6½"	65.00	95.00	Sugar Shaker	75.00	85.00
Open, hs, 5", sq.	55.00	75.00	Toothpick	35.00	65.00
Open, hs, 7"	45.00	80.00	* Tumbler	32.50	45.00
Open, hs, jelly	55.00	75.00	* Wine	35.00	65.00
Creamer	40.00	50.00			

CANADIAN

Non-flint, made by Burlington Glass Works, Hamilton, Ontario, Canada, c1870.

	Clear		Clear
Bowl, 7" d, 4½" h, ftd	65.00	Goblet	45.00
Bread Plate, 10"	45.00	Mug, small	45.00
Butter, cov	85.00	Pitcher	
Cake Stand, 9¼"	85.00	Milk	90.00
Celery Vase	65.00	Water	125.00
Compote		Plate, 6", handles	32.50
Cov, hs, 6"	90.00	Sauce	
Cov, hs, 7"	100.00	Flat	15.00
Cov, hs, 8"	110.00	Footed	20.00
Cov, ls, 6"	50.00	Spooner	45.00
Open, ls, 7"	35.00	Sugar, cov	90.00
Creamer	65.00	Wine	45.00

CANE

Non-flint made by Gillinder Glass Co. and McKee Glass Co., c1885. Goblets and toddy plates with inverted "buttons" known.

	Amber	Apple Green	Blue	Clear	Vaseline
Bowl, 9½", oval	15.00	—	—	—	—
Butter, cov	45.00	60.00	75.00	40.00	60.00
Celery Vase	38.00	40.00	50.00	32.50	40.00
Compote, open, ls, 5¾"	28.00	30.00	35.00	25.00	35.00
Cordial	—	—	—	25.00	—
Creamer	35.00	40.00	50.00	25.00	30.00
Finger Bowl	20.00	30.00	35.00	15.00	30.00
Goblet	25.00	40.00	35.00	20.00	37.50

	Amber	Apple Green	Blue	Clear	Vaseline
Honey Dish.	—	—	—	15.00	—
Match holder, kettle .	18.00	—	35.00	30.00	35.00
Pickle	25.00	20.00	25.00	15.00	20.00
Pitcher, milk	60.00	55.00	65.00	40.00	55.00
Pitcher, water	60.00	75.00	65.00	40.00	55.00
Plate, toddy, 4½" . . .	20.00	25.00	30.00	16.50	20.00
Salt & Pepper	60.00	50.00	80.00	30.00	70.00
Sauce, flat	—	9.50	—	7.00	—
Slipper	30.00	—	25.00	15.00	30.00
Spooner	42.00	35.00	30.00	20.00	30.00
Sugar, cov	45.00	45.00	45.00	25.00	45.00
Tray, water	35.00	40.00	50.00	30.00	45.00
Tumbler	24.00	30.00	35.00	20.00	25.00
Waste Bowl, 7½" . . .	32.50	30.00	35.00	20.00	30.00
Wine	35.00	40.00	35.00	20.00	35.00

CAPE COD

Non-flint, attributed to Boston and Sandwich Glass Co., c1870.

	Clear		Clear
Bowl, 6", handled	30.00	Marmalade Jar, cov	85.00
Bread Plate	45.00	Pitcher	
Butter, cov	65.00	Milk.	65.00
Celery Vase	45.00	Water	90.00
Compote		Plate	
Cov, hs, 6" d	50.00	5", handles	30.00
Cov, hs, 8"	100.00	10"	45.00
Cov, hs, 12"	175.00	Platter, open handles.	45.00
Cov, ls, 6"	50.00	Sauce, ftd.	17.50
Open, hs, 7"	50.00	Spooner	35.00
Creamer	45.00	Sugar, cov	55.00
Decanter	160.00	Wine	35.00
Goblet	45.00		

CARDINAL

Non-flint, c1875, attributed to Ohio Flint Glass Co., Lancaster, OH. There were two butter dishes made, one in the regular pattern and one with three birds in the base - labeled in script Red Bird (cardinal), Pewit, and Titmouse. The latter is less common. Goblet and creamer reproduced.

	Clear		Clear
Butter, cov		Pitcher, water	150.00
Regular	65.00	Sauce	
Three birds in base	100.00	Flat, 4"	10.00
Cake Stand	75.00	Footed, 4½" or 5½"	15.00
* Creamer	35.00	Spooner	35.00
* Goblet	30.00	Sugar, cov	60.00
Honey Dish, 3½"			
Cov.	45.00		
Open	20.00		

CAROLINA (Inverness)

Made by Bryce Brothers and later by U. S. Glass Co., as part of the States series, c1903. Ruby stained pieces often are souvenir marked. Some clear pieces found with gilt or purple stain.

	Clear	Ruby Stained		Clear	Ruby Stained
Bowl, berry	15.00	—	Pitcher, milk	45.00	—
Butter, cov	35.00	—	Plate, 7½".	10.00	—
Cake Stand	35.00	—	Relish.	10.00	—
Compote			Salt Shaker.	15.00	35.00
Open, hs, 8", beaded	35.00	—	Sauce		
Open, hs, 9½"	20.00	—	Flat.	8.00	—
Open, jelly	10.00	—	Footed	10.00	—
Creamer	20.00	—	Spooner	20.00	—
Goblet	25.00	45.00	Sugar, cov	25.00	—
Mug	20.00	35.00	Tumbler	10.00	—
			Wine	20.00	35.00

CATHEDRAL (Orion)

Non-flint pattern made by Bryce Bros., Pittsburgh, PA., in the 1880s and by U. S. Glass Co. in 1891. Also found in ruby stained, add 50% to clear prices.

	Amber	Amethyst	Blue	Clear	Vaseline
Bowl, berry, 8"	48.00	60.00	50.00	25.00	42.50
Butter, cov	60.00	110.00	62.00	45.00	60.00
Cake Stand	50.00	75.00	60.00	40.00	68.00
Celery Vase	35.00	60.00	40.00	30.00	38.00
Compote					
Cov, hs, 8"	80.00	125.00	100.00	70.00	90.00
Open, hs, 9½"	50.00	85.00	65.00	55.00	—
Open, ls, 7"	45.00	80.00	35.00	25.00	48.00
Open, jelly	—	—	—	25.00	—
Creamer					
Flat, sq	50.00	82.00	—	35.00	48.00
Tall	45.00	80.00	50.00	30.00	45.00
Cruet, os	80.00	—	—	45.00	—
Goblet	48.00	70.00	50.00	40.00	60.00
Lamp, 12¾" h	—	—	185.00	—	—
Pitcher, water	75.00	110.00	75.00	60.00	100.00
Relish, fish shape	40.00	50.00	50.00	—	45.00
Salt, boat shape	20.00	30.00	24.00	15.00	24.00
Sauce					
Flat	16.00	30.00	20.00	12.00	16.00
Footed	18.00	35.00	22.00	15.00	20.00
Spooner	40.00	65.00	50.00	35.00	45.00
Sugar, cov	70.00	100.00	60.00	50.00	60.00
Tumbler	32.50	40.00	35.00	25.00	40.00
Wine	40.00	60.00	55.00	28.00	50.00

CHAIN WITH STAR

Non-flint, made by Portland Glass Co, Portland, ME, and U. S. Glass Co., c1890.

	Clear		Clear
Bread Plate, 11", handles ..	30.00	Pickle, oval............	12.50
Butter, cov	35.00	Pitcher, water	55.00
Cake Stand		Plate, 7"..............	25.00
8¾"..................	30.00	Relish...............	10.00
10½"................	35.00	Salt Shaker............	25.00
Compote		Sauce	
Cov, hs	55.00	Flat.................	10.00
Cov, ls..............	45.00	Footed	12.00
Open, hs.............	30.00	Spooner..............	24.00
Open, ls	30.00	Sugar, cov	35.00
Creamer...............	25.00	Syrup................	45.00
Goblet	25.00	Wine	25.00

CHANDELIER (Crown Jewel)

Non-flint, O'Hara Glass Co., Pittsburgh, PA, c1880, continued by U. S. Glass Co. Also attributed to Canadian manufacturer. Sauce bowls made in amber, $35.00.

	Etched	Plain		Etched	Plain
Banana Stand.....	—	100.00	Pitcher, water	125.00	115.00
Bowl, 8" d, 3¼" h ..	35.00	37.50	Salt, Master	—	40.00
Butter, cov	85.00	65.00	Salt & Pepper.....	75.00	65.00
Cake Stand, 10" ...	85.00	65.00	Sauce, flat	—	15.00
Celery Vase	40.00	40.00	Sponge Dish.......	—	30.00
Compote			Spooner..........	30.00	35.00
Cov, hs	80.00	75.00	Sugar, cov	75.00	85.00
Open, hs, 9½" ...	70.00	68.00	Sugar Shaker	125.00	110.00
Creamer.........	60.00	45.00	Tray, water	70.00	50.00
Finger Bowl	40.00	30.00	Tumbler	45.00	35.00
Goblet	60.00	65.00	Violet Bowl	—	40.00
Inkwell, dated hard					
rubber top	—	85.00			

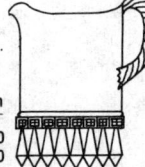

CHECKERBOARD (Bridal Rosette)

Made by Westmoreland Glass Co., early 1900s. Reproduced since the 1950s in milk glass and in recent years with pink stain. The Cambridge "Ribbon" pattern, usually marked Nearcut, is similar.

	Clear		Clear
Bowl, 9", shallow.........	20.00	Plate	
Butter, cov	40.00	7".................	15.00
Celery Tray.............	20.00	10"................	20.00
Celery Vase	30.00	Punch Cup	5.00
Compote, open, ls, 8"	25.00	Salt and Pepper	40.00
Creamer................	25.00	Sauce, flat	5.00
Cruet, os	40.00	Spooner..............	20.00
Cup	8.00	Sugar, cov	35.00
Goblet	28.00	Tumbler	
Honey, cov, sq, pedestal ...	45.00	Iced Tea	15.00
Pitcher		Water	18.00
Milk..................	40.00	Wine	18.00
Water	35.00		

CLASSIC

Clear and frosted non-flint produced by Gillinder and Sons, Philadelphia, PA, in the late 1870s. Pieces with log feet instead of a flat or collared base are worth more.

	Clear		Clear
Bowl, 7″, cov, log feet	145.00	Pitcher, water	
Butter, cov, log feet	185.00	Collared	200.00
Celery Vase		Log feet	250.00
Collared	115.00	Plate	
Log feet	125.00	Jas G. Blaine.	185.00
Compote		Pres. Cleveland	180.00
Cov, 6½″, collared	150.00	Thomas H. Hendricks. . . .	170.00
Cov, 6½″, log feet	250.00	John A. Logan	225.00
Cov, 7½″d, log feet.	225.00	Warrior	165.00
Cov, 8½″, collared	175.00	Sauce	
Cov, 12½″, collared	325.00	Flat.	25.00
Open, 7¾″, log feet	100.00	Log Feet	30.00
Creamer		Spooner	
Collared	100.00	Collared	95.00
Log feet	150.00	Log feet	125.00
Creamer.	125.00	Sugar, cov	
Goblet	250.00	Collared	150.00
Marmalade Jar, cov	350.00	Log feet	185.00
Pitcher, milk, log feet	450.00	Sweetmeat Jar	175.00

CLEAR DIAGONAL BAND

Non-flint, c1880. Also has been found in light amber.

	Clear		Clear
Bread Plate, Eureka	28.00	Marmalade Jar	35.00
Butter, cov	35.00	Pitcher, water	40.00
Cake Stand	30.00	Plate	15.00
Celery Vase	20.00	Relish, oval.	8.00
Compote		Salt & Pepper.	30.00
Cov, hs	45.00	Sauce, flat	7.50
Cov, ls.	30.00	Spooner	15.00
Creamer.	25.00	Sugar, cov	30.00
Dish, oval.	10.00	Wine	20.00
Goblet	15.00		

COLORADO (Lacy Medallion)

Non-flint States pattern made by U. S. Glass Co. in 1898. Made in amethyst stained, ruby stained, and opaque white with enamel floral trim, all of which are scarce. Some pieces found with ornate silver frames or feet. Purists consider these two as separate patterns, with the Lacy Medallion restricted to souvenir pieces. Reproductions have been made.

	Blue	Clear	Green
Banana Stand.	45.00	25.00	40.00
Bowl			
6″	35.00	20.00	30.00
7½″, ftd	40.00	25.00	35.00
8½″, ftd	65.00	45.00	60.00

	Blue	Clear	Green
Butter, cov	200.00	60.00	125.00
Cake Stand	70.00	55.00	65.00
Celery Vase	65.00	35.00	48.00
Compote			
Open, ls, 6"	45.00	20.00	42.00
Open, ls, 9¼" . . .	95.00	35.00	65.00
Creamer			
Individual.	45.00	24.00	40.00
Regular.	95.00	45.00	70.00
Mug	40.00	20.00	30.00
Nappy	40.00	20.00	35.00
Pitcher			
Milk.	145.00	—	100.00
Water	375.00	125.00	185.00
Plate			
6"	50.00	18.00	45.00
8"	65.00	20.00	60.00
Punch Cup	30.00	18.00	25.00
Salt Shaker.	65.00	30.00	40.00
Sauce, ruffled	30.00	15.00	25.00
Sherbet	50.00	25.00	45.00
Spooner	65.00	40.00	60.00
Sugar			
Cov, regular.	80.00	65.00	75.00
Open, individual. .	35.00	24.00	30.00
Toothpick	60.00	30.00	45.00
Tray, Calling Card . .	45.00	25.00	35.00
Tumbler	35.00	18.00	30.00
Vase, 12"	85.00	35.00	60.00
Violet Bowl	60.00	—	—
Wine	—	25.00	40.00

COMET

Flint made by Boston and Sandwich Glass Co in the late 1840s and early 1850s.

	Clear		Clear
Butter, cov	200.00	Pitcher, water	500.00
Compote, open, ls.	140.00	Spooner	95.00
Creamer.	175.00	Sugar, cov	175.00
Goblet	135.00	Tumbler	110.00
Mug	135.00	Whiskey	165.00

CONNECTICUT

Non-flint. One of the States patterns made by U. S. Glass Co., c1900. Found in plain and engraved. Two varieties of ruby stained toothpicks ($90.00) have been identified.

	Clear		Clear
Biscuit Jar	25.00	Butter, cov	35.00
Bowl		Cake Stand	40.00
4"	10.00	Celery Tray.	20.00
8"	15.00	Celery Vase	25.00

	Clear		Clear
Compote		Relish.	12.00
Cov, hs	40.00	Salt & Pepper	35.00
Open, hs, 7″	25.00	Spooner	25.00
Creamer	28.00	Sugar, cov	35.00
Dish, 8″, oblong	20.00	Sugar Shaker	35.00
Lamp, enamel dec.	85.00	Toothpick	40.00
Lemonade, handled	20.00	Tumbler, water	15.00
Pitcher, water	40.00	Wine	35.00

CORD AND TASSEL

Non-flint, made by La Belle Glass C., Bridgeport, OH, and patented by Andrew Baggs in 1872. Also made by Central Glass Co. and other companies. Heavily reproduced.

	Clear		Clear
Bowl, oval	20.00	* Goblet	35.00
Butter, cov	65.00	Lamp, ah, pedestal	100.00
Cake Stand, 10″	65.00	Mug, ah	65.00
Castor Bottle	25.00	Mustard Jar, cov	45.00
Celery Vase	35.00	Pitcher, water, ah	95.00
Compote		Salt & Pepper	45.00
Cov, hs, ...	90.00	Sauce	10.00
Open, ls	35.00	Spooner	25.00
Cordial	45.00	Sugar, cov	65.00
Creamer	25.00	Syrup	125.00
Egg Cup	35.00	Tumbler, water	45.00
Dish, oval, vegetable	25.00	* Wine	35.00

CORD DRAPERY

Made by National Glass Co., Greentown, IN, from 1899 to 1903; later by Indiana Glass at Dunkirk, IN, after 1907.

	Amber	Blue	Clear	Emerald Green
Bowl, 7½″	25.00	25.00	20.00	30.00
Butter, cov	85.00	85.00	80.00	175.00
Cake Stand	50.00	55.00	45.00	75.00
Compote				
Open, 6″	45.00	60.00	48.00	85.00
Open, 7″	75.00	75.00	60.00	95.00
Open, jelly	—	55.00	45.00	—
Creamer	65.00	95.00	45.00	85.00
Cruet, os	265.00	100.00	90.00	125.00
Cup	18.00	18.00	15.00	25.00
Goblet	50.00	50.00	55.00	65.00
Jelly, cov	85.00	95.00	65.00	115.00
Pickle, 9¼″, oval . . .	40.00	—	25.00	—
Pitcher, water	175.00	195.00	65.00	200.00
Plate	35.00	40.00	25.00	40.00
Relish	25.00	25.00	22.00	30.00
Sauce, flat	15.00	15.00	10.00	15.00
Spooner	50.00	60.00	45.00	65.00

	Amber	Blue	Clear	Emerald Green
Sugar, cov	125.00	95.00	60.00	100.00
Syrup	295.00	—	120.00	—
Sweetmeat, cov, 6½" d, 5¼" h	165.00	—	—	—
Toothpick	500.00	500.00	80.00	500.00
Tumbler	45.00	50.00	40.00	65.00
Wine	95.00	110.00	90.00	120.00

CORDOVA

Non-flint made by the O'Hara Glass Co., Pittsburgh, Pa. It was exhibited for the first time at the Pittsburgh Glass Show, December 16, 1890. Toothpick has been found in ruby stained, valued at $35.00.

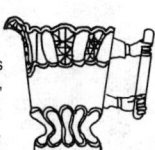

	Clear	Emerald Green		Clear	Emerald Green
Bowl, Berry, cov . . .	30.00	—	Water	48.00	—
Butter, cov, handled .	50.00	—	Punch Bowl	87.50	—
Cake Stand	45.00	—	Punch Cup	15.00	30.00
Celery Vase	45.00	—	Nappy, handled, 6"d	12.00	—
Cologne Bottle	20.00	—	Salt Shaker	20.00	—
Compote			Spooner	35.00	45.00
Cov, hs	40.00	—	Sugar, cov	40.00	80.00
Open, hs	35.00	—	Syrup	125.00	40.00
Creamer	35.00	45.00	Toothpick	20.00	—
Finger Bowl	16.00	—	Tumbler	18.00	—
Inkwell, metal lid . . .	80.00	—	Vase	12.00	—
Mug, handled	17.50	30.00			
Pitcher					
Milk	30.00	—			

COTTAGE (Dinner Bell)

Non-flint made by Adams and Co., Pittsburgh, PA, in the late 1870s and U. S. Glass Co. in the 1890s. Known to have been made in emerald green, amber, light blue, and amethyst. Add 50% for amber, 75% for other colors.

	Clear	Ruby Stained		Clear	Ruby Stained
Banana Stand	55.00	—	Cov, hs 7"	85.00	—
Bowl			Cov, hs hs, 8" . . .	90.00	—
7 ½, oval	15.00	—	Cov, hs, 8¼"	80.00	—
9½, oval	20.00	—	Open, hs, 8¼"d . .	65.00	—
Butter, cov			Jelly	35.00	45.00
Flat	45.00	—	Creamer	35.00	50.00
Footed	45.00	—	Cruet, os	55.00	—
Cake Stand			Cup and Saucer . . .	35.00	—
9"	38.00	—	Dish, oval, deep . . .	20.00	—
10"	42.00	—	Finger Bowl	25.00	—
Celery Vase	35.00	—	Goblet	25.00	—
Champagne	65.00	75.00	Pitcher		
Compote			Milk	35.00	—
Cov, hs 6"	75.00	—	Water	50.00	—

	Clear	Ruby Stained		Clear	Ruby Stained
Plate			Saucer	15.00	40.00
5″	10.00	20.00	Spooner	20.00	—
6″	15.00	—	Sugar, cov	45.00	—
7″	15.00	—	Syrup	85.00	—
8″	15.00	—	Tray, water	35.00	—
9″	20.00	—	Tumbler	25.00	—
Relish.	10.00	—	Waste Bowl.	20.00	—
Salt Shaker.	35.00	—	Wine	35.00	—

CROESUS

Made in clear by Riverside Glass Works, Wheeling, WV, in 1897. Produced in amethyst and green by McKee Glass in 1899. Some pieces trimmed in gold; prices are for examples with gold in very good condition. Reproduced.

	Amethyst	Clear	Green
Bowl			
4″, ftd	65.00	10.00	30.00
6¼″, ftd.	200.00	65.00	115.00
8″, flat	165.00	—	120.00
8″, ftd	115.00	25.00	115.00
8″, ftd, cov.	145.00	35.00	115.00
10″, ftd	165.00	—	120.00
* Butter, cov	175.00	85.00	165.00
Cake Stand, 10″ . . .	175.00	40.00	140.00
Celery Vase	275.00	65.00	135.00
Compote			
Cov, hs, 5″.	115.00	28.00	115.00
Cov, hs, 6″.	115.00	28.00	115.00
Cov, hs, 7″.	135.00	30.00	125.00
Open, hs, 5″	65.00	18.00	60.00
Open, hs, 6″	75.00	18.00	60.00
Open, hs, 7″	80.00	20.00	75.00
Compote, jelly	225.00	20.00	185.00
Condiment Set (cruet, salt & pepper on small tray). . . .	225.00	185.00	185.00
Creamer			
Individual.	185.00	—	100.00
Regular	150.00	55.00	65.00
Cruet, os	325.00	135.00	185.00
Pitcher, water	350.00	80.00	235.00
Plate, 8″, ftd	75.00	20.00	65.00
Relish, boat shaped.	70.00	30.00	60.00
Salt & Pepper	135.00	40.00	125.00
Sauce			
Flat.	40.00	15.00	37.50
Footed	45.00	18.00	40.00
Spooner	80.00	60.00	70.00
Sugar, cov	175.00	85.00	125.00
*Toothpick	100.00	25.00	85.00
Tray, condiment . . .	75.00	25.00	30.00
*Tumbler	65.00	20.00	50.00

CRYSTAL WEDDING

Non-flint made by Adams Glass Co., Pittsburgh, PA, in the late 1880s and U. S. Glass Co. in 1891. Also found in frosted, amber stained, and cobalt blue (rare). Heavily reproduced in clear, ruby stained, and milk with enamel trim.

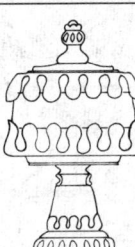

	Clear	Ruby Stained		Clear	Ruby Stained
Banana Stand.	85.00	—	Pitcher		
Bowl			Milk, round	110.00	—
4½", ind berry . . .	15.00	—	Milk, sq.	125.00	—
6", sq, cov.	65.00	—	Water, round	110.00	195.00
7", sq, cov.	75.00	—	Water, sq.	165.00	—
8", sq, master			Plate, 10"	25.00	40.00
berry	50.00	—	Relish.	20.00	—
8", sq, cov.	60.00	—	Salt		
Butter, cov	75.00	125.00	Individual.	25.00	—
Cake Plate, sq	45.00	85.00	Master	35.00	—
Cake Stand, 10" . . .	65.00	—	Salt Shaker.	65.00	—
Celery Vase	45.00	75.00	Sauce	15.00	20.00
Champagne	65.00	—	Spooner.	30.00	60.00
Compote			Sugar, cov	70.00	85.00
Cov, hs, 7 x 13". .	100.00	—	Syrup.	150.00	200.00
Open, hs, 7", sq. .	60.00	—	Toothpick	50.00	—
Open, ls, 5", sq . .	50.00	—	Tumbler	35.00	45.00
Creamer.	50.00	75.00	Vase		
Cruet	125.00	—	Footed, twisted . .	25.00	—
Goblet	55.00	85.00	Swung	25.00	—
Nappy, handle.	25.00	—	Wine	45.00	—
Pickle.	25.00	—			

CUPID AND VENUS

Non-flint made by Richards and Hartley Glass Co., Tarentum, PA, in the late 1870s. Also made in vaseline, rare.

	Amber	Clear		Amber	Clear
Bowl			Cruet, os	—	135.00
8", cov, ftd	—	35.00	Goblet	—	65.00
9", oval	—	32.00	Marmalade Jar, cov.	—	85.00
Bread Plate	75.00	40.00	Mug		
Butter, cov	—	55.00	Miniature.	—	40.00
Cake Plate	—	45.00	Medium, 2½"	—	35.00
Cake Stand	—	60.00	Large, 3½"	—	40.00
Celery Vase	—	40.00	Pitcher		
Champagne	—	90.00	Milk.	175.00	75.00
Compote			Water	195.00	65.00
Cov, hs, 8".	—	100.00	Plate, 10", round . . .	75.00	40.00
Cov, ls, 7"	—	90.00	Sauce		
Cov, ls, 9"	—	100.00	Flat.	—	10.00
Open, ls, 8½",			Footed, 3½", 4"		
scalloped	135.00	35.00	and 4½".	—	15.00
Open, hs, 9¼" . . .	—	45.00	Spooner.	—	35.00
Cordial, 3½"	—	85.00	Sugar, cov	—	65.00
Creamer.	—	36.50	Wine, 3¾".	—	85.00

CURRANT

Non-flint, made by Campbell, Jones and Co., and patented in 1871.

	Clear		Clear
Bowl, 7", vegetable	18.00	Goblet	30.00
Butter, cov	75.00	Pitcher	
Cake Stand		Milk, ah.	125.00
9¼".	60.00	Water, ah.	95.00
11".	85.00	Plate, oval	
Celery Vase	48.00	5" x 7".	25.00
Compote		6" x 9".	30.00
Cov, hs, 8".	100.00	Salt, ftd	30.00
Cov, hs, 9".	135.00	Sauce, ftd, 4"	12.00
Cov, hs, 12".	195.00	Spooner	25.00
Cov, ls, 8"	45.00	Sugar, cov	55.00
Cordial	45.00	Tumbler, ftd	30.00
Creamer, ah	45.00	Wine	25.00
Egg Cup.	25.00		

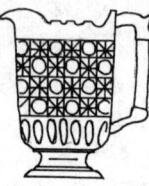

CURRIER AND IVES

Non-flint made by Bellaire Glass Co. in Findlay, OH, in 1890. Known to have been made in colors, but rarely found. A decanter is known in ruby stained.

	Clear		Clear
Bowl, oval, 10", canoe		Plate, 10".	20.00
shaped	30.00	Relish.	18.00
Butter, cov	50.00	Salt Shaker.	30.00
Compote		Sauce, oval	12.00
Cov, hs, 7½"	95.00	Spooner	30.00
Open, hs, 7½", scalloped .	50.00	Sugar, cov	45.00
Creamer.	30.00	Syrup	75.00
Cup and saucer	30.00	Tray	
Decanter	35.00	Water, Balky Mule	65.00
Dish, oval, boat shaped, 8" .	27.50	Wine, Balky Mule.	50.00
Goblet, knob stem	25.00	Tumbler	45.00
Lamp, 9½", hs	75.00	Water Bottle, 12" h, os.	55.00
Pitcher		Wine, 3¼".	18.00
Milk.	60.00		
Water	70.00		

CURTAIN (Sultan)

Clear non-flint pattern made by Bryce Brothers, Pittsburgh, Pennsylvania, late 1870s.

	Clear		Clear
Bowl		Castor Set, salt, pepper, and	
7½".	20.00	mustard, stand.	115.00
8".	25.00	Celery Tray.	30.00
Butter, cov	55.00	Celery Vase	30.00
Cake Stand		Compote, open, hs, 10". . . .	45.00
8".	40.00	Creamer.	25.00
9½".	45.00	Cruet, os	45.00

	Clear		Clear
Finger Bowl	30.00	Salt Shaker	25.00
Goblet	30.00	Sauce, 4¾"	8.00
Mug	25.00	Spooner	25.00
Pickle	10.00	Sugar, cov	35.00
Pitcher, water	75.00	Tray, water	35.00
Plate, 7", sq	20.00	Tumbler	20.00

CURTAIN TIE BACK

Clear non-flint pattern made in the mid 1880s.

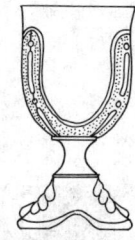

	Clear		Clear
Bowl, 7½", sq	18.00	Relish	10.00
Bread Plate	35.00	Salt & Pepper, pr.	35.00
Butter, cov	40.00	Sauce	
Celery Vase	25.00	Flat	5.00
Compote, cov, hs	40.00	Footed	8.00
Creamer	25.00	Spooner	30.00
Goblet		Sugar, cov	35.00
Fancy base	30.00	Tray, water	30.00
Flat base	20.00	Tumbler	15.00
Pickle	12.00	Wine	20.00
Pitcher, water	45.00		

DAHLIA

Non-flint, made by Portland Glass Co, Portland, ME, c1865, and Canton Glass Co., c1880. Also attributed to a Canadian manufacturer.

	Amber	Apple Green	Blue	Clear	Vaseline
Bowl	30.00	25.00	25.00	18.00	30.00
Bread Plate	55.00	50.00	60.00	45.00	55.00
Butter, cov	80.00	70.00	85.00	40.00	80.00
Cake Plate	60.00	45.00	60.00	24.00	60.00
Cake Stand, 9"	72.50	50.00	50.00	25.00	72.50
Champagne	65.00	85.00	75.00	55.00	75.00
Compote					
Cov, hs, 7"	100.00	85.00	85.00	55.00	80.00
Open, hs, 8"	60.00	45.00	45.00	30.00	60.00
Cordial	55.00	50.00	50.00	35.00	55.00
Creamer	40.00	35.00	35.00	25.00	40.00
Egg Cup					
Double	80.00	65.00	65.00	50.00	80.00
Single	55.00	40.00	40.00	25.00	55.00
Goblet	55.00	85.00	75.00	40.00	65.00
Mug					
Large	55.00	55.00	55.00	35.00	55.00
Small	50.00	45.00	40.00	30.00	50.00
Pickle	35.00	30.00	30.00	20.00	35.00
Pitcher					
Milk	70.00	55.00	55.00	40.00	70.00
Water	100.00	90.00	90.00	55.00	90.00

	Amber	Apple Green	Blue	Clear	Vaseline
Water, applied handle	—	—	—	125.00	—
Plate					
7"	45.00	40.00	40.00	20.00	45.00
9", handles	35.00	45.00	50.00	18.00	50.00
Platter	50.00	45.00	45.00	30.00	50.00
Relish, 9½" l.	20.00	20.00	20.00	15.00	25.00
Salt, ind, ftd	35.00	30.00	30.00	5.00	35.00
Sauce					
Flat.	15.00	12.00	15.00	10.00	15.00
Footed	20.00	15.00	15.00	10.00	20.00
Spooner	50.00	45.00	50.00	35.00	50.00
Sugar, cov	75.00	60.00	60.00	40.00	75.00
Syrup.	75.00	—	—	55.00	—
Wine	45.00	40.00	45.00	25.00	45.00

DAISY AND BUTTON

Non-flint pattern made in the 1870s by several companies in many different forms. In continuous production since inception. Also found in amberina, amber stain, and ruby stained.

	Amber	Apple Green	Blue	Clear	Vaseline
Bowl, triangular	40.00	45.00	45.00	25.00	65.00
Bread Plate, 13" . . .	35.00	60.00	35.00	20.00	40.00
Butter Chip	10.00	24.00	15.00	8.00	25.00
Butter, cov					
Round.	70.00	90.00	70.00	65.00	95.00
Square	110.00	115.00	110.00	100.00	120.00
Butter Pat.	30.00	40.00	35.00	25.00	35.00
Canoe					
4"	12.00	24.00	15.00	10.00	24.00
8½".	30.00	35.00	30.00	25.00	35.00
12"	60.00	35.00	28.00	20.00	40.00
14"	30.00	40.00	35.00	25.00	40.00
Castor Set					
4 bottle, glass std.	90.00	85.00	95.00	80.00	75.00
5 bottle, metal std	105.00	100.00	110.00	100.00	95.00
Celery Vase	45.00	50.00	40.00	30.00	48.00
Compote					
Cov, hs, 6".	35.00	50.00	45.00	25.00	50.00
Open, hs, 8"	75.00	65.00	60.00	40.00	65.00
Creamer.	35.00	40.00	40.00	18.00	35.00
Cruet, os	100.00	60.00	55.00	45.00	60.00
Egg Cup.	20.00	30.00	25.00	15.00	30.00
Finger Bowl	30.00	50.00	35.00	30.00	42.00
Goblet	40.00	50.00	40.00	25.00	40.00
Hat, 2½".	30.00	35.00	40.00	20.00	40.00
Ice Tub.	—	—	—	—	75.00
Inkwell	40.00	50.00	45.00	30.00	45.00
Parfait	25.00	35.00	30.00	20.00	35.00
Pickle Castor	125.00	90.00	150.00	75.00	150.00
Pitcher, water					
Bulbous, reed handle	125.00	95.00	90.00	75.00	90.00

	Amber	Apple Green	Blue	Clear	Vaseline
Tankard	62.00	65.00	62.00	60.00	65.00
Plate					
5", leaf shape . . .	20.00	24.00	16.00	18.00	25.00
6", round	10.00	22.00	15.00	6.50	24.00
7", square	24.00	35.00	25.00	15.00	35.00
Punch Bowl, stand .	90.00	100.00	95.00	85.00	100.00
Salt & Pepper	30.00	40.00	30.00	20.00	35.00
Sauce, 4"	18.00	25.00	18.00	15.00	25.00
Slipper					
5"	45.00	48.00	50.00	45.00	50.00
11½"	40.00	50.00	30.00	35.00	50.00
Spooner	40.00	40.00	45.00	35.00	45.00
Sugar, cov	45.00	50.00	45.00	35.00	50.00
Syrup	45.00	50.00	45.00	30.00	45.00
Toothpick					
Round	40.00	55.00	25.00	40.00	45.00
Urn	20.00	25.00	20.00	10.00	35.00
Tray	65.00	65.00	60.00	35.00	60.00
Tumbler	18.00	30.00	35.00	15.00	25.00
Vase, wall pocket . .	125.00	—	—	—	—
Wine	15.00	25.00	20.00	10.00	45.00

DAISY AND BUTTON WITH CROSSBARS (Mikado)

Non-flint pattern made by Richards and Hartley, Tarentum, PA, c1888.

	Amber	Blue	Clear	Vaseline
Bowl				
6"	20.00	30.00	15.00	25.00
9"	40.00	40.00	25.00	35.00
Bread Plate	30.00	45.00	25.00	35.00
Butter, cov				
Flat	55.00	55.00	45.00	55.00
Footed	—	75.00	25.00	60.00
Celery Vase	36.00	40.00	30.00	50.00
Compote				
Cov, hs, 8"	55.00	65.00	45.00	55.00
Open, hs, 8"	45.00	50.00	30.00	45.00
Open, ls, 7"	30.00	—	20.00	45.00
Creamer				
Individual	25.00	30.00	18.00	30.00
Regular	42.50	45.00	35.00	40.00
Cruet, os	75.00	85.00	35.00	100.00
Goblet	40.00	40.00	25.00	40.00
Mug, 3"h.	15.00	18.00	12.50	20.00
Pitcher				
Milk	45.00	60.00	35.00	60.00
Water	85.00	70.00	45.00	65.00
Salt & Pepper	40.00	50.00	30.00	45.00
Sauce				
Flat	15.00	18.00	10.00	15.00
Footed	18.00	25.00	15.00	24.00
Spooner	35.00	35.00	25.00	35.00
Sugar, cov				
Individual	25.00	35.00	10.00	25.00
Regular	50.00	60.00	25.00	55.00

	Amber	Blue	Clear	Vaseline
Syrup	100.00	125.00	65.00	125.00
Toothpick	40.00	40.00	28.00	35.00
Tumbler	20.00	25.00	18.00	25.00
Wine	30.00	35.00	25.00	30.00

DAISY AND BUTTON WITH NARCISSUS (Daisy and Button with Clear Lily)

Non-flint made in late 1890s. Later made by Indiana Glass Co. Dunkirk, IN, into 1920s. Sometimes found with flowers flashed with cranberry flashing and pieces trimmed in gold. Many pieces have been reproduced.

	Clear	Flashed Color		Clear	Flashed Color
Bowl, 6" w, 9¼" l,			Salt Shaker	18.00	—
oval, ftd	25.00	—	Sauce		
Butter, cov	50.00	—	Flat	10.00	—
Celery Vase	20.00	—	Footed, 4"	15.00	—
Compote, open, ls . .	35.00	—	Spooner	30.00	—
Creamer	25.00	—	Sugar, cov	38.00	42.50
Decanter, os	40.00	62.50	Tray, water, 10"	30.00	40.00
Goblet	25.00	—	Tray, wine	32.50	42.50
Pitcher, water	50.00	70.00	Tumbler	18.00	20.00
Punch Cup	10.00	18.00	Wine	22.00	25.00

DAISY AND BUTTON WITH V ORNAMENT (Van Dyke)

Made by A. J. Beatty & Co., 1886–1887.

	Amber	Blue	Clear	Vaseline
Bowl				
9"	30.00	40.00	25.00	35.00
10"	30.00	40.00	25.00	35.00
Butter, cov	75.00	95.00	65.00	85.00
Celery Vase	50.00	55.00	30.00	55.00
Creamer	30.00	50.00	30.00	50.00
Finger Bowl	28.50	45.00	22.50	55.00
Goblet	35.00	45.00	25.00	50.00
Mug	20.00	30.00	20.00	35.00
Pickle Castor	120.00	120.00	85.00	100.00
Pitcher, water	65.00	90.00	48.00	60.00
Punch Cup	12.00	20.00	12.50	25.00
Sauce, flat	20.00	20.00	12.00	30.00
Spooner	40.00	38.50	35.00	45.00
Sugar, cov	50.00	75.00	45.00	65.00
Toothpick	32.50	40.00	28.50	35.00
Tray, water	55.00	65.00	35.00	55.00
Tumbler	25.00	28.00	15.00	35.00

DAKOTA (Baby Thumbprint, Thumbprint Band)

Non-flint made by Ripley and Co., Pittsburgh, PA, in the late 1880s and early 1890s. Later reissued by U. S. Glass Co. as one of the States patterns. Prices listed are for etched fern and berry pattern; also found with fern and no berry, and oak leaf etching, and scarcer grape etching. Other etchings known include fish, swan, peacock, bird and insect, bird and flowers, ivy and berry, stag, spider and insect in web, buzzard on dead tree, and crane catching fish. Sometimes ruby stained with or without souvenir markings. There is a four piece table set available in a "hotel" variant, prices are about 20% more than the regular type.

	Clear Etched	Clear Plain	Ruby Stained
Basket, 10 x 2", metal bail	250.00	225.00	275.00
Bottle, 5½"	45.00	35.00	—
Bowl, berry	45.00	30.00	—
Butter, cov	65.00	40.00	125.00
Cake Cover, 8"	300.00	200.00	—
Cake Stand			
9½"	58.00	35.00	—
10½"	65.00	45.00	—
Celery Tray	35.00	25.00	—
Celery Vase	40.00	30.00	—
Compote			
Cov, hs, 5"	60.00	—	—
Cov, hs, 7"	65.00	—	—
Cov, hs, 8"	75.00	—	—
Cov, hs, 9"	75.00	—	—
Cov, hs, 12"	95.00	75.00	—
Cov, 6", jelly	65.00	50.00	—
Open, hs, 7"	55.00	40.00	—
Open, hs, 10" . . .	75.00	60.00	—
Condiment Tray, metal handles . . .	—	75.00	—
Creamer	60.00	28.50	65.00
Cruet	90.00	55.00	135.00
Goblet	35.00	28.00	75.00
Pitcher			
Milk	100.00	80.00	200.00
Tankard	125.00	95.00	225.00
Water	95.00	75.00	190.00
Plate, 10"	85.00	—	—
Salt Shaker	65.00	50.00	125.00
Sauce			
Flat	20.00	18.00	—
Footed	25.00	20.00	—
Spooner	30.00	25.00	65.00
Sugar, cov	65.00	55.00	85.00
Tray, water	100.00	75.00	—
Tumbler	35.00	30.00	55.00
Waste Bowl	75.00	45.00	—
Wine	30.00	20.00	55.00

DART

Clear non-flint pattern made in Ohio in the 1880s.

	Clear		Clear
Bowl	10.00	Open, jelly	18.00
Butter, cov	25.00	Creamer	25.00
Compote		Goblet	28.00
Cov, hs, 8½" d, 12½" h. . .	60.00	Pitcher, water	35.00

	Clear		Clear
Sauce, ftd.	12.50	Sugar, cov	35.00
Spooner	20.00	Tumbler	15.00

DEER AND DOG

Non-flint pattern made in the c1870s. Pattern identified by frosted dog finial. Found in both etched and non-etched styles.

	Clear		Clear
Butter, cov	125.00	Mug	40.00
Celery Vase	95.00	Pitcher, water, ah	150.00
Compote, cov, 7″, ls, non-		Sauce, ftd.	20.00
etched.	150.00	Spooner	60.00
Creamer.	75.00	Sugar, cov	125.00
Goblet	65.00	Wine	75.00
Marmalade Jar, cov.	125.00		

DEER AND PINE TREE (Deer and Doe)

Non-flint pattern, made by Belmont Glass Co., and McKee Glass Co. 1883. Souvenir mugs with gilt found in clear and olive green. Also made in canary (vaseline). The goblet has been reproduced.

	Amber	Apple Green	Blue	Clear
Bread Plate	100.00	125.00	125.00	75.00
Butter, cov	125.00	425.00	125.00	95.00
Cake Stand	—	—	—	75.00
Celery Vase	—	—	—	75.00
Compote				
Cov, hs, 8″, sq . . .	—	—	—	100.00
Open, hs, 7″	—	—	—	45.00
Open, hs, 9″	—	—	—	55.00
Creamer.	95.00	85.00	90.00	65.00
Finger Bowl	—	—	—	55.00
* Goblet	—	—	—	55.00
Marmalade Jar	—	—	—	90.00
Mug	40.00	45.00	50.00	40.00
Pickle.	—	—	—	24.00
Pitcher				
Milk.	—	—	—	90.00
Water	125.00	125.00	125.00	125.00
Platter, 8 x 13″	—	—	80.00	60.00
Sauce				
Flat.	—	—	—	20.00
Footed	—	—	—	28.00
Spooner	—	—	—	65.00
Sugar, cov	—	—	—	85.00
Tray, water	100.00	—	90.00	60.00

DELAWARE (Four Petal Flower)

Non-flint pattern made by U. S. Glass Co. c1899. Also found in amethyst (scarce), clear with rose trim, custard, and milk glass. Prices are for pieces with perfect gold trim.

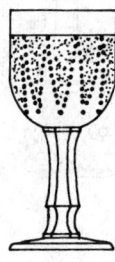

	Clear	Green With Gold	Rose With Gold
Banana Bowl	50.00	55.00	65.00
Bowl			
8″	30.00	40.00	50.00
9″	25.00	60.00	75.00
Bottle, os	90.00	150.00	185.00
Bride's Basket, SP frame	—	115.00	165.00
Butter, cov	60.00	125.00	145.00
Claret Jug, tankard shape	110.00	195.00	200.00
Celery Vase, flat . . .	75.00	90.00	95.00
Creamer.	45.00	65.00	70.00
Cruet, os	90.00	200.00	250.00
Finger Bowl	25.00	50.00	75.00
Lamp Shade, round.	—	—	75.00
Pin Tray	30.00	55.00	95.00
Pitcher, water	50.00	150.00	125.00
Pomade Box, jeweled	—	250.00	350.00
Puff Box, bulbous, jeweled	—	200.00	315.00
Punch Cup	18.00	30.00	35.00
Sauce, 5½″, boat . .	15.00	35.00	30.00
Spooner	45.00	60.00	55.00
Sugar, cov	65.00	85.00	100.00
Toothpick	40.00	125.00	150.00
Tumbler	20.00	45.00	48.50
Vase			
6″	—	45.00	70.00
8″	—	55.00	75.00
9½″	—	80.00	85.00

DEWDROP WITH STAR

Non-flint made by Campbell, Jones and Co., Pittsburgh, PA, in 1877. There was no goblet made in this pattern. This pattern has been reproduced in color.

	Clear		Clear
Bowl		Cov, ls, 5″	60.00
6″	8.00	Open, hs.	35.00
7″	15.00	Creamer, ah	35.00
9″, ftd	20.00	Honey, underplate	75.00
Bread Plate motto, sheaf of		Lamp, patented 1876.	85.00
wheat center	85.00	Pitcher, water, ah	125.00
Butter, cov, dome lid	50.00	*Plate	
Cake Stand	40.00	5″	12.00
Celery Vase	40.00	7″	15.00
Cheese Dish, cov, dome lid .	135.00	9″	20.00
Compote		Relish.	15.00
Cov, hs, dome lid	75.00	*Salt, ftd	20.00

	Clear		Clear
Sauce		Spooner	35.00
Flat	10.00	Sugar, cov, domed lid	50.00
Footed	12.00		

DIAGONAL BAND

Made in c1875-1885, maker unknown.

	Amber	Apple Green	Clear
Bread Plate	30.00	35.00	24.00
Butter, cov	60.00	80.00	35.00
Cake Stand	40.00	55.00	30.00
Celery Vase	45.00	50.00	25.00
Compote			
Cov, hs, 7"	65.00	80.00	55.00
Cov, ls, 8"	62.50	70.00	45.00
Open, hs, 7½" . . .	45.00	50.00	20.00
Creamer	40.00	50.00	30.00
Goblet	30.00	45.00	28.00
Pitcher			
Milk	50.00	—	32.00
Water	65.00	95.00	40.00
Plate, 6"	—	—	12.50
Relish, 6⅞" oval . . .	14.00	18.00	10.00
Sauce			
Flat	—	—	6.00
Footed	—	15.00	12.50
Spooner	24.00	40.00	20.00
Sugar, cov	40.00	50.00	30.00
Wine	35.00	45.00	20.00

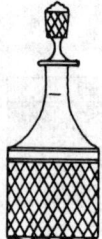

DIAMOND POINT

Flint, originally made by Boston and Sandwich Glass Co., in the 1830-1840 period, and by the New England Glass Co. Many other companies manufactured this pattern throughout the 19th century.

	Flint	Non-Flint		Flint	Non-Flint
Bowl			Open, hs, 11",		
7", cov	60.00	20.00	scalloped rim . .	110.00	—
8", cov	60.00	20.00	Open, ls, 7½" . . .	50.00	40.00
8", open	45.00	15.00	Cordial	165.00	—
Butter, cov	95.00	50.00	Creamer, ah	115.00	—
Cake Stand, 14" . . .	185.00	—	Decanter, qt. os. . . .	165.00	—
Candlesticks, pr . . .	145.00	—	Egg Cup	40.00	20.00
Celery Vase	75.00	30.00	Goblet	45.00	35.00
Champagne	85.00	—	Honey	15.00	—
Claret	90.00	—	Mustard, Brittania		
Compote			cov	25.00	—
Cov, hs, 8"	135.00	—	Pitcher		
Open, hs 10½",			Pint	185.00	—
flared	100.00	—	Quart	275.00	—

	Flint	Non-Flint		Flint	Non-Flint
Plate			Spooner	45.00	25.00
6"	30.00	—	Sugar, cov	65.00	—
8"	50.00	—	Syrup.	150.00	—
Salt, master, cov . . .	75.00	—	Tumbler, bar	65.00	35.00
Sauce, flat	14.00	—	Whiskey, ah	85.00	—
Spillholder	45.00	—	Wine	75.00	30.00

DIAMOND QUILTED

Non-flint, c1880. Heavily reproduced.

	Amber	Amethyst	Blue	Clear	Vaseline
Bowl					
6"	10.00	20.00	—	—	—
7"	18.00	—	—	—	25.00
Butter, cov	50.00	100.00	100.00	40.00	75.00
Celery Vase	35.00	60.00	50.00	40.00	40.00
Champagne	—	36.00	—	21.00	38.00
Compote					
Cov, hs, 8"	140.00	120.00	120.00	45.00	90.00
Open, ls, 9"	—	—	—	15.00	35.00
Creamer	45.00	40.00	70.00	25.00	55.00
*Goblet	40.00	40.00	40.00	30.00	35.00
Mug	—	30.00	40.00	—	—
Pitcher, water	75.00	85.00	80.00	50.00	75.00
Sauce					
Flat	12.00	—	16.50	8.00	18.00
Footed	16.00	18.00	18.00	12.00	22.00
Spooner	35.00	40.00	40.00	30.00	50.00
Sugar, cov	50.00	75.00	55.00	40.00	60.00
Tray	55.00	70.00	75.00	30.00	65.00
*Tumbler	45.00	40.00	40.00	25.00	32.50
Vase, 9"	—	—	—	48.00	—
* Wine	20.00	40.00	35.00	15.00	20.00

DIAMOND SPEARHEAD

Made by Northwood-Dugan Glass Co., Indiana, PA, around 1900. No cruet reported. A cake stand has been found, but it was not listed in early catalogues. Also made in canary opalescent, prices same as blue opalescent. A cake stand, 10", $65.00, and a carafe, $180.00 are known in canary opalescent.

	Clear	Cobalt Blue Opal	Green Opal	Sapphire Blue Opal	White Opal
Bowl, berry	20.00	—	40.00	40.00	35.00
Butter, cov	40.00	150.00	85.00	75.00	—
Carafe	—	—	180.00	—	—
Celery Vase	20.00	—	45.00	40.00	35.00
Compote					
Cov, hs	—	—	35.00	30.00	32.00
Cov, ls, jelly	—	—	60.00	50.00	—
Creamer	20.00	70.00	35.00	30.00	32.00

	Clear	Cobalt Blue Opal	Green Opal	Sapphire Blue Opal	White Opal
Cup and Saucer . . .	—	—	60.00	60.00	—
Goblet	—	—	90.00	90.00	—
Mug	20.00	—	55.00	65.00	—
Pitcher, water	50.00	200.00	195.00	75.00	—
Plate, 10″	—	—	80.00	—	—
Relish.	—	—	25.00	20.00	—
Sauce	—	—	15.00	10.00	—
Spooner	20.00	—	50.00	40.00	—
Sugar, cov	30.00	—	50.00	45.00	—
Syrup	—	230.00	195.00	65.00	—
Toothpick	—	125.00	85.00	″″ s ″″″″	—

DIAMOND THUMBPRINT

Flint, attributed to Boston and Sandwich Glass Co., and other factories from 1840 to 1850s. Compotes are being reproduced for Sandwich Glass Museum.

	Clear			Clear
Bitters Bottle, orig pewter pourer, applied lip, polished pontil	450.00	Quart, os.		225.00
		Finger Bowl		100.00
		* Goblet		350.00
Butter, cov	200.00	Honey Dish.		25.00
Celery Vase, scalloped top. .	185.00	Pitcher, water		650.00
Champagne	285.00	Sauce, flat		25.00
Compote		* Spooner		85.00
Cov, hs, 8″.	150.00	* Sugar, cov		150.00
Open, ls, scalloped, 8″ . . .	50.00	Tumbler, bar		125.00
Cordial	325.00	Whiskey, ah		300.00
Creamer.	225.00	* Wine		250.00
Decanter				
Pint, ns	175.00			

DOLLY MADISON (Jefferson's #271)

Made by Jefferson Glass Co., Follansbee, WV, c1907

	Clear	Blue Opal	Green Opal	White Opal
Bowl, berry, 9¼″ . . .	35.00	50.00	45.00	35.00
Butter, cov	40.00	120.00	125.00	75.00
Creamer.	35.00	65.00	90.00	80.00
Pitcher, water	45.00	150.00	140.00	125.00
Sauce	18.00	45.00	50.00	45.00
Spooner	30.00	75.00	85.00	75.00
Sugar, cov	45.00	65.00	100.00	45.00
Tumbler	30.00	40.00	60.00	40.00

DRAPERY (Lace)

Non-flint made by Doyle and Co., Pittsburgh, PA, in the 1870s. Reportedly made by Sandwich Glass Co. at an earlier period. Pieces with fine stippling have applied handles; pieces with coarse stippling have pressed handles.

	Clear		Clear
Butter, cov	45.00	Plate, 6″	30.00
Compote, ls	55.00	Sauce, flat	10.00
Creamer, ah	30.00	Spooner	25.00
Egg Cup.	25.00	Sugar, cov	40.00
Goblet	35.00	Tumbler	30.00
Pitcher, water, ah	85.00		

EGG IN SAND (Bean)

Non-flint, c1880. Has been reported in colors, but rare.

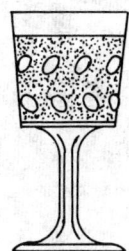

	Clear		Clear
Bread Plate, octagonal	25.00	Salt and Pepper	65.00
Butter, cov	40.00	Sauce	5.00
Compote, cov, jelly	45.00	Spooner, flat rim	28.00
Creamer.	30.00	Sugar, cov	35.00
Dish, swan center	40.00	Tray, water	40.00
Goblet	35.00	Tumbler	33.00
Pitcher, water	45.00	Wine	35.00
Relish.	12.00		

EGYPTIAN

Non-flint, attributed to Boston and Sandwich Glass Co., c1870.

	Clear		Clear
Bowl, 8½″	50.00	Creamer.	50.00
Bread Plate		Goblet	45.00
Cleopatra	65.00	Honey	14.00
Mormon Temple.	300.00	Pickle, oval	20.00
Butter, cov	85.00	Pitcher, water	185.00
Celery Vase	75.00	Plate, 12″, handles,	
Compote		Pyramids.	90.00
Cov, hs, 7″, Sphinx base. .	250.00	Relish.	20.00
Cov, hs, 8″ d (11″ h),		Sauce, ftd, 4½″	18.50
Sphinx base.	275.00	Spooner	40.00
Open, hs, 7½″, Sphinx		Sugar, cov	80.00
base	75.00		

EMPRESS

Made by Riverside Glass Works, Wellsburg, WV, c1898. Also found in amethyst (rare). Clear and emerald green pieces trimmed in gold; prices are for pieces with gold in very good condition.

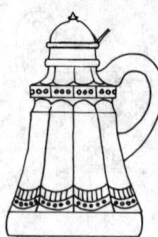

	Clear	Emerald Green		Clear	Emerald Green
Bowl, 8½"........	—	45.00	Pitcher, water	65.00	150.00
Breakfast Set, ind creamer and			Salt Shaker........	30.00	50.00
			Spooner.........	40.00	70.00
sugar	40.00	85.00	Sugar, cov	45.00	125.00
Butter, cov	50.00	100.00	Sugar Shaker	55.00	110.00
Celery Vase	55.00	—	Syrup..........	60.00	350.00
Creamer.........	40.00	80.00	Toothpick	—	150.00
Cruet	50.00	175.00	Tumbler	32.50	55.00
Oil Lamp, atypical ..	60.00	225.00			

ESTHER (Tooth and Claw)

Non-flint made by Riverside Glass Works, Wellsburg, WV, c1896. The green has gold trim. Also found in ruby stained and amber stained with enamel decoration.

	Clear	Green	Ruby Stained
Bowl, 8"	25.00	50.00	—
Butter, cov	65.00	100.00	150.00
Cake Stand, 10½"..	60.00	80.00	—
Celery Vase	40.00	90.00	—
Compote, jelly, hs ..	30.00	75.00	—
Cracker Jar.......	—	—	200.00
Creamer.........	45.00	70.00	75.00
Cruet, os	45.00	245.00	—
Goblet	40.00	95.00	75.00
Pitcher, water	65.00	165.00	250.00
Plate, 10"	—	60.00	—
Relish...........	20.00	25.00	40.00
Salt & Pepper	50.00	100.00	—
Spooner.........	35.00	50.00	60.00
Sugar, cov	55.00	70.00	100.00
Syrup...........	—	200.00	—
Toothpick	48.00	85.00	—
Tumbler	25.00	48.50	55.00
Wine	35.00	—	—

EUREKA

Flint made by Mckee & Bros in Pittsburgh, PA, in the late 1860s. Pieces have applied handles and bud finials. Made in flint and non-flint.

	Clear		Clear
Bowl		Creamer..............	45.00
6", round	25.00	Egg Cup..............	30.00
7", oval	30.00	Goblet	30.00
8", oval	35.00	Pitcher, water	95.00
Butter, cov	60.00	Salt, ftd	30.00
Champagne	35.00	Sauce, flat	10.00
Compote		Spooner..............	40.00
Cov, hs	85.00	Sugar, cov	50.00
Open, hs.............	50.00	Tumbler, ftd	25.00
Cordial...............	40.00	Wine	25.00

EVERGLADES (Carnelian)

Made by Harry Northwood Co., Wheeling, WV, c1903. Add 200% to White Opal Prices for green opalescent.

	Blue Opal	Canary Opal	Custard	White Opal
Banana Dish......	175.00	170.00	—	150.00
Bowl, berry, master .	175.00	100.00	150.00	80.00
Butter, cov	200.00	150.00	300.00	125.00
Compote, jelly.....	85.00	90.00	200.00	67.50
Creamer.........	90.00	75.00	145.00	45.00
Cruet, os	325.00	300.00	550.00	175.00
Pitcher, water	350.00	375.00	500.00	200.00
Salt Shaker.......	95.00	75.00	125.00	—
Sauce	35.00	25.00	50.00	25.00
Spooner.........	75.00	65.00	125.00	45.00
Sugar, cov	175.00	145.00	165.00	75.00
Tumbler	65.00	65.00	110.00	25.00

EXCELSIOR

Flint made by several firms, including Sandwich and McKee, from 1850s-1860s. Quality and design vary. Prices are for high quality flint.

	Clear		Clear
Bar Bottle.............	85.00	Single..............	40.00
Bowl, 10″, open.........	125.00	Goblet, Maltese Cross.....	50.00
Bitters bottle	95.00	Lamp, hand	95.00
Butter, cov	100.00	Mug.................	30.00
Candlestick...........	125.00	Pickle Jar, cov..........	45.00
Celery Vase, scalloped top..	85.00	Pitcher, water	350.00
Champagne	60.00	Salt, master	30.00
Claret................	45.00	Spillholder	75.00
Compote		Spooner..............	60.00
Cov, ls..............	125.00	Sugar, cov	85.00
Open, hs.............	85.00	Syrup................	125.00
Cordial...............	40.00	Tumbler, bar...........	50.00
Creamer..............	85.00	Whiskey, Maltese Cross....	65.00
Egg Cup		Wine	45.00
Double	55.00		

EYEWINKER

Non-flint made in Findlay, OH, in 1889. Reportedly made by Dalzell, Gilmore and Leighton Glass Co., who were organized in 1883 in West Virginia, moved to Findlay in 1888. Made only in clear glass; colors have been reproduced. A goblet and toothpick were not originally made in this pattern.

	Clear		Clear
Banana Stand, hs	135.00	Cake Stand, 8″	55.00
Bowl		Celery Vase	45.00
6½″.................	25.00	Compote	
9″, cov	75.00	Cov, hs, 6½″	60.00
* Butter, cov	70.00	Cov, hs, 9½″	90.00

	Clear		Clear
Open, 7¼", with fluted edge	65.00	9", sq, upturned sides. . . .	65.00
Open, 4½", jelly	45.00	10", upturned sides	85.00
Creamer.	65.00	Salt Shaker.	35.00
Cruet	65.00	Spooner	35.00
Lamp, kerosene	125.00	Sauce	15.00
Nappy, folded sides, 7¼" . . .	30.00	Sugar, cov	55.00
Pitcher, water	95.00	Syrup, pewter top	125.00
Plate		Tumbler	40.00
7"	30.00		

FEATHER (Doric)

Non-flint made in Indiana in 1896 and by McKee Glass. Later the pattern was reissued with variations and quality differences. Also found in amber stain (rare).

	Clear	Emerald Green		Clear	Emerald Green
Banana Boat, ftd . . .	75.00	175.00	Open, ls, 6"	20.00	—
Bowl, oval			Open, ls, 7"	30.00	—
8½"	25.00	—	Open, ls, 8"	35.00	—
9¼"	18.00	75.00	Cordial	125.00	—
Bowl, round			Creamer.	40.00	85.00
4"	15.00	—	Cruet, os	45.00	250.00
4½"	15.00	—	Dishes, nest of 3: 7",		
6"	20.00	—	8", and 9"	40.00	—
7"	25.00	75.00	Goblet	55.00	150.00
8"	30.00	85.00	Honey Dish.	15.00	—
Bowl, sq			Marmalade Jar	125.00	—
4½"	15.00	—	Pickle Castor	145.00	—
8"	30.00	—	Pitcher		
Butter, cov	55.00	130.00	Milk.	50.00	165.00
Cake Plate	65.00	—	Water	75.00	250.00
Cake Stand			Plate, 10"	35.00	—
8"	40.00	125.00	Relish.	18.00	—
9½"	50.00	125.00	Salt Shaker.	35.00	70.00
11"	70.00	175.00	Sauce	12.00	—
Celery Vase	35.00	85.00	Spooner	25.00	60.00
Champagne	65.00	—	Sugar, cov	45.00	80.00
Compote			Syrup.	125.00	300.00
Cov, hs, 8½"	125.00	250.00	Toothpick	85.00	165.00
Cov, ls, 4¼", jelly	100.00	150.00	Tumbler	45.00	85.00
Cov, ls, 8¼"	150.00	—	Wine		
Open, ls, 4"	15.00	—	Scalloped border .	40.00	—
			Straight border. . .	25.00	—

FESTOON

Non-flint, 1890-1894. No goblet or wine was made in this pattern.

	Clear		Clear
Bowl		9", rect	30.00
7 x 4½", rect	25.00	Butter, cov	40.00
8", Berry	25.00	Cake Stand, 10"	40.00

	Clear		Clear
Compote, open, hs	65.00	Sauce, flat	7.50
Creamer.	35.00	Spooner	35.00
Marmalade Jar, cov.	60.00	Sugar, cov	50.00
Pickle Castor, cov	110.00	Tray, water, 10″.	35.00
Pitcher, water	65.00	Tumbler	22.00
Plate, 7, 8, 9″.	30.00	Waste Bowl.	38.00
Relish, 9 x 5½″.	30.00		

FINECUT

Non-flint made by Bryce Bros., Pittsburgh, PA, c1879, and by U. S. Glass Co. in 1891.

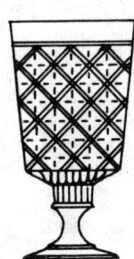

	Amber	Blue	Clear	Vaseline
Bowl, 8¼″.	15.00	20.00	10.00	15.00
Bread Plate	50.00	60.00	25.00	50.00
Butter, cov	55.00	75.00	45.00	60.00
Cake Stand	—	—	35.00	—
Celery Tray.	—	45.00	25.00	40.00
Celery Vase, SP holder	—	—	—	115.00
Creamer.	38.00	40.00	35.00	75.00
Goblet	45.00	55.00	22.00	42.00
Pitcher, water	95.00	95.00	50.00	75.00
Plate				
6″	—	20.00	8.00	—
7″	25.00	40.00	15.00	20.00
10″	30.00	50.00	21.00	45.00
Relish.	15.00	25.00	10.00	20.00
Sauce, flat	14.00	15.00	10.00	14.00
Spooner	30.00	45.00	18.00	40.00
Sugar, cov	45.00	55.00	35.00	45.00
Tray, water	50.00	55.00	25.00	50.00
Tumbler	—	—	18.00	28.00
Wine	—	—	24.00	30.00

FINECUT AND BLOCK

Made by King Glass Co., Crystal Glass Co. in c1890, and by McKee Glass Co. c1894. Also attributed to Portland Glass Co. Made in clear, solid colors of amber, blue, and yellow (all comparable in price), and in clear with color blocks.

	Clear	Solid Colored Pieces	Colored Block: Amber	Colored Block: Blue	Colored Block: Yellow or Pink
Bowl, 9″	35.00	—	—	—	—
Butter, cov					
Flat.	65.00	—	—	—	—
Footed	75.00	165.00	—	—	—
Cake Stand					
Large	40.00	—	—	—	—
Small	35.00	—	—	—	—
Celery Tray.	30.00	45.00	50.00	60.00	65.00

	Clear	Solid Colored Pieces	Colored Block: Amber	Colored Block: Blue	Colored Block: Yellow or Pink
Compote					
Cov, ls	35.00	—	—	—	—
Open, ls, 8½"	30.00	—	45.00	40.00	45.00
Open jelly	18.00	50.00	75.00	75.00	75.00
Cordial	—	—	—	65.00	—
Creamer	45.00	65.00	70.00	60.00	75.00
Goblet					
Lady's	45.00	—	—	50.00	—
Regular	32.00	65.00	60.00	65.00	60.00
Pitcher					
Milk	45.00	85.00	95.00	95.00	125.00
Water	45.00	85.00	95.00	95.00	125.00
Plate, 5¾"	12.50	—	—	—	—
Punch Cup	12.00	—	—	20.00	—
Relish, rect	12.00	—	55.00	50.00	55.00
Salt, individual	12.00	—	—	—	—
Salt, master	—	—	35.00	—	—
Sauce					
Flat	10.00	16.00	16.00	12.00	16.00
Footed	12.00	18.50	18.00	14.50	—
Spooner	30.00	45.00	55.00	65.00	50.00
Sugar, cov	45.00	—	120.00	130.00	120.00
Tray					
Ice Cream	55.00	—	—	—	—
Water	60.00	—	—	—	—
Tumbler	20.00	50.00	50.00	45.00	45.00
Wine	30.00	—	45.00	45.00	45.00

FINECUT AND PANEL

Non-flint pattern made by many Pittsburgh factories in the 1880s. Reissued in the early 1890s by U. S. Glass Co. An aqua wine is known.

	Amber	Blue	Clear	Vaseline
Bowl				
7"	28.00	35.00	15.00	30.00
8", oval	40.00	—	18.00	30.00
Bread Plate	50.00	45.00	30.00	—
Butter, cov	65.00	75.00	40.00	60.00
Cake Stand, 10"	50.00	75.00	30.00	50.00
Compote				
Cov, hs	125.00	135.00	75.00	130.00
Open, hs	65.00	65.00	35.00	60.00
Creamer	35.00	50.00	25.00	40.00
Goblet	40.00	48.00	20.00	35.00
Pitcher				
Milk	65.00	—	—	50.00
Water	85.00	85.00	40.00	45.00
Plate				
6"	25.00	30.00	15.00	25.00
7¼"	25.00	30.00	15.00	25.00
Platter	30.00	50.00	25.00	30.00
Relish	20.00	25.00	15.00	20.00
Sauce, ftd	15.00	25.00	8.00	15.00

	Amber	Blue	Clear	Vaseline
Spooner.........	35.00	45.00	20.00	30.00
Sugar, cov	37.50	42.50	30.00	32.50
Tray, water	60.00	55.00	50.00	60.00
Tumbler	25.00	30.00	20.00	38.00
Waste Bowl.......	30.00	35.00	20.00	35.00
Wine	30.00	35.00	20.00	35.00

FINE RIB

Flint made by New England Glass Co. in the 1860s. Later made in non-flint, which has limited collecting interest and priced at approximately one third the value of flint.

	Clear Flint		Clear Flint
Bitters Bottle............	65.00	Lamp	150.00
Bowl, 7", cov............	85.00	Mug..................	55.00
Butter, cov	75.00	Pitcher, ah	
Castor Set	200.00	Milk	250.00
Celery Vase	85.00	Water	350.00
Champagne	125.00	Plate, 6" or 7"	20.00
Compote		Salt	
Cov, hs, 8"............	110.00	Cov, ftd..............	85.00
Open, hs, 7¾"..........	60.00	Individual.............	35.00
Open, ls, 9"...........	75.00	Spooner..............	65.00
Cordial................	85.00	Sugar, cov	75.00
Creamer, applied handle ...	125.00	Tumbler, bar...........	85.00
Decanter, quart bar lip.....	75.00	Tumble-up	125.00
Egg Cup...............	40.00	Whiskey, handled	75.00
* Goblet	60.00	Wine	55.00
* Honey Dish, 3½"d........	16.00		

FISHSCALE (Coral)

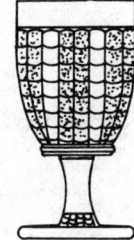

Non-flint made by Bryce Brothers, Pittsburgh, PA, in the mid-1880s and by U. S. Glass Co. in 1891.

	Clear		Clear
Bowl		Creamer..............	30.00
Cov, 7"	45.00	Goblet	25.00
Cov, 9½".............	55.00	Lamp, Finger	75.00
Open, 8"	20.00	Mug, large	35.00
Bread Plate	30.00	Pitcher	
Butter, cov	45.00	Milk................	35.00
Cake Plate	55.00	Water	55.00
Cake Stand		Plate	
9"..................	30.00	7", round	25.00
10½"................	35.00	9", square	30.00
Celery Vase	30.00	Relish................	17.50
Compote		Salt Shaker............	65.00
Cov, hs, 8"...........	85.00	Sauce	
Open, hs, 8"	30.00	Flat................	12.00
Open, hs, 9"	40.00	Footed	15.00
Open, jelly...........	18.00	Spooner..............	25.00

	Clear			Clear
Sugar, cov	50.00	Tray, condiment, rect.		35.00
Tray, attached Daisy & But-		Tumbler		75.00
ton shoe	100.00	Waste Bowl.		35.00

FLAMINGO HABITAT

Maker unknown, etched pattern.

	Clear			Clear
Bowl, 10″, oval	35.00	Open, 6″		40.00
Celery Vase	45.00	Creamer.		40.00
Champagne	45.00	Goblet		45.00
Cheese Dish, blown, folded		Sauce, ftd.		15.00
rim, dome lid	95.00	Spooner		25.00
Compote		Sugar, cov		50.00
Cov, 4½″.	75.00	Tumbler		30.00
Cov, 6½″.	95.00	Wine		40.00
Open, 5″, jelly	35.00			

FLEUR-DE-LIS AND DRAPE (Fleur-de-Lis and Tassel)

Non-flint made by U. S. Glass Co., c1892. Clear and emerald green pieces often trimmed with gilt. Also made in milk glass (rare).

	Clear	Emerald Green		Clear	Emerald Green
Bowl.	15.00	30.00	Cup	15.00	25.00
Butter, cov	45.00	55.00	Cup and Saucer . . .	25.00	35.00
Cake Stand	35.00	55.00	Goblet	25.00	45.00
Claret.	35.00	50.00	Honey Dish, cov . . .	40.00	55.00
Compote			Mustard Jar, cov . . .	35.00	50.00
Cov, ls			Pitcher		
5″	30.00	40.00	Milk.	40.00	60.00
6″	35.00	40.00	Water	50.00	65.00
7″	35.00	45.00	Plate, 8″.	20.00	35.00
8″	45.00	60.00	Salt Shaker.	20.00	35.00
Open, hs			Spooner	25.00	40.00
5″	25.00	30.00	Sugar, cov	30.00	55.00
6″	25.00	30.00	Syrup, metal top . . .	50.00	125.00
7″	30.00	35.00	Tumbler	20.00	30.00
8″	30.00	40.00	Waste Bowl.	30.00	40.00
Creamer.	25.00	40.00	Water Tray, 11½″ . .	24.00	50.00
Cruet, os	45.00	85.00	Wine	25.00	45.00

FLORIDA (Emerald Green Herringbone, Paneled Herring-bone)

Non-flint made by U. S. Glass Co., late 1880s-1890s. One of States patterns. Reproduced in green and other colors.

	Clear	Emerald Green		Clear	Emerald Green
Berry Set, master, 6			Nappy	15.00	25.00
sauces	65.00	100.00	Pitcher, water	50.00	75.00
Bowl			Plate		
7¾"	20.00	25.00	7½"	10.00	18.00
9"	20.00	25.00	9¼"	15.00	25.00
Butter, cov	50.00	85.00	Relish		
Cake Stand			6", sq	10.00	15.00
Large	60.00	72.00	8½", sq.	15.00	22.00
Small	30.00	40.00	Salt Shaker.	25.00	50.00
Celery Vase	30.00	35.00	Sauce	8.00	15.00
Compote, open, hs,			Spooner	20.00	35.00
6½", sq	—	40.00	Sugar, cov	32.00	50.00
Creamer	30.00	45.00	Syrup	60.00	175.00
Cruet, os	40.00	110.00	Table set	125.00	185.00
*Goblet	25.00	40.00	Tumbler	20.00	30.00
Mustard Pot, attach-			Wine	25.00	50.00
ed underplate, cov	25.00	45.00			

FLUTE

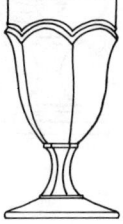

More than 15 Flute variants were produced in flint and non-flint glass from the 1850s through the 1880s. Some of the flint variants are Beaded Flute, Bessimer Flute, New England Flute, etc., all with comparable prices. Prices listed are for flint.

	Clear		Clear
Ale Glass	50.00	Single	30.00
Bitters Bottle	75.00	Goblet	25.00
Butter, cov, ls	60.00	Honey	15.00
Candlestick, 4"	50.00	Lamp	75.00
Claret	45.00	Mug	35.00
Compote		Pitcher, water	90.00
Open, ls, 8½"	40.00	Sauce, flat	15.00
Open, ls, 9½"	45.00	Sugar, cov	50.00
Creamer	45.00	Tumbler	15.00
Decanter, bar lip	75.00	Whiskey, handled	30.00
Egg Cup		Wine	25.00
Double	50.00		

FRANCES WARE

Made by Hobbs, Brockunier & Co., Wheeling, West Virginia, c1880. A clear frosted hobnail or swirl pattern glass with amber stained top rims. It may be pressed or mold blown. Swirl pieces are noted, otherwise they are hobnail.

	Clear	Frosted/ Amber Stain		Clear	Frosted/ Amber Stain
Bowl, 7½"	50.00	75.00	Creamer	50.00	85.00
Box, 5¼", round,			Cruet, os	—	175.00
cov	45.00	65.00	Finger Bowl, 4"	40.00	50.00
Butter, cov	80.00	110.00	Mustard, cov, swirl. .	—	135.00

	Clear	Frosted/ Amber Stain		Clear	Frosted/ Amber Stain
Pitcher			Syrup, swirl	85.00	175.00
8½"	90.00	150.00	Toothpick	75.00	125.00
11"	150.00	185.00	Tray		
Salt Shaker			Leaf shape, 12".	75.00	125.00
Hobnail	50.00	65.00	Rect, rounded		
Swirl	30.00	75.00	edges, 14 x		
Sauce, 4", sq	18.00	32.00	9½"	110.00	150.00
Spooner	45.00	60.00	Water, oval	—	150.00
Sugar, cov	60.00	85.00	Tumbler	35.00	45.00
Sugar Shaker, swirl .	65.00	125.00			

FROSTED CIRCLE

Produced by Bryce Bros., Pittsburgh, Pennsylvania, from 1876 to c1885. Later by U. S. Glass Co. in the late 1890s. Reproduced.

	Clear Circle	Frosted Circle		Clear Circle	Frosted Circle
Bowl, cov			* Goblet	35.00	45.00
7"	20.00	25.00	Juice	15.00	30.00
8"	25.00	30.00	Pitcher, water	55.00	80.00
Butter, cov	55.00	65.00	Plate		
Cake Stand			4"	10.00	22.00
8"	30.00	35.00	9"	22.00	25.00
9½"	40.00	50.00	Punch Cup	15.00	20.00
Champagne	35.00	55.00	Salt Shaker	25.00	35.00
Compote			Sauce	8.50	10.00
Cov, 7", hs.	30.00	65.00	Spooner	30.00	35.00
Cov, 8", hs.	45.00	75.00	* Sugar, cov	42.50	50.00
* Open, 7", hs	20.00	30.00	Sugar Shaker	40.00	65.00
* Open, 10", hs . . .	45.00	55.00	Syrup	95.00	135.00
Creamer	35.00	45.00	Tumbler	25.00	35.00
Cruet, os	45.00	65.00	Wine	35.00	45.00
Cup and Saucer . . .	25.00	40.00			

FROSTED LEAF

Flint pattern made c1850. Later production attributed to Portland Glass Co in 1863 and 1874.

	Clear		Clear
Butter, cov	135.00	Lamp, oil	500.00
Celery Vase	145.00	Pitcher, water	400.00
Champagne	160.00	Salt, ind	50.00
Compote, cov	250.00	Sauce, flat	28.00
Creamer	300.00	Spooner	85.00
Decanter, os, qt.	250.00	Sugar, cov	175.00
Egg Cup	100.00	Tumbler	150.00
Goblet	75.00	Wine	150.00

FROSTED STORK

Non-flint made by Crystal Glass Co, Bridgeport, OH, c1880. Now reproduced. Details of the stork's activities differ from scene to scene on the same piece.

	Clear		Clear
Bowl, 9″	50.00	Platter, 11½ x 8″	
Bread Plate, oval.	50.00	101 border	70.00
Butter, cov	80.00	Scenic border	68.00
Creamer.	45.00	Relish.	45.00
Finger Bowl	50.00	Sauce, flat	20.00
* Goblet	65.00	Spooner	40.00
Jam Jar, cov	125.00	Sugar, cov	95.00
Pickle, cov, stork finial	125.00	Tray, water	100.00
Pitcher, water	200.00	Waste Bowl.	50.00

GALLOWAY

Non-flint made by U. S. Glass Co., 1904. Clear glass with and without gold trim; also known with rose stain and ruby stain.

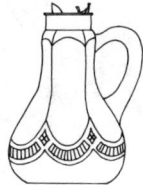

	Clear w/ Gold	Rose Stained		Clear w/ Gold	Rose Stained
Basket, no gold. . . .	75.00	—	Pitcher		
Berry Set, master, 6			Milk.	60.00	—
sauces	65.00	135.00	Tankard	75.00	—
Bowl			Water, ice lip	65.00	175.00
6½″.	25.00	—	Plate, 8″, round	40.00	65.00
8½″, oval.	25.00	—	Punch Bowl	160.00	—
8½″, round	25.00	—	Punch Bowl Plate,		
9¾″.	35.00	50.00	20″	80.00	—
11″ d, 3″ h.	45.00	—	Punch Cup	10.00	15.00
Butter, cov	65.00	125.00	Relish.	20.00	30.00
Cake Stand	65.00	90.00	Rose Bowl	25.00	—
Carafe, water	55.00	85.00	Salt Dip	25.00	—
Celery Vase	35.00	75.00	Salt & Pepper, pr. . .	35.00	—
Champagne	65.00	—	Sauce		
Compote			Flat.	10.00	—
Open, hs, 4¼″ . . .	35.00	—	Footed	12.00	—
Open, hs, 10″,			Sherbet	25.00	—
scalloped	85.00	—	Spooner	30.00	80.00
Creamer.	30.00	50.00	Sugar, cov	55.00	75.00
Cruet	45.00	—	Sugar Shaker	40.00	—
Egg Cup.	35.00	—	Syrup.	65.00	135.00
Finger Bowl	40.00	—	Toothpick	30.00	55.00
Goblet	80.00	—	Tumbler	25.00	—
Lemonade	35.00	—	Vase, swung.	30.00	—
Mug	38.00	50.00	Waste Bowl.	38.00	—
Nappy, tricorn	—	50.00	Water Bottle	40.00	—
Olive, 6″	20.00	30.00	Water Set, pitcher, 6		
Pickle Castor, sp			tumblers	225.00	350.00
holder and lid . . .	65.00	—	Wine	45.00	—

GARFIELD DRAPE

Non-flint pattern issued in 1881 by Adams & Co., Pittsburgh, Pennsylvania, after the assassination of President Garfield.

	Clear		Clear
Bread Plate		Honey Dish.	15.00
Memorial, portrait of		Goblet	40.00
Garfield	65.00	Pitcher	
"We Mourn Our Nation's		Milk.	70.00
Loss", portrait	75.00	Water, ah.	75.00
Butter, cov	60.00	Water, strap.	100.00
Cake Stand, 9½".	75.00	Relish, oval.	20.00
Celery Vase	45.00	Sauce	
Compote		Flat.	8.50
Cov, hs, 8".	100.00	Footed	12.00
Cov, ls, 6"	85.00	Spooner	30.00
Open, hs, 8½"	40.00	Sugar, cov	60.00
Creamer.	40.00	Tumbler	35.00

GEORGIA (Peacock Feather)

Probably Richards and Hartley, but reissued by several glass companies, including U. S. Glass Co. in 1902 as part of their States series. Rare in blue. (Chamber lamp, pedestal base, $275.00). No goblet known in pattern.

	Clear		Clear
Bon bon, ftd	25.00	Decanter	70.00
Bowl, 8"	25.00	Lamp	
Butter, cov	45.00	Chamber, pedestal.	85.00
Cake Stand, 10"	50.00	Hand, oil, 7"	80.00
Celery Tray, 11¾"	35.00	Mug	22.50
Compote		Nappy	28.00
Cov, hs, 8".	50.00	Pitcher, water	70.00
Open, hs, 7"	30.00	Plate, 5¼".	15.00
Open, hs, 8"	42.50	Relish.	15.00
Open, ls, 10"	30.00	Salt Shaker.	70.00
Open, jelly.	20.00	Sauce	12.50
Condiment Set, tray, oil cruet,		Spooner.	35.00
salt and pepper	75.00	Sugar, cov	45.00
Creamer.	35.00	Syrup, metal lid.	65.00
Cruet, os	55.00	Tumbler	35.00

GIANT BULL'S EYE (Bull's Eye and Spearhead)

Made by Bellaire Glass Co., Findlay, Ohio, and continued by U. S. Glass Co. after 1891.

	Clear		Clear
Bowl, 8"	25.00	Claret Jug, tankard shape . .	60.00
Brandy bottle, os, tall,		Compote, cov	75.00
narrow	55.00	Creamer.	30.00
Butter, cov	45.00	Cruet, os	60.00
Cake Stand	30.00	Decanter, os	50.00
Cheese Dish, cov	45.00	Goblet	45.00

	Clear		Clear
Lamp, handled	125.00	Tumbler	30.00
Pitcher, water	75.00	Vase	35.00
Relish.	15.00	Wine	30.00
Tray, wine, 7¼"	45.00		

GOOSEBERRY

Non-flint of the 1880s. Made by Boston and Sandwich Glass Co. and others in clear and milk glass. Reproduced in milk glass.

	Clear	Milk Glass		Clear	Milk Glass
Butter, cov	50.00	75.00	Mug	35.00	40.00
Compote			Pitcher, water, ah . .	165.00	225.00
Cov, hs, 6"	60.00	65.00	Sauce	10.00	15.00
Cov, hs, 7"	70.00	75.00	Spooner	25.00	30.00
Cov, hs, 8"	75.00	90.00	Sugar, Cov	45.00	55.00
Creamer	30.00	50.00	Syrup, ah	75.00	135.00
Goblet	35.00	45.00	Tumbler	35.00	40.00

GOTHIC

Flint made by Boston and Sandwich Glass Co., c1860s.

	Clear		Clear
Bowl, 7"	70.00	Creamer, ah	75.00
Butter, cov	85.00	Egg Cup.	50.00
Castor Set, pewter frame. . .	125.00	Goblet	65.00
Celery Vase	90.00	Sauce, flat	15.00
Champagne	165.00	Spooner	40.00
Compote		Sugar, cov	85.00
Cov, hs, 8"	110.00	Tumbler	95.00
Open, ls, 7"	65.00	Wine	125.00

GRAND (Diamond Medallion)

Non-flint, made by Bryce, Higbee and Co. 1885. Stemware comes in plain and ringed stems.

	Clear		Clear
Bowl, 6", cov.	30.00	Compote	
Bread Plate, 10"	25.00	Cov, hs, 5½"	60.00
Butter, cov		Cov, hs, 7½"	75.00
Flat.	35.00	Open, hs, 9"	65.00
Footed	45.00	Cordial	50.00
Cake Stand		Creamer.	25.00
8"	30.00	Goblet	25.00
10"	35.00	Pitcher, water	40.00
Celery Vase, pedestal	25.00	Plate, 10"	25.00

	Clear		Clear
Relish, 7½", oval	12.00	Spooner	20.00
Salt Shaker	30.00	Sugar, cov	35.00
Sauce		Syrup, metal top	90.00
Flat	10.00	Waste Bowl, collared	30.00
Footed	12.00	Wine	25.00

GRAPE AND FESTOON WITH STIPPLED LEAF

Non-flint pattern made by Doyle & Company, Pittsburgh, PA, in the early 1870s.

	Clear		Clear
Bowl	15.00	Mug	20.00
Butter, cov	50.00	Pitcher	
Buttermilk Goblet	30.00	Milk, ah	75.00
Celery Vase	40.00	Water, ah	90.00
Compote		Plate, 6"	18.00
Cov, hs, 8"	115.00	Relish	12.50
Open, ls, 8"	75.00	Salt, ftd	24.00
Creamer, ah	50.00	Sauce, flat, 4"	10.00
Egg Cup	30.00	Spooner	35.00
Goblet	35.00	Sugar, cov	50.00
Lamp, oil, 7½"	65.00	Wine	45.00

GRASSHOPPER (Long Spear)

Maker unknown; over 40 pieces documented. Pieces without the grasshopper bring 40–50% less. Creamer and sugar known in vaseline and blue. Goblet is modern.

	Amber	Clear		Amber	Clear
Bowl			Pitcher, water	125.00	75.00
Covered	55.00	35.00	Plate		
Open, ftd	—	25.00	8½", ftd	—	25.00
Butter, cov	90.00	65.00	9", ftd	—	20.00
Celery Vase	90.00	50.00	10½", ftd	—	25.00
Compote			Salt Dip	—	40.00
Cov, hs, 7"	—	50.00	Salt Shaker	—	35.00
Cov, hs, 8½"	—	65.00	Sauce		
Creamer	60.00	40.00	Flat	—	15.00
Marmalade Jar, cov,			Footed	—	18.00
insert	—	125.00	Spooner	75.00	40.00
Pickle	—	20.00	Sugar, cov	80.00	70.00

HAIRPIN (Sandwich Loop)

Flint pattern made in the Sandwich factory c1850. Finials are acorn shaped, handles are applied.

	Clear		Clear
Bowl, 6¼" d	100.00	Compote, cov hs	225.00
Celery Vase	40.00	Creamer, ah	55.00
Champagne	80.00	Decanter, os, qt.	90.00

	Clear		Clear
Egg Cup	30.00	Sugar, cov	95.00
Goblet	40.00	Tumbler	50.00
Salt, cov, ftd	85.00	Whiskey, handled	45.00
Sauce, flat	15.00	Wine	50.00
Spooner	40.00		

HALLEY'S COMET (Etruria)

Clear non-flint pattern made by Model Flint Glass Co, c1880. The tail of the comet forms continuous loops. A ruby stained wine is known.

	Clear		Clear
Bowl		Goblet	35.00
4", cov, 3 ftd	40.00	Mustard, cov, ftd	45.00
8"	25.00	Pitcher, water	100.00
9"	25.00	Punch Cup	25.00
Butter, cov	80.00	Relish	25.00
Cake Stand	75.00	Salt & Pepper, pr	45.00
Celery Vase	30.00	Spooner	45.00
Compote		Sugar, cov	65.00
Cov, hs, 10"	60.00	Syrup	85.00
Open, hs, 8"	40.00	Tumbler	25.00
Creamer	35.00	Wine	25.00
Cruet, os	60.00		

HAND (Pennsylvania #2)

Made by O'Hara Glass Co., Pittsburgh, Pennsylvania, c1880. Covered pieces have a hand holding bar finial, hence the name.

	Clear		Clear
Bowl		Goblet	45.00
9"	37.50	Marmalade Jar, cov	90.00
10"	40.00	Pickle	20.00
Butter, cov	85.00	Pitcher, water	75.00
Cake Stand	55.00	Sauce	
Celery Vase	48.00	Flat	12.00
Compote		Footed	15.00
Cov, hs, 7"	60.00	Spooner	30.00
Cov, hs, 8"	95.00	Sugar, cov	75.00
Open, hs, 7¾"	45.00	Syrup	125.00
Open, ls, 9"	20.00	Tumbler	85.00
Cordial, 3½"	85.00	Wine	55.00
Creamer	40.00		

HANOVER (Block With Stars #2, Blockhouse)

Originally made by Richards and Hartley, of Tarentum, Pennsylvania, in 1888 and possibly earlier. Made in many pieces. Also made in blue.

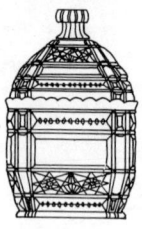

	Clear	Dark Amber		Clear	Dark Amber
Bowl, 10", berry. . . .	20.00	40.00	Ketchup Bottles, pr .	50.00	75.00
Bread Plate, 10" . . .	20.00	30.00	Mug		
Butter, cov	35.00	80.00	Large	24.00	48.00
Cake Stand, 10" . . .	42.00	62.00	Small	20.00	40.00
Celery Vase	27.00	38.00	Pitcher, water	50.00	85.00
Cheese Dish, cov,			Plate		
10"	50.00	95.00	4"	25.00	40.00
Compote			6"	25.00	40.00
Cov, hs	45.00	90.00	10"	18.00	45.00
Open, hs.	40.00	—	Puff Box, glass lid . .	45.00	—
Open, ls	40.00	45.00	Sauce, ftd.	10.00	15.00
Creamer.	30.00	45.00	Spooner	25.00	37.00
Cruet, os	50.00	—	Sugar, cov	45.00	55.00
Goblet	25.00	55.00	Tumbler	25.00	30.00

HARTLEY (Paneled Diamond Cut With Fan)

Non-flint pattern made by Richards and Hartley in 1880s, and by U. S. Glass Co in 1891. Trilobed form has either plain or engraved panels. Twenty-three pieces documented.

	Amber	Blue & Vaseline	Clear
Bowl, berry			
7", ftd	30.00	35.00	15.00
9"	30.00	35.00	15.00
Bread Plate, trilobed	30.00	40.00	20.00
Butter, cov	50.00	60.00	40.00
Cake Stand, 10" . . .	45.00	50.00	40.00
Celery Vase	30.00	40.00	25.00
Compote			
Cov, ls, 7¾".	65.00	75.00	45.00
Open, 7" and 8". .	30.00	40.00	18.00
Creamer.	30.00	35.00	20.00
Dish, centerpiece . .	40.00	45.00	20.00
Goblet	35.00	40.00	25.00
Pitcher			
Milk, qt	80.00	85.00	75.00
Water, ½ gal	90.00	90.00	85.00
Plate	45.00	50.00	30.00
Relish.	18.00	20.00	15.00
Spooner	28.00	30.00	18.00
Sugar, cov	40.00	50.00	30.00
Tumbler	30.00	35.00	20.00
Wine	40.00	45.00	20.00

HEART WITH THUMBPRINT (Bull's Eye in Heart)

Non-flint, made by Tarentum Glass Co. 1898. Some emerald green pieces have gold trim. Made experimentally in custard, blue custard, opaque nile green and cobalt. Some pieces are found with ruby stain. (Creamer $175.00)

	Clear	Emerald Green		Clear	Emerald Green
Banana Boat	75.00	—	Oil, 8″	50.00	160.00
Barber Bottle	115.00	—	Mustard, SP cov	95.00	100.00
Bowl			Nappy, turned up		
7″ sq	35.00	—	edges	32.50	65.00
9″	42.00	—	Pitcher, water	200.00	—
9½″ sq	35.00	—	Plate		
10″ scalloped	45.00	—	6″	25.00	75.00
Butter, cov	125.00	175.00	10″	35.00	—
Cake Stand, 9″	150.00	—	Powder Jar, SP cov.	65.00	—
Carafe, water	100.00	—	Punch Cup	20.00	35.00
Card Tray	20.00	45.00	Rose Bowl		
Celery Vase	65.00	—	Large	60.00	—
Compote			Small	30.00	—
Open, hs, 7½″,			Salt & Pepper	95.00	—
scalloped	150.00	—	Sauce, 5″	20.00	35.00
Open, hs, 8½″	100.00	—	Spooner	50.00	—
Cordial, 3″ h	125.00	—	Sugar		
Creamer			Ind	25.00	35.00
Ind	22.50	45.00	Regular, cov	85.00	90.00
Regular	60.00	110.00	Syrup	95.00	—
Cruet	75.00	—	Tray, 8¼″ l, 4¼″ w.	35.00	—
Finger Bowl	45.00	—	Tumbler	45.00	—
Goblet	58.00	125.00	Vase		
Hair Receiver, metal			6″	35.00	65.00
lid	65.00	—	10″	65.00	—
Ice Bucket	60.00	—	Wine	45.00	—
Lamp					
Finger	65.00	115.00			

HICKMAN (La Clede)

Non-flint pattern made by McKee Glass Co., Pittsburgh, Pennsylvania, c1897. Also made in ruby stain (rare).

	Clear	Emerald Green		Clear	Emerald Green
Banana Stand, ftd	65.00	—	Compote		
Bon bon, 9″, sq	15.00	—	Cov, hs, 7″	75.00	—
Bottle, Pepper	25.00	—	Open, hs, 8″	45.00	—
Bowl			Open, ls, 4½″,		
Round, or with			jelly	40.00	45.00
scalloped top			Condiment Set, han-		
4″	12.00	—	dled tray, cruet,		
4½″	12.00	—	pepper bottle,		
5″	14.00	18.00	open salt	85.00	110.00
6″	15.00	25.00	Cordial	24.00	—
7″	15.00	—	Creamer	25.00	35.00
8″	18.00	—	Cruet, os	45.00	—
Square, 7″	15.00	18.00	Cup, Custard	12.00	—
Butter, cov	35.00	58.00	Dish, 4″ sq	16.00	—
8½″	30.00	—	Goblet	30.00	40.00
9½″	32.50	—	Ice Bucket	60.00	—
Celery	25.00	32.00	Lemonade	15.00	—
Champagne	25.00	—	Mustard Jar, under-		
Cologne Bottle, fac-			plate, cov	45.00	—
eted stopper	30.00	—	Nappy, 5″	10.00	—

	Clear	Emerald Green			Clear	Emerald Green
Olive, 4", handle . . .	10.00	20.00	Round, squat. . . .		20.00	30.00
Pickle.	15.00	20.00	Square		20.00	—
Pitcher, water	55.00	—	Sauce		8.50	10.00
Plate, 9¼".	15.00	—	Spooner.		27.00	—
Punch Bowl	175.00	375.00	Sugar, cov		42.00	50.00
Punch Cup	10.00	15.00	Sugar Shaker		45.00	—
Punch Glass, ftd . . .	30.00	—	Toothpick		45.00	75.00
Relish.	18.00	15.00	Tumbler		30.00	—
Rose Bowl	25.00	—	Vase, 10¼".		12.00	45.00
Salt, individual, flat, sloping sides	10.00	—	Wine		30.00	35.00
Salt Shaker, single Round, long cut neck	15.00	—				

HIDALGO (Frosted Waffle)

Non-flint made by Adams and Co., Pittsburgh, Pennsylvania, in the early 1880s and U S Glass Co in 1891. This pattern comes etched and clear, and also with part of pattern frosted. Add 20% for frosted. Rare in color.

	Amber Stained	Clear		Amber Stained	Clear
Bowl, 10", sq	35.00	20.00	Pickle, boat shaped.	18.00	12.00
Bread Plate, cupped, sq, 10"	75.00	60.00	Pitcher		
Butter, cov	—	50.00	Milk.	—	40.00
Celery Vase	35.00	20.00	Water	—	45.00
Compote			Plate, 10"	—	35.00
Cov, hs, 7½"	85.00	65.00	Salt, master, sq. . . .	—	25.00
Cov, ls, 6"	—	50.00	Salt & Pepper.	—	40.00
Open, hs, 10" . . .	—	45.00	Sauce, handled. . . .	—	10.00
Open, hs, 11" . . .	—	50.00	Spooner.	—	20.00
Creamer.	—	40.00	Sugar, cov	—	48.00
Cruet	—	65.00	Sugar Shaker	—	45.00
Cup and Saucer . . .	—	40.00	Syrup.	—	60.00
Egg Cup.	—	30.00	Tray, water	—	55.00
Goblet	40.00	20.00	Tumbler	—	25.00
Nappy, handled, sq .	—	18.00	Waste Bowl.	—	25.00

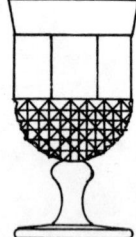

HINOTO (Diamond Point With Panels)

Flint made by Boston and Sandwich Co in the late 1850s.

	Clear		Clear
Butter, cov	90.00	Pitcher, tankard.	110.00
Celery Vase	65.00	Salt	35.00
Champagne	75.00	Spooner.	35.00
Cologne Bottle, os.	48.00	Sugar, cov	75.00
Creamer, ah	75.00	Tumbler	45.00
Egg Cup.	35.00	Whiskey	50.00
Goblet	60.00	Wine	65.00

HOLLY

Non-flint made by Boston and Sandwich Glass Co., late 1860s, early 1870s.

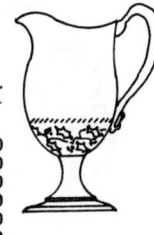

	Clear		Clear
Butter, cov	150.00	Salt	
Cake Stand, 11″	135.00	Flat, oval.	65.00
Celery Vase	85.00	Ftd	60.00
Compote, cov, hs	165.00	Sauce, flat	20.00
Creamer, ah	125.00	Spooner.	60.00
Egg Cup.	65.00	Sugar, cov	125.00
Goblet	100.00	Tumbler	125.00
Pitcher, water, ah	225.00	Wine	125.00

HONEYCOMB

A popular pattern made in flint and non-flint glass by numerous firms, c1850–1900, resulting in many minor pattern variations. Rare in color.

	Flint	Non-Flint		Flint	Non-Flint
Ale Glass	50.00	25.00	Finger Bowl	48.00	—
Barber Bottle	45.00	25.00	Goblet	25.00	15.00
7¼″, oval, base mkd "Mould pat'd May 11, 1869," acorn finial on cov	90.00	40.00	Honey, cov	—	25.00
			Lamp		
			All Glass	—	45.00
			Marble base	—	40.00
10″	—	40.00	Lemonade	40.00	20.00
Butter, cov	65.00	45.00	Mug, half pint	25.00	15.00
Cake Stand	55.00	35.00	Pitcher, water, ah . .	165.00	60.00
Castor Bottle.	25.00	18.00	Plate, 6″	—	12.50
Celery Vase	45.00	20.00	Pomade Jar, cov . . .	48.00	20.00
Champagne	50.00	—	Relish.	30.00	—
Claret.	35.00	—	Salt, master, cov, ftd.	35.00	30.00
Compote, cov, hs			Salt & Pepper	—	40.00
6½″ x 8½″h	100.00	50.00	Sauce	12.00	7.50
9¼ x 11½″h.	110.00	65.00	Spillholder	24.00	—
Compote, open, hs			Spooner	65.00	35.00
7 x 5″h	35.00	25.00	Sugar		
7 x 7″h	60.00	40.00	Frosted rosebud finial	—	50.00
7½″, scalloped top.	40.00	—	Regular.	75.00	45.00
8 x 6¼″h	65.00	—	Tumbler		
11 x 8″h	135.00	—	Bar.	35.00	—
Compote, open, ls,			Flat.	—	12.50
7½″, scalloped. . .	40.00	—	Footed	—	15.00
Cordial, 3½″	25.00	—	Lemonade.	40.00	—
Creamer, ah	35.00	20.00	Vase		
Decanter			7½″.	45.00	—
Pint.	55.00	18.50	10½″.	75.00	—
Quart, os.	70.00	65.00	Whiskey, handled . .	125.00	—
Egg Cup.	20.00	15.00	Wine	35.00	15.00

HORN OF PLENTY

A fine flint glass pattern reputed to have been first made by Boston and Sandwich Glass Co. in the 1850s. Later made in flint and non-flint by other firms.

	Clear Flint		Clear Flint
Bar Bottle, pewter spout, 8″ .	135.00	Quart	165.00
Bowl, 8½″	145.00	Egg Cup	45.00
Butter, cov		* Goblet	75.00
Conventional finial	125.00	* Lamp	200.00
Shape of Acorn	130.00	Mug, small, applied handle .	150.00
Butter Pat	20.00	Pepper Sauce Bottle, pewter	
Cake Stand	350.00	top	200.00
Celery Vase	150.00	Pitcher, water	600.00
Champagne	145.00	Plate, 6″	100.00
Compote		Relish, 7″ l, 5″ w	45.00
Cov, hs, 6¼″	175.00	Salt, master, oval, flat	75.00
Cov, hs, 8¼″ d, 5¾″ h,		Sauce	
oval	350.00	4½″	20.00
Open, hs, 7″	125.00	5¼″	25.00
Open, hs, 8″	115.00	Spillholder	65.00
Open, hs, 9¼″	200.00	Spooner	45.00
Open, hs, 10½″	140.00	Sugar, cov	125.00
Open, ls, 8″	55.00	Tumbler	
Open, ls, 9″	85.00	Bar	85.00
Cordial	150.00	Water	75.00
Creamer, ah		Whiskey	
5½″	235.00	Applied handle	235.00
7″	175.00	Shot glass, 3″	100.00
Decanter, os		Wine	125.00
Pint	150.00		

HORSESHOE (Good Luck, Prayer Rug)

Non-flint made by Adams & Co. and others in the 1880s.

	Clear		Clear
Bowl, cov, oval		Creamer, 6½″	55.00
7″	150.00	Doughnut Stand	75.00
8″	195.00	Finger Bowl	80.00
Bread Plate, 14 x 10″		Goblet	
Double horseshoe		Knob Stem	40.00
handles	65.00	Plain Stem	38.00
Single horseshoe handles .	40.00	Marmalade Jar, cov	110.00
Butter, cov	95.00	Pitcher	
Cake Plate	40.00	Milk	110.00
Cake Stand		Water	85.00
9″	70.00	Plate	
10″	80.00	7″	45.00
Celery Vase, knob stem	40.00	10″	55.00
Cheese, cov, woman		Relish, 5 x 7″	20.00
churning	275.00	Salt	
Compote		Ind, horseshoe shape	20.00
Cov, hs, 7″, horseshoe		Master, horseshoe shape	100.00
finial	95.00	Sauce	
Cov, hs, 8 x 12¼″	125.00	Flat	10.00
Cov, hs, 11″	135.00	Footed	15.00

	Clear			Clear
Spooner	35.00		Waste Bowl, ...	45.00
Sugar, cov	65.00		Wine	150.00
Vegetable Dish, oblong	35.00			

HUBER

(Straight Huber) Flint pattern made by Boston and Sandwich Glass Co, Sandwich, MA, and Bakewell, Pears and Co, Pittsburgh, PA, in the 1860s. Also found in non-flint, values would be 35% of prices shown.

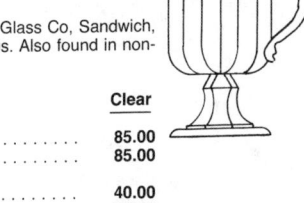

	Clear			Clear
Ale Glass	20.00		Stopper, pt.	85.00
Bitters Bottle	50.00		Stopper, qt.	85.00
Bowl			Egg Cup	
6"	40.00		Handle	40.00
7", cov	70.00		Regular	30.00
Butter, cov	85.00		Goblet	35.00
Celery	65.00		Lemonade	25.00
Champagne	35.00		Mug	35.00
Claret	50.00		Pitcher, water	150.00
Compote			Plate, 7½"	30.00
Cov, hs, 8"	100.00		Salt, ftd	25.00
Cov, hs, 10"	100.00		Sauce, flat	15.00
Cov, ls, 8"	100.00		Spooner	35.00
Open, 7"	60.00		Sugar, cov	70.00
Open, 8", engraved	75.00		Tumbler	
Cordial	40.00		Jelly	25.00
Creamer	80.00		Water	20.00
Decanter			Whiskey	35.00
Bar Lip, pt	70.00		Wine	30.00
Bar Lip, qt	75.00			

ILLINOIS

Non-flint. One of the States patterns made by U. S. Glass Co., c1897. Most forms are square. A few items are known in ruby stained, including a salt, $50.00, and a lidless straw holder with the stain on the inside, $95.00.

	Clear	Emerald Green		Clear	Emerald Green
Basket, ah, 11½". . .	100.00	—	Pitcher, water		
Bowl, 8"	35.00	—	Square	65.00	—
Butter, cov	60.00	—	Tankard, round, SP rim	75.00	135.00
Candlesticks, pr . . .	80.00	—	Plate, 7", sq	25.00	—
Celery Tray, 11" . . .	40.00	—	Relish		
Cheese, cov	75.00	—	7½" x 4"	18.00	—
Creamer			8½ x 3"	18.00	—
Ind	30.00	—	Salt		
Regular	40.00	—	Ind	15.00	—
Cruet	65.00	—	Master	25.00	—
Marmalade Jar	135.00	—	Salt and Pepper, pr	40.00	—
Olive	18.00	—	Sauce	20.00	—
Pitcher, milk, round, SP rim	175.00	—	Spooner	35.00	—

	Clear	Emerald Green		Clear	Emerald Green
Straw Holder, glass			Plain	30.00	—
cov	175.00	400.00	Tray, 12 x 8″, turned		
Sugar			up sides	50.00	—
Ind	30.00	—	Tumbler	30.00	40.00
Regular, cov	55.00	—	Vase, 6″, sq	35.00	45.00
Sugar Shaker	65.00	—	Vase, 9½″.	—	125.00
Syrup, pewter top . .	95.00	—			
Toothpick					
Adv emb in base .	45.00	—			

INTAGLIO (Flower Spray with Scroll)

Made by Northwood Co., Indiana, Pennsylvania, c1899. Also reported in custard trimmed in green and gold. Creamers in blue opalescent were used as premiums in 1901 by Arbuckle Coffee.

	Blue Opal	Custard	Vaseline Opal	White Opal
Bowl, berry	50.00	50.00	60.00	45.00
Butter, cov	165.00	235.00	170.00	150.00
Compote, jelly	45.00	100.00	60.00	35.00
Creamer	60.00	100.00	50.00	40.00
Cruet, os	100.00	210.00	110.00	95.00
Pitcher, water	200.00	—	225.00	125.00
Sauce	35.00	90.00	42.00	25.00
Spooner	75.00	115.00	80.00	50.00
Sugar, cov	150.00	100.00	100.00	85.00
Tumbler	65.00	70.00	58.00	45.00
Wine	—	—	—	20.00

INVERTED FAN AND FEATHER

Made by Northwood Co., Wheeling, West Virginia, c1900. Also known in carnival and canary opalescent. See Pink Slag.

	Blue Opal	Clear Opal	Custard	Green With Gold
Bowl, berry				
Individual.	40.00	—	40.00	15.00
Master	125.00	100.00	225.00	110.00
Butter, cov	275.00	195.00	245.00	200.00
Compote, jelly	200.00	195.00	175.00	195.00
Creamer	80.00	65.00	175.00	85.00
Cruet	200.00	195.00	575.00	195.00
Pitcher, water	325.00	200.00	500.00	215.00
Rose Bowl, ftd	150.00	—	—	—
Salt Shaker, single .	—	—	95.00	—
Spooner	100.00	75.00	100.00	75.00
*Sugar, cov	145.00	95.00	125.00	100.00
*Tumbler	80.00	25.00	80.00	35.00

INVERTED FERN

Flint, c1860. Attributed to Boston and Sandwich Glass Co. Goblets reproduced in color.

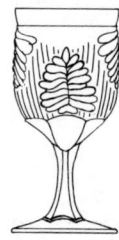

	Clear		Clear
Bowl, 7″	45.00	Plate, 6″	100.00
Butter, cov	95.00	Pitcher, water	250.00
Champagne	125.00	Salt, master, ftd.	35.00
Compote, open, hs, 8″	55.00	Sauce, flat	10.00
Creamer, ah	125.00	Spooner	40.00
Egg Cup.	30.00	Sugar, cov	80.00
Goblet, rayed base	45.00	Tumbler	95.00
Honey Dish.	18.00	Wine	75.00

IOWA (Paneled Zipper)

Non-flint made by U. S. Glass Co. c1902. Part of the States pattern series. Available in clear glass with gold trim (add 20%) and ruby or cranberry stained. Also found in amber (goblet $65.00), green, canary, and blue. Add 50% to 100% for color and amber stained.

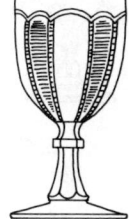

	Clear		Clear
Bowl, berry	12.00	Olive	15.00
Bread Plate, motto	80.00	Pitcher, water	50.00
Butter, cov	40.00	Punch Cup	15.00
Cake Stand	35.00	Salt Shaker, single	24.00
Carafe	35.00	Sauce, 4½″.	6.50
Compote, cov, 8″	40.00	Spooner	30.00
Corn Liquor Jug, os.	60.00	Sugar, cov	35.00
Creamer	30.00	Table Set, 4 pc	125.00
Cruet, os	30.00	Toothpick	20.00
Cup	15.00	Tumbler	25.00
Goblet	28.00	Wine	32.50
Lamp	125.00		

IRIS WITH MEANDER (Iris)

Made by Jefferson Glass Co., Steubenville, Ohio, c1903. Available in gold trim in clear, apple green, amethyst (toothpick $50.00; water pitcher $115.00), and blue. Also found in amber opalescent (rare) and green opalescent (usually found in berry sets and toothpicks).

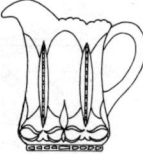

	Blue Opal	Canary Opal	White Opal
Bowl, berry	95.00	80.00	50.00
Butter, cov	310.00	195.00	125.00
Compote, jelly, 5″ . .	85.00	75.00	50.00
Creamer	145.00	100.00	60.00
Cruet, os	200.00	150.00	100.00
Pickle	30.00	30.00	20.00
Pitcher, water	225.00	200.00	125.00
Plate, 7″	50.00	60.00	35.00
Salt & Pepper	100.00	100.00	85.00
Sauce	30.00	30.00	30.00

	Blue Opal	Canary Opal	White Opal
Spooner	75.00	65.00	50.00
Sugar, cov	150.00	100.00	80.00
*Toothpick	85.00	60.00	50.00
Tumbler	60.00	45.00	30.00
Vase, 11″	60.00	35.00	25.00

IVY IN SNOW (Ivy in Snow-Red Leaves, Forrest Ware)

Non-flint pattern made by Co-operative Flint Glass Co., Beaver Falls, Pennsylvania, in the 1880s. Phoenix Glass of Monaco, Pennsylvainia, also produced this pattern from 1937 to 1942 and was called Forrest Ware. Ivy In Snow-Red Leaves is the name used for pieces where the leaves are ruby stained. Some pieces have a ruby stained band. Also known in amber stained. Widely reproduced pattern.

	Clear	Ruby Stained		Clear	Rose Stained
Bowl			Mug	25.00	40.00
7″	20.00	—	Pitcher		
8 x 5½″	30.00	—	Milk	—	200.00
Butter, cov	55.00	—	Water	55.00	—
Cake Stand, 8″	45.00	—	Plate		
Celery Vase	30.00	75.00	6″	20.00	—
Compote			7″	25.00	—
Cov, hs, 8″	75.00	—	10″	30.00	—
Open, jelly	30.00	—	Relish	20.00	—
Creamer			Sauce	12.00	—
Regular	28.00	75.00	Spooner	35.00	60.00
Tankard	35.00	135.00	Sugar, cov	50.00	75.00
Finger Bowl	25.00	—	Syrup	70.00	275.00
Goblet	32.00	65.00	Tumbler	25.00	45.00
Marmalade Jar	35.00	—	Wine	32.00	55.00

JACOB'S LADDER (Maltese)

Non-flint made by Portland Glass Co, Portland, ME, and Bryce Bros, Pittsburgh, PA, in 1876, and U. S. Glass Co in 1891. A few pieces found in amber, yellow, blue, pale blue, and pale green.

	Clear		Clear
Bowl		Cologne Bottle, Maltese	
6″ x 8¾″	15.00	cross stopper, ftd	85.00
6¾″ x 9¾″	20.00	Compote	
7½″ x 10¾″	20.00	Cov, hs, 6″	60.00
9″, berry, ornate SP holder,		Cov, hs 7½″	60.00
ftd	125.00	Cov, hs, 9½″	125.00
Butter, cov	65.00	Open, hs, 7½″	35.00
Cake Stand		Open, hs, 8½″, scalloped .	30.00
8″ or 9″	50.00	Open, hs, 9½″, scalloped .	38.00
11″ or 12″	60.00	Open, hs, 10″	40.00
Castor Bottle	18.00	Creamer	35.00
Castor Set, 4 bottles	100.00	Cruet, os, ftd	85.00
Celery Vase	35.00	Goblet	60.00

	Clear		Clear
Honey, 3½".	10.00	Footed, 4"	12.00
Marmalade Jar	75.00	Spooner	35.00
Mug	100.00	Sugar, cov	60.00
Pitcher, water	150.00	Syrup	
Plate, 6¼".	20.00	Knight's Head finial	125.00
Relish, 9½ x 5½"	15.00	Plain top	100.00
Salt, master, ftd.	20.00	Tumbler, bar	85.00
Sauce		Wine	35.00
Flat, 4", and 5".	8.00		

JERSEY SWIRL (Swirl)

Non-flint pattern made by Windsor Glass Co., Pittsburgh, Pennsylvania, c1887. Heavily reproduced in color. The clear goblet also reproduced.

	Amber	Blue	Canary	Clear
Bowl, 9¼".	55.00	55.00	45.00	35.00
Butter, cov	55.00	55.00	50.00	40.00
Cake Stand, 9"	75.00	70.00	45.00	30.00
* Celery Vase	42.00	42.00	35.00	30.00
* Compote, hs, 8" . . .	50.00	50.00	45.00	35.00
Creamer.	45.00	45.00	40.00	30.00
Cruet, os	—	—	—	25.00
* Goblet				
Buttermilk	40.00	40.00	35.00	30.00
Water	40.00	40.00	35.00	30.00
Marmalade Jar	—	—	—	50.00
Pickle Castor, SP				
frame and lid	—	—	—	125.00
Pitcher, water	50.00	50.00	45.00	35.00
Plate, round				
6"	25.00	25.00	20.00	15.00
8"	30.00	30.00	25.00	20.00
10"	38.00	38.00	35.00	30.00
Salt, Ind	20.00	20.00	18.00	15.00
Sauce, 4½", flat . . .	20.00	20.00	15.00	10.00
Spooner	30.00	30.00	25.00	20.00
Sugar, cov	40.00	40.00	35.00	30.00
Tumbler	30.00	30.00	25.00	20.00
Wine	50.00	50.00	40.00	15.00

KANSAS (Jewel With Dewdrop)

Non-flint originally produced by Co-Operative Flint Glass Co., Beaver Falls, Pennsylvania. Later produced as part of the States pattern series by U. S. Glass Co. in 1901. Also known with jewels stained in pink or gold. Mugs have been reproduced in vaseline, amber, and blue.

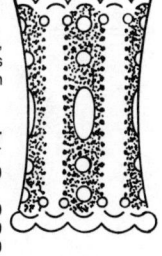

	Clear		Clear
Banana Stand.	90.00	Cake Plate	45.00
Bowl		Cake Stand	
7", oval	35.00	7⅝".	45.00
8½".	45.00	9"	50.00
Bread Plate, ODB	45.00	10"	85.00
Butter, cov	65.00	Celery Vase	45.00

	Clear			Clear
Compote			Water	60.00
Cov, hs, 7″	80.00		Relish, 8½″, oval	20.00
Cov, hs, 8″	125.00		Salt Shaker	50.00
Open, hs, 6½″, jelly	50.00		Sauce, flat, 4″	15.00
Open, hs, 9½″	60.00		Sugar, cov	65.00
Open, ls, 6½″	45.00		Syrup	125.00
Creamer	40.00		Toothpick	65.00
Goblet	55.00		Tumbler	45.00
Mug, regular	45.00		Whiskey	15.00
Pitcher			Wine	65.00
Milk	50.00			

KENTUCKY

Non-flint made by U. S. Glass Co., c1897, as part of the States pattern series. The goblet is found in ruby stained ($50.00). A footed, square sauce ($30.00) is known in cobalt blue with gold. A toothpick holder is also known in ruby stained, $150.00.

	Clear	Emerald Green		Clear	Emerald Green
Butter, cov	50.00	—	Punch Cup	10.00	15.00
Cake Stand, 9½″	40.00	—	Salt & Pepper	50.00	—
Creamer	25.00	—	Sauce, ftd, sq	8.00	12.00
Cruet, os	45.00	—	Spooner	35.00	—
Cup	10.00	20.00	Sugar, cov	30.00	—
Goblet	20.00	50.00	Toothpick, sq	35.00	85.00
Nappy	10.00	15.00	Tumbler	20.00	30.00
Pitcher, water	55.00	—	Wine	28.00	38.00
Plate, 7″, sq	15.00	—			

KING'S CROWN (Ruby Thumbprint; X.L.C.R.)

Known as Ruby Thumbprint when pieces are ruby stained. A non-flint pattern made by Adams and Co., Pittsburgh, Pennsylvania, in the 1890s and later. Made in clear and with the thumbprints stained amethyst, gold, green, and yellow, and in clear with etching and trimmed in gold. It became very popular after 1891 as ruby stained souvenir ware. Cobalt blue pieces reported as very rare. Approximately 87 pieces documented. NOTE: Pattern has been copiously reproduced for the gift-trade market. New pieces are easily distinguished: in the case of Ruby Thumbprint, the color is a very pale pinkish red; green and blue pieces have an off-color. Reproduced in milk glass. Available in amethyst stained in goblet ($30.00) and wine ($10.00) and in green stained in goblet ($25.00) and wine ($15.00). Add 30% for engraved pieces.

	Clear	Ruby Stained		Clear	Ruby Stained
Banana Stand, ftd	85.00	135.00	Castor Bottle	45.00	70.00
Bowl			Castor Set, glass		
9¼″, pointed	35.00	90.00	stand, 4 bottles	175.00	325.00
10″, scalloped	45.00	95.00	Celery Vase	40.00	60.00
Butter, cov	50.00	90.00	Claret	35.00	50.00
Cake Stand			Compote		
9″	68.00	125.00	Cov, hs, 6″	85.00	—
10″	75.00	125.00	Cov, hs, 7″	45.00	195.00

	Clear	Ruby Stained		Clear	Ruby Stained
Cov, hs, 8″	55.00	245.00	Pitcher		
Cov, ls, 12″	90.00	225.00	Milk, tankard	75.00	100.00
Open, hs, 5½″ . . .	55.00	65.00	Water, bulbous. . .	95.00	225.00
Open, hs, 7½″ . . .	45.00	—	Water, tankard . . .	110.00	200.00
Open, hs, 8¼″ . . .	75.00	95.00	Plate, 7″	20.00	—
Open, ls, 5¼″ . . .	30.00	45.00	Punch Bowl, ftd. . . .	275.00	—
Open, ls, 9″	40.00	—	Punch Cup	15.00	30.00
Cordial	45.00	—	Salt, master, sq	25.00	60.00
Creamer			Salt, ind, oblong . . .	16.00	30.00
Ind	30.00	35.00	Salt & Pepper	40.00	70.00
Regular.	50.00	65.00	Sauce, 4″	15.00	20.00
Cup & Saucer.	55.00	70.00	Spooner	45.00	50.00
Honey, cov, sq	100.00	175.00	Sugar, cov	50.00	85.00
Goblet	30.00	45.00	Toothpick	20.00	35.00
Lamp, oil, 10″	135.00	—	Tumbler	20.00	35.00
Mustard, cov.	35.00	75.00	Wine	25.00	40.00
Pickle, lobed.	18.00	40.00			

KING'S #500

Made by King Glass Co. of Pittsburgh, Pennsylvania in 1899. It was made in clear, frosted, and a rich, deep blue, known as Dewey Blue, both trimmed in gold. Continued by U. S. Glass Co. in 1891 and made in a great number of pieces. A clear goblet with frosted stem ($50.00) is known. Also known in dark green and a ruby stained sugar is reported ($95.00).

	Clear w/Gold	Dewey Blue w/Gold		Clear w/Gold	Dewey Blue w/Gold
Bowl			Lamp		
7″	10.00	30.00	Hand.	45.00	—
8″	12.00	35.00	Stand	65.00	—
9″	14.00	45.00	Pitcher, water	55.00	200.00
Butter, cov	65.00	125.00	Relish.	20.00	30.00
Cake Stand	40.00	60.00	Rose Bowl	20.00	45.00
Celery Vase	20.00	—	Salt Shaker, single . .	15.00	40.00
Compote			Sauce	15.00	35.00
Covered	45.00	—	Spooner	30.00	70.00
Open	30.00	—	Sugar, cov	45.00	75.00
Creamer.	30.00	50.00	Syrup.	55.00	225.00
Cruet	45.00	175.00	Tumbler	25.00	35.00
Cup	15.00	15.00			
Decanter, locking top	100.00	—			

KLONDIKE (Amberette, English Hobnail Cross)

This pattern reported to have been made originally by A. J. Beatty And Co., c1885. It was also made by Hobbs, Brockunier Co., and Dalzell, Gilmore and Leighton Co. Made in colors other than clear and amber stained, which are the original colors. Made to commemmorate the Alaskan Gold Rush. The frosted panels depict snow; the amber bands, gold. Found clear and frosted, with or without scrolls, depending on the maker. Prices are listed for frosted; clear prices would be approximately 20% of those shown.

	Frosted Amber Stain		Frosted Amber Stain
Bowl, berry, 8″	200.00	Salt Shaker, single	100.00
Butter, cov	300.00	Sauce, flat	75.00
Cake Stand, 8″, sq	450.00	Spooner	175.00
Celery Tray	200.00	Sugar, cov	250.00
Celery Vase	225.00	Syrup, pewter lid	650.00
Condiment Set, cruet and shaker on tray	1,000.00	Toothpick	350.00
Creamer	250.00	Tray, 5½″, sq	200.00
Cruet, os	450.00	Tumbler	135.00
Goblet	400.00	Vase, trumpet shape	
Pitcher, water	650.00	8″	225.00
Punch Cup	100.00	10″	250.00
		Wine	400.00

KOKOMO (Bar and Diamond, R and H Swirl Band)

Made in clear glass by Richards & Hartley, Tarentum, Pennsylvania in the late 1880s to 1891. Found in ruby stained and etched. About 54 pieces manufactured.

	Clear	Ruby Stained		Clear	Ruby Stained
Bowl, 8½″, ftd	24.00	—	Finger Bowl	25.00	35.00
Bread Tray	30.00	45.00	Goblet	25.00	45.00
Butter, cov	35.00	—	Lamp, hand, atypical—has no diamonds	50.00	100.00
Cake Stand	45.00	165.00			
Celery Vase	30.00	45.00			
Compote			Pitcher, water, tankard	55.00	95.00
Cov, hs, 7½″	35.00	165.00			
Open, hs, 5″	20.00	—	Salt & Pepper in holder	45.00	—
Open, hs, 6″	25.00	—			
Open, hs, 7″	30.00	—	Sauce, ftd, 5″	8.00	10.00
Open, hs, 8″	35.00	—	Spooner	25.00	45.00
Open, ls, 7½″	20.00	—	Sugar, cov	45.00	65.00
Condiment Set, oblong tray, shakers, cruet	80.00	195.00	Sugar Shaker	35.00	75.00
			Syrup	45.00	130.00
Creamer, ah	35.00	50.00	Tray, water	35.00	90.00
Cruet	35.00	—	Tumbler	20.00	35.00
Decanter, 9¾″, wine	55.00	95.00	Wine	20.00	35.00

LEAF AND DART (Pride)

Made by Boston and Sandwich Glass Co., Sandwich, Massachusetts, and Richards and Hartley Flint Glass, Pittsburgh, Pennsylvania, c1860. Shards have been found at Burlington Glass Works, Hamilton, Ontario.

	Clear		Clear
Bowl, 8¼″, ftd	25.00	Honey Dish	8.00
Butter, cov	60.00	Pitcher, water, ah	80.00
Celery Vase	30.00	Relish	15.00
Creamer, ah	40.00	Salt, master, ftd	
Cruet, pedestal, ah	100.00	Cov	65.00
Egg Cup	20.00	Open	30.00
Goblet	28.00	Sauce, 4″, flat	8.50

	Clear		Clear
Spooner	30.00	Tumbler, ftd	25.00
Sugar, cov	45.00	Wine	30.00
Syrup	90.00		

LIBERTY BELL (Centennial)

Made by Gillinder and Co., Philadelphia, Pennsylvania for the Centennial Exposition, 1876. Some items also made in milk glass. Reproduced. Some reproductions bear the year "1976" and "200 Years" instead of the original inscriptions.

	Clear		Clear
Bowl, 8", ftd	100.00	Plate	
Bread Plate, 13⅜ x 9½"		6", dated	75.00
Clear, no signatures	85.00	8"	60.00
Milk glass, sgd John Han-		10"	80.00
cock	200.00	Platter, 13 x 8", twig handles,	
Butter, cov	145.00	13 states	65.00
Creamer		Relish, oval	60.00
Applied handle	95.00	Salt Dip, ind, oval	30.00
Reed handle	100.00	Salt Shaker	95.00
Goblet	40.00	Sauce, ftd	20.00
Mug, snake handle	350.00	Spooner	60.00
Pickle	45.00	Sugar, cov	90.00
Pitcher, water, ah	425.00		

LILY OF THE VALLEY

Non-flint pattern made by Boston & Sandwich, Sandwich, Massachusetts, in the 1870s. Shards have also been found at Burlington Glass Works, Hamilton, Ontario. Lily of the Valley on Legs is a name frequently given to those pieces having three tall legs. Legged pieces include a covered butter, covered sugar, creamer and spooner. Add 25% for this type.

	Clear		Clear
Butter, cov	70.00	Pitcher	
Buttermilk Goblet	35.00	Milk	125.00
Cake Stand	65.00	Water	135.00
Celery Tray	40.00	Relish	15.00
Celery Vase	55.00	Salt, master	
Champagne	80.00	Cov	125.00
Compote		Open	50.00
Cov, hs, 8½"	85.00	Sauce, flat	12.00
Open, hs	50.00	Spooner	35.00
Creamer, ah	65.00	Sugar, cov	75.00
Cruet, os	110.00	Tumbler	
Egg Cup	40.00	Flat	50.00
Goblet	55.00	Footed	65.00
Honey	12.00	Vegetable Dish, oval	30.00
Nappy, 4"	20.00	Wine	100.00
Pickle, scoop shape	20.00		

LION

Made by Gillinder and Sons, Philadelphia, Pennsylvania, in 1876. Available in clear (20% less). Many reproductions.

	Frosted		Frosted
Bowl, oblong		Cordial	175.00
6½ x 4¼"	55.00	* Creamer.	65.00
8 x 5"	50.00	Egg Cup, 3½" h	65.00
Bread Plate, 12" including		* Goblet	70.00
lion handles, GUTDODB. .	100.00	Marmalade Jar, rampant	
Butter, cov		finial	85.00
Lion's head finial	90.00	Pitcher	
Rampant finial	125.00	Milk.	450.00
Cake Stand	85.00	Water	350.00
Celery Vase	85.00	Relish, lion handles	38.00
Champagne	175.00	Salt, master, rect lid.	250.00
Cheese, cov, rampant lion		* Sauce, 4", ftd	25.00
finial	400.00	* Spooner	70.00
Compote		Sugar, cov	
Cov, hs, 7", rampant finial .	150.00	Lion head finial	85.00
* Cov, hs, 9", rampant finial,		Rampant finial	95.00
oval, collared base	150.00	Syrup, orig top	400.00
Cov, 9", hs.	185.00	Wine	250.00
Open, ls, 8"	75.00		

LOG CABIN

Non-flint made by Central Glass Co. Wheeling, West Virginia, c1875. Also available in color, but rare. Creamer, spooner, and covered sugar reproduced in clear and cobalt blue.

	Clear		Clear
Bowl, cov, 8 x 5¼ x 3⅝" . . .	400.00	Pitcher, water	300.00
Butter, cov	300.00	Sauce, flat	75.00
Compote, hs, 10½"	275.00	* Spooner	120.00
* Creamer.	100.00	* Sugar, cov	275.00
Marmalade Jar, cov.	275.00		

LOOP (Seneca Loop)

Flint, c1850s–1860s; later in non-flint. Made by several firms. Sandwich produced fiery opalescent pieces. Yuma Loop is a contemporary with comparable values.

	Flint	Non-Flint		Flint	Non-Flint
Bowl, 9"	50.00	25.00	Cordial, 2¾" h.	40.00	20.00
Butter, cov	60.00	40.00	Creamer, ah	70.00	35.00
Cake Stand	95.00	50.00	Egg Cup.	30.00	20.00
Celery Vase	65.00	20.00	Goblet	20.00	15.00
Champagne	35.00	25.00	Pitcher, water, ah . .	170.00	60.00
Compote			Salt, master, ftd. . . .	25.00	18.00
Cov, hs, 9½"	135.00	—	Spooner	30.00	24.00
Open, hs, 9"	115.00	40.00	Sugar, cov	70.00	30.00

	Flint	Non-Flint		Flint	Non-Flint
Syrup	95.00	—	Water	40.00	20.00
Tumbler			Wine	30.00	12.00
Footed	25.00	15.00			

LOOP AND DART

Clear and stippled non-flint pattern of the late 1860s and early 1870s. Made by Boston & Sandwich, Sandwich, Massachusetts, and Richards & Hartley, Tarentum, Pennsylvania. Pattern related to Loop and Dart with Diamond Ornament and Loop and Dart with Round Ornament. Flint add 25%.

	Clear		Clear
Bowl, 9″, oval	25.00	Pitcher, water	75.00
Butter, cov	45.00	Plate, 6″	35.00
Cake Stand, 10″	40.00	Relish	18.00
Celery Vase	35.00	Salt, master	50.00
Compote		Sauce	5.00
Cov, hs, 8″	85.00	Spooner	30.00
Cov, ls, 8″	65.00	Sugar, cov	50.00
Creamer	35.00	Tumbler	
Cruet, os	95.00	Footed	30.00
Egg Cup	25.00	Water	25.00
Goblet	25.00	Wine	35.00
Lamp, oil	85.00		

LOOP AND DART WITH DIAMOND ORNAMENT

Clear and stippled non-flint pattern of the late 1860s and early 1870s. Made by Boston & Sandwich, and Richards & Hartley. Pattern related to Loop and Dart and Loop and Dart with Round Ornament. Flint add 25%.

	Clear		Clear
Bowl, 9″, oval	20.00	Sauce, flat	4.50
Butter, cov	45.00	Spooner	30.00
Celery Vase	35.00	Sugar, cov	40.00
Creamer	35.00	Tumbler	
Egg Cup	24.00	Footed	35.00
Goblet	32.00	Water	40.00
Relish	15.00	Wine	35.00
Salt, master	18.00		

LOOP AND DART WITH ROUND ORNAMENT

Clear and stippled non-flint pattern of the late 1860s and early 1870s. Made by Boston & Sandwich, and Richards & Hartley, also attributed to Portland Glass Co, Portland, ME. Pattern related to Loop and Dart and Loop and Dart with Diamond Ornaments. Flint add 25%.

	Clear		Clear
Bowl, 9″, oval	28.00	Butter Pat	15.00
Butter, cov	80.00	Celery Vase	35.00

	Clear		Clear
Champagne	85.00	Plate, 6″	35.00
Compote		Relish	15.00
Cov, hs, 8″	85.00	Salt, master	28.00
Cov, ls, 8″	65.00	Sauce, flat	8.00
Open, hs, 8″	45.00	Spooner	30.00
Creamer	35.00	Sugar, cov	50.00
Egg Cup	30.00	Tumbler	
Goblet		Footed	30.00
Buttermilk	20.00	Water	35.00
Water	32.00	Wine	35.00
Pitcher, water	90.00		

LOOP AND JEWEL (Jewel and Festoon; Venus)

Non-flint made by Beatty Glass and National Glass Co. then continued by Indiana Glass Co. Made until 1915. About 40 pieces known. A few rare pieces available in milk white.

	Clear		Clear
Bowl, 8″	15.00	Relish, 8″	22.00
Butter, cov	55.00	Salt & Pepper	32.00
Champagne	40.00	Sauce, flat, 4″	5.00
Compote, 6½″	20.00	Sherbet	45.00
Creamer	25.00	Spooner	30.00
Dish, 5″ sq	15.00	Sugar, cov	40.00
Goblet	20.00	Syrup	55.00
Pickle, 8″, rect.	18.00	Vase, 8¾″	40.00
Pitcher, water	45.00	Wine	30.00
Plate, sq.	15.00		

LOUISIANA (Sharp Oval and Diamond, Granby)

Made by Bryce Bros., Pittsburgh, Pennsylvania in 1870s, continued later (about 1892) by U. S. Glass Co. as one of the States patterns. Also available with gold and also comes frosted.

	Clear		Clear
Bowl, 9″, berry	20.00	Mug, handled, gold top	25.00
Butter, cov	65.00	Nappy, 4″, cov.	30.00
Cake Stand	45.00	Pitcher, water	65.00
Celery Vase	30.00	Relish	15.00
Compote		Spooner	30.00
Cov, hs, 8″	75.00	Sugar, cov	45.00
Open, hs, 5″, jelly	40.00	Tumbler	20.00
Creamer	30.00	Wine	35.00
Goblet	30.00		
Matchholder, attached			
saucer	30.00		

MAGNET AND GRAPE (Magnet and Grape with Stippled Leaf)

Flint first made by Boston and Sandwich Glass Co., c1860. Later non-flint versions have grape leaf in either clear or stippled. Reproduced by Metropolitan Museum, New York with frosted leaf.

	Flint Frosted Leaf	Non-Flint Stippled or Clear Leaf		Flint Frosted Leaf	Non-Flint Stippled or Clear Leaf
Bowl, cov, 8″	175.00	75.00	Low Stem	75.00	—
Butter, cov	185.00	40.00	Regular stem	70.00	30.00
Celery Vase	150.00	25.00	Pitcher		
Champagne	135.00	45.00	Milk, ah	—	75.00
Compote			Water, ah	350.00	75.00
Cov, hs, 4½″	125.00	—	Relish, oval	35.00	15.00
Open, hs, 7½″	110.00	65.00	Salt, ftd	50.00	25.00
Cordial, 4″	125.00	—	Sauce, 4″	20.00	7.50
* Creamer	175.00	40.00	Spill	65.00	—
Decanter, os			Spooner	95.00	30.00
Pint	150.00	75.00	* Sugar, cov	125.00	80.00
Quart	200.00	85.00	Syrup	125.00	55.00
Egg Cup	80.00	20.00	* Tumbler, water	110.00	30.00
* Goblet			Whiskey	140.00	25.00
American Shield	300.00	—	* Wine	90.00	50.00

MAINE (Paneled Stippled Flower)

Non-flint made by U. S. Glass Co., Pittsburgh, Pennsylvania c1890. Researchers dispute if goblet was made originally. Sometimes found with enamel trim or overall turquoise stain.

	Clear	Emerald Green		Clear	Emerald Green
Bowl, 8″	30.00	40.00	Mug	35.00	—
Bread Plate, oval, 10			Pitcher		
× 7¾″	30.00	—	Milk	65.00	85.00
Butter, cov	48.00	—	Water	50.00	125.00
Cake Stand	40.00	60.00	Relish	15.00	—
Compote,			Salt Shaker, single	30.00	—
Cov, jelly	50.00	75.00	Sauce	15.00	—
Open, hs, 7″	20.00	30.00	Sugar, cov	45.00	75.00
Open, ls, 8″	38.00	55.00	Syrup	75.00	225.00
Open, ls, 9″	30.00	35.00	Toothpick	125.00	—
Creamer	30.00	—	Tumbler	30.00	45.00
Cruet, os	80.00	—	Wine	50.00	75.00

MANHATTAN

Non-flint with gold, made by U. S. Glass Co., c1902. A depression glass pattern also has the "Manhattan" name. A table sized creamer and covered sugar are known in true ruby stained, and a goblet is known in old marigold carnival glass. Heavily reproduced.

	Clear	Rose Stained		Clear	Rose Stained
Biscuit Jar, cov	60.00	85.00	Plate		
Bowl			6"	6.50	30.00
6"	18.00	—	8"	15.00	—
8¼", scalloped	20.00	—	10¾"	20.00	—
9½"	20.00	—	Punch Bowl	125.00	—
10"	22.00	—	Punch Cup	10.00	—
12½"	25.00	—	Relish, 6"	12.00	—
Butter, cov	55.00	—	Salt Shaker, single	20.00	35.00
Cake Stand, 10"	40.00	50.00	Sauce	14.00	20.00
Carafe, water	40.00	65.00	Spooner	20.00	—
Celery Vase	25.00	—	Straw Holder, cov	65.00	—
Cheese, cov, 8⅜" d.	—	115.00	Sugar		
Compote, cov, hs,			Individual, open	12.00	—
9½"	45.00	—	Regular, cov	40.00	65.00
Creamer			Syrup	48.00	175.00
Individual	20.00	—	Toothpick	30.00	—
Regular	30.00	60.00	Tumblers		
Cruet			Ice Tea	30.00	—
Large	65.00	115.00	Water	20.00	—
Small	50.00	—	Vase, 6"	18.00	—
* Goblet	25.00	—	Violet Bowl	20.00	—
Ice Bucket	—	65.00	Water Bottle	40.00	—
Olive, Gainsborough	30.00	—	Wine	20.00	—
Pitcher, water, tank-					
ard, ½ gal	60.00	125.00			

MAPLE LEAF

Non-flint pattern made by Gillinder & Sons, c1850. Heavily reproduced in clear and colors.

	Amber	Blue	Canary/ Vaseline	Clear	Frosted
Bowl					
5½", oval	—	—	45.00	25.00	—
6", ftd	45.00	60.00	50.00	35.00	40.00
Bread Plate	70.00	85.00	75.00	75.00	85.00
Butter, cov	75.00	80.00	75.00	65.00	70.00
Cake Stand, 11"	60.00	65.00	60.00	45.00	50.00
Celery	45.00	50.00	45.00	35.00	40.00
Compote					
Cov, hs, 9"	65.00	90.00	65.00	85.00	100.00
Jelly	50.00	60.00	50.00	40.00	45.00
Creamer	65.00	65.00	68.00	50.00	55.00
Goblet	85.00	100.00	95.00	65.00	90.00
Pitcher					
Milk	80.00	95.00	85.00	65.00	75.00
Water	85.00	100.00	90.00	75.00	80.00
Platter, 10½"	45.00	50.00	50.00	40.00	45.00
Relish	18.00	22.00	18.00	12.00	15.00
Sauce					
5"	14.50	18.00	15.00	10.00	12.00
6", ftd	28.00	30.00	28.00	15.00	20.00
Spooner	60.00	75.00	60.00	40.00	45.00
Sugar, cov	50.00	100.00	80.00	65.00	75.00
Tumbler	40.00	45.00	40.00	35.00	45.00

MARDI GRAS (Duncan and Miller #42, Paneled English Hobnail with Prisms)

Made by Duncan and Miller Glass Co., c1898. Available in gold trim and ruby stained.

	Clear	Ruby Stained		Clear	Ruby Stained
Bowl, 8″, berry	18.00	—	Water	75.00	200.00
Butter, cov	65.00	145.00	Plate, 6″	10.00	—
Cake Stand, 10″ . . .	65.00	—	Punch Cup	10.00	—
Celery Tray, curled			Relish.	12.50	—
edges	25.00	—	Sherry, flared or		
Champagne, saucer	32.00	—	straight	35.00	—
Claret.	35.00	—	Spooner	25.00	—
Compote			Sugar, cov	35.00	65.00
Cov, hs	55.00	—	Syrup, metal lid. . . .	65.00	—
Open, jelly, 4½″ . .	30.00	55.00	Toothpick	35.00	125.00
Cordial	35.00	—	Tumbler		
Creamer			Bar	25.00	—
Ind, oval	20.00	—	Champagne.	20.00	—
Regular.	35.00	60.00	Water	30.00	40.00
Finger Bowl	25.00	—	Vase, trumpet shape,		
Goblet	35.00	—	3 sizes	20.00	—
Lamp Shade.	35.00	—	Wine	30.00	65.00
Pitcher					
Milk.	50.00	—			

MARYLAND (Inverted Loop and Fan; Loop and Diamond)

Made originally by Bryce Brothers, Pittsburgh, Pennsylvania. Continued by U. S. Glass Co. as one of their States patterns.

	Clear w/gold	Ruby Stained		Clear w/gold	Ruby Stained
Banana Dish.	35.00	—	Olive, handled.	12.00	—
Bowl, berry	15.00	—	Pitcher		
Bread Plate	25.00	—	Milk.	42.50	—
Butter, cov	65.00	—	Water	50.00	100.00
Cake Stand, 8″	40.00	—	Plate, 7″, round. . . .	25.00	—
Celery Tray.	20.00	—	Relish, oval.	15.00	—
Celery Vase	28.00	—	Salt Shaker, single .	30.00	—
Compote			Sauce, flat	14.00	20.00
Cov, hs	65.00	100.00	Spooner	30.00	—
Open, hs, 7½″ . . .	40.00	—	Sugar, cov	45.00	60.00
Open, jelly.	25.00	—	Toothpick	125.00	175.00
Creamer.	25.00	55.00	Tumbler	25.00	50.00
Goblet	30.00	48.00	Wine	40.00	75.00

MASCOTTE (Minor Block)

Non-flint made by Ripley and Co., Pittsburgh, Pennsylvania, in the 1870s. Reissued by U. S. Glass Co. in 1898. The butter dish shown on Plate 77 of Ruth Webb Lee's *Victorian Glass* is said to go with this pattern. It has a horsehoe finial and was named for the famous "Maude S," "Queen of the Turf" trotting horse during the 1880s. Apothecary jar and pyramid jars made by Tiffin Glass Co. in the 1950s.

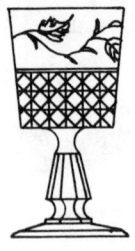

	Clear	Etched
Bowl		
Cov, 5"	—	35.00
Cov, 6"	—	35.00
Cov, 7"	—	45.00
Cov, 8"	—	50.00
Cov, 9"	—	55.00
Open 9"	35.00	40.00
Butter Pat........	10.00	15.00
Butter, cov		
"Maude S"	100.00	—
Regular........	50.00	65.00
Cake Basket, handle.	80.00	65.00
Cake Stand	35.00	50.00
Celery Vase	35.00	40.00
Cheese, cov	70.00	80.00
Compote		
Cov, hs, 5"......	—	40.00
Cov, hs, 6"......	—	45.00
Cov, hs, 7"......	—	55.00
Cov, hs, 8"......	75.00	85.00
Cov, hs, 9".....	—	90.00
Open, hs, 5"	—	25.00
Open, hs, 6"	—	25.00
Open, hs, 7"	—	30.00
Open, hs, 8"	—	35.00

	Clear	Etched
Open, hs, 9"	—	35.00
Open, ls, 8"	30.00	45.00
Creamer.........	30.00	45.00
Goblet	40.00	45.00
Pitcher, water	55.00	65.00
Plate, turned in sides..........	38.00	—
Pyramid Jar, 7" d, one fits into other and forms tall jar-type container with lid, three sizes with flat separators	40.00	—
Salt Dip	25.00	—
Salt Shaker, single .	25.00	25.00
Sauce		
Flat............	8.00	15.00
Footed	12.00	16.00
Spooner.........	30.00	35.00
Sugar, cov	40.00	45.00
Tray, water	40.00	55.00
Tumbler	20.00	35.00
Wine	25.00	30.00

MASSACHUSETTS (Geneva #2, M2-131)

Made in 1880s, maker unknown, and continued in 1898 by U. S. Glass Co. as one of the States series. The vase ($45.00) and wine ($45.00) are known in emerald green. Some pieces reported in cobalt blue and marigold carnival glass. Reproduced in clear and colors.

	Clear
Bar Bottle, metal shot glass for cover	75.00
Basket, 4½", ah	50.00
Bowl	
6", sq	17.50
9", sq	20.00
* Butter, cov	70.00
Celery Tray.............	28.00
Cologne Bottle, os........	37.50
Compote, open..........	35.00
Cordial................	55.00
Creamer...............	28.00
Cruet, os	
Regular.............	40.00
2 oz	55.00
Goblet	45.00
Mug.................	24.00
Olive	8.50

	Clear
Pitcher, water	75.00
Plate, 8"..............	32.00
Punch Cup	15.00
Relish, 8½"............	25.00
Rum Jug	110.00
Spooner..............	22.00
Sugar, cov	40.00
Toothpick	40.00
Tumbler	
Champagne or Juice	25.00
Water	30.00
Whiskey (shot)........	15.00
Vase	
6½", trumpet	25.00
7"..................	25.00
9", trumpet	35.00
Wine	40.00

MELROSE

Non-flint pattern made by Greensburg Glass Co., Greensburg, Pennsylvania, in 1887 in clear, etched, and ruby stained. Add 20% for etching.

	Clear		Clear
Bowl, berry	20.00	Plate	
Butter, cov	45.00	7″	15.00
Cake Plate	30.00	8″	10.00
Cake Stand	32.00	Salt, individual	6.00
Celery Vase	25.00	Salt Shaker	15.00
Compote		Sauce, flat	8.00
Cov, hs, 8″	90.00	Spooner	30.00
Open, hs, 7″	25.00	Sugar, cov	38.00
Open, jelly	18.00	Tray, water 11½″	45.00
Creamer	30.00	Tumbler	15.00
Goblet	20.00	Waste Bowl	20.00
Pitcher, water	45.00	Wine	20.00

MICHIGAN (Loop & Pillar)

Non-flint made by U. S. Glass Co., c1893. One of the States pattern series. The 10¼″ bowl ($42.00) and punch cup ($12.00) are found with yellow or blue stain. Also found with painted carnations. Other colors include "Sunrise," gold, and ruby stained.

	Clear	Rose Stained		Clear	Rose Stained
Bowl			Olive, two handles	—	35.00
7½″	15.00	—	Pickle	12.00	20.00
9″	35.00	60.00	Pitcher		
10¼″	35.00	62.00	8″	50.00	—
Butter, cov	60.00	125.00	12″	70.00	150.00
Celery Vase	40.00	85.00	Punch Bowl, 8″	50.00	—
Compote			Punch Cup	8.00	—
Jelly, 4½″	25.00	—	Relish	20.00	—
Open, hs, 9¼″	65.00	—	Salt Shaker, single, 3		
Creamer			types	20.00	30.00
Ind, 602 tankard	20.00	65.00	Sauce	12.00	22.00
Regular	30.00	50.00	Sherbet, cup,		
Cruet, os	60.00	225.00	handled	12.00	15.00
Crushed Fruit Bowl	75.00	—	Spooner	50.00	72.00
Finger Bowl	15.00	—	Sugar, cov	50.00	75.00
Goblet	35.00	65.00	Syrup	95.00	—
Honey Dish	10.00	—	* Toothpick	45.00	125.00
Lemonade Mug	24.00	40.00	Tumbler	30.00	40.00
Nappy, Gainsbor-			Vase, bud	35.00	35.00
ough handle	35.00	—	Wine	35.00	50.00

MINERVA

Non-flint made in the United States and probably in Canada in the 1870s. There are two forms.

	Clear		Clear
Bowl		Open, hs, octagonal ftd . .	95.00
Footed	40.00	Creamer.	40.00
Rectangular		Goblet	80.00
7″	25.00	Marmalade Jar, cov.	150.00
8 x 5″.	30.00	Pickle.	25.00
9″	45.00	Pitcher	
Bread Plate	65.00	Milk.	75.00
Butter, cov	85.00	Water	185.00
Cake Stand		Plate	
8″	95.00	8″	55.00
9 x 6½″.	100.00	10″, handled	60.00
10½″.	120.00	Platter, oval, 13″	65.00
13″	145.00	Sauce	
Champagne	85.00	Flat.	15.00
Compote		Footed, 4″	20.00
Cov, hs, 7″.	90.00	Spooner	50.00
Cov, ls, 8″	85.00	Sugar, cov	65.00
Open, hs, 10″	60.00	Waste Bowl.	50.00

MINNESOTA

Non-flint made by U. S. Glass Co., late 1890s. One of the States patterns. A two-piece flower frog has been found in emerald green ($46.00).

	Clear	Ruby Stained		Clear	Ruby Stained
Basket	65.00	—	Mug	25.00	—
Biscuit Jar, cov	55.00	150.00	Olive	15.00	25.00
Bowl, 8½″, flared. . .	30.00	100.00	Pitcher, water, tank-		
Butter, cov	55.00	—	ard	85.00	200.00
Carafe	35.00	—	Plate		
Celery Tray, 13″ . . .	25.00	—	5″, turned up		
Compote			edges	25.00	—
Open, hs, 10″,			7⅜″ d	15.00	—
flared.	60.00	—	Relish.	20.00	—
Open, ls, 9″, sq . .	55.00	—	Sauce, boat shape .	15.00	35.00
Creamer			Spooner	25.00	—
Individual.	20.00	—	Sugar, cov	40.00	—
Regular.	30.00	—	Syrup	65.00	—
Cruet	35.00	—	Toothpick, 3 handles	35.00	150.00
Cup	18.00	—	Tumbler	20.00	—
Goblet	35.00	50.00	Wine	40.00	—
Hair Receiver	30.00	—			

MISSOURI (Palm and Scroll)

Non-flint made by U. S. Glass Co. c1899, one of the States pattern series. Also made in amethyst and canary.

	Clear	Emerald Green		Clear	Emerald Green
Bowl, berry, 8″.	15.00	35.00	Celery Vase	30.00	—
Butter, cov	45.00	65.00	Cordial	55.00	—
Cake Stand, 9″	35.00	45.00	Creamer.	25.00	40.00

	Clear	Emerald Green		Clear	Emerald Green
Cruet	55.00	130.00	Water	75.00	85.00
Dish, cov 6″	65.00	—	Relish.	10.00	12.50
Doughnut stand, 6″ .	40.00	—	Salt Shaker, single .	35.00	45.00
Goblet	50.00	60.00	Sauce, flat, 4″	10.00	16.00
Mug	35.00	45.00	Spooner	25.00	48.00
Pickle Dish, rectan-			Sugar, cov	50.00	65.00
gular	18.00	27.50	Syrup	85.00	—
Pitcher			Tumbler	30.00	38.00
Milk.	40.00	85.00	Wine	40.00	45.00

MOON AND STAR (Palace)

Non-flint and frosted (add 30%). First made by Adams & Co., Pittsburgh, Pennsylvania, in 1874 and later by several manufacturers, including Pioneer Glass who probably decorated ruby stained examples. Six different compotes documented. Also found with frosted highlights. Heavily reproduced in clear and color.

	Clear		Clear
Bowl		Cruet	125.00
6″	25.00	Egg Cup.	35.00
8″, Berry	30.00	Goblet	45.00
12½″, Round	42.00	Lamp	140.00
Bread Plate, rect.	45.00	Pickle, oval	20.00
Butter, cov	70.00	Pitcher, water, ah	175.00
Cake Stand, 10″	50.00	Relish.	20.00
Carafe	42.50	Salt, ind	10.00
Celery Vase	35.00	Salt & Pepper, pr.	70.00
Champagne	75.00	Sauce	
Claret.	47.50	Flat	8.50
Compote		Footed	12.00
Cov, hs, 8″.	75.00	Spooner	45.00
Cov, hs, 10″	68.00	Sugar, cov	65.00
Cov, ls, 6½″	55.00	Syrup	150.00
Cov, ls, 10″	68.00	Tray, water	65.00
Open, hs, 9″	40.00	Tumbler, ftd	60.00
Open, ls, 7½″	25.00	Wine	60.00
Creamer, ah	55.00		

NAILHEAD (Gem)

Non-flint, made by Bryce, Higbee, and Co., in 1880s. Also found in ruby stained (goblet at $30.00, pitcher at $65.00).

	Clear		Clear
Bowl, 6″	15.00	Open, hs, 6½″	25.00
Butter, cov	40.00	Open, 9½″, hs	40.00
Cake Stand		Creamer	25.00
9½″.	30.00	Goblet	25.00
10½″.	35.00	Pitcher, water	35.00
Celery	30.00	Plate	
Compote		Round, 9″	20.00
Cov, 8″, hs.	45.00	Square, 7″	15.00
Cov, ls, 7″	45.00	Relish, 5¼ × 8¾″	10.00

	Clear			Clear
Sauce, flat	10.00	Tumbler		25.00
Spooner	24.00	Wine		20.00
Sugar, cov	40.00			

NEVADA

Non-flint made by U. S. Glass Co. as a States Pattern. Pieces are sometimes partly frosted and have enamel decoration. Add 20% for frosted.

	Clear		Clear
Biscuit Jar	45.00	Salt	
Butter, cov	68.00	Ind	15.00
Cake Stand, 10″	35.00	Master	20.00
Celery	25.00	Salt Shaker, single, two	
Compote, cov, 8″, hs	45.00	types	20.00
Creamer	30.00	Sauce	10.00
Cruet	35.00	Spooner	35.00
Cup, custard	12.00	Sugar, cov	35.00
Pickle, oval	10.00	Syrup, tin top	45.00
Pitcher, water, tankard, ½		Toothpick	38.00
gal	40.00	Tumbler	15.00

NEW ENGLAND PINEAPPLE

Flint made by Boston and Sandwich Glass Co. in early 1860s. Rare in color. The goblet has been reproduced in clear and color.

	Flint	Non-Flint		Flint	Non-Flint
Bowl, 8″, scalloped	85.00	—	Pitcher, water	450.00	—
Cake Stand	135.00	—	Plate, 6″	90.00	—
Castor Bottle	50.00	—	Salt		
Castor Set, 4 bottles,			Ind	24.00	—
complete	300.00	—	Master	45.00	40.00
Champagne	175.00	—	Sauce		
Cov, hs, 5″	175.00	—	Flat	15.00	10.00
Cov, hs, 8″	225.00	—	Footed	28.00	—
Open, hs, 7″	90.00	—	Spillholder	60.00	—
Open, hs, 8½″	125.00	—	Spooner	60.00	35.00
Creamer, ah, 2			Sugar, cov	150.00	75.00
sizes	185.00	70.00	Sweetmeat, cov	225.00	—
Decanter, qt, os	225.00	—	Tumbler		
Egg Cup	50.00	35.00	Bar	125.00	—
Lady's	100.00	—	Water	85.00	—
Regular	65.00	—	Whiskey, handled	145.00	—
Mug	95.00	—	* Wine	150.00	—

NEW HAMPSHIRE (Bent Buckle, Modiste)

Non-flint made by U. S. Glass Co. in the States Pattern series. There is a large ruby mug ($50.00), 5½″ bowl ($25.00), syrup ($48.00), toothpick ($40.00), and tumbler ($40.00). A vase is known in green stain ($30.00).

	Clear w/gold	Rose Stained		Clear w/gold	Rose Stained
Bowl			Goblet	25.00	45.00
Flared, 8½"	15.00	25.00	Mug, large	20.00	45.00
Round, 8½"	18.00	30.00	Pitcher, water, tank-		
Square, 8½"	25.00	35.00	ard	70.00	90.00
Butter, cov	45.00	70.00	Relish.	18.00	—
Cake Stand, 8¼". . .	30.00	—	Sugar		
Carafe	60.00	—	Cov.	45.00	60.00
Celery Vase	35.00	50.00	Ind, open.	20.00	25.00
Compote, open	38.00	55.00	Syrup	75.00	—
Creamer			Toothpick	25.00	40.00
Ind	20.00	30.00	Tumbler	20.00	35.00
Regular.	30.00	45.00	Vase	35.00	50.00
Cruet	55.00	135.00	Wine	30.00	50.00

NEW JERSEY (Loops and Drops)

Non-flint made by U. S. Glass Co. in States Pattern Series. Items with perfect gold are worth more than those with worn gold. An emerald green 11" vase is known, value $75.00.

	Clear w/gold	Ruby Stained		Clear w/gold	Ruby Stained
Bowl			Pitcher		
8", flared	25.00	50.00	Milk, ah	75.00	—
9"	32.50	65.00	Water		
10", oval	30.00	—	Applied handle .	80.00	210.00
Bread Plate	30.00	—	Pressed handle	50.00	185.00
Flat.	75.00	100.00	Plate, 12"	30.00	—
Footed	125.00	—	Salt & Pepper		
Cake Stand, 8"	65.00	—	Hotel.	50.00	—
Celery Tray, rect . . .	25.00	—	Small	35.00	55.00
Compote			Sauce	14.00	30.00
Cov, hs, 5", jelly. .	45.00	55.00	Spooner	27.00	75.00
Cov, hs, 8".	75.00	—	Sugar, cov	60.00	80.00
Open, hs, 6¾" . . .	30.00	—	Sweetmeat, 8", open,		
Open, hs, 8"	60.00	—	ftd.	40.00	—
Creamer.	35.00	60.00	Syrup, no gold	90.00	—
Cruet	50.00	—	Toothpick	55.00	225.00
Goblet	40.00	—	Tumbler	30.00	50.00
Olive, pointed,			Wine, straight or		
flared	18.00	—	flared	40.00	65.00
Pickle, rect	15.00	—			

O'HARA DIAMOND (Sawtooth and Star)

Non-flint, made by O'Hara Glass Co. in 1928 and by U. S. Glass Co. in 1898.

	Clear	Ruby Stained		Clear	Ruby Stained
Bowl, berry			base	45.00	125.00
Individual.	—	25.00	Compote		
Master	25.00	75.00	Cov, hs	40.00	185.00
Butter, cov, ruffled			Open, hs, jelly . . .	48.00	145.00

	Clear	Ruby Stained		Clear	Ruby Stained
Condiment Set, pr salt and pepper, sugar shaker, tray	—	250.00	8″	30.00	—
			10″	40.00	—
Creamer	30.00	60.00	Salt, master	15.00	35.00
Cruet	55.00	150.00	Salt Shaker	20.00	35.00
Cup and Saucer	40.00	60.00	Spooner	20.00	55.00
Goblet	25.00	50.00	Sugar, cov	35.00	90.00
Lamp, Oil	50.00	—	Sugar Shaker	55.00	150.00
Pitcher, water, tankard	—	165.00	Syrup	55.00	200.00
Plate			Tumbler	30.00	45.00
7″	20.00	—			

ONE HUNDRED ONE

Non-flint made by the Bellaire Goblet Co., Findlay, Ohio, in the late 1870s.

	Clear		Clear
Bread Plate, 101 border, Farm implement center, 11″	75.00	Pitcher, water, ah	125.00
		Plate	
Butter, cov	40.00	6″	15.00
Cake Stand, 9″	65.00	7″	15.00
Celery Vase	50.00	8″	15.00
Compote		Relish	15.00
Cov, hs, 7″	60.00	Sauce	
Cov, ls	60.00	Flat	10.00
Creamer	45.00	Footed	15.00
Goblet	40.00	Spooner	25.00
Lamp, hand, oil, 10″	80.00	Sugar, cov	45.00
		Wine	60.00

OPEN ROSE

Non-flint, c1870. Attributed to Boston and Sandwich Glass Co.

	Clear		Clear
Bowl, oval, 9″ x 6″	25.00	Regular	30.00
Butter, cov	55.00	Pitcher, water, ah	165.00
Compote		Relish	15.00
Cov, hs, 8″	75.00	Salt, ind, ftd	30.00
Cov, hs, 9″	90.00	Sauce	10.00
Open, ls, 7½″	35.00	Spooner	40.00
Creamer, ah	45.00	Sugar, cov	50.00
Egg Cup	25.00	Tumbler	50.00
Goblet			
Lady's	30.00		

OREGON #1 (Beaded Loop)

Non-flint. First made in the 1880s. Reissued in 1907 as one of the States series. Reproduced in clear and color by Imperial.

	Clear
Berry Set, master, 6 sauces.	72.00
Bowl	
7″	15.00
8″	15.00
9″, berry, cov	25.00
Bread Plate	35.00
Butter, cov	
English	65.00
Flanged.	50.00
Flat.	40.00
Cake Stand	35.00
Carafe, water	35.00
Celery Vase	30.00
Compote	
Open, hs, 8″	50.00
Open, ls, 9″	40.00
Creamer	
Flat.	30.00
Footed	35.00
Cruet	50.00
Goblet	35.00

	Clear
Honey Dish.	10.00
Mug	35.00
Pickle Dish, boat shape	15.00
Pitcher	
Milk.	40.00
Water	60.00
Relish.	15.00
Salt, master	20.00
Sauce	
Flat, 3½ to 4″.	10.00
Footed, 3½″.	15.00
Spooner	
Flat.	24.00
Footed	26.00
Sugar, cov	
Flat.	25.00
Footed	30.00
Syrup.	55.00
Toothpick	55.00
Tumbler	25.00
Wine	40.00

PALMETTE

Non-flint, late 1870s. Syrup known in milk glass.

	Clear
Bowl	
8″	25.00
9″	15.00
Bread Plate, handled, 9″	30.00
Butter Dish, cov	60.00
Butter Pat.	35.00
Cake Stand	80.00
Castor Bottle.	20.00
Castor Set, 5 bottles	125.00
Celery Vase	55.00
Champagne	75.00
Compote	
Cov, hs, 7″.	65.00
Cov, hs, 8½″	75.00
Cov, hs, 9¾″	85.00
Open, ls, 5½″	25.00
Open, ls, 7″	30.00
Creamer, ah	65.00

	Clear
Cup Plate	45.00
Egg Cup.	40.00
Goblet	35.00
Lamp, 8½″, all glass	80.00
Pickle, scoop shape	18.00
Pitcher, water, ah	120.00
Relish.	18.00
Salt, master, ftd.	22.00
Salt Shaker.	55.00
Sauce, flat, 6″	10.00
Shaker, saloon, oversize	80.00
Spooner	35.00
Sugar, cov	55.00
Syrup, ah	125.00
Tumbler	
Bar	75.00
Water, ftd.	40.00
Wine	110.00

PANELED FORGET-ME-NOT (Regal)

Non-flint, made by Bryce Bros., Pittsburgh, Pennsylvania, c1870. Made in limited production in amethyst and green.

	Amber	Blue	Clear
Bread Plate	—	—	30.00
Butter, cov	50.00	60.00	45.00

	Amber	Blue	Clear
Cake Stand, 10″ . . .	70.00	90.00	45.00
Celery Vase	45.00	70.00	36.00
Compote			
Cov, hs, 7″.	—	—	65.00
Cov, hs, 8″.	80.00	100.00	68.00
Open, hs, 8½″, scalloped rim . .	—	—	55.00
Open, hs, 10″ . . .	—	—	40.00
Creamer.	45.00	60.00	35.00
Cruet, os	—	—	45.00
Goblet	50.00	65.00	32.00
Marmalade Jar, cov.	60.00	80.00	50.00
Pickle, boat shape. .	25.00	35.00	15.00
Pitcher			
Milk.	—	—	50.00
Water	90.00	110.00	75.00
Relish, scoop shape	—	—	65.00
Salt & Pepper, pr. . .	—	—	65.00
Sauce, ftd.	18.00	25.00	12.00
Spooner.	40.00	50.00	25.00
Sugar, cov	60.00	80.00	40.00
Wine	55.00	70.00	60.00

PANELED "44" (Athenia, Reverse "44")

Non-flint made by U. S. Glass Co., c1912. Most pieces bear intertwined U. S. Glass Co. mark in base. Forms include pedestals and handles. Comes trimmed in gold and untarnishable platinum. Lemonade set (six piece set $150.00), goblet, and covered butter ($95.00) in rose or green staining. Some pieces in plain blue.

	Clear w/ platinum		Clear w/ platinum
Bon Bon, trifid ftd, cov	35.00	Olive, flat, handless.	30.00
Bowl, 8″, flat	50.00	Pitcher, water	
Butter, cov, flat	55.00	Flat, bulbous, ½ gal	90.00
Candlestick, 7″	65.00	Footed, tankard	95.00
Cruet	65.00	Salt & Pepper, pr.	75.00
Creamer		Sugar, cov, flat, handled. . . .	60.00
Flat.	45.00	Sugar, powdered, flat, no	
Footed	55.00	handles.	55.00
Finger Bowl	35.00	Toothpick	55.00
Goblet	45.00	Tumbler, water	30.00
Lemonade Set, pitcher, 6 tumblers	200.00	Vase, loving cup shape	40.00
		Wine	50.00

PANELED THISTLE (Delta)

Non-flint made by J. P. Higbee Glass Co., Bridgeville, Pennsylvania, in the early 1900s. The Higbee Glass Co. often used a bee as a trademark. This pattern has been heavily reproduced with a similar mark. Occasionally found with gilt. A covered sugar in ruby stained is known.

	Clear		Clear
Basket, small size	65.00	Water	70.00
Bowl		Plate	
8", bee mark	25.00	7"	20.00
9", bee mark	30.00	10", bee mark	30.00
Bread Plate	40.00	Punch Cup, bee mark	20.00
Butter, cov, ...	60.00	Relish, bee mark	24.00
Cake Stand, 9"	35.00	Rose Bowl, 5"	50.00
Candy Dish, cov, ftd	30.00	Salt, ind	20.00
Celery Tray	20.00	Sauce	
Celery Vase	40.00	Flared, bee mark	14.00
Champagne, bee mark	40.00	Footed	20.00
Compote		Spooner	25.00
Open, hs, 8"	30.00	Sugar, cov	45.00
Open, hs, 9"	35.00	Toothpick, bee mark	45.00
Open, ls, 5", jelly	30.00	Tumbler	25.00
Creamer, bee mark	40.00	Vase	
Cruet, os	50.00	5"	25.00
Doughnut Stand, 6"	25.00	9¼"	25.00
Goblet	35.00	Wine, bee mark	30.00
Honey, cov, sq, bee mark . . .	80.00		
Pitcher			
Milk	60.00		

PAVONIA (Pineapple Stem)

Non-flint made by Ripley and Co. in 1885 and by U. S. Glass Co. in 1891. This pattern comes plain and etched.

	Clear	Ruby Stained		Clear	Ruby Stained
Bowl, 9"	20.00	—	Plate, 6½", etched . .	17.50	—
Butter, cov, flat	75.00	125.00	Salt		
Cake Stand, large, etched	55.00	—	Ind	15.00	50.00
			Master	28.00	50.00
Celery Vase, etched	45.00	75.00	Salt Shaker	25.00	—
Compote			Sauce, ftd, 3½" or 4"	15.00	—
Cov, hs, 6"	65.00	—	Spooner, pedestal . .	45.00	50.00
Cov, hs, 8"	75.00	—	Sugar, cov, flat	55.00	75.00
Open, jelly, etched .	38.00	—	Tray, water, etched .	75.00	—
Creamer, etched . . .	48.00	65.00	Tumbler, etched bellflowers	35.00	50.00
Cup and Saucer . . .	35.00	—			
Finger Bowl, ruffled underplate	48.00	110.00	Waste Bowl	70.00	—
			Water Set, tankard pitcher, 6 tumblers	285.00	325.00
Goblet, etched	35.00	60.00			
Mug	—	50.00	Wine, etched	35.00	40.00
Pitcher					
Lemonade	125.00	135.00			
Water	75.00	195.00			

PENNSYLVANIA (Balder)

Non-flint issued by U. S. Glass Co., 1898. Also known in ruby stained. A ruffled jelly compote documented in orange carnival.

	Clear w/gold	Emerald Green
Biscuit Jar, cov	65.00	100.00
Bowl		
8", berry	25.00	35.00
8", sq	20.00	40.00
Butter, cov	60.00	85.00
Carafe	45.00	—
Celery Vase	45.00	—
Cheese Dish, cov ..	65.00	—
Compote, hs, ruffled,		
jelly...........	50.00	—
Creamer		
Ind	15.00	35.00
Regular........	25.00	50.00
Cruet, os	41.00	—
Decanter, handle,		
os...........	100.00	—

	Clear w/gold	Emerald Green
Goblet	24.00	—
Juice Tumbler.....	10.00	20.00
Pitcher, water	60.00	—
Punch Bowl	175.00	—
Punch Cup	10.00	—
Salt Shaker.......	10.00	—
Sauce	10.00	—
Shot Glass	12.00	—
Spooner.........	24.00	35.00
Sugar, cov	40.00	55.00
Syrup...........	50.00	—
Table Set, 3 pcs ...	125.00	185.00
Toothpick	35.00	90.00
Tumbler	28.00	40.00
Whiskey	15.00	—
Wine	15.00	40.00

PICKET

Non-flint made by the King Glass Co., Pittsburgh, Pennsylvania in the 1870s. Pattern has five different size compotes. Toothpick holders are known in apple green, vaseline, and purple slag.

	Clear
Bowl, 9½", sq	30.00
Bread Plate	70.00
Butter, cov	45.00
Celery Vase	40.00
Compote	
Cov, hs, 6"...........	65.00
Cov, hs, 8"...........	85.00
Cov, ls, 8"	95.00
Open, hs, 6"	30.00
Open, hs, 7", sq.	35.00
Open, hs, 8"	35.00
Open, hs, 10", sq.	70.00
Open, ls, 7"..........	50.00
Creamer.............	45.00

	Clear
Goblet	30.00
Pitcher, water	75.00
Salt	
Ind	10.00
Master	35.00
Sauce	
Flat...............	15.00
Footed	20.00
Spooner.............	30.00
Sugar, cov	45.00
Toothpick	35.00
Tray, water	65.00
Waste Bowl...........	30.00
Wine	85.00

PINEAPPLE AND FAN #1 (Heisey's #1255)

Made by A. H. Heisey and Co., Newark, Ohio, c1897, before the Heisey trademark was used. Came in about 70 pieces. Pieces often trimmed in gold. Also known in custard and ruby stained (toothpick at $125.00).

	Clear	Emerald Green		Clear	Emerald Green
Banana Stand.....	50.00	—	Compote		
Biscuit Jar, cov	65.00	150.00	Open, hs, 8"	50.00	225.00
Bowl, 5½"........	15.00	30.00	Open, jelly, 5" ...	35.00	—
Butter, cov	50.00	175.00	Creamer		
Cake Stand	45.00	75.00	Individual........	25.00	50.00
Celery Tray, flat....	25.00	—	Regular.........	35.00	95.00

	Clear	Emerald Green		Clear	Emerald Green
Cruet	60.00	295.00	Spooner	30.00	65.00
Custard Cup	15.00	30.00	Sugar, cov		
Goblet	18.00	—	Individual	25.00	50.00
Mug	30.00	45.00	Regular	45.00	125.00
Pitcher, water	80.00	225.00	Syrup	60.00	250.00
Rose Bowl	35.00	75.00	Toothpick	75.00	150.00
Salt, ind	25.00	—	Tumbler	25.00	60.00
Salt Shaker	20.00	—	Vase, 10", trumpet	25.00	45.00

PORTLAND

Non-flint pattern made by several companies c1880–1900. An oval pintray in ruby souvenir ($20.00) is known, and a flat sauce ($25.00).

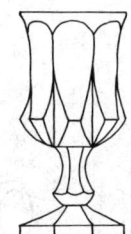

	Clear w/gold		Clear w/gold
Basket, handled	85.00	Lamp base, 9"	75.00
Biscuit Jar, cov	90.00	Pitcher, water, straight sides.	55.00
Bowl		Pomade Jar, SP top	30.00
Berry	20.00	Puff Box, glass lid	35.00
Small, flat, cov	30.00	Punch Bowl, 13⅝", ftd	150.00
Butter, cov	50.00	Punch Cup	10.00
Cake Stand, 10½"	45.00	Relish	15.00
Carafe, water	45.00	Salt Shaker	16.00
Celery Tray	25.00	Sauce	8.00
Compote		Spooner	30.00
Cov, hs, 6"	60.00	Sugar, cov	45.00
Open, hs, 8¼"	40.00	Sugar Shaker	40.00
Open, hs, 9½"	45.00	Syrup	50.00
Open, ls, 7"	45.00	Toothpick	25.00
Creamer	30.00	Tumbler	18.00
Cruet, os	48.00	Vase	25.00
Decanter, qt, handled	50.00	Water Bottle	40.00
Goblet	35.00	Wine	30.00

PRIMROSE

Non-flint made by Canton Glass Co., Canton, Ohio, c1880. Also made in milk glass. Apple green is scarce.

	Amber and Yellow	Blue and Green	Clear
Bowl, 8"	32.00	35.00	24.00
Butter, cov	50.00	60.00	35.00
Cake Stand, 10"	50.00	65.00	40.00
Celery Vase	35.00	40.00	25.00
Compote, cov, ls, 6"	40.00	45.00	30.00
Creamer	35.00	48.00	30.00
Egg Cup	30.00	35.00	20.00
Goblet			
Knob Stem	40.00	45.00	30.00
Plain Stem	35.00	40.00	25.00

	Amber and Yellow	Blue and Green	Clear
Lamp, finger	—	—	195.00
Pickle	18.00	20.00	14.00
Pitcher			
Milk	45.00	55.00	35.00
Water	55.00	50.00	48.00
Plate			
4½"	15.00	20.00	12.00
9", handled	30.00	35.00	20.00
Platter, 12 x 8"	35.00	45.00	30.00
Relish	18.00	20.00	14.00
Sauce, ftd	18.00	25.00	15.00
Spooner	25.00	30.00	20.00
Sugar, cov	40.00	55.00	35.00
Tray, water	50.00	60.00	35.00
Waste Bowl	32.00	35.00	28.00
Wine	40.00	45.00	28.00

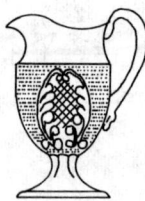

PRINCESS FEATHER (Rochelle)

Non-flint made by Bakewell, Pears & Co. in the late 1870s. Occasional pieces made in flint. Later by U. S. Glass Co. in the 1890s. Also made in milk glass. A rare blue opaque tumbler has been reported.

	Clear		Clear
Bowl		Goblet	45.00
7", cov, pedestal	35.00	Pitcher, water	75.00
7", oval	20.00	Plate	
8", oval	25.00	6"	30.00
9", oval	30.00	7"	35.00
Butter, cov	50.00	8"	40.00
Cake Plate, handled	35.00	9"	45.00
Celery Vase	40.00	Relish	20.00
Compote		Sauce	8.00
Cov, hs, 7"	50.00	Spooner	30.00
Cov, hs, 8"	50.00	Sugar	
Open, ls, 8"	35.00	Cov	55.00
Creamer, ah	55.00	Open	25.00
Dish, oval	20.00	Wine	45.00
Egg Cup	40.00		

PRISCILLA #1 (Findlay)

Non-flint made by Dalzell, Gilmore & Leighton, Findlay, Ohio, in the late 1890s and continued by National Glass Co. Fenton reproduced pattern in clear, colors, and opalescent in 1951. Also introduced many forms different from the original such as 12½" plate, goblet, wine, 6" handled bonbon, and sugar and creamer.

	Clear		Clear
Banana Stand	80.00	10¼", straight sides	50.00
Biscuit Jar	145.00	Butter, cov	65.00
Bowl		Cake Stand, 9½"	60.00
8½"	15.00	Celery Vase	55.00

	Clear			Clear
Compote			Tankard	85.00
Cov, hs, 9″	75.00		Plate	25.00
Open, hs, 7″	45.00		Sauce	8.00
Open, hs, 10″, scalloped	60.00		Spooner	30.00
Creamer	25.00		Sugar, open	20.00
Cruet, os	65.00		Syrup	90.00
Doughnut Stand	60.00		Toothpick	40.00
Goblet	40.00		Tumbler	25.00
Mug	20.00		Wine	35.00
Pitcher, water				
Bulbous	90.00			

QUARTERED BLOCK (Duncan & Miller #24)

Made by Duncan & Miller Co. c1903.

	Clear	Ruby Stained		Clear	Ruby Stained
Bowl	25.00	60.00	Sauce	7.50	—
Butter, cov	45.00	125.00	Spooner	20.00	45.00
Cake Stand, 9″	50.00	—	Sugar, cov	40.00	45.00
Celery Vase	30.00	—	Syrup	50.00	—
Compote, open, hs	35.00	—	Toothpick	30.00	85.00
Creamer	30.00	55.00	Tumbler	20.00	40.00
Goblet	35.00	—	Vase	18.00	—
Lamp	75.00	—	Water Bottle	35.00	—
Pitcher, water	45.00	150.00	Wine	30.00	—

QUEEN ANNE (Bearded Man)

Non-flint made by LaBelle Glass Co., Bridgeport, Ohio, c1879. Finials are Maltese cross. At least 28 pieces documented. A table set and water pitcher are known in amber.

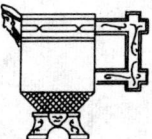

	Clear			Clear
Bowl, cov			Egg Cup	45.00
8″, oval	45.00		Pitcher	
9″, oval	55.00		Milk	75.00
Bread Plate	50.00		Water	85.00
Butter, cov	65.00		Spooner	40.00
Celery Vase	35.00		Sugar, cov	55.00
Compote, cov, ls, 9″	75.00		Syrup	100.00
Creamer	40.00			

QUESTION MARK (Oval Loop)

Made by Richards and Hartley in 1895 and later by U. S. Glass Co., 1891. An 1888 catalog lists 32 pieces. Scarce in ruby stained.

	Clear			Clear
Bowl			7″, oblong	18.00
4″, round, ftd	15.00		7″, round, ftd	20.00

	Clear		Clear
8", oblong	25.00	Goblet	25.00
8", round, ftd	25.00	Nappy, ftd	20.00
9", oblong	30.00	Pitcher	
10", oblong	25.00	Milk, bulbous	40.00
Butter, cov	30.00	Milk, tankard	45.00
Candlestick, chamber, finger		Water, bulbous	50.00
loop	45.00	Water, tankard	55.00
Celery Vase	28.00	Salt Shaker	15.00
Compote		Sauce, 4", collared	10.00
Cov, hs, 7"	50.00	Spooner	20.00
Cov, hs, 8"	65.00	Sugar Shaker	35.00
Open, hs, 7"	25.00	Sugar, cov	25.00
Open, ls	15.00	Tumbler	20.00
Cordial	20.00	Wine	20.00
Creamer	30.00		

RED BLOCK (Late Block)

Non-flint with red stain made by Doyle and Co.; later made by five companies plus U. S. Glass Co. in 1892. Prices for clear 50% less.

	Ruby Stained		Ruby Stained
Bowl, 8"	75.00	Rose Bowl	75.00
Butter, cov	90.00	Sauce, flat, 4½"	20.00
Celery Vase, 6½"	85.00	Salt Dip, ind	50.00
Creamer		Salt Shaker, single	60.00
Individual	45.00	Spooner	45.00
Regular	70.00	Sugar, cov	75.00
Decanter, 12", os, variant	175.00	Tumbler	35.00
*Goblet	45.00	Water Set, pitcher, 6	
Mug	40.00	tumblers	285.00
Pitcher, water, 8" h	175.00	*Wine	35.00

REVERSE TORPEDO (Bull's Eye Band, Bull's Eye with Diamond Point #2, Pointed Bull's Eye)

Made by Dalzell, Gilmore & Leighton Glass Co., Findlay, Ohio, c1888–1890. Also attributed to Canadian factories. Sometimes found with etching.

	Clear		Clear
Banana Stand, 9¾"	100.00	Cov, hs, 6"	80.00
Biscuit Jar, cov	135.00	Open, hs, 10½" d, V shape	
Bowl		bowl	90.00
8½", shallow	30.00	Open, hs, 7"	65.00
9", fruit, pie crust rim	70.00	Open, hs, 8⅜" d	45.00
10½", pie crust rim	75.00	Open, hs, jelly	50.00
Butter, cov	75.00	Open, ls, 9¼", ruffled	
Cake Stand	85.00	edge	90.00
Celery Vase	55.00	Goblet	85.00
Compote		Honey Dish, sq, cov	145.00
Cov, hs, 7"	80.00	Pitcher, water, tankard,	
Cov, hs, 10"	125.00	10¼"	150.00

	Clear		Clear
Sauce, flat, 3¾"	20.00	Syrup	165.00
Spooner	30.00	Tumbler	30.00
Sugar, cov	85.00		

RIBBED IVY

Flint, late 1850s. Attributed to Boston and Sandwich Glass Co.

	Clear		Clear
Bowl, 6"	15.00	Salt, master	
Butter, cov	100.00	Cov	125.00
Castor Bottle	35.00	Open, scalloped rim	40.00
Celery Vase	300.00	Sauce	12.00
Champagne	100.00	Spooner	40.00
Compote		Sugar, cov	80.00
Cov, hs, 6", jelly	125.00	Sweetmeat, cov, on stand	165.00
Open, hs, 9", scalloped		Tumbler	
edge	85.00	Bar	75.00
Creamer	125.00	Water	70.00
Decanter, quart, os	150.00	Whiskey	
Egg Cup	30.00	Handled	100.00
Goblet	45.00	Plain	70.00
Hat	350.00	Wine	100.00
Pitcher, water, ah	250.00		

RIBBON

Non-flint, usually frosted, made by Bakewell, Pears, Pittsburgh, Pennsylvania, in the late 1860s. It has been erroneously called "Frosted Ribbon" at times, which can be confusing. Other Ribbon patterns are Clear Ribbon, Frosted Ribbon, Double Ribbon, Fluted Ribbon, and Grated Ribbon. Compotes have been reproduced in clear and color by Fostoria for the Henry Ford Museum gift shop, and are usually sgd "HFM."

	Frosted		Frosted
Butter, cov	70.00	Pitcher, water	75.00
Cake Stand, 8½"	50.00	Platter, 9" x 13", oblong, cut	
Celery Vase	40.00	corners	62.50
Cheese, cov	95.00	Salt Shaker	40.00
Cologne Bottle, os	65.00	Sauce	
Compote		Footed	18.00
Cov, hs, 8"	75.00	Tab-handled	18.00
Cov, ls, 7"	45.00	Spooner	35.00
Open, hs, 10½", SP, Dol-		Sugar, cov	65.00
phin stand	250.00	Tray, water, 15"	100.00
Open, ls, 7"	35.00	Waste Bowl	45.00
Creamer	30.00	Wine	125.00
*Goblet	35.00		

RIBBON CANDY (Bryce)

Non-flint, made by Bryce Brothers, Pittsburgh, Pennsylvania, 1880s. Reissued by U. S. Glass Co. in 1890s. Bowls come in a variety of sizes: open or with lids; flat or with a low collared foot. Also known in emerald green.

	Clear		Clear
Bowl		Open, ls, 8″	25.00
3½″, round	10.00	Cordial	55.00
4″, round	10.00	Creamer	25.00
8″, oval	25.00	Cruet, os	65.00
8″, round	25.00	Cup and Saucer	40.00
Butter, cov		Goblet	65.00
Flat	50.00	Honey, cov, sq	75.00
Footed	55.00	Lamp, oil	75.00
Cake Stand		Pitcher	
8″	30.00	Milk	45.00
10½″	45.00	Water	75.00
Claret	65.00	Plate	
Compote		6″	18.00
Cov, ls, 5″	30.00	8″	25.00
Cov, ls, 6″	30.00	9½″	30.00
Cov, ls, 7″	40.00	11″	35.00
Cov, ls, 8″	40.00	Relish	10.00
Open, hs, 5″	20.00	Salt Shaker	35.00
Open, hs, 6″	25.00	Sauce	
Open, hs, 7″	30.00	Flat, 4″	10.00
Open, hs, 8″	35.00	Footed, 4″	12.00
Open, ls, 3″	12.00	Spooner	30.00
Open, ls, 4″	12.00	Sugar, cov	40.00
Open, ls, 5″	12.00	Syrup	90.00
Open, ls, 6″	15.00	Tumbler	25.00
Open, ls, 7″	20.00	Wine	55.00

ROMAN KEY (Frosted Roman Key)

Flint glass pattern of the 1860s made Union Glass Co. and by others in several variants. Available in clear but not as popular. Sometimes erroneously called "Greek Key."

	Flint Frosted		Flint Frosted
Bowl		Egg Cup	45.00
8″	45.00	Goblet	50.00
10″	50.00	Pitcher, water	225.00
Butter, cov	80.00	Plate, 6″	28.00
Celery Vase, ftd	80.00	Salt, ftd	45.00
Champagne	90.00	Sauce, 4″	18.00
Compote		Spooner	45.00
Open, hs, 8″, cable rim . . .	60.00	Sugar, cov	85.00
Open, ls, 7″	95.00	Tumbler, bar	45.00
Creamer, ah	115.00	Wine	85.00
Decanter, os	150.00		

ROMAN ROSETTE

Non-flint made by Bryce, Walker and Co. 1875–1885. Reissued by U. S. Glass Co. in 1892 and 1898. Attributed to Portland Glass Co. Also seen with English registry mark. Also known in amber stained.

	Clear	Ruby Stained		Clear	Ruby Stained
Bowl			Mug	35.00	—
6″	12.00	—	Pitcher		
8½″.	15.00	50.00	Milk.	45.00	150.00
Bread Plate	30.00	75.00	Water	50.00	140.00
Butter, cov	50.00	125.00	Plate, 7½″.	35.00	65.00
Cake Stand, 9″	45.00	—	Relish, oval, 9″	20.00	40.00
Celery Vase	30.00	95.00	Salt & Pepper, glass		
Compote			tray	40.00	100.00
Cov, hs, 4½″, jelly	50.00	—	Sauce	15.00	20.00
Cov, hs, 6″.	65.00	—	Spooner	25.00	45.00
Creamer.	32.00	45.00	Sugar, cov	40.00	80.00
Cordial	50.00	—	Syrup	85.00	125.00
*Goblet	40.00	—	Wine	45.00	65.00
Lemonade Mug. . . .	35.00	—			

ROSE-IN-SNOW

Non-flint made by Bryce Bros., Pittsburgh, Pennsylvania in the square form, c1880. Also made in the more common round form by Ohio Flint Glass Co. and after 1891 by U. S. Glass Co.

	Amber and Canary	Blue	Clear
Butter, cov			
Round.	50.00	125.00	45.00
Square	60.00	150.00	50.00
Cake Stand, 9″	—	—	90.00
Compote			
Cov, hs, 8″.	125.00	175.00	80.00
Cov, ls, 7″	100.00	150.00	75.00
Open, ls, 5¾″ . . .	40.00	120.00	35.00
Creamer			
Round.	60.00	100.00	45.00
Square	65.00	120.00	45.00
* Goblet	40.00	55.00	35.00
* Mug, "In Fond			
Remembrance" . .	45.00	110.00	32.00
* Pickle Dish			
Double, 8½″ x 7″ .	45.00	110.00	100.00
Single, oval, handles at end. . . .	25.00	95.00	20.00
Pitcher, water, ah . .	175.00	200.00	125.00
Plate			
5″	—	—	35.00
6″	20.00	80.00	18.00
7″	22.00	82.00	20.00
Platter, oval.	—	—	125.00

	Amber and Canary	Blue	Clear
Sauce			
Flat...........	15.00	20.00	12.00
Footed	8.00	48.00	18.00
Spooner			
Round.........	30.00	80.00	25.00
Square	38.50	100.00	35.00
Sugar, cov			
Round.........	55.00	120.00	50.00
Square	50.00	140.00	45.00
Tumbler, bar......	60.00	100.00	50.00

ROSETTE (Magic)

Non-flint made by Bryce Bros., Pittsburgh, Pennsylvania, in the late 1870s. Continued by the U. S. Glass Co. Later made in Ohio in 1898.

	Clear		Clear
Bowl, 7¼″, cov	30.00	Pickle................	12.00
Bread Plate, 9″, handles ...	25.00	Pitcher	
Butter, cov	35.00	Milk, qt	50.00
Cake Stand		Water, ½ gal	65.00
7″...................	24.00	Plate, 7″..............	12.00
10″..................	26.00	Relish, fish shape	15.00
11″..................	35.00	Salt Shaker.............	25.00
Celery, 8″..............	20.00	Sauce, flat, handled.......	8.00
Compote		Spooner...............	25.00
Cov, hs, 6″............	40.00	Sugar, cov	35.00
Cov, hs, 8″............	70.00	Sugar Shaker	35.00
Cov, hs, 11½″..........	50.00	Tray, 10¼″.............	35.00
Open, hs, 7″	30.00	Tumbler, 5″.............	18.50
Open, hs, 4½″, jelly	25.00	Waste Bowl............	25.00
Creamer...............	25.00	Wine	25.00
Goblet	25.00		

ROYAL IVY ("New" Jewel)

Non-flint made by Northwood Glass Co. in 1889. Made in cased spatter, clear and frosted rainbow cracquelle, clear with amber, stained ivy, and clambroth opaline. These last mentioned were experimental pieces, not made in sets.

	Clear Frosted	Rubena Clear	Rubena Frosted
Bowl, berry, small ..	20.00	30.00	45.00
Butter, cov	100.00	175.00	275.00
Creamer, ah	60.00	150.00	200.00
Cruet	90.00	225.00	325.00
Marmalade Jar, SP cov...........	125.00	—	—
Miniature Lamp....	—	—	350.00
Pickle Castor, SP frame	125.00	—	375.00
Pitcher, water, ah ..	110.00	175.00	275.00
Rose Bowl	55.00	70.00	85.00

	Clear Frosted	Rubena Clear	Rubena Frosted
Spooner	45.00	70.00	95.00
Sugar, cov	150.00	165.00	180.00
Sugar Shaker	65.00	135.00	150.00
Syrup	120.00	225.00	300.00
Toothpick	50.00	90.00	125.00
Tumbler	35.00	50.00	75.00

ROYAL OAK (Acorn)

Non-flint made by Northwood Glass Co., Martins Ferry, Ohio, c1899. In early 1900s, it was made in opaque, white with colored tops and colored acorns and leaves. Milk-white pieces are rare.

	Clear Frosted	Rubena Clear	Rubena Frosted
Butter, cov	150.00	175.00	185.00
Creamer	75.00	125.00	150.00
Cruet, os	150.00	425.00	480.00
Mustard Jar, cov . . .	90.00	—	—
Pickle Castor	100.00	150.00	225.00
Pitcher, water	100.00	350.00	350.00
Salt Shaker, single .	40.00	45.00	65.00
Spooner	50.00	90.00	100.00
Sugar, cov, acorn finial	85.00	150.00	180.00
Sugar Shaker	75.00	135.00	165.00
Syrup	135.00	200.00	275.00
Tumbler	40.00	60.00	80.00

SAWTOOTH (Mitre Diamond)

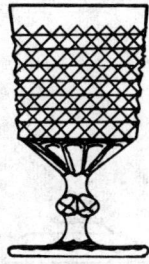

An early clear flint-glass pattern made in the late 1850s by the New England Glass Co., Boston and Sandwich Glass Co., and others. Later made in non-flint by Bryce Brothers and U. S. Glass Co. Also known in milk glass, clear deep blue, and canary yellow.

	Flint	Non-Flint		Flint	Non-Flint
Butter, cov	75.00	45.00	Plain Stem	—	20.00
Cake Stand, 10″ . . .	85.00	55.00	Pitcher, water		
Celery Vase, 10″ . . .	60.00	30.00	Applied handle. . .	150.00	95.00
Champagne	65.00	30.00	Pressed handle . .	—	55.00
Compote			Plate, 6½″.	45.00	30.00
Cov, hs, 9½″	85.00	48.00	Pomade Jar, cov . . .	50.00	35.00
Open, ls, 8″, saw-			Salt		
tooth edge	50.00	30.00	Cov, ftd	65.00	40.00
Cordial	50.00	30.00	Open, smooth		
Creamer			edge	25.00	20.00
Applied handle. . .	75.00	40.00	Spooner	70.00	30.00
Pressed handle . .	—	30.00	Sugar, cov	65.00	35.00
Cruet, acorn stopper	100.00	—	Tumbler, bar	50.00	25.00
Egg Cup.	45.00	25.00	Wine, knob stem . . .	35.00	20.00
Knob Stem	45.00	25.00			

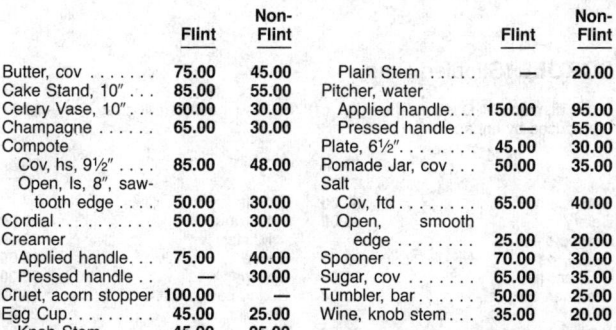

SCALLOPED DIAMOND POINT (Late Diamond Point Band, Panel with Diamond Point, Diamond Point With Flute)

Non-flint pattern. Not to be confused with early flint Diamond Point. Made by Central Glass Co., Wheeling, West Virginia. Also made by U. S. Glass Co. after 1891. A wine ($75.00) is known in electric blue, and in amber ($50.00).

	Clear		Clear
Bowl, oval, 9″	20.00	Goblet	30.00
Butter Dish, cov	55.00	Mustard Jar, cov	30.00
Cake Stand		Pickle Dish, oval	20.00
8″	30.00	Pickle Jar, cov.	45.00
12″	45.00	Plate	
Cheese Dish, cov, 8″	50.00	5″	12.00
Compote		9″	20.00
Cov, hs, 8″.	75.00	Sauce, ftd, 4″	10.00
Open, hs, 7″ d	40.00	Spooner	25.00
Cov, 5″, jelly	35.00	Sugar, cov	40.00
Creamer	50.00	Wine	35.00

SCALLOPED TAPE (Jewel Band)

Non-flint, c1880. Maker unknown. Occasionally found in amber, blue, canary, and light green.

	Clear		Clear
Bread Plate, oval, "Bread Is		Pitcher	
The Staff of Life"	45.00	Milk.	35.00
Butter, cov	35.00	Water	55.00
Cake Stand	35.00	Plate, 6″	15.00
Celery Vase	30.00	Relish.	10.00
Compote		Sauce	
Cov, hs, 8″.	55.00	Flat, 4″	8.50
Open, hs.	40.00	Ftd	12.00
Creamer	25.00	Spooner	20.00
Dish, rect, cov, 8″	45.00	Sugar, cov	35.00
Egg Cup.	25.00	Tray, 6 x 7″.	25.00
Goblet	25.00	Wine	20.00

SCROLL (Stippled Scroll)

Non-flint, made by Duncan Glass Co., c1870s. Also made in milk glass. Some items reproduced by Imperial.

	Clear		Clear
Butter, cov	50.00	Salt, ftd	
Celery	30.00	Individual.	20.00
Compote		Master	25.00
Cov, hs	65.00	Sauce	10.00
Open, hs	35.00	Spooner	30.00
Creamer, ah	40.00	Sugar, cov	45.00
Goblet	35.00	Tumbler, ftd	25.00
Pitcher, water, ah	75.00	Wine	30.00

SCROLL WITH FLOWERS

Non-flint. Attributed to Central Glass Co. in the 1870s and Canton Glass Co. Occasionally found in amber, apple green, and blue.

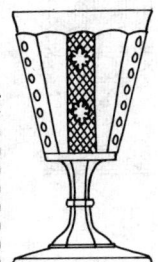

	Clear		Clear
Butter, cov	40.00	Mustard Jar, cov	50.00
Cake Plate, 10½", handled	25.00	Pickle, handled	18.00
Celery	36.00	Pitcher, water	45.00
Compote, cov	45.00	Plate, double-handled, 10½"	40.00
Cordial	35.00	Sauce, double-handled	10.00
Creamer	40.00	Spooner	28.50
Egg Cup, handled	20.00	Sugar, cov	45.00
Goblet	25.00	Wine	30.00

SEDAN (Paneled Star and Button)

Clear non-flint pattern made in the 1870s.

	Clear		Clear
Bowl	20.00	Pitcher, water	35.00
Butter, cov	30.00	Relish	10.00
Celery Tray	15.00	Salt Shaker	20.00
Celery Vase	25.00	Sauce, flat	8.00
Compote		Spooner	15.00
Cov, hs, 8½"	35.00	Sugar, cov	35.00
Open, hs	20.00	Tumbler	20.00
Creamer	20.00	Wine	15.00
Goblet	15.00		

SHRINE (Jewel with Moon and Star)

Non-flint made by Beatty & Indiana Glass Co., Dunkirk, Indiana, c. late 1880s.

	Clear		Clear
Bowl		Jumbo Size	100.00
4"	15.00	Platter	40.00
6½"	25.00	Relish	15.00
9½"	30.00	Salt Shaker	30.00
Butter, cov	50.00	Sauce	15.00
Cake Stand, 8½"	40.00	Spooner	30.00
Celery	45.00	Sugar, cov	50.00
Creamer	40.00	Tumbler	
Goblet	45.00	Lemonade	40.00
Mug	25.00	Water	35.00
Pickle	20.00		
Pitcher, water			
Normal Size	50.00		

SHUTTLE (Hearts of Loch Haven)

Made by Indiana Tumbler and Goblet Co., Greentown, Indiana, between 1894 and 1903. Some items reproduced.

	Clear	Cara-mel		Clear	Cara-mel
Bowl, berry	25.00	—	Mug	25.00	95.00
Butter, cov	50.00	150.00	Pitcher, water	50.00	—
Cake Stand	115.00	—	Spooner	20.00	—
Celery Vase	30.00	—	Sugar, cov	40.00	—
Cordial	32.00	—	Tumbler	25.00	80.00
Creamer	30.00	—	Wine	20.00	50.00
Cruet, os	75.00				

SKILTON (Oregon #2)

Made by Richards & Hartley of Tarentum, Pennsylvania in 1888 and by U. S. Glass after 1891. This is not one of the U. S. Glass States pattern series and should not be confused with Beaded Loop, which is Oregon #1, named by U. S. Glass Co. It is better known as Skilton (named by Millard) to avoid confusion with Beaded Loop.

	Clear	Ruby Stained		Clear	Ruby Stained
Bowl			Creamer	30.00	55.00
4″, round	10.00	—	Dish, oblong, sq	25.00	—
5″, round	15.00	—	Goblet	35.00	50.00
6″, round	20.00	—	Olive, handled	20.00	—
7″, rect	20.00	—	Pickle	15.00	—
8″, rect	25.00	—	Pitcher		
9″, rect	30.00	—	Milk	45.00	125.00
Butter, cov	45.00	110.00	Water	50.00	125.00
Cake Stand	35.00	—	Salt & Pepper, pr.	45.00	—
Celery Vase	35.00	95.00	Sauce, ftd	12.00	20.00
Compote			Spooner, flat	25.00	55.00
Cov, hs, 7″	45.00	—	Sugar, cov	35.00	85.00
Cov, hs, 8″	45.00	—	Tray, water	45.00	—
Open, ls, 4″	10.00	—	Tumbler	25.00	40.00
Open, ls, 7″	25.00	—	Wine	30.00	45.00
Open, ls, 8″	30.00	75.00			

SNAIL (Compact, Idaho, Double Snail)

Non-flint made by George Duncan & Sons, Pittsburgh, Pennsylvania, c1880, and by U. S. Glass Co. in the States Pattern series. Ruby stained pieces date after 1891. Add 30% for engraved pieces.

	Clear	Ruby Stained		Clear	Ruby Stained
Banana Stand	145.00	225.00	Bowl		
Basket, cake or fruit			4″	20.00	90.00
9″	85.00	—	4½″	20.00	—
10″	95.00	—	7″, cov	60.00	45.00

	Clear	Ruby Stained		Clear	Ruby Stained
7", oval	28.00	45.00	Pitcher		
7", round	28.00	45.00	Milk, tankard	100.00	—
8", cov	60.00	45.00	Water, bulbous	125.00	—
8", oval	28.00	45.00	Water, tankard	135.00	250.00
8", round	28.00	45.00	Plate		
9", oval	30.00	—	5"	35.00	—
9", round	30.00	—	6"	35.00	—
10"	35.00	45.00	7"	40.00	—
Butter, cov	75.00	160.00	Punch Cup	35.00	—
Cake Stand			Relish, 7", oval	25.00	—
9"	85.00	—	Rose Bowl		
10"	95.00	—	3"	50.00	—
Celery Vase	35.00	85.00	5"	45.00	—
Cheese, cov	95.00	—	6"	45.00	—
Compote			7"	50.00	—
Cov, hs, 6"	50.00	—	Salt		
Cov, hs, 7"	50.00	100.00	Ind	35.00	—
Cov, hs, 8"	80.00	135.00	Master	35.00	75.00
Cov, hs, 10"	125.00	—	Salt Shaker		
Open, hs, 6"	30.00	—	Bulbous	65.00	90.00
Open, hs, 7"	45.00	—	Straight sides	60.00	90.00
Open, hs, 8"	35.00	—	Sauce	25.00	45.00
Open, hs, 9", twist-			Spooner	45.00	75.00
ed stem, scal-			Sugar		
loped	75.00	—	Ind, cov	50.00	—
Cracker Jar, cov	85.00	—	Regular, cov	60.00	100.00
Creamer	65.00	75.00	Sugar Shaker	85.00	200.00
Cup, Custard	30.00	—	Syrup	125.00	225.00
Cruet, os	100.00	275.00	Tumbler	55.00	65.00
Finger Bowl	50.00	—	Vase	50.00	—
Goblet	65.00	95.00	Violet Bowl, 3"	50.00	—
Marmalade, cov	90.00	125.00	Wine	65.00	—

SPIREA BAND

Non-flint made by Bryce, Higbee & Co., Pittsburgh, Pennsylvania, c1885.

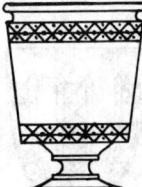

	Amber	Blue	Clear	Vaseline
Bowl, 8"	25.00	40.00	20.00	30.00
Butter, cov	50.00	55.00	35.00	45.00
Cake Stand, 11"	45.00	55.00	40.00	45.00
Celery Vase	40.00	50.00	25.00	40.00
Compote, cov, hs, 7"	44.00	65.00	40.00	44.00
Cordial	38.00	42.00	20.00	38.00
Creamer	32.50	44.00	35.00	35.00
Goblet	25.00	30.00	20.00	35.00
Pitcher, water	65.00	80.00	35.00	60.00
Platter, 10½"	32.00	42.00	20.00	32.00
Relish	30.00	35.00	18.00	30.00
Sauce				
Flat	10.00	12.00	5.00	9.00
Ftd	15.00	18.00	8.00	14.00
Spooner	30.00	35.00	20.00	35.00
Sugar, open	32.00	40.00	25.00	32.00
Tumbler	24.00	35.00	20.00	30.00
Wine	30.00	35.00	20.00	30.00

SPRIG

Non-flint made by Bryce, Higbee & Co., Pittsburgh, Pennsylvania, mid-1880s.

	Clear		Clear
Bowl, 10", scalloped	35.00	Pitcher, water	50.00
Bread Plate	40.00	Relish	12.00
Butter, cov	65.00	Salt, master	55.00
Cake Stand, 8"	35.00	Sauce	
Celery Vase	40.00	Flat	12.00
Compote		Ftd	15.00
Cov, hs	60.00	Spooner	25.00
Open, hs	45.00	Sugar, cov	40.00
Creamer	30.00	Wine	40.00
Goblet	30.00		

STAR ROSETTED

Non-flint made by McKee Brothers, Pittsburgh, PA, c1875.

	Clear		Clear
Bread Plate	50.00	Goblet	25.00
Butter, cov	48.00	Pickle	14.00
Compote		Pitcher, water	50.00
Cov, hs, 8½"	60.00	Plate, 7"	15.00
Cov, jelly	55.00	Relish, 9"	14.00
Cov, sweetmeat	55.00	Sauce	
Open, hs, 6½"	18.00	Flat	8.50
Open, hs, 7½"	20.00	Footed	12.00
Open, hs, 8½"	35.00	Spooner	25.00
Creamer	35.00	Sugar, cov	48.00

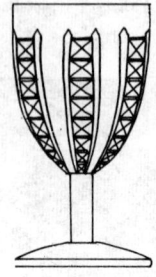

STARS AND STRIPES (Brilliant)

Made by Jenkins Glass Co., Kokomo, Indiana, in 1899. Appeared in 1899 Montgomery Ward catalog as "Brilliant."

	Clear		Clear
Bowl, berry	15.00	Pitcher, water	35.00
Butter, cov	30.00	Salt Shaker	15.00
Celery Vase	15.00	Sauce	6.00
Cordial	15.00	Spooner	15.00
Creamer	18.00	Sugar, cov	20.00
Cruet Set	35.00	Tumbler	15.00
Cup, sherbert, handled	12.00	Wine	15.00
Goblet	20.00		

STATES, THE (Cane and Star Medallion)

Non-flint made by the U. S. Glass Co. in 1908. Also found in emerald green; add 50%.

	Clear w/ gold		Clear w/ gold
Bowl		Punch Cup	8.00
7", round, 3 handles	25.00	Relish, diamond shape	35.00
9¼", round	30.00	Salt & Pepper	40.00
Butter, cov	65.00	Sauce, flat, 4", tub shape	10.00
Celery Tray	20.00	Spooner	25.00
Cocktail	25.00	Sugar	
Compote		Covered	40.00
Open, hs, 7"	30.00	Open, ind	15.00
Open, hs, 9"	40.00	Open, table	20.00
Creamer		Syrup	65.00
Ind, oval	18.00	Toothpick, flat, rectangular,	
Regular, round	30.00	curled lip	45.00
Goblet	35.00	Tray, 7¼" l, 5½" w	18.00
Pitcher, water	45.00	Tumbler	22.00
Plate, 10"	25.00	Wine	30.00
Punch Bowl, 13" d	75.00		

STIPPLED DOUBLE LOOP

Clear and stippled non-flint pattern of the 1880s.

	Clear		Clear
Butter, cov	50.00	Salt Shaker	20.00
Cake Stand	40.00	Spooner	20.00
Celery Vase	40.00	Sugar, cov	25.00
Creamer	30.00	Tumbler	30.00
Goblet	60.00	Wine	25.00
Pitcher, water	55.00		

STIPPLED GRAPE AND FESTOON

Non-flint made by Doyle and Co, Pittsburgh, PA, c1870. Pieces have applied handles and acorn finials.

	Clear		Clear
Butter, cov		Pickle	30.00
Flange	60.00	Pitcher	
Regular	45.00	Milk, ah	75.00
Celery Vase	45.00	Water	90.00
Compote		Relish	30.00
Cov, hs, 8"	45.00	Sauce, flat	12.00
Cov, ls, 8"	35.00	Spooner	30.00
Cov, ls, 9"	55.00	Sugar	
Open, ls	35.00	Cov	60.00
Creamer	50.00	Open	40.00
Egg Cup	35.00	Wine	45.00
Goblet	32.50		

STRAWBERRY AND CURRANT (Multiple Fruits)

One of a non-flint series of fruit patterns which has become known as Multiple Fruits (Cherry and Fig, Loganberry and Grape, Blackberry and Grape, and Cornucopia with Sprig of Cherries). They were made by Dalzell, Gilmore, and Leighton in Findlay, Ohio. A Loganberry and Grape jelly goblet, with "U" shaped bowl; is of inferior quality and not part of the pattern.

There are matching pieces in all forms, although whether or not all forms were made in all four patterns is not known. Reproduction goblets and other items are found in clear, opalescent, and colors.

	Clear		Clear
Butter, cov	50.00	Pitcher	
Celery Vase	35.00	Milk	40.00
Cheese, cov	50.00	Water	50.00
Compote		Sauce, ftd	10.00
Cov, hs, 8″ d	70.00	Spooner	35.00
Open, hs	35.00	Sugar, cov	40.00
Creamer	40.00	Syrup	80.00
* Goblet	35.00	Tumbler	25.00
Mug	35.00		

STRIGIL

Non-flint pattern made in the 1880s by Tarentum Glass Co, Tarentum, PA. May be gilded.

	Clear		Clear
Bowl, 8″	20.00	Water	35.00
Butter, cov	35.00	Punch Cup	10.00
Celery Tray	15.00	Sauce, flat	5.00
Celery Vase	25.00	Spooner	18.00
Creamer	15.00	Sugar, cov	32.00
Cruet, os	25.00	Table Set, 5 pcs	90.00
Egg Cup	20.00	Tumbler	18.00
Goblet	40.00	Wine	25.00
Pitcher			
Milk	30.00		

SWAG WITH BRACKETS

Made by Jefferson Glass Co., Steubenville, Ohio, c1904. Also found in non-opalescent, gold trimmed, amethyst, blue, and vaseline.

	Blue and Canary Opal	Green Opal	White Opal
Butter, cov	175.00	150.00	100.00
Compote, Jelly	45.00	55.00	30.00
Creamer	80.00	75.00	55.00
Cruet, os	150.00	110.00	—
Pitcher, water	185.00	200.00	130.00
Salt Shaker, single	50.00	40.00	35.00
Spooner	72.00	65.00	40.00

	Blue and Canary Opal	Green Opal	White Opal
Sugar, cov	135.00	85.00	50.00
* Toothpick	125.00	85.00	40.00
Tumbler	65.00	50.00	35.00

TEARDROP AND TASSEL (Sampson)

Non-flint made by the Indiana Tumbler & Goblet Co., Greentown, Indiana, c1890, to celebrate Admiral Sampson's victory in the Spanish-American War.

	Clear	Cobalt Blue	Emerald Green	Nile Green Opaque
Bowl, 7½".	40.00	55.00	50.00	75.00
Butter, cov	55.00	95.00	155.00	325.00
Celery Vase	40.00	—	—	—
Compote				
Cov, hs, 7"	75.00	90.00	80.00	125.00
Cov, jelly	65.00	—	—	—
Open, ls, 5".	20.00	—	—	—
Open, ls, 8".	30.00	45.00	35.00	65.00
Creamer.	45.00	100.00	45.00	90.00
Goblet	110.00	125.00	175.00	95.00
Pickle.	20.00	55.00	40.00	55.00
Pitcher, water	50.00	150.00	150.00	900.00
Salt Shaker, single .	50.00	75.00	60.00	70.00
Sauce	15.00	20.00	20.00	—
Spooner	30.00	45.00	35.00	65.00
Sugar, cov	60.00	135.00	70.00	90.00
Tumbler	40.00	50.00	45.00	65.00
Wine	65.00	80.00	70.00	110.00

TENNESSEE (Jewel and Crescent; Jeweled Rosette)

Made by King Glass Co., Pittsburgh, Pennsylvania, and continued by U. S. Glass Co., in 1899, as part of the States series.

	Clear	Colored Jewels		Clear	Colored Jewels
Bowl, berry	20.00	30.00	Creamer.	30.00	—
Bread Plate	40.00	75.00	Goblet	40.00	—
Butter, cov	55.00	—	Mug	35.00	—
Cake Stand			Pitcher		
9½".	38.00	—	Milk.	55.00	—
10½".	45.00	—	Water	65.00	—
Celery Vase	35.00	—	Relish.	20.00	—
Compote			Spooner	35.00	—
Cov, 5", jelly	40.00	55.00	Sugar, cov	45.00	—
Open, hs, 8"	45.00	—	Syrup	90.00	—
Open, hs, 9"	45.00	—	Toothpick	80.00	80.00
Open, hs, 10" . . .	45.00	—	Tumbler	35.00	—
Open, ls, 7"	35.00	—	Wine	65.00	85.00

TEXAS (Loop with Stippled Panels)

Non-flint made by U. S. Glass Co., c1900, in the States Pattern series. Occasionally pieces found in ruby stained. Reproduced in solid colors.

	Clear w/gold	Rose Stained		Clear w/gold	Rose Stained
Bowl			Pickle, 8½″	25.00	—
7″	20.00	40.00	Pitcher, water	125.00	—
9″, scalloped	35.00	50.00	Plate, 9″	35.00	60.00
Butter, cov	75.00	125.00	Sauce		
Cake Stand, 9½″	60.00	80.00	Flat	10.00	18.00
Celery Tray	30.00	—	Footed	20.00	—
Celery Vase	40.00	—	Spooner	35.00	—
Compote			Sugar		
Cov, hs, 6″	60.00	—	Individual, cov	45.00	—
Cov, hs, 8″	75.00	—	Regular, cov	65.00	—
Open, hs, 5″	40.00	—	Toothpick	25.00	95.00
Creamer			Tumbler	25.00	—
Individual	20.00	—	Vase		
Regular	40.00	—	6½″	25.00	—
Cruet, os	60.00	165.00	9″	35.00	—
Goblet	85.00	95.00	Wine	50.00	100.00

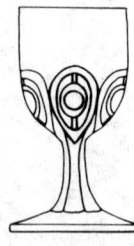

TEXAS BULL'S EYE (Filley, Bull's Eye Variant)

Originated by Bryce Bros., Pittsburgh, Pennsylvania, and continued by Findlay Glass, Findlay, Ohio. Also made in Canada. Originally made in semi-flint (no bell tone, but some lead content).

	Clear		Clear
Butter, cov	55.00	Spooner	25.00
Creamer	35.00	Sugar, cov	45.00
Egg Cup	30.00	Tumbler	50.00
Goblet	30.00	Wine	25.00
Pitcher, water	55.00		

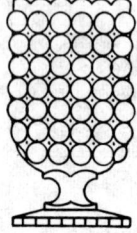

THOUSAND EYE

The original pattern was non-flint made by Adams Glass Co, Tarentum, PA, 1875, and by Richards and Hartley, 1888. (Their Pattern No. 103). It was made in two forms: Adams with a three knob stem finial, and Richards and Hartley with a plain stem with a scalloped bottom. Several glass companies made variations of the original pattern and reproductions were made as late as 1981. Crystal Opalescent was produced by Richards and Hartley only in the original pattern. (Opalescent celery vase $70.00; open compote, 8″, $115.00; 6″ creamer, $85.00;¼ gallon water pitcher, $140.00;½ gallon water pitcher, $180.00; 4″ footed sauce, $40.00; spooner, $60.00; and 5″ covered sugar, $80.00). Covered compotes are rare and would command 40% more than open compotes. A 2″ mug in blue is known.

	Amber	Apple Green	Blue	Clear	Vaseline
ABC Plate, 6″, clock center	50.00	55.00	52.00	45.00	52.00

	Amber	Apple Green	Blue	Clear	Vaseline
Bowl, large, carriage shape	—	—	85.00	—	85.00
Butter, cov					
6¼".	65.00	75.00	70.00	45.00	90.00
7½".	65.00	75.00	70.00	45.00	90.00
Cake Stand					
10"	50.00	78.00	55.00	30.00	84.00
11"	50.00	78.00	55.00	30.00	84.00
Celery, hat shape . .	50.00	65.00	60.00	35.00	55.00
Celery Vase, 7"	50.00	60.00	52.00	45.00	55.00
Christmas Light. . . .	27.00	45.00	35.00	25.00	40.00
Cologne Bottle	25.00	45.00	35.00	20.00	45.00
Compote, cov, ls, 8", sq.	—	100.00	100.00	—	—
Compote, open					
6"	35.00	40.00	38.00	25.00	38.00
7"	38.00	44.00	40.00	30.00	40.00
8", round	40.00	50.00	44.00	35.00	48.00
8", sq, hs.	39.00	50.00	48.00	38.00	55.00
9"	48.00	56.00	52.00	40.00	52.00
10"	55.00	65.00	60.00	45.00	60.00
Cordial	35.00	52.00	40.00	25.00	58.00
Creamer					
4"	32.00	40.00	36.00	25.00	38.00
6"	38.00	75.00	55.00	35.00	72.00
Creamer & Sugar Set	—	—	—	100.00	—
*Cruet, 6".	40.00	58.00	47.00	35.00	60.00
Egg Cup.	65.00	85.00	70.00	45.00	90.00
*Goblet	37.00	42.00	38.00	35.00	45.00
Honey Dish, cov, 6 × 7¼"	85.00	95.00	90.00	70.00	92.00
Inkwell	45.00	—	75.00	35.00	80.00
Jelly Glass	20.00	25.00	22.00	15.00	23.00
Lamp, Kerosene					
hs, 12"	120.00	150.00	130.00	100.00	140.00
hs, 15"	125.00	155.00	135.00	110.00	150.00
ls, handled	110.00	115.00	110.00	90.00	120.00
Mug					
2½".	23.00	30.00	25.00	20.00	32.00
3½".	23.00	30.00	25.00	20.00	32.00
Nappy					
5"	34.00	—	39.00	30.00	45.00
6"	39.00	—	44.00	35.00	52.00
8"	45.00	—	50.00	42.00	60.00
Pickle.	25.00	30.00	27.00	20.00	29.00
Pitcher					
Milk, cov, 7"	85.00	110.00	105.00	70.00	105.00
Water, ¼ gal	70.00	85.00	80.00	55.00	80.00
Water, ½ gal	80.00	92.00	84.00	65.00	85.00
Water, 1 gal.	90.00	100.00	95.00	85.00	95.00
*Plate, sq, folded corners					
6"	24.00	28.00	26.00	20.00	26.00
8"	26.00	30.00	28.00	22.00	30.00
10"	34.00	50.00	36.00	25.00	34.00
Platter					
8 × 11", oblong. .	40.00	48.00	42.00	38.00	45.00
11", oval	75.00	80.00	55.00	40.00	75.00

	Amber	Apple Green	Blue	Clear	Vaseline
Salt Shaker, pr					
Banded........	60.00	66.00	62.00	58.00	62.00
Plain.........	50.00	60.00	55.00	40.00	56.00
Salt, ind........	80.00	95.00	90.00	50.00	90.00
Salt, open, carriage shape.........	—		—	50.00	—
Sauce					
Flat, 4"........	10.00	22.00	12.00	8.00	15.00
Footed, 4"......	12.00	25.00	15.00	10.00	20.00
Spooner........	32.00	48.00	40.00	27.00	45.00
*String Holder	35.00	60.00	45.00	29.00	40.00
Sugar, cov, 5".....	52.00	70.00	54.00	45.00	55.00
Syrup, pewter top ..	80.00	100.00	70.00	55.00	70.00
Toothpick					
Hat..........	35.00	52.00	58.00	30.00	45.00
Plain.........	35.00	50.00	55.00	25.00	40.00
Thimble.......	55.00	—	—	—	—
Tray, water					
12½", round	64.00	78.00	65.00	55.00	60.00
14", oval	65.00	80.00	75.00	60.00	74.00
*Tumbler.........	26.00	62.00	34.00	21.00	30.00
*Wine	35.00	50.00	40.00	20.00	40.00

THREE-FACE

Non-flint made by George E. Duncan & Son, Pittsburgh, Pennsylvania, c1872. Designed by John E. Miller, a designer with Duncan, who later became a member of the firm. Companies in the Pittsburgh area produced many patterns in expectation of the 1876 Philadelphia Centennial Exposition. It has been heavily reproduced.

	Clear		Clear
Biscuit Jar, cov	300.00	Cov, ls, 4"	150.00
Butter, cov	140.00	Open, hs, 7"	75.00
Cake Stand		Open, hs, 8"	75.00
9"	150.00	Open, hs, 9"	135.00
10"	160.00	Open, ls, 6"	75.00
11"	165.00	Open, jelly, paneled	
Celery Vase		"Huber" top	85.00
Plain...............	95.00	Creamer..............	135.00
Scalloped	95.00	Goblet	85.00
Champagne		Lamp, Oil	150.00
Hollow stem..........	250.00	Marmalade Jar	200.00
Saucer type..........	150.00	Pitcher, water	375.00
Claret.................	100.00	Salt Dip	35.00
Compote		Salt & Pepper...........	75.00
Cov, hs, 7"..........	165.00	Sauce, ftd.............	25.00
Cov, hs, 8"...........	175.00	Spooner	80.00
Cov, hs, 9"..........	190.00	Sugar, cov	110.00
Cov, hs, 10"..........	225.00	Wine	150.00
Cov, ls, 6"	160.00		

THREE PANEL

Non-flint made by Richards & Hartley Co., Tarentum, Pennsylvania, c1888, and by U. S. Glass Co. in 1891.

	Amber	Blue	Clear	Vaseline
Bowl				
7″	25.00	40.00	20.00	45.00
8½″	25.00	40.00	20.00	45.00
10″	40.00	50.00	35.00	48.00
Butter, cov	45.00	50.00	40.00	50.00
Celery Vase, ruffled top	55.00	65.00	35.00	55.00
Compote, open, ls, 7″	35.00	55.00	25.00	40.00
Creamer	40.00	45.00	25.00	40.00
Cruet	250.00	—	—	—
Goblet	30.00	40.00	25.00	35.00
Mug	35.00	45.00	25.00	35.00
Pitcher, water	100.00	125.00	40.00	110.00
Sauce, ftd	15.00	15.00	10.00	15.00
Spooner	42.50	45.00	30.00	40.00
Sugar, cov	55.00	60.00	48.00	70.00
Tumbler	35.00	40.00	20.00	30.00

THUMBPRINT, EARLY (Argus, Giant Baby Thumbprint)

Flint originally produced by Bakewell, Pears and Co, Pittsburgh, PA, c1850-60. Made by several factories in various forms. Reproduced in color by Fenton.

	Clear		Clear
Ale Glass	40.00	Creamer	60.00
Banana Boat	150.00	Decanter, qt, os	
Berry Set, 7 pcs	195.00	Pattern base	125.00
Bitters Bottle	140.00	Plain base	85.00
Bowl, 6″	35.00	Egg Cup	40.00
Cake Stand	50.00	Goblet	50.00
Celery Vase		Honey Dish	10.00
Patterned base	100.00	Plate, 8″	50.00
Plain base	90.00	Salt, master, ftd	35.00
Champagne	100.00	Spooner	45.00
Claret	70.00	Sugar, cov	65.00
Compote		Tumbler	45.00
* Cov, 4″	80.00	Wine	75.00
* Cov, ls, 7″	100.00		
Open, 8″, scalloped top, flared	125.00		

TOKYO

Made by Jefferson Glass Co., Steubenville, Ohio, c1905. Also found in clear, blue, and apple green—all with gold trim. Some reproductions made by and signed Fenton.

	Blue Opal	Green Opal	White Opal
Bowl, berry	55.00	45.00	35.00

	Blue Opal	Green Opal	White Opal
Butter, cov	135.00	100.00	70.00
Compote, jelly	40.00	45.00	35.00
Creamer	80.00	60.00	50.00
Cruet	185.00	140.00	90.00
Dish, 6½"	40.00	45.00	40.00
Pitcher, water	185.00	150.00	100.00
Salt Shaker, single	50.00	40.00	30.00
Sauce	30.00	25.00	20.00
Spooner	45.00	40.00	30.00
Sugar, cov	95.00	75.00	60.00
Toothpick	110.00	80.00	50.00
Tumbler	50.00	45.00	35.00
Vase	60.00	60.00	45.00

TORPEDO (Pigmy)

Non-flint made by Thompson Glass Co., Uniontown, Pennsylvania, c1889. A black amethyst master salt ($150.00) also known.

	Clear	Ruby Stained		Clear	Ruby Stained
Banana Stand	75.00	—	Marmalade Jar, cov	85.00	—
Bowl			Pickle Castor, sp		
Cov, 7" d, 7¼" h	65.00	—	holder	125.00	—
Cov, 8"	40.00	—	Pitcher		
Open, 4"	—	20.00	Milk, 8½"	75.00	150.00
Open, 7"	18.00	—	Water, 10½"	85.00	175.00
Open, 8"	20.00	—	Punch Cup	25.00	—
Open, 9"	20.00	45.00	Salt		
Open, 9½", flared			Ind	20.00	—
rim	38.00	—	Master	35.00	—
Butter, cov	85.00	—	Salt Shaker, single, 2		
Cake Stand, 10"	85.00	—	types	50.00	—
Celery Vase, scal-			Sauce, 4½", collared		
loped top	40.00	—	base	15.00	—
Compote			Spooner, scalloped		
Cov, hs, 13¾"	165.00	—	top	45.00	—
Cov, hs, 4", jelly	65.00	—	Sugar		
Open, jelly	48.00	—	Cov	65.00	—
Creamer	50.00	—	Open	30.00	—
Cruet, os, ah	80.00	—	Syrup	95.00	175.00
Cup and Saucer	65.00	—	Tray, water		
Decanter, os, 8"	85.00	—	10", round	85.00	—
Finger Bowl	55.00	—	11¾", clover		
Goblet	45.00	85.00	shaped	75.00	—
Lamp			Tumbler	45.00	55.00
3", handled	75.00	—	Wine	90.00	—
8", plain base, pat-					
tern on bowl	85.00	—			

TRUNCATED CUBE (Thompson's #77)

Non-flint made by Thompson Glass Co., Uniontown, Pennsylvania, c1892. Also found with engraving.

	Clear	Ruby Stained		Clear	Ruby Stained
Bowl			Pitcher, water, tankard	50.00	110.00
4", berry	—	15.00	Spooner	30.00	50.00
8"	—	40.00	Salt Shaker, single	15.00	30.00
Butter, cov	50.00	90.00	Sugar, cov	30.00	70.00
Celery Vase	40.00	55.00	Syrup	40.00	100.00
Creamer			Table Set, 5 pcs	135.00	200.00
Ind	20.00	35.00	Toothpick	30.00	40.00
Regular	35.00	75.00	Tumbler	22.50	35.00
Decanter, os, 12" h	60.00	150.00	Wine	25.00	40.00
Goblet	30.00	50.00			

TULIP WITH SAWTOOTH

Originally made in flint glass by Bryce Bros., Pittsburgh, Pennsylvania, c1860. Later made in non-flint.

	Flint	Non-Flint		Flint	Non-Flint
Bottle, bar	70.00	—	No handle	—	45.00
Bottle, pint	—	45.00	Egg Cup	40.00	—
Butter, cov	125.00	82.00	Goblet	65.00	30.00
Celery Vase	85.00	24.00	Mug	80.00	—
Champagne	75.00	35.00	Pitcher, water	150.00	—
Compote			Plate, 6"	60.00	—
Cov, hs, 6"	90.00	—	Pomade Jar	45.00	—
Cov, hs, 8½"	95.00	—	Salt, master, plain		
Cov, ls, 8½"	85.00	—	edge	28.00	15.00
Open, hs, 8"	—	60.00	Spooner	35.00	—
Open, ls, 9"	60.00	—	Sugar, cov	95.00	—
Creamer	85.00	—	Tumbler		
Cruet			Bar	85.00	28.00
Applied handle	60.00	—	Footed	50.00	—
Pressed handle	—	40.00	* Wine	60.00	20.00
Decanter, os					
Handle	150.00	—			

TWO PANEL

Non-flint in oval forms made by Richards and Hartley Glass Co., Tarentum, Pennsylvania, 1880–1886, and by U. S. Glass Co. in 1891.

	Amber	Apple Green	Blue	Clear	Vaseline
Bowl					
5½"	35.00	40.00	40.00	15.00	25.00
8"	35.00	40.00	40.00	20.00	35.00
10 x 8½ x 3"	—	50.00	—	—	—
Butter, cov	50.00	55.00	55.00	30.00	40.00
Celery Vase	45.00	50.00	50.00	25.00	40.00
Compote, cov hs,					
6½", oval	55.00	—	—	35.00	75.00
7⅜ x 9 x 12¾"	—	100.00	—	—	—
8"	85.00	85.00	95.00	35.00	95.00
10 x 8½ x 3"	—	100.00	—	—	—

	Amber	Apple Green	Blue	Clear	Vaseline
Creamer.........	60.00	65.00	65.00	35.00	45.00
* Goblet	30.00	35.00	45.00	28.00	40.00
Lamp, high standard	85.00	125.00	100.00	45.00	115.00
Mug, 2 sizes......	30.00	35.00	40.00	20.00	30.00
Pitcher, water	60.00	60.00	65.00	35.00	50.00
Platter	25.00	—	—	—	—
Salt					
Ind	15.00	18.00	15.00	5.00	15.00
Master	20.00	25.00	20.00	10.00	12.00
Salt Shaker.......	40.00	45.00	40.00	25.00	30.00
Sauce					
Flat, oval.......	10.00	10.00	10.00	8.00	10.00
Footed	12.00	14.00	15.00	10.00	12.00
Spooner.........	45.00	50.00	45.00	25.00	35.00
Sugar, cov	65.00	70.00	72.00	40.00	60.00
Tray, water	50.00	55.00	55.00	45.00	50.00
Tumbler	35.00	42.50	35.00	15.00	40.00
Waste Bowl.......	40.00	45.00	40.00	20.00	30.00
*Wine	40.00	45.00	40.00	20.00	30.00

U. S. COIN

Non-flint frosted, clear, and gilted pattern made by U. S. Glass Co. in 1892 for three or four months. Production was stopped by U. S. Treasury because real coins, dated as early as 1878, were used in the molds. 1892 coin date is the most common.

	Clear	Frosted		Clear	Frosted
Bowl			Cruet, os	375.00	500.00
6"..............	170.00	220.00	Epergne..........	—	1,000.00
9"..............	215.00	325.00	Goblet	250.00	400.00
Bread Plate	175.00	325.00	Goblet, dimes	—	550.00
Butter, cov, dollars			Lamp		
and halves	250.00	450.00	Round font	275.00	450.00
Cake Stand, 10" ...	225.00	400.00	Square font	300.00	—
Celery			Mug, handled	185.00	300.00
Tray	200.00	—	Pickle...........	200.00	—
Vase, quarters...	135.00	350.00	Pitcher, water, dol-		
Champagne	—	400.00	lars...........	400.00	800.00
Compote			Sauce, ftd, 4", quar-		
Cov, hs, 7"......	300.00	500.00	ters...........	100.00	185.00
Cov, hs, 8", quar-			Spooner, quarters ..	225.00	325.00
ters and dimes .	—	415.00	Sugar, cov	225.00	350.00
Open, hs, 7", quar-			Syrup, dated pewter		
ters and dimes .	200.00	300.00	lid.............	—	525.00
Open, hs, 7", quar-			* Toothpick	180.00	275.00
ters and halves.	225.00	350.00	Tray, water, 8", rect .	275.00	—
Open, 8⅜" d,			Tumbler	135.00	235.00
6½" h.	—	240.00	Waste Bowl.......	225.00	—
Creamer.........	350.00	500.00	Wine	225.00	375.00

U. S. SHERATON (Greek Key)

Made by U. S. Glass Co in 1912. This pattern was made only in clear, but can be found trimmed with gold or platinum. Some pieces are marked with the intertwined U. S. Glass trademark

	Clear		Clear
Bon Bon, 6", ftd.	15.00	Squat, medium	30.00
Bowl		Tankard	35.00
6", ftd, sq	15.00	Plate, sq	
8", flat.	12.00	4½".	8.00
8", ftd, sq	14.00	9"	12.00
Bureau Tray	30.00	Pomade Jar	14.00
Butter, cov	35.00	Puff Box.	14.00
Celery Tray.	30.00	Punch Bowl, cov, 14".	90.00
Compote		Ring Tree	25.00
Open, 4", jelly	12.00	Salt Shaker	
Open, 6"	14.00	Squat	12.00
Creamer		Tall.	15.00
After dinner, tall, sq ft	12.00	Salt, ind	17.00
Berry, bulbous, sq ft	15.00	Sardine Box	35.00
Large	18.00	Spooner	
Cruet, os	25.00	Handled	15.00
Finger Bowl, underplate. . . .	24.00	Tray	12.00
Goblet	18.00	Sugar, cov	
Lamp, miniature	50.00	Individual.	15.00
Marmalade Jar	35.00	Regular.	20.00
Mug.	15.00	Sundae Dish.	10.00
Mustard Jar, cov	30.00	Syrup, glass lid	35.00
Pickle.	10.00	Tumbler	
Pin Tray	12.00	Iced Tea	15.00
Pitcher, water		Water	12.00
One half gallon	30.00		

UTAH (Frost Flower, Twinkle Star)

Non-flint made by U. S. Glass Co. in 1901 in the States Pattern series. Add 25% for frosting.

	Clear		Clear
Bowl		Creamer.	30.00
Cov, 6"	20.00	Goblet	25.00
Open, 8"	18.00	Pickle.	12.00
Butter, cov	35.00	Pitcher, water	45.00
Cake Plate, 9".	20.00	Salt & Pepper, pr.	40.00
Cake Stand		Salt & Pepper, in holder. . . .	45.00
8"	20.00	Sauce, 4"	8.50
10"	30.00	Spooner.	15.00
Celery Vase	20.00	Sugar, cov	35.00
Compote		Tumbler	15.00
Cov, ls, 6", jelly	25.00	Wine	25.00
Open, ls, 6", jelly	18.00		

VALENCIA WAFFLE (Block and Star #1)

Made by Adams & Co., c1885–1895; continued by U. S. Glass after 1891.

	Amber	Apple Green	Blue	Clear	Vaseline
Bowl, berry	15.00	25.00	20.00	12.00	15.00
Bread Plate	30.00	—	30.00	25.00	35.00
Butter, cov	55.00	65.00	45.00	40.00	42.50
Cake Stand, 10″ . . .	60.00	40.00	45.00	38.00	40.00
Celery Vase	30.00	38.00	42.50	28.00	32.00
Castor set, complete	60.00	—	65.00	50.00	60.00
Compote					
Cov, hs, 7″ d	60.00	75.00	75.00	50.00	70.00
Cov, ls.	40.00	50.00	65.00	30.00	40.00
Creamer.	35.00	—	45.00	30.00	32.50
Dish.	20.00	—	25.00	10.00	20.00
Goblet	40.00	—	40.00	30.00	35.00
Pitcher					
Milk.	50.00	60.00	55.00	40.00	50.00
Water	65.00	60.00	55.00	40.00	50.00
Relish or Pickle. . . .	20.00	20.00	25.00	15.00	20.00
Salt Dip	35.00	—	—	—	—
Sauce, ftd, 4″, sq. . .	12.00	—	18.00	10.00	15.00
Spooner.	30.00	—	35.00	20.00	35.00
Sugar, cov	40.00	—	50.00	35.00	45.00
Syrup.	100.00	125.00	125.00	60.00	—
Tray, 10½ x 8″	—	35.00	—	—	—
Tumbler	25.00	—	30.00	18.00	25.00

VERMONT (Honeycomb with Flower Rim; Inverted Thumbprint with Daisy Band)

Non-flint made by U. S. Glass Co., 1899–1903. Also made in custard (usually decorated), chocolate, caramel, and novelty slag, milk glass, and blue. Toothpick has been reproduced in clear and opaque colors.

	Clear w/gold	Green w/gold		Clear w/gold	Green w/gold
Basket, handle	30.00	45.00	Pitcher, water	50.00	125.00
Bowl, berry	25.00	45.00	Sauce	15.00	20.00
Butter, cov	40.00	75.00	Spooner.	25.00	75.00
Celery Tray.	30.00	35.00	Sugar, cov	35.00	80.00
Creamer.	30.00	55.00	*Toothpick	35.00	60.00
Goblet	40.00	50.00	Tumbler	20.00	40.00

VIKING (Bearded Head)

Non-flint, made by Hobbs, Brockunier, and Co. in 1876 as their centennial pattern. No tumbler or goblet originally made.

	Clear		Clear
Apothecary Jar, cov.	45.00	Cov, 9″, oval	65.00
Bowl		Bread Plate	70.00
Cov, 8″, oval	55.00	Butter, cov	75.00

	Clear		Clear
Celery Vase	45.00	Marmalade Jar	85.00
Compote		Mug, ah	50.00
Cov, hs, 9".	95.00	Pitcher, water	100.00
Cov, ls, 8", oval	75.00	Relish	20.00
Open, hs	60.00	Salt, master	40.00
Creamer, 2 types	50.00	Sauce	15.00
Cup, ftd	35.00	Spooner	35.00
Egg Cup	40.00	Sugar, cov	65.00

WAFFLE AND THUMBPRINT

Flint made by the New England Glass Co. and Boston & Sandwich Glass Co., c1850. Later by Bryce, Walker & Co., Pittsburgh, Pennsylvania.

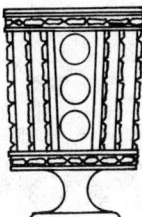

	Clear		Clear
Bowl, 5 x 7"	30.00	11", whale oil	175.00
Butter, cov	95.00	Pitcher, water	400.00
Celery Vase	105.00	Salt, master	45.00
Champagne	90.00	Spooner	45.00
Claret	110.00	Sugar, cov	125.00
Compote, cov, hs	150.00	Sweetmeat, cov, hs, 6"	150.00
Creamer	125.00	Tumbler	
Decanter, os		Flip Glass	125.00
Pint	100.00	Water, ftd	75.00
Quart	145.00	Whiskey	95.00
Egg Cup	45.00	Wine	85.00
Goblet, knob stem	65.00		
Lamp			
9½"	115.00		

WASHINGTON (Early)

Flint made by New England Glass Co., c1869.

	Clear		Clear
Ale Glass	125.00	Egg Cup	75.00
Bowl, 6 x 9", oval	45.00	Goblet	110.00
Bottle, bitters	85.00	Honey Dish, 3½"	30.00
Butter, cov	175.00	Lamp	150.00
Celery Vase	95.00	Pitcher, water	375.00
Champagne	125.00	Plate, 6"	60.00
Compote		Salt, master	55.00
Cov, hs, 6"	125.00	Sauce	25.00
Cov, hs, 10"	175.00	Spooner	75.00
Cordial	150.00	Sugar, cov	125.00
Creamer	200.00	Tumbler	85.00
Decanter, os	150.00	Wine	125.00

WASHINGTON CENTENNIAL (Chain with Diamonds)

Non-flint made by Gillinder & Co., Philadelphia, Pennsylvania, for centennial celebration.

	Clear		Clear
Bread Plates		Egg Cup	45.00
"Carpenter's Hall"	90.00	Goblet	45.00
"George Washington"	90.00	Pitcher, ah	
"Independence Hall"	90.00	Milk	85.00
Butter, cov	80.00	Water	100.00
Cake Stand		Relish, claw handle, dated	48.00
8½"	45.00	Salt, master, oval, flat	35.00
10"	60.00	Sauce, flat	12.00
Celery Vase	40.00	Spooner	35.00
Champagne	65.00	Sugar, cov	70.00
Compote		Syrup, metal lid	150.00
Cov, hs, 9"	75.00	Tumbler	40.00
Open, hs, 8"	45.00	Wine	50.00
Creamer, ah	80.00		

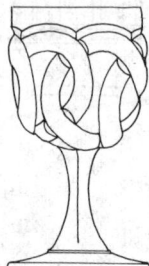

WEDDING RING (Double Wedding Ring)

Flint, c1860; non-flint, c1870s. Toothpick, frequently seen in muddy purple, not originally made. Reproduced in various colors.

	Flint		Flint
Butter, cov	100.00	Pitcher, water	175.00
Celery Vase	80.00	Relish	60.00
Champagne	95.00	Sauce	20.00
Cordial	85.00	Spooner	80.00
Creamer	85.00	Sugar, cov	100.00
Decanter, os	125.00	Tumbler	85.00
Goblet	60.00	Wine	90.00

WESTWARD HO! (Pioneer)

Non-flint, usually frosted, made by Gillinder & Sons, Philadelphia, Pennsylvania, late 1870s. Molds made by Jacobus who also made Classic. Has been reproduced.

	Clear		Clear
Bread Plate	175.00	Marmalade Jar, cov	175.00
Butter, cov	185.00	Mug	
Celery Vase	125.00	2"	225.00
Compote		3½"	175.00
Cov, hs, 5"	225.00	Pitcher, water	250.00
Cov, hs, 9"	275.00	Sauce, ftd, 4½"	35.00
Cov, ls, 5"	150.00	Spooner	85.00
Open, hs, 8"	125.00	Sugar, cov	175.00
Creamer	95.00	Wine	200.00
Goblet	90.00		

WHEAT AND BARLEY (Duquesne)

Non-flint made by Bryce Bros., Pittsburgh, Pennsylvania, in the late 1870s. Later made by U. S. Glass Co., 1891.

	Amber	Blue	Clear	Vaseline
Bowl, 8″, cov	35.00	40.00	25.00	35.00
Butter, cov	45.00	60.00	35.00	55.00
Cake Stand				
8″	30.00	45.00	20.00	30.00
10″	40.00	50.00	30.00	40.00
Compote				
Cov, hs, 7″	45.00	55.00	40.00	45.00
Cov, hs, 8″	50.00	55.00	45.00	50.00
Open, hs, jelly . . .	32.50	40.00	30.00	35.00
Creamer	30.00	40.00	28.00	35.00
Goblet	35.00	47.50	25.00	40.00
Mug	30.00	40.00	20.00	35.00
Pitcher				
Milk.	70.00	85.00	40.00	95.00
Water	85.00	95.00	45.00	100.00
Plate				
7″	20.00	30.00	15.00	25.00
9″, closed han-dles	25.00	35.00	20.00	40.00
Salt & Pepper	45.00	55.00	35.00	45.00
Sauce				
Flat, handle	12.00	15.00	10.00	15.00
Footed	15.00	15.00	10.00	15.00
Spooner	30.00	40.00	24.00	30.00
Sugar, cov	40.00	50.00	35.00	40.00
Syrup	175.00	195.00	85.00	—
Tumbler	30.00	35.00	18.00	30.00

WILDFLOWER

Non-flint made by Adams & Co., Pittsburgh, Pennsylvania, c1874, and by U. S. Glass Co., c1898. This pattern has been heavily reproduced.

	Amber	Apple Green	Blue	Clear	Vaseline
Bowl, 8″, sq	25.00	35.00	35.00	18.00	20.00
Butter, cov					
Collared base . . .	40.00	50.00	50.00	35.00	45.00
Flat	35.00	45.00	45.00	30.00	40.00
Cake Stand, 10½″ . .	50.00	80.00	75.00	45.00	50.00
Champagne	40.00	55.00	50.00	25.00	45.00
Celery Vase	55.00	60.00	55.00	35.00	55.00
Compote					
Cov, hs, 8″, oblong	80.00	85.00	85.00	50.00	75.00
Cov, ls, 7″	—	—	70.00	—	—
Open, hs	80.00	—	—	—	—
Creamer	35.00	50.00	45.00	40.00	48.00
* Goblet	30.00	40.00	40.00	25.00	40.00
Pitcher, water	55.00	95.00	65.00	40.00	70.00
Plate, 10″, sq	30.00	30.00	45.00	25.00	30.00
Platter					
10″, oblong	40.00	45.00	40.00	30.00	30.00
11 x 8″, deep scalloped edges . . .	—	—	45.00	—	—
Relish	20.00	22.00	20.00	18.00	20.00
* Salt, turtle	45.00	50.00	50.00	30.00	40.00

	Amber	Apple Green	Blue	Clear	Vaseline
Salt Shaker........	35.00	55.00	40.00	20.00	45.00
Sauce, ftd, 4", round	17.50	18.00	18.00	15.00	17.50
Spooner.........	30.00	35.00	30.00	20.00	40.00
Sugar, cov	45.00	45.00	50.00	30.00	45.00
Syrup...........	125.00	150.00	140.00	65.00	150.00
Tray, water, oval ...	50.00	60.00	60.00	40.00	55.00
Tumbler	40.00	35.00	35.00	25.00	35.00
Wine	45.00	45.00	45.00	25.00	45.00

WILLOW OAK (Wreath)

Non-flint made by Bryce Bros. Pittsburgh, Pennsylvania, c1880, and by U. S. Glass Company in 1891.

	Amber	Blue	Canary	Clear
Bowl, 8"	25.00	40.00	48.00	20.00
Butter, cov	55.00	65.00	80.00	40.00
Cake Stand, 8½"...	60.00	65.00	70.00	45.00
Celery Vase	45.00	60.00	75.00	35.00
Compote				
Cov, hs, 7½"	50.00	65.00	80.00	40.00
Open, 7"	30.00	40.00	48.00	25.00
Creamer.........	40.00	50.00	60.00	35.00
Goblet	40.00	50.00	60.00	35.00
Mug...........	35.00	45.00	54.00	30.00
Pitcher				
Milk...........	50.00	60.00	72.00	45.00
Water	55.00	60.00	72.00	50.00
Plate				
7"...........	35.00	45.00	50.00	25.00
9", closed handles.........	32.50	35.00	40.00	25.00
Salt Shaker.......	25.00	40.00	55.00	20.00
Sauce				
Flat, handle, sq ..	15.00	20.00	24.00	10.00
Footed, 4"	20.00	25.00	30.00	15.00
Spooner.........	35.00	40.00	48.00	30.00
Sugar, cov	68.50	70.00	75.00	40.00
Tray, water, 10½" ..	35.00	50.00	60.00	30.00
Tumbler	30.00	35.00	45.00	25.00
Waste Bowl.......	35.00	40.00	40.00	30.00

WISCONSIN (Beaded Dewdrop)

Non-flint made in Pittsburgh, Pennsylvania, in the 1880s. Later made by U. S. Glass Co. in Indiana, 1903. One of States patterns. Toothpick reproduced in colors.

	Clear		Clear
Banana Stand...........	75.00	6", oval, handled, cov....	40.00
Bowl		7", round	42.00
4½ x 6½"	28.00	8", oblong, preserve.....	42.00

	Clear			Clear
Butter, flat flange	75.00		Marmalade Jar, straight	
Cake Stand			sides, glass lid	125.00
8½"	45.00		Mug	35.00
9½"	55.00		Pitcher	
Celery Tray	45.00		Milk	55.00
Celery Vase	45.00		Water	70.00
Compote			Plate, 6¾"	25.00
Cov, hs, 6"	45.00		Punch Cup	12.00
Cov, hs, 7"	55.00		Relish	25.00
Cov, hs, 8"	65.00		Salt Shaker, single	30.00
Open, hs, 9½"	35.00		Spooner	30.00
Open, hs, 10½"	35.00		Sugar, cov	55.00
Open, jelly	20.00		Sugar Shaker	90.00
Condiment Set, SP, horse-			Sweetmeat, 5", ftd, cov	35.00
radish on tray	100.00		Syrup	110.00
Creamer	50.00		*Toothpick	55.00
Cruet, os	80.00		Tumbler	40.00
Cup & Saucer	50.00		Wine	75.00
Goblet	65.00			

WYOMING (Enigma)

Made by U. S. Glass Co., in the States Pattern series, 1903.

	Clear			Clear
Bowl, 8"	15.00		Goblet	65.00
Butter, cov	50.00		Mug	40.00
Cake Plate	55.00		Pitcher, water	75.00
Cake Stand	70.00		Relish	15.00
Compote, cov, hs, 8" d	85.00		Spooner	30.00
Creamer			Sugar, cov	45.00
Covered	50.00		Syrup, small	65.00
Open	35.00		Wine	85.00

X-RAY

Non-flint made by Riverside Glass Works, Wellsburgh, West Virginia, 1896 to 1898. Prices are for pieces with gold trim. A toothpick holder is known in amethyst ($125.00). Also, a toothpick holder with marigold iridescence is known ($35.00).

	Clear	Emerald Green		Clear	Emerald Green
Bowl, berry, 8",			Goblet	20.00	35.00
beaded rim	25.00	45.00	Pitcher, water	40.00	75.00
Butter, cov	40.00	75.00	Salt & Pepper, pr.	25.00	45.00
Celery Vase	—	50.00	Sauce, flat	8.00	10.00
Compote			Spooner	25.00	40.00
Cov, hs	40.00	65.00	Sugar		
Jelly	—	40.00	Ind, open	20.00	32.50
Creamer			Regular, cov	35.00	45.00
Individual	15.00	30.00	Syrup	—	265.00
Regular	30.00	60.00	Toothpick	30.00	60.00
Cruet	—	140.00	Tumbler	12.00	25.00
Cruet Set, 4 leaf clo-					
ver tray	125.00	350.00			

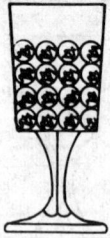

YALE (Crow-foot, Turkey Track)

Non-flint made by McKee and Brothers Glass Co., Jeannette, Pennsylvania, patented, 1887.

	Clear		Clear
Butter, cov	45.00	Relish, oval.	10.00
Bowl, berry, 10½"	20.00	Salt Shaker, single	30.00
Cake Stand	55.00	Sauce, flat	10.00
Celery Vase	35.00	Spooner	20.00
Compote		Sugar, cov	35.00
Cov, hs	50.00	Syrup	65.00
Open, scalloped rim	25.00	Tumbler	20.00
Creamer.	30.00	Water set, pitcher, 6	
Goblet	30.00	tumblers	165.00
Pitcher, water	50.00		

ZIPPER (Cobb)

Non-flint made by Richards & Hartley, Tarentum, Pennsylvania, c1880.

	Clear		Clear
Bowl, 7"	15.00	Pitcher, water, ½ gal	40.00
Butter, cov	30.00	Relish, 10"	10.00
Celery Vase	25.00	Salt Dip	5.00
Cheese, cov	55.00	Sauce	
Compote, cov, ls, 8"	45.00	Flat	7.50
Creamer	25.00	Footed	12.00
Cruet, os	42.00	Spooner	20.00
Goblet	20.00	Sugar, cov	35.00

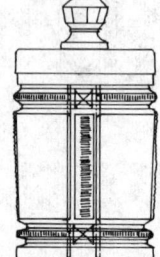

ZIPPERED BLOCK (Cryptic, Nova Scotia Ribbon & Star, Duncan #90)

Non-flint made by George A. Duncan & Sons, Pittsburgh, Pennsylvania, in the late 1870s and later by U. S. Glass. Also made in Canada. Comes frosted and frosted with cut stars. Add 20% for frosting.

	Clear	Ruby Stained		Clear	Ruby Stained
Butter, cov	75.00	150.00	Pitcher, water	125.00	175.00
Celery	40.00	—	Salt Shaker	50.00	80.00
Compote, cov, hs . .	125.00	—	Sauce	15.00	25.00
Creamer	45.00	100.00	Spooner	30.00	60.00
Goblet	40.00	60.00	Sugar, cov	60.00	100.00
Lamp	85.00	—	Tumbler	30.00	45.00
Pickle, oblong	25.00	35.00			

S. E. G.
PAUL REVERE POTTERY

History: Paul Revere Pottery, Boston, Massachusetts, was an outgrowth of a club known as "The Saturday Evening Girls." The S.E.G. was a group of young female immigrants who met on Saturday nights for reading and crafts such as ceramics.

Regular production began in 1908. The name Paul Revere was adopted because the pottery was located near the Old North Church. In 1915 the firm moved to Brighton, Massachusetts. Known as the "Bowl Shop," the pottery grew steadily. In spite of popular acceptance and technical advancements, the pottery required continual subsidies. It finally closed in January, 1942.

Items produced ranged from plain and decorated vases to tablewares to illustrated tiles. Many decorated wares were incised and glazed either in an Art Nouveau matte finish or an occasional high glaze.

In addition to the impressed mark, paper "Bowl Shop" labels were used prior to 1915. Pieces also can be found dated with P.R.P. or S.E.G. painted on the base.

References: Paul Evans, *Art Pottery of the United States, Second Edition,* Feingold & Lewis Publishing Corp, 1987; Ralph and Terry Kovel, *The Kovels' Collector's Guide to American Art Pottery,* Crown Publishers, Inc., 1974.

Collectors' Club: American Art Pottery Association, 9825 Upton Circle, Bloomington, MN 55431.

Teapot, marked "S. E. G.," $60.00.

Bowl
4" d, 2½" h, white band with blue stylized lotus, early signature and initials, c1910	110.00
6" d, green band of repeating squirrels, white ground, marked "S. E. G."	300.00

Creamer
2", blue bands and squirrel dec	150.00
3½", mountains, trees, and sky, beige ground, marked "S.E.G."	260.00

Egg Cup, underplate, yellow chick dec, blue ground, marked "S.E.G."	165.00
Hatpin Holder, incised daisy motif, blue ground, gold trim, marked "S.E.G."	165.00
Jug, 4½", rabbit dec, yellow ground, border marked "David–His Jug"	175.00
Pitcher, 7" h, bulbous, angled handle, circular medallion, initials "E. L. C." on blue ground, sgd "S. E. G.", dated 1923	50.00

Plate
6", green spatter, dark blue ground	32.00
8", dancing yellow chicks, blue band dec, marked "S.E.G."	325.00
8½", floral border, three color dec, marked "S.E.G."	45.00

Tile, 4 x 6", incised scene of paul Revere on horse, dog at his side, inscription "A Glimmer & then a Gleam of Light," shades of blue, green, brown, and white, artist sgd "Rose Buchini, 1911"	500.00
Trivet, 5½" sq, stylized mustard yellow crocus, green leaves in corners, darker green ground, artist sgd "Albina Mangini, 1911," partial paper label	900.00
Vase, 7" h, bulbous, band of light blue and green stylized water lilies and leaves, outlined in black, light and dark blue ground, sgd "S. E. G.," dated	635.00

PEACHBLOW

History: Peachblow, an art glass which derives its name from a fine Chinese glazed porcelain, resembles a peach or crushed strawberries in color. Three American glass manufacturers and two English firms produced peachblow glass in the late 1880s. A fourth American firm renewed the process in the 1950s. The glass from each firm has its own identifying characteristics.

Hobbs, Brockunier & Co., Wheeling peachblow: Opalescent glass, plated or cased with a transparent amber glass; shading from yellow at the base to a deep red at top; glossy or satin finish.

Mt. Washington "Peach Blow": A homogeneous glass, shading from a pale gray-blue to a soft rose color. Pieces may be enhanced with glass appliques, enameling, and gilting.

New England Glass Works, New England peachblow [advertised as "Wild Rose," but called "Peach Blow" at the plant]: Translucent, shading from rose to white; acid or glossy finish. Some pieces enameled and gilted.

Thomas Webb & Sons and Stevens and Williams, England: Around 1888 these two firms made a peachblow style art glass marked "Peach Blow" or "Peach Bloom." A cased glass, shading from yellow to red. Occasionally found with cameo-type designs in relief.

Gunderson Glass Co.: About 1950 produced peachblow type art glass to order; shades from an opaque faint tint of pink, which is almost white, to a deep rose.

Reference: John A. Shuman III, *The Collector's Encyclopedia of American Glass,* Collector Books, 1988.

Note: All pieces listed below are satin finish unless otherwise noted.

GUNDERSON

Compote, 7⅛" d, 6⅞" h, swirled knob, widely scalloped rim	175.00
Creamer, ftd	65.00
Cruet, 6½"	175.00
Sugar, ftd, open	65.00
Tumbler, 4"	125.00
Vase, 9½", lily form, deep color	150.00

MT. WASHINGTON

Perfume Bottle, ribbed, hp, apple blossom dec, orig stopper	1,850.00
Pitcher, 6⅞", bulbous, sq handle	3,700.00
Vase, 8¼", lily form, satin finish	1,800.00

NEW ENGLAND

Darner, 6" l	150.00
Celery Vase, 6¼", crimped top, glossy	800.00
Finger Bowl, 5¼ x 2½", wide ruffled top	335.00
Pitcher, hobnail, applied frosted ribbed handle	700.00
Punch Cup, applied white opaque reeded handle	125.00
Salt and Pepper Shakers, metal holder, orig tops, pr	850.00
Spooner, 4", ribbon candy rim	100.00
Toothpick, sq top, shiny finish	385.00
Tumbler, 3⅞", shiny, faint traces of agata type black mottling and gold tracery	385.00

Vase

2½" h, 2¾" d, acid finish, rolled over top edge, slightly raised white stripes on deep rose round	325.00
5", bulbous, satin finish, ruffled rim	75.00

6½", satin finish, applied clear handles, ruffled rim	125.00
7⅞", lily form, shiny finish	850.00
8½", gourd form, wide cup shaped top, shiny finish	600.00
8⅞", lily form, satin finish	1,000.00
Whimsey, pear shape, 4¾" h, Sandwich	120.00

WEBB

Bowl, 8", sq, shiny finish	225.00
Celery Vase, 6½", acid finish	175.00
Punch Cup, shiny finish, cream lining	115.00
Rose Bowl, 3⅛" d, 3" h, acid finish, deep red shaded to warm pink–amber, cream int., eight crimp top	225.00

Vase

5" h, 3½" d, glossy, deep rose shading to pink, off white int., two small birds in flowering branches, propeller mark	500.00
5¼" h, 2¾" d, glossy, deep rose shading to pink ext., off white int., gold prunus blossoms and dragonfly	300.00
11½" h, 6½" d, acid finish, rose to cream shading, deep pink int., blue and white flowers, green leaves, and gold trim, propeller mark, pr	1,200.00

Wheeling, vase, acid finish, 7¾" h, $665.00.

WHEELING

Creamer, 4", shiny finish, applied amber handle	400.00
Decanter, 9" h, applied twisted amber handle, amber stopper, slight annealing imperfection	550.00
Fairy Lamp, 5½" d, 5" h, wide ruffled base	650.00
Pitcher, 8½" h, matte, red top shading	

to light pink base, sq mouth, white int., applied frosted handle **400.00**
Punch Cup, 2⅝″ d, 2½″ h, glossy, deep shading, off white int., applied amber ring handle **300.00**
Salt Shaker, bulbous, orig SP top **200.00**
Sugar Shaker, 5½″, orig SP top **60.00**
Tumbler
  3³⁄₁₆″, shiny finish **425.00**
  3¾″ h, 2¾″ d, glossy, deep shading, off white int. **300.00**
Vase
  6″ d, 6½″ h, bulbous **600.00**
  7″, cylindrical, flared, gently ruffled top, Drape pattern, narrow amber border **650.00**
  8″, stick, excellent color **565.00**
  8½″, stick, ring of amber rigaree around base of neck **350.00**
  10″, Morgan, orig amber glass stand, satin finish **3,100.00**

PEKING GLASS

History: Peking glass is a type of cameo glass of Chinese origin. Its production began in the 1700s and continued well into the 19th century. The background color of Peking glass may be a delicate shade of yellow, green, or white. One style of white background is so delicate and transparent that it often is referred to as the "snowflake" ground. The overlay colors include a rich garnet red, deep blue, and emerald green.

Snuff Bottle, pastel colored leaves, green jade top, 2⅜″ h, $185.00.

Bowl, 6¼″, bell form, inset ring foot, deeply carved with chrysanthemum branch and long tailed bird, prunus branch and two song birds on reverse, yellow, pr **4,125.00**
Cup, 3″ d, flaring, everted rim, engraved, dragon and cloud motif, blue, silver holder, 19th C **225.00**

Jar, 5⅛″, cov, globular, four shaped medallions containing flower springs, ruyi band on shoulders, opaque white, red overlay, floriform knops, late 19th C, pr **800.00**
Snuff Bottle
  2½″, flattened ovoid body, horses dec, camphor ground, blue overlay, blue glass stopper with aventurine **175.00**
  3″, floral form, camphor ground, six color overlay floral dec, green glass stopper, late 19th C **200.00**
Vase
  9″ h
    Baluster, Chinese red cameo, deep cut leaves and berries, white ground, c1900 . . . . **550.00**
    Cased, emerald green, opal glass int., Bird's Eye pattern **45.00**
  13″ h, Chinese red tropical fish, green lotus and pond dec, white ground, c1900 . . . . **850.00**

PELOTON

History: Wilhelm Kralik of Bohemia patented Peloton art glass in 1880. Later it also was patented in America and England.

Peloton glass is found with both transparent and opaque grounds with opaque being more common. Opaque colored glass filaments (strings) are applied by dipping or rolling the hot glass. Generally, the filaments (threads) are pink, blue, yellow, and white (rainbow colors) or a single color. Items also may have a satin finish and enamel decorations.

Biscuit Jar, 6¾″, ribbed body, pale blue ground, multicolored filaments, white lining, SP rim, cover, and bail handle **500.00**
Bowl, 3½ x 2½″, pinched top, ribbed sides, clear ground, white, pink, blue,

Vase, bulbous, cranberry and red strings, clear ground, 7″ h, $250.00.

and olive green filaments, fiery opal pastel orchid lining **175.00**

Finger Bowl, clear, multicolored filaments **65.00**

Rose Bowl, 2½ x 2¼", crimped top, opaque white ground, pink, yellow, blue, and white filaments **250.00**

Toothpick
2½", clear ground, green filaments . **100.00**
3", clear, white filaments **125.00**

Tumbler, 3¾", clear ground, yellow, pink, red, light blue, and white filaments **125.00**

Vase
3 x 3¼", ball shape, flared ruffled top, orchid pink ground, blue, pink, yellow and white filaments **175.00**
3 x 6¾", stick, yellow ground, white, rose, blue, and yellow filaments, white lining **225.00**
4¾ x 4¼", squat, ribbed, tricorn folded down rim, clear ground, rose, yellow, blue and white filaments, white lining **300.00**

Water Set, blown water pitcher, polished pontil, five tumblers, light yellow amber ground, multicolored filaments . . **650.00**

PERFUME, COLOGNE, AND SCENT BOTTLES

History: Decorative bottles to hold scents have been made in various shapes and sizes. They reached a "golden age" during the second half of the 19th century.

An atomizer is a perfume bottle with a spray mechanism. Cologne bottles usually are larger and have stoppers which also may be used as applicators. A perfume bottle has a stopper that often is elongated and designed as an applicator.

Scent bottles are small bottles used to hold a scent or smelling salts. A vinaigrette is an ornamental box or bottle with a perforated top used to hold aromatic vinegars or smelling salts. Fashionable women of the late 18th and 19th centuries carried them in purses or slipped them into gloves in case of a sudden fainting spell.

Reference: Hazel Martin, *A Collection Of Figural Perfume & Scent Bottles,* published by author, 1982; Jacquelyne Jones-North, *Commercial Perfume Bottles,* Schiffer Publishing, 1987; Jacquelyne North, *Perfume, Cologne, and Scent Bottles,* Schiffer Publishing, 1987; Jean Sloan, *Perfume and Scent Bottle Collecting With Prices, Second Edition,* Wallace-Homestead, 1989.

ATOMIZERS

Art Deco, 3" h, opaque black ground, gold dec **65.00**

Baccarat, 6" h, amberina, swirled body **75.00**

Czechoslovakian, 8" h, cobalt blue glass, large enameled and faceted crystal stopper finial, c1930 . . . . . . **85.00**

DeVilbiss, black amethyst art glass, goldstone spiderweb dec, bulb missing **80.00**

Moser, 4½" h, sapphire blue melon ribbed glass body, tiny gold florals, leaves, and swirls, orig gold top and bulb **250.00**

Steuben, 7" h, Aurene, gold **360.00**

COLOGNES

Apple Green, 5¼" h, hexagonal, cut bull's eyes and punty dec, ground stopper **525.00**

Aurene, blue irid, three lug feet, unsigned Steuben **800.00**

Cameo Glass, English
2½" d, 3⅜" h, round body, white florals and butterfly, frosted vaseline ground, hallmarked silver hinged cap **800.00**
5¾" h, white florals and butterfly, raisin ground, hallmarked silver hinged cap **1,350.00**

Cranberry Glass, floral dec, gold trim, clear stopper **200.00**

Cut Glass, 3½" d, 7" h, slim cut neck, bulbous body, Cane pattern, pointed stopper **100.00**

Malachite, 6½" h, sgd "Moser" **240.00**

Paperweight Type
5½" h, clear, pink, blue, yellow, and white flowers with bubble centers, green ground, marked "St Clair Glass Works, Elwood, IN" **65.00**
7½" h, clear glass, brass filigree ftd frame, brass cap, crystal stopper . **125.00**

Ruby, 6¾" h, sanded gold, enameled green foliage, pink roses, three opal jewels, orig ruby ball stopper **125.00**

PERFUMES

Cameo, 1¼" d, 1⅞" h, morning glory blossom, white cut to deep blue to powder blue body, white lining, hallmarked SS top, English **700.00**

Cased Glass, 2½" d, 4⅛" h, pink, gold bands, enameled gold florals and flower garlands, orig clear ball stopper **100.00**

China, figural
1¼" w, 2" d, 3⅜" h, lady and parrot, blue, white, black, yellow, green, and orange, metal and cork stopper **70.00**
2" d, 4¼" h, child, seated in yellow bag, purple collar and black hat, metal and cork stopper, Germany **40.00**

Perfume, Art Deco, triangular motif, intaglio stopper, brass collar, 3¾" h, $80.00.

Cranberry Glass
2" d, 5¼" h, gold bands, small blue and white florals, gold ball stopper ... 120.00
2⅜" d, 3¾" h, bulbous, enameled blue and gray flowers, blue, orange, and white leaves, clear flattened ball stopper 90.00
Cut Glass
6½" h, Button and Star pattern, faceted stopper, rayed base, Brilliant period, American 100.00
8½" h, amber, cut panels and designs, matching stopper 180.00
Czechoslovakian, 1¾" d, 2½" h, overall filigree florals and mesh, white enameled florals, blue mirrored faceted stones, jeweled screw on cap and dauber 50.00
Pairpoint, 5½" h, heavy crystal, controlled bubbles 60.00
Satin Glass, 6" l, MOP, DQ, shading yellow to white, lay down horn shape . 400.00

SCENTS

Burmese, 4¾" h, 3⅜" d, acid finish, salmon pink to yellow, heavy gold leaves and birds, silver gilt screw on top, hallmarked 825.00
Czechoslovakian, lay down, multicolored jewels, enameled top 100.00
Enameled flowers, 3" l, pale blue body, hinged metal cap, finger ring, c1900 65.00
Ruby Glass, cylindrical, SS cap dated 1884 .... 90.00
Sterling Silver, 1¼" d, head of bearded man, wearing helmet, head of classical woman on reverse, hallmarked, chain handle 60.00
Webb, 7" l, opaque white body, covered

with stylized bamboo plant dec, burnished gold, lush tropical foliage of palm trees, ferns and cacti, long neck with gold bamboo like dec on dark green ground, hallmarked "JG & S" SS top, SS chain **485.00**

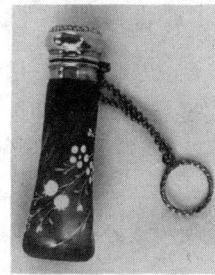

Scent, cylindrical, flared base, frosted and cut glass, light to dark blue, gold plated cap and chain, orig dauber, 2¾" l, $150.00.

VINAIGRETTES

Cut Glass, 3⅞" l, SS overlay, cobalt glass, yellow flashing, emb SS cap . **125.00**
Gold
1⅛" l, rect, hinged cov, florals, engraved grill, scrolling foliage, marked "A J Strachan, London, 1800" **1,320.00**
2½" l, flattened cartouche shape, putto playing lute, another playing with hound, carnelian intaglio base with two lovebirds and chaplet, inscribed "Vivons Fidelle," English, mid 18th C **650.00**
Silver, 1" l, purse shape, florals at clasp, engraved basketwork body, hallmarks for John Lawrence & Co, Birmingham, England, 1819 .... **450.00**

PETERS AND REED POTTERY

History: J. D. Peters and Adam Reed founded their pottery company in South Zanesville, Ohio, in 1900. Common flowerpots, jardinieres, and cooking wares comprised their early major output. Occasionally art pottery was attempted, but it was not until 1912 that their Moss Aztec line was introduced and widely accepted. Other art wares included Chromal, Landsun, Montene, Pereco, and Persian.

Peters retired in 1921 and Reed changed the

name of the firm to Zane Pottery Company. Marked pieces of Peters and Reed Pottery are unknown.

Bowl, 8½", Landsun, blue, yellow, and green	36.00
Candlesticks, pr, 10" h, mirror black glaze	24.00
Ewer, 11" h, brown, raised grapes, orange and yellow dec	40.00
Jardiniere, 6½ x 7½", green lion's head dec, beige ground	75.00
Jug, bulbous, grape clusters and vine dec, standard glossy brown glaze, single handle	50.00
Mug, 5½", grape clusters and vine dec, standard glossy brown glaze	35.00
Pitcher, 4", man with banjo, standard glossy brown glaze	35.00
Rose Bowl, wreath and vine dec, standard glossy brown glaze, three small feet	40.00

Vase, Art Nouveau, leaf and lily pattern, green striated leaves, purple flowers, high glaze, 5" h, $135.00.

Vase	
6 x 4", hexagonal, pinched sides, floral medallion dec, standard brown glaze	60.00
8½", Shadow Ware, blue and cream drip glaze, olive green ground	40.00
9¾", pine cones and needles, green wash glaze, terra cotta ground	65.00
13", chromal scene, Mt Fujiyama	200.00
Wall Pocket	
7¾", Pereco, Egyptian dec	70.00
8", Moss Aztec, emb grape cluster dec, sgd "Ferrell"	50.00
Window Box, 13", Moss Aztec, depicting Homer and two nudes, sgd "Ferrell"	150.00

PEWTER

History: Pewter is a metal alloy, consisting mostly of tin with small amounts of lead, copper,

antimony, and bismuth added to improve formability and hardness. The metal can be cast, formed around a mold, spun, easily cut, and soldered to form a wide variety of utilitarian articles.

Pewter ware was known to the ancient Chinese, Egyptians, and Romans. English pewter supplied the major portion of the needs of the American colonies for nearly 150 years before the American Revolution. The Revolution ended the embargo on raw tin and allowed the small American pewter industry to flourish. This period lasted until the Civil War.

The listing concentrates on the American and English pewter forms most often encountered by the collector.

Reference: Donald L. Fennimore, *The Knopf Collectors' Guides to American Antiques, Silver & Pewter,* Alfred A. Knopf, Inc., 1984.

Collectors' Club: Pewter Collector's Club of America, 740 Highview Drive, Wyckoff, NJ 07481.

Lamp, double font, handle, Morey and Smith, Boston, 6" h, $300.00.

Basin	
Danforth, Samuel, Hartford, CT, c1800, minor pitting, 8"	175.00
Evans, Humphrey, Exeter, England, c1760, minor pitting, 11" d	350.00
Graham & Wardrop, Glasgow, Scotland, 10", int. pitted	150.00
Hamlin, Samuel, Providence, RI, 1769–1810, 5¾"	700.00
Jones, Gershom, Providence, RI, 1774–1809, 7¾"	850.00
Townsend & Compton, London, 1785–1801, 11½", hammered booge	300.00
Unmarked, American, 7⅞", rampant lion touch mark of Thomas Danforth II	250.00
Beaker	
Boardman and Hart, NY, c1830, 5¼"	850.00
Flagg, Asa F, and Henry Homan, Cincinnati, OH, whiskey size	225.00

Yale, Hiram, Wallingford, CT, 1820–30, 3″, sgd "Yale" and "Britannia" ... **300.00**

Bedpan, Samuel Hamlin, Sr and Jr, Providence, RI, 10½″ d **250.00**

Bowl, Baptismal, Trask, Oliver, Beverly, MA, 10¾″, broad scooped rim, domed feet **2,750.00**

Box, Coldwell, George, New York, NY, 1787–1811, oval, hinged engraved lid, 2⅞″ l **575.00**

Candlestick
Hopper, Henry, New York, 1842–47, 9⅞″, trumpet shape, straight line touch **350.00**
Unmarked
American, 9⅜″, orig insets, pr ... **325.00**
Dutch, c1700, 6½″, provision for snuffer, weighted base **225.00**
English, 1800–25, 8¾″, push up ejectors, pr **375.00**

Chalice, Leonard, Reed & Barton, Taunton, MA, 1835–40, 7″ h **175.00**

Charger
Austin, Richard, Boston, MA, c1800, cleaned and polished, 13⅜″ **230.00**
Boyd, Parks, Philadelphia, PA, c1800, knife marks and pitting, 12″ d ... **125.00**
Hamlin, Samuel, Sr, Providence, RI, c1790, heavy pitting on upper surface, 13½″ d **225.00**
Spackman & Grant, London, c1715, repair in center, knife marks and denting, 15″ d **125.00**

Coffeepot
Boardman & Hart, NY, c1935, bulbous, finial resoldered, 11″ h **415.00**
Dunham, Rufus, Westbrook, ME, 1837–61, 10¾″, lighthouse shape **350.00**
Gleason, Roswell, Dorchester, MA, 1822–71, 10¼″, lighthouse shape **450.00**
Porter, Allen, Westbrook, ME, 1830–40, 11¾″, bulbous, bold straight line "A. Porter" touch in rect on bottom **600.00**
Putnam, James, Malden, MA, 1830–35, 11¼″, lighthouse shape, flared base, straight line name touch in rect **550.00**
Simpson, Samuel, Yalesville, CT, 1835–52, 11¼″, minor pitting in foot ring **500.00**
Smith & Co, Boston, MA, c1840, restoration at base and top of handle, handle repainted, 9½″ h **150.00**

Communion Plate, Gleason, Roswell, Dorchester, MA, c1850, 10¾″ d **250.00**

Communion Service, Boardman, Thomas Danforth, New York City and Hartford, CT, 11″ h flagon, two 10⅛″ d plates **650.00**

Cream Pitcher, H Joseph, 3¾″, pyriform **1,750.00**

Cuspidor, Gleason, Roswell, Dorches-ter, MA, c1850, well preserved, few minor dents, 8″ d **200.00**

Dish, Deep
Boyd, Parks, Phila, PA, 1795–1819, 12″, large eagle touch **800.00**
Griswold, Ashbil, Meriden, CT, 1802–42, 11⅛″, double struck with large eagle touch **250.00**
Townsend, John and Thomas Giffin, London, 1777–1801, 12″, hammered booge, numerous knife marks **250.00**

Flagon
Boardman & Co, New York, c1825, lighthouse shape **900.00**
Calder, William, Providence, RI, 1817–56, 11″ **850.00**
Trask, Oliver, Boston, MA, c1830, 10⅞″ **550.00**

Funnel, unmarked, English, c1800, 3½″ d, 4½″ l **175.00**

Goblet, unmarked, American, attributed to Israel Trask, early 19th C, 5⅛″ .. **200.00**

Inkwell, unmarked, c1800, 3¼″ d, circular, ironstone china inset with slight blue discoloration, lid, age and glaze cracks **100.00**

Ladle
Hall & Cotton, Middlefield, CT, c1840, 12¾″, straight line rect touch **300.00**
Kruiger, Lewis, Phila, PA, c1830, 14″, turned wood handle **250.00**
Lee, Richard, early 19th C, 13⅜″, punchwork dec on int. and ext. of bowl, turned hardwood handle ... **300.00**
Palethrop, John H, Phila, PA, 1820–40, soup, double rect straight line touch **350.00**
Stedman, S, Eastern CT or RI, c1800, 14″, curved wood handle with finely turned finial, marked "N" on shank **450.00**
Unmarked, American, 16″, turned wood handle, minor damage **100.00**
Yates, John, England, mid 19th C, 14¼″, soup, fiddle handle **200.00**

Lamp
Camphene, Gleason, Roswell, Dorchester, MA, c1840, double brass camphene burners with caps, cylindrical font **200.00**
Chamber, unmarked, American, attributed to Meriden Brittania Co, c1840, 5¾″, whale oil burners, pr . **350.00**
Gimball, unmarked, American, 8″, double camphene burner and ring handle, one cap missing **300.00**
Hand
Morey & Smith, Boston, c1850, double whale oil burners, strong touch marks, bell shaped, "C" shaped handle, 3½″ h **150.00**
Unmarked American, New England

or New York, c1840, double whale oil burner, bell shaped lamp, "C" shaped handle, re-soldered handle, 2⅝" h **100.00**

Sparking, whale oil

Putnam, James, Malden, MA, 1830–65, straight line "Putnam" touch, saucer base with ring handle, minor denting, 2⅝" h **125.00**

Unmarked, American, c1850, saucer base with ring handle, cylindrical font, 2¾" h **100.00**

Whale Oil

Dunham, Rufus, Westbrook, ME, 1837–61, c1840, straight line "Dunham" touch, brass double whale oil burner, cylindrical foot, several small base holes, 5½" h **100.00**

Gleason, Roswell, Dorchester, MA, c1840, unmarked, weighted base, single plated silver over copper bull's eye lens, 8½" ... **225.00**

Putnam, James, Malden, MA, 1830–65, straight line "Putnam" touch, minor resoldering at seam, 6" h **175.00**

Taunton Britannia Mfg Co, Taunton, MA, 1830–35, straight line touch "T. B. M. Co.," brass double whale oil burner, acorn font, resoldered under font, minor denting, 7¼" h **275.00**

Unmarked American, New England, c1840, double whale oil burner, acorn shaped font, trumpet base, 7⅝" h **175.00**

Loving Cup, James Dixon & Sons, England, 7" h, two handles **125.00**

Measure, unmarked, English

Half Pint, c1700, baluster, cov **350.00**

Set, bellied, c1830–50, ten measures ranging from ½ of pint to ½ gallon, Type IV, assembled **2,200.00**

Miniature

Porringer, Lee, Richard, Springfield, VT, late 18th C, minor dents, 2⅜" d **700.00**

Tea Service, child's, attributed to James Tufts, Boston, MA, c1870, cov 4" h teapot, sugar, creamer, waste bowl, six cups and saucers **275.00**

Mug

Austin, Nathaniel, Charlestown, MA, 6" h, late 18th C **1,350.00**

Bassett, Frederick, NY, c1780, 4½" h **1,600.00**

Kilbourn, Samuel, Baltimore, MD, early 19th C, 4" h **750.00**

Unmarked, American

Attributed to Thomas Danforth Boardman, Hartford, CT, c1820, 2¹¹⁄₁₆", one gill **325.00**

Attributed to Samuel Danforth,

Hartford, CT, 1795–1816, 4½", pint **650.00**

Unmarked, English, mid 19th C, owner's name inscribed on front, quart **100.00**

Pitcher

Boardman, Thomas Danforth, CT, 1840, 6¼", two quarts, cider type, "X" quality mark, minor denting and resoldering **500.00**

Curtis, Daniel, Albany, NY, c1830, 8" h **725.00**

Dunham, Rufus, Westbrook, ME, c1850, straight line touch, two quarts **400.00**

Gleason, Roswell, Dorchester, MA, c1850, two quarts, lidded, slight loss of foot ring **225.00**

McQuilkin, William, Phila, PA, 10", baluster shape, scrolled handle .. **950.00**

Plate, Thomas Danforth, Philadelphia, 8¾" d, $350.00.

Plate

Austin, Richard, Boston, MA, 1792–1817, 8½" **200.00**

Badger, Thomas, Boston, MA, 1787–1815

7⅞", name touch and Boston scroll touch **225.00**

8½" **350.00**

Barns, Blakslee, Phila, PA, 1812–17, 7⅞", second touch of straight line touch "B Barnes/Philad'a," stamped "DM" in rim **225.00**

Belcher, Newport, RI, 1769–84, 8" .. **350.00**

Billings, William, Providence, RI, c1800, 11½" **775.00**

Calder, William, Providence, RI, 1817–56, 7⅞", eagle touch **350.00**

Curtis, Daniel, Albany, NY, 1822–40, 7⅞", "X" quality mark, faint touch, pitted, ... **150.00**

Danforth, Edward, Middletown and Hartford, CT, 1788–94, 8" **150.00**

Jones, Gershom, Providence, RI, 1774–1809, 8⁵⁄₁₆", few knife marks and gouges on back **300.00**

Lightner, George, Baltimore, MD,
1806–15, 7⅞″ **275.00**

Melville, David or Thomas, Newport,
RI, 1790–95, 8¼″ **200.00**

Pierce, Samuel, Sr, Greenfield, MA,
8″, earliest eagle touch **250.00**

Whitmore, Jacob, Middletown, CT,
1758–90, 7⅞″, two small areas of
pitting **200.00**

Will, Henry, NY, late 18th C, 15″ . . . **1,450.00**

Platter, Thomas Compton, London, 20
x 15⅜″, oval **500.00**

Porringer

Boardman, Thomas D and Sherman,
Hartford, CT, 1830, 4″, old English
style handle, straight line touch . . **550.00**

Danforth, Samuel, Hartford, CT,
1795–1816, 3⅝″, basin type, old
English style handle **850.00**

Gleason, Roswell, Dorchester, MA,
c1850, heart and crescent handle,
3¼″ d **425.00**

Green, Samuel, Boston, 1790–1810,
5⁷⁄₁₆″, crown handle, reverse "SG"
signature **200.00**

Hamlin, Samuel E, Providence, RI,
1790–1810, 5¼″ **600.00**

Hamlin, Samuel E, Jr, Providence, RI,
1801–56

5¼″, flower handle, bold touch on
top of handle **550.00**

5⅜″, flower handle, strong eagle
touch on top of handle **700.00**

Lee, Richard, Springfield, VT, late
18th C, 3¾″ d **800.00**

Melville, David, Newport, RI, 1755–
93, 5″, geometric handle, Newport
style bracket **500.00**

Salt, English, 3⅜″ d, pedestal, octagonal base, candlestick standard **185.00**

Snuff or Spice Box, George Coldwell,
NY, 4¾″, bright cut engraving, straight
line touch **400.00**

Shaving Dish, Griswold, Ashbil, Meriden, CT, 1802–42, 4⅜″, circular, cov **250.00**

Sugar Bowl

Boardman, Thomas Danforth, Hartford, CT, 5¾″, baluster shape,
scrolled handles **500.00**

Will, William, 4¾″, double bellied,
beaded rim and foot **3,500.00**

Unmarked, New England, c1825–40,
6¾″ h, cov, strap handles **100.00**

Syrup Pitcher, unmarked, American,
5⅞″, lighthouse shape, reversed "C"
handle, old resoldering on spout . . . **75.00**

Tankard

Griffin, Thomas, London, late 18th C,
7½″ h **475.00**

Redhead, Anthony, English, Stuart,
6½″, flat lid, wriggle work engraving **485.00**

Young, Peter, 6¾″, cylindrical,
molded base, flat top **4,500.00**

Teapot

Boardman & Hart, New York, 1830–
40, 8¼″, "X" quality mark **225.00**

Calder, William, Providence, RI,
c1825, globular, minor surface
scratches, some int. pitting, 8¼″ . **275.00**

Curtiss, Lemuel, Meriden, CT, 1836–
49, c1840, globular, 8¼″ h **250.00**

Gleason, Roswell, Dorchester, MA,
c1830–40, 7″, inverted mold, minor
pitting **250.00**

Locke, J D, New York, NY, 1835–60,
c1840, good touch mark, minor pit-
ting and denting, 7½″ h **125.00**

Richardson, George, Sr, Cranston,
RI, 1828–45, 8″, tapered **400.00**

Smith, Eben, Beverly, MA, 1813–56,
7″, pear shape, Queen Anne style **1,550.00**

Waste Bowl, unmarked, New England,
c1825–40, 4¾″ **175.00**

PHOENIX BIRD CHINA

History: Phoenix Bird pattern is a blue and
white china exported from Japan during the 1920s
to 1940s. A limited amount was made during the
"Occupied Japan" period.

Initially it was available at Woolworth's 5 & 10,
through two wholesale catalog companies, or by
selling subscriptions to needlecraft magazines.
Myott Son & Co., England, also produced this pattern under the name "Satsuma," c1936. These
earthenware items were for export only.

Once known as "Blue Howo Bird China," the
Phoenix Bird pattern is the most sought after of
seven similar patterns in the Hō-ō bird series.
Other patterns are: Flying Turkey (head faces forward with heart-like border); Howo (only pattern
with name on base); and Twin Phoenix (border
pattern only, center white). The Howo and Twin
Phoenix patterns are by Noritake and are occasionally marked "Noritake." Flying Dragon (bird-
like), an earlier pattern, comes in green and white
as well as the traditional blue and white and is
marked with six oriental characters. A variation of
Phoenix Bird pattern has a heart-like border and
is called Hō-ō.

Phoenix Bird pattern has over 500 different
shapes and sizes. Also varying is the quality found
in the execution of design, shades of blue, and
shape of the ware itself. All these factors must be
considered in pricing. The maker's mark tends to
add value; over 90 marks have been cataloged.

Post 1970 pieces were produced in limited
shapes with precise detail, but are on a milk white
ground and usually don't have a maker's mark.
When a mark does appear on a modern piece, it
appears stamped in place.

Reference: Joan Collett Oates, *Phoenix Bird Chinaware*, published by author, *Book One*, 1984, *Book Two (A Through M)*, 1985, *Book Three (N through Z and Post 1970)*, 1986; *Book Four With A Section On Flying Turkey*, 1989.

Collectors' Club: Phoenix Bird Collectors of America, 5912 Kingsfield Drive, West Bloomfield, MI 48233.

Additional Listings: See *Warman's Americana & Collectibles* for more examples.

Advisor: Joan Oates.

Plate, 9¼″ d, $20.00.

Cake Tray, #3	48.00
Children's Dishes	
Tea Set, #4, 3 pc	65.00
Tureen, #2	45.00
Chocolate Pot, scalloped, tall	125.00
Coffeepot, post 1970	35.00
Condensed Milk Holder	75.00
Creamer and Sugar, #20	50.00
Custard Cup	15.00
Egg Cup, double	18.00
Fruit Dish, 5½″ d, scalloped, wide border	10.00
Gravy Boat, attached plate	60.00
Hair Receiver	65.00
Pitcher, buttermilk	55.00
Plate	
9¼″ d, breakfast	30.00
9¾″ d, dinner	45.00
Platter	
7¾ x 5″, scalloped	25.00
12¼ x 9″	45.00
15 x 9¾″	60.00
Rice Bowl, "A"	10.00
Rice Tureen, #3-A	85.00
Salt and Pepper Shakers, pr	25.00
Sauce Boat, #2	45.00
Sauce Boat Underplate, #2	20.00
Soup Bowl, 7¼ x 1½″ h	20.00
Syrup, #1	35.00
Teapot	
Pre 1970	45.00
Post 1970, rattan handle	25.00
Tile, 6″ d	25.00

PHOENIX GLASS

History: Phoenix Glass Company, Beaver, Pennsylvania, was established in 1880. Known primarily for commercial glassware, the firm also produced a molded, sculptured, cameo-type line from the 1930s until the 1950s.

Lamp, white ground, red berries, green leaves, brown stems, bronze plated base, 22″ h, $125.00.

Bowl	
9½ x 5½″, bittersweet, white ground	150.00
13½″, canoe shape, sculptured blue lovebirds, opal ground	325.00
Candlesticks, pr, 3¼″, blue, bubbles and swirls	48.00
Centerpiece, 14″, sculptured diving nudes, three colors	200.00
Compote, 8½″, dragonflies and water lilies dec, butterscotch ground	80.00
Console Bowl, diving ladies, blue figures, white ground	235.00
Lamp, table	
17½″, green peacock feather pattern, irid blue, sgd "Phoenix Studios, Tom Arnold, #197"	185.00
20″, red cardinals on tree branches, green berries, ivory ground	225.00
Plate	
6¾″, dancing nudes, frosted and clear	38.00
8½″, cherries, frosted and clear	55.00
Powder Box, cov	
6¾ x 3¾″, sculptured roses, humming bird, amethyst	125.00
7¼ x 4½″, sculptured white violets, pale lavender ground	100.00
Vase	
6½″, rect, opal sculptured lovebirds on branch, white ground	100.00
7½″, blown out pearlized white fern	

fronds and narrow leaves, salmon
pink ground, orig label **250.00**
8⅜", fan shape, sculptured praying
mantis, foliage, pearlized and
frosted, pale blue-gray ground ... **150.00**
9½", heavily gilted roses, white
ground **125.00**
10", dogwood, blue, white ground,
partial paper label **80.00**
10¼", Madonna, blue ground, sculptured head, white irid **240.00**
11", sculptured, coral, green, and
brown dogwoods, white ground .. **275.00**

PHONOGRAPH RECORDS

History: With the advent of the more sophisticated recording materials, such as 33⅓ RPM long
playing records, 8-track tapes, cassettes, and
compact discs, earlier phonograph records became collectors' items. Most have little value. The
higher priced examples are rare (limited production) recordings. Condition is critical.

References: L. R. Docks, *1915-1965 American
Premium Record Guide, 3rd Edition,*, Books
Americana, 1986; Jerry Osborne, *The Official
Price Guide To Records, Eighth Edition,* House of
Collectibles, 1988; Neal Umphred, *Goldmine's
Price Guide To Collectible Record Albums,*
Krause Publications, 1989.

Collectors' Club: Association For Recorded
Sound Collectors, P.O. Box 75082, Washington,
DC 20013; International Association of Jazz
Record Collectors, Box 10208, Oakland, CA
94610.

Periodicals: *Discoveries,* P.O. Box 255, Port
Townsend, WA 98368; *Goldmine,* 700 E. State
Street, Iola, WI 54990.

Additional Listings: See "Records" in *Warman's Americana & Collectibles* for those recordings in price range from: $5.00 to $25.00.

Note: Most records, especially popular recordings, have a value of less than $3.00 per disc. *The
records listed here are classic recordings of their
type and in demand by collectors.*

Alabama Harmony Boys, Sweet Pa-
tootie, Silvertone 5139 .... **100.00**
Slim Barlett & His Orchestra, Asphalt
Walk, Superior 2692 .... **75.00**
Irene Beasley, You'll Come Back To Me
Someday, Victor 40173 .... **10.00**
Blue Rhythm Orchestra, Keep Your
Temper, Pathe-Actuelle 36364 .... **30.00**
California Poppies, What A Wonderful
Time, Sunset 506/507 .... **80.00**
Bud Carlton's Orchestra, Rainy
Weather Rose, 81308 .... **10.00**
Clifford's Louisville Jug Band, Dancing
Blues, Okeh, 8221 .... **60.00**

Julia Davis, Black Hand Blues, Para-
mount 122498 .... **25.00**
Down Home Serenaders, Cootie
Stomp, Champion 15399 .... **75.00**
Erwing Brothers' Orchestra, The Erwing
Blues, Vocalion 2564 .... **15.00**
Woody Herman & His Orchestra, The
Goose Hangs High, Decca, 1056 .. **10.00**
The Ink Spots, Your Feets Too Big, Vic-
tor 24851 .... **25.00**
Al Jolson, That Haunting Melody, Victor
17037 .... **10.00**
Freddie Keppard's Jazz Cardinals,
Stock Yards Strut, Paramount 12399 **80.00**
Alfred Lewis, Friday Moan Blues, Vo-
calion 1498 .... **25.00**
Guy Lombardo, & His Royal Canadians,
So This Is Venice, Gennett 5416 ... **30.00**
The Melody Sheiks, Mighty Blue, Okeh
40484 .... **20.00**
Joe "King" Oliver, King Porter, Auto-
graph 617 .... **350.00**
Original Tuxedo Jazz Orchestra, Black
Rag, Okeh 8198 .... **100.00**
Red Onion Jazz Babies, Terrible Blues,
Gennett 5607 .... **150.00**
Bud Richie & His Boys, Slappin' The
Bass, Champion 16109 .... **40.00**

**Bing Crosby, Favorite Hawaiian Songs,
Vol 2, album, 10″ records, Decca
#A-461, 1946, $25.00.**

Savoy Bearcats, Senegalese Stomp,
Victor 20182 .... **25.00**
Noble Sissle, Slow River, Okeh 40824 **10.00**
Alphonse Trent & His Orchestra, Louder
and Funnier, Gennett 6664 .... **60.00**
George Tucker & His Novelty Band,
Doin' The New Low Down, Champion
15638 .... **40.00**
The Wanderers, I Ain't Got Nobody,
Bluebird 5869 .... **10.00**

Lawrence Welk & His Orchestra, Shanghai Honeymoon, Gennett 20341 . . . . **40.00**

PHONOGRAPHS

History: Early phonographs were commonly called "talking machines." Thomas A. Edison invented the first successful phonograph in 1877. Other manufacturers followed with their variations.

Collectors' Club: Antique Phonograph Collectors Club, 502 E. 17th Street, Brooklyn, NY 11226.

Periodical: *Horn Speaker,* Box 53012, Dallas, TX 75253.

Edison, Home, cover, brass plated, c1897–1903, $450.00.

Amberola Model 75, diamond reproducer **375.00**
Baltiphone, console, 38″ h, 78 rpm . . . **250.00**
Berliner Trade-Mark Gramophone . . . **2,000.00**
Britannia, key wind, open mechanism, c1910, Germany **200.00**
Busy Bee, disc model **400.00**
Columbia AA, cylinder, oak case, orig horn **300.00**
Edison
  Amberola Model 30, table model, four minute cylinder, oak case, 11 x 12½ x 14¼″ **300.00**
  Fireside Model, oak case, bentwood cover, oak cygnet horn, 9¾″ w . . . **800.00**
  Gem, Model A, metal case **375.00**
  Standard Model B, Model C reproducer, nickel plated winding handle, oak case, one cylinder, 13″ l **275.00**
  Triumph Model, morning glory horn, oak case, c1901 . . . . **1,250.00**
Heywood Wakefield, wicker **1,750.00**
Reginaphone, Style 155, oak serpentine cabinet, double comb, oak horn **4,500.00**
Robeyphone, disc type, large horn, English **500.00**
Standard X Talking Machine, large blue horn **425.00**

Thorens, portable, brown leather case, Switzerland **125.00**
Vanitrola, portable Victrola **175.00**
Victor
  Model O, orig case **875.00**
  Monarch Senior, brass bell horn, ornate oak case **850.00**
  Schoolhouse, oak case **1,400.00**
  Type MS Disc, 10″ d, turntable, carved oak cabinet, brass bell, 25½″ h **725.00**

PICKARD CHINA

History: The Pickard China Company was founded by Wilder Pickard in Chicago, Illinois, in 1897. Originally the company imported European china blanks, principally from the Havilands at Limoges, which they then hand painted. The firm presently is located in Antioch, Illinois.

Biscuit Jar, 6½″, hp chrysanthemums, cream ground, gold trim, SP bail and cov **80.00**
Bowl, 10½″, ruffled, poppies and leaves, gold trim, artist sgd, 1905 . . . . **175.00**
Cake Plate, 10¾″, sq, Oriental birds, sgd "Nichols," c1919 . . . . **180.00**

Celery Dish, gold floral design, marked "Pickard Deco, U.S.A.," #418," 11¾″ l, 5½″ w, $70.00.

Coffee Set, cov coffeepot, creamer, and sugar, artist sgd, 3 pcs **300.00**
Compote, 10½″, fruit and flower dec, gold border, handle, and pedestal base, artist sgd **175.00**
Creamer and Sugar, birds, butterflies, and flowers, artist sgd **140.00**
Cup and Saucer, enamel beading, artist sgd **80.00**
Hatpin Holder, all-over gold design of etched flowers, c1925 . . . . **45.00**

Lemonade Set, tankard pitcher, five tumblers, bluebells and foliage, lemon colored ground **100.00**

Marmalade Jar, 6", matching cov and underplate, hp, dogwoods and leaves, gold trim, artist sgd **85.00**

Mug, 5½", berries, gold handle and rim, artist sgd **150.00**

Perfume Bottle, yellow primroses, shaded ground, artist sgd and dated 1905, Limoges blank, gold stopper . **200.00**

Pitcher
  7¼", cherry clusters, gold trim, artist sgd **200.00**
  8½", bulbous, hexagonal, colored fruit, blossoms, and foliage, silver bands, gold trim, artist sgd, c1912 **285.00**
  10", tulips, artist sgd **265.00**

Plate
  7½", hp, currants, 1898 . . . . **75.00**
  8⅜", handles, Art Nouveau dec, gold and light turquoise **50.00**
  8¼", poppies, gold tracery and rim, sgd "Challinor" **150.00**
  8½", violets, green leaves, shaded purple ground, scalloped gold rim, 1905 mark **90.00**

Platter, 12" d, hp, landscape, sgd "Marker" **225.00**

Powder Box, 4" d, roses, artist sgd . . . **100.00**

Punch Bowl, 14", artist sgd "Schoner," Limoges blank **665.00**

Relish Dish, 9½ x 4¼", pink and green leaves, open handles, maple leaf mark **70.00**

Salt and Pepper Shakers, pr
  All-over gold etched design **30.00**
  Pink rosebuds, blue forget-me-nots, gold scrolls, 1905 mark **40.00**

Stein, 7", large bunches of grapes and leaves, black ground, gold handle, rim, and base, artist sgd, c1898 . . . **275.00**

Tea Set, ftd cov teapot with dolphin's head spout, tankard creamer, cov sugar, 11" d tray, pearlized ground, turquoise blue, pink, and rose tulips, gold tracery and trim on rims and handles, artist sgd **650.00**

Tray, 11" d, circular, bisque, teal blue, gold grapes and leaves, engraved, sgd "Coufall," 1905 mark **200.00**

Urn, 11½", all-over gold, 3" band of grapes and strawberries, artist sgd, Belleek blank **500.00**

Vase
  6", Spring scene, handles, matte finish, sgd "Challinor," maple leaf mark **300.00**
  6½", Deserted Garden scene, gold ground, sgd "Vokral" **200.00**
  7¾", cylindrical, moonlight lake and pine forest scene, artist sgd "Challinor," Nippon blank **250.00**
  8½", glossy finish, gold to rust shaded chrysanthemums, turquoise ground, gold scrolling, rim, and base, artist sgd, c1905 . . . . **150.00**
  9", large golden yellow, pink, and deep rose chrysanthemums and green leaves, soft turquoise blue shaded to green ground, gold trim, artist sgd, 1898 . . . . **300.00**

PICKLE CASTORS

History: A pickle castor is a table accessory used to serve pickles. It generally consists of a silver plated frame fitted with a glass insert, matching silver plated lid, and matching tongs. Pickle castors were very popular during the Victorian era. Inserts are found in pattern glass and colored art glass.

Daisy and Button with V Bar, blue pattern glass insert, silver plated Wilcox frame, matching lid and tongs, $235.00.

Blue, 11", IVT insert, white enamel flowers, orig tongs **250.00**

Cranberry, 13", thumbprint, enameled daisies, twig feet, elaborate floral cutout sides, top and tongs **325.00**

Crown Milano, 9" h, creamy white body, swags of pastel pink and white blossoms, resilvered floral emb lid and holder, 3¾ x 4½" h DQ glass insert, sgd on base "Pairpoint Mfg Co, New Bedford Quadruple Plate 661" **845.00**

Northwood, Netted Apple Blossom insert, ornate SP ftd frame **275.00**

Pigeon Blood, Beaded Drape insert, Consolidated Glass Co, orig cov and frame **425.00**

Pattern Glass

Beaded Dart, sapphire blue insert, re-silvered ftd Meriden frame and tongs **250.00**

Cupid and Venus, clear insert, ftd Pairpoint frame, stylized swan head tongs **85.00**

Daisy and Button, blue insert, SP Wilcox frame, lid and tongs **235.00**

Rubena, vertical optic pattern insert, Pairpoint, ornate ftd fretwork frame and bail handle **225.00**

Vaseline, white opal design, polished pontil, orig ruffled cov shaped as emb flower, stem finial, ornate ftd frame . **450.00**

PIGEON BLOOD GLASS

History: Pigeon blood refers to the deep orangish-red colored glass ware produced around the turn of the century. Do not confuse it with the many other red glass wares of that period. Pigeon blood has a very definite orange glow.

Pickle Castor, quadruple Empire Mfg Co frame, matching lid, and fork, $275.00.

Biscuit Jar, Torquay, SP rim, cover, and handles **275.00**

Bowl, 9″, master berry, Torquay, SP rim **110.00**

Butter Dish, cov, Venecia, enameled dec **350.00**

Celery, 6″, Torquay, SP rim **225.00**

Creamer, Venecia, enameled dec **125.00**

Decanter, 9½″, orig stopper **75.00**

Pickle Castor, Beaded Drape insert, SP

cov and frame, Consolidated Glass Co **425.00**

Pitcher, water

Diamond Quilted, 10½″, tankard shape **185.00**

Torquay, SP trim **325.00**

Salt and Pepper Shakers, Bulging Loops, orig tops, pr **145.00**

Sugar Shaker, Bulging Loops, orig top **150.00**

Syrup, Beaded Drape, Consolidated Glass Co., orig hinged lid **245.00**

Toothpick, Bulging Loops **125.00**

Tumbler, 3¼″, alternating panel and rib **75.00**

Vase, 6″, gourd shape, cased, gold leaf dec, applied elephant head handles, Webb, pr **375.00**

PINK SLAG

History: True pink slag is found only in the molded Inverted Fan and Feather pattern. Quality pieces shade from pink at the top to white at the bottom.

Reproduction Alert: Recently pieces of pink slag, made from molds of the now defunct Cambridge Glass Company, have been found in the Inverted Strawberry and Inverted Thistle pattern. This is not considered "true" pink slag and brings only a fraction of the Inverted Fan and Feather pattern prices.

Punch Cup, footed, $275.00.

Bowl, 9″ d, ftd **500.00**

Butter, cov **650.00**

Compote, jelly **375.00**

Creamer **450.00**

Cruet, 6¾″ h **950.00**

Jam Jar **875.00**

Pitcher, water **750.00**

Punch Cup, 2½″ h, ftd **275.00**

Salt Shaker **300.00**

Sauce Dish, 4½″ w, 2½″ h, four ball feet **285.00**

Sugar, cov **550.00**

Toothpick **400.00**

Tumbler **450.00**

PIPES

History: The history of pipe making dates as early as 1575. Almost all types of natural and man-made materials, some which retained smoke and some that did not, were used to make pipes. Among the materials were amber, base metals, clay, cloisonné, glass, horn, ivory, jade, meerschaum, parian, porcelain, pottery, precious metals, precious stones, semi–precious stones, assorted woods, *inter alia*. Chronologically the four most popular materials and their generally accepted introduction dates are: c1575, clay; c1700, woods; c1710, porcelain; and, c1725, meerschaum.

National pipe styles exist around the globe, wherever tobacco smoking is custom or habit. Pipes reflect a broad range of themes and messages, e.g., figurals, important personages, commemoration of historical events, mythological characters, erotica and pornographica, the bucolic, the bizarre, the grotesque, and the graceful.

Pipe collecting began in the mid-1880s; William Bragge, F.S.A., Birmingham, England, was an early collector. Although firmly established through the efforts of free-lance writers, auction houses, and museums (but not the tobacco industry), the collecting of antique pipes is an amorphous, maligned, and misunderstood hobby. It is amorphous because there are no defined collecting bounds; maligned because it is conceived as an extension of pipe smoking, now socially unacceptable [many pipe collectors are avid non-smokers]; and, misunderstood because of its association with the "collectibles" field.

References: R. Fresco-Corbu, *European Pipes*, Lutterworth Press, 1982; E. Ramazzotti and B. Mamy, *Pipes et Fumeurs des Pipes. Un Art, des Collections, Sous le Vent*, 1981; Benjamin Rapaport, *A Complete Guide To Collecting Antique Pipes*, Schiffer Publishing, 1979.

Collectors' Club: Pipe Collectors International, Inc., P.O. Box 22085, Chattanooga, TN 37422.

Periodicals: Pipe Collectors Of The World, Box 11652, Houston, TX 77293; Universal Coterie of Pipe Smokers, 20-37 120th Street, College Point, NY 11356.

Museums: Museum of Tobacco Art and History, Nashville, TN; National Tobacco-Textile Museum, Danville, VA; U.S. Tobacco Museum, Greenwich, CT.

PIPES

Clay, 18″ l, figural, young man with curly
   hair, wooden slim stem, French,
   Gambier **65.00**
Briar
   Man, 7″ l, bearded, tasseled hat and
     pipe, carved, marked "G.B.D." . . . **55.00**
   Queen Victoria, head, 6¼″, carved,
     silver trim, case, hallmarked **75.00**

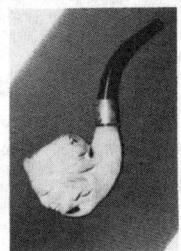

Meerschaum, Indian head, 5″ l, $125.00.

Glass, large ovoid bowl, long shaped
   stem, red and ivory dec **75.00**
Meershum
   Boy with mandolin, 12″, carved **200.00**
   Carved man lid, 6″ **50.00**
   Dog, long hair, amber stem, case . . **45.00**
   Horses, 14″, carved **100.00**
   Maiden, 7¾″ l, full figural, seated,
     flowing gown, garlands of roses,
     basket weave bowl, amber stem,
     orig case **185.00**
   Negro, 8″, figural, cream, bust bowl . **900.00**
   Wild Animal, 17″, carved, dated 1800 **150.00**
Opium, 7¾″, cranes, reed stem, brass
   fittings, Oriental, c1800 . . . . **85.00**
Porcelain
   Character, 10″, man under barrel . . **60.00**
   Family Crest 1847, 30″, marked
     "Made by Cmielow Factory, Po-
     land" **75.00**
   Floral, 12″, relief **125.00**
   Graf Zeppelin, 9″, P.O.G. **125.00**
   Hunter, 24″, sleeping **125.00**
   Occupational, 12″, machine, stem
     chips **75.00**
   Stag, 12″, marked "P.O.G." **75.00**
Pottery
   Man with pipe, set on lid, post war . **60.00**
   Monk, post war **45.00**
   Ram, post war **65.00**
Regimental
   4 Field Art. Regt. Magdellburg 1896–
     98, 36″ l **260.00**
   149 Inft. regt. 1881, blacksmith tools
     in rear, 10″ l **85.00**
Soapstone, Eskimo man, 9″, skinning
   animal, late 19th C **140.00**

TAMPS

Boot, 1½″, wood **35.00**
Column, 2¾″, ivory **15.00**
Man, 1⅝″, bending at waist, SP, marked
   "E.P.N.S." **25.00**
Napoleon, 2⅜″, brass **25.00**

Robin Hood, 2¼", brass, marked "England" **35.00**

POCKET KNIVES

History: Alcas, Case, Colonial, Ka-Bar, Queen,
and Schrade are the best of the modern pocket
knife manufacturers, with top positions enjoyed by
Case and Ka-Bar. Knives by Remington and Winchester, firms no longer in production, are eagerly
sought.

Form is a critical collecting element. The most
desirable forms are folding hunters (1 and 2
blades), trappers, peanuts, Barlows, elephant
toes, canoes, Texas toothpicks, Coke bottles, gun
stocks, and Daddy Barlows. The decorative aspect
also heavily influences prices. Values are for
pocket knives in mint condition.

References: James F. Parker, *The Official Price
Guide to Collector Pocket Knives, 9th Edition,*
House of Collectibles, 1987; Jim Sargent, *Sar-
gent's American Premium Guide To Pocket
Knives: Identification and Values,* Books Ameri-
cana, 1986; Ron Stewart and Roy Ritchie, *The
Standard Knife Collector's Guide,* Collector
Books, 1986.

Periodical: *Knife World,* P. O. Box 3395, Knox-
ville, TN 37917.

Collectors' Clubs: American Blade Collectors,
P.O. Box 22007, Chattanooga, TN 37422; Cana-
dian Knife Collectors Club, 3141 Jessuca Court,
Mississauga, ON L5C1X7; The National Knife Col-
lectors Association, P.O. Box 21070, Chattanooga,
TN 37421.

Museum: National Knife Museum, Chattanooga, TN.

Additional Listings: See *Warman's Americana
& Collectibles* for more examples.

CASE

Case uses a numbering code for its knives. The
first number (1–9) is the handle material; the second number (1–5) designates the number of
blades; the third and fourth number (0–99) the
knife pattern. Stage (5), pearl (8 or 9), and bone
(6) are most sought in handle materials. The most
desirable patterns are 5165—folding hunters,
6185—doctors, 6445—scout, muskrat—marked
muskrat with no number, and 6254—trappers.

In the Case XX series a symbol and dot code is
used to designate a year.

1920-40
5254, stag handle, 4⅛", stamped
"Tested XX" **1,350.00**
6111½, green bone, long pull,
stamped "Tested XX" **400.00**
6265, green bone, 5¼", flat blade,
stamped "Tested XX" **300.00**

6465, green bone, 5¼", saber blade,
bail in handle stamped "Tested
XX" **1,750.00**
9265, imitation pearl, 5¼", flat blade,
stamped "Tested XX" **400.00**
1940-65
3254, yellow composition 4⅛",
stamped "XX" **125.00**
42057, white composition, 3⅜"
marked on handle "OFFICE
KNIFE" **90.00**
6246R, green bone, 4⅜", bail in handle, stamped "Tested XX," rigger's
knife **150.00**
6265, red bone, 5¼", flat blade,
stamped "XX" **250.00**
8271, genuine pearl, 3¼", long pull
stamped "XX" **220.00**
Fly Fisherman **150.00**
1965-70
4200, white composition, 5½", serrated master blade, stamped
"USA," melon testor **125.00**
5265, stag, 5¼", saber ground, bols-
ters drilled stamped "USA" **85.00**
62009, bone, 3⁵⁄₁₆", master blade in
front, stamped "USA," Barlow ... **35.00**
6265, red bone, 5¼", flat blade,
stamped "XX" **225.00**
Muskrat, bone 3⅞", 10 dot **50.00**
1970-80 (Number of dots indicate year)
5111½, genuine stag, 4⁷⁄₁₆", lockback,
Cheetah, large stamp **175.00**
62009, bone stag, 3⁵⁄₁₆", Barlow ... **35.00**
6265, stag, 5¼", saber ground, bols-
ters drilled, 10 dot **75.00**
Fly Fisherman **100.00**
Muskrat bone, 3⅞", 10 dot **40.00**

Ka-Bar, trapper, pearl handle, $40.00.

KA-BAR (Union Cut. Co., Olean, New York)

The company was founded by Wallace Brown
at Tidioute, PA in 1892. It was relocated in Olean,
NY, in 1912. The products have many stampings
including Union [inside shield]; U-R Co. Tidoute
[variations]; Union Cutlery Co. Olean, NY; Alcut
Olean, NY; Keenwell, Olean, NY; and Ka-Bar. The
larger knives with a profile of a dog's head on the
handle are the most desirable. Pattern numbers
rarely appear on a knife prior to the 1940s.

22156	500.00
24107	1,000.00
31187, 2 blades	150.00
61161, light celluloid handle	100.00
61126L, dog's head	850.00
61187, Daddy Barlow	150.00
6191L	600.00
6260KF	100.00

KEEN KUTTER (Simons Hardware, St. Louis, MO)

K02220, office knife	50.00
K1881, Barlow	70.00
K1920	300.00
6354, Scout	100.00

REMINGTON, last made in 1940

R293, Field and Stream Bullet, bone, long pull, 5¼″	1,750.00
R953, toothpick, bone, 5″	225.00
R3273, Cattle, brown bone, equal end, 3¾″	235.00
R4233, Junior Scout, brown bone, scout shield, pinched bolsters, 3⅜″	200.00
R4353, Bullet/Big Muskrat, brown base, 4¼″	1,300.00

RUSSELL, Turner Fall, MA

60, 1 blade	100.00
55, 2 blades	125.00
600, Daddy Barlow	200.00

WINCHESTER

1051, Texas Jack, celluloid, 4¼″	300.00
1621, Budding, ebony, 4¾″	130.00
1920, Folding Hunter, bone, 5⅜″	1,000.00
2337, Senator, pearl, 3¼″	100.00
2703, Barlow, brown bone, 3½″	140.00
3944, Whittler, bone, 3¼″	225.00
4961, Premium Stockman, bone, 4″	285.00

OTHER MANUFACTURERS

Elephant Toe
Ibberson, pearl work back	300.00
Kutwell, Olean, NY	200.00
Primble, John	250.00

Folding Hunter
Case, Nantucket Sleigh Ride	125.00
Marble Arms Co	350.00
Neft Saftey	220.00
New York Knife Co.	400.00
Novelty Cutlery Co., pictured handle	125.00
Queen Cutlery Co. Titusville, PA, buffalo horn	200.00
Robeson	175.00
Russell	150.00
Schrade, Trail of Tears	150.00

Union Cutlery Co., Tidioute, PA	100.00
Valley Forge Cutlery Co., NJ	215.00

POISON BOTTLES

History: Poison bottles were designed to warn and prevent accidental intake or misuse of their poisonous substances, especially in the dark. Poison bottles generally were made of colored glass, embossed with "Poison" or a skull and crossbones, and sometimes were coffin-shaped.

John H. B. Howell of Newton, New Jersey, designed the first safety closure in 1866. The idea did not become popular until the 1930s when bottle designs became simpler and the user had to read the label to identify the contents.

References: Ralph and Terry Kovel, *The Kovels' Bottle Price List, 8th Edition,* Crown Publishers, Inc., 1987; Carlo and Dorothy Sellari, *The Standard Old Bottle Price Guide,* Collector Books, 1989.

Periodical: *Antique Bottle and Glass Collector,* P.O. Box 187, East Greenville, PA 18041.

Cash Boots Chemist, emb "Not To Be Taken," green, 4⅛″ h, $12.00.

Baker, Chester, A, Boston, cobalt blue, emb	45.00
Carbolic Acid, ring top, cobalt, poison crosses all around, 5″	15.00
Durfee Embalming Fluid Co, amethyst, 8¾″	25.00
Ikey Einstein Poison, rect, ring top, clear, 3¾″	25.00
JTM & Co, three cornered, "Poison" on one side, ring top, amber, 10″	80.00
Lin Saponis, green, 6¾″	20.00
Liq Morph Hydrochl Poison, cobalt, label, 4½″	40.00

Melvin & Badger Apothecaries, Boston,
MA, irregular hexagon, cobalt blue, 6″ **30.00**
Norwich, IGA, cobalt blue, 8″ **75.00**
Owl Poison Ammonia, three cornered,
cobalt, label, 5¼″ **25.00**
Spirits, silver, milk glass, 9″ **20.00**
Tinct Opii, poison on base, cobalt, 7″ . **40.00**
Victory Chemical Co, Quick Death In-
secticide, 148 Fairmount Ave, Phila,
PA, 8 oz, clear, 7″ **12.00**

POLITICAL ITEMS

History: Since 1800 the American presidency always has been a contest between two or more candidates. Initially souvenirs were issued to celebrate victories. Items issued during a campaign to show support for a candidate were actively being distributed in the William Henry Harrison election of 1840.

Campaign items cover a wide variety of materials—buttons, bandannas, tokens, pins, etc. The only limiting factor has been the promoter's imagination. The advent of television campaigning has reduced the emphasis on individual items. Modern campaigns do not seem to have the variety of materials which were issued earlier.

References: Herbert Collins, *Threads of History,* Smithsonian Institution Press, 1979; Stan Gores, *Presidential and Campaign Memorabilia With Prices, Second Edition,* Wallace-Homestead, 1988; Theodore L. Hake, *Encyclopedia of Political Buttons, United States, 1896–1972,* Americana & Collectibles Press, 1985; Theodore L. Hake, *Political Buttons, Book II, 1920–1976,* Americana & Collectibles Press, 1977; Theodore L. Hake, *Political Buttons, Book III, 1789–1916,* Americana & Collectibles Press, 1978; Edmund B. Sullivan, *American Political Badges and Medalets, 1789–1892,* Quarterman Publications, Inc., 1981. (Note: Theodore L. Hake issued a revised set of prices for his three books in 1984.)

Collectors' Club: American Political Items Collectors, P.O. Box 340339, San Antonio, TX 78234.

Periodical: *Political Collector,* 444 Lincoln Street, York, PA 17404.

Museum: Smithsonian Museum, Washington, D.C.

Note: The abbreviation "h/s" is used to identify a head and shoulder photo or etching of a person.

Additional Listings: See *Warman's Americana & Collectibles* for more examples.

Advisor: Theodore L. Hake.

Ashtray, 5″ d, china, white, gold band, "Vote Republican In '52" inscription, man hitchhiking next to exhausted Democratic donkey with GOP elephant lumbering down road cartoon, "My Ass Is Tired" caption **15.00**

Badge
1896, McKinley-Hobart, ribbon, celluloid jugate attached, "Sound Money/No Repudiation/Republican/Traveling Men's/Club/Peoria, Ill," 8 x 2½″ **50.00**
1910, Taft, Wisconsin Republican Convention, Badge, inscribed on black ribbon "We oppose men who are Republicans for office and Democrats in office," Taft medal on bottom, delegate label on top, 5 x 2″ **45.00**
1949, Truman, Truman-Barkley inauguration jugate, gray ribbon attached, "Democrats/from/Cambria-Indiana/Armstrong-Somerset/Counties/Johnstown, PA," 4 x 2″ **175.00**
Bandanna
1896, Bryan, cotton, 17¾ x 18¼″, black and white, jugate of Bryan and Sewall, eagle and shield at top, coin and rooster in center, White House at bottom, numerous slogans **80.00**
1928, Hoover, 17 x 18″, linen, white ground, blue oval bust portrait in center, "Our President," surrounded by state seals in red . . . **60.00**
29″ sq, red, white, and blue, "I Like Ike" slogan repeated four times, white stars on red and white elephants on blue border **35.00**
Bank, 1½ x 3½ x 2½″, cast iron, still, "Teddy" on one side, orig gold paint, c1908 . . . . **80.00**
Blotter, Willkie, 4 x 9″, black and white, campaign slogans, inscription "Contributed By A Citizen Of Amsterdam NY 1940" **15.00**
Book Cover, Goldwater, 13 x 20″, plastic lamination, portrait, Declaration of Independence signers on back **10.00**
Bookmark, Taft, 2½ x 2¾″, Taft, diecut,

Button, McKinley and Roosevelt, blue and gold, 1900, $25.00.

aluminum, teddy bear shape, portrait on cutout heart, back Sherman portrait, The Bear-Still In Evidence-But In Charge Of A New Keeper" slogan . . **75.00**

Bottle Stopper, figural, LB Johnson, 2½ x 3 x 4", three dimensional head, red foil "Japan" sticker, c1964 . . . . **20.00**

Bumper Sticker, 4 x 7", orange and black, license plate design, inscribed "Elect JFK-60 President" **8.00**

Button
1896, 1¾", sepia portrait of Bryan, St Louis Button Company **30.00**
1900, 2⅛", jugate, McKinley and TR, black and white portraits on red, white, and blue flag motif, gold border **50.00**
1900, 1¼", McKinley and Roosevelt, blue and gold **25.00**
1904, Parker-Davis, jugate, multicolor, ribbon center, 1¼" **50.00**
1912, Progressive, head of moose, "Progressive," white and gold on light blue **15.00**
1916, Wilson,⅞", black and white portrait, blue rim with "Progressive Policies Become Law Under Wilson" **15.00**
1920, Coolidge-Dawes, jugate,⅞", black and white, text above and below oval portrait **45.00**
1924, Smith, gray tone, h/s, rim "For President/Alfred E. Smith," ⅞" . . . **20.00**
1924, Hoover, oval, red, white, and blue, "100%/HOOVER/AMERICAN" **10.00**
1932, Roosevelt-Garner, jugate, black and white, "Return our country to the People" **200.00**
1940,⅞", "I'M FOR WILLKIE AND McNARY," jugate, black and white, lettering on right is lighter **55.00**
1948, Dewey-Warren, jugate,⅞" . . . **20.00**
1952, Stevenson, 1¾", brown and white, portrait, name across bottom **10.00**
1968, 1⅝" Goldwater, black, white, and blue, bust portrait, "I'll Back Barry" **6.00**

Coolidge,¾", litho, white on blue **15.00**

Car Attachment, 2½" d, silvered metal holder, tin plate with black and white portrait and slogan "Keep Coolidge", threaded shaft **250.00**

Cigar, 1928, Al Smith, 8½", black, white, gold, red, and green label picturing Smith, orig box **22.50**

Cigarettes, 1952, Eisenhower, h/s, "I Like Ike," red, white, and blue stripes **15.00**

Gearshift Knob, 2" d, Woodrow Wilson, solid amber celluloid, metal ring surrounds rubber disk with Wilson's portrait, c1916 . . . . **50.00**

Glass
1896, McKinley-Hobart, clear, tumbler, 3¾", etched pictures in wreath, names below **45.00**
1902, Roosevelt, clear, punch cup, 2¾", etched "President Roosevelt/ 1902/Oyster Bay," on bottom "Bloomingdales New York" **35.00**

Inaugural Item
Invitation, 1885, Cleveland-Hendricks, ball, 7 x 9¾" **45.00**
Periscope, 3 x 4 x 16", white and green cardboard box, JFK's name and picture on two sides, capitol on other two sides, two built in mirrors **50.00**

Program
1881, Garfield-Arthur, 16 pgs **35.00**
1957, Eisenhower, Rockwell cov, 50 pgs **15.00**

Letter Opener, 1¾ x 8", plastic, white, blue image and red lettering, "Vote Demo! Hubert Humphrey For President!", 1968 . . . . **7.00**

License Plate
1940, Willkie, white key on composition, "Good/Willkie/to White House/ 1940," made by Kuleness Co, Paulding, OH, 5½ x 10" **30.00**
1952, Eisenhower-Nixon, jugate, "I Like/Ike/and Dick," h/s of both red, white, and blue, 5¼ x 12" **25.00**
1964, Wallace, "Johnson for King/ Wallace for President," red, white, and blue, 6 x 12" **12.00**

Match Holder, 1½ x 2¼", Jefferson portrait, "National Democratic Club April 13, 1907" slogan, ART Mfg Co New York, 1904 patent date **20.00**

Medal, copper, 1⅞", Buchanan, buck leaping over cannon and "Ann/Breckinridge," rev with portrait of Washington and slogan **150.00**

Megaphone, 7½" l, cone shape, plastic, white, blue inscription "President Nixon. Now More Than Ever," 1972 . **10.00**

Mirror, Taft, 2¼" d, black and white, bust of Taft, "Its Up To The Man On The Other Side To Put This Tried & Safe Man At The Head Of The Government" **125.00**

Mug
1896, Bryan, milk glass, 3¾", oval transfer of h/s with name on right shoulder, floral dec border **60.00**
1928, Hoover, 7" toby, face with seating posture base, cream color, facsimile signature on side **50.00**

Note Pad, 2 x 2¾", Cleveland picture of front with wife, Baldwin & Gleason 1886 copyright **10.00**

Notebook, 2 x 3", celluloid, 1927 calendar on back, "Vote The Straight

Republican Tickets-Republican State Committee Women's Division" slogan ... **10.00**

Pen, 5½" l, dark blue, silver inscription "Businessmen For Humphrey/Thank You/Hubert H. Humphrey" **8.00**

Pencil, mechanical, 5½" l, light gray point end, transparent plastic covering JFK portrait clip end, diecut "109" PT boat that floats back and forth, skyline background scene **30.00**

Pennant
1912–16, Wilson, h/s to left with "Our/President," name in center, white and flesh tones, blue ground, 8½ x 21" **25.00**
1948, Truman, oval with Truman h/s and name on left "For President" in center, white, red ground, 4½ x 12" **25.00**

Pin
1896, McKinley, Nose Thumber, gold color, push heels to reveal Mckinley thumbing nose, on reverse "McKinley to Democrats and Populists, 1⅞" **200.00**
1928, Smith, enamel, donkey with derby **15.00**
1936, Landon, brass, sunflower, "Landon/Knox" in pedals **12.00**
1956, Eisenhower, bar, "IKE" above, "volunteer" inscribed, and "56" in relief **7.50**

Plate, Howard Taft and James S. Sherman, 1908, 9½" d, $70.00.

Plate
1884, Blaine, china, 9", black on white, floral motif beneath **35.00**
1912, Wilson, china, 9½", White House in center, oval h/s of all presidents up to Wilson on border ... **35.00**
1948, Dewey, 6½", white, glazed, portrait and "New York State Fair-

Chamber of Commerce-Farm Dinner-Syracuse-1949" **12.00**
Platter, 9 x 11½", oval, china, jugate portraits of W. H. Taft and JS Sherman, surrounded by red, white and blue flags, and purple roses, eagle with shield below, gold floral design border **35.00**

Postcard
1896–1900, Bryan, speaking from train platform label reads "Much Ado Abt Nothing," multicolored .. **15.00**
1908, Hopefuls, "Watching the Presidential Game," Hughes, Foraker, Cannon, Taft, and Fairbanks on one side of fence, T. Roosevelt on other, cartoon, multicolored **20.00**
1908, Taft, mechanical, black, white, and yellow elephant with rope tail, black and white portrait slides out when pulled by tail, October 24, 1908 postmark, brief message ... **25.00**
1940, "No More Fireside Chats," red, white, and blue **5.00**
1960, Kennedy, h/s, election day card, black and white **10.00**

Ribbon
1880, Hancock and English, 2¾ x 6", jugate, black and white, beige cloth, marked "Junior/Hancock/Club/of Chambersburg" **125.00**
1888, Cleveland, center "Cleveland/And/Truman," bandanna design top and bottom, red on white, 5 x 1¾" **50.00**
1904, Roosevelt, h/s of Roosevelt, above "For President/1904," signature at base, black on white, 4¼ x 2" **65.00**

Salt and Pepper Shakers, pr, ceramic, beige and tan, Ike's head lifts off for one shaker, body serves as other, c1952 .... **15.00**

Sheet Music
1856, "Fremont's Great Republican March," woodcut of h/s, black on white, 6 pgs **25.00**
1912, Wilson, "Its Woodrow Wilson, That's All," side h/s of Wilson imposed on Capitol dome, 6 pgs **20.00**
1952, Eisenhower, "For Eisenhower," h/s photo, peach, orange, and black, 4 pgs **7.50**

Soap, 1964, Goldwater, bath size, wrapper with black, silver, and white on gold **7.50**

Stereocard, McKinley And His Eight Chosen Advisors-Cabinet Room, Executive Mansion, 1900 .... **5.00**

Stickpin
Blaine, 1884, cardboard photo **50.00**

Coolidge, 1920, green and silver license plate logo, "Cal/24/Coolidge," ¼ x 1" **15.00**
Benjamin Harrison, 2" l, brass **15.00**
McKinley, 2", 1" d gold and silver engraved dish, mounted, c1896 . . . . **20.00**
Stud, 1896, "How The Farmer Loves Gold Bugs," lapel, three insects impaled on points of pitchfork, black ground **150.00**
Tape Measure, 1¾" d, gold glass case, metal measure, red, white, and blue inscription "President Nixon Now More Than Ever," orig plain gold box **5.00**
Tapestry, 19½ x 38", JF Kennedy with American flag and US Capitol, inscribed back "Made In Italy" **20.00**
Tab
1928, "HOOVER-CURTIS," White letters on blue metal tab **7.00**
1936, Landon-Knox, diecut elephant **10.00**
Tie, 1936, Landon, "For President/h/s/ Alfred M. Landon," brown ground, white lettering, round picture **25.00**
Tie Clip, brass, hat shape, "LBJ" in black lettering, orig dark blue card . . **5.00**
Token
1838, Hard Times Token, copper, front tortoise and safe, black donkey, 28mm **8.00**
1860, Lincoln, copper, h/s on front, Lincoln as rail splitter and log cabin on back, 28mm **40.00**
1893, Grover Cleveland, brass, luster, inscription "United States Mint Exhibit/World's Columbian Exposition Chicago/1893, 1" **12.00**
1845, James Garfield, brass, White House and canal boat, inscription "Canal Boy 1845/President 1881" inauguration souvenir, 1" **10.00**
T-Shirt, 1956, Eisenhower, children's size, h/s, "I'm Safe With Ike," gray picture, red letters, white shirt **20.00**
Watch Fob
William J Bryan, 1¼" black and white celluloid, mounted, black leather fob with strap **30.00**
Taft, silvered brass, red and blue enamel pennant design, 1908 patent date on back **25.00**

POMONA GLASS

History: Pomona glass, produced only by the New England Glass Works and named for the Roman goddess of fruit and trees, was patented in 1885 by Joseph Locke. It is a delicate lead, blown art glass which has a pale, soft beige ground and a top one–inch band of honey amber.

There are two distinct types of backgrounds.

First ground, made only from late 1884 to June 1886, was produced by fine cuttings through a wax coating followed by an acid bath. Second ground was made by rolling the piece in acid resisting particles and acid etching. Second ground was made in Cambridge until 1888 and until the early 1900s in Toledo where Libbey moved the firm after purchasing New England Glass works. Both methods produced a soft frosted appearance, with fine curlicue lines more visible on first ground pieces. Designs are used on some pieces, which were etched and then stained in color. The most familiar design is blue cornflowers.

Do not confuse Pomona with "Midwestern Pomona," a pressed glass with a frosted body and amber band.

Reference: Joseph and Jane Locke, *Locke Art Glass: A Guide For Collectors,* Dover Publications, 1987.

Pitcher, Cornflower pattern, first grind, light amber collar, 4½" h, $450.00.

Beverage Set, 8½" tankard pitcher, six glasses, second grind, Cornflower, DQ **600.00**
Bowl, ruffled, first grind, amber edge . **65.00**
Carafe, second grind, Cornflower **200.00**
Celery, first grind, Cornflower **300.00**
Creamer, second grind, Daisy and Butterfly, applied clear handle, three applied clear feet **275.00**
Cruet, 5½", first grind, Blueberry, gold leaves, applied clear handle, clear ball stopper **285.00**
Lemonade Mug, 5¾", first grind
Cornflower, blue flowers **275.00**
Optic Diamond Quilt pattern, irid, clear handle and upper border . . . **165.00**
Pitcher, milk, second grind
Blueberry **200.00**
Cornflower, sq top **225.00**
Punch Cup, first grind, Cornflower, blue flowers **100.00**
Toothpick, first grind, Cornflower **245.00**
Tumbler, 3⅝", first grind, Cornflower, blue flowers **200.00**
Vase, 10⅞", lily form, second grind . . . **400.00**

PORTRAIT WARE

History: Plates, vases, and other articles with portraits on them were popular in the second half of the 19th century. Although male subjects, such as Napoleon or Louis XVI, were used, the ware usually depicted a beautiful woman, often unidentified.

A large number of English and Continental China manufacturers made portrait ware. Because most ware was hand painted, an artist's signature often is found.

Additional Listings: KPM and Royal Vienna.

Ewer, oval portrait of maiden, one with diaphanous red gown, floral sash, standing before classical architecture, flowing brown hair, titled "Sehnsucht," other with red dress, holding white shawl, dark hair, entitled "Echo," elaborate palmette and Greek key gilt tooled reserves, shaded brown to copper luster ground, three large foliate scroll and spray registers, molded scrolled handle and leaf tip spout, socle base, circular plinth, scrolled feet, obscured factory mark, blue pseudo Vienna shield mark, black titles, artist sgd "Wagner," pr . **4,125.00**

Pedestal, 41″ h, tapering cylindrical column, bleu-do-roi painted by Rochette, three quarter standing portrait of Emperor Napoleon, wearing uniform, tooled gilt rect border, gilt palmettos, laurel garlands, scrolled leafage and rosettes above letter "N," leaf cast capital, gilt bronze molded base, amber veined white onyx sq top, Sevres, late 19th C **4,500.00**

Plate

7″, young woman, long hair, shaded green ground, wide lacy gold border, marked "R. C. Bavaria" **30.00**

8½″, maidens and cherub frolicking in garden, magenta border **75.00**

9½″, Napoleon and Josephine, three quarter youthful portrait, Napoleon with white and olive green uniform, medals, blue edged crimson ribbon, dark gray-brown ground, artist sgd "K. Ray," Josephine with pale crimson gown, shaded blue drape, pale crimson flower in hair, pale shaded gray ground, artist sgd "Wagner," marked "Vienna," c1900, giltwood shadowbox frame **850.00**

9⅝″, Carl Magnus Hutschenreuther, c1900, Mme. Recamier, white dress, blue ribbon sash, red cloak, brown eyes, upswept black hair, gray ground, green scrolled border, gilt scaled scrolls, floral sprays, and

Plate, Princess De Lamballe, blue mark "L S & S, Carlsbad, Austria," 8½″ d, $30.00.

flower filled urns, imp blue factory mark "Lamb Dresden 135.K," title in black, artist sgd "A. Lormin" . . **825.00**

10″, cherubs pulling wheel cart in garden, etched gold border, marked "Hutschenreuther, Bavaria" **110.00**

Urn, cov, 30″ h, elongated waisted cylindrical neck painted in reserve with bust portrait of Marie Antonionette on one, Louis XVI on other, gilt border with foliage scrollwork, drum form body painted with continuous landscape frieze depicting aristocratic ladies and gentlemen in 18th C costumes, waisted lobed base and foot, gilt highlights and rims, pierced dome cov with gilded pineapple knob, bleu celeste ground, marked "Serves," pr **1,250.00**

Vase

6⅜″, bud, cylindrical, oval self portrait, after Vigee Librun, flanked by molded gilt scrolls, green ground, gilt vertical banding, floral sprigs, and foliate scrolls, gilded asymmetrical rim and foot, crowned Dresden mark, "34927" in black, c1900 . . . . **250.00**

8¼″, young woman, pale red dress, white shawl and gloves, upswept blond hair, holding large lilac spray, gilt and silver tooled stylized floral sprig and scroll borders, copper luster ground, obscured factory mark, underglaze blue pseudo Vienna mark, underglaze blue title "Flieder (Lilac)" and "DEC .786 Depose" in black, gilt numerals, artist sgd "Wagner" **935.00**

8¾″, young woman, white dress, pink shawl, gilt tooled floral spray borders, copper luster ground, reserve with gilt foliage medallion, laurel sprigs in upswept brown hair, obscured factory mark, pseudo Vienna shield mark in blue, red title "Laurel, Germany," artist sgd "Wagner" **725.00**

POSTERS

History: The poster was an extremely effective and critical means of mass communication, especially in the period before 1920. Enormous quantities were produced, helped in part by the propaganda role posters played in World War I.

Print runs of two million were not unknown. Posters were not meant to be saved. Once they served their purpose, they tended to be destroyed. The paradox of high production and low survival is one of the fascinating aspects of poster history.

The posters of the late 19th century and early 20th century represent the pinnacle of American lithography printing. The advertising posters of firms such as Strobridge or Courier are true classics. Philadelphia was one center for the poster industry.

Europe pioneered in posters with high artistic and aesthetic content. Many major artists of the 20th century designed posters. Poster art still plays a key role throughout Europe today.

References: John Barnicoat, *A Concise History of Posters*, Harry Abrams, Inc., 1976; George Theofiles, *American Posters of World War I: A Price and Collector's Guide*, Dafram House Publishers, Inc.; Walton Rawls, *Wake Up, America!: World War I and The American Poster*, Abbeville Press, 1988; Stephen Rebello and Richard Allen, *Reel Art: Great Posters From The Golden Age of The Silver Screen*, Abbeville Press, 1988.

Collectors' Club: Poster Society, Inc., P.O. Box 43171, Montclair, NJ 07043.

Additional Listings: See *Warman's Americana & Collectibles* for more examples.

Advisor: George Theofiles.

ADVERTISING

"Arrow Shirts," J. C. Leyendecker, 11 x 21", c1915, man in smoking jacket and tie reading book **125.00**
"Ivory Soap," 11 x 21", Art Deco, two women inspecting garment **90.00**
"Lippincott's," March 1895, J. J. Gould, 12 x 18", woman in Victorian winter attire **200.00**
"R. R. Donnelley & Sons, Printers and Binders, Chicago," Ostertag, 13 x 21", three women posing like Art Nouveau "Three Kings," floral motif dec, metallic gold background, beautifully printed, 1894 .... **150.00**
"Salamander Shoes," Frank Weiss, 33 x 24", pink locomotive issues pale green salamanders, casual shoes in

Entertainment, Texas Guinan, c1935, 27 x 41", $225.00.

foreground, pink, green, brown, black, gray **120.00**
"Valmya Wine, Monnier," 63 x 47", girl in orange striped dress offers toast to Chateau De Valmya seen in background, 1937 .... **250.00**

CIRCUS, SHOWS, AND ACTS

Barnum and Bailey, combined shows, "Presenting 150 Horses In The Fete Of Garlands," 30 x 40", c1919–20 .. **175.00**
Christy Bros Big 5 Ring Wild Animal Shows, "The Wonder Show," 27 x 41", litho, camels in foreground with trained bison, oxen and deer, Christy Bros in vignette at upper left, c1925 **150.00**
Downey Bros Big 3 Ring Circus, "Leaps-Revival Of That Astounding And Sensational Exhibition," 41 x 27", group of elephants, camels and horses in line, aerial artist leap over them, crowd view background, c1925 **125.00**
Kay Bros, "Saijiro Kitchie-The Greatest Of All Japanese Head Balancers," 28 x 40", yellow and blue, Kitchie in litho, vignettes of acts all around, photo at left side, c1935 .... **135.00**
Ringling Bros Barnum & Bailey, "Rudy Rudynoff, Peerless Equestrian," 28 x 41", Rudynoff in Cossack-like uniform, close-up of steed on one side, Great Dane on other **200.00**

MOVIE

One Sheet, Silent
"Chase Me," Otis litho, Fox Sunshine Comedy, Arbuckle at beach with two ladies **300.00**
"Dawn Of Revenge," 1922, 41 x 27",

Richard Travers, Otis litho, linen backed **150.00**
"Second Hand Line," Charles Jones, c1915, man in boat wooing girl .. **135.00**
One sheet, 27 x 41"
"A Hard Days Night," 1964, The Beatles **200.00**
"Doomed Caravan," 1940, William Boyd, western design, orig Paramount **80.00**
"Head Over Heels In Love," 1936, Jessie Matthews, litho, blue, yellow, brown, green, black **90.00**
"Kidnapped," 1948, Roddy McDowall, Sue England, monogram design . **60.00**
"Most Precious Thing In Life," 1934, Jean Arthur, Richard Cromwell, litho, bust portraits, red, blue, orange, flesh tones, brown, and gray, yellow background **125.00**
"Partners In Time," 1946, Lum and Abner, pastel designs **60.00**
"The Glass Webb," 1955, Edward G. Robinson **70.00**
"The Last Time I Saw Paris," 1954, Elizabeth Taylor, Van Johnson, bust portraits **50.00**
Three Sheets
"Leave It To Me," 42 x 80", c1916, William Russell and woman **175.00**
"The Stowaway," 40 x 80", 1936, Shirley Temple, close-up **450.00**

THEATRICAL

"Bunco In Arizona," 30 x 40", 1907, saloon scene, man shooting pistol from hand of another **200.00**
"Child Slaves Of New York," 20 x 30", Strobridge Litho, Arab holding man in front pointing Kaldah The Mystic, frightened victorian beauty, bottom "He Is The Detective—You Know What To Do!", 1903 .. **165.00**
"Fogg's Ferry, Don't Kill Me Mammy," c1905, woman at beach hitting black child **100.00**
"Life's Shop Window," 40 x 80", litho, perplexed woman looking to baby, handed her by Indian woman in field, c1900 .... **210.00**
"Nip and Tuck, Detectives Out Of The Window Into The Water," 28 x 21", JM Jones Co, man falling from up-ended rain barrel into jaw's of ferocious mastiff, c1880 .... **225.00**
"The Beautiful Indian Maidens," 20 x 27", Enquirer Co, fourteen Victorian ladies dressed in tights and head dresses, catching duck dressed in tuxedo, lobster with smiling man's' face, 1898 .... **200.00**

"The Gambler Of The West," Strobridge, 20 x 30", 1906, comedic bad man **190.00**

TRANSPORTATION

"Automobiles," Bayard A Clement, 75 x 51", Bayard tears past viewer, aerodynamic wood speedboats background, c1909 .... **975.00**
"Fisk Tires, Easy To Ride. Safe To Buy," 16 x 22", c1900, Art Nouveau, woman on cycle **125.00**
"Peter's Union Pneumatic Tires," Ludwig Hohlwein, 28 x 36", sailor walks away from viewer toward cabriole and waving people, one hand a tube, other a tire, "The Lifesaver" at bottom, c1915 .... **675.00**
"Orix Bicycles," Fillipo Romoli, 28 x 39", beautiful blonde woman in green bathing suit, leaning against her Orix cycle, 1940 .... **300.00**
"Take The Union Pacific Railway To Denver and San Francisco," Omaha Republican Print, 9 x 24", two huge letters U and P with names of towns serviced, 1883 .... **135.00**

WORLD WAR I

"All Together. Enlist In The Navy," 40 x 29", sailors of all nations beckon standing beside each other **165.00**
"Be A US Marine," 29 x 40", marine image, no-nonsense pose, looming stars and stripes **375.00**
"First Call-I Need You In The Navy This Minute!" 10 x 11", Uncle Sam, full color, Navy recruiting use **275.00**
"I Want Your For The US Navy," 27 x 41", appealing blonde in Navy jacket looks seductively to viewer, 1917 .. **500.00**
"Learn To Ride-Learn To Handle A Military Motorcycle-Become A Crack Shot," 28 x 40", cavalryman at top in circle, surrounded by deep blue, red, and white design, motorcyclists and massive armored car at bottom **150.00**
"Men Wanted For The Army," 30 x 40", chromolithograph, fortress, gun crew, and sergeant preparing to fire toward distant sea **175.00**
"Over There! Skilled Workers On The Ground Behind The Lines In The Air Service," 30 x 38", three color lithograph, American Doughboy with hand in air beckoning to silhouette of biplane near hanger, 3" black and gray bottom border, rebuilt **375.00**
"You-Help My Boy Win The War, Buy A

Liberty Bond," 21 x 11", close-up of
mother in front young Doughboy . . . **100.00**

WORLD WAR II

"Buy War Bonds," N. C. Wyeth, 22 x
14", patriotic image, Uncle Sam holding billowing flag in one hand, pointing sternly toward unseen enemy with
other **150.00**
"Enlist In The Waves/Release A Man To
Fight At Sea," 42 x 28", recruiting im-
age **100.00**
"Every Child Needs A Good School
Lunch," 1944, 27 x 19", promoting nation's school lunch program, blue,
brown, green, yellow, black, photo im-
age **70.00**
"From Mine to Firing Line/More Produc-
tion," 40 x 28", stylized image, coal
dust proceeded from mine to artillery
shell casings **80.00**
"Japs In Alaska! Nazis In Egypt! Where
Next?" 38 x 25", red, white, and blue **60.00**
"Nurses Are Needed Now," 1944, 19 x
13", recruiting registered nurses,
Army Nurse Corps **60.00**
"Our Fighters/Deserve Our Best," 1942,
40 x 29", US Army Ordinance, defiant
soldier helping wounded buddy, flam-
ing and devastated landscape **85.00**
"Strong In The Strength Of The Lord,"
1942, 28 x 22", three strong arms lift
weapons in support of people's cause **75.00**
"The United Nations Fight For Freedom," 28 x 20", colorful image, flags
of Allied Nations surrounding Statue
of Liberty **125.00**

POT LIDS

History: Pot lids are the lids from pots or small
containers which originally held ointments, po-
mades, or soap. Although a complete set of pot
and lid is desirable to some collectors, lids are the
most collectible. The lids frequently were decorated with multicolored underglaze transfers of rural and domestic scenes, portraits, florals, and
landmarks.

The majority of the containers with lids were
made between 1845–1920 by F. & R. Pratt, Fenton, Staffordshire, England. In 1920, F. & R. Pratt
merged with Cauldon Ltd. Several lids were reissued by the firm using the original copper engraving plates. They were used for decoration and
never served as actual lids. Reissues by Kirkhams
Pottery, England, generally have two holes for
hanging and often are marked as reissues. Cauldon, Coalport, and Wedgwood were other firms
making reissues.

References: Susan and Al Bagdade, *Warman's
English & Continental Pottery & Porcelain, 1st Edi-
tion,* Warman Publishing Co., Inc., 1987; A. Ball,
*The Price Guide to Pot-Lids And Other Under-
glaze Multicolor Prints On Ware, Second Edition,*
Antique Collectors' Club, 1980; Ronald Dale, *The
Price Guide To Black and White Pot–Lids,* Antique
Collectors' Club; Barbara and Sonny Jackson,
American Pot Lids, published by authors, 1987.

Note: Sizes are given for actual pot lids; size of
any framing not included.

**Uncle Toby, Pratt, polychrome, 4¼" d,
framed, $100.00.**

Anchovy Paste, black label, white iron-
stone, 3½", marked "England" **25.00**
Arctic Expedition, multicolored, T J & J
Mayer, 3", rim chip **320.00**
Battle Of The Nile, Pratt, ebonized oak
frame, 4" **250.00**
Bloater Paste, black label, white iron-
stone, 4½" d, marked "England" . . . **25.00**
Deer Drinking, multicolored, 4" **25.00**
Dr. Johnson, multicolored, 4" **125.00**
Dublin Industrial Exhibition, multico-
lored, 3¾" **50.00**
Embarking For The East, multicolored,
Pratt, 4⅛", orig jar **100.00**
Farriers At Work, sgd "Wouvermann
Pinx," Pratt, 4¾" **65.00**
I See You My Boy, multicolored, 4½" . **20.00**
Lady Brushing Hair, multicolored, 3" . . **220.00**
Landing The Catch, Pratt type, 4⅛" . . **100.00**
Napirima, Trinidad, T J & J Mayer,
c1853, medium **165.00**
No By Heaven I Exclaimed..., multico-
lored, 4½" **175.00**
Peace, multicolored, 5½", rect, lobed
corners **25.00**
Persuasion, multicolored, 4⅛" **150.00**
Philadelphia Exhibition, 1876, multico-
lored, 4" **65.00**
Picnic On The Banks Of The River,
Gothic Ruins, Pratt, 4¾" **90.00**

Residence of Anne Hathaway, 4"	100.00
Residence of the Late Sir Robert Peel, Pratt	150.00
Tam O'Shanter and Souter Johnny, 4", framed	275.00
Transplanting Rice, 4⅛", framed	375.00
Trysting Place, The, small	165.00
Queen Victoria on Balcony, T J & J Mayer, large	265.00
View of Windsor Castle, Pratt, 6½" ..	150.00
Village Wedding, The, multicolored, Pratt, 4¼"	50.00
Ville De Strasbourg, Pratt type	75.00
Walmer Castle, Kent, Tatnell & Son, 4½"	200.00
Washington Crossing the Delaware, Pratt, orig jar	225.00
Wellington, T J & J Mayer, c1850, medium	100.00
Woman With Lamb, multicolored, William Wood, 4", orig jar	135.00

PRATT

PRATT
FENTON

PRATT WARE

History: The earliest Pratt earthenware was made in the late 18th century by William Pratt, Lane Delph, Staffordshire, England. In 1810–1818, Felix and Robert Pratt, William's sons, established their own firm, F. & R. Pratt, in Fenton in the Staffordshire district. Potters in Yorkshire, Liverpool, Sunderland, Tyneside, and Scotland copied the ware.

The wares consisted of relief molded jugs, commercial pots and tablewares with transfer decoration, commemorative pieces, and figure and animal groups.

Much of the early ware is unmarked. The mid-19th century wares bear several different marks in conjunction with the name Pratt, including "& Co."

References: Susan and Al Bagdade, *Warman's English & Continental Pottery & Porcelain, 1st Edition,* Warman Publishing Co., Inc., 1987; John and Griselda Lewis, *Pratt Ware 1780–1840,* Antique Collectors' Club, 1984.

Additional Listing: Pot Lids

Bowl, 9⅞" d, 3½" h, dark brown int., green transfer of Dr Syntax Drawing After Nature, polychrome	100.00
Compote, 56¼ x 9½", Spanish dancer scene, gold border	250.00
Cup Plate, 3⅛", white Dalmatian, black spots	65.00

Pitcher, molded form, green, yellow, orange, and brown enameled dec, 5⅞" h, $150.00.

Figure	
Four Seasons, 9½" h, matched set of four, late 18th C	1,700.00
Mother and her children, 8½" h, late 18th C	300.00
St. Mark, 9" h, late 18th C	275.00
Flask, 7¾", The Late Duke of Wellington on front, Rt Hon Sir Robt Peel on reverse, multicolored print, reserved on malachite ground, gilt borders, c1865	400.00
Jar, 7¾", molded oval panels of peacocks in landscapes, blue, brown, green, and ochre, lower section with vertical leaves, band of foliage on rim, c1790	600.00
Jug, 11", figural, Bacchus and Pan, sea lion handle, 1800	685.00
Mug, 4¼", multicolored scenes, maroon ground	135.00
Mustard Jar, dark blue hunt scene, tan ground	55.00
Pipe, 8", neatly coiled in concentric circles, 1800	1,100.00
Plaque, pierced for hanging	
5¾" d, relief of bird with insect perched on cherry branch, brown, ochre, and green, c1775	350.00
11" l, oval, relief of two recumbent lions, yellow ochre, brown, and green, blue border, c1800	570.00
Plate, 9", Haddon Hall, classical figure border	100.00
Tea Caddy, 4¾", relief bust of King George III, polychrome	175.00
Toby Jug, 10¾", Hearty Goodfellow, blue jacket, yellow-green vest, blue and yellow striped pants, blue and ochre sponged base and handle, stopper missing, slight glaze wear, c1770–80	1,500.00
Watch Holder, 10", figural, tall case clock, attended by two figures, early 19th C	700.00

PRINTS

History: Prints serve many purposes. They can be a reproduction of an artist's paintings, drawings, or designs. Prints themselves often are an original art form. Finally, prints can be developed for mass appeal as opposed to aesthetic statement. Much of the production of Currier & Ives fits this latter category. Currier & Ives concentrated on genre, urban, patriotic, and nostalgia scenes.

Prints are beginning to attract a wide following. This is partially because prices have not matched the rapid rise in oil and other paintings.

References: Frederic A. Conningham and Colin Simkin, *Currier & Ives Prints, Revised Edition*, Crown Publishers, Inc., 1970; Michael Ivankovich, *A Price Guide to Wallace Nutting Pictures*, Cheetah Prints, 1984; Denis C. Jackson, *The Price & Identification Guide to J. C. Leyendecker & F. X. Leyendecker*, published by author, 1983; Carl F. Luckey, *Collector Prints Old and New*, Books Americana, 1982; Craig McClain, *Currier & Ives: An Illustrated Value Guide,* Wallace-Homestead, 1987; Wallace Nutting, *The Wallace Nutting Expansible Catalog* (reprint of 1915 catalog), Diamond Press, 1987; Ruth M. Pollard, *The Official Price Guide To Collector Prints, 7th Edition,* House Of Collectibles, 1986.

Collectors' Clubs: American Historical Print Collectors Society, Inc., 25 West 43rd St., Suite 711, New York, NY 10036. *Imprint*; Prang-Mark Society, Century House, Old Irelandville, Watkins Glen, NY 14891.

Reproduction Alert: Reproductions are a problem, especially Currier & Ives prints. Check the dimensions before buying any print.

Allen, James, Spider Boy, etching, sgd, fine impression, hinged to mat in top corners, 11 x 8½" **1,500.00**
Audubon, James
  Belted King Fisher, aquatint and engraving, fine impression, minor discoloration, small edge losses, minor water stains, 25⅞ x 20¾" . . . **3,200.00**
  White Headed Pigeon, No. 36, elephant folio, engraved, printed, and colored by R Havell, London, 1833, full margins **1,700.00**
Bacon, Peggy
  Highbrows Flint 274, litho, sgd, dated, and titled, 10 x 7¾", 1952 . . . . . . **600.00**
  Priceless Find, The, litho, sgd and titled, hinged to mat in top corners, 8 x 6", 1943 . . . . **550.00**
Beham, Hans Sebald, Job and His Comforters B 16, etching, 1547, fine impression, some discoloration and fading, trimmed margins, hinged to mat, 2¾ x 4" **800.00**
Benson, Frank W.
  Herons at Rest, etching, sgd, fine

impression, marked "Trial Proof A– 1," hinged to mat, 11⅞ x 6¾" . . . **900.00**
Old Tom, etching, sgd, edition of 150, 1926, fine impression, minor discoloration, 14¾ x 8¾", framed . . . **800.00**
Benton, Thomas Hart
  Cows in Pasture, litho, sgd, 1952, fine impression, hinge remnants along top edge, 11 x 14" **650.00**
  Letter from Overseas, litho, sgd, edition of 250, 1943, fine impression, 9¾ x 13", framed **1,000.00**
Birch, Thomas
  Bethlehem, Pennsylvania, hand colored aquatint, fine impression, some discoloration, fading, and soiling, hinged to mat, 12 x 18¾" . **475.00**
  View of the Water Gap and Columbia Glass Works, River Delaware, fine impression, heavily soiled, uneven margins, hinged to mat, 12¾ x 19½" **250.00**
Bishop, Isabelle, Idle Conversation, etching, sgd and titled, fine impression, minor discoloration, 5 x 5⅞", framed **2,100.00**
Bohrod, Aaron, Pennsylvania Highway, litho, sgd, fine impression, minor discoloration, hinged to mat in top corners, 9¼ x 13½" **200.00**
Bone, Muirhead, Stockholm, etching and drypoint, sgd, fine impression, 9 x 11¼", framed **600.00**
Braque, Georges
  Nature Morte, color litho, minor discoloration, 10½ x 13½", framed . . **300.00**
  Oiseau, Lune et Soleil, aquatint, sgd and numbered 12/70, 1960, fine impression, 8¾ x 5½", framed . . . **500.00**
Buffet, Bernard
  Fish, color litho, 1953, numbered 143/ 220, small split in margin on left side, minor soiling, 12½ x 20½" . . **1,800.00**
  Rearing Horse, color litho, sgd and numbered 33/120, 27 x 18" **800.00**
Calder, Alexander
  Bird's Nest, color etching, sgd and numbered 12/90, fine impression, 10⅝ x 14½", framed **450.00**
  Moon & Star, color litho, sgd and numbered 37/90, 23¾ x 35", framed **500.00**
Cassat, Mary, Blanche without her Hat, engraving, sgd in pencil, fine impression, some discoloration and soiling, laid down and sandwiched between mat, scattered creases and foxing, framed **9,500.00**
Catlin, George
  Ball–Play Dance, hand colored litho, published by Day and Haghe, London, fine impression, diagonal tear

across upper left quadrant, some fading and discoloration, 14¼ x 18¼", framed **200.00**

Bison–Dance of the Mandan Indians, hand colored litho, published by Day and Haghe, London, good impression, some fading and discoloration, 14 x 18¼", framed . . . **2,000.00**

Buffalo Hunt, Chase, hand colored litho, published by Day and Haghe, London, good impression, some fading and discoloration, 12¾ x 18¼", framed **1,400.00**

Buffalo Hunt, Chasing Back, hand colored litho, published by Day and Haghe, London, good impression, some fading and discoloration, 12¾ x 18¼", framed **900.00**

Cezanne, Paul, The Bathers, litho, small plate, trial proof printed in black, scattered rippling and creasing, scotched taped to mat on sides, minor soiling, 9¼ x 12¼", framed **1,900.00**

Chagall, Marc, Parrot and King, etching, sgd and numbered 96, some discoloration and mat burn, 11½ x 9⅛", framed **550.00**

Crawford, Ralston, Overseas Highway, color litho, edition of 25, sgd, titled, and numbered 17/25, 1940, fine impression, minor fading and discoloration, scattered light foxing, lower left corner missing, hinge remnants in other three corners, hinged to mat in top corners, 10 x 15⅞", framed **35,000.00**

Currier & Ives
American Country Life, Pleasures of Winter, large folio, good margins, paper toned, minor foxing **1,200.00**

American Homestead, Winter, Spring, Summer, and Autumn, color litho, browned and faded, scattered creasing and paper tears, 11½ x 15¾", framed, set of 4 . . . . **500.00**

Harvesting, The Last Load, small folio, overall toning, lightly foxed, tear in upper margin, small scuff left upper margin, orig Empire frame . . . **225.00**

New England Winter Scene, hand colored litho, fine impression, scattered foxing, 16⅝ x 23½", framed **7,500.00**

Noah's Ark, small folio, good margins, minor foxing, orig Empire mahogany frame **250.00**

Leaders, The, hand colored litho, some discoloration and fading, 18 x 27½", framed **1,000.00**

Eby, Kerr
Night March, litho, sgd, fine impression, some soiling, creasing, losses in margins, hinged to mat at top corners, 15¾ x 20¼" **400.00**

No. 1 Wall Street, etching, sgd, titled and inscribed "Ed. 90," fine impression, hinged to mat at top, 16 x 10⅜" **350.00**

Fiene, Ernest, New York Skyline, litho, sgd, titled, dated '32, numbered 6/40, fine impression, hinge remnants on left and right side, minor soiling in margins, hinged to mat in top corners, 13 x 17¼" **550.00**

Freeman, Mark, 2nd Avenue El, litho, sgd, titled, dated "33," inscribed "Ed 75," fine impression, hinged to mat at top corners, 10¼ x 14¼" **850.00**

Gardiner, Eliza
Young Woman with Poppies, color woodcut, sgd, fine impression, old glue traces throughout margins, hinge remnants on reverse, taped to mat in top corners, 7⅞ x 9⅞" . . **650.00**

Young Yachtsman, color woodcut, sgd, fine impression, rag paper, uneven margins, hinged to mat at top, 7 x 9¾" **700.00**

Geerlings, Gerald, Black Magic, etching and aquatint, sgd and titled, 1929, fine impression, stain in margin, minor creases in corners, 11⅝ x 6⅝" . **1,800.00**

Gorsline, Douglas, Express Stop, etching, sgd, 1948, fine impression, hinged to mat in top corners, 6¼ x 5¾" **400.00**

Gropper, William, The Defense, litho, green, black, and white, sgd, fine impression, 14 x 17¾", framed **225.00**

Haden, Seymour, Towing Path, etching and drypoint, sgd, fine impression, 5½ x 8½", framed **450.00**

Hartley, Marsden, Pears in a Basket, litho, sgd and dated 1923, fine impression, some rippling, 13¾ x 17⅞", framed **2,100.00**

Hassam, Childe
Chimneys, Portsmouth, New Hampshire, etching, sgd with monogram and inscribed "imp," 1915, fine impression, slight rippling, 5 x 8⅛", framed **1,300.00**

Lion Gardner House, etching, sgd in pencil with monogram and "imp," 1920, pin holes in uneven margins, minor discoloration, hinged to mat along top edge, 9¾ x 14⅛", framed **14,000.00**

Oak and Old House in Springs, etching, sgd in pencil with monogram and "imp", 1931, framed **2,000.00**

Porte St. Martin, Paris, etching, sgd with monogram and inscribed "imp," c1898, fine impression, slight rippling, 11 x 7⅜", framed . . **3,200.00**

Icart, Louis
Casanova, 1928, color etching and

drypoint, cream wove paper, sgd in pencil, artist's blindstamp, titled in another hand, margins slightly trimmed, 21 x 14", framed **1,760.00**

Cinderella, Cendrille, 1927, color etching and drypoint, cream wove paper, sgd in pencil, artist's blindstamp, margins, faint traces of surface soiling, 14¾ x 18½", framed . **1,775.00**

Icart, Louis, Love's Blossom, unframed, $1,750.00.

Flower Seller, Marchande De Fleurs, c1928, color etching and drypoint, cream wove paper, sgd in pencil, artist's blindstamp, margins, small tear, old tape on verso, faint traces of foxing in margins, 18½ x 14¼" . **1,650.00**

Human Grenade, La Grenade, c1917, color etching and drypoint, Japan paper, sgd in pencil and annotated epreuve d'artiste, numbered, margins, 17 x 21", framed . **2475.00**

Hydrangeas, Le Hortensias, 1929, color etching and drypoint, cream wove paper, sgd in pencil, artist's blindstamp, full margins, 16½ x 20½", framed **2,000.00**

Shezeazade, c1927, color etching and drypoint, printed on Rives B. F. K. paper, sgd in pencil, artist's blindstamp, full sheet, 13½ x 20¼", framed **3,000.00**

The Broken Jug, Cruche Cassee, c1924, etching and drypoint, printed on Rives B. F. K. paper, sgd in pencil, full sheet, 17¼ x 12½", framed **1,100.00**

Waiting, Attente, 1927, color etching and drypoint, cream wove paper, sgd in pencil and annotated epreuve d'artiste, artist's blindstamp, margins slightly trimmed, 14¾ x 19¼", framed **1,650.00**

Lee, Doris

Afternoon Train, litho, sgd, fine impression, 9½ x 11¾", framed .. **100.00**

Vegetable Garden, litho, sgd, some mat burn, discoloration, laid down on cardboard, 8¾ x 11¾", framed **85.00**

Leighton, Clare, Breadline, New York, litho, sgd, titled, and numbered 77/100, fine impression, hinged to mat in top corners, 11¾ x 7⅞" **650.00**

Lindenmuth, Tod, Moonlight on Cape Cod, color linoleum cut, sgd and titled, fine impression, 9⅛ x 7", framed **1,800.00**

Lozowick, Louis

First Avenue Market, litho, sgd, 1935, fine impression, two small tears in left margin extending into image, 11¾ x 8¾" **1,400.00**

Under the El, litho, sgd and dated 1929, fine impression, 7½ x 11⅛", framed **9,000.00**

Lucioni, Luigi

Pomfret Church, etching, sgd, fine impression, minor discoloration, 7¾ x 10¼", framed **125.00**

Spreading Maple, The, etching, sgd, fine impression, some mat burn and discoloration, laid down on cardboard, 10¾ x 15½", framed .. **150.00**

Vermont Pastoral, etching, sgd, fine impression, 7¼ x 12½", framed .. **100.00**

Markham, Kyra, Bleecker St. Fire Hydrant, litho, sgd, titled, dated '42, inscribed "Ed. 25," fine impression, hinged to mat in top corners, 9¾ x 10½" **1,700.00**

Marini, Marina, Le Chevalier Noir, color litho, sgd and numbered 11/50, fine impression, slight rippling, 23 x 18½", framed **550.00**

Marsh, Reginald, Merry–Go–Round, etching, sgd and numbered 29, fine impression, 6⅞ x 9⅞", framed **3,400.00**

Miro, Joan, Adam and Eve, litho, sgd and numbered 2/5, dated 1944, some discoloration, 27 x 19¾", framed ... **7,500.00**

Moore, Henry, Three Sheep, color litho, sgd and numbered 36/50, 8½ x 10", framed **850.00**

Nutting, Wallace, framed, matted, 8 x 10"

Chimney Corner, The **90.00**

New England Uplands **50.00**

Wayside Inn Corner **72.00**

Picasso, Pablo

Head of a Bacchus, aquatint, sgd and numbered 231/300, fine impression, 11¾ x 9¾", framed **2,900.00**

Le Vieux Roi, color linocut, sgd and numbered 7/160, 1963, 26⅕ x 20¾", framed **12,000.00**

Vieux Roi, litho, edition of 1,000,

printed signature, minor soiling, good condition, 1959, 25¼ x 19¼" **850.00**

Rauschenberg, Robert, Artist's Rights Today, color litho, sgd, numbered 19/125, dated '76, good condition, 30 x 22" **1,200.00**

Renoir, Auguste, Claude Renoir Stella 39, litho, second state, edition of 1,000, scattered minor creases, 8½ x 7½", framed **2,100.00**

Riggs, Robert, On The Ropes, litho, sgd and titled, fine impression, 14⅞ x 19⅞", framed **2,900.00**

Rosenquist, James, Tide, color silkscreen, sgd, numbered 74/125, dated 1976, inscribed "for Artists," good condition, 30 x 22" **2,000.00**

Rouault, Georges
Ballerinas, aquatint printed in colors, initialed and dated 1934 in plate, fine impression, 12 x 8", framed .. **6,000.00**
Circus Clowns, color litho, sgd in the plate, good condition, hinge remnants in top corners, 22¾ x 17⅞" **3,250.00**

Rungius, Carl, King of the Mountain, etching and drypoint, sgd, fine impression, 7⅞ x 10⅝", framed **1,600.00**

Shokler, Harry, Coney Island, color serigraph, sgd in plate, hinged to mat at top corners, 12½ x 16" **500.00**

Sloan, Joan, Night Windows, etching, sgd, titled and inscribed "100 Proofs," 1910, fine impression, pin holes on sides, minor discoloration and soiling, hinged along top edge, framed **6,000.00**

Spruance, Benton, The Homecoming, litho, edition of 30, sgd by his wife, bearing estate stamp, titled, fine impression, 1935, 9 x 13⅞" **1,100.00**

Toulouse–Lautrec, Henri de, Zamboula–Polka, litho, first state before lettering, 9½ x 8½", framed **2,100.00**

Warhol, Andy
Campbell's Soup Can Shopping Bag, silkscreen, 1964, some discoloration and creasing, framed **4,000.00**
Happy Bug Day, offset litho, hand coloring, sgd and titled, heavy creasing, minor soiling, split in upper right corner, 14 x 9⅜", framed ... **1,200.00**

Wengenroth, Stow
Elms, litho, sgd, fine impression, good condition **225.00**
Fog Bell, litho, sgd, fine impression, good condition, 10 x 15¾" **1,100.00**

Wesselman, Tom, The Smoker, color litho, sgd and numbered 7/175, fine condition, 16 x 16" **1,600.00**

Whistler, James Abbott McNeill, Little Evelyn, litho, 1896, fine impression, some discoloration, crease in upper

right quadrant of image, hinged to mat in top corners, scattered foxing . **150.00**

Weinrich, Agnes, Grazing Cattle, color wood block, sgd in image and on mat, later state, fine impression, good condition, 10 x 10½", framed **3,000.00**

Wood, Grant
Family Doctor, litho, sgd and titled, edition of 300, 1940, hinged to mat at top corners, 10 x 11¾", framed **3,000.00**
February, litho, sgd, edition of 250, 1941, fine impression, full margins, 8⅞ x 11¾", framed **4,000.00**
January, litho, sgd, edition of 250, 1939, fine impression, discoloration, laid down on cardboard, 8⅞ x 11¾" **1,000.00**
Seed Time and Harvest, litho, sgd, edition of 250, 1937, fine impression, full margins, 7½ x 12½", framed **1,900.00**

PRINTS—JAPANESE

History: Buying Japanese woodblock prints requires attention to detail and skilled knowledge of the subject. The quality of the impression (good, moderate, or weak), the color, and condition are critical. Various states and strikes of the same print cause the price to fluctuate. Knowing the proper publisher and censor's seals are helpful in identifying an original print.

Most prints were recopied and issued in popular versions. These represent the vast majority of the prints found in the marketplace. These popular versions should be viewed solely as decorative since they have little value.

A novice buyer should seek expert advice before buying. Talk with a specialized dealer, museum curator, or auction division head.

The listings below concentrate on details to show the depth of data needed for adequate pricing. Condition and impression are good, unless indicated otherwise.

O = Oban, 10 x 15"	C = Chuban,
t = tat-e, large in width	7 x 10"
	H = Hosoban,
y = yoke-e, large in length	5½ x 13"
	T = Triptyck

Reference: Sandra Andacht, *Oriental Antiques & Art: An Identification And Value Guide,* Wallace-Homestead, 1987.

Buncho, courtesan *Nishikigi* of the Kanaya standing before a *tokonoma* with a spray of plum blossoms in her hand, scroll on wall sgd *Ippitsusai* and seal *Mori uji*, minor fading, one set of three

entitled *Wrestling Match or Battle of
Flowers,* H **3,500.00**

Eisen

Imayo jibin sankumimai, high ranking
courtesan, sgd *Keisai Eisen-ga,*
with *kiwame* and publisher's seals,
fair impression and color, center
crease, fair state **175.00**

Ukiyo nijuyonko series, Yang Hsiang
shown teasing cat, sgd *Keisai Eisen-ga,* with *kiwame* and publisher's seal, good impression, slight
wrinkling, Ot **725.00**

Eizan, Kakemono-E, humorous tiger
emerging from behing large stalk of
bamboo, sgd *Kikugama Eizan hitsu,*
good impression, fair color, good condition **375.00**

Gakutei, seated geisha playing the
biwa, from *Hanazo bantsuki* series,
sgd *Gakutei,* color slightly faded, C . **950.00**

Hausi, 15¼ x 10⅛", $300.00.

Harunobo, courtesan showing the neck
of her kamoro before a screen dec
with farmers harvesting rice, entitled
Jin, Virtue, from *The Five Cardinal
Virtues* series, sgd *Suzuki Harunobo
ga,* Ct **7,750.00**

Hiroshige

Fishing boats at Tsuikudajima in
Buyp Province, *Shokoku meisho*
series, "Famous Places in Various
Provinces," sgd *Hiroshiga ga,* published by Dansendo, *unchima-e*
center fold, margins slightly soiled,
backed **5,750.00**

Kanagawa-Dai no tei, hilltop view,
from *Tokaido Gojusan-tsugi* series,

sgd *Hiroshige-ga,* red gourd
shaped seal with *kiwame* and *Tak-
enouchi* seals, fair impression,
good color, backed, left margin
trimmed, Oy **125.00**

Mishima asagiri, "Morning Mist,
Mishima," from *Toto meisho* series,
"Famous Places of the Eastern
Capital," sgd *Hiroshege ga,* with
Hoseido/Senkakudo, publisher's
seals, margins trimmed, slightly
rubbed, and soiled, Oy **675.00**

Hiroshige II, Chuban Album, complete
set of series *Edo meisho yonju hak-
kei/Forty-eight famous Sights of Edo,*
each sgd *Hiroshige-ga,* some margins with *aratame/negetsu* (c1860)
and publisher *Tsuta-ya Kichizo* seals,
good states, laid down, Ct **1,350.00**

Hokuji, *omocha-e* with inset *okubi-e*
portrait of *Ichimura Kakitsu* next to
eight scappered depictions of various
hair styles and hats, individual label
cartouches, sgd *Shunkosai Hokushu-
ga* with artist, carver, and publisher
Toshijura-ya Shinbei seals, fair
impression, Ot **325.00**

Hokusai

Aoyama enza matsu, "The cushion
pine at Aoyama," from *Fugaku sanjurokkei* series, "Thirty-six views of
Mt Fuji," sgd *Hokusai Iitsui hitsu,*
slightly faded, center fold, Oy ... **2,650.00**

Sinsho Suwa-ko, "Lake Suma in
Shinano Province," from *Fugaku
sanjurokkei* series, "Thirty-six
views of Mt Fuji," sgd *Zen Hokusai
Iitsui hitsu,* publisher's seal *Eijudo,*
Oy **4,250.00**

Uki-e depicting the Oji Inari Shrine,
sgd *Hokusai ga,* slightly faded and
trimmed, Oy **300.00**

Kawase Hasui

*Ebisu Harbor, Sado Island in Winter,
Tabi miyage dinishi* series, sgd
Hasui, seated *kawase,* dated
Taishi 10 (1921), *Watanabe* pub-
lisher's seal, Oy **1,200.00**

*Okayamajo no Asahi/Dawn at Okay-
ama Castle,* dated Showa 30
(1955), misty view of castle, sgd
Hasui, circular *Watanabe Shosa-
buro* seal, good impression, color,
and state, Ot **350.00**

Kikumaro, courtesan seated by hibachi,
surrounded by female attandants,
blossoming prunus and sparrow, sgd
Kikumaro hitsu, fair impression, poor
color, stained, Ot **275.00**

Kunisada

Kakemono-e, high ranging courtesan
walking in elaborate kimono, sgd

Kochoro Kunisada hitsu, with ara-tame/negetsu seal, c1865, good impression, fair color, faded, toned, trimmed, backed 225.00

Three bijin walking with long sword and flute under flowering cherry trees at night, sgd Kochoro/Ichiyo-sai Toyokuni ga, two nanushi and publisher seals, good impression, toned, backed Ot 200.00

Kotondo, Beauty in sudden shower, sgd Genjin ga,, dated Showa 4 (1929), numbered 84/200, published by Sakai-Kawaguchi, large Ot 1,000.00

Kuniyoshi

Giyu hakken-den series, depicting In-yuama Dosetsu, sgd Ichiyasi Ku-niyoshi-ga, two naushi and pub-lisher seals, fair impression and color, faded, fair state, Ot 100.00

Tanuki print showing four drunken badgers dancing and singing, illus text passage, sgd Ichiyusai Kuni-yoshi-giga, and one nanushi and anonymous publisher's seal, fair impression and color, slightly faded, Ot 150.00

Oda Kazuma, entitled Matsue Ohashi/The Great Bridge of Mat-sue, group of figures crossing bridge in snow storm, sgd Kazuma hitsu, red artist's seal, right margin with title and dated Taisho 13 (1924), very good impression and color, Oy 850.00

Tori Kyonagi, from series Hinagata wakana no hatsumoyo, sgd Kiyonaga ga, fair impression and color, faded, rough margins, Ot 750.00

Toyokuni I, three courtesans and their attendants strolling on busy street, sgd Toyokuni-ga, kiwame and Iwato-ya Kisaburo publisher's seal, fair impression, pool color, faded, fair state, Ot 400.00

Utamaro, one courtesan standing over another in front, sgd Utamaro hitsu, with kiwame, negetsu, (1806) and publisher's seals, fair impression, poor color, faded, wrinkled, Ot 300.00

Utamaro II, Beauty, half length, holding up her baby who plays with ball, sgd Utamaro hitsu, kiwame seal, publish-er's seal Iwatoya Kisaburo, and cen-sor's seal of Kisabura, Ot 2,000.00

Yakamura Koko (Toyonari), three quar-ter view of actor Matsumoto Koshiro as Sekibei, sgd Koka-ga, publisher's seal and blind printed date Taisho 8 (1919), good impression and color, Ot 900.00

Yoshikawa Kampo, actor Nakamura Ganjiro as Kamiya Jihei (c1922), sgd,

publisher Sato Shotaro, reverse with additional publisher cartouche, edi-tion 51/200, good impression and color, foxed, slightly toned, Ot 375.00

Yoshitoshi

Diptych Set, from series Shinsen Azuma Nishiki-e/Newly Selected Edo Color Prints, entitled Tamiya Botaro no Hanashi/the Story of Ta-miya Botaro, sgd Yoshitoshi, one seal reading Taiso, left margin dated Meiji 19 (1886) and publisher Tsunanshima Kamekichi car-touche, good impression and colors, margins partially trimmed, Ot 650.00

Triptych Set, entitled Taiheiki 'Sen-gatake' honjun no zu, showing sa-murai Takuma Morimasa bound in ropes held by warriors, sgd Ikahai-sai Yoshitoshi hutsu with aratame/negetsu (c1867) and publisher Tsunajima Kamekuchi seals, fair impression and color, fair state, Ot 300.00

PURPLE SLAG (MARBLE GLASS)

History: Challinor, Taylor & Co., Tarantum, Pennsylvania, c1870s–80s, was the largest pro-ducer of purple slag in the United States. Since the quality of pieces varies considerably, there is no doubt other American firms made it as well.

Purple slag also was made in England. English pieces are marked with British Registry marks.

Other color combinations, such as blue, green, or orange, were made, but are rarely found.

Additional Listings: Greentown Glass (choco-late slag) and Pink Slag.

Reproduction Alert: Purple slag has been heavily reproduced over the years and still is re-produced at present.

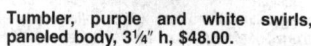

Tumbler, purple and white swirls, paneled body, 3¼″ h, $48.00.

Bowl, 10¾", scalloped, hp orange and
gold flowers **50.00**
Cake Stand, Flute **75.00**
Celery Tray, 12 x 4⅛ x 2½" h, rowboat
shape, Daisy Block **135.00**
Compote, 4½", crimped top **65.00**
Creamer, Flower and Panel **85.00**
Cruet, 7", Imperial Glass **45.00**
Goblet, Flute **40.00**
Match Holder, Daisy and Button **40.00**
Mug, rabbit **65.00**
Plate, 10½", closed lattice edge **100.00**
Salt, 2½ x 4" **50.00**
Spooner, Scroll with Acanthus **65.00**
Sugar, cov, Flute **200.00**
Tumbler, 3¼", Flute **48.00**

Quezal

QUEZAL

History: The Quezal Art Glass Decorating Company, named for the "quetzal," a bird with brilliant colored feathers, was organized in 1901 in Brooklyn, New York, by two disgruntled Tiffany workers, Martin Bach and Thomas Johnson. They soon hired two more Tiffany workers, Percy Britton and William Wiedebine.

The first products, unmarked, were exact Tiffany imitations. In 1902 the "Quezal" trademark was first used. Quezal pieces differ from Tiffany pieces in that they are more defined and the decorations more visible and brightly colored. No new techniques came from Quezal.

Johnson left in 1905. T. Conrad Vahlsing, Bach's son–in–law, joined the firm in 1918, but left with Paul Frank in 1920 to form Lustre Art Glass Company which copied Quezal pieces. Martin Bach died in 1924; and, by 1925 Quezal ceased operations.

Wares are signed "Quezal" on the base of vases and bowls and rims of shades. The acid-etched or engraved letters vary in size and may be found in amber, black, or gold. A printed label of a quetzal bird was used briefly in 1907.

Bowl, 12", peacock blue, hammered silver base, marked "Oscar B Bach,
NY" **465.00**
Candlesticks, 7¾", blue irid, sgd, pr . . **550.00**
Cruet, white opal ground, green pulled
feather design, clear yellow stopper
and applied handle **2,300.00**
Lamp Shade, gold ribbed, sgd, matched
set of 3 . . . . **225.00**
Perfume Bottle, 5", flattened teardrop
shape, bulbous stopper, Gorham SS
monogrammed foliate mounts **585.00**
Salt, 2¾", irid gold, ribbed **175.00**

Cruet, pulled green feather, white opalescent ground, clear yellow handle and stopper, 6½" h, $2,300.00.

Toothpick, 2¼", melon ribbed, pinched
sides, irid blue, green, purple, and
gold, sgd **185.00**
Vase
4¼", slender body, circular ft, folded
back surface, gold irid, green and
gold threads, sgd "Quezal 167" . . **1,000.00**
6⅜", squatty, irid gold neck, white
body, irid gold feather pulled dec,
green zigzag band around shoulder, sgd "Quezal 861" **900.00**
6⅝", ivory and green, platinum pulled
feather design, sgd "Quezal 739" . **1,100.00**
6⅞", irid blue, abstract gold threading,
opaque white hearts, sgd **500.00**
Wall Sconce, 14", irid floriform shade,
white ground, gold pulled feather design, gold int., molded brass sconce,
foliage and mirror dec, sgd at base of
shade **175.00**

QUILTS

History: Quilts have been passed down as family heirlooms for many generations. Each is an individual expression. The same pattern may have hundreds of variations in both color and design.

The advent of the sewing machine increased, not decreased the number of quilts which were made. Quilts still are being sewn today.

The key considerations for price are age, condition, aesthetic beauty, and design. Prices are now at a level position. The exception is the very finest examples which continue to bring record prices.

References: American Quilter's Society, *Gallery of American Quilts, 1849–1988,* Collector Books, 1988; Cathy Florence, *Collecting Quilts: Investments In America's Heritage,* Collector Books, 1985; William C. Ketchum, Jr., *The Knopf Collec-*

tors' Guides to American Antiques: Quilts, Alfred A. Knopf, Inc., 1982; Lisa Turner Oshins, *Quilt Collections: A Directory For The United States And Canada,* Acropolis Books, Ltd., 1987; Rachel and Kenneth Pellman, *The World of Amish Quilts,* Good Books, 1984; Schnuppe von Gwinner, *The History of the Patchwork Quilt,* Schiffer Publishing Ltd, 1988.

Collectors' Club: The American Quilter's Society, P.O. Box 3290, Paducah, KY 42002.

Periodical: Quilter's Newsletter Magazines, Box 394, Wheat Ridge, CO 80033.

Album, pieced, calico, red and various shades of yellow, blue field, each white center sq with pen and ink signature and date 1858, white homespun backing, minor age stains, 76 x 89" **500.00**

Amish

Appliqued, crib, cotton, four geometric cross motifs in pale gray, black ground, pale gray primary border, subsidiary large black border, pale gray edge, chain, foliate vine, and vertical bar quilting, Ohio, c1930, 45 x 37" **350.00**

Pieced, cotton, central large six pointed star, lavender and pale lavender, black ground, lavender and black borders, concentric feathered wreath, leaf, potted plant, and chain quilting, Lancaster County, PA, late 19th C, 77 x 84" **3,850.00**

Bear Paw, pieced, cotton, white geometric and printed orange and blue squares, chintz floral patterned border with blue piping, diagonal bar quilting, 85 x 76" **1,150.00**

Blossom, Bud, and Berry pattern, pieced and appliqued, cotton, red, bright green, and yellow, white cotton field, feather wreath, diamond, and outline quilting, PA, 19th C, 80 x 88" **900.00**

Carolina Lily, applique, red and blue calico, white field, machine applique, hand quilted, minor stains, 73 x 73" . **350.00**

Crazy, pieced, random patches of velvet, satin, cotton, and calico, shades of yellow, blue, green, brown, red, purple, white, and black, fifty-six squares joined by turkeywork stitching, embroidered floral sprigs, flowerheads, and foliage, brown border, Victorian, 75 x 69" **425.00**

Double Irish Chain, pink and green, white field, c1920 .... **185.00**

Feathered Star, pieced olive green and yellow calico, white cotton field, tulips, hearts, wreaths, and meandering vines quilting, American, 19th C, 96" sq **2,650.00**

Grandma's Fan, multicolored prints, 1930 .... **170.00**

Honeycomb Star, patchwork, 96" sq, American, 19th C **950.00**

Monkey Wrench, pieced, cotton, yellow stylized pinwheel motif, white ground, square, stylized floral sprig and berry, and triangular quilting, yellow edge, Missouri, 1930, 78 X 59" **675.00**

Ocean Waves, pieced, multicolored triangular calico patches, printed red and white borders, Missouri, early 20th C **500.00**

Optical Star, pieced, white, yellow, and purple, lavender machine sewn binding, 72 x 82" **200.00**

Pinwheel, applique, four large pinwheels and vining border, red and yellow-green, 96 x 96" **600.00**

Postage Stamp, pieced, cotton and calico, green, black, blue, brown, and gray diamond patches, diamond quilting, Iowa, third quarter 19th C, 81 x 67" **850.00**

Princess Feather, pieced and appliqued, bright green and orange patches, white field, wreath, flowerhead, and blossom quilting, swag leaf border, PA, 19th C, 84" sq **1,500.00**

Rainbow, pieced cotton, 86 x 84", $950.00.

Schoolhouse, pieced, cotton, four rows of pink schoolhouse squares, white trim, blue band borders, white intersecting squares, concentric semi-circle quilting, minor wear, late 19th C, 65 x 74" **725.00**

Star Flower, applique, vining floral border, red, blue, and goldenrod, red and goldenrod puffed berries and circles,

machine stitched vine on border, red
binding very worn, 68 x 78″ **500.00**
Star Medallion, pieced, twelve stars in
solid green and goldenrod, pink calico, white field, feather wreath and
meandering vine quilting, minor wear,
84 x 85″ **475.00**
Tree of Life, pieced, cotton, five rows of
four green, brown, and white stylized
diagonal tree motifs within red bar
borders, green intersection squares,
triangular, bar, and band quilting, minor fading and patches, c1875, 81 x
69″ **500.00**
Wrench, pieced, multicolored prints,
pink calico field, 64 x 72″ **250.00**

QUIMPER

History: Quimper faience, dating back to the
17th century, is named for Quimper, a French town
where numerous potteries were located. Several
mergers resulted in the evolution of two major
houses—the Jules Henriot and Hubaudiébre–
Bousquet factories.

The peasant design first appeared in the 1860s,
and many variations exist. Florals and geometrics,
equally popular, also were produced in large quantities. During the 1920s the Hubaudiébre–Bousquet factory introduced the Odetta line which utilized a stone body and Art Deco decorations.

The two major houses merged in 1968, each
retaining its individual characteristics and marks.
The concern suffered from labor problems in the
1980s and recently was purchased by an American group.

Marks: The HR and HR Quimper marks are
found on Henriot pieces prior to 1922. The HenRoit
Quimper mark was used after 1922. The HB mark
covers a long span of time. The addition of numbers or dots and dashes refers to inventory numbers and are found on later pieces. Most marks
are in blue or black. Pieces ordered by department
stores, such as Macy's and Carson Pirie Scott,
carry the store mark along with the factory mark,
making them less desirable to collectors. A comprehensive list of marks is found in Bondhus's
book.

References: Susan and Al Bagdade, *Warman's
English & Continental Pottery & Porcelain, 1st Edi-
tion,* Warman Publishing Co., Inc., 1987; Sandra
V. Bondhus, *Quimper Pottery: A French Folk Art
Faience,* published by author, 1981; Millicent Mali,
Quimper Faience, Airon, Inc., 1979; Marjatta Ta-

buret, *La Faience de Quimper,* Editions Sous le
Vent, 1979, French text.

Museums: Musee des Faiences de Quimper,
Quimper, France; Victoria and Albert Museum,
French Ceramic Dept., London, England.

Advisors: Susan and Al Bagdade.

Ashtray, 4½″ d, center with blue painted
male peasant dressed as fisherman,
"Normandie" below, white ground,
marked "Henriot Quimper France" . **38.50**
Basket, 8½″ l, 6″ h, gold basketweave
pattern, male peasant on int., brown
handle, HB Quimper mark **275.00**
Bell, 4⅞″ h, figural male peasant, blue
jacket, black vest, brown striped shirt,
marked "Henriot Quimper France,"
repaired **72.00**
Bowl
9″ d, light green and rose geometric
pattern, marked "Henriot Quimper
France" **265.00**
12″ d, male peasant on int., blue,
gold, violet banded border, pierced
for hanging, marked "HB Quimper"
inside bowl **435.00**
Box, 3¼″ l, 3″ w, male figure on lid,
marked "Henriot Quimper France" . **110.00**
Butter Dish, 8″ l, 6″ w, bagpipe shape,
woman with distaff on cov, decor
riche, marked "Henriot Quimper" . . **525.00**
Cigarette Holder, 3½″ l, 2½″ h, camel
on each side, scalloped base, marked
"Henriot Quimper France" **235.00**
Cup and Saucer
Blue and orange typical floral designs, marked "Henriot Quimper
France" **135.00**
Blue, green, pink, and orange–yellow,
panels of seated male and female
peasants on cup with cross hatching panels, hexagonal shape,
marked "Henriot Quimper France" **190.00**
Red, blue, and green, overall floral
designs, marked "Henriot Quimper
France" **65.00**
Dish, 14″ handle to handle, 3″ h, scalloped rim, green and gold handles,
multicolored dancing couple, Brittany
coat–of–arms above, decor riche bor-
ders, HR Quimper mark **625.00**
Egg Set, six floral pattern cups, 9½″ d
platter with seated peasant woman
with basket, Henriot Quimper mark . **525.00**
Figure
7″ h, St. Anne and Mary, multicolored,
marked "St. Anne" on base, HB
Quimper mark **225.00**
13″ h, mother wit child on knees, Art
Deco colors and style, sgd "J. E.
Sevellec," Henriot Quimper mark . **525.00**
Fish Plate, fish head, fins, and tail

molded and detailed, frontal female peasant on one, male peasant on other, multicolored, Henriot Quimper marks, pr **110.00**

Fish Platter, 19½″ l, 8½″ w, shaped rim, outlined in blue, male and female peasants, floral wreath border, HB Quimper mark **410.00**

Holy Water Font, 5″ h, fleur-de-lis shape, kneeling peasant woman before cross, scattered green, rust, and blue florals, blue sponged outline, Henriot Quimper mark **880.00**

Inkstand, 11″ l, 6½″ w, double wells with center sander, male and female peasants in pen tray section, molded blue scrolls outline body, marked "Henriot Quimper France" **710.00**

Inkwell, 5″ w, heart shape, brown, blue, green, and pink florals, cream ground, HB Quimper mark **165.00**

Jug, 6″ h, small spout, two blue sponged strap handles, blue and burnt orange floral wreath on body, yellow bands top and bottom, HB mark on base . . **55.00**

Liqueur Set, 7¾′ d tray with male peasant in center flanked by florals, sponged rim, six small cups with floral bands and sponged rims, HB Quimper marks, hairlines **125.00**

Pitcher, 8½″ h, male peasant with florals, blue bands on base, fleur-de-lis shaped spout, marked "HR Quimper" under handle **300.00**

Planter, green sponged rim, red, blue, yellow, and green figures and florals, four small feet, "Henriot Quimper France" mark, 9½″ handle to handle, $225.00.

Planter, 9½″ handle to handle, green sponged rim, red, blue, yellow, and green figures and florals, four small feet, marked "Henriot Quimper France" **225.00**

Plate
7″ d, male peasant on one, female peasant on other, green ground, marked "Henriot Quimper France," pr **125.00**

7½″ sq, octagonal, male peasant, florals, marked "Henriot Quimper France" **55.00**

8″ d, male peasant in center with florals, blue and yellow banded border, marked "Henriot Quimper France" **65.00**

8¼″ d, sq, octagonal, female peasant in center, cross hatched and paneled border, marked "HB Quimper" **135.00**

9¼″ d, female peasant in center with florals, blue and yellow banded border, marked "Henriot Quimper France" **80.00**

9½″ d
Female peasant in center, floral border, scalloped rim, marked "Henriot Quimper France" **75.00**

Female peasant in center, single stroke floral border, marked "Henriot Quimper France" **130.00**

9¾″ d, peasant woman in center, floral border, marked "HR Quimper" **245.00**

10″ d
Exotic bird in center, multicolored, marked "Henriot Quimper France" **185.00**

Overall floral pattern, red, blue, and green, HR Quimper mark **135.00**

11″ d, three red and blue flowers in center, flowers on border, marked "Henriot Quimper France," pr . . . **150.00**

12½″ d, painted busts of male and female peasants, Breton Broderie border, HB Quimper mark **395.00**

Porringer, 6″ d, frontal view of female peasant, circle of flowers on lip, tiny side handles, marked "Henriot Quimper France" **110.00**

Quintal, 5″ h, four outside fingers, center finger, Mayflower in colors in bowl, multicolored scattered flowers, marked "Henriot Quimper France" . **360.00**

Ramekin, 5¼″ handle to handle, two with male peasants, two with female peasants, dashed on open knobs and handles, marked "Henriot Quimper France," set of 4 . . . . **360.00**

Salt, double, fleur-de-lis shape, center handle, male peasant on one section, female peasant on other, marked "Henriot Quimper France" **120.00**

Sardine Dish, 6½″ l, 5″ w, seated female peasant with basket on lid, sardine knob, decor riche, HB Quimper mark **795.00**

Snuff Bottle, 2⅞″ h, 5″ w, seated female peasant on front, rooster on reverse, French inscription, unmarked **440.00**

Sugar Bowl, 5¼″ l, 6¼″ handle to handle, swirled designs on cov and bowl rim, male peasant on one side, female peasant on other, striped open handles, Henriot Quimper mark **235.00**

Teapot, 8" h, 10½" 2, green and yellow dragon spout and handle, blue fleur–de–lis knob, female peasant with scattered florals in red, blue, yellow, and green, marked "Henriot Quimper France" **1,210.00**

Toy Dishes, blue and red peasant and floral dec, shaped rims, "Henriot Quimper France" marks, 3⅞" d, pr, $90.00.

Toy Dishes, 3⅞" d, blue and red peasant and floral designs, shaped rims, marked "Henriot Quimper France," pr **90.00**

Vase
4" h, 8¼' d, relief of three dancing women, Art Deco colors, sgd "J. E. Sevellec," Henriot Quimper mark . **375.00**

15" h, medallion of peasant with flute on one, female peasant on other, tan–cream ground, sponged borders, Henriot Quimper marks, pr . **695.00**

16" h, decor riche top and base, dancing couple on sides, florals on reverse, blue and orange, ermine tails and cross hatching, Grecian type handles, HB Quimper mark . **650.00**

Wall Pocket, 12¼" h, bellows shape, blue and yellow decor riche borders, two peasants with musical instruments framed in center, Henriot Quimper mark, repaired **880.00**

RADIOS

History: The radio was invented over 100 years ago. Marconi was the first to assemble and employ the transmission and reception instruments that permitted sending electric messages without the use of direct connections. Between 1905 and the end of World War I many technical advances were made to the "wireless," including the invention of the vacuum tube by DeForest. By 1920 technology progressed. Radios filled the entertainment needs of the average family.

Changes in design, style, and technology brought the radio from the black boxes of the 1920s to the styled furniture pieces and console models of the 1930s and 1940s, to midget models of the 1950s, and finally to the high-tech radios of the 1980s.

References: Philip Collins, *Radios: The Golden Age,* Chronicle Books, 1987; Alan Douglas, *Radio Manufacturers of the 1920's, Volume 1,* Vestal Press Ltd., 1988; Robert Grinder and George Fathauger, *Radio Collectors Directory And Price Guide,* Ironwood Publishing, 1986; David and Betty Johnson, *Antique Radios: Restoration and Price Guide,* Wallace-Homestead, 1982.

Periodicals: *Antique Radio Classified,* 9511 Sunrise Boulevard, Cleveland, OH 44133; *Antique Radio Topics & The Classic Radio Newsletter,* Box 28572, Dallas, TX 75228; *Radio Age,* 636 Cambridge Road, Augusta, GA 30909.

Collectors' Clubs: Antique Radio Club of America, 81 Steeplechase Road, Devon, PA 19333; Antique Wireless Association, Main Street, Route 3, Holcomb, NY 14469.

Museums: Antique Wireless Museum, East Bloomfield, NY; Caperton's Radio Museum, Louisville, KY; Muchow's Historical Radio Museum, Elgin, IL; Museum of Wonderful Miracles, Minneapolis, MN; New England Museum of Wireless and Steam, East Greenwich, RI; Voice of the Twenties, Orient, NY.

Additional Listings: See *Warman's Americana & Collectibles* for more examples.

RCA Victor, Model 65XI, red plastic case, electric, 11 x 7 x 6½", $95.00.

Atwater Kent, Model 318, table model, dome	**100.00**
Columbia, table model, oak	**135.00**
Crosley	
Model 4-29, battery operated, 1926 .	**110.00**
Model 10-135	**45.00**
Fada, 5½ x 10½ x 6", Art Deco style yellow case, red trim	**200.00**
General Electric, Model 81, 8 tube, 1934	**195.00**
Metrodyne Super 7, 1925	**250.00**
Philco	
Model 37-84, Cathedral, schematic design, 1937	**85.00**
Model 551, 1928	**125.00**
RCA, Radiola 20, 1925	**135.00**
Spartan, Model 5218	**85.00**

Stromberg Carlson, Model 636A, console, 1928 . . . . **120.00**
Westinghouse, Model WR-602 . . . . . . **45.00**
Zenith, Zephr, 6-S-147, multiband **85.00**

RAILROAD ITEMS

History: Railroad collectors have existed for decades. The merger of the rail systems and the end of passenger service made many objects available to private collections. The Pennsylvania Railroad sold its archives at public sale.

Railroad enthusiasts have organized into regional and local clubs. Join one if interested. Your local hobby store can probably point you to the right person. The best pieces pass between collectors and rarely enter the general market place.

References: Stanley L. Baker, *Railroad Collectibles: An Illustrated Value Guide, 4th Edition*, Collector Books, 1990; Phil Bollhagen, *The Pictorial Value Guide to Railroad Playing Cards*, published by author, 1987; Arthur Dominy and Rudolph A. Morgenfruh, *Silver At Your Service*, published by authors, 1987; Richard Luckin, *Dining On Rails*, published by author, 1983, out-of-print.

Collectors' Clubs: Railroad Enthusiasts, 456 Main Street, West Townsend, MA 01474; Railroadiana Collectors Association, Box 58A, Prairie View, IL 60069; Railway and Locomotive Historical Society, 3363 Riviera West Drive, Kelseyville, CA 95451.

Periodicals: Key, Lock and Lantern, P.O. Box 15, Spencerport, NY 14559; U.S. Rail News, P.O. Box 7007, Huntington Woods, MI 48070-7007.

Museums: Baltimore and Ohio Railroad, Baltimore, MD; Museum of Transportation, Boston, MA; New York Museum of Transportation, Albany, NY; California State Railroad Museum, Sacramento, CA.

Additional Listings: See *Warman's Americana & Collectibles* for more examples.

Advisor: Alan H. Altman.

Mug, NYC, cream ground, rust brown dec, stamped mark "Shenango China, New Castle, PA," $30.00.

Ashtray, Clinchfield RR, Southern Potteries **10.00**
Baggage Checks, brass
Baltimore & Ohio Southwestern Railroad, 4¾ x 2¼", reads "B&OSWRR CINCINNATI, O.," manufactured by American Railway Supply **65.00**
Missouri Kansas & Texas Railway, 4¾ x 2¼", reads MISSOURI KAN & TEX RY COMPANY" **70.00**
Bell, brass, steam type **425.00**
Business Document, ALS, Pennsylvania Railroad stationery, Office of Superintendent, 1860, orig envelope . . **40.00**
China
Ashtray, Norfolk & Western, Dogwood, 3¾", no backstamp, Syracuse China **65.00**
Butter Pat, Atchinson, Topeka & Santa Fe, Black Chain, 3¼" d, no backstamp, Sterling China **20.00**
Celery Tray, Chicago, Burlington & Quincy, Violet & Daisies, 10¾ x 4¾", no backstamp, Syracuse China **75.00**
Cup and Saucer
Baltimore and Ohio, Capital, both pieces have top logo, no backstamp, Shenango China **225.00**
Southern Pacific, Prairie Mountain Wildflower, backstamp, Syracuse China **75.00**
Plate
6¼", Chesapeake and Ohio, Greenbrier, no backstamp, Shenango China **25.00**
9", Baltimore and Ohio, Derby, no backstamp, Shenango China . . **65.00**
Platter, oval, Missouri Pacific, Eagle, 10½ x 7¼", top logo, backstamp, Syracuse China **65.00**
Sauce Dish, Great Northern, Mountain & Flowers, 5", backstamp, Syracuse China **35.00**
Soup
Reading, Bound Brook, 8", backstamp, Lamberton China **350.00**
Southern, Pelican, 9", top marked, no backstamp, Lamberton China **100.00**
Fire Grenades, 18" l, Northwestern RR, c1870, pr **125.00**
Glassware
Cordial, 4½" h, stemmed, gold NEW YORK CENTRAL" in oval logo . . . **50.00**
Water, New York Central, 4½" h, 2¾" d, black and gold diesel engine and cars, "NEW YORK CENTRAL SYSTEM" in black log, "ROUTE TO THE WORLD'S FAIR NEW YORK WORLD'S FAIR 1964–1965" in black and gold **25.00**
Wine, Baltimore & Ohio, 4" h,

stemmed, gold line around top, series of train cars running around glass, "B &O" on side of one gold and one white train car **35.00**

Handbook, *Railroad Handbook for Track Foreman,* 1902 . . . . **5.00**

Hats with Cap Badges

Delaware & Hudson, old style hat with two gold bands running around outside, enameled badge with circle at top with "the D&H" "CONDUCTOR" in gold at bottom **175.00**

Louisville & Nashville, old style hat with two gold buttons marked "L&N" with cord running between buttons, domed style badge with red "L&N" in rect box and black enamel "CONDUCTOR" at bottom **95.00**

Seaboard Airline, old style hat with two "SEABOARD" buttons and silver band running between buttons, cap badge with silver "SEABOARD AIRLINE" at top and "FLAGMAN" at bottom **75.00**

Lantern, Tall Globe

Colorado & Southern Railway, Adams & Westlake Company "The Adams," last patent date Nov. 30, 1897, framed marked in large letters "C&S Ry," double horizontal wire guards, twist-off pot and burner, 5⅜" unmarked cobalt blue globe **250.00**

Lehigh Valley Railroad, Keystone Lantern Co. "The Casey," last patent date June 2, 1903, frame marked in large letters "L.V.R.R.," single horizontal wire guard, 5⅜" L.V.R.R. extended base globe . . . **350.00**

Lantern Globes

Canadian National Railroad, 5⅜", clear cast, extended base, globe has cast "CNR" in serifs **85.00**

Louisville & Nashville, 5⅜", amber, etched "L&N RR," goble is extended base, manufactured by MacBeth Pearl Glass 220 . . . . . . **210.00**

Northern Pacific, 5⅜", amber, etched "N.P.R.R.," globe also etched on backside "SAFETY ALWAYS" . . . **150.00**

Union Pacific, 5⅜", amber, etched "Southern Ry" **65.00**

Pocket Mirror, Frisco **90.00**

Silver, Flatware

Fork, dinner, Missouri Pacific, top and bottom marked with logo, Century, International Silver **12.00**

Knife

Dinner, Northern Pacific, top and bottom marked with logo, Embassy, Reed & Barton **18.00**

Steak, Soo Line, bottom marked with logo, Vasser, Reed & Barton **28.00**

Spoon

Grapefruit, California Zephyr, bottom marked with logo, Century, International Silver **15.00**

Teaspoon, Union Pacific, bottom marked "U.P.R.R.," Zephyr, International Silver **8.00**

Serving, Rock Island Lines, top marked, Empire, Gorham **18.00**

Silver, Holloware

Bouillion Cup Holder, Lehigh Valley, 4", hammered mounts, side logo is raised "LVRR" in diamond, Barth . **135.00**

Creamer, Great Northern, 4 oz, #05082, side logo is incised over "G" and "N," International Silver . **50.00**

Gravy Boat, Pullman, 2 oz, #SL0688, backstamped with name of railroad, International Silver **65.00**

Ice Bucket, double handled, Southern, 7½", #1833-S, side logo incised "Southern," Reed & Barton . **400.00**

Tip Tray, Western Pacific, 6½", #05090, backstamped with name of railroad, International Silver . . . **65.00**

Switch Keys

BELT, Adlake, 3756 . . . . **20.00**

MK&TRY, Slaymaker, 28928, fat barrel **35.00**

SANTA FE ROUTE, A & W, football hallmark **28.00**

WP&BRR, C, tapered barrel **175.00**

Tablecloth, Baltimore & Ohio **20.00**

Ticket and envelope, Milwaukee Road, 1930 . . . . **5.00**

RAZORS

History: Razors date back several thousand years. Early man used sharpened stones. The Egyptians, Greeks, and Romans had metal razors.

Razors made prior to 1800 generally were crudely stamped WARRANTED or CAST STEEL, with the maker's mark on the tang. Until 1870 almost all razors for the American market were manufactured in Sheffield, England. Most blades were wedge shaped; many were etched with slogans or scenes. Handles were made of natural materials: various horns, tortoise shell, bone, ivory, stag, silver, and pearl. All razors were handmade.

After 1870 razors were machine made with hollow ground blades and synthetic handle materials. Razors of this period usually were manufactured in Germany (Solingen) or in American cutlery factories. Hundreds of molded celluloid handle patterns were produced.

Cutlery firms produced boxed sets of two, four, and seven razors. Complete and undamaged sets are very desirable. Most popular are the 7-Day sets with each razor etched with a day of the week.

The fancier the handle or more intricately etched the blade, the higher the price. Rarest handle materials are pearl, stag, sterling silver, pressed horn, and carved ivory. Rarest blades are those with scenes etched across the entire front. Value is increased by certain manufacturer's names, e.g., H. Boker, Case, M. Price, Joseph Rogers, Simmons Hardware, Will & Finck, Winchester, and George Wostenholm.

hgb = hollow ground blade

wb = wedge blade

References: Robert A. Doyle, *Straight Razor Collecting, An Illustrated Price Guide*, Collector Books, 1980, out-of-print; Phillip L. Krumholz, *Value Guide For Barberiana & Shaving Collectibles*, Ad Libs Publishing Co., 1988.

Periodical: *Blade Magazine*, P.O. Box 22007, Chattanooga, TN 37422.

Additional Listings: See *Warman's Americana & Collectibles* for more examples.

American, Geneva Cutlery Co, Geneva, NY, carved bone handle, 6¼" I, $45.00.

AMERICAN BLADES

American Knife Co, Plymouth Hollow, Conn, wb, stamped "A Real American," black horn handle	55.00
Case Brothers, Little Valley, NY, blade stamped "Tested XX," yellow wrapped rope pattern handle	30.00
Golden Rule Cutlery Co, Chicago USA, blade ground slightly out of shape, four beautiful women in bathing suits on handle	65.00
Ontario Cutlery Co, Geneva, NY, blade etched with two crossed American flags, crown above and "The Mighty" below, black and white striped handle	25.00
Schrade Cutlery Co, Walden, NY, hg, etched "Everlasting Sharp," green swirl handle with German silver ends, gray and green orig box with model number 158-R	135.00
Waterville Cutlery Co, Waterville, Conn, blade "Waterville Hand Forged," black celluloid handle with raised floral pattern, oak leaf and acorn scroll	65.00

ENGLISH BLADES, SHEFFIELD

Joseph Allen, medium hg, ivory handle with inlaid escutcheon plate of German silver	30.00
Chris Johnson, wide hgb, plated brass handle	55.00
Joseph Rodgers & Sons, wb, stag handle with inlaid rect escutcheon plate	125.00
Turniss Cutler & Stacey Sheffield, pressed horn handle, two intertwined snakes, marker's mark on blade	615.00
Wade & Butcher, hg, etched in ribbon "Wade & Butcher," Art Nouveau handle stamped "Sterling," raised scroll across front and back, monogrammed	320.00
Geo Wostenholme, blade etched with adv, ivory handle emb	30.00

GERMAN BLADES

Boker, H & Co, Solingen, emb celluloid handle, scene of touring car, two passengers, blade etched "King Cutter"	190.00
Cosmos Mfg Co, hgb, ivory handle, raised nude picking purple grapes, green leaves	95.00
Henckels, corn, rounded and shaped bone handle, plain blade, orig box with silver emb adv "J A Henckels Twin Works, Germany"	48.00
Imperial Razor, blade etched with ship *US Battleship Oregon* scene, dark blue celluloid handle	40.00
F. A. Koch & Co, Made In Germany, ivory handle, colored scene of branches, oak leaves, and deer dec	45.00
Lewis Razor Co, hgb, celluloid handle, stork eating fish and standing in cattails	50.00
Chas T. Scott, hgb, marbleized green celluloid handle	12.00
Wadsworth Razor Co, semi wb, carved bone handle, c1870	55.00
Zartina Cutlery Works, hgb, floral SS handle	275.00

SWISS BLADE

Joh. Engstrom, frameback, seven interchangeable "wafer" blades, black horn handle, c1880	65.00

Tornablom, hgb, ivory handle **27.00**

SETS OF RAZORS

Pair, G. W. Ruff's Peerless, hg, ivory
handles, leather over wood case with
"Gentlemen's Companion Containing
2 Razors Special Hollow Ground," red
lining **55.00**
7-Day Set, Crown and Sword, blades
etched "The Crown & Sword Razor
Extra Hollow Ground," black handles
with raised "Crown and Sword,"
home-made felt lined wood case,
plaque with "RAZORS emb on top .   **45.00**

RED WING POTTERY

History: The Red Wing pottery category covers
several potteries from Red Wing, Minnesota. In
1868 David Hallem started Red Wing Stoneware
Co., the first pottery, with stoneware as its primary
product and with a red wing stamped under the
glaze as its mark. The Minnesota Stoneware Co.
started in 1883. The North Star Stoneware Co.,
1892–1896, used a raised star and the words Red
Wing as its mark.

The Red Wing Stoneware Co. and the Minnesota Stoneware Co. merged in 1892. The new
company, the Red Wing Union Stoneware Co.,
made stoneware until 1920 when it introduced a
pottery line which it continued until the 1940s. In
1936 the name was changed to Red Wing Potteries, Inc. During the 1930s it introduced several
popular lines of hand painted pattern dinnerware
which were distributed through department stores,
Sears, and gift stamp centers. Dinnerware declined in the 1950s, being replaced with hotel and
restaurant china in the early 1960s. The plant
closed in 1967.

References: Dan and Gail DePasquale and
Larry Peterson, *Red Wing Collectibles,* Collector
Books, 1985; David A. Newkirk, *A Guide To Red
Wing Markings,* Monticello Printing, 1979; Dolores
Simon, *Red Wing Pottery With Rumrill,* Collector
Books, 1980; Gary and Bonnie Tefft, *Red Wing
Potters and Their Wares, Second Edition,* Locust
Enterprises, 1987; Lyndon C. Viel, *The Clay
Giants, The Stoneware of Red Wing, Goodhue*
County, Minnesota, Book 2 1980, *Book 3,* 1987,
Wallace-Homestead.

Collectors' Club: Red Wing Collectors Society,
Route 3, Box 146, Monticello, MN 55362.

Additional Listings: See *Warman's Americana
& Collectibles* for more examples.

**Vase, tapered cylinder, straight neck,
relief floral design, red matte glaze,
stamped "Red Wing/Union/Stoneware
Co, Red Wing/Minn," 8¼" h, $50.00.**

Ashtray, 7¼" d, marked "Red Wing Pot-
tery" **25.00**
Bean Pot, lid, Saffron **75.00**
Beater Jar, adv for "H. L. Sander, Ar-
lington, MN," marked "Red Wing Saf-
fron Ware" **90.00**
Bowl
  7", four blue stripes, adv for "T. C.
  Johnson, Latimer, IA" **50.00**
  10", two blue stripes, marked "10 Red
  Wing USA" **70.00**
  11", stoneware, paneled, sponged
  rust and blue ext. dec **115.00**
Butter Jar, deep blue lettering, 20 lb . .   **200.00**
Canteen, stoneware, 1900–08 . . . . . .   **350.00**
Casserole, all-over sponge dec, lid . . .   **150.00**
Churn, molded blue elephant ear
leaves, 3 gal, sgd "Minnesota" oval
on bottom **400.00**
Clock, figural, wall, electric, marked
"Tik-Tok Baker" **40.00**
Crock, 20 gal, marked "Red Wing Union
Stoneware" **225.00**
Cuspidor, mold seam, brown and white,
unsigned **100.00**
Jar, ball lock, self-sealing, 3 gal **75.00**
Jug
  Beehive, 5 gal, large wing **135.00**
  Funnel top, salt glaze, 1 gal, marked
  "Minnesota" **70.00**
  Shoulder, birchleaf, molded, 4 gal, sgd   **125.00**
Measure, Convention Commemorative,
acid proof **65.00**

Nappy, white, marked "Minnesota" ...	60.00
Pitcher, cherry band, medium size ...	30.00
Salt Box, spongeband, lid, hanging	450.00
Snuff Jar, white glaze, 1 quart, marked "RW"	75.00
Spittoon, salt glaze, "Red Wing Stoneware Company" stamped on side ..	275.00
Umbrella Stand, blue sponge dec, unsigned	500.00

Vase
- 6½" h, Art Pottery, paper label, pr .. — **35.00**
- 9¾", four relief panels with brown semi-glaze trees, gray matte ground, marked .... — **45.00**

Wash Bowl and Pitcher, blue and white, lily	350.00
Water Cooler, "Ice Water," lid, #4, orig cork	265.00
Water Pitcher, Saffronware adv	125.00

REDWARE

History: The availability of clay, the same used to make bricks and roof tiles, accounted for the great production of red earthenware pottery in the American colonies. Redware pieces are mainly utilitarian—bowls, crocks, jugs, etc.

Lead glazed redware retained its reddish color, but a variety of colored glazes were obtained by the addition of metals to the basic glaze. Streaks and mottled splotches in redware items resulted from impurities in the clay and/or uneven firing temperatures.

"Slipware" is a term used to describe redwares decorated by the application of slip, a semi–liquid paste made of clay. Slipwares were made in England, Germany, and elsewhere in Europe for decades before becoming popular in the Pennsylvania German region and elsewhere in colonial America.

Apple Butter Jar, 7¼" h, strap handle, mottled green glaze, amber spots, hairlines and old flakes .... — **120.00**

Bank, 5¼" h, ovoid, tooled lines at shoulder, knob finial, slightly amber glaze with brown flecks, minor wear — **125.00**

Bottle, 5½" l, keg shaped, bung hole, gray glaze, brown and green spots, hairlines and minor chips .... — **250.00**

Bowl
- 5¼ x 3⅛", crown like molded handles, mottled brownish black glaze, minor wear and small edge flakes .. — **375.00**
- 9¼ x 4⅞", flared, scalloped rim and tooled lines, mottled brownish amber glaze, black spots, wear and edge chips .... — **300.00**
- 12 x 5", protruding lip and tooled line, sponged brown rim and three vertical bands, minor wear and flakes — **185.00**

15½ x 2½", coggled edge, three and four line yellow slip dec, minor wear and old flakes	1,800.00
Charger, 11½", yellow slip crossed wavy lines, worn and chipped	475.00
Creamer, 3¾", strap handle, running black splotches, clear glaze, minor wear, small flakes, close fitting mismatched lid	175.00
Cup, 3¾", flared lip, applied handle, clear glaze with mottled amber, minor wear and glaze flakes	85.00
Cup and Saucer, dark brown glaze, small flakes, handle glued	50.00
Cuspidor, 8 x 4¼", tooled bands, brown and green running glaze with brown dashes, some wear and edge chips	250.00
Dish, oval, 10¾ x 14 x 2", coggled edge, yellow slip dec of wavy lines, rim hairline, edge chipped	350.00

Figure
- 1½" h, bird, simple molded detail, white slip, amber glaze, edge wear — **75.00**
- 9¼" l, 6½" h, dog, reclining, cold dec, attributed to John Bell .... — **250.00**

Flask, 6½" h, tooled lines and brown splotched glaze, old hairline in side, chip on lip .... — **220.00**

Flower Pot, attached base, crimped edges, green and brown glaze, I. S. Stahl, 1938, 4½" d, 2¼" h, $85.00.

Flower Pot
- 4⅝", tooled lines, crimped lip, brown flecked glaze, brown sponging, attached saucer, wear and edge chips .... — **155.00**
- 5¼" h, wheel turned foot, applied crimped dec on base and rim, yellow slip and running dark glaze with mottled black, edge wear and small ships, drainage hole in bottom ... — **115.00**
- 8½" h, edge tooling on rim and attached saucer base, yellow slip int., ext. with yellow slip and splotches of brown and green, clear shiny

glaze, Shenandoah, some wear
and chips **500.00**

Jar

4⅝", ovoid, protruding lip, amber
glaze, brown sponging, minor
flakes **355.00**

5⅝", well shaped, tooled lines, flaring
lip, mottled greenish glaze, brown
sponging, rim chips **200.00**

6¼", ovoid, tooled lines at shoulder,
flared lip, mottled brown glaze, minor wear and chip on base **225.00**

7"

Ovoid, simple tooled line, flaring lip,
black fleck glaze, dark brown
sponging, green spots, closely
mismatched lid, wear and edge
chips **165.00**

Sloping shoulder, tooled lip, dark
green glaze, brown splotching,
bottom incised "Pickle," wear
and edge chips **425.00**

7¾", ovoid, tooled lines and applied
handles, shiny glaze with amber
highlights, dark brown splotches,
wear and edge chips **400.00**

8¼ x 6¾", imp label "John W. Bell,
Waynesboro, Pa.," brown int. glaze,
unglazed ext. with good patina, mi-
nor wear, small flakes **80.00**

9½", flared lip, yellow slip stripes,
green highlights, brown wavy lines,
rim hairline and small rim chips, two
old chips on base **1,350.00**

Jug

6⅝" h, ovoid, wide ribbed strap handle, black shiny glaze, minor wear,
small edge flakes **200.00**

6¾", tooled line at shoulder, strap
handle, shiny glaze with few brown
splashes, hairline in shoulder **125.00**

Loaf Pan

9½ x 13½", coggled edge, four line
yellow slip dec, old surface and
edge flakes **825.00**

11½ x 15½ x 3", coggled edge, three
line yellow slip dec, old edge flakes,
good wear, minor flakes in slip . . . **950.00**

Milk Bowl, 7 x 3¼", tooled dot line and
bulbous lip, brown sponged glaze, mi-
nor wear **225.00**

Mug

4½", rich brown sponging, imp "John
Bell" **775.00**

5¼", butter print-like applied star design, strap handle and tooled lip,
clear glaze with greenish highlights, good patina, minor glaze
flakes and wear **125.00**

Pie Plate

6½", coggled edge, yellow slip stylized tulip design, hint of green, old
chips **950.00**

6⅞", yellow slip X and O design,
brown spots, old edge chips **675.00**

7⅝", coggled edge, yellow slip double
tulip, highlighted in rich green, old
chips **1,625.00**

8⅛", yellow slip wavy lines, imp "W.
Smith, Womelsdorf," two old rim
chips **500.00**

8½", yellow slip dec, green highlights,
imp "W. Smith, Womelsdorf," small
rim flakes **1,300.00**

8⅞", three line yellow slip dec, small
edge flakes **325.00**

9¾", coggled edge, wear and small
chips **250.00**

9⅞", coggled edge, three line yellow
slip dec, wavy lines and dots, worn,
center slip chipped, small old edge
chips **150.00**

Pipe Bowl, 5¼", greenish amber glaze,
brown flecks **100.00**

Pitcher

4½ x 5⅛", yellow slip int., ext. with
three deep rim scallops in brown
glaze bordered and dec with yellow
slip designs on rim and handle,
hairlines, chips and glaze flakes,
some old rim flakes colored in . . . **55.00**

6¼", squat, ovoid, tooled dotted line,
ribbed strap handle, slightly greenish glaze, three brown vertical
slashes, wear and glaze flakes,
mismatched lid **150.00**

6¾", tooled lines and strap handle,
dark brown sponged glaze, bottom
incised "10," wear and old chips . **250.00**

7¾", applied handle, tooling at rim
and shoulder, clear slightly greenish glaze, sponged brown vertical
bands, edge wear and flakes **250.00**

8 x 4⅝", cup shape, tooled dotted
line, ribbed strap handle, brown
sponging on rim, four vertical
bands, hairlines and glued break
out on bottom **150.00**

Plate, 7" d, coggled edge, yellow slip
dec **650.00**

Preserving Jar

6", tooled lines just below shoulder,
protruding lip, black fleck glaze,
three vertical bands of brown
sponging, wear and small chips . . **150.00**

7", tooled lines, wide vertical brushed
brown bands, some wear, small
chips **200.00**

Salt

2 x 1⅜", mottled greenish amber
glaze, brown circles and sponging,
edge chips **165.00**

3" l, scroddle ware, marbleized yellow

slip with brown and green, cast
from lacy salt **325.00**
Slip Cup, 1⅞″ h, single hole for quill, int.
glazed **115.00**
Turk's Head Mold
8 x 2¼″, scalloped rim, greenish amber glaze, brown sponging, wear
and small flakes **115.00**
9¼″, scalloped rim and black
sponged glaze, some filled in rim
chips and small flakes **65.00**
Watch Holder, 4″ h, dark brown glaze,
scalloped rims **200.00**

RELIGIOUS ITEMS

History: Objects for the worshiping or expression of man's belief in a superhuman power are
collected by many people for many reasons.

Icons are included since they are religious mementos, usually paintings with a brass encase-
ment. Collecting icons dates from the earliest period of Christianity. Most antique icons in today's
market were made in the late 19th century.

Reproduction Alert: Icons are heavily reproduced.

**Cross, Russian Orthodox, early 19th C,
brass, 3¼″ h, $175.00.**

Altar Candlestick, 27½″ h, parcel giltwood, leaf carved baluster form, entwined berry laurel, triangular base,
three scroll and relief carved feet, late
Baroque, Italian, early 18th C **1,650.00**
Altar Stick, pr, 15″ h, Gothic Revival,
mounted turrets and angels, late
19th C **140.00**
Bible Box
21¾″ l, oak, carved front panel with
"1725," iron lock, hasp, and strap
hinges, minor damage, English . . **150.00**
23 x 16 x 7¼″, oak, carved front
panel, dated "1676" **550.00**

23¹⁄₁₂ x 15½ x 8″, oak, slant lid, carved
front panel dec, butterfly hinges,
orig lock and hasp, dated 1703 . . **350.00**
Communion Items
Chalices, pr, pewter, Leonard, Reed
& Barton, 1835–40 . . . . **350.00**
Flagon, 14½″ h, pewter, silver plating,
marked "Reed & Barton" **45.00**
Service, 5 pcs, 10½″ flagon, pair chal-
ices, and two 10″ d plates, pewter,
straight line touch marks, Reed &
Barton **400.00**
Token, 1″ d, pewter, marked "A. C. of
Hebron" on one side, "J.I. 1824" on
other **25.00**
Crucifix, 19″ h, wood, Gesso and poly-
chrome repaint **200.00**
Icon, 15½ x 8½″, pr, wood, painted, Ma-
donna and child, 20th C **10.00**
Figure
25¼″ h, angels, carved wood, polychrome, light blue gilt trimmed dal-
matic over white gown, short wavy
golden hair, wings and halos missing, restorations, wormed and
chips to base, paint, and gesso,
later ivory painted circular base, cylindrical shaft and lamp wiring,
early Baroque, Italian, c1600, pr . **11,000.00**
26″ h, Mary at the tomb, carved wood,
parcel gilt and polychrome, standing figure, red tunic, Renaissance,
South Germany, early 16th C **8,850.00**
50″ h, Christ holding child, gesso and
painted wood, carved, sq base,
19th C **3,200.00**
68″ h, St. Barbara, carved pine, wear-
ing a tiara and flowing robes, minor
losses and cracks **2,475.00**
Painting, Polish, 27½ x 19½″, Icon Trip-
tych, oil on panel, Jozef Borkowski,
20th C **190.00**
Statue, Saint, wearing monk's habit,
holding christ child, cross backing, silver mounted marble base, sgd "J
DAMPT. Sc" and "Cartier" **1,320.00**

REVERSE PAINTING ON GLASS

History: The earliest examples of reverse painting on glass were produced in the 13th century
Italy. By the 17th century the technique had spread
to Central and Eastern Europe. It spread westward
as the glass industry center moved to Germany in
the late 17th century.

The Alsace and Black Forest region developed
a unique portraiture style. The half and three–
quarter portraits often were titled below the portrait. Women tend to have general names. Most
males are of famous men.

The English used a mezzotint method, rather

than free–style, to create their reverse paintings. Landscapes and allegorical figures were popular. The Chinese began working in the medium in the 17th century, eventually favoring marine and patriotic scenes.

Reverse painting was done in America. Most were by folk artists, unsigned, who favored portraits, patriotic and mourning scenes, floral compositions, landscapes, and buildings. Known American artists include Benjamin Greenleaf, A. Cranfield, and Rowley Jacobs.

In the late 19th century commercially produced reverse paintings, often decorated with mother–of–pearl, became popular. Themes included the Statue of Liberty, the capitol in Washington, D.C., and various world fairs and expositions.

PORTRAITS

Apostles, three, landscape background, Italian, giltwood frames, 3¼ x 7¼", minor flaking and losses, pr **125.00**
Chinese Export, Mandarin, seated, smoking, attendant standing, 19 x 21" **3,200.00**
George and Martha Washington, bust portrait, white wig, frilled stock, white shawl, shaded brown ground, 19th C, 28 x 24", pr **350.00**
Napoleon, three quarter length portrait, white uniform, gold and red, green oval, black rect background, gilt flowers, beveled frame, worn black paint, 12½ x 14½" **1,000.00**
Nikolaus, Kaizer Aller Russina, green uniform, blue sash, gold highlights, brown ground, 9½ x 12" orig frame . **225.00**

SCENES

A Visit To The Grandmother, scene of three generations of women and cat,

European scene, house and bridge along river, gilded 23 x 17″ frame, 19 x 13½″ oval image, $165.00.

black border, title on back, orig gilt frame, 21¾ x 27¾" **225.00**
Flowers, large cream white peonies and buds, green leaves, blue ground, 17¾ x 15½", later gilt gesso carved frame, artist sgd "Drian" **4,400.00**
H.M.S. Marlborough, Victorian, three masted ship, sails furled, small boat approaching, oval border, four pierced and dec corners, 13½ x 12¼", gilt lined rect outer border, ogee maple frame **220.00**
Naval Battle, "Perry's Lake Erie Victory, Sept 10th, 1813," multicolored, 7 x 9" **250.00**
Three couples, picnic scene, discovering bird's nest, 4½ x 6" **250.00**

RIDGWAY

History: Throughout the 19th century the Ridgway family, through a series of partnerships, held a position of importance in Shelton and Hanley, Staffordshire, England. The connection began with Job and George, two brothers, and Job's two sons, John and William. In 1830 John and William separated with John retaining the Cauldon Place factory and William the Bell Works. By 1862 the porcelain division of Cauldon was carried on by Coalport China Ltd. William and his heirs continued at the Bell Works and the Church [Hanley] and Bedford [Shelton] works until the end of the 19th century.

Many early pieces are unmarked. Later marks include the initials of the many partnerships.

References: Susan and Al Bagdade, *Warman's English & Continental Pottery & Porcelain, 1st Edition,* Warman Publishing Co., Inc., 1987; G. A. Godden, *Ridgway Porcelains,* Antique Collectors' Club.

Additional Listings: Staffordshire, Historical, and Staffordshire, Romantic.

Bowl, cov, Humphrey's Clock pattern . **140.00**
Cup and Saucer, green transfer, children at play **85.00**
Dinner Service, underglaze blue, enamels, and gilding, printed coat of arms, marked "Imperial Stone China," 54 pcs, minor damage and staining . . . **950.00**
Dish, 10¼" d, Oriental scenes, blue ground **25.00**
Jug, 5" h, soft paste, white griffins and cherubs, brown body, mask spout . . **150.00**
Pitcher, 10" h, salt glaze, raised scenes of Burns poems, marked "Ridgway & Company, design published Oct 1, 1835" **225.00**
Plate, 7½", gray transfer, Columbian Star pattern, imp "John Ridgway" . . **25.00**
Platter, 17", Asiatic Places, dark blue, two people on mound in foreground

Plate, Coaching Days and Coaching Ways, silver trim, 9″ d, $35.00.

scene, vase with flowers to left, temple background, cartouche enclosing label "Ridgways Asiatic Palaces" .. 155.00
Saucer, 5¼″, blue, small child petting lamb, imp "Ridgway" on back 90.00
Soup Tureen, 13½″, black transfer, Indus pattern, marked "Ridgway, Sparks & Ridgway" 145.00
Teapot, 4¾″ h, molded formal and fluted borders, mid 19th C 30.00
Tray, 12½″ d, Pickwick Series, "Mr. Pickwick at the Election," black transfer, caramel ground, silver scalloped edge 100.00
Waste Bowl, light blue, University pattern, cartouche border, scholar in cap and gown standing in front of university 65.00

RING TREES

History: A ring tree is a small, generally saucer shaped object made of glass, porcelain, metal, or wood with a center post in the shape of a hand, branches, or cylinder for hanging or storing finger rings.

Hand Painted, pink flowers, green leaves, center gold tree, artist sgd "E Wolff," R. S. Germany blank, 5¼″ l, 2¾″ h, $48.00.

GLASS

Cranberry, floral dec, gold trim 115.00
Cut Glass, tapering center post, diamond cut saucer 40.00
Fenton, turtle 20.00
Opaline, blue, hp gold, blue, and white floral dec, ftd, 4½″ 70.00
Ruby Stained, Button Arches pattern . 50.00
Spatter, yellow, white, and clear, 3¾″h 65.00

PORCELAIN

Child's hand, fingers extended, 4″, Parian Ware 45.00
German, hand on saucer, dec 22.50
Limoges, multicolored blossoms, white ground, marked "T & V Limoges ... 40.00
Minton, 3″ h, pastel flowers on top, gold edge and knob, marked "Minton, England" 40.00
Nippon, gold hand, rim dec 35.00
Schlegelmilch, RS Poland, violets, pearlized finish 90.00

POTTERY

Irid gold, 3½″, Zsolnay 75.00
Pink and green flowers, gold, hp, marked "M Z Austria" 65.00

WOOD

Tramp Art, carved fruitwood, hand shape 25.00

ROCKINGHAM AND ROCKINGHAM BROWN GLAZED WARES

History: Rockingham ware can be divided into two categories. The first consists of the fine china and porcelain pieces made between 1826 and 1842 by the Rockingham Company of Swinton, Yorkshire, England, and its predecessor firms: Swinton, Bingley, Don, Leeds, and Brameld. The Bramelds developed the cadogan, a lidless teapot. Between 1826 and 1842 a quality soft paste body with a warm, silken feel was developed by the Bramelds. Elaborate specialty pieces were made. By 1830 the company employed 600 workers and listed 400 designs for dessert sets and 1,000 designs for tea and coffee services in their catalog. Unable to meet its payroll, the company closed in 1842.

The second category of Rockingham ware includes pieces produced in the famous Rockingham brown glaze, that became an intense and vivid purple-brown when fired. It had a dark, tortoise shell mottled appearance. The glaze was copied by many English and American potteries. American manufacturers who used Rockingham glaze include D. & J. Henderson of Jersey City, New Jersey, United States Pottery in Bennington, Vermont, potteries in East Liverpool, Ohio, and several potteries in Indiana and Illinois.

Reference: Susan and Al Bagdade, *Warman's English & Continental Pottery & Porcelain, 1st Edition,* Warman Publishing Co., Inc., 1987.

Additional Listings: Bennington and Bennington–Type.

Toby Jug, basketweave body, tricorn hat, Rockingham glaze, 6″ h, $225.00.

Bowl, 6½″ d, 3½″ h, emb, diamond quilted band near base, Rockingham glaze 80.00
Creamer, 6¼″, cow shape, brown Rockingham glaze 100.00
Dish, 8¼ x 9⅛″, rect, emb rim dec, Rockingham glaze 125.00
Foot Warmer, brown Rockingham glaze 85.00
Pie Plate, 10¼″ d, Rockingham glaze . 125.00
Pitcher, Rockingham glaze
  8⅜″ h, emb scene of cranes, acorns, and oak leaves, serpent handle, animal head spout 100.00
  9¼″ h, emb hunter, dog, and game . 1255.00
Platter, 15″ l, emb scalloped rim, Rockingham glaze 350.00
Potpourri Garniture, pair of 6⅞″ campana form vases, center 11¼″ vase, Howick Hall and still life of shells on center vase, landscapes on others, applied trailing vines, flowerheads, and green leaves, relief molded acanthus border at base, raised waisted scroll and leaf molded feet, applied gilded handles with double scroll terminals, pierced cov with applied flowering vines, puce griffin mark "Rockingham Works/Brameld/Manufacturer to the King," title in iron–red, c1831–41 . . . . 1,100.00
Tea Service, part, 6¼″ h teapot, dolphin form spout, scroll handle, dome cov, rosebud finial, two handled sugar bowl with dome cov, rosebud finial, matching creamer, waste bowl, nine tea cups, five coffee cups, twelve saucers, transfer printed, beige acanthus leaves, polychrome floral sprays, gilt, white ground 425.00
Teapot, 9¾″ l, figural, duck, emb detail, rect lid, Rockingham glaze 225.00
Tobacco Jar, 9″ h, cov, emb dec, Gothic Arches pattern, Rockingham glaze . 225.00

ROCKWELL, NORMAN

History: Norman Rockwell (February 3, 1894–November, 1978) was a famous American artist and illustrator. During the time he painted, from age 18 until his death, he created over 2,000 works.

His first professional efforts were illustrations for a children's book. He next worked for *Boy's Life,* the Boy Scout magazine. His most famous works were used by *Saturday Evening Post* for their cover illustrations.

Norman Rockwell painted everyday people in everyday situations, mixing a little humor with sentiment. His paintings and illustrations are treasured because of this sensitive approach. Rockwell painted people he knew and places with which he was familiar. New England landscapes are found in many of his illustrations.

References: Denis C. Jackson, *The Norman Rockwell Identification And Value Guide To: Magazines, Posters, Calendars, Books, 2nd Edition,* published by author, 1985; Mary Moline, *Norman Rockwell Collectibles, Sixth Edition,* Green Valley World, 1988.

Museums: Corner House, Stockbridge, MA; Norman Rockwell Museum, Northbrook, IL.

Reproduction Alert: Because of the popularity of his works, they have been reproduced on many objects. These new collectibles should not be confused with original artwork and illustrations. However, they do allow a collector more range in collecting interests and prices.

Additional Listings: See *Warman's Americana & Collectibles* for more examples.

Poster, Checkup, autographed, c1957, 11 x 14″, $75.00.

HISTORIC

Advertising Tray, Green Giant, 17½ x 12¾″, c1940	48.00
Book, Mark Twain, *The Adventures of Tom Sawyer*, 1936	50.00
Calendar, 1922, Warren National Bank, Music Master	300.00
Poster, The Saturday Evening Post 100th Year of Baseball, 22 x 28″, 1939	175.00

MODERN

Bell	
Danbury Mint, Doctor and Doll, 1975	55.00
Royal Devon, Butter Girl, 1976	40.00
Coin, Ford Motor Co, 50th Anniversary	35.00
Figure	
Gorham Fine China	
Batter Up	50.00
Four Seasons, Childhood, 1973, set of four	500.00
Pride of Parenthood	60.00
Grossman Designs, Inc.	
Barbershop Quartet, 1975	125.00
Tom Sawyer, Series No. 1, 1976	100.00
Ingot, Franklin Mint, tribute to Robert Frost, 1974	275.00
Plate	
Ages of Love, Gorham Fine China, 1973, Four Seasons series, set of 4	300.00
Doctor and Doll, Royal Devon, 1975, Mother's Day	90.00
Scotty Gets His Tree, Rockwell Society of America, 1974, Christmas	175.00
Under The Mistletoe, Franklin Mint, SS, 1971	175.00
Print	
Circle Fine Arts, limited edition, sgd and numbered	
Dressing Up, pencil sgd	2,800.00

Ichabod Crane	5,000.00
Music Hath Charms	3,000.00
Wet Paint, 24 x 30″, collotype	1,550.00
Eleanor Ettinger, Inc.	
After The Prom, 24 x 26¾″, litho	4,500.00
Gilding The Eagle, 21 x 25½″, litho	3,225.00
The Swing, 20 x 21″, litho	4,750.00
Young Spooners, 1977, 20 x 24″, litho	4,000.00

ROGERS & SIMILAR STATUARY

History: John Rogers, born in America in 1829, studied sculpturing in Europe and produced the first plaster-of-paris statue, "The Checker Players," in 1859. It was followed by "The Slave Auction" in 1860.

His works were popular parlor pieces of the Victorian era. He produced at least 80 different subjects and the total number of groups made from the originals is estimated to be over 100,000.

Casper Hennecke, one of Rogers' contemporaries, operated C. Hennecke & Company from 1881 until 1896 in Milwaukee, Wisconsin. His statuary often is confused with Rogers' work since both are very similar.

It is difficult to find a statue in undamaged condition and with original paint. Use the following conversions: 10% minor flaking; 10% chips; 10–20% piece or pieces broken and reglued; 20% flaking; 50% repainting.

References: Paul and Meta Bieier, *John Rogers' Groups of Statuary*, published by author, 1971; Betty C. Haverly, *Hennecke's Florentine Statuary*, published by author, 1972; David H. Wallace, *John Rogers: The People's Sculptor*, Wesleyan Univ., 1976.

Periodical: *Rogers Group*, 4932 Prince George Avenue, Beltsville, MD 20705.

ROGERS

Balcony, The, 32½″ h, 11/4/1879, orig paint, some flaking, violin repaired	600.00
Courtship in Sleepy Hollow, 2/8/1870, 16½″	750.00
Council of War	
Type A, 24½″ h, 3/31/1868	875.00
Type B, 3/31/1868, orig paint, flaked, chair cov chipped, document cracked	500.00
Type C, 24″ h, minor flaking	475.00
Faust & Marguerite–Leaving The Garden, 25½″ h, 1890	400.00
Mail Day, 16″ h, 1864	650.00
One More Shot, 24″ h, 1865	425.00
Referee, The, 22″ h, 1880, repainted	350.00
School Days, 21½″ h, 1877	700.00
Union Refugees, spelter, 1864, one of seven known, hammer of rifle chipped	1,200.00

Rogers, Council of War, Type C, 24″, $450.00.

ROGERS TYPE

After The Case, 20″ h	110.00
By Jingo, 17″ h, orig paint, minor chipping	125.00
Can't You Talk, 10½″ h	135.00
First Love, 13″ h, repainted	165.00
Holy Family, 18″ h	225.00
Romeo and Juliet, 16″ h	150.00
Wounded Scout, 6/23/1864, 23″ h	900.00

ROOKWOOD POTTERY

History: Mrs. Marie Longworth Nicholas Storer, Cincinnati, Ohio, founded Rookwood Pottery in 1880. The name of this outstanding American art pottery came from her family estate "Rookwood," named for the rooks (crows) which inhabited the wooded grounds.

There are five elements to the Rookwood marking system—the clay or body mark, the size mark, the decorator mark, the date mark, and the factory mark. Rookwood art pottery can best be dated from factory marks.

In 1880–1882 the factory mark was the name "Rookwood" incised or painted on the base. Between 1881 and 1886 the firm name, address, and year appeared in an oval frame. Beginning in

1886, the impressed "RP" monogram appeared and a flame-mark was added for each year until 1900. After 1900 a Roman numeral, indicating the last two digits of the year of production, was added at the bottom of the "RP" flame-mark monogram. This last mark is the one most often found on Rookwood pottery today.

Though the Rookwood pottery filed for bankruptcy in 1941, it was soon reorganized under new management. Efforts at maintaining the pottery proved futile, and it again was sold in 1956 and in 1959. The pottery was moved to Starkville, Mississippi, in conjunction with the Herschede Clock Co. It finally ceased operation in 1967.

Rookwood wares changed with the times. The variety is endless, in part because of the great variations in glazes and designs due to the creativity of the many talented artists.

References: Herbert Peck, *The Book of Rookwood Pottery*, Crown Publishers, Inc., 1968; Herbert Peck, *The Second Book of Rookwood Pottery*, published by author, 1985.

Collectors' Club: American Art Pottery Association, 9825 Upton Circle, Bloomington, MN 55431.

Basket, 7 x 4 x 4″, two handles, four feet, upfolded sides, underglaze slip painted flowers, standard brown glaze, artist sgd "Edith Regina Felton, 1887"	400.00
Bookends, pr	
Dachshund, brown, tan highlights, 1927, artist sgd "Louise Abel"	200.00
Elephant, walking, white glaze, 1921	175.00
Rook, chocolate brown glaze, artist sgd "William McDonald"	165.00
Bowl, 5½ x 6″, yellow and green flowers, standard reddish-brown glaze, marked with "U" and "7" on bottom	50.00
Cologne Bottle, 4½″ h, gray glaze, incised design of butterflies and berry vine, sgd, numbered, and dated "AP (Albert Pons)/19S/Rookwood/1883" on base, remains of cologne label	200.00
Compote, 8¼″ d, 5⅜″ h, three eagles with spread wings form base under shallow bowl, black glaze, blue bowl int., sgd, dated 1923, numbered	175.00
Creamer, 3″, underglaze slip painted leaf and berries, standard glaze, shape #655, artist sgd "Sallie E. Coyne, 1903"	250.00
Cup and Saucer, 2½ x 4½″, holly leaves and berries, standard glaze, artist sgd "Sara Sax, 1897"	300.00
Desk Set, Arts and Crafts style double inkwell, matching letter holder, high glaze, 1926	300.00
Ewer, 6¾″, four cherries and leaves, Eliza C Lawrence, c1900, handle repaired	100.00

Figure
4" l
    Cat, medium blue, matte finish, 1929, various marks **80.00**
    Elephant, ivory glaze, matte finish, artist sgd "William McDonald, 1926" **75.00**
    5¼", rooster, green, yellow, brown, and red matte finish, artist sgd "Charles T. McLaughlin, 1928" with various other marks **225.00**
Flower Frog, 6" h, figural, raven, black glaze, 1923 . . . . **200.00**
Jug
    4⅝", shades of brown, white, and gold, bird, pine boughs, and clouds, artist sgd "Martin Rettig, 1884" with various other marks **300.00**
    4¾", blue, turquoise, black, green, brown, ivory, and gold spiders and webs dec, artist sgd "William P. McDonald, 1883," with various other marks **250.00**
Mug
    4¾", pint, dark and light brown, yellows, and flesh tones, elderly Flemish lady dec, artist sgd "Grace Young, 1897" with various other marks **1,000.00**
    5", dog portrait, standard glaze, artist sgd "MAD, 1897" **1,000.00**

Tile, titled "The Lake," artist Elizabeth F. McDermott, blue and green pastels, artist's initials in lower right corner, 6½ x 8" image, 9½ x 13½" frame, $2,500.00.

Plaque
    5 x 8", rect, titled "The Bay," artist sgd "Lenore Asbury, 1920," framed . . **750.00**
    7¼ x 9¼", scenic vellum, winter landscape, artist sgd "Sara Sax, 1917" **1,200.00**
Plate, 7⅛", yellow, pansies and swirl

dec, standard glaze, artist sgd "Laura A. Fry, 1887" **240.00**
Tea Tile, 5¾", ftd, parrot perched in flowering tree, four pastel colors, 1920 . . . . **80.00**
Teapot, 7¼", thistle dec, standard glaze, artist sgd "OGR, 1892" **575.00**
Tile
    4½ x 4¼", blue-green, emblem of Packard Motor Co, 1910 . . . . **75.00**
    12 x 12", architectural, standing cherubs **300.00**
Vase
    4½", medium and dark brown, yellow-brown nasturtiums, sgd "Laura E. Lindeman, 1907" with various other marks **200.00**
    5¼", yellow and green blossoms, wax matte glaze, artist sgd "Margaret Helen McDonald, 1930" with various other marks **200.00**
    6¼", wisteria, standard glaze, artist sgd "BH, 1893" **375.00**
    6⅝", background shaded from green to soft peach, blue at top, violet flowers, wax matte glaze, unidentified signature, miscellaneous other marks, 1938 . . . . **450.00**
    6¾", Art Deco motif, wax matte, artist sgd "LA, 1923" **300.00**
    7", dogwood border, vellum glaze, light green int., sgd, numbered and dated "KH (Katharine Hickman)/ XIV (1914)/V/1124/E" on base . . . **300.00**
    8", stylized blue peacock feathers, green ground, vellum, artist sgd "Sara Sax, 1910" **800.00**
    8¼", Iris, berries and leaves, shaded gray to orchid to black ground, artist sgd "Sara Sax," shape #909C **1,000.00**
    9", blue glaze, sgd and numbered, c1924 . . . . **200.00**
    9½", shaded blues and tans landscape dec, vellum glaze, artist sgd "Edward Diers, 1921," faint age cracks in bottom **300.00**
    12½", yellow breasted birds and blue flowers, salmon ground, sgd and dated 1949 on base, artist sgd and numbered, factory second, heavy crackling to glaze **450.00**

ROSE BOWLS

History: A rose bowl, a decorative open bowl with a crimped, pinched, or petal top, held fragrant rose petals or potpourri which served as an air freshener in the late Victorian period. Practically every glass manufacturer made rose bowls in a variety of patterns and glass types, including fine art glass.

Additional Listings: See specific glass categories.

Opalescent, Swirl pattern, blue, $75.00.

Cameo, 3¼", enameled three petal top, mottled gold, river landscape cutting, acid cut, sgd "Daum Nancy"	**625.00**
Cranberry, 6", opalescent, hobnail . . .	**60.00**
Cut Velvet, 3¾", rose, DQ, white lining	**175.00**
Opalescent, Swirl, blue	**75.00**
Peachblow, 4", six crimps	**125.00**
Rubena Overshot, 3¾", eight crimps . .	**70.00**
Satin	
4⅜" d, 2⅜" h, DQ, MOP, pink, blue, and yellow rainbow stripes shade to white base, cream glossy int., six crimp top, marked "Patent"	**950.00**
4½" d, 3⅛" h, beige, mauve pull–up feathers, soft blue–green int., closely crimped top	**900.00**
5½" d, 5" h, DQ, MOP, shaded peach to ivory, white int., eight crimp top, dimpled sides	**275.00**
Spangled, 6", cased, lavender, silver veining, attributed to Cape Cod Glass Works	**90.00**
Stevens and Williams, 3", satin glass, DQ, MOP, rainbow, alternating stripes of pastel yellow, pink, and blue, imp sgd "Stevens & Williams, Stourbridge Glass"	**1,100.00**

ROSE CANTON, ROSE MANDARIN, ROSE MEDALLION

History: The pink rose color has given its name to three related groups of Chinese export porcelain. Rose Mandarin was produced from the late 18th century to approximately 1840. Rose Canton began somewhat later extending through the first half of the 19th century. Rose Medallion originated in the early 19th century and was made through the early 20th century.

Rose Mandarin derives its name from the Mandarin figure(s) found in garden scenes with women and children. The women often feature gold decorations in their hair. Polychrome enamels and birds separate the scenes.

Rose Medallion has alternating panels of figures and birds and flowers. The elements are four in number, separated evenly around the center medallion. Peonies and foliage fill voids.

Rose Canton is similar to Rose Medallion except the figure panels are replaced by flowers. People are present only if the medallion partitions are absent. Some patterns have been named—Butterfly and Cabbage, Rooster, etc. The category actually is a catchall for all pink enamel ware not fitting into the first two groups.

Reference: Sandra Andacht, *Oriental Antiques & Art: An Identification And Value Guide,* Wallace-Homestead, 1987.

Reproduction Alert: Rose Medallion is still made, although the quality does not match the earlier examples.

ROSE CANTON

Bowl, 11½", green, alternating sections of florals and figures	**285.00**
Brush Pot, 4½", scenic, ladies, reticulated, gilt trim	**265.00**
Charger, 13", floral panels, 19th C . . .	**200.00**
Compote, flower and butterfly medallions, pedestal base	**300.00**
Plate, 8½", floral dec	**75.00**
Soup Tureen, cov, lozenge shape, gilt floral ground, figural scenes	**300.00**
Sugar, cov, handle	**100.00**
Teapot, 5", flowers and butterflies	**135.00**

ROSE MANDARIN

Bough Vase, 7" h, elongated, flaring, hexagonal section over stepped foot, panels of figures, birds, and landscape, red, black, and gilt fish scale ground, five apertures on cov	**2,000.00**
Chamber Stick, 5½" d, snuffer missing, Canton, Chinese, 19th C	**100.00**
Cup and Saucer, scenic panels, butterfly and floral border	**150.00**
Fruit Bowl, 11⅛" l, matching undertray, Canton, Chinese, 19th C	**1,300.00**
Plate, 9⅞", Canton, Chinese, 19th C .	**50.00**
Teapot, 7½", enamel, orange, pink, green, lavender, and yellow, mandarin panels, gilding	**675.00**
Vegetable Dish, scalloped cov, flowers, butterflies,and bird panels and borders, boating scene on cov	**650.00**

ROSE MEDALLION

Bouillon Cup and Saucer, cov, handle . **75.00**
Bowl
  9½″ d, int. painted with reserve panel
    of flowers and figures, gilt floral
    ground, ext. with unusual frieze of
    figures, 19th C, pr **1,500.00**
  10″ d, notched sq form, int. single
    rose spray, ornate border, ext. fi-
    gural vignettes, Chinese, 19th C . **400.00**
  13¼″, reserve panels of figures, gilt
    thunder borders, 19th C **1,600.00**
Dish, 15″ d, figural panels, flowers and
  objects ground, 19th C **550.00**
Flower Pot, 3¼″, three small feet **175.00**
Ginger Jar, 10½″ h, pr, figural reserve
  dec **200.00**

**Rose Medallion, plate, marked "Made
in China," 10⅛″ d, $40.00.**

Punch Bowl, 23″ d, reserve panels of
  int. scenes, elaborate gilt ground of
  flowers, insects, and birds, 19th C . **5,000.00**
Pomade Jar, 2½ x 2¼″, cylindrical, sce-
  nic lid, man and woman at window . **125.00**
Sauce Boat, 4¼″, int. border with rose
  and butterfly dec, ext. with household
  scenes, orange glaze **150.00**
Tray, 15″ l, twin strap handles, 19th C . **900.00**
Tureen, 14½″ l, cov, 16″ l undertray,
  bombe shape, twin strap handles,
  double domed lid, gilt finial, 19th C . **1,800.00**
Vase
  18″ h, baluster form, applied handles,
    late 19th C **1,000.00**
  32½″, baluster, gilt relief dragons on
    shoulders, gilt foo dog handles,
    scalloped rim, reserve panels of fig-
    ures and birds, gilt ground, green
    vine, pr **3,000.00**
Vegetable Dish, 11″ l, cov, alternating
  figural and floral reserve dec,
  Chinese, late 19th C **200.00**

MARKE

ROSENTHAL

History: Rosenthal Porcelain Manufactory began operating at Selb, Bavaria in 1880. Specialities were tablewares and figurines. The firm is still
in operation.

Reference: Susan and Al Bagdade, *Warman's
English & Continental Pottery & Porcelain, 1st Edition,* Warman Publishing Co., Inc., 1987.

**Butter Pat, Moss Rose pattern, gilded
edges, 4″ d, $12.00.**

Bowl, 9″, hp, clusters of cherries, green
  ext., gold trim, double handles, artist
  sgd **85.00**
Cake Plate, 10¼″ d, open handles, hp,
  multicolored roses, cobalt blue
  ground, gold border, artist sgd **50.00**
Chocolate Set, chocolate pot, cov, 10″
  d plate with handle, four cups and
  saucers, transitional Art Deco–Art
  Nouveau dec, brown shaded to
  beige, cream ground, gold trim, artist
  sgd, 1922, 10 pcs **135.00**
Compote, 13 x 8¾″, oblong, blue Delft
  dec, ornately scrolled blank, marked
  "Rosenthal, Delft, Savoy, Germany" **150.00**
Cup and Saucer
  Donatello pattern, light green, dark
    green, and gold, white ground . . . **10.00**
  Portrait, woman, gold trim, artist sgd **50.00**
Demitasse Cup and Saucer, medallion
  portrait **45.00**
Figure
  6″, young boy frolicking with lamb, art-
    ist sgd **200.00**
  10½″, group of birds, bright blue,
    green, orange, yellow and brown,
    underglaze green factory mark, imp
    "J Feldtmann," numbered **425.00**

15¾", Oriental dancer, right leg raised, ornate yellow, blue, mauve, green, black, and gilt costume, Oriental man seated at base **1,215.00**
Hatpin Holder, 5½", figural, stylized bust **30.00**
Model
  6" h, Dachshund, seated **150.00**
  8 x 6", Pointer dog, black and white **125.00**
  8 x 8", Poodle, standing, white, green collar, artist sgd **235.00**
  10 x 6 x 5", reclining deer **350.00**
Plate
  4", white glaze, SS rim **10.00**
  8¾", bearded Dutch fisherman, lavender trousers and cap, pale blue ground **38.00**
Urn, cov, 10½", portrait of woman, garden setting, multicolored **240.00**
Vase
  7", shaded tan and rust foliage, crackle glaze, artist sgd, 1946 . . . . . . **90.00**
  8", blue and white Dutch scene **80.00**
  10¼", Copenhagen series, SS overlay, marked, c1890 . . . . **385.00**
Wall Mask, 10" l, stylized female face, cutout eyes, long arched eyebrows, sgd "Gerhard Schliepstein," printed factory mark, imp "402," c1920 . . . . **1,430.00**

Roseville
U.S.A.

ROSEVILLE POTTERY

History: In the late 1880s a group of investors purchased the J. B. Owens Pottery in Roseville, Ohio, and made utilitarian stoneware items. In 1892 the firm was incorporated and joined by George F. Young who became general manager. Four generations of Youngs controlled Roseville until the early 1950s.

A series of acquisitions began: Midland Pottery of Roseville in 1898, Clark Stoneware Plant in Zanesville (formerly used by Peters and Reed), and Muskingum Stoneware (Mosaic Tile Company) in Zanesville. In 1898 the offices also moved from Roseville to Zanesville.

In 1900 Roseville introduced its art pottery—Rozane. Rozane became a trade name to cover a large series of lines. The art lines were made in limited amounts after 1919.

The success of Roseville depended on its commercial lines, first developed by John J. Herald and Frederick Rhead in the first decades of the 1900s. In 1918 Frank Ferrell became art director and developed over 80 lines of pottery. The economic depression of the 1930s brought more lines, including Pine Cone.

In the 1940s a series of high gloss glazes were tried to revive certain lines. In 1952 Raymor dinnerware was produced. None of these changes brought economic success. In November 1954 Roseville was bought by the Mosaic Tile Company.

References: Sharon and Bob Huxford, *The Collectors Encyclopedia Of Roseville Pottery*, Collector Books, 1976; Sharon and Bob Huxford, *The Collectors Encyclopedia Of Roseville Pottery, Second Series*, Collector Books, 1980.

Collectors' Club: American Art Pottery Association, 9825 Upton; Circle, Bloomington, MN 55431.

Additional Listings: See *Warman's Americana & Collectibles* for more examples.

Ashtray, Bushberry, berries and leaves, blue bark textured ground **60.00**
Basket
  Apple Blossom, 8", white relief apple blossoms, brown tree branch handles, green ground **85.00**
  Bleeding Heart, 12", pointed overhead handle, pink blossoms, green leaves, shaded green ground, matching flower frog **100.00**
  Imperial, 6" **42.00**
  Pine Cone, blue **300.00**
  Rozane, 3", two handles **50.00**
  Waterlily, green, 8" **50.00**
Bookends, White Rose, 6½", pr **75.00**
Bowl
  Ferrella, 12", brown **200.00**
  Magnolia, green **35.00**
  Pine Cone, 6", brown **45.00**
  Snowberry, green and brown **35.00**
Candlestick
  Baneda, pr **200.00**
  Donatello, 6½" **65.00**
  Luster, 12", pr **85.00**
  Rozane, pr **75.00**
Children's Dishes
  Creamer, 3", chicks dec **45.00**
  Feeding Dish, 5", rolled rim, five chicks **135.00**
  Mush Set, bowl and pitcher, chicks dec **75.00**
Compote, Donatello, 9" **110.00**
Console Bowl, Sunflower **75.00**
Ewer
  Bushberry, 10", blue **100.00**
  Magnolia, 10" **70.00**
  Water Lily, brown **75.00**
Flower Frog, Magnolia, blue and gray, handle **30.00**
Flower Pot, Cherry, 4" **100.00**
Hanging Basket
  Apple Blossom, pink, orig chains . . . **85.00**
  Cherry **300.00**
Jardiniere
  Blackberry **250.00**
  Donatello, 6½" **45.00**
  Futura, 6", gray and pink **100.00**

Jardiniere and Pedestal

Jonquil, 29"	550.00
Normandy	750.00

Jug

Blackberry, 5"	100.00
Cherry, 4½"	90.00

Lamp, Vista, 10" base	225.00

Mug

Dutch, 4½"	45.00
Rozane, cherries dec, artist sgd "L"	125.00

Pitcher, Freesia, blue	55.00
Planter, Pine Cone, green, 4½ x 4½"	40.00
Powder Box, Donatello	260.00
Rose Bowl, Tourmaline, 4"	22.00
Sand Jar, Pine Cone, green	525.00
Tea Set, Apple Blossom, green	125.00
Umbrella Stand, blended majolica	170.00

Urn

Monticello, double handles, blue	125.00
Sunflower, 6½"	130.00

Vase

Blackberry

4"	85.00
8"	180.00
Bushberry, green	85.00
Cherry Blossom, 7", pink	120.00
Cosmos, 10", green	90.00
Foxglove, pink	65.00
Fuchsia, 10", blue, double handles	110.00
Futura, 7", pink	300.00
Imperial II, 5½"	75.00
Jonquil, 6½", double handles	70.00
Monticello, 5 x 7", double handles	100.00
Morning Glory	135.00
Orian, 10½", blue	70.00
Pine Cone, 12", blue	175.00
Tourmaline, 6", blue, silvery streaks	50.00
Zephyr Lily, blue	50.00

Wall Pocket

Apple Blossom	35.00
Bushberry, 8", blue ground	85.00

Wall Pocket, Blackberry, 8½" h, $375.00.

Corinthian

8"	65.00
12"	110.00
Dogwood I	75.00
Donatello, 10"	85.00
Floran	65.00
Imperial II	225.00
White Rose, blue	90.00

ROYAL BAYREUTH

History: In 1794 the Royal Bayreuth factory was founded in Tettau, Bavaria. Royal Bayreuth introduced their figural patterns in 1885. Designs of animals, people, fruits, and vegetables decorated a wide array of tablewares and inexpensive souvenir items.

Tapestry ware, rose and other patterns, were made in the late 19th century. The surface of the ware feels and looks like woven cloth. Tapestry ware was made by covering the porcelain with a piece of fabric tightly stretched over the surface, decorating the fabric, glazing the piece, and firing.

The Royal Bayreuth crest mark varied in design and color. Many wares were unmarked. It is difficult to verify the chronological years of production due to the lack of records.

Royal Bayreuth still manufactures dinnerware. It has not maintained production of earlier wares, particularly the figural items.

Reference: Susan and Al Bagdade, *Warman's English & Continental Pottery & Porcelain, 1st Edition,* Warman Publishing Co., Inc., 1987.

Corinthian

Humidor, cov	200.00
Pitcher, 6", classical figures, black ground, yellow bands, leaf dec around neck and base	125.00
Toothpick, three handles	75.00

Devil and Cards

Ashtray	125.00
Creamer, 4"	120.00
Demitasse Cup and Saucer	135.00
Humidor, 7¾" h, winged finial	675.00
Pitcher, water, green mark	500.00
Wall Pocket, figural	200.00

Grape Cluster

Creamer, white MOP, marked "Germany"	85.00

Lobster, sugar bowl, large, $115.00.

Mustard, pink MOP, Tettau mark . . .	100.00
Relish, white MOP	80.00

Lobster

Ashtray, 6¼" l	50.00
Creamer, 4"	50.00
Pitcher, water, blue mark	425.00
Sugar, cov	115.00

Miscellaneous Patterns

Ashtray, swan scene, twisted handle	45.00
Bread Plate, figural, oak leaf, white satin finish	175.00
Candleholder, farm scene, ring handle	80.00
Candy Dish, oval, Bavarian women and horses	60.00
Chocolate Pot, dome shaped lid, ornate handle, floral and fruit dec . .	175.00
Cigarette Set, box and matching holder, musicians dec	150.00

Creamer, figural

Bear	300.00
Bo Peep	55.00
Crow, black, tan beak, blue mark .	200.00
Dachshund	140.00
Duck, marked "Deponiert"	90.00
Eagle, blue mark	275.00
Fish, open mouth, blue mark	160.00
Geranium	130.00
Goat, head	100.00
Hound Dog, brown	85.00
Iris, unmarked	290.00
Lamplighter	165.00
Robin	115.00
Seal	225.00
Strawberry	70.00

Creamer and Sugar, Apple, blue mark	375.00
Marmalade Jar, cov, figural, strawberry	175.00
Match Holder, hanging, shell, MOP, green and gold	60.00
Mug, long horned steer dec	75.00
Mustard, Lemon, cov, orig spoon . . .	75.00

Pitcher, figural

Clown, 4½", red	250.00
Parrot, 4¼"	150.00
Pelican	750.00

Plate, Lettuce, 7" d, yellow flowers, ring handle	40.00
Powder Dish, cov, figural, elk	85.00
Relish, figural, poinsettia, 7½" l	100.00
Salt Shaker, Bellringer, figural	235.00

Toothpick

Brittany woman dec, three gold feet	125.00
Colonial dining room scene, three handles, blue mark	125.00
Elk, figural, blue mark	125.00

Vase

3⅜", two handles, Dutch girl and boats scene, silver top rim, hallmarks	45.00
4½", floral	45.00
Wall Pocket, figural, strawberry	225.00

Murex Shell

Cigarette Vase	90.00
Creamer	50.00
Pitcher, water, blue mark	375.00
Salt Shaker, marked "Bavaria"	30.00
Sherbet	70.00

Nursery Rhyme

Creamer, Little Jack Horner	55.00
Jug, 6½", Babes in Woods, two little girls talking to troll	300.00
Match Holder, girl and dog	200.00
Mug, Little Jack Horner, blue mark .	125.00
Vase, 3¼", girl with candle, silver rim, green mark	50.00

Poppy

Biscuit Jar, red, blue mark	650.00
Bowl, 6"	85.00
Demitasse Creamer and Sugar, red .	150.00
Match Holder, wall, red	115.00
Mustard, spoon, Deponiert and green mark	100.00
Plate, 5¾"	50.00
Teapot	175.00

Sand Babies

Dresser Tray	150.00
Planter, 3" h, two handles	100.00
Sugar	75.00
Vase, 2¾" h, brown ground, ball feet	100.00
Wall Pocket	175.00

Snow Babies

Cereal Set, sledding	150.00
Creamer and Sugar	185.00
Plaque, pierced, 9"	175.00
Plate, babies on ice	75.00
Vase, 3¼" h, brown ground	100.00

Sunbonnet Babies

Candlesticks, pr, washing	325.00
Cereal Set, bowl, 7" underplate, washing and ironing	385.00
Creamer and Sugar, boat shape, cleaning	300.00
Cup and Saucer, sewing	145.00

Dish

Diamond shape, sewing	155.00
Heart shape, farming	165.00
Spade shape, sweeping	155.00

Hair Receiver, babies sweeping, three high gold legs, blue mark .. **450.00**
Pitcher, milk, washing, pinch nose .. **235.00**
Plate
  7", cleaning **100.00**
  8", washing **100.00**
Relish, 8", open handle, fishing **175.00**
Vase, 3¼" h, washing clothes **100.00**
Wall Pocket, cleaning **500.00**
Tomato
  Biscuit Jar **265.00**
  Box, cov, 4½ x 3¾" **50.00**
  Pitcher, water **275.00**
  Plate, 8¾" **30.00**
  Tea Set, leaf base **185.00**

Rose Tapestry, bowl, blue mark, 11" d, $725.00.

ROSE TAPESTRY

Box, cov, 4 x 1¾", pink and yellow roses **285.00**
Cake Plate, 10½", pink roses **200.00**
Creamer, 3½", pinched spout, blue mark **225.00**
Demitasse Mug, three color roses, blue mark **80.00**
Dresser Tray, blue mark **350.00**
Fernery, flared, three color roses, pink, white, and yellow, tiny gold handles, orig insert, blue mark **245.00**
Hair Receiver, blue mark **250.00**
Hatpin Holder, blue mark **450.00**
Mustard Jar, spoon, pink and white roses **225.00**
Pitcher, 3½", gold trim **165.00**
Plate, 6" d, three colored roses, gold rim **150.00**
Powder Box, blue mark **250.00**
Ring Tree, saucer base **425.00**
Vase, 5½", four color roses, soft green ground, apricot, yellow, pink, and white roses, narrow base, bulbous center, narrow top **300.00**

TAPESTRY, MISCELLANEOUS

Box, cov, 2½", five sheep **185.00**

Cake Plate, 10", handles, mountain goats among aspens **140.00**
Chocolate Pot, mountain goats, pastoral scene **415.00**
Clock, Christmas Cactus pattern, dresser type, blue mark **400.00**
Hair Receiver, goats gracing, blue mark **225.00**
Humidor, 6¾", scenic, gold trim, mushroom finial **350.00**
Pitcher, court lady and cavalier, formal garden setting, blue mark **425.00**
Toothpick, woman in large hat, fur coat and muff, four gold feet, gold handles **350.00**
Vase
  4", chateau scene, blue mark **225.00**
  6¼", portrait of lady, wearing bonnet **275.00**

ROYAL BONN

Bonn

History: In 1836 Franz Anton Mehlem founded a Rhineland factory that produced earthenware and porcelain, including household, decorative, technical, and sanitary items. In 1890 the name Royal was added to the mark. All items made after 1890 include the name "Royal Bonn." The firm reproduced Hochst figures between 1887 and 1903. These figures, produced in both porcelain and earthenware, were made from the original molds from the defunct Prince-Electoral Mayence Manufactory in Hochst. The factory was purchased by Villeroy and Boch in 1921 and closed it in 1931.

Reference: Susan and Al Bagdade, *Warman's English & Continental Pottery & Porcelain, 1st Edition,* Warman Publishing Co., Inc., 1987.

Bowl, 10" × 5" hp, roses, heavy gold trim **200.00**
Cake Plate, 10¼" d, dark blue floral transfer **20.00**
Celery Tray, floral dec, gilt trim **80.00**
Cheese Dish, cov, multicolored floral dec, cream ground, gold trim **75.00**
Cracker Jar, multicolored enamel floral dec **100.00**
Ewer, 12" h, pink, yellow, and blue flowers, cream ground, gold trim **175.00**
Jardiniere, 15" d, 12" h, hp, multicolored flowers **365.00**
Marmalade Jar, 5" h, floral dec, beige ground, SP cov and bail handle ... **65.00**
Plate, 9" d, floral dec, gilt tracery **60.00**

Vase, bulbous, floral design, light yellow–green ground, burgundy neck, gilding at top, impressed and painted marks, 9" h, $185.00.

Relish, 10" l, handle, three sections, hp, florals, gold trim **125.00**

Teapot, 4½" h, red, black, and light blue, gilding, marked "1755" in cartouche with crown **75.00**

Urn, cov, 13" h, hp, multicolored flowers, green and yellow ground, two gold handles, artist sgd **100.00**

Vase
7½" h, deep pastel florals, ivory ground, gilt tracery, gilt collar and side ring handles **225.00**

8¼" h, 8" d, shaded brown and gold ground, gold emb dec, portrait of lady with wreath of roses in hair, cream dress, artist sgd "G Muller" . . **550.00**

10½" h, 5" d, shaded brown and gold ground, gold emb dec, gold handles, portrait of lady in purple dress and scarf, light brown hair, artist sgd "G Muller" **550.00**

13½" h, portrait medallion, raised gold trim, artist sgd **350.00**

ROYAL COPENHAGEN

History: Franz Mueller established a porcelain factory at Copenhagen in 1775. When bankruptcy threatened in 1779, the Danish king acquired ownership, appointing Mueller manager and adopting the name "Royal Copenhagen." The crown sold its interest in 1867; the company remains privately owned today.

Blue Fluted, Royal Copenhagen's most famous pattern, was created in 1780. It is of Chinese origin and comes in three styles: smooth edge, closed lace edge, and perforated lace edge (full lace). Many other factories copied it. Flora Danica, named for a famous botanical work was introduced in 1789 and remained exclusive to Royal Copenhagen. Botanical illustrations were done free hand; all edges and perforations were cut by hand.

Royal Copenhagen porcelain is marked with three wavy lines which signify ancient waterways and a crown, the latter added in 1889. Stoneware does not have the crown mark.

Reference: Susan and Al Bagdade, *Warman's English & Continental Pottery & Porcelain, 1st Edition,* Warman Publishing Co., Inc., 1987.

Additional Listings: Limited Edition Collectors' Plates.

Butter Pat, Symphony pattern, set of 6 **20.00**

Candle Bobeches, 3½" d, Full Lace pattern, blue, pr **65.00**

Candlesticks, 7" h, white and gilt, circular columns molded with foliate swags suspended from tied ribbons enriched in gilding, lower and upper parts with shallow grooves, bases with stylized foliage, matched set of four **1,000.00**

Cup and Saucer, Half Lace pattern, blue, fluted **25.00**

Dinnerware, Flora Danica pattern, pink and green, botanical specimen, gilt dentil rim, underglaze blue triple wave mark, numbered, printed mark, green painter's mark, black botanical inscription

Chocolate Cup and Saucer, 5½" d, gilt highlighted scalloped reticulated border, molded beading, gilt roundels, buds, and leaves on rim, inscribed numbers, set of 8 . . . . . **3,575.00**

Compote, 6", pink and gold molded beadwork border, pr **1,250.00**

Creamer and Sugar, branch handles **900.00**

Fish Plates, 10⅛", various fish species in aquatic setting, green and gold molded beadwork border, set of 12 . . . . **4,500.00**

Fruit Bowl, 5⅝" d, set of 6 . . . . **1,760.00**

Pickle Dish, 6" l, shaped, everted rect handle **300.00**

Plate, set of 12
5⅝", bread and butter **2,200.00**
7⅞", salad **3,575.00**
10⅛", dinner **4,125.00**

Platter
14", round **825.00**

16⅛", oval	1,125.00
17¼", oval	1,650.00
Salad Bowl, 9½"	900.00
Soup Plate, 8¾" d, set of 6	2,000.00
Vegetable Dish, cov, 9½", twig handles with flowerhead terminals, molded rim, inscribed artist's ciphers, black inscription	1,550.00
Wine Cooler, 6½", oval, twig handles with flowerhead terminals, inscribed artist's ciphers	1,775.00

Figure

5½", cat, sitting, gray and white, green eyes	125.00
7¼", boy with teddy bear	200.00
8½", faun, perched on half columns, holding pipes, rabbit at base, No. 433	125.00
11", polar bear, hunting	250.00

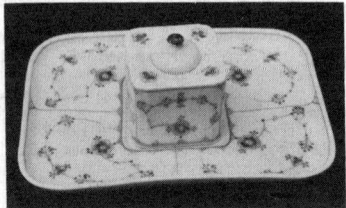

Inkwell, Blue Fluted pattern, 6" w, 8½" l, $100.00.

Inkwell, 6 x 8½", Blue Fluted pattern, matching undertray	125.00
Jar, 16½", flat sided circular shape, rocky seascape dec, bronze cov, oval bronze base, knop feet	450.00
Pitcher, 4", cobalt blue ground, floral dec	50.00
Plate, 8", hp, fruit center	35.00
Tureen, cov, 18" l, Blue Fluted pattern, c1897	275.00

Vase

6", bulbous, celadon green, molded leaves, applied frog, 19th C	200.00
7¾", floral and dragonfly dec, c1890	175.00

ROYAL CROWN DERBY

History: Derby Crown Porcelain Co., established in 1875 in Derby, England, had no connec-

tion with earlier Derby factories which operated in the late 18th and early 19th centuries. In 1890 the company was appointed "Manufacturers of Porcelain to Her Majesty" (Queen Victoria) and from that date has been known as "Royal Crown Derby."

Derby porcelains from 1878 to 1890 carry only the standard crown printed mark. After 1891 the mark carries the "Royal Crown Derby" wording; and, in the 20th century "Made in England" and "English Bone China" were added to the mark.

A majority of these porcelains, both tableware and figures, were hand decorated. A variety of printing processes were used for additional adornment. Today, Royal Crown Derby is a part of Royal Doulton Tableware, Ltd.

References: Susan and Al Bagdade, *Warman's English & Continental Pottery & Porcelain, 1st Edition,* Warman Publishing Co., Inc., 1987; John Twitchett and Betty Bailey, *Royal Crown Derby,* Antique Collectors' Club.

Ewer, swan, white, long neck forms handle, maroon egg shaped body, green foliage on base and handle, marked "Made for Tiffany & Co," crown mark, c1878–1890, 11½" h, $250.00.

Bowl, 11" d, hp floral dec, cobalt blue rim	90.00
Cake Basket, 12" h, rect, meandering roses, polychrome and gilt, ftd, marked, c1830	150.00
Creamer, 1⅛", miniature, cobalt, orange, and white floral dec, marked .	110.00
Cup and Saucer, Imari pattern, iron red, cobalt blue, burnished gilt, set of 22	1,200.00
Dessert Set, Imari type dec, 35 pcs . .	450.00
Dinner Set, Japanese pattern, Imari palette, marked, c1870, 30 pcs	1,400.00
Dish, 9", scattered rose sprays, floral border, late 18th C	150.00

Entree Dish, cov, lozenge form, Imari
  pattern, iron red, cobalt blue, bur-
  nished gilt, set of 3 . . . . **1,500.00**
Plate
  8½", #2451 pattern **60.00**
  10¼", Imari pattern, iron red, cobalt
  blue, burnished gilt, set of 48 . . . . **9,500.00**
Sauce Dish, matching stand, Imari pat-
  tern, iron red, cobalt blue, burnished
  gilt, pr **1,200.00**
Soup Plate, 10", Imari pattern, iron red,
  cobalt blue, burnished gilt, set of 16 **3,250.00**
Toothpick Holder, 3½", green, hp floral
  reserve **135.00**
Urn
  7" h, apple green, scenic reserve, figures, landscape, handles terminating at masks, sq pedestal base,
  c1880 . . . .   **300.00**
  11½" h, cobalt blue, red, and gold
  floral pattern, painted red crown
  mark **400.00**
Vase
  4¼", pink, gold floral, two gold han-
  dles **200.00**
  7", dark red and gold, two handles,
  c1884 . . . .   **185.00**
  8½", broad baluster shape, yellow,
  painted Oriental florals, iron-red,
  green, and gilt, Japanese style,
  1892 . . . .   **370.00**

ROYAL
DOULTON
FLAMBE

ROYAL DOULTON

History: Doulton pottery began in 1815 under
the direction of John Doulton at the Doulton &
Watts pottery in Lambeth, England. Early output
was limited to salt-glazed industrial stoneware.
John Watts retired in 1854. The firm became Doulton and Company, and production was expanded
to include hand decorated stoneware such as figurines, vases, dinnerware, and flasks. In 1872 the
firm began marking their ware "Royal Doulton."

In 1878, John's son, Sir Henry Doulton, purchased Pinder Bourne & Co. in Burslem and the
companies became Doulton & Co., Ltd. in 1882.
Decorated porcelain was added to Doulton's earthenware production in 1884. The Royal Doulton
mark was used on both wares.

Most Doulton figurines were produced at the
Burslem plants from 1890 until 1978, when they
were discontinued. A new line of Doulton figurines
was introduced in 1979.

Beginning in 1913, an "HN" number was assigned to each new Doulton figurine design. The
"HN" numbers refers to Harry Nixon, a Doulton
artist. "HN" numbers were chronological until
1940, after which blocks of numbers were assigned to each modeler. From 1928 until 1954, a
small number appeared to the right of the crown
mark; this number added to 1927 gives the year
of manufacture of the figurines.

Dickens ware, in earthenware and porcelain,
was introduced in 1908. The ware was decorated
with characters from Dickens' novels. The line was
withdrawn in the 1940s, except for plates which
continued until 1974.

Character jugs, a 20th century revival of early
Toby models, were designed by Charles J. Noke
for Doulton in the 1930s. They come in 4 major
sizes and feature fictional characters from Dickens, Shakespeare and other English and American novelists, and historical heroes.

Doulton's Rouge Flambee (also Veined Sung)
is a highly glazed, strong colored ware noted most
for the fine modeling and exquisite colorings, especially in the animal items. The process used to
produce the vibrant colors in this ware is a Doulton
secret.

Production of stoneware at Lambeth ceased in
1956; production of porcelain continues today at
Burslem.

References: Susan and Al Bagdade, *Warman's
English & Continental Pottery & Porcelain, 1st Edi-
tion*, Warman Publishing Co., Inc., 1987; Ralph
and Terry Kovel, *The Kovels' Illustrated Price
Guide to Royal Doulton*, Crown, 1980; Jocelyn
Lukins, *Collecting Royal Doulton Character &
Toby Jugs*, Venta Books, 1985; Kevin Pearson,
*The Character Jug Collectors Handbook, 3rd Edi-
tion*, Kevin Francis Publishing Ltd, 1986; Kevin
Pearson, *The Doulton Figure Collectors Hand-
book*, Kevin Francis Publishing Ltd, 1986; Ruth M.
Pollard, *The Official Price Guide To Royal Doulton,
Fifth Edition*, House of Collectibles, 1986; Princess
and Barry Weiss, *The Original Price Guide to
Royal Doulton Discontinued Character Jugs, Sixth
Edition*, Harmony Books, 1987.

Periodicals: *Collecting Doulton*, BBR Publish-
ing, 2, Strattford Avenue, Elsecar, Barnsley, S.
Yorkshire, S74 8AA, England; *Jug Collector*, P.O.
Box 91748, Long Beach, CA 90809.

Collectors' Club: Royal Doulton International
Collectors Club, P.O. Box 1815, Somerset, NJ
08873.

Animal Mold
  Mallard, HN 807 . . . .   **45.00**
  Setter with Pheasant, HN 2529, sgd
  "JB" **325.00**
  Terrier, reclining, front paws crossed,
  HN 1101 . . . .   **65.00**
Ashtray, Barleycorn **90.00**

Child's Feeding Dish, boy pushing wheelbarrow at beach, c1908 ..... 60.00

Biscuit Jar, 6½ x 5½", SP cov, rim and handle, Coaching Days Series 225.00

Bowl
3½, 8" d, Oasis in the desert 100.00
9¼" d, 2¼" h, marked "Rosalind" .. 70.00

Busts, mini
Sairey Gamp 65.00
Tony Weller 65.00

Candleholder, rural scene 65.00

Candlestick, silicon, tan and brown, pr 135.00

Character Jug, tiny, 1¼"
Auld Mac 210.00
Fat Boy 100.00
John Peel 250.00
Mr. Micawber 85.00

Character Jug, miniature, 2¼ to 2½"
Dick Turpin, masked 20.00
Gondolier 350.00
John Barleycorn 65.00
Mad Hatter 25.00
Mr. Pickwick 55.00
Pied Piper 20.00
Sancho Panzo 25.00
Viking 115.00
Walrus 40.00

Character Jug, small, 3½ to 4"
Captain Hook 320.00
Falstaff 25.00
Fortune Teller 350.00
Gardener 40.00
Punch and Judy 375.00
Scaramouche 350.00
Robin Hood, feather handle 60.00
Sgt Buz Fuz 120.00
Simon the Cellarer 65.00
Trapper 40.00

Character Jug, large, 5¼ to 7"
Aramis 50.00
Baccus 50.00
Capt Hook 275.00
Clown, white hair 850.00
Don Quixote 50.00
Gondolier 475.00
Granny 50.00
Parson Brown, A mark 135.00
Vicar of Bray 165.00

Creamer and Sugar, florals, gold outline 45.00

Cup and Saucer, hp, c1892 .... 80.00

Demitasse Cup and Saucer, hp, c1880 80.00

Dickens Ware
Bowl, 7¾" d, 3⅞" h, three characters, marked 145.00
Demitasse Cup and Saucer, Mr. Pickwick on 2⅛" cup, Sam Weller on 4" d saucer 55.00
Jug, Bill Sykes, 3", miniature 95.00
Mug, Cap'n Cuttle, 4" d, 4¼" h, two handles, marked 145.00
Pitcher, pottery, sq shape 5¾" h, 2⅞" d, Mr. Micawber 95.00

6⅝" h, 3¼" d, Trotty Veck 115.00
7⅜" h, 3½" d, Alfred Jingle 125.00

Sandwich Tray, 5⅝ x 11", rect shape, Bill Sykes 85.00

Sauce Dish, Fat Boy, 5¼" 45.00

Vase
Alfred Jingle, 7⅝", 5" d, sq flattened shape, two handles 135.00
Old Peggoty, 5¼" h, 4⅛" d, pottery, two handles 75.00
Sydney Carton, 7 × 3¾", handle . 135.00

Ewer
7 x 3¾", cream, pansies, maroon, yellow with green leaves, gold handle, pink collar 195.00

Figurine
A Courting 400.00
Autumn Breezes, 1913 .... 185.00
Balloon Man, HN1954 .... 130.00
Biddy Penny Farthing, HN1843 .... 130.00
Bridget, HN2070 .... 210.00
Clockmaker 170.00
Cobbler 225.00

Pitcher, bulbous, cream ground, dark blue and rust floral dec, cobalt blue neck band with gold floral outlines, cobalt blue handle with gold stripes, gold rim band, c1882–1890, $225.00.

Darby 175.00
Delight, #1772 .... 155.00
Favorite, #2249 .... 120.00
First Waltz, #2862 .... 145.00
Granny's Heritage, HN2031 ...... 300.00
Johnny Appleseed 305.00
Lunch Time, #2485 .... 150.00
Mary Had A Little Lamb, #2048 ... 75.00
Old Balloon Seller, HN1315 ...... 130.00
Owd William, HN2042 .... 200.00
Paisley Shawl, 9" 175.00
Pensive Moments, #2704 .... 125.00
Queen of the Ice, 2435 .... 110.00
Sairey Gump, HN1896 .... 250.00

Votes For Women, #2816 .... 150.00
Flambe
Animal Mold, fish, 12½" 800.00
Bowl, 9¾ x 3", Oriental style, handled 225.00
Jardiniere, blue and white, woman
playing guitar scene 210.00
Plate, 6", landscape scene 45.00
Jardiniere, 7⅛" h, 7¼" d, Welsh ladies
and children walking toward church,
marked "Welsh Ladies Series Ware" 325.00
Jug
Golfer 250.00
Gondolier, large 400.00
Quaker Oats 495.00
Rip Van Winkle 250.00
Simple Simon 475.00
Mug
Captain Ahab 55.00
Parson Brown 120.00
Santa, 1st edition 100.00
Pitcher
5½", Coaching Days 85.00
8", Old Bob Ye Guard, pinch-in type 95.00
12" h, 6" d, country scene 180.00
Plate
6¾", Coaching Days 60.00
7¾", Coaching Days 65.00
8", Coaching Days, scalloped edge . 80.00
9½", The Gleaners, reticulated border 35.00
10"
Romeo 65.00
Shakespeare Plays 45.00
10¾", Coaching Days, irregular edge 80.00
13½", Tony Weller 125.00
Punch Bowl, 18" d, creamware, transfer
dec, sepia vine and insect design,
marked "Doulton, Burslem," late
19th C 350.00
Tankard, 12" h, 6" d, rural scene 170.00
Tea Caddy, 4 x 3", old woman drinking
tea, SS lid, Kingsware 350.00
Teapot, creamer and sugar, Burslem,
set 145.00
Toby Jug
Beefeater, D6233 .... 45.00
Bacchus, wreath of grapes and
leaves on head, twisted vine handle, 7" h 80.00
Stoneware, 6½" h, blue coat, double
XX, Harry Simeon 375.00
Tray, 5 x 11", Robin Hood Series 85.00
Tumbler, 4", Jackdaw of Rheims Series 125.00
Vase
3", squatty bulbous body, short cylin-
drical neck, running lavender blue
crystalline glaze over yellow, gilt
factory mark, cursive script "Royal
Doulton" 165.00
9 x 3¾", goats, incised in black on
beige center, green and brown borders top and bottom, sgd "Hannah
Barlow 500.00

ROYAL DUX

History: Royal Dux porcelain was made in Dux, Bohemia (Czechoslovakia) by E. Eichler at the Duxer Porzellan-Manufaktur, established in 1860. Many items were exported to the United States. By the turn of the century Royal Dux figurines, vases, and accessories were captivating consumers, especially Art Nouveau designs.

A raised triangle with an acorn and the letter "E" plus Dux, Bohemia was used as a mark between 1900 and 1914.

Reference: Susan and Al Bagdade, *Warman's English & Continental Pottery & Porcelain, 1st Edition,* Warman Publishing Co., Inc., 1987.

Vase, applied peaches and leaves, dark peach ground, 5" h , $100.00.

Bust, 16¾" h, young woman, smiling,
lily bud and blossom in long hair,
more lilies and lilypads at dress,
glazed rose, celery green, tan, ivory,
and peach, traces of gilding, incised
"H Schuberty," triangle factory mark,
numbered, c1900 .... 1,000.00
Candleholder, lady in pants suit, pink
triangle mark 250.00
Centerpiece
7¾ x 4¼ x 11", Art Deco, off white,
two nudes kneeling by center vase,
cobalt blue and gold trim, raised
pink triangle, marked "Royal Dux
Bohemia" 475.00
11 x 11½", beige, maiden overlooking
pool 525.00
Figure
7¾", woman getting dressed, #3396,
sgd "Eli Straback" 125.00
11½, courting scene, pink mark ... 165.00

14", young Greek athlete standing on
backs of two horses **500.00**
14¾ x 4½" d, shepherdess, rose
toga, beige sheepskin robe, green
turban, two white and tan goats on
green grass, semi-gloss finish,
marked "Royal Dux Bohemia" . . . **575.00**
17", camel with rider, pink triangle
mark **395.00**
18", fisherman, carrying net, over the
knee boots and hat, green and
brown, pink triangle mark **635.00**
19", lady reading book **750.00**
21" h, harvester and wife, cobalt blue
and white, gold trim, both holding
sheath of wheat, man with sickle,
pink triangle mark, paper label, pr **725.00**
23" h, hunter with dog **475.00**
Jug, 9½", woman at fountain **175.00**
Mantle Set, 12½" d double handled
bowl, two 12½" vases, applied pink
roses, yellow and green ground . . . **145.00**
Tray, figural, irid blue, center maiden
holding basket on her back **300.00**
Vase
5", dark peach coloring, applied
peaches and leaves **100.00**
8" h, orange and green, flowers and
cherries, pr **85.00**
11", green, rose, and ivory, maiden
holding conch shell **300.00**

ROYAL FLEMISH

History: Royal Flemish was produced by the
Mount Washington Glass Co., New Bedford, Mas-
sachusetts. The process was patented by Albert
Steffin in 1894.

Royal Flemish has heavy raised gold enamel
lines on frosted transparent glass that separates
areas into sections, often colored in russet tones.
It gives the appearance of stained glass windows
with elaborate floral or coin medallions in the design.

Advisors: Clarence and Betty Maier.

Biscuit Jar, 8" h, cylindrical, pale red
roses and gold leaves over typical
lines of raised gold which create
panels in shades of tan, emb SP lid
and bail, sgd **1,200.00**
Jar, cov, 9½" h, olive green and gold
sections, Roman motif medallions,
gold scrolls and leaves, fancy pointed
swirled finial, unsigned **2,250.00**
Vase
8½" h, sq, rounded corners, two delicate applied handles, raised gold
borders separate mauve and olive
green panels, Roman coin motif
dec, unsigned **1,300.00**

**Vase, globular, Roman head within sgd
medallion, additional medallions and
dec, orig label, 6″ d, $2,500.00.**

11" h, bulbous stick shape, gold and
green panels, dragon and floral
medallions, unsigned **1,600.00**
12½" h, bulbous stick shape, raised
gold enamel lines and circles,
winged creatures and multicolored
shadow floral design outlined in
gold, unsigned **1,400.00**

ROYAL RUDOLSTADT

History: Johann Fredrich von Schwarzburg-Ru-
dolstadt was the patron of a faience factory located
in Rudolstadt, Thuringen, East Germany, from
1720 to c1790. The pottery's mark was a hayfork
and later crossed two-prong hayforks in imitation
of the Meissen mark.

In 1854 Ernst Bohne established a factory in
Rudolstadt. His pieces are marked "EB."

The "Royal Rudolstadt" designation originated
with wares imported by Lewis Straus and Sons
(later Nathan Straus and Sons) of New York from
the New York and Rudolstadt Pottery between
1887 and 1918. The factory's mark was a diamond
enclosing the initials "RW" and which was surmounted by a crown. The factory manufactured
several of the Rose O'Neill (Kewpie) items.

Reference: Susan and Al Bagdade, *Warman's
English & Continental Pottery & Porcelain, 1st Edition,* Warman Publishing Co., Inc., 1987.

Bowl, 9", scalloped gold rim, hp roses
and grapes, green leaves **60.00**

Cake Plate, 12", pink, white roses, gold
handles and trim **75.00**
Candlesticks, 7", ivory, emb acanthus
leaves, petal shape cups, marked on
base "Crown Mark," pr **50.00**
Celery Dish, 13", hp yellow rose, gold
trim, handled, artist sgd **80.00**
Child Set, teapot, creamer and sugar
with lid, four cups, saucers, and
plates **275.00**
Dresser Set, tray, hatpin holder, hair re-
ceiver, ring tree, cov jar, rose dec, 6
pcs **250.00**
Ewer, 10", ivory, floral dec, gold handle
and trim **100.00**
Figure, 5½" h, begger girl holding tam-
bourine, white, c1905 . . . .   **100.00**
Hair Receiver, 4¼" d, shaded yellow
ground, yellow roses, green leaves,
gold trim **75.00**
Hatpin Holder, lavender and roses . . .   **25.00**

**Vase, ivory ground, orange and pink
flowers, green and brown leaves, gold
details, blue mark and #6230 on base,
13½" h, $125.00.**

Inkwell, 6 x 3½", cream, multicolored
flowers, attached saucer, sgd **60.00**
Nut Set, master bowl, six small bowls,
white and green roses, fluted, ftd, B
under crown mark, set **250.00**
Pin Tray, 5", clover dec **25.00**
Pitcher
8" h, 5" d, cream, gray and gold birds,
coral and pink leaves, raised mark   **75.00**
11", bulbous, floral dec, gold handle   **125.00**
Plate
8½", pink, yellow, and white roses,
gold pie crust molded rim **30.00**
Relish Dish, 8¾", hp floral dec **25.00**
Teapot, cov, 5½", ivory, pink, lavender,
and green hp floral dec **95.00**

Urn on stand, cov, 10", mythological
scene, Hector and Andro crowning
maiden, gold handled, cobalt blue
ground, artist sgd **125.00**
Vase
4" h, floral dec, elephant handles . .   **90.00**
6½", enameled florals, gold beading,
elaborate gold handles, flower form
opening, cobalt ground **155.00**
10", shaded cream to beige ground,
multicolored pastel floral spray, reticulated gold neck and handles,
blue mark **165.00**

ROYAL VIENNA

History: Production of hard paste procelain in
Vienna began in 1720 with Claude Innocentius du
Paquier, a runaway employee of the Meissen factory. In 1744 Empress Maria Theresa brought the
factory under royal patronage; subsequently the
ware became known as Royal Vienna. The firm
went through many administrative changes until it
closed in 1864. The quality of its workmanship
always was maintained.

Many other Austrian and German firms copied
the Royal Vienna products, including the use of
the "Beehive" mark. Many of the pieces on today's
market are from these firms.

Reference: Susan and Al Bagdade, *Warman's
English & Continental Pottery & Porcelain, 1st Edition,* Warman Publishing Co., Inc., 1987.

Box, 8½" d, 4½" h, slightly domed lid
with hp scene of "Rape of Europa,"
maiden with white robe, gilt zig–zag,
diaper and foliate scroll borders, cobalt blue ground, artist sgd "K. W.,"
Turn EW factory mark, late 19th C .   **500.00**
Charger, 13⅜" d, octagonal, gilding,
center scene of maiden and companion being crowned, paneled ground,
blue shield mark, c1900 . . . .   **660.00**
Chocolate Pot, burgundy and gold, bust
of lady, beehive mark **185.00**
Demitasse Cup and Saucer, portrait,
lady and dog, scalloped green border
with gold design, blue beehive mark   **75.00**
Dish, 8", shell shape, flower sprigs, gilt
zig-zag on blue border, c1773 . . . . .   **360.00**
Ewer, 6¼" h, maiden and cupid in re-
verse, gold, maroon, and dark green,
sgd "Kauffmann," beehive mark . . .   **195.00**
Figure, 7" h, young boy, period dress,
enameled colors, imp beehive mark   **285.00**
Jug, 8½", portrait, mother and small
child, mask shape lip, sgd "LCF,"
c1920 . . . .   **275.00**

Urn, two paintings, artist sgd "Homer," 9½" h, $1,175.00.

Plaque, 12", portrait, woman with child, gilt tracery, raised gold and jewels, pink border, artist sgd, beehive and "Flora" mark 425.00

Plate
   9", maiden draped in white center, band of flowers in hair, serenaded by angel playing lute, cobalt border with gold dec, artist sgd, under-glaze beehive mark 350.00
   9½", portrait, Reflexion, downcast gaze, brown flowing curls, claret cov drapery, gilt band, luster pink border with reserves of shaped claret panels, gilded, late 19th C . 900.00

Tray, 8¼ x 12", pale green, hp violet dec, gold trim 175.00

Urn
   5¼", crimson and green, gold bordered cartouche on front, handles, beehive mark 265.00
   13" h, cov, man and woman in classic garden setting, cupid on reverse, multicolored, sgd "Wagner" 550.00

Vase
   7", bottle shape, gold, brown, and blue, Terra Sita portrait, sgd "Wagner," beehive mark 500.00
   15½", baluster, everted rim, slender neck and foot, two portraits of classical women with doves, heavily jeweled gilt scrolls, pink and green luster ground, sgd "Feuer," beehive mark 1,550.00

ROYAL WORCESTER

History: In 1751 the Worcester Porcelain Company, led by Dr. John Wall and William Davis, acquired the Bristol pottery of Benjamin Lund and moved it to Worcester. The first wares were painted blue under the glaze, followed closely by painting on the glaze in enamel colors. Among the most famous 18th century decorators were James Giles and Jefferys Hamet O'Neale. Transfer-print decoration was developed by the 1760s.

A series of partnerships took over upon Davis's death in 1783: Flight (1783–93), Flight & Barr (1793–1807), Barr, Flight & Barr (1807–13), and Flight, Barr & Barr (1813–40). In 1840 the factory was moved to Chamberlain & Co. in Diglis. Decorative wares were discontinued. In 1852 W. H. Kerr and R. W. Binns formed a new company and revived the ornamental wares.

In 1862 the firm became the Royal Worcester Porcelain Co. Among the key modelers of the late 19th century were James Hadley and his three sons and George Owen, expert at pierced clay pieces. Royal Worcester absorbed the Grainger factory in 1889 and the James Hadley factory in 1905. Modern designers include Dorothy Boughty and Doris Lindner.

References: Susan and Al Bagdade, *Warman's English & Continental Pottery & Porcelain, 1st Edition,* Warman Publishing Co., Inc., 1987; David, John, and Henry Sandon, *The Sandon Guide To Royal Worcester Figures, 1900–1970,* The Alderman Press, 1987.

Museum: Charles William Dyson Perrins Museum, Worcester, England.

Basket, 5¾" h, cane weave base, twisted reed handle, tan, gold highlights, purple mark, Reg #26402/1080, c1891 .... 450.00

Biscuit Jar, 6" h, cov, underplate, flowers, beige ground 325.00

Bone Dish, 5¾", cream, blue floral dec 55.00

Bowl
   5¾", scalloped rim, matte ext., glazed int., hp floral, ivory ground, wide gold bands on rim and base, c1890 120.00
   7¾", boat shape, pedestal base, gold handles, floral dec, gilt trim, date mark 1918 .... 385.00
   9", beige, emb basketweave, large pink and green grape leaves, gold trim, c1896 .... 350.00

Candle Snuffer, white, pink plume ... 60.00

Candlesticks, 11⅜" h, 3¾" d, figural, classic lady wears gold laurel wreath, semi-gloss, cream, gold trim, 1862, pr 900.00

Chocolate Pot, 9" h, hp yellow thistles, purple mark 65.00

Cologne, 3¾", pansies, lavender, rust, and pale yellow, green leaves, SP cap, sgd, 1887 .... 220.00

Creamer and Sugar, cov, blue, pink, and yellow floral, green and rust leaves, gold outlining, sgd, c1888 .... 275.00

Cup and Saucer, polychrome Imari dec, matching 8¾" plate, imp "FBB" with crown 115.00

Creamer, bone china, face below spout, leaf motif on body, green mark, 4″ h, $35.00.

Demitasse Cup and Saucer, blue and white, crescent mark **95.00**

Dish, 5½″, shell, blue and white, bird on rockwork, flowering plants and insects, foliage border, c1755 ...... **350.00**

Ewer
6″ h, floral sprays, gold coiled handle, c1889 .... **140.00**
6½″ h, flowers, gold trim, horn handle, white ground **180.00**
17½″ h, cream, flowers and butterflies, gold handle, spout, and rim . **750.00**

Figurine
Boy and girl getting water from cistern, 6½″ w, 7½″ h, Hadley, dated 1882 .... **350.00**
Irishman, 2⅝ x 2⅞″, 6⅞″ h, Countries of the World Series, beige, satin finish, marked 1891 .... **395.00**
John Bull, 2⅝ x 2⅞″, 6⅞″ h, beige, satin finish, marked, 1891 ...... **400.00**
Sweet Anne #3630 .... **150.00**
Wednesday Child **85.00**

Jug, 10″, mask spout, floral dec, gold trim **375.00**

Lamp, figural, 13″ Elizabethan era woman playing lute, 18″ tree base, supports 14″ brass arm that holds two Clarke Cricklites, orig inserts and shades, dated 1898, marked "Clarke and Worcester" **2,475.00**

Mug, 3¼″, white, holly dec, gold trim, purple mark, 1892 .... **75.00**

Pitcher
8″, fluted top, gold handle, florals, artist sgd, 1889 .... **200.00**
8½″ h, 7″ w, tobacco leaf shape, cream, gold outlining, curled leaf handle, green mark, purple im-

porters mark "French & Co, Boston," c1885 .... **175.00**

Plate
9½″, man fishing in pond, trees, and castled mountain top scene **250.00**
10½″, eagle, gold trim, Bicentennial, Ltd Edition **85.00**

Rose Jar, 4⅜″ h, cov, pink, gold outline, purple mark **125.00**

Serving Dish, 11″ l, oval, Imari dec, gilt, unmarked **175.00**

Soup Bowl, cov, 6″ d, pink leaf and berry design, cream ground, gold handles and knob **150.00**

Spill Vase, 5¼″, emb full figures of girls, sunflowers and cattails, pr, 1908 ... **450.00**

Sugar Bowl, 5¼″ h, porcelain, swirled ribs, purple and green enameled foliage with gilt, imp "BFB" with crown **75.00**

Tankard, 10″, gold mask face under spout, gold handle, floral dec **350.00**

Teapot, 5″ h, pastel floral sprays, gold leaves, purple mark **265.00**

Urn, 12″ h, hp bird, white ground, reticulated handle and top **965.00**

Vase
3¼″ h, butterflies on front and back, gilt foliage, double handles, green mark, c1883 .... **95.00**
7½″, double walled top, reticulated pink top and base with blue and ivory enameled dots, reserved with gilt birds, butterflies, and ducks, all-over gold gilt dots, sgd, c1890 ... **950.00**
10¼″, robin's egg, blue, raised gilt daisies, slender ivory neck, mask handles, marked, c1902 .... **375.00**
12″ h, Water Carrier, cream and gold **80.00**
15¼″, sheep in mountainous landscape, gilt foliage, handles terminating in lotus flowers, pierced cov, crown finial, green mark, early 20th C **900.00**
23⅜″, reserve of three peacocks perched on gnarled tree in garden, blue matte ground, applied scroll griffin handles, molded griffin base, sgd "E Salter," date mark 1901 .. **1,150.00**

ROYCROFT

History: Elbert Hubbard, founder of the Roycrofters in East Aurora, New York, during the turn of the 19th and 20th centuries, was considered a genius in his day. He was an author, lecturer, manufacturer, salesman, and philosopher.

Hubbard established a campus which included a printing plant where he published "The Philistine," "The Fra," and "The Roycrofter." His most famous book was "A Message to Garcia," published in 1899. His "community" also included a furniture manufacturing plant, a metal shop, and a leather shop.

References: Nancy Hubbard Brady, The Book of The Roycrofters, House of Hubbard, 1977; Nancy Hubbard Brady, Roycroft Handmade Furniture, House of Hubbard, 1973; Charles F. Hamilton, Roycroft Collectibles, A. S. Barnes & Company, Inc., 1980; Paul McKenna, A New Pricing Guide For Materials Produced by The Roycroft Printing Shop, Tona Graphics, 2nd edition, 1982.

Additional Listing: Arts and Crafts Movement and Copper.

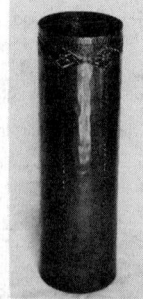

Vase, hammered copper, dark patina, #212, 1919, 10″ h, $325.00.

Ashtray, 6 x 4″, copper, brass finish, attached match holder, pedestal	**85.00**
Book, Sesame and Lilies, John Ruskin, Roycroft Publication, 1897	**165.00**
Bookends, pr	
6 x 6″, leather, tooled design, marked with orb on back	**150.00**
7 x 6″, wood, carved orb mark on front	**200.00**
10 x 5″, copper, fleur-de-lis design, large orb mark	**100.00**
Candlesticks, pr, 20½″, hammered copper, twisted standard with two applied candleholders, orb mark	**300.00**
Cigarette Box, hinged cov	**60.00**
Furniture	
Desk, oak, four drawers on left, 30 x 60 x 30″	**650.00**
Hall Chair, 46″ h, oak, wood seat, carved orb mark	**475.00**
Rocker, 38″ h, mahogany, leather seat, orb mark	**275.00**
Table, library, oak, two drawers, 52 x 33 x 30″	**750.00**
Lamp, 18″, hammered copper, round base, helmet shade	**465.00**
Letter Opener, hammered copper	**30.00**
Platter, 22″, oval, handles	**175.00**
Vase	
7½″, bud, pyramid base, Steuben Aurene glass insert	**265.00**
19″, American Beauty, hammered copper	**450.00**
Wall Sconces, pr, 8¾″ h, rect, copper, Style 402, marked	**165.00**

RUBENA GLASS

History: Rubena crystal is a transparent blown glass which shades from clear to red. It also is found as the background for frosted and overshot glass. It was made in the late 1800s by several glass companies, including Northwood and Hobbs, Brockunier & Co. of Wheeling, West Virginia.

Rubena was used for several patterns of pattern glass including Royal Ivy and Royal Oak.

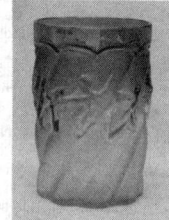

Tumbler, Royal Ivy, 2½″ d, 3¾″ h, $48.00.

Bowl, 4½″, Daisy and Scroll	**60.00**
Celery Vase, threaded, Northwood . . .	**72.00**
Compote	
8½ x 12¾″, rubena overshot bowl, white metal bronze finished figural standard	**125.00**
9 x 14″, rubena overshot bowl, white metal bronze finished figural standard	**150.00**
Creamer, Medallion Sprig, applied clear handle	**160.00**
Decanter, 9″, bulbous base, narrow neck, applied clear handle	**140.00**
Marmalade Jar, cov, enamel dec, sgd "Moser"	**315.00**
Perfume, 3¼″ h, SP top rim, cranberry cut stopper	**125.00**

Pickle Castor, vertical optic insert, fancy
fretwork on ftd Pairpoint SP frame . . **225.00**
Sugar, cov, Royal Ivy, frosted **135.00**
Sugar Shaker, 6½", sq, cut diagonal
stripes, Georgian style SP top **140.00**
Tumbler, Royal Ivy, 3¾" h **48.00**
Vase
6", bud, bank of cut diamonds, enam-
eled floral dec **60.00**
9½", six crimp gold trim top, chrysanthemum dec, gold foliage, pr **265.00**
Water Set
Hobnail, opalescent, pitcher, applied
clear handle, six matching tumblers **750.00**
Swirl, opalescent, pitcher, sq ruffled
mouth, four matching tumblers . . . **350.00**

RUBENA VERDE GLASS

History: Rubena Verde, a transparent glass that
shades from red in the upper section to yellow-
green in the lower, was made by Hobbs, Brockunier & Co., Wheeling, West Virginia, in the late
1880s. It is often found in the inverted thumbprint
(IVT) pattern, termed "Polka Dot" by Hobbs.

**Tumbler, Inverted Thumbprint pattern,
3⅛" h, $60.00.**

Bowl, 9" d, ftd, rolled rim, Honeycomb **100.00**
Butter Dish, cov, Daisy and Button base,
Thumbprint cov **225.00**
Celery Vase, 6¼", IVT **225.00**
Compote, 6", Honeycomb **125.00**
Creamer, IVT, bulbous, reeded handle **265.00**
Cruet, 6", Hobnail, clear faceted stopper **250.00**
Pitcher
Hobnail, 7½" h, bulbous base, sq
mouth, Hobbs, Brockunier & Co . . **400.00**
Reverse Thumbprint, sq top, applied
vaseline handle, Hobbs, Brocku-
nier & Co **250.00**
Salt and Pepper Shakers, orig tops, pr **200.00**

Sugar Shaker, enameled floral dec,
metal lid, Hobb's Coloratura series . **295.00**
Syrup, 6¾", IVT, orig hinged pewter cov **300.00**
Tumbler, 3¾", paneled **95.00**
Vase
4", threaded dec **225.00**
7", bulbous, scalloped rim, enameled
floral dec **225.00**
13", trumpet, enameled gold scrolling,
wafer connection to flaring domed
foot **100.00**

RUBY STAINED GLASS, SOUVENIR TYPE

History: Ruby stained glass was produced in
the late 1880s and 1890s by several glass manufacturers, primarily in the area of Pittsburgh,
Pennsylvania.

Ruby stained items were made from pressed
clear glass which was stained with a ruby red
material. Pieces often were etched with the name
of a person, place, date, or event and sold as
souvenirs at fairs and expositions.

In many cases one company produced the
pressed glass blanks; a second company stained
and etched them. Many patterns were used, but
the three most popular were Button Arches, Heart
Band, and Thumbprint.

Reference: William Heacock, *Encyclopedia of
Victorian Colored Pattern Glass, Book 7: Ruby-
Stained Glass From A to Z*, Antique Publications,
Inc., 1986.

Reproduction Alert: Ruby staining is being
added to many pieces through the use of modern
stain glass coloring kits. A rash of fake souvenir
ruby stained pieces was made in the 1960s, the
best known example is the "bad" button arches
toothpick.

Bell, Button Arches, Elkhorn Fair, 1913,
clear paneled handle, 6½" h **65.00**
Bread Tray, Triple Triangle, Cape Cod **65.00**
Butter Dish, Button Arches, Atlantic City,
1919 . . . . **75.00**

**Creamer, Button Arches, etched "Sou-
venir of Kane, Pa," 2¼" h, $20.00.**

Candy Dish, cov, Columbia Expo, 1893	**65.00**
Goblet	
Ruby Thumbprint, Mother	**30.00**
Triple Triangle, 1906	**30.00**
Mug	
Button Arches, Charles Bray	**25.00**
Heart, World's Fair, 1904	**20.00**
Napkin Ring, Diamond with Peg, 1907	**85.00**
Pitcher, Button Arches, tankard, Pittsburgh	**125.00**
Punch Cup, Button Arches, Chicago . .	**20.00**
Sauce Dish, Cathedral, Niagara Falls .	**18.00**
Spooner, York Herringbone, World's Fair, 1893	**45.00**
Toothpick Holder	
King's Crown, Atlantic City, 1899 . . .	**25.00**
Shamrock, Coney Island	**30.00**
Tumbler	
Inverted Strawberry pattern, Deshler, OH	**30.00**
Red Block, World's Fair, 1893	**35.00**
Whiskey Glass, Ruby Thumbprint, 1907	**25.00**
Wine	
Asbury Park, NJ	**35.00**
Button Arches, World's Fair	**25.00**
Triple Triangle, Christmas	**35.00**

RUSSIAN ITEMS

History: During the late 19th and early 20th centuries Russia contained skilled craftsmen in lacquer, silver, and enamel wares. Located mainly in Moscow during the Czarist era, 1880–1917, were a group of master craftsmen, led by Faberge, who created exquisite enamel pieces. Faberge also had an establishment in St. Petersburg and enjoyed the patronage of the Russian Imperial family and the royalty and nobility from throughout Europe.

Almost all enameling was done on silver. Pieces are signed by the artist and the government assayer.

The Russian Revolution in 1917 brought an abrupt end to the century of Russian craftsmanship. The modern Soviet government has exported some inferior enamel and lacquer work, usually lacking in artistic merit. Modern pieces are not collectible.

ENAMEL

Bell Push, 1½", nephrite sq, white guilloche enameling and moon stone, IGK, Moscow, 1895	**1,400.00**
Bonbonniere, 1¾" d, shaded, pastel colors en suite, 11th Masters Artel, Moscow, 1900	**1,500.00**
Box, cov, 2" d, Pan Slavic style, slip on lid, Anton Kuzmichev, Moscow, 1900	**1,000.00**
Caviar Bowl, 3¼" d, Pan Slavic style	

Cup, champleve enamel, marked "84" in circle and "BA" in square, 5" l, 2¾" h, $3,600.00.

enameling, geometric and floral patterns, A E, Moscow, 1900	**1,250.00**
Cigarette Case, 4 x 3" w, shaded enamel en suite, pastel floral pattern, Pavel Ovchinnikov, Moscow, 1899 . .	**3,500.00**
Creamer and Sugar and Tongs, Pan Slavic enameling, geometric and floral patterns, swing handle on sugar bowl, Nikolai Zverev, Moscow, 1900, 3 pcs	**3,000.00**
Crucifix, 12¼" h, silver gilt, arms enameled with multicolored foliate dec, blue ground, Cyrillic marker's mark "F R," c1910	**4,650.00**
Demitasse Spoon, 4½" l, shaded enamel, geometric pattern, twisted knop handle, Ivan Saltykov, Moscow, 1900	**200.00**
Kovsh, 5" l, Art Nouveau style, enameled flowers on gilded silver, Pavel Ovchinnikov, Moscow, 1890	**2,500.00**
Salt	
Champleve enamel, 2" l, gilded silver, Anton Kuzmichev, Moscow, 1894 .	**800.00**
Shaded enamel on gilded silver, circular, three ball feet, Maria Semenova, Moscow, 1908	**800.00**
Scent Flask, 1¾" d, Atomizer, En Plein floral, shaded on reverse side, gilded silver, C.B., Moscow, 1890	**2,500.00**
Serving Spoon, 7¾" l, Pan Slavic style, Anton Kuzmichev, Moscow, 1889 . .	**800.00**
Sugar Shovel, 4½" l, all–over shaded enamel pastel floral pattern, Ivan Khlebnikov, Moscow, 1899	**1,000.00**
Tabernacle, 24¾" h, silver, three sides emb and chased with figures of Christ, front with hinged doors, multicolored foliage on enameled columns, superstructure with five turquoise enameled onion domes, four bracket supports, Nicholai Tarabrov, Moscow, c1910	**8,250.00**
Tea Holder, glass, shaded enamel, gilded silver, reticulated edges, pastel	

colors, Maria Semenova, Moscow,
1895 . . . . **2,900.00**
Teapot, 6½″ h, hinged cov, silver gilt
and shaded enamel, lobed body with
multicolored enameled panels of
plumed birds and foliage, sky blue,
white, avocado, and sea green
grounds, scroll handle, swan's neck
spout, Dmitri Smirnov, Moscow,
c1900 . . . . **6,675.00**

MISCELLANEOUS

Dessert Cup, liner, handled, c1893 . . . **35.00**
Figure, Troika with Driver, 10″, brass,
two passengers, sgd "Gratchen" and
foundry marks **2,900.00**
Plate, 10″, Imperial Russian Porcelain,
gilt on cobalt blue ground, four hp floral panels, Alexander III, dated 1893 **200.00**
Vase, 12″ h, cut glass, 5″ base flares
out to 10″ d **900.00**

SILVER

Basket, cake, 9¼″, chased cornucopia
border, swing handle, gilt int., Mos-
cow, c1910 . . . . **525.00**
Candleholder, figure, flared shell shape
saucer, molded flower at handle, attached matchbox, marked "84" and
artist initials **125.00**
Dessert Spoon, 6⅝″, vermeil bowl, floral
engraving, reverse side gold, marked
"84" **30.00**
Goblet, 3″, mid 19th C **75.00**
Soup Ladle, Fiddle pattern, Moscow,
1891–96 . . . . **150.00**
Toasting Mug, Slavic design, marked
"St George and the Dragon," 1885 . **475.00**
Tray, 22½″, oval, two handles, raised
pierced edge, Cyrillic maker's mark
"Ya P," Assaymaster Mikhail Karpin-
ski, Moscow, 1806 . . . . **1,875.00**
Vase, 4″ h, curved sides, bulbous base,
two handles with satyr's mask and
foliage, Cyrillic marker's mark "N Ya,"
St Petersburg, c1890, pr **1,225.00**

SABINO GLASS

History: Sabino glass, named for its creator Ernest Marius Sabino, originated in France in the
1920s and is an art glass which was produced in
a wide range of decorative glassware: frosted,
clear, opalescent, and colored glass. Both blown
and pressed moldings were used. Hand sculpted
wooden molds that were cast in iron were used
and are still in use at the present time.

In 1960 the company introduced a line of figurines, one to eight inches high, plus other items in
a fiery opalescent glass in the Art Deco style. Gold
was added to the batch to attain the fiery glow.
These pieces are the Sabino that is most commonly found today. Sabino is marked with the
name in the mold, an etched signature, or both.

Rooster, 6½″ w, 7⅜″ h, $400.00.

Ashtray, shell, 3½ x 5½″ **30.00**
Bird
  Babies, two chubby babies perched
    closed on twig with berries and
    leaves, 3″ h, opal, oval molded
    base, relief molded "Sabino" **22.00**
  Mocking, 4½ x 6″ **100.00**
Blotter, rocker type, 6 x 3″, crossed
American and French flags **275.00**
Butterfly, opal, relief molded "Sabino" . **20.00**
Cat, 2″ **20.00**
Chick, drinking **45.00**
Dog
  Collie, 2″ **50.00**
  Pekingese, sitting up begging, 1¼″ h,
    opal, relief molded "Sabino" **24.00**
Elephant **25.00**
Fox **25.00**
Hand, left **200.00**
Hen **30.00**
Knife Rest, duck **20.00**
Mouse, 3″ **50.00**
Napkin Ring, birds, opal **45.00**
Owl, 4½″ **65.00**
Powder Box, small **40.00**
Rooster, large **400.00**
Scent Bottle, Petalia **50.00**
Snail, opal, relief molded "Sabino" . . . **22.00**
Squirrel, eating acorn, 3½″ h, opal, oval
molded base, relief molded "Sabino" **24.00**
Statue, Venus de Milo, large **65.00**
Vase, Art Deco, topaz, 12″ **500.00**

ℂ 𝒮 SALOPIAN

SALOPIAN WARE

History: Salopian ware was made at Caughley Pot Works, Salop, Stropshire, England, in the 18th century by Thomas Turner. The ware is poly-chrome on transfer. One time classified as Poly-chrome Transfer, it retains the more popular name of Salopian. Wares are marked with an "S" or "Salopian" impressed or painted under the glaze. Much of it was sold through Turner's Salopian warehouse in London.

Cup and Saucer, Cottage pattern, 3⅝ x 2⅛" h handleless cup, 5⅞" d saucer, $120.00.

Bowl, 6¼, milkmaid and cow scene, multicolored **125.00**
Charger, 11", Bird on Branch pattern, blue transfer **400.00**
Coffeepot, 9½" h, multicolored stag scene, woodland setting **1,000.00**
Creamer, 5¼" h, milkmaid and cow scene **180.00**
Cup and Saucer, handleless
  2⅞" d cup, 4¾" d saucer, Bird on Branch pattern **175.00**
  3⅝" d cup, 5⅞" d saucer, cottage scene **120.00**
Cup Plate, 4½", double deer **350.00**
Dish, 10", oval, milkmaid and cow scene, scalloped edge, blue transfer **200.00**
Mug, 2½", double deer, five colors ... **400.00**
Plate, 8⅝" d, fishermen on bank, painted centers, dark blue and gold borders, palmettos, scrolls and loops, imp "Salopian" **120.00**
Punch Bowl, 9⅝" d, 4¼" h, brown mon-ochrome, wide border of flowers and leaves on int. and ext., Willow pattern, applied blue enamel rim **175.00**
Sauce Dish, 4⅝", polychromed scene of woman and two children, manor

house in background, brown transfer with yellow, blue, pink, and green ap-plied highlights **150.00**
Sugar Bowl, 5" h, cov, yellow bird, blue, yellow, and orange dec **325.00**
Teapot, 8¼" h, boy carrying lamb, blue and white **450.00**

SALT AND PEPPER SHAKERS

History: Collecting salt and pepper shakers, whether late 19th century glass forms or the con-temporary figural and souvenir types, is becoming more and more popular. The supply and variety is practically unlimited; the price for most sets is within the budget of cost conscious, young collec-tors. Finally, their size offers an opportunity to as-semble a large collection in a small amount of space.

One can specialize in types, forms, or makers. Great art glass artisans such as Joseph Locke and Nicholas Kopp, designed salt and pepper shakers in the normal course of their work. Arthur Goodwin Peterson's *Glass Salt Shakers: 1,000 Patterns* provides the reference numbers given below. Pe-terson made a beginning; there are hundreds, per-haps thousands of patterns still to be cataloged.

The clear colored and colored opaque sets com-mand the highest prices, clear and white sets the lowest. Although some shakers, e.g., the tomato or fig, have a special patented top and need it to hold value, it is not detrimental to the price to replace the top of a shaker.

The figural and souvenir type is often looked down upon by collectors. Sentiment and whimsy are prime collecting motivations. The large variety and current low prices indicate a potential for long term price growth.

Generally older shakers are priced by the piece, figural and souvenir types by the set. The pricing method is indicated at each division. All shakers are assumed to have original tops unless noted. Identification numbers are from Peterson's book.

References: Gideon Bosker, *Great Shakes: Salt and Pepper For All Tastes*, Abbeville Press, 1986; Melva Davern, *The Collector's Encyclope-dia of Salt & Pepper Shakers: Figural And Novelty*, Collector Books, 1985; Melva Davern, *The Collec-tor's Encyclopedia of Salt and Pepper Shakers, Second Series*, Collector Books, 1990; Helene Guarnaccia, *Salt & Pepper Shakers*, Collector Books, 1984; Helene Guarnaccia, *Salt & Pepper Shakers II: Identification & Values*, Collector Books, 1989; Mildred and Ralph Lechner, *The World of Salt Shakers*, Collector Books, 1976; Ar-thur G. Peterson, *Glass Salt Shakers: 1000 Pat-terns*, Wallace-Homestead, 1970.

Collectors' Clubs: Antique and Art Glass Salt Shaker Collectors Society, 348 N. Hamilton Street,

Painted Post, NY 14870; Salt Shaker Collectors Club, 2832 Rapidan Trail, Maitland, FL 32751.

Additional Listings: See *Warman's Americana & Collectibles* for more examples.

ART GLASS (PRICED INDIVIDUALLY)

Barrel, ribbed, Mt Washington, Burmese, floral motif, satin finish, 2 pc pewter top with finial, Peterson 154-A	200.00
Bulging Loop, Rib #8, 3", pigeon blood, orig brass top, 37-C	65.00
Fig, enameled pansy dec, satin, orig prong top, Mt Washington	110.00
Inverted Thumbprint, reverse amberina, pewter top	165.00
Knobby, heavy opaque white, hp pastel flowers, shading to pale yellow, orig pewter top	42.50
Lob #5, satin, hp, orange floral spray, pewter top with finial, Mt. Washington, 33-C	62.50
Melon, squatty, enameled daisy dec, satin, orig two piece top, Mt Washington	55.00
Medallion Sprig, 3¼", shaded cobalt blue to white, orig brass top, 33-S	67.50

FIGURAL AND SOUVENIR TYPES (PRICED BY SET)

Black Cooks, man in white hat, lady in white apron and turban, pottery, red and white underglaze dec, stove size	25.00
Ducks, 2½", sitting, glass, clear bodies, blue heads, sgd "Czechoslovakia"	35.00
Lobsters, 3", marked "Made in Japan"	15.00
Nipper, RCA Dog, marked "Lenox"	35.00
Refrigerator, 2⅞", old G.E. refrigerator shape, white opaque glass, black trim, chrome plated top, 36-N	30.00
Squirrels, 3½", standing, metal, SP top	37.50

OPALESCENT GLASS (PRICED INDIVIDUALLY)

Argonaut Shell, Northwood, blue	55.00
Circle Scroll, Northwood, blue, tin top, 5", 156-S	72.00
Fluted Scrolls, Northwood, vaseline	40.00
Jewel and Flower, Northwood, blue, 164-J, replaced top	35.00
Ribbed, 3", white, brass top, 36-W	42.50
Seaweed, Hobbs, cranberry	45.00
Windows, Hobbs, blue, pewter top	45.00

OPAQUE GLASS (PRICED INDIVIDUALLY UNLESS OTHERWISE NOTED)

Acorn, Hobbs, shaded pink to white, tin top, 3", 21-A	45.00

Apple Blossom, milk glass	25.00
Brownie, 2⅜" h, rounded cube, four vertical sides, Palmer-Cox Brownies in different postures on each (F448)	75.00
Creased Waist, yellow, milk glass	30.00
Diamond Point and Leaf, 2¾" h, blue, diamond point ground broken by compound leaf extending up side of shaker (F489)	35.00
Everglades, Northwood, purple slag, white, gold highlights, pewter top, 160-K	70.00
Melon Ribbed, red, floral dec, pewter top	72.50
Punty Band, Custard	42.50
Sunset, Dithridge, white, 3", 40-U	30.00
Winged Scroll, Custard	87.50

Opaque Glass, Rib and Scroll pattern, pink cased glass, orig tin top, made by Consolidated Lamp & Glass Co, $45.00.

PATTERN GLASS (PRICED INDIVIDUALLY)

Actress, pewter top	40.00
Beautiful Lady, Bryce, Higbee and Co, 1905, clear	20.00
Block and Fan, US Glass Co, 1891, clear	15.00
Cane, Gillinder Glass Co, c1885, apple green, non-flint	25.00
Crown Jewel, O'Hara Glass Co, c1880, etched	35.00
Croesus, McKee Glass, 1899, amethyst, gold trim	75.00
Diamond Horseshoe, Brilliant Glass Works, 1888, ruby stained	40.00
Diamond Point, Boston and Sandwich Glass Co, 1830–40, clear, flint	25.00
Francesware, Hobbs, Brockunier & Co, c1880, hobnail, frosted, amber stained	30.00
Mikado, Richards and Hartley, c1888, vaseline, non-flint	20.00
Whirligig, US Glass Co, clear, tin top, 3½", 177-A,	15.00

SALTGLAZED WARES

History: Saltglazed wares have a distinctive "pitted" surface texture, made by throwing salt into the hot kiln during the final firing process. The salt vapors produce sodium oxide and hydrochloric acid which react on the glaze.

Many Staffordshire potters produced large quantities of this type of ware during the 18th and 19th centuries. A relatively small quantity was produced in the United States. Saltglazed wares still are made today.

Reference: Susan and Al Bagdade, *Warman's English & Continental Pottery & Porcelain, 1st Edition,* Warman Publishing Co., Inc., 1987.

Teapot, sheaf of wheat finial, $175.00.

Basket, 12½", relief molded grapes and
leaves, open twig handles, English,
c1750–60, faint age crack **1,400.00**
Cream Pitcher, 5" h, cov, loop handle,
three paw feet, applied grape and leaf
design, Chinese lion finial, English,
c1730–40 . . . . **3,200.00**
Dessert Plate, 8⅜", basketweave border, center relief band of pears, English, c1755 . . . . **950.00**
Dish, 9⅛" d, molded, gadroon rim, polychrome enamel and gilt, scene of
fisherman and wife, multicolored floral sprays border, English, c1760 . . **4,500.00**
Figure, sheep, Rockingham, c1830, pr **400.00**
Fruit Dish, 9" l, oval, molded, reticulated,
yellow, turquoise, and strawberry, English, c1760–65, chip on foot ring . . **5,200.00**
Jar, cov, 2¼" d, handle **250.00**
Jug, 7", pyriform, strainer spout, polychrome enamels and gilding, bird,
butterfly, and floral dec, floral dec
handle, English, c1760, lid missing,
two hairline cracks in rim **3,000.00**
Mug, tavern, stoneware, strap handle,
applied raised deer hunt dec, inscribed "Jno Coldre at Whiteham,
1716," English, attributed to Vauxhall
area of London **4,600.00**
Pitcher, 7⅜" h, straight sides, slightly

sloping shoulder, cylindrical neck, incised presentation label "Matilda
Dundors from Harry," blue, gray, and
green pebbly highlights **265.00**
Sauceboat, 4" h, three mask and paw
feet, scrolls, shells, and trellis relief
dec, English, c1750–60, age crack at
bottom, one toe chipped **1,150.00**
Teapot
3¾", slightly oval body, rose sprig
painted in rose, pale pink, green,
yellow, and black, blue ground,
crabstock spout and handle, Staffordshire, England, c1760, minor
chips **2,000.00**
5¼", spherical, floral bouquet and
small sprigs painted in iron–red,
rose, blue, yellow, green, and
black, deep pink ground, crabstock
spout and handle, Staffordshire,
England, c1870, spout tip repaired **4,675.00**

SALTS, OPEN

History: When salt was first mined, the supply was limited and expensive. The necessity for a receptacle in which to serve the salt resulted in the first open salt, a crude, hand-carved, wooden trencher.

As time passed salt receptacles were refined in style and materials. In the 1500s both master and individual salts existed. By the 1700s firms such as Meissen, Waterford, and Wedgwood were making glass, china, and porcelain salts. Leading manufacturers in the 1800s included Libbey Glass Co., Mount Washington, New England Glass Company, Smith Bros., Vallerysthal, Wavecrest, Webb, and many outstanding silversmiths in England, France, and Germany.

Open salts were used as the only means of serving salt until the appearance of the shaker in the late 1800s. The ease of procuring salt from a shaker greatly reduced the use and need for the open salts.

References: William Heacock and Patricia Johnson, *5,000 Open Salts: A Collectors Guide,* Richardson Printing Corporation, 1982; L. W. and D. B. Neal, *Pressed Glass Dishes Of The Lacy Period 1825–1850,* published by the author, 1962; Allan B. and Helen B. Smith have authored and published ten books on open salts beginning with *One Thousand Individual Open Salts Illustrated* (1972) and ending with *1,334 Open Salts Illustrated: The Tenth Book* (1984). Daniel Snyder did the master salt sections in Volumes 8 and 9. In 1987 Mimi Rudnick compiled a revised price list for the ten Smith Books.

Collectors' Club: New England Society of Open Salt Collectors, 587 Dutton Road, Sudbury, MA 01776.

Note: The numbers in parentheses refer to plate numbers in the Smith's publications.

CONDIMENT SETS WITH OPEN SALTS

Metal, collie pulling ricksaw, contains salt, pepper, and mustard dishes, blown glass liners, Oriental (461)	350.00
Porcelain, Limoges, double salt and mustard, sgd "JM Limoges" (388)	65.00
Pottery, Quimper, double salt and mustard, white with blue and green floral dec, sgd "Quimper" (388)	95.00

Individual, glass, squirrel on tree trunk, Portland Glass Co, $65.00.

INDIVIDUALS

China
Austria, tub shape, floral dec, sgd "Brothers" and "O&EG Royal Austria" (441)	38.00
Noritake, oval, int. dec in blue and gold (382)	35.00
Royal Bayreuth, lobster claw, unsgd (87)	65.00

Colored Glass
Amber, pedestal, Decagon, Cambridge (468)	32.50
Cobalt Blue, Moser, pedestal, gold bands, applied flowers, sgd (380)	55.00
Cameo Glass, E. Galle, green pedestal, enamel dec, sgd, early (205)	275.00
Cranberry, ruffled salt held by rigaree in wire holder, unmarked (373)	185.00
Ruby, dolphin in center (451)	85.00

Cut Glass
Hexagonal, twelve point star in bottom, sgd "Libbey" (464)	48.00
Octagonal, curved sides, polished cut bottom (470)	20.00
Pedestal, Hawkes, sgd with trefoil emblem (86)	55.00

Double Salts
China, boat shaped bowls, anchor handle of floral dec (392)	185.00
Baccarat, pedestal, paneled sides,	

one salt frosted panels, sgd (395)	125.00
Clear, octagonal, Thumbprint, attributed to Sandwich (394)	75.00

In Metal Frames
Amber intaglio, Webb butterfly, brass stone-studded frame (248)	85.00
Cobalt blue liner, round SS, hallmarked, mkd "Made in Dublin, Ireland 1795" (412)	215.00

Metals
German Silver, dolphin feet, German, c1890–1910 (353)	95.00
Silver plated, pot, hallmarked "Wilcox Silver Plate Co" (414)	35.00
Sterling, Georg Jensen, Denmark, porringer (238)	200.00

Pressed Glass
American, Fostoria, round, gold rim, rayed bottom (465)	47.50
Hawaiian Lei, Higbee (477)	25.00
Mt. Vernon, Cambridge (80)	28.50
Wood, bucket, white porcelain int. (232)	45.00

FIGURALS

Goat, hauling green milk glass cart, sgd "Baccarat," 6" l (458)	135.00
Peacock, glass, amethyst wings, green base (462)	55.00
Seahorse, brilliant turquoise, white base, supports shell salt, mkd with first Belleek black mark (458)	350.00

INTAGLIOS

Scene of Niagara Falls (368)	65.00
Tree, six intaglios showing Venus and Cupid (423)	110.00

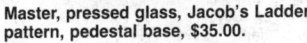

Master, pressed glass, Jacob's Ladder pattern, pedestal base, $35.00.

MASTERS

China
Germany, pedestal, girl sitting on grass, mkd "Printemps, Monbijou, Germany" (387)	55.00

Moss Rose, white (320) 45.00
Colored Glass
  Blue, opalescent, silver rim, Registry
    number "176566" (384) 110.00
  Cranberry, geometrically cut to clear
    (384) 120.00
  Green, light, dark green ruffled top,
    open pontil (449) 75.00
  Purple Slag, leaf and flower print
    (313) 60.00
  Raspberry, heavy, sq, Pairpoint (444) 65.00
  Satin Glass, tulip shaped, silver leaf
    holder (312) 80.00
Cut Glass, heart shape, alternating dia-
  mond and fan pattern (404) 65.00
Lacy
  Clear
    Double, beaded rim and handles
      (329) 60.00
    Eagle (EE7b:327) 180.00
      Lafayette Boat (BT6:329) 260.00
      Oblong Double (OG12:326) 70.00
      Staghorn (SN1:328) 100.00
    Colored
      Lyre, green (LE1:324) 225.00
      Mount Vernon, light citron
        (MV1a:324) 375.00
      Strawberry Diamond, yellow green
        (SD7:324) 280.00
Metal
  Gold, pedestal, mkd "1880" (349) . . 80.00
  Pewter, pedestal, cobalt blue liner
    (349) 60.00
  Silver, plated, applied legs, triple
    plate, Simpson Hall Miller & Co
    (312) 47.50
Sterling Silver
  Boy with bow and arrow holding
    salt on head, blue glass insert,
    mkd "800" Germany (355) 400.00
  Pedestal, four medallion profiles,
    monogrammed "S.C.W.," made
    in 1865, mkd with Gorham hall-
    mark and number 520
    (358) 95.00
Pressed Glass
  Bakewell Pears, clear 20.00
  Barberry, oval berries, clear 30.00
  Basketweave, sleigh (397) 110.00
  Grasshopper, clear 30.00
  Horizontal Framed Ovals, clear 22.00
  Sawtooth Circle, clear 30.00
  Snail (348) 30.00
  Toboggan (397) 175.00
  Viking, clear 25.00
Pressed Glass, Pedestal
  Barberry (344) 35.00
  Eyewinker (346) 82.50
  Gothic Arches variant, (3606) 2½" h,
    2⅝" d, c1865, clear 25.00
  Paneled Diamond (331) 47.50
  Sunflower (346) 35.00

SAMPLERS

History: Samplers served many purposes. For a young child they were a practice exercise and permanent reminder of stitches and patterns. For a young woman they demonstrated her skills in a "gentle" art and preserved key elements of family genealogy. For the mature woman they were a useful occupation and functioned as gifts or re-membrances, e.g., mourning pieces.

Schools for young ladies of the early 19th century prided themselves on the needlework skills they taught. The Westtown School in Chester County, Pennsylvania, and the Young Ladies Seminary in Bethlehem, Pennsylvania, are two examples. These schools changed their teaching as styles changed. Berlin work was introduced by the mid-19th century.

Examples of samplers date back to the 1700s. The earliest ones were long and narrow, usually done only with the alphabet and numerals. Later examples were square. At the end of the 19th century, the shape tended to be rectangular.

The same motifs were used throughout the country. The name is a key element in determining the region. Samplers are assumed to be on linen unless otherwise indicated.

References: Glee Krueger, *A Gallery of American Samplers: The Theodore H. Kapnek Collection,* Bonanza Books, 1984 edition; Betty Ring, *American Needlework Treasures; Samplers and Silk Embroideries From The Collection of Betty Ring,* E. P. Dutton, 1987; Anne Sebba, *Samplers: Five Centuries of a Gentle Craft,* Thames and Hudson, 1979.

1836, H. Croll, red and blue alphabet on natural linen, unfinished, 15 x 15½", $250.00.

1801, Sally Cane, Hagarstown, NJ, scene of girl and two lambs beside river, sailboats, large pinnacled building with trees, inscribed below "Sally Cane is my name/America is my nation/Hagarstown is my dwelling place/ and Christ is my salvation/Finished this September 17 1801," zig zag border with flowerhead and buds, shades of brown, green, blue, and white, faded, giltwood frame, 8 x 9½" **1,870.00**

1802, Elizabeth Dursee, needlework, linen, "Elizabeth Dursee's Sampler Wrought in the 9 year of her age AD 1802," green, white, pink, blue, and yellow silk stitches, alphabet bands, house, trees, ladies, and gentlemen, stylized floral border, 24¾ x 17½" .. **3,300.00**

1805, Hannah Davis, needlework, linen, verse and "Hannah Davis AE 11 years Roxbury September 27, 1805," blue, green, rose, yellow, beige and black silk stitches, bands of alphabets, men seated on river banks fishing and men in boats **26,400.00**

1808, Hannah Wiley and Eliza Wiley, needlework, linen, "The above wrought by Eliza Wiley now dec, Hannah Wiley, aged 13, 1808" and verse, green, blue, black, and pink silk stitches, alphabet bands, flowers, pots of flowers, and birds perched in trees border, 17¼ x 13" **1,980.00**

1811, Mary Ann M. Holtzbecher, needlework, linen, "Mary Ann M. Holtzbecher's work, Anno Domini, 1811," green, blue, yellow, rose, and white silk stitches, alphabet bands, tulips, leaping rabbits, rose spray outer border, framed, 14¾ x 15" **6,050.00**

1812, Rachel Borton, needlework, linen, blue, gold, pink, and rose silk stitches, alphabet bands, slower twined wreath, blue birds, roses, and basket of fruit, strawberry border, 18 x 12¼" **1,320.00**

1814, Sarah Wells, needlework, linen, "Sarah Wells, 1813" and "Token of Love SW to EW, 1814," olive green stitches, random octagonal cartouches, birds, swan, orses, stars, tulips, snowflakes, and carnations patterns, framed, 17 x 21" **1,980.00**

1818

Gibson, Hannah, needlepoint, "Hannah Gibson aged 9 years, Thorp School," colorful alphabets, house birds, plants, framed, 16¼" h, 20" w **700.00**

Jackson, Mary, homespun, "By this work of mine, you may plainly see, what pains my parents took with me. Mary Jackson worked this in

the 8th year of her age 1818.," birds, flowers, animals angels, ship, house design, minor wear, framed, 18" h, 23½" w **800.00**

1822, Harriet Tupper, Sandwich, MA, dated March 1822, alphabets, meandering vine house, verses over center house, 12¾ x 10", framed **1,000.00**

1823, Mary Martin, crewel embroidered, cross stitched "Mary Martin, aged 10 years, 1823," blue, white, pink, green, yellow, and brown wool, black ground, compote filled with roses and lilies, stenciled frame, 10⅜ x 9" **990.00**

1824

Noel, Elizabeth, needlework, linen, "Elizabeth Noel, Her Work Aged 11 Years, 1824," red, yellow, purple, magenta, green, and orange silk stitches, house, shepherd, polka dot stags, trees and parrots, meandering pink carnation border, 25 x17" **16,500.00**

Owston, Mary Ann, age 11, Adam and Eve in the Garden of Eden, numbers, alphabets, flowers, etc., 12" sq, framed **300.00**

Pader, Catharine A., homespun, verse "Admonition...Catherine A. Pader, aged-years, New York Bethel School No 2, A.D. 1824," floral dec, vine border, 18" h, 18" w, tear, stains, and fading **210.00**

Unidentified Maker, homespun, "Hannah—ton, April 28, 1824", colorful alphabets, verse, animal border, 12½" h, 12½" w, framed, bleeding and fading **435.00**

1826, Hannah Ann Pryer, NY, age 7, green, gold, blue, and white silk stitches, linen ground, religious verse, undulating strawberry vine flanked by bellflowers, second inscription with name and date, flower filled urns above and below, framed, 17⅛ x 13⅞" **1,210.00**

1827, Clarissa Squire, needlework, linen, verse, family genealogy, and memorial, green, blue, white, and pink silk stitches, alphabet bands, trees and flower border, 17¼ x 18" . **2,200.00**

1828, Christina C. Robb, needlework, woven homespun, inscription, red, green, yellow, and blue stitches, alphabet bands, central star, and flowering trees in corners, 17½" × 16½" **1,980.00**

1829, Julia Sargeant, needlework, linen, "Julia Sargeant wrought in her 9 year 1829" and verse, blue, green, yellow, white, and pink silk stitches, alphabet bands, landscape scene, meandering bud border, 17 x 16½" . **7,700.00**

1830, Ann S. Deputron, needlework, linen, verse, red, pale blue, navy blue, beige, and green stitches, basket of flowers center, red and yellow birds, mother with infant in arms, child, dog, strawberry border, 15½ x 20" **2,420.00**

1831, Mary A. Fawcett, needlework, verse with names "Mary A. Stanford, Mary A. Ross, Eliza Fawcett, John Fawcett, Joseph Fawcett, and Elanor Fawcett," green, pink, white, blue, and yellow, silk stitches, house, pine trees, birds, baskets of fruit, fruit and flower border, 22 x 17¼" **13,200.00**

1835, Jane Wild, sq linen panel, birds in flight, trees, recumbent stag, animals, figures, three story brick manor house, religious verse above, green, brown, red, and tan, some discoloring to borders, mahogany frame, 20¼ x 21" **1,760.00**

1846, M. A. Bottomley, needlework, verse, maker's name and "Aged 8 1846," red, green, blue, yellow, and green silk stitches, linen ground, red carnations, urns with flowers, baskets of fruit, paired birds and tulips, blue roofed house, strawberry border, 16 x 15½" **2,310.00**

SANDWICH GLASS

History: In 1818 Deming Jarves was listed in the Boston Directory as a glass factor. The same year he was appointed general manager of the newly formed New England Glass Company. In 1824 Jarves toured the glass-making factories in Pittsburgh, left New England Glass Company, and founded a glass factory in Sandwich.

Originally called the Sandwich Manufacturing Company, it was incorporated in April 1826 as the Boston & Sandwich Glass Company. From 1826 to 1858 Jarves served as general manager. The Boston & Sandwich Glass Company produced a wide variety and quality of wares. The factory used the free-blown, blown three-mold, and pressed glass manufacturing techniques. Clear and colored glass both were used.

Competition in the American glass industry in the mid-1850s forced a lowering of quality of the glass wares. Jarves left in 1858, founded the Cape Cod Glass Company, and tried to maintain the high quality of the earlier glass. At the Boston & Sandwich Glass Company emphasis was placed on mass production. The development of a lime glass (non-flint) led to lower costs for pressed glass. Some free-blown and blown-and-molded pieces, mostly in color, were made. Most of this Victorian era glass was enameled, painted, or acid etched.

By the 1880s the Boston & Sandwich Glass Company was operating at a loss. Labor difficulties finally resulted in the factory closing on January 1, 1888.

References: Raymond E. Barlow and Joan E. Kaiser, *The Glass Industry In Sandwich*, Vol. 2, Vol. 3 and Vol. 4, distributed by Schiffer Publishing, Ltd.; George S. and Helen McKearin, *American Glass*, Crown Publishers, Inc., 1941 and 1948; Ruth Webb Lee, *Sandwich Glass. The History Of The Sandwich Glass Company*, Charles E. Tuttle, 1966; Ruth Webb Lee, *Sandwich Glass Handbook*, Charles E. Tuttle, 1966; L. W. and D. B. Neal, *Pressed Glass Dishes Of The Lacy Period 1825–1850*, published by author, 1962; Catherine M. V. Thuro, *Oil Lamps II: Glass Kerosene Lamps*, Wallace-Homestead, 1983.

Periodical: *The Sandwich Collector*, McCue Publications, P. O. Box 340, East Sandwich, MA 02537.

Museum: Sandwich Glass Museum, Sandwich, MA.

Additional Listings: Blown Three Mold and Cup Plates.

Vase, Loop and Bull's Eye, sapphire blue, gauffered rim, Lee 200–3, c1840, 7¼" h, $375.00.

Bowl, 9¼", Gothic Arches, clear, lacy, Lee 129 .... **150.00**

Candlestick, 9" h, dolphin, clear, dolphins and shells on socket, McKearin 204–65 .... **800.00**

Celery Vase, 7¾" h, Excelsior pattern, clear, flint **70.00**

Cologne Bottle, amber, gilded floral dec, orig gilded lily stopper **400.00**

Compote
7¼" d, 5" h, Waffle pattern, clear, flint, minute under rim roughage **50.00**
8½" d, 6¼" h, Excelsior pattern, clear, flint **100.00**
12 x 9", Sandwich Star, electric blue **5,000.00**

Creamer, Gothic Arches, deep purple– blue, lacy **800.00**

Cup Plate, Lee–Rose 440–B, deep
  blue, heart **325.00**
Decanter, 12″ h, 1½–2 pint capacity,
  Sandwich Star, canary yellow, period
  stopper, pr **3,300.00**
Dish, 12 x 9 x 1¾″, oblong, Peacock
  Eye **800.00**
Jewel Casket, cov, 6½″ l, oblong, clear,
  lacy, Lee 162 .... **1,100.00**
Lamp, 10⅝″, whale oil, free blown tear-
  drop shape font, triangular scrolled
  base, paw feet **700.00**
Lamp Shade, 8½″ d, 5½″ h, 3¾″ fitter
  ring, white, all over ruby threading, 4″
  ruby threaded floral band, ruffled trim **250.00**
Miniature
  Bowl, cov, 1⅝″ d, pattern around base **100.00**
  Cup and Saucer, handleless, lacy,
    Lee 80–7 .... **250.00**
  Flat Iron, blue–green **600.00**
  Plate, opal, lacy, Lee 81–5 ...... **150.00**
  Tray, 2¾ x 2″, oval, paneled **100.00**
  Wash Bowl and Pitcher, clear, Lee
    80–3 .... **350.00**
Ointment Jar, opaque white, orig pewter
  lid, oval, concave panels, 3″ d **125.00**
Plate, 7⅛″, Peacock Eye, translucent
  moonstone, lacy, Lee 108–2 ...... **150.00**
Scent Bottle
  Deep emerald green, violin shape,
    orig pewter screw top, McKearin
    241–31 .... **225.00**
  Medium purple–blue, McKearin 241–
    55 .... **130.00**
Sugar, cov, Gothic Arches, fiery opal,
  Lee–158–4 .... **500.00**
Sweetmeat, cov, Waffle pattern, clear,
  flint, one scallop rim chipped **90.00**
Tray, 10″ l, Butterfly, clear, lacy, Lee
  95–3 .... **300.00**
Vase
  7¼″, Bull's Eye and Ellipse, dark em-
    erald green, gauffered rims, pr ... **3,000.00**
  9¾″, tulip shape, honey amber, flint,
    Lee 198–2, pr **2,000.00**
Vegetable Dish, cov, 10½″, clear, lacy,
  grape border, Lee 151–1 .... **5,500.00**
Whiskey Glass, 2⅜″, hexagonal, deep
  cobalt blue, flint **225.00**

SARREGUE MINES

SARREGUEMINES CHINA

History: Sarreguemines ware is a faience porcelain, i.e., tin-glazed earthenware. The factory
was established in Lorraine, France, in 1770, under the supervision of Utzcheider and Fabry. The
factory was regarded as one of the three most

prominent manufacturers of French Faience. Most
of the wares found today were made in the 19th
century. Later wares are impressed Sarreguemines and Germany due to a change of boundaries
and location of the factory.

Reference: Susan and Al Bagdade, *Warman's
English & Continental Pottery & Porcelain, 1st Edition,* Warman Publishing Co., Inc., 1987.

Bowl, basketweave, relief tomatoes,
  handles **30.00**
Box, 6″ d, multicolored dec of children
  in Kate Greenaway type dress **60.00**
Compote, 9½″, majolica, series of five
  different raised fruits, natural colors . **65.00**
Creamer, 5″, row of ducks, frog, flower
  border **48.00**

**Dish, shallow, strawberriers and
leaves, brown interior, marked, 5 x 9¼″,
#25.00.**

Dish, cov, 8½″, majolica, basketweave,
  white egg lid finial **175.00**
Pitcher
  8″, shoemaker scenes **145.00**
Plate
  7½″, multicolored French comic
    scene **20.00**
  8½″, majolica, strawberries and floral
    trim, aqua ground **70.00**
Toby Jug
  6½″, majolica, shaded beige flesh
    tones, ruddy cheeks **85.00**
  8″, majolica, The Scotsman **125.00**
Vase, 20″, pyriform, pearlware, Moorish
  influence, painted shaped panel of
  cavaliers in tavern, reverse painted
  with fortress on banks of river, emerald green ground, multicolored enam-
  els, and gilding, printed mark, pr ... **2,750.00**

SARSAPARILLA BOTTLES

History: Sarsaparilla refers to a number of tropical American, spiny, woody vines of the lily family
whose roots are fragrant. An extract was obtained
from these dried roots and used for medicinal purposes. The first appearance in bottle form dates

from the 1840s. The earliest bottles were stoneware, later followed by glass.

Carbonated water often was added to sarsaparilla to make a soft drink or to make consuming it more pleasurable. For this reason, sarsaparilla and soda became synonymous even though they were two different entities.

References: Ralph & Terry Kovel, *The Kovels' Bottle Price List, 8th Edition,*, Crown Publishers, 1987; Carlo & Dot Sellari, *The Standard Old Bottle Price Guide,* Collector Books, 1989.

Periodical: *Antique Bottle and Glass Collector,* P. O. Box 187, East Greenville, PA 18041.

Additional Listings: See *Warman's Americana & Collectibles* for a list of soda bottles.

Stollo Co, Troy, NY, "The Temperance Beverage," paper label, 12 oz, $7.50.

Ayer's Sarsaparilla, deeply whittled, pontil	50.00
Belding's, Dr Ira, Honduras Sarsaparilla, clear, 10½"	20.00
Bull's Extract Of Sarsaparilla, beveled corner, 7 x 2"	385.00
Compound Extract Of Sarsaparilla, amber, gallon	125.00
Foley's Sarsaparilla	15.00
Green's, Dr	15.00
Guysott's Yellow dock & Sarsaparilla	35.00
Lancaster Glassworks, barrel, golden amber	120.00
Murray's, Burnham, ME, aqua	20.00
Riker's Compound Sarsaparilla, rect, beveled corners, aqua	30.00
Skoda's Sarsaparilla, amber	20.00
Townsend's, Dr, Sarsaparilla, olive green, pontil	80.00
Warren Allen's Sarsaparilla Beer, tan, pottery	125.00

SATIN GLASS

History: Satin glass, produced in the late 19th century, is an opaque art glass with a velvety matte (satin) finish, achieved through treatment with hydrofluoric acid. A large majority of the pieces were cased or had a white lining.

While working at the Phoenix Glass Company, Beaver, Pennsylvania, Joseph Webb perfected Mother-of-Pearl (MOP) satin glass in 1885. Similar to plain satin glass in respect to casing, MOP satin glass has a distinctive surface finish and an integral or indented design, the most common being diamond quilted (DQ).

The most common colors are yellow, rose, or blue. Rainbow coloring is considered choice. Satin glass, both plain and MOP, has been widely reproduced.

Additional Listings: Cruets, Fairy Lamps, Miniature Lamps, and Rose Bowls.

Miniature Lamp, pink DQ, MOP, 8½", $1,325.00.

Basket, 8½ x 9½", herringbone, MOP, pink–salmon ext., tightly crimped edge, frosted clear twisted thorn handle	635.00
Bowl, 5¼" d, 4¼" h, DQ, MOP, tricorn, blue, crystal applique edge, marked "Patent"	750.00
Bride's Basket, 11 x 15½", deep rose, enamel swan and floral dec, heavy bronze holder with birds perched at top	400.00
Cologne Bottle, 5½", globular, peach, SS top	250.00
Cruet, 7" h, DQ, MOP, blue, matching satin stopper, applied clear reeded handle	630.00
Dish, 5¾", raspberry, ivory ruffled rim	50.00
Ewer, 9½", DQ, MOP, deep apricot shading to light, thorn handle	255.00

Jar, cov, 6¼", DQ, MOP, salmon, applied clear flower finial **325.00**
Perfume Bottle, 4", globular, ivory, SS top, gold dec **115.00**
Pitcher, 8¼", Coinspot, MOP, blue, applied frosted handle **150.00**
Rose Bowl
  5¼ d, 6" h, pale green, pink floral dec, green leaves **180.00**
  5½" d, 5" h, DQ, MOP, shaded peach, white int., eight crimp top, dimpled **275.00**
Toothpick, 2½", DQ, MOP, yellow **150.00**
Tumbler, DQ, MOP, deep blue to pearly white, heavy enameled pink blossoms, multicolored foliage **285.00**
Vase
  3" d, 5" h, DQ, MOP, shaded apricot, white int., ruffled top with frosted binding, five frosted applied wishbone feet **225.00**
  3" d, 5½" h, peach, brown feather pull up dec, robin's egg blue int., Northwood **750.00**
  4½" d, 9¾" h, herringbone, MOP, blue, white int., applied frosted thorny handles and feet, ruffled tops, pr **750.00**
  5½" h, hobnail, MOP, blue, folded in sq top **610.00**
  10" h, pr, frosted, bulbous, pinched neck, enameled orange, green, and yellow flowers, white leaves, gold trim, pr **125.00**

SATSUMA

History: Satsuma, named for a war lord who brought skilled Korean potters to Japan in the early 1600s, was a hand-crafted Japanese faience glazed pottery. It is finely crackled, has a cream, yellow-cream, or gray-cream color, and is decorated with raised enamels in floral geometric and figural motifs.

Figural satsuma was made specifically for export in the 19th century. Later satsuma, referred to as satsuma-style ware, is Japanese porcelain also hand decorated in raised enamels. From 1912 to the present, satsuma-style ware has been mass produced. Much of the ware on today's market is of this later period.

References: Sandra Andacht, *Oriental Antiques & Art: An Identification And Value Guide,* Wallace-Homestead, 1987; Sandra Andacht, *Treasury of Satsuma,* Wallace-Homestead, 1981.

Belt Buckle, cobalt blue ground, enameled lavender and blue iris, green foliage, gilt outlines, SS mounting, c1905 . . . . **225.00**
Bowl, 4¾", octagonal, int. scene of geis-

has, figural reserves on ext., ornate border, c1870 . . . . **275.00**
Box, cov, 3½", circular, three ball feet, ladies and children by river on cov, landscape sides, int. with sprigs of flowering plum, sgd "Kinkozan," late 19th C **250.00**
Brush Holder, 5", cream, flowers and butterflies **50.00**
Cache Pots, 10½", hexagonal, scenic, earth tones, figural handles, 19th C, pr **1,350.00**
Charger, 12½", Thousand Warriors pattern, diaper border of dragons, multi-colored, c1850 . . . . **1,500.00**
Figure, Kannon, 7½", diety molded in royal ease posture, holding rosary, serene face, jet black coiffure, floral diadem, gilt patterned cowl flowing over shoulders and back, partially opened robes scattered with gilt and pastel floral patterns, base inscribed "Satsuma 'Iwaida'" **175.00**

Incense Burner, courtesans on one side, Mandarins on obverse, c1875, 4" w, 3¾" h, $250.00.

Incense Container (Kogo)
  3¾", compressed circular body, flat lid with gilt and bright polychrome enameled figural arhats scene, backdrop of celestial mansions, straight ext., sides painted with brocade band of scalloped edge roundels, scattered Satsuma mon, black ground, gilt spirals and granulation, base cartouche reading "Satsuma-yaki Kotoen" **475.00**
  5" d, compressed circular body, convex lid, inset high ring foot, top with minute gilt and polychrome enamels, sq reserve of country cottage, abstract patterned roundel, wide band of millefleur, gilt granulated ground, gilt edged border, int. painted with overall pattern of scat-

tered brocade patterned maple leaves and stylized waves, base cartouche inscribed "Kinkozan-zu-kuri," Meiji period **700.00**

Koro, 30¼" h, compressed hexagonal form, five footed stand molded with lioness mask heads and feet, high shouldered body painted with Japanese scholars and sages, molded chrysanthemum and swag mock ring handles, shoulders painted with fronted phoenix on diaper and shippo–tsunagi ground, applied two standing Chinese children supporting flared rim, bell shaped top with karashishi finial, Japanese, Meiji period **2,475.00**

Plate
8¾", fan shape, colored enamels of large phoenix in flight, cloud scrolls, multicolored and gilt ribs, monogrammed "EGS," set of 16 ..... **400.00**

9⅝", cream crackle glaze, brush fence, chrysanthemums, bamboo, stylized foliate rim, sgd, late 19th C **385.00**

Urn, 6¼", rect, two molded elephant head handles, bright polychrome enamels, gilt, rect reserve of spring scene with mother and children, blossoming landscape reserves, gilt keyfret band, gilt painted baskets of ferns, dark blue ground, recessed dome shaped lid, gilt knob finial, base imp "Kinkozan-zukui," Meiji period .. **900.00**

Vase
7¼", cobalt blue collar and base, lavender flowers and gold trim, body with garden of blue flowers, two orange and lavender pheasants, trees, stream, and hills, marked .. **325.00**

9¾", baluster, high waisted neck, rolled rim, high flared foot, polychrome enamels and gilt, continuous frieze of blossoming wisteria vines, flowering iris plants, gilt geometric patterned bands, base cartouche "Ryuzan," Meiji period ... **250.00**

15¼", hexagonal, rolled rim with keyfret band, recessed high circular foot, bright polychrome enamels, large rect reserves, family on spring excursion, two samurai watched by maiden alternating with gilt painted panels of blossoming plants on dark blue ground, gilt shippo-tsunagi bands, base inscribed "Takarayama" **1,650.00**

SCALES

History: Prior to 1900 the simple balance scale commonly was used for measuring weights. Since then scales have become more sophisticated in design and more accurate. A variety of styles and types include beam, platform, postal, and pharmaceutical.

Collectors' Club: International Society of Antique Scale Collectors, 111 N. Canal St., Chicago, IL 60606.

Egg Grader, Zenith, O. W. Bedell, Earlville, NY, 1925, $18.00.

Apothecary Scale, brass pans, walnut base **160.00**

Baby, wicker **45.00**

Balance
Cast Iron, 14" l, nickel plated brass pans, orig red paint with black and yellow trim, marked "Henry Troemner, Phila, No 5B, Baker's" **100.00**

Butter, 27" w, wood, carved handle, worn black paint **75.00**

Wrought Iron, 22" h, cast iron base, tin pans **60.00**

Candy
Dayton, brass pan, metallic orange . **300.00**

National Store Co, tin pan, c1910 .. **85.00**

Coin Operated, 69" h, floor model, porcelain top and bottom, mirrored front, wood back, marked "National Weighing Machine, NY" **175.00**

Counter, blue and chrome with tan, marked "Toledo" **165.00**

Egg, Oaks Mfg Co **7.50**

Grain, brass **235.00**

Hand Held, wide side gauge, unusual cylinder, marked "Chatillon, NY" ... **20.00**

Jeweler, brass pans, brass standard, ten brass weights, green velvet lined box **150.00**

Photographer, brass pans, brass weights, marked "Made in Germany" **145.00**

Postal, 4¼" h, desk, SS, cased, mono-

gram, marked "Shreve & Co," c1900–
22 . . . .   **250.00**
Steelyard, wood, weighted bulbous end,
turned shaft, 18th C **200.00**
Store
  Hanson Weighmaster, 6 x 14 x 10",
  cast iron, gold case with ground,
  black lettering and indicator **25.00**
  Howe, cast iron, red base, gold highlights, brass pan, five weights, patent June 18, 1867 . . . .   **80.00**
  National Store Specialty Co, green
  base **175.00**
  Toledo Computing Scale Co, 26 x 28
  x 11", gold paint, pan, patent Sept
  11, 1906 . . . .   **35.00**

SCHLEGELMILCH PORCELAINS

History: Erdmann Schlegelmilch founded his porcelain factory in Suhl in the Thuringia region in 1861. Reinhold, his brother, established a porcelain factory at Tillowitz in Upper Silesia in 1869. In the 1860s Prussia controlled Thuringia and Upper Silesia, both rich in the natural ingredients needed for porcelain.

By the late 19th century an active export business was conducted with the United States and Canada due to a large supply of porcelain at reasonable costs achieved through industrialization and cheap labor. Both brothers marked their pieces with the RSP mark, a designation honoring Rudolph Schlegelmilch, their father. Over 30 mark variations have been discovered.

The Suhl factory ceased production in 1920, unable to recover from the effects of World War I. The Tillowitz plant, located in an area of changing international boundaries, finally came under Polish socialist government control in 1956.

References: Susan and Al Bagdade, *Warman's English & Continental Pottery & Porcelain, 1st Edition,* Warman Publishing Co., Inc., 1987; Mary Frank Gaston, *The Collector's Encyclopedia Of R.S. Prussia and Other R.S. and E.S. Porcelain*, Collector Books, 1982; George W. Terrell, Jr., *Collecting R.S. Prussia Identification and Values*, Books Americana, 1982; Clifford S. Schlegelmilch, *Handbook Of Erdmann And Reinhold Schlegelmilch, Prussia-Germany And Oscar Schlegelmilch, Germany, 3rd Edition*, published by author, 1973.

Reproduction Alert: Many "fake" Schlegelmilch pieces are appearing on the market. These reproductions have new decal marks, transfers, or recently hand painted animals on old, authentic R.S. Prussia pieces.

R. S. GERMANY

Basket, oval, rust and green Chinese

R. S. Germany, sugar bowl, cov, floral dec, shaded ground, 5″ h, $35.00.

pheasants and trees, dark cream
ground **245.00**
Biscuit Jar, 6", loop handles, roses dec,
satin finish, gold knob **95.00**
Bonbon Dish, 7¾" l, 4½" w, pink car-
nations, gold dec, silver-gray ground,
looped inside handle **30.00**
Bowl, Oriental pheasant **275.00**
Bread Plate, Iris variant edge mold, blue
and white, gold outlined petal and rim,
multicolored center flowers, steeple
mark **115.00**
Brides Bowl, ornate, floral center, ftd . .   **45.00**
Cake Plate, deep yellow, two parrots on
hanging leaf vine, open handle, green
mark **225.00**
Candy Dish, 7", sq, gray-green, orange
roses, wide scalloped rim, pierced
handles **35.00**
Celery Tray, 11" l, 5¾" w, lily dec, gold
rim, open handles, blue label **100.00**
Chocolate Pot, demitasse, white rose
florals, blue mark **85.00**
Creamer and Sugar, pedestal, sheep-
herder scene, overall dec, red mark   **650.00**
Cup and Saucer, plain mold, swan, blue
water, mountain and brown castle
background, red mark **235.00**
Demitasse Cup and Saucer, 3", pink
roses, gold stenciled design, satin fin-
ish, blue mark **55.00**
Gravy Boat, white, blue flowers, gold
rim, handle, blue mark **30.00**
Hatpin Holder **75.00**
Inkwell, 3", pink roses, gold scroll, hp,
artist sgd, blue mark **70.00**
Mustard Pot, cov, pink roses **25.00**
Napkin Ring, green, pink roses, white
snowballs **45.00**
Nut Bowl, 5¼" d, 2¾" h, cream, yellow
roses, green scalloped edge **55.00**
Pin Tray, woman with oxen scene, at-
tached powder box **200.00**

Pitcher, 5¾", light blue, chrysanthemums, pink roses, gold trim **65.00**

Planter, green, white tulips, blue mark .   **125.00**

Plate

  6½" d, dessert, yellow and cream roses, green and rich brown shades, set of 6 . . . .   **125.00**

  9¾", white flowers, gold leaves, gilded edge, green ground, marked "RS Germany" in dark green, script sgd "Reinhold Schlegelmilch/Tillowitz/Germany" in red **40.00**

10", hp flowers **40.00**

Powder Box, cov, green poppies, green mark **45.00**

Salt and Pepper Shakers, shaded green, peach floral dec, gold trim, pr   **45.00**

Sauce Dish and Underplate, green, yellow roses, blue mark **40.00**

Syrup, cov, 6", bluebells **65.00**

Tea Tile, peach and tan, greenish white snowballs, red mark over faint blue mark **150.00**

Toothpick Holder, White Rose, three handles **55.00**

Vase, 4", bottle shape, shaded green to cream, cottage scene, marked **65.00**

R. S. POLAND

Candleholder, floral dec, marked **115.00**

Creamer, soft green, chain of violets, applied fleur-de-lis feet, red mark . .   **100.00**

Flower Holder, pheasants, brass frog insert **675.00**

Vase

  8¾" h, 4" d, pink and white roses, gold band top with garlands of gold roses and leaves, cream ground, marked **165.00**

  12" h, 6¼" d, white poppies, cream shaded to brown ground, pr **750.00**

R. S. PRUSSIA

Berry Bowl, 10", Iris mold, blown–out, pink roses and daisies, red mark . . .   **285.00**

Berry Set, poppies, iris mold, 5 pc . . .   **300.00**

Biscuit Jar, Sunflower mold, red mark .   **400.00**

Bowl

  10" d, sheepherder scene, mold 155   **750.00**

  13 x 9", oval, masted ship scene, mold 207 . . . .   **910.00**

Butter Dish, porcelain insert, cream, gold shading, pink roses, raised enamel, red mark **700.00**

Cake Plate, handles

  10", floral dec, red mark **85.00**

  10½", basket of flowers, pearl luster ground, Medallion mold **275.00**

Celery Tray

  12", flowers in bowl dec **125.00**

R. S. Prussia, cake plate, pink, white flowers, yellow, purple, white, and gold highlights, green wreath mark, 10⅞" d, $150.00.

12½", pink and yellow roses, green shadows, Lily mold, unmarked . . .   **75.00**

Chocolate Pot, cobalt blue, white flowers, hp, transfer, applied gold, gold handle **1,000.00**

Chocolate Set

  10 pcs, chocolate pot, four cups and saucers, dark green, pink Bachelor Button type flowers, fancy handles, red mark **800.00**

  17 pcs, fluted pot with lid, cov sugar and creamer, six cup and saucers, pink roses, yellow daisies, light blue and peach ground, gold trim, ftd **3,000.00**

Compote, 4", green florals **85.00**

Creamer and Sugar, lilac satin ground, red mark **145.00**

Cup, roses, ftd, ornate, red mark **25.00**

Demitasse Cup and Saucer, dainty flowers **100.00**

Demitasse Set, surreal dogwood and leaf dec, red mark **950.00**

Dresser Tray

  Pale blue, Tiffany dec rim **650.00**

  Poppies, Carnation mold, satin finish, blown–out, red mark **330.00**

Ewer, 8¼", small roses, gold leaves, pedestal base, red mark, satin finish   **400.00**

Hair Receiver, green Lilies of the Valley, white ground, red mark **110.00**

Hatpin Holder, 4¾", scalloped base, roses, luster finish, red mark **215.00**

Plate

  6", Melon Eater, keyhole mold, red mark **450.00**

  8½", Gibson girl "Evelyne," sgd Prussia **350.00**

Relish Dish, 9", blown–out mold, lav-

ender and pink gloss finish, pink and
white roses, two handles, red mark . . 80.00
Shaving Mug, mirrored, green shadows,
pink poppies, red mark 275.00
Spoon Holder, 14" l, pink and white
roses 200.00
Sugar Shaker, 5", scalloped base, pearl
finish, roses, red mark 235.00
Teapot, brown cottage scene, red mark 450.00
Toothpick Holder, green shadows, pink
and white roses, six ftd jeweled, red
mark 250.00
Tray, 10¼ x 7", blown–out iris mold, hidden image, woman's head, floral cen-
ter 300.00
Vase
 5¼", cobalt, flowers and leaves 225.00
 6", pearl jeweled, satin finish, pink
 and white roses, purple bottom,
 shadow leaves at top, solid gold
 handles, red mark 325.00
 9", portrait, three handles, Greek Key
 design, sgd "LeBrun" 650.00
 9½", six sheepherder, pink flowering
 trees, red mark 700.00

**R. S. Suhl, dish, light green exterior,
interior with green ground, classical ladies in white, pink, and yellow, 8" l, 4⅝"
w, $475.00.**

R. S. SUHL

Coffee Set, 9" h coffeepot, creamer,
sugar, six cups and saucers, figural
scenes dec, some marked "Angelica
Kauffmann" 1,675.00
Jar, cov, 7", tapestry dec 135.00
Pin Tray, 4½", round, Nightwatch 375.00
Plate, 8½", windmill scene and water,
green mark 100.00
Vase, 8", four pheasants, green mark . 265.00

R. S. TILLOWITZ

Bowl, 7¾", slanted sides, open handles,
four leaf shape feet, matte finish, pale

**R. S. Tillowitz, bowl, roses, gold border,
marked "R & S" in green wreath and
"Reinhold Schlegelmilch/Tillowitz/Ger-
many," 9½" d, $45.00.**

green ground, roses and violets, gold
flowered rim, marked 100.00
Creamer and Sugar, soft yellow and
salmon roses 45.00
Plate, 6½", mixed floral spray, gold
beading, emb rim, brown wing mark 100.00
Relish Tray, 8" l, oval, hp, shaded green,
white roses, green leaves, center
handle, blue mark 35.00
Syrup, pastel pink snowballs, blue mark 35.00
Teapot, creamer and sugar, stacking,
yellow, rust, blue flowers, gold trim,
ivory ground, marked "Royal Silesia,"
and green mark in wreath 75.00
Vase, 10", pheasants, brown and yellow, two curved handles 115.00

Schneider

SCHNEIDER GLASS

History: Brothers Ernest and Charles Schneider, founded a glassworks at Epiney-sur-Seine,
France, in 1913. Charles, the artistic designer, previously had worked for Daum and Galle.

Although Schneider art glass is best known, the
firm also made table glass, stained glass, and
lighting fixtures. The art glass exhibits simplicity of
design; bubbles and streaking often are found in
larger pieces. Other wares include cameo cut and
hydrofluoric acid etched designs.

Schneider signed their pieces with a variety of
script and block signatures, "Le Verre Francais,"
or "Charder." Robert, son of Charles, assumed art
direction in 1948. Schneider moved to Loris in
1962.

Compote, cobalt blue center, citron edge, blue pedestal base, metal holder with three curled feet and applied foliate dec, 10¼" d, 8¾" h, $350.00.

Bowl
  6", amethyst, shallow, sgd **175.00**
  9¼", mottled, red and purple, sgd . . **175.00**
  10 x 4", red rim, mottled yellow ftd center, wrought iron handled holder with roses and leaves, sgd **225.00**
Charger, 29¼", bowl shape, satin finish, opaque, rust–reds and browns, sgd "Schneider France, Ovington, NY" . **625.00**
Compote
  8¼", deep amethyst, knobbed stem and pedestal, sgd **115.00**
  15 x 5", purple and red, sgd **275.00**
Dish, 13½ x 5½", mottled orange and dark blue, amethyst with white ribbing pedestal base **260.00**
Ewer, 6½", mottled blue and gray, applied black amethyst handle **225.00**
Lamp Shade, 18", Art Deco style, sgd . **1,050.00**
Pitcher
  6", raspberry body, mottled handle and spout **350.00**
  7½", maroon, white, and pink, sgd . **325.00**
Plate, 4", mottled, deep pink **75.00**
Vase
  5½", cased, blue, black, and clear, orange lining, wrought iron ftd base, c1925, sgd **250.00**
  9½", round, handles, orange with lavender and lemon pulls at raised neck, sgd **325.00**
  17", trumpet, ftd, clear with streaks of pink and raspberry, controlled bubbles, sgd **325.00**

SCHOENHUT TOYS

History: Albert Schoenhut, son of a toymaker, was born in Germany in 1849. In 1866 he ventured to America to work as a repairman of toy pianos for Wanamaker's, Philadelphia, Pennsylvania. Finding the glass sounding bars inadequate, he perfected a toy piano with metal sounding bars. His piano was an instant success, and the A. Schoenhut Company had its beginning.

From that point, toys seemed to flow out of the factory. Each of his six sons entered the business. The business prospered until 1934 when misfortune forced the company into bankruptcy. In 1935 Otto and George Schoenhut contracted to produce the Pinn Family Dolls.

At the same time, the Schoenhut Manufacturing Company was formed by two other Schoenhuts. Both companies operated under a partnership agreement that eventually led to O. Schoenhut, Inc., which continues today.

Some dates of interest: 1872-toy piano invented; 1903-Humpty and Dumpty and Circus patented; 1911–1924-wooden doll production; 1928–1934-composition dolls.

Reference: Richard O'Brien, *Collecting Toys, 5th Edition*, Books Americana, 1990.

Rhinoceros, 9" l, $200.00.

Animals
  Bear, brown painted eyes **125.00**
  Buffalo, painted eyes **150.00**
  Bulldog, brown painted eyes **225.00**
  Camel, painted eyes, two humps, 8" **175.00**
  Cat, glass eyes, leather ears, 7" . . . **215.00**
  Donkey, small, painted eyes **50.00**
  Hippopotamus, glass eyes **250.00**
  Lion, glass eyes, 9" **165.00**
  Ostrich, painted eyes **250.00**
  Sea Lion **480.00**
  Tiger, glass eyes **185.00**
  Zebra, glass eyes **225.00**
Building Blocks, orig box **175.00**
Building Toy, Little Village Builder, orig box **75.00**
Circus, Humpty Dumpty
  Accessories
    Barrel **20.00**
    Chair **20.00**
    Platform **18.00**
    Tent, 25 x 35" **350.00**
  Performers
    Acrobat, man **325.00**
    Bare back rider on white horse, 6½" **200.00**
    Lion Tamer, wooden head **175.00**

Ringmaster, wooden head, 8½" ..	**150.00**
Weight, 50 lbs	**50.00**

Doll, carved wooden socket head and painted facial features, wooden spring jointed body, marked "Schoenhut Doll Pat. Jan 17, 1911, USA"

13", Nature Baby, domed head, bent limb baby body, painted baby hair, almond shaped green eyes, c1915	**375.00**
19", blonde mohair wig, blue painted intaglio eyes, closed pouty mouth, 2 pc linen suit, c1915	**325.00**
Exploding Battleship, painted wood, set of three	**75.00**

Farm Characters

Farmer	**135.00**
Goat, painted eyes	**150.00**
Goose, painted eyes	**200.00**
Horse, painted eyes, 10"	**150.00**
Lamb, painted eyes	**150.00**
Milkmaid	**75.00**
Pig, glass eyes	**160.00**
Movie Camera, marked "Spirit of Hollywood," orig box	**75.00**

Personalities

Barney Google	**175.00**
Felix, 7 pc ball jointed body, Patent 1925, 4"	**200.00**
Golfer, orig skirt	**375.00**
Hobo	**125.00**
Jiggs and Maggie, pr	**750.00**
Teddy Roosevelt, 8"	**485.00**
Piano, 8½ x 9½ x 16", 15 keys	**125.00**
Railway Station	**325.00**

SCIENTIFIC INSTRUMENTS

History: Chemists, doctors, geologists, navigators, and surveyors used precision instruments as tools of their trade. Such objects are well designed and beautifully crafted. The principal medium is brass. Fancy hardwood cases also are common.

References: Crystal Payton, *Scientific Collectibles Identification & Price Guide*, published by author, 1978; Anthony Turner, *Early Scientific Instruments, Europe 1400–1780*, Sotheby's Publications, 1987.

Chronometer

Ship, orig case, 5" d, Hamilton	**400.00**
Yacht, 6" sq case, Hamilton	**300.00**
Compass, mahogany, boxed, orig lamp, marked "John Bliss & Co"	**425.00**
Globe, 13" d globe, 24" h, celestial and terrestrial, horizon ring band, later tiger maple stand, compass below, marked "J Wilson & Sons, Albany St, NY," dated 1826 and 1828 respectively, pr	**12,000.00**
Heeling Error Instrument, orig case, marked "Pratt No. 5"	**100.00**

Microscope, E. Leitz–Wetzler, No. 34459, 170 mm to 250 mm, 6 objective, orig wood case, $175.00.

Inclinometer, cased, French, marked "Made by H Bellieni of Nancy," dated 1900	**125.00**
Measuring Device, compensated, measures in meters, marked "Made by Troughton & Simms, London," 19th C	**25.00**
Quadrant, ebony, case label "Frederic W Lincoln, Jr, Boston"	**500.00**
Sextant, brass, pr binoculars, case with certificate of Examination from "National Physical Laboratory at Surrey, dated October, 1905," marked "Heath & Co Ltd, Crayford, London"	**650.00**
Stadimeter, cased	**50.00**
Surveyor's Compass, 4¾" sq case, removable handle, 19th C	**225.00**
Telegraph, 45¼" h, brass, marked "Made by J W Ray & Co"	**550.00**

Telescope

Floor Model, brass, orig tripod, sighting scope, tripod marked "Stanley," English, early 19th C	**2,400.00**
Table Model, tapered wood tube, brass tripod, Dollond, London, late 18th to early 19th C	**1,300.00**
Thermograph, cased, USD Navy Mark 2, Barth	**195.00**

SCRIMSHAW

History: Norman Flayderman defined scrimshaw as "the art of carving or otherwise fashioning useful or decorative articles as practiced primarily by whalemen, sailors, or others associated with nautical pursuits." Many collectors expand this to include the work of Eskimos and War of 1812 French POWs.

Collecting scrimshaw was popularized during the presidency of John F. Kennedy.

References: E. Norman Flayderman, *Scrimshaw, Scrimshanders, Whales And Whalemen,* N. Flayderman & Co., 1972, out-of-print; Richard C. Malley, *Graven By The Fishermen Themselves,* Mystic Seaport Museum, Inc., 1983.

Periodical: *Whalebone,* P. O. Box 2834, Fairfax, VA 22031.

Museums: Cold Spring Harbor Museum, Long Island, NY; Kendall Whaling Museum, Sharon, MA; Mystic Seaport Museum, Mystic, CT; National Maritime Museum, San Francisco, CA; Old Dartmouth Historical Society, New Bedford, MA; Whaling Museum, Nantucket, MA.

Reproduction Alert: The biggest problem in the field is fakes. A very hot needle will penetrate the common plastics used in reproductions. Ivory will not generate static electricity when rubbed, plastic will. Patina is not a good indicator; it has been faked with tea, tobacco juice, burying in raw rabbit hide, and other ingenious ways. Usually an old design will not be of consistent depth of cut as the ship rocked and tools dulled; however, skilled forgers have even copied this.

Bodkin
    3″ l, clenched hand at one end, multi-sided cuff, abalone inlays, early to mid 19th C **275.00**
    4⅛″ l, walrus ivory, carved and turned, mid 19th C **100.00**
Cane
    32⅝″ l, whalebone shaft, ivory handle in claw hammer form, mid 19th C **450.00**
    35″ l, bone shaft and ivory handle, part twist and part octagonal whale bone shaft terminates with wood palm on turned ivory handle **350.00**
    36″ l, rope carved whalebone shaft, walrus ivory and rubber top and bottom, handle fits deeply into shaft and pinned with two whale ivory pins, American, mid 19th C **1,300.00**
    36½″ l, whalebone shaft, L shape handle, separated from shaft by teak and whale ivory rings, mid 19th C **250.00**
Coat Rack
    23⅞″, panbone mounted on pine, three sperm whale teeth hangers, early to mid 19th C **900.00**
    31¾″ l, molded hardwood, four large sperm whale teeth hangers, early to mid 19th C **600.00**
Corset Busk
    12¾″ l, light colored bone, age crack to center, engraved on both sides with ships, whales, and ladies, colored **500.00**
    13½″ l, reddish-brown inked, unusual engraving **800.00**
Cribbage Board, 17½″ l, walrus tusk,

engraved, game animals, hunting scenes, and map, late 19th C **450.00**
Cup, 4⅝″ h, animal leg bone, engraved with semi nude female figure, European, early 19th C **175.00**
Ditty box, 7″ l, engraved, baleen, landscape of buildings, willow trees and figure of man with walking stick detail, orig mahogany cov with whalebone and wood finial, second quarter 19th C **600.00**
Egg Cup, 3⅝″, turned, mid 19th C, one minor age crack **125.00**
Fid, bone, light yellow to gray, 7½″ l .. **200.00**
Jackknife, 5½″ l open, whalebone handle, pinned blade, early to mid 19th C **170.00**
Jagging Wheel, 5″ l, whale ivory, comma shape handle, baleen ring and hear inlays, American, second quarter 19th C **450.00**
Knitting Needles, 12″ l, whalebone, alternating whale ivory and island wood rigs, carved clenched hands at top, second quarter 19th C, pr **2,600.00**
Letter Opener, 7½″, whale shape, whale and gaff rigged schooner on one side, "18 E.C. 37″ on other, good patina . **250.00**
Mantle Ornament, 10½″ l, 7½″ h, two carved and engraved teeth, eagle's head form engraved with ship, mounted on wood base with whalebone black splash, simulated whalebone drawer, turned whalebone feet, two whale ivory and baleen star inlays, rope carved circular frame, mid 19th C **1,100.00**
Model, 7″ l, 5¼″ h, sailor made bone ship model, full rigging, all whalebone, some rigging slack **900.00**
Panbone, 10½ × 9 × 6″, engraved, whaling scene, William Perry, New Bedford, c1920–30 .... **1,200.00**
Pincushion, 6¾″ d, octagon shape, mounted on walnut, ebony, whalebone, and mother-of-pearl inlay base, mid 19th C **175.00**
Rolling Pin, 20″, turned mahogany cylinder, acorn shape, whale ivory handles, c1825–40 .... **1,100.00**
Scribe, 9″ l, whalebone, American, second quarter 19th C **400.00**
Seam Rubber, 4½″ l, ebony separator between whale bone handle and blade **225.00**
Sewing box, 12″ l, 9″ w, exotic woods, whale ivory and wood inlays, ebony and whale ivory drawer pulls, third quarter 19th C **550.00**
Sewing Knife, lady's, bone, walking sailor's figure **70.00**
Spoon, 10⅜″ l, tortoiseshell bowl,

Ship Model, rigged, baleen water line, ivory cradle, detailed helm, side lights, and life boat, 8½" l, 7" h, $1,200.00.

whalebone handle, handle riveted to bowl, early to mid 19th C 150.00
Sewing Stand, 7 × 5¼ × 7", turned bone finials, single drawer, third quarter 19th C 200.00
Swift
   15¾" h, double whalebone and whale ivory, abalone shell heart inlay on upper clamp, mid 19th C 1,350.00
   23¼" h, whalebone and whale ivory, cup at top supported by standard with pewter band, mid 19th C ... 1,100.00
Table, 17¾ × 18¼ × 26", tapered turned legs, cherry wood, 29 individual whale ivory, baleen, and abalone inlays, orig hand written label on bottom 1,500.00
Tongue Depressor, 7¼" l, 1" w, ivory, eagle under words "Union Forever" on one side, wreath and "BP to LB 1841 AD" on other 250.00
Walking Stick, 34¾" l, lady's, tapered whalebone shaft, turned whale ivory knob, circular dark wood set in top, mid 19th C 200.00
Walrus Tusk, 14½", cribbage board and engravings of game and bird on one side, Eskimo hunting seal on other side 225.00
Watch Holder, 9 × 6⅜ × 10", dovetailed, whale ivory and baleen inlays, engraved flowers, curved scrolled supports, single drawer, other whale ivory and abalone shell inlays, American Waltham railroad watch with name "Nicholas Eisboa" 3,250.00
Whale Tooth
   3¼" l, pinpoint and regular engraving, half figure portraits, stylish dressed ladies, mid 19th C, pr 500.00
   4¾", carved, deep relief nude, third quarter 19th C 550.00

5" l, engraved, full figure portrait of young couple on one side, full rigged ship and sun ray bearing a face on other, second quarter 19th C 1,100.00
6¾", red blue, and black design on both sides, Prince of Servia on front, Princess with two natives, sailing ship, flowers, begging dog, etc, on back 600.00

SEBASTIAN MINIATURES

History: Sebastians are hand painted, lightly glazed figurines of characters from literature and history. They range in size from 3 to 4 inches. Each figurine is made in limited numbers. Other series include children and scenes from family life.

Prescott W. Baston, the originator and designer of Sebastian figures, began production in 1938 in Marblehead, Massachusetts. Sebastian Studios are located in Hudson, Massachusetts. Prescott Baston died on May 25, 1984.

Each year a Sebastian Auction is held in Boxborough, Massachusetts, at the Sebastian Collector's Society meeting. Prices are determined from this source plus the work of the Sebastian Exchange Board which develops a price list that is the standard reference for the field.

Reference: Dr. Glenn S. Johnson, *The Sebastian Miniature Collection & A Guide To Identifying, Understanding, and Enjoying Sebastian Miniatures*, Lance Corp., 1982.

Collectors' Club: Sebastian Collector's Society, 321 Central Street, Hudson, MA 01749. *Sebastian Miniature Collectors Society News* (quarterly) and *The Sebastian Exchange*.

Aunt Betzy Trotwood, Marblehead label   **50.00**
Baby Buggy of 1850 ....   **85.00**

Lobsterman, Marblehead paper label, $45.00.

Colonial Carriage	75.00
Crockett, Davy, #249	225.00
Evangeline, #12	125.00
Family Sing, #371	200.00
Gabriel, #11	135.00
Gibson Girl, #316-A	85.00
House of Seven Gables, #111	100.00
Hudson, Henry, #311	175.00
Jackson, Andrew, #159-A	250.00
Jefferson, Thomas, #124	85.00
Kennel Fresh, ashtray, #239	300.00
Lincoln, Abraham, seated	125.00
Mary Had A Little Lamb, #137	100.00
Parade Rest, #216	100.00
Peggotty, #52-A	85.00
Ross, Betsy, #129	85.00
Santa Claus, #123	100.00
Shaker Man, #1	150.00
St Joan of Arc, bronzed	275.00
Twain, Mark, #315	100.00
Victorian Couple, #89-B	85.00
Washington, George, pen holder, sgd "PW Baston, 1961"	22.50
Weaver and Loom, Marblehead label	50.00

SEVRES

History: The principal patron of the French porcelain industry in early 18th century France was Jeanne Antonette Poisson, Marquise de Pompadour. She supported the Vincennes factory of Gilles and Robert Dubois and their successors in its attempt to make soft paste porcelain in the 1740s. In 1753 she moved the porcelain operations to Sevres near her home, Chateau de Bellevue.

The Sevres soft paste formula used sand from Fontainbleau, salt and saltpeter, soda of alicante, powdered alabaster, clay, and soap. Louis XV allowed the firm to use the "double L's." Many famous colors were developed, including a cobalt blue. The great scenic designs on the ware were painted by such famous decorators as Watteau, La Tour, and Boucher. In the 18th century Sevres porcelain was the world's foremost diplomatic gift.

In 1769 kaolin was discovered in France, and a hard paste formula developed. The baroque gave way to rococo, a style favored by Jeanne du Barry, Louis XV's next mistress. Louis XVI took little interest in Sevres. Many factories began to turn out counterfeit copies. In 1876 the factory was moved to St. Cloud and was eventually nationalized.

Reference: Susan and Al Bagdade, *Warman's English & Continental Pottery & Porcelain, 1st Edition,* Warman Publishing Co., Inc., 1987.

Reproduction Alert.

Figurines, unglazed white pair, marble and gilt metal bases, 8" h, $3,000.00.

Bowl on Stand, 22¼" l, 15¼" h, oval bowl painted with two oval reserves, one of three maids and boy fishing in 18th C costume, other with multicolored floral spray, gilt borders, bleu–du–roi ground, obverse with gilt diapering, foliate forms, and scrollwork, white int. with floral spray and garland border, reticulated gilt bronze rim, two lion mask and ring handles with extended acanthus and scroll terminals, gilt bronze socle on oval base with four scroll feet **3,350.00**
Bust, 18 and 19½" h, portraits of George Washington and Benjamin Franklin, white biscuit, Washington with pronounced forehead and receding hairline, shoulder drapery over blouson, Franklin with long curling hair, furrowed brow, buttoned vest and cravat, imp "Sevres S1914, Presented to Whitney Warren By The French Government MCDXV," white biscuit socle bases, pr **18,700.00**
Cache Pot, 12¼" h, cylindrical, molded foot, two rect reserves, one painted with two maids and shepherd in 18th C costumes, obverse with large spray of flowers, gilt borders, gros bleu ground, four scroll feet, gilt bronze acanthus and scroll mounts with lion mask terminal, pierced rim, beaded collar, restoration to base, blue crossed L's mark **1,450.00**

Urn

24" h, ovoid, bust portrait of Marie Antoinette wearing straw hat, other with Mme Elizabeth holding a bouquet of flowers, pastel shades, wide gilt border, white ground dec with trophies and pr of flanking putti holding drapery, reverse with musical trophy or dove, pale green and gilt circular base, mounted as lamp, c1900, pr **1,870.00**

28½" h, cov, amorous couple in garden, obverse with landscape and architectural monuments, two gilt bronze handles cast with beading and foliate scroll terminals, circular gilt bronze cast base, painted by Marant, sgd, c1900, pr **11,000.00**

29" h, ovoid, heart shaped gilt bordered panel with young couple in Grecian costume, classical landscape background, gros bleu ground, gilt foliate scrollwork borders, diapered cartouches, foliate cast handles headed by female bust, waisted pedestal with molded gilt line borders, reticulated gilt bronze spreading circular cast base, c1900 . . . . **3,850.00**

30½" h, cov, cylindrical, historical frieze sgd "E Lattermann," two colorful scenes of mid 16th C trimuphal entry into European city, reverse with int. scene of presentation before bishop, applied molded guilloche border above, acanthus below, swirl molded porcelain socle and sq base, painted panels of Venus and cupids in landscape, gros bleu ground, swirl molded domed cov, large gilded pineapple knop, extensive cracking and restoration to base, c1900 . . **2,250.00**

Vase

5⅛" h, oviform tapering to narrow waisted neck, white ground, pale green line dec, allover honeycomb pattern, gray sunbursts with yellow centers, overlapping leaftips on shaded yellow neck band, printed date mark for 1911, decorator's mark for 1912, inscribed monogram in iron–red **100.00**

37¼" h, cov, ovoid, panel with two rustic maids and boy on riverbank playing with doves, reverse with riverscape and building, gilt floral and foliage borders, gros bleu ground, foliate handles, leaf garland rings, shaped sq gilt bronze base, gilt bronze pineapple knop, sgd "A Grisare," pseudo interlaced L's mark on lid, c1900 . . . . **4,450.00**

SEWING ITEMS

History: As late as 50 years ago, a wide variety of sewing items were found in almost every home in America. Women of every economic and social status were skilled in sewing and dress making. Even the most elegant ladies practiced the art of embroidery with the aid of jeweled gold and silver thimbles. Sewing birds, an interesting convenience item, were used to hold cloth (in the bird's beak) while sewing. Made of iron or brass, they could be attached to table or shelf with a screw-type fixture. Later models featured a pincushion.

References: Joyce Clement, *The Official Price Guide To Sewing Collectibles*, House of Collectibles, 1987; Victor Houart, *Sewing Accessories: An Illustrated History*, Souvenir Press (London), 1984; Gay Ann Rogers, *An Illustrated History of Needlework Tools*, John Murray (London), 1983; Estelle Zalkin, *Zalkin's Handbook Of Thimbles & Sewing Implements, First Edition*, Warman Publishing Co., 1988.

Collectors' Club: Thimble Collectors International, P. O. Box 2311, Des Moines, IA 50310.

Periodical: *Thimbletter*, 93 Walnut hill Road, Highlands, MA 02161.

Museums: Fabric Hall, Historic Deerfield, Deerfield, MA; Museum of American History, Smithsonian Institution, Washington, D.C.; Shelburne Museum, Shelburne, VT.

Additional Listings: See *Warman's Americana & Collectibles* for more examples.

Sewing Bird, silver plated, patent dated 1853, 3⅝" l bird, 5¼" h, $135.00.

Advertising Trade Card

Clark's Thread, business man **8.00**

Merrick's Thread, titled "In Search of the North Pole," balloon **5.00**

Box, 4½" l, straw work, abstract design on sides, cottage on cov, English, 19th C **150.00**

Darning Egg, 5¾" l, ebony egg, SS handle with raised floral and Scroll dec . **45.00**

Embroidery Hoop, 5¼" d, SS **35.00**
Hem Gauge, cast iron, marked "Pe-
louze," c1894 . . . . **30.00**
Needle and Pin Case
  Leather, 2 x 1⅞", black, emb gold . . **45.00**
  Wood, 2½", carved, silk-lined, c1870 **55.00**
Needle Case
  Adv, Nipper and phonograph, 2½ x
    1½", RCA Victor **30.00**
  Ivory, ornate, marked "Stanhope" . . **90.00**
Needle Threader, metal, Champion Oil
  adv **10.00**
Pincushion
  Beaded, 4½ x 5 x 8", figural, red,
    beaded, two strawberries, thimble
    pocket **150.00**
  Doll, porcelain head, 4", flapper . . . **75.00**
Scissors
  Embroidery, 3", silverplated, emb flo-
    ral dec on handles, patent 1864 . . **20.00**
  Tailor's, 10", steel, japanned handles,
    bent trimmers **15.00**
Sewing Bird
  Iron, one pincushion, bird with long
    sweeping curved tail which turns
    under **290.00**
  Silver Plated, double pincushion, emb
    bird and clamp **165.00**
Sewing Kit, 3" h, "Ladies Companion,"
  leather, stainless steel thimble, scis-
  sors, needle case, and punch, stain-
  less steel hinges on oval box, late
  1700s **110.00**
Sewing Machine
  Fristen–Rossman, hand crank, hard-
    wood case **125.00**
  Singer, hand operated, japanned,
    gold trim, c1820 . . . . **175.00**
  Wilcox and Gibbs, portable, orig
    booklet **75.00**
Sewing Table, bird's eye maple, walnut
  pedestal base, two drawers, pull out
  slide, glass knobs, carved foliate
  scrolls with floral band around stem,
  Baltimore, early 19th C, 22 x 17 x 33" **4,200.00**
Spool Cabinet
  Brooks, two drawer, reversed glass
    insert **265.00**
  Clark's Christmas, six drawer **650.00**
Tape Measure
  Advertising, Lydia Pinkham Medi-
    cines **30.00**
  Brass, pig, tail turns to pull out tape **95.00**
Thimble Case
  Crochet, basket shape, handle and
    cov **20.00**
  Mother-of-Pearl, hinged top **65.00**
  Papier Mache, floral design, gilded
    hinged top **40.00**
Thimble
  Brass, applied butterfly with rhine-
    stone insets, fret band, amethyst
    top **45.00**
  China, floral dec, hp, artist sgd **15.00**
  Gold, engraved leaf border, 14K . . . **85.00**
  Tortoise Shell, inset band **80.00**

SHAKER

History: The Shakers, so named because of a
dance used in worship, are one of the oldest com-
munal organizations in the United States. This religious group was founded by Mother Ann Lee who
emigrated from England and established the first
Shaker community near Albany, New York, in
1784. The Shakers reached their peak in 1850
with 6,000 members.

Shakers lived celibate and self-sufficient lives.
Their philosophy stressed cleanliness, order, simplicity, and economy. Highly inventive and moti-
vated, the Shakers created many utilitarian household forms and objects. Their furniture reflected a
striving for quality and purity in design.

In the early 19th century, the Shakers produced
many items for commercial purposes. Chairmak-
ing and the packaged herb and seed business
thrived. In every endeavor and enterprise, the
members followed Mother Ann's advice: "Put your
hands to work and give your heart to God."

References: Charles R. Muller and Timothy D.
Rieman, *The Shaker Chair,* The Canal Press,
1984; Don and Carol Raycraft, *Shaker, A Collector's Source Book II,* Wallace-Homestead, 1985;
June Sprigg and David Larkin, *Shaker Life, Work,
and Art,* Stewart, Tabori & Chang, 1987.

Periodical: *The Shaker Messenger,* P.O. Box
45, Holland, MI 49423.

**Chair, ladderback, hardwood, splint
seat, sgd "Sick, 1840," $1,200.00.**

Basket, 9¾ x 17 x 17″, splint black ash,
curved handles, sq bottom **250.00**
Bonnet, dark brown palm and straw,
black ribbons, 9″ flounce, KY **385.00**
Bottle, 9″, aqua, emb "Shaker Pickles,"
base labeled "Portland, Maine, E. D.
P. & Co" **90.00**
Box, cov, utility
7½ x 3½″, painted chrome yellow,
oval bentwood form, lid, printed paper label inscribed "Isaac N.
Youngs," first half 19th C **6,600.00**
10¾ x 4½″, painted green, oval bent-
wood form, 19th C **2,000.00**
Brush, 10¾″, horsehair, turned wooden
handle **85.00**
Carpet Beater, 41½″ l, bent willow,
turned beech handle **85.00**
Clothing, dress, homespun linen, pale
brown, wide double collar, twelve later
buttons, late 19th C **200.00**
Dough Scraper, 4½″, wrought iron . . . **40.00**
Dry Measure, 14½″ d, 7¾″ h, pine, cylindrical bentwood body, nailed end,
metal band rim, cast iron semi-circular handles, int. with stenciled Shaker
label, late 19th C **175.00**
Display Case, 8 x 10 x 10″, pine, red
stain, sliding lid, dovetailed, Mt Leb-
anon **375.00**
Furniture
Apothecary Cabinet, stained wood,
rect, front fitted with twelve small
drawers, molded white glazed porcelain handles, identification labels,
drawer sides inscribed with various
content titles, New England, 19th
C, 66 x 13″ **400.00**
Blanket Chest, red painted wood,
hinged rect top with molded edge,
int. till, paneled front and sides
raised on tapering cylindrical legs,
lid int. inscribed in pencil "Blooms-
burg, C B Hutton, Box 105, Oran-
gevill," midwestern, 19th C, 37 x
24¾″ **1,000.00**
Chair
Counter, painted and dec, single
arched slat back, rush seat,
turned legs, turned stretchers,
ochre dec, stamped "FW" on top
right front leg, Freegift Wells, Wa-
tervliet, NY, c1845 . . . . **8,800.00**
Clothes Rack, red painted wood,
three horizontal bars, top bar
mounted on either side with three
hooks, rect uprights continuing to
form arched feet, New England,
late 19th C, 36½″ w, 72″ h **2,500.00**
Rocker, curly maple, lemon form fini-
als, four arched graduated back
slats, mushroom capped arms,

rush seat, turned legs and stretchers, rockers, Enfield, CT, first half
19th C **14,300.00**
Table
Dining, maple, drop leaf, rect top,
hinged rect leaves, single
drawer, sq tapering legs, first half
19th C, 34¾ x 35½ x 28″ **6,600.00**
Side
Birchwood, rect top, frieze with
molded drawer, slightly turned
circular tapering legs, New
Lebanon Community, c1830,
painted red, 42 x 23 x 28″ . . . **6,600.00**
Cherry, red stained, two board
scrubbed rect top, single
drawer, turned wood pull, tapering sq legs, 19th C, 36 x
28⅞″ **1,250.00**
Work, painted birchwood and pine,
rect top and splash board, single
molded drawer, circular tapering
legs, orig red paint, New Lebanon Community, first half 19th C,
37½ x 23 x 25½″ **8,800.00**
Yarn Winder, 18″ l, 20¼″ h, movable
winder with rect bars joined by
block and cylindrical shaft, slightly
arched trestle base joined by
stretchers, dark green paint, late
19th C **350.00**
Hanger, 24″, bentwood, chestnut **65.00**
Pantry Box, bentwood, oval, lappet construction
Blue painted, single lappet on rim and
body, off-white painted int., 6 x 2¼″ **325.00**
Matched set of four, sgd "S. Mar-
mouth Kegsilk, August 1848," New
England, 4⅝″, 7⅞″, 11½″, and
13½″ **3,575.00**
Scoop, 11¾″, walnut **275.00**
Sewing Box, pink cotton lining and pin
cushion, stamped "Shaker Goods,
Alfred, Maine" **100.00**
Sock Stretcher, 26″ l, wood **20.00**
Whisk, 14½″ l, wood, primitive **45.00**

SHAVING MUGS

History: Shaving mugs hold the soap, brush,
and hot water used to prepare a beard for shaving.
They come in a variety of materials including tin,
silver, glass, and pottery. One style is the scuttle,
so called because of its "coal scuttle" shape, with
separate compartments for water and soap.
Shaving mugs were popular between 1880 and
1925, the period of the great immigration to the
United States. At first barber shops used a common mug for all customers. This led to an epidemic
of a type of eczema, known as barber itch.

Laws were passed requiring each individual to have his own mug. Initially names and numbers were used. This did not work well for those who could not read. The occupational mug developed because illiterate workers could identify a picture of their trade or an emblem of its tools. Fraternal emblems also were used and were the most popular of the decorative forms. Immigrants especially liked the heraldry of the fraternal emblems since it reminded them of what they knew in Europe.

European porcelain blanks were decorated by American barber supply houses. Prices ranged from fifty cents for a gold name mug to two dollars and fifty cents for an elaborate occupational design. Most of the art work was done by German artists who had immigrated to America.

The invention of the safety razor by King C. Gillette, that was issued to three and one-half million servicemen during World War I, brought an end to the shaving mug era.

References: Susan and Al Bagdade, *Warman's English & Continental Pottery & Porcelain, 1st Edition,* Warman Publishing Co., Inc., 1987; Phillip L. Krumholz, *Value Guide For Barberiana & Shaving Collectibles,* published by author, 1988; Robert Blake Powell, *Occupational & Fraternal Shaving Mugs of The United States,* published by author, 1978.

Collectors' Club: National Shaving Mug Collectors Association, 818 South Knight Avenue, Park Ridge, IL 60068.

Advisor: Edward W. Leach.

Fraternal, Jr. O. U. A. M., gold trim, red, white, and blue flags, green wreath, marked "T & V Limoges/France," $225.00.

BARBER SHOP: FRATERNAL

Ancient Order Of Foresters, deer head, crossed American flags, shield, lodge #7995 . . . . 275.00
B.L.E.E., Brotherhood of Locomotive Eng, "BLE" monogram 90.00
Elks, B.P.O.E., double emblem, Dr. title 300.00
Fraternal Order of Eagles, eagle holding F.O.E. plaque 250.00
International Brotherhood of Paper

Makers, paper making machine, clasped hands, IB of PM 265.00
International Order of Mechanics, ark ladder, I.O.M. 250.00
Jr. Order United American Mechanics, arm, hammer, compass, square, and crossed flags 275.00
Loyal Knights of America, eagle, flags, and six pointed star 275.00
Retail Clerks Union, red star, clasped hands, initials, ARCIP 175.00
United Mine Workers of America, picks and shovels, hand clasp 350.00

Occupational, musician, trumpet, gold trim, aqua ground, multicolored flowers, $250.00.

BARBER SHOP: OCCUPATIONAL

Baker, hp, baker putting bread in red brick oven, detailed background . . . 950.00
Barber, hp, pair of hair clippers, worn name 125.00
Bartender, hp, bartender pouring drink, mirrored back bar, two patrons drinking and smoking 400.00
Brewery, man pulling dolly, vaulted ceiling, row of kegs 400.00
Butcher, man standing with prize steer 500.00
Caboose, B.R.R.T. 400.00
Cavalry, Lt. 6th, eagle, crossed flags and sabers 750.00
Chicken Farmer, rooster crowning . . . 225.00
Coal Miner, an in mine shoveling coal into cart 350.00
Coke Kiln, man with poker pulling coke chunks out of kiln 375.00
Cooper, man working on wooden barrel 400.00
Dentist, upper false teeth 350.00
Hand Car Operator on track, two men pumping 350.00
Hotel Clerk, clerk at desk, guest signing register 375.00
Hotel Owner, picture of hotel, owner's name 575.00
Ice Cream Parlor, metal dish of strawberry ice cream with spoon, worn gold trim 250.00

Livery Stable, horse drawn wagon with
driver in front of stable **275.00**
Marksman, crossed rifles, target eagle
wreath **225.00**
Musical, banjo, owner's name **350.00**
Oyster House Proprietor, hp, oysters
and clams in foreground, sailing ships
and birds in background, gilt vines
and name, marked "Royal China In-
ternational," 1929 adv for oyster
house **1,200.00**
Painter, two men on scaffold painting
house **385.00**
Phonograph, outside horn phono **350.00**
Photographic
Dog trainer, man showing pit bull dog **375.00**
Man with beard **250.00**
Plasterer, hp, mortar board and two
trowels, gilt sprigs, marked "TECD
Co, Semovit" **150.00**
Poultry Farmer, rooster, hen, and
chicks, worn gold trim **100.00**
Shepherd, sheep standing in field **350.00**
Shoemaker, tapering cylindrical body,
spreading gilt foot, gilt swags around
name, hp colored scene of shoe-
maker in shop **75.00**
Soldier, 22nd Inf. Div., crossed rifles,
bayonets **400.00**
Theater Owner, movie entrance scene,
patrons on side walk, hand bills . . . **750.00**
Trolley, overhead lines **400.00**
Trolley Repair Wagon, horse drawn,
scaffolding **1,250.00**
Truck, chain driven, early **375.00**
Tugboat in water, crew and captain, title **750.00**
Waiter, hp, patron sitting at table, waiter
serving drink, red and light yellow
ground, floral dec, worn gilt **1,000.00**

BARBER SHOP: OTHER

Bluebird, holding ribbon, owner's name **65.00**
Drape and Flowers, purple drape, pot
of flowers, gold name **85.00**
Flowers, purple, wheatheads, gold
name **65.00**
Horses In Storm, white and black
horses, copied from painting **100.00**
Pansies, blue and gold flowers on either
side of name **95.00**

GOLDEN SPORTSMAN MUGS

Father in top hat, Victorian ice skating
scene **65.00**
The Bartender, three customers, saloon
scene **75.00**
The Dentist, pulling teeth, patient in
chair **100.00**
The Engineer, locomotive tender **75.00**

The Iceman, horse drawn ice wagon,
driver, man on back **85.00**

SCUTTLES

Character
Chinese Man's Head, beige skin,
black mustache and queue,
marked "P. M. Bavaria," 3¾" h . . . **175.00**
Fish shape, green and brown **45.00**
Skull shape **75.00**
Rose Decorated, mirror, R.S. Prussia . **175.00**
Scuttle
Moss and rose, green leaves, gold
dec **50.00**
Ribbed, multicolored flowers, gold
dec **65.00**
Silver Plated **150.00**

SHAWNEE POTTERY

History: The Shawnee Pottery Co. was founded
in 1937 in Zanesville, Ohio. The company acquired
a 650,000 square foot plant that formerly housed
the American Encaustic Tiling Company and
where it produced as many as 100,000 pieces of
pottery per day until 1961, when the plant closed.

Shawnee limited its chief production to kitchenware, decorative art pottery, and dinnerware. Distribution was primarily through jobbers and chain-
stores.

Shawnee can be marked "Shawnee," "Shawnee U.S.A." "USA #—," "Kenwood," or with character names, e.g., "Pat. Smiley," "Pat. Winnie,"
etc.

Reference: Mark Supnick, *Collecting Shawnee
Pottery: A Pictorial Reference And Price Guide,*
L-W Book Sales, 1989.

Advisor: Mark Supnick.

**Granny Anne, lady, blue bow, gold
apron, white ground, 7½" w, 8½" h,
$25.00.**

Bank, bulldog **45.00**
Casserole, Corn King, small, marked
  "Shawnee #73" **35.00**
Creamer
  Elephant, marked "Pat. USA" **18.00**
  Puss 'N Boots, gold trim, decals
    marked "Pat. Puss 'N Boots" **110.00**
Cookie Jar
  Clown, seal **75.00**
  Dutch Girl **120.00**
  Elephant **45.00**
  Winnie The Pig, marked "Pat. Winnie
    USA or USA" **75.00**
Figure
  Gazelle **35.00**
  Puppy **20.00**
  Tumbling Bear **22.00**
Mug, Corn King **25.00**
Pitcher
  Birds on perch **30.00**
  Bo Peep, marked "Pat. Bo Peep" .. **35.00**
  Buddha **12.00**
  Canopy Bed **30.00**
  Smiley Pig, marked "Pat. Smiley" .. **45.00**
Planter
  Canopy Bed, marked "Shawnee
    #734" **32.00**
  Doe, seated next to log, #766 .... **19.00**
  Dutch boy and girl at well **12.00**
Platter, Corn King, 12" **35.00**
Salt and Pepper Shakers, pr
  Duck **18.00**
  Sailor Boy **10.00**
  Wheelbarrow **8.00**
Relish, Corn King **20.00**
Teapot
  Corn King, 30 oz **40.00**
  Tom Tom the Piper's Son, marked
    "Tom the Piper's Son #44" **35.00**
Utility Jar, Corn King **25.00**
Wall Pocket
  Bird House **14.00**
  Mantle Clock **16.00**
  Telephone **15.00**

SILHOUETTES

History: Silhouettes (shades) are shadow profiles, produced by hollow cutting, mechanical tracing, or painting. They were popular in the 18th and 19th centuries.

The name came from Etienne de Silhouette, a French Minister of Finance, who tended to be tight with money and cut "shades" as a pastime. In America the Peale family was one of the leading silhouette makers. An impressed stamp marked "PEALE" or "Peale Museum" identifies their work.

Silhouette portraiture lost popularity with the introduction of daguerreotype prior to the Civil War. In the 1920s and 30s a brief revival occurred when tourists to Atlantic City and Paris had their profiles cut as souvenirs.

Reference: Blume J. Rifken, *Silhouettes in America, 1790–1840, A Collectors' Guide,* Paradigm Press, 1987.

Lady and gentleman, hollow cut, 4 x 3¼", $200.00.

Children
  6½ x 10¼", pair of full length children,
  gilded detail, simple ink wash
  ground, labeled "Master Hubbard,"
  framed **200.00**
  10 x 13¾", full length of girl in garden,
  bird in one hand, flower in other, ink
  wash ground, pen and ink inscription "Annabelle Wallace, Aug.
  Edouart fecit 1842," walnut shadow
  box frame, gilded liner **675.00**
  12½ x 15", full length of standing boy,
  black paper, gilt detail on ink wash
  ground, labeled "D. W. R. Buchanan 1847", gold frame **215.00**
Gentleman
  8¼ x 11½", Sea Captain, black backing, white litho ground showing window, ship, black cut paper ink set
  and cap on floor, highlighted in pencil, red, and gold on spyglass, sgd
  "Sam'l Metford, Newport, RI," identified on back in pencil as Charles
  Procter, framed **2,350.00**
  10¾ x 13½", full length cleric in pulpit,
  cut and pasted on paper, ink wash
  church int. scene, attributed to
  Edouart, bird's eye maple veneer
  ogee frame **235.00**
Group
  3½ x 2¾", oval, watercolor and cut
  paper mounted on black fabric, inscribed on reverse: "Samuel Fish
  and Mrs. Elvira Fish, Gov Went-
  worth's family, NH," repousse
  brass frames, c1825 .... **4,000.00**
  13½ x 15½", family, brushed white
  highlights on each, black backing,
  white ink wash ground of room int.,
  fireplace, entitled "The Lesson

1840," printed paper label "Clay Turner, Profiles From Life," inscription "George Walters and his family, Jan 7th, 1840" on back of paper visible through window in backing, bird's eye veneer ogee frame ...   **900.00**

Women

3⅞ x 2⅜", young woman, emb signature of Peales Museum, framed   **75.00**

4⅞ x 5⅞", young woman, hollow cut, black cloth backing, eglomise glass with worn gilded frame **75.00**

5¼ x 6¼", bust portrait of woman, black paper, brushed black, white, and gold details, white ground, c1840, framed **100.00**

SILVER

History: The natural beauty of silver lends itself to the designs of artists and craftsmen. It has been mined and worked into an endless variety of useful and decorative items. Pure silver is too soft to be fashioned into strong, durable, and serviceable utensils. Therefore, a way was found to give silver the required degree of hardness by adding alloys of copper and nickel.

Silversmithing in America goes back to the early 17th century in Boston and New York. It began in the early 18th century in Philadelphia. Boston was influenced by the English styles, New York by the Dutch.

References: Frederick Bradbury, *Bradbury's Book of Hallmarks*, J. W. Northend, Ltd, 1987; Louise Bilden, *Marks Of American Silversmiths in the Ineson-Bissell Collection*, Univ. of VA Press, 1980; Rachael Feild, *Macdonald Guide To Buying Antique Silver and Sheffield Plate*, Macdonald & Co., 1988; Donald L. Fennimore, *Silver & Pewter*, Alfred A. Knopf *Knopf Collector's Guides To American Antiques*, 1984; *Jewelers' Circular Keystone Sterling Flatware Pattern Index, 2nd Edition*, Chilton Company, 1989; Dorothy T. Rainwater, *Encyclopedia of American Silver Manufacturers, 3rd Edition*, Schiffer Publishing Ltd., 1986; Dorothy T. and H. Ivan Rainwater, *American Silverplate*, Schiffer Publishing, Ltd., 1988; Jeri Schwartz, *The Official Indentification And Price Guide To Silver and Silver-Plate, Sixth Edition*, House of Collectibles, 1989; Peter Waldon, *The Price Guide To Antique Silver, 2nd Edition*, , Antique Collectors' Club, 1982 (price revision list 1988); Seymour B. Wyler, *The Book Of Old Silver, English, American, Foreign*, Crown Publishers, Inc., 1937 (available in reprint).

Periodicals: *Silver*, P.O. Box 1243, Whittier, CA 90609; *Silver Collector*, 170 Fifth Avenue, 12th Floor, New York, NY 10010.

Additional Listings: See Silver Flatware in *Warman's Americana & Collectibles* for more examples in this area.

American, Coin, tablespoon, marked "J. Brenise," York County, PA, 9¾" l, $85.00.

AMERICAN, 1790–1840
Mostly Coin

Coin silver is slightly less pure than sterling silver. Coin silver has 900 parts silver to 100 parts alloy. Sterling silver has 925 parts silver. American silversmiths followed the coin standards. Coin silver also is called Pure Coin, Dollar, Standard, or Premium.

Beaker, 3⅜" h, tapered cylindrical form, molded borders, base engraved "W. P. to Nannie," stamped on base, John Adam, Alexandria, VA, c1820, 4 ozs   **825.00**

Bowl, 6¼" d, circular, pedestal base, beaded borders, marked on base twice, Christian Wittberger, Philadelphia, c1795 ....   **1,500.00**

Cann, good clear mark, Jacob Hurd, Boston, MA, 1740–50, 12½ oz **3,900.00**

Caster, 5½" h, baluster, domed lid, spiral turned flame finial, engraved and pierced drum, body inverted pyriform, spreading circular foot, lid and body with three gadrooned moldings, initial punch on one side, mark illegible, few bruises **500.00**

Coffeepot, 15½", vase form, incurved neck, pedestal base, beaded borders, swan neck leaf capped spout, reel shaped cov with vase finial, wood scroll handle, marked on base, Christian Wittberger, Philadelphia, c1795, split in cov, 42 ozs **4,500.00**

Creamer, spheroid body, scrolled handle, flaring open concave spout, conforming circular stepped base, monogrammed, Bailey & Kitchen, Philadelphia, 1833–46 ....   **250.00**

Cup, 4¼", beaker form, two S scroll handles, monogrammed, Ebenezer Moulton, Newburyport, MA, c1810, 5 ozs **475.00**

Fish Server, reticulated panel of acorns and leaves, incised monogram "H," orig ivory handle, Joseph Lownes, Philadelphia, PA, c1780, 4½ oz, needs minor repair where handle joins silver **300.00**

Ladle

Sauce, feather edge stem, bright cut, terminal monogrammed, spirally fluted bowl, marked twice on lower back of stem, William Hollingshead, Philadelphia, c1775 . . . . **800.00**

Soup, 13¼" l, circular bow, curved flaring handle, pointed oval grip, handle engraved with bright cut border forming oval reserves, one with pendant bellflower, other with monogrammed, roulette work border, marked Christian Wittberger, Philadelphia, c1790, 5 ozs **1,000.00**

Lemon Strainer, 3⅝" d, hemispherical bowl pierced in flowerhead pattern below border of lozenges, single incised line rim, side applied with scrolled strap clip for attachment to rim of bowl, marked, Adrian Bancker, NY, c1760, 2 ozs **1,650.00**

Mug, engraved initials "MAA," William Carrington, 6 oz **200.00**

Pepper Box, 3" h, cylindrical form, molded borders, domed foot, fluted scroll strap handle, domed cov pierced in flowerhead pattern, domed finial, marked on base three times, Miles Beach, Litchfield and Hartford, CT, c1780, 20 ozs, 5 dwts **1,250.00**

Porringer

5", engraved with initials "WL" on the handle, straight line mark with eagle in circle, Abel Moulton, Newburyport, MA, c1800, 6½ oz **2,600.00**

7½", pierced unornamented handle, deep bowl, John & Peter Targee, NY, 1811–25, 9 ozs, 2 dwts **1,450.00**

Spoon

Tablespoon

Boelin, Joseph, NY, upturned midrib handle, fluted rattail bowl, terminal engraved with initials, marked on back of stem, c1720, 2 ozs **375.00**

Brasher, Ephraim, NY, mid 19th C, strong marks, single drop, 2 ozs **225.00**

Frederick Curtis & Co, Burlington, VT, c1786, engraved "Badgley," set of four, 5 ozs **100.00**

Sargeant, Jacob, Hartford, CT, c1761, raised sheaf of wheat on handle, appears unused, 2 oz . **150.00**

Teaspoon, Myer Myers, NY, 1723–95, engraved initials on handle **225.00**

Sugar Nippers, 4¼" l, scissor form, spurred ring grips, shaped arms, shell tips, circular hinge engraved on each

side with initials, marked on inside of each tip, Jacob Hurd, Boston, c1750, 10 dwts **3,150.00**

Teapot

10" h, spheroid body, stepped domed top, acorn finial, scrolled handle, leaf capped swan like spout, conforming circular stepped base, Bailey & Kitchen, Philadelphia, 1833–46 . . . . **600.00**

12" l, Federal style, oval body, banded design engraved on shoulder, hinged lid, urn finial, wood handle, maker's mark, R & H Farnam, Boston, post 1807, 18 ozs **500.00**

Tongs, engraved "PK," Matthew Petit, New York, NY, c1790, 2 oz **100.00**

Waste Bowl, 7½", globular body, lobed sides, concave paw and ball feet terminating in acanthus leaves, ring handles attached over lion mask roundels, William Thomson, NY, 1811–25, 23 ozs, 14 dwts **350.00**

American, Sterling, cigarette case, raised floral motif, patent Dec 4, 1888, 3 x 2", $100.00.

SILVER, AMERICAN, 1840–1920
Mostly Sterling

There are two possible sources for the origin of the word sterling. The first is that it is a corruption of the name Easterling. Easterlings were German silversmiths who came to England in the Middle Ages. The second is that it is named for the starling (little star) used to mark much of the early English silver.

Sterling silver has 925/1000 parts pure silver. Copper comprises most of the remaining alloy. American manufacturers began to switch to the sterling standard about the time of the Civil War.

Alvin Corp., Providence, RI, salts, 3⅜", set of four, oval, pierced sides, ball and claw feet, cobalt blue glass liners, 4 ozs **200.00**

Bailey, Banks and Biddle Co., basket, 9½", Art Nouveau, oval, pierced, flared sides, swing handle, monogrammed, 11 ozs, 10 dwts **350.00**

Baltimore Silversmiths Mfg Co., Baltimore, 1903–05, soup cup frames and liners, set of twelve, 3½" d, 1¾" h, double handles, threaded rims, engraved with scrolls suspending medallions, monogrammed, set of twelve porcelain Lenox liners, gilt trim, 30 ozs, 6 dwts **500.00**

Barbour Silver Co., Hartford, CT, box, cov, 7¼", sq, Rococo style rose and foliate sections, handle set with green stone, raised on four thread edged feet, gilt int., monogrammed, 19 ozs **350.00**

Cartier, basket, 6" sq, 7¼" h, hand made, woven with silver strips, strap handle, 12 ozs, 16 dwts **600.00**

Dominick & Haff, Newark, NJ
Cake Plate, 13¾", plain face, emb rim with basket of flowers motif, 31 ozs, 6 dwts **450.00**
Compote, 8" h, shaped and chamfered sq top pierced and chased in floral designs, inverted trumpet form stand, pierced rim at bottom, monogrammed, 11 ozs, 8 dwts . . **385.00**
Flatware, seventy-three pcs, Renaissance pattern, monogrammed, orig filled oak case, 114 ozs, 10 dwts . **1,450.00**
Service Plates, 11", set of twelve, plain, rolled edges and rims pierced with Greek key design spaced with medallions of hanging leaves and bell flowers, monogrammed, 151 ozs, 18 dwts **2,200.00**

Duhme Co, Cincinnati, OH, 1898–1907, punch bowl, 14" d, chased and pierced with floral border at rim and feet, 76 ozs **2,750.00**

Wm. B. Durgin Co., Concord, NH, center bowl, 15½ x 7¾", flaring pierced sides, pedestal stem, domed base, spreading circular foot, rims of bowl and base with applied frieze of chased scrolling leafage, central face monogrammed and dated 1913, 50 ozs, 18 dwts **1,430.00**

Elgin Silversmith Co, Inc., candelabra, 9¾" h, chamfered flaring central shaft supporting arm with nozzle on either side, circular base with engraved cypher monogram, c1945, pr **175.00**

Gorham Mfg Co., Providence, RI
Bread and Butter Plates, 6½", set of ten, Florenz pattern, monogrammed, 1929, 59 ozs, dwts . . . **950.00**
Cheese Dish, cov, 11¼", Maintenon pattern, 1924, retailed by Spaulding & Co., Chicago, 34 ozs, 12 dwts **475.00**

Coffee Set, four pcs, 12" h Turkish form coffeepot, creamer, open sugar, and 14¾" tray, Iris pattern, wavy strapwork leaves and iris blossoms chased and worked on repousse, lobed wavy feet, hollow ware pcs monogrammed, tray with worked border, plain face, Martele silver, 950 standard, retailed by Theodore B. Starr, NY, 81 ozs, 8 dwts **9,350.00**

Dressing Table Set, lady's, twenty pcs, two salve jars, two scent bottles, two powder jars, two cov puff jars, cov jewelry box, cov hatpin tray, engraved with swags of cloth and flowers, matte ground, center circular reserve with monogram on each pc, orig fitted case, retailed by Anderson & Randolph, San Francisco, 1877, 42 ozs, 10 dwts **2,575.00**

Epergne, 23¼ x 6¼, Rococo style, four multiple scrolled feet, connecting aprons of scrolling foliage centering leafy spray, supporting platform with collet base for large glass bowl (cut with scrolling foliage), four leaf capped scrolling arms supporting smaller matching glass bowls, 85 ozs **4,125.00**

Fruit Bowl, 11 x 3½", spreading circular form, ringed foot, monogrammed, 27 ozs, 18 dwts **275.00**

Meat Platter, 16½ x 22½", Plymouth pattern, well at both ends, groove at sides, monogrammed, 80 ozs, 8 dwts **935.00**

Salver, 14¼", circular, quatrefoil form, emb and flat chased border, plain face, 35 ozs, 6 dwts **300.00**

Tea and Coffee Set, six pcs, Maintenon pattern, 14" hot water kettle (1929) on stand (1930), 11" coffeepot (1926), teapot, cov sugar, creamer, and waste bowl, 164 ozs, 18 dwts **5,000.00**

Tea Tray, 25¼", Maintenon pattern, 1930, 162 ozs **2,750.00**

Vase, 9", pierced lap-over mouth, threaded rim, ovoid body, circular domed pedestal base, pierced foot, plated gilt frog, 26 ozs, 6 dwts . . . **360.00**

Graff, Washbourne & Dunn, NY
Center Bowl, 14¾", French border, hand chased, shaped circular form, fold-over pierced skirt rim, pierced frog cover, inscription on underside, for J. E. Caldwell & Co., 39 ozs . . **650.00**
Service Plates, 11½", set of eleven, French border, hand chased, retailed by Theodore B. Starr, Inc., NY, 221 ozs, 12 dwts **6,000.00**

International, Meriden, CT, flatware, 63 pcs, Frontenac pattern, monogrammed, c1903 . . . . **750.00**

Kalo Shops, Park Ridge, IL
Compote, 10⅝″ d, 5¼″ h, shallow bowl, scalloped border, five floriform sections, slender neck, circular base, slightly peened finish, marked "Sterling/Hand Wrought/At/The Kalo Shop," c1920, 23 ozs, 4 dwts **1,250.00**
Platter, 12″ w, 19½″ l, oval, folded over border, convex moldings form handles, applied crescent borders, peened surface, marked "Kalo Shops, Sterling/Hand Beaten," c1905, 34 ozs, 8 dwts **5,500.00**

Samuel Kirk & Son, Inc., Baltimore. flatware, service for twelve, Florentine pattern, 72 pcs **900.00**

Matthews Co, Newark, NJ, 1907–30, child's set, three pcs, 5½″ d plate, mug, and brush, acid etched with scenes and names of nursery rhymes, 5 ozs, 10 dwts **250.00**

Meriden Britannia Co., Meriden, CT
Dessert Plate, 10½″ d, shaped circular form, wide applied cast reticulated border with winged masks, foliate scrolls, and flowers, 19 ozs **200.00**
Flower Basket, 14½″ d, cylindrical body, wavy open mouth, threaded rim, swelling shoulder, swinging strap handle, pierced with flat chased floral design, monogrammed, 62 ozs **1,650.00**

Pratt, 20th C, pitcher, water, 6″ d, 8½″ h, hand hammered, plain melon form body, curved handle, helmet form lip, rolled over edge, ring foot, monogram, 29 ozs, 10 dwts **825.00**

Reed & Barton, Tauton, MA, garniture, 11″ trumpet shaped vase with fluted rim, three 6½″ vases attached by chains, fourth vase and chain lacking monogram, weighted bases **220.00**

Schofield Co., Baltimore, MD, center bowl, late Georgian style, lozenge form, shaped lip over pierced panel of diaperwork and acanthus border, lug handles, lion masks and garlands on body, scrolling feet, c1920, 158 ozs **7,500.00**

Shreve & Co, San Francisco
Bread and Butter Plates, 7⅛″, set of sixteen, German Iris pattern, chased borders in heavy relief, monogrammed, 80 ozs, 8 dwts . . **1,650.00**
Cocktail Shaker, 10½″ h, cylindrical body, peened surface, fish tail removable pourer, side set with gilt

and enameled medallion, bell mark, 20 ozs, 4 dwts **500.00**

Flower Bowl, 11½″ d, 4⅜″ h, deep sides, flat base, concave center, everted wavy border pierced and applied with sinuous vines and poppy medallions, Art Nouveau, c1900, 22 ozs **500.00**

Garniture, 3 pcs, 15½″ h cov center vase, two 11¼″ h flanking vases, inverted pyriform bodies, domed circular feet, flaring lip above, domed lids with upright stiff leaf finial, applied chased bearded iris dec on shoulder, base, and lip, Art Nouveau, c1909, bell mark, 75 ozs, 12 dwts **2,475.00**

Ice Bucket, 6″ h, flaring cylindrical body, applied horizontal staves, swing handle with finger strap below at back, hammered surface, applied monogram on spout, Arts and Crafts, c1910, 17 ozs, 6 dwts **360.00**

Presentation Tray, 16¾″, unadorned peened surface with inscription and date 1915, bell mark, 52 ozs **365.00**

Sandwich Plate, 11¼″, flat, chased, scrolling flower and tendril design, monogrammed, bell mark, 19 ozs, 18 dwts **225.00**

Teapot, 9½″, Art Nouveau style, undulating vines, 19 ozs, 10 dwts . . **385.00**

Vase
9½″, SS collar with chased German bearded iris on neck, modified Art Nouveau pierced border at lip, faceted polygonal glass base **1,000.00**
13″, champagne bucket shape, fold-over lip pierced and engraved with scrolling flowers, matching underplate, bell mark, 92 ozs **1,870.00**

Spaulding & Co., Chicago, 1888–1920, dish, 11″, grape leaf form, tendril and leaf handle, 25 ozs **400.00**

Tiffany & Co, NY, pitcher, water, 11¾″, ovoid body, tapering neck, diagonally shaped spout joining strap handle, ring foot, inscribed on underside, dated 1958, 50 ozs, 8 dwts **1,210.00**

R. Wallace & Sons Mfg Co., Wallingford, CT, roast carving set, La Reine pattern, 3 pcs **100.00**

Wood & Hughes, NY, c1870
Hot Water Urn, 20″ h, Renaissance Revival style, trumpet shaped body ending in pressed band of leaves and berries, lid engraved with scrolling design on matted surface, twisted post finial, handles with foliate ends and capped with figure of putto on each side, spigot handle

topped with bust of female beauty, legs of attached stand cast openwork foliage, orig burner, 82 ozs, 10 dwts **935.00**

Soup Ladle, 15″ l, Medallion pattern, silver-gilt bowl, scalloped edge, fitted leather case with purple velvet lining, 9 ozs, 18 dwts **660.00**

Woodside Sterling Co (for Richard M Woods,) NY, fruit bowl, 8⅝″ d, 6½″ h, Jensen style, flaring circular body, pierced stem of grape clusters and flowering plants on stiff leaves, circular rising base, c1920, 22 ozs, 14 dwts **715.00**

SILVER, CONTINENTAL

Continental silver does not have a strong following in the United States. The strong feeling of German silver cannot compete with the lightness of the English examples. In Canada, Russia silver finds a strong market.

Austrian

Centerpiece, 22½ x 16½″, diamond shaped bowl on four feet, one foot on each side with heart shaped leaf flowing to reeded supports, ends with figures of Venus and Cupid, four straps issuing from ends and sides joining by four angled stalks and robed figure of Flora, holding clusters of grapes, marked AB, 800 standard, 116 ozs, 10 dwts **7,150.00**

Hot Water Kettle, 10¾″, inverted pyriform kettle, scrolling handle, hinged lid with ivory finial, matching stand with heating pan, ivory handle, and three extra ivory knobs, M & K, Vienna, 1862, 66 ozs, 10 dwts **1,210.00**

Danish

Bowl, 6½″ d, 3¾″ h, bowl resting on stem chased with overlapping palmettos, polygonal base applied with beads, Georg Jensen, c1925, 7 ozs, 18 dwts **1,000.00**

Cake Knife, Cactus pattern, Georg Jensen, c1945 . . . . **195.00**

Carving Set, 3 pcs, fork, knife, and steel, presentation box, Cactus pattern, Georg Jensen, c1945 . . . . . **450.00**

Coffee Set, three pcs, 7″ coffeepot with ivory handle, creamer with ivory handle, cov sugar, Blossom pattern, Georg Jensen, 26 ozs, 10 dwts **2,750.00**

Compote, 12½″ h, bowl applied with threaded band alternating with leaves, bulbous pedestal engraved with band of foliage, cushion foot with circular medallions in re-

pousse encircled with strapwork and foliage, Michelsen, Copenhagen, 1851, assayer's mark for P. R. Hinnerup, zodiac marks for Libra and Scorpio, 39 ozs **800.00**

Flatware, 84 pcs, Cactus pattern, Georg Jensen, c1933, 76 ozs, 10 dwts **5,225.00**

Dutch

Creamer, 6″, pyriform body, three inverted cabriole legs, branch form scrolling handle, neck engraved and bright cut foliage dec, HB, Amsterdam, 1793, 6 ozs **250.00**

Marrow Scoop, 9¼″, plain design, double ends, Amsterdam, 18th C, 1 oz **360.00**

Salad Fork and Spoon, bowl of spoon with crowned double lion crest, fork with basket of fruit flanked by birds, spoon marked Amsterdam, import mark, and rubbed assay mark, fork marked Embden, assay mark for Leeuwarden, both handles marked 833 standard, 1909, 9 ozs, 8 dwts **250.00**

Wedding Cup, 13″, silver-gilt, goblet shape, repousse with trellis supporting foliage and flowers on matte ground, ship finial on inverted goblet, body made from seashell, silver deck, mast sail, tiller, and anchor, 14 ozs **500.00**

French

Asparagus Tongs, 10″, engine turned dec, 950 standard, J. G., late 19th C **200.00**

Bowl, 17½ x 4⅜″, shell shape, fluted sides, four scroll feet with fluted palmette terminals, rim applied with alternating ball and bead pattern within a meander, A. Aucol, 950 standard, 49 ozs **1,450.00**

Dessert Bowls, 4¼ x 2¾″, plain, threaded bands at rim and circular ftd base, monogrammed, Paris, post 1879, 950 standard, 82 ozs, 6 dwts, set of 12 . . . . **1,650.00**

Dish Stands, 6 x 3″, ring form, four scroll feet terminating in leafage, suspending floral garlands, 950 standard mark post 1879, return mark post 1888, 31 ozs, pr **425.00**

Tea and Coffee Service, 14″ h hot water kettle on stand, coffeepot, teapot, hot milk jug, cov sugar, and creamer, paneled pyriform body, scrolling spout, conforming lid with gadrooned edge, pineapple finial, scrolling treen handles, maker's mark GF, first half 19th C, 102 ozs **4,000.00**

German

Bread Basket, 15″, oval, pierced

openwork and repousse ornaments, floral garland borders entwining flower filled baskets at ends holding agricultural implements, draped over ribbons tied in French knots, alternating with cartouche at either side with scene of kneeling suitor and intended in Alpine landscape, each scene spaced with facing pair of birds and flowers, base with medallion of two infants playing with baby ducks, 19th C, 800 standard, 15 ozs **525.00**

Ewer, 10¼", Baroque taste, silver-gilt, emb and chased bird and floral garlands, scrolling foliage and bands of strapwork on pricked ground, domed circular foot, double C scroll handles, marked B & Z, post 1888, 800 standard, 26 oz, 10 dwts ... **1,210.00**

Salver, 10" d, 2¾" h, circular piecrust molded border with plain center, flaring standard, molded foot, Augsburg, mid 18th C, 16 ozs ... **3,600.00**

Table Ornament, owl, 9¼" h, chased plumage, glass eyes, marked sterling, retailed by I. F. and Son, Ltd, 30 ozs, 4 dwts **1,100.00**

Tea and Coffee Service, silver gilt, pyriform bodies and domed tops, elaborately chased all–over with panels of scrolling foliage and flowers, pricked ground, floral swags centering cartouche on either side, scrolling finial, domed spreading feet, 14½" h hot water kettle on stand with burner, 12" h coffeepot, teapot, two handled sugar and creamer, marked W. W. H., post 1888, 160 ozs, 14 dwts, coffeepot handle loose **5,500.00**

Norwegian

Coffee Set, 3 pcs, engine turned, cobalt blue enamel, gilt int., ivory handle on 7" coffeepot, David Andersen **800.00**

Liqueur Goblets, 3¾" h, set of twelve, engine turned and enameled, stems and feet of plain silver, gilt bowl ints. **465.00**

Unmarked

Caster, 7½" h, Baroque style, bulging globular body, cylindrical neck and stem, domed circular foot and cap, dolphin finial, applied relief and chased flowers, scrolling leaves and armorial, 19th C, pseudo hallmarks, 9 ozs, 18 dwts, pr **365.00**

Table Ornament, pair of pheasants, hinged wings, 19" l, 31 ozs, 10 dwts **1,450.00**

Vase, 16½", inverted pyriform shape, scalloped trumpet motifs, domed

circular foot, all–over scrolling foliage and floral sprays, pricked ground, cartouche on either side, one in reserve, other with genre scene of peasants outside tavern, late 19th C, English import marks of I. F. & Son, Ltd., London, 1928, pr **4,500.00**

SILVER, ENGLISH

From the 17th century to the mid-19th century, English silversmiths set the styles which American silversmiths copied. The work from the period exhibits the highest degrees of craftsmanship. Active collection of English silver takes place in the American antiques marketplace.

Charles II, tumbler, 3" d, hammered sides, slightly convex bottom, marks rubbed, 2 ozs **250.00**

Edwardian, center bowl, 10" d, 10" h, Baroque style, truncated baluster form, repousse with acanthus leaf tips, scrolling acanthus form lug handles, stepped socle base, Mapin and Webb, London, c1903, 72 ozs **2,200.00**

George I, caudle cup, 5" h, plain lip, cast S scroll handles, reeded and gadrooned body, socle base, maker's mark rubbed, London, c1725, 9 ozs **200.00**

George II

Candlesticks, pr, segmented shafts on circular convex shaped feet, maker's mark stamped twice, Thomas England, London, c1725–39, 27 ozs, 4 dwts, lacking nozzles **900.00**

Inkstand, 8" l, oblong tray, gadrooned edge, baluster form inkwell and pounce pot, tapered stand of differing origin, raised on ball and claw feet, Magdeline Feline, London, c1758, 14½ ozs **900.00**

Sauce Boat, boat form, flying double C scroll leaf capped handles, tripod shell feet, shell terminals, repousse sides with flowers, lip edge with gadrooning, armorial under spout, marks partially rubbed off, William Grundy, London, 1759, 16 ozs, 6 dwts, pr **2,750.00**

Tankard, 4¾", plain baluster form, double scroll handle, William Kidney, London, 1742, 14 ozs, 6 dwts **715.00**

George III

Basin, 16½" w, 3½" h, oval, gadrooned lip quartered by shell form clasps, plain body, engraved coronet, William Simmons, London, c1809, 50 ozs **3,250.00**

Basket, 14½ x 3½", oval, threaded swing handle, scalloped rim, threaded with pierced border, oval pierced foot, bright cut armorial and monogram on face, Peter and Anne Bateman, London, 1795, 22 ozs, 18 dwts **1,320.00**

Butter Dish, 7" d, slightly compressed dome form, gadrooned acorn form finial, dished base with reeded edge, unidentified maker's mark, London, c1802, 12 ozs **850.00**

Candlesticks, pr, 5½" h, plain cylindrical columnar form, beaded nozzle, stepped beaded base, treen lined, Robert Makepeace and Richard Carter, London, c1777 ...... **750.00**

Calling Card Tray, 6¾" d, shell and S scroll molded border enclosing plain surface, raised on double C scroll legs, pad feet, attributed to Edward Capper, London, c1768, 7 ozs **175.00**

Center Bowl, 8½ x 3½", shallow, applied rim with branches and flowers, Victorian dec on sides in repousse of flowers and foliage, monogram in central cartouche, domed ring foot, caryatid handles, Paul Storr, London, 1805, 18 ozs, 10 dwts **665.00**

Chocolate Pot, 11½" h, pyriform, leaf capped scroll handle, hinged lid, foliate finial, circular foot, body engraved with cartouches centered by scrolling foliate medallions, one inscribed 1847, Robert Gray & Son, Glasgow, Edinburgh mark, 1804, 23 ozs, 4 dwts, foot repaired **800.00**

Cup, 8" h, urn form, plain scrolling S handles, socle base, John Langlands, Newcastle, 29 ozs **600.00**

Epergne, 22" h, triple tiered frame supported by four multiple foliate scrolled feet linked by side aprons of floral sprays, center of lowest tier open with four foliage scrolling strap form stretchers supporting pineapple, enclosed by four reserve swelling leaf capped arms on second oval tier, central detachable boat shaped pierced basket, six detachable circular paterae form shallow armorial engraved baskets, leaf capped scrolling branches ending in beaded circular supports, Thomas Powell, London, 1771, 194 ozs, 14 dwts **11,000.00**

Hot Water Urn, 15" h, heavily molded lid with gadrooned border, loop handles with acanthus terminals, projecting reeded spout, sq base, angled monopodia, John Edwards, London, c1810, 122 ozs **4,500.00**

Ladle, rubbed Irish maker's marks, Dublin, c 1775, 3 ozs **250.00**

Marrow Scoop, 9" l, feather edge, Thomas Chawner, London, 1774, 1 oz **250.00**

Salt
3½" d, Neoclassical style, border of Greek Key, three loop carrying handles, basin form body, reeded legs, ball feet, attributed to Joseph Heriot, London, c1770, 24 ozs, set of 4 .... **2,000.00**

5½" l, Neoclassical style, lozenge form, gadrooned border, angular loop handles, conforming stepped base, parcel gilt int., marker's mark WA, London, c1803, 14 ozs, set of four **1,400.00**

Salver, 10", shaped piecrust top, beaded border, three claw and ball feet, chased armorial of later date, Hester Bateman, London, 1781, 18 ozs **1,540.00**

Sauce Boat, 5" l, open scrolling handle, William Caldecott, London, c1763, 3 ozs **300.00**

Snuff Box, 3½" l, oblong lid, cast floral rim, engraved turned surface above conforming case, band of scrolling floral engraving, Joseph Willmore, Birmingham, c1818, 3½ ozs **285.00**

Spoon, berry, gilt, repousse chased bowl, handles chased with flowers and strapwork, Hester Bateman, London, 1786, set of six, 11 ozs, 14 dwts **525.00**

Sugar Stand, 3" h, inverted slightly compressed dome form, stepped socle with gadrooned edges, Samuel Taylor, London, c1769, contemporary armorial, 6 ozs **500.00**

Toast Rack, 8½" l, wirework lozenges, skeletal boat form base with gadrooned border, winged shell form feet, Emes and Barnard, London, c1810, 11 ozs **500.00**

Urn, 13½"h, Neoclassical style, molded lid with acorn finial, inverted cone form body with bands of bright cut floral dec within loop handles, ornamented socle base, partly effaced marks of John Emes, London, c1800, 36 ozs **2,100.00**

George IV
Fruit Basket, 14¾", pierced basket with applied border chased with scrolls and fluted garlands, sides of fluted swirls terminating in acanthus leaves, swing openwork handle, pierced band of flowers and scrolls base, central face engraved

with rampant cat, inscribed below "Touch Not The Cat Bot A Glove," Robert Hennell, London, 1820, 45 ozs, 16 dwts **5,000.00**

Grape Shears, 6" l, gilt handles, shells, flowers, and fruit on matte ground, Jonathan Hayne, London, 1822, 3 oz, 10 dwts **500.00**

Salt, 3¾" d, double border of scrolls and flowers, tripod hoof feet, gilt int., Charles Price, London, 1822, 15 ozs, set of 4 . . . . **375.00**

Stand, 8½" l, rect, rounded corners, scrolling gadrooned border, bellied body heavily repoussed with scrolling foliage and flower heads, center armorial within foliate clasps, paw feet, treen base, marker's mark AK, London, c1824, 14 ozs **200.00**

Georgian Style, jug, 9¾" h, baluster form, C scroll spout, S scroll handle, stepped circular foot, marker's mark RC, London, c1828, retailed by Tiffany and Company, NY, 43 ozs **1,600.00**

Victorian

Creamer, 4", pyriform, shaped flaring lip, C scroll handle, incurvate legs ending in pad feet, J. Whipple and Co., Exeter, c1878, 2 ozs **75.00**

Cruet Stand, 7½ x 10", boat shaped bulging body, spiral gadrooned border, four scrolled leafy feet, segmented columnar handle with heart shaped handle, cut plate to hold bottles, wooden platform below, monogram on body, six glass bottles, diaper cut band, James Edwards, London, 1845 . . . . **900.00**

Dressing Spoon, Fiddle, Thread, and Shell pattern, Samuel Hayne & Dudley Cater, London, 1844, 6 oz, 10 dwts **350.00**

Roast Dish, cov, 24" l, oval, heavily molded lid, pomegranate and fruit finial, base with removable tray fitted with bombe jacket with pierced sides, scrolling legs, parcel gilt, J E Terry & Co, London, c1865, tops and bases engraved with contemporary armorials and motto, 656 ozs, pr **21,000.00**

Stand, 12½" w, 18" h, stile and rail construction, surmounted by fully modeled crown, tubular crest rail supported by fluted stiles resting on stepped molded bases, marker's mark HI, Edinburgh, c1897, 70 ozs **1,600.00**

Tea and Coffee Service, teapot, 10" coffeepot, creamer, and cov sugar, Rococo style, pyriform bodies, leafy reserved cartouches, fluted quatrefoil sections, handles of double leafy S curves, tea and coffee spouts of matte work still leaves, acanthus feet, J. W. & J. W., Edinburgh, 1850, 86 ozs **3,125.00**

Tea Kettle, 14" h, indented ovoid shape, highly worked emb, chased, and engraved surface, Elizabethan figures in village dec, hinged lid with male sitting on keg, leaf capped spout terminating in bearded mask, matching stand applied with cast and reticulated floral swags headed by female masks, three cabriole legs, leafy feet, strut branching from each leg to support fuel container, I. Foligno, London, 1867, 80 ozs, 10 dwts **1,450.00**

Wine Coaster, 5½ x 6¾", bulging boat shaped body, repousse and chased with scrolls and flowers, four tab feet emb with anthemia, monogrammed, William K. Read, London, 1856 . . . . **300.00**

Wine Cooler, 9½ x 11½", Greek vase shape, bulging lobed body with acanthus leaves, emb and chased border of English rose, Scotch thistle, and Irish shamrock at top, overhanging lip with alternating leaves, squat stem with border of tongues and leaves, circular foot chased with acanthus on matted ground, S curved handles ending in acanthus leaf terminals, Edward, Edward Jr, John, and W. Barnard, London, date letter rubbed, c1840s, 74 ozs **3,850.00**

Edward VII

Asparagus Tongs, 9" l, crested Fiddle, Thread, and Shell pattern, W. W. BT. London, 1903, 6 oz . . . **175.00**

Cup, cov, 5" h, lid fitted with feet to act as stand, cylindrical cup, flared lip, scrolling handles, dec at base with geometric anthemion, maker's mark rubbed, London, c1901–2, 16 ozs **200.00**

George V, kettle on lampstand, 12¾" h, pyriform body, faceted leaf capped swan neck spout, domed hinged cov, knob finial, turned wood and C scroll handle, stand of four scrolled and pad supports, threaded skirt, detachable burner, EJG, London, 1931, 54 ozs . **625.00**

SILVER, ENGLISH, SHEFFIELD

Sheffield Silver, or Old Sheffield Plate, was made by a fusion method of silver plating used from the mid-18th century until the mid-1880s when the silver electroplating process was introduced.

English, Sheffield, soup tureen, fluted bombe oval form raised on four shell and acanthus scrolled feet, reeded bracket handles, shell and scroll molded borders, fitted with liner, domed lid with handle of intertwined foliage, crested, marked "T & J Creswick," c1820, 15½" l, $2,000.00.

Sheffield plate was discovered in 1743 when Thomas Boulsover of Sheffield, England, accidentally fused silver and copper. The process consisted of sandwiching a heavy sheet of copper between two thin sheets of silver. The result was a plated sheet of silver which could be pressed or rolled to a desired thickness. All Sheffield plate articles were worked from these plated sheets.

Most of the silver plated items found today marked "Sheffield" are not early Sheffield plate. They are later wares made in Sheffield, England.

Biscuit Box, 6½" h, sq, hinged lid, lion mask and loose ring handles, faux tray base with paw supports, gadroon borders, unmarked, English, 19th C, replated **250.00**
Candelabra, pr, 19½", tapering turned column form, heavily gadrooned banding, surmounted by twin scrolling candle arms **900.00**
Candlesticks, pr, 11½" h, late Neoclassical style, tapering shaft, fluted base, stepped socle, Matthew Bolton & Co, 19th C **1,600.00**
Casserole, cov, 6½ x 5½", Baroque style, oval body standing on four scroll feet terminating in shell flanked leaves, leaf capped handles terminating in leaves, covs with leaf capped entwined branch handles, armorial on sides and cov, unmarked, early 19th C, pr, copper showing ... **825.00**
Entree Dish, cov, 12½ x 9", gadrooned borders, shells and flowers at corners, covs with fluted borders and conforming borders, detachable handle with double bound branch terminating on calyx of acanthus leaves, armorial engraved on side, unmarked, first or second quarter, 19th C, pr **1,320.00**
Inkstand, 9", rect tray, twin pen channels, faceted crystal pounce pot and inkwell, central chamberstick, 19th C **425.00**
Plateau, 17½", Rococo style, mirror plate in shell and scroll border, conforming spreading border, spreading shell form sides, mask, and scroll feet, possibly T. J. Creswick, mid 19th C, feet cut down **625.00**
Sauce Dish, cov, 5½ x 6½", form of cov calyx craters, disc shaped lids with gadrooned handles, spoon openings on rim, bowl with spiral gadrooned border, hot water reservoir, pair of double threaded handles, lobed sides, conforming circular foot with spiral gadrooned ring, early 19th C, pr **715.00**
Tea Urn, 16" h, heavily gadrooned lid, flattened urn form body, everted leaf tip collar, scrolling hand fitted with molded petcock, sq molded base with ruffled foliate feet **700.00**
Tureen, cov
13½ x 11", Rococo taste, elongated lobed oval body, four scrolling foliage feet, pair of reeded bracket handles terminating in leaves, lip gadrooned and spaced with shells and leaves, fitted cov rising to chased foliage handle terminating with spreading foliate, marked GD **2,100.00**
14 x 20", turtle shape, detachable hinged lid, unmarked **1,760.00**
Wine Cooler, pr, 9½" h, campana form, broad bands of acanthus leaves, loop handles, 19th C **1,800.00**

SILVER, PLATED

Plated silver production by an electrolytic method is credited to G. R. and H. Ekington, England, in 1838.

In electroplating silver, the article is completely shaped and formed from a base metal and then coated with a thin layer of silver. In the late 19th century, the base metal was Britannia, an alloy of tin, copper, and antimony. Other bases are copper and brass. Today the base is nickel silver.

In 1847 the electroplating process was introduced in America by Rogers Bros., Hartford, Connecticut. By 1855, a number of firms were using the method to mass produce silver plated items in large quantities.

The quality of the plating is important. Extensive use or polishing can cause the base metal to show through. The prices for plated silver items are low, making it a popular item with younger collectors.

Bowl, 17¾ x 6¾″, Neoclassical style, plain body, four paw feet with acanthus terminals, lion mask ring handles, band of spiral gadrooning, unmarked **600.00**

Butler's Tray, 18½ x 28″, crescent shape, threaded edge, solid galleried sides imp with repeating rect band of flowers and leaves, face bright cut in Egyptianizing floral motif, large circular medallion with traces of acid etched design of Athena drawn in chariot in reserve at center, large bracket handles with lotus terminals, unmarked, late 19th C **665.00**

Butter Dish, three pcs, base, lid, insert, delicate tiny double rows of beading around base, on edges, and dome lid, cut glass drip tray, Meriden Silver Plate Co **50.00**

Candelabra, pr, 20″ h, Neoclassical style, fluted pedestal shaft, draped urn supporting four lights, scrolling reeded branches and urn form nozzles, molded and reeded base **1,500.00**

Candlesticks, pr, 9½″ h, paneled baluster form standard, turned nozzle, molded base, Georgian style **350.00**

Champagne Bucket, 9″, cylindrical, bracket handles, applied scroll border band, monogrammed, Simpson, Hall, Miller & Co **250.00**

Cheese Ball Frame, 5″ d, mechanical, vitriculture border, E. G. Webster & Sons **75.00**

Cigar Holder, 10½″ h, champagne bottle with beaded trim, engraved "CIGARS," marked Graham Silver **75.00**

Desk Set, four pcs, inkstand, letter holder, letter opening, and half moon blotter, raised design of Rococo flowers, scrolls, trellis, and stork, marked J. B. **75.00**

Egg Caddy, emb floral platform holding six egg cups, dec prongs, feet with raised lion's masks, heart shaped bail handle, six egg spoons with shell shaped bowls, marked Simpson Hall Miller **225.00**

Epergne, 18½″ h, figural, central shaft with applique supporting spread winged eagle carrying partially draped maiden holding cornucopia with glass dish, two plated petal form dishes on either side rising from curvilinear foliate tendrils, domed base chased with applied flowers, four feet of curving elongated leaves, Art Nouveau, English, c1895 .... **2,750.00**

Flatware, After Dinner, four berry spoons, two nutcrackers, and grape shears, gilt bowls, emb and chased berries, English, H. H. & Co., retailed by Marshall and Sons, 87 George St., Edinburgh, orig fitted presentation case **300.00**

Frame, 9¾ x 17½″, 2″ wide border with raised figures, dancing and seated peasants, trees, houses, and fences in village scene, rough textured finish **90.00**

Fruit Stand, 16″ d, slightly dished shaped circular bowl, emb with vitricultural dec, four ftd base, International **200.00**

Ice Bucket, cov, Baroque pattern, thermos lined, Wallace **225.00**

Jardiniere, 25½″, Baroque style, oblong, pair of leaf capped scroll handles, body emb with broad band of acanthus leaves and foliate scrollwork, supported by pair of griffins, stepped oval platform base, metal liner **1,200.00**

Meat Cover, 18 x 10½″, domed body, bright cup with panel of foliage swags and roses, beaded base edge, twisted branch handle, monogrammed, maker's marks, Victorian . **225.00**

Pitcher, 12″, cov, ice water, tankard form, branch handle terminating in leaves, figural thumbpiece, hinged lid surmounted by swan, body with bright cut dec of diamond panels, dogwood blossoms in reverse, inscription on center panel, Reed & Barton **275.00**

Punch Bowl Set, 20¼ x 8″ punch bowl, twelve cups, circular waiter, Harvest pattern, Wallace **250.00**

Sardine Box, small Greek key border on box, lid with figural fish finial, fancy feet, monogrammed, glass liner ... **75.00**

Serving Dish, 15¾″ l, 10¾″ d, 2½″ h, rect, deep vertical sides, flanged everted border with double grooves on ends and sides, peened finish, four ivory ball feet, marked "Dirk Van Erp, San Francisco," Arts and Crafts, c1930 .... **1,760.00**

Syrup, 8″, geometric and floral strap work body, figural lady's head on lid and handle, Meriden, 1865, replated **85.00**

Tea and Coffee Service, five pcs, 10¾″ h coffeepot, teapot, cov sugar, creamer, and waste bowl, King George pattern, plain pyriform shape, four hoof feet terminating in a shell, International **250.00**

Tea Tray, 35″ l, oval, heavily cast border, engraved scrollwork center, Victorian **750.00**

Tea Urn, 16″ h, Regency, oblong stepped lid with fan form finial, con-

forming bowl with scrolling handles, slender reeded legs, paw feet, plinth base with ball feet **1,300.00**
Tray, 25¼", Winthrop pattern, shaped rect, Rococo form, flat chased surface, bracket handles, Reed & Barton **200.00**
Umbrella Stand, 20½", elongated trumpet shape, interlaced flowering branches, H. Wilkinson & Co., copper showing **225.00**
Watch Holder, 6", cherub holds bird aloft, stands on raised base, emb trim around edge, Meriden Co **125.00**
Wine Coasters, pr, 5¾", sides emb with repeating repousse frieze of female mask crowned with grapes, scrolling grape vines and leaves on pricked ground, base of wood, engraved armorial central plug, English **550.00**

SILVER DEPOSIT GLASS

History: Silver deposit glass, consisting of a thin coating of silver actually deposited on the glass by an electrical process, was popular at the turn of the century. The process was simple. The glass and a piece of silver were placed in a solution. An electric current was introduced which caused the silver to decompose, pass through the solution, and remain on those parts of the glass on which a pattern had been outlined.

Cologne Bottle, bulbous, floral and flowing leaf motif, 3⅜" h, $165.00.

Bowl, 10½", cobalt blue, flowers and foliage, silver scalloped edge **85.00**
Compote, 7 x 7", clear, floral dec **75.00**
Decanter, 13¼", crystal, Continental silver mounts, grape clusters and leaves dec, orig stopper **80.00**
Ice Tub, closed tab handles, floral and foliage dec, matching SS ice tongs . **125.00**
Perfume Bottle, 4½", clear, vine and grape leaf dec **40.00**
Plate, 12", crystal, floral dec **75.00**
Sugar Shaker, vine and grape leaf dec, silver plate top **60.00**

Tray, 11", cobalt blue, vine and grape leaf dec **100.00**

SILVER OVERLAY

History: Silver overlay is silver applied directly to a finished glass or porcelain object. The overlay is cut and decorated, usually by engraving, prior to being molded around the object.

Glass usually is of high quality, either crystal or colored. Lenox used silver overlay on some porcelain pieces. The majority of design motifs are from the Art Nouveau and Art Deco periods.

Vase, blue iridescent ground, attributed to Loetz, 5½" h, $650.00.

Bowl, 8½ x 12½", heavy clear glass, scalloped rim, floral and scroll silver overlay int. **70.00**
Calling Card Tray, 9½" d, ruffled upturned edge, black, ftd **35.00**
Compote, 5½" d, 3¼" h, dark amethyst, floral silver overlay, marked "Rockwell" **135.00**
Cruet, 7½" h, amber, Art Nouveau flowers and leaves **140.00**
Decanter, 6½" h, clear, squatty, scroll dec, shaped spout, applied handle, matching bulbous stopper, marked "Hawkes" **290.00**
Loving Cup, 3½" h, cranberry, three handles, marked "999" **525.00**
Pitcher, 10½" h, clear, silver overlay on top half, applied handle **125.00**
Vase
3¾" h, ovoid, flared raised rim, amber glass, floral overlay design, hallmark, c1900 . . . . **375.00**
7¼" h, deep amethyst, marked "T & V" **325.00**
8" h, trumpet shape, green, silver overlay floral dec and name shield, sgd **275.00**

SILVER RESIST

History: Silver resist ware was first produced about 1805. It is similar to silver luster in respect to the silvering process and differs in that the pattern appears on the surface.

The outline of the pattern was drawn or stenciled on the ware's body. A glue or sugar-glycern adhesive was brushed over the part not to be lustered, causing it to "resist" the lustering solution which was applied and allowed to dry. The glue or adhesive was washed off. When fired in the kiln, the luster glaze covered the entire surface except for the pattern.

Pitcher, peacock and floral motif, 6⅝" h, $350.00.

Bough Pot, cov, 8½" l, 7" h, semicircular, reserve polychrome enameled river scene with fisherman, floral designs ... **300.00**
Cup and Saucer, flower and vine dec . **85.00**
Flower Horn, 6⅝" h, three spouts, floral design **355.00**
Goblet, 4½" h, vintage design **90.00**
Jug, 4⅜", shield shape, painted florals, blue ground, c1820 .... **260.00**
Mug, child's, girl reading, floral dec ... **100.00**
Pitcher
  5⅞" h, emb ribs and floral rim, polychrome enamel highlights **145.00**
  6¼" h, floral design, putty ground, white int. **225.00**
  7⅜" h, floral design **450.00**
Pot, 8½" l, 5⅛" h, semicircular, vintage designs **200.00**
Teapot, 5½", flower and vine dec **285.00**
Vase, 7½", Leeds, ovoid, flared rim, flowering vines and foliage, rect base, c1810 .... **300.00**

SMITH BROS. GLASS

History: After establishing a decorating department at the Mount Washington Glass Works in 1871, Alfred and Harry Smith struck out on their own in 1875. Their New Bedford, Massachusetts, firm soon became known worldwide for its fine opalescent decorated wares, similar in style to those of Mt. Washington.

Their glass often is marked on the base with a red shield enclosing a rampant lion and the word "Trademark."

Reproduction Alert: Beware of examples marked "Smith Bros."

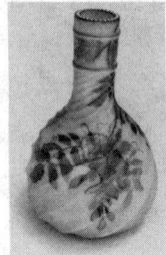

Vase, hand decorated, wisteria dec, beaded rim, swirled ribbed body, rampant lion mark, $575.00.

Bowl, 4¼", melon ribbed, yellow daisies dec, cream white satin ground **235.00**
Creamer and Sugar, individual size, 2¾" h creamer, 3¼ x 3½" cov sugar, slightly ribbed satin glass, tiny yellow and orange flowers, silver plated trim, sugar marked **410.00**
Mustard jar, 2", ribbed, gold prunus dec, white ground **300.00**
Potpourri Vase, 10", enameled chrysanthemums and leaves, gold outlines, satin ground, sgd **950.00**
Rose Bowl, 4¼", pink and rose pansies, green leaves, cream ground, sgd .. **300.00**
Salt, open, melon ribbed, beaded rim, hp florals, white satin ground **90.00**
Sweetmeat Jar, cov, 5¼" d, 5¼" h, melon ribbed body and lid, tiny blue flowers, white satin ground, silver plated collar and braided bail handle **625.00**
Toothpick, columned ribs, pansies dec, blue enameled dots around rim, white ground **115.00**
Vase
  7¼" h, 8" w, double, pilgrim, lavender wisteria, traced in gold, gold beading on top **1,215.00**
  12" h, 7" d, enameled birds, long branch, moon and sun overlapping behind birds **200.00**

SNOW BABIES

History: Snow babies, small bisque figurines spattered with glitter sand, were made originally in Germany and marketed in the early 1900s. There are several theories about their origin. One is that German doll makers copied the designs from the traditional Christmas candies. Another theory, the most accepted, is that they were made to honor Admiral Peary's daughter who was born in Greenland in 1893 and was called the "Snow Baby" by the Eskimos.

Reference: Ray and Eilene Early, *Snow Babies*, Collector Books, 1985.

Sitting baby, arms raised, 1⅛″ h, $45.00.

Babies
Holding camera, one arm extended, 1½″	85.00
Ice Skating, boy and girl, 2″, pr	250.00
Playing musical instruments, seven babies, 2″	325.00
Riding bear, 2⅞″, red, blue, and maroon	150.00
Seated	
1″, arm extended	40.00
2″, one leg tucked under	30.00
3½″, one arm extended, black face, googly eyes, marked "Germany"	200.00
Sledding, 2¾″, pulled by huskies	75.00
Christmas Tree Ornament, snow angel, 1¾″	200.00
Figure	
Elf, 1½″	50.00
Kitten, 1½″	48.00
Snow Man	50.00
Sheep, 2″	45.00
Match Holder, 3½″	125.00
Planter, 8″	175.00

SNUFF BOTTLES

History: Tobacco usage spread from America to Europe to China during the 17th century. Europeans and Chinese preferred to grind the dried leaves into a powder and sniff it into their nostrils. The elegant Europeans carried their snuff in boxes and took a pinch with their finger tips. The Chinese upper class, because of their lengthy fingernails, found this inconvenient and devised a bottle with a fitted stopper and attached spoon.

In the Chinese manner, these utilitarian objects soon became objects d'art. Snuff bottles were fashioned from precious and semi-precious stones, glass, porcelain and pottery, wood, metals, and ivory. Glass and transparent stone bottles often were enhanced further with delicate hand paintings, some done on the interior of the bottle.

Reference: Sandra Andacht, *Oriental Antiques & Art, An Identification and Value Guide*, Wallace-Homestead, 1987.

Collectors' Club: International Chinese Snuff Bottle Society, 2601 North Charles Street, Baltimore, MD 21218.

Agate, moss, fish and lotus carving, fern like inclusions, c1800	2,500.00
Amber, Baltic, natural pebble form, gold tone, swirls	650.00
Amethyst, 2¼″, pear shape, carved, matching stopper, flat foot	175.00
Aquamarine, 1¾″, carved leaves, butterfly, rose tourmaline stopper, wood stand, 20th C	1,750.00
Chalcedony, 3″, butterscotch, medium high relief, Shou symbol, early 19th C	100.00
Cinnabar, 2¾″, deep blood red, carving of figures, scenic design, matching stopper, apocryphal seal of Chien Lung, 20th C	100.00
Enamel on Metal, 2⅜″, prunus blossoms, flowers, mid 20th C	100.00
Interior Painted Glass, 3¼″, four children playing under a tree, sgd Yung Shao-t'ien, c1898	175.00
Jade, 2″, brown, peacock carved in white coloration of stone, 20th C	225.00
Lapis Lazuli, 2″, carved foo dog holding coral ball stopper in mouth, 20th C	350.00

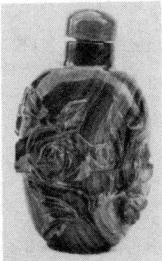

Malachite, carved roses, 2½″ h, $265.00.

Peking Glass, 3⅛", five color overlay, fish and aquatic plants, early 19th C **350.00**

Porcelain, 2⅜", Famille rose enamels, silver mounted jade stopper, late 18th C **150.00**

Quartz, 3", rose, relief carving of two birds, blossoms, carved foot, matching carved stopper, late 18th C **325.00**

Tourmaline, 2⅝", rose, Kuan Yin carving, matching stopper, 20th C **350.00**

Turquoise, 2⅞", highly polished, 20th C **115.00**

Wood, silver wire inlaid inscription, 19th C **1,200.00**

SOAPSTONE

History: The mineral steatite, known as soapstone because of its greasy feel, has been utilized for carved figural groups and other designs by the Chinese and others. Utilitarian pieces also were made. Soapstone pieces were very popular during the Victorian era.

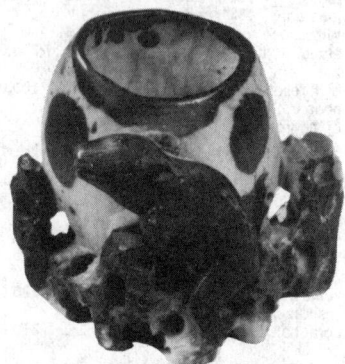

Vase, carved rodent, tan and brown, 2½" h, $75.00.

Bowl, 11½", irregular oval, flat bottom, carved figure ext., carved teak stand, Chinese, 19th C **225.00**

Candlesticks, 5⅛" h, red tones, flowers and foliage, pr **80.00**

Figure
Geisha, 3½ × 3¼", kneeling, Chinese, c1880 .... **125.00**

Lion **65.00**

Loon, 8½" h, carved, green, sgd "Pauloosie" **300.00**

Polar Bear, 10" l, 8¾" h, carrying a seal, mounted on turntable, dated **1,300.00**

Walrus, 11" l, carved, green, sgd "Nooveya Ipeelie" **400.00**

Plaque, 9½" h, birds, trees, flowers, and rocks. stand **115.00**

Sculpture, 11" h, four dancing figures in circle **110.00**

Teapot, 5 x 3", carved, figures, vines, and flowers **350.00**

Toothpick Holder, two containers with carved birds, animals, and leaves .. **80.00**

Vase, 8½", double, carved monkey, pig, and bird, dark mahogany brown, Chinese, 19th C **150.00**

SOUVENIR AND COMMEMORATIVE CHINA AND GLASS

History: Souvenir, commemorative, and historical china and glass includes those items produced to celebrate special events, places, and people.

Among the china plates, those by Rowland and Marcellus and Wedgwood are most eagerly sought. Rowland and Marcellus, Staffordshire, England, made a series of blue and white historic plates with a wide rolled edge depicting scenes beginning with the Philadelphia Centennial in 1876 and continuing to the 1939 New York World's Fair. Wedgwood collaborated in 1910 with Jones, McDuffee and Stratton to produce a series of historic dessert–sized plates depicting scenes throughout the United States.

Many localities issued plates, mugs, glasses, etc., for anniversary celebrations or to honor a local historical event. These items seem to have greater value when sold in the region from which they originated.

Commemorative glass includes several patterns of pressed glass which celebrate persons or events. Historical glass includes campaign and memorial items.

References: Bessie M. Lindsey, *American Historical Glass,* Charles E. Tuttle Company, Inc., 1967; Frank Stefano, Jr., *Wedgwood Old Blue Historical Plates And Other Views Of The United States Produced For Jones, McDuffee & Stratton Co., Boston, Importer; A Check–List with Illustrations,* published by author, 1975.

Periodical: *Travel Collector,* P.O. Box 40, Manawa, WI 54949.

Collectors' Club: Souvenir China Collectors Society, Box 562, Great Barrington, MA 01230.

Additional Listings: Cup Plates, Pressed Glass, Political Items, and Staffordshire, Historical. Also see *Warman's Americana & Collectibles* for more examples.

CHINA

Creamer
3⅛" h, bulbous base, straight neck, black basalt, hp enamel crest of

Plate, University of Chicago, Ida Noyes Hall, 1931, marked "Copeland Spode, England," 10½" d, $30.00.

Ontario, Canada, green maple leaf, side trim, orange Ontario banner underneath, green enamel rim and handle trim, marked "Wedgwood, England"	250.00
6" h, white ground, blue illus of Williamsburg, VA scenes, English ...	25.00

Pitcher

Masonic Hall, Chester, PA, blue and white transfer, tankard shape	225.00
William Penn, coral Indian handle, Lenox	150.00

Plate

Rowland and Marcellus, 10½" d	
Atlantic City, NJ	45.00
Garfield Memorial	40.00
Williamsport, PA, city hall	40.00
Staffordshire, 10" d, Lewis & Clark Centennial Expo 1905, flow blue, marked	50.00

Unknown Maker

Lincoln Sesquicentennial, white ground, black illus, 1959, 10" ..	20.00
Pennsylvania Turnpike, George Washington	35.00

Wedgwood, 7½" d, blue

King Edward VII Coronation, dated June 26, 1902	50.00
Marietta College 125th Anniversary, 1960	20.00
Signing of the Declaration of Independence, blue	45.00
Vase, 6½" h, scrolled enameled panel of Niagara Falls with scenic background, all-over enameled pink apple blossoms, purple highlights, brass base	425.00

GLASS

Bottle, Statue of Liberty, milk glass ...	175.00
Butter Dish, Liberty Bell	140.00

Creamer and Sugar, breakfast size, Georgia Gem, custard glass, marked "Illinois State Pentientiary–Joliet" ..	85.00
Dish, cov, Remember the *Maine*, green	125.00
Goblet, G. A. R., 1887, 21st Encampment	100.00

Mug

Bryan, William Jennings, milk glass .	30.00
Independence Hall	70.00
Washington and Lafayette, milk glass	50.00

Paperweight

Plymouth Rock, clear	65.00
Washington Monument, deep blue, sq base, bust of Washington on oval medallion sq and compass medallion on opposite corner, top inscribed "Cornerstone, July 4th–48, Dedicated Feb 21, '85," 5½" h ...	165.00
Pitcher, Garfield Drape	75.00

Plate

5½", Old Glory	25.00
7", Washington Centennial, center emb "Centennial Exhibition 1876"	250.00
9", Columbus, emb "1892"	50.00
9½", sq, Grant, emb "Patriot & Soldier," amber	50.00
Platter, clear and frosted, three presidents, remembrance center	55.00
Tile, 4" d, Detroit Women's League, multicolored irid	130.00

Tumbler

Dewey, Banded Icicle pattern, portrait base	50.00
McKinley, William and Theodore Roosevelt, prosperity and protection slogan	75.00
Spanish American War, five frosted busts	75.00

SOUVENIR AND COMMEMORATIVE SPOONS

History: Souvenir and commemorative spoons have been issued for hundreds of years. Early American silversmiths engraved presentation spoons to honor historical personages or mark key events.

In 1881 Myron Kinsley patented a Niagara Falls spoon; and, in 1884 Michael Gibney patented a new flatware design. M. W. Galt, Washington, D.C., issued commemorative spoons for George and Martha Washington in 1889. From these beginnings a collecting craze for souvenir and commemorative spoons developed in the late 19th and first quarter of the 20th century.

References: Dorothy T. Rainwater and Donna H. Fegler, *American Spoons, Souvenir and Historical*, Everybodys Press, Inc., 1977; Dorothy T. Rainwater and Donna H. Fegler, *A Collector's Guide To Spoons Around The World*, Everybodys

Press, Inc., 1976; *Sterling Silver, Silverplate, and Souvenir Spoons With Prices*, L-W Inc., 1988.

Collectors' Club: American Spoon Collectors, 4922 State Line, Westwood Hills, KS 66205.

Additional Listings: See *Warman's Americana & Collectibles* for more examples.

US Battleship *Indiana*, sp, 4¼" l, $25.00.

Alaska Indian Totem Pole, emb on handle reverse, demitasse	24.00
Atlantic City, NJ, Steel Pier, chased floral handle, demitasse	32.00
Bar Harbor, emb bowl, fish handle, Shepard mark	35.00
Boulder, CO, name in bowl, Indian head handle	34.00
California, Golden Gate emb in bowl, bear handle, marked "Watson"	15.00
Canada, SS	25.00
Decatur, IL, SS	40.00
Denver, mule handle, SS	15.00
Fort Dearborn, SS	12.00
Grand Army of Republic, engraved bowl	65.00
Huron, SD, Ralph Voorhees Hall	35.00
Jamestown Expo	35.00
Keokuk, IA, SS	52.00
King Cotton	30.00
Lake Okaboji, cut-out Indian head handle	45.00
Memorial Arch, Brooklyn, round oak stove	30.00
Mt. Vernon	45.00
Nebraska, Omaha, high school emb in bowl, SS, Watson	25.00
New Orleans, SS	35.00
Palm Springs Aerial Tramway, SP, John Brown, marked "Antico"	100.00
Pasadena, Golden Gate, diecut bear finial	40.00
Philadelphia, SS	35.00
Portland, Oregon, SS	25.00
Prophet, veiled	135.00
Queen Elizabeth, 1953 Coronation	15.00
Richmond, MO, SS	25.00
Rip Van Winkle	30.00
Rushville, IL, SS	30.00
Salem, witch	40.00
San Antonio, TX, SS	35.00
San Francisco, CA, SS	35.00
Silverton, CO, SS	25.00
Statue of Liberty, NY	40.00

Teddy Roosevelt, riding horse, full figure handle	85.00
Thousand Islands, fish handle, engraved bowl, SS, Watson	40.00
Williamsport, emb shield, knight's head on handle, teaspoon	35.00
Winona Hotel, IN, SS	35.00
World's Fair, Chicago 1893, SS	50.00
Yale Boat House, engraved bowl, oar shaped handle, Towle	15.00

SPANGLED GLASS

History: Spangled glass is a blown or blown molded variegated art glass, similar to spatter glass, with the addition of flakes of mica or metallic aventurine. Many pieces are cased with a white or clear layer of glass. Spangled glass was developed in the late 19th century and still is being manufactured.

Originally spangled glass was attributed only to the Vasa Murrhina Art Glass Company of Hartford, Connecticut, which distributed the glass for Dr. Flower of the Cape Cod Glassworks, Sandwich, Massachusetts. However, research has shown that many companies in Europe, England, and the United States made spangled glass, and attributing a piece to a specific source is very difficult.

Basket, 5 x 6 x 6½", pink and gold, mica flecking, clear thorn handle	225.00
Beverage Set, bulbous pitcher, six matching tumblers, rubena, opalescent mottling, silver flecks, attributed to Sandwich, c1850–60	250.00
Bride's Bowl, 10⅜", multicolored, ruby, cranberry, and green, ivory-yellow ground, silver flecks	100.00
Candlesticks, pr, 8⅝" h, pink and white spatter, green Aventurine flecks, cased white int.	110.00
Condiment Set, cranberry, green flecks, SP holder, 3 pcs	200.00
Creamer and Sugar, cov, blue, gold mica flecks	225.00
Cruet, Leaf mold pattern, cranberry, mica flecks, white casing, Northwood	450.00
Fairy Lamp, 6⅜", multicolored, gold mica flecks, Clarke insert	200.00
Finger Bowl, 4¼ x 2½", ftd, swirled streaks of white, gold, and emerald green, clear body, foot drawn from body, applied clear handles imp with cherub's face	75.00
Pitcher, 7½", bulbous, four sided top, apricot, gold mica flecks form diamond pattern, white casing, pontil	165.00
Rose Bowl, 6" d, lavender, silver veining, attributed to Cape Cod Glass Works	80.00

Tumbler, rainbow spatter of pink, pale blue, butterscotch, green, beige, white, and silver spangles, cased white interior, 3¾" h, $90.00.

Sugar Shaker, cranberry, mica flecks, white casing, Northwood **115.00**
Tumbler, 4", pink, white, orange, red, yellow, and silver spangles **75.00**
Vase
  7⅞" h, pink and green, swirl pattern body, cased white int., ruffled top . **180.00**
  8", modified baluster, tulip shaped lip, deep cranberry casing, clear casing with gold foil flecks in wide vertical swath, brown, green, yellow, and red spatter **225.00**
  8½", cased pink, ruffled crimped top, gold mica flecks, applied cherries and leaf rigaree, pr **550.00**
  14½", melon ribbed, ruffled, pink, white, and green mica flakes **250.00**

SPATTER GLASS

History: Spatter glass is a variegated blown or blown molded art glass. It originally was called "End-of-Day" glass, based on the assumption that it was made from leftover batches of glass at the end of the day. However, spatter glass was found to be a standard production item for many glass factories.

Spatter glass was developed at the end of the 19th century and still is being produced. It was made in the United States and Europe.

Reproduction Alert: Many modern examples come from Czechoslovakia.

Basket
  5" w, 6½" h, aqua, brown, and white spatter, swirled ribbed body, ruffled edge, applied clear thorn handle . **240.00**
  6 x 5½", blue, white casing, applied clear thorn handle **185.00**
Box, 7½ x 4½", egg shaped, hinged, white casing, yellow and blue flowers,

gold and white leaves, three applied clear feet **275.00**
Candlestick, 7½", yellow, red, and white streaks, clear overlay, vertical swirled molding, smooth base, flanged socket **50.00**
Creamer, 4¾", pink and white, applied clear handle, Northwood **45.00**
Cologne Bottle, 8½", etched adv "Rich Secker Sweet Cologne, New York," applied clear handles **60.00**
Cruet, amber and white spatter, polished pontil **50.00**
Darning Egg, multicolored, attributed to Sandwich Glass **125.00**
Fairy Lamp, 3¼ x 2⅞", pyramid shape, pink, yellow, and white, white casing, clear base marked "Clarke" **100.00**
Jar, cov, 6½ x 3¼", gold, maroon, white, and green, yellow casing, leaf finial . **75.00**
Pitcher, pink and white, white int., applied reeded handle **65.00**
Rose Bowl, 4½", pink and blue, pontil . **40.00**
Salt, master, 3 x 3¼", white, maroon, green, blue, and yellow, white casing, applied crystal rigaree and leaf dec . **65.00**
Tumbler, 3¾", royal blue and white . . . **35.00**

Vase, hexagonal, purple and yellow spatter, cased white interior, marked "Czechoslovakia," 4⅝" h, $25.00.

Vase
  7½", bulbous, ruffled rim, ruby, white spatter, gold butterflies, flowers, and foliage, etched mark, pr **450.00**
  9¼", jack in the pulpit, ruffled, DQ, white and peach spatter top, green base **100.00**
Whimsey, 3½" l, 1¾" h, figural, pig, vaseline ext., red and white spatter int. **125.00**

SPATTERWARE

History: Spatterware is made of common earthenware, although occasionally creamware was used. The earliest English examples were made about 1780. The peak period of production was 1810–1840. Marked pieces are rare. Firms known to have made spatterware are Adams, Barlow, and Harvey and Cotton.

The amount of spatter decoration varies from piece to piece. Some objects simply have decorated borders. These often are decorated with a brush, requiring several hundred touches per square inch to achieve the spatter effect. Other pieces have the entire surface covered with spatter. Aesthetics of the final product is a key to value.

Collectors today focus on the patterns—Cannon, Castle, Fort, Peafowl, Rainbow, Rose, Thistle, Schoolhouse, etc. On flat ware the decoration is in the center. On hollow pieces it occurs on both sides.

Color of spatter is another price key. Blue and red are most common. Green, purple, and brown are in a middle group. Black and yellow are scarce.

Like any soft paste, spatterware was easily broken or chipped. Prices are for pieces in very good to mint condition.

References: Susan and Al Bagdade, *Warman's English & Continental Pottery & Porcelain, 1st Edition,* Warman Publishing Co., Inc., 1987; Carl and Ada Robacker, *Spatterware and Sponge,* A. S. Barnes & Co., 1978.

Reproduction Alert: "Cybris" spatter is an increasing collectible ware made by Boleslow Cybris of Poland. The design utilizes the Adams type peafowl and was made in the 1940s. Many contemporary craftsmen also are reproducing spatterware.

Bowl, blue, pink, and green, pink band, white ground, lion and shield mark, Staffordshire, 6¼″ d, 3⅛″ h, $40.00.

Beaker, 2½″ h, blue, brown, and yellow rainbow spatter	275.00
Bowl	
5⅞″, Peafowl, blue spatter	275.00
18¾″, Tulip, blue spatter	300.00
Chamber Pot, 8½ x 6″, rose dec in red, green, and black, blue spatter	250.00
Creamer	
Peafowl, blue spatter	400.00
Rainbow, red and blue, 5½″ h	265.00

Cup and Saucer	
Acorn, blue spatter	250.00
Castle, purple spatter	185.00
Peafowl, red, blue, yellow, and black, handleless	130.00
Schoolhouse, five colors	550.00
Thistle, purple spatter	245.00
Cup Plate, 3⅜″ d, Peafowl, red, Cybis	45.00
Honey Pot, Schoolhouse, red, yellow, and blue	3,000.00
Mustard Pot, Peafowl, green spatter	785.00
Pitcher, Rainbow, green and red spatter	475.00
Plate	
American Eagle, underglaze blue, eagle clasping arrows in talons, perched before shield with 13 stars, purple spatter border rim, 3⅞″ d, c1840	375.00
Dahlia, red, blue, and green, blue spatter, 8⅜″ d	275.00
Flora, purple floral transfer, enameling, 10″ d, marked "T. Walker, Flora"	125.00
Fort, blue spatter, 5⅛″ d	175.00
Peafowl, blue spatter, 8¼″ d	300.00
Rainbow	
5⅛″ d, blue and red spatter	200.00
9½″ d, blue and purple	125.00
Star, red and black, 8¾″ d	75.00
Tulip, purple spatter, 6¼″	275.00
Platter, Rainbow, red and blue spatter	500.00
Sugar, cov	
Dahlia, red, blue, and green, 4½″ h, mismatched lid	90.00
Peafowl, blue spatter	450.00
Tea Bowl and Saucer	
Coxcomb, red, blue spatter	235.00
Peafowl, three color rainbow spatter	175.00
Teapot	
Peafowl, blue, green, yellow, and black, red spatter, 7″	150.00
Tulip, blue and purple, 10″ h	175.00
Toddy Plate, Acorn, brown, and black, green and purple spatter, 5⅛″	375.00
Wash Bowl and Pitcher, Peafowl, red, blue, green, yellow, and black, 14½ x 13¼″	1,000.00
Waste Bowl	
Peafowl, red, green, blue, and yellow, 2⅝ x 5″	420.00
Rainbow, red and blue, 3½ x 5⅜″	250.00

SPONGEWARE

History: Spongeware is a specific type of decoration, not a type of pottery or glaze.

Spongeware decoration is found on many types of pottery bodies—ironstone, redware, stoneware, yellow ware, etc. It was made in both England and the United States. Marked pieces indicate a starting date of 1815, with manufacturing extending to the 1880s.

Decoration is varied. In some pieces the sponging is minimal with the white underglaze dominant. Other pieces appear to be sponged solidly on both sides. Pieces from 1840–1860 have sponging which appears in either a circular movement or a streaked horizontal technique.

Examples are found in blue and white, the most common colors. Other prevalent colors are browns, greens, ochres, and greenish-blue. The greenish-blue results from blue sponging which has been overglazed in a pale yellow. A red overglaze produces a black or navy color.

Other colors are blue and red (found on English creamware and American earthenware of the 1880s), gray, grayish-green, red, dark green on stark white, dark green on mellow yellow, and purple.

References: Susan and Al Bagdade, *Warman's English & Continental Pottery & Porcelain, 1st Edition,* Warman Publishing Co., Inc., 1987; Earl F. and Ada Robacker, *Spatterware and Sponge,* A. S. Barnes & Co., 1978.

Bank, 6", pig, blue and brown sponging, cream ground	175.00
Batter Bowl, 7½ x 4¼", pour spout, blue sponging, yellow ware ground, replaced wire bail handle	120.00
Bean Pot, cov, green, brown, and ochre sponging	150.00
Bowl	
6" d, blue sponging, white ground	55.00
6½" d, blue and rust sponging, cream ground, Iowa adv	50.00
6¾" d, 3" h, brown and green sponging, cream ground	40.00
10¾" d, 4⅛" h, light blue sponging, tan ground, arch molded sides	210.00
13¾" d, blue and white sponge spatter	275.00
Creamer, 4", green, corset shape	65.00
Cup and Saucer, blue and white, straight sides	110.00
Cuspidor, blue sponging, white ground, molded basketweave dec	150.00
Inkwell, green	180.00
Jar, cov, 6", blue sponging, cream ground, wire handle	215.00
Jug	
3", green, brown, and ochre sponging	125.00
7¼", flared top, blue sponged bands, cream ground, applied handle	125.00
Mug, 1¾", red sponging, cream ground	125.00
Nappy, 8½", rect, blue sponging, white ground, only int. sponged	175.00
Pie Plate	85.00
Pitcher	
5", brown, blue, red, and white sponging, cream ground	125.00
8⅞" h, blue and white sponge	325.00

Pitcher, cobalt and tan, 8″ h, $200.00.

9⅝" h, blue and white sponge spatter	425.00
Plate, 10¼", blue sponging, white ground, scalloped rim	120.00
Soap Dish, blue and cream	60.00
Sugar, blue and red sponging, cream ground	175.00
Wash Bowl and Pitcher, 11⅝ x 8½", blue and olive green sponging, blue bands, white ground	325.00

STAFFORDSHIRE ITEMS

History: A wide variety of ornamental pottery items originated in England's Staffordshire district, beginning in the 17th century and extending to the present. The height of production was from 1820 to 1890.

These naive pieces are considered folk art by many collectors. Most items were not made carefully; some were even made and decorated by children.

The types of objects are varied, e.g., animals, cottages, and figurines (chimney ornaments). The key to price is age and condition. The older the piece, the higher the price is a general rule.

References: Susan and Al Bagdade, *Warman's English & Continental Pottery & Porcelain, 1st Edition,* Warman Publishing Co., Inc., 1987; Pat Halfpenny, *English Earthenware Figures, 1740–1840,* Antique Collectors' Club; P. D. Gordon Pugh, *Staffordshire Portrait Figures Of The Victorian Era,* Antique Collectors' Club; Dennis G. Rice, *English Porcelain Animals Of The 19th Century,* Antique Collectors' Club.

Bank, eagle, multicolored	225.00
Bust	
Clergyman, black marbleized plinth, 8½" h	200.00
Washington, George, yellow floral coat, marked "Wood/Caldwell," 8" h	750.00
Wesley, John, soft paste, multicolored, 12" h, minor edge flakes	300.00
Chimney Ornament	
Cat, 5½" h, black spotted white bod-	

ies, orange cushions, green collars, mid 19th C, pr **1,200.00**

Dog

4″ h, Poodle, coleslaw coat, standing, ftd plinth **125.00**

8″ h, King Charles Spaniels, black and brown–gray, c1820–30, pr . **450.00**

Commemorative Cup, 4⅜″ h, Admiral Hood, black–gray, green, and flesh tones, brown eyes, c1780–90 . . . . . **550.00**

Cow Creamer, 5½″ h, spotted ochre and indigo glazes, hobbled back legs, green milkmaid on base, orig cov, c1785–1800 . . . . **1,500.00**

Figure

Cat, 5¾″ h, enamel sponged yellow and brown, oval blue banded base, c1775–85 . . . . **1,800.00**

Cupid astride lioness, Ralph Wood, 8⅝″ h, restored **2,000.00**

Death of Monrow, Obadiah Sherratt, 15″ l, restored **1,600.00**

Deer, 6″ h, bocage, naturalistic colors, stag missing antlers, c1820–35, pr **225.00**

Ewe, 3⅞″ h, reclining, relief textured, pale blue eyes, green glazed base, c1780–90 . . . . **300.00**

Female Fish Peddler, 8¾″ h, glazed enamel gaudy dec, carries basket with sign "Haddies," c1800 . . . . . **275.00**

Franklin, Benjamin, dark blue jacket, gold trim, 14″ h **750.00**

Group

Robin Hood **150.00**

Tenderness, bocage, man and woman in front of tree, titled, naturalistic colors, sgd "John Walton," c1820, 7″ h, repairs **325.00**

Hound, chasing hare, multicolored, 10½″ h **300.00**

Owl, 7¾″ h, cream ware, raised wings, molded relief feathers, sponged manganese dec, possibly by Thomas Whieldon, c1770–80 . **13,000.00**

Ram and Ewe, 5″ w, 4″ h, relief textured, sponged blue manganese and yellow, green glazed bases, c1780–90, pr **3,200.00**

Shepherd, sheep and harp, white, 12½″ h **120.00**

Widow of Zarephath, Obadiah Sherratt, 11½″ h **500.00**

Flower Pot, pearl ware, emb leaves and acorns, matching saucer, 6¾″ h . . . **250.00**

Inkstand

3½″ h, swan, coleslaw dec, wings with pink highlights **175.00**

4½″ l, dog, red–brown whippet, cobalt blue base **200.00**

5½″ l, greyhound, cobalt blue base . **150.00**

Mantel Vase, 8″ h, pearl ware, cov, diapered pattern with medallions of

Chinese scenes, polychrome enamels, c1790–1810 . . . . **950.00**

Mug

3½″ h, pearl ware, underglaze blue dec "Beer," and floral sprays, c1800 . . . . **500.00**

5½″ h, cream ware, hand colored transfer printed dec of gentry on outing, c1790–1810 . . . . **300.00**

Pastile Burner, cottage, black and yellow roof, red chimney, white, gold trim, multicolored flowers, c1840, 5 x 5 x 5″, $500.00.

Pastile Burner, 4½″ h, two part, porcelain, four gilt edge windows and door in front, heavily encrusted multicolored blossoms, pink roses, single leaf painted inside base, c1835, repairs to flowers **2,000.00**

Sauce Tureen, 8″ l, 4″ h, cov, pearl ware, duck, relief textured, feathers, green, yellow, blue, and brown, c1770–80 . . . . **1,300.00**

Tea Service, strawberry luster, cov teapot, creamer, spill bowl, large dish, eight cups and saucers, c1820–40, 20 pcs **475.00**

Teapot, 5″ h, cream ware, matching cov, floral finial, blue, green, yellow, and rose stylized leaves, splattered iron–red ground, chinoiserie scenes, c1780–1800 . . . . **500.00**

Toy Figure

Cat, 2½″ h, agate ware, c1740–50 . **450.00**

Lion, 2½″ h, pink, iron–red, and black, green base, c1800 . . . . **325.00**

Vase, 8″ h, boy and maiden with basket, 8″ h **100.00**

Watch Holder, 8¼″ h, pearl ware, monument, two children wearing classical dress, blue, brown, yellow, green, and ochre, c1785–1800 . . . . **1,000.00**

STAFFORDSHIRE, HISTORICAL

History: The Staffordshire district of England is the center of the English pottery industry. There were eighty different potteries operating there in 1786, with the number increasing to 179 by 1802. The district includes Burslem, Cobridge, Eturia, Fenton, Foley, Hanley, Lane Delph, Lane End, Longport, Shelton, Stoke, and Tunstall. Among the many famous potters were Adams, Davenport, Spode, Stevenson, Wedgwood, and Wood.

In historical Staffordshire the view is the most critical element. American collectors pay much less for non-American views. Dark blue pieces are favored. Light views continue to remain undervalued. Among the forms, soup tureens have shown the highest price increases.

References: David and Linda Arman, *Historical Staffordshire: An Illustrated Check List,* published by author, 1974, out-of-print; David and Linda Arman, *First Supplement, Historical Staffordshire: An Illustrated Check List,* published by author, 1977, out-of-print; Susan and Al Bagdade, *Warman's English & Continental Pottery & Porcelain, 1st Edition,* Warman Publishing Co., Inc., 1987; Ada Walker Camehl, *The Blue China Book,* Tudor Publishing Co., 1946, (Dover, reprint); A.W. Coysh and R. K. Henrywood, *The Dictionary Of Blue And White Printed Pottery, 1780–1880,* Antique Collectors' Club, 1982; Ellouise Larsen, *American Historical Views On Staffordshire China, 3rd Edition,* Dover Publications, 1975.

Notes: Prices are for proof examples. Adjust prices by 20% for an unseen chip, a faint hairline, or an unseen professional repair; by 35% for knife marks through the glaze and a visible professional repair; by 50% for worn glaze and major repairs.

The numbers in parentheses refer to items in the books by Linda and David Arman, which constitute the most detailed list of American historical views and their forms.

W.ADAMS&SONS ADAMS

ADAMS

The Adams family has been associated with ceramics from the mid 17th century. In 1802 William Adams of Stoke–upon–Trent produced American views.

In 1819 a fourth William Adams, son of William of Stoke, became a partner with his father and was later joined by his three brothers. The firm became William Adams & Sons. The father died in 1829 and William, the eldest son, became manager.

The company operated four potteries at Stoke and one at Tunstall. American views were produced at Tunstall in black, light blue, sepia, pink,

and green in the 1830–40 period. William Adams died in 1865. All operations were moved to Tunstall. The firm continues today under the name of Wm. Adams & Sons, Ltd.

Adams, plate, Mitchell & Freeman's China & Glass Warehouse, Chatham Street, Boston, dark blue, c1804–40, (444), 10″ d, $400.00.

Log Cabin, medallions of Gen. Harrison on border, teapot, pink (458)	**275.00**
Seal of United States, dark blue, pitcher, 7½″ (443)	**1,000.00**
U.S. Views	
Lake George, U.S., brown, vegetable dish (448)	**225.00**
Shannondale Springs, Virginia, U.S., pink, 8″ plate (451)	**60.00**

CLEWS

From sketchy historical accounts that are available, James Clews took over the closed plant of A. Stevenson in 1819. His brother Ralph entered the business later. The firm continued until about 1836 when James Clews came to America to enter the pottery business at Troy, Indiana. The venture was a failure because of the lack of skilled workmen and the proper type of clay. He returned to England but did not re–enter the pottery business.

Cities Series, dark and medium blue	
Albany, 10″ plate (16)	**275.00**
Chillicothe, 10½″ platter (20)	**3,200.00**
Washington, 7¾″ plate (30)	**275.00**

Clewes, plate, Picturesque Views Series, Near Fishkill, Hudson River, brown, 10¼″ d, (111), $175.00.

Doctor Syntax, dark blue
Doctor Syntax setting out on his first
  tour, 12″ covered dish (35) **1,750.00**
Doctor Syntax and the gypsies, soup
  tureen (51) **3,000.00**
Doctor Syntax turned nurse, 7¾″
  plate (56) **165.00**
Don Quixote Series, dark blue
Don Quixote's Library, vegetable dish
  (68) **600.00**
Sancho Panza's debate with Teresa,
  9″ plate (78) **150.00**
Landing of Lafayette at Castle Garden,
  dark blue (1)
Cup Plate, 3½″, oval medallion **400.00**
Pitcher, 5½″ **800.00**
Plate, 7½″ **275.00**
Platter, 21¾″, well and tree **1,200.00**
Teapot **700.00**
Picturesque Views Series
Bakers Falls, Hudson River, pink, 9″
  plate (101) **60.00**
Fort Edward, Hudson River, light blue,
  4⅛″ cup plate (102) **75.00**
Hudson, Hudson River
  Gravy Tureen, black (107) **250.00**
Penitentiary in Allegheny, near Pitts-
  burgh, pink, 15½″ tray (117) **275.00**
Troy From Mount Ida, light blue, 6″
  pitcher (120) **200.00**
Peace and Plenty, dark blue (34)
Cup Plate, 4½″ **900.00**
Platter, 17″ **500.00**
Pittsfield Elm, dark blue, soup, 10½″
  (33) **250.00**
States or America and Independence
  Series, dark blue
Building, Deer on Lawn, 10½″ plate
  (2) **250.00**
Dock, large building and ships, 19½″
  platter (4) **1,500.00**

Mansion, small boat with flag in foreground, 13½″ bowl (12) **1,500.00**

J.&J. JACKSON

J. & J. JACKSON

Job and John Jackson began operations at the Churchyard Works, Burslem, about 1830. The works formerly were owned by the Wedgwood family. The firm produced transfer scenes in a variety of colors, such as black, light blue, pink, sepia, green, maroon and mulberry. Over 40 different American views of Connecticut, Massachusetts, Pennsylvania, New York, and Ohio were issued. The firm is believed to have closed about 1844.

J & J Jackson, plate, American Scenery Series, The Race Bridge, Philadelphia, (486), $60.00.

American Scenery Series, all colors
Albany, NY, 20″ platter (462) **275.00**
At Richmond, VA, 7″ plate (465) . . . **60.00**
Bunker Hill Monument, 6½″ plate
  (468) **150.00**
Hartford, CT, 10″ soup (476) **60.00**
Iron Works at Saugerties, 12″ platter
  (478) **250.00**
Water Works, Phila, 9″ plate (487) . . **60.00**
Yale College, deep dish (493) **125.00**

THOMAS MAYER

In 1829, Thomas Mayer and his brothers, John and Joshua, purchased Stubbs' Dale Hall Works of Burslem. They continued to produce a superior grade of ceramics.

Arms of the American States, dark blue
CT, gravy tureen (498)	**4,500.00**
DE, 17" platter (499)	**3,000.00**
PA, 21" platter (506)	**12,000.00**
Lafayette at Franklin's Tomb, dark blue, sugar bowl (510)	**700.00**

CHARLES MEIGH

Job Meigh began the Meigh pottery in the Old Hall Pottery, in 1780. Later his sons and grandsons entered the business. The firm's name is recorded as Job Meigh & Sons, 1823; J. Meigh & Sons, 1829; Charles Meigh, 1843.

The American Cities and Scenery series was produced by Charles Meigh between 1840 and 1850. The colors are light blue, brown, gray, and purple. Sometimes the colors appear in combination.

Albany, 7½" pitcher (544)	**200.00**
Baltimore, wash bowl (546)	**225.00**
Capitol at Washington, tureen, round, cover (550)	**500.00**
City Hall, New York, 10¼" plate (551)	**65.00**
Hudson City, 10¼" soup (552)	**60.00**
Utica, cup plate (556)	**90.00**
Village of Little Falls, 8¼" plate (558)	**60.00**
Yale College, New Haven, 9½" plate (560)	**60.00**

MELLOR, VENEABLES & CO.

Little information is recorded on Mellor, Veneables & Co. except that they were listed as potters in Burslem in 1843. Their Scenic Views series with the Arms of the States Border does include the arms for New Hampshire. This state is missing from the Mayer series. However, the view was known in England and collectors search for a Mayer example.

Arms of States, white body, light color transfers (529)
MD, teapot	**250.00**
PA, sugar bowl	**200.00**
Scenic Views, Arms of States Border, light blue, pink, brown, purple	
Albany, 15" platter (516)	**275.00**
The President's House from the River, 14" pitcher (520)	**250.00**
Tomb of Washington, Mt. Vernon, 7½" plate	**85.00**
View of Capitol at Washington, 11", vegetable dish (526)	**225.00**

J.W.R.

Stone China

W. RIDGWAY

J. & W. RIDGWAY AND WILLIAM RIDGWAY & CO.

John and William Ridgway, sons of Job Ridgway and nephews of George Ridgway who owned Bell Bank Works and Couldon Place Works, produced the popular Beauties of America series at the Couldon plant. The partnership between the two brothers was dissolved in 1830. John remained at Couldon.

William managed the Bell Bank works until 1854. Two additional series were produced based upon the etchings of Bartlett's American Scenery. The first series had various borders including narrow lace. The second series is known as Catskill Moss.

Beauties of America is in dark blue. The other series are found in the light transfer colors of light blue, pink, brown, black, and green.

John & William Ridgway, plate, American Scenery Series, Harper's Ferry from the Potomac Side, light blue, (284), $60.00.

American Scenery
Albany, wash bowl (279)	**275.00**
Columbia Bridge on the Susquehanna, soup tureen (281)	**450.00**
Peekskill Landing, Hudson River, teapot (287)	**200.00**
Valley of the Shenandoah from Jefferson's Rock, 7" plate (289)	**60.00**
Wilkes–Barre, Vale of Wyoming, coffeepot (294)	**275.00**
Beauties of America, dark blue	
Almshouse, Boston, soup tureen (254)	**2,500.00**

Bank, Savannah, gravy tureen (257) **1,200.00**
City–Hall, New York, 10″ plate (260) **125.00**
Exchange, Charleston, vegetable dish (265) **900.00**
Octagon Church, Boston, 10″ soup (271) **175.00**
Catskill Moss
  Anthony's Nose, 6″ plate (295) **60.00**
  Caldwell, Lake George, 5″ sauce dish (298) **60.00**
  Kosciusko's Tomb, 10″ plate (305) . **75.00**
  Valley of Wyoming, cup (317) **35.00**
Columbia Star, Harrison's Log Cabin
  End View, plate (276) **90.00**
  Side View, cup with handles (277) .. **65.00**

ROGERS

ROGERS

John Rogers and his brother George established a pottery near Longport in 1782. After George's death in 1815, John's son Spencer became a partner and the firm operated under the name of John Rogers & Sons. John died in 1816. His son continued the use of the name until he dissolved the pottery in 1842.

Boston Harbor, dark blue (441)
  Cup Plate **1,000.00**
  Cup and Saucer **375.00**
  Waste Bowl **600.00**
Boston State House, dark blue (442)
  Creamer **450.00**
  Platter, 19″ **550.00**
  Soup Tureen **3,000.00**

R.S.W.

STEVENSON

As early as the 17th century the name Stevenson has been associated with the pottery industry. Andrew Stevenson of Cobridge introduced American scenes with the flower and scroll border. Ralph Stevenson, also of Cobridge, used a vine and leaf border on his dark blue historical views and a lace border on his series in light transfers.

The initials R. S. & W. indicate Ralph Stevenson and Williams are associated with the acorn and leaf border. It has been reported that Williams was Ralph's New York agent and the wares were produced by Ralph alone.

Ralph Stevenson and Williams, plate, Park Theater, New York, acorn and leaf border, medium blue, (357), 10″ d, $425.00.

Acorn and Oak Leaves Border, dark blue
  Columbia College, New York, 7½″ plate (350) **450.00**
  State House, Boston, 5″ plate (360) **500.00**
  Water Works, Phila, 10″ soup (363) . **375.00**
Floral and Scroll Border, dark blue
  Almshouse, New York, 10″ plate (394) **750.00**
  Catholic Cathedral, New York, 7½″ plate (395) **1,400.00**
  Troy from Mt. Ida, 9¾″ platter (402) . **1,750.00**
  View of New York From Weekawk, soup tureen (404) **10,000.00**

Stevensons, platter, Alms House, Boston, vine border, dark blue, (365), 12½ x 16¼″, $1,250.00.

Lace Border
  Erie Canal at Buffalo, 10″ soup (386) **150.00**
  New Orleans, Sugar Bowl (387) ... **225.00**
  Riceborough, GA, wash bowl (388) . **450.00**
Vine Border
  Almshouse, New York, 7″ pitcher (366) **900.00**
  Battery, New York, 7¾″ plate (367) . **550.00**
  Columbia College, New York, 8″ plate (372) **475.00**

Hospital, Boston, 9" plate (378) **225.00**
Pennsylvania Hospital, Phila, soup
 tureen (383) **8,500.00**

STUBBS

In 1790 Stubbs established a pottery works at Burslem, England. He operated it until 1829 when he retired and sold the pottery to the Mayer brothers. He probably produced his American views about 1825. Many of his scenes were from Boston, New York, New Jersey and Philadelphia.

Rose Border, dark blue
 Boston State House, 7" pitcher (335)   **600.00**
 City Hall, New York, plate, 6" (336) .   **350.00**
Spread Eagle Border, dark and medium
 blue
 City Hall, New York, 6½" plate (323)   **325.00**
 Fair Mount Near Phila, platter, 22"
  (324) **1,200.00**
 Highlands, North River, 10" plate
  (325) **1,500.00**
 Hoboken in New Jersey, salt shaker
  (326) **600.00**
 State House, Boston, 14½" platter
  (331) **700.00**
 Upper Ferry Bridge over the River
  Schuylkill (332)
  Dish, round **500.00**
  Platter, 19" **750.00**
  Vegetable Dish **650.00**
  Wash Pitcher **600.00**

S. TAMS & CO.

The firm operated at Longton, England. The exact date of its beginning is not known, but believed to be about 1810–15. The company produced several dark blue American views. About 1830 the name became Tams, Anderson, and Tams.

Capitol, Washington
 Bowl, deep (514) **1,500.00**
 Wash Pitcher (514) **1,700.00**
United States Hotel, Phila, soup, 10"
 (515) **750.00**

WOOD

Enoch Wood, sometimes referred to as the Father of English Pottery, began operating a pottery at Fountain Place, Burslem, in 1783. A cousin Ralph Wood was associated with him. In 1790 James Caldwell became a partner and the firm was known as Wood and Caldwell. In 1819 Wood and his sons took full control.

Enoch died in 1840. His sons continued under the name of Enoch Wood & Sons. The American views were first made in the mid 1820s and continued through the 1840s.

It is reported that the pottery produced more signed historical views that any other Staffordshire firm. Many of the views attributed to unknown makers probably came from the Woods.

Marks vary, although always with the name Wood. The establishment was sold to Messrs. Pinder, Bourne & Hope in 1846.

Wood, Enoch, plate, Catskill Mountains, shell border, dark blue, (162), 7½", $350.00.

Celtic China, light transfer colors
 Columbus, GA, 3⅞" cup plate (238)   **350.00**
 Shipping Port on the Ohio, KY, 12"
  platter (249) **450.00**
 Transylvania University, Lexington,
  KY, 10" soup (250) **100.00**
 West Point, Military Academy, open-
  work dish (252) **350.00**
Floral Border, irregular, dark blue
 Commodore MacDonnough's Victory
  (154)
  Coffeepot **1,750.00**
  Cup and Saucer **325.00**

Entrance of the Erie Canal into the
Hudson at Albany (156)
Plate, 6″ 750.00
Soup, 10″ 825.00
Erie Canal, Aqueduct Bridge at Roch-
ester, pitcher, with first canal view,
5½″ (157) 1,200.00
Wadsworth Tower, sugar bowl (155) 450.00
Four Medallion, Floral Border Series,
light transfers
Castle Garden, 8″ plate (225) 60.00
Monte Video, 7½″ plate (229) 60.00
Race Bridge, Phila, gravy tureen
(233) 275.00
General Jackson (224)
Cup Plate 500.00
Pitcher, luster, 4″ 1,500.00
Plate, 7″ 750.00
Shell Border, circular center, dark blue
Belleville on the Passaic River, soup
tureen (159) 6,000.00
Castle Garden Battery, New York,
18½″ platter (160) 1,500.00
Catskill Mountains, Hudson River,
custard cup with handle (162) ... 500.00
City of Albany, State of New York, 10″
plate (163) 375.00
Highland, Hudson River, vegetable
dish (167) 1,000.00
Mount Vernon, 5¾″ plate (173) 600.00
Railroad, Baltimore and Ohio, incline,
9″ plate (182) 600.00
West Point Military Academy, 12″ plat-
ter (188) 1,200.00
White House, Washington, cup plate
(189) 1,750.00
Shell Border, irregular center, dark blue
Cadmus, 10″ soup (125) 375.00
Commodore MacDonnough's Victory,
coffeepot (130) 1,500.00
Constitution and Guerriere, 10″ plate
(131) 1,000.00
Erith on the Thames, vegetable dish
(136) 750.00
Union Line, 10″ soup (144) 375.00
Wadsworth Tower (147)
Coffeepot 1,500.00
Cup and Saucer 275.00
Waste Bowl 450.00
Washington's Tomb, dark blue (190B)
Creamer 550.00
Soup, 10″ 750.00
Sugar Bowl 650.00
Teapot 750.00

UNKNOWN MAKERS

Anti–slavery, light blue, 9¼″ plate (608) 150.00
Erie Canal inscription (597)
Cup Plate, 3¾″ 1,750.00
Pitcher, 5¼″ 1,500.00

Famous Naval Heroes
Pitcher, 7″ (604) **750.00**
Washbowl (604) **1,000.00**
Franklin Flying a Kite, light blue, 3¾″
platter, miniature (603) **95.00**
Great Fire, City of New York, series,
plates, each (605–607) **125.00**
Mount Vernon, Washington's Seat, 8″
pitcher (600) **1,000.00**

STAFFORDSHIRE, ROMANTIC

History: The Staffordshire district of England
produced dinnerware with romantic scenes between 1830 and 1860. A large number of potters
were involved and over 800 patterns have been
identified.

The dinner services came in a variety of colors
with light blue and pink perhaps the most popular.
Usually the pattern is identified on the back of the
piece. It was not uncommon for two potters to
issue pieces with the same design. Therefore,
check the pattern name as well as the maker's
name.

It would be impossible to list all patterns. A rep-
resentative selection follows. Some price ranges
to keep in mind are: cups and saucers (handleless)
$35–50; cup plates $40–75; plates, 9–10″, $10–
50; platters $25–75.00.

References: Petra Williams, *Staffordshire: Romantic Transfer Patterns,* Fountain House East,
1978; Petra Williams, *Staffordshire II,* Fountain
House East, 1986.

**Spanish Convent pattern, Adams, plat-
ter, brown, 9⅛ x 11⅛″, $55.00.**

Asiatic Plants, maker unknown
Bowl 75.00
Cup and Saucer 65.00
Plate, 10½″ 85.00
Vegetable Bowl, cov, ornate handles,
finial, light blue, 12 x 9½″ 135.00
Canova, Thomas Mayer, c1834–1848
Cup and Saucer 45.00

Cup Plate, green	30.00
Plate, 7½", pink	20.00
Platter, 18 x 11½"	85.00
Soup Plate	35.00
Vegetable Bowl, 8½", blue, cov with floral finial	120.00
Waste Bowl, 4"	40.00

Corinthian, E Challinor

Bowl, 5½"	45.00
Gravy Boat, attached underplate	95.00
Plate	40.00
Sauce Dish, 4"	20.00
Saucer	15.00
Vegetable Dish, open	45.00

Damacus, blue and white, Wm Adams and Sons

Bowl, 4"	20.00
Creamer, paneled	125.00
Cup Plate	50.00
Custard Cup	30.00
Plate	
8½"	60.00
9¾"	65.00
Tureen, cov, oval	130.00

Friburg, Davenport, c1844

Bowl	45.00
Cup and Saucer, handleless	60.00
Plate, 10½"	55.00
Platter	100.00
Teapot, tall, paneled, fruit finial	200.00
Tureen, matching underplate	150.00

Medici, Mellor, Veneables & Co., 1834–1851

Bowl	30.00
Cup and Saucer	40.00
Gravy Boat	80.00
Plate, 12 sided	37.50
Platter	75.00
Sugar Bowl, tab handles	80.00

Palestine, John Ridgway, c1830–1855

Bowl	27.00
Creamer	55.00
Cup and Saucer, handleless	50.00
Plate	45.00
Platter, 16½ x 10"	65.00
Sugar, cov	80.00
Vegetable Bowl, open, matching underplate	130.00

Rhone Scenery, T. J. & J. Mayer, c1850

Dish, 5½", oblong	40.00
Plate	
8½"	48.00
9¼", 12 sided, brown	35.00
Platter, 7 x 5"	45.00
Toothbrush holder	50.00

Siam, J. Clementson, c1839–1864

Bowl	35.00
Creamer	55.00
Cup and Saucer	35.00
Gravy Boat	60.00
Plate, 9"	45.00
Sauce Dish, 4"	27.00

Sugar, cov	75.00
Tureen with matching underplate, cov	125.00

STAINED AND/OR LEADED GLASS PANELS

History: American architects in the second half of the 19th century and the early 20th century used stained and leaded glass panels as a chief decorative element. Skilled glass craftsmen assembled the designs, the best known being Louis C. Tiffany.

The panels are held together with soft lead cames or copper wraps. When purchasing a panel, check the lead and have any repairs made to protect your investment.

Collectors' Club: Stained Glass Association of America, 1125 Wilmington Avenue, St. Louis, MO 63111.

Window, center yellow, red, and green tulip, horizontal pale yellow and blue band, frosted glass panes, 23 x 14½", orig 26 x 17¾" frame, $85.00.

Leaded

29" h, 27½" w, Tiffany, central tiny white blossoms radiating towards larger mottled brown and white pebbled blossoms, pink and green stamens, amber glass surround, geometric green glass border	18,000.00
30¼" h, 13¼" w, Gothic interlocking arch motif, etched design inside arched sections, beveled orig frame	200.00
96" h, 20" w, Prairie School, c1910, rect panel of textured, rippled, and opaque glass, turquoise, white, and avocado, clear glass ground, stylized flowering plant motif, set of six panels	6,000.00

Stained

36" h, 144" w, designed by John

LaFarge, central rect panel finely plated with overflowing cornucopia, three winged cherubs, painted features, sinous blossoms, stems and leaves, rect jeweled panel set with six fractured glass reserves, identical flanking panels with jeweled diamond, surrounded by ornate wreaths, c1885 . . . . .35,000.00

96″ h, American, designed and executed by Alice D Laughlin, Gloucester, MA, divided into eight panels depicting scenes of medieval clergy, surrounded by multicolored foliate border **850.00**

#3444, Cardinal, $75.00.

STANGL POTTERY BIRDS

History: Stangl ceramic birds were produced from 1940 until the Stangl factory closed in 1972. The birds were produced at Stangl's Trenton plant and shipped to their Flemington, New Jersey, plant for hand painting.

During World War II the demand for these birds and Stangl pottery was so great that 40 to 60 decorators could not keep up with the demand. Orders were contracted out to private homes. These orders then were returned for firing and finishing. Colors used to decorate these birds varied according to the artist.

As many as ten different trademarks were used. Almost every bird is numbered; many are artist signed. However, the signatures are used only for dating purposes and add very little to the value of the birds.

Several birds were reissued between 1972 and 1977. These reissues are dated on the bottom and valued at approximately one half of the older birds.

References: Harvey Duke, *The Official Identification And Price Guide To Pottery And Porcelain, Seventh Edition,* House of Collectibles, 1989; Joan Dworkin and Martha Horman, *A Guide To Stangl Pottery Birds,* Willow Pond Books, Inc., 1973; Norma Rehl, *The Collectors Handbook of Stangl Pottery,* Democrat Press, 1982.

Additional Listings: See Stangl pottery in the American Dinnerware category in *Warman's Americana & Collectibles* for more examples.

3276 Bluebird	**65.00**
3276–D Bluebirds, double, 8½″	**125.00**
3402–D Orioles	**85.00**
3404 Lovebirds, pr	**95.00**
3405 Cockatoo, 6¼″	**45.00**
3406 Kingfisher	**60.00**
3408 Bird of Paradise	**80.00**
3431 Duck, standing, 8″	**300.00**
3443 Duck, flying, 9″	**220.00**
3444 Cardinal	**75.00**
3445 Rooster, gray, 9″	**135.00**
3446 Hen, 7″	**145.00**
3447 Prothonotary Warbler	**60.00**
3448 Blue Headed Vireo	**40.00**
3453 Key West Quail Dove	**225.00**
3583 Parula Warbler	**38.00**
3589 Indigo Bunting	**36.00**
3595 Bobolink	**125.00**
3598 Kentucky Warbler	**40.00**
3626 Broadtail Hummingbird, 6″	**90.00**
3629 Broadbill Hummingbird, 6″	**85.00**
3635, Goldfinch family, 12″ l, 4½″ h . .	**150.00**
3634 Allen Hummingbird	**48.00**
3747 Canary, facing left, blue flower, 6¼″	**155.00**
3754–D White Wing Crossbill, 8¾″ . . .	**325.00**
3810 Blackpoll Warbler	**100.00**
3811 Chestnut Backed Chickadee . . .	**80.00**
3813 Evening Grosbeak	**120.00**
3815 Western Bluebird	**145.00**
3848 Golden Crowned Kinglet, 4″	**50.00**
3852 Cliff Swallow	**60.00**

STATUES

History: Beginning with primitive cultures, man produced statues in the shape of people and animals. During the Middle Ages most works were religious and symbolic in character and form. The Renaissance rediscovered the human and secular forms.

During the 18th and 19th centuries it was fashionable to have statues in the home. Many famous works were copied for popular consumption.

Statuette or figurine denotes smaller statues, one-fourth life size or smaller.

Reference: Anita Jacobsen (ed.), *Jacobsen's Painting and Bronze Price Guide,* published by author.

Additional Listings: Bronzes and Busts.

Bronze
    13½″, water carrier, slave dressed in ballooning costume and cap, carrying water jug on right shoulder,

rust and black polychrome dec, rect leaf molded base, labeled "Aguador," inscribed Louis–Auguste Hiolin, late 19th C **675.00**

25", seated philosopher, draped man holding tablet and pen, rich brown patina, inscribed "P DuBois, F. Barbedienne Fondeur Paris 337," stamped "Reduction Mechanique" seal, France, late 19th C **8,250.00**

44½", Sophocles Celebrating the Victory at Salamis, nude, holding tortoiseshell and horn lyre, rect plinth base inscribed in Greek, after J Donoghue, also inscribed "F. Barbedienne Fondeur, Paris," brown patina, c1900 . . . . **44,000.00**

Bronze, equestrian, Emmanuel Fremiet, French, 1824–1910, 14" h, $400.00.

Cast Iron, 27", Victory, winged figure wearing swirling tunic, resting on marble sphere, sienna marble plinth, French, early 19th C **850.00**

Gilt, silvered, patinated bronze, and carved marble, 24½", girl, carved white marble face and hands, ruffled bonnet, laced bodice beneath shawl, lifting skirt as she steps across stream, oval base, inscribed "Monginot," French, c1900 . . . . **2,250.00**

Ivory, 7", three Grecian nude women embracing each other, sgd "G.R." . . **85.00**

Ivory and gilt bronze, 14½", fashionable woman, carved ivory head and forearms, lace and ribbon dec bodice and wide skirt with train, hat with wide, undulating brim, incised "Armand Quenard," mounted on shaped sq black and white striated marble plinth, c1900 . . . . **725.00**

Marble

36", Summer, young maiden, revealing robes, holding bunch of wheat in left hand, leaning on wheat bundle resting on tree stump, late 19th C, weathered **1,425.00**

45", young maiden, partially draped figure resting on rocky base, floral garland in her hair, circular base, weathered **2,250.00**

Porcelain, 7⅜", blacksmith, pale green vest under brown apron, Meissen, attributed by J. J. Kaendler, incised "99," c1750, hammer and sword repaired **1,200.00**

Silvered Bronze, 32½", Cupid and Psyche, cloth draped around naked figure, winged Cupid gazing over her shoulder, circular base **3,000.00**

Terra Cotta, 24⅝" h, La Comtesse de Sabran, classically draped, looking left, after Jean Antonie Houdon, France, 19th C, separate terra cotta socle, 2 pcs, restored **6,000.00**

STEIFF

History: Margarete Steiff, GmbH, established in Germany in 1880, is known for very fine quality stuffed animals and dolls as well as other beautifully made collectible toys. It is still in business, and its products are highly respected.

The company's first products were wool-felt elephants made by Margaret Steiff. In a few years the elephant line was expanded to include a donkey, horse, pig, and camel.

By 1903 the company also was producing a jointed mohair Teddy Bear, whose production dramatically increased to over 970,000 units in 1907. Margarete's nephews took over the company at this point. The bear's head became the symbol for its label, and the famous "Button in the Ear" round, metal trademark was added.

Newly designed animals were added: Molly and Bully, the dogs, and Fluffy, the cat. Pull toys and kites also were produced, as well as larger animals on which children could ride or play.

Become familiar with genuine Steiff products before purchasing an antique stuffed animal. Plush in old Steiff animals was mohair; trimmings usually were felt or velvet. Unscrupulous individuals have attached the familiar Steiff metal button to animals that are not Steiff.

References: Peggy and Alan Bialosky, *The Teddy Bear Catalog*, Workman Publishing, 1984, revised edition; Shirley Conway and Jean Wilson, *Steiff Teddy Bears, Dolls, and Toys With Prices*, Wallace-Homestead, 1984; Margaret Fox Mandel, *Teddy Bears And Steiff Animals*, Collector Books, 1984; Margaret Fox Mandel, *Teddy Bears, Annalee Animals & Steiff Animals, Third Series*, Collector Books, 1990; Jean Wilson, *Steiff Toys Revisited,* Wallace-Homestead, 1989.

Periodical: *Steiff Collectors' Anonymous*, 1308 Park Avenue, Piqua, OH 45356.

Additional Listings: Teddy Bears. See Stuffed Toys in *Warman's Americana & Collectibles* for more examples.

Bambi, deer, 1939, 32″ h, $400.00.

Camel, 13½″, Cosy, orig tags **90.00**
Cat
  5″, Tom, black velvet body, mohair tail, glass eyes, sewn nose and mouth, c1960 . . . .   **85.00**
  6½″, Mama Kitty, fully jointed, c1950   **65.00**
  9″, Siamese, mohair, jointed neck, orig leg tag, c1950 . . . .   **125.00**
Dog
  Cocker Spaniel, 6½″, long and short mohair, jointed head, black sewn nose, felt mouth, squeaker **65.00**
  Collie, 20½ x 10″, long and short mohair, glass eyes, sewn nose, felt mouth **125.00**
  Poodle, 8″, Snobby, long and short mohair, jointed glass eyes, c1960   **90.00**
Duck, Mallard, 8″, pull toy, felt and velvet, metal wheels **275.00**
Fish, 14″, mohair body, glass eyes, felt fins, tail, and mouth **85.00**
Frog, 4″, felt, orig neck tag **45.00**
Goat, 5 x 6″, mountain, gray mohair, glass eyes, felt horns, c1950 . . . . .   **50.00**
Lion, 45″, Leo, mohair, reclining, orig tag, c1955 . . . .   **600.00**
Monkey, 19″, white mohair, felt face, hands, and feet, green glass eyes, c1905 . . . .   **700.00**
Pony, 5½″, white and brown mohair, felt ears, red vinyl saddle and bridle, c1950 . . . .   **85.00**
Seal, 6″, Floppy Robby, buff Dralon, soft stuffing, sewn eyes, c1950 . . . .   **65.00**
Teddy Bear, 11″, Zotty, tan curly mohair, jointed body, glass eyes, sewn nose, felt mouth, c1950 . . . .   **150.00**

Tiger, 16″, mohair, reclining, orig button, #0910/60 . . . .   **400.00**
Turtle, 5″, mohair body, vinyl shell, glass eyes, c1950 . . . .   **65.00**
Zebra, 5″, black and white felt, c1950 .   **40.00**

STEINS

History: A stein is a mug especially made to hold beer or ale, ranging in size from the smaller ³/₁₀ liters and ¼ liters to the larger 1, 1½, 2, 3, 4, and 5 liters, and in rare cases to 8 liters. (A liter is 1.05 liquid quarts.)

Master steins or pouring steins hold 3 to 5 liters and are called krugs. Most steins are fitted with a metal hinged lid with thumblift. The earthenware character-type steins usually are German in origin.

References: Susan and Al Bagdade, *Warman's English & Continental Pottery & Porcelain, 1st Edition,* Warman Publishing Co., Inc., 1987; John L. Hairell, *Regimental Steins,* published by author, 1984; Gary Kirsner and Jim Gruhl, *The Stein Book,* Glentiques, Ltd., 1984; Dr. Eugene Manusov, *Encyclopedia of Character Steins,* Wallace-Homestead, 1976; Eugene V. Manusov and Mike Wald, *Character Steins: A Collector's Guide,* Cornwall Books, 1987; Mike Wald, *HR Steins,* SCI Publications, 1980.

Collectors' Club: Stein Collectors International, P.O. Box 463, Kingston, NJ 08528.

Additional Listings: See Mettlach.

Advisor: Ron Fox

Fraternal, Lulu, Atlantic City, shaded brown to light brown ground, marked "Thos. Maddock Sons Co, Trenton, NJ," 1904, 4″ d, 4⅞″ h, $35.00.

Brass, 17½″, relief, coins and faces, fancy figural handle, rampant lion finial **1,150.00**
Faience, ¾ L, verse between trees, Hannoverisch Munden Factory, 1810 . . .   **440.00**

Glass

Blown

1/2 L, enameled floral and verse, c1850	**275.00**
1 L, cut circle design, stag under prism lid, pewter base rim	**320.00**
Blown with pewter,1/2 L, amber glass, elaborate pewter faces, serpent handle	**575.00**
Mold Blown,1/2 L, flashed cranberry panels, porcelain inlay, turquoise inset thumblift	**210.00**
Glass and Pewter, relief,1/2 L, Alpine scene	**275.00**
Ivory, 9½", hand carved, three scenes, reattached finial, sgd "B. Rudolph Stuttgart"	**2,475.00**
Lithophane,1/2 L, clown	**350.00**
Pewter,1/2 L, relief, eagles and angles faces, eagle finial	**155.00**

Porcelain

Bohne,1/2 L, bisque, indian	**275.00**
Regimental, 1 L, Naval S.M.S. Von Der Tann 1909–12, four naval scenes, bolt hinge, naval litho, rear roster	**1,290.00**
Schierholz,1/2 L, rabbit E.C.S. #62	**2,255.00**

Pottery

Relief, 1 L	
Cavaliers drinking	**115.00**
Man with two women, man as lid, sgd "KB"	**75.00**
Russian Enamel, 6½", on silver, turquoise, light and dark blue, violet, white, and red enamel, gold wash, silver marks on base and lid, Silversmith Gustau Klingert, Moscow, 1889	**6,000.00**

Stoneware

Character,1/2 L, monk, E.C.S. #357	**115.00**
Dreihausen, 13", red metallic glaze, minor rim chips, thumblift missing	**600.00**
Print over glaze,1/2 L, Munich child and city side scenes	**175.00**
Relief	
½ L, Occupational, fireman, strap repair	**80.00**
1 L, Enameled Apostle, worn	**165.00**

STEUBEN GLASS

History: Frederick Carder, an Englishman, and Thomas G. Hawkes of Corning, New York, established the Steuben Glass Works in 1904. In 1918 the Corning Glass Co. purchased the Steuben Company. Carder remained with the firm and designed many of the pieces bearing the Steuben mark. Probably the most widely recognized wares are "Aurene," "Verre De Soie," and "Rosaline," but many other types were produced.

The firm continues operating, producing glass of exceptional quality.

References: Paul Gardner, *The Glass of Frederick Carder*, Crown Publishers, 1971; Paul Perrot, Paul Gardner, and James S. Plaut, *Steuben: Seventy Years Of American Glassmaking*, Praeger Publishers, 1974.

Museum: The Corning Museum of Glass, Corning, NY.

ACID CUT BACK

Bowl, 8 x 7¼", green jade, cut chrysanthemums and leaves dec	**600.00**
Candlesticks, pr, 14", black cut to clear, Poussin pattern, flowers and leaves	**2,250.00**
Jar, cov, 5½", apple green leaves and flowers, white ground	**800.00**
Vase, 9½", urn shape, chartreuse, cased with green, scroll, fern, and classic medallion motif, sgd	**1,300.00**

ANIMALS

Dinosaur, 12¾" l, modeled by James Houston	**600.00**
Elephant, 8½"	**350.00**
Penguin, 6½", numbered	**175.00**
Rabbit, numbered	**125.00**
Rooster, 10" h, modeled by Donald Pollard, inscribed "Steuben"	**600.00**
Sea Horse, 9¼" h, modeled by Lloyd Atkins, numbered	**265.00**
Songbird, 4½", numbered	**185.00**
Squirrel, 5" h, modeled by Lloyd Atkins, inscribed "Steuben"	**250.00**

AURENE

AURENE

Atomizer, 7", gold	**360.00**
Basket, 6" h, gold, mirror finish, sgd, #455	**825.00**
Bowl, 10" d, 3¾" h, flaring rim, int. heightened with pink, crackled rim, low molded purple shaded foot, inscribed "Steuben Aurene/2851"	**600.00**
Candlesticks, 5¼", gold, sgd "Aurene 6637," pr	**1,000.00**
Cigarette Holder, 4¼" l, blue, ribbed	**350.00**
Compote	
5¾" h, 12" d, circular dish, double guard stem, circular foot, brilliant	

peacock irid blue, inscribed "Aurene 6150" 550.00

6" h, shallow circular cup, slender cylindrical stem, gold with pink shading, circular foot shading to purple rim, inscribed "Aurene/2642," set of 4 .... 800.00

Finger Bowl and Underplate, millefiori, irid gold, green vines and leaves, applied white flowers, sgd "Aurene/Haviland & Co" 1,150.00

Flower Frog, 4¾", irid blue, sgd "Aurene 2775" 300.00

Plate, 8½", gold, sgd and numbered 3059 .... 220.00

Vase
5½ x 5⅞", red, irid gold and opaque white feather design, sgd "Aurene/548" 3,900.00

8", baluster, short cylindrical neck everted at rim, gold irid shaded with pink on shoulder and base, incised "Steuben Aurene 5687" 935.00

CALCITE

Centerpiece Bowl, 12", blue, sgd 500.00
Goblet, 6", gold 250.00
Rose Bowl, 6½" x 4", calcite ext., gold Aurene int., shape no. 2687 ...... 350.00
Sherbet and Underplate, blue Aurene lining 500.00

CLUTHRA

Vase
6", shouldered ovoid, everted rim, frothy mottled Pamona green, acid stamped "Steuben" 200.00
10½", shouldered ovoid, everted rim, frothy mottled Pamona green, acid stamped fleur–de–lis mark 625.00

IVORINE

Candlestick, 4 x 3", foliate form, ftd .. 125.00
Lamp Shade, 5" h 75.00
Vase
3", green edge trim 175.00
4⅜", flaring, sgd "Steuben" 220.00
12", triple, two lily form with center trumpet vase, sgd "Steuben" 900.00

MISCELLANEOUS

Bottle, crystal, teardrop stopper 85.00
Candlesticks, 4½", mushroom shape, green, sgd, pr 135.00
Candy Jar, 7" h, Art Deco, black thread dec and multifaceted lid, etched mark base, c1920 .... 200.00

Champagne, 4⅝", opal striped pink bowl and stem 100.00
Cigarette Holder, 4½" l, Alabaster 190.00
Decanter, 11" h, engraved Thistle pattern, ring stopper 175.00
Goblet, 8¼" h, opal striped pink bowl, green stem and foot, sgd 300.00
Plate, 8½" d, Cintra, opalescent body, blue and red Cintra edge 175.00

ORIENTAL POPPY

Champagne, green stem 375.00
Compote, 7", twisted green stem 700.00
Cordial, green stem and foot, sgd 300.00
Perfume Bottle, 10½", opal, rose, c1925 .... 1,150.00
Sherbet, 4½" 250.00

Vase, Verre de Soie, purple iridescent threading, scalloped top, 8¼" h, $250.00.

VERRE DE SOIE

Basket, 9½ x 4½", engraved 225.00
Cocktail Shaker, 10", turquoise prunts . 300.00
Compote, 10 x 6", ruffled edge, twisted stem 375.00
Nut Dish, 4", green rim 35.00
Plate, 8½", sgd "F Carder" 125.00
Sherbet and Underplate, engraved florals 250.00
Tumbler, 5", sgd 75.00
Vase, 7", aquamarine, turquoise band on rim, shape #938 .... 225.00

STEVENGRAPHS

History: Thomas Stevens of Coventry, England, first manufactured woven silk designs in 1854. His first bookmark was produced in 1862, followed by the first Stevengraphs, perhaps in 1874, but definitely in 1879 at the York Exhibition. The first "portrait" Stevengraphs (of Disraeli and Gladstone) were produced in 1886, and the first postcards incorporating the silk woven panels in 1903. Stevens offered many other items with silk panels, including valentines, fans, pin cushions, needle cases, etc.

Stevengraphs are miniature silk pictures, matted in cardboard, and usually having a trade announcement, or "label," affixed to the reverse. Thomas Stevens' name appears on the mat of the early Stevengraphs directly under the silk panel. Many of the later "portraits" and the larger silks (produced initially for calendars) have no identification on the front of the mat other than the phrase "woven in pure silk" and have no label on the back. Other companies, notably W. H. Grant of Coventry, copied this technique. Their efforts should not be confused with Stevengraphs.

American collectors favor the Stevengraphs of American interest, such as "Signing of the Declaration of Independence," "Columbus Leaving Spain," "Landing of Columbus." Sports related Stevengraphs such as "The First Innings" (baseball), and "The First Set" (tennis) are also popular, as well as portraits of Buffalo Bill, President and Mrs. Cleveland, George Washington, and President Harrison.

The bookmarks are longer than they are wide, have mitered corners at the bottom, and are finished with a tassel. Originally, Stevens' name was woven into the fold-over at the top of the silk, but soon the identification was woven into the fold-under mitered corners. Almost every Stevens bookmark has such identification, except the ones woven at the World's Columbian Exposition in Chicago, 1892–93.

Postcards with very fancy embossing around the aperture in the mount almost always have Stevens' name printed on them. Embossed cards from the "Ships" and "Hands Across The Sea" series generally are not printed with Stevens' name. The most popular postcard series in the United States are "Ships" and "Hands Across the Sea," the latter incorporating two crossed flags and two hands shaking. Seventeen flag combinations have been found, but only seven are common. Stevens produced silks that were used in the "Alpha" Publishing Co. cards. Many times the silks were the top or bottom half of regular bookmarks.

References: Geoffrey A. Godden, *Stevengraphs and Other Victorian Silk Pictures,* Associated University Presses, Inc., 1971; Chris Radley, *The Woven Silk Postcard,* privately printed, 1978; Austin Sprake, *The Price Guide to Stevengraphs,* The Antique Collectors' Club, Baron Publishing, 1972.

Collectors' Club: Stevengraph Collectors' Association, 2829 Arbutus Road, #2103, Victoria, British Columbia, V8N 5X5, Canada.

Museum: Coventry, England.

Note: Prices are based on pieces in mint or close to mint condition.

Advisor: John High.

Bookmark, Many Happy Returns of Thy Birthday, Loves Offering, orig card, $50.00.

BOOKMARK

Assassinated At Washington, President Lincoln	150.00
For A Good Boy, I had a little doggy	60.00
For A Good Girl, Sweet Maggie had a little bird	60.00
Little Bo-Peep	50.00
Little Jack Horner	50.00
Little Red Riding Hood	50.00
The Late Earl Of Beaconsfield, Peace With Honour	25.00

POST CARD

Anne Hathaway's Cottage	40.00
Hands Across The Sea, man and woman's hands	
R.M.S. Carmania, GB and USA flags	40.00
U.S.M.S. Philadelphia, USA and Norway flags	100.00
Houses Of Parliament	60.00
Princes Street, Edinburgh	60.00
R.M.S. Hilary	125.00
R.M.S. Lusitania	70.00
R.M.S. Saxonia	40.00
Shakespeare's Birthplace	40.00

STEVENGRAPH

Are Your Ready?	150.00
John L. Sullivan, story label	100.00
Rt. Hon. J. Chamberlain, M.P., flower spray	125.00
The Final Spurt	175.00
The First Innings	300.00
The First Over	250.00
The First Set	250.00

STEVENS AND WILLIAMS

History: In 1824 Joseph Silvers and Joseph Stevens leased the Moor Lane Glass House at "Briar Lea Hill" (Brierley Hill), England, from the Honey-borne family. In 1847 William Stevens and Samuel Cox Williams took over, giving the firm its present name. In 1870 the firm moved to its Stourbridge plant. In the 1880s the firm employed such renowned glass artisans as Frederick C. Carder, John Northwood, other Northwood family members, James Hill, and Joshua Hodgetts.

Stevens and Williams made cameo glass. Hodgets developed a more commercial version using thinner-walled blanks, acid etching, and the engraving wheel. Hodgetts, an amateur botantist, was noted for his brilliant floral designs.

Other glass products and designs manufactured by Stevens and Williams include intaglio ware, Peach Bloom (a form of peachblow), moss agate, threaded ware, "jewell" ware, tapestry ware, and Silveria. Stevens and Williams made glass pieces covering the full range of late Victorian fashion.

After WWI the firm concentrated on refining the production of lead crystal and achieving new glass colors. In 1932 Keith Murray came to Stevens and Williams as a designer. His work stressed the pure nature of the glass form. Murray stayed with Stevens and Williams until WWII and later followed a career in architecture.

Reference: R.S. Williams-Thomas. *The Crystal Years*, Stevens and Williams Limited, England, Boerum Hill Books, 1983.

Additional Listings: Cameo Glass.

Biscuit Jar, 5½" d, 7¾" h, creamy opaque ground, applied amber and

Vase, ftd, blue body, applied amber rim, rigaree, and feet, sgd, 6½" w, 7½" h, $325.00.

green leaves, deep pink lining, SP rim, cov, and handle **275.00**

Bowl
3¾" d, 3½" h, box pleated top, plain panels alternating with raised emb beaded panels, white shaded to cranberry, frosted cranberry lining, satin finish **175.00**

6¾" d, 3¼" h, box pleated top, pink MOP satin, Swirl pattern, cream lining **500.00**

Calling Card Receiver, 10" l, applied amber handle, rolled edge, translucent opalescent ground, three applied berries, blossoms, and green leaves, three applied amber feet **725.00**

Cruet, 3½" d, 9½" h, amber, opaque Arboresque pattern, applied amber handle, amber pedestal foot, orig flattened amber stopper **150.00**

Pitcher, 10½", applied green handle forms leaves and yellow flower, cranberry overlay, blue int., applied amber rim and feet **600.00**

Plate, 4¾" d, ruffled shell shape, shaded pink to green, MOP satin, Swirl pattern **175.00**

Rose Bowl, 3", DQ, MOP, rainbow, alternating stripes of pastel yellow, pink, and blue, imp "Stevens & Williams, Stourbridge Glass," crown logo, patent **1,045.00**

Vase
5¾", egg shape, opal and cranberry vertical stripes, gold and black floral dec, applied clear rigaree extends to three feet, pr **125.00**

8¼", shaded pink, white lining, applied amber and green leaves and branches, applied soft blue and cream flowers, amber centers, applied amber loop feet **300.00**

10", slender refined shape, six medallions of applied clear glass, trailing stems swirling to base, engraved ornate stylized petals and foliage, sgd in pontil "Frederick Carder," Stevens and Williams logo **745.00**

12", baluster, Silveria, green threading on shaded pink and white silver speckled ground, bright green lining **725.00**

STICKLEYS

History: There were several Stickley brothers: Albert, Gustav, Leopold, George, and John George. Gustav often is credited with creating the Mission style, a variant of the Arts and Crafts style. Gustav headed Craftsman Furniture, a New York firm, much of whose actual production took place near Syracuse. A characteristic of Gustav's furniture is exposed tenon ends. Gustav published *The Craftsman*, a magazine supporting his anti-machine points of view.

Originally Leopold and Gustav worked together. In 1902 Leopold and John George formed the L. and J. G. Stickley Furniture Company. This firm made Mission style furniture and cherry and maple early American style pieces.

George and Albert organized the Stickley Brothers Company, located in Grand Rapids, Michigan.

Reference: David M. Cathers, *Furniture Of The American Arts and Crafts Movement*, New American Library, 1981; Bruce Johnson, *The Official Identification And Price Guide To Arts And Crafts*, House of Collectibles, 1988.

Periodical: *Arts and Crafts Quarterly*, P.O. Box 3592, Station E, Trenton, NJ 08629.

Book, *Craftsman Homes,* 1909, orig buckram cov, 11 x 8¼" **175.00**
Chandelier, 20¼", hammered copper and glass dome, hanging chain, c1910 . . . . **6,875.00**
Furniture
  Bed, #923, double, orig medium brown finish, vertical strap hardware, c1912 . . . . **11,000.00**
  Book Case, #645, orig finish, L & J G Stickley **4,675.00**
  Book Stand, #46, orig finish, L & J G Stickley **2,475.00**
  Chest of Drawers
    #905 with mirror, orig medium brown finish, vertical strap hardware, c1912 . . . . **26,500.00**
    #906, tall chest of drawers with mirror, orig medium brown finish, vertical strap hardware, c1912 . **22,000.00**
  Chair
    Arm, oak, ladder back, four horizontal slats, red Gustav Stickley decal, model no. 352A, c1904–12, 39½" h, pr **1,800.00**
    Morris
      #322, straight arms, orig finish, Gustav Stickley decal **4,675.00**
      #762, orig finish, L & J G Stickley mark **4,000.00**
    Side, oak, red Gustav Stickley decal, model no. 352, c1904–12, 37¼" h, set of 10 . . . . **7,500.00**
  China Cabinet, oak, two doors, each with eight panes, hammered "V" pulls, arched apron, red Gustav Stickley decal, model no. 815, c1904 . . . . **9,000.00**
  Desk, oak, recessed top section, lower gallery, ten cubbyholes, central drawer, two stacked drawers on either side, hammered back plates, riveted back plates on four sq legs,

unsigned, c1904–12, 42" w, 24" d, 37" h **2,225.00**
Magazine Stand, oak, four shelves, curved apron, two demilune handles, model no. 79, 39⅝" h **2,200.00**
Rocker, oak
  Model #317, Gustav Stickley **2,475.00**
  Model #803, L & J. G. Stickley decal **275.00**
Sideboard, oak, hammered copper hardware, plate rack, through tenons on front , red Gustav Stickley decal, model no. 814, c1904–12, 60¼" w, 21" d, 48" h **6,000.00**
Table
  Library, oak, hexagonal, stained stretchers joined by faceted central knob, exposed tenons with keys, red Gustav Stickley decal, model no. 625, c1902–03, 43¾" w, 27" h **9,500.00**
  Serving, oak, two drawers, arched apron, lower shelf, overhanging top, red Gustav Stickley decal, model no. 802, c1904–12, 42" w, 18" d, 39" h **3,500.00**
  Trestle, orig finish, Gustav Stickley decal, 60 x 36" **4,125.00**
Lamp, table, 15" h, copper standard, conical wicker shade, marked "G. Stickley" **375.00**
Sconce, 10 x 15", copper, brass accents, separate bobeches for candles, marked "342, Stickley Bros." . . **425.00**
Wastebasket, oak, conical, vertical slats attached to two int. circular metal stays, model no. 94, c1910, 13¾" h **1,900.00**

STIEGEL TYPE GLASS

History: Baron Henry Stiegel founded America's first flint glass factory at Manheim, Pennsylvania, in the 1760s. Although clear glass was the most common color made, amethyst, blue (cobalt), and fiery opalescent are found. Products included bottles, creamers, flasks, flips, perfumes, salts, tumblers, and whiskeys. Prosperity was short lived. Stiegel's extravagant living forced the factory to close.

It is very difficult to identify a Stiegel-made item. As a result the term "Stiegel type" is used to identify glass made at that time period in the same shapes and colors.

Enamel decorated ware also is attributed to Stiegel. True Stiegel pieces are rare. An overwhelming majority is of European origin.

Reference: Frederick W. Hunter, *Stiegel Glass*, 1950, available in Dover reprint.

Reproduction Alert: Beware of modern reproductions, especially in enamel wares.

Creamer, ftd, Expanded Diamond pattern, fiery opalescent, 3½" h, $800.00.

ENAMELED

Bride's Bottle, clear, enameled dec
5¾", sprays of flowers, red, yellow,
white, green, and baby blue **250.00**
yellow, black, green, and baby blue,
remnants of orig pewter collar ... **500.00**
6", long neck, rolled mouth, Carpenter's Arms, reverse inscribed "Vivat
der Schreiner 1825," red, white,
yellow, and blue **200.00**
6½", pewter collar, bright dec **200.00**
6⅞", large spray of flowers, white,
red, yellow, blue, and black, slight
haze on bottom **275.00**
8⅜", pewter collar, bright dec **225.00**
Flip, 6½", basket of flowers and leaves **375.00**
Whiskey, man on prancing horse **265.00**

ENGRAVED

Bottle, 7⅞" h, blown clear glass, engraved large tulip on each side, monogram and date 1837, chemical deposit on bottom **150.00**
Flip, clear
6 x 7¾", clear, Phoenix bird between
two tulips **150.00**
6⅜ x 7¼", lovebirds in sunburst,
frosted **400.00**
Mug, cov, floral motif, strap handle ... **400.00**
Vase, 9¾", clear, hollyhocks and ferns
dec, hollow base, hollow stem, pontil **100.00**

OTHER

Bowl, amethyst, fifteen expanded diamond patter, miniature **425.00**
Christmas Light, 4", yellow–green, expanded diamond, metal fixture **125.00**
Creamer, 4⅛", cobalt blue, twenty expanded diamonds **300.00**
Perfume Bottle, daisy in hexagon pattern, flake on neck **4,000.00**

Salt, blue, checkered diamond **750.00**
Sugar, cov, deep sapphire blue, eleven
expanded diamond pattern **2,500.00**

STONEWARE

History: Made from dense kaolin clay and commonly salt-glazed, stonewares were hand-thrown and high-fired to produce a simple, bold vitreous pottery. Stoneware crocks, jugs, and jars were produced for storage and utility purposes. This use dictated shape and design—solid, thick-walled forms with heavy rims, necks, and handles with little or no embellishment. When decorated, the designs were simple: brushed cobalt oxide, incised, slip trailed, stamped, or tooled.

Stoneware has been made for centuries. Early American settlers imported stoneware items at first. As English and European potteries refined their earthenware, colonists began to produce their own wares. Two major North American traditions emerged based only on the location or type of clay. North Jersey and parts of New York comprise the first area; the second was eastern Pennsylvania spreading westward and into Maryland, Virginia, and West Virginia. These two distinct locations, style of decoration, and shape are discernible factors in classifying and dating early stoneware.

By the late 18th century, stoneware was manufactured in all sections of the country. During the 19th century, this vigorous industry flourished until glass "fruit jars" appeared and the widespread use of refrigeration. By 1910, commercial production of salt-glazed stoneware came to an end.

References: Georgeanna H. Greer, *American Stoneware: The Art and Craft of Utilitarian Potters,* Schiffer Publishing, Ltd., 1981; Don and Carol Raycraft, *Country Stoneware And Pottery,* Collector Books, 1985; Don and Carol Raycroft, *Collector's Guide To Country Stoneware & Pottery,* 2nd Series, Collector Books, 1990.

Periodical: *Stoneware Collectors' Journal,* 670 Mix Avenue #5L, Hamden, CT 06514.

Batter Jug, W J & E O Schror, cov, handle, Albany slip, sgraffito birds, imp
label, incised 1873 .... **450.00**
Bowl
Hermann, P, Baltimore, 10", milk, cobalt blue leaf motif **200.00**
Hickerson, J H, Strasburg, VA, 8¼",
cobalt blue foliage dec on rim, floral
sides **225.00**
Butter Churn
Ballard, A K, 6 gal, cobalt blue, floral
and leaf motif **245.00**
Unidentified Maker, 19½", 6 gal,
slightly ovoid, molded rim, eared
handles, brushed cobalt blue stylized florals and "6" **250.00**

Butter Crock
  Bell, Samuel and Solomon, Strasburg, VA, 6", applied handles, brown slip floral motif, imp mark on shoulder, c1834–82 . . . .   **250.00**
  Ratcliff, D L, and Co, Wheeling, WV, 5¾", straight sides, stenciled cobalt blue label **120.00**
  Unidentified Maker, 10", feather motif, matching lid **300.00**
Canning Jar
  Clark, N, and Co, Mount Morris, NY, cobalt blue leaf dec **165.00**
  Rouston, Wooster, OH, 8", narrow mouth, Albany slip, three brushed white flowers **125.00**
  Weymon and Bros, Pittsburgh, PA, 9¾", stenciled label, leaf motif . . .   **100.00**
Churn, 14", blue bands, wood lid, stamped "Davis Bros" **45.00**

Crock, H. J. Heinz, 6¼" d, 5¼" h, $250.00.

Crock
  Burger and Long, Rochester, NY, 3 gal cobalt tulip and leaves **125.00**
  Donaghho, A P, stenciled cobalt blue label, 1 gal **60.00**
  Fort Edward Pottery Co, Fort Edward, NY, 19th C, 5 gal, straight sided, standing stag flanked by pine and elm tree, flattened eared handles, some rim chips, 12⅝ x 12" **5,775.00**
  Hamilton and Jones, Greensboro, PA, 7", stenciled cobalt label, straight sides **160.00**
  Irvine, S, Newville, 4 gal, ovoid, three flowers **425.00**
  Lewis and Cady, Fairfax, VT, 9 x 9½", 2 gal, ovoid, brushed cobalt blue design **285.00**
  Maquoid and Co, Wm A, 10", 3 gal, cylindrical, projecting rim, applied handles, cobalt blue figure of farmer, wide brim hat, holding rake and sickle, imp label, "Wm A Maquoid & Co, Little Wst 12th St. 3," c1860 . . . .   **7,150.00**

Unidentified Maker
  9¼", stenciled cobalt blue shaking hands dec, imp "2" **275.00**
  13½", ovoid, double tulips **300.00**
West Troy Pottery, 3 gal, cobalt blue chicken pecking corn **375.00**
Cuspidor, 11" d, 6¾" h, cobalt blue dec ext., brown Albany slip int., marked "Livingston House" in bold letters . .   **70.00**
Flask, 5½", flattened ovoid **85.00**
Jar
  Bouchner, A and W, 12¼", 4 gal, eared handles, cobalt blue tulips and foliage, imp label **725.00**
  Crolius, C, Manhattan-Wells, NY, 7½", ovoid, eared handles, imp swags and single flower, cobalt blue wash **1,100.00**
  Hamilton and Jones
    13¾" h, ovoid, cobalt blue stenciled and free hand label, flowers, marked "Hamilton & Jones, Greensboro, Pa 3" **275.00**
    14½" h, ovoid, cobalt blue stenciled and freehand label, "Hamilton and Jones, Greensboro, PA 4" .   **200.00**
  Reppert, T F, Eagle Pottery, Greensboro, PA, 14½", 4 gal, eared handles, stenciled cobalt label and spread winged eagle, brushed "4" and wavy lines **625.00**
  Unidentified Maker
    8¾" h, ovoid, brushed cobalt blue flower, applied handles **235.00**
    8⅝" h, cobalt blue floral dec, open handles **175.00**
Jug
  Cowden and Wilcox
    2 gal, 12¾" h, semi–ovoid, strap handle, brushed cobalt blue leafy floral sprig, imp "Cowden & Wilcox, Harrisburg, Pa, 2," c1870, minor flakes **275.00**
    4 gal, large cluster of grapes **500.00**
  Edmands and Co, 3 gal, cobalt slip dec of drapes, two minor chips . .   **150.00**
  Farrar and Co, W H, Geddes, NY, 11", 1 gal, cobalt blue bird, sprouted flower to left, continuous curving line with dots to right, imp label, c1841 . . . .   **4,620.00**
  Heilbronner, H, Schnectady, NY, 2 gal, bird on leafy branch **475.00**
  Jones, Evan B, 13" h, cobalt blue slip bird on branch, imp label "Evan B. Jones, Pittston, PA" **400.00**
  Lyman and Clark, 12½" h, ovoid, brushed brown floral design, impressed label "Lyman & Clark, Gardiner" **485.00**
  Norton and Co, J E, Bennington, VT, 11" h, semi–ovoid, slip quilled co-

balt blue bird perched on scrolling branch **325.00**

Ottman Bros and Co, Fort Edward, NY, 2 gal, flower **100.00**

Purdy, Henry, Mogadore, OH, 2 gal, 14¼″ h, ovoid, strap handle, brushed cobalt blue stylized flower, daub of blue on imp label "H. Purdy, Ohio 2," c1840, minor chips and short hairline in base **500.00**

Ruckel, Viall, Middlebury, OH, 19¼″ h, semi–ovoid, applied loop handles at rim, fine slip quilled cobalt blue script inscription "Viall Ruckel & Co, Middlebury, O" **2,000.00**

Somerset Potters, 11½″ h, cobalt blue quill work, stylized floral design, imp label "Somerset Potters' Works" **200.00**

Unidentified Maker
7½″ h, ovoid, gray salt glaze, brown highlights, imp "Charlestown" .. **250.00**
12″ h, ovoid, cobalt blue slip dash marks, marked "1840" **325.00**

Webster and Berge, 13¼″, 2 gal, cobalt blue stenciled griffins, imp label **135.00**

White, 13¾″ h, cobalt blue slip bird on branch, imp label "White's Utica, 2″ **300.00**

Match Holder, 2¾″ h, cone shaped, gray body, imp narrow bands around top and base with cobalt blue wash, serrated striking surface **75.00**

Milk Bowl, 12¾″ d, 6¼″ h, pouring spout, applied handles, brushed cobalt blue "2″ with foliate detail, brown Albany slip int., imp label "Lyons" .. **475.00**

Mug, 4¾″ h, cylindrical, applied strap handle, slip quilled cobalt blue blossoms, attributed to Daniel P. Shenfelder, Marion Township, Berks County, PA, c1869–80 .... **450.00**

Pitcher, H Prudy, 4 gal, cobalt blue double flower **500.00**

Preserving Jar
Enrix, J F, 6¼″ h, slightly ovoid, stenciled cobalt blue label, blurred, "J F Enrix, New Geneva, PA" **75.00**
McCarthey and Hayless, Louisville, KY, 8″, stenciled cobalt blue label . **200.00**
Janson Bros, "Pure French Mustard, Cinti, OH," 9½″, stenciled cobalt blue label **150.00**
Sonner, S H, Strasburg, VA, 9″ h, cylindrical, molded rim, mottled two tone green–gray and red–tan glaze, simple brushed cobalt blue three part leaves at rim, imp label **100.00**

Salt Box, 6¾″ w, 6½″ h, hanging, emb basketweave design and "SEL," wood lid **55.00**

Smoking Stand, 8″ d, blue and brown

sponging, white ground, match and cigar containers, striking surface edge, ink mark "Geo Oliver Moody, Robinson Clay Products, Akron, Ohio 1910" **80.00**

Spittoon, 8″, cobalt blue leaf and floral motif **175.00**

Wash Board, 13¾ x 24½″, dark brown Albany slip wash board insert in wooden frame, scrubbed finish, insert chipped **50.00**

Water Cooler, Cyrus Fenton, 24½″, domed cov, ovoid, applied loop handles, incised florals, cobalt blue highlights **650.00**

Whimsey, 5¾″ h, tree stump, applied vine, crude spread winged bird on top, tan salt glaze **275.00**

STONEWARE, BLUE AND WHITE

History: Blue and white stoneware refers to molded, salt glazed, domestic, utilitarian earthenware with a blue glaze produced in the late 19th and early 20th centuries. Earlier stoneware was usually handthrown and either undecorated, hand decorated in Spencerian script floral and other motifs, or stenciled. The stoneware of the blue and white period is molded with a design impressed, embossed, stenciled, or printed.

Although known as blue and white, the base color is generally grayish in tone. The blue cobalt glaze may coat the entire piece, appear as a series of bands, or accent the decorative elements.

All types of household products were available in blue and white stoneware. Bowls, crocks, jars, pitchers, mugs, and salts are just a few examples. The ware reached its height between 1870 and 1890. The advent of glass jars, tin containers, and chilled transportation brought its end. The last blue and white stoneware was manufactured in the 1920s.

Reference: Kathryn McNerney, *Blue & White Stoneware*, Collector Books, 1981.

Collectors' Club: Blue & White Pottery Club, P. O. Box 297, Center Point, IA 52213.

Reproduction Alert: A vast majority of the blue and white stoneware found in antiques shops and flea markets is unmarked reproductions from Rushville Pottery, Rushville, OH.

Batter Jug, 8″ h, pinched top, sponged dec **185.00**

Berry Bowl, 4½″ d, 2½″ h, diffused blues **50.00**

Bowl
5″ d, Wedding Ring **50.00**
9½″ d, 5″ h, currants and diamonds dec **75.00**
10½″ d, 5½″ h, feather dec **100.00**

Butter Crock
Butterfly **100.00**

Crock, cov, Grape pattern, glazed interior, marked "Robinson Clay, Akron, OH," 7¾" d, $200.00.

Panel	80.00
Cake Crock, four blue bands, "cake" stencil, replaced tin lid	325.00
Chamber Pot, Beaded Rose Cluster and Spear Points	100.00
Coffeepot, 11½" h, 6" d, swirl, blue tipped finial knob, spurs handle, iron base cap	350.00
Cookie Jar, 8" h, 7¼" d, grooved blue, orig lid	125.00
Cup, 2½" d, 4½" h, Wildflower, emb ribbon and bow	60.00
Ice Crock, 6" d, 4½" h, Rope Bands, ice tongs, and ice block dec, late 1800s	125.00
Mug	
Cattails	115.00
Rose, decal	50.00
Pickle Crock, blue band, barrel shape, bail handle	60.00
Pie Plate, 10½", blue walled, brick edge base, imp star shaped mark	100.00
Pitcher	
Butterfly, 9", large butterfly surrounded by raised rope medallion, diffused blues, small butterflies between raised rope bands top and bottom	150.00
Grapes, 7¾", emb	100.00
Indian Chief, 8", feather headdress medallion on waffle ground	200.00
Old Fashioned Garden Rose, 10"	125.00
Peacock, 7¾", emb spout	250.00
Rolling Pin, 13" l, swirl design, orig wood handles	200.00
Salt	
Apricot	140.00
Lovebirds, wooden lid	125.00
Soap Dish	
Cat's Head	125.00
Indian War Bonnet	140.00
Spittoon, emb, sponged blue earthworm pattern	120.00

Toothbrush Holder, blue band, rolled rim	35.00
Toothpick Holder, Swan	55.00
Wash Bowl and Pitcher, Feather and Swirl	250.00

STRETCH GLASS

History: Stretch glass was produced by many glass manufacturers in the United States between the early 1900s and the 1920s. The most prominent makers were Cambridge, Fenton (who probably manufactured more stretch glass than any of the others), Imperial, Northwood, and Steuben. Stretch glass can be identified by its iridescent, onionskin-like effect. Look for mold marks. Imported pieces are blown and show a pontil mark.

Reference: Berry Wiggins, *Stretch Glass,*, Antique Publications, n.d.

Collectors' Club: Stretch Glass Society, 1221 Andrews Avenue, Lakewood, OH 44107.

Bowl, fluted body, vaseline, flat rim with applied gold band of peasants in medallions and floral motif, 9¾" d, 3¼" h, $45.00.

Bobeches, scalloped, vaseline, pr	40.00
Bowl	
10 x 4½", yellow irid, Imperial	85.00
12", white, Fenton	40.00
Candlesticks, 10½", vaseline, pr	50.00
Candy Dish, topaz, Fenton	60.00
Compote, 7⅝ x 4½", green irid, clear stem, amber base	65.00
Creamer and Sugar, Rings pattern, tangerine	75.00
Nappy, 7", vaseline, Fenton	32.00
Pitcher, lemonade, celeste blue, cobalt handle	200.00
Plate	
6", red, paneled, Imperial	50.00
8¼", Aurene, gold	70.00
Rose Bowl, 3½ x 5", pink, melon ribbed	50.00
Sherbet, 4", red, melon ribbed	50.00
Vase	
5½", pink, Imperial	75.00

6", fan shape, ribbed, green **35.00**
10", blue, vertical cut **50.00**

STRING HOLDERS

History: The string holder developed as a utilitarian tool to assist the merchant or manufacturer who needed tangle-free string or twine to tie packages. The early holders were made of cast iron, some patents dating to the 1860s.

When the string holder moved to the household, lighter and more attractive forms developed, many made of chalkware. The string holder remained a key kitchen element until the early 1950s.

Cast Iron, beehive, 6½" d, 4½" h, $18.00.

Brass, desk, emb roses and scrollwork, 3" h, 2" d, ornate, marked "The DM Read Company Fair Week 1909" .. **15.00**
Cast Iron
  Advertising, "Use Higgins German Laundry Soap. It is the Best," black, four wall or counter mounts, 6" h . **60.00**
  Counter type, openwork beehive, three legs **35.00**
  Girl ice skating, polychrome paint, 7" h **375.00**
  Woman, string comes out of mouth, repainted **350.00**
Ceramic, bear **10.00**
Chalkware
  Baby **35.00**
  Mexican Man **25.00**
  Scotty Dog **45.00**
  Spanish Senor and Senorita, pr ... **50.00**
Glass
  Beehive, 4¾", tin enclosure **38.00**
  Cut, notched prisms, Gorham sterling silver top **185.00**
Plaster, cat, cream, red ball **20.00**
Porcelain, rooster, Royal Bayreuth ... **220.00**
Pottery, figural, dog, Bennington **165.00**
Silver Plated, 3⅝" h, 3¾" d, dome shape, repousse wreath around body, Pairpoint **65.00**
Stoneware, cobalt blue bird dec **50.00**

SUGAR SHAKERS

History: Sugar shakers, sugar castors, or muffineers all served the same purpose: to "sugar" muffins, scones, or toast. They are larger than salt and pepper shakers, were produced in a variety of materials, and were in vogue in the late Victorian era.

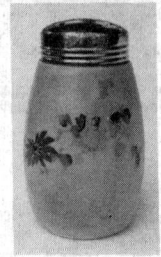

Hand Painted, floral motif, orig sp top, 4¾" h, $55.00.

CHINA

Austrian, 4½", border of delicate pink roses, shaded blue ground, marked "MZ Austria" **55.00**
Nippon, 3⅛ x 4⅞", panels of pink and red roses, cream ground, gold dec handle **65.00**
Schlegelmilch, RS Prussia, 5", scalloped base, pearl finish, roses, red mark **235.00**
Wedgwood, blue ground, classic white dec **50.00**

GLASS

Milk Glass
  Apple Blossom **85.00**
  Bulbous, three Palmer Cox Brownies dec, pale blue ground **175.00**
  Challinor's Forget–Me–Not, white, opaque, orig top **100.00**
Mt Washington
  Egg shape
    Daisies dec, yellow shading to brown ground **150.00**
    Pansies dec, peach shading to yellow ground **250.00**
  Lighthouse shape, 5½", IVT, bluerina, orig metal top **270.00**
  Melon ribbed, blue and white forget–me–nots, yellow ground **200.00**
Opalescent Glass
  Reverse Swirl, cranberry, 6" **125.00**

Ribbed Lattice, blue **75.00**
Pattern Glass
  Acorn, opaque pink **165.00**
  Coin Spot, cranberry, SP top **75.00**
  Inverted Thumbprint, vaseline, orig
    top **60.00**
  Leaf Umbrella, cranberry spatter,
    white casing **225.00**
  Medallion Sprig, rubena **165.00**
  Royal Oak, rubena, frosted **225.00**
  Wisconsin, orig top **65.00**
Satin
  Diamond Quilted, MOP, blue **225.00**
  Herringbone, MOP, apricot **200.00**

SWANSEA

History: This superb pottery and porcelain was
made at Swansea (Glamorganshire, Wales) as
early as the 1760s with production continuing until
1870.

Marks on Swansea vary. The earliest marks
were SWANSEA impressed under glaze and DILL-
WAN under glaze after 1805. CAMBRIAN POT-
TERY was stamped in red under glaze from 1803-
1805. Many fine examples, including the Botanical
series in pearlware, are not marked, but may have
the botanical name stamped under glaze.

Fine examples of Swansea often may show im-
perfections, such as firing cracks. These pieces
are considered mint because they left the factory
in this condition.

Reference: Susan and Al Bagdade, *Warman's
English & Continental Pottery & Porcelain, 1st Edition,* Warman Publishing Co., Inc., 1987.

Reproduction Alert: Swansea porcelain has
been copied for many decades in Europe and England. Marks should be studied carefully.

Cake Plate, 12½″, painted florals, gilt
  rim and handles, c1813 .... **375.00**

**Plate, floral dec, marked "Swansea"
underglaze, 8½″ d, $150.00.**

Creamer, 6½″, cow, cov, pink splash luster, rect base, c1825 .... **425.00**
Cup and Saucer, 4¼″, pink roses, turquoise and gilt ground, printed mark,
  c1820 .... **375.00**
Goblet, 5″, copper luster, three polychrome rose sprigs, green band with
  black edge, c1830 .... **65.00**
Pitcher, 6½″, Chinese pattern, multicolored **300.00**
Plate
  8¼″, floral dec, printed mark, artist
    sgd "William Pollard," c1820 .... **600.00**
  9⅝″, blue transfer, scattered bou-
    quets, c1820 .... **135.00**
Serving Dish
  9¾″, oval, botanical series, cyclamen,
    artist sgd "Thomas Pardoe," imp
    "Swansea" **375.00**
  10¼″, oval, center floral bouquet, full
    blown roses on rim, gilt dentil, imp
    mark **465.00**

SWORDS

History: The first swords in America came from
Europe. The chief cities for sword manufacturing
were Solingen in Germany, Klingenthal in France,
and Hounslow and Shotley Bridge in England.
Among the American importers of these foreign
blades was "Horstmann" whose mark is found on
many military weapons.

New England and Philadelphia were the early
centers for American sword manufacturing. By the
Franco-Prussian War, the Ames Manufacturing
Company of Chicopee, Massachusetts, was ex-
porting American swords to Europe.

Sword collectors concentrate on a variety of
styles: commission vs. non-commission officers'
swords, presentation swords, naval weapons, and
swords from a specific military branch such as
cavalry or infantry. The type of sword helped identify a person's military rank and, depending on how
he had it customized, his personality as well.

Following the invention of repeating firearms in
the mid-19th century, the sword lost its functional
importance as a combat weapon and became a
military dress accessory. Condition is a key criterion determining value.

Reference: Harold L. Peterson, *The American
Sword 1775–1945,* Ray Riling Arms Books Co,
1965.

Collectors' Club: Japanese Sword Society of
the United States, Inc., P.O. Box 4387, Grasso
Plaza Branch, St. Louis, MO 63123.

AMERICAN

Artillery, Light, Saber, Model 1840,
  stamped at obverse ricasso "U.S./

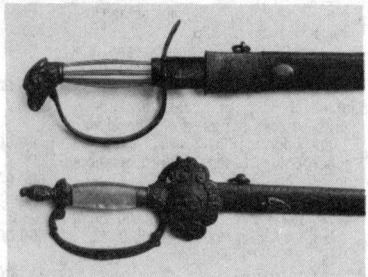

Top: Foot Officer's saber, non-regulation, 1810, $350.00; bottom: Artillery Officer's Indian head pommel, 1821-50, $250.00.

C.E.W./1864," reverse with faint "AMES" etc. markings, orig scabbard ... **350.00**

Cavalry, Saber, Model 1840, stamped on obverse ricasso "US JH" and on reverse "N.P. AMES CABOTVILLE 1846," crisp brass hilt, steel scabbard with some polishing marks **800.00**

Cavalry, Saber, Model 1840, stamped "US/WD" on obverse, reverse with "AMES MFG. CO./CABOTVILLE/ 1849," scabbard with moderate uniform age patina **525.00**

Confederate, Officer's, 83½" overall, 33¼" unmarked blade with unstopped fuller, brass basket guard with large "CS" in counterguard surrounded by floral patterns, leather grip wound with twisted brass wire, complete with part of orig scabbard, brass throat mount Serial No. 47 and engraved "MADE BY/James Coning/Mobile/ Ala," brass middle mount unmarked, drag missing **5,000.00**

Fraternal, Ames, deluxe, 27" blade, etched against gilt ground for 18½", obverse with profuse scrolls, a standing knight in armor and "Wilson Daniel Rau," reverse with scrolls, a panel showing knights jousting with a castle at the side, a trophy of flags, and "AMES/Sword Co/CHICOPEE/ MASS," fancy cast and silvered hilt with black painted grips, silvered scabbard with fancy openwork mounts with enameled crown and cross, Maltese cross **100.00**

Halberd, Colonial, steel head, 17" overall, 12" leaf shaped blade, 29½" straps for attachment to shaft, deep age patina, small areas of light cleaning, scattered pitting, fitted to restoration 87½" oak shaft **125.00**

Non-commissioned Officer, Model 1840, obverse stamped "US/DFM/ 1860," reverse "EMERSON/&/SILVER/TRENTON, N.J.," orig brass mounted black leather scabbard ... **300.00**

Polearm, military

97" overall, 6" iron tip, heavy 4½" point square in cross-section, forged one piece with 17" straps, butt a 2½" iron cone with 8½" straps, again forged as one piece, straps all attached to heavy oak shaft with screws, shaft marked "U.S." and "T.H." **500.00**

98½" overall, 14¼" forged iron tip, 8½" spear point blade, 11¾" attaching straps, all forged as one piece, forged iron butt 9½" overall made of two iron straps attached to a 3" cone, all forged in one piece, orig heavy wood shaft with period black painted surface, first half of 19th C **225.00**

EUROPEAN

Continental

Halberd Head, 21¼" head, 47" overall including orig straps for attaching to pole, pole cut off just before end of straps, pierced blade unmarked **500.00**

Sword, Presentation, German silver scabbard with high raised cast brass mounts in oak leaf and acorn pattern, orig script inscription between throat and middle mount, "Presented to/Lt. H. H. Dumont,/By Co. F 189th O.V.I./1865," sword 40" overall, 34" curved "W.CLAUBERG/ SOLINGEN" blade, deeply etched for 15½" on each side with trophies of arms, scrolls, etc., hollow silver plate casting grip in dot and leaf pattern **2,100.00**

MIDDLE EAST

Eastern, 30⅝" overall, 25½" blade engraved overall with large figures of various animals, iron hilt with gold damascened dec and ivory scales that are mellowed old replacements, engraved animals with considerable traces of gold dec **125.00**

Persian, Saber, 36" overall, 31" curved blade, damascened panel containing Farsi writing, iron hilt with stylized lion head pommel dec with gold damascening, orig black leather cov wood scabbard with iron drag **375.00**

TEA CADDIES

History: Tea once was a precious commodity. Special boxes or caddies were used as containers to accomodate different teas, including a special cup for blending.

Around 1700 silver caddies appeared in England. Other materials, such as Sheffield plate, tin, wood, china, and pottery, also were used. Some tea caddies became very ornate.

Burl walnut, two compartments, line inlay, ivory key inlay, chamfered corners, brass hinges, 4⅜ x 7½ x 4¾", $575.00.

Brass, coffin shape, hasp, Chinese . . . **40.00**
Ivory, rect, carved, scholars, boats, pavilions, and tree scenes, bamboo carved edges, sliding top, Chinese, 19th C **1,250.00**
Lacquer, 10⅜ x 6¾", octagonal, hinged lid with oval monogrammed medallion, two borders of overlapping foliate vines, divided int. fitted with two removable wells, circular covs, Chinese Export, c1830–40 . . . . **550.00**
Silver, 3" h, rect cross section, gadrooned lip and foot, ivory pineapple finial, George III, John Edwards, London, c1797–98, approx 19.5 ounces, pr **1,900.00**
Porcelain, 5½" h, Chinese Export, polychrome floral enameled crest, fruit finial **125.00**
Tin, 4", oval, red, yellow, and green floral dec, orig black paint **125.00**
Wood
    Mahogany, 6¼ x 5", octagonal, cross banded mahogany, polychrome paper rolls form design on foil grounds, each panel under glass, hinged cov with flowerhead flanked by floral sprigs, side panels with oval and geometric motifs, floral bouquet on front and back panel, George III, late 18th C **1,650.00**

Rosewood
    6 x 11 x 6", rect top, compartment int., English, 19th C **275.00**
    6 x 13 x 6½", rect top, three covered compartments, English, 19th C **375.00**
Satinwood
    7 x 8½ x 5½", Federal style, inlaid, tapering rect form, hinged lid, turned feet, 19th C **500.00**
    12 x 6½", tapering rect, hinged rect lid inlaid with elliptical shell medallion, int. with six pointed star, two removable rect lidded tea bosses, cross banding, gilt metal lion mask ring handles, late George III, early 19th C **1,320.00**
Walnut, 5¾ x 4½", oval, hinged cov with marquetry inlaid, central shell medallion, two tied lily sprigs on front, George III, c1800 . . . . **950.00**

TEA LEAF IRONSTONE CHINA

History: Tea Leaf Ironstone china flowed into America from England in great quantities in the 1860 to 1910 period and graced the tables of working class America. It traveled to California and Texas in wagons and by boat down the Mississippi River to Kentucky and Missouri. It was too plain for the rich homes; its simplicity and strength appealed to wives forced to watch pennies. Tea Leaf found its way into the kitchen of Lincoln's Springfield home; sailors ate from it aboard the *Star of India*, now moored in San Diego and still displaying Tea Leaf.

Tea Leaf was not manufactured exclusively by English potters in Staffordshire, contrary to popular opinion. Although there were more than 30 English potters producing Tea Leaf, at least 21 American potters helped satisfy the demand. However, American potters perpetuated the myth by using backstamps bearing the English coat-of-arms and the marking "Warrented." The American housewife favored imported ware to that made by Americans.

Anthony Shaw (1850–1900) first registered the pattern in 1856 as Luster Band and Sprig. Edward Walley (1845–56) already was decorating ironstone with luster trefoil leaf, a detached bud, and trailing green vine. Walley's products are designated Pre-Tea Leaf and are sought by eclectic collectors. Other early variants include "Morning Glory" and "Pepper" by Elsmore & Forster (Foster) (1853–57) and "Teaberry" by Clementson Bros. (1832–1916). Clover leaf, cinquefoil, and pinwheel all may be found in a collection specializing in early ware.

The most prolific Tea Leaf makers were Anthony Shaw and Alfred Meakin (1875–). Johnson Bros. (1883–), Henry Burgess (1864–92) and Arthur J. Wilkinson (1897–), all of whom shipped much of their ware to America and followed close behind Shaw and Meakin.

Although most of the English Tea Leaf is copper luster, Powell & Bishop (1868–78) and their successors, Bishop & Stonier (1891–1936), worked exclusively in gold luster. Beautiful examples of gold luster by H. Burgess still are being found. Mellor, Taylor & Co. (1880–1904) used gold luster on their children's tea sets.

J. & E. Mayer, Beaver Falls, Pennsylvania, were English potters who immigrated to America and produced a large amount of copper luster Tea Leaf. The majority of the American potters decorated with gold luster, with no brown underglaze like that found under the copper luster.

East Liverpool, Ohio, potters such as Cartwright Bros. (1864–1924), East End Pottery (1894–1909), Knowles, Taylor & Knowles (1870–1934), and others decorated only in gold luster. Since no underglazing was used with the gold, much of it has been washed away.

By the 1900s Tea Leaf's popularity had waned. The sturdy ironstone did not disappear. It was stored in barns and relegated to attics and basements. Much of it was disposed in dumps, where one enterprising collector has dug up some beautiful pieces.

A frequent myth about Tea Leaf is that pieces marked "Wedgwood" are THE Wedgwood, Josiah. This is not true! Dealers and collectors who perpetuate this myth should be confronted. Enoch Wedgwood was the only potter of that name to produce Tea Leaf. Enoch Wedgwood's product is beautiful with large showy leaves. He deserves full credit for his work.

Reference: Annise Doring Heaivilin, *Grandma's Tea Leaf Ironstone*, Wallace-Homestead, 1981.

Museums: Lincoln Home, Springfield, IL; Sherman Davidson House, Newark OH; Ox Barn Museum, Aurora, OR.

Reproduction Alert: There are reproductions that are collectible, and there are *reproductions*! Avoid the latter. Collectible reproductions were made by Cumbow China Decorating Co. of Abington, Virginia, from 1932 to 1980. Wm. Adams & Sons, an old English firm, made reproduction Tea Leaf from 1960 to 1972. Red Cliff, who decorated Hall China blanks with Tea Leaf and clearly marked them, worked in the late 1960s and early 1970s.

Ruth Sayer started making Tea Leaf reproductions in 1981. Although her early pieces were not marked, all of it now is marked with a leaf and the initials "RS" on the bottom. In 1968 Blakeney Pottery, a Staffordshire firm, manufactured a poor quality reproduction of Meakin's Bamboo pattern and marked it "Victoria." It was distributed through a Pennsylvania antiques reproduction outlet.

Baker, open
  Pepper Leaf variant, Elsmore & Foster, 9 x 7″ **60.00**

Platter, marked "Royal Ironstone China, Alfred Meakin, England," 8½ x 12″ l, $25.00.

Tea Leaf, Meakin, individual, 5½ x 3⅝″ **22.00**
Bone Dish, Tea Leaf
  J & E Mayer, impressed stem pattern **65.00**
  Meakin, scalloped edge **40.00**
Butter Dish, 3 pcs (base, lid, liner), Tea Leaf
  J & E Mayer **70.00**
  Shaw, Lily Of The Valley **190.00**
  Wedgwood **115.00**
Butter Pats
  Clover Leaf variant, 3″ d **7.00**
  Tea Leaf
    Meakin, 3⅛″ d **9.00**
    Wilkinson, 2¹⁵⁄₁₆″ d **8.00**
Cake Plate, Tea Leaf
  J & E Mayer, emb **60.00**
  Shaw, Daisy **90.00**
Chamber Pot, Tea Leaf, Meakin, Bamboo, cov **150.00**
Children's Ware, Tea Leaf
  Mug, unmarked, 2¾″ h **225.00**
  Set, 15 pcs, Knowles, Taylor, Knowles **1,200.00**
  Sugar Bowl, Mellor Taylor **250.00**
Coffeepot
  Cinquefoil variant, unmarked, emb wheat, repairs **110.00**
  Tea Leaf
    J & E Mayer, 9″ h **145.00**
    Meakin, Fish Hook, 8¾″ h **120.00**
    Shaw, Chinese shape, 9⅝″ h **245.00**
Creamer, Tea Leaf
  Edge, Malkin **85.00**
  J & E Mayer **65.00**
  Meakin, Fish Hook, 5⅛″ h **110.00**
Cup and Saucer
  Pepper Leaf variant, unmarked, 3″ d handled cup **60.00**
  Teaberry, unmarked, 3″ d handled cup **65.00**
  Tea Leaf
    W & E Corn, gold luster, 3″ d handled cup **55.00**

Grindley, 3¾" d handled cup	57.50
Shaw, Chinese shape, 3½" d handleless cup	80.00
Cup Plate, Tea Leaf	
Meakin	35.00
Royal Burslem Pottery	30.00
Doughnut Stand, Tea Leaf, Meakin . .	255.00
Plate	
Pinwheel variant, 10" d	12.00
Pre-Tea Leaf variant, 10" d	12.50
Tea Leaf	
Meakin, 9" d	9.00
Shaw, Lily Of The Valley, emb, 9¾" d	16.00
Teaberry, Clementson, 4½" d	27.50
Pitcher, wash, Tea Leaf, Davenport, pink luster	850.00
Sauce Tureen, Tea Leaf, 3 pcs, sauce dish, lid, underplate	
Mellor Taylor, Lionhead	300.00
Shaw, Cable, orig ladle	500.00
Shaw, Lily Of The Valley	480.00
Shaving Mug, Tea Leaf	
Grindley	100.00
Shaw	130.00
Shaw, Lily Of The Valley	155.00
Soap Dish, Tea Leaf	
Shaw, Lily Of The Valley, liner	220.00
Wilkinson, open	50.00
Soup Tureen, Tea Leaf, Shaw, Cable, 3 pcs (base, lid, ladle)	550.00
Toothbrush Holder, Tea Leaf	
Meakin, Chelsea	210.00
Powell & Bishop, gold luster, 5" h . .	45.00
Shaw, round	115.00
Wedgwood	45.00
Vegetable Dish, cov	
Tea Leaf	
Meakin, Fish Hook	80.00
Shaw, hexagon shape	120.00
Wilkinson	50.00
Teaberry, Clementson	140.00
Sugar Bowl, Tea Leaf, J & E Mayer . .	65.00
Wash Bowl and Pitcher, Tea Leaf	
J & E Mayer	350.00
Mellor Taylor, ribbed	300.00

TEDDY BEARS

History: Originally thought of as "Teddy's Bears," the name comes from President Theodore Roosevelt. These stuffed toys are believed to have originated in Germany and in the United States during the 1902–03 period.

Most of the earliest Teddy Bears had humps on their backs, elongated muzzles, and jointed limbs. The fabric used was usually mohair; the eyes were either glass with pin backs or black shoe buttons. The stuffing was generally excelsior. Kapok (for softer bears) and wood-wool (for firmer bears) also were used as stuffing materials.

Quality older bears often had elongated limbs, sometimes with curved arms, oversize feet, and felt paws. Noses and mouths were black and embroidered onto fabric.

The earliest Teddy Bears are believed to have been made by the original Ideal Toy Corporation in America and a German company, Margarete Steiff, GmbH. Bears made in the early 1900s by other companies can be difficult to identify because they had a strong similarity in appearance and because most tags or labels were lost through childhood play.

Teddy Bears are rapidly increasing as collectibles and their prices are increasing proportionately. As in other fields, desirability should depend upon appeal, quality, uniqueness, and condition. One modern bear already has been firmly accepted as a valuable collectible among its antique counterparts: the Steiff Teddy put out in 1980 for the company's 100th anniversary. This is a reproduction of that company's first Teddy and has a special box, signed certificate, and numbered ear tag; 11,000 of these were sold worldwide.

References: Peggy and Alan Bialosky, *The Teddy Bear Catalog*, Workman Publishing, 1984, revised edition; Shirley Conway and Jean Wilson, *Steiff Teddy Bears, Dolls, and Toys With Prices*, Wallace-Homestead, 1984; Margaret Fox Mandel, *Teddy Bears And Steiff Animals*, Collector Books, 1984; Margaret Fox Mandel, *Teddy Bears, Annalee Animals & Steiff Animals, Third Series*, Collector Books, 1990; Helen Sieverling (comp.) and Albert C. Revi (ed.), *The Teddy Bear And Friends Price Guide*, Hobby House Press, Inc., 1983.

Periodical: *The Teddy Bear And Friends*, Hobby House Press, Inc., 900 Frederick Street, Cumberland, MD 21502.

Collector's Clubs: Good Bears Of The World, P. O. Box 8236, Honolulu, HI 96815; Teddy Bear Collectors Club, P. O. Box 601, Harbor City, CA 90710.

Additional Listing: See Steiff.

BEARS

4½ d, 14" h, Knickerbocker, brown plush, jointed at hips and shoulders, head turns, c1930	125.00
7", gold mohair, squeaker, hump, shoe button eyes, jointed at hips and shoulders, swivel head, long upturned nose, elongated torso, thin limbs, black sewn nose and mouth, straw stuffed	85.00
8", mohair, squeaker, glass eyes, hump, jointed at hips and shoulders, swivel head with long nose, felt paws, brown sewn nose	110.00
12", mohair, squeaker, shoe button eyes, humps, jointed at hips and shoulders, swivel head, felt paw, straw stuffed, Steiff, early 1900s . . .	165.00

Ideal, brown mohair, felt pads, c1920, 24″ h, $325.00.

13″, dark brown plush, jointed at hips and shoulders, long nose, high set ears, felt paws, black sewn nose and mouth, solidly stuffed	25.00
14″ l, articulated limbs and head, yellow haircloth, recovered paw pads, replaced button eyes, embroidered features, repairs	75.00
17″, brown plush, cream paws, squeaker in tail, plastic eyes, molded nose and mouth, soft stuffed, label "Ideal"	40.00
20″, light mohair, squeaker, glass eyes, jointed at hips and shoulders, swivel head, felt paws, brown sewn nose and mouth, straw stuffed, Steiff, 1920s	150.00
21″, gold mohair, glass stick pin eyes, pear shape torso, jointed at hips and shoulders, swivel head, felt paws, brown sewn nose and mouth, straw stuffed, 1930s	100.00

BEAR RELATED ITEMS

Jack–in–the–Box, 8″, tin, teddy bear with parasol, wood handle, plays music, bear bobs up and down	150.00
Paper Doll, 10½″, cardboard tab for stand–up, four color outfits and hats, orig printed envelope, c1910	350.00
Perfume Bottle, 3¾″, mohair, black button eyes, jointed at hips and shoulders, head removes to show glass bottle	65.00
Spoon, sterling silver, sculptured three dimensional teddy bear on handle, "Teddy Bear" emb down handle . . .	80.00

TELEPHONES

History: The deregulation of the nation's telephone industry and increasing interest in antique telephones has led to increasing values for old telephones and equipment.

Lovers' telegraphs and other crude sound operated and unpatented telephones existed prior to Alexander Graham Bell's 1876 patent. However, it is generally accepted that Bell invented the telephone powered by electricity.

The most valuable antique telephones come from the pre-1895 period and must be marked, dated, or easily documented. Instruments also must be unaltered and have all major original parts. Telephones marked Charles Williams, Jr., a Boston manufacturer whose factory was the "birthplace" of the infant Bell Telephone Company, are among the most valued.

Post 1895 telephones have value if modified or converted to be compatible with today's modern phone network. Conversions should be done by an expert who will supply additional parts without removing any of the major components to accomplish conversion.

Refinishing also requires expert skills. Do not remove original circuitry. Restoring nickel and black baked enamel finishes is most desirous. Buffing original parts to expose the brass beneath will make it difficult to distinguish those parts from the many dated and old fashioned marked, solid brass fake parts and whole telephones which have been flooding the market for a decade. No mass produced telephone made in the United States prior to 1950 was offered with a shiny brass finish!

References: R.H. Knappen, *History And Identification Of Old Telephones,* 2 volumes, published by author, 1978; R.H. Knappen, *Old Telephones Price Guide And Picture-Index To History Of Old Telephones,* published by author, 1981.

Collectors' Clubs: Antique Telephone Collectors Association, Box 94, Abilene, KS 67410; Telephone Collectors International, P.O. Box 700165, San Antonio, TX 78270.

Advisor: Dan Golden.

Automatic, Dialing Telephones	
Couch, S. H., Autophone	250.00
Globe Automatic, wall model	950.00
Lorimer Automatic, all models	1,500.00
Monson Automatic, wall model	1,200.00
National Automatic, wall model	1,500.00
Ness Automatic, wall model	700.00
Select-O-Phone	200.00
Strowger Patent	
Automatic Electric, candlestick model	1,200.00
Pre-1898 models	2,500.00
Wall Model, large	1,500.00
Wall Model, small	650.00
Double Box Telephones	
48″ l, tandem, any manufacturer . . .	550.00

Western Electric, candlestick, marked "Pat. in USA, Aug 04, Jan 15, Chicago, USA," $90.00.

49 to 60″ l, tandem two boxes	**750.00**
60 to 70″ l, tandem two boxes	**1,200.00**
71″ and longer	**1,500.00**
Oak, plain, Stromberg-Carlson type, c1899	**350.00**
Unusual in any way, any manufacturer	**450.00**

Fiddleback Telephones
Gillian, American Bell, Blake or Charles Williams transmitter	**1,000.00**
Vought Berger, Kellogg, Western Electric, Stromberg Carlson, Dean, Diamond, etc	**275.00**

Pay Phones
Common 1950s style	**165.00**
Gray Pay Station	
Desk Model, wood, slots for coins up to dollar, marked	**3,000.00**
Wall Phone, wood	**2,500.00**
Wall Phone, 72″	**3,000.00**
1920s style (Known as Laurel & Hardy style)	**400.00**
Pay Box, cast iron, small, c1910 . . .	**150.00**

Single Box Wall Telephones, wood
Picture Frame Front
Cathedral Top, lightning arrestors at top	**300–400.00**
1910–15	**225.00**
Plain Front, 1915–20	**200.00**
Unusual style	**450–600.00**

Stands
Gossip Benches, approx	**70.00**
Ornate, carvings	**600.00**
Plain, 1920s style	**150.00**

Switchboards
Hotel Annunciators	**50–400.00**
Mansion Annunciators, depending on size and ornateness	**75–450.00**
Pre-1894, wall mount, marked American Bell-Blake, Gillian, Edison, National Bell, or Charles Williams . .	**2,000.00**
Pre-1910, wall mount	**500.00**
Pre-1935	
Light Bulbs	**250.00**
Transmitter broom	**400.00**
1935 to present	**Surplus Value**

Telephone Booths
1890s, leaded glass	**2,000–3,500.00**
1910 to 1912, single door	**2,000.00**
1914 to 1940, folding door	
Oak	**1,200.00**
Walnut	**1,100.00**

Triple Box
American Bell, Edison, Blake, Berliner on transmitter	**1,700.00**
American Electric, Kokomo	**1,200.00**
Bell Telephone	**1,200.00**
Chicago	**950.00**
Elliott	**1,200.00**
Gilliand	**2,000.00**
Keystone	**900.00**
Mianus	**900.00**
Molecular	**1,400.00**

Note: If any of these sets are missing the 7″ long exposed terminal receiver, subtract $150.00.

Upright Desk Stands (Candlestick Phones)
Hour Glass or Potbelly shape	**750.00**
Oil Can shape	**500.00**
Straight Pipe, regular style	
Dial type	**185.00**
No dial	**95.00**
With magneto box	**160.00**

Notes: Extremely unusual candlestick phones made of wood or in an outrageous style may be worth in excess of $1,000.00. All phones mass produced from the WWI to 1950 were made in black. The Western Electric model is now being reproduced in solid shiny brass.

TEPLITZ CHINA

History: Around 1900 twenty-six ceramic manufacturers were located in Teplitz, a town in the Bohemian province of Czechoslovakia. Other potteries were located in the nearby town of Turn. Wares from these factories were molded, cast, and hand decorated. Most are in the Art Nouveau and Art Deco styles. Most pieces do not carry a specific manufacturer's mark. They are simply marked "Teplitz," "Turn-Teplitz," and "Turn."

Reference: Susan and Al Bagdade, *Warman's English & Continental Pottery & Porcelain, 1st Edition,* Warman Publishing Co., Inc., 1987.

Basket, Arab motif **60.00**
Bowl
  3", enameled boy and dog, gray ground, marked "Stellmacher" . . . **75.00**
  6¾", ecru, enameled flowers, c1912 **175.00**
Box, cov, 6 x 7¾ x 5½", turtle shape, children on cov, green, gray, and natural colors, satin finish, marked "Ernst Wahliss Turn Vienna," c1918 . . . . . **375.00**
Candlestick, 5¼", figural, woman in flowing gown, c1905 . . . . **135.00**
Ewer
  6½", hp, pink and gold flowers, light green ground, light pink neck, gold twig handle **85.00**
  9½", cream, red roses, gold trim, marked "Royal Teplitz" **60.00**
  9¾" h, c1900, earthenware, gold paint, faint irid, free form dec of squares and flowing lines, red painted berries, curving handle, stamped "Turn–Teplitz," c1900 . . **300.00**
Figure
  12½", young girl, peasant clothes, basket resting on tree stump **350.00**
  15", man and woman, court clothes, multicolored, pr **250.00**
Jug, 8", classical man, smoking pipe, bronze ground, marked "Stellmacher, Teplitz" **175.00**
Pitcher, 9½", lily pad dec, green and pink, c1895 . . . . **185.00**
Tobacco Jar, 4 x 8", Boxer dog dec . . **400.00**
Vase
  5", bud, relief rooster head in medallion, multicolored geometric dec . . **90.00**
  5½", reticulated top, two handles, portrait of girl **135.00**

Vase, two handles, brown ground, gold highlights, marked "Stellmacher, Teplitz, Austria," 7½" h, $150.00.

  7" h, four handles, pierced rim panels of poppies, drip enamel cobalt blue and green dec, gold trim **250.00**
  16" h, 5" d base, turned down pierced flared lip flows into handle on shoulder, hp florals, heavy gold panel, cream ground, marked "Teplitz Amphora" **475.00**
Window Box, 12 × 3 × 4", boat shape, rose dec, spider web ground, orig liner **125.00**

TERRA COTTA WARE

History: Terra cotta is ware made of a hard, semi-fired ceramic clay. The color of the pottery ranges from a light orange-brown to a deep brownish red. It is usually unglazed, but some pieces can be found partially glazed or decorated with slip designs, incised, or carved. Examples include utilitarian objects as well as statuettes and large architectural pieces. Fine early Chinese terra cotta pieces recently have brought substantial prices.

Wall Plaque, marked "C. Conrad, Charlottenstutte, Salzburg," 8½" h, $25.00.

Bust, 24½" h, French Aristocrat, draped shoulders revealing lacy cravat falling from silk neckerchief, liver veined marble socle, patinated **3,575.00**
Figure
  19¾", Hercules, seated, folding fragments of serpents, stepped shaped plinth, inscribed "R. J. Auguste F. 1744," remains of paper label and wax seal, some restoration **20,000.00**
  29" h, nude Omphale, hands raised above her head holding Hercules' lion pelt, Hercules crouches on ground behind her, dark brown patination, oval base inscribed "A Carrier–Belleuse" **6,000.00**
Jug, 7½" h, marked "Cambridge Ale" . **150.00**

Pipe Holder, 5 x 9", Chinese boy, black
glaze **80.00**
Plaque, 12 x 22", relief neoclassical fig-
ures **35.00**
Tobacco Jar, 11", figural, Bismark, sit-
ting in easy chair **250.00**
Vase, 6" h, 4½" d, raised daisy dec,
green glazed int. **35.00**
Wall Plaque, 8½", sgd "C Conrad, Salz-
burg" **25.00**

TEXTILES

History: Textiles are cloth or fabric items, especially anything woven or knitted. Those that survive usually represent the best since these were
the objects that were used carefully and stored by
the housewife.

Textiles are collected for many reasons—to
study fabrics, understand the elegance of an historical period, and for decorative and modern use.
The renewed interest in clothing has sparked a
revived interest in textiles of all forms.

References: William C. Ketchum, Jr., *The Knopf
Collectors' Guides to American Antiques, Quilts,*
Alfred A. Knopf, Inc., 1982; Betty Ring, *Needlework: An Historical Survey,* Main Street Press,
1984, revised edition; Helene Von Rosenstiel,
*American Rugs And Carpets: From The Seven-
teenth Century To Modern Times,* William Morrow
And Company, 1978; Carleton L. Safford and Robert Bishop, *America's Quilts And Coverlets,* Bonanza Books, 1985.

Collectors' Club: Costume Society of America,
P.O. Box 761, Elizabethtown, NJ 07726.

Additional Listings: See Clothing, Linens,
Quilts, and Samplers.

Blanket
Homespun, wool, natural white and
pink, yellow and brown pinstripes,
hand sewn hems, 56 x 78" **155.00**
Wool, embroidered, attributed to
Chester County, PA, panels of linen
homespun, central floral circle enclosing small bird, borders with random design of birds, hearts, leaves,
pineapples, flowerheads, candlestand with vase of flowers, houses,
inscribed "Remember Me, Forget
Me Not, S. R., Sarah, 1852," 100 x
84" **725.00**
Bolster Cover, trapunto, basket of flow-
ers with vintage and floral designs,
finely quilted ground, lace trim, worn
ball fringe on three sides, stains,
wear, and small holes, 23 x 42" . . . **200.00**
Chair Seat Cover, needlepoint, English,
19th C, trapezoidal shape, bright
colors, vignettes of shepherds and
shepherdesses, travelers, and farmers, petit and gros point, red, rust,
gold, lavender, and brown, teal
ground, set of nine **3,000.00**
Coverlet
Bride's, trapunto, all white, cotton
American, early 19th C, field with
luxuriant pendant blossoms and
meandering vines, oval reserve
of urn with climbing floral vines,
heightened with seed stitching,
white cotton fringe, 88 x 90" . . . **2,450.00**
Baltimore, early 19th C, center area
with elegant urn mounted on
pedestal, topped with pineapple,
feathered tassels pendant from
floral chains, borders with undulating grapevines, daisy sprigs,
and clover leaves, 100 x 104" . **1,200.00**
Jacquard
One piece, double weave, Centennial design, Capitol building, floral border with birds, light green,
lavender, dark brown, and natural, minor overall and edge wear,
bottom fringe loose, 75 x 78" . . **175.00**
One piece, double weave, central
floral urn flanked by two pheasants, floral borders, natural
white, tomato red, olive, and
gray–green, 86 x 90", minor wear **250.00**
One piece, single weave, small
center floral medallions, border
of two rows of stars and meandering foliage vine, two shades
of blue, red, and narrow green
stripe, corners sgd "Rebecca
Funk 1896," 76 x 88", some wear
and loss to fringe **200.00**
Two piece, double weave, blue and
white, eagle corners, dated
1848, 80 x 88" **700.00**
Two piece, double weave, blue and
white snowflake and circle design, sewn on fringe, minor age
stains, 78 x 86" **350.00**
Two piece, single weave, compotes
of flowers and floral border with
corners sgd "Susanna Zech,"
red, blue, green, and natural, minor age stains, bit of edge wear,
80 x 90" **375.00**
Two piece, single weave, large
center floral medallions, meandering feather borders, abstract
tulips in corners, Magdalene Har-
ham 1867, blue and white, 72 x
90" **300.00**
Two piece, single weave, medal-
lions, birds and floral border, red,
olive green, and natural, corners
sgd "Jacob Stephen Springvil,

Seneca County, Ohio, 1853," 78 x 88" **500.00**

Overshot, two piece, four block and optical plaid design, dark blue and white, Shelburne Falls, MA, early 19th C, 71 x 86" **650.00**

Dresser Scarf, drawn work border of ducks, eight pointed star in corners, 17 x 33" **40.00**

Handkerchief, homespun cotton, tricorner, muted plaid design, c1830, 24 x 35" **40.00**

Mattress Cover, blue and white homespun, one seam, white homespun backing, 60 x 104", very minor wear and age stains **115.00**

Rug
Hooked
11 x 39", yarn, pictorial, scene of red barn, purple house, green tree, pond in foreground with ducks and chicks, birds in flight in distance, PA, early 20th C .. **275.00**

24 x 46", yarn, sheared, all-over triangular motifs, shades of gray, blue, red, black, and purple, American, late 19th C **285.00**

26 x 47½", yarn, eight point stars in green, orange and blue, green trellis border with orange intersection points, American, c1900 **250.00**

31 x 86", yarn, fiery sunburst design, minor edge wear **200.00**

34 x 56", rag, black dog, beige and gray ground, tan grid and light blue dots **750.00**

Penny, felt, overlapping tan and brown petals, embroidered blue and red edges, center with applied oval brown panel embroidered with vase filled with three red and green floral sprigs, American, early 20th C, 28 x 34½" **475.00**

Rag
Braided, 52 x 78", alternating gray and blue squares, border of red and black squares **85.00**

Woven, 65 x 33", pink, blue, and green squares, American **85.00**

Sheet, homespun linen, two piece, hand hemmed, Ephrata, PA, 76 x 100" .. **45.00**

Show Towel
Homespun, cross stitch and cut work, tied fringe, gray and several shades of brown embroidery floss, 10 x 10" plus fringe, framed, 12¾ x 16¾" **475.00**

Homespun, linen and cotton cut work, floral embroidery with "C. L.," minor stains, 13½ x 51" **100.00**

Linen, embroidered in pink threads with numerous stars, flowerheads, birds, reindeer, dogs, potted flowering shrubs, zig-zag crochet panel with fringe below, sgd "Anna Marie Nies, 1816," 15 x 60" **350.00**

Tablecloth, linen, cutwork and filet lace inserts, twelve matching napkins, tablecloth 76 x 116" **310.00**

Towel, homespun linen, natural color, natural and white embroidery, 11½ x 32" **20.00**

Tapestry, Brussels, second half 17th C, silk, wool, and silver thread, depicting departure of Meleager for the Hunt of the Calydonian Boar, central field filled with equestrians, attendants and hunting dogs, foliate border woven with flower filled urns, fruits, arrowfilled quivers, and masks in rust, burgundy, gold, green, olive, ivory, umber, blue, and pink, 16'3" × 11'10" . **21,000.00**

THREADED GLASS

History: Threaded glass is glass decorated with applied threads of glass. Before the English invention of a glass threading machine in 1876, threads were applied by hand. After this invention, threaded glass was produced in quantity by practically every major glass factory.

Threaded glass was revived by the art glass manufacturers, such as Durand and Steuben, and continues to be made today.

Bowl, 16", clear, topaz threaded edge, controlled air bubbles, Steuben **125.00**

Candlestick, 9⅞" clear, cut, flared base, bell nozzle with frosted floral and beaded dec, amethyst rim and threading in stem **175.00**

Candy Jar, green, Steuben **80.00**

Finger Bowl, matching underplate, yellow green opal, pr **75.00**

Epergne, four purple lilies, white trim . **375.00**

Goblet, pink, threaded bowl, clear base and stem, Steuben **80.00**

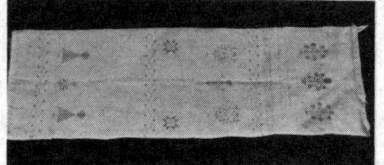

Show Towel, rose color, 16½ x 50½", $185.00.

Compote, threaded clear top, light green threads, controlled bubbles dec, unsigned, 8⅛″ d, 7″ h, $130.00.

Lemonade Mug, 5⅜″, clear glass, cranberry threading, Sandwich	**125.00**
Mayonnaise, underplate, cranberry, ground pontil	**70.00**
Perfume Bottle, 5½″, clear, pink threading	**175.00**
Pitcher, 6″, clear, red and clear applied threading over entire body and neck, applied clear ruffles around base of neck, applied clear solid handle, polished pontil, attributed to Sandwich	**150.00**
Rose Bowl, 5 x 6″, clear, pink threading	**48.00**

Vase
7″, peacock blue, blue threading and
white hearts, sgd "Quezal" **625.00**
8″, petal top, cranberry, white threading, sgd "Stevens and Williams" .   **130.00**

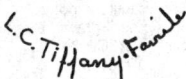

TIFFANY

History: Louis Comfort Tiffany (1849–1934) established a glass house in 1878 primarily to make stained glass windows. There he developed a unique type of colored iridescent glass called Favrile. His Favrile glass differed from other art glass in manufacture as it was a composition of colored glass worked together while hot. The essential characteristic is that ornamentation is found within the glass. Favrile was never further decorated. Different effects were achieved by varying the amount and position of colors which project movement in form and shape.

In 1890, in order to utilize surplus materials at the plant, Tiffany began to design and produce "small glass" such as iridescent glass lamp shades, vases, and stemware and tableware in the Art Nouveau manner.

Commercial production began in 1896. Most Tiffany wares are signed with the name L. C. Tiffany or the initials L.C.T. Some pieces also carry the word "Favrile" as well as a number. A number of other marks can be found, e.g., Tiffany Studios and Louis C. Tiffany Furnaces.

Louis Tiffany and the artists in his studio also are well known for the fine work in other areas—bronzes, pottery, jewelry, silver and enamels.

References: Victor Arwas, *Glass, Art Nouveau and Art Deco,* Rizzoli International Publications, Inc., 1977; Vivienne Couldrey, *Tiffany: The Art of Louis Comfort,* Wellfleet Press, 1989; *The Art Work of Louis C. Tiffany,* Apollo Books, 1987; Robert Koch, *Louis C. Tiffany, Rebel In Glass,* Crown Publishers, Inc., 1966; John A. Shuman III, *The Collector's Encyclopedia of American Art Glass,* Collector Books, 1988.

Note: All glass is of the Favrile type unless otherwise noted.

Stirrup Cup, Art Nouveau, three handles, etched copper, bronze patina, sterling silver insert with vermeil finish, marginal top rim dec in silver, marked "Tiffany & Co/Makers 4578/ Sterling Silver/925/1000/T/And/Other Metals," 2 pint, 5⅜″ h, $825.00.

BRONZE

Ashtray, 7″ d, circular, cast low relief, graduated band of rect border, three curving cigarette rests, imp "Tiffany Studios/New York/186," c1900	**200.00**
Candlesticks, pr, 17¾″ h, Queen Anne's Lace pattern, spherical green Favrile glass candle holder, reticulated bronze mount, slender stem, circular base cast with floral sprigs, stamped "Tiffany Studios New York 30055" . .	**2,600.00**
Desk Clock, 3¾″ w, Adam pattern, gilt bronze, circular gilt dial, black hands and Arabic numerals, hexagonal case, cast low relief, printed on face	

"Tiffany Studios/New York," imp mark, c1920 .... **250.00**

Desk Set

Six Pcs

Chinese pattern, 12" l pen tray, rocker blotter, double inkwell, desk calendar, magnifying glass, rect pen holder, intaglio pseudo–Chinese linear devices, each pc numbered and imp "Tiffany Studios," c1900–28 .... **1,100.00**

Pine Needle pattern, 10" l paper rack, 7¾" l rect box, sq inkwell, rect perpetual desk calendar, and pen, polished gilt bronze over opaque amber and white marbleized favrile glass, each pc imp "Tiffany Studios/New York" and numbered **1,325.00**

Ten pcs, Zodiac pattern, 19¼" l blotter ends, utility box, perpetual calendar, pen tray, large paper rack, ink stand, pen brush holder, memoranda pad, paper knife, low relief casting of zodiac signs and interlacing strapwork, green patina, each pc numbered and imp "Tiffany Studios/New York," c1900–28 **1,540.00**

GLASS

Bowl

7½" d, 3⅝" h, brilliant allover blue irid **750.00**

8" d, ribbed, scalloped rim, gold irid, stems and leaves etched int., inscribed "L. C. Tiffany Favrile" ... **1,200.00**

Candlesticks, pr, 4" h, urn form nozzle, downward curving drip pan, spherical standard, quilted circular foot, inscribed "L. C. Tiffany–Favrile 1846," orig paper label **1,800.00**

Candy Dish, 4" h, translucent foot and stem, shallow dish, widely flaring scalloped rim, white linear dec, crackled blue irid, inscribed "L. C. T. Favrile 1924" **950.00**

Centerpiece, 12¼" d, widely flaring circular rim, gently ribbed, raised leaves, allover crackled gold and mirror irid, inscribed "1925 L. C. Tiffany–Favrile," **1,155.00**

Compote, 4½" h, slender translucent stem and foot, crackled lemon yellow irid, white petal dec, numbered and inscribed "L. C. T. Favrile" **400.00**

Cordial, conical, etched frieze of grape clusters, vines, and leaves, slender stem, gold irid, inscribed "L. C. T.," set of 7 .... **1,800.00**

Decanter Set, Moravignian pattern, 9" h peacock irid stoppered double gourd decanter, applied lily pads and tendrils dec, eleven matching gold irid globular cordials, each pc inscribed "L. C. T." **2,000.00**

Juice Glass, applied lily pad and trailing stems, inscribed "L. C. T.," set of 11 **2,400.00**

Perfume Bottle, 4¼" h, globular, short cylindrical neck, everted lip, ball shaped stopper, irid green trailing vine and ivy leaves dec, irid amber ground, shaded with pink, numbered, inscribed "L. C. Tiffany, Favrile," c1916 .... **1,000.00**

Tile, 6" h, turtle back, rect form, rounded corners, green, molded undulating surface, shaded amber, blue, and violet irid dec **250.00**

Vase

3¾" h, irregular shaped oviform, pinched sides, four large and four small alternating dimples, quatrefoil mouth, amber irid, shaded pink highlights, inscribed "L. C. Tiffany, Favrile/142D," c1909 .... **550.00**

4" h

Bud, irregular shaped pinched ribbed body, scalloped rim, blue irid, numbered and inscribed "L. C. Tiffany–Favrile," orig paper label **1,200.00**

Waisted cylindrical, bright amber irid Favrile, intaglio cut with fruiting grape vine, base etched "L. C. Tiffany–Favrile" **500.00**

5¼" h, candlestick, swirl ribbed shaft, spreading circular base, amber dec, pink shaded amber irid, incised "L. C. T." **450.00**

5⅝" h, Tel El Amarna, bulbous, circular foot, circular neck, deep red, crackled irid collar, irid blue and green drawn threading, inscribed "4516C L. C. Tiffany–Favrile," c1912 .... **15,000.00**

6¼" h, Lava, heavy walls, irreg shaped circular section, amber irid, crackled midnight blue irid, thick gold irid globules dec, inscribed "L. C. Tiffany–Favrile Inc. Exhibition Piece 9333M," c1918 .... **12,000.00**

7⅛" h, flattened oviform, slender neck, eight applied spouts, brilliant gold irid, inscribed "2605D L. C. Tiffany Favrile," c1909 .... **1,800.00**

8¾" h, paperweight, baluster, translucent silver irid body, stems, free form leaves and tiny white millefiore dec, inscribed "L. C. T. R2131," c1902 .... **4,000.00**

14¼" h, slender baluster, internally dec with tall shaded green lily leaves, crimson flowerheads with green centers, clear opal ground,

sgd "L. C. Tiffany, Inc., Favrile/
6401N," c1919 . . . . **11,000.00**

LAMPS

Chandelier, 22" d, domed leaded glass
shade, geometric mottled green glass
squares, circular frieze of irid glass
spheres, orig ceiling cap and light
cluster, stamped "Tiffany Studios
New York" **9,500.00**
Desk, 14½", turtle back shade, peacock
surface irid, white opaque int., rotating bronze mount cast with petals, circular frieze of irid glass spheres,
stamped "Tiffany Studios New York" **7,000.00**
Table
22" h, 16" d rounded conical shade,
four horizontal bands of large
shaped rect tiles, small diamond
tiles, narrow shaped rect border,
light lime green and amber, edge
imp "Tiffany Studios/New York," gilt
bronze finial, gilt bronze slender
hexagonal stem, domed gently
dished base, imp "Tiffany Studios/
New York/534" **7,800.00**
24¼" h, dome shade, wide medial
band, meandering lemon yellow
and green swirled vine leaves, mottled green ground, wide borders of
rect tiles, imp "Tiffany Studios/New
York," gilt bronze baluster form
base, spreading circular foot, lon-
gitudinal graining, etched finish,
brown patinated bronze finial, imp
mark **8,875.00**

SILVER

Cake Basket, 19 oz, marked "Tiffany &
Co" **700.00**
Flatware Service
English King pattern, 83 pcs, 177 oz **4,000.00**
Flemish pattern, 213 pcs, 362 oz . . **9,250.00**
Gravy Boat and Underplate, 21 oz,
c1873–91 . . . . **700.00**
Relish Tray, 9 oz, marked "Tiffany &
Co" **275.00**
Vegetable Dish, cov, 15 oz, marked "Tif-
fany & Co" **425.00**

TIFFIN GLASS

History: A. J. Beatty & Sons built a glass manufacturing plant in Tiffin, Ohio, in 1888. On January
1, 1892, the firm joined the U. S. Glass Co. and
was known as factory "R". Quality and production
at this factory were very high and resulted in fine
depression era glass.

Beginning in 1916 wares were marked with a
paper label. From 1923 to 1936, Tiffin produced a
line of black glassware, called Black Satin. The
company discontinued operation in 1980.

References: Fred Bickenheuser, *Tiffin Glassmasters, Book I*, Glassmasters Publications, 1979;
Tiffin Glassmasters, Book II, Glassmasters Publications, 1981; Fred W. Bickenheuser, *Tiffin Glassmasters, Book III*, Glassmasters Publications,
1985.

Collectors' Club: Tiffin Glass Collectors Club,
P.O. Box 554, Tiffin, OH 44883.

**Vase, bulbous, frosted, light blue, pop-
pies and bird motif, 8" d, 8" h, $75.00.**

Ashtray, 6", Carnegie National Bank, 1902–1928	**30.00**
Basket, Black Satin	**40.00**
Cake Plate, Shaggy Rose	**15.00**
Candy Jar, cov, vaseline, frosted stripes	**40.00**
Champagne	
Classic Shawl Dancer, crystal, puffed stem	**25.00**
Flanders, topaz	**25.00**
Persian Pheasant	**20.00**
Claret, Persian Pheasant	**30.00**
Cocktail	
June Night	**25.00**
Persian Pheasant	**20.00**
Console Bowl, Amberina	**70.00**
Creamer and Sugar, Flanders, crystal .	**30.00**
Cup and Saucer, Primo, green	**6.00**
Goblet	
Cherokee Rose	**22.00**
Classic Shawl Dancer, crystal, puffed stem	**20.00**
June Night	**22.00**
Persian Pheasant	**24.00**
Iced Tea Tumbler	
Byzantine, crystal, black base	**15.00**
Flanders, topaz, ftd	**22.50**
Jug, Classic Shawl Dancer, crystal . . .	**175.00**
Marmalade Jar, cov, Jungle pattern, green satin, painted parrots dec and floral sprays, handles	**100.00**

Parfait, Persian Pheasant 24.00
Perfume, Black Satin, hp florals, tong
  applicator, 6" h 75.00
Pitcher, La Fleur, topaz 225.00
Plate
  Flanders, crystal, 6", ruffled 6.00
  Othello Ebony, 10¾", dinner 25.00
Tray, Birch Tree, Deerwood pink, center
  handle 45.00
Tumbler, Flanders, topaz, 9 oz, ftd ... 15.00
Vase
  Dahlia, 10½", green satin 35.00
  Heliotrope, 7¼" 30.00
  Poppy, pink 40.00
Whiskey, La Fleur, topaz, ftd 12.50

TILES

History: The use of decorated tiles peaked during the latter part of the 19th century. Over one hundred companies in England alone were producing tiles by 1880. By 1890 companies had opened in Belgium, France, Australia, Germany, and the United States.

Tiles were not limited to adorning fireplaces. Many were installed into furniture, such as wash stands, hall stands, and folding screens. Since tiles were easily cleaned and, hence, hygienic, they readily were used on the floors and walls of entry halls, hospitals, butcher shops, or any place where sanitation was a concern. Many public buildings and subways also employed tiles to add interest and beauty.

Condition is an important fact in determining price. A cracked, badly scuffed and scratched, or heavily chipped tile has very little value. Slight chipping around the outer edges of a tile is, at times, considered acceptable by collectors, especially if these chips can be covered by a frame.

It is not uncommon for the highly glazed surface of some tiles to have become crazed. Crazing is not considered a deterent as long as it does not detract from the overall appearance of the tile.

References: J. & B. Austwick, *The Decorated Tile,* Pitman House Ltd., 1980; Susan and Al Bagdade, *Warman's English & Continental Pottery & Porcelain, 1st Edition,* Warman Publishing Co., Inc., 1987; Julian Barnard, *Victorian Ceramic Tiles,* N. Y. Graphic Society Ltd., 1972; Terence A. Lockett, *Collecting Victorian Tiles,* Antique Collectors Club, 1979; Hans Van Lemmen, *Tiles: A Collectors' Guide,* Seven Hills Books, 1985.

Collectors' Club: Tile & Architectural Ceramics Society, Ironbridge Gorge Museum, Ironbridge, Telford, Shropshire, England TF8 7AW.

American Encaustic Tiling Co, Zanesville, OH
  3" sq, President McKinley, orig label
    with biography, slight glaze crazing **50.00**

Rozenburg Den Haag, windmill scene in blues and greens, orig paper labels, 6" sq, 9½" wood frame, $300.00.

  4¼" sq, white, black design of horseman riding through brush 30.00
  6" sq
    Cherub band, highly emb, brown . 160.00
    Jack and Jill, polychrome 75.00
  6 x 24", set of four tiles in frame,
    flower in pot design, brown 90.00
California Art
  5¾", landscape, tan and green 50.00
  7½ x 11½", peacock and grapes, multicolored 120.00
Cambridge Art Tile, Covington, KY, 6 x 18"
  Goddess and Cherub, amber, pr ... 200.00
  Night and Morning, pr 475.00
J. & J. G. Low, Chelsea, MA
  4¼" sq
    Blue, putti carrying grapes, pr ... 60.00
    Teal Blue, swirled foliate 50.00
    Yellow–green, floral 25.00
  6" d, circular, yellow, minor edge nicks
    and glaze wear 30.00
  6" sq
    Geometric pattern, pale blue 20.00
    Woman wearing hood, brown ... 85.00
  6⅛ x 4½", rect, blue–green, picture
    of woman, titled "Autumn" 75.00
  7⅞ x 5⅜", rect, blue–green, portrait
    of stylish lady, small chip on corner 75.00
Kensington, 6", sq, classic female head,
  brown 40.00
KPM, 5¾ x 3⅜", portrait of monk, titled "Hieronymus of Ferrara sends this image of the prophet to God," small nicks to corners 225.00
Marblehead, 4⅝" sq, ships, blue and white, pr 100.00

Minton China Works
6" sq
   Aesops Fables, Fox and Crow, black and white **60.00**
   Cows crossing stream, brown and cream **75.00**
   Girl feeding pigeons, blue and white **60.00**
6 x 12", Wild Roses, polychrome slip dec **48.00**
8", Rob Roy, Waverly Tales, brown and cream **85.00**
Minton Hollins & Co
6" sq
   Daisies, polychrome **20.00**
   Urn and floral relief, green ground **30.00**
8" sq, Morning, blue and white **100.00**
Mosaic Tile Co, Zanesville, OH
6" sq
   Fortune and the Boy, polychrome . **75.00**
   Leo, Zodiac series, polychrome . . **25.00**
8", Delft windmill, blue and white, framed **45.00**
Pardee, C.
4¼", chick and griffin, blue–green matte **175.00**
4½", white rabbit, light green ground, sgd **100.00**
6" sq, portrait of Grover Cleveland, gray–lavender **120.00**
Paul Revere Pottery
3⅞" sq, green trees and landscape, circular mark, part of orig label . . **150.00**
4⅜" d, circular
   Paul Revere Trademark, blue, green, black, yellow, and brown on white **200.00**
   Swan, yellow, brown, green, and white, slight age crack **125.00**
Providential Tile Works, Trenton, NJ
   Round, stove type, hole in center, flowered **10.00**
   Square, 6", raspberries **20.00**
Rookwood
4½ x 4¼", blue–green, emblem of Packard Motor Co, 1910 . . . . **75.00**
5¾" d, circular, seagulls in flight, two colors, 1943 . . . . **60.00**
Sherwin & Cotton
6" sq, dog head, brown, artist sgd . . **100.00**
6 x 9", Abraham Lincoln, brown . . . **135.00**
6 x 12", Quiltmaker and Ledger, orange, pr **250.00**
Trenton Tile Co, Trenton, NJ
6" sq
   Grant, portrait, yellow–green **110.00**
   Leaf, emb, green **5.00**
U. S. Encaustic Tile Works, Indianapolis, IN
6" sq
   Boy with umbrella, amber **75.00**
   Wreath, flowered, emb, light green **12.00**

6 x 18", panel, Dawn, green, framed **150.00**
Wedgwood, England
6" sq
   Red Riding Hood, black and white **100.00**
   November, boy at seashore, peacock blue **85.00**
8"
   Shakespeare's Mid–Summer Night's Dream, moth **100.00**
   Tally Ho, man riding horse, blue and white **75.00**

TINWARE

History: Beginning in the 1700s many utilitarian household objects were made of tin. Tin is nontoxic, rust resistant, and fairly durable, so it can be used for storing food. It often was plated to iron to provide strength. Because it was cheap, tinware and tin plated wares were in the price range of most people.

An early center of tinware manufacture in the United States was Berlin, Connecticut. Almost every small town and hamlet had its own tinsmith, tinner, or whitesmith. Tinsmiths used patterns from which to make items. They cut out the pieces, hammered and shaped them, and soldered the parts. If a piece was to be used with heat, a copper bottom was added because of the low melting point of tin. The Industrial Revolution brought about machine made, mass produced tinware pieces. The hand made era ended by the late 19th century.

This category is a catchall for tin objects which do not fit into other categories in our book.

Additional Listings: See Advertising, Kitchen Collectibles, Lanterns, Lamps and Lighting, and Tinware: Decorated.

Box, 4¼" h, hanging, semicircular, hinged lid, rounded crest, beaded brass trim **55.00**

Cheese Strainer, ftd, heart shape, 5¾ x 5⅜ x 3⅝", $85.00.

Campaign Torch

22½" h, flared conical font, recessed
burner, turned wood handle **40.00**
46¾" l, halberd shape, wood handle **85.00**
48" l, wood pole **45.00**
54" l, wood pole **55.00**

Candle Mold

Eight tubes, 6" h **225.00**
Six tubes, handle, 10½" h **70.00**
Twenty four tubes, 11" h **160.00**

Centerpiece, 12" d, twelve candle sock-
ets **475.00**

Chamberstick, 7½ x 9¾", oblong shape
pan, replaced brass pushup knob . . **100.00**

Chandelier, 24" h, two tiers, fifteen candle arms, crimped pans **400.00**

Coffeepot, 23" h, oversized **450.00**

Conical Torch, 6" h, spout, handle, and
chain hanger, emb label "P. Wall,
Pittsburgh" **35.00**

Decoy

13¾" l, mallard hen, worn orig paint **350.00**
14" h, folding, shore bird, orig paint
traces, pellet holes **55.00**

Grease Lamp, 1⅝" h, colorful glaze . . **150.00**

Lamp

8" h, acorn font, weighted base, mis-
matched whale oil burner **55.00**
11" h, green paint, reflector, brass
kerosene burner, clear chimney . . **90.00**

Lantern

5½" h, kerosene burner **75.00**
7⅝" h, marked "Dietz Sport," globe
marked "Dietz Scout" **55.00**
10" h, candle type, crown top, ring
handle **185.00**
11" h, star and diamond shape air
holes, clear globe, orig font and
whale oil burner, wire guard, ring
handle **90.00**
12¼" h, clear blown globe, pierced
vent holes, orig glass font and
whale oil burner, brown japanning,
ring handle, marked "Union glass" **350.00**

Match Box, 2½" h, English Post Office
dec, ivory socket **85.00**

Muffin Pan, hearts **35.00**

Sconce, candle

10" h, rect, crimped crest, round
stamped out reflector **200.00**
14" h, pr, crimped circular crests . . . **300.00**

TINWARE: DECORATED

History: Decorating sheet iron, tin, and tin
coated sheet iron sheet dates back to the mid-
18th century. The Welsh called the practice pon-
tipool, the French To'le Peinte. In America the
center for tin decorated ware in the late 1700s was
Berlin, Connecticut.

Several styles of decorating techniques were
used: painting, japanning, and stenciling. Designs
were done by both professionals and itinerants.
English and Oriental motifs strongly influenced
both form and design.

A special type of decoration was the punch work
on unpainted tin practiced by the Pennsylvania
tinsmiths. Forms included coffeepots, spice boxes,
and grease lamps.

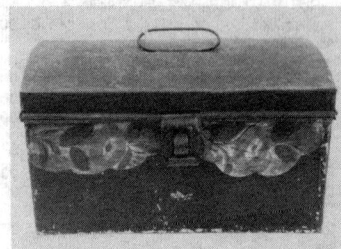

**Document Box, dome lid, black
ground, white band trim, red flowers,
and green leaves, 4 x 7¾ x 4½",
$185.00.**

Box, 9¼" l, dome top, orig dec **160.00**

Bread Box, green paint and dec, Victo-
rian **800.00**

Bread Tray, 12¾" l, oblong, painted fruit
and leaf motif border, brown ground,
19th C **3,025.00**

Candle Sconces, pr, 15½" h, polychrome sailing ship withAmerican flag
scene, shield shape reflectors **100.00**

Chocolate Pot, 10½" h, painted dec, inscribed "Lizzie Lefever 1875" **1,600.00**

Coal Scuttle, painted and dec, Victorian **550.00**

Coffeepot

8½" h, conical body, painted fruit and
floral motifs, brown ground, hinged
lid, strap handle, 19th C **4,125.00**
10½" h, painted bird and leaf and fruit
motifs, brown ground, hinged
domed lid, brass finial, strap han-
dle, 19th C **1,550.00**
11" h, stylized, punched tulip design,
worn black paint **2,600.00**

Deed Box, 9½" l, painted floral and leaf
motifs, black ground, hinged domed
lid, brass bail handle, 19th C **3,850.00**

Foot Warmer

6¼" h, punched heart and diamond
design, replaced wood base **175.00**
7¾ x 8½", punched diamonds and
circles, mortised hardwood case,
turned corner posts, old cherry fin-
ish **145.00**

9½ × 9½", punched dec, mortised cherry frame, turned posts **150.00**

12½ x 15", punched circles and diamonds, mortised cherry frame, turned corner posts **375.00**

Lamp, 19½" h, dished circular base, central cylindrical standard, ring finial, two adjustable scroll form candle arms, dished wax pans and candle holders, flared nozzles, adjustable flared circular shades with reticulated tops and gilt sprig trim, green ground **350.00**

Lantern, 14" h, candle, Revere type, ring handle **75.00**

Sign, rect black reserve, gilt dec, top hat flanked by scrolls, inscription below for Richmond gentlemen's hat store, sgd in small print "L. A. Woodside, Phila," gilt and crimson highlighted floral borders, maple frame, 16½ x 12½" **450.00**

Spice Box, 7" d, six int. canisters and grater, brown japanning with gold striping, stenciled labels **150.00**

Tea Caddy, 4¼" h, orig floral dec, black ground **90.00**

Wall Pocket, 7¾" h, punch hear designs **250.00**

Watering Can, 18½" h, painted morning glories, pomegranates and roses, reddish-brown metallic ground, d-shape handles, 19th C **1,980.00**

TOBACCO CUTTERS

History: Before pre-packaging, tobacco was delivered to merchants in bulk form. Tobacco cutters were used to cut the tobacco into desired sizes.

Counter , wood base, cast iron cutter, 6¼ x 7¼ x 11½", $45.00.

Black Beauty, figural, horse head **300.00**
Brown's Mule, iron, counter top **55.00**
Climax, 17" l **50.00**
Cupples Arrow & Superb **50.00**
Drummond Tobacco Co **65.00**
John Finzer & Brothers, Louisville, KY **45.00**

Griswold Tobacco Cutter, Erie, PA ... **55.00**
E C Simmons Keen Kutter **225.00**
Sprague Warner & Co **75.00**
Unmarked, graduated 6¼ to 7¼" w, 10½" l, cast iron cutter, wood base . **45.00**

TOBACCO JARS

History: A tobacco jar is a container for storing tobacco. Tobacco humidors were made of various materials and in many shapes, including figurals. The earliest jars date to the early 17th century. However, most examples in today's market were made in the late 19th or early 20th centuries.

Reference: Deborah Gage and Madeleine Marsh, *Tobacco Containers & Accessories,* Gage Bluett & Company, 1988.

Owl's Head, dressed in pink bonnet with blue ribbon, multicolored, high glaze, marked "JS" in acorn, 4½" h, $115.00.

Bisque, 4⅝ x 6", figural, monkey's head, light brown, glossy gray cap, eyeglasses, white collar and bowtie, yellow and brown bee finial **175.00**

Brass, 5½", int. tin case, early 19th C . **40.00**

Cream Ware, 9" h, 6" d, plum colored transfers on side, one titled "Success to the British Fleet," striped orange, blue, and yellow molding, domed lid **900.00**

Doulton, galleon pattern, reglued lid .. **60.00**

Jasper Ware, raised white Indian chief on cov, Indian regalia on front, green ground **185.00**

Majolica, figural
American Indian, bust, 5" **135.00**
Bear, smoking pipe, 6" **125.00**

Milk Glass, hp, hunting dogs, green and maroon ground, metal top, Handel Ware **525.00**

Porcelain, figural
Arab Head **100.00**

Humpty Dumpty	**115.00**
Skull, marked "Carlsbad, Austria"	**150.00**
Pottery, 4½ x 5½", Oriental man, black mustache and goatee, hat cov	**120.00**
Wavecrest, 5" sq	**425.00**

TOBY JUGS

History: A toby jug is a drinking vessel usually depicting a full-figured, robust, genial drinking man. They originated in England in the late 18th century. The term "Toby" probably related to the character Uncle Toby from *Tristam Shandy* by Laurence Sterne.

References: Susan and Al Bagdade, *Warman's English & Continental Pottery & Porcelain, 1st Edition,* Warman Publishing Co., Inc., 1987; Vic Schuler, *British Toby Jugs,* Kevin Francis Publishing Ltd. (London), 1986.

Additional Listings: Royal Doulton.

Reproduction Alert: Within the last 100 years or more, tobies have been reproduced copiously by many potteries in the United States and England.

Rockingham Type, 10¾" h, $175.00.

Cream Ware, 10½", man seated on barrel, yellow, black, green and rasberry, orig cracked hat lid, possibly Scottish, 19th C **200.00**
Delft, 11¼", man seated on barrel, green hat, green and black sponged coat, blue and yellow pants, old cork stopper, c19th C **350.00**
Pearl Ware, Yorkshire, 10", satyr handle, small toby jug resting on gentleman's left knee, goblet in right hand, grotesque dwarf standing between knees, underglaze dec of blue jacket,

yellow neckpiece, brown trousers, black shoes, black and white sponged hair, inner rim of hat and base sponged blue, ochre, and rasberry **3,750.00**
Pratt, 10¾", Hearty Good Fellow, blue jacket, yellow-green vest, blue and yellow striped pants, blue and ochre sponged base and handle, stopper missing, slight glaze wear, c1770–80 **1,500.00**
Staffordshire
9", pearl ware, seated figure, sponged blue jacket, ochre buttons, ochre and lavender speckled vest and trousers, brown hair and hat, green glazed base, shallow flake inside hat rim, attributed to Ralph Wood, c1770–80 .... **1,900.00**
9¼", Thin Man, full chair, green, blue, and brown, holding pipe and foaming mug, attributed to Ralph Wood, c1765–75 .... **5,000.00**
11¾", Rodney's Sailor, black hat, green coat, white trousers with blue stripes, imp "65" on base, Ralph Wood, lid missing, c1765–75 .... **5,700.00**
Whieldon, 9½", pearl ware, seated figure, yellow greatcoat, green vest, blue trousers, holding brown jug in left hand, raises foaming glass of ale towards mouth, lid missing, c1770–80 **1,500.00**
Wilkinson, 11¾", Winston Churchill, multicolored, designed by Clarice Cliff, black printed marks, number, and facisimile signature, c1940 .... **765.00**
Yorkshire, 10", seated, holding jug and goblet, blue coat, copper luster on hat, waistcoat, and breeches, c1830 **375.00**

TOOLS

History: Before the advent of assembly line and mass production, practically everything required for living was handmade at home or by a local tradesman or craftsmen. The cooper, the blacksmith, the cabinet maker, and the carpenter all had their special tools.

Early examples of these hand tools are collected for their workmanship, ingenuity, place of manufacture, or design. Modern day craftsman often search out old hand tools for use to authentically recreate the manufacture of an object.

References: Ronald S. Barlow, *The Antique Tool Collector's Guide to Value,* Windmill Publishing Company, 1985, 1987 value update; Kathryn McNerney, *Antique Tools, Our American Heritage,* Collector Books, 1979; R. A. Salaman, *Dictionary of Tools,* Charles Scribner's Sons, 1974.

Collectors' Club: Early American Industries Association, P.O. Box 2128, Empire State Plaza Station, Albany, NY 12220; Mid-West Tool Collectors

Association, 2825 Jackson Street, La Crosse, WI 54601.

Museum: Shelburne Museum, Shelburne, VT.

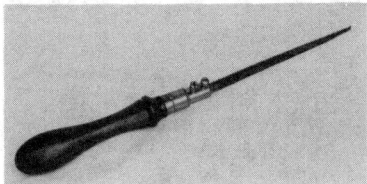

Key Hole Saw, tip tooth, British, 15½″ l, $30.00.

Adze, carpenter	20.00
Anvil, hand forged, 8″	50.00
Auger, 17″ wood cross handle	15.00
Barn Beam Drill	50.00
Beader, hand, Stanley Universal #66, single blade	40.00
Bench Press, 9½ x 6″, Sherman, solid brass, 12 lbs	60.00
Clamp, wood, 13½″ jaws, pr	110.00
Chisel, 22½″ l, blade stamped "E Connor"	45.00
Claw Hammer, Winchester	55.00
Drill, hand, Goodel and Pratt, brass ferrules	24.00
File, 20″, half round	10.00
Hammer, claw, iron, wood handle, c1880	30.00
Hay Rake	
62″ l, wood	190.00
67″ l, wood, branded "M B Young"	200.00
Knife, pruning, hand forged iron blade, wood handle, c1800	30.00
Level, wood and brass, patent Dec 1886, marked "Davis & Cook"	40.00
Mallet, 34″ l, burl, hickory handle	200.00
Mitre Box, laminated maple, birch, and oak, graduated quadrant, Stanley	25.00
Plane	
Chaplin #1210	60.00
Keen Kutter K110	20.00
Stanley, #10½	100.00
Plumb Bob, Bruning	25.00
Router, Stanley #71½″, patent date 1901	35.00
Rule	
K & E, parallel, German silver and ebony	25.00
Lumkin #1085, brass, folding	42.00
Stanley, folding	15.00
Saw	
Band, 76″ h, mortised and pinned wood frame, orig red paint with blue and white striping, blade and blade	

guides, laminated cherry and maple top	300.00
Buck, 30″, wood, worn varnish finial, marked "W T Barnes"	35.00
Keyhole, 9″, well shaped wood handle	25.00
Screwdriver, 9″ blade, flat wood handle, round sides	18.00
Scribe	
7½″ l, hewn wood handle	35.00
21″ l, curly maple, adjustable fence and arm	65.00
Square, cherry, iron, brass bound blade, marked "Set Try"	45.00
Surveyor's Tape, 50 ft, steel and brass, wind handle	25.00
Trammel, 29¾″ l, wrought iron, sawtooth	65.00
Wheel Measure, 14½″ l, wrought iron	40.00
Whetstone, 4″ d, round, fitted case	15.00
Wrench, alligator, hand forged	12.00

TOOTHPICK HOLDERS

History: Toothpick holders, indispensible table accessories of the Victorian era, are small containers used to hold toothpicks.

They were made in a wide range of materials: china (bisque and porcelain), glass (art, blown, cut, opalescent, pattern, etc.), and metals, especially silver plate. Makers include both American and European firms.

Toothpick holders were used as souvenir items by applying decals or transfers. The same blank may contain several different location labels.

References: William Heacock, *Encyclopedia Of Victorian Colored Pattern Glass, Book I, Toothpick Holders From A To Z*, Antique Publications, 1981; William Heacock, *1,000 Toothpick Holders: A Collector's Guide*, Antique Publications, 1977; William Heacock, *Rare & Unlisted Toothpick Holders*, Antique Publications, 1984.

Collectors' Club: National Toothpick Collector's Society, P. O. Box 246, Sawyer, MI 49125.

Additional Listings: See *Warman's Americana & Collectibles* for more examples.

Advisor: Judy Knauer.

China
Bisque, skull, blue anchor shape mark	55.00
Meissen, clown	55.00
Royal Bayreuth, elk	100.00
Royal Doulton, Santa scene, green handles	65.00
Schlegelmilch, R. S. Germany, mother of pearl luster	35.00
Unmarked	
Flower form mold	30.00
Raised beaded dec, Moriage	35.00

Art Glass, Alexandrite, attributed to Thomas Webb, 2½" h, $1,250.00.

Glass
Cut Glass
| Pedestal, chain of hobstars . . . . . | **135.00** |
Star, clear, Federal Glass, c1910–
| 14 . . . . | **45.00** |
Figural
Baby Bootie, amber, c1890–95 . .	**38.00**
Elephant, amber, c1890	**65.00**
Pig, pink	**75.00**
Milk Glass
Alligator, c1885	**50.00**
Parrot and Top Hat, c1895	**28.00**
Rose Urn, dec, two handles, Fos-
toria Glass Co, c1905	**38.00**
Scroll, claw ftd, light pink and blue
dec, c1900	**40.00**
Opalescent, Reverse Swirl, blue,
speckled	**85.00**
Pattern glass
Arched Fleur-de-lis, clear	**30.00**
California, green with gold	**60.00**
Florette, opaque, turquoise	**100.00**
Intaglio Sunflower, clear	**25.00**
Kansas	**45.00**
Michigan, clear, yellow stain	**175.00**
Monkey, clear, 3¾" h	**45.00**
Spearpoint Band, ruby stained	**80.00**
Teardrop and Cracked Ice, c1900–
03	**75.00**
Texas, gold	**27.00**
Wisconsin	**40.00**
Ruby Stained Glass
Button Arches, souvenir Battleview,
NJ	**30.00**
Truncated Cube	**35.00**

TORTOISE SHELL ITEMS

History: For many years amber and mottled colored tortoise shell has been used in the manufacture of small items such as boxes, combs, dresser sets, and trinkets.

Note: Anyone dealing in the sale of tortoise shell objects should be familiar with the Endangered Species Act and Amendment in its entirety. As of November, 1978, antique tortoise shell objects can be legally imported and sold with some restrictions.

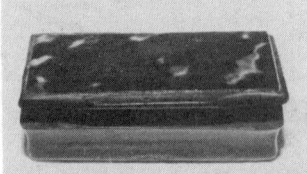

Box, hinged lid, 1½ x 3½", $135.00.

Box
| 1½ x 3½", hinged cov . . . . | **135.00** |
4½ x 8½ x 6", Baroque, inlaid trailing
ivy foliage, domed lid, late 17th C,
| early 18th C . . . . | **500.00** |
| 11 x 7½ x 4", rect, fitted int. . . . . . | **150.00** |
Cigarette Box, SS mounts, hallmarked
| "Birmingham," c1925 . . . . | **275.00** |
Hair Comb, carved crest, five oval
cameo relief medallions with pierced
| borders, 19th C . . . . | **375.00** |
Inkwell, SS mounts, marked "V C Vick-
erey, 179–81–3 Regent St W, Lon-
| don," c1900 . . . . | **275.00** |
Ladle, 10", tortoise shell bowl, agate,
coral, and amber mounted handle,
| 19th C . . . . | **200.00** |
Razor, straight, faux tortoise shell han-
| dle, Landers . . . . | **30.00** |
| Salt and orig spoon, SS rivets . . . . . | **20.00** |
Stickpin, carved fly perched on coral
| branch, gold filled pin . . . . | **75.00** |
Tea Caddy, Regency, first quarter
19th C
5½" h, rect, hinged rect cov with silver
monogrammed plaque, curved reverse breakfront frieze, slightly
| curved sides, ball feet . . . . | **1,980.00** |
6½" w, slightly domed panel, rect
hinged lid, central plaque, two lid-
| ded compartments . . . . | **990.00** |
7¾" l, 5¼" h, rect, hinged stepped
canted top with canted corners,
conforming base, projecting plinth,
| ball feet . . . . | **2,250.00** |

TOYS

History: In America the first cast iron toys began to appear shortly after the Civil War. Leading 19th century manufacturers include Hubley, Dent, Kenton, and Schoenhut. In the first decades of the

20th century, Arcade, Buddy L, Marx, and Tootsie Toy joined the earlier firms. Wooden toys were made by George Brown and other manufacturers who did not sign or label their work.

In Europe, Nürmberg, Germany, was the center for the toy industry from the late 18th through the mid 20th century. Companies such as Lehman and Marklin produced high quality toys.

Several auction houses, e.g., Lloyd Ralston Toys, have specialty auctions consisting entirely of toys.

Every toy is collectible. The key is the condition and working order if mechanical. Examples listed are considered to be in good to very good condition to mint condition unless otherwise specified.

References: Linda Baker, *Modern Toys, American Toys, 1930–1980*, Collector Books, 1985; Robert Carter and Eddy Rubinstein, *Yesterday's Yesteryears: Lesney "Matchbox" Models*, Haynes Publishing Group (London), 1986; Jurgen and Marianne Cieslik, *Lehmann Toys*, New Cavendish Books, 1982; Constance King, *Metal Toys & Automata*, Chartwell Books, 1989; Gordon Gardiner and Alistair Morris, *The Illustrated Encyclopedia of Metal Toys*, Harmony Books, 1984; Lillian Gottschalk, *American Toy Cars & Trucks*, Abbeville Press, 1985; Ernest & Ida Long, *Dictionary of Toys Sold in America*, 2 vols, published by author; David Longest, *Character Toys and Collectibles*, Collector Books, 1984; David Longest, *Character Toys and Collectibles, Second Series*, Collector Books, 1987; David Longest, *Toys: Antique & Collectible*, Collector Books, 1990; Albert W. McCollough, *The Complete Book of Buddy "L" Toys: A Greenberg Guide*, I. Greenberg Publishing Co., 1982; Brian Moran, *Battery Toys*, Schiffer Publishing, 1984; Richard O'Brien, *Collecting Toys: A Collectors Identification and Value Guide, 5th Edition*, Books Americana, 1990; Maxine A. Pinsky, *Greenberg's Guide To Marx Toys, Volume I*, Greenberg Publishing Co., 1988; Martyn L. Schorr, *The Guide To Mechanical Toy Collecting*, Performance Media, 1979; Peter Viemeister, *Micro Cars*, Hamilton's, 1982; Blair Whitton, *Paper Toys of The World*, Hobby House Press, Inc., 1986; James Wieland and Dr. Edward Force, *Tootsie Toys, World's First Die Cast Models*, Motorbooks International, 1980; Blair Whitton, *The Knopf Collector's Guide to American Toys*, Alfred A. Knopf, 1984.

Periodicals: *The Antique Toy World*, P.O. Box 34509, Chicago, IL 60634; *Professor Pug Frog's Newsletter*, 3 Hillside Avenue, Peabody, MA 01960; *Toy Shop*, 700 East State Street, Iola, WI 54990; *Wheel Goods Trader*, P.O. Box 435, Fraser, MI 48026; *YesterDaze Toys*, P.O. Box 57, Otisville, MI 48463.

Collectors' Club: Antique Toy Collectors of America, Two Wall Street, New York, NY 10005.

Museums: American Museum of Automobile Miniatures, Andover, MA; Museum of the City of New York, New York, NY; Smithsonian Institution, Washington, D.C.; Margaret Woodbury Strong Museum, Rochester, NY; Toy Museum of Atlanta, Atlanta, GA.

Additional Listings: Disneyana and Schoenhut. Also see *Warman's Americana & Collectibles* for more examples.

Carette, German, battleship, lithographed tin, red and light green, paint flaked, dented, 9″, $400.00.

Arcade, Freeport, IL, 1893–1946
Bus, Greyhound Lines GMC, cast iron, 1933, 10″ l	125.00
Chester Gump Cart, painted cast iron, 7½″ l	325.00
Coupe, rumble seat, c1920, 5″	150.00
Gas Pump, painted cast iron, mechanical, 6¼″ h	115.00
Ice Truck, red, white rubber tiers, 6¾″ l	100.00
Yellow Cab Taxi, cast iron, Century of Progress, orig black and orange paint, 7″ l	350.00

Auburn Rubber, Auburn, IN, 1913–1968
Bulldozer and Earthmover, 8″ l bulldozer, 8″ l earthmover, orig 18 x 5″ box	40.00
Early American Frontier Set, 44 pcs of Indians, Frontiersmen, wild animals, cabins, and accessories, orig box, 17 x 12″	115.00
Public Service Set, 17 pcs, soft rubber, seven vehicles, ten figures, c1950, orig box	75.00

Bing, German
Airplane and Tower, painted and litho tin, 7½″	250.00
Automobile, litho tin windup, 5″	125.00
Combination Railroad Coach, litho and hp tin	100.00
Postcard Projector, painted tin, 9″ h, smokestack missing	50.00
Yacht, painted tin, canopy, live steam attachment, 16″	1,750.00

Buddy L, American, 1921–Present, painted pressed steel
Aerial Towers Tramway, orig labels rough, incomplete	7,500.00

Airport, orig plane, spring loaded, 12"   **325.00**
Baggage Line, orig labels **1,500.00**
Bus, orig labels **2,000.00**
Camper, MIB **85.00**
Coal Hopper, doors open, coal chutes
  missing, black rubber tires **3,600.00**
Coal Truck, labels and paint restored   **900.00**
Dump Truck, Robotoy, mechanical,
  orig labels, electrical hookup, orig
  box **1,400.00**
Fire Truck
  Aerial **700.00**
  Hook and Ladder, hose reel, orig
    labels **1,300.00**
  Steam Pumper, nickel plated, orig
    labels **850.00**
  Water Tower, nickel plated hose
    tower, incomplete **2,300.00**
Hanger, two BL12 mono–airplanes,
  motors missing, orig labels incom-
  plete **650.00**
Ice Delivery Truck, orig canvas top   **900.00**
International Harvester Truck, red,
  spoked wheels, orig labels **2,500.00**
Overhead Crane **1,900.00**
Texaco Tanker, MIB **95.00**
Wrecker, orig labels, 1 gear broken,
  hook missing **2,000.00**

Chein, J., Harrison, NJ, c1930
  Army Truck, tin, cannon, 8½" **30.00**
  Clown in Barrel, litho tin windup, 7½"   **150.00**
  Mother Goose Tea Set, tin litho, 7 pcs   **35.00**
  Organ, Cathedral Player, litho tin
    windup, multicolored, hand crank .   **70.00**
  Ride–A–Rocket, litho tin windup, 9" h   **135.00**
  Roadster, litho tin windup, c1925, 8½"   **65.00**
  Space Ride, litho tin windup, 9" **225.00**
  Walking Popeye, litho tin windup,
    6" h **150.00**

Dent
  Bus, Public Service, painted cast iron,
    13½" l, 2nd series **375.00**
  Coupe, painted cast iron, 9½" l, 2nd
    series **450.00**
  Zeppelin, painted cast iron, 12½" l,
    2nd series **275.00**

Fisher Price, East Aurora, NY, 1930–
  Present
  Barky Dog, pull toy **25.00**
  Donald Duck Choo Choo, pull toy, 4
    x 8 x 7", c1940 . . . .   **80.00**
  Elsie's Dairy Truck, two milk bottles,
    pull toy **150.00**
  Hot Diggety, windup, Black boy, col-
    orful cloth outfit, painted wooden
    head, cardboard body, black metal
    ski–like feet, feet shuffle back and
    forth, 6" h, c1934, orig box **700.00**
  Peter Bunny Cart, bunny rings bell,
    pull toy **100.00**
  Puffy Train, pull toy, paper on wood,

plastic arms, multicolored, 6" l,
  c1950, orig box **90.00**
Squeaky the Clown, pull toy **60.00**
Woodsy–Wee Circus, nine paper litho
  on wood animals, one clown and
  circus wagon, 1931, orig 16 x 12"
  box, unplayed with condition **600.00**

**Gong Bell Toy Co, Keene, NY, cat and
dog bell toy, $1,250.00.**

Gong Bell Toy
  Black Boy Baiting Alligator, painted
    cast iron, mechanical, 8" l **1,600.00**
  Trix, pull toy, litho paper on wood, me-
    chanical, 16¼" **150.00**
Gunthermann, Martin, German
  Bettle, litho tin windup, 7" l **50.00**
  Clown and Acrobatic Dog, litho and
    hp tin windup, working, clown miss-
    ing one leg **200.00**
  Fiddler, black man playing fiddle, 8½"
    h, repainted **150.00**
  Musicians, litho and painted tin,
    windup, cloth dressed, paper ac-
    cordion, 8½" base **2,000.00**
  Playing Boy, hp tin windup, vibrating
    movement, side to side body action
    swings celluloid ball in circular mo-
    tion, c1910, 7½" **200.00**
Horsman, E. I., Golden ABC Cubes,
  block set litho paper on wood, c1883,
  orig wood framed 14½ x 9½ x 2" box,
  40 pcs **340.00**
Hubley, Lancaster, PA, 1894–1965
  Bell Telephone Khaki Mack Truck,
    orig accessories, 10" l **350.00**
  Circus Chariot, painted cast iron,
    three horses, Kenton clown figure,
    10" l **300.00**
  Crash Car, motorcycle with rider, 9½"
    l, worn paint **425.00**
  Elephant, painted cast iron, howdah   **350.00**
  Life Saver Truck, holds pack in back,
    c1930 . . . .   **80.00**
  Limousine, c1920, 7" **65.00**
  Motorcycle, cast iron, red, policeman,
    black rubber tires, 4" l **80.00**

Royal Circus Bear Cage, 12½" l ... **125.00**

Sedan, painted cast iron, nickel plated grill and bumper, white rubber tires, red hubcaps, 7" l **175.00**

Steam Shovel, Panama, red paint, dual label, 9" l **525.00**

Street Sweeper, cast iron, 8" **675.00**

Ives, Bridgeport, CT

Cannon, painted cast iron, Hotchkiss, firecracker, 9½" l **175.00**

Fire Engine, pumper, painted cast iron, 23" **2,150.00**

General Butler, mechanical, cloth clothing, 9½" h **1,500.00**

Magic Snake Toy, japanned and painted cast iron, 4" h **400.00**

Katz, Red Arrow Airplane, litho tin, copy of Spirit of St. Louis, framed box lid, missing tin tab **250.00**

Kenton, Kenton, OH

Buckboard, horse drawn wagon, painted cast iron, 13" l **125.00**

Cabriolet, painted cast iron, rubber tires under horse, 16" l, 2nd series, orig box **275.00**

Carriage, painted cast iron, silver wheels and shafts, cream body, black trim, orig lady rider, 17" l ... **900.00**

Log Wagon, painted cast iron, 15" l . **375.00**

Overland Cage Wagon, painted cast iron and tin, orig white bear and reins, 14" l **300.00**

Overland Calliope, painted cast iron, iron wheels under horse, 1 wheel and outriders missing, 14" l **400.00**

Sulky, painted cast iron, 7½" l **100.00**

Keystone, painted pressed steel, marked "Packard"

American Railway Express, screen sides, orig labels, rubber tires ... **2,300.00**

Dump Truck, scissors action, coal chute, orig labels, all metal wheels **450.00**

Fire Truck

Aerial Ladder, rubber tires, ladders missing, old repaint **325.00**

Chemical Pump Engine, incomplete **800.00**

Water Tower, rubber tires and hoses **1,200.00**

Koaster Truck, orig labels, rubber tires **1,000.00**

Moving Van, rubber tires, orig labels rough **300.00**

Police Patrol, 28" l **575.00**

Steam Roller, orig string for bell, labels, orig box **1,100.00**

Wrecker, rubber tires, orig labels, mechanical, 1 brace and hook missing **350.00**

Kilgore, roadster, painted and nickel plated cast iron, 6" l **400.00**

Kingsbury, Keene, NH, painted pressed steep, windup

Biplane, white rubber tires, 16" l, 12" wingspan **375.00**

Bus, Greyhound, white rubber tires, 18" l, restored **125.00**

Fire Truck

Aerial Ladder, airflow design, black rubber tires, 24" l **60.00**

Ladder, red and yellow, ladder extends to 37", 18" **100.00**

Pumper, cast iron and wood details, not working, 10" l **100.00**

Sunbeam Racer, yellow, driver, black rubber tires, plastic windshield, rubber bumper, c1930 .... **340.00**

Lehmann, Nürnberg, Germany, 1881–Present

Adam, porter with trunk, litho and painted tin, 1912 .... **950.00**

Anxious Bride, litho tin windup **1,250.00**

Balky Mule, litho tin windup, cloth dressed **160.00**

Daredevil, litho tin windup **450.00**

Going To The Fair, painted and litho tin, momentum **600.00**

Mandarin, painted and litho tin windup, orig braids, 7½" l **1,000.00**

Mars Captive Balloon, 1896 ...... **2,225.00**

Na–Nu, litho tin windup, 7" h **500.00**

Oh My Alabama Coon Jigger, litho tin windup, 4½ x 3 x 2" litho tin base, 10" h **375.00**

Wild West, bucking bronco and rider **375.00**

Linemar

Campus Express, litho tin, multicolored, working crank sound, 4½" l **65.00**

Disneyland Roadster, litho tin friction, 1½" celluloid Nephew Duck driver, plastic windshield, c1950, 4½" ... **160.00**

Dockyard Crane, litho tin windup, 8 x 3" base, c1950 .... **50.00**

Donald Duck In His Convertible, litho tin friction, celluloid Donald at wheel, orig cartoon box, c1950 .. **275.00**

Figaro, litho tin friction, multicolored, 3" l, c1950 .... **90.00**

Goofy, multicolored litho tin windup . **250.00**

Jalopy Car, litho tin, graffiti filled, siren sound, 4½" l **60.00**

Jam Licking Bear, mechanical, plush body, tin base, reaches into litho tin strawberry jam can and then licks paw, c1950, orig box **100.00**

Mickey Mouse Crazy Car, litho tin windup, orig tin ears and arms, not working **150.00**

Sam The City Gardener, litho tin windup, red, white, and brown plastic figure pushes litho tin cart with seven plastic garden tools, red pressed steel base, c1950, orig box **125.00**

Marklin, German
Armored Car, hp tin, clockwork, 14½"
l, c1930 . . . . **975.00**
Ocean Liner, painted tin, red, black,
and white deck, clockwork, marked
on rudder, c1910, 15" l **1,750.00**

Marx, American, 1921–Present
Airplane, WWII, US Army, litho tin
windup, 8" w **60.00**
Dick Tracy Police Car, litho tin, plastic, windup, electric, rubber tires,
10" l **225.00**
G–Man Pursuit Car, litho tin windup,
no key, 14" l **375.00**
Hey–Hey the Chicken Snatcher, black
man, litho tin windup, c1920 . . . . **650.00**
Hopalong Cassidy, rocking horse,
litho tin windup **175.00**
Lazy Daisy Dairy Truck **50.00**
Liberty Bus, litho tin friction, black and
red, green metal wheels, c1930,
5" l **100.00**
Moon Mullins & Kayo Dynamite
Handcar, litho tin windup, not work-
ing **300.00**
Pinocchio, litho tin windup, blinking
eyes, nose glued, 8½" h **200.00**
Police Motorcycle with Sidecar, litho
tin windup, celluloid pieces, 8½" l . **175.00**
Popeye, with parrots, litho tin windup,
8¼" h **200.00**
Racer, litho tin windup, red, yellow,
and black, black tin tires, c1930,
5" l **100.00**
Rocket Racer, litho tin windup, rubber
front bumper **225.00**
Touring Auto, green and yellow tin,
emb side louvers and doors, red tin
tires, grill marked "103," red and
black litho tin uniformed figure, 10"
l, c1920 . . . . **275.00**
Schieble, c1920, car, Hillclimber Roads-
ter Coupe, pressed steel, friction,
black, 17" l **375.00**
Schuco, marked "U.S. Zone Germany,"
c1940
Car
2002, painted tin body, chrome trim **60.00**
3000, cream colored tin, chrome
grill and five gears, 4" l **65.00**
Fex 1111, windup, dark orange tin
body, chrome grill, tin litho name
plate **115.00**
Microracer 1043, windup, gray cast
body, red int., gray rubber tires,
white grill marked "Schuco," orig
box, 4" l **100.00**
Old Timer Ford Coupe, 1917 T, tin
and plastic, windup, 6" l, orig box . **50.00**
Steelcraft
Fire Truck, painted pressed steel,
rubber tires, orig labels

Combination Hook and Ladder and
Hose Reel **900.00**
Mack Chemical Wagon **2,000.00**
**Strauss, Ferdinand, New York City,
20th C**
Leaping Lena Car, litho tin windup,
1920s **275.00**
Scissors Grinder, litho tin windup, MIB **175.00**
Tip–Top Porter, litho tin windup, porter pushing blue and yellow cart, 6"
l, c1930 . . . . **165.00**
Tombo–The Alabama Coon Jigger,
litho tin windup, multicolored, 5 x 3
x 2" base **400.00**
Trikauto–The Circus Wonder, litho tin
windup, bright yellow and red, orig
7½" box with circus motif artwork,
c1920 . . . . **425.00**
Unidentified Maker
American
Tricycle, painted and stenciled
wood, cast iron hardware, 34" l,
c1860 . . . . **1,200.00**
Velocipede, painted and stenciled
wood, cast iron, 40" l, c1870 . . **1,000.00**
German
Balloonist, painted tin, clockwork,
straw basket, 15" h **1,750.00**
Ferris Wheel, painted tin, live
steam attachment, 15" h **1,600.00**
Minstrel Drummer, painted tin
windup, 8½" **700.00**
Pool Player, penny–toy, litho tin
man hits metal cue ball, spring
operated pool stick, c1920, 2½ x
4" **200.00**
Unique Art
Dogpatch Band, litho tin windup . . . **400.00**
GI Joe and K9 Pups, litho tin windup,
9½" h **175.00**
Kiddy Cyclist, litho tin windup **100.00**
Lincoln Tunnel, litho tin windup, 24" **200.00**
Police Motorcycle, litho tin windup,
multicolored, uniformed officer,
8½" l **150.00**
Rodeo Joe, litho tin windup **150.00**
Sky Rangers, litho tin windup, orig
box **250.00**
Wolverine
Jet Roller Coaster, litho tin windup . **85.00**
Luxury Liner, litho tin windup, MIB . . **80.00**
Merry–Go–Round, litho tin, spring ac-
tion, horses and airplanes, 12" h . **160.00**
Wyandotte
Hoky Poky, litho tin windup, multico-
lored, 6" red pressed steel base,
two clowns, c1930 . . . . **200.00**
Humphrey Mobile, litho tin windup,
MIB **500.00**
Speed King, boy riding scooter, litho
tin windup, 1930 . . . . **250.00**

Super Mainliner, airplane, painted
pressed steel **75.00**

TRAINS, TOY

History: Railroading has always been an important part of childhood, largely because of the
romance associated with the railroad and the emphasis on toy trains.

The first toy trains were cast iron and tin; windup motors added movement. The Golden Age of
toy trains was 1920–1955 when electric powered
units were available and names such as Ives,
American Flyer, and Lionel were household words.
The construction of the rolling stock was of high
quality. The advent of plastic in the late 1950s
lessened this quality considerably.

Toy trains were designated by a model scale or
gauge. The most popular are HO, N, O and standard. Narrow gauge was a response to the modern
capacity to miniaturize. Its popularity has lessened
in the last few years.

Condition of trains is critical. Items in fair condition (scratched, chipped, dented, rusted or
warped) and below generally have little value to a
collector. Restoration is accepted, provided it is
done accurately. It may enhance the price one or
two grades. Prices listed below are for very good
to mint condition unless noted.

References: John O. Bradshaw, *Greenberg's
Guide To Kusan Trains,* Greenberg Publishing Co,
1987; Bruce Greenberg, (edited by Christian F.
Rohlfing), *Greenberg's Guide To Lionel Trains:
1901–1942, Volume 1* (1988), *Volume 2* (1988),
Greenberg Publishing Co.; Bruce Greenberg (edited by Roland La Voie), *Greenberg's Guide To
Lionel Trains:1945-1969, Volume 1* (1990), *Volume
2* (1988), Greenberg Publishing Co.; John Hub-
bard, *The Story of Williams Electric Trains,* Greenberg Publishing Co., 1987; Steven H. Kimball,
*Greenberg's Guide To American Flyer Prewar O
Gauge,* Greenberg Publishing Co., 1987; Roland
La Voie, *Greenberg's Guide To Lionel Trains,
1970–1988,* Greenberg Publishing Co., 1989; Dal-
las J. Mallerich, III, *Greenberg's Guide to Athearn
Trains,* Greenberg Publishing Co., 1987; Eric J.
Matzke, *Greenberg's Guide To Marx Trains, Vol-
ume 1,* Greenberg Publishing Co., 1989; Al Mc-
Duffie, et. al., *Greenberg Guide to Ives Trains,*
1901-1932, Greenberg Publishing Co, 1984; Rob-
ert P. Monaghan, *Greenberg's Guide to Markin
OO/HO,* Greenberg Publishing Co., 1989; John R.
Ottley, *Greenberg's Guide To LGB Trains,* Green-
berg Publishing Co., 1989; James Patterson and
Bruce C. Greenberg, *Greenberg's Guide To
American Flyer S Gauge, Third Edition,* Green-
berg Publishing Co., 1988; Vincent Rosa and
George J. Horan, *Greenberg Guide To HO Trains,*
Greenberg Publishing Co., 1986.

Note: Greenberg Publishing Company (7543
Main Street, Sykesville, MD 21784) is the leading

publisher of toy train literature. Anyone interested
in the subject should write for their catalog and
ask to be put on their mailing list.

Collectors' Clubs: Lionel Collector's Club, P.O.
Box 11851, Lexington, KY 40578; The National
Model Railroad Association, P.O. Box 2186, Indianapolis, IN 46206; The Toy Train Operating Society, Inc., 25 West Walnut Street, Suite 305, Pas-
adena, CA 91103; The Train Collector's
Association, P.O. Box 248, Strasburg, PA 17579.

Additional Listings: See *Warman's Americana
& Collectibles* for more examples.

AMERICAN FLYER

Car
631, T & P, gondola, red **90.00**
934, caboose, S **38.00**
962, Vista Dome, Silver Rocket,
 green stripe **50.00**
3007, gondola, litho, O gauge **20.00**
4041, American, pullman, light green,
 S gauge **75.00**
24047, Great Northern, box, S gauge   **100.00**
Locomotive
283, engine with tender, S gauge . .   **40.00**
290, steam, S gauge **65.00**
360, 361, diesel, S gauge, pr **125.00**
375, GM American Flyer, 1953, S
 gauge **300.00**
L2002, Burlington Route, S gauge . .   **185.00**
Set
Locomotive 429, tender, four cars,
 orig box, O gauge **450.00**
Locomotive 4670, tender, three Lone
 Scout coaches, S gauge **850.00**

IVES

Car
51, Newark, coach, O gauge, yellow
 litho, gray roof **75.00**
67, Caboose, four wheels **50.00**
184, Club Car, std gauge, olive,
 c1927 . . . .   **100.00**
Locomotive
1118, steam engine with tender, O
 gauge **125.00**
1132, steam engine with tender, wide
 gauge, 1921–26, excellent condi-
 tion **750.00**
3241, electric, std gauge, dark green,
 c1925, excellent condition **250.00**
3243, electric, wide gauge, 1921–28,
 good condition **175.00**
3251, electric, O gauge, orange with
 brown trim **100.00**
4637, electric, std gauge, restored,
 new wheels **550.00**
Set, American, cast iron, black and red
 locomotive, tender, 1182 passenger
 car, 1193 royal blue line passenger

cars, finished in blue and red roofs, c1895 .... **950.00**

LIONEL

Car

50, gang car, 027 gauge, 1955–65 . **45.00**
58, rotary snowplow, 027 gauge, 1959–61, excellent condition **400.00**
514, ventilated refrigerator car, white with green, orig box, paint flaking . **100.00**
602, baggage, dark green body and roof, wood litho doors, O gauge .. **50.00**
6457, O gauge, caboose, lighted ... **45.00**

Lionel, electric, No. 233, "O" gauge, engine #262, hopper car #803, gondola #902, cattle car #806, caboose #802, orig box, $175.00.

Locomotive

5, B & O gauge, Tunnel, maroon finish, c1904 .... **3,700.00**
150, O gauge, maroon, green windows **160.00**
251E, O gauge, red with cream trim, brass plates **120.00**
252, electric, O gauge, 1926–32, peacock **90.00**
380, electric, std gauge, 1923–27 .. **250.00**
1668, steam engine with tender, O gauge, 1937–41 .... **70.00**
2378, Milwaukee, AB diesel, O gauge **350.00**
Set
Locomotive 262, 262T, 602, 600, and 601, O gauge, diecast and pressed steel, rusting **175.00**
Locomotive 402E, three coaches, std gauge **1,150.00**

Locomotive 773, tender, New York Central, coaches 2625, 2627, and 2628, O gauge **1,250.00**

TRAMP ART

History: Tramp art was prevalent in the United States from 1875 to the 1930s. Items were made by itinerant artists who left no record of their identity. They used old cigar boxes and fruit and vegetable crates. The edges of items were chip-carved and layered, creating the "Tramp Art" effect. Finished items usually were given an overall stain. Today they are collected primarily as folk art.

Reference: Helaine Fendelman, *Tramp Art: An Itinerant's Folk Art Guide,* E. P. Dutton & Co., 1975.

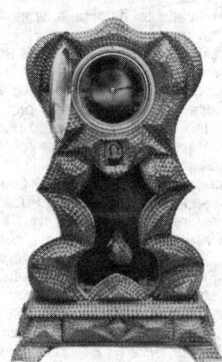

Clock, wooden, chip carved, portrait medallion below clock face, 27″ h, $500.00.

Box

5 x 6¼″, five dec sides **65.00**
8¼ x 11″, three tiers, geometric designs, brown finish, inlay, carved initials "L D," three drawers in top . **300.00**
8½″ l, hinged lid, dark varnish finish **55.00**
11″ l, pedestal base **45.00**
12″ w, 12″ h, hanging, bottom crest, old brown paint, black trim **45.00**
Frame, 19½″ h, 17¼″ w, holds German diploma, Philadelphia, 1915 ...... **45.00**
Miniatures
Chest
6 x 10 x 12″, three drawers, scalloped crest, natural finish, carved green trim edge **160.00**

12" l, three drawers, old varnish finish **100.00**
Desk, 21 x 15", pine, multi-layered chip carved stars, compasses, circles, and geometric shapes, slant front hinged lid, compartment int. lined with blue paper, six drawers, c1930 .... **990.00**
Dresser, 10½" w, 22" h, miniature, Gothic arch mirror, triptych-like back, three drawers, old varnish finish **225.00**
Mirror, 20½" h, 12¼" w, pine carved, multi-layered moons, circles, hearts, and geometric designs, c1930 .... **935.00**
Stand, 30⅜" h, removable planter top with diamond sides **325.00**

TRUNKS

History: Trunks are portable containers that clasp shut for the storage or transportation of personal possessions. Normally "trunk" means the ribbed flat, or dome top models of the second half of the 19th century. Unrestored they sell between $50 and $150. Refinished and relined the price rises to $200 to $400, with decorators being a principal market.

Early trunks frequently were painted, stenciled, grained, or covered with wallpaper. These are collected for their folk art qualities and as such experience high prices.

Reference: Martin and Maryann Labuda, *Price & Identification Guide to Antique Trunks,* published by authors, 1980.

Flat Top, tin on wood, brass banding on ends, wood rim, interior shelf missing, 16¼ x 29¼ x 15½", $90.00.

DOME TOP

Leather covered wood, 16" l, brass studding dec, bail handle **30.00**
Oak, immigrant type, 46¾" l, dovetail, wrought iron strap hinges, banding, end handles and lock, dark finish .. **270.00**

Pine
11 x 32 x 16", rect, brass bound, English, early 19th C **50.00**
25" l, orig dark green paint with orange striping and yellow dots, orig iron hinges and end handles, replaced lock **65.00**

FLAT TOP

Campaign, 46", brass bound leather, c1850 .... **400.00**
Camphor wood, 39⅓ x 19¼", rect, dovetail, brass bound corners, shaped hasp, escutcheon and carrying handles, fitted int. **550.00**
Pigskin, 14 x 8", red, painted Oriental maidens and landscapes within quatrefoils on front and sides, brass loop handles and lock, Chinese, 19th C . **125.00**

VAL SAINT–LAMBERT

History: Val Saint–Lambert, a twelfth century Cistercian abbey, was located during different historical periods in France, Netherlands, and Belgium (1930 to present). In 1822 Francois Kemlin and Auguste Lelievre, along with a group of financiers, bought the abbey and opened a glassworks. In 1846 Val Saint–Lambert merged with the Société Anonyme des Manufactures de Glaces, Verres à Vitre, Cristaux et Gobeletaries. The company bought many other glassworks.

Val Saint–Lambert developed a reputation for technological progress in the glass industry. In 1879 Val Saint–Lambert became an independent company employing 4,000 workers. Val Saint–Lambert concentrated on the export market making table glass, cut, engraved, etched, and molded pieces, and chandeliers. Some pieces were finished in other countries, e.g., silver mounts added in the United States.

Val Saint–Lambert executed many special commissions for the artists of the Art Nouveau and Art Deco periods. The tradition continues. The company also made cameo–etched vases, covered boxes, and bowls. The firm celebrated its 150th anniversary in 1975.

Ashtray, shell, gold label **5.00**
Bowl, cov, 6½" d, deep cut purple florals, frosted ground, sgd "Val St Lambert" **750.00**

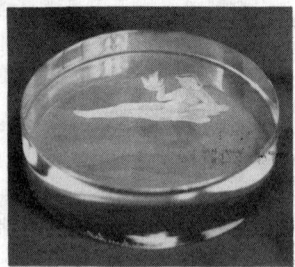

Paperweight, intaglio etched nude, seated, holding flame, script sgd, 4″ d, $50.00.

Chest Set, crystal, clear crystal half, green and clear crystal remaining half, each pc labeled and sgd, 6½″ h tallest pc **300.00**
Dresser Jar, cov, 4¾″, double cut, ruby cut to clear, sgd **100.00**
Pitcher, clear, paneled, diamond shaped cuttings, sgd **85.00**
Vase
   10″ h, ribbed body, hp wine blossoms connected by gold branches of thorns, gold accents, ruffled top . . **120.00**
   23¾″, slender neck, wide sloping foot, cameo, clear glass overlaid with white, brown, and green, c1900 . . **5,000.00**
Wine Glass, intaglio cut, ribbons, bows, and cranberry cameos, gold trimmed stems, set of 12 . . . . **480.00**

VALENTINES

History: Early cards were handmade, often containing both handwritten verses and hand drawn pictures. Many cards also were hand colored and contained cutwork.

Mass production of machine made cards featuring chromolithography began after 1840. In 1847 Esther Howland of Worcester, Massachusetts, established a company to make valentines which were hand decorated with paper lace and other materials imported from England. They had a small "H" stamped in red in the top left corner. Howland's company eventually became the New England Valentine Company (N.E.V. Co.).

George C. Whitney and his brother founded a company after the Civil War which dominated the market from the 1870's through the first decades of the twentieth century. They bought out several competitors, one of which was the New England Valentine Company.

Lace paper was invented in 1834. The 1835 to 1860 period is known as the "golden age" of lacy cards.

Embossed paper was used in England after 1800. Embossed lithographs and woodcuts developed between 1825–40, with early examples being hand colored.

References: Ruth Webb Lee, *A History of Valentines*, reprinted by National Valentine Collectors Association; Frank Staff, *The Valentine And Its Origins*, out-of-print.

Collectors' Club: National Valentine Collectors Association, Box 1404, Santa Ana, CA 92702. **Additional Listings:** See *Warman's Americana & Collectibles* for more examples.

Advisor: Evalene Pulati.

Sailor's Valentine, shell encrusted, mirror, 4¾ x 5¾″, $95.00.

Aquatint, English, 8 x 10″, 1840 . . . . . **75.00**
Cameo, Berlin and Jones, 5 x 7″, 1860 **35.00**
Cobweb, Dobbs, 8 x 10″, hand colored, 1860 . . . . **35.00**
Comic, English, 5 x 7″, lithographed center with verse, 1860 . . . . **18.00**
Cutwork, Pennsylvania German, 16″ sq, handcolored, 1820 . . . . **350.00**
Easel Back
   6 x 9″, fancy cutwork border, 1900 . **10.00**
   8½″, girl carrying red honeycomb paper parasol **50.00**
Lacy Folder, 3 x 5″
   Hand assembled, emb, 1850 . . . . . **15.00**
   Howland, signed, 1855 . . . . **25.00**
   N.E.V. Co., layered, 1875 . . . . **18.00**
Layered, 5″, hearts and flowers, c1860 **20.00**
Mechanical, R. Tuck, large paper doll, 1900 . . . . **25.00**
Pulldown, German
   5 x 10″, five layers, 1920 . . . . **20.00**
   8 x 12″, large ship, 1910 . . . . **75.00**
Sheet, emb, Union soldier embracing girl, c1860 . . . . **50.00**

Stand Up, diecut, 9", adv, girl riding in
Woods car, "If you love your wife, give
her a Woods" **25.00**

VALLERYSTAHL GLASS

History: Vallerystahl (Lorraine), France, has
been a glass producing center for centuries. In
1872 two major factories, Vallerystahl glassworks
and Portieux glassworks, merged and produced
art glass until 1898. Later, pressed glass covered
animal dishes were introduced. The factory continues operation today.

**Candy Dish, cov, basketweave, rope
edging, handles, and finial, white milk
glass, 4⅛" d, $25.00.**

Animal Dish, cov
  Dog, patterned quilt top, raised flow-
    ers on base, milk white, sgd **165.00**
  Rabbit, 6", white, frosted **60.00**
  Snail, figural strawberry base, milk
    white, sgd **90.00**
  Swan, blue milk glass **100.00**
Breakfast Set, hen cov dish, six egg
  cups, basket form master salt, and
  tray, milk white, 9 pcs **450.00**
Butter Dish, cov, turtle, snail finial, milk
  white **100.00**
Candlesticks, Baroque pattern, amber,
  pr **75.00**
Compote, 6¼" d, 6¼" h, sq, blue milk
  glass **75.00**
Dish, cov, figural, lemon, milk white, sgd **65.00**

Mustard, cov, swirled ribs, scalloped,
  matching cov with slot for spoon, blue
  milk glass **25.00**
Plate, 6", Thistle pattern, green **65.00**
Salt, cov, hen on nest, white opal **35.00**
Sugar, cov, 5" h, Strawberry pattern, sal-
  amander finial, milk white, gold trim . **75.00**
Tumbler, 4", blue **40.00**
Vase, 8", cylindrical, Optic Diamond pat-
  tern, green, painted rose thistles, sgd **150.00**

VAN BRIGGLE POTTERY

History: Artus Van Briggle, born in 1869, was a
talented Ohio artist. He joined Rookwood in 1887
and studied in Paris under Rookwood's sponsor-
ship from 1893 until 1896. In 1899 he moved to
Colorado for his health and established his own
pottery in Colorado Springs in 1901.

Van Briggle's work was influenced heavily by
the Art Nouveau "school" he saw in France. He
produced a great variety of matte glazed wares in
this style. Colors varied.

The "AA" mark, a date, and "Van Briggle" were
incised on all pieces prior to 1907 and sometimes
into the 1910s and 20s. After 1920, "Colorado
Springs, Colorado" or an abbreviation was added.
Dated pieces are the most desirable.

Artus died in 1904. Anne Van Briggle continued
the pottery until 1912.

References: Barbara Arnest (ed.), *Van Briggle
Pottery: The Early Years*, The Colorado Springs
Fine Art Center, 1975; Scott N. Nelson, Lois
Crouch, Euphemia Demmin, and Robert Newton,
Collector's Guide To Van Briggle Pottery, Halldin
Publishing, 1986.

Collectors' Club: American Art Pottery Association, 9825 Upton Circle, Bloomington, MN
55431.

Museum: Pioneer Museum, Colorado Springs,
CO.

Reproduction Alert: Van Briggle pottery still is
made today. These modern pieces often are confused with older examples. Among the glazes used
are Moonglo (off white), Turquoise Ming, Russet,
and Midnight (black).

1901–1920

Bowl
  3", dragonfly design, deep plum, 1917 **100.00**
  5¾ x 2", buff colored clay body, flow-
    ers in panels, shaded light blue
    glaze, Pattern 322, 1906 .... **300.00**

Candlesticks, pr, 9¼″, figural, facing
children, light green, medium blue
glaze, late teens **90.00**
Figure
Elephant, raised trunk, turquoise, AA
mark **90.00**
Rabbit, early **45.00**
Plaque
Indian, pr **175.00**
Mermaid, 10″, AA mark **65.00**

**Vase, Design 503, Flowers and Leaves,
eggplant matte glaze, marked, 1918,
9¼″ h, $450.00.**

Vase
3¾″, robin's egg blue wash, buff colored clay, 1908–11 .... **120.00**
4¼′, olive green, rose brushed around
bottom, Pattern 549, 1907 ..... **225.00**
4½″, poppy seed pods, matte moss
green curdled to yellow–green,
some smooth areas, Shape 452,
1907 .... **275.00**
5″, copper clad, shape #696, c1907 **1,000.00**
6¼″, dark green long slender leaves,
deep dark blue, matte glaze on
leathery texture, Shape 636, 1908–
11 .... **275.00**
7¼″, brown glaze, shape #296, 1906 **475.00**
7½″, medium blue, cream colored
clay body, thistle flowers, 1918 .. **225.00**
Wall Pocket, 7½″, turquoise matte, relief, AA mark **75.00**

1921–1968

Ashtray, 6½ x 6½″, Hopi Indian maiden
kneeling, grinding corn, turquoise
Ming glaze **75.00**
Boot, 2½″ **35.00**
Bust, 6½″, child reading book **45.00**

Indian Maiden, 4 x 6″, bent over rock,
ear of corn in hands, blue-green ... **50.00**
Lamp, Damsel of Damascus **175.00**
Paperweight, 3″, rabbit, maroon **60.00**
Pitcher, conical, plain, blue, Pattern 435 **100.00**
Rose Bowl, 5″ d, spade shaped leaves
around top, blue–green **30.00**
Vase
3″, butterfly **45.00**
5″, rect, blue flower, rose ground ... **40.00**

Vasart

VASART

History: Vasart is a contemporary art glass
made in Scotland by the Streathearn Glass Co.
The colors are mottled, and sometimes shade from
one hue to another. It is readily identified by an
engraved signature on the base.

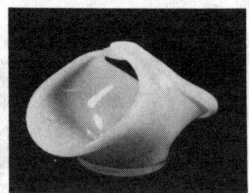

**Basket, green shading to pink, 8¼″ l, 5″
h, $90.00.**

Ashtray, 4½″ d, mottled blue to pink, sgd **40.00**
Basket
4 x 6″, mottled blue **72.00**
8¼ x 5″, green shading to pink **85.00**
Bowl
6½″, pierced handle, pink and green **30.00**
8″, green-gray, gold stone flecks ... **75.00**
Hat, sgd **25.00**
Mug, mottled white and lavender **35.00**
Plate, 8″, green-gray, gold stone flakes **75.00**
Rose Bowl, mottled white and green .. **40.00**
Vase
8½″, mottled blue shading to pink .. **100.00**
9″, ftd, jade green, sgd **75.00**

VENETIAN GLASS

History: Venetian glass has been made on the
island of Morano, near Venice, since the 13th century. Most of the wares are thin walled. Many types
of decoration have been used: embedded gold
dust, lace work, and applied fruits or flowers.

Reproduction Alert: Venetian glass continues to be made today.

Barber Bottle, green overlay, cut to clear	125.00
Bowl, cranberry, pie crust edge	55.00
Candleholders, 3¾", flower form, aqua, opalescent, and clear, gold dec, pr .	80.00
Candlesticks, pr	
12", clear, gold dust	135.00
15¾", pink, clear glass shot with gold, dolphin standard	125.00
Centerpiece, 13 x 9", figural, swan, blue, flower frog	35.00
Chalice, 9", DQ aqua bowl and pedestal, clear trim, gold handles and stem, gold int., 19th C	135.00
Cologne Bottle, 10¾", pink, flower form stopper with long applicator, pr	125.00

Vase, latticino, white, gold dust, clear ground, two clear applied reeded handles, $225.00.

Compote
6⅜" d, 7½" h, pink, clear glass, gold dec, dolphin standard	100.00
8½" h, blue bowl, gold flecked ball stem, applied gold leaf prunts . . .	75.00
Cruet, lavender, double swirled, orig stopper	100.00
Flower Frog, 13 x 9", swan, blue	35.00
Goblet, 6¼", green, pink rigaree	40.00
Plate, 7", pink and white alternating latticino stripes	60.00
Rose Bowl, ruffled, ftd, pink, gold flecks	100.00
Salt, swan shape, pink, gold trim	35.00
Vase, 10½", ftd, goblet shape, quilted pattern, petals, stem, and applied berries, pale green, gold trim	48.00

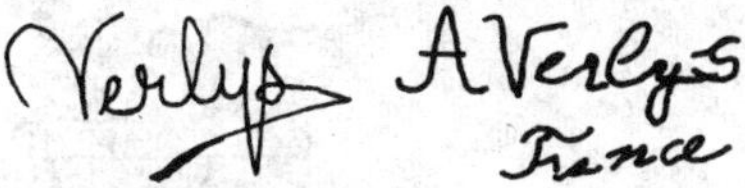

VERLYS GLASS

History: Verlys glass is an art glass originally made in France after 1930. For a period of a few months, Heisey Glass Co., Newark, Ohio, produced the identical glass, having obtained the rights and formula from the French factory.

The French-produced glass can be distinguished from the American product by the signature. The French is mold marked; the American is etched script signed.

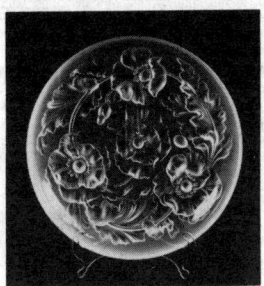

Bowl, Poppy pattern, script sgd, 13½" d, $125.00.

Ashtray, 4½", frosted doves, floral border, script mark	50.00
Bowl	
6", Pinecone, French blue	100.00
13½", Poppy, frosted	125.00
14", Dragonfly, etched mark	150.00
Box, 6½", butterflies, script mark	100.00
Candy Dish, 7", sculptured florals on cov, opal	375.00
Candlesticks, pr, 5½" d, leaftip molded nozzle, spreading circular foot with molded nasturtiums, etched signature on base, minor chips on rim	90.00
Centerpiece, 19¼" l, 4⅞" h, oval, high relief molded ext., four exotic fish with long swirling fins and tails, each molded with shaped handle formed by extended fan shaped tails, wavy ground scattered with bubbles, relief molded signature	350.00
Charger, 13", Waterlily	145.00
Plate, 11¾", bird dec	165.00
Powder Box, lovebirds, frosted	65.00
Vase, 9¾" h, clear and frosted, high relief molded stalks of wheat, inscribed "Verlys"	150.00

VILLEROY & BOCH

History: Pierre Joseph Boch established a pottery near Luxemburg, Germany, in 1767. Jean Francis, his son, introduced the first coal–fired kiln in Europe and perfected a water–power–driven potter's wheel. Pierre's grandson, Eugene Boch, managed a pottery at Mettlach; Nicholas Villeroy also had a pottery nearby.

In 1841 the three potteries were merged into the firm of Villeroy & Boch. Early production included a hard paste earthenware comparable to English ironstone. The factory continues to use this hard paste formula for its modern tablewares.

Reference: Susan and Al Bagdade, *Warman's English & Continental Pottery & Porcelain, 1st Edition,* Warman Publishing Co., Inc., 1987.

Additional Listings: Mettlach.

Plaque, blue inner circle, profile of woman in white, four masks, four love birds on ochre outer edge, brown trim, marked "V & B" on bottom, imp #879, c1885, 13¾" d, $400.00.

Bowl, 10½", blue floral dec, handles ..	100.00
Bread Board, 5½ x 8½", white	115.00
Coffeepot, 8", Virginia pattern	85.00
Creamer, Aragon pattern	20.00
Jug, 14¼", brown earthenware, peasants in field, white relief, pewter mounts, 19th C	175.00
Mug, elk dec, sgd	40.00
Plaque, 10¼", boat scene, blue and white, matte finish	85.00
Plate, 10", gaudy stick spatter, polychrome floral design	25.00
Punch Bowl, cov, underplate, 3 quart, blue, scene of dancing figures, #2087	750.00
Ramekin, underplate, blue and white .	40.00
Salt Box, 9½", wood lid, blue dec	150.00

Stein, ½ l, 6½" h, blue ground, five white figures, Mercury mark	225.00
Tile, blue and white Dutch scene with windmills	50.00
Vase	
6¼", Art Deco, green and brown, gold outlining, white ground, pr	185.00
7½", tan, beige relief figure, silver luster trim	250.00
15", incised dec of four seasons, sgd "C Gorig"	250.00

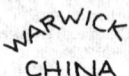

WARWICK

History: Warwick China Manufacturing Co., Wheeling, West Virginia, was incorporated in 1887 and continued until 1951. The company was one of the first manufacturers of vitreous glazed wares in the United States. Production was extensive and included tableware, garden ornaments, and decorative and utilitarian items.

Pieces were hand painted or decorated by decals. Collectors seek portrait items and fraternal pieces for groups such as the Elks, Eagles, and Knights of Pythias.

Some experimental, eggshell–type porcelain was made before 1887. A few examples are in the market.

Mug, Seaman, brown glaze, white int., marked "IOGA, Warwick," 5" h, $80.00.

Basket, cavalier portrait, two handles .	75.00
Bone Dish, scenic flow blue dec, marked "Warwick China"	48.00
Egg Cup, large, Tudor Rose	15.00
Gravy Boat, red currants, green leaves, gold trim	50.00

Marmalade Jar, cov, handles, pale yellow florals, brown ground **100.00**

Mug, 4½", singing monk, brown ground **45.00**

Plate
9½", monk drinking wine, brown ground **75.00**

10", herons, green ground **135.00**

Portrait Plate, 10", gypsy lady, multicolored, white ground **65.00**

Spooner, platinum banded dinnerware **60.00**

Tea Set, teapot, creamer, and cov sugar, gold banded dinnerware **115.00**

Vase
9¼", charcoal ground, verbena, marked "LG #1" **200.00**

10½"
Bouquet shape, portrait, girl, flamingo shaded ground, twig handles **275.00**

Urn shape, gypsy girl portrait, blue blouse and hair ribbon, brown shaded ground, twig handles .. **150.00**

11", red hibiscus, brown ground ... **75.00**

11½", bouquet shape, portrait, lady with white rose, brown ground ... **170.00**

13½", trumpet shape, yellow chrysanthemums, green foliage **200.00**

WATCHES, POCKET

History: Pocket watches can be found from flea markets to the specialized jewelry sales at Butterfield & Butterfield, William Doyle Galleries, and Sothebys. Condition of movement is first priority; design and detailing of case is second.

In pocket watches, listing aids are size (18/0 to 20), number of jewels in movement, open or closed (hunter) face, and whether the case is gold, gold filled, or some other metal. The movement is the critical element since cases often were switched. However, an elaborate case, especially of gold, adds significantly to value.

Pocket watches designed to railroad specifications are desirable. They are 16 to 18 in size, have a minimum of 17 jewels, adjust to at least five positions, and conform to many other specifications. All are open faced.

Study the field thoroughly before buying. The literature is vast including books and newsletters from clubs and collectors. Abbreviations: S = size; gf = gold filled; yg = yellow gold; j = jewels.

References: Michael Balfour, *The Classic Watch,* The Wellfleet Press, 1989; August C. Bolino,*The Watchmakers of Massachusetts,* Kensington Historical Press, 1987; Howard Brenner, *Collecting Comic Character Clocks and Watches,* Books Americana, 1987; Roy Ehrhardt & William Meggers, *American Pocket Watches Identification And Price Guide: Beginning To End...1830–1980,* Heart of America Press, 1987; Cedric Jagger, *The Artistry Of The English Watch,* Charles E.

Tuttle Co., 1988; Reinhard Meis, *Pocket Watches: From the Pendant Watch To The Tourbillon,* Schiffer Publishing, 1987, orig published in German; Cooksey Shugart and Tom Engle, *The Official Price Guide To Watches, Eighth Edition,* House of Collectibles, 1988.

Collectors' Club: National Association of Watch & Clock Collectors, 514 Poplar Street, Box 33, Columbia, PA 17512. *Bulletin* (bi-monthly) and *Mart* (bi-monthly).

Museums: American Clock & Watch Museum, Bristol, CT; Hoffman Clock Museum, Newark, NY; National Association of Watch and Clock Collectors Museum, Columbia, PA; The Time Museum, Rockford, IL.

Elgin, 17 jewel, hunter, 12 size, 25 year, gold filled case, $150.00.

Character
Babe Ruth, wrist **175.00**

Big Bad Wolf, pocket, slogan on reverse, Ingersoll, Disney, c1930 .. **400.00**

Donald Duck, wrist, rect face, 1940s **100.00**

Richard Nixon, wrist, Nixon on dial . **40.00**

Pendant
Belforte, 18K gold, oval shaped case, white enamel and gold key motif border, oblong shaped link chain with applied translucent peach colored enamel over quilloche ground, pendant loop and bow set with small diamond, c1910 .... **1,250.00**

Hamilton, 16 S, 17j, #962, open face, bridge plate **800.00**

Swiss, 30 S, 15j, 12¾ Ligne brass cylinder escapement, 14K yg enameled (black) hunter **450.00**

Pocket
Railroad
Blinn, 24j **650.00**

Bunn (Illinois), 16 S, 23j, 10K gf case **325.00**

Hampden, 18 S, 23j, gold jewel set-
ting, adjusted to heat, cold, iso-
chronism, and five positions, nickel
plate case, double roller, two tone | **275.00**
Rockford, 18 S, 21j, open face,
Railway King . . . . | **550.00**
Seth Thomas, 18 S, 15j, locomotive
engraved on silveroid case . . . . | **65.00**
Waltham Watch Co, 18 S, 17j,
M#1883 . . . . | **260.00**
Regular
American Watch Co, 16 S, 17j,
#1899, yg filled hunter case, . . | **165.00**
Berlington, 19j, Montgomery dial . | **180.00**
Chicago Watch Co, 18 S, 11j, key
wind . . . . | **450.00**
Elgin, 8 S, hunter, 14K, #1141341,
lever set, machine turned case . | **465.00**
Eureka, 18 S, 11j . . . . | **115.00**
Hamilton, 16 S, 17j, #987, gold
filled open face, Masonic em-
blems . . . . | **125.00**
Hampden, 18 S, 7j, open face,
stem wind . . . . | **75.00**
Howard, open face, 16 S, 17j, gf . | **135.00**
Illinois, 16 S, hunter, 17j, nickel le-
ver movement #1923165, yg
filled case #537918 . . . . | **250.00**
Ingersoll, 16 S, 17j, white base
metal, Reliance . . . . | **55.00**
Movado, 17j, open face, movement
#1617359, 14K yg case . . . . . | **500.00**
National Watch Co, 18 S, 15j, coin
silver, hunter case, key wind . . . | **175.00**
New York Standard, yellow playing
card dial . . . . | **650.00**
Patek Philippe, 18j, open face, cir-
cular dial, raised gold bar nos.,
subsidiary second dial, nickel le-
ver movement, 18K plain case,
sgd, #882371 . . . . | **950.00**
Rockford, 16 S, 21j, gold jewel set-
ting, open face . . . . | **650.00**
South Bend, 18 S, 21j, gold jewel
setting, hunter case, full plate . . | **425.00**
Tiffany, 3/0 S, 15j, 18K, open face,
swing out . . . . | **400.00**
Waltham, 18 S, 17j, silveroid case,
lever set, 1903 . . . . | **90.00**
Washington, 18 S, 17j, 25 year, yg
filled, open face, single sunk dial,
lever set, Senate . . . . | **175.00**
Wristwatch, Lady's
Bucherer, 18K, white gold, 12 dia-
monds with brick work solid band
and cov over dial . . . . | **2,200.00**
Bulova, 14K, 23j, yg, surrounded by
24 diamonds . . . . | **665.00**
Girod, 14K . . . . | **150.00**
Le Roy & Fils, London, platinum and
diamond, rect, strap set at intervals
with six old European cut dia-

monds, each .65 carat, numerous
rose cut diamonds . . . . | **2,000.00**
Longines, 14K . . . . | **200.00**
Nicolet, 17j, flexible band, cabochon
crystal, small diamond on each
side of ½ sq face . . . . | **85.00**
Wristwatch, Man's
Baylor, 14K, yg, rect fancy case, small
diamond set in white gold on dial . | **185.00**
Corum, 18K, rect, heavy case . . . . | **600.00**
Elgin, 14K, automatic, c1960 . . . . | **250.00**
Hamilton, 17j, gf, #987, stem wind,
leather band . . . . | **75.00**
Jules Jergensen, quartz, day and
date, leather band . . . . | **150.00**
Patek Philippe, 18j, nickel lever
movement, optionally adjusted to
heat cold, and isochronism, and
five positions, sgd, #794679 . . . | **850.00**

WATERFORD

History: Waterford crystal is quality flint glass
commonly decorated with cuttings. The original
factory was established at Waterford, Ireland, in
1729. Glass made before 1830 is darker than the
brilliantly clear glass of later production. The factory closed in 1852. After 100 years it reopened
and continues in production.

Goblet, 5¼" h, $15.00.

Ashtray, 7" . . . . | **80.00**
Bowl, 9", leaf cut border over trellis work
sides . . . . | **100.00**
Creamer and Sugar, diamond cut . . . . | **50.00**
Cruet, 5", waisted body, short fluted
neck, fluted rim, strawberry leaves
and fan cutting, faceted stopper . . . | **100.00**
Decanter, 10", deep cut Sawtooth Rib
pattern, double rope ring neck, orig
stopper . . . . | **250.00**
Jar, cov, 6", diamond cut body, triple

sprig chain bordering thumb cut rim and star cut lid, faceted knob finial . **100.00**
Letter Opener **45.00**
Salt, 3", cut, star base **30.00**
Vase, 7", fluted neck, flared rim, hobnail cut, triple sprig chains, star cut centered base **85.00**
Water Set, 6" pitcher, six tumblers, diamond cut **600.00**
Wine Glass, diamond and flute cut, star base **25.00**

WAVE CREST WARE

WAVE CREST

History: The C. F. Monroe Company of Meriden, Connecticut, produced the opal glassware known as Wave Crest from 1898 until World War I. The company bought the opaque, blown molded glass blanks for decoration from the Pairpoint Manufacturing Co. of New Bedford, Massachusetts, and other glass makers including European factories. Florals were the most common decorative motif. Trade names used were "Wave Crest Ware," "Kelva," and "Nakara."

References: Wilfred R. Cohen, *Wave Crest: The Glass of C.F. Monroe,* Collector Books, 1987; Elsa H. Grimmer, *Wave Crest Ware,* Wallace-Homestead, 1979.

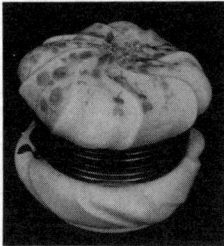

Box, cream ground, blue floral enamels, 3¾" d, $115.00.

Ashtray, 4¼" d, 1¾" h, golf club and ball rest on open glass tray, blue flower dec **355.00**
Bishop's Hatbox, ftd, small, cobalt ground, marked "Nakara" **450.00**
Biscuit Jar, robins, violets, pink and blue ground **300.00**
Bowl, 5¼", Embossed Rococo mold hp cherubs and enameled florals, ormolu rim and foot, sgd **315.00**

Box, hinged lid
4 x 3", octagonal, mottled sage green, hp orange and white flowers, ormolu fittings, orig lime green lining, sgd "Kelva" **335.00**
5¼ x 3", Embossed Rococo mold, creamy white ground, cupids and flowers, sgd **535.00**
8", Queen Louise, marked "Nakara" **800.00**
Calling Card Tray, 4½ x 2½", Embossed Rococo mold, white ground, pastel flower dec, brass rim **150.00**
Cigarette Box, 4" h, Embossed Rococo mold, creamy white ground, enameled flowers, ornate ormolu ftd base and rim, tab handles **325.00**
Ferner, 8 x 4½", octagonal, blue and cream ground, hp flowers, sgd **300.00**
Finger Bowl, matching underplate, florals and foliage, shaded yellow to white ground **300.00**
Hair Receiver, 6", Embossed Rococo mold, blue daises, orig ormolu cov, sgd **250.00**
Ice Bucket, 6¼" d, 13¼" h, wild roses, light blue ground, ornate lid and handle **1,000.00**
Jardiniere
6¾", sq, Egg Crate mold, white ground, blue florals, shaded branches, green leaves, round ormolu collar, sgd **225.00**
7¼ x 8½", Embossed Rococo mold, pink ground, yellow and pink flowers, plain ormolu rim and base, cupid's masks at feet **700.00**
Jewelry Box, 7 x 6½", puffy Egg Crate mold, ftd, satin finish, hp lid, child with bow and arrow, orig lining **1,200.00**
Letter Holder, 4 x 5½ x 3", puffy, blue floral dec, white beading, brass ormolu rim **275.00**
Mirror Tray, 3 x 2¼" oval mirror, 6¼" h overall, pink flowers, blue ground, marked "Kelva" **500.00**
Pin Tray, 4¼" w, yellow trim, white dots, pink ground, orig lining **255.00**
Powder Jar, cov, 3 x 3", blown mold full relief rose on lid, sgd "Kelva" **300.00**
Salt and Pepper Shakers, pr, swirled necks, bulbous bottom, bust of cat surrounded by wreath of green foliage **110.00**
Vase, 12", blue flower panels, shadow flowers, lavender scrolls, white ground **1,000.00**

WEATHER VANES

History: A weather vane indicates wind direction. The earliest known examples were found on late 17th century structures in the Boston area. The vanes were handcrafted of wood, copper, or tin. By the last half of the 19th century, weather vanes adorned farms and houses throughout the nation. Mass produced vanes of cast iron, copper, and sheet metal were sold through mail order catalogs or at country stores.

The champion vane is the rooster. In fact, the name weathercock is synonymous with weather vane. The styles and patterns are endless. Weathering can affect the same vane differently. For this reason, patina is a critical element in collecting vanes.

Whirligigs are a variation of the weather vane. Constructed of wood and metal, often by unskilled craftsmen, whirligigs not only indicate the direction of the wind and its velocity, but their unique movements served as entertainment for children, neighbors, and passersby.

Reproduction Alert: Reproduction of early models exist, are being aged, and sold as originals.

Weathervane, rooster, copper, wooden base, 22″ l, 21½″ h, $750.00.

Bull, 40″ l, 26″ h, copper and cast iron, full bodied, black metal base, 19th C **12,650.00**
Cow
  28½″ l, copper, gilded, c1880 . . . . . **3,700.00**
  32″ l, copper, full bodied, standing, molded, cast zinc head, black metal stand, 19th C **4,950.00**
Deer, 31 x 36″, copper, molded, leaping over rockwork, black metal base, 19th C **22,000.00**
Dragon, 78″ h, 38″ d, copper, scrolled wrought iron direction, wood pedestal, restored, mid 19th C **1,400.00**
Eagle, 31″ h, 35″ w, copper, perched on globe, outstretched wings, American, c1800 . . . . **1,800.00**
Horse
  26″ l, 18″ h, running, galvanized sheet

metal, wire reinforcement, dark red paint traces **550.00**
  36″ l, 26¼″ h, cast iron, standing, raised left leg, sheet iron tail, black metal base, Rochester Iron Works, 19th C **35,200.00**
Horse and Rider, 28½″ l, 26¼″ h, copper, molded, gilded, repousse, mounted on rod on black metal base, A L Jewell & Co, Waltham, MA, 19th C **19,800.00**
Horse and Sulky
  40″ l, 27″ h, copper and zinc, molded, mounted on rod, black metal base J. W. Fiske & Co, c1880 . . . . **11,000.00**
  49½″ l, 24½″ h, copper, molded, gilded, running horse pulling sulky with seated driver, mounted on rod, Harris & Co, Boston, MA, 19th C . **15,400.00**
Mermaid, 40¼″ h, gilded sheet iron, pointing finger, orig paint, mounted on pedestal, 19th C **7,500.00**
Plow, 52 x 23″, copper and cast zinc, mounted on rod in black metal base, c1860 . . . . **5,500.00**
Rooster
  22 x 14″, sheet iron, stylized, sawtooth comb, pierced eye, brush-like tail, 19th C **1,650.00**
  37 x 43″, copper and sheet metal, molded, perched on arrow, mounted on rod, black metal base, 19th C **3,300.00**
Sea Captain, 43½″ h, copper, black coat and top hat, pointing right forefinger, spyglass under left arm, mid 19th C **22,500.00**
Seaman, 44″ l, wood, blowing foghorn, 19th C **2,500.00**
Ship, 33″ l, wood, copper wire rigging, black hull, white and black gunports, green undersides, late 19th C **1,600.00**
Whale, 50″ l, wood, carved, late 19th C **600.00**

WEBB, THOMAS & SONS

History: Thomas Webb & Sons was established in 1837 in Stourbridge, England. The company probably is best known for its very beautiful English cameo glass. However, many other types of colored glass were produced including enameled glass, iridescent glass, pieces with heavy glass ornamentation, cased glass, and other art glass besides cameo.

Additional Listings: Burmese, Cameo, and Peachblow.

Bowl
  3″ d, 2½″h, tricorn, satin, shaded brown, gold prunus blossoms and butterfly dec, creamy int., gold trim **325.00**

4⅞" d, 4¼" h, DQ, MOP, satin, apple green, rich cream lining, six crimp top, applied frosted feet, frosted flower prunt **550.00**

10", butterscotch, gold floral dec, two handles **165.00**

Bride's Basket, 10", pink satin, DQ, MOP, ruffled edge, metal base, sgd . **300.00**

Claret Jug, opaque white body, brilliant gold palm trees and bamboo stalks, rust and dark green ferns and tropical foliage, SP flip top lid, collar, and handle, hallmarked and numbered **335.00**

Cologne Bottle, 5½" h, globular, peach satin, SS screw top **250.00**

Flower Holder, 12 1 2 x 8¾", gold irid glass foot, brass leaves and branches, four irid gold ribbed flower shaped vases **500.00**

Jar, 5" d, DQ, MOP, blue, berries dec, SP hallmarked collar, lid, and bail handle **450.00**

Perfume Bottle, 3½", globular, carved white blossoms, blue satin ground, SS screw on cap **875.00**

Rose Bowl

2½" d, 2⅜" h, shaded brown to ivory, satin, cream int., eight crimp top . **325.00**

3⅛" d, 3" h, rose overlay, white int., four crimp top, clear wafer foot, heavy gold flowers and branches, enameled "E" and spider web on base **265.00**

3¾" d, blue swirled MOP satin glass bowl, green satin glass leaf shaped base **220.00**

Salt, master, frosted, Adam and Eve, butterfly signature **65.00**

Scent Bottle

1¼ x 4¼", lay down, gold prunus blossoms, green shaded to yellow satin ground, hallmarked SS domed monogrammed cap **400.00**

3½", black satin, white floral dec, small label reads "Lily of the Valley" **80.00**

Toothpick, Alexandrite, ruffled edge . . **1,000.00**

Vase

5¼", stick top, bulbous, blue satin glass **115.00**

6⅛" h, 3½" d, yellow satin, cream int., gold prunus and butterfly dec . . . **325.00**

6⅞", peach blow, acid finish, deep cream lining, shaded rose to cream, heavy gold daisies and leaves, large gold dragonfly on back **650.00**

8¾", brown satin, fluted, elaborate gold filigree dec, blue and white enamel highlights, pr **600.00**

9" h, 4¼" d, deep coral red overlay, white lining, heavy gold flowers and branch dec **350.00**

WEDGWOOD

WEDGWOOD

History: In 1754 Josiah Wedgwood entered into a partnership with Thomas Whieldon of Fenton Vivian, Staffordshire, England. Products included marbled, agate, tortoise shell, green glaze, and Egyptian black wares. In 1759 Wedgwood opened his own pottery at the Ivy House works, Burslem. In 1764 he moved to the Brick House (Bell Works) at Burslem. The pottery concentrated on utilitarian pieces.

Between 1766 and 1769 Wedgwood built the famous works at Etruria. Among the most renowned products of this plant were the Empress Catherina of Russia dinner service (1774) and the Portland Vase (1790s). Product lines were caneware, unglazed earthenwares (drabwares), piecrust wares, variegated and marbled wares, black basalt (developed in 1768), Queen's or creamware, Jasperware (perfected in 1774), and others.

Bone china was produced under the direction of Josiah Wedgwood II between 1812 and 1822 and revived in 1878. Moonlight luster was made from 1805 to 1815. Fairyland luster began in 1920. All luster production ended in 1932.

A museum was established at the Etruria pottery in 1906. When Wedgwood moved to its modern

Vase, hp, woman seated on rock, light brown flowing robe, holding rose, valley and mountains background, clear blue applied dragon handles, 13¼" h, $800.00.

plant at Barlaston, North Staffordshire, the museum was continued and expanded.

References: Susan and Al Bagdade, *Warman's English & Continental Pottery & Porcelain, 1st Edition,* Warman Publishing Co., Inc., 1987; David Buten and Jane Clancy, *Eighteenth–Century Wedgwood: A Guide For Collectors And Connoisseurs,* Main Street Press, 1980; Robin Reilly, *The Collector's Wedgwood,* Portfolio Press/A Robert Campbell Rowe Book, 1980; Robin Reilly and George Savage, *Dictionary Of Wedgwood,* Antique Collectors Club, 1980; Geoffrey Wills, *Wedgwood,* Chartwell Books, Inc., 1989.

Periodical: American Wedgwoodian, 55 Vandam Street, New York, NY 10013.

Collectors' Club: The Wedgwood Society, 246 N. Bowman Avenue, Merion, PA 19066; The Wedgwood Society, The Roman Villa, Rockbourne, Fordingbridge, Hents, England, SP 6 3PG.

Basalt, teapot, classic design, 8½″ h, $65.00.

BASALT

Bust
   2⅛″ d, 4¼″ h, Aristophanes, marked
      "Wedgwood" **400.00**
   18½″, Mercury, sgd "Wedgwood" on
      bust and plinth **125.00**
Coffeepot, 9¼″, basketweave, Widow
   Warburton finial, unmarked **325.00**
Creamer
   2¾ x 2″, black, one side classic figural
      scene of old man with serpent and
      young man with dish in his hand,
      reverse side classical figure of old
      woman washing young woman's
      feet **130.00**
   3⅛″, bulbous base, straight neck,
      black, hp enamel crest of Ontario,
      green maple leaf, side trim, orange
      Ontario banner underneath, green
      enamel rim and handle trim,
      marked "Wedgwood, England" and
      painter's no. **250.00**

Figure
   4¾″ bulldog, standing, amber glass
      eyes, black, modeled by Hubert
      Light, imp "Wedgwood," c1914 . . **300.00**
   5⅞ x 9⅜″, Cleopatra, nude, sitting,
      asp on her wrist, marked "Wedg-
      wood" **650.00**
Pendant, oval, black, lion chasing
   horse, beaded SS frame and chain . **75.00**
Pitcher
   4¾″, tankard shape, black, classical
      women and children scene, black,
      grape and vine border, large mark with "8″
      in circle **155.00**
Tea Set, 5¾″ teapot, 4¼″ sugar, 4½″
   creamer, Strawberry pattern **450.00**
Urn, cov, 11″, pedestal, sq base, swags,
   acanthus leaves at base and cov,
   c1860 . . . . **1,700.00**
Vase, 7¾″, urn shape, cov, high relief
   floral swags suspended from rams'
   heads enclosing flower head motifs,
   knob finial, scroll handles with foliage
   motif, sq pedestal, imp mark, c1770 . **875.00**
Wine Ewer, 16″ h, figural models by
   John Flaxman on shoulders, swags
   of vine and water reeds, stiff leaves,
   bands of overlapping foliage, gadrooned stems, sq bases, imp mark,
   c1860, pr **900.00**

CANEWARE

Bowl, drabware dec of ferns and stars,
   c1810 . . . . **425.00**
Dish, 9¾″, rect, molded with overlap-
   ping leaves, imp mark, letter "L",
   c1790 . . . . **250.00**
Fruit Stand, 12⅜″, foliate scroll handles,
   rect flaring foot, imp "Wedgwood,"
   early 19th C **200.00**
Sugar, cov 6″, smear glaze, prunus
   blossoms, c1800 . . . . **300.00**
Teapot, c1820, smear glaze Arabesque
   scene, dog finial **225.00**
Vase, 8¾″, sq, pierced domed lid, con-
   cave sides, relief brown classical figures, brown foliage caryatid corner
   supports suspending swags, four
   brown paw feet, stepped shaped sq
   base, imp mark, c1800 . . . . **1,200.00**
Waste Bowl, 5½″ d, Wicker pattern, imp
   mark, c1820 . . . . **100.00**

CREAMWARE

Basket, 9″ d, round, reticulated, c1790 **200.00**
Compote, 8¼″ d, 4¾″ h, basketweave,
   reticulated foliate scroll, rope twist rim
   handles **175.00**

Cup and Saucer, daisies, enameled dec 65.00

Dish, 10¼", oval, clusters of fruit, green printed rim transfer, scrolling flowering branches, gilt rims, artist sgd "F. H. Cox," imp mark, Pat #G4744, c1880 .... **150.00**

Fruit Bowl, oval, wide brown and plum border pattern **550.00**

Plate, 9½", black printed transfer, green enamel crustacean, shaped rim with green line, imp mark, c1780 ...... **95.00**

Sauce Dish, cov, attached underplate, oval, two handles, glazed **250.00**

Serving Dish
  11" l, lozenge form, Neo–Classical, painted sepia dec, early 19th C, pr **300.00**
  11¾" l, shaped rect, brown edged scalloped rim, low relief int. molded with two fish, small painted swan below banner, inscribed "AI SIDERA VULTUS," imp "Wedgwood," minor chips **200.00**
  13½" l, oval, Neo–Classical, painted sepia dec, early 19th C **200.00**

Soup Plate, 10", wide brown and plum border pattern **125.00**

Sugar, cov, 8", stand, painted iron-red, green, blue, and yellow bands of flowering foliage, disc finial and flower head motif cov, imp mark, iron-red mark "Pat #1173," c1860 .... **235.00**

Teapot, 9", swelled cylindrical, dome cov, knop finial, brown dec, circular band and floral sprigs, scrolling vines, imp "Wedgwood" **250.00**

Tray, 6¼" w, diamond shape, transfer printed and painted, embracing cupids among clouds, sgd "EL," imp mark, letters "C," "AVO," c1865 ... **250.00**

Tureen, cov, 17" l, Neo–Classical, painted sepia dec, loop handles, fitted undertray, early 19th C **650.00**

Urn, 6", mottled blue and brown, glazed, mounted on basalt plinth, marked "Wedgwood and Bentley," c1768–80 **475.00**

Water Tray, 4 pcs, pitcher, two tumblers, and tray, dog handles, gilt, Victorian **850.00**

DRABWARE

Child's Tea Set, 3½" teapot, cov sugar bowl, milk jug, waste bowl, basketweave, button knobs, imp mark, early 19th C **275.00**

Cup and Saucer, applied blue bands of flowering foliage **100.00**

Jug, 8", classical women emb on panels, loop handle, Wedgwood mark, c1820 .... **2,250.00**

Teapot, 8½", Gothic dec, bearded man faces on lower section, imp "Wedgwood" **225.00**

Vase, 10", blue and white, three sections, figural swan handles **400.00**

JASPERWARE

Ashtray, 4½", spade shape, dark blue, cupids dec, marked "Made in England" **30.00**

Biscuit Jar, 5¼ x 7¾", white floral dec, lavender ground, acorn finial, artist sgd "Barnard" **710.00**

Box, cov, 4" sq, dark blue, white classical figures, flower heads on corners of lid, vine border, marked, c1860 .. **165.00**

Cake Plate, 9", black, raised white classical ladies border, orig box **48.00**

Candlesticks, pr, 6¼", blue, white coat of arms of St. Andrews, inscribed name and motto, scrolling foliage, circular column, flaring feet, imp marks **325.00**

Comb Tray, 9 x 6½", dark blue, classical scenes, floral border, marked "Wedgwood, England" **185.00**

Jasperware, sugar, cov, dark blue ground, white figure of woman at altar and women in garden, 6" l, 4" h, $150.00.

Cup and Saucer, tri-color, green ground, white relief rams' heads suspending floral swags enclosing oval medallions of classical figures on lilac ground, imp marks, 19th C **250.00**

Dish, 4½", heart shape, dark blue, classical dec, marked "Made in England" **130.00**

Hair Receiver, cov, heart shape, medium blue, large white angel dec, numbered only **250.00**

Jardiniere, 7", oval, blue, white trailing vine and circles, scrolling vine rim band, flower head handles **900.00**

Loving Cup, 4 x 4½", three handles, olive green, white cameo medallions of Washington, Franklin, and Lafayette, marked "Wedgwood, England" **450.00**

Mantle Lusters, 11½" h, cylindrical, light blue and white jasper base, silver-plated mounts, relief dec of cupids, festoons and rams' heads, two center trophies and oval medallions in violet, molded and cut glass bobeche hung with drops, glass floriform nozzle, pr **600.00**

Mug, 4⅞", dark blue, white classical figures and medallion, SS rim, marked "Wedgwood, Elkington & Co, Ltd" .. **140.00**

Mustard Jar, 3½", yellow, black grape swags and lion's heads, two white bands around base, SP lid, marked Wedgwood only **250.00**

Pin Tray, 2½ x 6", dark blue, classical dec, marked "Wedgwood, England" **40.00**

Pitcher
  6", blue ground, white classical dec . **100.00**
  7¾", sage green, classical figures, cupid, and cherubs, marked "Wedgwood, England" **85.00**

Plaque, 9 x 7", oval, white Virgin Mary cameo medallion, flowers and vine border, lilac, marked "Made in England" **135.00**

Plate, 9", Shell, solid white **200.00**

Preserve Jar, 6", cov, dark blue, matching underplate, four classical Muses in cartouches, marked "Wedgwood, England" **200.00**

Ring Tree, dark blue, rose border, classical scenes, unmarked **175.00**

Sweetmeat, cov, 3¼", cylindrical, dark blue, white horses and figures, knob finial, marked "Wedgwood" **185.00**

Tablet, 2 x 5", black and white **225.00**

Tea Set, teapot, creamer, cov sugar, sage green, straight sided Brewster shape, cameo medallions of Washington and Franklin, marked "Wedgwood, England" **575.00**

Toothpick Holder, 2¼", dark blue, white bust of Josiah Wedgwood, marked "Wedgwood, Made In England" ... **75.00**

Urn
  6¼" h, shouldered ovoid body, frieze of Three Graces dancing, waisted neck with two applied handles, domical foot with acanthus dec, sq gilt bronze base, pr **500.00**
  7½", cov, tri-color, white ground, green swags and acanthus leaves, lilac rams' masks, two green medallions with white classical figures on lilac ground, floral lilac shoulder band, flared foot, ball finial, scroll handles, imp mark, mid 19th C .. **900.00**

Vase, 8¼", light blue, white classical figures cameos, white handles, bolted pedestal base with white scrolling vine dec, marked **375.00**

LUSTERS

Butterfly
  Bowl, 2¾ x 1¾", octagonal, gold outlined multicolored butterflies, gold trim, mottled MOP luster ext., mottled flame int., Portland vase mark **115.00**
  Mug, 2", three handles, blue, tan, and pink, gold butterflies, coral int., marked "Wedgwood Lustre" **200.00**

Dragon
  Box, cov, 5¾ x 4⅞", mottled green luster ext., gold dragons, ornate gold bands, MOP luster int., three jewels on base, maroon luster widow finial, Portland vase mark . **450.00**
  Garniture Set, 11" center vase, two 8" sq vases, flying cranes and dragon breathing flames, 3 pcs **900.00**
  Salt, 2¼", orange dog's head in bowl, blue ext. **130.00**
  Vase, 4¾ x 9¾", gold outlined dragon breathing flames, ornate gold designs at top, base, and rim int., mottled powder blue luster ext. **450.00**

Fairyland
  Bowl, 6⅜ x 3", gold outlined green eyed Firbolgs, ruby ext., green luster int., center scene of Thumbelina, Portland vase mark **1,000.00**
  Melba Cup, 4⅞" d, 3½" h, green MOP int. with two elves on branch, midnight luster ext., gold stars, green grass, leapfrogging elves and fairies, Portland vase mark **700.00**
  Plate, 10¾", elves on bridge, gold center, lacy gold fairies and florals on gold border, mottled blue back **1,700.00**
  Vase, 8⅜ x 4¼", "Candlemas," multicolored, gold details, Portland vase mark and "Z5157, Wedgwood" **1,275.00**

Hummingbird
  Jar, cov, 9", gold outlined multicolored hummingbirds, mottled green ext., gold trim, marked "Wedgwood" .. **725.00**
  Vase, 2½ x 5⅛", gold outlined multicolored hummingbirds, mottled blue luster ground, mottled flame luster int. **200.00**

Moonlight
  Goblet, 3¼", pink with yellow and green splashes, gilt rim, imp mark, c1810 .... **300.00**
  Plate, 9¾", purple luster splotches, c1810 .... **200.00**
  Vase, 3¼ x 8⅛", "Boys on Bridge" dec, Portland vase mark **1,150.00**

MAJOLICA

Bowl, 9 x 4⅛", white and brown, emb

white seashells, rose and gold seaweed, turquoise int., SP rim band, imp mark 125.00
Creamer, 3", Strawberry pattern, turquoise int., imp mark 160.00
Match Holder, 4¾ x 3½", green and brown, striker on base, imp mark .. 90.00
Pitcher, 8½", jug shape, jeweled design, turquoise int., c1860 .... 350.00
Plate, 6½", butterflies, florals, and fans dec 65.00
Platter, 12½", basketweave center, bamboo edge 100.00
Sugar, 7", Fan pattern, flowering prunus, gray-green, yellow, and pink, turquoise int., two branch handles, imp mark, 1878 .... 165.00
Teapot, cov, 6¼", Bamboo pattern, imp mark, 1871 .... 625.00
Water Bottle, 10", multicolored florals, horizontal blue stripes, cream ground, 1879 .... 300.00

MISCELLANEOUS

Bulb Pot, 9½", figural, hedgehog, light blue, glazed, imp mark 475.00
Calendar Tile, 1910, The Mayflower Approaching Land, brown and white .. 65.00
Compote, 5⅝ x 4", green luster scrollwork, copper luster trim, yellow luster ext., two handles, pedestal base, c1920 .... 100.00
Honey Pot, cov, 3¾", stoneware, beehive shape, translucent smear glaze, c1820 .... 225.00
Pepper Pot, 3½", bulbous, relief grapes and leaves, white, imp mark 100.00
Pitcher, brown transfer, ivory ground, 1878 .... 85.00
Tray, 15¾", oval, smear glaze, rim relief molded, band of scrolling flowering foliage, imp mark, early 19th C 280.00
Vase, 4¾", flaring, bands of brown ovals below band of flower heads, yellow glazed brown ground, imp mark, mid 19th C 165.00

PEARLWARE

Bough Pot, 9", pierced cov, D-shape, speckled, molded floral swags, still foliage border, gilt, imp mark, c1810, pr 1,200.00
Compote, 10¾ x 6¼", Havelock pattern, floral border, imp mark, c1840–68 .. 265.00
Jug, 4½ x 5¾", blue, scenic transfer, gold wreath with initials under spout, gold rim, imp mark, c1820 .... 275.00
Plate, 8½", shell shape, ribbon handle, 1882 .... 75.00
Soup Tureen, cov, ladle, blue dahlias,

green foliage, black rope edge, imp mark 400.00
Vase, cov, 6⅝", tan slip, engine turned gadroons, relief beadwork and swags, imp mark, late 18th C 425.00

Pearlware, platter, ftd, imp "Wedgwood/Pearl," marked "Havelock," c1840–68, 8½ x 11¼ x 2", $150.00.

QUEEN'S WARE

Box, 4 x 5", powder blue, relief berries, marked "Wedgwood England" 100.00
Crocus Pot, 6", rect, bombe shape, classical motifs in oval medallion 115.00
Cup and Saucer, relief vintage rim border, #2223 .... 25.00
Tea Set, Edward VIII Coronation, blue, c1937, 3 pcs 400.00

ROSSO ANTICO

Bowl, Egyptian 385.00
Creamer, 6", applied center black band of scrolling flowering foliage, imp mark, mid 19th C 225.00
Inkwell, 4⅛", pavilion shape 125.00
Jug, 6", pinched spout, applied black formal foliage and bellflowers, c1820 200.00
Teapot, cov, 10½", squatty, band of hieroglyphs at shoulder, crocodile finial, 1810 .... 420.00

TERRA COTTA WARE

Ashtray, 4½", classical dec, marked "Made in England" 35.00
Box, heart shaped 85.00
Compote, jasper 125.00
Pin Dish, 4", oval, cupids playing, marked "Made in England" 30.00
Teapot, black dec, limited edition of 500 325.00
Vase, 5¼", Portland shape, black relief lilies and foliage, flaring rim, band of grass, angular handles, applied mask terminals, imp mark, mid 19th C ... 300.00

WELLER POTTERY

History: In 1872 Samuel A. Weller opened a small factory in Fultonham, near Zanesville, Ohio, to produce utilitarian stoneware, such as milk pans and sewer tile. In 1882 he moved his facilities to Zanesville. In 1890 Weller built a new plant in the Putnam section of Zanesville along the tracks of the Cincinnati and Miskingum Railway. Additions followed in 1892 and 1894.

In 1894 Weller entered into an agreement with William A. Long to purchase the Lonhuda Faience Company, which had developed an art pottery line under the guidance of Laura A. Fry, formerly of Rookwood. Long left in 1895, but Weller continued to produce Lonhuda under a new name, Louwelsa. Replacing Long as art director was Charles Babcock Upjohn. He, along with Jacques Sicard, Frederick Hurten Rhead, and Gazo Fudji, developed Weller's art pottery lines.

At the end of World War I, many prestige lines were discontinued and Weller concentrated on commercial wares. Rudolph Lorber joined the staff and designed lines such as Roma, Forest, and Knifewood. In 1920 Weller purchased the plant of the Zanesville Art Pottery and claimed to be the largest pottery in the country.

Art pottery enjoyed a revival when the Hudson Line was introduced in the early 1920s. The 1930s saw Coppertone and Graystone Garden ware added. However, the Depression forced the closing of the Putnam plant and one on Marietta Street in Zanesville. After World War II, cheap Japanese imports took over Weller's market. In 1947 Essex Wire Company of Detroit bought the controlling stock. Early in 1948 operations ceased.

Reference: Sharon and Bob Huxford, *The Collectors Encyclopedia Of Weller Pottery*, Collector Books, 1979; values updated 1989.

Collectors' Club: American Art Pottery Association, P. O. 9825 Upton Circle, Bloomington, MN 55431.

Additional Listings: See *Warman's Americana & Collectibles* for more examples.

Basket, Eocean, 6½", florals, glossy
   gray to black ground 150.00
Bowl
  Ardsley, 5", sword shaped green
   leaves forming handles, water lily
   form 55.00

Blue Drapery, 5½", clusters of roses,
   vertical folded blue matte ground . 20.00
Coppertone, 10½ x 2", lilypads, applied frog on edge 135.00
Glendale, 16", birds and nests, flower
   frog 275.00
Malvern, 10", matching flower frog . 55.00
Candlesticks, pr
  Blue Drapery, 9", double gourd form,
   clusters of roses 85.00
  Roma, 9", triple candelabra, pink
   flowers, cream ground 160.00
Chalice, Rosemont, 10", robins, butterflies, flowers, and branches, black
   ground 240.00
Console Bowl, Silvertone, frog, sgd
   "DE" 200.00
Ewer
  Dickensware, 2nd line, 11½", incised
   fish, matte green ground, sgd
   "E. L. Pickens" 565.00
  Louwelsa, green 350.00
Figure
  Canaries, two on branch, textured
   Brighton base 160.00
  Cocker Spaniel, 10½ x 14", ink stamp
   mark 800.00
Hanging Basket
  Cameo 30.00
  Souevo, 6½" 175.00
Jardiniere
  Aurelian, pedestal base, slip painted
   florals, glossy brown glaze, artist
   sgd 1,250.00
  Blueware, 8½ x 7" 150.00
  Cameo Jewel, 8", applied jewels and
   female heads, light gray shading to
   dark ground, imp block lettered
   mark 200.00
  Dickensware, Line I, portrait of cavalier, caramel ground 500.00

Mug, Indian Chief, marked "Louwelsa,"
5⅞" h, $2,600.00.

Woodcraft, 9½", figural squirrel and woodpecker, tree trunk ground . . . **275.00**
Lamp, oil, Turada, blue **650.00**
Mug, Louwelsa, blue, cherries dec . . . **275.00**
Pitcher
Aurelian, 12", tankard, slip painted berries, glossy brown glaze, artist sgd **350.00**
Dickensware, 3rd line, 12½", molded full figure of man, long coat and hat, gray, marked "Weller" by hand, sgd "LM" **350.00**
Zona, 8", kingfisher, half kiln ink stamp mark **175.00**
Tobacco Jar, Louwelsa, brass lid **175.00**
Umbrella Stand, Flemish, 12½", panels of vines and pink morning glories, blended brown and green ground, imp block lettered mark **350.00**
Vase
Aurelian, 12 x 10", pillow shape, slip painted blackberries, glossy brown glaze, artist sgd **350.00**
Dickensware, 11", gourd shape, deep brown ground, autumn colored leaves and berries on branch, artist sgd "A. G." **245.00**
Coppertone, 11" **225.00**
Grape, 6" **100.00**
Silvertone, 6¾", bud **35.00**
Wild Rose, 9½" **35.00**
Wall Pocket
Blue Drapery, 9", clusters of roses, blue ground **50.00**
Glendale, 7½", multicolored molded bird and nest, ink stamp mark . . . **200.00**
L'Art Nouveau, 6½", blown-out floral, matte green and yellow glaze . . . **165.00**

WHALING

History: Whaling items are a specialized part of nautical collecting. Provenance is of prime importance since whaling collectors want assurances that their pieces are from a whaling voyage. Since ship's equipment seldom carries the ship's identification, some individuals have falsely attributed a whaling provenance to general nautical items. Know the dealer, auction house, or collector from whom you buy.

Special tools, e.g., knives, harpoons, lances, spades, etc., do not overlap the general nautical line. Makers' marks and condition determine value for these items.

Richard Bourne, Hyannis, Massachusetts, and Chuck DeLuca, York, Maine, regularly hold auctions featuring whaling material.

Reference: Thomas G. Lytle, *Harpoons And Other Whalecraft*, Old Dartmouth Historical Society, 1984.

Periodical: *Whalebone,* P. O. Box 2834, Fairfax, VA 22031.

Museums: Cold Spring Harbor Museum, Long Island, NY; Kendall Whaling Museum, Sharon, MA; Mystic Seaport Museum, Mystic, CT; National Maritime Museum, San Francisco, CA; Old Dartmouth Historical Society, New Bedford, MA; Whaling Museum, Nantucket, MA.

Additional Listings: Nautical Items and Scrimshaw.

Branding Iron, cast and wrought iron, E. S. Mitchell, Dartmouth, c1850, 32¾" l, $65.00.

Book
Nantucket Whalers and Their Voyages From 1815 to 1870, Nantucket, 1876, orig paper covers . . **500.00**
Whale Ships and Whaling, George Francis, Marine Research Society Salem, MA, 1925, First Edition, orig cloth binding **250.00**
Whaling Masters, Old Dartmouth Historical Society, New Bedford, MA, 1938, orig paper jacket and cloth binding **225.00**
Chest
Liquor, captain's, contains 18 engraved blown clear bottles **1,000.00**
Medicine, mahogany, contains 32 bottles, 3 jars, and medical instruction book with orig labels, orig label "James Folsom (ship druggist), 140 Commerical Street, Boston" . **1,250.00**
Deck Slate, 10 x 14", *Commodore Morris,* records sightings, positions, and remarks, 19th C **400.00**
Journal
Gideon Barstow, voyage to South Atlantic, June 15, 1836 to January 24, 1838 off Block Island, 26 whale stamps, rebound leather covers . . **3,250.00**
Nye, voyage to South Pacific Ocean, August 29, 1847 to March 19, 1849, contains entry of captain bur-

ied at sea on January 5, 1848 and
8 whale stamps, orig paper covers ... **650.00**
Sea Fox, voyage from New Bedford,
MA, April 18, 1871 to May 31,
1874, kept by Thomas McLane,
357 drawings, whale stamps, orig
leather covers, orig label "Barba-
dos" **87,500.00**
Susan, voyage departing from Nantucket, September 14, 1837 to May
27, 1841, contains 83 stamps and
drawings, rebound and boxed ... **20,000.00**
Quarterboard
154" l, *Maggie Abbott,* carved,
19th C **1,400.00**
79½" l, *Montclair,* scroll carved ends,
19th C **800.00**
Sailing Card, framed
Cutwater, 6½ x 4⅛" **525.00**
Fearless, 6⅝ x 4⅛", mid 19th C ... **500.00**
Table, 60 x 22¾ x 27¼", oak, from New
Bedford whaleship **950.00**
Whale Stamp
2", whale ivory, whale's tail shape,
coffin stamp, engraved "BARK/
ELLA/1841" **600.00**
2⅛" l, pine, carved, American, 19th C **300.00**
3¾" l, pine, carved sperm whale on
left side, whale's tail on other side,
American, 19th C **700.00**
Whalebone Products
Cane, 60" l, five pc sections, 19th C **200.00**
Clothespin, 4¾" l, carved **100.00**
Measure, 10⅞" l, 19th C **75.00**
Spatula, 13½" l, 19th C **300.00**
Toy
Crossbow, 15¼" l, spring steel bow,
brass mountings, 19th C **1,400.00**
Doll, 4¾" h, jointed, painted and
carved hair, eyes, and mouth,
19th C **2,750.00**
Yardstick, 36" l, inlaid tortoiseshell di-
visions, mid 19th C **400.00**

WHIELDON

WHIELDON

History: The Staffordshire potter, Thomas
Whieldon, established his shop in 1740. He is best
known for his mottled ware, molded in forms of
vegetables, fruits, and leaves. Josiah Spode and
Josiah Wedgwood, in different capacities, had connections with Whieldon.

Whieldon ware is a generic term. His wares
were never marked and other potters made similar
items. Whieldon ware is agate–tortoise shell earthenware, in limited shades of green, brown, blue
and yellow. Most pieces are utilitarian items, e.g.,
dinner ware and plates, but figurines and other
decorative pieces are found.

Reference: Susan and Al Bagdade, *Warman's
English & Continental Pottery & Porcelain, 1st Edition,* Warman Publishing Co., Inc., 1987.

**Tea Caddy, Cauliflower pattern, oval
base, 4" h, $575.00.**

Charger, 13⅞", rim molded with bands
of stars and dots, leaf form cartouches, mottled gray and green
glaze, yellow and brown sponging,
two rim firing cracks, c1760–70 .... **1,200.00**
Coffeepot, 9", green, yellow, and brown
streaky glaze, repaired **800.00**
Cradle, 3¾" l, mottled green, yellow,
and brown, c1770 .... **385.00**
Dish, leaf, 5½" l, gray and brown mottling, splashes of green and yellow on
white, three small feet, c1770 ..... **400.00**
Pitcher, cov, 8¾", green, brown, and
gray–blue glaze, applied flower and
scroll design, three mask and paw
feet, matching cov with bird finial,
c1755–60, finial repaired **8,000.00**
Plate
8½", octagonal, splashed manganese, raised rope twist rim,
c1755, pr **1,000.00**
9½", splashed manganese, blue,
green, and ochre, feather molded
edge, pr **600.00**
Spill Bowl, 5¾" d, mottled brown and
white glaze, vertical yellow, green,
and blue stripes, c1770 .... **450.00**
Tea Caddy, 5½" h, rect, canted corners,
flat shoulder, splashed brown glaze,
c1755 .... **425.00**
Teapot, Cauliflower pattern, deep
green, c1760 .... **1,100.00**

WHISKEY BOTTLES, EARLY

History: The earliest American whiskey bottles
were generic form bottles blown by pioneer glass
makers in the 18th century. The Biningers (1820–

1880s) were the first bottles specifically designed for whiskey. After the 1860s distillers favored the cylindrical 'fifth' form.

The first embossed brand name bottle was the amber E. G. Booz Old Cabin Whiskey bottle which was issued in 1860. Many stories have been told about this classic bottle. Unfortunately, most are not true. Research has proved that "booze" was a corruption of the words "bouse" and "boosy" from the 16th and 17th centuries. It was only a coincidence that the Philadelphia distributor also was named Booz. This bottle has been reproduced extensively.

Prohibition (1920–1933) brought the legal whiskey industry to a standstill. Whiskey was marked "medicinal purposes only" and distributed by private distillers in unmarked or paper label bottles.

The size and shape of whiskey bottles are standard. Colors are limited to amber, amethyst, clear, green, and cobalt blue (rare). Corks were the common closure in the early period, with the inside screw top being used in the 1880–1910 period.

Bottles made prior to 1880 are the most desirable. In purchasing a bottle with a label, condition is a critical factor. In the 1950s distillers began to issue collectors' special edition bottles to help increase sales.

References: Ralph & Terry Kovel, *The Kovels' Bottle Price List, 8th Edition*, Crown Publishers, 1987; Carlo and Dorothy Sellari, *The Standard Old Bottle Price Guide*, Collector Books, 1989.

Periodical: *Antique Bottle and Glass Collector*, P. O. Box 187, East Greenville, PA 18041.

Additional Listings: See *Warman's Americana & Collectibles* for a listing of Collectors' Special Editions Whiskey Bottles.

Atherton, Julius Kessler & Co., Distillers, indented, gold paint, backbar	35.00

Troyka Vodka, Siberian Vodka Co, San Francisco, CA, ⅘ qt, 12″ h, $15.00.

Booth & Sedgewicks Cordial Gin, iron pontil, sq, green, 10″	95.00
Brown, Thompson & Co, Louisville, KY, amber, 1860–90	18.00
Casper's, round, paneled shoulder, cobalt blue, 12″	210.00
Chestnut Grove, jug, pontil, amber, applied seal, 8¾″	90.00
Cutter, J. F., star and shield, olive green, whittled	150.00
Davis Rye, pinch bottle, gold paint	55.00
Eagle Liqueur Distilleries, olive	50.00
G. & B Whiskey, decanter, bulbous shape, gold letters, backbar	35.00
Hotaling, A. P., light amber, whittled, four pcs	50.00
Imperial, aqua, ½ pint	20.00
Lacey, W. A. Whiskey, stenciled, two tone, threaded stopper, 4½″	50.00
Macy & Jenkins, NY, handled, amber	18.00
Melchers Finest Canadian, Geneva, dark green	28.00
Moonshine, cylinder, smiling moon face, amber	300.00
Old Club Whiskey, Mach & Jenkins, NY, applied handle, amber	15.00
Peacock, Honolulu, monogram, cylinder, light amber	65.00
Pharazyn, H., figural, Indian warrior, yellow amber, 12¼″	625.00
Turner Brothers, New York, Buffalo, & San Francisco, sq, deep olive green, 9¾″, 1860	70.00
Weltys Private Stock Rye Whiskey, heavily emb, amber	25.00

WHITE PATTERNED IRONSTONE

History: White patterned ironstone is a heavy earthenware, first patented in 1813 by Charles Mason, Staffordshire, England, using the name "Patent Ironstone China." Other English potters soon began copying this opaque, feldspathic, white china.

All white ironstone dishes first became available in the American market in the early 1840s. The first patterns had simple Gothic lines similar to the shapes used in transfer wares. Pattern shapes, such as New York, Union, and Atlantic, were designed to appeal to the American housewife. Motifs, such as wheat, corn, oats, and poppies, were embossed on the forms as the American western prairie influenced design. Eventually over 200 shapes and patterns, with variations of finials and handles, were made.

White patterned ironstone is identified by shape names and pattern names. Many potters only named the shape in their catalogs. Pattern names usually refer to the decoration motif.

References: Jean Wetherbee, *A Look At White*

Ironstone, Wallace-Homestead, 1980; Jean Wetherbee, *A Second Look At White Ironstone,* Wallace-Homestead, 1985.

Baker, oval, 9⅜" l, Hebe shape, Alcock	**50.00**
Butter, cov, Athens, Podmore Walker, 1857	**80.00**
Cake Plate, 9", Brocade, Mason, handles	**125.00**
Chamber Pot, Wheat & Blackberry, Meakin	**35.00**
Coffeepot, Washington Shape, John Meir	**125.00**
Creamer	
Fig, Davenport	**60.00**
Wheat in the Meadow, Powell & Bishop, 1870	**40.00**
Cup and Saucer	
Ceres, Elsmore & Forster, handleless	**48.00**
Oak Leaf, Pankhurst, 1863, handleless	**50.00**
Paris, Alcock	**30.00**
Ewer, Scalloped Decagon, Wedgwood	**140.00**

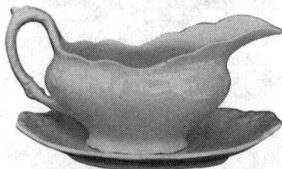

Gravy Boat, marked "Royal Ironstone China, Johnson Bros England," 9 x 4½" gravy boat, 5 x 8½" underplate, $75.00.

Gravy Boat	
Bordered Fuchsia, Anthony Shaw	**40.00**
Wheat & Blackberry, Meakin	**25.00**
Pitcher	
Berlin Swirl, Mayer & Elliot	**115.00**
Japan pattern, Mason, c1815	**275.00**
Syndenham, T & R Boote, 7⅞" h	**185.00**
Wheat, W E Corn	**65.00**
Plate	
Ceres, Elsmore & Forster, 8½"	**12.00**
Gothic, Adams, 9½"	**18.00**
Platter	
Columbia, 20 x 15", octagonal	**125.00**
Wheat, Meakin, 20¾ x 15⅜"	**50.00**
Punch Bowl	
Adriatic, scalloped edge	**335.00**
Berry Cluster, J Furnival	**125.00**
Relish	
Ceres, Elsmore & Forster, 1860	**40.00**
Wheat, W E Corn	**30.00**
Sauce, Vintage, Challinor	**15.00**
Soup Tureen, cov, Lily of the Valley, Shaw	**225.00**

Sugar, cov, Hyacinth, Wedgwood	**40.00**
Teapot	
Hyacinth, Wedgwood	**85.00**
Ivy, imp "William Adams," 10"	**75.00**
Niagara, Walley	**110.00**
Trent, T & R Boote	**90.00**
Toothbrush Holder	
Bell Flower, Burgess	**45.00**
Cable and Ring, Cockson & Seddon	**40.00**
Vegetable, cov	
Blackberry	**45.00**
Cable and Ring, Savoy shape, T & R Boote	**50.00**
Prairie Flowers, Livesley & Powell	**85.00**
Ribbed Bud, J W Pankhurst	**80.00**

WILLOW PATTERN CHINA

History: Josiah Spode developed the first "traditional" willow pattern in 1810. The components, all motifs taken from Chinese export china, are: a willow tree, "apple" tree, two pagodas, fence, two birds, and a three figures crossing a bridge. The legend, in its many versions, is an English invention based on the design components.

By 1830, there were over 200 plus makers of willow pattern china in England. The pattern has remained in continuous production. Some of the English firms that still produce willow pattern china are: Burleigh, Johnson Bros. (Wedgwood Group), Royal Doulton's continuation of the Booths pattern, and Wedgwood.

By the end of the 19th century, pattern production spread to France, Germany, Holland, Ireland, Sweden, and the United States. In the United States, Buffalo Pottery made the first willow pattern beginning in 1902. Many other companies followed, developing willow variants using rubber–stamp simplified patterns as well as overglaze decals. The largest American manufacturers of the traditional willow pattern were Royal China and Homer Laughlin, usually preferred because it is dated. Shenango pieces are most desired among restaurant quality ware.

Japan began producing large quantities of willow pattern china in the early 20th century. Noritake began about 1902. Its early pieces used a Nippon "Royal Sometuke" mark. Most Japanese pieces are porous earthenware with dark blue pattern using the tradition willow design, usually with no inner border. Noritake did put the pattern on china bodies. Unusual forms include salt and pepper shakers, one–quarter pound butter dishes, and canisters. "Occupied Japan" may add a small percentage to the value of common table wares. Maruta and Moriyama marked pieces are especially valued. The most sought after Japanese willow is the fine quality NKT Co. ironstone with a copy of the old Booths pattern. Recent Japanese willow is a paler shade of blue on a porcelain body.

The most common dinnerware color is blue. However, pieces can also be found in black (with clear glaze or mustard–color glaze by Royal Doulton), brown, green, mulberry, pink (red), and polychrome. Although colors other than blue are hard to find, there is less demand; thus, prices may not necessarily be higher.

The popularity of the willow design has resulted in a large variety of willow–decorated products: candles, fabric, glass, graniteware, linens, needlepoint, plastic, tinware, stationery, watches, and wall coverings. All this material has collectible value.

References: Mary Frank Gaston, *Blue Willow: An Identification & Value Guide,* Collector Books, 1983, revised prices, 1986; Veryl Marie Worth and Louise M. Loehr, *Willow Pattern China: Collector's Guide, 3rd Edition,* H. S. Worth Co, 1986.

Periodical: *American Willow Report,* 1733 Chase Street, Cincinnati, OH 45223.

Reproduction Alert: The Scio Pottery, Scio, Ohio, currently manufactures a willow pattern set sold in variety stores. The pieces have no marks or back stamps, and the transfer is of poor quality. The plates are flatter in shape than those of other manufacturers.

Additional Listings: Buffalo Pottery. See *Warman's Americana & Collectibles* for more examples.

Toby Jug, black hat, gray hair, flesh tones, willow coat, green vest, yellow britches, gray socks, black shoes, Staffordshire Ware, marked with rope knot and "W," 5½" h, $225.00.

Bowl, 9¾ x 7⅝", oval, Ridgway	24.00
Cake Stand, porcelain, Royal Worcester	225.00
Child's Feeding Dish, 5" d, divided, single border, marked "Made In Japan"	25.00
Child's Set, Japanese, 15 pcs	150.00
Cup and Saucer	
Allerton, scalloped edge	25.00
Booths	25.00
Buffalo Pottery	20.00
Homer Laughlin	6.00
Japanese, NKT Co., Booths copy	16.00
Shenango	12.00
Ginger Jar, cov, 4¼" h, Mason, England	20.00
Gravy Boat, Buffalo Pottery	75.00
Pepper Pot, 19th C	115.00
Pitcher, English, 1 qt	55.00
Plate, 10"	
Allerton, plain edge	20.00
Johnson Bros	15.00
Royal China	8.00
Royal Doulton, gold trim	55.00
Platter	
Allerton, 9 x 12"	45.00
Homer Laughlin, 13" d	15.00
Soup Plate, Booth, old mark	18.00
Syrup Jug, pewter lid, Royal Doulton	125.00
Tea Caddy, Rington	175.00
Teapot	
Homer Laughlin	35.00
Johnson Bros	55.00
Tumbler, glass, frosted	10.00
Wash Bowl and Pitcher, Royal Doulton	400.00

WITCH BALLS

History: A witch ball simply is a hollow sphere of colored or multicolored glass. There are various myths surrounding the origin and purpose of the witch ball. Some say they were displayed by the fireplace to catch demon spirits as they descended the chimney and then were taken outside for cleaning. Others contend they were used to store salt by the chimney to keep it dry.

In all probability a witch ball was a glassmaker's whimsey, used strictly for decorative purposes atop an unfilled flower vase.

Don't confuse witch balls with Christmas tree ornaments, target balls, floats, or early glass fire extinguishers. Witch balls come in a variety of sizes. They cannot be attributed to one specific glass maker or company.

Reference: Joyce E. Blake, *Glasshouse Whimsies,* published by author, 1984.

Amber Glass, 4" d ball, white loopings, matching 4¾" ribbed baluster form holder	425.00
Aqua, 4¼" d ball, white loopings	190.00
Cranberry Glass, 4½" d ball	90.00
Green, 5" d ball, opalescent swirls	115.00
Nailsea Type, 6½" d ball, 10½" h vase, clear, red, white, and blue loopings, flared bowls, scalloped rims, pedestal vases, pr	3,500.00
Pittsburgh Glass, 10¼" h, clear, white loopings, scalloped matching stand	225.00
Sapphire Blue Glass, 2½" d ball	125.00

Goblet and witch ball, Lutz type lattice glass, pink, white, and gold design, 7″ h goblet, 4″ d witch ball, $375.00.

Spatter Glass, 4½″ d, white ground, red, pink and green flecks **115.00**

WOODENWARE

History: Many utilitarian household objects and farm implements were made of wood. Although they were used heavily, these implements were made of the strongest woods and well taken care of by their owners.

This category serves as a catch–all for wood objects which do not fit into other categories.

Additional Listings: See *Warman's Americana & Collectibles* for more examples.

Box, utility, sliding cover, green felt base, 7½ x 4 x 2½″, $60.00.

Apple Peeler, 15½″ h, red varnish finish, hand crank flywheel, marked "Patented" **65.00**
Barn Lantern
  10¼″ h, pine, glass sides, hinged door, replaced tin candle socket . . **325.00**
  11″ h, beech, oak, and pink, glass sides, hinged door, replaced tin candle socket **225.00**

Baton, 40″ l, orange paint, red and black dec **75.00**
Bootjack, 19″ l, fish shape, relief carving, red stain **30.00**
Bowl, 15½″ d, old dark finish **40.00**
Box
  10¼″ l, brass studs, handle, and escutcheons, traces of leather covering **65.00**
  18¾″ l, dovetailed poplar, dec, orig red and black flame graining, wrought iron lock and hasp, brass escutcheon **450.00**
Butter Paddle, 9½″ l, curly maple, dark patina **45.00**
Candle Box
  13½″ w, 20″ h, hanging, pine, relief carved, old natural finish **250.00**
  14″ l, walnut, dovetailed, sliding lid, worn finish **120.00**
  15″ l, pine, black stenciled stylized flowers, orig green paint, wrought iron nail construction, sliding lid with molded edge **300.00**
Candle Dryer, 32″ h, turned post, two rows of cross arms, red **475.00**
Candlestick, 8″ h, silver stick shape, worn silver gilt over gesso **300.00**
Canteen
  5″ d, 4¼″ h, keg shape, red **175.00**
  6⅝″ d, stave constructed, laced bands, branded "O E" and carved initials, old patina **175.00**
Chamber Stick, 4⅞″ h, pushup **185.00**
Cheese Box, 15½″ d, 11½″ h, "Monarch Chicago" label **55.00**
Cobbler's Bench, 42″ l, pine, nut brown finish, five drawers, worn leather set, one drawer dated "1806" **450.00**
Doll, 17½″ l, articulated arms and legs, old paint traces **250.00**
Dough Box
  12 x 31″, poplar, red finish **65.00**
  15½ x 26¾″, pine, reddish brown stain, gothic arch feet, lid, refinished **175.00**
  19 x 34″, pine and poplar, splayed base, turned legs, dovetailed, replaced lid, refinished **295.00**
Drying Rack, 24 x 60″, folding, poplar, gray patina, mortised construction . . **200.00**
Figure
  Eagle
    7½″, carved, old green and yellow paint **275.00**
    11¾″ h, relief carved feathers, gold repaint **200.00**
  Pig, 7″ h, carved **225.00**
Footstool, 16″ l, pine, old worn green repaint **65.00**
Frame, 12½ × 16½″, pine, molded, old green repaint **10.00**

Glove Box, ornate	45.00
Jar	
5¾", walnut, barrel shape, varnish finish	40.00
8" h, keg shaped, poplar, turned detail, old finish	200.00
Lamp, betty, 7¾" h, turned detail, adjustable shelf	225.00
Lighting Trammel, iron candle sockets, adjusts from 36" l, late 19th C	265.00
Padlock, 7¾ x 12", orig red and black paint, marked "Souvenir Marquette Prison, made by Jale Lock Co"	250.00
Pipe Box, 18½" h, oak, dark finish, English	170.00
Plate, 7½" d, turned, painted winter landscape scene	145.00
Printing Block, carved, deep cut "W H J" initials	40.00
Shelf, 12½" w, pine, carved rayed back, old brown finish	425.00
Spice Box, 10½" w, 14" h, hanging, pine, shaped crest, divided two part int., drawer, molded edge, dovetail corners, old gray paint	300.00
Sugar Bucket	
9¾" h, stave constructed, stenciled mark "18XX" on handle	85.00
10" h, stave construction, two-tone brown stain	75.00
Towel Bar, 15" l, oak, cut out bird, bird head brackets, 20th C	50.00
Towel Rack, 25¾ x 32", folding, poplar, dark brown finish, peaked finials . . .	400.00
Toy, pull, 6½" h, cart with wheels, brown flocked papier mache rabbit, marked "Germany"	35.00
Tray	
16 x 24½", polychrome stenciled children at play scene, orig black lacquer	45.00
18¾ x 19", pine, scalloped sides with cut out designs, orig green paint, red striping	200.00
Watch Hutch, 2¼ x 3¼ x 4⅞", oak, sliding lid with round lens	110.00
Whirligig, 29" l, man and kicking mule, polychrome paint, 20th C	225.00
Writing Box, 1⅜ x 8¾ x 15¼", pine, old brown patina, drawer in end	45.00

WORLD WAR I COLLECTIBLES

Collecting Hints: Most veterans of World War I have died, so nostalgia does not play as large a part in this collecting area as it does for World War II. Also, America's involvement was much more limited both in time and personnel. Equipment was not as sophisticated and patches to differentiate units were not used until the end of the war.

Reenactment groups have been organized; several mock encounters have been staged on the European battlefields.

Try to obtain as much information as you can about the source of the material you buy. Many uniform and equipment pieces were prewar models and some forms lasted into the peace time army. Purists want equipment that was "over there."

History: The assassination of Archduke Ferdinand of Austria in 1914 set in motion a series of internal conflicts within Europe that eventually led to full-scale war. After initial German successes, the war evolved into a series of trench engagements. In 1917 America entered the war. After a series of military defeats, Germany and its allies surrendered on November 11, 1918.

Periodicals: *Military Collectors News,* P.O. Box 702073, Tulsa, OK 74170.

Collectors' Clubs: American Society of Military Insignia Collectors, 1331 Bradley Avenue, Hummelstown, PA 17036; Association of American Military Uniform Collectors, 446 Berkshire Road, Elyria, OH 44035.

Silk, white, black, maroon border, 15 × 15", 16½ × 16½" frame, $35.00.

Belt, web	8.00
Belt and Buckle, "Hate Belt," button and cap insignias around belt, German, Wurttenburg	95.00
Canteen, Army	10.00
Certificate, 9½ x 12½", Liberty Loan, multicolored	25.00
Cigarette Lighter, trench, German	30.00
Coat, US Army	75.00
Gas Mask, carrying can, shoulder strap, canister attached to bottom, German	40.00
Handkerchief, 11" sq, "Remember Me,"	

soldier and girl in center, red, white, and blue edge **12.00**
Helmet
  German, leather, spiked **225.00**
  US, 3rd Army insignia **45.00**
Jacket, Sergeant's **40.00**
Periscope, wood, used in trenches ... **40.00**
Picture Frame, iron, emb dec, dated
  1917 .... **35.00**
Pillow cover, 16 x 17½", full color printed soldier portrait surrounded by flags and American eagle, gold lettering "Forget Me Not," full color Miss Liberty holding stone table reads "World War Service" **35.00**
Pin
  ¾ x 1⅜", Rainbow Division 166/1917; almond shape, 10k gold, openwork, two crossed rifles in center . **35.00**
  1", Victory Loan, bond seller, 1919 . **15.00**
Plaque, 20 x 14½", bronze, Democracy and Patriotism poems **40.00**
Pocket Mirror, 2¾", oval, "Leaders of the World War For Democracy," world leaders and flags **25.00**
Print, 156th Field Artillery, Col. Miller Commanding Camp Sheridan, AL, Nov 22, 1917, 52" l **87.50**
Ribbon, 2 x 5", "Welcome Home 26th Division" **12.00**
Stickpin, porcelain, wounded German soldier, 1914–1918 .... **25.00**
Sword, cipher on handle, folding clamshell guard, blackened, fittings, Imperial **125.00**
Tobacco Jar, cov, 6½", ceramic, brown glaze, General Pershing **125.00**
Toy
  Machine gun, wood and tin, magazine on top holds wood bullets, turn crank to fire **50.00**
  War camp, miniature, dated 1917 .. **45.00**
Wings, German fliers, set of 24 ..... **240.00**
Yardlong, framed, USS Sibenoy Arriving At US Naval Base, Aug 8, 1919 ... **125.00**

WORLD WAR II COLLECTIBLES

Collecting Hints: World War II material still is plentiful. Collectors should specialize either in actual military equipment or material issued for children and adults on the home front. Many collectors narrow the topic further by focusing on one form, e.g., manuals, patches, sheet music, toys, etc.

Uniforms and cloth material should be stored and cleaned carefully. Remember that World War II items are now forty-five or more years old; the cloth may not hold up in a modern washing machine.

The more personal information about an object you can obtain the better. Whenever possible identify the military unit and theater of operation. Collectors tend to favor materials related to the United States. The principal foreign collectible is Nazi items.

History: Although America's formal involvement in World War II lasted from 1941 to 1945, World War II collectors focus on the 1936 to 1948 period. The early dates cover America's response to the German military activities in Europe and Japan's invasion of Korea and China. The later period covers the time of American military occupation in Europe and Japan.

Besides equipping and supplying American Armed Forces abroad, the U. S. government and industry produced a wealth of material to prepare America for possible invasion and to bolster American morale. Any collectible field active during World War II should be checked for related material.

Periodicals: *Military Collectors News,* P.O. Box 702073, Tulsa, OK 74170.

Collectors' Clubs: American Society of Military Insignia Collectors, 1331 Bradley Avenue, Hummelstown, PA 17036; Association of American Military Uniform Collectors, 446 Berkshire Road, Elyria, OH 44035.

Atlas
  Global Atlas of World At War,
    Mathews-Northup, 1944 .... **7.50**

Sheet Music, *Any Bonds Today,* **by Irving Berlin, copyright by Henry Morgenthau Jr, Sec'y of Treasury, theme song of the National Defense Savings Program, $8.00.**

Liberty World Atlas, Pictorial History of World War II, Hammond, cutout globe assembly . . . . | **10.00**

1942 War Atlas, Pure Oil . . . . | **7.50**

Binoculars, Army, M-17, field type, 7½" l, olive drab, 7 x 50 power, clear, fixed optics . . . . | **85.00**

Book, *World War II in Headlines and Pictures,* Philadelphia, "Evening Bulletin," 10½ x 14", softbound, 1956 . . | **32.00**

Booklet, US Navy 150th Anniversary . | **6.00**

Bracelet, AAF P-47, Sweetheart, gilt metal body, side view of P-47, gilt wrist chain . . . . | **14.00**

Card Game, "Navy Aircraft Squadron Insignia," 4 x 5 x 1" box . . . . | **20.00**

Drinking Glass, silk screen design, 4⅝" h, 2⅝" d, "Remember Pearl Harbor–Dec. 7, 1941," multicolored . . . . . | **22.00**

Flight Suit, Army Air Force, Type A-4, olive drab gaberdine, matching belt, zipper front, size 38 . . . . | **65.00**

Gas Mask, Japanese, head straps, attached canister . . . . | **40.00**

Letter Opener, brass, rifle diecut, "Compliments of Dreifus & Co" . . . . | **25.00**

Magazine, "Sea Power," 1945 . . . . . . | **6.50**

Map, silk, AAF rayon escape map, Holland, Belgium, France, and Germany, 1944, orig carrying case, mint . . . . . | **35.00**

Paper Airplane, Crestcraft Co, Chicago, copyright 1943, 11 x 14", multicolored pgs showing four different planes, Brewster Buffalo, Model F2A2, Curtiss Warhawk P-40, Flying Fortress B-19, Lockheed Lightning P-38 . . . . . | **25.00**

Paperweight, 2½ × 4 × 3", wood, syroco, showing three military men riding in jeep scene . . . . | **24.00**

Pencil holder, 3½", plastic, red, white, and blue, "Victory," back lumber yard adv . . . . | **10.00**

Pin, ¾", stamped brass, "Remember Pearl Harbor," small simulated pearl in center . . . . | **10.00**

Poster

20 x 28½", American flag, "Give It Your Best," full color, unsigned . . . | **55.00**

22 x 28, Sailor looking out port hole, "This Man May Die If You Talk Too Much," full color, artist sgd "Sarra" | **65.00**

25 x 38", B-17 with American flag waving overhead, "Keep Em Flying - Do Your Part," full color, artist sgd "D. V. Smith & A. Dorne" . . . . . . | **200.00**

Shovel, fox hole type . . . . | **8.00**

Sign, Dunhill Service Lighter, 5¼ x 7", cardboard . . . . | **10.00**

Sweater, sleeveless, olive drab, "V" neck . . . . | **18.00**

Tank, miniature, copper colored metal, 3" l, green felt bottom . . . . | **20.00**

Toy Airplane, Hubley

P-38, 12¾" wing span, 9" l body, silver color, red pilot cockpit and undercarriage, twin fuselage . . . . . . | **30.00**

P-40, die cast, 8¼" wing span, 7¾" l body, yellow wings, orange balance and propeller, rubber wheels | **35.00**

Wall Plaque, "Victory-Liberty," "God Bless those In Our Service," 9", red, white, blue, and gold, octagonal cardboard, 1943 . . . . | **6.00**

Window Banner, "Welcome Home," 8 x 12", red, white, and blue, cloth brown eagle, gold fringe . . . . | **7.00**

WORLD'S FAIRS AND EXPOSITIONS

History: The Great Exhibition of 1851 in London marked the beginning of the World's Fair and Exposition movement. The fairs generally feature exhibitions from nations around the world displaying the best of their industrial and scientific achievements.

Many important technological advances have been introduced at world's fairs. Examples include the airplane, telephone, and electric lights. The ice cream cone, hot dog, and iced tea were products of vendors at fairs. Art movements often were closely connected to fairs with the Paris Exhibition of 1900 generally considered to have assembled the best of the works of the Art Nouveau artists.

References: *American Art, New York World's Fair 1939,* Apollo Books, 1987; Carl Abbott, *The Great Extravaganza: Portland and the Lewis and Clark Exposition,* Oregon Historical Society, 1981; Stanley Appelbaum, *The New York World's Fair, 1939/1940,* Dover Publications, Inc., 1971; Patricia F. Carpenter and Paul Totah, *The San Francisco Fair, Treasure Island, 1939–1940,* Scottwall Associates, 1989; Kurt Krueger, *Meet Me In St. Louis—The Exonumia Of The 1904 World's Fair,* Krause Publications, 1979; Howard Rossen and John Kaduck, *Columbia World's Fair Collectibles,* Wallace-Homestead, 1976, revised price list 1982.

Periodical: *World's Fair,* P.O. Box 339, Corte Madera, CA 94925.

Collectors' Clubs: Expo Collectors & Historians Organization (ECHO), 1436 Killarney, Los Angeles, CA 90065; World's Fair Collectors' Society, Inc., P. O. Box 20806, Sarasota, FL 33583.

1876, Philadelphia, Centennial

Paperweight, glass, scenes of exposition buildings . . . . | **75.00**

Worker's Passbook, 3 x 4", stiff paper, 4 pgs, black and white photo of employee . . . . | **65.00**

1893, Chicago, Columbian Exposition

Advertising Trade Card, oversized,

Clark's O.N.T. Thread, Electrical
Building 8.00
Badge, 1½ x 2½", emb brass link
badge, Columbus on U.S. shore
with Indians, "400th Anniversary/
Discovery Of America/Oct. 1892" . 60.00
Fan, 12¼" h, 23" w opened, full color
illus of fairgrounds, mounted on flat
wood swivel pieces 55.00
Sheet Music, *Columbus or World's
Fair Grand March,* Frank Drayton,
National Music Co, Chicago, 1892 15.00

**Chicago, change purse, white metal
top, nautical and patriotic motifs, roll
bars to allow change to enter, leather
pouch, 2¾ x 1⅞", $50.00.**

1901, Buffalo, Pan-American Exposition
Pin, pan shape, 2¼" l, diecut litho tin,
"C Klinck's Daisy Leaf Lard," red,
white, and blue, full color lard pail
in center 27.50
Matchsafe, 1½ x 2½", silvered brass,
ladies outstreached arms as crest
of Niagara Falls, Manufacturers &
Liberal Arts Building on back 70.00
1904, St. Louis, Louisiana Purchase Exposition
Ashtray, Cascade Gardens 10.00
Paperweight, 3", domed, sepia photo
of Cascades Building and lagoon . 35.00
Pin, Heinz Pickle, 1¼" l, composition,
"Heinz" in raised letters on one
side, "St. Louis '04" on other, brass
hanging loop 17.50
Vase, 5" h, irid blue and purple, double handles, Electricity Bldg picture, numbered 45.00
1909, Alaska-Yukon Pacific Exposition,
plate 55.00
1915, San Francisco, Panama-Pacific
International Exposition, book, *Red
Book of Views of the Panama Intl Exposition in San Francisco* 18.00

1933, Chicago, Century of Progress
Ashtray, Travel & Transportation Bldg 8.00
Bottle Opener, 5" h, figural, copper-
colored metal, mythological Egyp-
tian lady and American Legion
logo, Fort Dearborn exhibit and
"Chicago 1933" on back 25.00
Puzzle, jigsaw, 11 x 16", "H. M. Pettit
Approved Bird's Eye View Of A Century Of Progress," 8½ x 8½ x 1" box 30.00
Tie Clip, 1 x 2", silvered metal, diecut,
silver and black enamel of fair building 20.00
Watch Box, 2¼ x 2½ x¾", for "Chicago
World's Fair Watch #9531," black and
white illus of early fort on lid 60.00
1939, New York, New York World's Fair
Bottle, 9¼", milk glass, molded, Hemisphere 40.00
Compact, 3" d, light colored wood,
hinged lid with brass border, full
color celluloid scene of Hall of
Communications 25.00
Flashlight, 3½" d, 2" silvered steel circular shape, foldup 3½" d ball, rev
with blue-enameled design of Trylon and Perisphere, official "NYWF
copyright" license, two "C" batteries 125.00
Jewelry Box, wood, 7½ x 9½ x 3",
heavily textured black finish, textured Art Deco design of Trylon and
Perisphere on lid, floral paper-lined
int. 75.00
Pencil, mechanical, 10½" l,¾" d, gold
colored wood barrel, cartoon illus
of person with camera clinging to
Trylon and lady sitting on Perisphere, marked "N.Y.W.F. Eagle
Pencil Co.," rubber eraser 30.00
1939, San Francisco, Golden Gate International Exposition
Guide Book, 5½ x 8", soft cover, 118
pgs, 16 x 19" foldout map, diecut
tab index, Junket Dessert adv on
back cov 20.00
Scarf, 27½ x 29", linen-like, light blue
and brown illus, off-white ground . 40.00
1964, New York, New York World's Fair,
guide book, *Official Guide New York
World's Fair* 18.00

WRIGHT, RUSSEL

Collecting Hints: Russel Wright worked for
many different companies in addition to creating
material under his own label, American Way.
Wright's contracts with firms often called for the
redesign of pieces which did not produce or sell
well. As a result, several lines have the same item
in more than one shape.

Wright was totally involved in design. Most collectors focus on his dinnerware; however, he also designed glassware, plastic items, textiles, furniture, and metal objects. Bleached and blonde furniture were part of his contributions. His early work in spun aluminum often is overlooked as is his later work in plastic for the Northern Industrial Chemical Company.

History: Russel Wright was an American industrial engineer with a design passion for domestic efficiency through simple lines. His streamlined influence is found in all aspects of living. Wright and his wife, Mary Small Einstein, wrote *A Guide To Easier Living* to explain the concepts.

Russel Wright was born in 1904 in Lebanon, Ohio. His first jobs included set designer and stage manager under the direction of Norman Bel Geddes. He later used this theatrical flair for his industrial designs, stressing simple clean lines. Some of his earliest designs were executed in polished spun aluminum. These pieces, designed in the mid-1930s, included trays, vases, teapots, and other items. Wright received awards from the Museum of Modern Art in 1950 and 1953. His designs garnered many other awards.

Among the companies for which Russel Wright did design work are Chase Brass and Copper, General Electric, Imperial Glass, National Silver Co., Shenango, and Steubenville Pottery Company. In 1983 a major exhibition of Wright's designs was held at the Hudson River Museum in Yonkers, New York, and at the Smithsonian's Renwick Gallery in Washington, D.C.

References: Ann Kerr, *Russel Wright And His Dinnerware: A Descriptive Price Guide,* privately printed, 1981; Ann Kerr, *The Steubenville Saga,* privately printed, 1979, out-of-print.

AMERICAN MODERN

Made by the Steubenville Pottery Company, 1939–59. Initially this pattern was issued in Seafoam Blue, Coral, Chartreuse Curry, Granite Gray, White and Bean Brown, also issued in Black Chutney, Cedar Green, Cantaloupe, and Glacier Blue. The Ideal Toy Co made a set of miniature dishes, which were distributed by Sears, Roebuck.

Creamer, Chartreuse Curry	**20.00**
Fruit Bowl, lug handle	
Cedar Green	**6.00**
Granite Gray	**7.50**
Plate	
6″, bread and butter, Seafoam Blue .	**3.00**
8¼″, salad, Coral	**5.00**
10″, dinner, Granite Gray	**6.00**
Salad Bowl, Cantaloupe	**24.00**
Salt and Pepper, pr	
Coral	**9.00**
Glacier Blue	**9.00**
Soup, lug handle, Granite Gray	**7.50**

IROQUOIS

Made by the Iroquois China Co and Garrison Products, 1946–60s. Initially it was issued in Ice Blue, Forest Green, Avocado Yellow, Lemon Yellow, Nutmeg Brown, and Sugar White. Also issued in Lettuce Green, Charcoal, Ripe Apricot, Pink Sherbet, Parsley Green, Cantaloupe, Oyster Gray, Aqua, Brick Red, and Grayed-Blue. A patterned line was offered in 1959.

Bowl	
5″	
Avocado Yellow	**4.00**
Charcoal	**5.00**
5½″	
Avocado Yellow	**4.50**
Charcoal	**5.50**
Parsley Green	**4.50**
10″, Ice Blue	**16.00**
Casserole, cov, Nutmeg Brown, 2 qt . .	**20.00**
Creamer and Sugar, stacking, Sugar	
White	**15.00**
Cup and Saucer	
Avocado Yellow	**5.00**
Brick Red	**10.00**
Plate	
7″, luncheon	
Brick Red	**7.00**
Lemon Yellow	**3.00**
Lettuce Green	**3.00**
Pink Sherbet	**3.00**
Turquoise	**7.00**
9″, dinner	
Avocado Yellow	**4.00**
Lettuce Green	**4.00**
Sugar White	**4.00**
10″, dinner	
Brick Red	**10.00**
Turquoise	**10.00**
Platter	
13″, Ice Blue	**10.00**
14″, Avocado Yellow	**14.00**

WHITE CLOVER

Made by Harker China, 1951–55. Initially it was issued in Meadow Green, Coral Sand, Golden Spree, and Charcoal.

Cereal Bowl	**5.00**
Cup	**6.00**
Plate, 10″ dinner	**8.00**

YELLOW WARE

History: Yellow ware is a heavy earthenware of differing weight and strength which varies in color from a rich pumpkin to lighter shades which are more tan than yellow. Although plates, nappies, and custard cups are found, kitchen bowls and other cooking utensils are most prevalent.

The first American yellow ware was produced at Bennington, Vermont. English yellow ware has additional ingredients which make its body much harder. Derbyshire and Sharp's were foremost among the English manufacturers.

References: John Gallo, *Nineteenth and Twentieth Century Yellow Ware,* Heritage Press, 1985; Joan Leibowitz, *Yellow Ware: The Transitional Ceramic,* Schiffer Publishing, 1985.

Bowl, brown bands, 6¼″ d, 2¾″ h, $30.00.

Bowl
8⅜″ d, 4¼″ h, blue and brown sponge
spatter with a touch of red, minor
wear 65.00
9½″ d, brown sponging 130.00
Box, 15½″ l, rect, emb vintage and urns
of fruit dec, clear glaze, running
brown and green 200.00
Casserole, 7¼″ d, cov, brown sponging 50.00
Creamer, 4½″ h, green and brown
sponging 75.00
Crock, 5½″, brown bands 30.00
Cuspidor, 5 x 7½″, green, blue, and tan
sponge glaze 60.00
Figure, 11⅜″ h, seated cat, oval base,
freestanding front legs, brown and
bluish green running glaze, minor
chips on edge of base 2,000.00
Grease Lamp, 14½″ h, bluish green running glaze, rayed circle with "W" ... 55.00
Jar
8¾″ h, brown slip dec 525.00
12¼″ h, brown running glaze, chipped
lid 85.00
Mug
3¼″, brown polka dots 675.00
3⅞″, white band with brown stripes . 115.00
Pitcher
4½″ h, emb ribs, rect area with transfer label "Equity Elev. & Trading
Co...Whitman, ND," green and
brown sponging 45.00
8½″ h, brown band, dark brown
stripes, repaired handle 210.00
Salt, 3″ d, 2⅛″ h, ftd, white band, blue
seaweed dec, blue stripe 155.00

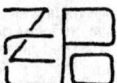

ZANE WARE
MADE IN U.S.A.

ZANE POTTERY

History: In 1921 Adam Reed and Harry McClelland bought the Peters and Reed Pottery in Zanesville, Ohio. The firm continued production of garden wares and introduced several new art lines: "Sheen," "Powder Blue," "Crystalline," and "Drip." The factory was sold in 1941 to Lawton Gonder.

Additonal Listings: Gonder and Peters and Reed.

Bowl
5″, brown and blue 45.00
5¼″, Wilse Blue, dragonfly dec 50.00
6½″, blue, marked "Zanesware" ... 25.00
Figure, 10⅛″, cat, black, green eyes .. 500.00

Vase, daisy motif, unglazed terra cotta, green glazed int., 4½″ d, 6″ h, $35.00.

Jardiniere, 34″ h, green matte glaze, artist sgd "Frank Ferreu" 300.00
Vase
5″, green, cobalt blue drip glaze ... 25.00
7″, flowing medium green over dark
forest green ground 85.00

LA MORO
ZANESVILLE POTTERY

History: Zanesville Art Pottery, one of several potteries located in Zanesville, Ohio, began production in 1900. A line of utilitarian products was first produced. Art pottery was introduced shortly thereafter. The major line was La Moro which was hand painted and decorated under glaze. The impressed block print mark La Moro appears on the high glazed and matte glazed decorated ware. The firm was bought by S. A. Weller in 1920 and became known as Weller Plant No. 3.

References: Louise and Evan Purviance and Norris F. Schneider, *Zanesville Art Pottery In Color*, Mid-America Book Company, 1968; Evan and Louise Purviance, *Zanesville Art Tile In Color*, Wallace-Homestead Book Co., 1972.

Vase, bulbous bottom, cone top and neck, two handles, La Moro, marked 2/802/4, 8¾″ h, $350.00.

Bowl, 6½″, fluted edge, mottled blue . .	45.00
Jardiniere, 8¼″ h, cream to light amber peony blossoms, ruffled rim, shaded brown ground	75.00
Plate, 4½″, applied floral dec	25.00
Teapot, 2¾″ h, souvenir, dark green, marked "Tyces Pottery/Zanesville/Ohio"	35.00
Tile, 6 x 18″, woman, blowing horn, cream ground	275.00
Vase, 10¼″, matte, white–gray portrait of horse, light olive green to blue–green ground, peachblow in back, high glaze brown int., sgd "R. G. Turner"	825.00

ZSOLNAY POTTERY

History: Vilmos Zsolnay (1828–1900) assumed control of his brother's factory in Pécs, Hungary,

in the mid-19th century. In 1899 Miklos, Vilmos's son, became manager. The firm still produces ceramic ware.

The early wares are highly ornamental, glazed, and have a cream color ground. "Eosin" glaze, a deep rich play of colors reminiscent of Tiffany's iridescent wares, received a gold medal at the 1900 Paris exhibition. Zsolnay Art Nouveau pieces show great creativity.

Originally no trademark was used. Beginning in 1878 a blue mark depicting the five towers of the cathedral at Pécs was used. The initials "TJM" represent the names of Miklos's three children.

Zsolnay's recent series of iridescent glazed figurines, which initially were inexpensive, now are being sought by collectors and show a steady increase in value.

Reference: Susan and Al Bagdade, *Warman's English & Continental Pottery & Porcelain, 1st Edition*, Warman Publishing Co., Inc., 1987.

Bowl	
9¾″, fan shape, rolled in sides, scrolled handle, reticulated, multicolored chrysanthemums int. dec, cobalt blue ground, gold trim	325.00
10″ d, carved, cherubs dec, curved leaf handles	500.00
Centerpiece, 16 x 4 x 5″, crescent shape, double walled, reticulated, irid florals, gold trim	285.00
Dish, 8½″, fan shape, rolled in edge, reticulated, beige, gold, and pink dec, steeple mark	185.00
Ewer, 7½″, cream, yellow, and beige dec, gold base, gold reticulated neck band, ornate handle	115.00

Figure, iridescent green–gold, marked "Made In Hungry, Zsolnay," and castle mark, 6¼″ h, $125.00.

Figure

3¾", fox, irid green, sgd	**50.00**
4", kitten, irid green	**75.00**
5", German Shepherd, irid	**50.00**
7½", polar bears, irid purple and green	**225.00**

Jug, 9", handles, multicolored enameled flowers, cream ground, lustered . . . **200.00**

Mug, 4½", irid blue luster **80.00**

Pitcher, 9" h, pink cherub design, c1870 **100.00**

Plate

8½" d, shell shape, reticulated, red and gold flowers, beige ground, steeple mark	**180.00**
10¾", Persian type design, red, blue, and silver luster	**300.00**

Puzzle Jug, 6½", pierced roundels, irid dec, cream ground, castle mark, imp "Zsolnay" **165.00**

Ring Tree, 3½", irid gold **75.00**

Vase

5½" h, applied simulated stone with thumbprints, irid red glaze	**155.00**
6" h, double walled, reticulated, pastels, marked	**135.00**
6½" h, double walled, reticulated, cobalt blue, beige, and gold dec . . .	**350.00**
9½" h, baluster, ftd, wide shaped handles, reticulated, ivory flowers, gilt ground, luster glaze, printed factory mark	**175.00**

PHOTO CREDITS

We wish to thank those who permitted us to photograph objects in their possession. Unfortunately, we are unable to identify the sources for all of our pictures; nevertheless, we are deeply appreciative for all who contributed to this and past editions, and to the editions of *Warman's Americana & Collectibles*.

California: Carlsbad, Dan Golden; Moor Park, Tony and Jackie Anello; Oceanside, Lois Misiewicz; San Francisco, Butterfields; Santa Ana, Evalene Pulati. **Connecticut**: New Canaan, Mildred Fishman; Sandy Hook, Bea Morgan; Stamford, Donna Schilero, West Hartford, Arnold Chase; Westport, Tom Gallagher; Woodbury, Daria of Woodbury; Woodstock, David and Linda Arman. **Delaware**: Lewes, The Price's, Sea Gert Antiques. **Florida**: Cape Coral, The Calico Cat, Elizabeth Clancey, The Collector's Den, Sandra Martz, Country Closet Antiques; Clearwater Beach, Bill Wheeler, The Oar House; Ft. Myers, Ft. Myers Antique Mall, Mina Tinsley, Things Unlimited; Hollywood, Cynthia and Joseph Klein; Miami Beach, Estelle Zalkin; Orlando, Peg Harrison, Harrison's Antiques. **Georgia**: Atlanta, Walter Glenn, Geode Ltd.; Jim Marin, Art Deco Atlanta. **Illinois**: Arlington Heights, T. Johnson; Chicago, Dick and Bindy Bitterman, Eureka! Antiques and Collectibles; Lislie, Susan Nicholson; Mapleton, White's Antiques and Furniture Finishing; Monmouth, David and Betty Hallam; Northbrook, Al and Susan Bagdade, Norman Rockwell Museum; Peotone, Kathy Wojciechowski. **Iowa**: Spencer, Paul and Paula Brenner; Spirit Lake, Gaylord and Margaret Franken. **Maine**: Kennebunk, Richard W. Oliver Auction & Art Gallery; Oxford, Oxford Common; Topsham, Allan and Helen Smith, The Country House. **Maryland**: Laurel, Ken Cohen, Julie Rich; Temple Hills, John Rosenberg; **Massachusetts**: Cambridge, Stan Tillotson; Hyannis Port, Richard A. Bourne, Inc.; Winchester, Lorry and Bruce Hanes, Dad's Follies; Worcester, Ralph R. Saarinen.

Michigan: Monroe, Herb and Joyce Krueger, Mostly Majolica; Utica, Virgil Rogers and David Graves, Avant-Garde; West Bloomfield, Joan Collett Oates. **Missouri**: Sedalia, Crystal and Leyland Payton. **New Hampshire**: Peterborough, Lee and Rally Dennis; Salem, Bea and Bill Laycock, B & B Antiques & Collectibles. **New Jersey**: Bellmawr, Angie Ricciardi Antiques; Demarest, Mimi Rudnick, The Salt Lady Antiques; Hackensack, Roz Albert; Madison, Don Fiore, The Toy Man; Magnolia, Carol Pollock, Custom Covers; Montclair, Susan Morse; Moorestown, Cindy and James Townes, Ladybug's Cupboard; Morris Plains, Elyce Litts; New Egypt, Red Barn Antiques; Old Bridge, Sue Theurich, Respectable Collectables; Paterson, Edward W. Leach; Short Hills, Cynthia Klein, Joseph Klein, C. J. K. Kollectibles; Stewartsville, Marcia and Bob Weissman, Neat Olde Things; Toms River, Shelley, Norman and Phyllis Galinkin; West Orange, Barbara and Melvin Alpern; Woodcliff Lake, Joan Raines Antiques. **New York**:

Auburn, Lower Lake Collectibles; Carmel, Bob Cahn, The Primitive Man; Elmsford, Gerald and Carol Newman; Fishkill, Robert A. Doyle, Livingston, Langes Steinworld; New Platz, Charlotte and Larry Settle; New York, John High; Queens, Flamingoes; Valley Stream, Craig Dinner; Webster, Richard and Joan Randles, From The Cutter's Wheel. **North Carolina**: Chapel Hill, Alda Horner, Whitehall Shop. **Ohio**: Akron, Betty Franks; Beachwood, Rita Orons; Canton, Lewis Bettinger; Cincinnati, Connie Rogers; Newton Falls, Bob and Kathy Wujcik; Novelty, Peggy Bialosky; Urbana, Parker's Antiques. **Oklahoma**: Tulsa, Phyllis Bess.

Pennsylvania: Adamstown, Dottie Freeman and Allan Teal; Allentown, The Borgmans, Wanamaker R.R. Depot Antiques, LeFevre's Antiques, Jim Lo Antiques, Phyllis and Alvin Kahn, The Pen Man's Antiques, Arlene Rabin, Edna Stauffer, Today & Yesterday; Bath, Roy Repsher; Bethlehem, Doris M. Squyres; Cabot, Clair Bargerstock; Coatesville, Chet Ramsay Antiques; Cogan Station, Roan Bros. Auction Gallery; Coopersburg, Neil and Clodogh Wotring; Danville, Lissa L. Bryan-Smith, Dick Smith, Holiday Antiques; Eagleville, Tyler's Antiques; Easton, Harold Mellor, Coach and Four Antiques; Elkins Park, Rose Sill, The Window Sill; Emmaus, Anna M. Benner; Glen Rock, Ron Lieberman; Johnstown, Precious Metals Co; Lampeter, James S. Maxwell, Jr.; Leola, R. C. Lauchnor's Collectables; Lititz, Doug Flynn and Al Bolton, Holloway House; Montgomeryville, Clarence and Betty Maier, Burmese Cruet; Montoursville, M. Jeanne Foust, Jeanne's Glass House; New Freedom, George Theofiles, Miscellaneous Man; New Hope, Debby Bogdan, Ferry Hill, Ted and Linda Freed; Northampton, David and Sue Irons, Irons Antiques; Oley, Mrs. Lena Eyrich; Orefield, Gloria Burkos, Gloria's Collectibles; Philadelphia, Shelly Hoffman, Ed Kelberg, Marcy Kula, Ed Volkrecht, Ed's Antiques, Inc., Murray and Selma Petersons; Pittsburgh, Regis and Mary Ferson, Edward Grzybowski; Pottsville, George and Tedi Hahn, Doorway To Glass; Quakertown, Doris Castellon, Brick House Antiques, Mary Webber, Webber's Antiques; Schnecksville, David Koch; Whitehall, Herb and Nancy Hallman, The Churn Antiques; Wilkes-Barre, Al Sallitt Antiques, Golden Webb Antiques; Williamsport, Michael Rath; Yardley, Ellie Archer; York, Lookenbill's Antiques.

South Dakota: Huron, Joan Hull. **Tennessee**: Elaine J. Luartes, Athena Antiques. **Texas**: Dallas, Ted Birbilis; Euless, The Stevensons. **Vermont**: Cavendish, Henry and Doris Sigourney, Sigourney's Antiques. **Virginia**: Portsmouth, Whitney LeCompte. **Virginia**: Arlington, Carolyn Smith; Crozet, Betty L. Loba, Rose Valley Antiques; Hopewell, Carolyn R. Morris, Yestermorrow's Collectibles and More; Portsmouth, Whitney Le Compte; Radford, Roy M. Collins. **Wisconsin**: Kaukauna, Ferill J. Rice.

PRICE LIST CREDITS

We wish to thank the following people who cooperated with us by sending us price lists and other useful information.

California: Big Bear City, Richard Hale; Burlingame, Ken Prag; Cedar Ridge, Bud and Sally's; Coronado, Coronado Coins; Covina, Jim Ducote; Fair Oaks, John Heleva; Los Angeles, Jim Solk Co., Inc., Manhattan Beach, Ruth Raymond; Oceanside, Abill; Santa Monica, Sam & Family; Sausalito, Bridgeway To Hollywood; Sunnyvale, L & B Acquisitions. **Colorado**: Golden, The Foss Co.; Pueblo, Sheila Malouff, Colorado Estates, Inc. **Connecticut**: Avon, Garland and Frances Pass. **Delaware**: Newark, Delaware Salt Box. **Florida**: Jacksonville, Ron Fairchild; Lantana, Past Present Future; Malabar, Toys; West Palm Beach, The Collector's Stop. **Georgia**: Richmond Hills, B. Kelly. **Hawaii**: Alea, A.T. Ralston. **Illinois**: Chicago, Mrs. Ernie Lawrence, Russell's Antiques, The Bradford Exchange; Evanston, Helen Reed; Northbrook, Norman Rockwell Museum; Peoria, Charles Amery; Roanoke, J. Getz. **Indiana**: Sullivan, Dee Boston. **Kansas**: Kansas City, Ron Manion.

Louisiana: Covington, Antique Imports. **Maryland**: Baltimore, Geppi's Comic World. **Massachusetts**: Boston, Phil Barber; Brewster, Muriel and Wendell Smith, Sunsmith House Antiques. **Michigan**: Bay City, L. Butterfield; Fraser, William Fagen. **Missouri**: Bridgeton, Woollard; La Clede, Missouri Country Quilts. **Nebraska**: Omaha, Mike and Elaine Lehn. **New Jersey**: Freehold, David Metz; Teaneck, Judy Posner; Union, John E. Bilane. **New York**: Guilderland, Veeder's Antiques; New Rochelle, Promenade Club; Rochester, Lew Hohn; Scarsdale, Lucid Antiques. **Ohio**: Akron, Anytime, David C. Pierson; Columbus, Giftique. **Oklahoma**: Del City, Dennis Ivy; Ponca City, Joyce Knight; Skiatook, Melvin Rozell; Tulsa, D.L. Hill, Shirley Robinson. **Pennsylvania**: Pittsburgh, Carol Jessen; Port Vue, Helen and Phil Rosso; Yardley, Artiques. **Tennessee**: Memphis, Pop Poppenheimer. **Texas**: Spring, Ray Johnson; Wimberly, Charles Warlick. **Washington**: Olympia, Frederick; Seattle, Accoutrements. **West Virginia**: Charleston, Lighthouse Antiques. **Wisconsin**: Oakfield, The Stationmaster.

INDEX

-XYZ-

HARRY L. RINKER is consulting editor for Wallace-Homestead Book Company, editor of *Warman's Antiques and Their Prices* and *Warman's Americana & Collectibles;* author of *Rinker on Collectibles* and *How to Make the Most of Your Investments in Antiques and Collectibles;* co-author with Frank Hill of *The Joy of Collecting with Craven Moore;* syndicated columnist of ''Rinker on Collectibles;'' and president of ''Rinker's Antiques and Collectibles Market Report.''

OTHER TOPICS COVERED BY WALLACE-HOMESTEAD

All the following books can be purchased from your local book store, antiques dealer, or can be borrowed from your public library. Books can also be purchased directly from **Chilton Book Company, Chilton Way, Radnor, PA 19089**. Include code number, title, and price when ordering. Add applicable sales tax and **$2.00** postage and handling for the first book plus $ .50 for each additional book shipped to the same address. VISA/Mastercard orders call **1-800-345-1214** and ask for Customer Service Department (AK, HI, & PA residents call **215-964-4000** and ask for Customer Service Department). Prices and availability are subject to change without notice. Please call for a current Wallace-Homestead catalog.

COLLECTOR'S GUIDE SERIES

Code	Title/Author	Price
W5339	Collector's Guide to Baseball Cards, *Troy Kirk*	$12.95
W5479	Collector's Guide to Early Photographs, *O. Henry Mace*	$16.95
W5320	Collector's Guide to American Toy Trains, *Susan & Al Bagdade*	$16.95
W5568	Collector's Guide to Autographs, *George Sanders, Helen Sanders, and Ralph Roberts*	$16.95
W5487	Collector's Guide to Comic Books, *John Hegenberger*	$12.95

COLLECTIBLES

Code	Title/Author	Price
W5258	American Clocks and Clockmakers, *Robert W. & Harriett Swedberg*	$16.95
W4529	British Royal Commemoratives with Prices, *Audrey Zeder*	$24.95
W4464	Check the Oil: Gas Station Collectibles with Prices, *Scott Anderson*	$18.95
W4723	Clock Guide Identification with Prices, *Robert W. Miller*	$14.95
W3786	Cocoa-Cola Collectibles, Wallace-Homestead Price Guide to, *Deborah Goldstein Hill*	$15.95
W4235	Collectible Clothing with Prices, *Sheila Malouff*	$14.95
W0175	Collecting Antique Marbles, *Paul Baumann*	$12.95
W5460	Commercial Aviation Collectibles: An Illustrated Price Guide, *Richard Wallin*	$15.95
W5177	Contemporary Fast-Food and Drinking Glass Collectibles, *Mark E. Chase & Michael Kelly*	$16.95
W4731	Dolls, Wallace-Homestead Price Guide to, *Robert W. Miller*	$16.95
W4936	Dr. Records' Original 78 RPM Pocket Price Guide, *Peter A. Soderbergh Ph.D.*	$12.95
W5118	Food and Drink Containers and Their Prices, *Al Bergevin*	$16.95
W4901	Girl Scout Collector's Guide: 75 Years of Uniforms, Insignia, Publications & Keepsakes, *Mary Degenhardt and Judy Kirsch*	$21.95
W5185	Guide to Old Radios: Pointers, Pictures, and Prices, *David & Betty Johnson*	$16.95
W5436	Herron's Price Guide to Dolls, *R. Lane Herron*	$16.95

Code	Title/Author	Price
W0060*	Illustrated Radio Premium Catalof and Price Guide, *Tom Tumbusch*	$34.95
W5371	Jigsaw Puzzles: An Illustrated History and Price Guide, *Anne D. Williams*	$24.95
W121X*	Oil Lamps: The Kerosene Era in North America, *Catherine M. V. Thuro*	$38.95
W5312*	Petretti's Coca-Cola Collectibles Price Guide, *Allan Petretti*	$29.95
W4944	Plastic Collectibles, Wallace-Homestead Price Guide to, *Lyndi Stewart McNulty*	$17.95
W5169	Presidential and Campaign Memorabilia with Prices, Second Edition, *Stan Gores*	$18.95
W541X	Psychedelic Collectibles of the 1960s and 1970s: An Illustrated Price Guide, *Susanne White*	$21.95
W5657	Space Adventure Collectibles, *T. N. Tumbusch*	$19.95
W4154	Steiff Teddy Bears, Dolls, and Toys with Prices, *Shirley Conway & Jean Wilson*	$17.95
W538X	Steiff Toys Revisited, *Jean Wilson*	$18.95
W4847*	Thimble Collector's Encyclopedia: New International Edition, *John von Hoelle*	$35.95
W1236	Thimble Treasury, *Myrtle Lundquist*	$12.95
W3972	Tins 'N' Bins, *Robert W. & Harriett Swedberg*	$16.95
W4642	Tobacco Tins and Their Prices, *Al Bergevin*	$16.95
W5584	Tomart's Illustrated Disneyana Catalog and Price Guide, Condensed Edition, *Tom Tumbusch*	$19.95
W5576	Warman's Americana & Collectibles, *Edited by Harry L. Rinker*	$14.95
W5606	Warman's Antiques and Their Prices, 24th Edition, *Edited by Harry L. Rinker*	$13.95
W0140*	Zalkin's Handbook of Thimbles & Sewing Implements, *Estelle Zalkin*	$24.95
W4383	Yesterday's Toys with Today's Prices, *Fred and Marilyn Fintel*	$14.95

COUNTRY

Code	Title/Author	Price
W524X	American Country Antiques, Wallace-Homestead Price Guide to, Ninth Edition, *Don & Carol Raycraft*	$14.95
W4499	Antiques From the Country Kitchen, *Frances Thompson*	$16.95
W5428	Baskets, Wallace-Homestead Price Guide to, Second Edition, *Frances Thompson*	$16.95
W5002	Country Sourcebook, Second Edition, *Elaine Hawley*	$19.95
W3956	Country Store 'N' More, *Robert W. & Harriett Swedberg*	$17.95
W3263	Graniteware Collector's Guide with Prices, *Vernagene Vogelzang & Evelyn Welch*	$16.95
W4588	Granite Ware, Book II, *Vernagene Vogelzang & Evelyn Welch*	$18.95
W3581	Kitchens and Gadgets: 1920 to 1950, *Jane Celehar*	$16.95
W4251	Kitchens and Kitchenware: 1900 to 1950, *Jane Celehar*	$15.95
W443X	Shaker: A Collector's Source Book II, *Don & Carol Raycraft*	$15.95

FURNITURE

Code	Title/Author	Price
W4758	American Oak Furniture, Revised Edition, *Robert W. & Harriett Swedberg*	$16.95
W4243	American Oak Furniture, Volume II, *Robert W. & Harriett Swedberg*	$16.95
W4928	American Oak Furniture, Volume III, *Robert W. & Harriett Swedberg*	$16.95
W4111	Country Furniture and Accessories with Prices, *Robert W. & Harriett Swedberg*	$16.95
W376X	Country Furniture and Accessories with Prices, Book II, *Robert W. & Harriett Swedberg*	$16.95
W3883	Country Pine Furniture, Revised Edition, *Robert W. & Harriett Swedberg*	$14.95
W5401*	Macdonald Guide to Buying Antique Furniture, *Rachael Feild*	$25.00
W393X	Victorian Furniture, Book I, Revised, *Robert W. & Harriett Swedberg*	$16.95
W3875	Victorian Furniture, Book II, *Robert W. & Harriett Swedberg*	$16.95
W3964	Victorian Furniture, Book III, *Robert W. & Harriett Swedberg*	$16.95
W5207	Wicker Furniture: Styles and Prices, Revised, *Robert W. & Harriett Swedberg*	$14.95

GENERAL

Code	Title/Author	Price
W4189	Antique Radios: Restoration and Price Guide, *Betty & David Johnson*	$14.95
W3921	Antiques, Wallace-Homestead Price Guide to, Eleventh Edition, *Dan D'Imperio*	$14.95
W5274	Antiquing in England: A Guide to Antique Centres, *Robert W. & Harriett Swedberg*	$16.95
W5126	The Complete Collector's Guide to Fakes and Forgeries, *Colin Haynes*	$15.95
W5592	Flea Market Handbook: Making Money in Antiques, Second Edition, *Robert G. Miner*	$12.95
W3913	Flea Market Price Guide, Fifth Edition, *Robert G. Miller*	$12.95
W4618	Joy of Collecting, *Harry Rinker & Frank Hill*	$ 6.95
W4855	Oriental Antiques & Art: An Identification and Value Guide, *Sandra Andacht*	$17.95
W5266	Rinker on Collectibles, *Harry L. Rinker*	$14.95

GLASS

Code	Title/Author	Price
W4308*	American Cut and Engraved Glass of the Brilliant Period, *Martha Louise Swan*	$35.00
W5452*	Early American Pattern Glass – 1850 to 1910: Major Collecible Table Settings with Prices, *Bill Jenks & Jerry Luna*	$29.95
W4626	Glass Signatures, Trademarks, and Trade Names, *Anne Geffken Pullen*	$16.95
W4421	Pattern Glass, Wallace-Homestead Price Guide to, Eleventh Edition, *Robert W. Miller & Dori Miles*	$15.95
W5444*	Perfume and Scent Bottle Collecting with Prices, Second Edition, *Jean Sloan*	$35.00

JEWELRY

Code	Title/Author	Price
W3697	Antique Jewelry with Prices, *Doris J. Snell*	$14.95
W5231*	Ladies' Compacts of The 19th and 20th Centuries, *Roselyn Gerson*	$34.95

PAPER EPHEMERA

Code	Title/Author	Price
W460X	A Collector's Guide to Autographs with Prices, *Bob Bennett*	$14.95
W4987	Currier & Ives: An Illustrated Value Guide, *Craig McClain*	$16.95
W5363	Hancer's Price Guide to Paperback Books, Third Edition, *Kevin Hancer*	$16.95
W5029	Military Postcards, 1870 to 1945, *Jack H. Smith*	$19.95
W5193*	Postcard Companion: The Collector's Reference, *Jack H. Smith*	$39.95
W5053	The Price Guide to Autographs, *George Sanders, Helen Sanders, & Ralph Roberts*	$18.95

POTTERY & PORCELAIN

Code	Title/Author	Price
80038*	British Studio Ceramics in the 20th Century, *Paul Rice and Christopher Gowing*	$45.00
7982X	A History of World Pottery, Revised and Updated Edition, *Emmanuel Cooper*	$24.95
W5398*	Macdonald Guide to Buying Antique Pottery & Porcelain, *Rachael Feild*	$25.00
W0116	Warman's English & Continental Pottery & Porcelain, *Susan & Al Bagdade*	$18.95

* Denotes hardcover, all others are paperback.